THE HERMENEUTICS
OF DOCTRINE

THE HERMENEUTICS
OF DOCTRINE

Anthony C. Thiselton

WILLIAM B. EERDMANS PUBLISHING COMPANY
GRAND RAPIDS, MICHIGAN / CAMBRIDGE, U.K.

Wm. B. Eerdmans Publishing Co.
2140 Oak Industrial Drive N.E., Grand Rapids, Michigan 49505 /
P.O. Box 163, Cambridge CB3 9PU U.K.

Printed in the United States of America

12 11 10 09 08 07   7 6 5 4 3 2 1

Library of Congress Cataloging-in-Publication Data

Thiselton, Anthony C.
The hermeneutics of doctrine / Anthony C. Thiselton.
p.   cm.
Includes bibliographical references and index.
ISBN 978-0-8028-2681-7 (cloth: alk. paper)
1. Hermeneutics — Religious aspects — Christianity.
2. Theology.   I. Title.

BR118.T487   2007
230.01 — dc22
2007028518

www.eerdmans.com

Contents

Contents

Contents

Acknowledgments

The last thirty-five years have witnessed a massive step forward in the exploration of hermeneutics as an interdisciplinary resource. This has made a considerable impact upon ways of reading the biblical writings. But it has yet to make a comparable impact on the formulation of Christian doctrine and our engagement with it, other than in one or two noteworthy cases. My aim is to try to make explicit some hermeneutical starting points and hermeneutical currencies that may perhaps serve to resource Christian doctrine. I explain this aim and my hopes for this book in the Introduction that follows.

My purpose here is to acknowledge the very great debt of gratitude that I owe to my typist and to my two proofreaders, and to explain why this debt is so very great. My birth in 1937 was considerably premature, and meningitis then struck in infancy. These two factors left me with very poor eyesight. I have always needed a magnifying glass as well as glasses to read Hebrew, and by the providence of God the then Bishop of Southwark in 1958 chose to ignore my pre-ordination medical report, which read: "This man will never be able to read enough books to exercise a useful parish ministry."

Over the years proofreading has taxed my eyes beyond measure. I have written all of my ten books to date by hand. This has imposed a huge burden on my typists, in the case of this latest work on Mrs. Carol Dakin. She has deciphered some eight hundred pages of poor writing over the last six months. Equally, my wife Rosemary and friend Mrs. Sheila Rees have checked printouts for corrections that I missed. They have freely given their time and concentration. If typographical errors still remain, I hope that potential reviewers will kindly bear our situation in mind.

Like many others who strive to think creatively, I also acknowledge the contributions of my students. Ten of the books cited in the text and bibliography are revisions of dissertations written by my Ph.D. candidates in the Universities of

Sheffield, Durham, and Nottingham. Currently I am teaching hermeneutics to M.A. and final-year students in Nottingham, and a course in Christian Theology and the Bible to M.A. and final-year students in the University of Chester. Questions and comments from students are vital ingredients for clarifying and developing one's thought.

Finally, I warmly thank Jon Pott of William B. Eerdmans Publishing Company for his kind support and friendship over the years. I hope that the present work will make a distinctive contribution to the shaping of Christian theology, and to the capacity of Christian doctrine under God to shape us.

January 2007

ANTHONY C. THISELTON
Department of Theology and Religious Studies
University of Nottingham,
Department of Theology and Religious Studies
University of Chester

NOTE: My husband was devastated by a major stroke August 4, 2007, before he had completed the indexing and the correcting of the proofs for this volume. We are grateful to Milton Essenburg of Eerdmans for finalizing the proof corrections, to Jenny Hoffman of Eerdmans for coordinating the indexing, and to Craig Noll and Holly Knowles for taking on the huge task of completing the indexes.

ROSEMARY THISELTON

Abbreviations

BDAG   W. Bauer, F. W. Danker, W. F. Arndt, and F. W. Gingrich, *A Greek-English Lexicon of the New Testament and Other Early Christian Literature*. Chicago: University of Chicago Press, 3d edn. 2000

BDB   F. Brown, S. R. Driver, and C. A. Briggs (eds.), *The New Hebrew-English Lexicon*. Lafayette, IN: Associated Publishers, 1980

FRLANT   Forschungen zur Religion und Literatur des Alten und Neuen Testaments

HTR   *Harvard Theological Review*

ICC   International Critical Commentary

JBL   *Journal of Biblical Literature*

JSNT   *Journal for the Study of the New Testament*

JSNTMS   Journal for the Study of the New Testament Monograph Series

JSNTSS   Journal for the Study of the New Testament Supplement Series

JSOT   *Journal for the Study of the Old Testament*

JTS   *Journal of Theological Studies*

KEKG   Kritisch-exegetischer Kommentar über das Neue Testament (Göttingen)

Neot.   *Neotestamentica*

NICNT   New International Commentary on the New Testament

NIGTC   New International Greek Testament Commentary

NTTS   New Testament Tools and Studies

SBLDS   Society of Biblical Literature Dissertation Series

SBLMS   Society of Biblical Literature Monograph Series

SJT   *Scottish Journal of Theology*

SNTSMS	Society for New Testament Studies Monograph Series
TDNT	*Theological Dictionary of the New Testament*
TDOT	*Theological Dictionary of the Old Testament*
WA	Weimarer Augabe (Martin Luther)
WBC	Word Biblical Commentary
WUNT	Wissenschaftliche Untersuchungen zum Neuen Testament
ZNW	*Zeitschrift für die neutestamentliche Wissenschaft und die Kunde der älteren Kirche*

INTRODUCTION

From Abstract Theory to Life-Related Hermeneutics

Alongside my teaching and research in five British universities I have been privileged to serve as Examining Chaplain or as Canon Theologian to the bishops of three English dioceses. This has involved my interviewing those recently ordained, those about to be ordained, and those seeking to test a call to ministry or to ministerial training.

In this context I have regularly asked clergy or ordinands, on behalf of the bishops, about their attitudes to the use of the Bible, to doctrine, to worship, and to everyday life. From time to time a small minority have become enthusiastic about doctrine, sometimes because they have engaged constructively with the writings of a specific creative theologian. They have mentioned Moltmann in this context most frequently. Apart from this, some saw doctrine only as a vehicle for establishing markers between true and false belief. Too many seemed to perceive doctrine as a theoretical system of truths received by the church that made little or no impact on their daily lives. By contrast, those who had acquired some understanding of the resources of biblical and philosophical hermeneutics held far higher expectations of how engaging with biblical texts could make a formative impact upon their thought and daily life.

All of this seemed to pose a question. Might not a more significant interaction between *hermeneutics* and *doctrine* play some part in rescuing doctrine from its marginalized function and abstraction from life, and deliver it from its supposed status as mere theory?

The most striking example of this theoretical conception of the nature of doctrine emerged from an interview with a former Roman Catholic priest who had married and was seeking to explore possible Anglican ordination. He clearly viewed doctrine as what he had "done" to meet the requirements for ordination, but since then he had left it well alone.

Lest it risk discourtesy to cite an example from a Christian tradition other than mine, I cite a similar expression of dismay from Karl Rahner. It is fair to note that the quotation that follows predates Vatican II. Rahner speaks of "the stagnation of our textbooks," and observes that people offer to doctrine "a reverential bow" without its making much difference to their lives.[1] Doctrine "is not very vividly alive."[2] It tends to become "esoteric," with little engagement with the Christian life.[3] Yet, Rahner concludes, it *ought* to be an art or science of *"understanding"* and especially of *"Listening,"* embodying "Truth," and actualizing "Love" (capital letters his).[4]

"Understanding," "listening," "love" in action, and respect for "the other" in life are precisely the major characteristics of serious hermeneutical inquiry identified by leading writers in the field. Looking back over some seventy years of publications, Hans-Georg Gadamer (1900-2002), the most influential writer on hermeneutics in the twentieth century, observes, "Hermeneutics is above all a *practice,* the art of *understanding....* In it what one has to exercise above all is *the ear,* the sensitivity for perceiving prior determinations, anticipations, and imprints that reside in concepts" (my italics).[5] Further, hermeneutical reflection, properly understood, is *formative:* it gives rise to formation (to *Bildung,* in a special sense that goes beyond *culture*). This in turn entails transformation because, in Gadamer's words, it involves "keeping oneself open to *what is the other* . . . to distance oneself from oneself and from one's private purposes," and to see as others or "the other" may see (my italics).[6]

Hermeneutics, for Gadamer, also draws on *communal* understanding and transmitted *wisdom,* just as Christian doctrine is not simply a matter of individual belief but also of *communal understanding,* transmitted traditions, wisdom, commitment, and action. Gadamer traces the roots of hermeneutical inquiry to the communal and historical emphasis of G. B. Vico and to *"sensus communis,"* in contrast to the timeless, individual-centered rationalism of Descartes.[7]

The other leading hermeneutical thinker of the late twentieth century, Paul Ricoeur (1913-2005), makes closely parallel points, and we shall interact with his work in more detail. Pannenberg rightly argues that while doctrine "does not rest on the consensus of church," nevertheless Christian doctrine entails a "commonality of knowledge" that leads to "the intersubjective identity of the subject mat-

1. Karl Rahner, "The Prospects for Dogmatic Theology," in Rahner, *Theological Investigations,* vol. 1, trans. C. Ernst (London: Darton, Longman & Todd, 1961), 4; cf. 1-18.

2. Rahner, "Prospects," 13.

3. Rahner, "Prospects," 16.

4. Rahner, "Prospects," 17.

5. Hans-Georg Gadamer, "Reflections on My Philosophical Journey," in Lewis E. Hahn (ed.), *The Philosophy of Hans Georg Gadamer* (Chicago and La Salle: Open Court, 1997), 17; cf. 3-63.

6. Hans-Georg Gadamer, *Truth and Method,* trans. J. Weinsheimer and D. G. Marshall (London: Sheed & Ward, 2d rev. edn. 1989), 17.

7. Gadamer, *Truth,* 19-30.

ter."[8] Some writers are more cautious about the role of epistemology in Christian doctrine but nevertheless urge its communal nature. George Lindbeck writes, "Like a culture or language, religion [or doctrine] is a communal phenomenon that shapes the subjectivities of individuals rather than being primarily a manifestation of those subjectivities."[9] It relates to a religious and communal tradition.[10]

All the major traditions of the Christian church formally define doctrine in communal terms, although the emphasis and nature of the community in question varies. We may briefly cite examples from Catholic, Anglican, Presbyterian, Methodist, and "high church Mennonite" writers or texts. According to the documents of Vatican II, "The Roman Pontiff, or the body of bishops together with him, defines a doctrine . . . in conformity with revelation itself."[11] The defining community in the Roman Catholic tradition is primarily the bishops "as successors of the apostles."[12] The emphasis is communal but also "hierarchical."[13] The Church of England Doctrine Commission, on which I served for more than twenty-five years, emphasizes the communal nature of Christian doctrine as a theological axiom. This emerged especially in our report, *Believing in the Church,* to which I contributed an essay on this particular subject.[14]

Kevin Vanhoozer acknowledges his Presbyterian tradition and emphasizes the communal nature of doctrine in his recent book, *The Drama of Doctrine.*[15] The importance of the communal dimension on the part of traditions within Methodism finds a passionate defense in Richard Heyduck's *The Recovery of Doctrine in the Contemporary Church.*[16] Stanley Hauerwas has lived and thought among diverse traditions and is a self-designated "high church Mennonite." His roots were United Methodist, but he has taught in a Lutheran college and in the Catholic University of Notre Dame.[17] Drawing on the work of Hans Frei,

8. Wolfhart Pannenberg, *Systematic Theology,* trans. G. W. Bromiley, 3 vols. (Grand Rapids: Eerdmans and Edinburgh: T&T Clark, 1991-98), vol. 1, 16.

9. George A. Lindbeck, *The Nature of Doctrine: Religion and Theology in a Postliberal Age* (London: SPCK, 1984), 33.

10. Lindbeck, *Doctrine,* 33; cf. 32-41 and 79-88.

11. Austin P. Flannery (ed.), *Documents of Vatican II* (Grand Rapids: Eerdmans, 1975), 380.

12. *Vatican II,* 378-79.

13. *Vatican II, Lumen Gentium,* in Flannery, *Documents* 369-413.

14. Report of the Doctrine Commission of the Church of England, *Believing in the Church: The Corporate Nature of Faith* (London: SPCK, 1981), including Anthony C. Thiselton, "Knowledge, Myth and Corporate Memory," 45-78; also essays by Tom Wright, J. V. Taylor, and V. H. Vanstone, "Where Shall Doctrine Be Found?" 108-58. See also John Bowker, "Religions as Systems," 159-89.

15. Kevin J. Vanhoozer, *The Drama of Doctrine: A Canonical-Linguistic Approach to Christian Theology* (Louisville: Westminster/John Knox, 2005), esp. 27-30 and 399-457.

16. Richard Heyduck, *The Recovery of Doctrine in the Contemporary Church: An Essay in Philosophical Ecclesiology* (Waco, TX: Baylor University Press, 2002), 51-137.

17. Stanley Hauerwas, *A Community of Character: Towards a Constructive Christian Ethic* (Notre Dame: University of Notre Dame Press, 4th edn. 1986), 6.

Hauerwas sees doctrine not only in terms of living out the "narrative of God" but also as focussing on "what kind of community the church must be to rightly tell the stories of God."[18]

Arguably, then, substantial points of resonance exist between hermeneutics and Christian doctrine, while misconceptions of doctrine and in many places its marginalization reflect a vacuum to which serious explorations of resources in hermeneutics might provide a constructive response. Richard Heyduck provides incontrovertible evidence concerning the marginalization and neglect of doctrine, with careful documentation. He diagnoses the primary cause of this marginalization as the emergence of individualism and an individual-centred epistemology. Here the supposed ground of doctrine is perceived to lie in personal "belief," at the expense of ecclesiology.[19] William Abraham similarly speaks of a widespread "forgetfulness" of Christian doctrine.[20]

I endorse Heyduck's diagnosis of the mistaken reduction of corporate doctrine to *individual-centered* belief. With regret, I must part company with him when he claims that epistemology in doctrine is also the most blameworthy culprit. I address his claim critically in this book. With appropriate modifications, "understanding" *(Verstehen)* includes "knowledge." Even if Gadamer retains only the pole of *Verstehen,* most exponents of hermeneutical traditions from Schleiermacher to Ricoeur and Apel stress the necessary role of both explanation *(Erklärung)* and understanding *(Verstehen).* This originates from, and is mediated through, revelation and *communal* wisdom *(phronēsis).* These together bring us to the heart of truth-claims in hermeneutics. Some of the postmodern writers whom Heyduck perceives as "liberating" doctrine too readily replace epistemology with a "rhetoric" of social or ecclesial self-construction.

Yet Heyduck is right to emphasize (as Rahner does) the destructive effects of isolating doctrine from life. This leaves the impression that doctrine constitutes only theory. Bernard Lonergan has argued convincingly that theology or Christian doctrine requires an *enlarged epistemology,* in contrast to narrower or more abstract epistemologies of any kind. This "knowing" embraces being attentive, being intelligent, being reasonable, and being responsible, and includes research, interpretation, historical understanding, and dialectic.[21] Lonergan, indeed, offers what amounts to the beginnings of a hermeneutic of Christian doctrine.

These characteristics of disciplined inquiry, then, are precisely those that

---

18. Hauerwas, *Community,* 1. Cf. also John B. Thomson, *The Ecclesiology of Stanley Hauerwas: A Christian Theology of Liberation* (Aldershot and London, U.K. and Burlington VT: Ashgate, 2003). This work is based on a dissertation under my joint supervision, and is favorably endorsed by Hauerwas.

19. Heyduck, *Recovery,* 1-50.

20. William J. Abraham, *Waking from Doctrinal Amnesia* (Nashville: Abingdon, 1986).

21. Bernard Lonergan, *Method in Theology* (London: Darton, Longman & Todd, 1972), esp. 28-56, 81-84, 155-265, and 311-37, but also throughout.

mark hermeneutical reflection and experience at a serious level. Thinkers who have engaged with the flood of literature on hermeneutics over the last forty or fifty years highlight these aspects when they draw on hermeneutical resources for biblical interpretation. But parallel applications of these resources to engagement with doctrine seem in many cases to lag behind. Sometimes stripped from the temporal flow of life out of which they were born, living questions that arise too often become transposed into static, freestanding, doctrinal "problems."

Biblical hermeneutics explores levels of meaning, strategies of reading, historical distance, appropriation, engagement, and formation, and often features *patient and attentive listening.* The relation between text, community, and tradition remains constantly in view. Can these *habits of mind,* with the historical, intellectual, and moral resources of hermeneutics, be placed at the service of understanding, exploring, appropriating, and applying Christian doctrine?

In Part I I attempt to set out the distinctive perspectives and methods that belong to a hermeneutical approach. The focus here is mainly upon method and upon exploring hermeneutical resources. Part II aims to anticipate potential objections to a hermeneutic of doctrine from the standpoint of the claims of coherence and system. I firmly endorse the need for system, but with significant qualifications, and I strongly urge the importance of coherence as a criterion of truth. On the other hand, I seek to distinguish between different notions of "system," and to balance the genuine need for coherence with a consideration of the role of polyphony, dialectic, and open systems that permit correction, modification, and further growth.

Part III expounds the content of specific Christian doctrines, but always from the specific standpoint of *hermeneutical starting points, hermeneutical resources,* and *hermeneutical currencies.* To write on theological method without applying it to specific Christian doctrines would leave everything in the air. Although they provide various insights, the widely respected work of Lindbeck, Tracy, Vanhoozer, and others who cover similar ground leaves me wondering how their discourses on theological method, valuable as they are, would work out when they turn to the theological content of a range of specific doctrines. Work on method can often seem like an overture without an opera.

The fourteen chapters of Part III explore *two different kinds of horizons of understanding.* I compare these with each other explicitly in 14.1, on the work of Christ. The first kind of hermeneutical horizon concerns the formulation of initial *preunderstandings* (or a readiness to understand) on the part of those who seek to understand. It relates to the attempt to identify *points of engagement* between the interpreter and the subject matter. The second kind of hermeneutical horizon is different. This seeks to identify *what the "otherness" of the doctrinal subject matter demands* as a horizon within which its claims will be heard *without distortion* and without the interpreter's *imposing alien questions, concepts, and conceptual worlds upon it.* In very provisional, inadequate, shorthand terms, the first horizon primarily concerns a hermeneutic of communication; the second horizon concerns a hermeneutic of truth. Both, however, interact, and one leads on to the other.

I am concerned to avoid any suggestion that other systematic theologies avoid the dimension of hermeneutics. My task is, rather, to make explicit what is involved in seeking to explore this hermeneutical dimension. The present book is not a "systematic theology" *as such;* it explores the content of Christian doctrine insofar as explicitly hermeneutical questions impinge upon it and resource it for its communication, understanding, and truth.

Among many theologians upon whose work I draw, that of Jürgen Moltmann and Wolfhart Pannenberg features probably more prominently than most. This is not only because since the late 1960s I have been drawn to their work, but also because I find in their work very considerable implicit hermeneutical concerns. Moltmann maintains notable sensitivity in relation to the "first" communicative horizon, which seeks to engage with people in life where they are, while Pannenberg constantly engages with rigorous questions about hermeneutics and horizons of truth. At the same time each also interacts with both hermeneutical horizons of meaning. I have also drawn on theologians of all traditions, from Balthasar and Rahner to Barth, Bonhoeffer, and Jüngel, as well as major American and British thinkers.

Hermeneutical inquiry is incompatible with overly easy generalization and categorization. I press this point in almost every chapter of this book. But this invites one personal comment. On occasion I read critical assessments of my work, and am dismayed to see it described as "Wittgensteinian" or "Gadamerian," or as a "follower" of some theological school. I do not intend to "follow" anyone. It is a trait of many British scholars, unlike some of their counterparts elsewhere in the world, to abhor any notion of belonging to a "school." I draw upon Moltmann, Pannenberg, Gadamer, Ricoeur, Wittgenstein, *and many other thinkers,* where I find in their writings resources that facilitate what I want to say, or sometimes ideas that inspire further vision. In such circumstances I fully document and openly acknowledge my sources, giving credit where credit is due.

In this respect I am grateful to Robert Knowles, who has produced a Ph.D. thesis for Cardiff University on my work, revised and to be published under the title *Anthony Thiselton and the Search for a Unified Theory: The Grammar of Hermeneutics.* This is contracted with Ashgate of Guildford, U.K., for publication in due course. Knowles criticizes those who have sought to classify me under the heading of some other thinker, arguing that this is the cardinal way to guarantee misunderstanding my work.

I have placed considerably more emphasis upon the need for careful biblical exegesis than tends to characterize many works on Christian doctrine. This is unavoidable for an exploration of the *hermeneutics* of doctrine. A hermeneutics of doctrine cannot proceed without careful engagement with "home language games," and this requires interaction with the questions of biblical specialists and biblical languages. The same principle applies to the exploration of conceptual grammar as it develops and changes amid ongoing historical traditions and interpretations. Every area of doctrine has been explored in relation to its biblical roots, its historical development, and its practical significance for life. Historical inquiries may sometimes appear uneven. Major attention has been focused on the Patristic period in many chapters; but in others mainly on the medieval or Reformation period; and in yet other chapters more especially the modern period from Schleiermacher to the present. This reflects the varying *hermeneutical* questions and sensitivities that each individual doctrine brings to the fore.

I turn now to Part I, to try to set out the hermeneutical groundwork that will pave the way for a hermeneutic of the content of Christian doctrine in Part III. If this hermeneutical approach could inject life into engagement with doctrine with as much effect as hermeneutics has resourced biblical reading, this would exceed my highest hopes for the present undertaking.

Reasons to Explore the Hermeneutics of Doctrine

CHAPTER 1

From Free-Floating "Problems"
to Hermeneutical Questions from Life

1.1. Gadamer's Contrast between "Problems" and "Questions That Arise"

I do not wish to imply that most recent expositions of Christian doctrine approach their subject at a high level of abstraction. Nevertheless a number of older works may seem to veer towards the abstract and overly general, and even many specialists in systematic theology or doctrine nowadays seem to agree that this perception of doctrine as abstract or theoretical is more widespread than is healthy. My concern relates more closely to the expectations and agenda of readers of doctrine than to most of its current exponents. I am not telling systematic theologians how to ply their craft. To cite a possible parallel, current research in biblical hermeneutics has brought about radically new expectations and assumptions in the *reading* of biblical texts without in any way seeking to change the *content* of the biblical writings. Hermeneutical resources have simply encouraged *reading with fresh eyes.*

The contrast, or "fresh eyes," indicated by the subheading of this section goes to the heart of hermeneutical understanding as Gadamer expounds it. He devotes a section of his *Truth and Method* to the contrast between approaching a set of issues as free-floating *"problems"* or the *"history of problems"* on one side, and reaching behind and beyond these, on the other side, in such a way that "reflection on hermeneutical experience transforms problems back to *questions that arise,* and that *derive their sense from their motivation."*[1] Gadamer's section under the heading "The Logic of Question and Answer" constitutes the culmination of his substantial Part II of *Truth and Method,* which relates questions of truth to

---

1. Gadamer, *Truth,* 377 (my italics); cf. 369-79.

understanding, and expounds his notion of the impact of the history of effects (*Wirkungsgeschichte*) upon the "historical" or temporal nature of human understanding.[2] What he calls "the recovery of the fundamental hermeneutical problem" includes the *"task of application"* that we have already recognized as a central theme of hermeneutics.[3] "Application" relates to the everyday *particularities* of human life, and exists only in relation to concrete forms of life.

Gadamer follows R. G. Collingwood in the belief that we can say that we *understand* "only when we understand the question to which something is the answer, but [conversely] the intention of what is understood in this does not remain foregrounded against our own intention."[4] This comment may initially appear obscure because Gadamer is compressing together three distinct points. First, he does not wish to imply that every statement or piece of subject matter presupposes some *single* question. It derives part of its meaning from a dialogical chain of questions and answers that shape and condition how it *"arises."* Second, the process of understanding concerns not one question or even one set of questions, but those from an earlier context in which the statement or subject matter arose *as well as* questions that emerge from within *present* horizons of understanding. These are questions that readers or interpreters *bring with them.* Third, these two horizons of understanding (the earlier context and the present context) serve *to modify each other* as they begin to merge to form a single, *larger* horizon which *moves beyond* the initial round of questions and questioning.

This complex process shapes the *flow* or *movement* that characterizes an ongoing engagement with understanding of (and in due course also appropriation of) the subject matter. Gadamer explains elsewhere in his work, "The horizon of the present cannot be formed without the past," and *"understanding is always the fusion of these two horizons supposedly existing by themselves"* (his italics).[5] But *"fusion"* of horizons denotes only one aspect of the process and is *never complete.* For "distance" must not be "covered up" in "a naïve assimilation of the two."[6] It is simply the case that in the dawning of understanding and in the process of appropriation, a horizon moves and expands as the reader or interpreter advances. Gadamer notes, "Horizons change for a person who is moving. Thus the horizon of the past . . . is always in motion."[7] This forms part of Gadamer's perception of the historical situatedness of each stage or aspect of this dialogical and dialectical process.[8] It

2. Gadamer, *Truth,* 341-69.

3. Gadamer, *Truth,* 315 (his italics); cf. 307-41.

4. Gadamer, *Truth,* 374.

5. Gadamer, *Truth,* 306.

6. Gadamer, *Truth,* 306.

7. Gadamer, *Truth,* 304.

8. I have discussed this further in Anthony C. Thiselton, "The Significance of Recent Research on 1 Corinthians for Hermeneutical Appropriation of the Epistle Today," *Neot.* 40:2 (2006) 91-123.

thus "transforms *problems* back into *questions that arise,* and that *derive from their motivation*" (my italics).[9] Gadamer ascribes the model of engaging with free-floating "problems" not to Aristotle, but to Kant. Problems, for Kant, become abstractions divorced from the situations that gave them birth, and they exist "like stars in the sky."[10] They are fixed, self-grounded, and unmoving. This, Gadamer concludes, is the paradigm of timeless, unhistorical rationalism, which cannot be sustained in the light of "hermeneutical experience."[11]

How, then, might all this relate to Christian doctrine? One recent study of doctrine serves to illustrate some of the issues by providing a positive, if brief, model. Justo L. González's recent work has the effect of demonstrating the strengths of a more hermeneutical approach to Christian doctrine than many other works.[12] He argues, for example, that the Christian doctrine of creation did not arise initially from asking questions about the origins of the world, but from gratitude for human life and existence set within the beauty of the world; from human awareness of finitude, creatureliness, and dependence upon God; and from a desire to celebrate God's goodness for his gifts and for the goodness of the world.[13] These questions and this agenda also recognize the role of stewardship of the earth accorded to God's people, and engage in worship of the one God of both creation and salvation. González concludes, "In short, the Christian doctrine of creation, like most doctrines, did not emerge originally from intellectual puzzlement, but rather from the experience of worship."[14] The creation of the sun, the moon, and the heavenly bodies in the Genesis account served to exclude notions among Israel's neighbors that the celestial bodies were divine.[15] "My help comes from the Lord, who made heaven and earth" (Ps. 121:2) celebrates the God of creation as the God of salvation. González writes, "Creation is not so much about the beginning of things as it is about their meaning."[16]

Admittedly we should not carry this too far. Bultmann is arguably guilty of this. In my earlier study of Bultmann's hermeneutics I stressed that while an emphasis upon creation as expressing human finitude, dependence upon God, and self-involving stewardship and accountability remains valid and constructive, the cognitive truth-claim that God performed an act of creation as Ground and Originator of all that is, cannot be reduced to a mere existential attitude of self-

---

9. Gadamer, *Truth,* 377.

10. Gadamer, *Truth,* 377.

11. Gadamer, *Truth,* 377.

12. Justo L. González, *A Concise History of Christian Doctrine* (Edinburgh: Alban, 2006 and Nashville: Abingdon, 2005).

13. González, *History,* 35-44.

14. González, *History,* 38.

15. González, *History,* 42. On the Babylonian background cf. Bruce Vawter, *On Genesis: A New Reading* (New York: Doubleday, 1977), 38-63, on this esp. 46-50.

16. González, *History,* 49.

awareness or self-understanding, without remainder.[17] In Barth's classic comment, "If God is the Lord of existence . . . our existence is sustained by Him . . . alone, above the abyss of non-existence."[18] God's lordship over "the abyss" (Hebrew תהום, *t*ᵉ*hôm*) occurs not only in Gen. 1:2 but also in Pss. 33:6-7 and 148:7-8. Here the context is that of celebrating God's lordship over all creation. This applies no less to God's lordship over *nothingness, waste, confusion,* or *chaos* (Hebrew תהו, *tōhû* — Gen. 1:2, of creation; Deut. 32:10, of protection and sustaining providence; Isa. 34:11, of destruction and non-being).

González expounds the Christian doctrine of being human and humanness along similarly hermeneutical lines. In contrast to many nineteenth-century systematic theologies, he writes concerning the earliest Christians, "Christians were not particularly concerned . . . about whether a human being is composed of body and soul, as some held, or of body, soul, and spirit or mind, as others . . . thought."[19] Charles Hodge begins his section "The Nature of Man: Scripture Doctrine" with the observation that the Scriptures "assume . . . that the soul is a substance . . . and that there are two, and not more than two, essential elements in the constitution of man."[20] Some of the biblical passages cited in support of this might not readily bear close contextual scrutiny from many biblical scholars today.[21] Hodge is not alone in this. Augustus Hopkins Strong includes a section on "The Dichotomous Thesis" and "The Trichotomous Theory."[22] Laidlaw's *The Bible Doctrine of Man* spends an inordinate proportion of time on trichotomy, dichotomy, and Hebrew "physiology," even if he is more alert than Hodge and Strong to examples of Hebrew poetic parallelism and other literary features.[23] Even several biblical specialists make relatively heavy weather out of such psychological terms as *heart* (לב, *lēbh*), *liver* (כבד, *kābhēdh*), *kidneys* (כליות, *k*ᵉ*lāyôth*), and *bowels* (מעים, *mē*ᶜ*îm*) than a more careful hermeneutic might suggest. Wheeler Robinson insists that these terms are used in a *non*metaphorical sense (his italics), to denote centers of consciousness.[24]

Such explorations are not entirely misguided. Much may be gained from examining the specific and varied meanings of *flesh* (Greek σάρξ, *sarx*) and *body*

17. Anthony C. Thiselton, *The Two Horizons: New Testament Hermeneutics and Philosophical Description* (Grand Rapids: Eerdmans and Exeter: Paternoster, 1980), 252-92.

18. Karl Barth, *Church Dogmatics*, I:1, trans. G. W. Bromiley (Edinburgh: T&T Clark, 1975) sect. 10, 389; cf. 384-90, from Karl Barth, *Church Dogmatics*, ed. G. W. Bromiley and T. F. Torrance, 14 vols. (Edinburgh: T&T Clark, 1957-75).

19. González, *History*, 91.

20. Charles Hodge, *Systematic Theology*, 3 vols. (New York: Scribner, 1871), vol. 2, 43.

21. For example, the use of Dan. 7:15.

22. A. H. Strong, *Systematic Theology*, 3 vols. (1907; repr. London: Pickering & Inglis, 1965), vol. 2, 483-88.

23. John Laidlaw, *The Bible Doctrine of Man* (Edinburgh: T&T Clark, 1895), 49-138.

24. H. Wheeler Robinson, *The Christian Doctrine of Man* (Edinburgh: T&T Clark, 1911), 21; cf. 20-27.

(Greek σῶμα, *sōma*) as Paul uses these terms in his epistles. The issue is not that they feature at all, but whether some writers abstract such terms from the agenda and contexts from which they arose to treat them as virtually self-contained "problems." The motivations and settings from which they "arise" (Gadamer's term) remain decisive for how we shape our discussion. González rightly observes that the overriding motivation for inquiry into humanness among the earliest Christians *arose* from humans being "called to a particular sort of communion with God. . . . Humans have an intellect that allows them to understand the world around them. Humans have control over much of the world. Humans are qualitatively different from the rest of creation."[25] In terms of our human relationship with God, as we shall argue in these chapters, questions about being *body* "arise" not in the context of asking, "Of what are we made?" but in the context of asking, "How does Christian discipleship become credible and communicable in the public domain?" Similarly, reflection on divine creation and on human relations with the nonhuman orders of creation "arises" not by asking about remote origins; it "arises" in the context of human praise for the privilege of being created in the image of God and sharing as co-vice-regents in the ordering and stewardship of the world (Ps. 8:3-8; cf. Gen. 1:26-27; 9:6; also 2 Cor. 4:4; Col. 1:15; 3:10; Heb. 1:3).

Further hermeneutical horizons emerge, most certainly, as controversies, debates, and conflicts that often attend, or lead to, the development of doctrine. In some cases conflict may constitute an originating horizon, as is the case, for example, in the emergence of Paul's doctrine of the Lord's Supper or Eucharist in 1 Cor. 11:17-34 and 10:14-22. These Pauline recitals of pre-Pauline tradition and Pauline theology served to correct misunderstandings and inappropriate practices in Corinth. Alister McGrath observes that potential conflict within the earliest biblical sources gave rise to "the inevitability of doctrine."[26] González shows with convincing clarity how, for example, Augustine's *Confessions,* written for the most part as "a hymn celebrating God's grace that brought him to salvation," embodies the statements and doctrines that provoked Pelagius into vigorous doctrinal controversy and polemic.[27]

Terrence Tilley goes further in reassessing the status of Augustine's language concerning divine grace and human fallenness. At this particular point Tilley formulates, in effect, a hermeneutics of doctrine. He writes, "The understanding of Augustine as a theodicist is mistaken."[28] *The City of God,* he argues, is often cited as part of Augustine's theodicy; but this is misleading. He comments, "The problematic is not the plausibility of theism, but a *hermeneutic of*

---

25. González, *History,* 94-95.

26. Alister E. McGrath, *The Genesis of Doctrine* (Oxford: Blackwell, 1990), 4.

27. González, *History,* 99-100.

28. Terrence W. Tilley, *The Evils of Theodicy* (Washington, D.C.: Georgetown University Press, 1991), 115.

history."[29] The *Confessions* are also frequently cited as "theodicy," but this work, Tilley continues, constitutes a *speech-act of confession, praise, and celebration of grace*. Only the *Enchiridion* counts strictly as a "defense" as such, although Tilley regards it as "an institutionally bound assertive, an instruction. It was not shaped by the needs of polemic or apology or ecclesial politics, but by the needs of a Christian for . . . guidance."[30] The speech-act of *"instruction,"* Tilley insists, is not to be confused with that of *"argument."*[31]

The Enlightenment and post-Enlightenment philosophical discussion of grace, or equally of the problem of evil, transposed Augustine's varied writings into the formulation of an abstract, generalized, theological doctrine. But "theodicies do not respond to complaints or laments. They are not addressed to people who sin and suffer. They are addressed to abstract individual intellects who hear purely theoretical problems. . . ."[32] This, in another context, is Gadamer's point. The paradigm of addressing "problems," fixed and abstracted "like stars in the sky," is different from that of a *hermeneutical dialectic* of question and answer. The latter explores motivation, context, particularity, and effects in life. González and Tilley provide two examples (among other possible instances) of what a hermeneutic of doctrine might begin to look like and perhaps to achieve.

1.2. Christian Confessions and Their Life-Contexts: From the New Testament to the End of the Second Century

Evidence about the nature of creeds, confessions, and earliest Christian doctrine suggests a remarkable convergence of understanding of doctrine with philosophical accounts of the "dispositional" dimension of belief. We shall argue that on the basis of participation in a common narrative this applies equally to communal expressions of doctrine. It seems astonishing that virtually no serious engagement with dispositional accounts of belief has taken place to facilitate our understanding of doctrinal development and of the relation between doctrine, life, and action. We shall explore dispositional accounts of belief in the next chapter, especially with reference to the later thought of Wittgenstein and to H. H. Price's systematic discussion of the subject.

First, however, we briefly explore the broad contours of confessions of faith and the emergence of doctrinal forms within the New Testament. Two of my former doctoral candidates have produced constructive published work on hymnic

---

29. Tilley, *Theodicy,* 228, my italics.
30. Tilley, *Theodicy,* 117.
31. Tilley, *Theodicy,* 121, my italics.
32. Tilley, *Theodicy,* 229.

and confessional forms in the New Testament, namely Stephen E. Fowl (Ph.D., Sheffield) and Richard S. Briggs (Ph.D., Nottingham).[33] Fowl pays particular attention to Phil. 2:6-11, Col. 1:15-20, and 1 Tim. 3:16b, arguing that in each case we must distinguish between hymnic or confessional *forms* and their uses or *functions.* This distinction, more widely, is central to Wittgenstein's approach to language. The three passages, Fowl writes, "are not used to present pictures of Christ for their own sake . . . as Christological definitions to be mastered. . . ."[34] In other words, they are not theoretical or *"freestanding"* expressions of Christological doctrine. They are "used" to initiate and to nurture appropriate *ethical attitudes and action,* primarily through the formal vehicle of doctrinal *narrative.* They operate with "practical force."[35]

Richard Briggs examines confessions of faith in Rom. 10:8-9, 1 Cor. 12:1-3, 15:3-5, Phil. 2:5-11, Heb. 4:15, and elsewhere. He draws particularly on the research of Oscar Cullmann, Vernon Neufeld, J. T. Sanders, Stephen Fowl, and Dietmar Neufeld's important work on the speech-acts of confessions in 1 John.[36] Briggs underlines the practical, participatory, first-person nature of these confessions of faith. He writes, "It is the self-involving nature of confession that is most significant. Confessions are strong illocutions with commissive force but which are also declarative. . . . They typically include a commitment to a certain definable content: 'Jesus is Lord' or 'Jesus is the Christ'. Credal forms in the New Testament are indications of . . . self-involvement."[37] Briggs rightly perceives that speech-acts, far from excluding cognitive truth-claims about states of affairs, *presuppose* such truth-claims. Those who perceive speech-acts as *excluding* propositional truth-claims impose "a false polarization" onto the debate. In the end, Briggs concludes, Alan Richardson (a distinguished predecessor who held my Nottingham Chair) is correct: "It is the business of Christian doctrine to interpret . . . facts. The Apostles' Creed, for example, strongly insists upon the historical facts."[38] All the same, creeds and confessions of faith are *also self-involving speech-acts.* I have strongly urged the same point over a number of years in a variety of my publications.[39]

One of the earlier modern studies (i.e., over the last half-century) on confes-

---

33. Stephen E. Fowl, *The Story of Christ in the Ethics of Paul: An Analysis of the Function of the Hymnic Material in the Pauline Corpus,* JSNTSS 36 (Sheffield: Sheffield Academic Press, 1990); and Richard S. Briggs, *Words in Action: Speech-Act Theory and Biblical Interpretation, Toward a Hermeneutic of Self-Involvement* (Edinburgh and New York: T&T Clark, 2001).

34. Fowl, *Story,* 197.

35. Fowl, *Story,* 201.

36. Briggs, *Words in Action,* 183-215.

37. Briggs, *Words in Action,* 214-15.

38. Alan Richardson, *Creeds in the Making: A Short Introduction to the History of Christian Doctrine* (London: SCM, 1935), 7 and 9.

39. Most of these are now collected in Thiselton, *Thiselton on Hermeneutics* (Aldershot, U.K.: Ashgate and Grand Rapids: Eerdmans, 2006), 51-149, spanning from 1970 to today.

sions and creeds in the New Testament is that of Oscar Cullmann, alongside the early first edition of J. N. D. Kelly's classic study *Early Christian Creeds*.[40] Cullmann first asks why the early Christians needed a common apostolic formula or summary of the faith, and then inquires what circumstances brought this need into being.[41] On the first issue, an apostolic "rule of faith" served to maintain coherence, integrity, and, in effect, Christian identity. On the second issue, Cullmann refuses to give undue privilege to my *single* cause, but suggests "five simultaneous causes," namely *baptism* and instruction through catechism; *worship*, including both liturgy and preaching; *exorcism*; situations of *persecution*; and *polemic* against heretics or unbelievers.[42] His allusion to baptism is corroborated in the New Testament when Philip's question to the Ethiopian official invites the baptismal confession: "I believe that Jesus Christ is the Son of God" (Acts 8:36-38). Ephesians, which largely expounds the theme of the one church, includes the confessional acclamation, "One Lord, one faith, one baptism, one God and Father of all, who is above all, and through all, and in all" (4:5-6). After the close of the New Testament the link with baptism also appears readily in Justin, Irenaeus, and other early sources.[43] By the third century a series of baptismal questions had been formulated to which the responses began a development that culminated in the Apostles' Creed. Cullmann alludes (as Kelly does) to the earlier observations of Seeberg in this context.[44]

Cullmann cites 1 Cor. 15:3-7 and Phil. 2:5-11 as examples of confessions evoked in the context of worship and preaching. This may apply in part, but we shall note that Stephen Fowl draws a contrast between form and function here. His claims about settings of exorcism may also remain only at the level of probability, although it is plausible to see these occasions as inviting the use of fixed formulae. The confession of Christ's total lordship (Phil. 3:10) would indeed be relevant to the situation, and by the time of Justin (c. 150) confessional formulations are in evidence on such an occasion: "to subjugate the demons in the name of the Son of God, the first-born of all creation, who was born of a Virgin, made man and suffered, crucified under Pontius Pilate, was dead, rose from the dead, and ascended into heaven."[45]

On the setting of possible threat or persecution, Cullmann is on firmer ground. He writes (with many others), "It is possible that the formula *Kyrios*

---

40. Oscar Cullmann, *The Earliest Christian Confessions*, trans. J. K. S. Reid (London: Lutterworth, 1949, from the French, 1943). Kelly published the first edition in 1950 and a second edition in 1960. We shall consider his work when we look at his expanded third edition of 1972.

41. Cullmann, *Confessions*, 8-34.

42. Cullmann, *Confessions*, 18; elaborated in 19-34.

43. Irenaeus, *Against Heresies* I:9:4; Justin, *1 Apology* 61.

44. A. Seeberg, *Der Katechismus der Urchristenheit* (Leipzig, 1903; repr. Munich: Kaiser, 1966).

45. Justin, *Dialogue with Trypho* 85:2; cf. also 76:6.

Christos was first fashioned in time of persecution and in opposition to the *Kyrios Kaisar*."[46] Hugh Williamson and others have endorsed and expounded this aspect.[47] We shall return to Cullmann's "causes" in due course. They cohere very closely, for the purposes of our argument, with claims about the "dispositional" dimension of belief and corporate doctrine, which we consider in the next chapter.

A more recent study by Larry Hurtado very broadly confirms Cullmann's identification of a variety of settings for these early Christian confessions. Hurtado discusses: "(1) hymnic practices; (2) prayer and related practices; (3) uses of the name of Christ; (4) confession of faith in Jesus; and (6) prophetic pronouncements of the risen Christ."[48] Hurtado also acknowledges that some scholars ascribe devotion to Christ to a later date, but offers a thorough discussion of the issues in the light of multiple New Testament passages.[49] As he notes, Arthur Wainwright also addressed this issue convincingly.[50]

It is worth pausing for a moment to look more closely at the confession "Jesus is Lord" (1 Cor. 12:3), which is widely understood as in effect the earliest Christian creed or mark of Christian identity. In my larger commentary on the Greek text of 1 Corinthians I alluded to Bousset's *Kyrios Christos*, and commented, "The best that can be drawn from Bousset's work is the proper recognition, shared by form criticism and by speech-act theory, that *'Jesus is Lord'* is no mere 'floating' fragment of descriptive statement or abstract proposition, but is a spoken act of personal devotion and commitment which is part and parcel of Christ-centred worship and life-style. . . . Further . . . Paul bases his argument on the premise of a shared tradition."[51] If, as Scott urges, this confession is "the one audible profession of faith which Paul requires for a would-be Christian, the only and sufficient condition for participating in salvation (Rom 10:9)," then clearly this confession of faith constitutes more than a theoretical and intellectual belief.[52] Kramer calls it "an acclamation" often "proclaimed with a shout" as a self-

46. Cullmann, *Confessions*, 27-28.

47. Hugh Williamson, *The Lord Is King: A Personal Rediscovery* (Nottingham: Crossway, 1993).

48. Larry W. Hurtado, *One God, One Lord: Early Christian Devotion and Ancient Jewish Monotheism* (London and New York: T&T Clark, 2d edn. 1998), 100. See further Larry W. Hurtado, *Lord Jesus Christ: Devotion to Jesus in Earliest Christianity* (Grand Rapids: Eerdmans, 2005).

49. Hurtado, *One God*, 101-13; and *Lord Jesus Christ* throughout.

50. Arthur W. Wainwright, *The Trinity in the New Testament* (London: S.P.C.K., 1962), 93-104.

51. Anthony C. Thiselton, *The First Epistle to the Corinthians: A Commentary on the Greek Text*, NIGTC (Grand Rapids: Eerdmans and Carlisle: Paternoster, 2000), 926; cf. Wilhelm Bousset, *Kyrios Christos: A History of the Belief in Christ from the Beginnings of Christianity to Irenaeus*, trans. J. E. Steely (Nashville: Abingdon, 1970), esp. 132-33.

52. C. A. Anderson Scott, *Christianity according to St. Paul* (Cambridge: Cambridge University Press, 1927), 250.

involving utterance.[53] Neufeld captures the first-person force of self-involving, commissive speech-acts. He writes that they are "personal declarations of faith."[54]

The confession "Jesus is Lord" performs multiple functions, of which two are especially important. One function is that of nailing one's colors to the mast as a self-involving act of Christian identity and commitment. Thus Weiss observes that what the confession means "in a practical sense will best be made clear through the correlative concept of servant or slave of Christ."[55] To "belong" to Jesus as Lord or to be under his care and responsibility, Bultmann points out, is a great assertion and celebration of freedom. The Christian, he writes, "lets this care go, yielding himself entirely to the grace of God" (Rom. 14:7-8).[56] All the same, the other function is to declare a belief that a state of affairs is the case. Bultmann neglects this dimension. Jesus is rightful Lord because God raised him from the dead and exalted him as Lord (Rom. 1:3-4; Phil. 2:5-11).

Neufeld, whose work we are about to consider, rightly underlines these complementary modes of discourse. A self-involving speech-act often depends for its efficacy on certain states of affairs being the case, or certain statements being true. A hermeneutics of doctrine constantly needs to keep in view the relation between the formative or self-involving and doctrinal truth-claims. The presupposition of many transformative speech-acts derives from common apostolic tradition and its truth-claims in the New Testament and the early church.[57]

Vernon Neufeld published a constructive treatment of this subject in 1963, under the same title as that used by Cullmann. He points out that earlier studies of confessions and creeds focus on their content, date, and authenticity rather than on their function and settings in life.[58] Neufeld explored the nature of the Greek terms for confession — ὁμολογία (homologia, noun) and ὁμολογεῖν (homologein, verb) — and their relation to μαρτυρεῖν (marturein) and other terms in this semantic field.[59] He then explores examples of confessions in Judaism, Paul, the Gospel and Epistles of John, and the Synoptic Gospels and Acts. The life-situations of the homologia in Paul, he concludes, concern worship, bap-

---

53. Werner Kramer, *Christ, Lord, Son of God* (London: SCM, 1966), 66-67.

54. Vernon H. Neufeld, *The Earliest Christian Confessions*, NTTS 5 (Leiden: Brill and Grand Rapids: Eerdmans, 1963), 144.

55. Johannes Weiss, *Earliest Christianity* (earlier English title, *History of Primitive Christianity*), Eng. ed. F. C. Grant, 2 vols. (New York: Harper, 1959), 2, 458.

56. Rudolf Bultmann, *Theology of the New Testament*, trans. K. Grobel, 2 vols. (London: SCM, 1952 and 1955), vol. 1, 331.

57. See further A. Eriksson, *Traditions as Rhetorical Proof: Pauline Argumentation in 1 Corinthians* (Stockholm: Almqvist & Wiksell, 1998) and Hans von Campenhausen, "Das Bekenntnis im Urchristentum," *ZNW* 63 (1972) 210-53.

58. Neufeld, *Christian Confessions*, 1-7.

59. Neufeld, *Christian Confessions*, 13-33.

tism, and preaching, as a part of the daily life of the Christian community, but from time to time also persecution, and the need to counter disruptive forces that distort or otherwise threaten the gospel or in effect the integrity of Christian identity.[60] Such passages as Rom. 10:9, 1 Cor. 15:3-5, Phil. 2:5-11, and 1 Cor. 8:6 and 12:3 play their part in showing this. The setting of 1 John more distinctly witnesses to the impact of "false prophets" and "antichrists" (1 John 4:1-3).

This research, no less than Cullmann's, paves the way for an understanding of a dispositional account of belief, as I shall argue. Neufeld also underlines the self-involving character of first-person utterances of confession. Confessions *declare a content*, but they *also* serve *to nail the speaker's colors to the mast* as an act of first-person testimony and commitment.

Kelly's third edition of his classic work on early Christian creeds appeared in 1972.[61] He begins by calling attention to the undervaluing of creeds and confessions, and scepticism about their place within the New Testament on the part of classical liberal writers in the last quarter of the nineteenth century and up to around 1914. This era was dominated by Adolf von Harnack (1851-1930) and likeminded liberal writers. Harnack believed that the teaching of Jesus revolved around only a few simple "core" truths, in particular that God was a loving Father, that humankind should live as brothers, and that the human "soul" was of infinite value.[62] He ascribed the strongest force for the genesis and development of doctrine to the process of "hellenizing" the simple gospel. This process allegedly imposed a metaphysical frame upon the simple ethical teaching of Jesus. Earlier Albrecht Ritschl (1822-89) had paved the way for this climate by a liberal interpretation of the gospel largely in terms of a community of believers motivated not by doctrines but by the higher ethics of Jesus.[63]

Kelly cites the research of Seeberg as a notable but neglected exception to this account of creeds and confessions in the New Testament, and also cites the work of Charles H. Dodd in this context with approval.[64] He convincingly argues that Harnack's contrast between a Spirit-led, dynamic, spontaneous Christian fellowship and an ordered institutional church is overdrawn. He writes, "It is impossible to overlook the emphasis on the transmission of authoritative doctrine which is to be found everywhere in the New Testament."[65] Other writers make

---

60. Neufeld, *Christian Confessions*, 61; cf. 60-68.

61. J. N. D. Kelly, *Early Christian Creeds* (London: Longman, 3d edn. 1972).

62. Adolf von Harnack, *What Is Christianity?* trans. T. B. Saunders (London: Ernest Benn, 5th edn. 1958), 54-59 and 200-210. The German title was *Das Wesen des Christentums* (1st edn. 1900).

63. On Ritschl's influence see James Richmond, *Ritschl: A Reappraisal* (London: Collins, 1978), 13-45 and 266-314.

64. Charles H. Dodd, *The Apostolic Preaching and Its Developments* (London: Hodder & Stoughton, 2d edn. 1944).

65. Kelly, *Creeds*, 8.

similar points.[66] Today, as James Dunn urged in 1998, "There is a substantial consensus on the use of preformed material" in the Pauline epistles.[67] Following Hunter, Neufeld, Wengst, and others, Dunn includes among his examples of "kerygmatic and confessional formulae": Rom. 1:3-4; 3:25; 4:24-25; 5:6, 8; 7:4; 8:11, 32; 10:9; 1 Cor. 6:14; 8:6, 11; 11:23; 12:3; 15:3-7; 2 Cor. 4:14; 5:14-15; Gal. 1:1; 4:5; Eph. 4:5; Phil. 2:5-11; Col. 2:6, 12; 1 Thess. 1:10; 4:14; 5:10; 1 Tim. 1:15; 2:6; 4:8-9; 2 Tim. 2:11; Tit. 3:5-8.[68] These include confessions of Christ and of his death and resurrection, and confessional formulae conveying apostolic traditions and ethical catechesis.

It may appear that this broader discussion of confessions in the New Testament and early second century has distracted us from pursuing the path indicated by Cullmann, Briggs, and Neufeld about confession as first-person, self-involving speech-acts called forth by specific settings or situations that prepare us to appreciate the logic of dispositional accounts of belief. In fact, Kelly's work also prepares us for a later discussion of how self-involving, formative expressions of belief or doctrine relate, in turn, to more systematic, descriptive truth-claims about states of affairs. Kelly rightly cites those passages that speak in more descriptive terms of "the faith once delivered to the saints" (Jude 3), and of "healthy doctrine" (2 Tim. 4:3; Tit. 1:9).[69] However, he also reviews the question of situational settings, dissenting from Cullmann only on whether Cullmann gives too much speculative attention to "baptismal" settings, and whether he is too cautious in recognizing very early Trinitarian formulations.[70] He underlines the settings of catechesis, preaching, polemic, and liturgy.[71] Kelly rightly observes that too many scholars are "mesmerized by the evolutionary maxim that the less complex must always precede the more complex, and there must be a line of progressive development."[72] He also calls attention to the use of narrative in the earliest confessions.

We come finally to Dietmar Neufeld's excellent and constructive study of New Testament research into confessional formulae, and especially of their place

66. Frederick W. Danker, *Creeds in the Bible* (St. Louis: Concordia, 1966), throughout; William A. Curtis, *A History of Creeds and Confessions of Faith in Christendom and Beyond* (Edinburgh: T&T Clark, 1911), 34-43; and Ethelbert Stauffer, *New Testament Theology,* trans. John Marsh (New York and London: Macmillan, 1955), 235-54; John Burnaby, *The Belief of Christendom: A Commentary on the Nicene Creed* (London: S.P.C.K., 1959), 1-10.

67. James D. G. Dunn, *The Theology of Paul the Apostle* (Edinburgh: T&T Clark and Grand Rapids: Eerdmans, 1998), 174, n. 66.

68. Dunn, *Paul,* 174-77; see K. Wengst, *Christologische Formeln und Lieder des Urchristentums* (Gütersloh: Gütersloher, 1972); and A. M. Hunter, *Paul and His Predecessors* (London: SCM, 2d edn. 1961). Cf. further Neufeld, *Confessions,* and Kramer, *Christ.*

69. Kelly, *Creeds,* 8-10; he cites further 2 Thess. 2:15; Heb. 3:1; 4:14; 10:23.

70. Kelly, *Creeds,* 13 and 26-29.

71. Kelly, *Creeds,* 13-23 and 30-99.

72. Kelly, *Creeds,* 27.

and function in 1 John.[73] Neufeld examines the passages in question "from the perspective of a modified version of J. L. Austin's speech-act theory," and includes language of confession and denial in relation to Christ (1 John 2:22-23, 26; 4:1-4, 16; 5:6); warnings about antichrists (2:18-22); and the so-called "boast" and "denial" slogans (1:6, 8, 10; 2:4, 6, 9; 4:20).[74] He concludes that texts exercise "power *to transform* the readers' *expectations, speech and conduct.*"[75] These speech-acts also imply and presuppose "the writer's perception, description, commitment and belief in what he has written. He bears witness to Jesus Christ."[76] The confessions of faiths are performative and participatory, again like nailing one's colors to the mast.

This understanding of first-person confessions in the New Testament leads with clear continuity to declarations of a "rule of faith" in subapostolic and early Patristic writings. Ignatius of Antioch (c. A.D. 104) makes a series of first-person belief-utterances declaring in what "I place my hopes" in a series of narrative affirmations. Ignatius declares, "Jesus Christ, who was of the family of David, and of Mary, who was truly born [Greek ἀληθῶς ἐγγενήθη], both ate and drank, and was truly persecuted under Pontius Pilate, was truly crucified and died [Greek ἀληθῶς ἐσταυρώθη καὶ ἀπέθανεν] in the sight of those in heaven and on earth and under the earth; who also was raised from the dead, when his Father raised him up, as . . . his Father shall raise up in Christ Jesus us who believe in him."[77] The context or setting of this particular example is clear. He adds that there are unbelievers who claim that "his [Christ's] suffering was a semblance" (Greek τὸ δοκεῖν, from which we derive *docetic*), but "it is they [who] are merely a semblance."[78] The notion that the denial of a belief may generate a personal expression of the belief is part and parcel of the dispositional view that we shall explore very shortly in Chapter 2.

Polycarp (c. 69-155) witnesses implicitly, although not with an explicit formula of confession, to the use of confessions of faith in situations of persecution, or, in Polycarp's case, imminent martyrdom (probably in February 155). He foresees his martyrdom and is joyfully ready for it. He is brought before the Proconsul, and asked, "What harm is there in saying 'Lord Caesar' (or 'Caesar is Lord')?" The Proconsul urges him to deny Christ, but Polycarp replies, "For eighty-six years have I served Christ, and he never did me wrong. How, then, can I blaspheme my King and my Saviour?" After increasing abuse, during which Polycarp asks why they still wait, the Proconsul's herald cries, "Polycarp has confessed that

---

73. Dietmar Neufeld, *Reconceiving Texts as Speech Acts: An Analysis of 1 John*, Biblical Interpretation Monograph Series 7 (Leiden and New York: Brill, 1994).

74. Neufeld, *Reconceiving Texts*, 3 and 82-132.

75. Neufeld, *Reconceiving Texts*, 133 (my italics).

76. Neufeld, *Reconceiving Texts*, 76.

77. Ignatius, *Epistle to the Trallians* 9:1-2 (Loeb Library edn., London: Heinemann, 1912).

78. Ignatius, *Epistle to the Trallians* 10:1.

he is a Christian."[79] This is not strictly a doctrinal formulation, but demonstrates well typical settings for the "dispositional" expression of belief (as explained in the next chapter).

Irenaeus (c. 130–c. 200) declares and formulates several instances of confessional forms or doctrinal creeds in his treatise *Against Heresies* (c. 190). In Book I, mainly against Valentinian gnosticism, he declares, "The church . . . has received from the apostles and their disciples this faith: 'in one God, the Father Almighty, Maker of heaven and earth . . . and in one Christ Jesus, our Lord, . . . our Lord and God and Saviour and King [to whom] every knee should bow . . . and every tongue confess . . . that he should execute last judgment towards all.'"[80] Irenaeus is addressing the concrete situation of the threat of gnostic belief, against which he affirms an early formulation of the Christian creed. He also addresses the potential disruption of the unity of the church.

In Book III he addresses more specifically the basis of Christian doctrine in Scripture and places a more explicit emphasis upon the public transmission of tradition in the church in contrast to the esoteric, inner, or "private" traditions among the gnostics. (This relates, too, to Wittgenstein's view of belief as a disposition with public currency rather than an "inner" or "private" mental state). We carefully preserve this public tradition, he writes, "believing in one God, the Creator of heaven and earth . . . by means of Christ Jesus the Son of God . . . who condescended to be born of the Virgin . . . suffered under Pontius Pilate, rising again, and having been received up in splendour, shall come in glory . . . the Judge of those who are judged."[81]

Confessions of faith in the "one God, Creator of heaven and earth," function not only to exclude polytheistic beliefs, but also to exclude two other systems of belief: to exclude a Marcionite distinction of identity between the God or demiurge of creation and God the Father of Jesus Christ, and to reject a gnostic disparagement of the earthly. God created both heaven and earth as good gifts. Thus in Book IV, where he addresses the errors of Marcion, Irenaeus includes a confession of faith that correlates the work of Father, Son, and Holy Spirit, not least in relation to creation: "Full faith in one God Almighty, of whom are all things, and in the Son of God, Jesus Christ our Lord, by whom are all things . . . and a firm belief in the Spirit of God . . . who dwells [Greek σκηνοβατοῦν] with every generation of humankind."[82] Other shorter confessions in Irenaeus underline the authenticity of public apostolic traditions.[83]

---

79. *Martyrdom of Polycarp* 8–11.

80. Irenaeus, *Against Heresies* I:10:1. Cf. Edward R. Hardy, "Introduction to Irenaeus' *Against Heresies*," in Cyril C. Richardson (ed.), *Early Christian Fathers*, Library of Christian Classics (London: SCM, 1953), 343-57.

81. Irenaeus, *Against Heresies* III:4:2.

82. Irenaeus, *Against Heresies* IV:33:7.

83. Irenaeus, *Against Heresies* V:20:1.

Clement of Alexandria (c. 150-215) is less concerned than Irenaeus about a rule of faith and apostolic tradition. His brief inclusion of a short summary narrative creed or confession in *The Stromata* serves more readily to define a communal Christian identity than to exclude anyone with different beliefs. When people hear of "him who made the universe, assumed flesh, and was conceived in the Virgin's womb . . . and subsequently, as was the case, suffered on the cross and rose again," some may perceive this as folly (1 Cor. 1:18), but others may see it as a parable of the truth.[84]

Tertullian (c. 160–c. 225) returns to the approach of Irenaeus and explicitly uses the phrase "the rule of faith" to denote an apostolic confession of faith or "catholic" creed. His *Prescription against Heretics (De praescriptione haereticorum)* attacks belief-systems that differ from the apostolic doctrine of the one true church, transmitted through public tradition guarded by its bishops. Tertullian perceives the situation behind his explicit formulation of a communal creed or confession as the need to counter both a Marcionite separation between the God of creation and the God of salvation, the Father of Jesus Christ, and equally gnostic docetism and dualism with its disparagement of the body and bodily life as unspiritual. Once again the form is that of narrative, narrative-drama, or narrative-plot. Tertullian declares, "There is only one God, and he is the Creator of the world, who produced all things out of nothing through his own word. . . . His word is called his Son . . . brought down by the Spirit and power of the Father into the Virgin Mary, and was made flesh in her womb. . . . Having been crucified, he rose again the third day, and ascended into heaven; he sat at the right hand of the Father; sent instead of himself the power of the Holy Spirit to lead such as believe; he will come with glory to take the saints to the enjoyment of everlasting life . . . after the resurrection. . . ."[85]

In the same treatise Tertullian celebrates the universal or catholic faith of the whole church, and clearly underlines *the communal nature of Christian doctrine*. He names Corinth in Achaia; Philippi and Thessalonica in Macedonia; Ephesus in Asia; Rome in Italy; "and [our] churches in Africa," and then declares that all as one "acknowledge one Lord God, the Creator of the universe, Jesus Christ [born] of the Virgin Mary, the Son of God the Creator; and the resurrection of the flesh."[86] This confession "unites the writings of the evangelists [the Gospels] and the apostles [the epistles], from which she [the universal church] drinks in her faith."[87]

The development of doctrine proceeds further in *Against Praxeas*. Here Tertullian not only expounds a Trinitarian formula (as arguably already occurs

---

84. Clement, *Stromata* VI:15.
85. Tertullian, *On Prescription against Heretics,* ch. 13.
86. Tertullian, *Against Heretics,* ch. 36.
87. Tertullian, *Against Heretics,* ch. 36.

in such passages as Matt. 28:19, 1 Cor. 12:4-6, 2 Cor. 13:13, and elsewhere), but also, anticipating later developments, attempts to offer a more precise account of intra-Trinitarian relations on the basis of Scripture and apostolic tradition. He writes, "We believe that there is one only God . . . that this one only God has also a Son, his Word, who proceeded from himself, by whom all things were made [i.e., the Son was not created as a creature]; we believe him to have been sent into the Virgin Mary, and to have been born of her — being both man and God . . . we believe him to have suffered, died, and been buried, according to the scriptures, and after he had been raised again by the Father and taken back into heaven, to be sitting at the right hand of the Father, and that he will come again to judge the living and the dead. He sent from heaven from the Father according to his prom-ise the Holy Spirit, the Paraclete, the sanctifier of the faith of those who believe in the Father, and in the Son, and in the Holy Spirit. This rule of faith has come down to us from the beginning of the gospel."[88]

With the writings of Clement of Alexandria and Tertullian we reach the end of the second century. After this, the first "systematic theology" emerges with Origen (c. 185-254). In 2.3 we shall return to this early era of the late first century and the second century, but in Chapter 2 we shall explore examples in the light specifically of a dispositional account of belief. We shall endeavour not to repeat the same instances of early doctrinal formulations, and to cite only what serves the argument of the second chapter. We have said enough, however, to lay down the starting points of our argument as a whole, and we turn next to dispositional accounts of belief.

---

88. Tertullian, *Against Praxeas*, ch. 2.

CHAPTER 2

Dispositional Accounts of Belief

2.1. Mental States and Dispositional Belief in Wittgenstein, and Belief in First John

The clearest and most systematic exposition of a dispositional account of belief comes from the philosopher H. H. Price.[1] Traditional accounts of belief, Price observes, tend to construe belief as an "occurrence," almost as a mental event. On the other hand, more recent approaches perceive belief as a "disposition." Price writes, "When we say of someone, 'he believes the proposition', it is held that we are making a dispositional statement about him, and that is equivalent to a series of conditional statements describing what he *would* be likely to say or do or feel if such and such circumstances were to arise. For example, *he would assert the proposition* (aloud or privately to himself) *if he heard someone else denying it* or expressing doubt of it. . . . If circumstances were to arise *in which it made a practical difference* whether *p* was true or false, he would *act as if it were true.* If *p* were falsified he would be surprised, and he would feel no surprise if it were verified."[2]

Before we pursue Price's argument in detail, two corollaries may serve to clarify the nature of this claim. The first is a positive point, which is also made in a broader context by Wittgenstein. It concerns the logical asymmetry of *first-person* utterances of belief ("I believe," "we believe") and *third-person* utterances ("he or she believes"). Wittgenstein, Price, and Dallas High make much of this logical asymmetry, or grammatical difference. The second point is more negative. On the basis of the traditional "mental occurrence" approach, how could we explain, for example, why we should *not* say of people who lose consciousness or

---

1. H. H. Price, *Belief,* Muirhead Library of Philosophy (London: Allen & Unwin and New York: Humanities, 1969).
2. Price, *Belief,* 20 (my italics).

fall asleep, "Now they have ceased to believe." Wittgenstein suggests that belief does not have genuine, specifiable duration, in the sense of an action that could be timed. It is more illuminating to ask what counts as a criterion of believing, or "what are the consequences of this belief, where it takes us."[3]

First-person utterances of the form "I believe" do not, it appears, simply, or more accurately and in most cases, primarily, denote an inner mental state or process. Wittgenstein explores the logic or "grammar" of the first-person utterance "We mourn our . . ." in a funeral oration. He remarks, "This is surely supposed to be an expression of mourning, not to tell anything to those who are present."[4] Similarly, in saying "I believe," he continues, "My own relation to my words is wholly different from other people's."[5] "Believing . . . is a kind of disposition of the believing person."[6] He observes, "If there were a verb meaning 'to believe falsely', it would not have any significant first person present indicative."[7] In other words, the utterance is inextricably *embodied* in patterns of *habit, commitment, and action,* which constitute endorsement, "backing," or "surroundings" for the utterance. Its logical grammar *cannot* (in the logical sense of *cannot*) be theoretical.

The second point emerges from Wittgenstein's observations in his *Zettel.* He writes, "One hardly ever says that one has believed . . . 'uninterruptedly' since yesterday. An interruption of belief would be a period of unbelief, not, e.g., the withdrawal of attention from what one believes, e.g., sleep."[8]

Price comments on the relation between the two points under discussion, "The difference between first-person and third-person belief-sentences is of considerable philosophical importance. . . . 'I believe that p' (still more . . . 'I believe in X') . . . is not usually giving us a piece of autobiographical information. . . . [The speaker] is expressing an attitude. . . . Sometimes he is taking a stand in the face of a hostile or sceptical audience."[9] The utterance, Price continues, has what J. L. Austin calls a "performatory" character.[10] Often "we are inviting our hearers to accept what we believe. . . . We are conveying to them . . . that they will be *justified* in accepting it" (Price's italics).[11] The utterance has "a guarantee-giving character."[12] Degrees of guarantee may be implicit in such a scale or spectrum as "I believe," "I think," "I suspect," "I rather think. . . ." Since the speaker is not

---

3. Wittgenstein, *Investigations,* sect. 578; see also sects. 571-94.

4. Wittgenstein, *Investigations,* II:ix, 189e.

5. Wittgenstein, *Investigations,* II:x, 192e.

6. Wittgenstein, *Investigations,* II:x, 191e.

7. Wittgenstein, *Investigations,* II:x, 190e.

8. Ludwig Wittgenstein, *Zettel,* ed. and trans. G. E. M. Anscombe and G. H. von Wright (German and English, Oxford: Blackwell, 1967), sect. 85.

9. Price, *Belief,* 29.

10. Price, *Belief,* 30.

11. Price, *Belief,* 30.

12. Price, *Belief,* 31.

seeking to describe an inner mental state *as such,* it would not make sense to claim that he or she has ceased to believe when they fall asleep.

Clearly all of this coheres closely with the examples of settings-in-life identified by Cullmann, Vernon Neufeld, Dietmar Neufeld, and others. Indeed, this New Testament research would have shown that in these settings we may best understand *believing* as a *disposition to respond* to situations both by expressing and by "standing behind" belief-utterances in *situations that challenge belief,* or that demand *action appropriate to belief.* If a Christian believer nails his or her colors to the mast in situations of persecution, hostile criticism, pledging oneself in baptism, liturgical doxology and declaration, kerygmatic proclamation, or the need to correct error, these are precisely the moments when the disposition to respond becomes *explicit, active, and public.* Conversely, if a believer remains silent in situations that do *not* necessarily call for explicit expressions of belief in the public domain, this would not necessarily imply unbelief.

Belief, then, is *action-orientated, situation-related,* and embedded in the *particularities and contingencies* of everyday living. Wittgenstein would call this relationship between belief, life, and action one of "internal" grammar. *Action, contingency, particularity,* and the *public world of embodied life* constitute part of the very grammar of what it is to *believe.* In the chapters that follow I argue that these features stand at the heart of a *hermeneutic* of doctrine. For hermeneutics is concerned with particularity and embodied life, as well as with a distinct dimension of coherence and with expanding horizons of understanding.

This starting point now invites further exploration in two directions. First, a dispositional account of belief relates closely to Wittgenstein's distinctive approach to questions about *"the inner"* and "inner states." He explicitly rejects the accusation that he is a behaviorist, and we, too, need to resist any suggestion that this approach reduces belief almost to the status of a causal mechanism akin to a conditioned reflex. The reverse is the case. To perceive the role of *habit and "training" or tradition* in belief is to enhance the moral and volitional dimension by relating it to the *formation of character.* We discuss positively the claims of Balthasar, Vanhoozer, and Samuel Wells on doctrine as drama in relation to training and performance in 4.2 and 4.3, and further in Chapter 5.

The second set of issues concerns the relation of a dispositional account of belief to *communal* doctrine rather than only to *individual* belief. In the course of a valid critique of *individual-centered* epistemology, Richard Heyduck, for one, perceives much of the modern Western shift to individualism to derive from redefining "doctrine . . . as 'beliefs.'"[13] I argue that "doctrine" must retain its epistemological status as necessarily embodying truth-claims that invite and indeed deserve belief, but on the other side I agree with Heyduck that doctrine also carries with it inextricably a *communal commitment* and *communal formation.*

---

13. Heyduck, *Recovery,* 18.

Hence we ask in Chapters 3 and 4 how a dispositional approach to belief applies to Christian doctrine as a communal phenomenon.

Wittgenstein's exposition of *belief* and *believing* is bound up with his attack on "private" language.[14] The heart of this argument is that language about "inner states," including language about pain and about sensations, cannot derive its currency merely from "private" introspection or "private" memory. Such language acquires working currency only in the context of intersubjective commonalities of regularized language uses together with their "backing" and anchorage in observable patterns of action in the public domain. In this respect the two distinct sets of issues that I have just outlined (i.e., the rejection of a *"behaviorist"* or stimulus-response account of belief, and the application of a dispositional account of belief to *communal* doctrine) closely converge in Wittgenstein's philosophical thought on private language.

A simile, image, or analogy may sometimes serve to clarify a difficult and complex concept, provided that it is valid and not overdrawn. Hence it may be helpful to introduce the "private language argument" with reference initially to Wittgenstein's simile of "the beetle in the box." He writes:

> Someone tells me that *he* knows what pain [or other sensations, perhaps belief] is only from his own case! — Suppose everyone had a box with something in it: we call it a "beetle." No one can look into anyone else's box, and everyone says he knows what a beetle is only by looking at *his* beetle. — Here it would be quite possible for everyone to have something different in his box. . . . But suppose the word "beetle" had a use in these people's language? If so, it would not be used as the name of a thing. The thing in the box has no place in the language-game at all; not even as a *something;* for the box might even be empty. No, one can "divide through" by the thing in the box; it cancels out, whatever it is. That is to say: if we construe the grammar of the expression of sensations [or the expression of belief] on the model of "object and designation," the object drops out of consideration as irrelevant.[15]

14. The main discussion in the *Philosophical Investigation* begins at sect. 243 and continues through to at least sect. 317, although the topic reappears elsewhere and in other works of Wittgenstein. There are a number of specialist discussions of this subject. We cannot list all of them, but see especially Paul Johnston, *Wittgenstein: Rethinking the Inner* (London and New York: Routledge, 1993); Saul A. Kripke, *Wittgenstein on Rules and Private Language* (Oxford: Blackwell, 1982, which takes a different view from that of Johnston); Fergus Kerr, *Theology after Wittgenstein* (Oxford: Blackwell, 1986), 77-100; O. R. Jones (ed.), *The Private Language Argument* (London: Macmillan, 1971), containing essays by P. F. Strawson, 3-42 and 127-53; Norman Malcolm, 45-81 and 215-26; and others; Rush Rhees, *Discussions of Wittgenstein* (London: Routledge and Kegan Paul, 1970), 55-70; Cyril Barrett, *Wittgenstein on Ethics and Religious Belief* (Oxford: Blackwell, 1991), 111-208; and Oswald Hanfling, Wittgenstein's Later Philosophy (London: Macmillan, 1989), 88-151.

15. Wittgenstein, *Investigations,* sect. 293 (his italics).

"Private language" is "unteachable" language because it does not yet have a "currency" in the public, intersubjective world. Its illusory paradigm is "I know . . . only from my *own* case."[16] Wittgenstein exclaims, "Imagine someone saying: 'But I know how tall I am!' and laying his hand on top of his head to prove it."[17] It is "as if someone were to buy several copies of the morning paper to assure himself that what it said was true."[18] It is like turning a knob that we think is part of a machine, but in actuality "it is a mere ornament, not connected with the mechanism at all."[19] The problem applies to even more than language and concepts. In several of his later works Wittgenstein declares, "If you go about to observe your mental happenings, you may alter them and create new ones, and this whole point of observing is that you should not do this."[20]

Wittgenstein's negative observations about inner states, together with the model of object and designation, and "incommunicable" or "private" language, lead to positive comments about the language of feeling, attitudes, or dispositions as internally "embedded" in the public, intersubjective world of action. He asks, "Why can't my right hand give my left hand money?"[21] My right hand can place bank notes or coins in my left hand; and my left hand can write a receipt and place it in my right hand. But this cannot *amount to* a "gift," for *giving* presupposes *action* between agents within an *intersubjective* world. Language about certain "inner" states depends for its currency on certain criteria derived from a person's behavior.[22] Wittgenstein anticipates a counterreply that he firmly rejects: "Are you not really a behaviorist in disguise? Aren't you at bottom really saying that everything except human behavior is a fiction?"[23] Wittgenstein does *not* claim that mental processes do not exist: "It looks as if we had denied mental processes. And naturally we don't want to deny them."[24] His concern is for "a particular way of looking at the matter"; to avoid buzzing around in conceptual confusion and perplexity by showing "the fly the way out of the fly-bottle."[25]

Although Wittgenstein's private language argument has often been controversial in some quarters, and although much of his other philosophical thought remains so, Paul Johnston rightly observes, "The one area of Wittgenstein's work which is still in some measure accepted is the so-called private language argu-

---

16. Wittgenstein, *Investigations,* sect. 295 (his italics).

17. Wittgenstein, *Investigations,* sect. 279.

18. Wittgenstein, *Investigations,* sect. 265.

19. Wittgenstein, *Investigations,* sect. 270.

20. Ludwig Wittgenstein, *Wittgenstein's Lectures on Philosophical Psychology, 1946-47* (Hemel Hempstead, U.K.: Harvester Wheatsheaf, 1988); cf. also Ludwig Wittgenstein, *Remarks on the Philosophy of Psychology,* vol. 1 (Oxford: Blackwell, 1980), sect. 643.

21. Wittgenstein, *Investigations,* sect. 268.

22. Wittgenstein, *Investigations,* sect. 269.

23. Wittgenstein, *Investigations,* sect. 307.

24. Wittgenstein, *Investigations,* sect. 308.

25. Wittgenstein, *Investigations,* sects. 308 and 309.

ment."[26] "The private linguist's case rests on the possibility of a private ostensive definition, or ostensive function."[27] As Wittgenstein notes, here "a great deal of stage-setting in the language is presupposed."[28] The key point on which most philosophers of language agree is the importance of a *practice in the public world.* Wittgenstein often calls this "following a rule," in contrast to supposed individual-centered subjective justification, without appeal to anything that is independent of this.[29]

We shall move in 2.2 from Wittgenstein's observations to Price's more systematic discussion. But meanwhile we may note how readily Wittgenstein's contrast between the logical grammar of pain or sensations and that of *believing,* and equally *loving,* pave the way for understanding more readily the dispositional character of these qualities or attitudes and their "internal" relations to life and life-settings especially as these emerge in the First Epistle of John. Wittgenstein's observations place us in the same universe of discourse as that inhabited at times by this epistle.

Wittgenstein writes in the *Zettel,* "Love is not feeling. Love is put to the test, pain not. One does not say, 'That was not true pain, or it would not have gone off so quickly.'"[30] On the other hand, as he observes in the *Investigations,* "Could someone have a feeling of ardent love or hope for the space of one second — *no matter what* preceded or followed this second? . . . (A smiling mouth *smiles* only in a human face)."[31] The "surroundings," Wittgenstein comments, give this language its importance, its logical grammar, and its working currency.

Although Gilbert Ryle, rather than Wittgenstein, introduced the technical term *"avowal"* into modern philosophy, writers often translate *Äusserung* or *Ausdruck* in Wittgenstein (expression, manifestation, or utterance) as *avowal* in contexts of first-person utterances or gestures. Smiling, frowning, raising an eyebrow, grimacing, shaking a fist, having trembling hands, or weeping may express emotions, attitudes, belief or disbelief, pain or joy, no less effectively than, or in place of, verbal utterances.[32] But few would be likely to claim that these avowals through gesture or facial expression are primarily *reports* of mental processes, rather than expressive communicative *actions.* We teach young chil-

---

26. Johnston, *Wittgenstein,* ix.

27. Johnston, *Wittgenstein,* 19.

28. Wittgenstein, *Investigations,* sect. 257.

29. Cf. Johnston, *Wittgenstein,* 20-21. See further O. R. Jones (ed.), *Private Language;* and for a different view from Johnston's, Kripke, *Wittgenstein on Rules and Private Language,* esp. 55-113.

30. Wittgenstein, *Zettel,* sect. 504.

31. Wittgenstein, *Investigations,* sect. 583; cf. *Zettel,* 53-68.

32. Wittgenstein, *Investigations,* II, 187-89; Ludwig Wittgenstein, *Remarks on the Philosophy of Psychology,* ed. G. E. M. Anscombe, G. H. von Wright, and H. Nyman, trans. A. E. M. Anscombe, C. G. Luckhardt, and M. A. E. Aue, 2 vols. (Oxford: Blackwell, 1980), vol. 1, sects. 633 and 693.

dren progressively to replace tears, screams, shouts, or throwing food onto the floor, by more appropriate linguistic behavior. Uses of language come to replace visual or acoustic actions by linguistic action. The focus, however, remains on *action*.

Much of the First Epistle of John addresses the relation between belief-claims and action, or patterns of behavior. But more is at stake than a merely laying down of moralizing warnings against hypocrisy or insincerity. John is helping his readers to understand *what counts as* genuine belief, or *what is at stake in* making belief-utterances. John says more than "if we *say* that we believe or that we love, our actions must match our words." This would transpose John's First Epistle into a simple Victorian moralizing tract. Wittgenstein's simile of actions "surrounding" a belief-utterance or a love-utterance resonates with the deeper understanding of Christian belief and how it relates to the discipleship that John seeks to convey. Dietmar Neufeld comments, "The cluster of merging antitheses dynamically depicts two contrasting spheres [or, in Wittgenstein's language, two sets of 'surroundings']. . . . In their confessing, denying, and believing, [readers] make plain to which sphere they belong."[33] Hence John writes, "Those who say, 'I love God', and hate their brothers or sisters [meaning here *fellow Christians*] are liars, for those who do not love a brother or sister whom they have seen, cannot love God whom they have not seen" (4:20). Here *"cannot"* is a *logical* cannot, not an *empirical* cannot. Vernon Neufeld takes up the contrastive terms "confess" (Greek ὁμολογεῖν, *homologein*) and "deny" (Greek ἀρνεῖσθαι, *arneisthai*). These operate together antithetically to formulate the "grammatical" axiom: "No one who denies the Son has the Father; everyone who confesses the Son has also the Father" (2:23).[34]

A relation with God the Father contributes to the "surroundings" that give currency to claims to *believe* in the Son: "If we say that we have fellowship with him while we are walking in darkness, *we lie* and do not *do* what is true" (1 John 1:6). Why should this be understood as a *"grammatical"* or logical utterance about *belief and action?* This is apparent because God is "in the light," and to "walk in the light" reflects and derives from walking with God (1 John 1:2).

This approach also sheds light on the logic of the otherwise notoriously problematic declaration: "No one who abides in him sins" (1 John 3:6), as well as the parallel, "We know that those who are born of God do not sin" (5:18). These cannot be empirical statements about "facts"; for the writer has stated, "If we say that we have no sin, we deceive ourselves" (1 John 1:8). It is a *grammatical* axiom that to declare settled belief in Christ, or that we "abide" in Christ, can retain no working currency if the speaker habitually and deliberately chooses the path of sin and alienation from God. How could both make sense at the same

---

33. Neufeld, *Reconceiving Texts*, 132.
34. Neufeld, *Confessions*, 70-71.

time?[35] It is not, then, a piece of mere moralizing when the writer declares, "Let us love, not in word or speech, but in truth and action" (3:18). *Action* provides criteria for the sense, credibility, and working currency here of the utterance "I love you." As Wittgenstein, we noted, observes, "Could someone have a feeling of ardent love . . . for the space of one second — no matter what preceded or followed this second?"[36]

The background or "surroundings" against which John writes is one of deceit, self-deceit, and the use of utterances that have no currency: "Do not believe every spirit, but test the spirits to see whether they are from God" (4:1). The confession "Jesus Christ has come in the flesh" derives from, and presupposes, the presence and action of God and the Spirit of God (4:2). In this sense John writes, "Everyone who believes that Jesus is the Christ has been born of God, and everyone who loves the parent loves the child" (5:1). All of this, John concludes, raises questions about "understanding," first-person testimony, and the currency of truth (5:20; cf. 5:9). Wittgenstein's perspective, then, appears to cohere with what we might have gleaned on other grounds. I urged this in *The Two Horizons* (as long ago as 1980) when I argued that "expecting" the *parousia* amounted to both an attitude or stance and public behavior in life, rather than having certain mental states.

I argued further that patterns of regularity observable in the public domain identified God as "the Father of Abraham, Isaac, and Jacob," "backed" the linguistic currency with patterned or "rule governed" grammar.[37] This is *not*, however, to adopt "Wittgenstein's" view of theology as a whole. Robert Knowles has shown conclusively that my approach is my own, not Wittgenstein's.[38] My approach is "Wittgensteinian" only strictly to the extent that I draw explicitly on Wittgenstein's observations concerning certain belief-utterances and a hermeneutical approach to language, meaning, and understanding. Nothing could be less "Wittgensteinian" or more indigestible than to try to swallow Wittgenstein whole. Fergus Kerr remarks, "The great question remains: why do we retreat from our world; why do we withdraw from the body . . . ? This is the hidden theological agenda of Wittgenstein's later writings."[39]

---

35. See Stephen S. Smalley, *1, 2, 3 John*, WBC (Waco, TX: Word, 1984), 21. Smalley imagines the person who makes illusory, self-deceptive claims to belief responding, "Sin does not affect me," as the man's counterclaims to John's series of declarations.

36. Wittgenstein, *Investigations*, sect. 583.

37. Anthony C. Thiselton, *The Two Horizons: New Testament Hermeneutics and Philosophical Description* (Grand Rapids: Eerdmans and Exeter: Paternoster, 1980), 379-85 and 422-27.

38. Robert Knowles, *The Grammar of Hermeneutics: Anthony C. Thiselton and His Search for a Unified Theory* (Aldershot, U.K.: Ashgate, 2007, in the press).

39. Fergus Kerr, *Theology after Wittgenstein* (Oxford: Blackwell, 1986), 147.

2.2. Dispositional Accounts of Belief in H. H. Price, and "Half-belief" in Jonah

We noted above H. H. Price's succinct definition of a dispositional account of belief. It is equivalent to "a series of conditional statements describing what [a believer] would be likely to say or do or feel if such and such circumstances were to arise. For example, he would assert the proposition . . . if he heard someone denying it. . . . He would act as if it [the belief] were true. . . . A belief shows itself or manifests itself in various sorts of occurrences."[40] Price underlines the "practical consequences" of belief and of expressions of belief. Like Wittgenstein, he also stresses the self-involving and action-related character of belief-utterances. Indeed, when a speaker declares a belief (using a verb in the first-person singular or plural), such an utterance belongs to the class identified by J. L. Austin as speech-acts, performatives, or illocutionary acts. It is the nature of first-person belief-utterances that in various ways they indicate and initiate a speaker's "taking a stand." The speaker actually does this in and through the utterance.[41]

Austin defines a "performative" utterance, unsurprisingly, as "the performing of an action."[42] But the issues are more complex than this. Austin writes, "An 'illocutionary' act" denotes "performance of an act *in saying something as opposed to performance of* an act of saying something."[43] The latter he designates "perlocutions," which, together with locutions and illocutions, are indicators of force, not of meaning.[44] Austin's work is too well known to require detailed exposition here. Numerous rehearsals and treatments of Austin's approach now abound. Our main concern in this chapter is to underline the action-related character of first-person belief-utterances, although we should not lose sight of Austin's careful but often neglected stipulations about their presupposed relation to certain states of affairs as being the case, and to some specified necessary conditions in given situations for their operative function.[45]

Price takes up this performative perspective. He points out that first-person belief-utterances remain self-involving speech-actions whether the belief is hesitant and reluctant (as when a speaker might say, "I rather believe that . . ."), or whether it is firmly confident, or directed to a trustworthy person or agent (as when a speaker might say, "I believe in . . ."). Price examines a variety of different situations in which belief may take many forms. For example, a person may in certain circumstances "take a stand" for a period of weeks, months, or years, and

---

40. Price, *Belief,* 20.

41. Price, *Belief,* 33.

42. John L. Austin, *How to Do Things with Words,* ed. J. O. Urmson (Oxford: Clarendon, 1962), 6-7.

43. Austin, *Things with Words,* 99.

44. Austin, *Things with Words,* 100-119.

45. Austin, *Things with Words,* 14-66.

then, after rethinking the grounds for belief, or the grounds for a counterbelief, may come to declare, "I no longer believe it," even with regret. In some situations, Price suggests, the point of saying "I believe" is not necessarily to declare a high degree of certainty, for "if one is completely sure that *p* (Price reminds us), one normally says just 'p.'"[46] "God exists" may in some contexts seem stronger than "I believe that God exists." But "I believe" may serve in certain contexts to indicate not only the truth of an assertion ("God exists"), but also *the speaker's personal endorsement of it, as one who "takes a stand."*

Doctrinal declarations often follow this pattern: "We believe in God . . ." indicates a personal or communal pledge on the part of a community; it is an illocutionary act of corporate testimony, as well as the recital of a narrative that the believer or believing community believes to be true. As Vernon Neufeld argues, and as we noted in the previous chapter, early Christian confessions of faith carried both a performative dimension of personal pledge, like nailing one's colors to the mast, and a claim to assert cognitive truth.

Price identifies one example of "dispositional" belief that may seem surprising. Is it possible to believe a proposition *without realizing that we believe it?* A belief may be dormant or buried in the subconscious until a new set of circumstances confronts us that brings it out, to self-awareness. Following F. P. Ramsey, Price suggests that to believe a proposition may be to add it to our stock of premises. It is available as a premise for our inferences, often alongside other premises. As Wittgenstein reminds us in *On Certainty*, such premises may lie unnoticed, as if "removed from traffic, . . . so to speak, shunted onto an unused siding. . . . It has belonged to the scaffolding of thoughts. (Every human being has parents)."[47] But it still "gets its meaning from the rest of our proceedings."[48] Price argues that the test of a "real" belief, in contrast to what we may merely claim to believe, lies not in whether such a belief lies consciously in the mind, but in the course of action, or in the habituated actions, which proceed from the belief. For example, suppose that someone says that he or she believes that no one can do a good day's work unless they have had a good night's sleep. If they stay up playing Bridge until 1:30 a.m., knowing that they have an important and heavy day following, and they do this regularly, what is the status of their claim to hold this belief? Price writes, "We do quite often judge a man's beliefs — his *real* beliefs as opposed to his professed ones — by observing the way he acts" (his italics).[49]

I suggest that in the development of Christian doctrine expressions of belief in the deity of the Holy Spirit and of the Holy Spirit's place within the Trinity emerged in such ways as have been outlined, although a fuller discussion is re-

---

46. Price, *Belief,* 36.
47. Wittgenstein, *On Certainty,* sects. 211 and 212.
48. Wittgenstein, *On Certainty,* sect. 229.
49. Price, *Belief,* 256; cf. 250-57.

served for 2.3 and Part III. In 18.3 we ask whether Origen, Athanasius, and Basil are examples of this process. Origen (c. 185-254) acted on the basis of a number of contributory factors that served as consciousness-raising markers on the way to a formulation of his "real" beliefs about the Holy Spirit. To offer praise and glory to the Spirit as a *liturgical act* would be idolatrous if the Spirit were a mere creature, part of God's created order. Hence Origen formulates the explicit belief that the Spirit is neither "born" nor "created." The Spirit is "ungenerated" (Greek ἀγέννητον, *agennēton*).[50] Origen seeks the guidance and wisdom of the Holy Spirit in reading Scripture, for he believes that the Spirit inspires the Scriptures and prompts prayer (Rom. 8:15).[51] Coherent action proves the authenticity of belief that becomes explicit through cumulative reflection, reaching the explicit belief that is implicit in Paul, that the Holy Spirit is co-worker in the co-operative and united work of the Trinity.[52]

The dispositional nature of belief can be seen more clearly in Athanasius and Basil.[53] In his *Letters to Serapion* (A.D. 358-59) Athanasius finds it necessary *to respond to explicit claims that the Holy Spirit is no more than a creature* (Greek κτίσμα, *ktisma*). Here is a classic example of a disposition to respond in public ways when a belief is denied. Athanasius brings into the open a more explicit formulation of belief in the deity and personhood of the Holy Spirit than had emerged formally hitherto. "If he were a creature," Athanasius responds, the Spirit would not be ranked with the Triad (οὐ συνετάσσετο τῇ Τριαδι, *ou sunetasseto tē Triadi*). For the whole Triad is one God (ὅλη γὰρ θεός ἐστι, *holē gar theos esti*).[54]

Basil's treatise *On the Holy Spirit* (c. 373) is equally a public *response* to a belief that is incompatible with his, and with Christian doctrine, namely the explicit belief that the Spirit is merely a creature, and part of the created order. Basil expounds a more explicit formulation of belief than probably hitherto. He appeals to the habituated *Christian action* of using the doxology of the threefold *"Gloria."* He further invokes the explicit concept of the procession of the Spirit, which is arguably implicit in 1 Cor. 2:12, and asserts explicitly the status of the Spirit as "Lord," which is implicit in 2 Cor. 3:17.[55] *The circumstances of challenge*

50. Origen, *De Principiis* IV:1:8; Greek, J.-P. Migne (ed.), *Patrologia Graeca* (Paris, 1857-66), vol. 11, 357C. Cf. also Justin, *Dialogue* 5:4; Greek, Migne, *Patrologia Graeca*, vol. 6, 488B; and Irenaeus, *Against Heresies*, IV:28:1 (Migne, *Patrologia Graeca*, vol. 7, 1105A).

51. Origen, *De Principiis* I:3:2-3; *Commentary on John*, 2:10 (Migne, *Patrologia Graeca*, vol. 14, 125D).

52. Origen, *De Principiis* I:5:3-5; he cites esp. 1 Cor. 12:3-7.

53. Among many useful resources on this subject, see esp. Michael A. G. Haykin, *The Spirit of God: The Exegesis of 1 and 2 Corinthians in the Pneumatomachian Controversy of the Fourth Century*, Supplement to *Vigiliae Christianae* 27 (Leiden and New York: Brill, 1994), throughout.

54. Athanasius, *Letters* 1:7; Greek, Migne, *Patrologia Graeca*, vol. 26, 569C.

55. Basil, *On the Holy Spirit* 12; 28; 16:37; 24:56 (Greek, in Migne, *Patrologia Graeca*, vol. 32, 117 A-172 C); also *Against Eunomius* 1:14 and 3:6 (Migne, *Patrologia Graeca*, vol. 32, 544B and 664C).

and denial draw forth belief that had remained latent and implicit into explicit formulations and confessions of faith.

Price uses the term "disposition" to denote the reservoir of knowledge, understanding, or conviction upon which the believer draws to perform appropriate belief-utterances or action.[56] This may include knowledge of facts, as well as ways of perceiving and understanding persons or situations. I argue in a subsequent chapter that this embraces "explanation" *(Erklärung)* and "understanding" *(Verstehen)* in the traditions of hermeneutics. It may also draw on testimony, which in the case of Christian doctrine rests on apostolic testimony and the transmission of apostolic tradition. This dispositional reservoir becomes operative and *counts* when the believer risks *staking himself or herself* on it *by manifesting an appropriate stance and by performing appropriate utterances and habituated actions in the public domain.* In this context mere "mental states" alone remain more like the ornamental knobs that are not part of the operation (to borrow Wittgenstein's simile), rather than providing hard currency for the authenticity of claims to belief. In Wittgenstein's terminology, pointing only to an inner state would be like attempting to provide an ostensive definition "only in private."

Sometimes "believing in," Price continues, is like adding one's personal signature and endorsement or evaluation to "belief that." Often the former can be cashed out in terms of the latter, but with the addition of "attaching importance to" the belief in question.[57] Beliefs can be supported by knowledge and by other beliefs, in spite of Bultmann's attempt to privilege and to elevate "bare" belief above reasonable belief.[58] Pannenberg regards Bultmann's type of approach as little more than "credulous" belief, and Wolterstorff associates it with belief that is less than "reasonable," and may lack moral or intellectual "entitlement."[59] Whether belief may be justified (in terms of a dispositional approach) may depend on whether the series of conditional statements on the basis of which the believer may speak and act are probable, reasonable, or proven, or whether they are unfulfilled counterfactual conditionals.[60] Thus Price makes it clear that a dispositional analysis of belief neither bypasses nor excludes issues of epistemology (*pace* Heyduck). At the same time, he removes "belief" from the realm of the theoretical and abstract, and places it in the public domain of inter-subjective behavior and action.

Moreover, dispositions relate closely to habit and character. In Wittgenstein's language, they relate to "training." We shall return to this subject when we ex-

---

56. Price, *Belief,* 42-91.

57. Price, *Belief,* 76.

58. Price, *Belief,* 92-129.

59. Wolfhart Pannenberg, *Basic Questions in Theology,* vol. 2, trans. G. H. Kehm (London: SCM, 1971), 1-64; and Nicholas Wolterstorff, *John Locke and the Ethics of Belief* (Cambridge: Cambridge University Press, 1996); cf. Price, *Belief,* 112-29.

60. There are certain parallels here with Price's "acting as if" (*Belief,* 267-89).

plore doctrine as drama and the relation between Wittgenstein on training and Samuel Wells on habit and improvisation. Sometimes a belief that awaits vindication or corroboration may invite the virtues of patience and resolution. A person or community may *believe* that they are on the right road, but no road sign may have appeared for some considerable time. Yet he or she continues in hope that the belief will be corroborated. Clearly this has parallels with exhortation to remain in settled belief (especially in the Epistle to the Hebrews) until eschatological vindication is at hand.[61] Belief is not incompatible with pilgrimage. Price writes, "Our beliefs are like posts which we plant in the shifting sands of doubt and ignorance."[62]

Belief, finally, is a "multiform disposition, which is manifested or actualized in many different ways: not only in . . . actions . . . but also in emotional states such as hope and fear; in feelings of doubt, surprise and confidence . . . and in inferences . . . in which a belief 'spreads itself' from a proposition to some of its consequences."[63] In this sense "this 'inner life' does matter. . . . But after all, the miscellaneous character of belief-manifestations is one of the most interesting and important things about them." Price continues, "If 'A' holds some belief, many *different* sorts of happenings in A's history . . . are tied together or made explicable by the fact that he holds it" (Price's italics).[64]

The book of Jonah provides a striking example of such varied "manifestations" of dispositional belief and unbelief, including what Price calls "half-belief." Jonah actively seeks to flee "away from the presence of the LORD" (Jon. 1:3). But when the polytheistic sailors ask him, in effect, to give his testimony, he shifts key to an orthodox-belief mode. He declares, "I worship the LORD, the God of heaven, who made the sea and the dry land" (1:9). What does Jonah *believe*? If God is omnipresent, sovereign Creator, how can Jonah "flee" from God's presence by taking ship to a distant place? The narrative next finds him seeking to die: "Throw me into the sea!" (1:12). But as soon as he plummets into the depths of the sea, Jonah begins to pray in careful, rhythmic, Psalmic, liturgical Hebrew, "I called to the LORD out of my distress, and he answered me; out of the belly of Sheol I cried, and you heard my voice. . . . Then I said, 'I am driven away from your sight; how shall I look again upon your holy temple?'" (2:2-4). Jonah continues, "As my life was ebbing away, I remembered the LORD. . . . Deliverance belongs to the LORD" (2:7-9). With masterly timing the narrator drives in the satire: "And the fish spat out Jonah upon the dry land" (2:10). Jonah has *beliefs that operate in some circumstances but not in others.* Price does not allude to Jonah, but he describes as *"half-belief"* a belief that operates "on some occa-

---

61. Price, *Belief,* 293.
62. Price, *Belief,* 293.
63. Price, *Belief,* 294.
64. Price, *Belief,* 295-96.

sions" as that of a genuine believer but "on other occasions" hardly at all, or like the outlook of an unbeliever.[65]

However, neither the satirical narrative nor Jonah has yet finished. Jonah preaches to the city of Nineveh, as God had commissioned him to do, but when the city and its king repent in dust and ashes, "this was very displeasing to Jonah, and he became angry" (4:1). Now Jonah has let the cat out of the bag: He explains, "This is why I fled to Tarshish at the beginning; for I knew that you are a gracious God and merciful, slow to anger . . . and ready to relent" (4:2). Jonah then proceeds to sulk under the shade of a bush. With heavy irony the narrator declares, "God appointed a bush" (4:6), but then "God appointed a worm that attacked the bush, so that it withered" (4:7). When the sun is at its height, and beats down upon Jonah, he exclaims once again, "It is better for me to die than live" (4:8). Throughout the entire narrative what has most concerned and moved Jonah has been his personal dignity, comfort, and reputation. Jonah expresses extreme anger at the loss of the bush. But is he not a Hebrew believer, even a commissioned prophet? God responds: "Should not I be concerned about Nineveh, that great city, in which there are more than a hundred and twenty thousand persons . . . and many animals?" (4:11).[66]

Does Jonah "believe"? A dispositional analysis of his belief reveals him as a "half-believer." In some situations he is a believer, but only when it seems to suit him. In other circumstances he manifests behavior more suggestive of unbelief. A dispositional analysis of belief helps us to see what is going on more clearly than any narrative of his inner processes abstracted from his actions and public behavior. If belief were not manifested in overt action in the public domain, resting upon *a disposition to respond to varied situations in varied ways,* could this matchless satire on a pompous prophet's half-belief have operated so incisively?

As a postscript to this chapter we may note that Price is not alone in adopting a dispositional approach to belief, although his is the fullest and probably the most judicious discussion. Dallas M. High approaches issues about "life," conduct, and the public domain from the angle of a Wittgensteinian approach to belief-utterances.[67] In Part I of his book he offers a basic textbook approach to the later Wittgenstein's observations on meaning and use, language games, and forms of life. He then moves on to a more distinctive account of belief-utterances in his Part II.[68] He rehearses the main arguments that we have already noted. These include the logical asymmetry between first-person belief-utterances and third-person utterances ("I or we believe" in contrast to "he or she believes");

65. Price, *Belief,* 305; cf. 302-14.

66. On the use of satire in Jonah, see J. C. Holbert, "Deliverance Belongs to Yahweh: Satire in the Book of Jonah," *JSOT* 21 (1981) 59-81.

67. Dallas M. High, *Language, Persons and Belief: Studies in Wittgenstein's Philosophical Investigations and Religious Use of Language* (New York: Oxford University Press, 1967).

68. High, *Language,* 133-212.

belief-utterances as giving "personal backing" through public commitments and observable conduct; and the implausibility of viewing belief-utterances as mere reports of mental events. The upshot is that he has demonstrated, alongside Wittgenstein and Price, the dependence of belief-utterances *upon extralinguistic factors in "bodily" life.*[69]

In his more detailed two chapters on belief, High expounds an expression of "believing *in*" as primarily an "act of self-involvement." On the other hand, "believing *that*" is *also* an "act of tentative assertion," while it still entails a self-involving dimension.[70] High then examines the language of classical creeds (the Apostles' Creed and the Nicene Creed) as aphoristic expressions of basic Christian doctrine, and concludes that these, too, share in the logic of belief-utterances. They function as "logically extended" uses.[71] This prepares for our argument that communal belief may also be understood in dispositional terms. High judiciously observes that they *both* signal personal "backing" or taking a stand, *and* additionally make truth-claims, but *they are not exhausted by any single category of language function or observable public criteria so far identified.*

Although he does not explicitly engage with their status as communal doctrine in an explicitly theological manner, High is right to urge that such utterances "can never be exhaustive of myself or my self-involvement."[72] They have "groundedness" beyond the self or even the community. In various writings I have urged that while Bultmann is right to suggest that *the practical currency* of calling Christ "Lord" comes most clearly to view in the absolute trust and service rendered by the believer, *the ultimate ground* for Christ's lordship does not lie in anyone's subjective or intersubjective recognition of it, but in God's act of naming Christ Lord at the resurrection (Rom. 1:3-4).[73] High notes further that the concept "person" similarly finds currency in intersubjective experience and publicly observable phenomena, but that this does not lead to a behaviorist account of persons.[74]

High argues that the credal form "I believe in God . . ." leads us "to adopt a category of otherness"; an otherness best expressed, as Martin Buber might say, as the "special otherness of a 'vocative category.'"[75] He rightly insists, however, that the first-person performative status of "I believe" does not imply a fideistic notion of belief. This is "scandalous to ordinary canons of thinking."[76] Belief-

---

69. High, *Language*, 133-63.

70. High, *Language*, 165-72.

71. High, *Language*, 173.

72. High, *Language*, 170.

73. Anthony C. Thiselton, *Thiselton on Hermeneutics: Collected Writings with New Essays* (Grand Rapids: Eerdmans and Aldershot, U.K.: Ashgate, 2006), 51-150.

74. High, *Language*, 174.

75. High, *Language*, 183; cf. Martin Buber, *I and Thou*, trans. Ronald Gregor Smith (Edinburgh: T&T Clark, 1984, and various other editions).

76. High, *Language*, 186; also 187-201.

utterances remain, in Pannenberg's language, "debatable" as claims to truth, and a dispositional account of belief remains entirely compatible with "giving reasons for beliefs."[77] We return to this subject especially in Chapter 8. Meanwhile, as Price notes, and as we saw from the example of the narrative of Jonah, a dispositional approach to belief helps us to see when a person "really" believes. Christian doctrine is the communal endorsement and transmission of such belief, as expressed in life, worship, and action.

2.3. From the New Testament to Patristic Doctrine: Continuities of Dispositional Responses

Since at least the era of F. C. Baur writers have sought to drive a wedge between the proclamation of Jesus and Paul on one side, and the supposedly "early catholic," or more ecclesial, writings of the later New Testament documents and the subapostolic and early Patristic writings on the other. Adolf von Harnack (1851-1930) in particular viewed the development of Christian doctrine in the second century as a hellenization of the "simple" teaching of Jesus.

Jesus, according to Harnack, conveyed the simple teaching of the fatherhood of God, the brotherhood and sisterhood of humankind, and the infinite value of a human being.[78] He writes, "The preaching of Jesus Christ was in the main . . . plain and simple."[79] Paul, he conceded, remained faithfully "Christocentric," and expanded the teaching of Jesus to include in more detail the abolition of the law, monotheism, a hope for the future, and an exhortation to love others and to promote social welfare. But Christianity soon became "transformed." Harnack writes, "The decisive thing was the conversion of the Gospel into a doctrine, into an absolute philosophy of religion."[80] The threat of gnosticism, he argues, lay not in the gnostic systems themselves, but in the response that they provoked. He declared, "The Gnostic systems represent the acute secularizing or Hellenizing of Christianity."[81] The gnostics were "the theologians of the first century. They were the first to transform Christianity into a system of doctrine (dogmas)."[82] Harnack concludes, "The religion of the heart passes into the religion of custom. . . . The influx of Hellenism . . . form[s] the greatest fact . . . in the second century."[83]

---

77. High, *Language*, 201-12.

78. Adolf von Harnack, *What Is Christianity?* trans. T. B. Saunders (London: Ernest Benn, 5th edn. 1958), 54-59.

79. Adolf von Harnack, *History of Dogma*, trans. from the 3d German edn. by Neil Buchanan, 7 vols. (London: Williams & Norgate, 1897), vol. 1, 61.

80. Harnack, *History of Dogma*, vol. 1, 252.

81. Harnack, *History of Dogma*, vol. 1, 226.

82. Harnack, *History of Dogma*, vol. 1, 227.

83. Harnack, *What Is Christianity?* 145.

Harnack is a classic exponent of liberal antipathy to doctrine, and of an attempt to divorce the "living" or "simple" texts of Jesus from the beginnings of doctrine in the late first-century and second-century church. Apart from the Reformation, Harnack sees the history of Christian doctrine as largely (although not in every respect) a tragic development.[84] His most lasting impact, after the dust had settled, was to leave the impression that the earlier writers of the New Testament (including Luke-Acts, to which he assigns an early date) were of a different cast of mind from that of the Apostolic Fathers and the early Patristic theologians.

In the 1930s and 1940s Albert Schweitzer and Martin Werner widened this divorce between the two mind-sets by postulating a process of "deeschatologization." On one side Jesus and the Paul of the four major epistles maintained an eschatological approach; on the other side the later Paul or "Deutero-Paul" and John promoted the rise of "early Catholic doctrine." Jesus and Paul, Schweitzer urged, lived in the world of Jewish apocalyptic. "Paul did not Hellenize Christianity."[85] Nevertheless, Schweitzer continues, Paul *paved the way* for such hellenization, and soon "the Hellenization of Christianity took place unobserved."[86] A version of Christianity emerged from which eschatology has been emasculated. This was replaced by a doctrine of the presence of Christ mediated through the Holy Spirit and the sacraments. Such a doctrine now appears in Ignatius (*Epistle to the Ephesians* 11:1), Polycarp (*Epistle to the Philippians* 5:2), Papias (*Historia Ecclesiastica* 3:39) and Justin (*Dialogue with Trypho* 28:2).[87] A dual emphasis upon the Spirit and the sacraments supposedly also finds expression in the Johannine writings.[88]

Martin Werner's *The Formation of Christian Dogma* first appeared in German in 1941, expounding a "consistent-eschatological" approach to the subject.[89] He took as his starting point Schweitzer's assumption (repeated by Bultmann) that "in consequence of the delay of the Parousia a contradiction between the eschatological scheme [i.e., of Jesus] and the actual course of history began to be apparent."[90] The delay of the Parousia led to the "deeschatologization" of the Christian message. In place of eschatological expectation, urgency, and hope of a

---

84. Alister E. McGrath, *The Genesis of Doctrine: A Study in the Foundations of Doctrinal Criticism* (Oxford: Blackwell, 1990), 149, notes Harnack's comparison with "a chronic degenerative illness."

85. Schweitzer, *The Mysticism of Paul the Apostle*, trans. W. Montgomery (London: Black, 1931 [German, 1930]), 334.

86. Schweitzer, *Mysticism*, 336.

87. Schweitzer, *Mysticism*, 336-37; cf. 338-59.

88. Schweitzer, *Mysticism*, 359-75. Schweitzer cites John 3:22-26; 4:1-2; 6:47-60; 13:7-8, and 20:21-23, and presupposes a late date.

89. Martin Werner, *The Formation of Christian Dogma*, trans. S. G. Brandon (London: Black, 1945), 9ff.

90. Werner, *Formation*, 22.

new creation, a new doctrine took its place, namely that "Christianity preserves the world."[91] Heresy, Werner claims, "became for centuries a general phenomenon," in reaction to which Catholic doctrine was largely negative and arbitrary. Doctrine was no more than a series of reactions against a series of heresies.[92] Both sides no longer knew or understood the true Paul, but only "a new interpretation of the Paul who had become a problem."[93] This view finds resonances with Walter Bauer's influential *Orthodoxy and Heresy in Earliest Christianity*, which first appeared in 1934.[94] Bauer argues that "heresy" was far more widespread than is usually acknowledged, especially in Asia Minor, Edessa, and Egypt. "Orthodoxy" was more closely associated with Rome.

At one level the claims of Harnack, Schweitzer, and Werner could hardly stand up for lack of evidence. A number of writers have offered decisive critiques. Martin Hengel, among others, demonstrated that Judaism and Hellenism never existed in self-contained compartments.[95] Alister McGrath has shown how "modern values" control Harnack's assessments, together with his self-contradictory rejection of metaphysics while relying upon theories of truth that presupposed them.[96] H. E. W. Turner argues in detail that Werner's thesis "involves a radical recasting not only of the theology and experience of the early Church, but also of the New Testament itself."[97] Other such criticisms could be cited, but dealing with them is not the main purpose of this section of our argument.

The main point that I seek to make here is that a *dispositional account of belief sheds a different light on these issues.* The most damaging effect of the hypotheses floated by Harnack and Werner is that even when their theories have been called into question, the impression remains that the New Testament belongs to an entirely different world of thought from that of the Apostolic Fathers and the Patristic church. It is true that the *creativity* of the New Testament writings and the experience of hearing God speak through the text make them qualitatively different from some later literature. This is reflected retrospectively in the formation of the canon. But these are different factors from those identified by Harnack. They have to do with the unique witness of "the apostolic circle" to the

91. Werner, *Formation*, 43.

92. Werner, *Formation*, 48-52.

93. Werner, *Formation*, 55.

94. Walter Bauer, *Orthodoxy and Heresy in Earliest Christianity*, ed. Robert A. Kraft and Gerhard Krodel, with Appendices by George Strecker (London: S.C.M., 1972, and Philadelphia: Fortress, 1971).

95. Martin Hengel, *Judaism and Hellenism: Studies in Their Encounter in Palestine during the Early Hellenistic Period*, trans. John Bowden (London: SCM, 1974).

96. McGrath, *The Genesis of Doctrine*, 148; cf. 146-51.

97. H. E. W. Turner, *The Pattern of Christian Truth: A Study of the Relations between Orthodoxy and Heresy in the Early Church* (London: Mowbray, 1954), 22.

person and work of Jesus Christ. This is why the Christian church came *to recognize (not to create)* the distinctive status of the New Testament as a "canonical" plurality of voices over a period of *"reception."*

It is not true that the New Testament writings do not include doctrine. Nor is it true that the theological formulations of the early Church Fathers are "hellenized" abstractions or metaphysical speculations that have little in common with the New Testament. *An understanding of the dispositional nature of belief reveals an evident continuity between confessions of faith in the New Testament and formulations of belief in response to the later claims of "heretics,"* whether these are gnostics, Marcionites, or those who held docetic views of Jesus Christ. *A dispositional account of belief suggests that belief becomes articulated precisely when someone denies it, distorts it, or attacks it in the hearing of Christian believers.*

Werner's notion that Christian doctrine emerged "merely" as a series of denials of heresies simply reveals a misunderstanding of the nature of belief as it has been discussed in modern philosophical discourse. If the expression and communication of belief entailed reconceptualizations in more "Hellenistic" idioms from time to time, this is what this same philosophical analysis would predict as probable. It reveals a necessary hermeneutical concern *to communicate* belief in terms that the doubter, denier, or inquirer can most readily understand.

The problem of a "transition" from the New Testament to early Christian doctrine has become so ingrained into much (although not all) theological scholarship that not only liberal writers like Harnack, or more radical writers like Schweitzer and Werner, voice this "problem," but also more moderate or conservative writers show concern about it. Recently three such writers, I. Howard Marshall, Kevin Vanhoozer, and Stanley Porter jointly produced a work that bears the subtitle, "Moving from Scripture to Theology."[98] Marshall opens the discussion by underlining the importance of hermeneutics, although his first chapter seems to speak more about "application" than "doctrine."[99] His second chapter seeks to address how we approach "the question of the development of doctrine from Scripture."[100] In positive terms Marshall asserts, "There is development in doctrine throughout the Bible."[101] But while he acknowledges "incompleteness" in Scripture, his discussion does not engage at all with the subapostolic writings or with the early Patristic era.[102]

Marshall's more significant contribution to this subject comes from a different book, namely his *New Testament Theology,* especially in his work on

---

98. I. Howard Marshall, with Kevin J. Vanhoozer and Stanley E. Porter, *Beyond the Bible: Moving from Scripture to Theology* (Grand Rapids: Baker Academic, 2004).

99. Marshall, *Beyond the Bible,* 11-32.

100. Marshall, *Beyond the Bible,* 45; cf. 33-54.

101. Marshall, *Beyond the Bible,* 44-54; cf. 64.

102. Marshall, *Beyond the Bible,* 78; cf. 55-79.

method.[103] Theological construction, he notes, takes place in the New Testament. He endorses P. Balla's critique of H. Räisänen's claims that imply the contrary. Marshall rejects any divorce between New Testament studies and systematic theology, noting that in the New Testament "there are such things as creeds and confessions."[104]

Vanhoozer takes Marshall to task for suggesting that there is relatively little literature on the problem, and cites the work of David Kelsey, George Lindbeck, Alister McGrath, and others, all of whom feature in the present volume.[105] Nevertheless, Vanhoozer does not seem to give the impression that he would dissent from Porter's verdict that this entire area is "one of the most demanding intellectual tasks imaginable."[106] It would not be entirely unfair to sum up the book's discussion as arguing for the complexity, difficulty, and urgency of the task, but as also hesitating to venture into many of the actual nuts and bolts of the issues, at least with regard to the period of transition between the New Testament writings and the late second century. This is not a criticism; but it suggests that this issue cannot be tackled in the abstract. What we need are (1) a better and more comprehensive explanatory hypothesis for the phenomena in question (we identify this in these chapters as a dispositional account of belief), and (2) a more explicit comparison of formulations of doctrine in the Apostolic Fathers and earliest Patristic period with confessions of faith in the New Testament writings (which we anticipate very briefly in the last few pages of this chapter as an example, but explore in detail in Part III).

(1) With regard to *explanatory hypotheses and conceptual formations*, if belief is a *disposition to respond* in overt ways appropriate to a situation in which belief is denied or distorted, it need not surprise us that Clement of Rome and Ignatius should express formulations through the medium of epistles, that Justin formulates ideas as an *Apologia*, that Irenaeus should write five treatises under the title *Against Heresies*, or that Tertullian should write five treatises *Against Marcion* and treatises *Against Hermogenes*, *Against the Valentinians*, and *Against Praxeas*, as well as other works. It is a mistake to regard these as a series of merely negative reactions in the interests of power politics or a static status quo.

During the period from the subapostolic writings to Irenaeus and Tertullian, doctrine takes the form of a series of *dispositional responses* to new situations that concern precisely the areas of theology that are already the subjects of confessions of faith in Old and New Testament traditions, with no dominating disparity of *content*. Only in those less characteristic or *later* instances when faith be-

---

103. I. Howard Marshall, *New Testament Theology: Many Witnesses, One Gospel* (Downers Grove, IL: InterVarsity Press, 2004), 17-48.

104. Marshall, *New Testament Theology,* 43.

105. Kevin Vanhoozer, "Into the Great 'Beyond,'" in Marshall, *Beyond the Bible,* 87.

106. Stanley Porter, "Hermeneutics, Biblical Interpretation and Theology," in Marshall, *Beyond the Bible,* 121.

gins to address *"freestanding problems"* rather than *"questions that arise"* does doctrine risk losing its contingent, temporal, narrative, life-related, dispositional character. In some respects it then begins to move toward a more abstract system. This is not to criticize system as *coherence*. This is necessary for the formulation of doctrine. I address different notions of *system* in 8.3, distinguishing between system as a *closed* circle incapable of expansion, and systems as mechanisms or devices for the transmission of identifiable belief. A second, closely related problem arises when third- and fourth-century theologians utilize quasi-Platonist or Hellenistic notions of Being, which is not the only way to promote ontological truth-claims and sits uncomfortably with biblical material.

(2) With reference to the *specific content* of late first-century and second-century writings, two different trends may be identified. To be sure, sometimes deviations, eccentricities, and disproportionate attention to particular details occur, for the church after the New Testament period remains fallible, as it does today. It is easy to pick out maverick instances, occasionally obsessional ones, of a "special agenda." However, a larger set of questions was raised by Walter Bauer. He asks, in effect, whether it is only in the light of a particular retrospective view of history that we fail to see that "orthodoxy" was largely defined not by apostolic tradition but by the church in Rome from Clement to Novatian, while "heresies" flourished in Asia Minor, Egypt, and Edessa.

If Bauer's hypothesis were valid, this would call into question our claim that a strong and stable continuity existed between the world of the New Testament and the subapostolic and earliest Patristic periods. Bauer writes, "Rome . . . was from the very beginning the center and chief source of power for the 'orthodox' movement within Christianity."[107] Heterodox Christianity could gain no foothold because "A united front composed of Marcionites and Jewish Christians, Valentinians, and Montanists is inconceivable."[108] In Asia Minor, he claims, Galatia had a reputation for heresy, and allegedly Philippi and Thessalonica embraced gnosticism. Here the nature of theological development becomes identified with issues of power and power play.

In spite of its immediate influence in the 1930s, and among some scholars more recently, a number of writers have drawn attention to Bauer's questionable use of arguments from silence. H. E. W. Turner is as incisive and cogent in his critique of Bauer as he is in his critique of Werner.[109] On Edessa, for example, Turner writes, "We know nothing, and can conjecture little more."[110] *The Gospel of the Egyptians* and *The Gospel of the Hebrews* "represent . . . splinter movements."[111] Turner concludes that Bauer has grossly oversimplified the issues, and

107. Bauer, *Orthodoxy and Heresy*, 229.
108. Bauer, *Orthodoxy and Heresy*, 231.
109. Turner, *The Pattern of Christian Truth*, 39-80; cf. 26-35.
110. Turner, *Pattern*, 41.
111. Turner, *Pattern*, 51.

pressed supposed evidence to fit his prior theory. A range of reviews and appraisals is included in appendix 2 of the English translation of 1971-72.

The second trend is more important. Specific doctrinal themes faithfully reflect what Irenaeus calls "the rule of faith" found in the theology of the apostolic circle. To be sure, the canon speaks a coherent gospel with polyphonic voices. In 7.3 we allude to this significant phenomenon of polyphonic discourse with reference to Mikhail Bakhtin and Hans Urs von Balthasar, as well as to the conservative scholar Vern Poythress.[112] We should probably have added Paul Ricoeur in this context. But in terms of doctrinal *content* the period of transition, often unduly exaggerated and mythologized as a "tunnel" period, constitutes a smoother transition manifesting a more broadly stable continuity than writers such as Harnack, Schweitzer, Werner, or, for that matter, Räisänen (whom we discuss in 7.3) would have us believe.

If there is truth in claims about Hellenistic metaphysics and about a different later mind-set, this applies mainly to the doctrine of God as immutable and absolute, as well as to certain related Christological and Trinitarian formulations. These sacrifice the notion of "event" transcendence, as Jüngel often calls it, or the horizon of dynamic, temporal narrative, to which Pannenberg and Moltmann call attention, to speculative and static notions of "Being" that are generally alien to the biblical writings. We discuss these issues in 19.1, on God as Trinity. But the core doctrines of the work of Christ, the atonement, and the resurrection, which constitute common pre-Pauline traditions of "first importance" (1 Cor. 15:3), do not significantly change up to the end of the second century and beyond. The same can broadly be claimed for the doctrine of creation, notions of the image of God, the human condition, human sin, and the person and work of the Holy Spirit. These stand in direct continuity with New Testament confessions of faith.

(i) On *the work of Christ,* Clement of Rome (c. 96) sees the death of Christ as the fruit of his love, shedding his blood for us by the will of God, "his flesh for our flesh and his life for our lives" (τὴν σάρκα ὑπὲρ τῆς σαρκὸς ἡμῶν καὶ τὴν ψυχὴν ὑπὲρ τῶν ψυχῶν ἡμῶν, *tēn sarka huper tēs sarkos hēmōn kai tēn psuchēn huper tōn psuchōn hēmōn*).[113] He writes, "Let us gaze on the blood of Christ, and let us know that it is precious to his Father, because it was poured out for our salvation."[114] *The Epistle of Barnabas* cites Isa. 53:7 as the context for understanding the substitutionary death of Christ: "so that we should be made holy through the

---

112. Cf. Mikhail Bakhtin, *Problems of Dostoevsky's Poetics,* ed. and trans. Caryl Emersson (Minneapolis: University of Minnesota Press, 1984); Hans Urs von Balthasar, *Truth Is Symphonic: Aspects of Pluralism,* trans. Graham Harrison (San Francisco: Ignatius, 1987); and Vern S. Poythress, *Symphonic Theology: The Validity of Multiple Perspectives in Theology* (Phillipsburg, NJ: Presbyterian and Reformed, 2001). Cf. also Ricoeur, *The Conflict of Interpretations: Essays in Hermeneutics,* ed. Don Ihde (Evanston: Northwestern University Press, 1974).

113. *1 Clement* 49:6.

114. *1 Clement* 7:4.

forgiveness of sins, which is by the sprinkling of his blood" (ἐν τῷ αἵματι τοῦ ῥαντίσματος αὐτοῦ, *en tō haimati tou rhantismatos autou*).[115] Christ is "a sacrifice for our sins."[116] Polycarp (c. 69–c. 155) quotes and expounds 1 Pet. 2:22, 24: "Christ who bore our sins in his own body on the tree, who did no sin, . . . endured all things for our sake that we might live. . . ."[117] Ignatius of Antioch (c. 35–c. 107) quotes and expounds 1 Cor. 1:18-25: "The cross is an affront (σκάνδαλον, *skandalon*) to those who do not believe, but to us it is salvation and eternal life."[118]

Justin sees the cross as divinely willed for our salvation.[119] He expounds Paul's use of Deut. 21:23 and Deut. 27:26 in Gal. 3:13 to make the point: "Although a curse lies in the law against persons who are crucified, yet no curse lies on the Christ of God by whom all . . . are saved."[120] In 16.1, we cite further examples from the *Epistle to Diognetus,* from Melito of Sardis, and from Irenaeus, Clement of Alexandria, and Tertullian.[121]

(ii) On *the doctrine of creation,* the *Didache* follows the biblical traditions in affirming that God the Almighty created all things (Greek τὰ πάντα, *ta panta*) for the enjoyment of humankind.[122] Tatian calls God "Creator . . . Father of things that can be perceived and seen."[123] Justin affirms that the Creator is Father and Lord, and that all things were created through Christ.[124] Irenaeus (c. 130-200), Clement of Alexandria (c. 150-215), and Tertullian (c. 160-225) express their belief in God as sole Creator *ex nihilo* in a series of dispositional responses to gnostic claims that the Creator was not the Father of Jesus Christ but a Demiurge. Irenaeus provides a bridge from the biblical writings to the creeds: "God is the Creator of the world . . . Maker of heaven and earth."[125] Tertullian explicates the implication: "God created the universe . . . neither out of matter . . . nor out of God."[126] We cite further evidence in Chapter 10.

(iii) On *humankind made in the image of God,* Clement of Rome (c. 96) gives a faithful exposition of Gen. 1:26-27.[127] Irenaeus follows the New Testament in looking forward to a "recovery" of the destined image of God "in Christ Je-

115. *Epistle of Barnabas* 5:1; cf. 5:2; 5:5.
116. *Epistle of Barnabas* 7:3.
117. Polycarp, *Epistle to the Philippians* 8:1; cf. 1:20.
118. Ignatius, *Epistle to the Ephesians* 18:1.
119. Justin, *Dialogue* 95:2.
120. Justin, *Dialogue* 95:1-2 and 96:1; cf. 91:4.
121. Cf. esp. Irenaeus, *Against Heresies* IV:6:2; V:1:1; V:2:1; V:17:2-3; Clement, *Paedagogus* 1:5; *Stromata* IV:7; and Tertullian, *Against Marcion* III:8.
122. *Didache* 10:2-3.
123. Tatian, *Orations* 4.
124. Justin, *Apology* II:6:1.
125. Irenaeus, *Against Heresies* II:9:1.
126. Tertullian, *Against Hermogenes* 15:1 and 17:1; cf. *Against Marcion* II:2.
127. *1 Clement* 33:4 (Greek τῆς ἑαυτοῦ εἰκόνος, *tēs heautou eikonos*).

sus."[128] Following Irenaeus, Tertullian elucidates biblical language about the image (Hebrew צלם, *tselem*) of God and God's likeness (דמות, *d*ᵉ*muth*).[129] We provide more detail in Chapter 11.

(iv) On *sin and ideas of a fall,* Tatian argues that sin led to the loss of God's image in humankind.[130] Clement of Alexandria and Irenaeus understand sin as "offending" (Greek προσκόπτω, *proskoptō*) against God and humankind.[131] Irenaeus perceives sin as breaking a relationship with God and bringing grief (Latin *dolor*) and death *(mors).*[132] Tertullian does indeed go beyond the biblical material in proposing a "traducian" view of the transmission of sin based on a quasi-material view of "the soul" (Latin *anima*), but he nevertheless understands sin as involving more than the single individual who commits sin.[133] We explore these issues in detail in Chapters 12–13.

It is hardly necessary to anticipate further samples of chapters on other doctrinal themes. This section performs a specific purpose, namely to indicate that a dispositional account of belief, as well as illuminating and facilitating a hermeneutic of doctrine, sheds light on the transition from the biblical writings to early Christian doctrine. The earliest Christian writings that follow the era of the New Testament do not reflect a radically different mind-set from the confessions of faith that we find in the biblical writings, at least on the themes considered above.

---

128. Irenaeus, *Against Heresies* V:19:1; cf. V:16:2; V:21:10; V:34:2.
129. Tertullian, *On Baptism* 5; cf. Irenaeus, *Against Heresies* V:6:1.
130. Tatian, *Orations* 7.
131. Clement, *Stromata* 2:2; Irenaeus, *Against Heresies* V:16:3.
132. Irenaeus, *Against Heresies* V:34:2.
133. Tertullian, *On the Soul* 5–6.

CHAPTER 3

Forms of Life, Embodiment, and Place

3.1. Communal Confessions in Israel's Life
and Embodiment in the Biblical Writings

We have already noted that confessions of faith in the New Testament and the early church are *communal* belief-utterances that share commonly transmitted and received apostolic testimony or doctrine. We shall examine this communal aspect further in the next chapter, where we shall argue that doctrine may be perceived as the corporate memory and communal celebration of the narratives and drama of God's action in the world and in the life of Israel and the church.

Our aim here is to establish three related claims. First, *communal* belief-utterances are no less *closely embedded in life-situations and actions* than are the expressions of individual belief considered in the previous chapter. This applies to recitals, celebrations, acclamations, and other multiform expressions of Israel's corporate faith in the context of her historical life. Second, many of these communal confessions of faith on the part of Israel and of the apostolic community of the church emerge in the context of *narratives of events.* In this way, too, they are embedded in *historical life and action.* Third, what emerges as a dispositional dimension serves in these communal examples also to underline the first-person *self-involvement, active participation,* and *endorsement or "taking a stand"* on the part of a believing community and successive generations of believing communities. These communities, even if separated in time or place, perceive themselves as taking their stand and as staking their identity through *sharing in the same narrative,* and through the recital and retelling of the same founding events.

In Judaism and in rabbinic thought the recital of the *Shema* morning and evening constitutes a participatory act of identification and practical self-involvement that "stands behind" Deut. 6:4, "Hear, O Israel, the LORD is our

God, the LORD alone" (Hebrew שמע ישראל יהוה אלהינו יהוה אחד, *Sh^ema'*, *Iśrāēl, Y-h-w-h 'elōhēynû Y-h-w-h 'echād*). The rabbinic injunction stems from Deut. 6:7: "Recite them to your children . . . when you lie down and when you rise." The custom of wearing phylacteries directly reflects the command of Deut. 6:8: "Bind them as a sign on your head, fix them as an emblem on your forehead." Marvin Wilson rightly observes, "The *Shema* is a theological confession, the *credo par excellence* of Judaism. . . . The Jewish community came to view its recitation as a distinct means . . . to bear witness to the essence of Jewish belief. . . . Martyrs and those on their deathbeds have also made proclamation of the *Shema* a practice."[1] We have cited the Hebrew text because its English translation is disputed. C. H. Gordon suggests, by way of example, "Yahweh is our God, Yahweh is 'One.'"[2]

The *communal* aspect of confessions of faith, then, consists especially in the Old Testament in what Gerhard von Rad identified some fifty years ago as "retelling." In the Old Testament, he writes, "Re-telling remains the most legitimate form of theological discourse"; he cites Stephen's speech in Acts 7:2-53 as an example of this genre in the New Testament.[3]

Even if the *Shema'* constitutes the paradigm case of a credal confession of faith in Israel's life, the biblical writings contain many other examples. In terms of general importance and scholarly consensus the confession of faith in Deut. 26:5-9, which begins "An Aramean ready to perish was my father, and he went down to Egypt and sojourned there," narrates the saving story embodied in the confessional form. The formula continues: "And the LORD brought *us* forth out of Egypt with a mighty hand. . . . He brought *us* into this place and gave *us* this land . . ." (my italics). The use of *"us"* clearly draws those who recite the confession *into the very narrative itself as active participants who were "there."* Gerhard von Rad and G. E. Wright note that precisely the same logic attaches to the recital of the Passover narrative in Deut. 6:20-24: "When your son asks you, 'What do these testimonies mean . . . ?' you shall say, '*We* were Pharaoh's bondmen in Egypt, and the LORD brought *us* out of Egypt with a mighty hand. . . .'"[4] These confessions, Gerhard von Rad adds, are "out and out a confession of faith. They recapitulate the main events in the saving history from the time of the patriarchs . . . down to the conquests. . . . As in the Apostles' Creed, there is no reference at

---

1. Marvin R. Wilson, "Shema," in *Dictionary of Old Testament Theology and Exegesis*, ed. W. A. VanGemeren, 5 vols. (Carlisle: Paternoster, 1997), vol. 4, 1217; cf. 1217-18.

2. C. H. Gordon, "His Name Is 'One,'" *Journal of New Eastern Studies* 29 (1970) 198-99; cf. also R. W. L. Moberly, "Yahweh Is One: The Translation of the *Shema*," *Supplements to Vetus Testamentum* 41 (1990) 209-15.

3. Gerhard von Rad, *Old Testament Theology*, trans. D. M. G. Stalker, 2 vols. (Edinburgh and London: Oliver & Boyd, 1962), vol. 1, 121.

4. Cf. G. Ernest Wright, *God Who Acts: Biblical Theology as Recital* (London: SCM, 1952), 71; Von Rad, *Theology*, vol. 1, 121.

all to . . . teaching . . . [but] a disciplined celebration of the divine acts . . . extolling God."[5]

This emphasis upon the self-involving functions of confessions of faith in the Old Testament should not be ascribed exclusively to a return to the distinctive methods and perspectives of the "salvation-history" approach associated with the biblical theology movement of the mid-twentieth century. New Testament writers bear witness to this same communal, self-involving perspective. The Passover setting of the Lord's Supper or the Eucharist in Pauline theology confirms that "participation in the communal narrative of salvation" is precisely the form that "proclaiming the Lord's death" (1 Cor. 11:26) takes in the central liturgical confession of faith in the Pauline churches. O. Hofius and F. J. Leenhardt rightly perceive the covenantal, participatory, narrative background of the Passover as the key semantic frame within which to understand in what sense Jesus declared "This is my body," and in what sense by participating in the Eucharist Christian believers corporately and individually "proclaim" his death by participating in the narrative.[6] As one of the Black spirituals expresses the matter, believers are "there" as participating witnesses to the crucifixion. I have long held this approach, and develop it in my commentary on the Greek text of 1 Corinthians.[7]

According to the Mishnah, "in every generation a man must so regard himself *as if he came forth himself* out of Egypt" (*m. Pesaḥim* 10:5, my italics).[8] Leenhardt comments, "Everyone had to participate in the great redemption. . . . The past reaches and joins the present." The "surprising innovation" is Jesus' insertion of "This is my body" in place of "This is the bread of affiliation that your fathers ate in the wilderness."[9] "Remembering" has a participatory dimension. In accordance with the dispositional character of belief, believers "proclaim the Lord's death" as those who *nail their colors to the mast* as *active participants* who see themselves as "there" in the redemptive event of the crucifixion of Christ. Certainly, as Vernon Neufeld adds, they *also* witness to the *content* of the event. Nothing brings this home more forcefully than reading the Eucharistic texts of the New Testament side by side with *Mishnah Pesaḥim* 10:1-7, and the Jewish Passover *Haggadah*, especially *Haggadah* 8.[10]

5. Von Rad, *Theology,* vol. 1, 122.
6. O. Hofius, "The Lord's Supper and the Lord's Supper Tradition: Reflections on 1 Cor. 11:23b-25," in B. Meyer (ed.), *One Loaf, One Cup: Ecumenical Studies of 1 Cor. 11 and Other Eucharistic Texts* (Macon, GA: Mercer University Press, 1993), 75-115; and F. J. Leenhardt, "This Is My Body," in Oscar Cullmann and F. J. Leenhardt, *Essays on the Lord's Supper* (London: Lutterworth, 1958), 39-40.
7. Thiselton, *First Epistle,* 848-99, esp. 871-88.
8. The most readily available text is Herbert Danby (ed.), *The Mishnah: Translated from the Hebrew with Notes* (Oxford: Clarendon, 1933), 151.
9. Leenhardt, "This Is My Body," 39-40.
10. A convenient edition is that of Cecil Roth, *The Haggadah: New Edition with Notes,* Hebrew and English (in parallel, London: Soncino, 1934).

Anders Eriksson has most helpfully demonstrated the importance of shared apostolic formulations as common premises for life and thought in the Pauline communities.[11] It is not "Paul's" tradition alone (contrary to the overly speculative claims of Hans Lietzmann), but *common apostolic tradition* to which appeal is made in 1 Cor. 11:17-26. Eriksson traces the history of research on this area from the work of Alfred Seeberg in 1903, to Eduard Norden, Ernst Lohmeyer, and more recently Neufeld, Hans von Campenhausen, Klaus Wengst, and Ferdinand Hahn, to whom we alluded in the first chapter.[12] He writes, "The traditions . . . constitute the common ground between Paul and the Corinthians, and can therefore be appealed to as the 'facts of the case.'"[13] We have already considered other examples of communal confessions in the New Testament and some in the second century in our first chapter.

These last paragraphs have served to address primarily the issue of how *dispositional accounts* of "belief" on the part of *individuals* relate to *communal and corporate expressions of doctrine*. The latter, too, focus primarily not on "inner states" or "mental processes," although, as Wittgenstein and Price readily concede, certain aspects indeed have effects that may involve sensations or experiences of joy, awe, imagination, or memory. But these qualifications do not detract from the main argument about dispositional accounts of belief. *The purpose of this philosophical analysis of dispositional approaches has been to demonstrate the inextricable internal logical grammar that connects Christian doctrine or communal belief with dispositional responses and habits of mind to live and act in a correlative way in the public domain.* We now turn to this dimension of "bodily life" in the New Testament.

In New Testament studies several writers have rightly seen that Paul's notion of living the Christian life in the "body" (Greek σῶμα, *sōma*) has decisive significance for the notion of the *embodied self* as the medium or arena for trustful, obedient response to God *in the public domain*. Ernst Käsemann expresses this principle very well. He rightly argues that the Cartesian, dualist notion of body and spirit as two separable "elements" of a human person is in general alien to the New Testament. He also rejects Rudolf Bultmann's problematic understanding of *body* in Paul as denoting a person's "being able to make himself the object of his own action or to experience himself as the subject to whom something happens."[14] By contrast, Käsemann declares, "'Body' for Paul mean[s] . . . *that piece of the world which we ourselves are* and for which we bear responsibility because it was the earliest gift of our Creator to us. 'Body' is not primarily to be re-

---

11. Anders Eriksson, *Traditions as Rhetorical Proof: Pauline Argumentation in 1 Corinthians*, Coniectanea Biblica, New Testament Series 29 (Stockholm: Almqvist & Wiksell, 1998).

12. Eriksson, *Proof*, 76-80.

13. Eriksson, *Proof*, 33.

14. Rudolf Bultmann, *Theology of the New Testament*, trans. K. Grobel, 2 vols. (London: SCM, 1952-55), vol. 1, 195.

garded and interpreted from the standpoint of the individual. For the apostle it signifies man in his worldliness [i.e., in his being part of the *world*] and therefore in his ability *to communicate*."[15]

In other words, the public domain of "the world" in which persons are embedded as "bodily" provides the conditions and necessary currency for intersubjective agency and personal interaction, for the communication of meaning and understanding, and for the capacity to identify and to recognize other persons as who they are. Thus the "reality of our being in the world" makes Christian faith and obedience *expressible* and *communicable* in public contexts. Käsemann continues, "*In the bodily obedience of the Christian,* carried out as the service of God *in the world of everyday,* the lordship of Christ finds *visible expression,* and only when this visible expression takes personal shape in our lives does the whole thing become *credible* as Gospel message" (all italics are mine).[16]

This is why Paul makes so much of the axiom "the body (σῶμα, *sōma*) belongs to the Lord, and the Lord to the body" (1 Cor. 6:13). When he enjoins the church in Corinth, "Glorify God in your body" (6:20), Paul refers to the whole person with special reference to what is at stake in their conduct and lifestyle. Käsemann makes the broader point that very "embodiment" of the self is the mode of existence given by God the Creator as a *gift* for the good of his people. In the sphere of salvation, the *living out* of faith, thought, and discipleship takes the form of a *visible, tangible, practical, bodily mode of existence; a disposition, habit, and action.* It is this, or it is nothing at all. Thus the whole of 1 Cor. 6:12-20 traces the meaning of embodiment for discipleship: "Your bodies are Christ's limbs and organs (v. 15); your body is a temple of the Holy Spirit (v. 19); show forth God's glory in how you live your bodily life."[17] Paul repeats the theme in Romans: "Present your bodies as a living sacrifice" (12:1).

It may seem at first sight as if the issue turns on human "physicality." Gundry argues for the importance of "the physical side of *sōma,*" highlighted by its proximity to "flesh" (σάρξ, *sarx*) in 6:14-20.[18] But Käsemann's notion of the self as sharing in the observable, visible, intelligible, communicable, tangible life of the "world" is broad and more faithful to the arguments of this and parallel Pauline passages. Gundry is not "wrong," but simply does not go far enough. B. Byrne, for example, stresses "personal communication" as a major aspect of bodiliness in these verses.[19]

---

15. Ernst Käsemann, "On the Subject of Primitive Christian Apocalyptic," in E. Käsemann, *New Testament Questions of Today,* trans. W. J. Montague (London: S.C.M., 1969), 135; cf. 108-37.

16. Käsemann, "Apocalyptic," 135.

17. Translation mine, in Thiselton, *First Epistle,* 458; the exegesis of these verses is discussed on 458-82.

18. Robert H. Gundry, *Sōma in Biblical Theology with Emphasis on Pauline Anthropology,* SNTSMS 29 (Cambridge: Cambridge University Press, 1976), 68.

19. B. Byrne, "Sinning against One's Own Body: Paul's Understanding of the Sexual Relationship in 1 Cor 6:18," *Catholic Biblical Quarterly* 45 (1983) 608-16.

The difficult v. 18 (sinning against one's own body in an illicit sexual relation) suggests that a sexual relationship is more than bio-physical, but also communicative, commissive, and, according to Loader, also creative of some new reality.[20] Be that as it may, Paul's concerns that relate to the "body" in 6:1-20 include more than issues of sexual conduct. They relate no less to the manipulative use of power (6:1-8) and to greed for possessions or wealth (6:8).[21]

In a recent report of the Church of England Doctrine Commission to which I was a contributor, we pointed out that power, money, sex, and time constitute precisely those areas of Christian and everyday living in which everyone has "high stakes."[22] On *power,* it matters greatly whether the vulnerable are powerless or empowered, and whether the influential use their power responsibly or abuse it to oppress and manipulate others. Power can also be life-giving, as when Jesus taught and acted "with authority and power" (Luke 4:36; cf. Matt 7:29; Mark 1:22). Mary the mother of Jesus reflects on divine power, "He has brought down the powerful from their thrones, and has lifted up the lowly" (Luke 1:52).

On *money,* it is clear from a comparison between the first three Gospels that Luke has a distinctive concern about how people use money, not least as a "public" indication of the seriousness of their claims to discipleship. This is part of Luke's special understanding of the public, "bodily," and historical nature of salvation. This is so clear that P. Vielhauer has even appealed to this feature to exaggerate "his distance from Paul," who was allegedly interested only in present existential address by comparison.[23] Luke anchors the events of the coming of Christ in a triple dating according to public offices of Roman Jewish-national and Jewish-religious officials (Luke 3:1-2); he traces geographical features relevant to the ministry of Jesus (cf. the travel narrative of chs. 9–19), and stresses the role of witnesses to public events (1:2-4). He addresses woes to the rich and beatitudes to the poor (6:20-26), and includes the parables of the two debtors, the rich fool, the tower builder, the rich man and Lazarus, and the pounds (7:40; 12:20; 14:28; and 16:20-25). There are several references to almsgiving (11:41; 12:33). Following Mark, he narrates the episode of the poor widow who gave her two copper coins (21:1-4; cf. Mark 12:41-44).[24] What people do with their pocketbooks provides

---

20. William Loader, *The Septuagint, Sexuality, and the New Testament: Case Studies on the Impact of the LXX in Philo and the New Testament* (Grand Rapids: Eerdmans, 2004), 90-92.

21. Paul's condemnation of a Christian initiating a civil lawsuit presupposes a situation of manipulation and the ability to offer a favor to the judge, that is, to manipulate the situation to gain advantage over a less wealthy or less influential fellow believer. See Thiselton, *First Epistle,* 418-38.

22. Doctrine Commission of the Church of England, *Being Human: A Christian Understanding of Personhood with Reference to Power, Money, Sex, and Time* (London: Church House Publishing, 2003).

23. P. Vielhauer, "On the 'Paulinisms' of Acts," in *Studies in Luke-Acts,* ed. L. E. Keck and J. L. Martyn (London: SPCK, 1968), 37; cf. 33-50.

24. For an outline of Lucan scholarship since the 1950s see Anthony C. Thiselton, "'Reading

currency (in both senses) for their claims to be believers. They manifest a believing disposition in the public domain.

To return to the publication of the Doctrine Commission, here we noted that while an abundance of money can seduce us into overestimating our self-worth, poverty may tempt both us and others into the illusion of underestimating it.[25] The possibility of monetary credit has opened up otherwise unimagined worlds of possible choice and human flourishing. But extended credit can also seduce us into believing the fantasy of a risk-free life, and lead us to over-resource the present on the basis of a future that we do not know.[26] Current crises in pension funds offer one small indication of this. Money not only makes possible the satisfaction of desires, but more subtly it often shapes, redirects, and extends the scope of these desires too far.[27] In the late twentieth century and in our twenty-first century a widening gap between money and real wealth-production, with the accelerating rise of fractional reserve banking, has not only expanded markets served by money, but has also increasingly expanded markets in which money is itself the commodity. All of this heightens further the huge personal and communal stakes held in a global money market, with its potential to bring either a degree of wealth or dire poverty to millions almost at the stroke of a pen, or at the click of a personal computer.

The Song of Solomon celebrates *love* as the strongest of all human qualities: "Love is strong as death. . . . If one offered for love all the wealth of one's house, it would be utterly scorned" (Song of Songs 8:6-7). Yet love is more than a matter of words. We wrote in our report, "Sexual engagement is mutually involving. It entails give-and-take, desire and delight, loss of control and self-surrender, and the assumption of responsibility for each other."[28] Yet in a fallen world the stakes remain very high in yet another sense: "Sexual union can be not only joyful and fulfilling, but also painful and disappointing. At worst it becomes a place of cruelty and perversion."[29]

Love derives from God because God chooses not to be self-contained but deeply involved with others. Hence sex is a gift of God, in which sexuality can be a

---

Luke' as Interpretation, Reflection and Formation," in Craig Bartholomew, Joel B. Green, and Anthony C. Thiselton (eds.), *Reading Luke: Interpretation, Reflection, Formation,* Scripture and Hermeneutics Series 6 (Carlisle: Paternoster and Grand Rapids: Zondervan, 2005), 3-17; cf. 3-52; on Luke's concerns, see Joel B. Green, *The Theology of the Gospel of Luke* (Cambridge: Cambridge University Press, 1995); R. Maddox, *The Purpose of Luke-Acts* (Edinburgh: T&T Clark, 1982); Robert J. Karris, "Poor and Rich: The Lukan Sitz im Leben," in C. H. Talbert, *Perspectives on Luke-Acts* (Edinburgh: T&T Clark, 1978), 112-25; and Luke T. Johnson, *The Literary Function of Possessions in Luke-Acts,* SBLDS 39 (Missoula: Scholars Press, 1977).

25. Doctrine Commission, *Being Human,* 62.

26. Doctrine Commission, *Being Human,* 72-75.

27. Doctrine Commission, *Being Human,* 67.

28. Doctrine Commission, *Being Human,* 86.

29. Doctrine Commission, *Being Human,* 86.

sacrament in the broadest sense of love, and "our bodies can be part of our spirituality, not an obstacle to it."[30] But openness to the other brings risk. Sexuality has also become one of the idols of our times. Sexual attractiveness may often be taken out of its context of a loving relationship. Sexual relations can become the subject of manipulative power and a source of deep disappointment or even torment. The intersubjective world of sexual behavior and action, like those of power and money, becomes a domain where everything becomes a matter of huge stakes. But all this, whether it results in delight or pain, forms part of the "bodily" domain (in Käsemann's sense) that gives currency to what our beliefs, attitudes, values, and doctrines actually amount to (in Wittgenstein's sense). They achieve working currency in this way. Jürgen Moltmann acutely observes concerning God's openness to go forth from his "private" world, to leave behind an "inner" world of self-protection to encounter others: "A God who cannot suffer cannot love either."[31] We postpone any discussion of time until we reach the next chapter.

3.2. Embodiment in Christian Traditions, Disembodiment, and Place

We shall shortly return to the role of "life" and "forms of life" in hermeneutical inquiry. However, we first note that the "bodily" or "public" understanding of belief and doctrine that we have observed in the New Testament should not be taken for granted as characterizing all religious belief, at least as this is perceived from within its own horizons. The New Testament writers draw their understanding from the Old Testament and develop it further, but in the ancient world very different evaluations of the body or of bodiliness were to be found among many Greek philosophical thinkers after Plato, and in the second and third centuries an even more explicit hostility toward the bodily or the earthly and material characterized gnostic writings. Marcionite thought shares this negative evaluation, for Marcion's separation of the Father of Jesus Christ from the Creator of the Old Testament undermined the very premise to which Käsemann rightly alluded, namely that the body is God's good gift to humankind as Creator, to be respected and valued.

Generalizations about Greek thought remain hazardous, in spite of Harnack's sweeping claims about the effects of "hellenization." Heidegger emphatically insists that the pre-Socratic philosophers never succumbed to Plato's temptation to see "being as mere idea . . . exalted to a suprasensory realm," thereby producing a dualist "chasm, *chōrismos*."[32] Plato indeed reflects a gener-

30. Doctrine Commission, *Being Human*, 90.

31. Jürgen Moltmann, *The Trinity and the Kingdom of God*, trans. Margaret Kohl (London: SCM, 1981), 38.

32. Martin Heidegger, *An Introduction to Metaphysics*, trans. Ralph Manheim (New Haven and London: Yale University Press, 1959), 106.

ally negative attitude toward the body and the material world, although even this should not be overstated. In his earlier work, especially in *Phaedo,* Plato sees the task of the soul as that of disengaging from, and resisting, the body and its needs.[33] Yet Skemp warns us not to make too much of this. He comments, "The down-drag of the body, even in Plato, is really to be interpreted as the self-assertion of immediate satisfactions . . . against the control of the soul."[34] Plato modified his earlier, sharper dualism in later writings, but still retained a generally negative view of the body and of matter. The material world could never be more than an inferior and imperfect copy of the world of spirit and Ideas. Aristotle and many of the Stoics held more complex, more unified, views of the self, but Stoic writers in general ascribed the "divine spark" exclusively to *pneuma.* Some regarded the body (sometimes with the soul, but not with mind or spirit) as disruptive of the cultivation of *apatheia,* freedom from emotional forces. Only πνεῦμα *(pneuma)* or νοῦς *(nous, mind),* not the body, could be re-united with the whole at death.

Gnostic writers held a more radical and far-reaching dualism. No gnostic could have written that the divine Word became *flesh* (John 1:14), nor could any have urged, "Glorify God in your *body*" (1 Cor. 6:20). The gnostic texts of the second and early third centuries witness to a radical disjunction between a transcendent realm of light or spirit (πνεῦμα, *pneuma*) on one side, and the realm of the bodily or material (ὕλη, *hulē*) on the other. The human self as an *embodied* being cannot be saved in gnosticism. Only the spirit can be saved by *gnōsis.* Revealed truth is handed down as an esoteric mystery to be explained only to the initiated. It is not accessible as part of a public and open tradition. Revelation and *gnōsis* take the form of aphorisms, abstract systems, or myths, not that of a narrative of occurrences in the public domain. If they draw on the narratives of Christian Gospels, gnostic writers interpret these in wholly "spiritual" terms.

Some gnostic writings share a range of vocabulary with the New Testament. The Valentinian meditation *The Gospel of Truth* speaks of the divine wisdom, the divine word, divine glory, and divine love.[35] The writer declares: "This is the Gospel revealed to the initiate through the mercies of the Father, the secret mystery, Jesus Christ, through whom it has illuminated them. It gave them a Way, and the Way is the Truth."[36] The words "Gospel," "Father," "mystery," "Jesus Christ," "enlighten," "way" and "truth" occur in the *Gospel of Truth.* Nevertheless, as Samuel Laeuchli insists, the meaning of this is different from that of the same

33. Plato, *Phaedo* 66B-66C.

34. J. B. Skemp, *The Greeks and the Gospel* (London: Carey Kingsgate, 1964), 85.

35. *Evangelium Veritatis* 23:18-26; text and commentary in Kendrick Grobel, *The Gospel of Truth: A Valentinian Meditation on the Gospel, Translation from the Coptic and Commentary* (London: A. & C. Black and Nashville: Abingdon, 1960) 88.

36. *Evangelium Veritatis* 18:12-20; Grobel, *Gospel,* 48-50.

terms in the New Testament because the frame of reference or context that determines the meaning remains radically different.[37]

Gnostic writers appeal to the Gospel of John and yet at the same time "reject the 'earthly Jesus.'"[38] They achieve this by the hermeneutical process of rejecting the "simple" reading of the gospel. Elaine Pagels writes, "The literal level of *any* text, then, including that of the gospels, offers only the outward manifestation of inner meaning; it contains the metaphorical form of the ineffable truth."[39] In this sense meaning remains "hidden," *almost* like "private" language, except that it retains a "soft" currency strictly within the community of the initiated. There can be no appeal to "public" truth. Irenaeus states that to refute gnostic teaching he has to expose false exegesis of John.[40] Laeuchli observes, "The familiar biblical concepts . . . hold the key to the reversal of meaning of seemingly biblical terms."[41] Most important of all, "There is no Incarnation! Where there seems to be, it is only a 'coming down.'"[42]

It would be tempting to explore further examples of gnostic texts, but this would begin to constitute a digression from our main argument, and there are many standard treatments of this subject.[43] Our purpose is to show that the biblical writings, especially the New Testament, the early Patristic writers, and mainline Christian doctrine cohere with confessions of faith embedded in action and life, and compatible with a dispositional approach to individual belief and communal doctrine, but this is not to be taken for granted amid alternative quasi-Platonic, gnostic, and docetic understandings of belief-claims and truth-claims. Indeed, the legacy of Platonism has lingered on in popular versions of Christianity. Heidegger echoes Friedrich Nietzsche's damning accusation: "In the chasm [between the mental and the bodily] Christianity settled down. . . . Nietzsche was right in saying that Christianity is Platonism for the people."[44]

---

37. Samuel Laeuchli, *The Language of Faith: An Introduction to the Semantic Dilemma of the Early Church* (London: Epworth, 1962), 15-93. Cf. also Elaine H. Pagels, *The Gnostic Paul: Gnostic Exegesis of the Pauline Letters* (Philadelphia: Fortress, 1975).

38. Elaine Pagels, *The Johannine Gospel in Gnostic Exegesis: Heracleon's Commentary on John* (Nashville and New York: Abingdon, 1973), 15.

39. Pagels, *Johannine Gospels*, 15-16.

40. Irenaeus, *Against Heresies* IV:11:7.

41. Laeuchli, *Language*, 43.

42. Laeuchli, *Language*, 47.

43. Hans Jonas, *The Gnostic Religion* (Boston: Beacon, 2d rev. edn. 1963); R. McL. Wilson, *The Gnostic Problem* (London: Mowbray, 1958); and Bertil Gärtner, *The Theology of the Gospel of Thomas* (London: Collins, 1961); and among many collections of texts: Grobel, *The Gospel of Truth;* Werner Foerster, *Gnosis: A Selection of Gnostic Texts,* trans. R. McL. Wilson, 2 vols. (Oxford: Clarendon, 1972); and Edgar Hennecke, *New Testament, Apocrypha,* ed. Wilhelm Schneemelcher, trans. R. McL. Wilson, 2 vols. (Philadelphia: Westminster, 1963).

44. Heidegger, *Metaphysics,* 106.

All the same, this is not the Christianity of the New Testament and of the early Fathers who guarded and transmitted apostolic tradition. We have earlier noted that already in 1 John a confession of faith includes the test of authenticity that "Jesus Christ has come in the flesh" (1 John 4:2).[45] Bultmann comments of the "deniers," "They deny that the Christ . . . has appeared in the historical Jesus. . . . It therefore appears to be a question of Docetism."[46] Ignatius of Antioch includes a full confession of faith concerning the public life and lineage of Jesus as "truly born, who ate and drank, . . . was truly crucified and truly died, *in full view of heaven, earth, and hell* (βλεπόντων τῶν ἐπουρανίων καὶ ἐπιγείων καὶ ὑποχθονίων, *blepontōn tōn epouraniōn kai epigeiōn kai hupochthoniōn*) and was truly raised from the dead" (my italics).[47] He adds, "If some . . . say he suffered in mere appearance (τὸ δοκεῖν πεπονθέναι αὐτόν, *to dokein peponthenai auton*) . . . why am I in chains?"[48]

Irenaeus follows this tradition in three ways. He affirms both the bodily humanity of Jesus Christ; the "public" nature of Christian tradition; and the historical-grammatical or "public" interpretation of Scripture. Thus he opposes Saturninus's denial of the true birth and true body of Jesus Christ.[49] He traces the apostolic tradition from Peter's first sermon onwards as a matter of public, open record, not a "secret" or "private" tradition.[50] Against the Valentinians he interprets the Scriptures as open to rational criteria of coherence in the light of apostolic tradition, rather than something to be manipulated in esoteric ways to defend some prior doctrine.[51] Tertullian takes up the apostolic tradition. He pours ridicule on the gnostic myths concerning the creation of matter by an ignorant or confused Demiurge.[52] He accuses Marcion and others of distorting and manipulating the Scriptures, and of an irrational contempt for the body.[53] Action, embodiment, and the public world find a prominent place in the biblical writings and early mainline Christian doctrine, in contrast to other approaches that privilege only mental states and "the inner."

David Brown traces in part through the Patristic and medieval periods an emphasis upon embodiment and place, although in a different theological context from that used hitherto here.[54] The subtitle of his book, "Reclaiming Human

45. Cf. Neufeld, *Reconceiving Texts*, 113-32.
46. Rudolf Bultmann, *The Johannine Epistles*, trans. R. P. O'Hara and others, Hermeneia (Philadelphia: Fortress, 1973), 62.
47. Ignatius, *Epistle to the Trallians* 9:1-2.
48. Ignatius, *Epistle to the Trallians* 10:1.
49. Irenaeus, *Against Heresies* I:24:2.
50. Irenaeus, *Against Heresies* III:12:1–15:3.
51. Irenaeus, *Against Heresies* I:8:1-2.
52. Tertullian, *Against the Valentinians* 15–24; and *Against Hermogenes* 22–37.
53. Tertullian, *Against Heretics* 40; and *Against Marcion* I:24-25.
54. David Brown, *God and the Enchantment of Place: Reclaiming Human Experience* (Oxford: Oxford University Press, 2004).

Experience," signals his concern at the church's tendency to narrow the expected channels through which we may experience divine presence and action. Every facet and activity of human life, he believes, may become (in the broadest sense) sacramentally or even in iconic ways a vehicle for such experience. In his Introduction he writes, "God is found in nature and gardens, in buildings and place, in music and bodies, in ways . . . now largely lost."[55] This book is an interim report *en route* to another book to be called *God and Grace of Body*.[56] Brown urges, "Sport, drama, humour, dance, architecture, place, and home . . . are all part of a long list of activities . . . where God can be encountered."[57] A partial theological basis for this argument arises from a discussion of a changing usage or understanding of "sacrament," and an exploration of the role of icons in Orthodox theology. Even Platonism, Brown argues, has not simply devalued the bodily. Even this seems to emerge in *Phaedo*. Plato celebrates the beauty of the human body in the *Symposium*.[58] Whether his arguments about the positive impact of Middle Platonism remain as convincing I am not sure, but others may judge. However, the upshot is to place questions about the public domain and everyday life in a large theological frame.

John Inge's recent study *A Christian Theology of Place* also affirms the importance of everyday life and action in Christian discipleship in specific terms that are often associated with the particularity of "place."[59] Place, unlike "space" (which is more general and abstract), underlines the specificity of Christian experience of God and practical living. Inge cites a wide range of thinkers from Heidegger and Foucault to David Harvey and Anthony Giddens for the view that Western thought has tended to dissolve away the particularities of place, not least by a "homogenization of space" that dulls our sense of place.[60] Drawing especially on Walter Brueggemann's volume *The Land*, Inge argues that land and place are central in the Old Testament, in contrast to a widespread sense today of anonymity, rootlessness, and generalizing abstraction that lends to "the undoing of our common humanness."[61] He comments, "The Lord, people, and place are inextricably woven together."[62] Place is "relational" both to God and to God's people.[63]

The New Testament reflects a possible tension. On one side it shows keen in-

---

55. Brown, *Place*, 2.

56. Brown, *Place*, 407.

57. Brown, *Place*, 9.

58. Brown, *Place*, 62.

59. John Inge, *A Christian Theology of Place* (Aldershot, U.K.: Ashgate, 2003).

60. Inge, *Place*, 21; cf. 5-32.

61. Inge, *Place*, 35; cf. 33-58. See also Walter Brueggemann, *The Land: Place as Gift, Promise and Challenge in Biblical Faith* (London: SPCK, 1978).

62. Inge, *Place*, 40.

63. Inge, *Place*, 47.

terest in place, especially in Luke-Acts. Yet it also at times prefers to focus on Christ as *the* "place" of meeting rather than on an earthly place as such. Even so, Christ enters the scene as the "*enfleshed* Word" (John 1:14), and as the *embodied* Christ. His "flesh" is the entire embodied medium of his deeds and words in life (Heb. 5:7). Inge alludes to "ongoing tension between place and placelessness (universality)," in which the incarnation of Christ emphasizes particularity.[64] As we shall see, this comes close to being a characteristic dialectic of hermeneutics between particularity and universality or coherence. Such a biblical perspective on place paves the way, Inge argues, for the concept of "the incarnation as sacrament."[65] Like David Brown, Inge explores the sacramental significance of place and particularity. The incarnate person of Christ witnesses to *embodiment*. Invisible grace is sacramentally mediated and lived out through the *visible, tangible, and everyday*.[66] Thus the importance of "place" broadens into the axiom that grace comes into being in visible, embodied form, in accordance with the classic definition of a sacrament. William Temple, Inge points out, pressed this point in terms of "the reality of matter and its place in the divine scheme."[67]

We explore temporality and time in the next chapter. Meanwhile three convergent lines of thought point to the nature of Christian doctrine as relating to life, action, and embodiment. These include the life-settings of confessions of faith in Israel and the early church; dispositional accounts of individual belief and of communal doctrine in narrative settings; and the importance of embodiment and place in the biblical writings and for Christian theology. All of this of necessity brings doctrine more closely within the domain of hermeneutics, which is above all concerned with particularity, contingency, life, intersubjectivity, and action.

3.3. "Life" and "Forms of Life" in Hermeneutics: Dilthey, Apel, and Wittgenstein

We return now to the role of "life" and "forms of life" in philosophical hermeneutics, although we have seen that even in the polemic between Irenaeus and gnostics on embodiment and public world, *hermeneutics* came already to the forefront. In these chapters we remain concerned to draw upon resources at hand in hermeneutical theory to nurture a more hermeneutical mind-set and more

---

64. Inge, *Place*, 54.

65. Inge, *Place*, 59; cf. 59-90.

66. See further Karl Rahner, *The Church and the Sacraments* (New York: Herder & Herder, 1963), and E. Schillebeeckx, *Christ: The Sacrament of Encounter with God* (London: Sheed & Ward, 1963).

67. William Temple, *Nature, Man, and God* (London: Macmillan, 1935), 478; cited by Inge, *Place*, 64.

appropriate expectations among readers who approach doctrine. In the historical tradition of hermeneutical inquiry Dilthey takes his place as a major successor to Schleiermacher, but with a stronger emphasis on *"life" (Leben)*, on *history* and historical understanding, on *social institutions,* and on individual or communal *action.* Even so, many argue that he did not fully escape Schleiermacher's focus on "inner" processes (although I have argued elsewhere that this criticism of Schleiermacher is too often overstated).[68] Dilthey stresses embodiment and the public domain more strongly than Schleiermacher, but we shall consider Karl-Otto Apel's well-argued criticism that he does not go far enough in this respect. Apel suggests that Wittgenstein's emphasis on "forms of life" serves largely to make up for this deficit in Dilthey's hermeneutics.

Wilhelm Dilthey (1831-1911) regards "life" *(Leben)* as a controlling category for "understanding" *(Verstehen).* He regards the philosophical traditions of the rationalists Descartes and Leibniz, of the empiricists Locke, Berkeley, and Hume, and even of the critical philosophies of Kant and Hegel, as too "mind-centered" or cerebral, and insufficiently grounded in human life as a whole. Alluding to these philosophical thinkers, he writes, "In the veins of the 'knowing subject' . . . *no real blood flows."*[69] Even Hegel's perceptive acknowledgment of the importance of history and "historical reason," Dilthey argues, still ascribed the privileged role in understanding to *mind* or *spirit (Geist).* Dilthey explicitly and consciously makes *Leben* his distinctive counterpart to the role played by *Geist* in Hegel. Hermeneutical reflection begins with *lived experience (Erlebnis).* He applied this axiom not only to language and texts, but also to the understanding of social institutions and communal practices.[70]

Dilthey's concept of "understanding" *(Verstehen),* then, seems at first sight to support philosophical caveats about the notion of belief as an inner mental event. Self-knowledge and understanding, he argues, do not come through introspection of inner states, but through the *historical flow of life in the public domain.*[71] Life as publicly observed reveals the similarities and differences of character, habit, and behavior that provide the frame of reference for understanding others. Dilthey suggests by way of example that we "understand" Luther's thought and beliefs through engaging not so much with his psychology as with

68. Thiselton, *New Horizons,* 204-28 and esp. 558-63.

69. Wilhelm Dilthey, *Gesammelte Schriften,* Bd. 5: *Die Geistige Welt: Einleitung in die Philosophie des Lebens* (Leipzig and Berlin: Teubner, 1927), 4 (my italics).

70. On Dilthey, cf. Anthony C. Thiselton, *New Horizons in Hermeneutics: The Theory and Practice of Transforming Biblical Reading* (Grand Rapids: Zondervan and Carlisle: Paternoster, 1992), 247-53.

71. Wilhelm Dilthey, *Gesammelte Schriften,* Bd. 7: *Die Aufbau der Geschichtlichen Welt in den Geisteswissenschaften* (Leipzig and Berlin: Teubner, 1927), 206; part translated in Wilhelm Dilthey, *Selected Writings,* ed. and trans. H. P. Rickman (Cambridge: Cambridge University Press, 1976), 279.

the public record of his letters, disputes, controversies, and actions. Here we perceive Luther's power and energy *in action.*[72] This is part of Dilthey's perception of the flesh-and-blood character of "historical reason" as embracing what is historically conditioned in life-situations, and reaches beyond Hegel. We understand "the other" only through a "life-relation" with the others. This emerges through the actual "interconnectedness" *(Zusammenhang)* of social and historical life. Dilthey's thought developed from a more individual-oriented perspective in *Einleitung in die Geisteswissenschaften* of 1883 to more communal and institutional concerns about "what people have in common" in the later *Der Aufbau der Geschichtlichen Welt in den Geisterwissenschaften.*

On this basis Dilthey formulates a hermeneutical dialectic of correspondence, analogy, or generality on one side, and uniqueness, particularity, and contingency on the other. We explore this dialectic in a later chapter as a model for a hermeneutics of Christian doctrine. Above all, Dilthey insists, the basis of hermeneutics is "not a logical abstraction."[73] Dilthey sees the "inner" life of human thought and belief transposed in terms of "always objectified and observable events."[74] This might seem to match our advocacy above of a dispositional account of belief in multiple public contexts.

Nevertheless Gadamer and Apel offer telling criticisms of Dilthey that suggest a degree of caution in seeing an adequate hermeneutic here. Gadamer attacks Dilthey's tendency to seek to establish hermeneutics as a kind of pseudo-science for the *Geisteswissenschaften,* or the "human sciences" of arts, humanities, and social sciences.[75] Gadamer writes, "Dilthey did not regard the fact that finite, historical man is tied to a particular time and place as any fundamental impairment of the possibility of knowledge in the human sciences. Historical consciousness was supposed to rise above its own relativity in a way that made objectivity in the human sciences possible."[76] Dilthey is too ready to find "historical" equivalents to Kant's *a priori* categories, and to ascribe too much to causal connections and generalizing, unifying patterns. Gadamer suggests that Dilthey came near to asserting that the idea of scientific progress could be extrapolated to the realm of human value.[77] Dilthey also shows too much sympathy with the Romanticist notion found in J. G. Herder that texts are merely objectified "deposits," to be distanced from the living fire of the mind that gave birth to them.

72. Dilthey, *Gesammelte Schriften,* vol. 7, 215-16.

73. See Dilthey, *Gesammelte Schriften,* vol. 5, 336; and "The Development of Hermeneutics," in *Selected Writings,* 262.

74. Zygmunt Bauman, *Hermeneutics and Social Science: Approaches to Understanding* (London: Hutchinson, 1978), 32.

75. Gadamer, *Truth,* 231-42.

76. Gadamer, *Truth,* 234.

77. Hans-Georg Gadamer, *Hermeneutics, Religion, and Ethics,* trans. J. Weinsheimer (New Haven and London: Yale University Press, 1999), 67.

Within the argument of this chapter, however, Karl-Otto Apel's critique is even more important. In his incisive essay "Wittgenstein and the Problem of Hermeneutic Understanding," Apel traces continuities and contrasts between Schleiermacher, Droysen, Dilthey, and Wittgenstein, but especially between Dilthey and Wittgenstein.[78] He argues that in spite of strong features in Dilthey's hermeneutics, especially in his attention to history and historical understanding, "the theory of hermeneutic understanding cannot be founded either on empathetic re-living *(Nacherleben)* or on the mental construction of someone else's creative acts which are expressed in the medium of the printed text (. . . or actions, or institutions)."[79] Apel believes that these "mental processes" or psychological states remain too important in Dilthey for his emphasis on observable life and action to compensate for them. Further, hermeneutical understanding is *not* a matter of *describing or observing* objectified life and action, but of *participating in it.*

Hence, Apel argues, Wittgenstein's explorations of *forms of life, situational contexts,* and *language games* constitute a way of approach that might "replace" the weaker aspects of Dilthey's thought.[80] Apel expands and illustrates what we discussed as "surroundings" in Wittgenstein in our previous chapter on belief. Wittgenstein insists that questions about meaning and understanding lead to confusion when asked *"outside* a particular language-game" (his italics), and "language-game" is his term for *"the whole,* consisting of language and *the actions into which it is woven"* (my italics).[81] The expression "the sun rises" may vary in its working currency depending on whether the actions into which it is woven are those of compiling a brochure for tourists or working in astronomy. The meaning in a tourist brochure has clear operational currency; in astronomy it is not "false," but in most astronomical contexts probably meaningless.[82] The word "exact" may denote a tolerance of not less than half a millimeter in the work of a carpenter or joiner, but "exact" would not denote this in talking of the distance between the earth and the sun.[83] To ask about meaning outside the language game, form of life, or extralinguistic situational context, Wittgenstein suggests, is like trying to do something with "the engine idling."[84]

The key factor, Apel declares, is "the entanglement of linguistic usage with the situational reference of the life-form in the language-game."[85] Only in the

78. Karl-Otto Apel, *Towards a Transformation of Philosophy,* trans. G. Adey and D. Frisby (London and Boston: Routledge & Kegan Paul, 1980), 1-45.

79. Apel, *Transformation,* 27.

80. Apel, *Transformation,* 7 and 22-35.

81. Wittgenstein, *Investigations,* sects. 47 and 7 (respectively).

82. Apel, *Transformation,* 22.

83. Wittgenstein, *Investigations,* sect. 88.

84. Wittgenstein, *Investigations,* sect. 88.

85. Apel, *Transformation,* 23.

larger unit of language-and-life-activity does a linguistic utterance acquire its meaning currency. So inconceivable is it to be otherwise that Wittgenstein observes, "To imagine a language means to imagine a form of life *(eine Lebensform vorstellen)*."[86] "The *speaking* of language is part of an *activity* or of a form of life" (first italics Wittgenstein's; second, mine).[87]

Apel insists that this is central to *hermeneutics*. He writes, "The model of the language-game implies both the immediate world (situational) understanding which is an aspect of 'meaning something' and, in the narrower sense, the 'hermeneutic' understanding of the intentions that reside in the immediate understanding of the world and are expressed in the actions and deeds of human beings."[88]

This comes to light more clearly when Wittgenstein selects certain examples of what it is to understand. If a person is wrestling with a mathematical problem or formula, and light dawns, that person may say, "Now I know how to proceed." But this utterance is not primarily a report on an inner psychological condition; it is an indication that further action now becomes possible; it is about competency and performance, not mental processes *as such*.[89] Wittgenstein, however, is at pains to say that this is not behaviorism, and that he is not a behaviorist.[90] He does not doubt that mental processes occur; but the *grammar* of understanding does not have these *as its focus*. Wittgenstein writes of the response "Now I know how to go on": "It would be quite misleading . . . to call the words 'a description of a mental state' — One might rather call them a 'signal.'"[91] Wittgenstein's careful distinctions between public "grammar" and behaviorism (which he rejects) also emerge clearly in several passages in *Philosophical Occasions*.[92]

One further factor links Wittgenstein closely with Gadamer, and distances him from Dilthey's notion of *describing* objectified phenomena. Apel identifies both aspects well. He writes, "One must presuppose not a detached description of the language-game as a whole but rather participation in the language-game, since — according to Wittgenstein's own maxim — . . . an understanding of meaning commonly exists within the framework of a functioning language-game."[93] "Understanding of meaning always presupposes *participation* in the language-game" (Apel's italics).[94]

86. Wittgenstein, *Investigations*, sect. 19.

87. Wittgenstein, *Investigations*, sect. 23.

88. Apel, *Transformation*, 24.

89. Wittgenstein, *Investigations*, sects. 179, 180, and 321; cf. also 154 and 308.

90. Wittgenstein, *Investigations*, e.g., sects. 307-8 and 318.

91. Wittgenstein, *Investigations*, sect. 180.

92. Ludwig Wittgenstein, *Philosophical Occasions: 1912-1951*, ed. J. Klagge and A. Nordmann (Indianapolis and Cambridge: Hackett, 1993), 50, 98-99, 297, 339-40, and 342-45.

93. Apel, *Transformation*, 28.

94. Apel, *Transformation*, 31.

If description were to replace *participation*, the dimension of *action* and "bodiliness" would vanish. This need not and should not be taken to imply a radically pluralist or fideistic interpretation of Wittgenstein. Wittgenstein sees some examples of communication and understanding as resting upon "the common behavior of mankind."[95] I have argued against a pluralist interpretation elsewhere, especially against the dubious application of the term "incommensurable" to different language games, and Apel, moreover, does not hold this view of Wittgenstein.[96] Gadamer, in a parallel way, speaks of entering into "play as play," not as a spectator; "a festival exists only in being celebrated"; engagement occurs when "one loses oneself as a spectator."[97] He comments, "Play fulfils its purpose only if the player loses himself in play."[98] However, Wittgenstein *also* leaves room to view language games as "objects of comparison," and allows room also for "a quiet weighing of linguistic facts."[99] Further, Apel, unlike Gadamer, leaves room for "abstraction" as a critical exercise. We explore this particular aspect of how hermeneutical participation and formation relate to critical assessment and even theological "science" in Chapter 8.

It would take us too far afield from our argument to trace those developments in linguistic theory that underline the indispensable role of "life," action, and embodiment in many instances (even if not perhaps in all) relating to meaning, communication, and understanding. We cite only one such. Recently the area of speech-act theory and pragmatics has undergone further particular development in terms of "Politeness Theory," pioneered by Penelope Brown and Stephen C. Levinson.[100] The heart of the approach turns on social and formal politeness as reflecting motivations for "face-saving" communication, common to a variety of cultures. Much of the research arises from conversational implicature.[101] We cannot describe this approach in detail here, but the regular terminology of the subdiscipline (face-threatening acts, face-saving acts, footing, weightiness, habitus, and field) indicate the irreducible significance of embodiment for this type of approach to meaning, understanding, and communicative events.

This chapter has sought to weave together pointers from theory to practice in Christian traditions, doctrine, hermeneutics, biblical studies, and philosophi-

---

95. Wittgenstein, *Investigations*, sect. 206.
96. Thiselton, *New Horizons*, 395-400.
97. Gadamer, *Truth*, 116, 124, and 128.
98. Gadamer, *Truth*, 102.
99. Wittgenstein, *Investigations*, sect. 130 and *Zettel*, sect. 447.
100. Penelope Brown and Stephen C. Levinson, *Politeness: Some Universals in Language Usage*, Studies in Interactional Sociolinguistics 4 (Cambridge: Cambridge University Press, 1987).
101. Stephen C. Levinson, *Pragmatics* (Cambridge: Cambridge University Press, 1983); and Geoffrey Leech, *The Principles of Pragmatics* (London and New York: Longman, 1983). Cf. also Gillian Brown and George Yule, *Discourse Analysis* (Cambridge: Cambridge University Press, 1983).

cal analysis. All point in a common direction. We conclude by calling attention to George Pattison's recent discussion of Christian doctrine. Pattison argues, first, that doctrine entails hermeneutics; and, second, that it involves action and bodiliness. Whether in orthodox, biblical, radical, or neo-orthodox treatments of doctrine, he writes, "Something rather important is being overlooked."[102] Too little is said about Christian doctrine as "a practice, an activity, a doing."[103] The implicitly hermeneutical nature of doctrine raises issues of "understanding," and of a concrete relation to life.[104] Appealing in part to Kierkegaard, on whom he has written elsewhere, he sees doctrine as "an open-ended process to communication" in which "the how" as well as "the what" of knowing, understanding, and communication performs a major role.[105] *Dialectic* occurs in doctrine, especially as it relates to *concrete situations.* God, as we have argued, is known only through God, but God is the living God who acts in human *life.*[106] Doctrine enables us "to be participants in the divine conversation."[107]

102. George Pattison, *A Short Course in Christian Doctrine* (London: S.C.M., 2005), 5.
103. Pattison, *Doctrine,* 6.
104. Pattison, *Doctrine,* 9.
105. Pattison, *Doctrine,* 11.
106. Pattison, *Doctrine,* 19-45.
107. Pattison, *Doctrine,* 41.

CHAPTER 4

The Hermeneutics of Doctrine as a Hermeneutic of Temporal and Communal Narrative

4.1. Time, Temporality, and Narrative: The Living God

Among major systematic theologians of acknowledged stature it is widely acknowledged that God alone is the ground and source of authentic Christian doctrine. Karl Barth offers the classic formulation: "God is known through God alone."[1] "God can be known only by God. . . . We know God in utter dependence, in pure discipleship and gratitude."[2]

This is not an exclusively "Barthian" starting point. Wolfhart Pannenberg writes, "The knowledge of God that is made possible by God and therefore by revelation is one of the basic conditions of the concept of theology as such. Otherwise the possibility of the knowledge of God is logically inconceivable; it would contradict the very idea of God."[3] Doctrine is in principle "discourse about God that God himself has authorized."[4] Jesus Christ, he adds, is the "only foundation" (1 Cor. 3:11), but this does not exclude the "debatability of the reality of God."[5] Karl Rahner writes, "Theology consists in a process of human reflection upon the revelation of God in Jesus Christ, and arising from this, upon the faith of the Church."[6] In the premodern era this same starting point for doctrine found widespread expression in the Patristic writers, in Thomas Aquinas, and in John Calvin.[7]

---

1. Barth, *Church Dogmatics*, II:1, sect. 27, 179.
2. Barth, *Church Dogmatics*, II:1, 183; cf. "The Hiddenness of God," 179-204.
3. Pannenberg, *Systematic Theology*, vol. 1, 2.
4. Pannenberg, *Systematic Theology*, vol. 1, 7.
5. Pannenberg, *Systematic Theology*, vol. 1, 61.
6. Karl Rahner, *Theological Investigations*, 22 vols. (English, London: Darton, Longman & Todd and New York: Seabury/Crossroad, 1961-91), vol. 13 (1975), 61.
7. Thomas Aquinas, *Summa Theologiae*, Latin and English, Blackfriars edn., 60 vols. (London:

Might this seem to cut across our arguments about the relation between doctrine and hermeneutics? Does it suggest that hermeneutics has little or no place in the understanding of Christian doctrine? For if doctrine is founded upon a definitive revelation from God, what room is there for the ambiguities, provisionality, contingencies, and particularities that characterize hermeneutical inquiry?

As we have noted, Pannenberg insists that knowledge "made possible by God" does not cease thereby to be "debatable" and capable of diverse interpretations. Barth fully acknowledges the role of the church in "criticising and revising its speech about God. . . . Theology is a fallible human work."[8] Moreover, revelation and Christian doctrine *come into being within a temporal frame and context.* As Barth expresses it, the Old Testament witnesses to a "time of expectation," and the New Testament reflects a "time of recollection."[9] González comments, "Doctrines . . . are ways in which the church through the ages has sought to clarify what it has heard from God. . . . One of the most common errors in the life of the church . . . has been to confuse doctrine with God."[10] Doctrines evolve often by responding to new challenges (as we have seen in our accounts of dispositional analyses of belief), or in the context of changing languages or situations. But they also *assume a living, dynamic, ongoing form, because God is the living, dynamic, ongoing God.* If doctrine reflects the nature of God and derives ultimately from God, *doctrine will be no less "living" and related to temporality than God,* who acts in human *history.* God's partial self-disclosure in Exod. 3:14 is best translated in a way that recognizes the temporally extended force of the Hebrew verb, suggesting: "I will be who I will be" (Hebrew אהיה אשר אהיה, *'ehyeh 'ᵃsher 'ehyeh,* imperfect with future force).[11] It does not quite convey the translation of the Septuagint: "I am who I am." This might be taken to imply: "I am a self-contained, incomprehensible being." Childs comments, "God's nature is neither static being, nor eternal presence, nor simply dynamic activity. Rather, the God of Israel makes known his being in specific historical moments, and confirms in his works his ultimate being by redeeming a covenant people."[12]

The *particularity, contingency,* and *temporality* of hermeneutical inquiry remain not only appropriate but also necessary for exploring the truth-claims, meaning, and life-related dimensions of Christian doctrine. To say that doctrine is derived ultimately from God, far from suggesting that doctrine inhabits an abstract, timeless, conceptually pure domain, underlines the temporal and narrative character of its subject matter.

Eyre & Spottiswood and New York: McGraw & Hill, 1963), Ia, Q. 2, arts. 1-3; and John Calvin, *Institutes of the Christian Religion,* trans. H. Beveridge, 2 vols. (London: James Clarke, 1957), I:1:1-3.

8. Barth, *Church Dogmatics,* I:1, sect. 1, 3-4.
9. Barth, *Church Dogmatics,* I:2, sect. 14, 45.
10. González, *History,* 7.
11. Brevard S. Childs, *Exodus: A Commentary* (London: SCM, 1974), 76; cf. 60-89.
12. Childs, *Exodus,* 88.

At certain points I have used the more cumbersome term *temporality* rather than *time* to avoid a possible misunderstanding. Temporality (*Zeitlichkeit* especially in Heidegger) denotes the transcendental ground for the possibility of time. The term allows for recognition of the truth that God is neither conditioned by "human" time nor "timeless" in the sense of being unrelated to time. God interacts with the world through actions marked by *purpose, duration, periodicity, tempo, and eventfulness*, even if "God's" time is not to be equated with "human" time, but relates to temporality as the transcendental ground for time.[13] Meaning and truth are not "timeless" in relation to God. "The truth of God," Pannenberg writes, "is not the result of logical necessity. . . . [It] must prove itself anew in the future. . . . Only trust can anticipate it."[14]

Karl Rahner, similarly, seeks to hold together the notion of a revelation from God that is both definitive in principle and enters into the conditions of temporal human life as occurrence or "happening." He comments, "Revelation is not the communication of a definite number of propositions, a numerical sum . . . but an historical dialogue between God and man in which something *happens*. [This is] related to the continuous 'happening' . . . of God."[15] Doctrine "must *necessarily* exist . . . through the medium of the historical process" (his italics).[16] Doctrine, in effect, reflects dialectic or what Rahner calls a "balance" between definitive truth ("how a proposition . . . can be explicated") and "living, growing . . . awareness in faith."[17]

Charles Scalise rightly perceives this dialectic as central to the relation between hermeneutics and Christian doctrine or theology. He places it in the context of eschatology. An overrealized eschatology will err on the side of conceiving of God (and doctrine) as "already defined." Here God becomes entirely "the God of propositional revelation" without as it were loose ends. The system is closed rather than open. On the other hand, a one-sided futurist eschatology risks conceiving of God as "not yet defined," akin to the God of process theology.[18] Scalise constructively alludes to the work of Jürgen Moltmann and Eberhard Jüngel as approaches that strive to sustain such a working dialectic. Moltmann insists, "Christianity is eschatology . . . forward looking and forward moving, and there-

13. See Anthony C. Thiselton, "Hermeneutics within the Horizon of Time: Temporality, Reception, Action" and esp. "Natural Time, Clock Time and Human Time: Temporality, Hermeneutics and Theology," in Roger Lundin, Clarence Walhout, and Anthony C. Thiselton, *The Promise of Hermeneutics* (Grand Rapids: Eerdmans and Carlisle: Paternoster, 1999), 183-209.

14. Wolfhart Pannenberg, "What Is Truth?" in Pannenberg, *Basic Questions in Theology*, trans. G. H. Kehm, 3 vols. (London: SCM, 1971-73), vol. 2, 8; cf. 1-27.

15. Rahner, "The Development of Dogma," in *Theological Investigations*, vol. 1, 48; cf. 39-77.

16. Rahner, *Investigations*, vol. 1, 47.

17. Rahner, *Investigations*, vol. 1, 76.

18. Charles J. Scalise, *Hermeneutics as Theological Prolegomena: A Canonical Approach*, Studies in American Hermeneutics 8 (Macon, GA: Mercer University Press, 1994), 118-21.

fore . . . transforming the present."[19] *Promise* takes its place in opposition both to "presumption" as premature fulfillment and to "despair" as premature anticipation of non-fulfillment.[20]

All of this sets the stage for exploring concepts of Christian doctrine as *narrative* or as *drama*. If doctrine may be perceived even in part as narrative or drama, the immediate relevance of hermeneutical theory becomes almost self-evident. Paul Ricoeur's magisterial three-volume *Time and Narrative* is one of the greatest works on both hermeneutics and narrative of the late twentieth century. Narration, he observes, "implies meaning" and invites hermeneutical inquiry.[21] This explores the parts played by issues of temporal logic, plot, narrative structure, narrative coherence, and *telos*. The coherence and continuity of narrative depend in part upon the mind's performing "three functions: those of expectation . . . attention . . . and memory"; these together make possible interactively the temporal hope of emplotment.[22] Christian doctrine relates closely to memory of God's saving acts in history; attention to God's present action in continuity with those saving acts; and trustful expectation of an eschatological fulfillment of divine promise. In 1980 I contributed an essay for the Church of England Doctrine Commission on the communal nature of doctrine under the title "Knowledge, Myth, and Corporate Memory."[23]

Aristotle, Ricoeur notes, speaks of *mythos* (which is very broadly equivalent to "emplotment" in his use of the term) as "the organization of events (Greek ἡ τῶν πραγμάτων σύστασις, *hē tōn pragmatōn sustasis*) into a system. However, this is *not a static, closed system of propositions*, but a system that is *open to the future* and *temporally conditioned*.[24] The emphasis is not on deductive or inductive logic, as if to construct a timeless system. Emplotment is to be understood in "a dynamic sense of *making (poiēsis)* a representation" in terms of *time and action*.[25] Aristotle sees agents within the narrative not primarily as "characters" in a passive sense, but as "persons engaged in action."[26] Ricoeur transposes this logic of action and temporality into "a hierarchy of levels of temporalization" reflecting "the dialectic of time and eternity."[27]

Ricoeur declares, "The composition of the plot is grounded in a pre-understanding of the world of action, its meaningful structures, its symbolic re-

---

19. Jürgen Moltmann, *Theology of Hope*, trans. J. Leitch (London: SCM, 1967), 16.

20. Moltmann, *Hope*, 23.

21. Paul Ricoeur, *Time and Narrative*, trans. K. McLaughlin and D. Peliauer, 3 vols. (Chicago and London: University of Chicago Press, 1984-88), vol. 1, 20.

22. Ricoeur, *Time*, vol. 1, 19 and 20.

23. Thiselton, "Knowledge, Myth and Corporate Memory," in *Believing in the Church*, 45-78.

24. Aristotle, *Poetics* 50A.15; cited in Ricoeur, *Time*, vol. 1, 33.

25. Ricoeur, *Time*, 33.

26. Aristotle, *Poetics* 48A.1; Ricoeur, *Time*, vol. 1, 35.

27. Ricoeur, *Time*, vol. 1, 28.

sources, and its temporal character."[28] Toward the end of his programmatic first three chapters Ricoeur cites several points of hermeneutical resonance with Martin Heidegger.[29] First, as in Heidegger, all interpretations and questions of meaning take place *within the horizon of time*. Second, Heidegger's philosophical understanding of "possibility" shapes its distinctive meaning for Ricoeur. Similarly, temporality *(Zeitlichkeit)* provides the transcendental ground for the *possibility* of time for both thinkers.[30] Third, "possibility" also indicates the *heuristic and imaginative scenarios of possible plots and possible* "worlds" of a projected future. This reflects Ricoeur's earlier thought in which he formulates the axiom, "Symbol *gives rise to* thought."[31] "Symbols give rise to an endless exegesis."[32] Symbol (at the level of word), metaphor (at the level of sentence), and emplotment (at the level of narrative) do not merely *reflect prior* thought; they *creatively generate, extend,* and *actualize* thought.[33]

"Plots," or "emplotment," allow for reversals, conflicts, surprises, complexities, hopes, frustrations, and fulfillment. They are the very stuff of human *life* (not theoretical thought) with which Christian doctrine interacts. A "grand narrative" (although not in the sense implied by Lyotard) may recount God's dealings with the world; "little" narratives may also portray the appropriation of divine acts on the scale of particular events and persons, with all the ambiguity and need for interpretation that characterizes a journey or narrative *en route*. There is room for what Ricoeur terms "a hierarchy of levels."

It is scarcely surprising, then, that many theologians have sought to expound the nature of Christian doctrine in terms of narrative, drama, or dramatic narrative. One part of the motivation for this doubtless arises from a sense of disenchantment with the more static and apparently more sterile models formulated by such writers as Charles Hodge, especially in the late nineteenth century. Hodge wrote, "The duty of the Christian theologian is to ascertain, collect, and combine all the facts which God has revealed . . . guided by the same rules as the man of science."[34] He rejoiced that while the Yale of his day flirted with novel

---

28. Ricoeur, *Time,* vol. 1, 54.

29. Ricoeur, *Time,* vol. 1, 60-64 and 83-87.

30. Martin Heidegger, *Being and Time,* trans. J. Macquarrie and E. Robinson (Oxford: Blackwell, 1962, rpt. 1973), Division II, sects. 61-83, esp. chs. 3 and 4, 349-423. For an exposition, see Thiselton, *The Two Horizons,* 181-87.

31. Paul Ricoeur, *The Conflict of Interpretations: Essays in Hermeneutics,* ed. Don Ihde (Evanston: Northwestern University Press, 1974), 288; and *Freud and Philosophy: An Essay on Interpretation,* trans. D. Savage (New Haven and London: Yale University Press, 1970), 543 (my italics).

32. Paul Ricoeur, *Interpretation Theory: Discourse and the Surplus of Meaning* (Fort Worth: Texas Christian University Press, 1976), 57.

33. For an exposition of Ricoeur's theory of symbol and metaphor, cf. Thiselton, *New Horizons,* 344-58.

34. Hodge, *Systematic Theology,* vol. 1, 11.

ideas, during his presidency at Princeton "a new idea never originated in this Seminary."[35] But the insight has a more positive grounding. Alister McGrath points out that an impetus for the construal of doctrine as narrative comes from the incontrovertible "narrative nature of the scriptural material itself."[36] The general point is too obvious to require confirmation. An increasing flood of studies call attention to the genre of narrative, drama, or dramatic narrative, and several argue for its significance as the chosen medium for theology and Christology on the part of John the Evangelist within the New Testament. R. Alan Culpepper's work is widely known, and we may add that of Derek Tovey, for which I was part-supervisor for a Ph.D. in the University of Durham.[37] Both works draw on narrative theory and narrative hermeneutics, especially in such literary theorists as Gérard Genette and Seymour Chatman.

In biblical studies narrative hermeneutics exploded into a fashionable area of research in the 1980s, with the fresh perspectives of Robert Alter, Wesley Kort, Ronald Thiemann, Stephen Crites, Meir Sternberg, and others.[38] In more theological terms, George Stroup and Hans Frei explored narrative in relation to communal Christian identity; Stephen Crites and Stanley Hauerwas underlined its primordial character for human experience and personhood; and Nicholas Wolterstorff explored the "projected worlds" of narrative and their self-involving dynamic, together with their refiguring, life-changing, formative character as "worlds" that draws readers into them as active *participants* rather than mere observers.[39] We discuss this participatory dimension in other chapters, especially in Chapter 3, in relation to Dilthey, Apel, Gadamer, and Wittgenstein.

35. Cited by Baird William, *History of New Testament Research*, 3 vols. (Minneapolis: Fortress, 2003), vol. 2, from A. A. Hodge, *The Life of Charles Hodge* (New York: Arno, 1969), 521.

36. Alister E. McGrath, *The Genesis of Doctrine: A Study in the Foundations of Doctrinal Criticism* (Oxford: Blackwell, 1990), 4.

37. R. Alan Culpepper, *Anatomy of the Fourth Gospel: A Study in Literary Design* (Philadelphia: Fortress, 1983); and Derek Tovey, *Narrative Art and Act in the Fourth Gospel*, JSNTSS 151 (Sheffield: Sheffield Academic Press, 1997).

38. For example, Robert Alter, *The Art of Biblical Narrative* (New York: Basic Books, 1981); Wesley A. Kort, *Story, Text and Scripture: Literary Interests in Biblical Narrative* (University Park, PA, and London: Pennsylvania State University Press, 1988); and Meir Sternberg, *The Poetics of Biblical Narrative: Ideological Literature and the Drama of Reading* (Bloomington, IN: Indiana University Press, 1985).

39. George Stroup, *The Promise of Narrative Theology* (London: SCM, 1984 [John Knox, 1981]); Hans Frei, *The Eclipse of Biblical Narrative: A Study in Eighteenth and Nineteenth Century Hermeneutics* (New Haven: Yale University Press, 1974); Nicholas Wolterstorff, *Divine Discourse: Philosophical Reflections in the Claim That God Speaks* (Cambridge: Cambridge University Press, 1985), esp. 1-129; Stanley Hauerwas, *A Community of Character* (cited above).

4.2. Christian Doctrine as Dramatic Narrative: Hans Urs von Balthasar

Among theologians of international stature Hans Urs von Balthasar has done more than others to unfold the explicit role of *drama* and *dramatic tension* as a model of Christian doctrine. In the Catholic tradition, Balthasar has nevertheless been influenced by Barth's emphasis upon God's dynamic and purposive action through the grand sweep of history from creation onward, through the revelation of God in Christ, through to the present, and finally but provisionally to the eschaton. He shares Barth's Trinitarian and Christological focus within a framework of an ongoing historical narrative of promise and grace. In his five-volume work *Theo-Drama: Theological Dramatic Theory,* near the beginning of the first volume he observes, "The shortcomings of the theology that has come down to us over the centuries have called forth new approaches and methods in recent decades."[40] Traditional forms and models risk an over-easy use of "slogans" and "catchphrases." More recent models are more aware of the problem, but seem slow to solve it. Balthasar writes, "All see theology stuck fast on the sandbank of rational abstraction, and want to get it moving again."[41] Nevertheless there are signs of more creative thinking. Hans Küng believes that since Vatican II there have been signs of a movement towards a new paradigm in theology.[42] David Tracy believes that a more serious turn to interpretation and hermeneutics heralds the beginnings of such a new paradigm.[43] Among recent more evangelical Protestant writers, Kevin Vanhoozer and Samuel Wells have explored this drama-oriented approach to doctrine and ethics, and we shall consider their work below.[44]

Balthasar is not entirely happy with a lack of comprehensiveness or balance in many late-twentieth-century attempts to identify more dynamic models of doctrine, even though he concedes that these make progress. He explores seven such models. The use of "events" as models takes us forward constructively, and Rahner makes use of this term. It does justice to the "lightning-flash" character of revelation, but in Balthasar's view it leaves too much room for both orthodox and liberal rationalism.[45] Models that stress "history" are also insufficient, for history may be understood in bland ways that do not preserve and convey the

---

40. Hans Urs von Balthasar, *Theo-Drama: Theological Dramatic Theory,* trans. G. Harrison, 5 vols. (San Francisco: Ignatius, 1988-98), vol. 1, *Prolegomena,* 25.

41. Balthasar, *Theo-Drama,* vol. 1, 25.

42. Hans Küng, "Paradigm Changes in Theology," in Hans Küng and David Tracy (eds.), *Paradigm Change in Theology: A Symposium for the Future* (Edinburgh: T&T Clark, 1989), 3-33.

43. David Tracy, "Hermeneutical Reflections in the New Paradigm," in Küng and Tracy, *Paradigm Change,* 34-62.

44. Vanhoozer, *The Drama of Doctrine* (cited above), and Samuel Wells, *Improvisation: The Drama of Christian Ethics* (London: SPCK, 2004).

45. Balthasar, *Theo-Drama,* vol. 1, 25-28.

"dramatic tension" that inheres in Christian doctrine.[46] An emphasis upon "orthopraxy" rightly fastens on action, embodiment, and the dimension of everyday human life. These indeed characterize doctrine, but they may too readily allow a reduction and dissipation of doctrine into ethics.[47] "Dialogue" again takes us further, and rightly gives prominence to *communal understanding.* God speaks, and the people of God address God as *"Abba."* Doctrine is indeed more than monologue, and characteristically entails communal responsibility, but this is only part of a wider picture.[48] "Political theology" takes up a particular dimension of Christian doctrine, but doctrine transcends this. "Futurist" theology takes up an important eschatological aspect of doctrine, but this too easily degenerates into liberal utopianism, or, on the other side, into apocalypticism. Christian doctrine is again wider.[49]

Finally, the seventh model brings us nearer to Balthasar's model of drama, dramatic tension, and narrative. It takes up the notion of *role* within a network of actions, especially in narrative grammar. But in some contexts, such as that of structuralism, narrative grammar has made "role" too fixed and formalized, while in Christian doctrine roles "overflow" into broader and more complex notions of divine and human agency. We must move beyond such structured categorizations to wrestle also with the genuine realities of darkness and evil that also belong to Christian doctrine.[50] Any approach that is too structured, fixed, or formalized will prove to be inadequate.

Balthasar argues that the search to do justice to the phenomenon of *dramatic tension* in Christian doctrine cannot achieve this goal simply by recasting the content of doctrine.[51] *Dialectic* comes into play. Further, doctrine as drama is played out upon the *"world stage."*[52] Some writers outside Christian traditions, notably Pindar and Aristotle, and then later Epictetus, have this sense of action or acting on a world stage. Certainly Paul the Apostle uses language of this kind in 1 Cor. 4:9, which is especially significant in the light of the ironic context of 4:8-13.[53] I cite my translation (in my two commentaries) of v. 9: "For it seems to me that God has put us apostles on display as the grand finale, as those doomed to die, because we have been made a spectacle in the eyes of the world, of angels, and of humankind."[54] The metaphor is that in which "criminals, prisoners, or

46. Balthasar, *Theo-Drama,* vol. 1, 28-31.
47. Balthasar, *Theo-Drama,* vol. 1, 31-34.
48. Balthasar, *Theo-Drama,* vol. 1, 34-37.
49. Balthasar, *Theo-Drama,* vol. 1, 37-46.
50. Balthasar, *Theo-Drama,* vol. 1, 46-50.
51. Balthasar, *Theo-Drama,* vol. 1: "Theology and Drama," 125-34.
52. Balthasar, *Theo-Drama,* vol. 1, under "World Stage," 135-257.
53. Balthasar, *Theo-Drama,* vol. 1, 136-51.
54. Translation from Anthony C. Thiselton, *The First Epistle to the Corinthians: A Commentary on the Greek Text,* NIGTC (Grand Rapids: Eerdmans and Carlisle: Paternoster, 2000), 344;

professional gladiators join in procession to the gladiatorial ring, with the apostles bringing up the rear as those who must fight to the death. . . . The Corinthians have a grandstand view . . . as spectators. . . . As the drama intensifies, finally the doomed criminal appears who must go to his death."[55] I translate 4:13b: "We have become, as it were, the world's scum, the scraping from everyone's shoes."[56] The Christians in Corinth simply lounge about in the best seats as spectators, and applaud or criticize as those who are not involved.

In a recent work L. L. Welborn goes into further details about Paul's use of drama and dramatic imagery. In particular he presses home the point that "Paul was governed by a social constraint in his discourse about the cross . . . and the sufferings of the apostles."[57] "Because . . . in the cross of Christ God has affirmed nothings and nobodies. . . . Paul's appropriation of the role of the fool is a profound . . . manoeuvre."[58] He emphasizes that Paul uses metaphors drawn from theatre and drama not only in 1 Cor. 4:8-13 but also in 2 Cor. 11:1–12:10 and Phil. 3:12–4:3. Welborn cites further literature in support of this claim.[59] He attempts also to argue the case for understanding the allusion in Acts 18:3 to Paul's occupation as σκηνοποιός (Greek skēnopoios, usually translated tentmaker, although as leatherworker by R. Hock) to denote *a maker of stage properties* or *prop maker*.[60] It is significant that in the third edition of the definitive Baur-Danker-Arndt-Gingrich *Greek Lexicon,* F. W. Danker argues that *tentmaker* has inadequate lexical support outside biblical literature, and that Luke's readers would most naturally understand his use of the term in Acts 18:3 "in reference to matters theatrical."[61] The "comic philosophical tradition," to which Welborn alludes, reflects a tradition that draws on Socratic dialectic, satire, mime, and dramatic tension.

Balthasar does not explore Pauline material in detail here, but underlines that doctrine as drama embodies not only dramatic tension but also *celebration,* especially in the context of festivals, which passes on to doxology. In the remainder of his first volume Balthasar explores elements of dramatic presentation.[62]

also in Anthony C. Thiselton, *1 Corinthians: A Shorter Exegetical and Pastoral Commentary* (Grand Rapids: Eerdmans, 2006), 73-74.

55. Thiselton, *First Epistle,* 360.

56. Thiselton, *First Epistle,* 344.

57. L. L. Welborn, *Paul, the Fool of Christ: A Study of 1 Corinthians 1–4 in the Comic Philosophical Tradition,* JSNTSS 293 (London and New York: T&T Clark International Continuum, 2005), 3.

58. Welborn, *Paul, the Fool,* 250.

59. Hans Windisch, *Der zweite Korintherbrief,* KEKG (Göttingen: Vandenhoeck & Ruprecht, 1924), 316 and 349; D. J. Williams, *Paul's Metaphors — Their Context and Character* (Peabody, MA: Hendrickson, 1999).

60. Welborn, *Paul, the Fool,* 11-12.

61. W. Bauer and F. W. Danker, *A Greek-English Lexicon of the New Testament and Other Early Christian Literature,* trans., ed., and rev. W. F. Arndt, F. W. Gingrich, and F. W. Danker (BDAG) (Chicago: University of Chicago Press, 3d edn. 2000), 929.

62. Balthasar, *Theo-Drama,* vol. 1, 259-478.

Balthasar devotes a substantial section of his second volume to *hermeneutics*.[63] He writes, "All theology is an interpretation of divine revelation. Thus, in its totality, it can only be hermeneutics. . . . God interprets himself," and this involves "giving an interpretation, in broad outline and in detail, of his plan for the world — and this knowledge is hermeneutical."[64] Various modes of communication become intelligible through the Holy Spirit, and this invites exploration through the general horizon of hermeneutics. This remains the case whether the subgenre is drama or symphony. "Ordinary horizons of understanding" in daily life may be inadequate, Balthasar recognizes, but they may be *extended*. This principle, we have noted, finds a key place in Gadamer, and (we may add) in Pannenberg. A viable theological hermeneutic will embody both *"retrospective"* understanding *in time*, and also projection *"forward"* on the basis of eschatological divine promise.[65]

This is not the place to try to offer a further exposition of Balthasar's sometimes difficult thought in detail. Before we move on, though, we may note that his conception of doctrine as drama reaches a definitive stage where he expounds the person and dramatic work of Christ as an integrated whole in his third volume. This holds a central place in the gospel and in Christian doctrine, and Balthasar (with Barth, Pannenberg, and Moltmann) places it firmly within a Trinitarian frame. Dramatic "tension" occurs "within the Christ-event itself."[66] The doctrine of the cross, indeed the cross itself, is not "external" to the events and process of salvation. The drama focuses on the climax of "the hour" of Jesus Christ. The Fourth Gospel emphasizes this narrative point of view (John 2:4; 4:21; 5:25; 7:30; 8:20; and especially 12:23, 27; 13:1; 16:32; 17:1).[67] The whole drama with its dramatic tension derives from the "drama in the very heart of God," in which God as Father *"sends"* the Son in mission; and the Son is *"obedient"* to the Father, even to his descent into the very jaws of hell, prior to his ascent in the climactic event of the resurrection and exaltation.[68] The drama of God's saving acts in the world reflects the "higher" drama or "super-drama" of the Trinitarian life of God.

Ben Quash, who is a well-known interpreter of Balthasar, notes that this movement forward from Balthasar's six-volume work *The Glory of the Lord* to his five-volume *Theo-Drama* "gives birth to discipleship, after the manner of the transition in Ignatian spirituality from contemplation to mission."[69] Quash also

---

63. Balthasar, *Theo-Drama*, vol. 2, *Dramatis Personae: Man in God*, 91-171.

64. Balthasar, *Theo-Drama*, vol. 2, 91.

65. Balthasar, *Theo-Drama*, vol. 2, 94-95 (my italics).

66. Balthasar, *Theo-Drama*, vol. 3, *Dramatis Personae: Persons in Christ* (San Francisco: Ignatius, 1992), 117.

67. Cf. Balthasar, *Theo-Drama*, vol. 3, 122.

68. Balthasar, *Theo-Drama*, vol. 3, 119.

69. Ben Quash, "Hans Urs von Balthasar," in David F. Ford (with Rachel Muirs), *The Modern Theologians* (Oxford: Blackwell, 3d edn. 2005), 112; cf. 106-23.

rightly links this with Balthasar's Christology in *Heart of the World:* "the drama of the passion of the eternal Son (with the cry from the cross sounding at its heart); the Son's subsequent descent into Hell, and his entry into resurrection life. It is in these events that both human action and the inner life of the Trinity, which is the condition of all human freedom, are displayed in the full depth of their interrelation."[70] Clearly, as in the theology of Jürgen Moltmann, we have moved away from more abstract formulations of "the immutability of God" as these are traditionally stated and too often understood, to a more dynamic and "personal" understanding of the divine nature and outgoing love.[71]

Ben Quash has formulated his own distinctive approach to doctrine as drama in *Theology and the Drama of History.*[72] His work takes place primarily in dialogue with Balthasar, but also with Hegel and Barth, and their respective approaches to history. In accordance with hermeneutical traditions Quash emphasizes provisionality and corrigibility of doctrinal formulation and development, but he ascribes this to his writing as an "Anglican theologian with Anglican habits of mind."[73] What may amount to a state of play or "settlement" in doctrine may stand in need of correction in the light of new historical circumstances. Also in line with Anglican theology and the argument of these chapters, Quash places greater emphasis upon particularities than Balthasar, whom he accuses of a "habitual neglect of historical particulars."[74] His critique of Balthasar's overreadiness to find analogical patterns may remind us of Gadamer's critique of Betti, but again Quash believes that this has more to do with the role of *analogia entis* in Thomas Aquinas and Catholic theology than with an appeal to hermeneutical theory.

These themes of drama, dramatic tension, and dramatic "world" find a place equally in the philosophical hermeneutics of Gadamer and in the narrative hermeneutics of Ricoeur. Gadamer's notion of art and of "worldhood" builds in part upon formulations in the earlier and later Heidegger.[75] The notions of epic narrative, lyric narrative, and drama or dialogue derive in part from the philosophy of Hegel, and both Balthasar and Quash give attention to this feature. Hegel

70. Quash, "Balthasar," 113.

71. Jürgen Moltmann, *The Trinity and the Kingdom of God,* trans. Margaret Kohl (London: SCM, 1981), 21-60; and Jürgen Moltmann, *The Crucified God: The Cross of Christ as the Foundation and Criticism of Christian Theology,* trans. R. A. Wilson and John Bowden (London: SCM, 1974), 200-290.

72. Ben Quash, *Theology and the Drama of History,* Cambridge Studies in Christian Doctrine (Cambridge: Cambridge University Press, 2005).

73. Quash, *Drama of History,* 8.

74. Quash, *Drama of History,* 196.

75. Heidegger, *Being and Time,* ch. 3, 91-148; and Martin Heidegger, "The Origin of the Work of Art," in *Heidegger: Poetry, Language, and Thought,* trans. A. Hofstadter (New York: Harper & Row, 1971), esp. 32-37, but also 15-87; cf. also Martin Heidegger, *On the Way to Language,* trans. P. Hertz (New York: Harper & Row, 1971), 111-36; and Gadamer, *Truth,* 84-129 and 476-77.

argues that "Epic as such . . . contains the universal in the sense of completeness of the world presented . . . the memory of an essential mode of being once directly present."[76] The content is an "act" or a "drama."[77] But epic or drama is directed toward an "other." In tragedy individuals destroy themselves through the one-sidedness of their will, for they are forced to resign themselves to a course of action to which they are opposed.[78]

On the theological side, such issues relating to drama find expression not only in Balthasar and Quash, but also among more recent broadly evangelical writers, including Kevin Vanhoozer, Samuel Wells, and Richard Heyduck.

4.3. Doctrine as Drama
in Kevin Vanhoozer's Canonical-Linguistic Approach

Kevin Vanhoozer's *The Drama of Doctrine* (2005) in part follows the pattern and agenda of Balthasar's work remarkably closely, except that it deploys the issues of doctrine and drama also to the American situation (to include, for example, a substantial critical discussion of Lindbeck, and the legacy of Hodge and "propositionalism"), and he expounds a firmer emphasis on biblical foundations, "the canonical-linguistic approach," and enters into dialogue with the evangelical world.[79] Vanhoozer begins his substantial volume by asserting, "The gospel — God's gracious self-communication in Jesus Christ — is intrinsically dramatic."[80] The neglect of this perspective, he argues, constitutes a major factor, if not *the* major factor, in the widespread perception of doctrine as dull, weak, and unimportant. "Doctrine no longer plays any meaningful role in the life and thought of ordinary Christians. . . . Gone are the arguments over doctrine and theology. . . . For many in our postmodern age 'feeling is believing.'"[81]

Yet doctrine, Vanhoozer argues, is indispensable for understanding and for truthful living. It is vital for the well-being of the church. He writes, "Doctrine, far from being unrelated to life, serves the church by directing its members in the project of wise living."[82] This has been a major theme of our argument for a more explicit hermeneutics of doctrine, and we shall return to it again. Vanhoozer writes, "Doctrine, far from being a matter of abstract theory, is actually *the stuff of*

---

76. G. W. F. Hegel, *The Phenomenology of Mind,* trans. with Notes by J. B. Baillie (New York: Harper & Row, 1967), 732.

77. Hegel, *Phenomenology,* 733.

78. Hegel, *Phenomenology,* 736-45.

79. Kevin J. Vanhoozer, *The Drama of Doctrine: A Canonical-Linguistic Approach to Christian Theology* (Louisville, KY: Westminster/John Knox, 2005).

80. Vanhoozer, *Drama,* xi.

81. Vanhoozer, *Drama,* xi.

82. Vanhoozer, *Drama,* xii.

life" (my italics).[83] This harmonizes with Archbishop Rowan Williams' three dimensions of theology as celebration or doxology, as communication and meaning, and as criticism to distinguish true from false witness.[84] In turn, these also cohere with Balthasar's emphasis and with the need for a hermeneutics of doctrine.

Vanhoozer combines his emphasis upon life and practice with the dynamic nature of doctrine stemming from the very early descriptions of Christianity as "the Way," and from the biblical and Puritan concept of holiness as "walking with God" in love (Eph. 5:2) and in wisdom (Col. 4:5; cf. Exod. 18:20; Deut. 28:9; Pss. 1:1; 119:1; 128:1; Rom. 8:4; Gal. 5:16; 1 John 1:7; Rev. 3:4).[85] Vanhoozer introduces his section "From Theory to Theater" by rightly declaring, "Doctrine seeks ... *to embody truth in ways of living,*" and an active and self-involving kind of discipleship is entailed in the Christian way as "fundamentally dramatic, involving speech and action on behalf of Jesus' truth and life."[86]

Doctrine, he argues, is a response to something *beheld,* to "what we have seen and heard" (1 John 1:3); and in terms of action, it is *a lived performance.* He comments, "Doctrines are less propositional statements or static rules than they are life-giving dramatic directions."[87] More specifically, he adds, "The remembered past is rendered through a plot," and this may assume a propositional form.[88] All of this, we note, involves issues of *narrative hermeneutics.* Hermeneutical perspectives are also implicit in Vanhoozer's further comment that doctrine has overcome equally the ditch between theory and *practice* and the ditch between exegesis and *theology.*[89]

Vanhoozer helpfully employs his notion of "canonical script" (which denotes the uses to which language is put in Scripture) to express caution about whether Lindbeck's model shifts too readily from the biblical canon to ecclesial communities. This does indeed remain a nagging concern about Lindbeck's work, even in spite of his explicit concern to respect the definitive status of Scripture, and the ecumenical context of his work. Lindbeck observes, for example, "It is the text, so to speak, which absorbs the world, rather than the world the text."[90] Believers not only find stories in the Bible, but they must also "make the story of the Bible this story. . . . It is the religion instantiated in the Scripture which defines being, truth, goodness, and beauty."[91] One cannot go much fur-

---

83. Vanhoozer, *Drama*, 2.
84. Rowan Williams, *On Christian Theology* (Oxford: Blackwell, 2000), xiii.
85. Vanhoozer, *Drama*, 14.
86. Vanhoozer, *Drama*, 15 (my italics).
87. Vanhoozer, *Drama*, 18.
88. Vanhoozer, *Drama*, 18.
89. Vanhoozer, *Drama*, 21.
90. George A. Lindbeck, *The Nature of Doctrine: Religion and Theology in a Postliberal Age* (Philadelphia: Westminster and London: SPCK, 1984), 32-41.
91. Lindbeck, *Nature of Doctrine*, 118.

ther than this. Thus when Vanhoozer states, "Neither tradition nor practice can be the supreme norm for Christian theology," it is doubtful whether Lindbeck would wish to contradict this.[92] Both writers stress that divine revelation recounts *an extended narrative of God's dealings with the world.*

As we have seen, communal confessions of faith and acclamations of praise often take this form in the Old and New Testaments. N. T. Wright stresses that "the narrative dimensions of Paul's thought [are] . . . one of the key elements of what has come to be known as the 'new perspective' on Paul. . . . It certainly does not reduce Paul's thought . . . to a world of 'story' *over against* doctrine . . ." (his italics).[93] Vanhoozer, in part following Ricoeur, stresses here the notion of "the plot" that has to be "performed." He reflects Balthasar's theme of an "all-embracing cosmic drama," but orients this toward an explicitly "evangelical" theology. He writes, "Evangelical theology deals not with disparate bits of ideas and information, but with divine doings — with the all-embracing cosmic drama that displays the entrances and exits of God."[94]

This perspective is not exclusive to evangelical theology, especially in the light of Balthasar's work, and G. E. Wright among many others earlier expounded a unitary sweep (arguably today, too unitary a sweep) of biblical history. On the other hand, such a view reflects the thought of several younger, more recent, evangelical writers. Vanhoozer is also right to trace a continuity of action, including dramatic action, between the word of God as divine communication through human language, the Word of God as Christ, the Word of God in gospel preaching, and the Word of God as Scripture.[95]

Vanhoozer follows earlier and more recent narrative patterns and dramatic patterns formulated by N. T. Wright and others against the theological background of Barth on "speech-acts" and of Balthasar in "deed-words."[96] The speech and action of Jesus "dramatically enacts the kingdom of God. Jesus and Paul carry forward the drama of creation, Israel's exile, the decisive, active Word

92. Vanhoozer, *Drama,* 22.

93. N. T. Wright, *Paul: Fresh Perspectives* (London: SPCK, 2005), 7; cf. 7-13. See esp. also Bruce W. Longenecker (ed.), *Narrative Dynamics in Paul: A Critical Assessment* (Louisville and London: Westminster John Knox, 2002); Richard B. Hays, *The Faith of Jesus Christ: The Narrative Substructure of Galatians 3:1–4:11* (Grand Rapids: Eerdmans, 1983, 2d edn. 2002); N. T. Wright, *The New Testament and the People of God,* vol. 1 of *Christian Origins and the Question of God* (London: SPCK and Minneapolis: Fortress, 1992), esp. 121-44; and N. T. Wright, *Jesus and the Victory of God,* vol. 2 of *Christian Origins and the Question of God* (London: SPCK and Minneapolis: Fortress, 1996). Cf. further Vanhoozer, *Drama,* 30-31; and N. T. Wright, "How Can the Bible Be Authoritative?" *Vox Evangelica* 21 (1991) 1-20, esp. 10-16.

94. Vanhoozer, *Drama,* 39.

95. Vanhoozer, *Drama,* 44-45.

96. Wright, *Paul: Fresh Perspectives,* 7-13; and Wright, *Christian Origins and the Question of God,* vol. 2, *Jesus and the Victory of God,* 130; and the other sources cited above. Cf. Vanhoozer, *Drama,* 52.

of God in Jesus Christ, and the "fourth act" of the era of the church, in which present participants in the gospel and its doctrine find themselves. The final *denouement* of the "five-act theo-drama" will culminate in the eschaton.[97]

In his more substantive chapters on theology in the theo-drama and the nature of doctrine, Vanhoozer presents divine communicative action primarily as that of *promissory action*. God's covenantal promise finds expression in "mission," and in "the missions of the Son and the Spirit."[98] "Drama works with *embodied personal relationships* (Vanhoozer's italics).[99] For the church becomes not simply audience, but is itself a *participant* in the dramatic action. In the period following the New Testament, the church of the second century decisively reaffirmed the continuity of the dramatic narrative in its first three "acts" by condemning Marcion's rejection of creation by the God and Father of Jesus Christ, the Old Testament as revelation of the one God, and the continuity between Israel and the church as the continuous narrative of the people of God. *Understanding* this drama requires interpretation or *hermeneutics*.

Too often writers formulate systematic theology or doctrine as if to try to mimic the voice of an impersonal and omniscient narrator. Here Vanhoozer draws, once again, on Balthasar for a distinction that goes back to Hegel between epic narrative on one side, which reflects a monological or declarative model of discourse, and lyric narrative, which is a more expressive mode, and dialogical narrative, which speaks with more than one single voice. If epic styles of narration speak declaratively with a single voice, this cannot but invite competing voices and competing interpretations to emerge.[100] Each is tempted to seek to make its *own* interpretation definitive, comprehensive, or absolute. "Propositionalist theology" is particularly vulnerable to this temptation. Indeed, Vanhoozer asserts, "Propositionalist theology at its worst is guilty of *de-dramatizing* Scripture" (his italics).[101] Charles Hodge comes in for particular criticism in this respect, although Vanhoozer seeks to rehabilitate the role of cognitive truth-claims through offering a more sophisticated account of propositions.[102]

Vanhoozer's Part II continues with what occupies Balthasar in his volume 2, namely *hermeneutics* (almost as if he were shadowing Balthasar's volumes). In practice Vanhoozer seldom uses the term *hermeneutics* (the index contains only three references to it), but he begins his chapter on "Word and Church" with an appeal to the "Gaza Road" experience of Acts 18:26-39. This turns on whether the Ethiopian official *understands* what he is reading from Isaiah (Acts 8:30).[103] He

97. Vanhoozer, *Drama*, 57.
98. Vanhoozer, *Drama*, 63-73.
99. Vanhoozer, *Drama*, 77.
100. Vanhoozer, *Drama*, 85-86.
101. Vanhoozer, *Drama*, 87.
102. Vanhoozer, *Drama*, 88-91.
103. Vanhoozer, *Drama*, 116-50.

needs someone *to interpret* the text, and Philip does this, Vanhoozer observes, in accordance with earliest traditions or the apostles' rule of faith. He lists several key components of hermeneutical inquiry, including the role of interpretation; the status of the text; the relevance of tradition; the community who reads; and the agency of the Holy Spirit. Nevertheless Vanhoozer's deepest and broadest concerns throughout the remainder of the book are, first, issues about the biblical canon, and, second, about the communal life of the church.

We may review a substantial number of common points of emphasis shared between Vanhoozer's approach and these present chapters. We share a common concern about the importance of doctrine and its current tragic neglect or apparent inability to inspire; a common emphasis on doctrine as practices of life, also expressed in worship; a common conviction about the foundations of the biblical writings defined in terms of canon, but also its continuity with an ongoing, developing tradition; a common belief that covenantal promise stands at the heart of divine communicative action and Christian theology, and that this grounds the currency of divine speech-action in the world; a common understanding of doctrine as formation that generates habits that generate performance; and the temporal logic of narrative embodying a coherent plot. The application of the term *drama* allows the dynamic and tensive nature of doctrine to remain prominently in view.

Yet it will be clear that our agenda for future progress and the contexts of thought that drive our concerns also reflect considerable differences. Vanhoozer rightly speaks of "believing practice" and of "practical belief," but I suggest that what this entails becomes very much clearer when we place confessions of faith in the New Testament and second-century church in the context of dispositional accounts of what it is to believe. The themes identified require larger contexts of thought to be convincing. The relation between doctrine and practice is more than a matter of "living it out," although it is not less than this. The biblical notion of embodiment derives from a distinctive mode of thought with which the biblical writings are saturated, and which manifests itself in the Bible and Christian tradition in the incarnation, sacramental theology, the importance of time and place, the contrast with gnostic thought, New Testament research on "body" and the public domain, and many other ways.

Vanhoozer emphasizes the role of hermeneutics for doctrine, but apart from his allusion to Ricoeur on narrative, he states this rather than expounding it in detail. While the place of habit and performance, drawn in part from Samuel Wells remains helpful, I shall argue in Chapter 6 that the relation between "training," understanding, and action in the later Wittgenstein provide this with a practical edge that gives it currency for doctrine. Vanhoozer offers many constructive insights, but often these lack a wider context and a longer explanation of how they might be followed through.

I have three other minor reservations concerning this generally constructive and useful study, with most of which I am in agreement. First, the problem with any picture or metaphor is that it can seduce us to overplay it. Vanhoozer speaks of God as a player or actor in the drama. He then suggests that, like all actors, God has his "entrances" and "exodus" or moment of exit. He writes, "The God of the gospel is free to come and go as he pleases."[104] But can we properly press the picture of a player to imply God's *absence* from the scene? Martin Luther, Jürgen Moltmann, Kornelis Miskotte, and a number of other writers all rightly draw a contrast between divine absence and times of divine "*hiddenness.*"[105] The two are not the same. Moltmann writes, "Hiddenness . . . presses forward . . . into that open realm of possibilities that lies ahead and is so full of promise."[106] Miskotte asserts, "To declare the hiddenness of God is in itself a confession of faith. . . . The hiddenness of God, pregnant with glad remembrance and full of happy promise, surrounds us, as it were, with the presence of an absence."[107] This is not the case if God chooses to be absent. The Luther scholar James Atkinson writes, "The hiddenness, the silence" has nothing to with "There is no God."[108] This difference does not compromise God's freedom, since through covenant promise God has chosen to pledge himself to remain present with his covenant people, just as Jesus Christ has promised, "I am with you always, to the end of the age" (Matt. 28:20). The drama model is helpful, but a picture can "hold us captive."[109]

Second, I warmly endorse Vanhoozer's attempts to reach behind what he calls the "propositionalist" debate by means of defining the issues with greater precision. I pursued a broadly similar line of argument in a paper delivered in Union University, Jackson, Tennessee, in 2002. But I suggest that two points are of even greater importance than Vanhoozer's reformulations. First, we cannot generalize about the role of propositions, metaphors, or poetry in the biblical writings as a whole. The issues depend on what genre the writer is using, the purpose of the passage in question, and whether a "closed" or "open" text is under consideration. Second, in my paper I suggested that what writers in the Hodge tradition were genuinely seeking would have been better expressed had they used the term "ontological" to denote biblical truth-claims rather than becoming sidetracked into a different universe of discourse about propositions and types of propositions.[110] Metaphor remains also a critical issue, as I (like Vanhoozer)

---

104. Vanhoozer, *Drama*, 40.

105. Martin Luther, *The Bondage of the Will*, trans. J. I. Packer and O. R. Johnston (London: Clark, 1957), 169-71.

106. Moltmann, *Theology of Hope*, 213.

107. Kornelis Miskotte, *When the Gods Are Silent*, trans. J. Doberstein (London: Collins, 1967), 51.

108. James Atkinson, *Faith Lost: Faith Regained* (Leiden: Deo, 2005), 203.

109. Wittgenstein, *Investigations*, sect. 115.

110. Anthony C. Thiselton, "Biblical Authority in the Light of Contemporary Philosophical

have argued elsewhere. Janet Martin Soskice, who began her postgraduate research on Wittgenstein's picture theory under my supervision, has demonstrated that metaphors may make valid cognitive truth-claims.[111] I have alluded to a misconceived polarity between Hodge and Horace Bushnell in a previous chapter. This has had devastating effects for American debates between conservatives and liberals until relatively recently.

Third, as we have noted already, Vanhoozer presents his "canonical-linguistic" approach to doctrine as if it were a modified version of George Lindbeck's "cultural-linguistic" model of doctrine. Few North American authors write on the nature of doctrine without some interaction with Lindbeck. Such frequent and regular allusions to the so-called Yale School of Lindbeck and Frei, or to the so-called Chicago School of David Tracy, may seem puzzling to European writers, especially since their most creative work appeared more than twenty years ago, or even more in some cases.[112] Both sets of writers place issues of value before us, but other agenda may by now have overtaken them that invite attention. Vanhoozer's volume of 2005 certainly owes much more to Balthasar's constructive ideas than to Lindbeck's.

Nevertheless Vanhoozer does have good cause to engage with Lindbeck's work, and concedes that his own approach "has much in common with its cultural-linguistic cousin."[113] Both Lindbeck and Vanhoozer share a common dissatisfaction, certainly in part, with "cognitive-propositional" models of doctrine, and a more pronounced dissatisfaction with "experiential-expressive" models, at least as *comprehensive* accounts of the nature of doctrine. Both see experiential-expressive models in older liberal theology as weak and unfit for purpose. Vanhoozer argues, on the other side, that Lindbeck gives ultimately more weight to "rules" that relate to church practice than to the biblical foundations of doctrine.

Although he draws on the thought of the later Wittgenstein on grammar and on linguistic and behavioral practices, Lindbeck arguably overextends the scope and prior application of his three chosen models (cognitive-propositional, experiential-expressive, and cultural-linguistic) in such a way as to accord with Wittgenstein's warnings about the need to look at *particular cases and to avoid generalization and generality.* For nearly a century writers have recycled either the descriptive-versus-address/volitional dichotomy that was the undoing of Bultmann, or Karl Bühler's overly generalized linguistic trichotomy between cognitive, expressive, and volitional uses of language.[114] But for three-quarters of

---

Hermeneutics," in Anthony C. Thiselton, *Thiselton on Hermeneutics: Collected Works and New Essays* (Grand Rapids: Eerdmans and Aldershot: Ashgate, 2006), 625-42.

111. Janet Martin Soskice, *Metaphor and Religious Language* (Oxford: Clarendon, 1985).

112. Vanhoozer introduces his description in *Drama,* 16-33; Lindbeck introduces his model in *The Nature of Doctrine,* 32-41.

113. Vanhoozer, *Drama,* 16.

114. Karl Bühler, *Sprachtheorie: Die Darstellungsfunktion der Sprache* (Jena: Fischer, 1934).

a century we have been aware (not only but not least) through the later Wittgenstein that language uses are *manifold* (not threefold); that they can *overlap;* and that they can perform numerous functions *concurrently.* One of several giveaways in Lindbeck is the phrase "A Cultural-Linguistic Alternative."[115] One reply might be to suggest that the multiplicity of language has been recognized within the cultural-linguistic model. But in this case is it quite an "alternative," or are we speaking of different logical categories of classification or explanation that are not of the same order.

I am not arguing that Vanhoozer is "wrong" here. My point is, rather, that his choice of a subtitle implies that we might continue with this well-worn agenda, when he has done his done his best to shift to a new agenda. We do not have to bother whether Lindbeck has given priority to the church or the biblical writings to give priority to Scripture. In the end my reservations about both Lindbeck and Vanhoozer would be parallel ones. They have formulated some excellent constructive insights and critiques, but stopped short just as these were becoming really significant. In Vanhoozer's case this applies most of all to hermeneutics. He gives us a few lines on the role of the Spirit, the role of apostolic tradition, the role of the church, the role of the canonical text, even on "otherness," but none of this engages with the resources of hermeneutical theory and practice. It is my hope that some of these pages may serve to fill in a part of a gap of this kind.

115. Lindbeck, *Nature of Doctrine,* 32.

CHAPTER 5

Formation, Education, and Training in Hermeneutics and in Doctrine

5.1. Formation, Education, and Training in Gadamer, Ricoeur, and Betti

It is almost commonplace nowadays for those who write on biblical hermeneutics to stress the formative and transformative impact of biblical texts. David Kelsey, George Lindbeck, and Frances Young all urge that, as Kelsey expresses it, biblical texts as Christian scripture serve *"to shape persons' identities so decisively as to transform them"* (his italics).[1] I have argued this throughout *New Horizons in Hermeneutics*, which carries the subtitle *The Theory and Practice of Transforming Biblical Reading*, in both senses of *transforming*.

It is less evident, however, that writers usually urge this about Christian doctrine. One exception is Philip Turner. He argues convincingly that the distinctive foundations of Anglican doctrine lie, as Thomas Cranmer saw it, not in an abstract collection of "core doctrines" but in the "formative power" of communal commitment to worship and life, expressed in "faithful lives . . . *formed and lived* through reading, marking, learning, and inwardly digesting the Holy Scriptures . . . as the practical 'organizer of life' for . . . an ordered community."[2] What is important, Turner urges, is the "liturgical and *formational* setting" of doctrine.[3] Whatever tensions may seem at first sight to exist between hermeneutical inquiry and Christian doctrine (particularities versus coherence; provisionality versus

---

1. David Kelsey, *The Uses of Scripture in Recent Theology* (London: S.C.M., 1975), 91. See also Lindbeck, *Doctrine*, 118; and Frances Young, *The Art of Performance: Towards a Theology of Holy Scripture* (London: Darton, Longman & Todd, 1990).

2. Philip Turner, "Tolerable Diversity and Ecclesial Integrity: Communion or Federation?" in *The Journal of Anglican Studies* 1:2 (2003) 32; cf. 24-46.

3. Turner, "Tolerable Diversity," 36 (my italics).

commitment), both are *formative;* both aim at *formation* of understanding, life, and character.

Philosophical hermeneutics in Gadamer's sense of the term also concerns formation. Gadamer draws on the notion of *Bildung*, but he does not equate this simply with *culture*. *Culture* is a matter of "developing one's own capacities or talents." But in the context of hermeneutics *Bildung* carries us beyond this.[4] He writes, "The Latin equivalent for *Bildung* is *Formatio*, with related words in other languages — e.g., in English (in Shaftesbury) 'form' and 'formation'. In German . . . '*Formierung*' and '*Formation*' have long vied with the word *Bildung*."[5] This carries with it the notion of seeking to be transformed into an "image" *(Bild)* of the human, but *also the educational goal* of *building* by *forming*. The heart of hermeneutical endeavor is learning how to be open to "the other," to come to respect "the other" on its own terms. Thereby it is "learning to affirm what is different from oneself." This ultimately leads to and involves the cultivation of *wisdom (phronēsis)*.[6] An "educated" *(Gebildete)* human being draws on a process of *character formation*, not just the learning of "skills," competences, and "techniques" *(technē)*.

The relation between hermeneutics and the recovery of tradition, history, and "the classic" in world literature plays an important part here, parallel with the retrieval of Scripture and of earlier classical (including Patristic) theological traditions in Christian doctrine. In her excellent study of Gadamer Georgia Warnke observes, "From the point of view of edification what is important is not 'the possession of truths' but our own development."[7] *Bildung* still entails "keeping oneself open to what is other," namely to *truth* rather than merely to "a *procedure*."[8]

Gadamer's approach at this point resonates closely with Kierkegaard's. Kierkegaard writes, "Everyone who has a result merely as such does not possess it; for he has not *the way*" (his italics).[9] Kierkegaard observes in a later work, "The objective accent falls on WHAT is said, the subjective accent on HOW it is said. . . . This 'how' is the passion of the infinite. . . . [It] is precisely subjectivity, and thus subjectivity becomes the truth" (Kierkegaard's capitals and italics).[10] In spite of his language about "the inner," Kierkegaard draws attention here not to

---

4. Gadamer, *Truth*, 11.

5. Gadamer, *Truth*, 11.

6. Gadamer, *Truth*, 14; also 20-22.

7. Georgia Warnke, *Gadamer: Hermeneutics, Tradition and Reason* (Cambridge: Polity, 1987), 157.

8. Gadamer, *Truth*, 17; cf. 11 (my italics).

9. Søren Kierkegaard, *The Concept of Irony*, trans. L. M. Capel (London and New York: Collins, 1966), 340.

10. Søren Kierkegaard, *Concluding Unscientific Postscript to the Philosophical Fragments*, trans. D. Swenson and W. Lowrie (Princeton: Princeton University Press, 1941), 181.

inner mental states but to active *participation,* which is transformative. Subjectivity denotes "being sharpened into an I" rather than "dulled into a third person" who merely absorbs information.[11] In this sense, communication, understanding, and active subjectivity entail *formation* and *training.* In the same vein Gadamer declares that in the independent position of a university, teachers and students co-jointly "learn to discover possible ways of shaping our own lives."[12] This is reminiscent of John Henry Newman's *The Idea of a University.* The goal of a university and university education, Newman writes, is "to open the mind, to correct it, to refine it, to enable it to know, and to digest . . . to give it application . . . sagacity. . . ." Newman adds that university education is not merely a technical, utilitarian resource for society or for the church to "use"; its value is "what it is in itself . . . an object as intelligible as the cultivation of virtue."[13]

Formation in hermeneutics, then, belongs to the vocabulary of *character* formation, judgment, *training, habit,* and human agency. In Hegel's view, Gadamer notes, it presupposes and nurtures a continuity of awareness on the part of the self that enables the self to transcend the particularity of the fleeting present moment. It endows the self with the capacity to deal "with something that is not immediate, something that is alien, with something that belongs to memory."[14]

Wittgenstein believes that *training (Abrichtung)* plays a necessary role in making it possible *to understand.* In learning to understand and to execute a series of orders, for example, "one learns . . . by receiving a training."[15] A seemingly self-contradictory dialectic is at work. On one side in the training regime a certain stable regularity provides a backcloth, almost achieving the status of a "tradition." On this basis a continuity of understanding and habits of interpretation emerge. However, on the other hand, each contingent or particular example of "actualizing" what is being learned takes a distinctive, nonreplicated form, which often requires independent judgment or even "improvisation." Wittgenstein writes, "*The possibility of getting him* [the learner] *to understand (die Möglichkeit der Verständigung)* will depend on his going on [in this particular example] to write it down (as a series) independently" (his italics).[16] The criterion of understanding is fulfilled in certain contexts when he declares, "Now I know how to go on!"[17]

---

11. Søren Kierkegaard, *The Journals of Søren, Kierkegaard,* ed. and trans. A. Dru (Oxford: Oxford University Press, 1938), 533.

12. Hans-Georg Gadamer, *Hans-Georg Gadamer on Education, Poetry, and History: Applied Hermeneutics* (Albany, NY: State University of New York Press, 1992), 59.

13. John Henry Newman, *The Idea of a University* (New York and London: Longmans, Green, 1947), 108.

14. Gadamer, *Truth,* 13-14.

15. Wittgenstein, *Investigations,* sect. 86.

16. Wittgenstein, *Investigations,* sect. 143.

17. Wittgenstein, *Investigations,* sect. 179; cf. also 151.

This has close parallels with Gadamer's dialectic between tradition and performance. Two games of the same kind will follow the same rules, and two musical performances of the same piece will follow the same score. But no two games, and no two performances, will or should replicate the other. A predictable replication would cease to be a game, or cease to be art, as the case may be.[18] Gadamer writes, "The being of art . . . is a part of the event of being that occurs in presentation, and belongs essentially to play as play."[19] Indeed, he comes very close to Wittgenstein's view of training, understanding, and application in the following comment: "The knowledge that guides action is demanded by the concrete situation in which we have to choose the thing to be done and cannot be spared the task of deliberation and decision by any learned or mastered technique."[20] Two of the best interpreters of Gadamer, Georgia Warnke and Joel Weinsheimer, both provide excellent expositions of Gadamer on "Understanding and Application" (Warnke) or "Understanding by Applying" (Weinsheimer).[21]

Is this explication of "understanding" also a matter of *"formation?"* It is precisely in the context of this "hermeneutical" discussion of understanding *(Verstehen)* that Wittgenstein observes concerning the effects of this "training," "I have changed his *way of looking at things* (seine *Anschauungsweise*)" (Wittgenstein's italics).[22] In terms subsequently used in the philosophy of language (for example, by John Searle and Jonathan Culler) the linguistic or conceptual *competency* of the person who is learning has been decisively enlarged.[23] In Gadamer's terms, formation includes an *enlargement of prior horizons* of understanding that makes *room for engagement with new horizons.*[24] What "arises" (for Gadamer) or "dawns" (for Wittgenstein) makes an irrevocable impact that shapes the perspective of the person in question.

Paul Ricoeur also regards hermeneutical experience as that which will be formative for the human agent, provided that it is authentic. When individual consciousness remains trapped in merely individual self-reflection (for example, of the kind perpetrated in the philosophical tradition of Descartes), this consciousness risks "narcissism," and it generates "resistance to truth."[25] Drawing

18. Gadamer, *Truth,* 110-29.

19. Gadamer, *Truth,* 116.

20. Hans-Georg Gadamer, *Reason in the Age of Science,* trans. F. Lawrence (Cambridge, MA: MIT, 1981), 92; the quotation comes from "Hermeneutics as Practical Philosophy."

21. Warnke, *Gadamer,* 91-106; and Joel C. Weinsheimer, *Gadamer's Hermeneutics: A Reading of Truth and Method* (New Haven and London: Yale University Press, 1985), 184-99.

22. Wittgenstein, *Investigations,* sect. 144.

23. Jonathan Culler, *Framing the Sign: Criticism and Its Institutions* (Oxford: Blackwell, 1988), 95; cf. Searle's related notion of "Background," in John Searle, *Intentionality: An Essay in the Philosophy of Mind* (Cambridge: Cambridge University Press, 1983), 19-20 and 144-59.

24. Gadamer, *Truth,* 355-79; esp. 358-62.

25. Paul Ricoeur, *Freud and Philosophy: An Essay on Interpretation,* trans. D. Savage (New Haven and London: Yale University Press, 1970), 427.

critically on Freud and Jung, Ricoeur perceives the human self not only as fallible and capable of self-deception, but also divided by a self-imposed barrier that disguises the self from the self. There is another "text" that lies *"beneath the text of consciousness"* (Ricoeur's italics).[26] "The subject is never the subject one thinks it is."[27] Mere *introspection* will not breach the barrier of disguise. But genuine hermeneutical engagement with "the other" may begin to erode this spell of idolatrous self-deception, and may begin to *re-form* and *form* an "intersubjective" self that is capable of relations with others, by reaching out beyond the isolated self. Formative self-identity arises in the context of acquiring "narrative identity"; this emerges "at once in its difference with respect to *sameness* and in its dialectical relation with *otherness*" (Ricoeur's italics).[28] The aim of hermeneutical endeavor and hermeneutical training is to overcome narcissistic self-projections composed and imposed by the disguised self. Ricoeur declares, "*The idols must die* — so that symbol [which points beyond] may live."[29]

In this process of formation, "Symbol gives rise to thought."[30] Symbols suggestively convey a multiplicity or even infinity of meaning that beckons beyond the here and now. Symbols may thus extend the original horizons of the isolated self in the process of re-forming a self who is open to "the other." The respective poles of a critical axis of "explanation" and a hermeneutical axis of "understanding" or retrieval serve to operate together almost like transformative forces of death and resurrection. Ricoeur comments, "An interpretation which began by abandoning the point of view of consciousness does not serve to eliminate consciousness, but in fact radically renews its meaning. What is definitely denied is not consciousness but its pretension to know itself completely from the very beginning, *its narcissism*."[31] As he argues in *Oneself as Another*, it is not so much that the Cartesian model of the self is "wrong" as that it needs dialectical supplementation and re-formation: individuation is a more complex process that goes beyond "basic particulars."[32]

Hence like Gadamer on *Bildung* with its context implying education, Ricoeur compares this process of formation with *"growing"* from childhood to adulthood. As the human person receives education, interaction occurs not only with other persons but with societal institutions, and a sense of the traditions and history to which one belongs. Ricoeur writes, "How does a man emerge from

26. Ricoeur, *Freud*, 392.

27. Ricoeur, *Freud*, 420.

28. Paul Ricoeur, *Oneself as Another*, trans. Kathleen Blamey (Chicago and London: University of Chicago Press, 1992).

29. Ricoeur, *Freud*, 531.

30. Paul Ricoeur, *The Conflict of Interpretations: Essays in Hermeneutics*, ed. Don Ihde (Evanston, IL: Northwestern University Press, 1974), 288.

31. Ricoeur, *Conflict*, 323-24.

32. Ricoeur, *Oneself as Another*, 27-55.

his childhood to become an adult? . . . Images and symbols guide this growth, this maturation. . . . Growth itself here appears at the intersection of two systems of interpretation . . . a movement which must be rediscovered in the . . . structure of institutions, monuments, works of art, and culture."[33] This educational path is indirect, through encounter with "the other," not in introspective self-reflection. He concludes his second essay, "The Hermeneutics of Symbols, II," by quoting Freud's aphorism, "Where *id* was, there *ego* shall be."[34]

As a major exponent of hermeneutical theory Emilio Betti (1890-1968) is arguably next in importance to Gadamer and Ricoeur, and certainly alongside Habermas, Jauss, and Apel as among the half-dozen most creative thinkers in philosophical and textual hermeneutics. Betti is less well known in English-speaking circles, probably in part because his massive two-volume *Teoria Generale della Interpretazione* appeared only in Italian (1955), with an abridged German translation but to date no English equivalent.[35] In continuity with the earlier tradition of Vico, Betti pays particular attention to *communal* understanding. Following Schleiermacher, Dilthey, Gadamer, and Ricoeur, he also explores the concept and processes of *understanding (Verstehen)*. With Gadamer, he stresses the key importance of "open-mindedness" *(Aufgeschlossenheit)*, which includes openness to listen and to "receive," namely to cultivate "receptiveness" *(Empfänglichkeit)*.[36] In common with Dilthey and Gadamer, Betti recognizes that both the interpreter and what the interpreter seeks to understand are equally conditioned by their own place in history and by their respective historical horizons.

Betti may stand nearer to Schleiermacher and to Dilthey than to Gadamer in insisting that to "understand" the interpreter needs *to reach behind* the text or behind a human institution to apprehend what led to *its* formation. However, Betti claims that this is less a psychological process than a *historical* or *reconstructive* one. He is critical of Schleiermacher's appeal to a psychological dimension, but he approves of Schleiermacher's concern for "the whole" in contrast to merely atomistic or analytical interpretation. Closer at this point to Wittgenstein, Betti insists that understanding entails *appreciation of the form of life out of which* an utterance or institution arises. The goal of interpretation includes reconstructing the train of thought, public events, and historical processes that lie behind the text or phenomenon to be understood.

Betti differs most clearly from Gadamer in at least two respects. First, he tries to integrate a hermeneutical approach with linguistic and semiotic theory. He is

---

33. Ricoeur, *Conflict*, 324-25.

34. Ricoeur, *Conflict*, 334.

35. Italian, 2 vols. (Milan: Giuffre, 1955); German, Emilio Betti, *Auslegungslehre als Methodik der Geisteswissenschaften* (Tübingen: Mohr, 1967, abridged in one volume). A smaller treatment is E. Betti, *Die Hermeneutik als allgemeine Methodik der Geisteswissenschaften* (Tübingen: Mohr, 1962).

36. Betti, *Allgemeine Auslegungslehre*, 21.

less wary of "science" than Gadamer, and is willing to attempt provisional *typifications* and classifications. Second, he distinguishes between three main types of interpretation: *recognitive, re-presentational,* and *normative.* (1) "Recognitive" interpretation seeks to apprehend or to *"re-cognize"* the intended meaning of a text within its social form of life and historical and dynamic flow of life. (2) "Re-presentational" interpretation aims so to understand what is to be understood that the interpreter can "re-present" it in terms that are understandable to another person. The hermeneutical task becomes that of *spokesperson or educator.* (3) The third mode, normative interpretation, seeks *to apply* the text to a particular situation. This task of application, however, unlike Gadamer's view, carries with it the responsibility for formulating norms, canons, or criteria of "right" interpretation. Like Gadamer, Betti draws on legal and theological hermeneutics to show the importance of "application," but in contrast to Gadamer he draws from this comparison the inference that criteria for valid or acceptable application are inevitable and appropriate.

All three aspects of this triple hermeneutical process are *formative.* For a person who seeks to understand, seeks to communicate the understanding, and seeks to apply it appropriately has thereby become "stretched" to make room for something new, namely "the other." Betti's German translator uses the term *Fremd,* what is "strange," "alien," or "not-me," to convey Betti's thought. This is not simply a matter of making room for "new information." Far from it: it is a matter of creating "another mentality" or mind-set.[37] This re-formed mind-set draws on qualities or virtues *of character:* it involves *listening, tolerance, patience, respect for the other,* and ultimately mutual understanding. The *educational* dimension of all this is transparent, and indeed Betti argues that hermeneutics should be an obligatory subject in universities precisely because "hermeneutical *training*" involves all these qualities that assist communities to live together in mutual respect, common understanding, and harmony.

In spite of his clear differences from Gadamer and Ricoeur, Betti shares with them (and with Schleiermacher and Dilthey) the "hermeneutical canons" of taking account of preunderstanding, of the hermeneutical circle, of dialectic and questioning, and of the transcendental level of inquiry into what it is to understand. Where Betti and Gadamer speak of openness to "the other," Ricoeur speaks of destroying narcistic idols. Wittgenstein also captures this element of self-discipline, if not self-denial, when he observes, "You can't think decently if you don't want to hurt yourself." All of these major thinkers state or imply that hermeneutical understanding involves *formation,* not merely information, indoctrination, or the communication of merely instrumental or technical data.

37. Betti, *Allgemeine Auslegungslehre,* 307.

5.2. Training and Application in Wittgenstein; Training and Performance in Wells

This dialectic between formation of character and "application" has remarkable affinities with some recent reformulations of the nature of Christian doctrine and ethics. One striking example comes from the recent work of Samuel Wells, which we noted above in the context of drama. A telling parallel arises from his contrast between habit, training, or formation, on one side, and the often unpredictable nature of performances or "improvisation" on the other, even if performance becomes possible only on the basis of training. His chapter "Forming Habits" offers a useful starting point.[38]

Wells introduces the role of habit and training in relation to ethics (and by implication doctrine) with reference to the Duke of Wellington's famous comment that the Battle of Waterloo was won on the playing fields of Eton. Wellington's point was that Eton had provided the *character formation, training, and habits of thought and action* that proved decisive for the later moment of decision and action in battle. Wells observes, "The moral life is more about Eton than it is about Waterloo. . . . The heart of ethics lies in the formation of character."[39] He adds, "The time for moral effort is the time of formation and training."[40] In ethical discourse this approach coheres well with the revival in recent years of "virtue" ethics. Virtue ethics looks back to the ethics of Plato and Aristotle, in contrast to the consequentialist ethics of Bentham's utilitarianism and the deontological ethics of Kant.

Shared worship and common listening to Scripture, Wells argues, constitute character-forming habits of action. Intercession contributes to the formation of the virtues of patience, of persistence, and of learning to put oneself in the place of others. The sacrament of baptism nurtures the attitude of coming before God naked in death and appropriating Christ's death and resurrection in a participatory act of identification with Christ. To share the peace in the Eucharist or the Lord's Supper is to learn the habit of living in a state of reconciliation with others, and of sharing collaboratively in a common mission and commitment. Participation in the bread and wine of the Eucharist nurtures the habit of seeking to be formed in the image of Christ. Like play within a game, worship has its own rules and customs, which Wells compares with the training ground of the playing fields of Eton, from which it also looks forward to eschatological fulfillment. Wells writes, "Heaven is the time when the game becomes reality."[41]

These habits of mind and this kind of training relate to Christian doctrine as

---

38. Samuel Wells, *Improvisation: The Drama of Christian Ethics*, 23-85.
39. Wells, *Drama*, 73 and 74.
40. Wells, *Drama*, 75.
41. Wells, *Drama*, 85; cf. 82-85.

well as to ethical decision and action. Wells observes, "Training in improvisation is an analogy for worship and discipleship."[42] On one side, improvisation and performance take place in a context where there is a communally accepted script. This broadly corresponds with the givenness of Scripture and agreed doctrinal traditions. On the other side, Wells draws on Shannon Craigo-Snell's concept of "rehearsal," and observes: "Craigo-Snell's notion of rehearsal and performance, a form of hermeneutics . . . is concerned with how a text and a tradition are realized by a community in new circumstances. It creates new examples, new aspects of the narrative in the course of its drama, and this contributes to the hermeneutical spiral of action, reflection, and new encounters with text and tradition."[43] In the context of hermeneutics I have tended to use the term *actualized*, where Wells and Craigo-Snell use *realized*.[44]

Wells argues that rather than investing all thought and effort in a single moment of decision and action, the grounding of appropriate action lies elsewhere, namely in the prior formative grounding of "where it is perceived to fit into the story of the way God deals with his people." What is at issue first and foremost is acting "in the light of the larger story."[45] Shared memory of the past, as I argued in the Church of England Doctrine Commission Report of 1981, is more fundamental than the passing moment of response only to the present.[46] Wells explores and draws on "memory" for the relation between improvisation and "reincorporation." He writes, "The key factor in reincorporation is memory. Memory is much more significant than originality. The improviser does not set out to create the future, but responds to the past, reinvigorating it to form a story. . . . The improviser looks back when stuck."[47] Wells draws a contrast between the attitude of the improviser and (especially in the context of ethics) the "consequentialist." The latter tends to disregard the past, looking only to the future. Yet, Wells continues, the story told by the consequentialist is far too short. Indeed, neither the historical or remembered past nor the eschatological future receives their proper due. Alluding in common with Vanhoozer and other writers to N. T. Wright's notion of God's dealings with the world on the analogy of a five-act play, Wells writes, "Consequentialists live in a one-act play with no awareness of Act Five — Their perception of the future seldom accounts for the final resolution of all things."[48]

42. Wells, *Drama*, 85.

43. Wells, *Drama*, 66. Wells cites Shannon Craigo-Snell, "Communal Performance: Rethinking Performance Interpretation in the Context of *Divine Discourse*," *Modern Theology* 16:4 (2000) 475-94, esp. 479-82 for the notion of "rehearsal" as the moment when roles are tried and tested, and interactions practiced, in an embodied, communal setting.

44. Thiselton, *New Horizons*, 11-12, 31-32, 63-68, and 517-19.

45. Wells, *Drama*, 130 and 131.

46. Thiselton, "Knowledge, Myth, and Corporate Memory," in *Believing in the Church*, 45-78.

47. Wells, *Drama*, 147 and 148.

48. Wells, *Drama*, 148.

The approach advocated by Wells is profoundly hermeneutical. It entails the notion of understanding in terms of "placing in a larger context" (with Schleiermacher); reincorporating the present within a living tradition (with Gadamer); exploring the relation between training and habit (Gadamer and Wittgenstein); and understanding "application" as that which cannot be pre-formulated in advance, but arises from a dialectic between habit and the capacity "to go on" independently (with Wittgenstein and also Gadamer). On the basis of habits of judgment and "training," Wittgenstein perceives criteria of understanding (for example, understanding a procedure or formula in mathematics) as expressed in some such exclamation as "Now I know how to go on."[49] Wittgenstein's observations in these paragraphs turn on what he explicitly calls "education" *(Erziehung)* and "training" *(Abrichtung)*.[50] It is difficult and complex to determine what counts as "understanding" or as "following a rule," because this does not clearly emerge *except "in actual cases."* Wittgenstein explains, "Everything turns here on 'a practice.'"[51] "The application *(Anwendung)* is still a criterion of understanding."[52] Depending upon a person's training, habits, concepts and practices, a teacher may be able to say "and so on."[53] Teaching or training may need to cite examples, but *also to "point beyond them."*[54] It seems that Well's hermeneutics, or his account of how "performance" (actualization) relates to training, precisely matches Wittgenstein's account of the relation between understanding *(Verstehen)*, practice *(Praxis)*, and application *(Anwendung)*.

In *Culture and Value* Wittgenstein dryly suggests a counter-example. A child might innocently fail to understand the role of "training and memory" in playing a game of drawing. He writes, "Philosophers often behave like little children who scribble some marks on a piece of paper at random and then ask the grown-up, 'What's that?' — It happened like this: the grown-up had drawn pictures for the child several times and said, 'this is a man', 'this is a house', etc. And then the child makes some marks and asks: What's *this,* then?"[55] The child's question is senseless because it has been abstracted from a regularity of process that depends on training and memory. At one point Wittgenstein applies the principle to understanding, practice, and application in theology. He asks, "How do I know that two people mean the same when each says he believes in God? And the same goes for belief in the Trinity. A theology that insists on the use of *certain particular* words or phrases, and outlaws others, does not make anything clearer (Karl

49. Wittgenstein, *Investigations,* sect. 179; cf. sects. 138-242.
50. Wittgenstein, *Investigations,* sects. 189 and 201.
51. Wittgenstein, *Investigations,* sect. 202.
52. Wittgenstein, *Investigations,* sect. 146.
53. Wittgenstein, *Investigations,* sect. 208.
54. Wittgenstein, *Investigations,* sect. 208.
55. Ludwig Wittgenstein, *Culture and Value,* Germ. and Eng. trans. Peter Winch, ed. G. H. von Wright (Oxford: Blackwell, 2d edn. 1978), 17.

Barth). It gesticulates with words, as one might say. . . . *Practice (die Praxis) gives the words their sense.*"[56]

All of this is remarkably close to Gadamer's view of the relation between understanding, practice, and application. We cannot specify *in advance* how to apply our understanding in terms of action, because this would entail our imposing an already-arrived-at understanding onto "the other" *prior to* our encounter with it. In Gadamer's view *application* remains fundamental in the hermeneutical endeavor. "Performative interpretation" is critical "in the cases of music and drama," which *"acquire their real existence only in being played."*[57] "Understanding always involves something like applying the text to be understood to the interpreter's present situation."[58] Hence Gadamer *rejects* the historical and Romanticist division between *subtilitas intelligendi* (understanding), *subtilitas explicandi* (interpretation), and *subtilitas applicandi* (application). This is because he insists that they cannot be separated. To take up Wells's analogy, it would be like sending troops into action who had never experienced the needed training. Gadamer thus appeals to the models of legal and theological hermeneutic for this emphasis on application, in a different direction from Betti.[59]

5.3. More on Education in Wittgenstein and Gadamer and Its Relevance to Doctrine

Gadamer's appeal to legal and theological hermeneutics as a paradigm for wider examples of hermeneutical understanding presupposes the role of a tradition embodying *continuities of practices and judgments* in law and in theological doctrine. These provide the framework within which practices or judgments may be extended to engage with new situations. In English law the application of legal fiction appears to offer a useful example.[60] If a law is strictly inapplicable to a new situation, in certain special circumstances an unforeseen state of affairs may be designated under a fictional categorization to permit the case to fall within the scope of the envisaged application. A fresh judgment, however, has to be made.

Habit and training become the central issue here. Edward Farley speaks of wisdom-based action and practice in Christian theology as *habitus*.[61] In the con-

---

56. Wittgenstein, *Culture*, 85.

57. Gadamer, *Truth*, 310 (my italics).

58. Gadamer, *Truth*, 308.

59. Gadamer, *Truth*, 310-11.

60. See Owen Barfield, "Poetic Diction and Legal Fiction" (1946), in Max Black (ed.), *The Importance of Language* (Englewood Cliffs, NJ: Prentice-Hall, 1962); also repr. in *Essays Presented to Charles Williams* (London: Oxford University Press), 106-27.

61. Edward Farley, "Theory and Practice outside the Clinical Paradigm," in Don S. Browning, *Practical Theology* (San Francisco: Harper & Row, 1983), 23 and 30; cf. 21-41.

text of medicine and psychology *habitus* usually denotes a particular "bodily build" (literally, a psycho-physical *formation*), which denotes the human person as an *integrated whole*. The term assumes an even greater relevance in the context of Bourdieu's social anthropology. Pierre Bourdieu (1930-2002) acknowledges Wittgenstein's influence upon his thought (together with Merleau Ponty's), and uses *habitus* to denote a person's historically shaped *disposition to act* on the basis of *the form of life* in which they participate.[62]

In his study *Jung's Hermeneutic of Doctrine* Clifford Brown identifies connections between *habitus,* stability, and integration of the human person. Jung, Brown argues, developed and retained a regard for Christian doctrine as offering an "enduring *stability*" that served "the need of safeguarding and nourishing a consciousness which was still young, fragile, and which remained in constant danger of *disintegration*" (my italics).[63] Jung perceives the role of habit, training, habituation, and stable regularity as *integrating and shaping character, will, and desires* as a coherent, well-ordered, healthy whole. The allusion to "sound doctrine" (AV/RJV) or "sound teaching" (NRSV, REB, NJB) in 1 Timothy 1:10 (Greek ὑγιαίνουσα διδασκαλία, *hugiainousa didaskalia*) uses an adjective cognate with the verb ὑγιαίνω *(hugiainō),* to *be in good health*. Mounce comments, "An elder must be able to teach healthy teaching" (Titus 1:5; cf. 1 Tim. 5:17).[64]

Pederito A. Aparece has published a constructive dissertation on the significance of Wittgenstein's work on understanding, training, rule following, and application, for the philosophy of education and for the practice of teaching.[65] Towards the end of his careful analysis of *training, habit,* and *understanding* Aparece reminds us that Wittgenstein pursued this work as *therapy* in the face of conceptual confusions, mistaken uses of logical grammar, and the application of misleading analogies that caused "mental cramp."[66] In a statement that resonates with Gadamer, Wittgenstein declares, "There is not *a* philosophical method, though there are indeed methods, like different therapies." He adds, "The philosopher's treatment of a question is like the trade-

---

62. Pierre Bourdieu, *Language and Symbolic Power,* ed. J. Thompson and trans. G. Raymond (Cambridge, MA: Harvard University Press, 1991), 1-42; and *Outline of a Theory of Practice,* trans. R. Nice (Cambridge: Cambridge University Press, 1977). Cf. also "Bourdieu and the Social Conditions of Wittgenstein's Language and Grammar," *International Journal of Applied Philosophy* 12 (1996) 15-21.

63. Clifford A. Brown, *Jung's Hermeneutic of Doctrine: Its Theological Significance,* AARDS 22 (Chico, CA: Scholars Press, 1981), 1-3 and 105.

64. William D. Mounce, *Pastoral Epistles,* WBC 46 (Nashville: Thomas Nelson, 2000), 42; cf. C. K. Barrett, *The Pastoral Epistles* (London: Oxford University Press, 1963), 42; and J. N. D. Kelly, *The Pastoral Epistles* (London: Black, 1963), 50; both "translate wholesome."

65. Pederito A. Aparece, *Teaching, Learning, and Community: An Examination of Wittgenstein Themes Applied to the Philosophy of Education,* Tesi Gregoriana 22 (Rome: Pontifical Gregorian University, 2005).

66. Aparece, *Teaching,* 39-46 and 155-93.

mark of an illness."[67] If illness is what impairs a person's ability to undertake certain "performances," to restore persons to health is to restore their capacities and competences for appropriate human activities, including *understanding*.

The most important aspect of Aparece's thesis concerns Wittgenstein's observations on training, habit, tradition, form of life, and "understanding" in relation to *teaching and learning*. Aparece is not alone in exploring this aspect, however. One of my former Ph.D. candidates in the University of Nottingham, Dr. Lin Hong-Hsin, Principal of Taiwan Theological Seminary, has also investigated this area with success.[68] Training and *praxis*, he concludes, are central to Wittgenstein's notion of understanding, and thereby to education.[69]

Aparece identifies features of Wittgenstein's thought that correspond reasonably closely with Samuel Wells's dialectic of habit, training, and wisdom on one side, and improvisation and performance on the other. Wittgenstein is interested in teaching and learning in the context of observations on linguistic competence.[70] Wittgenstein asks, "How do I teach?" How do such expressions as "and so on" *(und so weiter)* feature in teaching *(Unterricht)*, especially if the one who seeks to learn does not yet possess the appropriate concepts?[71] "How did we *learn* *(gelernt)* the meaning of this word?"[72] Aparece notes, "Basic pedagogical terms such as pupil *(Schüler)*, teacher *(Lehrer)*, teaching *(lehren)*, learning *(lernen)*, training *(Abrichtung)*, explanation *(Erklärung)*, instruction *(Unterricht)*, understanding *(Verstehen)*, and others, are found in Wittgenstein's later writings."[73] Of the two major terms *training* and *explanation*, *training* is the foundation of explanation, and the difference between them is of fundamental importance.[74]

Gilbert Ryle draws a useful distinction between *training* (in Wittgenstein's sense of the term) and *drill* (in a quasi-behaviorist sense).[75] *Drill* is like *conditioning* by sheer repetition and replication, and would lead to a stimulus-response or behaviorist philosophy of education. *Training* is more flexible, innovative, and critical, and stimulates the pupil *to make his or her judgment independently*. The "cultural" aspect of training (as Gadamer also implies in his comments on *Bildung*) entails "one's initiation into a form of life — as a preparation

67. Wittgenstein, *Investigations*, sects. 133 and 255.

68. Hong-Hsin Lin, *The Relevance of Hermeneutical Theory in Heidegger, Gadamer, Wittgenstein, and Ricoeur for the Concept of Self in Adult Education* (Nottingham Ph.D. diss., August 1998), esp. 154-88 on Wittgenstein.

69. Hong-Hsin Lin, *Relevance*, esp. 176-77.

70. Aparece, *Teaching*, 90-92.

71. Wittgenstein, *Investigations*, sect. 208.

72. Wittgenstein, *Investigations*, sect. 77.

73. Aparece, *Teaching*, 92.

74. Aparece, *Teaching*, 93-94.

75. Gilbert Ryle, *The Concept of Mind* (London: Hutchinson, 1949, and Penguin Books, 1963), 42.

for one's further application . . . and participation within that particular *Lebensform.*"[76] This is equally akin to the respective parts that Wells assigns to the playing fields of Eton and to the Battle of Waterloo. As in dispositional accounts of believing, the pupil's way of reacting and responding to extended or to new situations will serve as a criterion of understanding. In the context of understanding the pupil may exclaim, "Now I can do it"; "Now I understand"; "Now I can go on." But these are, in terms of Wittgenstein's "grammar," not "a mental process"; they are more like "a glad start."[77]

Explanation (Erklärung) plays a different role, which is not entirely dissimilar from that of *explanation* in Ricoeur and Karl-Otto Apel. In mainline hermeneutical tradition (although *not* in Gadamer) explanation provides a critical check *against misunderstanding,* but it does not initiate creative *understanding.* Citing Wittgenstein on "explanation" in his "identity of Moses" example, Aparece observes, "An explanation serves to remove or avert a misunderstanding."[78] By contrast teaching that serves to initiate *understanding* depends upon participation in a life-form that yields "practices, customs, and institutions."[79] Education and formation are related to the *habit* of "obeying a rule," not in a prescriptive or mechanical sense, but in the sense of being "at home" amidst certain regularities of the kind that Jung ascribed to the integrating "stability" of communal doctrine. Wells and Gadamer associate it with traditions and habits of *wisdom.*[80] Wittgenstein observes amidst his discussion of "rules": "I shall teach him . . . by means of *examples* and by *practice (durch Beispiele und durch Ubung gebrauchen lehren,* his italics).[81] Aparece notes, "We need *training* in order to engage ourselves in *practice*" (his italics).[82]

Wittgenstein's notion of understanding *(Verstehen)* comes close to Gadamer's, also, in terms of this shared conviction that in order to teach and to understand a person needs to be "an *educated person*" (*Gebildete,* cognate with *Bildung).* Such a person is not fully equipped already, but is one who has received *training (Abrichtung).*[83] Gadamer speaks of nurturing "a hermeneutically trained" consciousness or awareness through hermeneutical "experience."[84] In the philosophy of education, this avoids either of two extremes: it avoids a purely instructional, rationalist, or "indoctrination" concept of education and understanding; and it avoids quasi-behaviorist stimulus-response philosophy and pro-

76. Aparece, *Teaching,* 95.
77. Wittgenstein, *Investigations,* sects. 151-55.
78. Aparece, *Teaching,* 100; citing Wittgenstein, *Investigations,* sect. 87.
79. Aparece, *Teaching,* 105.
80. Cf. Wittgenstein, *Investigations,* sects. 196-208.
81. Wittgenstein, *Investigations,* 208.
82. Aparece, *Teaching,* 108; cf. Wittgenstein, *Investigations,* sects. 185, 198, and 208.
83. Gadamer, *Truth,* 9-19; and Wittgenstein, *Investigations,* sect. 86.
84. Gadamer, *Truth,* 300-324 and 346-62.

cedure. Lin Hong-Hsin has argued this point.[85] Jeff Astley has also developed this further.[86] Indoctrination, he argues, does not necessarily stop the growth in children of the capacity to think for themselves. This view depends on a narrow, mechanistic definition of the term. But it nevertheless risks defining learning outcomes too specifically and too clearly in advance, as well as veering towards overauthoritarianism and an overvaluation of a quest for certainty. On one side, it is a matter of wisdom to try to nurture *"right"* beliefs; on the other side, education is also about self-criticism and creativity. Astley writes: "Formative initiation into the ways of a culture or tradition is inevitably the major element in the education of young children."[87] Formation, he adds, includes a dimension of character formation, ethical attitudes, and life-practices; it is not only informational or intellectual. Corresponding in some degree to *explanation* and *understanding* in hermeneutics, education includes *both* a critical pole *and* a formative one. Of the two the latter is perhaps the more important. Astley observes, "Formative education is (or should be . . .) whole person education. . . . Formative education forms not only cognitions in the learner, but also attitudes, dispositions, values, emotions, and lifestyle as both products and processes."[88] Like Betti, Astley sees this formative pole as inviting "receptive" understanding, but education also entails the rational process of "thinking" to bring "critical evaluation" to bear.

Astley mentions "dispositions" among these formative processes. The entire argument of this chapter, but especially of this third and last section of it, clarifies one criterion of the "dispositional" approaches to belief discussed in Chapter 2. Whereas temporal duration might in principle be ascribed to certain "mental processes" (for example, a doctor may ask us for how long we have been in pain), understanding and believing do not normally function in quite the same way. If someone asks, "How long have you been a believer?" this will usually apply to such public phenomena as taking a stance as a Christian, or becoming a member of a church, rather than to continuous or interrupted mental processes. Believing, learning, and understanding are interwoven with life and practice. In the *Zettel* Wittgenstein asks us to compare two imagined cases of speaking about pain and love. Can we imagine someone saying, "I love you so much — oh, it's alright, it's gone off now"? On the other hand, "One does not say, 'That was not true pain, or it would not have gone off so quickly.'"[89] *"Love is not a feeling"*: like believing, it draws its currency from all the gestures, attitudes, behavior, and ac-

85. Hong-Hsin Lin, *Relevance*, 20-53 and 222-54 on the philosophy of education; see 128-53 on Gadamer, and 171-88 on Wittgenstein.

86. Jeff Astley, *The Philosophy of Christian Religious Education* (Birmingham, AL: Religious Education Press, 1994), 33-107.

87. Astley, *Education*, 73; cf. 44-77.

88. Astley, *Education*, 85.

89. Wittgenstein, *Zettel*, sect. 504.

tion that "back" the utterance in each case, perhaps including "a friendly mouth, friendly eyes."[90] The category of gestures to which Gilbert Ryle gave the technical philosophical term "avowals," Wittgenstein calls simply "surroundings."

The processes of formation and formative education, then, involve training and the cultivation of *habits and practices*. In philosophical terms this recognition forms part of Wittgenstein's concern to explore deep-seated assumptions about the nature of human life that education and training have built up into a settled, stable stance or mind-set. Let us suppose, he suggests, that we meet someone who believes that the world has existed for only fifty years. To "teach" such a person otherwise would not be a matter of providing some overly easy "explanation" of the world, but of *changing* that person's picture of the world *(Weltbild)* ". . . through a kind of *persuasion (Überredung)*."[91] Such a *formative* process would involve not information about a single isolated belief, but reconfiguring a whole network of shared beliefs and practices. Sometimes this might be a slow process. Hence formation cannot be superficial. Wittgenstein observes, "In philosophizing we may not *terminate* a disease of thought. It must run its natural course, and *slow* cure is all important (that is why mathematicians are such poor philosophers)" (his italics).[92]

Wittgenstein's simile of *changing* a worldview *(Weltbild)* brings us back to the notion in Gadamer and Betti of "openness to the other." This openness carries with it an acknowledgment that (in Gadamer's phrase) "some things are against me."[93] If a response is made to what is "against me," change in formation, re-formation, or re-figuration will occur. This reminds us of Martin Luther's experience that Scripture addresses us most formatively when God's word confronts us as "our adversary."[94] This is exactly the principle that Wittgenstein had in mind when he declared (to cite this aphorism once again): "You can't think decently if you don't want to hurt yourself."[95] Being open to re-formation may be painful, but ultimately it may lead to health.

Do these considerations apply to the formative nature of Christian doctrine? It is difficult to see how it could be otherwise. We began this chapter by noting comments by David Kelsey and Frances Young about the formative power of Scripture, and Philip Turner's observation that Thomas Cranmer perceived doctrine as formative for life and character, especially as embodied in

---

90. Wittgenstein, *Zettel*, sects. 504-6.

91. Ludwig Wittgenstein, *On Certainty — Über Gewissheit*, ed. G. E. M. Anscombe and G. H. von Wright, Germ. and Eng. (Oxford: Blackwell, 1969), sect. 262; the same example occurs in sect. 92.

92. Wittgenstein, *Zettel*, sect. 382.

93. Gadamer, *Truth*, 361.

94. Cited in Gerhard Ebeling, *Introduction to a Theological Theory of Language*, trans. R. A. Wilson (London: Collins, 1973), 17.

95. Cited also above, from Norman Malcolm, *Ludwig Wittgenstein: A Memoir*, 40.

communal liturgy and worship. In the Church of England, if not in the whole of the Anglican Communion, after Scripture itself the Book of Common Prayer serves as a primary source of doctrine, which is indissolubly interwoven with practices and a form of life, rather than simply with the cognitive content of a confessional formula of "right beliefs," associated more distinctively with the Continental Reformers.

Our chapters on dispositional accounts of belief and on embodiment have laid theological and hermeneutical foundations for the argument of this chapter. The new turn in the argument has been to show that a stable tradition of doctrine, far from inhibiting innovative thought and action, and far from discouraging improvisation, provides the very ground for it. Only within a tradition of firm communal identity-markers can constructive "going on independently" be distinguished from maverick idiosyncrasy and self-indulgence. Our chapter has shown, however, that this point does not rest upon theological special pleading. We have seen how "following a rule" and participating in a form of life in Wittgenstein, and standing within a tradition on Gadamer, provide the frame of reference within which belief, understanding, practices, and performance intelligibly arise. But there is more to the matter than even this. For as we noted in Gadamer, Ricoeur, and Betti, an openness to what lies beyond the narcissistic horizons of the isolated self makes it possible to experience new horizons that are formative for a new self. The nurture of such formative change and growth within a stable life-form defined in terms of shared communal beliefs is the business of Christian doctrine. The notion that doctrine is unimportant, repressive, or merely theoretical would run against the grain of this chapter, as well as others.

CHAPTER 6

Formation through a Hermeneutic
of Alterity and Provocation

6.1. Formation through Encounter with the Other:
Jauss on Reception and Provocation

Hans Robert Jauss (1921-77) explores the concepts of "otherness" and "provocation" in the context of his exposition of reception history. He is a former student of Heidegger as well as of Gadamer, and approaches the reading of texts from the standpoint of their place in history, and especially in literary history. From 1966 Jauss was involved in founding a multidisciplinary research center in the newly founded University of Constance. He established his international reputation with a programmatic inaugural lecture in 1967 under the title "Literary History as a Challenge (or Provocation) to Literary Theory" (*Literaturgeschichte als Provokation der Literaturwissenschaft*).[1]

Jauss takes as his point of departure the concept of historicity or historicality (*Geschichtlichkeit*) to denote especially being conditioned by one's finite place in history. But Jauss develops the notion of history of effects (*Wirkungsgeschichte*) in a different or modified way from that followed by Gadamer. *Changing situations* make *their impact or effect on successive readings and rereadings of texts.* These may include texts of Scripture, doctrine, or literature. Conversely, successive rereadings of texts serve to *reshape* readers' *horizons of expectations,* with the result that the impact of *texts* has *an effect upon situations.* The history of effects is two-sided or bi-directional.

Jauss recognizes that Marxist literary theory, especially as it was practiced in

---

1. Hans Jauss Robert, *Toward an Aesthetic of Reception,* trans. T. Bahti, Theory and History of Literature 2 (Minneapolis: University of Minnesota Press, 1982), contains the English translation in 3-45.

East Germany, acknowledges the historical dimension of literature and of interpretation. But he argues that it ascribes too much to social patterns of society in a
quasipositivist, causal, or purely historical way. On the other hand, literary formalism restricts its attention too narrowly to immanent forces within the text.
Both offer limited insights, but need to complement each other, and invite further development in accounting for the history of effects or effective history as
working in two reciprocal directions: *texts have a formative influence upon readers and society; but changing situations also have effects on how texts are read.*

In his inaugural lecture Jauss postulates seven theses for a program of reception theory. Like Collingwood and Gadamer, he rejects the notion of a "closed
past."[2] In the history of reception a dialectic emerges "between the production of
the new and the reproduction of the old."[3] Prior and subsequent readings of
texts reveal a continuous but not unchanged thread of causes and effects that
connect the experiences of earlier and later readers.

(1) In his first thesis Jauss argues that a new focus on literary history reveals
the shallowness of a "historical objectivism" that seeks merely to construct "literary facts" *after the event.* What is important is "the preceding experience of the
literary work *by its readers*" (my italics).[4] To illustrate and to reinforce the point
Jauss draws on an important concept from Russian formalism: that of
defamiliarization or estrangement. A reading of a text may have become routin-
ized, automatic, or "passive." But a sudden *disruption* that occurs *unexpectedly*
will turn such passive reading into active engagement as a reader seeks to wrestle
with what seems strange or unfamiliar.[5] *Defamiliarization* disrupts normal ways
of seeing, perceiving, and understanding, to make room for new ways of apprehending and understanding the text. This first emerged as a technical term in the
formalist literary theory of V. Schkovsky, and I have discussed this term in *New
Horizons in Hermeneutics.*[6]

Jauss comments that within an ongoing but also "changing horizon-of-
experience" such an event "enters . . . a continuity in which . . . inversion occurs
. . . from passive to active reception, from recognized aesthetic norms to a new
production that surpasses them."[7]

(2) This leads to Jauss's second thesis. He writes, "The literary experience of
the reader [takes place] . . . within the objectifiable *systems of expectations* that
arise for each work."[8] "Expectation" and especially "horizon of expectation" are
key critical terms for Jauss. Each horizon of expectation is defined and shaped

2. Jauss, *Reception*, 5.
3. Jauss, *Reception*, 12.
4. Jauss, *Reception*, 20.
5. Jauss, *Reception*, 16.
6. Thiselton, *New Horizons*, 117-18.
7. Jauss, *Reception*, 19.
8. Jauss, *Reception*, 22 (my italics).

with reference not only to a prior "preunderstanding" (his word here), but also to "the historical moment of its appearance," that is, the moment when it comes into being, but may shortly be reshaped or changed.[9] The *formative* effect of a text may operate when the reader's expectations are frustrated or changed. The text encounters the reader, causing an experience of surprise. Alternatively, on the other hand, in some circumstances a habit of reading and understanding may be affirmed and even intensified.

(3) Jauss's third thesis touches more specifically on the literary and aesthetic dimensions of successive reading experiences. A reader may appreciate and appropriate the literary form and impact of a text, or be shocked by it and seek to resist it. However, the reader's horizons are constantly undergoing *reshaping, change, and re-formation.* Jauss writes, "The way in which a literary work . . . satisfies, surpasses, disappoints, or refutes the expectations of the first audience. . . . [This] provides a criterion . . . of its aesthetic value."[10]

(4) The fourth thesis draws more explicitly on Gadamer's notion of the logic of question and answer. To what kinds of questions might the text under consideration suggest a response? "Reconstruction" entails more than merely reconstruction of a historical situation without reference to any hermeneutical context. The major concept of *provocation* or *challenge* begins to emerge here more clearly. Jauss declares, "The reconstruction of the horizon of expectations in the face of which a work was created and received in the past enables one . . . to pose questions that the text gave an answer to, and *thereby to discover how the contemporary reader could have . . . understood the work.*"[11] This must without doubt "correct" overly easy "modernizing" understandings that assimilate a text to the spirit of the age. Almost replicating Gadamer's comment about "not covering up" the tension between the past and the present horizon, Jauss observes, "It brings to view the hermeneutic difference between the former and the current understandings of a work."[12]

(5) The fifth thesis explicates further the historical dimension and process of successive modes of understanding linked with successive readings from within successive situations. It addresses "the historical unfolding of the understanding."[13]

(6) (7) The sixth and seventh theses move to the notion of "lived praxis" in contrast to value-neutral "representation." These last two theses underline "the *socially formative* function" of literary texts (his italics).[14] *Formation* has become an explicit concern in the exposition of these seven programmatic theses.

9. Jauss, *Reception,* 22.
10. Jauss, *Reception,* 25.
11. Jauss, *Reception,* 28 (my italics).
12. Jauss, *Reception,* 28.
13. Jauss, *Reception,* 32.
14. Jauss, *Reception,* 45.

David Tracy utilizes the notion of *provocation* in his discussion of hermeneutics. He discusses how a work "allows the meaning to become sharable by provoking expectations and questions in the reader."[15] Tracy does not appear to allude to Jauss in the study, although there are multiple references to Gadamer and Ricoeur, and he uses the term in a sense more akin to Gadamer than Jauss.[16] If this work is "a classic," Tracy argues, it may yield questions "enduring . . . and demanding of constant interpretation and application."[17] All of this, too, is part of its *formative* function and effect. We shall shortly discuss David Tracy's works.

Jauss, too, insists that "classic" works continually provoke horizons of expectation. Thereby they *enlarge and reshape* the horizons of readers, and make a transformative impact upon how they think and how they live. However, in other works he goes further. Like Collingwood, Bakhtin, and Gadamer, he explores not only dialectic but also dialogue. "Monologue," he argues, threatens to silence "the other" by imposing the agenda, questions, and conceptual grid of the reader upon the other rather than respecting and hearing another voice. Monologue is symptomatic of "closed" discourse, or of static system. Jauss draws a contrast between monologic "myth" and the dialogic genre of the Hebrew-Christian biblical writings. In Gen. 3:9 God poses a question to Adam: "Adam, where are you?" In the book of Job, Job poses the question "Why?" (Job 3:11-12, 20; 10:18, 20; 13:24).[18]

In this context Jauss introduces his "hermeneutics of the Other." His concept of *the other* combines two elements that we find respectively in Gadamer and Betti, and in Paul Ricoeur. Like Gadamer and Betti, Jauss conceives of *the other* as deserving sufficient respect to understand the other *on the other's terms,* without seeing the other through the lens of the self, and imposing on the other the self's conceptual expectations and categories. Like Ricoeur, Jauss also understands *the other* as a catalyst for understanding the self. Jauss insists far more strongly than Gadamer that it is impossible actually to reach a "fusion of horizons" (*Horizontverschmelzung),* arguing that "the other" *cannot and should not undergo full assimilation into the horizons of the self.* A differentiation of horizons, not assimilation between them, irreducibly remains. *Alienation* and *provocation* (or a challenge experienced on the basis of difference) are part of Jauss's *"hermeneutics of alterity."* Like Luther's maxim cited above, it is whatever confronts us as most strange, adversarial, challenging, or provocative that encounters us with the most creative, formative, transformative, and life-changing effects.[19]

15. David Tracy, *The Analogical Imagination: Christian Theology and the Culture of Pluralism* (London: SCM, 1981), 129.

16. Tracy, *Imagination,* esp. 99-153.

17. Tracy, *Imagination,* 129.

18. Hans Robert Jauss, *Question and Answer: Forms of Dialogic Understanding,* trans. M. Hays, Theological History of Literature 68 (Minneapolis: University of Minnesota Press, 1989), 51-94.

19. Hans Robert Jauss, *Wege des Verstehens* (Munich: Fink, 1994), 11-28. See further Hans-

Ormond Rush has convincingly and incisively demonstrated the relevance of Jauss's "hermeneutics of Alterity" to theological hermeneutics or to the hermeneutics of doctrine. After an exposition of Jauss in the first half of his book, he turns to issues of doctrine. He examines the notion of "reception" and "reception of doctrine" in A. Grillmeier and Y. Congar, and concludes his study with a final chapter under the title "A Hermeneutics of Doctrine."[20] Grillmeier sees theological reception as "an ongoing hermeneutical task for theology."[21] Alluding to the Christology of Chalcedon Grillmeier argues that like the task of hermeneutics itself, reception is in one sense never ended, yet must also allow for a fundamental truth that each generation must state afresh in its understanding of it.[22]

Rush places Jauss's dialectic of a fusion and differentiation of horizons in the context of successive readings of doctrine "in a rich plurality of ongoing discovery of further meaning."[23] Rush also endorses Ricoeur's affirmation of the mutual inclusion of philosophical and theological hermeneutics for the specific task of interpreting theological texts.[24] He also accords a role to the "conversation model" of hermeneutics developed by David Tracy, alongside other resources.[25] Rush concludes, *The task of theology is a hermeneutical one, i.e., to interpret for today theological texts from the past.*[26]

This brings us to the theological heart of Rush's argument. Openness to *the other* together with the importance of questions and of "differentiation" derives from the given of "Divine Alterity."[27] This also comes close to the main concerns of Jauss. With particular reference to medieval texts Jauss speaks not only of "the otherness of a departed past," but also (with Rush) of "the surprising otherness of God."[28] "Otherness" embraces both "vertical alterity" (the otherness of God) and "diachronic alterity" (the otherness of the past). Rush writes, "There is both the 'surprising otherness' of graced liberation and the negative otherness of contrast[ing] experience of suffering, aggression and marginalization (synchronic

---

Ulrich Gehring, *Schriftprinzip und Rezeptionsästhetik: Rezeption in Martin Luther's Predigt und bei Hans Robert Jauss* (Neukirchen-Vluyn: Neukirchener, 1999).

20. Ormond Rush, *The Reception of Doctrine: An Appropriation of Hans Robert Jauss' Reception Aesthetics and Literary Hermeneutics,* Tesi Gregoriana, Serie Teologia 19 (Rome: Pontifical Gregorian University, 1997), 277-36 on a hermeneutics of doctrine. On Grillmeier see 127-47; on Congar see 147-61.

21. Rush, *Reception,* 146.

22. A. Grillmeier, "The Reception of Chalcedon in the Roman Catholic Church," *Ecumenical Review* 22 (1970) 383-411.

23. Rush, *Reception,* 280.

24. Rush, *Reception,* 283.

25. Rush, *Reception,* 284.

26. Rush, *Reception,* 286 (my italics).

27. Rush, *Reception,* 291-315.

28. Hans Robert Jauss, "The Alterity and Modernity of Mediaeval Literature," in *New Literary History* 10 (1978-79) 182-83; cf. 181-229; and Rush, *Reception,* 297.

otherness)."[29] He concludes, "Alterity therefore names the otherness or strangeness in the horizon of understanding God in the horizon of understanding the past, within understanding meaning in both positive and negative human experience."[30]

This coheres, Rush comments, with Grillmeier's notion of "exogenous" reception, in which what is received comes "from without." In theological language this is understood in terms of the *gift* and the giver, or as divine grace. He writes, "True reception takes place when each partner in the reception dialogue *is open to being changed in the process*" (my italics).[31] This involves appropriation, or participatory application.

This relates very closely to the nature of doctrine. Rush continues, "The horizons from which doctrines are understood, interpreted, and applied, change from generation to generation. . . . *Past doctrinal formulation functions to provoke and ultimately change limited human horizons of expectation*."[32] Rush notes that Jauss is aware of the negative tendency to reduce back again what was once perceived as "other" into the routine, manageable, ordinary, and unsurprising. Jauss comments that even where there is "tension, surprise, disappointment, irony" in the reception of a poem, understandings may be re-familiarized and "canonized," with the result that provocation and challenge are domesticated and reduced.[33] In such circumstances *"rereadings" of a tradition become necessary*. Scripture and doctrine require "rereadings" that restore the dimensions of surprise and alterity. This is part of the agenda of a hermeneutics of doctrine.

Vanhoozer includes a short section on "Formation" in his *Drama of Doctrine*. His main focus is to extrapolate from his metaphor of doctrine as drama, not to draw upon Jauss, or upon a hermeneutic of otherness. However, points of resonance with Jauss's approach arise. Vanhoozer begins his section by repeating the point, "Mental assent to information by itself stops short of having a decisive impact on our lives."[34] This is akin to Jauss's assessments, as well as to Kierkegaard's, of "passive" reading with a predictable horizon of expectation that will not undergo or bring about change. I have discussed this issue explicitly in *New Horizons in Hermeneutics*, although there is no mention of my discussion in Vanhoozer's work; Jauss is not mentioned at all; and Kierkegaard receives mention only in passing and in one or two other contexts.[35]

---

29. Rush, *Reception*, 299.

30. Rush, *Reception*, 300.

31. Rush, *Reception*, 302.

32. Rush, *Reception*, 308 (my italics).

33. Jauss, "The Poetic Text within the Change of Horizons of Reading," in *Reception*, 145 and 147.

34. Vanhoozer, *Drama*, 370.

35. Thiselton, *New Horizons*, 272-79 and esp. 563-66. In spite of helpful and constructive content and an impressive index of names Vanhoozer's acknowledgments of earlier ideas and sources

Vanhoozer also touches upon the area that we noted in our discussion of Wittgenstein and "therapy." He argues that doctrine "helps disciples to become spiritually fit."[36] He declares, "Doctrine contributes to spiritual fitness by *forming* our thinking and spirits, those *habitual patterns* of *communicative action* that define and *character* so that we conform to Christ" (my italics).[37] He writes, "Habits are dispositions or tendencies toward certain kinds or patterns of thinking and behavior" (my italics).[38] The fact that he mentions Wittgenstein only in other contexts does not detract from the validity of these points.

Vanhoozer, then, rightly brings together formation, habit, action, and disposition, as we have done throughout these chapters. He also links these with *wisdom*, which has also been a theme in Gadamer and in these chapters. "Habits" of seeing and perceiving, he continues, also belong to the picture. He writes, *"Doctrines are . . . habits that draw upon the . . . power of the imagination to enable us to see the world in otherworldly — which is to say, eschatological — terms"* (his italics).[39] This is perhaps the nearest that Vanhoozer comes to drawing upon, or expounding, a hermeneutics of otherness. There is some common ground between our hermeneutic of doctrine and Vanhoozer's approach. Both of us, for example, have drawn briefly on the recent work of Samuel Wells, as well as certain other common sources.

However, there are two main differences, in addition to those cited in an earlier chapter (where, for example, I questioned extrapolating about divine absence). First, my reading of Wittgenstein, Ian Ramsey, and others makes me cautious about extrapolating quite so much *from a single model or picture,* namely that of doctrine as drama. I see this as *one* picture or resource among many others. Second, I attempt to draw upon a wider range of resources found in hermeneutical theory and practice, notably theories of understanding in Gadamer, Ricoeur, Betti, Jauss, Wittgenstein, Apel, Habermas, and speech-act theory as well as a wider dialogue with theological writers on the nature of doctrine.

6.2. Formation, Hermeneutics, and Public Discourse in Doctrine: Tracy and the Classic

David Tracy (b. 1939) writes from within the Roman Catholic tradition, and attempts to take serious account of the impact of hermeneutical theory, especially the approaches of Gadamer and Ricoeur, for Christian theology. Those who, like

that contribute to his arguments seem at best a little selective and patchy. Even Balthasar seems a little short-changed in spite of some brief allusions to his *Theo-Drama.*

36. Vanhoozer, *Drama,* 373; cf. 374-80.

37. Vanhoozer, *Drama,* 376.

38. Vanhoozer, *Drama,* 376.

39. Vanhoozer, *Drama,* 377.

the sociologist Peter Berger, are trained to typify and to categorize perceive him as representing the so-called Chicago School (with Schubert Ogden and Langdon Gilkey) in contrast to the Yale School of George Lindbeck and Hans Frei. It is probably more instructive, however, to note that his main theological mentor was initially Bernard Lonergan, who also respects the epistemological dimensions of hermeneutical theory, although over the years Tracy has moved, with Ogden, in a more pluralist direction than Lonergan sustains. Tracy's emphasis upon analogy resonates with his Catholic roots and the Thomist background that is never far distant in most Catholic theology.

Categorizations into "schools" have always met with hostility and suspicion in British theology. This arises in part because individual thinkers deserve not to be bracketed with others. This often owes its origin to crude didactic purposes. Is Nicholas Wolterstorff, for example, to be bracketed with Frei, in the light of his meticulous work on authorial agency and reference? It also arises in part because most British universities (unlike some German or American counterparts) try to expose students (whether doctoral or undergraduate) to a variety of views within the same university.

I make this brief digression because if I share certain selected themes in common with Tracy, this has no bearing on whether I find selected aspects of Lindbeck's approach to doctrine attractive or otherwise. To introduce a related issue (as I have witnessed it done) as "The Yale School *versus* the Chicago School" is to violate a genuinely hermeneutical approach by deciding in advance how to conceptualize and to *understand* the contributions of individual thinkers. Surprisingly, even as sophisticated and thoughtful a theologian as Hans Frei chooses to entitle a volume *Types of Christian Theology,* and to head a chapter of it "Five Types of Theology."[40] In the event, the five *types* of theology turn out to be five *theologians:* Kaufman, Tracy, Schleiermacher, Barth, and D. Z. Phillips. But does it serve theology or hermeneutics well to force these individual thinkers to fit into the prior categorizations and fuzzy edges of "types" with an implicit invitation to view them as founders of competing, imperializing "schools"? *To subscribe to a "school" is to give up independent thought,* and to *reduce* a complex debate into a smaller-than-valid number of *pre-packaged* options. The diagnosis of this reductive and polemical method in theology has been a major contribution of Nancey Murphy's utilization of Lakatos. We argue this in detail in Chapter 8, section 4, although we also identify certain differences from Murphy.

Our arguments in this book share certain strong hermeneutical features with Tracy, especially his emphasis upon doctrine as formative, even as I also find a certain strong sympathy with Lindbeck on doctrine as praxis and his use of Wittgenstein on language and forms of life. But in neither case do I buy into the

---

40. Hans Frei, *Types of Christian Theology* (New Haven, CT: Yale University Press, 1992), ch. 4, 28-55.

system of thought as a whole, or even into the precise sense in which we should speak of *formation* or *praxis*. I have drawn on the metaphor or model of *horizons* since the late 1970s, primarily in the light of Gadamer's use of the term, and Tracy also makes much of the term *horizon*. But in Tracy's work the term comes first especially from Lonergan, although ultimately for all of us it derives from Husserl and Heidegger. Tracy is also deeply concerned not only to do justice to the formative power of doctrine, but also to explore its relation to "fundamental" theology.

In the distinctive sense in which the terms are used in modern catholic theology, Tracy also distinguishes between *fundamental* theology and *systematic* theology. "Fundamental" theology embodies apologetics or issues of argument and "debatability"; "systematic" theology relates more closely to the church, and roughly corresponds to our use of the word *doctrine*. Our argument in these chapters shares this same concern to explore how the *formative* power of doctrine relates to debating or establishing the *truth-claims* of Christian theology. Is it good enough to assign *drama, narrative, and hermeneutics to ecclesiology* (with Heyduck) or to matters of *"grammar" and praxis* (with Lindbeck), while assigning the role of *argument, debate, coherence,* and logical *inference* to fundamental theology? I shall argue in due course that in principle this is artificial, but that at the same time this contrast very roughly reflects a legitimate hermeneutical distinction between explanation and understanding.

Tracy, like me in the argument of these present chapters, emphasizes the importance of *public* theology. But he tends to seek a solution to the problem just outlined by postulating the hypothesis that fundamental, systematic, and practical theology address, and are shaped to the needs of, *three distinct audiences respectively.* Indeed, he expresses reservations about Lonergan's supposed "foundational" approach to fundamental theology, on the basis of a sharper distinction between *hermeneutical* questions about *meaning* and *epistemological* criteria of *truth.*

The first of Tracy's three major works on the nature of theology, *Blessed Rage for Order,* comes from the 1970s when processes of secularization led many thinkers to write of a "crisis of belief." It is fair to remark now that I find this work less constructive from the standpoint of the arguments of these chapters than Tracy's later two works. Tracy urges that what since Victorian times had been designated *a crisis of belief* "can now be designated the crisis of *cognitive claims.*"[41] Many critical writers, from A. J. Ayer and R. B. Braithwaite in the 1930s through to the 1950s, insisted that religious language conveyed only emotive meaning that could not be verified or falsified in cognitive terms. Tracy is aware of this debate, and, taking his cue from Ian Ramsey, Frederick Ferré, and Max Black, he begins with a case for the need for models.[42]

---

41. David Tracy, *Blessed Rage for Order: The New Pluralism in Theology* (New York: Seabury, 1975), 5.

42. Tracy, *Blessed Rage,* 22-25.

In the 1970s numerous theistic writers sought to place the truth-claims of Christian theology on a rational basis that embodied cognitive meaning. This forms the background to Tracy's concerns in this first volume. In 1971 Anders Nygren had re-traveled the ground of his earlier work to wrestle with the problem of whether theology could remain "scientific," in the sense of dealing in critical and "objective" argument, while *also* letting faith speak as faith. He attempted a method of "motif research" that transposed theology almost into a history of ideas.[43] In spite of various insights in Nygren's commentary on Romans and in *Agapē and Eros,* Hall is probably correct to observe, "Nygren at times comes across to his readers as a rather naïve believer in the virtues of science."[44] Lonergan and Wolfhart Pannenberg held no such naïve view of science, but they nonetheless wrestled with issues regarding the credibility of the cognitive truth-claims of Christian theology. Both succeeded in giving a greater place to the problem of understanding *(Verstehen),* but also addressed issues of coherence, knowledge, and truth. Pannenberg explicitly explored these issues in relation to "science" in the German sense of *Wissenschaft.*[45] Lonergan recognized the role of hermeneutical understanding, but he placed it within the frame of a very broad epistemology.[46]

In *Blessed Rage for Order* Tracy wrestles with the relationship between these two different sides of the problem. He explores method, meaning, and understanding. In Schleiermacher, Dilthey, Ricoeur, and Apel, this turns in part on the relation between explanation *(Erklärung)* and understanding *(Verstehen).* Tracy acknowledges that Lonergan admirably brings these together in his model of self-transcendence, formulated in his aphorism, "Be attentive, be intelligent, be rational, be responsible, develop, and if necessary change."[47] The first three relate especially to critical epistemology or *explanation;* the second three, especially to hermeneutics or *understanding* (although "attentiveness" is also a hermeneutical feature). Nevertheless Tracy has one reservation: does Lonergan still stand too close to Enlightenment "foundationalism"?

We have noted our disappointment above that both Lindbeck and Frei too readily divide theology and theologians into pre-packaged broad "types." Almost unbelievably for the world health of theology, Tracy does almost the same thing. He offers a brief survey of five "models" of theology: (1) orthodoxy, with special reference to Catholic tradition; (2) the older liberal theology of Schleiermacher and Harnack; (3) the neo-orthodox theology of Barth; (4) radical theology in the

---

43. Anders Nygren, *Meaning and Method: Prolegomena to a Scientific Philosophy of Religion and a Scientific Theology* (London: Epworth, 1972).

44. Thor Hall, *Anders Nygren* (Waco, TX: Word, 1978), 209.

45. Wolfhart Pannenberg, *Theology and the Philosophy of Science,* trans. F. McDonagh (Philadelphia: Westminster, 1976).

46. Bernard Lonergan, *Insight: A Study of Human Understanding* (New York: Harper & Row, 1978) and *Method of Theology* (cited above).

47. Tracy, *Blessed Rage,* 12; from Lonergan, *Method,* 53-55 and 231-32.

form of Thomas Altizer's "death of God" theology; and (5) a "revisionist" model that draws on a modified principle of correlation, and reflecting certain continuities with Reinhold Niebuhr, Karl Rahner, and Paul Tillich.[48]

It as a pity that theologians from both Yale and Chicago follow the tried and tested but profoundly unhermeneutical method of defining a series of generalized "positions," with the writer's favored one described last, as if it were the only option left after the others have been unmasked as inadequate. For all the supposed differences between "Chicago" and "Yale" this is precisely the classificatory method that marks Lindbeck's work on the nature of doctrine and Frei's five "types." Lindbeck outlines three categories, out of which the cultural-linguistic model waits in the wings until he has exposed the inadequacies of the other two models. The preferred model rushes to the rescue, as if competitive consumerism were the only way to *understand* theology.

So, too, Tracy now outlines the major features of his last, preferred model. "Common human experience," "critical correlations," and history and hermeneutics are foci that are thought to do justice to "a basic reconciliation" between "postmodern consciousness and a reinterpreted Christianity."[49] The last fits well with our current concern about *formation,* but how should we assess the model as a whole?

At first sight hermeneutics appears to feature strongly. Tracy writes, "The Christian theologian must . . . find a hermeneutic method capable of discovering *at least* the central message of the principal textual expressions of Christianity" (his italics).[50] But this tends to reduce the very hermeneutical dimension of otherness, alterity, distance, and the avoidance of premature or complete assimilation between the horizons of the human and God as Other. Jauss and Rush have shown this to be *essential if hermeneutical encounter is to be seriously transformative.* If Tracy had produced only this first book, it would have contributed relatively little to the hermeneutics of doctrine. Indeed, it has a decidedly "sixties" feel, in spite of being written in the seventies. Everyone, including Tracy himself, has moved forward from that more barren era, with its liberal mythologies about the "secular" mind.

Tracy's second major work, *The Analogical Imagination,* brings us far closer to the issue of *formation, transformation,* and a *hermeneutic of doctrine,* while his later work *Plurality and Ambiguity* consolidates his later, mature, hermeneutical approach. The third work also revisits the relation between hermeneutical questions of meaning and formation, and questions about coherence, "science," and truth.[51]

---

48. Tracy, *Blessed Rage,* 24-34.

49. Tracy, *Blessed Rage,* 32-33.

50. Tracy, *Blessed Rage,* 49.

51. David Tracy, *The Analogical Imagination: Christian Theology and the Culture of Pluralism* (London: SCM, 1981); and David Tracy, *Plurality and Ambiguity: Hermeneutics, Religion, Hope* (London: SCM, 1987).

Much of Tracy's second major work concerns *"systematic theology,"* which he defines (as we have already noted) as closely akin to our use of the word *doctrine,* in contrast to *fundamental theology* in the traditional Roman Catholic sense. *"Fundamental* theology," Tracy writes, relates "primarily to the public represented but not exhausted by the academy"; *"systematic* theologies" relate "primarily to the public represented but not exhausted in the church . . . as a community of moral and religious discourse and action," *practical* theologies related primarily to the public of society, or "more exactly to the concerns of some particular social, political, cultural, or pastoral movement."[52] Tracy concludes that the major concern of doctrine or systematics enhances "the *reinterpretation*" of what is perceived to be "ever-present, disclosing, and *transformative*" in its power (my italics).[53] "*Fundamental* theology," meanwhile, involves the truth criterion and answers to Pannenberg's concerns about "debatable" theology. *Practical* theology overlaps with the other two areas, and impinges in hermeneutical discussions between Gadamer and Jürgen Habermas concerning the notion and role of contemporary *praxis.*[54] Theology has to become collaborative and interdisciplinary.[55]

Tracy's arguments become more clearly constructive when he expounds the quasi-normative status of "the classic" with particular reference to Gadamer.[56] He declares, "The word 'hermeneutical' best describes this realized experience of understanding in conversation."[57] Participation and processes of questioning play a fundamental part. Approaching nearer to the concept of *"otherness,"* Tracy urges that genuine conversation "occurs only *when our usual fears about our own self-image die.* . . . Understanding *happens* in . . . intersubjective shareable, public, indeed historical movement of authentic conversation."[58]

6.3. More Explicit Language on Doctrine as Formative: Evaluation and Critique

Tracy uses a number of significant terms that imply formation. These include *participation, hermeneutical, public* (i.e., embodied), *the death of self-image,* and even *provocation.* He implicitly speaks of openness to *the other.* He writes, "Every classic lives as a classic only if it finds readers willing *to be provoked* by its claim to

52. Tracy, *Imagination,* 56-57 (his italics).
53. Tracy, *Imagination,* 57.
54. Tracy, *Imagination,* 73.
55. Tracy, *Imagination,* 81.
56. Tracy, *Imagination,* 99-153.
57. Tracy, *Imagination,* 101.
58. Tracy, *Imagination,* 101 (my italics). Tracy alludes here to Hans-Georg Gadamer, *Dialogue and Dialectic: Eight Hermeneutical Studies on Plato* (New Haven, CT: Yale University Press, 1980).

attention."[59] The *questions* brought to the classic by interpreters are shaped, in turn, by the *history of its effects,* within "a temporal horizon."[60] Tracy concludes, "All contemporary systematic theology [i.e., all doctrine] can be understood as fundamentally hermeneutical."[61] The reader must allow his or her "present horizon to be vexed, provoked, challenged, by the claim to attention of the text itself."[62] Tracy does not appear to refer to Jauss. However, very much like Jauss, he portrays the formative impact of the text as an experience of surprise, when expectations are reversed, and "we are startled into thinking that 'something else may be the case.'"[63] Jauss has probably been filtered through the broader ethos of American literary theory. Gadamer stands behind Tracy's work, but "provocation" does not carry the same sense, as we have seen, in Gadamer and in Jauss.

"Classics" may take the form of texts, events, images, rituals, persons, or symbols that match the criteria for being judged a classic. They convey what is recognized as truth with an impact that is lasting rather than fleeting, and convey an excess or surplus of meaning. They are "recognized," Tracy urges, and function as disclosure events that create or project a "world" of *mimesis.* Clearly there are affinities with Paul Ricoeur's hermeneutics of "surplus of meaning" here, as well as with Ian Ramsey's notion of disclosure events.[64] Tracy declares, "The classics endure as provocations awaiting the risk of reading."[65] The image of "risk" is also relevant, as Claude Geffré reminds us in his work *The Risk of Interpretation,* which also reflects some common ground with Tracy.[66] Geffré writes, "The movement from theology as knowledge to theology as interpretation is inseparable from the emergence of . . . Christian praxis, which is both a place of production of the meaning of the Christian message and a place of verification of that message. Theology can therefore be defined as hermeneutics, giving a contemporary interpretation to the Word of God."[67]

Tracy rehearses some of the standard conceptual resources of hermeneutics, especially as these are found in Ricoeur: explanation and understanding; suspicion and retrieval; preunderstanding and reception; tradition and transformation; the transcending of my preunderstanding; and the model of dialogue, *praxis,* and larger understanding.[68] Like Ricoeur and Nicholas Wolterstorff, he speaks of

---

59. Tracy, *Imagination,* 102 (my italics).

60. Tracy, *Imagination,* 103.

61. Tracy, *Imagination,* 104.

62. Tracy, *Imagination,* 105.

63. Tracy, *Imagination,* 107.

64. Tracy, *Imagination,* 113.

65. Tracy, *Imagination,* 115.

66. Claude Geffré, *The Risk of Interpretation: On Being Faithful to Christian Tradition in a Non-Christian Age,* trans. David Smith (New York: Paulist, 1987).

67. Geffré, *Risk,* 19.

68. Tracy, *Imagination,* 118-24.

"possible worlds" and "forms of life." Doctrine "allows the meaning to become shareable by provoking expectations and questions in the reader . . . demanding interpretation and application. . . ."[69] In his conclusion to his discussion of "the classic," Tracy sees the theologian of doctrine as engaging in a five-stage process: preunderstanding; exposure to the claim of religious classics; initiating dialogue with it; reflecting on its history of influences or effects; and communicating this process in the public domain.

Tracy's emphasis upon formation and the transformative becomes still more explicit in his chapter "Interpreting the Religious Classic." Theologians, he argues, must risk interpretation of the meaning and truth of classic texts of theology and doctrine, not least because their history of effects or effective history forms the horizon of our own attempts to understand and to appropriate them. In his Notes at the end of the chapter he observes, *"Hermeneutics challenges exactly this will to mastery and control* present in mere controversy by its challenge to every participant *to enter a conversation where the subject matter is allowed primacy."*[70] This is precisely Gadamer's point in his *Truth and Method.* The stakes are higher, Tracy adds, when we interpret religious classics rather than simply classics of art or literature. The task of interpretation remains finite and historical, but "disclosure" is at stake. Hence in his chapter "The Religious Classic," revelation, truth, and limit situations come under consideration. A word of address may occur, often with a prophetic or ethical "defamiliarizing focus and power."[71]

In the Christian tradition or in Christian doctrine a personal response to the Christ-event becomes a *communal* response, and in spite of certain fallible human distortions faithfulness to the original apostolic witness is mediated in and through the historical tradition. "Explanation" should play a corrective role, which may entail historical reconstruction, and social-scientific methods may contribute to such explanation. But other hermeneutical resources are also appropriate, Tracy adds, including demythologizing and de-ideologizing.[72] He engages with Ricoeur, with Eric Auerbach, with Hans Frei, and with others, for a hermeneutic of narrative that relates to the Christian classic and entails "distanciation" and intensification.[73] In his discussion on the sources and foundations of Christian doctrine, Tracy engages with the specificities of New Testament scholarship to ground Christian tradition and interpretation in the historical particularities and implicit motivations that may be traced within the biblical canon. Tracy writes, "The cross discloses the power, pain, seriousness, and scandal of the negative: the conflict, destruction, contradiction, the suffering of love

69. Tracy, *Imagination,* 129.
70. Tracy, *Imagination,* 178, n. 1 (my italics).
71. Tracy, *Imagination,* 215.
72. Tracy, *Imagination,* 238-41.
73. Tracy, *Imagination,* 249-65.

which is the actuality of life."[74] The resurrection vindicates, confirms, and trans-forms the journey and grounds hope in an authentic future, leading to "Paul's 'logic of superabundance' — his logic of 'so much more.' . . ."[75]

Hermeneutics remains at the heart of Tracy's concerns, not least because "there is no one central interpretation around which all interpretations focus."[76] There is no one simple question with which to approach the text of Scripture or doctrine. Other than the "systems" formulated by individuals (Aquinas, Calvin, Schleiermacher, or Hegel) so-called systematic theology or doctrine works not to produce "systems" but only "assemblages."[77] Yet certain symbols and doctrines remain simply "there": God, Christ, grace, sin, revelation, creation, and eschatol-ogy, even if the range of responses to them has become multiform. Tracy returns to the effective dynamic of doctrine. This reveals "the presence of a power not one's own."[78] Like truth in hermeneutics, systematic theologians or doctrines may be inadequate or incomplete, but relatively sufficient for the situation of the time, and open to testing by coherence and existential meaningfulness.[79] They point, Tracy concludes, to God's self-manifestation in grace and love. This pro-vides understanding of the self, but also *forms and re-forms the self* in a power that both demands and heals.[80]

In *Plurality and Ambiguity* Tracy explicitly brings together hermeneutical theory and hermeneutical practice. Good theory, he writes, "is both an abstrac-tion from, and enrichment of, our current experience."[81] Like Ricoeur he argues that classic texts yield "excess" or (in Ricoeur's words) surplus of meaning, and continuing or permanent relevance to later times.[82] Hedging such texts around by restricting their impact to that urged by an individual scholar as a piece of ac-ademic "private property" domesticates and diminishes them. The use of "ana-logical imagination" beckons us beyond, but yields (like analogy) "similarity-in-difference." Underlining this formative and transformative impact, Tracy com-ments, "Conversation occurs if, and only if, *we will risk ourselves by allowing the questions of the text.*"[83] Engagement with classic texts (the Old and New Testa-ments) and with classic persons (Jesus and Paul) sets in motion interactive, dialogical, and intersubjective acts of formative communication.

All the same, Tracy points out, argument is also intersubjective and interac-

---

74. Tracy, *Imagination*, 281.
75. Tracy, *Imagination*, 283.
76. Tracy, *Imagination*, 346.
77. Tracy, *Imagination*, 373.
78. Tracy, *Imagination*, 374.
79. Tracy, *Imagination*, 407.
80. Tracy, *Imagination*, 429-38.
81. Tracy, *Plurality*, 9.
82. Tracy, *Plurality*, 12.
83. Tracy, *Plurality*, 20.

tive. Argument may test coherence and rationality, and we should abandon argument for rhetoric. Indeed, there is less tension between hermeneutics and "science" than we imagine. The critique of "method" mounted in Gadamer's hermeneutics is less urgent given that natural sciences are now entering "a post positivist stage."[84] Tracy cites the familiar impact of quantum theory, quasars, and the recognition of the role of the scientific interpreter in all experiment, to underline that "all data are theory-laden," not value-free.[85] He concludes, "Science has become again both historical and hermeneutical."[86] Even literary critics require "the occasional interruption of argument, theory, explanation, and method."[87] These can only "link every conversation with every text."[88] This paves the way for our discussion in the next chapter.

Tracy's emphasis upon the hermeneutical dimension of Christian doctrine in *The Analogical Imagination* and in *Plurality and Ambiguity* accords in some serious measure with the arguments put forward in these pages, even if we have expressed stronger reservations about *Blessed Rage for Order*. Nevertheless some aspects of his view of theology have less in common with ours. Two factors in particular signal a clear difference of approach. First, we do not agree with Tracy's excessively positive evaluation of "autonomy." As Pannenberg rightly insists, Augustine understood human fallenness in terms of the self seeking self-gratification, which could be expressed as "an autonomy of the will that puts the self in the center and uses everything else as a means to the self as an end."[89] "Autonomy" in many contexts probably owes more to Kant and to the secular Enlightenment than to Christian theology. Second, Tracy too readily designates all experience as "religious" if or when it reflects the kind of attitude or implicature that Paul Tillich called "ultimate concern."[90] I have argued elsewhere that Tillich regularly slides between an ontological and psychological notion of ultimate concern.[91] This critique might fall under the heading of reservation about an overenthusiasm for the method of correlation. If the widespread habit of distinguishing between a "Yale" school and "Chicago" school has any justification outside the realm of oversimplifying slogans, it justifiably comes into play here in terms of Hans Frei's rejection of models of Christian doctrine based on the principle of correlation.[92]

Whatever plays the role of the "ultimate" is not necessarily Christian or reli-

---

84. Tracy, *Plurality*, 33.
85. Tracy, *Plurality*, 33.
86. Tracy, *Plurality*, 33.
87. Tracy, *Plurality*, 41.
88. Tracy, *Plurality*, 46.
89. Pannenberg, *Systematic Theology*, vol. 2, 243.
90. Tracy, *Blessed Rage*, 108; cf. 91-109.
91. Anthony C. Thiselton, "The Theology of Paul Tillich," *Churchman* 88 (1974) 86-107.
92. Frei, *Types of Christian Theology*, 33-34 and 61-69; cf. 70-91.

gious, if this is understood (as Tillich understands it) to denote what is ultimate *for the person concerned.*[93] Tillich writes, "'God' . . . is the name for that which concerns man ultimately. This does not mean that first there is a being called God and then the demand that man should be ultimately concerned about him. It means that whatever concerns a man ultimately becomes god for him."[94] It is clear from transcripts of Tillich's conversations with his students in the University of California that he relishes the fact that "The term ultimate concern, like the German phrase of which it is a translation, is intentionally ambiguous. It indicates on the one hand *our* being ultimately concerned . . . on the other hand the *object* of our ultimate concern" (Tillich's italics).[95]

Nevertheless Tracy achieves three important goals. First, he allows *the resources of hermeneutical theory* to engage with Christian *doctrine.* In particular he draws on Gadamer and Ricoeur, and Habermas, even if Apel, Betti, and Jauss do not feature, and Wittgenstein hardly at all in this context. Second, he demonstrates the *formative effect* of hermeneutical understanding in life, thought, and concrete action, including the role of *difference-and-similarity and otherness in formation.* He includes an emphasis upon life and praxis without disengaging from epistemology. Third, with Ricoeur, but against Gadamer, Tracy accords a positive role to both *explanation* and *understanding* in hermeneutics and in doctrine. This paves the way for our exploring more explicitly in the next chapter how the "explanatory" axis of doctrine as "argument," "truth-claim," and even "science" relates to more formative and hermeneutical understanding of the nature of doctrine. If doctrine entails *argument,* criteria of *coherence,* and even a *"scientific"* dimension, does this not have a reductive or even destructive effect on the aspect of *"understanding," "appropriation,"* and *"application,"* with its related appeals to *narrative, drama,* and *speech-action?*

Gadamer would claim that this dimension is inimical to hermeneutics. On the other hand, Ricoeur and Apel, in accord here with Schleiermacher and Dilthey, maintain that only critical distance and an explanatory axis can prevent understanding and appropriation from degenerating into mere credulity with its related risk of self-affirming "narcissism" (Ricoeur's term). Paul Ricoeur comments, "Distanciation is the condition of understanding"; and adds, "Explanation and interpretation are indefinably opposed and reconciled."[96] In the lan-

---

93. Paul Tillich, *Systematic Theology,* 3 vols. (Chicago: University of Chicago Press, 1951-64 and London: Nisbet 1953-64), vol. 1, 234 and 267; cf. 234-79.

94. Tillich, *Systematic Theology,* vol. 1, 234.

95. Paul Tillich, *Ultimate Concern: Dialogues with Students,* ed. D. Mackenzie Brown (London: SCM, 1965), 11; see also 7-18, 24-25, 72-74, and 182-87; see also John P. Clayton, *The Concept of Correlation: Paul Tillich and the Possibility of a Mediating Theology* (Berlin: Walter de Gruyter, 1980).

96. Paul Ricoeur, *Hermeneutics and the Human Sciences,* ed. and trans. J. B. Thompson (Cambridge: Cambridge University Press, 1981), respectively 144 and 164; cf. 131-64. See also

guage of doctrine, the hermeneutical axis alone might be seen as a sellout on the part of epistemology and truth to some self-projected or self-constituted ecclesiology. On the other hand, would any concession to the notion that doctrine could or should entail abstraction and "science" serve to undermine Gadamer's hermeneutical liberation from the tyranny of prior "method," or Wittgenstein's attack on generality and his defense of the particular case?

Ricoeur, *Freud and Philosophy*, 20-36, 112-34, and 230-60; and Paul Ricoeur, *The Conflict of Interpretations: Essays in Hermeneutics*, ed. Don Ihde (Evanston, IL: Northwestern University Press, 1974), 287-334. See further Karl-Otto Apel, *Understanding and Explanation* (cited above), throughout, but esp. 11-79; and Schleiermacher, *Hermeneutics*, 205-8.

PART II

Replies to Possible Objections

CHAPTER 7

Dialectic in Hermeneutics and Doctrine: Coherence and Polyphony

7.1. Coherence and Contingency: A Possible Source of Tension?

Up to this point we have been offering reasons why there is a need to explore, and to try to formulate, a hermeneutics of doctrine. We have expressed the hope that this might be as formative in its impact on perceptions of the nature of doctrine as more recent insights into the hermeneutics of biblical texts have proved to be over the last twenty-five years. The shape and expectations of biblical reading has changed. Might we expect a parallel shift in the expectations and perceptions with which we approach Christian doctrine?

It would be naïve to assume that such a hope would encounter no difficulty or counterargument. Hans Küng and David Tracy call for a "paradigm change" in theology and in the study of doctrine, and both writers include in this the need for a deeper engagement with hermeneutics and with human life than has hitherto characterized more traditional doctrine.[1] Alongside their recognition of the need for a more sophisticated model of the problem of understanding, however, they leave open the question of how this might be achieved; how it might relate to more traditional concerns about "knowledge," including the possible status of theology as a "science," and complex questions about continuity, tradition, and coherence on one side, and discontinuities, plurality, and the particularities of human life on the other.[2]

Matthew Lamb articulates the problems of a dialectic between theory and

---

1. Hans Küng and David Tracy (eds.), *Paradigm Change in Theology: A Symposium for the Future*, trans. Margaret Köhl (Edinburgh: T&T Clark, 1989), 3-62, esp. 35-57.

2. Küng, "Paradigm Change in Theology," in Küng and Tracy, *Paradigm Change*, 18-21 and 29-33; and Tracy, "Hermeneutical Reflections in the New Paradigm," ibid., 43-56.

praxis in the third programmatic essay in Küng and Tracy's volume on paradigm change. He writes, "Ordinary discourse tends to ascribe objectivity to such generalities as reason, truth, criticism, science, while subjectivity is ascribed to such generalities as myth . . . [and] religion."[3] If doctrine is perceived as an institutionally or ecclesiologically defined body of "objective" truth, can doctrine leave room for the formative and transformative roles that a hermeneutics of doctrine carries with it?

Lamb does not leave this dichotomy unchallenged. He goes as far as to insist, "Hermeneutics . . . is intrinsic to the natural sciences."[4] He shows, however, that questions about the relations between theory and *praxis* are complex, and his discussions of coherence, rationality, and relations between subject and object lead him to engage in some detail with the status of "science" and "knowledge" in such writers as Paul Feyerabend, Habermas, Apel, Karl Popper, Thomas Kuhn, Michael Polanyi, Imre Lakatos, and Bernard Lonergan.[5] We engage with most of these thinkers over the next two chapters.

Concerns have been expressed both from the side of hermeneutics and from the side of Christian doctrine that engagement between the two disciplines can lead to compromising the distinctiveness of one or the other. One of the most distinctive contributions of Friedrich Schleiermacher (1768-1834) was to argue that hermeneutics could not serve theology as a critical and creative resource unless it was allowed to stand on its own feet as an independent critical discipline. Too often in the past, he argued, "hermeneutics" was called in by theologians who wanted to justify an understanding of biblical texts at which they had *already arrived*. The discipline was seen as an *instrumental* and *retrospective* way of validating what theologians or philologists thought they had already understood.

Such a procedure, Schleiermacher insists, emasculates the discipline of hermeneutics to a point where it cannot serve theology except as a self-affirming rhetorical tool. He declares, "Hermeneutics is part of the art of thinking."[6] It involves "listening" and stepping "out of one's frame of mind."[7] Hermeneutics is not concerned with merely correcting "*mis*-understanding," but with *initiating* understanding.[8] Hence he writes, "Special hermeneutics can be understood only in terms of general hermeneutics."[9] Yet Schleiermacher also lays out the ground

---

3. Matthew Lamb, "The Dialectics of Theory and Praxis," in Küng and Tracy, *Paradigm Change*, 69; from 63-109.

4. Lamb, "Dialectics," 75.

5. Lamb, "Dialectics," 63-86.

6. Friedrich Schleiermacher, *Hermeneutics: The Handwritten Manuscripts*, ed. H. Kimmerle and trans. J. Duke and J. Forstman; American Academy of Religion Text and Translation 1 (Missoula, MT: Scholars Press, 1977), 97.

7. Schleiermacher, *Hermeneutics*, 42 and 109.

8. Schleiermacher, *Hermeneutics*, 41 and 49.

9. Schleiermacher, *Hermeneutics*, 67.

for a possible and understandable unease on the part of theologians. Complete understanding, he concedes, would presuppose an understanding of "the whole," which in principle is virtually infinite. He explains, "The provisional grasp of the whole . . . will necessarily be incomplete. . . . Our initial grasp of the whole is only provisional and imperfect."[10] Schleiermacher continues, "Even after we have revised our initial concept of a work, our understanding is still only provisional."[11] He writes, "Only in the case of insignificant texts are we satisfied with what we understand on first reading."[12] Would many exponents of Christian doctrine be satisfied with such provisionality?

Jens Zimmermann puts the case for a distinctive "theological" hermeneutics that would not compromise the shape of Christian doctrine in this way.[13] He rightly urges that Christian interpretation and Christian doctrine share the goal of "communion with God."[14] However, he argues that from Kant and Schleiermacher onward philosophical hermeneutics brought about "the Silencing of the Word."[15] He writes, "Philosophical hermeneutics suffers from the illusion that secularisation is a purely positive development because it does away with the pre-modern universe and allows for an interpretative approach . . . without reference to God."[16] Such a generalization is too sweeping, and further, Zimmermann's exposition of Schleiermacher may be questioned on grounds of strict accuracy. Curiously, "the interpreter's superiority over the text" is precisely *not* a dominant theme of philosophical hermeneutics. Gadamer, Betti, and Ricoeur seek to establish precisely the reverse, even if this trend does characterize much nineteenth-century biblical criticism. Strangely, after all this polemic, Zimmermann then suggests that the thought of Heidegger and Gadamer "contains resources for a workable theory of interpretation."[17] He even adds, "Gadamer is a helpful ally in recovering theological hermeneutics."[18] Although he has castigated Schleiermacher for advocating the universality of hermeneutics, he praises Gadamer for doing precisely the same thing.[19]

From this point onward Zimmermann proceeds to support many of the concerns expressed in these chapters. He attacks "disembodied" knowledge and argues that Gadamer "presents the best possible starting point for a recovery of theologi-

---

10. Schleiermacher, *Hermeneutics*, 200.

11. Schleiermacher, *Hermeneutics*, 203.

12. Schleiermacher, *Hermeneutics*, 113.

13. Jens Zimmermann, *Recovering Theological Hermeneutics: An Incarnational-Trinitarian Theory of Interpretation* (Grand Rapids: Baker Academic, 2004), throughout.

14. Zimmermann, *Theological Hermeneutics*, 18.

15. Zimmermann, *Theological Hermeneutics*, 135-293 (his title for this section).

16. Zimmermann, *Theological Hermeneutics*, 18.

17. Zimmermann, *Theological Hermeneutics*, 160.

18. Zimmermann, *Theological Hermeneutics*, 161.

19. Zimmermann, *Theological Hermeneutics*, 161.

cal hermeneutics."[20] He shares much common ground with my concerns in these chapters in arguing for "incarnational" hermeneutics.[21] In this context he expresses some wise reservations about the approaches of Jacques Derrida and John Caputo, although to suggest that "radical hermeneutics" constitutes "Dancing with the Devil" is an unguarded overstatement that I should not have expressed in such terms.[22] Overstatement tends to mark this volume from time to time.

In the end, the "objections to philosophical hermeneutics" turn out to be objections *only to philosophical hermeneutics of a certain kind,* from which, interestingly, Gadamer and Heidegger (the latter surprisingly) are exempted. Ricoeur receives only a single mention, not in his own right but astonishingly as contributing to Jean Grondin's thought. Wittgenstein receives one mention only, again not in his own right but as contributing to Gadamer's thought. Apel, Betti, Jauss, Vanhoozer, and Tracy appear to receive no mention at all. In the light of all this, it is not easy to see how Zimmermann understands the scope of "philosophical hermeneutics" at all.

In the end we might perhaps imagine that the only serious source of incompatibility between hermeneutical theory and Christian doctrine arises from the *provisionality* and *corrigibility* of judgments in hermeneutics. But in Protestant traditions, in both conservative and liberal Protestantism alike, the doctrine of *the fallibility of the church* finds clear and unambiguous expression. In conservative Protestantism this stands in contrast to claims in Roman Catholic traditions for an ecclesial *magisterium.*[23] In liberal Protestantism all human thought is fallible. In mainline Anglican tradition the Book of Common Prayer of the Church of England states simply, "General Councils may err, and sometimes have erred, even in things pertaining unto God."[24] Is doctrine less fallible than hermeneutical judgments, especially when much Protestant doctrine depends precisely on judgments about the meaning and application of biblical texts as foundations for doctrinal construction?

Roman Catholic traditions, on the other hand, are sufficiently confident in doctrinal reception to encourage engagement with Gadamer, Ricoeur, and philosophical hermeneutics not only through such individual thinkers as Lonergan and Tracy, but also in official pronouncements. The Pontifical Biblical Commission's Document *The Interpretation of the Bible in the Church* (1993) was published with the blessing of Pope John Paul II, and under the chairmanship of the present Pope Benedict (then Joseph Cardinal Ratzinger).[25] The section entitled

20. Zimmermann, *Theological Hermeneutics,* 179.

21. Zimmermann, *Theological Hermeneutics,* 150 and 274-84.

22. Zimmermann, *Theological Hermeneutics,* 252-58.

23. The classic work, which is detailed but highly polemical, is George Salmon, *The Infallibility of the Church* (London: John Murray, 1888, 2d edn. 1890).

24. The Book of Common Prayer, Article XXI of the Thirty-Nine Articles of Religion.

25. Joseph A. Fitzmyer (ed.), *The Biblical Commission's Document "The Interpretation of the*

"Hermeneutical Questions" cites the work of Schleiermacher, Dilthey, Heidegger, Gadamer, and Ricoeur under "Philosophical Hermeneutics" and commends their value and usefulness for the church, Scripture, and theology. The report states, "Contemporary hermeneutics is a healthy reaction to historical positivism and to the temptation to apply to the study of the Bible the purely objective criteria used in the natural sciences."[26] The report continues: "Biblical hermeneutics, for all that it is part of the general hermeneutics applying to every literary and historical text, constitutes a unique instance of general hermeneutics."[27]

Does this apply to doctrine? The report includes a section on the relationship between biblical exegesis and systematic theology. It recognizes that "tensions" exist between specialist scholars in each area, because "the points of view of both disciplines are in fact different, and rightly so."[28] The role of the theologian is "more systematic," but theologians must not regard the biblical writings "as a store of *dicta probantia* serving to confirm doctrinal theses. In recent times theologians have become more keenly conscious of the importance of the literary and historical context . . . and they are much more ready to work in collaboration with exegetes."[29] The first point underlines Schleiermacher's concern about the very nature of hermeneutics; the second point underlines the hermeneutical nature of doctrine itself. This is confirmed by the positive evaluation of the report concerning the *History of Influence (Wirkungsgeschichte)* of the Text, Feminist Approaches, Canonical Approaches, and the use of Patristic Exegesis.[30] In sum, "Dialogue with Scripture in its entirety . . . must be matched by dialogue with the generation of today. Such dialogue will mean establishing a relationship of continuity. It will also involve acknowledging differences."[31]

This accords entirely with a specific point put forward by a British Catholic theologian, Nicholas Lash. In his *Change in Focus* he shows how, since the earlier work of Rahner and Schillebeeckx, "increasing attention" has been given to "problems of hermeneutics."[32] Further, he argues, Bernard Lonergan combines "starting from where we are" (i.e., respecting particularity and contingency) with trying "to see all things in their relationship to each other" (i.e., in terms of their

---

Bible in the Church": Text and Commentary (Rome: Editrice Pontificio Instituto Biblico, 1995); also text only, Pontifical Biblical Commission, *The Interpretation of the Bible in the Church* (Sherbrooke, QC: Éditions Paulines, 1994).

26. Fitzmyer, *Document,* 109; also Biblical Commission, *Interpretation,* 73.

27. Fitzmyer, *Document,* 116; also Biblical Commission, *Interpretation,* 77.

28. Fitzmyer, *Document,* 166; also Biblical Commission, *Interpretation,* 110-11.

29. Fitzmyer, *Document,* 168; also Biblical Commission, *Interpretation,* 111.

30. Fitzmyer, *Document,* 79-81, 96-101, and 142-50; also Biblical Commission, *Interpretation,* 55-57, 66-69, and 93-97.

31. Fitzmyer, *Document,* 141; also Biblical Commission, *Interpretation,* 92.

32. Nicholas Lash, *Change in Focus: A Study of Doctrinal Change and Continuity* (London: Sheed & Ward, 1973), 136.

coherence).[33] In a later essay Lash argues convincingly that the hermeneutical task of "understanding" cannot be apportioned out as two self-contained "stages" to the biblical exegetic and systematic theologians, like sequential runners who pass on the baton in a relay race. The theological task is shared, and it is not to be divided into "descriptive" and "evaluative" stages.[34] The alleged tension between the legitimate concern for coherence in systematic theology and doctrine and the respect for particularity that characterizes hermeneutics and biblical exegesis is more apparent than real. For in hermeneutics it is axiomatic that understanding entails a dialectic between attention to the details of language, situations, and texts, and a provisional understanding of "the whole" that the details presuppose. To elaborate this point would be to repeat material already expounded both in *The Two Horizons* (especially in the section on hermeneutics and theology) and in *New Horizons in Hermeneutics* (especially on Schleiermacher and on the interpretation of Pauline texts).[35]

Schleiermacher holds these two poles together as central to hermeneutics. On one side, "Only historical interpretation can do justice to the rootedness of the New Testament authors in their time and place."[36] On the other side, "complete" understanding requires in principle "a complete knowledge of the language" and "a complete knowledge of the person."[37] Further, since the generation of meaning depends on linguistic choice, "One must know all the possibilities that were at the author's disposal."[38] In summary, "Complete knowledge always involves an apparent circle: that each part can be understood only out of the whole to which it belongs and vice versa."[39]

In *New Horizons* I pointed out that J. Christiaan Beker had approached Pauline exegesis and Pauline theology in these terms, although some scholars have since criticized this approach. It is true that in the history of Pauline research different scholars have identified a series of "centers" of Pauline thought: for Marcion it was freedom from the Jewish law; for Albert Schweitzer it was eschatology; for Rudolf Bultmann and John A. T. Robinson it was Paul's theology of human being or "body"; for Anderson Scott it was "salvation"; for E. P. Sanders it was what became broadly known as "covenantal nomism." All of this led Wayne Meeks to speak of Paul as "the Christian Pastor."[40]

Beker fully recognizes that "the 'core' is for Paul not simply a fixed, frozen,

---

33. Lash, *Change in Focus*, 137.

34. Nicholas Lash, "What Might Martyrdom Mean?" in Nicholas Lash, *Theology on the Way to Emmaus* (London: S.C.M., 1986), 79; see also 75-92.

35. Thiselton, *Two Horizons*, 104-14 and elsewhere; and *New Horizons*, 204-47.

36. Schleiermacher, *Hermeneutics*, 104.

37. Schleiermacher, *Hermeneutics*, 100.

38. Schleiermacher, *Hermeneutics*, 91.

39. Schleiermacher, *Hermeneutics*, 113.

40. The sources are documented in Thiselton, *New Horizons*, 242-47.

message that must . . . be imposed as immutable doctrine. For Paul, tradition is always interpreted tradition."[41] The search for a "center" does not entail pushing everything else to the periphery. But Paul himself sets an exemplary hermeneutical pattern: "the one gospel of 'Christ crucified and risen'" stands at the center by his own explicit acknowledgment; and this "achieves incarnational [i.e., embodied] depth and relevance in every particularity and variety of the human situation."[42] Beker writes, "Paul's . . . hermeneutic consists of the constant interaction between the coherent center of the gospel and its contingent interpretation."[43]

The only "objections" that can be made to our argument seem to depend on one side on a style of biblical scholarship that retreats from theology and ultimately rejects the main axioms of philosophical hermeneutics in favor of a piecemeal quasi-positivist approach. On the other side, it might fail to satisfy an older style of systematic theology that tends toward a fixed, static, and closed system. In practice both extremes seem to be losing ground.

On the side of systematic theology, few have placed greater emphasis upon coherence than Wolfhart Pannenberg. "*Truth as coherence,*" he writes, entails "the mutual agreement of all that is true" (his italics).[44] It is a legitimate and necessary concern "to defend the truth of Christianity by generally accepted criteria"; otherwise it could hardly stand on its own feet in the university, and "this would be a severe setback for the Christian understanding of truth."[45] Nevertheless this does not suggest, for Pannenberg, that the truth of Christian doctrine constitutes a "finished" system. First, all truth remains *provisional* upon the realization of the eschaton. It is precisely this point that marks one of Pannenberg's greatest differences from Hegel. Second, if truth is derived from the living God who acts in *ongoing history,* the truth of doctrine and truth of God is disclosed "'in a *contingent* manner.' . . . Contingent events are the basis of a historical experience. . . . The truth of God must prove itself anew in the future . . . [even if] the truth of God embraces all other truth."[46]

---

41. J. Christiaan Beker, *Paul the Apostle: The Triumph of God in Life and Thought* (Edinburgh: T&T Clark, 1980), 33.

42. Beker, *Paul,* 35.

43. Beker, *Paul,* 11.

44. Pannenberg, *Systematic Theology,* vol. 1, 21.

45. Pannenberg, *Theology and the Philosophy of Science,* 13.

46. Pannenberg, "What Is Truth?" in Pannenberg, *Basic Questions in Theology,* vol. 2, 8 (my italics).

7.2. Does a Communal, Contingent, Hermeneutical Approach Exclude Epistemology?

Wolfhart Pannenberg insists on the very first page of his *Systematic Theology* that knowledge of God "is made possible by God"; it is "knowledge" mediated by "revelation."[47] He rightly insists that the truth of doctrine, therefore, does not rest upon "a mere consensus theory of truth," even if ecclesial consensus plays a role in the development of doctrine.[48] It is not that the consensus of churches *creates* Christian doctrine, but that "conviction of the divine *truth* of the Christian religion can establish and justify the continual existence of Christian churches."[49]

This brings us into serious collision with a work that we commended in our first chapter for other features, namely Richard Heyduck's *The Recovery of Doctrine*. We wholeheartedly applauded his attempt to correct the marginalization of doctrine in the mainline churches, together with his attack on the de-historicization of doctrine, his defense of the narrative nature of doctrine, and especially his insistence that doctrine is a *communal* phenomenon, not simply an aggregate of individualistic belief-systems.

However, in Chapter 2 we expressed serious reservations about his ascription of *"belief"* to individuals in contrast to *practice* on the part of communities. "Individualism," he claims, depends on the view that "doctrine must be redefined as 'belief.'"[50] Part of the purpose of our chapter on dispositional accounts of beliefs was to demonstrate that this alleged contrast between authentic belief and habits of practice was entirely artificial and logically unsustainable. This is part of the message of the Epistle of James, as well as an implicate of some of Wittgenstein's observations, and I touched on this reading of James in *The Two Horizons*.[51]

Heyduck staggers into murky waters when he then associates "epistemology" necessarily with "foundationalism" and "modernity," and perceives Christian doctrine as based upon ecclesiology rather than publicly debatable truth-claims. *The disastrous step is the assimilation of "epistemology" to "foundationalist epistemology."* He writes, "Foundationalist epistemology marginalizes the particular and local in favor of the general and universal," and if doctrine is bound up with history, then "history was found to be too messy, too varied, too undependable, and most of all too contingent" for historical understanding to interact with epistemology.[52]

47. Pannenberg, *Systematic Theology*, vol. 1, 2.
48. Pannenberg, *Systematic Theology*, vol. 1, 12-16 and 24-26.
49. Pannenberg, *Systematic Theology*, vol. 1, 7 (his italics).
50. Heyduck, *Recovery*, 18.
51. Thiselton, *Two Horizons*, 422-27.
52. Heyduck, *Recovery*, 19.

Yet the burden of this chapter so far has been to show that such a contrast between coherence and contingency is vastly overdrawn. Whether we recall Beker on the contingencies of biblical scholarship, or Pannenberg on the coherence of systematic theology, each pays respect to a working dialectic between coherence and contingency. A further very good example comes from the British scholar Richard Bauckham, who began as a specialist in Christian theology and moved into the area of New Testament studies. Bauckham perceives the biblical writings and Christian doctrine as embodying a coherent account or even "grand narrative" of God's dealings with the world. Nevertheless he shows that the Christian narrative is *not* the kind of "grand narrative" that invites the rejection and condemnation of grand narrative expressed by J.-F. Lyotard. Lyotard attacks narratives that are "totalizing" and thereby oppressive. Bauckham cites Marxist economics, Freudian views of the human, global capitalism, and the myth of scientific progress as examples of such "grand narratives."[53] The Christian narrative is different. For although the biblical writings and Christian doctrine do offer an overreaching narrative of God's dealings with the world from creation to the end-time, alongside this drama the Bible offers "little narratives" about *particular people* in *particular places* at *particular times*. A dialectical interplay of coherence and contingency characterizes these texts.

Heyduck's antipathy toward epistemology cannot rest, then, merely upon the legitimate recognition that particularity, contingency, and forms of life characterize communal doctrine. Doctrine and hermeneutics both leave room for, and indeed nurture, dialectic between coherence and contingency. Two further factors seem to seduce Heyduck to move along a perilous path. The first arises from the near-obsessional concern among some, especially in North America, to debate and to attack what they loosely generalize under the *all-embracing term "foundationalism."* This in turn is loosely and uncritically linked with *modernity,* as if to suggest that all who have reservations about the one also reject the other, and thence turn toward the postmodern.

The second factor arises from reading too much into the legitimate insight that a *shared communal narrative* and shared communal doctrine becomes a mark of *community identity.* This insight by itself is valid. But it becomes extended to imply that *ecclesiology steps into the place traditionally occupied by epistemology or testable claims to truth.* In the mood of postmodern loss of nerve about *entitled* belief, the validity of Christian doctrine no longer rests upon "this is true," but upon "look who we are!" Heyduck's laudable aim of "recovering" respect for doctrine is supposedly won at the expense of retreating from what Pannenberg describes as its claim to credibility in the world and in the university. Doctrine becomes little more than a mark of ecclesial identity. Heyduck declares,

53. Richard J. Bauckham, *Bible and Marxism: Christian Witness in a Postmodern World* (Carlisle: Paternoster, 2003), 89.

"Ecclesiology regains its place in theology."[54] But there is more to both truth and to ecclesiology than this.

Almost needless to say, this fits all too well with Lindbeck's third preferred model of doctrine formulated some twenty years earlier, and amazingly influential in proportion to its relatively slim volume of exposition. Lindbeck's model, Heyduck writes, "breaks the tie to individualism (directly) and epistemology (indirectly). Cultures and languages are social institutions. . . . What ecclesial communities put forth as doctrines *look* like [Heyduck's italics] propositions. They are not about objective reality, however, but rather are second-order utterances used to regulate the first-order ones."[55] Although he "positions himself as postliberal . . . he is postmodern in his decentering of epistemology . . . and in his philosophy of language."[56] Thus Heyduck regards Lindbeck as his ally in attacking "epistemology and individualism."[57]

The major problem with Heyduck's argument is that he brackets together positive and constructive themes with questionable ones, as if the former necessarily entail the latter. Hence a major chapter follows in which he commends the model of speech-act theory as well as that of doctrine as drama and narrative, as if this were a "postmodern" replacement for epistemology. *But while I have spent more than thirty years commending speech-act theory as formative and relevant to biblical exegesis and doctrine, I have consistently argued in every publication that its operational currency depends on certain states of affairs actually being the case.* Some of this work is now available in a section on speech-act theory in *Thiselton on Hermeneutics.*[58] The other "constructive" features mixed in with a postmodern attack in ecclesiology are those of community, narrative, drama, formation, embodiment, action, particularity, and history. I stand behind all these positive features, but they have nothing to do with the demise of epistemology, the testing of truth-claims, or the astonishing imperializing of the very English, Oxford-like J. L. Austin as "postmodern."[59]

The worst source of serious confusion in all this discussion is the overly loose, ill-defined, sloppy use of the term *foundationalism.* It is so badly abused that together with *incommensurability* I generally ban its use from my classes unless the speaker defines in what sense he or she is using the term with some preci-

54. Heyduck, *Recovery,* 29.

55. Heyduck, *Recovery,* 27-28 and 29.

56. Heyduck, *Recovery,* 33.

57. Heyduck, *Recovery,* 36.

58. Thiselton, *Thiselton on Hermeneutics,* "Part II, Hermeneutics and Speech-Act Theory," 51-150, from 1974 through to 2004/5. I might also have included my essay on Fuchs in *Scottish Journal of Theology* 23 (1970) 437-68.

59. If this is not asserted as an explicit proposition, Austin features under the heading "Postmodern Philosophy [singular] of Language" (Heyduck, *Recovery,* 57-67), which also includes Wittgenstein. I recall D. Z. Phillips orally protesting with Welsh fervor on behalf of Wittgenstein that Wittgenstein and Austin were utterly and entirely different. Certainly in temperament, passion, and agenda they were quite unlike each other.

sion. I have tried to disentangle some threads in my *Concise Encyclopedia of the Philosophy of Religion.*[60] It is necessary to distinguish the thoroughgoing or "hard" foundationalism of *rationalist* thought in Descartes from the "softer" foundationalism of *empiricist* thought in John Locke. Descartes sought truth that is "absolutely indubitable"; "truth so certain that sceptics were not capable of shaking it."[61] This forms part of the celebrated argument concerning "self-evident" knowledge, which includes his proposition, *cogito, ergo sum.*[62]

Descartes does indeed speak explicitly of "foundations." In his *Meditations* of 1641, he formulates arguments designed to cast doubt on all that he already or formerly believed, with the aim of identifying "certain" truth as against mere opinions, prejudices, or illusory beliefs. He begins, there, with *individual* self-consciousness: the *cogito.* This thinking self discovers the idea of God, who is thought to guarantee that human reason can be trusted. The "certainties" discovered through reason are thought to be "clear and distinct." It is sometimes thought that Descartes commended a perpetual method of doubt about traditions and opinions. In fact he wrote, "Once in a life-time" we must "demolish everything and start again right from the foundations. . . . Then there remains nothing but what is indubitable."[63] Heyduck associates what he calls *foundationalism* with a purely deductive method of inference. But, as Gadamer observes, Descartes exempts both "God" and moral values from this realm of prior doubt.[64]

Nevertheless Descartes represents the "hard" or "classical" foundationalism that belongs to the rationalist tradition. The certainties are as absolute as that which belongs to the realm of the formal logician or pure mathematician. In the empirical tradition it is utterance. John Locke promotes *not rationalism but reasonableness.* "Certainty" becomes a relative matter, depending on whether evidential support for an argument is "reasonable." Even at the beginning of his *Essay concerning Human Understanding,* Locke writes that his purpose is to inquire into "the certainty and extent of human knowledge, together with the grounds and degrees of belief, opinion, and assent."[65] He rejects the search for the kind of certainty sought by Descartes, which was based on "innate ideas." The certainty based on consensus is also no certainty.[66]

---

60. Anthony C. Thiselton, *A Concise Encyclopedia of the Philosophy of Religion* (Grand Rapids: Baker Academic and Oxford: Oneworld, 2002), 106-7.

61. René Descartes, *Discourse on Method,* Part IV, 53-54. The standard English edition of Descartes's works is René Descartes, *The Philosophical Writings of Descartes,* ed. and trans. J. Cottingham and others, 3 vols. (Cambridge: Cambridge University Press, 1984-91).

62. Descartes, *Method,* 53.

63. Descartes, *Meditations* (La Salle: Open Court, 1901), Part II, 31.

64. Gadamer, *Truth,* 279.

65. John Locke, *An Essay concerning Human Understanding,* ed. Peter H. Nidditch (Oxford: Clarendon edn., Oxford University Press, 1975 [1690]), I:1.

66. Locke, *Essay,* I:2:3.

Book IV of Locke's *Essay* is different in character from Books I-III, and was often neglected until recently. However, Nicholas Wolterstorff has recently reinterpreted this part to expound the notion of "reasonable" or "entitled" belief.[67] Wolterstorff writes, "Locke was the first to develop with profundity and defend the thesis that we are all responsible for our believings, and that . . . reason must be our guide."[68] Locke gives us "a theory of entitled belief."[69] What Locke means by "reason," however, is that which serves "for the enlargement of our knowledge."[70] Deductive reason through the syllogisms of formal logic may even be unhelpful and restrictive, inhibiting "enlargement" of mind.[71] Locke's notion of reason and reasonableness has far more in common with Lonergan's notions of insight and understanding, even perhaps with Christian writers in "wisdom" than with the abstract reason of Descartes. Locke concedes that faith may concern what is "above reason."[72] Nevertheless "reasonable belief" includes *a multitude of criteria* including responsible evaluation of evidence and the quality of being reasonable. This may well exclude the claims of a fanatical pietism, but not reasonable, debatable, grounds for belief.

Alvin Plantinga and Nicholas Wolterstorff concede that "Reformed Epistemology" arose in response to the exaggerated claims of "classical," "narrow," or "strong" foundationalism in the tradition of Descartes.[73] Against any quasi-positivist empiricism Reformed thinkers also reject a "narrow" or "hard" evidentialism. If evidentialism is to yield the "basic" propositions of "hard" foundationalism, these basic propositions will need to derive directly from sense data. Usually, however, the issue in debates turns upon what W. K. Clifford called sufficient or "insufficient" evidence. Even belief in God cannot properly be "basic" or underived in the "hard" foundationalist tradition. Yet in a different sense, for theists, can any proposition be more "basic" than one expressing theistic belief? Hence Plantinga proposes a "softer" or "broader" foundationalism that retains criteria of reasonableness, but rejects the notion of "basic" beliefs upon which belief in God is said to rest. Wolterstorff earlier showed more reserve about any form of foundationalism, but during the middle and late 1990s he came to believe that their earlier attack even on classical foundationalism "remained too superficial."[74] In Locke, he declares, there is the "depth" for which he was looking.

---

67. Nicholas Wolterstorff, *John Locke and the Ethics of Belief* (Cambridge: Cambridge University Press, 1996).

68. Wolterstorff, *John Locke*, xiv.

69. Wolterstorff, *John Locke*, xv.

70. Locke, *Essay*, IV:17:2.

71. Locke, *Essay*, IV:17:4-7.

72. Locke, *Essay*, IV:18:7.

73. Alvin Plantinga and Nicholas Wolterstorff, *Faith and Rationality* (Notre Dame, IN: University of Notre Dame Press, 1983).

74. Wolterstorff, *John Locke*, xi.

Heyduck's bracketing together of "foundationalism," epistemology, and modernity simply cuts across all this and sets it on one side as irrelevant. Yet he is not alone in paying insufficient attention to these finer but vital distinctions. Stanley Grenz, for example, whose book *The Social God and the Relational Self* is more thorough and of an altogether higher order, hurries over these distinctions in his less careful *Beyond Foundationalism,* let alone in his popular-level *A Primer of Postmodernism.*[75] On the other hand, several works from within an evangelical tradition judiciously explore these distinctions to advantage. One such is W. Jay Wood's *Epistemology* (1998); another is James Beilby, *Epistemology as Theology* (2005) on Plantinga's epistemology; a third is J. Wentzel Huyssteen, *Essays in Postfoundationalist Theology.*[76]

We have been obliged to engage with Heyduck's arguments, however, because of a radical disparity. (1) On one side: a hermeneutic of doctrine affirms almost every feature that he commends: community, embodiment, narrative, drama, practices, wisdom, community identity, the place of the church as an interactive community; the significance of Wittgenstein, Gadamer, and their "participating" hermeneutics; and the recovery of the importance of doctrine in the setting of a wider theory of understanding. (2) On the other side: none of this could be commended or accepted if it were to entail a retreat from epistemology; a consensus or social theory of truth; and an uncritical appropriation of the postmodern as such. The entire mainline Christian tradition from the New Testament through Irenaeus, Clement, Origen, Augustine, Aquinas, and Calvin supports Pannenberg's axiom: "Only conviction of the divine *truth* of the Christian religion can establish and justify the continual existence of the churches."[77]

It is all the more necessary to underline this point because in postmodern thought such writers as Richard Rorty have offered a version of "hermeneutics" precisely as a strategy of "coping" in a pluralistic era, when allegedly no claims to "truth" in any but a neo-pragmatic sense can thought to be sustainable. Even in 1979 in his relatively early volume *Philosophy and the Mirror of Nature,* Rorty entitled his penultimate chapter "From Epistemology to Hermeneutics."[78] As a qualification he states, "I am not putting hermeneutics forward as a 'successive

---

75. Stanley J. Grenz and John R. Franke, *Beyond Foundationalism: Shaping Theology in a Postmodern Context* (Louisville: Westminster John Knox, 2001); cf. Grenz, *The Social God and the Relational Self* (Louisville: Westminster John Knox, 2001) to which we allude positively in Chapters 9.1 and 11.2, below.

76. W. Jay Wood, *Epistemology: Becoming Intellectually Virtuous* (Downers Grove: InterVarsity Press and Leicester: Apollos, 1998), 77-104; James Beilby, *Epistemology as Theology: An Evaluation of Plantinga's Religious Epistemology* (Aldershot, U.K.: and Burlington, VT: Ashgate 2005); and J. Wentzel van Huyssteen, *Essays in Postfoundationalist Theology* (Grand Rapids: Eerdmans, 1997), esp. 73-90.

77. Pannenberg, *Systematic Theology,* vol. 1, 7.

78. Richard Rorty, *Philosophy and the Mirror of Nature* (Princeton, NJ: Princeton University Press, 1979), 315-56.

subject' to epistemology."[79] Indeed, much of his attack on traditional notions of truth is at this stage an attack on the correspondence theory of truth.[80] He uses "hermeneutics" as a polemical term, and interprets Gadamer as meaning that "hermeneutics is not 'a method for attaining truth' which fits into the classic picture of man."[81] But Rorty adds, "Hermeneutics is what we get when we are no longer epistemological."[82] Hermeneutics has more to do with "edification" or "coping" than with knowing or with understanding. Here Rorty seems to think that he is expounding *Bildung* as borrowed from Gadamer, but Gadamer uses the term to denote more than mere competence to carry on. We examined this concept in Chapter 5 (5.1 and 5.3).

Rorty's interpretation of Gadamer (and of Wittgenstein) remains open to question, as some have quickly pointed out.[83] Gadamer does indeed reject the kind of epistemology associated with the individualism and "hard" foundationalism of Descartes and Leibniz, and with the individualism of Locke, Berkeley, and Hume. But he goes back to the *sensus communis* of classical Roman culture and to the *phronēsis* of Greek philosophy to trace a communal understanding *(Verstehen)* through Vico, Shaftesbury, and more recent thinkers to a hermeneutical mode of engaging with *truth*. Truth is not understood in Gadamer's title to denote Rorty's *neo-pragmatic, functional, instrumental* notion of truth. This is different even from the tradition of William James and John Dewey to which Rorty appeals. The one point in common between Gadamer and Rorty, Warnke argues, is that "knowledge is bound to a tradition . . . closer to forms of 'making' than to forms of 'finding.'"[84] But "Hermeneutics is not as subjectivistic as Rorty makes it out to be. . . . Rorty overlooks Gadamer's emphasis on *die Sache*."[85] She concludes, "The connection between *Bildung* and a certain kind of knowledge remains fundamental."[86] Gadamer uses "judgment" as a form of knowledge that can differentiate between the appropriate and inappropriate, or between right and wrong, in more than merely pragmatic terms.

We do not have space to trace these themes in Rorty's later writings. I have attempted this in several essays, some now collected in the section on postmodernity in the volume *Thiselton on Hermeneutics*.[87] His three volumes of

---

79. Rorty, *Mirror*, 315.

80. Rorty, *Mirror*, 332 and 333-42.

81. Rorty, *Mirror*, 357.

82. Rorty, *Mirror*, 325.

83. Warnke, "Hermeneutics and the 'New Pragmatism,'" in Warnke, *Gadamer*, 139-66; and Jane Heal, "Pragmatism and Choosing to Believe," in Alan Malachowski (ed.), *Reading Rorty* (Oxford: Blackwell, 1990), 101-14.

84. Warnke, *Gadamer*, 141.

85. Warnke, *Gadamer*, 146.

86. Warnke, *Gadamer*, 159.

87. Thiselton, *Thiselton on Hermeneutics*, Part VI, "Philosophy, Language, Theology, and

Philosophical Papers, culminating in *Truth and Progress,* do not significantly change his approach to knowledge and truth, although in certain respects they radicalize it and say more about community. The third volume might almost be summed up in his statement that there is no such task as "the task of getting reality right" because "there is no Way the World Is."[88] He cites William James's pragmatic understanding of truth with approval: "The true is the name of whatever proves itself to be good in the way of belief."[89] However, what emerges in the later writings more clearly is Rorty's emphasis upon *community.* This community is defined in "ethnocentric" terms, that is, a community of liberal pluralist thinkers "like me," or, better, "like us." For if truth is merely a matter of justification, *to whom* is the question about "What proves itself to be *good*" to be addressed? In Rorty's view they can only be our "local" community. This amounts, in effect, to a nontheist's counterpart to Heyduck's ecclesial community. In postmodern terms, there *is* no other court of appeal *beyond* "*my*" *community.*

I have argued elsewhere that while this appears to promote a tolerant liberal pluralism, in actuality it risks becoming an authoritarian and manipulative strategy whereby truth for *other* communities becomes defined, understood, and cashed out in the image of "my" or "our" community. In view of Robert Corrington's incisive and brilliant diagnosis of pragmatic, community-based hermeneutics as distinctively "American" (traced through Royce, James, and Dewey), it is not altogether foolish to wonder, if only for a moment, whether what Richard Bauckham has called "the Americanization of the world" might perhaps owe something to these pragmatic-communal-philosophical roots.[90] At the very least it suggests that Heyduck's disengagement of epistemology from doctrine and from hermeneutics leaves open certain problematic areas, including the very dimension urged by Karl Barth as essential for "churchly" theology and doctrine, namely the capacity for self-criticism. To promote a hermeneutics of doctrine does not entail unacceptable consequences in relation to epistemology or for the status of claims to truth in Christian doctrine.

As a footnote to this section it is worth noting that many writers within the Evangelical and Reformed traditions (in addition to Alvin Plantinga and Nicholas Wolterstorff) hold their nerve about the status of epistemology. We have al-

Postmodernity," 523-681. The main essay on Rorty is "Two Types of Postmodernity," my Presidential Paper for the Society for the Study of Theology (1998), 581-606; but I have modified and supplemented my argument in "A Retrospective Reappraisal" (1995), 663-81.

88. Richard Rorty, *Truth and Progress: Philosophical Papers 3* (Cambridge: Cambridge University Press, 1998), 25.

89. Rorty, *Truth,* 21.

90. Robert S. Corrington, *The Community of Interpreters: On the Hermeneutics of Nature and the Bible in the American Philosophical Tradition,* Studies in American Biblical Hermeneutics 3 (Macon, GA: Mercer University Press, 1987); cf. Bauckham, *Bible and Mission,* 89.

ready noted one such constructive example, namely W. Jay Wood's *Epistemology,* from Wheaton College. This explores the subject with reference to a context of ethical responsibility and ethical virtue, and distinguishes between "strong" foundationalism and what Wood calls "modest" foundationalism.[91] Wood rightly argues that engagement with epistemology relates to "wisdom, understanding, foresight, and love of truth," while holding at bay "gullibility, willful naïveté, closed-mindedness and intellectual dishonesty."[92] This useful work includes sections on coherence, evidentialism, and Reformed epistemology.[93]

7.3. Different Understanding of *Dialectic, Systems, Polyphony,* and *Canon:* Bakhtin

We have used the term "dialectic" in various contexts, especially in this chapter to denote dialectic between coherence and contingency and once or twice in relation to polyphonic meaning. Yet Mikhail Bakhtin (1895-1975) is deeply suspicious about the use of the term *dialectic* in most of its more traditional contexts, for example, in the context of Plato, Hegel, or Marx. Their uses of this term, he insists, are ultimately "monologic," that is to say, they combine two "separate thoughts" into what grows into a *single* "system of thoughts."[94] Monologic discourse, for Bakhtin, consists of thoughts, assertions, or propositions that are separable from the text, communicator, or writer to whom they belong.[95] "The content of these thoughts is not materially affected by their source."[96]

It is undeniable that many uses of the term *dialectic* function less to sustain the dramatic tension of two viewpoints expressed by two different agents than to hold together two complementary points within a single discourse. Socrates uses a dialectic of question and answer in the earlier dialogues of Plato. But are these more than exploratory devices to expose false opinions by *demonstration* rather than by a process of question and answer that "arises" without a prior determination and goal? Bakhtin concedes that the earlier Socratic dialogues respect "the dialogic nature of human thinking about truth"; truth here is not prepackaged or ready-made; "it is born between people collectively searching for the truth."[97] But Plato later "monologized" the Socratic dialogue, with the effect that

---

91. Wood, *Epistemology,* 77-104, as cited above.

92. Wood, *Epistemology,* 7.

93. Wood, *Epistemology,* 105-19 and 162-74.

94. Mikhail Bakhtin, *Problems of Dostoevsky's Poetics,* ed. and trans. Caryl Emerson (Minneapolis: University of Minnesota Press, 1984), 93.

95. Bakhtin, *Problems,* 80; see also Morson, Gary Saul, and Caryl Emerson, *Mikhail Bakhtin: Creation of a Prosaics* (Stanford, CA: Stanford University Press, 1990), 235.

96. Morson and Emerson, *Mikhail Bakhtin,* 235.

97. Bakhtin, *Problems,* 110.

it becomes almost a catechism of correct truths. In Plato it is not dialectic in the fullest sense of the term. It serves a prior system of thoughts.

In the writings of Aristotle dialectic becomes little more than a rhetorical device to assert the *demonstration* of Aristotle's views. After Aristotle the term becomes a largely pejorative one, often used to cast doubt on the validity of the empty rhetoric of the Second Sophistic. The term broadly fades out until its recovery by J. G. Fichte (1762-1814), and then especially G. W. F. Hegel (1770-1831), Søren Kierkegaard (1813-55), and Karl Marx (1818-83). In Hegel and in Marx we find instances of "systems" put together out of separate thoughts.[98] Bakhtin sees the "dialectic" of Hegel and Marx as ultimately "monologic" rather than "dialogic," primarily because their "systems" can "be comprehended and fully contained by a *single* consciousness — in principle, by *any* consciousness with sufficient intellectual power."[99]

This holds considerable significance for our attempts to explore the possibility of a hermeneutics of doctrine. Three major consequences follow if Bakhtin's view is to receive attention and respect. First, discourse that is genuinely dialogic is both *produced and "owned" by a collective, intersubjective, mutually responsible community of persons.* In the context of the Russian Orthodox Church, in which Bakhtin was brought up in his early years, as well as diffused in Russian culture, the concept of *sobornost, togetherness-in-solidarity,* underlines the interaction between multiple voices and a coherent collectivity. This coheres with the *communal* nature of Christian doctrine, transmitted through the plurality of the apostolic circle and mediated through both a college of bishops or elders and the whole people of God. Hermeneutics, too, rests upon a framework of understanding that presupposes shared language and shared forms of life in the public domain. Doctrine is not a matter of monologic discourse produced by a single person and addressed to individuals in abstraction from corporate worship and the life of the church.

Second, Bakhtin distinguishes between the *participatory* dimension of dialogic discourse and the observer status of monologic discourse. As Kierkegaard also insisted, speech and communication abstracted from subjectivity too readily offers a pre-packaged, pre-formed set of objective propositions, which a person may examine and to which they express uninvolved assent or rejection. Kierkegaard speaks of the participatory dimension that entails staking one's life, which one avoids doing if one is a third person.[100] He writes, "Everyone who has a result merely as such does not possess it; for he has not the way."[101] Bakhtin states the aphorism: "Only error individualizes."[102]

98. Bakhtin, *Problems,* 93.

99. Morson and Emerson, *Mikhail Bakhtin,* 236.

100. Søren Kierkegaard, *The Journals of Søren Kierkegaard,* ed. and trans. A. Dru (London: Oxford University Press, 1938), 533.

101. Søren Kierkegaard, *The Concept of Irony,* ed. and trans. H. V. Hong and E. H. Hong (Princeton, NJ: Princeton University Press, 1989), 340.

102. Bakhtin, *Problems,* 81.

Third, Bakhtin regards the *intersubjectivity of genuine multiple voices* as the paradigm of dialectic, dialogue, or polyphony. Morson and Emerson, who are acknowledged authorities on Bakhtin, lament the frequency and lack of precision with which the notion of "polyphonic voices" is too readily ascribed to Bakhtin. They write, "Polyphony is one of Bakhtin's most intriguing and original concepts. Unfortunately, as Bakhtin wrote to his friend . . . polyphony 'has more than anything else given rise to . . . misunderstanding.'"[103] Bakhtin, they point out, never defines polyphony, but he "clearly states that Dostoyevsky invented polyphony."[104] It does presuppose "dialogic" discourse and a dialogic sense of truth. But it is not synonymous with Bakhtin's term *heteroglossia,* which denotes only a diversity of linguistic styles of speech. Polyphony, Morson and Emerson continue, does not exclude an authorial point of view and commitment and does not exclude coherence.[105] But it does embrace changes in view or perspective. It steers between "systems" and relativism or chaos: Bakhtin writes, "The polyphonic approach has nothing in common with relativism. . . . Relativism and dogmatism equally exclude all . . . authentic dialogue by making it unnecessary (relativism) or impossible (dogmatism)."[106]

Why is this so important for the argument of the present book? One clue comes in the comment by Morson and Emerson that Bakhtin regarded Dostoyevsky's *The Brothers Karamazov* as *more than one book.* But this is precisely the case in the example of *the biblical canon.* Bakhtin argues that it is possible to conceive of coherent truth "that requires a plurality of consciousness . . . full of event potential . . . born among various consciousnesses."[107] The notion "event potential" denotes a particularity within a temporal process that is not exhausted by its own moment of existence, and in this sense is not "finalized." The development of the biblical canon and its continuity as a *coherent plurality* that generates Christian tradition and doctrine reflects this plurality-in-coherence that characterizes a hermeneutic of doctrine. A *hermeneutic* of doctrine prevents doctrine from becoming only monologic discourse; a hermeneutic of *doctrine* prevents hermeneutics from becoming only relativistic. As Bakhtin observes, either relativism or dogmatism prevents and undermines dialogic discourse.

Hans Urs von Balthasar also draws attention to the significance of polyphonic discourse, or, to use his preferred term, "symphonic truth."[108] He begins with the simile of the symphony orchestra in which the difference between the instruments must be as striking as possible. Each keeps its utterly distinctive tim-

---

103. Morson and Emerson, *Mikhail Bakhtin,* 231.

104. Morson and Emerson, *Mikhail Bakhtin,* 231.

105. Morson and Emerson, *Mikhail Bakhtin,* 232-33.

106. Bakhtin, *Problems,* 69 (cited by Morson and Emerson, *Mikhail Bakhtin,* 233).

107. Bakhtin, *Problems,* 819 (cited by Morson and Emerson, *Mikhail Bakhtin,* 236).

108. Hans Urs von Balthasar, *Truth Is Symphonic: Aspects of Pluralism,* trans. Graham Harrison (San Francisco: Ignatius, 1987), 7-15 and 37-64; cf. also Poythress, *Symphonic Theology,* 69-91.

bre.[109] The orchestra must be "pluralist." Today, he urges, we must "take to heart that Christian truth is symphonic."[110] God is the faithful God of covenant promise, but God also reveals himself in sovereign freedom. Knowledge of God tells us more about *who* he is than about *what* he is. Because God acts both in judgment and grace, and speaks in many ways through history, law, and prophecy, "a pluralism of statements . . . comes into being."[111] These cannot be neatly ordered and pre-packaged in advance of God's actual dealings with the world. Both tears and delight characterize relationships with God.

Balthasar sees the Person of Christ as the paradigm of symphonic truth. On one side he enfolds "in-finite" truth, which cannot be "delimited" into a single set of statements. On the other side he is "the higher integration of all God's individual self-revelations known through history, . . . this center . . . and organizing focus of truth."[112] In accordance with what we have said about Bakhtin and the biblical canon, the polyphony or dialectic has a unity and coherence, but not a static, monologic, reductive unity.

These considerations also shed fresh light on the need for logical and semantic clarifications in the use of the terms *dialectic, systems, polyphony,* and *canon. Such clarifications contribute replies to possible objections or difficulties about a hermeneutics of doctrine.* For the suggestion that hermeneutical explorations stand in tension with systematic theology may rest upon prior understandings of *system,* while the contentions of Heikki Räisänen, for example, that theological construction cannot proceed on the basis of the pluriformity and "contradictions" found within the New Testament *canon* simply sidestep the subtle understanding of coherence and dialogic discourse found in Bakhtin and, for that matter, Balthasar. Indeed, while I should not wish to endorse without reserve every detail associated with "canon criticism" or with a "canonical approach," such work offers a useful corrective to ill-informed criticisms of appeals to the biblical canon. Bakhtin's approach facilitates a greater appreciation of the relevance of "canon" for the genesis and development of Christian doctrine.[113] A more disciplined exploration of *dialectic* also facilitates a more adequate understanding of the *self-involving or participatory* dimensions of a hermeneutics of doctrine.

System is used in hermeneutical and theological debate in at least three different senses. In some writers it denotes a *finished* or *closed* system of thought. We do not need to explore this use further because we have excluded this use from our discussion on the grounds of the fallibility of the church, of the as-yet-

---

109. Balthasar, *Truth,* 7.

110. Balthasar, *Truth,* 15.

111. Balthasar, *Truth,* 24.

112. Balthasar, *Truth,* 34.

113. Craig Bartholomew et al. (eds.), *Canon and Biblical Interpretation,* Scripture and Hermeneutics Series 8 (Grand Rapids: Zondervan, 2006 and Carlisle: Paternoster, 2007) including Anthony C. Thiselton, "Canon, Community and Theological Construction," 1-30.

future fulfillment of the eschaton, and of other factors identified above. Kierkegaard clearly regards Hegel as implying this kind of system. Kierkegaard feigns the identity of a baffled inquirer, and writes: "I shall be as willing as the next man to fall down in worship before the System, if only I could manage to set eyes on it. . . . Once or twice I have been on the verge of bending the knee. But at the last moment, when I made a trusting appeal. . . . 'Tell me now sincerely, is it entirely finished . . . ?' I received the same answer: 'No, it is not quite finished.'"[114] Kierkegaard's irony rests on the conviction that only a purely logical system could ever be "closed" or complete. If it touches upon human life, it can only remain ongoing. He declares, "A logical system is possible. . . . An existential system is impossible."[115]

One major difference between system as "final" or absolute and system as coherence can in part be further clarified with reference to the respective roles played by dialectic, negation, and otherness in Hegel's system in contrast to their role in Kierkegaard or in Bakhtin. In the first volume of his *Lectures on the Philosophy of Religion*, Hegel discusses in three short sections "The Moment of Universality," "The Moment of Particularity or the Sphere of Differentiation," and "The Annulling of the Differentiation, or Worship."[116] The universality of religion "does indeed take the first place. . . . *Thought thinks itself.* The object is universal, which, as active, is Thought" (Hegel's italics).[117] "Particularization" is *within* the sphere of the universal, but when it manifests itself outwardly it "constitutes the Other as against the extreme of Universality. . . . In thinking I lift myself up to the Absolute above all that is finite, and an infinite consciousness, while at the same time finite consciousness."[118] This "movement" or process, Hegel writes, "is just that of the notion of God, of the Idea, in becoming objective to itself. We have this before in the language of ordinary thought in the expression 'God is Spirit'. Spirit . . . is Spirit only in being objective to itself, in beholding itself in 'the Other' as itself."[119]

Hegel sees this movement in terms of *a dialectic of identity and difference.* It involves separation through negation and mediation through a negation of the negation. But how "other" is the otherness of "the Other"? Dialectic comes to be subsumed with "sublation" *(das Aufheben).* Hegel makes it utterly clear that the verb *aufheben,* often used to denote *to lift up,* also means *abolition, assimilation,* and *absorption.* The clearest example comes in the third volume of his *Lectures*

114. Søren Kierkegaard, *Concluding Unscientific Postscript to the Philosophical Fragments,* translated by W. Lowrie and others (Princeton, NJ: Princeton University Press, 1941), 97-98.

115. Kierkegaard, *Concluding Unscientific Postscript,* 99 and 107.

116. Georg W. F. Hegel, *Lectures on the Philosophy of Religion,* trans. E. B. Spiers and J. B. Sanderson, 3 vols. (London: Kegan Paul, Trench, Trübner, 1895), vol. 1, 61-75.

117. Hegel, *Lectures,* 61.

118. Hegel, *Lectures,* 63.

119. Hegel, *Lectures,* 66.

on the Philosophy of Religion, where he describes the death of Jesus Christ as not only a particularization of God but also God's negation. He writes, "This death is thus at once *finitude* in its most extreme form, and at the same time the *abolition and absorption* of natural finitude."[120] He declares, "God has died, God is dead. . . . God maintains himself in . . . the death of death. God comes to life again, and thus things are revised."[121] This is a system when neither dialectic nor otherness nor difference can sustain the kind of role that Kierkegaard and (differently) Bakhtin envisage for them.

These paragraphs are not merely too long a digression into Hegel's thought; they help us to differentiate between three senses of *system*. In two other senses of the term, but not in the one just discussed, *system* may still allow a measure of genuine diversity and pluriformity of a particular kind. This is the kind that characterizes particularity in hermeneutics, for which Christian doctrine clearly leaves room.

We have explored this second sense of system, namely *system as coherence*, with particular reference to the theology of Wolfhart Pannenberg, among others. We noted that while he places great weight on the coherence of truth (not only within theology, but more widely with other disciplines) Pannenberg leaves room for the contingent "proving anew" of God's truth within an ongoing history. Pannenberg explicitly dissociates himself from Hegel's approach, which leaves insufficient room for *provisionality* and surprise.

A third and highly significant meaning of *system* derives from *systems theory*, and can be found in classic form in Talcott Parsons and Jürgen Habermas.[122] In the later work of Parsons and more especially in Habermas, the concern for system is for a *self-regulating organism that maintains stability, identity, and boundaries*. Habermas speaks of them as "being able to maintain their boundaries relative to a hypercomplex environment."[123] Parsons formulates a sociological theory that seeks to extend the phenomenology of E. Husserl to make possible an "objective" account of human social action, which supposedly has transcendental validity. He utilizes systems theory in his later work to account for habitual continuities in human social behavior. Although he attempts to draw issues of "understanding" *(Verstehen)* into his social theory, he veers too far toward a quasi-positivist objectivism for his approach to be considered a contribution to hermeneutics.

Habermas, however, is a major exponent of hermeneutical theory, as his earlier work *Knowledge and Human Interests* shows, and his dialogue with Gadamer confirms. He wrestles with the relation between understanding and truth, and

120. Hegel, *Lectures*, vol. 3, 93 (my italics).

121. Hegel, *Lectures*, vol. 3, 91.

122. Jürgen Habermas, *The Theory of Communicative Action: The Critique of Functionalist Reason*, trans. T. McCarthy, 2 vols. (Cambridge: Polity, 1987); Talcott Parsons, *The Social System* (Glencor, Ill.: Free Press, 1951).

123. Habermas, *Communicative Action*, vol. 2, 225.

with the transcendental conditions for their validity. I devoted two sections of *New Horizons in Hermeneutics* to Habermas's work, and need not retrace these discussions here.[124] Habermas reveals his appreciation of the particularities and contingencies of hermeneutics by giving the concept of *life-world* as prominent a place as *system*. Indeed, his main criticism of Parsons is that Parsons (and before him Max Weber) has "uncoupled" system from life-world in an attempt to arrive at an overly scientific, quasi-positivist, objectified account of human behavior. It is not enough to speak of "the structure of a tradition" or of "a cultural system of values," for human beings regulate interpersonal, intersubjective relations as agents and actors in terms of individual life-histories as well as in collective forms.[125]

Habermas accepts that in the integration of society *life-world* also becomes "objectified as a system." This can remain healthy and retain validity as a social and hermeneutical analysis, however, *only* if system and life-world are not "uncoupled," but function interactively and reciprocally.[126] He lays a firm emphasis upon the historically conditioned nature of human reason, and, like Heidegger and Gadamer (and Lonergan in a different tradition), understands reason in a more than instrumental, technical, or functional sense. His work has a strongly emancipatory or moral dimension. The oppressive features of state-oriented and government-oriented cultures in "modernity" thrive on the basis of a progressive uncoupling of system and life-world.[127] In the smaller-scale context of the ancient clan, family, or tribe, the human life-world was less likely to be assimilated into a bureaucratic system.

Nevertheless systems function *to preserve* communal boundaries, societal order, and *stability*. We noted earlier that this also served as a function of *doctrine*, as Jung, among others, noted. In the second and third centuries, the *communal identity* of the apostolic church, founded upon biblical writings, could be publicly discerned through what Irenaeus and Tertullian called "the rule of faith." The everyday experiences of Christians enlarged or developed the "system" of doctrine through their expanding and changing life-worlds, but the interaction between life-world and system guaranteed a continuity of recognizable corporate identity as *this trans-local church*. In our Church of England Doctrine Commission Report of 1981, we appealed to systems theory in this context, primarily through the initiative of John Bowker.[128]

Bowker begins almost where Habermas stands by expressing sympathy with those who deeply suspect "the institutions, the bureaucracies, — the Juggernauts

124. Thiselton, *New Horizons*, 378-93.

125. Habermas, *Communicative Action*, vol. 2, 140-48 and 225-34.

126. Habermas, *Communicative Action*, vol. 2, 233-34.

127. Habermas, *Communicative Action*, vol. 2, 153-97.

128. John Bowker, "Religions as Systems," in Doctrine Commission of the Church of England, *Believing in the Church: The Corporate Nature of Faith* (Carlisle, U.K.: SPCK, 1981), 159-89.

— . . . which control our lives."[129] Yet systems provide channels through which energy flows: channels through which information is protected and organized; in religions "systems to protect information which is believed to be of vital (indeed, saving) importance"; and the maintenance and continuity of a system demands "some sense of a boundary — some way of marking what the system is, who belongs to it . . . and how the system is related to its environment."[130]

Even the human organism has the dual organic mechanisms of continuity and change. The genotype preserves identity and continuity; the phenotype yields diversification. Although the very notion of "boundaries" may seem oppressive or restrictive, "without a boundary we do not have a system."[131] It may well come about that in such an institution as the Christian church subsystems evolve with different patterns of ministry or sacramental theology, but there remain sufficient family resemblances to identify them as part of the main system, unless there is a radical parting of the ways, and a new system is evolved. Richard Hooker reminds us that chaos might ensue if "the Church did give every man licence to follow what he himself imagineth that 'God's Spirit doth reveal' unto him. . . . What other effect could hereupon ensure, but the utter confusion of his Church?"[132]

In the agenda of a hermeneutics of doctrine, then, there is room for "system" both as coherence (argued above) and as a provision for boundary markers and identity markers in interaction with ongoing history, experience, and hermeneutical life-worlds. The notion of a "final" system is excluded. However, a little more perhaps needs to be said about whether the interaction between coherence and particularity on one side and contingency, particularity, pluralism, and polyphony on the other constitutes a genuine or imagined dialectic. We conclude this part of our argument by comparing the relation between coherence and plurality in Bakhtin with coherence and plurality in the biblical canon.

We have seen that Bakhtin's notion of any "coherence" on the part of dialogic discourse is highly complex. It has nothing whatever to do with a synthesis of differing forces or viewpoints, as Hegel or Marx might be said to imply. Although many writers appeal to the notion of *sobornost*, togetherness, or conciliarity as holding together difference, my Nottingham colleague Malcolm Jones points out that in the context of Bakhtin's concept of polyphony in Dostoyevsky some writers (here Avril Pyman) perceive a polyphonic form of *sobornost* in Dostoyevsky as tragically *unresolved*.[133]

---

129. Bowker, "Systems," in *Believing*, 159.

130. Bowker, "Systems," in *Believing*, 161.

131. Bowker, "Systems," in *Believing*, 171.

132. Richard Hooker, *Of the Laws of Ecclesiastical Polity*, 7th edn., arr. John Keble and rev. R. W. Church, 3 vols. (Oxford: Clarendon, 1888), Preface, 1:1.

133. Malcolm Jones, *Dostoevsky and the Dynamics of Religious Experience* (London: Anthem, 2005), 41.

Clark and Holmquist shed a fascinating light on the *possible* relation between coherence and difference in Bakhtin by introducing the early influence upon Bakhtin of new scientific models and the changing nature of the philosophy of science brought about by the work of Albert Einstein.[134] Einstein's own concerns in physics related to the complex unity of differences, to the relation between space and time, and to problems of temporal simultaneity. Only different systems of reference permit two different events of a certain kind to be brought into a conceptual unity. *Differences are relativized as differences,* but their *possible unity remains potential* rather than actual. *Yet each "different" entity cannot be "itself" except in relation to "the Other";* for only in relation to the other can its meaning be signified. In a more recent study Michael Holmquist goes further. He discusses Bakhtin's interest in Max Planck, Einstein, and Niels Bohr (as well as in neo-Kantianism) in his earlier years in St. Petersburg, and that although this influence is not direct and explicit, "dialogism is a version of relativity."[135] Motion has meaning only in dialogue with another body. We regard the world and each other from different centers in cognitive space-time. "'Being' for Bakhtin, then, is not just an event, *but an event that is shared.* Being . . . is always *co*-being."[136]

This understanding of dialogic discourse and of the need on occasion to hear polyphonic voices places some of the traditional "difficulties" about the biblical canon in a fresh light. It suggests, for example, that Heikki Räisänen's objections are superficial and contrived when he attacks Brevard Childs and Peter Stuhlmacher for postulating an illusory unity in a way that "runs counter to the rules of sound scholarship."[137] Räisänen believes that we cannot construct Christian doctrine on the foundations of the New Testament because "the New Testament has turned out to be filled with theological contradictions."[138] There is a methodological gap, Räisänen argues, between "everyday exegesis" and "theological syntheses" or "New Testament theologies."[139]

The very word "contradiction," however, betrays the narrowness of the horizons of a writer who appears to work largely within a single discipline (*historical* and phenomenological biblical-critical scholarship) and seems unable to explore whether the biblical canon might be other than monologic discourse, intended

---

134. Katrina Clark and Michael Holmquist, *Mikhail Bakhtin* (Cambridge, MA: Harvard University Press, 1984), 69-70 and 277; cf. also Tzvetan Todorov, *Mikhail Bakhtin: The Dialogical Principle,* trans. W. Godzich, Theory and History of Literature 12 (Minneapolis: University of Minnesota Press, 1984), 14-24.

135. Michael Holmquist, *Dialogism: Bakhtin and His World* (London and New York: Routledge, 1990), 20; cf. 5-6, 21, 25, 116-17, and 156-62.

136. Holmquist, *Dialogism,* 25.

137. Heikki Räisänen, *Challenges to Biblical Interpretation: Collected Essays 1991-2000,* Biblical Interpretation Series 59 (London and Boston: Brill, 2001), 231.

138. Räisänen, *Challenges,* 229.

139. Räisänen, *Challenges,* 229.

as third-person, nonparticipatory utterance, capable of being mediated by, or reduced to, the scope of a single mind. Or to express the matter more accurately, he seems to believe that theological construction can be undertaken with validity only if the canon has this monologic character. But how would such an assumption cohere with our work in Chapter 2 on dispositional accounts of belief? Might someone with a sharper philosophical awareness be tempted to suggest that such an assumption could "run counter to the rules of sound scholarship"? This apparent blind spot is all the more surprising since Räisänen's volume of essays includes a constructive essay on *Wirkungsgeschichte* and another on tradition and experience, and elsewhere he produces work of considerable insight.[140] All the same, Peter Balla seems successfully to have challenged and attacked many of Räisänen's methodological assumptions one by one.[141]

I do not propose to retrace the argument of my recent essay "Canon, Community and Theological Construction," written for the *Scripture and Hermeneutics Series* in conjunction with our Consultation held in the Pontifical Gregorian University, Rome, in June 2005.[142] I cited a range of primary sources to underline the point that such writers as Brevard Childs, James Sanders, Rolf Rendtorff, and Gerald Sheppard respect the pluriformity of the biblical writings, and do not reject the methods of modern biblical criticism. They reflect a dynamic, historical, and dialectical understanding of relations between texts, traditions, and communities of faith. They allow the distinctive traditions to speak in their own right. Yet they also, at a different level, attempt to "hear" what, in Bakhtin's language, an intersubjective plurality of voices may be saying *together* in ways that transcend any single voice.

Two points are especially important for a hermeneutics of doctrine. First, the canon is no artificially contrived set of books awaiting decision or imprimatur from the third of fourth centuries. The canon identifies those "voices" through which address from God was experienced in speaking to the church and the world from the first century onward. Second, in the remaining essays of the volume *Canon and Biblical Interpretation,* to which we have alluded, the writers in question both demonstrate their respect for the integrity of specific voices without attempts at artificial harmonization, and let the interaction between very different viewpoints speak *together* as *different* (but not contradictory) voices. Thus Ecclesiastes and Job are seen as different from, but also complemen-

---

140. Räisänen, *Challenges,* 251-82.

141. Peter Balla, *Challenges to New Testament Theology: An Attempt to Justify the Enterprise* (Peabody, MA: Hendrickson, 1997), esp. 86-209.

142. Anthony C. Thiselton, "Canon, Community and Theological Construction," in *Canon and Biblical Interpretation,* ed. Scott Hahn and others, Scripture and Hermeneutics Series 7 (Grand Rapids: Zondervan, 2006 and Carlisle: Paternoster, 2007), 1-30. See, e.g., Brevard Childs, *Old Testament Theology in a Canonical Context* (Philadelphia: Fortress and London: SCM, 1985); idem, *Exodus: A Commentary* (London: SCM, 1974).

tary to, Deuteronomy and Proverbs in their treatment of the philosophy of providence. Tremper Longman and Ryan O'Dowd show that the Wisdom literature is not all of a piece, but that different traditions within this genre address different situations. Gordon McConville identifies distinctive themes in the Book of the Covenant, the Holiness Code, and the Deuteronomic Code within the Pentateuch, while Gordon Wenham distinguishes different "voices" within the Psalms.[143]

None of this suggests that the biblical writings are too "contradictory" to serve as a foundation for the genesis and development of Christian *doctrine*. Arguably they pose for the development of doctrine not a series of free-floating "problems" but "questions that arise." Within a framework of the hermeneutics of doctrine, such agenda play their part as *hermeneutically motivated questions that arise from life,* and the development of the theological traditions to which each voice gives rise will be traced in its *embodied* forms of life. The ultimate aim remains for these polyphonic voices to have *formative effects* upon readers of successive generations, whose situations in turn are *also varied.*

---

143. These are authors of essays in this volume.

CHAPTER 8

Can Doctrine as "Science" Remain Hermeneutical and Promote Formation?

8.1. Science, Theological Science, and Hermeneutical Formation in T. F. Torrance

We have endorsed the relevance of criteria of coherence for doctrine, and affirmed that the two poles of "explanation" *(Erklärung)* and understanding *(Verstehen)* belong together within hermeneutics. The former provides a critical or "checking" dimension that serves what Ricoeur terms a hermeneutic of suspicion alongside the more creative and formative dimension that he calls a hermeneutic of retrieval.[1] Schleiermacher explicitly described the critical aspect as the "masculine" principle of comparison and rational inquiry, in contrast to a "divinatory" or "feminine" principle of more creative interpersonal understanding. Each, he argued, complements the other.[2]

The history of philosophical hermeneutics confirms that these two angles of approach perform complementary tasks rather than undermining each other, although Gadamer is the one dissenting voice on this issue, placing everything, in effect, under hermeneutics as *Verstehen*. But does this "explanatory" or critical dimension allow for the application of the traditional term "science" to doctrine? We need to define more carefully what the terms "science" and "scientific" may be thought to denote in this context. Clearly the use of scientific *method* does not presuppose or entail a "scientific" or positivist *worldview*. Such a point is axiom-

---

1. Pannenberg, *Systematic Theology,* vol. 1, 16-26; *Basic Questions in Theology,* vol. 1, 1-27; and *Theology and the Philosophy of Science,* 326-45; and Ricoeur, *Hermeneutics and the Human Sciences,* 145-64; and *Interpretation Theory,* 71-88; cf. also Apel, *Understanding and Explanation,* throughout.

2. Schleiermacher, *Hermeneutics,* 150-51.

atic for most students of the philosophy of religion, and Paul Ricoeur implies such a working distinction in his discussion of interpretation in Sigmund Freud.[3] To use certain mechanistic *methods* for the purpose of understanding *empirical data* is different from assuming a mechanistic *worldview* of all reality, as if to imply that everything without remainder can be fully explained in mechanistic or positivist terms. Theists rightly regard this view as reductionist. The grounds for extending scientific method into a scientific worldview take us beyond the limits of scientific methods into a positivist metaphysic and thereby rest upon a category mistake. To elucidate the possibility of understanding theological science in a way that is not only compatible with hermeneutics, but also explicitly acknowledges and even calls for hermeneutical endeavor and formative understanding, we shall look briefly at the claims of Thomas F. Torrance and in more detail at the work of Bernard Lonergan.

Thomas F. Torrance (b. 1913) offers a profoundly hermeneutical conception of both theological and natural sciences when he observes that they "share the same basic problem: how to refer our thoughts and statements genuinely beyond ourselves, how to reach knowledge of reality *in which we do not intrude ourselves distortingly into the picture,* and yet how to retain the full and *integral place of the human subject* in it all."[4] The words that I have italicized sum up the overriding reason for Gadamer's suspicion of "method." Older notions of "science" as merely a process of perceiving empirical objects in a value-neutral way, often within positivist horizons, no longer hold sway after the advances of twentieth-century scientific inquiry.[5] In relation to the problem of subjectivity and objectivity Torrance continues, "Genuine critical questions as to the *possibility* of knowledge cannot be raised *in abstracto,* but only *in concreto,* not *a priori* but only *a posteriori*" (his italics).[6]

Torrance appeals to Kierkegaard here, although the words might perhaps have come equally well as a principle of hermeneutics from Gadamer. He writes, "It is false, Kierkegaard argued, to answer a question in a medium in which the

---

3. Ricoeur, *Freud and Philosophy,* 230-54 and 375-418.

4. Thomas F. Torrance, *Theological Science* (London and New York: Oxford University Press, 1969), xvii.

5. Of a multitude of possible sources, see, e.g., Arthur R. Peacocke, *Creation and the World of Science* (Oxford: Clarendon, 1979), esp. 52-77; Arthur Peacocke, *Theology for a Scientific Age: Being and Becoming — Natural and Divine* (Oxford: Blackwell, 1990), 1-43; Robert J. Russell, Nancey Murphy, and C. J. Isham (eds.), *Quantum Cosmology and the Laws of Nature: Scientific Perspectives on Divine Action,* (Berkeley, CA: Center for Theology and the Natural Sciences, and Vatican City: Vatican Observatory Publications, 2d edn. 1996), esp. 1-34 but also throughout; Harold K. Schilling, *The New Consciousness in Science and Religion* (London: SCM, 1973), 15-119; Ian G. Barbour, *Religion and Science: Historical and Contemporary Issues* (London: SCM, 1998), 115-251; and John Polkinghorne, *Science and Theology: An Introduction* (London: SPCK and Minneapolis: Fortress, 1998), 1-48.

6. Torrance, *Theological Science,* 1.

question cannot arise, and therefore it is wrong to pose the question as to possibility in abstraction from the reality which alone can give rise to it."[7] This leads to a fundamental point about the very nature of science and scientific method, whether we apply it to the natural sciences or to theological science. Torrance declares, "It is important to distinguish this understanding of objectivity from a commonly held view that objectivity means detachment, impartiality, indifference toward the object — that is to say, the attitude in which we stand off from the object in order to contemplate it calmly and dispassionately, in which we suspend active relation to the object in order to prevent our commitment from warping our judgement or even to exclude the influence of our subjectivity upon the object."[8]

Much of this resonates with Gadamer's exploration of the phenomenon of "understanding." Where Torrance speaks of the involvement of an active participant, Gadamer speaks of both participation and historical finitude and prejudgments in the light of prior horizons and pre-given traditions. There is even a certain degree of convergence about "otherness" in Gadamer, Jauss, Ricoeur, and Tracy, although Torrance states it more explicitly in terms of divine transcendence and divine holiness. In relation to knowing God, Torrance writes, "God gives Himself to our knowing, only in such a way that He . . . distinguishes Himself from us and makes Himself known in this divine otherness even when he draws us into communion with Himself. . . . He never resigns knowledge of Himself to our mastery, but remains the One who is Master over us, who resists, and objects to, every attempt on our part to subdue or redact the possibility of knowledge grounded in His divine freedom. . . ."[9] "To know God in His Holiness means that our human subjectivity is opened out and up toward that which infinitely transcends it."[10] If we were using Gadamer's language, we should say that our horizons were *enlarged, transcended, and re-formed* in *engaging with the Other* with *transformative* effect, even if a necessary degree of distanciation always remains.

Torrance carefully considers the impact of developments in the natural sciences, including especially those of relativity and quantum mechanics. These have involved a radical change in the structure of scientific consciousness. Albert Einstein wrestled with issues deriving from Newtonian and Kantian conceptions of space and time, while advances in nuclear physics through the work of Maxwell and Rutherford forced physicists like Bohr "to carry through a change in the whole structure of knowledge, as it lay embedded in classical physics and mechanics."[11] Abstract objectivism underwent severe criticism. Arthur Edding-

---

7. Torrance, *Theological Science*, 2.
8. Torrance, *Theological Science*, 35.
9. Torrance, *Theological Science*, 53.
10. Torrance, *Theological Science*, 53.
11. Torrance, *Theological Science*, 92-93.

ton, Michael Polanyi, and C. F. von Weizsäcker, Torrance continues, "have successfully shown how the personal factor inevitably enters into scientific knowledge, for the very fact of our knowing explicitly enters into what we know."[12] This does not imply that the human subject obtrudes distorting judgments into the content of truth (in the sense that Gadamer strenuously strives to avoid as "method"). Nevertheless Torrance quotes Werner Heisenberg's aphorism, "Natural science does not simply describe and explain nature; it is part of the interplay between nature and ourselves."[13]

The other side of the picture, Torrance continues, is that the theories of relativity and quantum physics have contributed startlingly to the unity of science, especially in "the notion of complementarity, which, as Oppenheimer has stated it, 'recognizes that various ways of talking about physical experience may each have validity and may be necessary . . . and yet may stand in a relation of mutually exclusive relationship to each other, so that to a situation to which one applies, there may be no consistent possibility of applying the other.'"[14]

In the light of such complexity, how are we still to understand the nature of "science" in the natural sciences and especially in theology or doctrine? In the light of his reappraisal of scientific method in the natural sciences, Torrance offers five criteria for a "scientific" theology.

(1) The first is "the utter lordship of the Object. . . . Knowledge of God entails an *epistemological inversion*" (his italics). This amounts to a theological version of Gadamer's attack on method, and is entirely in accord with the nature of hermeneutical inquiry. The human subject must not impose upon God as our Object of thought any prior categorization or fixed horizon that will distort understanding by speaking before we have listened. James Robinson introduces Gadamer's hermeneutics (and indeed theological hermeneutics from Barth to Fuchs) in precisely such terms. He writes, "The flow of the traditional relation between subject and object in which the subject interrogates the object and, if he masters it, obtains from it his answer, has been significantly reversed. For it is now the object — which should henceforth be called the subject matter — that puts the subject in question."[15] God speaks, and humankind hears. The impact of broad and sophisticated traditions of hermeneutical epistemology should serve to guard against any mistaken notion that such an epistemology derives

---

12. Torrance, *Theological Science*, 93.

13. From Werner Heisenberg, *Physics and Philosophy: The Revolution in Modern Science* (London: Allen & Unwin, 1959), 80; cf. Karl Heim, *The Transformation of the Scientific World View*, trans. N. H. Smith (London: SCM, 1953).

14. Torrance, *Theological Science*, 111.

15. James M. Robinson, "Hermeneutics Since Barth," in James M. Robinson and John B. Cobb Jr. (eds.), *New Frontiers in Theology: 2, The New Hermeneutic* (New York and London: Harper & Row, 1964), 23-24; from 1-77. Cf., similarly, Robert W. Funk, *Language, Hermeneutic and Work of God* (New York and London: Harper & Row, 1966), 10-18.

solely from Karl Barth, as if this alone would somehow provide grounds to suspect or to discount it.

(2) The second requirement for theological science derives from an acknowledgment of the *personal nature* of the "Object" of theology and doctrine. This is Jesus Christ as both "Person and Word."[16] The relationship between the theological interpreter and Christ operates within a "dialogical" framework. This reminds us of Bakhtin's observations on monological and dialogical discourse (discussed in 7.3). But it also underlines the artificial nature of the disjunction posed by Heyduck between epistemology and communion with God, stressed as the object of engagement with Scripture and doctrine not only in Calvin but also in the Eastern Fathers. According to Torrance, no such disjunction exists in responsible, Christ-centered, Christian doctrine. Less directly this is supported further by Paul Ricoeur's notion of the multidimensional character of hermeneutical discourse. In Scripture and doctrine this includes not only didactic propositions and prophetic declarations, but also prayer, doxology, lament, Psalmic praise, and celebration of narrative.[17]

(3) A third mark of "scientific" theology or doctrine expands this notion of dialogue and conversation. The word of God creates "a community of conversation" that corresponds as far as possible with the "objectivity of the Object" and God's glory. God gives himself as Lord, but in human form "within our space and time."[18] This section coheres well with our chapters on a *hermeneutic* of doctrine as *formative, communal,* and *embodied.*

(4) The fourth "scientific requirement" for theology arises from "the *centrality* of Jesus Christ as the self-objectification of God for us in our humanity," which explicates the sense in which theological *coherence* grows. This comes about "only through relation to Christ." It "cannot be abstracted, and turned into an independent principle."[19] Coherence in doctrine depends upon relating all theology ultimately to Christ. It loses its authenticity if it becomes abstracted from our dialogical encounter with God.

(5) Torrance's fifth principle tends to repeat his earlier point about the need for science to accord with its Object. However, he adds that the dimension of critique and self-critique (which we have broadly related to "explanation," *Erklärung*) retains a necessary place, given the "historical objectivity" of the incarnation of Jesus Christ. This aspect does not undermine the others.

All of these arguments about the nature of "theological science" place "scientific" theology firmly within a hermeneutical framework that *not only allows, but also positively nurtures formative, transformative, embodied, and dynamic doc-*

---

16. Torrance, *Theological Science*, 133-35.

17. Paul Ricoeur, *Essays on Biblical Interpretation*, ed. Lewis S. Mudge (London: SPCK, 1981 and Minneapolis: Fortress, 1980), 73-118.

18. Torrance, *Theological Science*, 136.

19. Torrance, *Theological Science*, 138.

trine. In *Theological Science* a "scientific" approach, as Torrance defines it, does not preclude, but initiates, transformative effects.

8.2. Coherence, Cognition, Formation, and Hermeneutics in Bernard Lonergan

Bernard Lonergan (1904-84) also contributes to a changing understanding of the nature of "science" in the context of hermeneutical understanding and Christian theology. Lonergan makes much of the concept of "horizon" within the framework of seeking to interpret, to understand, and to reach reasonable and rational judgments. The pre-given horizons from within which we perceive, imagine, inquire, reflect, interpret, and judge, render the process of perceiving and judging more complex than "naïve realism" might suggest. Lonergan attacks a merely perceptual view of knowledge. His recognition of the sheer complexity of ways of knowing and understanding the world is bound up with his working distinction between "classic" and "contemporary" science. "Classic" views of science sought *certainty;* "contemporary" sciences work with *probability.* Classical sciences, including an Aristotelian approach, proceeded on the assumption of working with *fixed objects* or essences; contemporary science presupposes the pervasive effects of *change* and development. In hermeneutical terms, they acknowledge the impact and role of *shifting horizons.*

Lonergan's magisterial work *Insight* was the first of two major works on theological method, almost a proto-"hermeneutics of theology."[20] As Frederick Crowe argues, in *Insight* Lonergan was prompted first by "the overwhelming advances of the scientific revolution," and second by the critical turn taken in Kant's philosophy together with controversy in Catholic thought concerning the interpretation of Thomas Aquinas for theology. Both areas touch on the central question of theories of cognition.[21] The straightforward empirical model of scientific inquiry associated with the paradigm of the Newtonian era of gathering empirical data and "taking a look" was demonstrably inadequate and simplistic in the light of scientific progress in the twentieth century. This "classic" view of science was individual-centered, and philosophically reflected the era of rationalism and empiricism from Descartes to Hume. Even Kant, with his new critical, transcendental questions, followed Hume in beginning with perception. More recent models of scientific inquiry are more *communal, collaborative, historical,* and relative to *interpretation* and to *human judgment.*

20. Bernard J. F. Lonergan, *Insight: A Study of Human Understanding* (New York and London: Harper & Row, 1978 [also Longman, 1957]; and *Method in Theology* (London: Darton, Longman, & Todd, 1971).

21. Frederick E. Crowe, *Lonergan* (London: Geoffrey Chapman, 1992), 62.

Lonergan tells us that he worked on *Insight* from 1949 through to 1953. He writes, "Rationalist and empiricist philosophers . . . cancel each other out in Kantian criticism. . . . The present work . . . is an account of knowledge."[22] The significance of "the transition from the old mechanism to relativity, and from the old determinism to statistical laws" finds clear expression, first, in "the relevance of mathematics and mathematical physics."[23] Hence Lonergan explores knowledge in mathematics in chapter 1 of *Insight*. Like Collingwood and Gadamer, he begins "the question": "the pure question is prior to insights. . . . It is the wonder which Aristotle claimed to be the beginning of all science and philosophy."[24] If we explore positive integers and addition tables, we reach "the need for a higher viewpoint," and indeed "successive higher viewpoints."[25] In the end even the attempt to abstract requires us "to see what is significant and set aside the irrelevant."[26]

Chapters 2 to 5 of *Insight* explore the *heuristic structures* of empirical method, including uses of statistical inquiry, within which processes of selection, operation, relevance, explanation, formulation, characterization, probability, and place and time all play a role.[27] Lonergan's exposure of the dependence of statistical analysis upon *selection* of data, *judgments* concerning relevance, and subsequent *interpretation* correspond precisely to those factors identified by Gadamer when Gadamer argued that statistics, contrary to widespread assumptions, demonstrate *the universality of hermeneutics,* even in empirical sciences.[28]

In chapters 6–8 Lonergan applies this principle to "common sense" phenomena. In the context of commonsense acts of perception, we might well assume that everything turns upon perception alone, or on "taking a look." But even at this modest level Lonergan points out that interpreting and judging data through acts of cognition are also involved. Lonergan addresses the phenomenon of "intelligence in every walk of life."[29] This goes beyond "taking a look," for it often involves "readiness in catching on, in getting the point, in seeing the issue, in grasping implications, in acquiring know-how . . . the act that released Archimedes' 'Eureka!' For insight is ever the same . . . rendered conspicuous by the contrasting, if reassuring, occurrence of examples of obtuseness and stupidity."[30]

22. Lonergan, *Insight,* xvii and xix.
23. Lonergan, *Insight,* xxi.
24. Lonergan, *Insight,* 9.
25. Lonergan, *Insight,* 15-19.
26. Lonergan, *Insight,* 30.
27. Lonergan, *Insight,* 33-172.
28. Lonergan, *Insight,* 56-79; cf. also Gadamer, "The Universality of the Hermeneutical Problem," in Gadamer, *Philosophical Hermeneutics,* 3-17.
29. Lonergan, *Insight,* 173.
30. Lonergan, *Insight,* 173. A helpful exposition of Lonergan's approach to this point can be found in Francis Schüssler Fiorenza, "Bernard Lonergan," in *Modern Christian Thought:* vol. 2, *The Twentieth Century,* ed. J. C. Livingston and F. Schüssler Fiorenza (New Upper Saddle River, NJ: Prentice Hill, 2d edn. 2000), 214-21.

Common sense, Lonergan argues, is "an intellectual development."[31] Imagination and intelligence collaborate in representing a projected course of action that invites reflection and critical judgment, and this is more akin to the "directedness" of a drama or dramatic narrative than to merely biophysical or mechanical processes.[32] Human persons are artists as well as intelligences. They use clothes, for example, not only for warmth and protection, but to project a "face" or mode of presence to those around them. From the very first (as Gadamer also notes) "common sense" presupposes, and interacts within, an intersubjective world of community. Human persons are committed by our human nature to "intersubjective spontaneity and intelligently devised social order."[33] We encounter "things" within a framework of law and system.[34]

This leads to the three central chapters (chs. 9–11) on judgment, reflective understanding, and the self-affirmation of the knower.[35] Concepts, definitions, and objects of thought are not enough: "We conceive in order to judge."[36] The cognitional process is a cumulative and complex process. *Cognition* involves "levels of consciousness." If a first level of consciousness concerns the *perception* of objects, a second level of knowing looks for *intelligible patterns* in their representations in moments of insight. In a third level of knowing, "*Reasonableness* is reflection in as much as it seeks groundedness for objects of thought; reasonableness discovers *groundedness*. . . . Balanced *judgement* . . . testifies to the dominance of reasonableness *in the subject*."[37] Lonergan declares, "Fact, then, combines with the correctness of experience, the determinateness of accurate intelligence, and the absoluteness of rational judgement. . . . It is the anticipated unity to which sensation, perception, imagination, inquiry, insight, formulation, grasp of the unconditional, and judgement, make their several, complementary, contributions."[38]

Lonergan traces five differences between his epistemology and that of Kant, and even more differences from relativist approaches.[39] On this basis many describe Lonergan as an advocate of "critical realism."[40] He agrees with Kant that the role of the subject is vital in processes of cognition, but against Kant retains a major role for the intersubjective community and an unconditional "reality."

Lonergan has shown over the first eleven chapters of *Insight* that even the

31. Lonergan, *Insight*, 175.
32. Lonergan, *Insight*, 188-89.
33. Lonergan, *Insight*, 215; cf. 211-44.
34. Lonergan, *Insight*, ch. 8, "Things," 245-70.
35. Lonergan, *Insight*, 271-347.
36. Lonergan, *Insight*, 273.
37. Lonergan, *Insight*, 323 (my italics).
38. Lonergan, *Insight*, 331.
39. Lonergan, *Insight*, 339-47.
40. Francis Schüssler Fiorenza, "Lonergan," 214-16.

natural sciences themselves are profoundly *hermeneutical*. He has achieved this in the context of a more affirming, positive, and focused dialogue than Gadamer achieves. He goes beyond merely disparaging abstraction, generality, and value-neutral objectivity. He shows that interpretation, understanding, and judgment reside within the very process of "scientific" inquiry as well as within broader inquiries about persons and God. In the second half of *Insight* he extends his inquiry to the dialectic of method in metaphysics, exploring Hegel's dialectic and broader questions of truth and of ethics. But these questions overlap substantially with the later magisterial volume *Method in Theology*, to which we now turn briefly.

The approach in this volume follows the pattern laid down in *Insight*, but applies it to theology or to doctrine. Theology concerns more than "experience." Many see experience as the primary "given" for Schleiermacher and for the liberal tradition identified by George Lindbeck as yielding an "experiential-expressive" conception of doctrine. But what *is* "experience" *until we interpret it, understand it, and bring it to judgment and to practical decision?* It is vital for Lonergan that we begin with a transcendental method that brings our conscious and intentional operations to light. Transcendental inquiry raises two questions for Lonergan: What am I doing when I "know"? "What do I know when I do it?"[41] In exploring feelings, judgments, and beliefs, he concludes that inquiry must follow certain "transcendental precepts." These are: "Be attentive, Be intelligent, Be reasonable, Be responsible."[42] This is part of a quest for a *transcultural* framework, which will not be overtaken by each new fashion in changing cultures. These processes of cognition, Lonergan argues, are successive and cumulative. Higher levels of knowing or understanding "sublate" lower ones. He calls specific processes "functional specialties."[43]

We now reach a crucial point in relation to our argument in these chapters. In *Insight* Lonergan addressed the relation between *"science"* and *formation*, and showed that far from being mutually in conflict, each process complemented the other. Now in *Method in Theology*, Lonergan makes out a parallel case in relation to "explanation" and "understanding," although through a slightly different vocabulary. He calls the two complementary theological dimensions *"declaring"* (or "explaining") and *"taking a stand"* (or "understanding"). "Declaring" includes research, explanation, interpretation, history, and dialectic; *taking a stand* includes foundations, doctrines, systematic theology, and communications, or, in other words, *understanding*, and *formative action*. The difference between these two approaches, however, is mainly one of *method* rather than content. Lonergan rightly says of doctrine, "It makes thematic what already is a part of *Christian liv-*

41. Lonergan, *Method*, 25.
42. Lonergan, *Method*, 55.
43. Lonergan, *Method*, 125-45.

ing" (my italics).[44] This might have been a description of our aim in Part III of this volume.

Theological method, then, begins with research, followed by interpretation. In common with the major traditions of hermeneutics Lonergan asserts that one approaches texts or questions with a necessary preunderstanding. He writes, "The principle of the empty head rests on a naïve intuitionism. So far from tackling the complex task . . . the principle of the empty head bids the interpreter to forget his own views."[45] Theoretical "objectivity" of this kind is based upon an illusion: the only "objective" datum is a series of signs. To understand these signs requires "the experience, intelligence, and judgement of the interpreter."[46] The less the experience, the less "cultivated" that intelligence, and the less" formed" that judgment, the greater the likelihood of misunderstanding. "It is *understanding* that surmounts the hermeneutical circle."[47]

Lonergan subscribes to the notion of "understanding" found in the hermeneutical tradition from Schleiermacher to Gadamer and Ricoeur. He writes, "Coming to understand is not a logical deduction. It is a self-correcting process of learning that spirals into the meaning of the whole by using each new part to fill out and qualify and correct the understanding reached in reading the earlier parts."[48]

Lonergan refuses to regard "hermeneutics" as some esoteric discipline reserved for American literary theorists and German theologians. This hermeneutical process, he insists, is "not only the way in which we acquire our own common sense, but also the way in which we acquire an understanding of other people's common sense."[49] This applies to understanding authors and texts, in which referential meaning also has its place. This does not suggest, however, that such understanding is always determinate, let alone exhaustive. Lonergan urges that we need constantly to labor. He endorses Friedrich Schlegel's dictum, "A classic is a writing that is never fully understood. But those that are educated and educate themselves must always want to learn more from it."[50] "Context" is "a nest of interlocked or interwoven questions and answers."[51]

History and historical inquiry not only does justice to the *life-related* content of doctrine or theology, but also places what needs to be understood within its wider social context. History provides a context for what contemporaries may not know. Lonergan explains, "In most cases, contemporaries do not know what

44. Lonergan, *Method*, 144.
45. Lonergan, *Method*, 157.
46. Lonergan, *Method*, 157.
47. Lonergan, *Method*, 159.
48. Lonergan, *Method*, 159.
49. Lonergan, *Method*, 160.
50. Lonergan, *Method*, 161; also cited by Gadamer, *Truth*, 290, n. 218.
51. Lonergan, *Method*, 163.

is going forward. . . . The actual course of events results not only from what people intend but also from their oversights, mistakes, failures to act."[52] The study of history has undergone a Copernican revolution and become both critical and constructive, drawing upon historical imagination. Appealing to Gadamer, Lonergan asserts that there is a widespread rejection "of the Enlightenment and Romantic ideal of presuppositionless history."[53] The historian works within pregiven "horizons."[54]

Dialectic also belongs within this process. Dialectic explores conflicting conclusions drawn from research, interpretation, and historical inquiry. The horizon is "the limits of one's field of vision," but as one moves about, "it recedes in front and closes in behind so that, for different standpoints, there are different horizons."[55] Horizons may differ in complementary ways. For example, engineers, doctors, lawyers, and professors may have different "worlds" of interests, but in principle *each is capable of enlargement to include the other.* There is no appeal to the dire notion of "incommensurability" here. Horizons may also differ as successive stages in a journey or a process of development. Each may presuppose earlier stages. Horizons may indeed differ in *dialectical* terms: "what in one horizon is found intelligible, in another is unintelligible. What for one is true, for another is false."[56] Nevertheless the whole process of interaction may become transposed into one of organic growth. The sweep of our knowledge is capable of adjustment, re-formation, and larger integration.

What Lonergan terms *foundations, doctrines, systematics,* and *communications* carry us from epistemological resources to *"stance-taking"* commitments. In doctrine these may take the form of confessions of faith, belief-utterances, and first-person speech-acts. Here theology takes "a much more personal stance."[57] It is no longer a matter of narrating what others have believed or do.

The material on *foundations* remains probably the most controversial of Lonergan's chapters. For in the turn away from "hard" or "classical" foundationalism in the early twenty-first century the very notion of "seeking the foundations of . . . doctrines, systematics, and communications" has become widely questioned.[58] On the other hand, Lonergan's earlier appeal to *groundedness, reasonableness,* and *responsible belief* is not too far removed from the "soft," non-Cartesian version of foundationalism that we have already discussed in the previous chapter. Arguably, Lonergan, too, regards "foundations" as serving in two quite different ways. They may serve "as a set of premises, of logically first propo-

52. Lonergan, *Method,* 179.
53. Lonergan, *Method,* 223.
54. Lonergan, *Method,* 220-33.
55. Lonergan, *Method,* 235.
56. Lonergan, *Method,* 236.
57. Lonergan, *Method,* 267.
58. Lonergan, *Method,* 267.

sitions."[59] The biblical writings can serve in this way. On the other hand, foundations may also be understood as identifying "a momentous change in the human reality that a theologian is."[60] "Conversion" entails moving from one *"set of roots"* to another. Francis Schüssler Fiorenza offers a helpful clarification here. He writes, "The crucial-turning point in Lonergan's division of the functional specialties is at the level of foundations. It is one's decision that provides the foundations for what follows. . . . Moral conversion entails . . . radical self-transcendence through the change of horizons."[61] If readers accept the argument of chapter 11 on "foundations," the chapters on doctrines, systematics, and communications flow on with less to cause hesitation.

Some critics argue that Lonergan is pinning everything on a decision here. We need not enter into this debate, but we note that in this context he also speaks of response to grace, and of the power of divine love. What relates directly to our argument is Lonergan's unambiguous emphasis upon the *formative* and *transformative* effect of hermeneutical engagement with Scripture and with theological understanding. This constituted my central concern (indicated by the title and especially the subtitle) in *New Horizons in Hermeneutics: The Theory and Practice of Transforming Biblical Reading*. Further, Lonergan's two books develop and sustain the fully complementary character of *"scientific"* theology and the *formative* role of doctrine as a *"stance-taking"* first-person (plural) speech-action. His questions about "groundedness" and "reasonable" belief form part of the "checking" or critical role played by "explanation" in the dialectic between explanation *(Erklärung)* and understanding *(Verstehen)*. He has proved that even a "scientific" theology, if understood within the frame of a very broad and duly rigorous and sophisticated epistemology, can remain profoundly hermeneutical and formative for life.

8.3. Coherence, System, and Scientific Criteria of Truth: Pannenberg

Wolfhart Pannenberg (b. 1928) views "the scientific status of theology" and its "right to be included among the sciences taught in a university" as resting at least in part on defending or debating its truth "by generally accepted criteria."[62] Such a tradition can be traced back to the thirteenth century. The scientific character of theology or doctrine involves on one side its "external relation to other disciplines on the common basis of their scientific character," and on the other side an ordered understanding of its own internal organization as a coherent set of subdisciplines.[63] Pannenberg does not regard Hermann Diem's proposal in the

---

59. Lonergan, *Method*, 269.
60. Lonergan, *Method*, 270.
61. Francis Schüssler Fiorenza, "Lonergan," 219.
62. Pannenberg, *Theology and the Philosophy of Science*, 13.
63. Pannenberg, *Science*, 5. On its internal organization see 346-440.

Barthian tradition to regard theology as *"kirchliche Wissenschaft"* as entirely adequate as a ground on which to claim its scientific status.

Emphatically "science," however, does not imply any compromise with positivist criteria of truth or meaning. Pannenberg addresses and rejects the criterion of verification associated with logical positivism, and expresses sympathy with Karl Popper's view that empirical research proceeds by a process of conjectures, models, and hypotheses.[64] However, even Popper's principle of falsification cannot be viewed as a universal criterion that can be independently applied, outside historically conditioned systems; nor even, in Thomas Kuhn's sense of the term, paradigms.[65] This applies equally to historical reconstruction, which retains critical importance in Christian theology. Pannenberg writes, "All that can be required of historical hypotheses in the interest of testability and possible refutability is the greatest possible clarity in construction, so that a particular historical reconstruction, with its main assumptions and selection of evidence, can be clearly distinguished from alternative hypotheses.[66] Two factors suggest a view of science that comes close to C. S. Peirce's fallibilism. First, as Gadamer and Lonergan urge, neither verification nor falsification can operate *independently of interpretation*. Second, in Pannenberg's view "ultimate" truth and meaning "can be discovered only with reference to the totality of reality and to the total context of human experience."[67] John Hick to some extent implies this when he explores the notion of "eschatological verification."[68]

In discussing the relationship between the material sciences and the *Geisteswissenschaften* Pannenberg introduces Dilthey's hermeneutical principle that meaning, including "the relationship between life's parts," changes in relation to "the whole."[69] However, in Christian theology this "whole" is not exhausted by notions of immanent purpose, such as that which is central for Troeltsch, but rather by the eschatology of the kingdom of God.[70] Pannenberg comments concerning the role of hermeneutics that Gadamer and Habermas (in spite of other differences) agree that "description by means of causal laws cannot deal with a particular but essential aspect of the human world, that of the perception of meaning."[71] Hence "scientific explanation in terms of laws is only a special form of understanding; or even a 'derivative mode.'"[72] Thus "explanation" may sometimes need to "burst through the framework of the familiar, current understand-

---

64. Pannenberg, *Science*, 32-43.

65. Pannenberg, *Science*, 50-58.

66. Pannenberg, *Science*, 67.

67. Pannenberg, *Science*, 70.

68. John Hick, *Faith and Knowledge* (London: Macmillan, 2d edn. 1988), 175-99.

69. Pannenberg, *Science*, 78.

70. Pannenberg, *Science*, 110; cf. 103-16.

71. Pannenberg, *Science*, 125.

72. Pannenberg, *Science*, 137.

ing of the world."[73] In this sense often deductive-nomological arguments that bring events under hypothetical laws "are in themselves not explanations at all."[74] Even systems theory has more to do with clarifying or maintaining the already known than with paving the way for fresh understanding. Systems theory may facilitate placing the "parts" into a pattern of meaning. The conclusion is a *hermeneutical* one: "*Understanding* operates within a frame of reference," and in *some* contexts *explanation* may provide a framework for understanding. "Understanding, however, does not always presuppose an explanation."[75]

The next stage of the argument explicitly carries the heading: "Hermeneutic: A Methodology for Understanding Meaning."[76] Pannenberg begins with the comment: "The aim of hermeneutic is the understanding of meaning, and meaning is to be understood in this context as the relation of parts to whole within a structure of life or experience."[77] He surveys the development of hermeneutical inquiry from Aristotle and the Stoics through Flacius and Schleiermacher to Dilthey, Gadamer, and Betti. Although he has some reservations about Betti, Pannenberg approves of Betti's search for greater objectivity than characterizes the work of Gadamer. He criticizes Gadamer especially on the ground that "Gadamer does not allow for the constitutive importance of the statement as the expression of the representational function of language for the specifically human relation to the world."[78]

When he addresses the subject of "hermeneutical theology," Pannenberg appears to have in view primarily, if not in effect only, the existentialist perspectives of Rudolf Bultmann, Ernst Fuchs, and Gerhard Ebeling, all of whom reflect the influence of Heidegger. Hence, once again, he understandably sees the movement as "devaluing the role of statement or of assertions about states of affairs."[79] The "content" of a speaker's utterance must be separable from the speaker in terms of a proposition or assertion. Moreover, just as positivism in the natural sciences is "narrow" in one direction, Pannenberg insists that existential philosophy is "narrow" in another direction.

Dialectic and hermeneutic, Pannenberg continues, share a common concern with the interrelation between wholes and parts. Habermas constructively explores this interaction of "depth hermeneutics" as that which transcends the mind of an individual author or reader alone, in relation to a broader, deeper, social structure. Pannenberg acknowledges Habermas's concern with the relation between the hermeneutical circle and concept formation. In the sciences "the

73. Pannenberg, *Science*, 139.
74. Pannenberg, *Science*, 142.
75. Pannenberg, *Science*, 153.
76. Pannenberg, *Science*, 156-224.
77. Pannenberg, *Science*, 156.
78. Pannenberg, *Science*, 168.
79. Pannenberg, *Science*, 177-79; cf. 169-84.

speaker's intentions are not the sole, exclusive, context within which his utterances are to be understood. The utterance enters a different context with each hearer."[80] Meaning embraces object relation and context relation, and this "corresponds strikingly to the two aspects of the concept of truth which have traditionally formed the basis for opposite interpretations, [namely] correspondence with the object, and coherence or consensus."[81] Pannenberg rejects a mere consensus approach, but concedes that a correspondence approach cannot function fruitfully without reference to the judgments of others who "speak the same language as us" (loc. cit.).

Pannenberg explores the senses in which theology has served as a "science" in the history of theology. Thomas Aquinas cited Aristotle's dictum that sciences pursued for the sake of knowledge itself were "higher" than "useful" sciences, and thus included theology among the "pure" sciences. On the other hand, Duns Scotus and William of Ockham saw theology as a "practical" science of knowledge of God, and Luther followed this path. The twists and turns in the status of theology from the seventeenth to the nineteenth century need not detain us for the purposes of our discussion.[82] The different evaluations of theology by Hegel and Schleiermacher are too well known to require repetition. The "historical" nature of Christianity as relating to a given community with a given history was firmly established by the mid-nineteenth century, and soon debates about "religion" and "theology" would come to dominate the scene, even as in a different form today they still do. Pannenberg repeats his conviction that the question of the truth of Christianity cannot be raised as a scientific concern *without inquiry into "the truth of all areas of human experience."*[83] The importance of *coherence* as a major criterion of truth and the *universality* of a hermeneutical framework of understanding provide strong reasons for maintaining this conclusion.

Even so, theology is not simply a science, but "the science of *God.*"[84] Pannenberg observes, "Today especially the reality of God seems to be mentioned only in the utterances of believers and theologians. This is a result of the disintegration of the traditional metaphysical doctrine of God. However, if the reality of God cannot be distinguished from the assertions of believers and theologians about it, such assertions can no longer be taken seriously as assertions."[85] He accepts two scientific criteria proposed by H. Scholz: first, the evaluation of the implications of statements; and second, the postulate of coherence as a minimum requirement. These must convey a genuinely cognitive content. Pannenberg concludes, "The presence of the all-determining reality in a historical phe-

---

80. Pannenberg, *Science*, 211.
81. Pannenberg, *Science*, 219.
82. Pannenberg, *Science*, 236-55.
83. Pannenberg, *Science*, 264 (my italics)
84. Pannenberg, *Science*, 297-345.
85. Pannenberg, *Science*, 329.

nomenon can be investigated only through an analysis of the totality of meaning implicit in the phenomenon."[86] Further, in relation to the internal organization of theology, "Investigation of truth is systematic by nature. . . . An investigation which seeks truth must be systematic to the unity of truth."[87] Within the specific subdiscipline of systematic theology the premises and implications of the traditions of Christian texts must be *made explicit,* and placed within their *appropriate context.*[88]

This brief summary of the main arguments in Pannenberg's *Theology and the Philosophy of Science* underlines his main concerns about the nature of theology, except that we do not have space to include his explication of this approach for his view that Christian theology belongs to the context of a theology of religions.[89] Our main concern has been whether, or to what degree, these concerns would undermine, or stand in conflict with, our emphasis upon contingency, particularity, embodiment, community, and especially the formative and transformative nature of Christian doctrine. We detect no serious conflict here.

First, Pannenberg's insistence that theology and doctrine is grounded upon *God,* and is not coextensive with expressions of *experience of God found among believers and theologians,* fulfills a fundamental condition for transformative doctrine.[90] For any reduction of "doctrine" to what is *already* implicit in "experience" will be self-affirming rather than transformative. Pannenberg's contrast between the "immanent" teleology of Troeltsch and an eschatology of the kingdom of God may represent a partial parallel.[91] Pannenberg writes, "It belongs to the task of theology to understand all being in relation to God."[92] If the Holy Spirit is the *"Beyond"* who is also "Within," transformation is *not self-generated* on the basis of "standing where I am." This is a different point from the equally valid dictum of "incarnational" theology that Christ (who comes to me from "beyond") *meets* me where I am. Lonergan's complex analysis of "experience" has already warned that encounters with *Christ* are not always the same as *experiences assumed to constitute* such encounters.

Dietrich Bonhoeffer stands in a tradition not to be identified wholly with Pannenberg's, but he underlines the unproductive effects of mere self-affirmation. He writes, "Either I determine the place in which I will find God, or I allow God to determine the place where he will be found. If it is I who say where God will be, I will always find there a God who in some way corresponds to me, is agreeable to me, fits in with my nature. But if it is God who says where He will be,

86. Pannenberg, *Science,* 338.
87. Pannenberg, *Science,* 347.
88. The comment is made with reference to G. I. Planck; Pannenberg, *Science,* 405.
89. Pannenberg, *Science,* 358-71 and elsewhere.
90. Pannenberg, *Science,* 329.
91. Pannenberg, *Science,* 103-16.
92. Pannenberg, *Basic Questions in Theology,* vol. 1, 1.

then that will likely be a place which . . . at first does not fit so well with me. That place is the cross of Christ."[93] It is above all *truth* that is transformative. If this is a self-generated truth-claim, even by the church, it will remain what Ricoeur has called (in terms already discussed above) "narcissistic."[94] It is for this reason that my critique of Don Cupitt's later writings has been more forceful than usually characterizes my style of writing.[95] A self-projected "God" cannot be a source of formative and transformative doctrine.

Second, Pannenberg explicitly provides a hermeneutical theory of meaning and understanding that is related to the hermeneutical tradition of Dilthey, Gadamer, Betti, and Habermas. Admittedly he attacks the devaluation of assertions or statements found in Dilthey, Gadamer, Bultmann, Fuchs, Ebeling, and Heidegger. Here, however, Pannenberg shares with Gadamer a key point, namely the possibility of *enlarged and expanding horizons of understanding.*[96] If doctrine and theology seeks "to understand all being in relation to God," a theological horizon of meaning will expand to embrace those of smaller contexts, interests, and concerns. This is why we are less certain than Nancey Murphy that the respective horizons of Hume and Pannenberg are "incommensurable," a subject we shall take up in the next section.[97] In discussing explanation and understanding Pannenberg observes that "something that surprises us" requires explanation, "precisely because it bursts through the framework of the familiar, current understanding . . . and is not intelligible within the framework of the already known."[98] We receive, or discover, "a new frame of reference." This is precisely the kind of hermeneutical experience that we have explored in terms of formation.

Third, in his writings as a whole Pannenberg places a strong emphasis upon resurrection and eschatology. It is precisely the bursting in of the future that provides the dynamic of Christian transformation in accordance with "being conformed to the image of Christ" (Rom. 8:29). "What we will be has not yet been revealed. What we do know is that when he is revealed we shall be like him" (1 John 3:2). Pannenberg questions the notion of God as *ens perfectissimum* without reference to a *temporal* dimension: "As the power of the future, God is no thing, no object presently at hand. . . . Man will participate in the glory of God

93. Dietrich Bonhoeffer, *Meditation on the Word,* trans. D. M. Gracie (Cambridge, MA: Cowley, 1986), 44-45.

94. Ricoeur, *Freud and Philosophy,* 129-32, 277-78, and esp. 426-27; also *The Conflict of Interpretations,* 242-43.

95. Anthony C. Thiselton, *Interpreting God and the Postmodern Self: On Meaning, Manipulation and Promise* (Edinburgh: T&T Clark and Grand Rapids: Eerdmans, 1995), 81-110.

96. Pannenberg, *Science,* 166-67, 118-205, and 333-78; cf. also Pannenberg, *Basic Questions in Theology,* vol. 1, 96-136; vol. 2, 1-27; and vol. 3, 1-79 and 192-210.

97. Nancey Murphy, *Theology in the Age of Scientific Reasoning,* Cornell Studies in the Philosophy of Religion (Ithaca and London: Cornell University Press, 1990), 43-44.

98. Pannenberg, *Science,* 139.

only in such a way that he will always have to leave behind again what he already is . . . by active transformation."[99] Alluding to the consummation of all things, Pannenberg writes: "The glorifying of believers . . . their transformation by the light of the divine glory, draws them into the eternal fellowship of the Father and the Son by the Spirit."[100]

Fourth, virtually all hermeneutical inquiry presupposes the distinct but complementary tasks of *explanation* and *understanding*. Pannenberg's main concern is with *truth* and willingness to *test* truth-claims. But we have already observed from Lonergan's works that we cannot draw sharp, rigid contrasts between *"facts" and "fact-stating propositions"* on one side, and *contexts, frames of reference*, and *horizons of understanding* on the other. However robust is Pannenberg's concern with system, coherence, propositions, truth-claims, and truth-criteria, his work remains profoundly *hermeneutical*. Because revelation is located not only in God, but indirectly in the ongoing words-and-events of history, and because truth is provisional upon the revealing of the eschaton, truth and understanding and their frame of reference remain dynamic, temporal, embodied, contingent, and provisional as well as coherent, and grounded in God. In summary, *meaning* in terms of both "*object-relation* and *context-relation* corresponds strikingly to . . . aspects of the concept of *truth*."[101] The three-volume *Systematic Theology* demonstrates this in practice even more clearly than *Theology and the Philosophy of Science*. This will soon become evident in Part III.

8.4. Proposals regarding Research Programs in the Sciences: Lakatos and Murphy

Nancey Murphy discusses Pannenberg's view of theological method in the course of her exposition and commendation of the approach of Imre Lakatos and his concept of the "research program." Murphy makes three kinds of comments about Pannenberg's work.

First, Murphy expresses approval of several features of Pannenberg's method. (i) He repudiates a sharp distinction between natural theology and "revelation" theology largely on the basis of assimilating the latter to history and to various texts and forms of life that include Scripture. (ii) He calls for "the adoption of scientific method for theology." (iii) He sees theology or doctrine as "the science of God," not merely "the science of the Christian religion."[102] Murphy commends these three features.

Second, however, Murphy argues that Pannenberg's critique of David

---

99. Pannenberg, "The God of Hope," in *Basic Questions*, vol. 2, 242 and 248; from 234 to 249.
100. Pannenberg, *Systematic Theology*, vol. 3, 626; cf. 622-46.
101. Pannenberg, *Science*, 219 (my italics)
102. Murphy, *Theology in the Age of Scientific Reasoning*, 208-9.

Hume's empiricism fails, on the ground that Hume's system and Pannenberg's are, in the terminology of Thomas Kuhn, "incommensurable."[103] Supposedly his critique could not be effective outside his own system, or "consistent with his own system."

Third, in language that combines approval with perhaps rather faint praise, Murphy concludes that if he were to transpose his method and approach into that of a Lakatosian research program, "Pannenberg's system when named as a theological research program (and if we ignore his own criteria for scientific success) looks [OK]."[104]

Pannenberg has responded positively and graciously to these suggestions. He writes, "I have no problems with this description. I could have used that notion myself . . . if the work of Lakatos had been available to me when I wrote my book *Theology and the Philosophy of Science* around 1970."[105] On the other hand, while he is relatively happy with a Lakatosian approach as a "systematic structure" for the framework of theological explanation, Pannenberg remains convinced that the question of *method* may not fit quite so easily with Lakatos' approach.[106]

On what grounds, then, does Nancey Murphy promote a Lakatosian notion of "the research program" for theology? Murphy writes from a dual background in the philosophy of science and in the philosophy of religion. Her doctoral mentor in the philosophy of science was Paul Feyerabend, and some will detect a number of features drawn from Feyerabend in Murphy's subsequent work. She rightly perceives that theology becomes impoverished when exponents of doctrine have little or no expertise in the philosophy of religion. Her adaptation of Feyerabend's aphorism is apposite: "Philosophy of religion without theology is empty; theology without philosophy of religion is blind," although *blind* is an overstatement, pardonable because it is an aphorism.[107] But the next point is more open to question. In the light of Feyerabend's overly pluralist interpretation of Wittgenstein, I am not surprised to find the use of the term "incommensurability" in Murphy's work. It is perhaps in part the overly ready application of this terminology that lends Murphy to a more hospitable approach to the postmodern than many might share.

Murphy rightly perceives the fruitlessness of the numerous polemical "posi-

---

103. Murphy, *Theology*, 47 and 43-50.

104. Murphy, *Theology*, 178.

105. Wolfhart Pannenberg, "Theological Appropriation of Scientific Understandings," in C. R. Albright and J. Haugen (eds.), *Beginning with the End: God, Science, and Wolfhart Pannenberg* (Chicago: Open Court, 1997), 430.

106. Pannenberg, "Theological Appropriation," 431. This dialogue is placed in the context of hermeneutics in Jacqui A. Stewart, *Reconstructing Science and Theology in Postmodernity: Pannenberg, Ethics and the Human Sciences* (Aldershot, U.K. and Burlington, VT: Ashgate, 2000), 140-46, although some have reservations concerning her specific discussion of Pannenberg.

107. Murphy, *Theology*, xii.

tions" so often taken up in theology. Her more recent work, *Beyond Liberalism and Fundamentalism*, makes this point in a wider context.[108] She rightly laments the reduction of too much theology and doctrine as "a two-party system" of "liberals and conservatives," often "marked by acrimony and stereotypes," especially since she also claims that these "positions" have been driven by philosophical positions . . . [now] called into question."[109] As her chapter headings suggest, the endlessly repeated alternatives "experience or Scripture," "description or expression," "immanence or intervention" presuppose a static, largely worn out, prepackaged agenda.[110] The rise of "modernity" in the forms expounded by Kant and Schleiermacher, she argues, has driven the forces of Liberalism; Reid and Princeton theology have been the forces behind conservative theology.

It would take us beyond the scope of the present argument to offer any assessment of Murphy's second book here. We might ask in passing, however, whether this rather schematic portrait applies to theologies in other parts of the world as well as it does to America. Few British conservatives have been greatly enamored with Hodge, who explicitly regarded all original ideas as subversive, and in Britain has often been regarded as rather dull and predictable. While we may wholeheartedly agree that outmoded philosophies have too often set the agenda for theology, is there more than a hint that it is a different type of philosophy that will gallop to the rescue, waving the flags of "nonfoundationalism" (without much distinction between "hard" and "soft" foundationalism) and "postmodernism"? The term "postmodern" does not denote *only* throwing off the controls of such Kant/Schleiermacher/Reid agenda of questions, nor simply an escape from the grand narrative/mythologies of high modernity. It also denotes a distinct turn toward pluralism, fragmentation, a pragmatic or instrumental and "local" understanding of rationality, and very much else besides.[111] Is the agenda of Part II of her later book quite as straightforward as Murphy perhaps suggests?[112]

None of this should detract from the constructive value of Murphy's basic thesis worked out in her earlier book on Lakatos, and her related claims about the need to move on in her second book. Much of the strength of Murphy's assimilation of the Lakatosian "research program" is to try to extricate theology from its endless obsession with "positions," "schools," polarizations, and polemical styles. I should like to think of my theological vocation as that of attempting to provide *cre-*

---

108. Nancey Murphy, *Beyond Liberalism and Fundamentalism: How Modern and Post-Modern Philosophy Set the Theological Agenda*, Rockwell Lecture Series (London and New York: Continuum/Trinity Press International, 1996).

109. Murphy, *Beyond Liberalism*, 1.

110. Murphy, *Beyond Liberalism*, 11-82.

111. See Anthony C. Thiselton, *Thiselton on Hermeneutics: Collected Works and New Essays*, Contemporary Thinkers on Religion (Aldershot, U.K.: Ashgate and Grand Rapids: Eerdmans, 2006), Part 6, 537-682.

112. Murphy, *Beyond Liberalism*, 85-153.

ative exploration (what Murphy and Lakatos tend to call a "heuristic" approach), although this is not to deny that sometimes a duty of attack and defense becomes a distasteful but necessary task in accordance with one's Christian commitment and the injunctions of the Pastoral Epistles.[113] *Prima facie* a Lakatosian research program looks ideally to cohere with a hermeneutics of doctrine.

Imre Lakatos (1922-74) was born in Hungary in a Jewish home. He converted to Calvinism, at least for a period of time.[114] He studied mathematics, physics, and philosophy, and completed his education in Budapest. He was active in Marxist politics and became a research student of Gyorgy Lukács. He traveled to Moscow University in 1949, but clashed with Stalinist orthodoxy as a "revisionist." Only with Stalin's death in 1953 could Lakatos begin a serious academic career in his thirties, working on probability theory in mathematics. It is no accident that during 1954-56 he raised questions about the Marxist *system* and its epistemology. In 1956 he supported the doomed Hungarian uprising, and with the arrival of Soviet troops, Lakatos escaped to Vienna and then to England. At King's College, Cambridge, he began Ph.D. research under the supervision of R. B. Braithwaite, the empiricist philosopher. He later revised and published his thesis as *Proofs and Refutations*. In 1960 he joined Karl Popper at the London School of Economics, where he worked until his death in his early fifties in 1974.

Many of Lakatos' seminal ideas come from his *Proofs and Refutations*.[115] He argued that *counterexamples*, for which he used the term *refutations*, play a major role in mathematics as well as in the sciences. A steady search for counterexamples leads not so much to the *rejection* of a theorem, but to its gradual *refinement and improvement*. Lakatos aimed to move beyond the more sharply bounded theories of philosophy of science expounded respectively by Karl Popper and Thomas S. Kuhn. Clearly such a model focused on *refinement and improvement* rather than with scoring points against opponents is what is needed also in Christian theology, especially when doctrine, as we argued above, is a corporate enterprise requiring Christian collaboration.

This finds clearest expression in the long essay by Lakatos, "Falsification and the Methodology of Scientific Research Programmes," published in the volume that he jointly edited with Alan Musgrave.[116] This volume reports the proceed-

---

113. See Anthony C. Thiselton, "Academic Freedom, Religious Commitment, and the Morality of Christian Scholarship," reprinted from 1982 in *Thiselton on Hermeneutics*, 685-700.

114. A summary of the life of Lakatos appears in Brendan Larvor, *Lakatos: An Introduction* (London and New York: Routledge, 1998), 1-7.

115. Imre Lakatos, *Proofs and Refutations: The Logic of Mathematical Discovery*, ed. J. Worrall and E. Zahar (Cambridge: Cambridge University Press, 1976, with additional material from 1963-64).

116. Imre Lakatos, "Falsification and the Methodology of Scientific Research Programmes," in Imre Lakatos and Alan Musgrave, *Criticism and the Growth of Knowledge* (Cambridge: Cambridge University Press, 1970).

ings of the International Colloquium in the Philosophy of Science held in London in 1965, and includes essays by Thomas Kuhn, Stephen Toulmin, Karl Popper, and Paul Feyerabend, among others. I drew on this work to expound the corporate foundations of knowledge in Christian doctrine in the Church of England Doctrine Commission Report, *Believing in the Church,* of 1981.[117]

Kuhn drew attention to the *social and historical factors* that underlie scientific theories and premises. This work is now too well known to bear repetition, although sadly too often in its unrevised form of Kuhn's early first edition of *The Structure of Scientific Revolutions.* His first essay in the 1970 volume edited by Lakatos and Musgrave takes issue with Popper on several counts. He cites Popper's first chapter in Popper's *Logic of Scientific Discovery* to the effect that the scientist tests his or her statements "step by step," and tests hypotheses "against experience by observation and experiment."[118] Kuhn calls this virtually a cliché, but detects ambiguity within it. In social and historical terms, in a period of "normal" research, "the scientist must *premise* current theory as the rules of the game. . . . Only his personal conjecture is tested. . . . These tests are of a peculiar sort."[119] In effect, a prevailing set of *accepted rules,* or a *dominant model or paradigm, restricts and constrains* what *constitutes "testing."* Genuine central discourse "recurs only at moments of crisis when the bases of the field are again in jeopardy."[120] The prevalence of a given paradigm means that "practitioners share criteria"; but these are *relative to particular times and particular groups of persons.* Kuhn observes, "This is the context in which Sir Karl's term 'falsification' must function."[121]

I have referred mainly to this essay rather than to Kuhn's *The Structure of Scientific Revolutions* because the essay provides the immediate context for the response of Popper and Lakatos in the same volume. Moreover, Kuhn's book has become endlessly summarized and repeated elsewhere.[122] Lakatos begins his response to Popper and Kuhn with an exposition of *fallibilism.* He writes, "For centuries knowledge meant proven knowledge. . . . Einstein's results again turned the tables and now very few philosophers or scientists still think that scientific knowledge is, or can be, proven knowledge. But few realize that with this the whole structure of intellectual values falls in ruins and has to be replaced."[123]

117. Thiselton, "Knowledge, Myth, and Corporate Memory," esp. the section "The Corporate Foundations of Knowledge," in *Believing in the Church,* 45-78, esp. 49-59.

118. Thomas S. Kuhn, "Logic of Discovery or Psychology of Research?" in Lakatos and Musgrave, *Criticism and Growth,* 4. Cf. 1-23.

119. Kuhn, "Logic," 4-5 (his italics).

120. Kuhn, "Logic," 6-7.

121. Kuhn, "Logic," 15.

122. See Thomas S. Kuhn, *The Structure of Scientific Revolutions* (Chicago: Chicago University Press, 2d rev. edn. 1970 [1st edn. 1962]). See further Thomas S. Kuhn, *The Essential Tension: Selected Studies in a Scientific Tradition and Change* (Chicago: University of Chicago Press, 1977), where Kuhn modifies his 1962 views.

123. Lakatos, "Methodology," in Lakatos and Musgrave, *Criticism and Growth,* 91-92.

Classical empiricists, Lakatos points out, accepted as axioms only a relatively small set of "factual propositions," which they expressed as "hard facts." They argued that "a hard fact" may "*disprove* a universal theory," although few thought that such a theory could be *proved* by inductive logic.[124] But if it is logically impossible to establish an inductive logic of the kind required, it turns out that "*all theories are equally unprovable*" (his italics).[125] By Popper's efforts, even *probability* becomes unviable for intellectual justification of theories. Hence, with Popper, "dogmatic falsificationism" recognizes that all theories are equally *conjectural*. All that can be shown with certainty is "the repudiation of what is false."[126] The implication is that the *growth* of knowledge depends upon the repeated overthrow of theories with the help of "hard facts."

Lakatos now turns to the attack. "Dogmatic falsificationism" depends on two false assumptions: the first is that "there is a natural, psychological borderline between theoretical or speculative propositions on the one hand and factual or observational (or basic) propositions on the other. . . . The second assumption is that if a proposition satisfies the psychological criterion of being factual or observational (or basic), then it is true . . . *proved* from facts. . . . *But both assumptions are false*."[127] It does not ease the problem to try to elaborate, with Popper, a "demarcation criterion" for what counts as "scientific," especially if this includes only what is falsifiable as an analytical statement on *Popper's* basis. "No factual proposition can ever be proved from an experiment. Propositions can only be derived from other propositions."[128] This brings us back to "square one."[129]

The second step in this attack is to separate the strategy of the "*methodological* falsificationist" from that of the "*dogmatic* falsificationist." The former separates *rejection* from *disproof*, and is *fallibilist*. But it is possible to combine hard-hitting criticism with fallibilism if, and *only if*, "*decisions* play a crucial role in this methodology" (Lakatos' italics).[130] The decisions arise when the methodological falsificationist digs his or her feet into the ground to avoid the supposed alternative of irrationalism. There remain, of course, numerous smaller-scale strategies for seeking to refine this position. Lakatos calls them strategies of "sophisticated methodological falsificationism."[131] But Lakatos insists that the issue has been fundamentally misconceived. He writes, "The problem is *not* what to do when 'theories' clash with 'facts'. *Only* the '*monotheoretical deductive model*' would suggest such a clash. Whether a proposition is a '*fact*' or a '*theory*' . . . depends on our method-

---

124. Lakatos, "Methodology," 94.
125. Lakatos, "Methodology," 95.
126. Lakatos, "Methodology," 96.
127. Lakatos, "Methodology," 97-98 (my italics)
128. Lakatos, "Methodology," 99.
129. Lakatos, "Methodology," 103.
130. Lakatos, "Methodology," 112.
131. Lakatos, "Methodology," 122.

ological decision. . . . In the pluralistic model the clash is not 'between theories and facts' but between two high-level theories: between an *interpretative theory* to provide the facts and an *explanatory theory* to explain these" (his italics).[132] This might well be applied to Räisänen's misconceived language about "contradictions" within the canon that allegedly preclude theological construction.

Does this bring us near to the perspective of Gadamer's essay on the universality of the hermeneutic problem? Lakatos declares, *"The problem is which theory to consider as the interpretative one which provides the 'hard' facts, and which the explanatory one which 'tentatively' explains them"* (all italics by Lakatos).[133] He adds, "No theory forbids a state of affairs specifiable *in advance*."[134] "We cannot articulate and include *all* 'background knowledge' . . . into our critical deductive model."[135] Gadamer comments, "What is established by statistics seems to be a language of facts, but which questions these facts answer and which facts would begin to speak if other questions were asked are *hermeneutical* questions. *Only a hermeneutical inquiry* would legitimate the meaning of those facts and thus *the consequences that follow from these*."[136] Equally Gadamer insists that the validity or propriety of a given hermeneutical content or frame cannot be determined in advance of the act or process of understanding itself. In Chapter 5 we made this point with a number of examples both from Gadamer and from Wittgenstein. Gadamer writes, "The knowledge that guides action is demanded by the concrete situations in which we have to choose [make a decision] . . . and cannot be spared the task of deliberation and decision by any learned or mastered technique."[137] In Chapter 5 we compared the role of training and habit with that of decision and performance in Wittgenstein and Samuel Wells.

I do not claim that the argument formulated by Lakatos is the same as that of Gadamer and Wittgenstein, but that it is *hermeneutical* in ways that resonate with their approaches. Lakatos has cleared the path for his proposals about *"research programs."* To my mind this affords a parallel in the philosophy of science to the fundamental contrast with which this book began: the contrast between *"problems"* and *"questions that arise."*

Lakatos disengages from the notion of pitting one-theory-at-a-time against another in competition. Discovery, he writes, involves "a succession of theories and not one theory. . . . such series of theories are usually connected by a remarkable continuity which welds them into *research programmes*."[138] He concludes,

132. Lakatos, "Methodology," 129.
133. Lakatos, "Methodology," 129.
134. Lakatos, "Methodology," 130 (my italics).
135. Lakatos, "Methodology," 132 (italics by Lakatos).
136. Gadamer, "The Universality of the Hermeneutical Problem," in *Philosophical Hermeneutics*, 11 (my italics); cf. 3-17.
137. Gadamer, *Reason in the Age of Science*, 92; also cf. *Truth and Method*, 110-29, esp. 116.
138. Lakatos, "Methodology," 132.

"The logic of discovery cannot be satisfactorily discussed except in the framework of a methodology of research programmes."[139]

This methodology elucidates what paths of research to avoid, which Lakatos terms "negative heuristic," and what paths to pursue, which he terms "positive heuristic." Refutations or counterexamples that cannot be explained in terms of a model or theory currently operative will not *falsify* the program but may serve as a *negative heuristic*. Anomalies may lead to changes in what Lakatos calls "the protective belt" of a hypothesis or theory. Sets of suggestions or hints on how to develop puzzle-solving ways forward constitute positive heuristics. A research program may be deemed successful or otherwise partly in terms of its "heuristic power."[140] Lakatos provides numerous examples of the operational currency of his proposed research program drawn from mathematics and physics with reference to the work of Newton, Prout, Bohr, Rutherford, and Michelson.[141]

Lakatos concludes his long essay by emphasizing once again the "heuristic power" of research programs that lead to continuous growth in knowledge, and rejects the pretensions to "instant rationality" that "justificationalists" seek from isolated theories.[142] His final half-dozen pages map out where he stands in the Kuhn-Popper debate. Kuhn is right to stress the continuity of scientific growth, but wrong to exclude *any* possibility of a rational reconstruction of the growth of science. In a key statement he observes, *"In Kuhn's view there can be no logic, but only psychology of discovery"* (italics by Lakatos).[143] Popper replaced *"the old problem of foundations* with *the new problem of fallible-critical growth"* (Lakatos' italics). Lakatos has sought to develop this program a step further.[144]

Nancey Murphy has drawn attention to a significant resource for theological method. An emphasis on creative discovery and on the growth of knowledge, rather than declaring premature war between rival theories, is critical for theology. In Chapter 6 I argued that the practice of assigning thinkers into classificatory boxes as broad "types" risked nurturing a mind-set of conceiving of theology in terms of competing "schools." I lamented that even Lindbeck, Frei, and Tracy were not entirely innocent of providing models of this "unhermeneutical" method. Lakatos and Murphy constructively illuminate the debate about the role of *scientific* procedure and rationality in doctrine. This contribution carries us *beyond* the tired, overworked appeal to paradigms in Kuhn and the wearisome repetition of the Kuhn-Popper debate that should be relegated now to the twentieth century.

---

139. Lakatos, "Methodology," 132.
140. Lakatos, "Methodology," 137; cf. 132-37.
141. Lakatos, "Methodology," 138-73.
142. Lakatos, "Methodology," 174-77.
143. Lakatos, "Methodology," 178.
144. Lakatos, "Methodology," 179.

One example of the importance of this comes from Rorty's misguided attempts to evaporate truth in any traditional sense of the term of all but a strictly pragmatic and "local" content. Rorty has tried to appeal to Kuhn's "socialization" (or in Lakatos' language, *"psychologization"*) of scientific or intellectual paradigms in the history of philosophy in order to support a neo-pragmatic, postmodern account of "new philosophical paradigms nudging old problems aside."[145] But we have already noted Jane Heal's critique of Rorty's overly pluralist reading of Wittgenstein as well as Georgia Warnke's critique of Rorty's reading of Gadamer in insufficiently "rational" terms. The debate has moved beyond Rorty, but, on his own premises, "progress" is all.

Whether or not we may agree with the details of Murphy's specific proposals for negative and positive heuristics in theology, the very notion of shaping theological programs in terms of *heuristics* offers a constructive contribution.[146] Even if there remains a notion of "competing" research programs, this steers a judicious middle path between (i) a Kuhnian notion that largely social and local factors drive a succession of dominant paradigms, in which arguably genuinely rational and scientific criteria are in danger of becoming marginalized to being assimilated into a pragmatic postmodernism; and (ii) a simplified polemical confrontation between fixed "positions" that, as Murphy has argued in her *Beyond Fundamentalism and Liberalism,* threaten to keep doctrine locked up in past controversies and constrained by worn-out agendas. A careful reappraisal of the different roles and different meanings of "rationality" and "science" in doctrine or theology *in fresh terms* has long been overdue.

Nevertheless Murphy's proposals arguably leave us with three puzzles or unresolved ambiguities. (i) The first arises from a lack of explicit engagement with the difference between "hard" or "classical" foundationalism as inherited from Descartes and rationalist traditions and "soft" or "moderate" foundationalism as recently discussed in Wolterstorff's rehabilitation of John Locke in terms of *"reasonable"* or *"entitled"* belief. I urged the importance of this distinction in Chapter 7. In the context of Lakatosian argument the latter coheres with fallibilism; the former does not. I cited Wood's work on this in his *Epistemology;* in the present context James Beilby's *Epistemology as Theology* and Wentzel van Huyssteen's *Essays in Postfoundationalist Theology* underline that this distinction is fundamental in relation to Murphy's argument.[147] Beilby comments, "It is important to see that Plantinga's argument against *classical* foundationalism is not an argument *against foundationalism in general.*"[148]

145. Rorty, *Philosophy and the Mirror of Nature,* 264.

146. See Murphy, *Theology,* 183-97.

147. James Beilby, *Epistemology as Theology: An Evaluation of Plantinga's Religious Epistemology* (Aldershot, U.K. and Burlington, VT: Ashgate, 2005), 45-67; and J. Wentzel van Huyssteen, *Essays in Postfoundationalist Theology* (Grand Rapids and Cambridge: Eerdmans, 1997), 73-90.

148. Beilby, *Epistemology,* 47.

It is unsettling that on one side Murphy commends "nonfoundationalist" approaches among such writers as James McClendon, but on the other side also offers a valid critique of self-grounded postmodern narrative theologies and of inadequate criteria of rational support for doctrine that is to meet scientific criteria of truth based on Scripture and coherence with other knowledge.[149] The latter seems to cohere more convincingly with her appeal to Lakatos.

(ii) This brings me to my second reservation, which perhaps reflects a difference of interpretation and judgment. This arises from Murphy's judgment that Pannenberg's critique of Hume's empiricism fails because his system of thought is *"incommensurable"* with Hume's.[150] She does not discuss in detail whether Pannenberg brings a *larger* or *more comprehensive horizon* of meaning and truth to the issue, which might be said to advance the argument in terms of coherence with a *wider range of data.* I do not know whether Lakatos favors the term *incommensurability,* but it seems to fit better with Kuhn, Rorty, and especially Paul Feyerabend. Indeed, Murphy writes, "In Paul Feyerabend's terms, the two systems are *incommensurable*" (her italics).[151] As Murphy is aware, this term denotes more than an inability to move forward without self-contradiction. It denotes *a total absence of sufficient shared language and conceptual grammar* to allow each "paradigm" or "local" system to communicate intelligibly with the other. But Pannenberg's theology can hardly be characterized in such terms. Cyril Barrett rightly complains about those who interpret the later Wittgenstein in such a way as to imply that some of his language games are "incommensurable." Barrett urges that this intelligibility gap would presuppose *untranslatability.*[152] He writes, "The crucial test of conceptual relativism is the possibility or otherwise of translation."[153]

It is no accident that the name of Paul Feyerabend appears at this point. We now (since 1999) have access to a fascinating correspondence between Feyerabend and Lakatos that reveals their differences on criteria of rationality. Both thinkers are fallibilists. Neither follows either Popper or Kuhn to the letter. But Feyerabend writes to Lakatos (in December 1967): "In some way you are much better off than I, and I envy you for it. You believe in something such as the truth, and you have some ideas how to reach it. . . . Right now, I am lost."[154] Lakatos' willingness and desire to move away from Feyerabend's radical conceptual relativism receives abundant confirmation in his *Mathematics, Science, and*

---

149. Murphy, *Theology,* 200-204; cf. van Huyssteen, *Essays,* 79-80.
150. Murphy, *Theology,* 43-48.
151. Murphy, *Theology,* 44.
152. Cyril Barrett, *Wittgenstein on Ethics and Religious Belief* (Oxford: Blackwell, 1991), 146.
153. Barrett, *Wittgenstein,* 147.
154. In Imre Lakatos and Paul Feyerabend, *For and Against Method: Including Lakatos's Lectures on Scientific Method and the Lakatos-Feyerabend Correspondence,* ed. M. Motterlini (Chicago and London: University of Chicago Press, 1999), 121.

Epistemology, while Feyerabend's pilgrimage finds expression in his *Against Method*, "Theses on Anarchism," and elsewhere.[155]

These factors may not determine decisively our answer to the specific question about whether Pannenberg's system is incommensurable with Hume's. However, they suggest a degree of strong caution about the very notion of incommensurability, which is more readily used by radical pluralists and by social pragmatists than by those who retain some modest confidence in transcontextual reasonableness. I simply place a sceptical question mark against this particular application of the term.

(iii) My third point of unease is not dissimilar to van Huyssteen's, if I am reading him and Murphy rightly. I entirely share Murphy's diagnosis of the constraining and unproductive legacy of the "high" modernity of Descartes and secular rationalism, and of the "modernity" of so-called scientific positivism and dominance of a related worldview. But it is a *non sequitur* to equate a turn *from* this specific *type* of "modernity" with a turn *to postmodernity*. Postmodernity involves infinitely more than a recognition of the need to be liberated from *this* type of "high" modernity.

Elsewhere I have written at length on the phenomenon of postmodernity. In particular I have argued that "two types of postmodernity" are damaging to theology and Christian doctrine in two specific ways respectively. American postmodernity, as instanced in Richard Rorty and Stanley Fish, leads to pragmatic self-affirmation on the part of "local communities" and their practices. It destroys hermeneutics, for in place of "listening to the Other" it imposes the truth-criteria constructed by its own community onto others. Without rational or ethical justification it claims the credentials of "liberal pluralism" and tolerance, but since all criteria are self-referring in relation to the community from which we derived, they lead to a dangerous and deceptive sociopolitical imperialism.

European postmodernism initially seems to leave room for self-criticism by unmasking truth-claims as disguised interests of power. Yet in the end the elevation of the "local" leads to radical scepticism about the possibility of hermeneutical dialogue at all. J.-F. Lyotard believes that assimilation of the weaker by the stronger is all the more likely to come about through the "pretence" of hermeneutical dialogue. I offered these two critiques in my Presidential paper for the Society for the Study of Theology in 1998, but I have recently modified some of the sharpness of my critique in my "Retrospective Reappraisal" of seven ear-

---

155. Imre Lakatos, *Mathematics, Science, and Epistemology: Philosophical Papers*, ed. J. Worrall and Gregory Currie, 2 vols. (Cambridge: Cambridge University Press, 1978), vol. 2, 110 and 136-37. See further Paul Feyerabend, *Against Method* (London: Verso, 3d edn. 1993), 158; Paul Feyerabend, "Theses on Anarchism," in Lakatos and Feyerabend (eds.), *For and Against Method*, 113-18; and "Consolations of the Specialist," in Lakatos and Musgrave, *Criticism and Growth*, 197-230. Cf. also Larvor, *Lakatos*, 82-85.

lier essays on this subject in *Thiselton on Hermeneutics*.[156] Although she does not commend postmodern thought as such, Murphy places many thinkers whom she regards as constructive under this overly broad heading, including Wittgenstein, Austin, and McClendon. It is surprising to find the two terms "foundationalism" and "postmodern" used so loosely in an otherwise rigorous philosophical thinker.[157] Arguably, it appears to add an unnecessary but confusing ambiguity to the line of argument.

Nevertheless, after all has been said, Murphy has constructively introduced Lakatos into a significant area of debate that cried out for fresh input. Above all, in relation to the argument of these chapters, Lakatos underlines in effect what amounts to the unavoidably *hermeneutical* dimension of truth-claims within "scientific" discourse. This allows for the necessity of interpretative judgment. Like most hermeneutical theorists, Lakatos acknowledges the provisionality of "fallibilist" judgments, but does not regard these as irrational. In accord with a hermeneutics of doctrine, he emphasizes a *"heuristic"* program in contrast to a closed system. Far from our needing to present a "reply" to anticipated difficulties about applying hermeneutics to "scientific" discourse, a Lakatosian research program appears positively to encourage this approach.

---

156. Both essays are published in Thiselton, *Thiselton on Hermeneutics*, 581-606 and 663-82 respectively. The Presidential paper first appeared in Marcel Sarot, *The Future as God's Gift: Explorations in Christian Eschatology* (Edinburgh: T&T Clark, 2000), 9-39. Five other essays in theology and postmodernity are published in *Thiselton on Hermeneutics*, 537-81 and 607-63.

157. Cf. also van Huyssteen, *Essays*, 83-90.

PART III

Major Themes in Christian Doctrine

CHAPTER 9

Varied Horizons of Understanding for the Hermeneutics of Being Human

9.1. Horizons of Understanding: First Example, the Hermeneutics of Relationality

This chapter is situated at a point of transition between our exploration of hermeneutics and theological method, and our remaining chapters in which the content of Christian doctrine is viewed in relation to hermeneutical horizons of understanding. Each of the following chapters explicitly offers a *hermeneutic* of specific doctrines rather than a systematic theology under another name. Nevertheless the doctrine of *humanness* or *being human* (traditionally a "doctrine of man") invites larger questions about horizons of understanding in hermeneutics. For comparability of size, these questions now form a separate chapter. This also constitutes a suitable transition into Part III, in which we consider a series of doctrines in greater detail.

In hermeneutical theory the notion of an appropriate horizon of understanding plays a critical role. This may operate in two distinct ways. First, within the universe of discourse of Christian doctrine, arguably some horizons of understanding are fundamental for avoiding confusions of meaning or of conceptual grammar, and for facilitating progress in the appropriation of truth. We might suggest a broad analogy with Wittgenstein's notion that we use language with least risk of confusion within its "home" setting or language game; language that generates confusion is that which slips from its moorings and *"goes on holiday."*[1] He writes, "Is the word ever actually used in this way in the language-game which is its original *home*? What *we* do is to bring words back . . . to their every-

---

1. Wittgenstein, *Philosophical Investigations*, sect. 38 (his italics)

day use."[2] Free-floating *problems* sometimes generate confusions when language uses slip from their moorings. This takes up Gadamer's contrast with which this study began, namely between "free-floating problems" and "questions that arise."

All the same, hermeneutical horizons may be used in a second context to make a second point also. How do supposedly "home" horizons engage or interact, if at all, with other more "foreign" horizons of understanding? Other inquirers may bring such horizons with them as prior "givens" to explore what they may perceive as a free-standing "problem." While the first sense of "horizon of understanding" relates to meaning or truth, the second sense also relates to communication.

If our concern here was not doctrine, but only to construct a "biblical theology," we might have restricted discussion only to the first issue, namely to the formation of "home" hermeneutical horizons. However, as our earlier discussions of Pannenberg and Lonergan indicate, in exploring Christian doctrine we are obligated to engage with a multiplicity of varied horizons in the public world. Some of these are generated within the "home" horizons of the biblical writings and Christian doctrine; others are horizons generated from within nontheistic thought, or within traditions that may appear to use quasi-biblical or quasi-Christian language, but arise from within different horizons of understanding. This chapter (unlike, I hope, most subsequent chapters) selects simple, perhaps simplified, examples for the purpose of making preliminary points about a hermeneutic of the doctrine of *being human*.

(1) First example: does an appropriate understanding of *being human* or of human personhood *depend upon a relational or reciprocal understanding of humankind and God, and upon a relational understanding of the self?*

Many authentic expositions of Christian doctrine presuppose that an adequate understanding of what it is to be human *depends upon a hermeneutical horizon that takes full account of the relation between humankind and God, or of human beings as relational.* Often this is expressed in terms of human creatureliness in relation to God as Creator. However, this may also suggest more than merely human finitude and dependency upon a power other than the human self. Moltmann and Pannenberg rightly associate this relation to the Creator as one of *being loved.* Moltmann succinctly comments, "When we say that God created the world 'out of freedom' we must immediately add 'out of love.'"[3] Pannenberg explicates the point as follows: "It is essential for the Christian understanding of God's freedom in his activity as Creator that he did not have to create the world out of some inner necessity of his own nature.... The creation of the world is an

---

2. Wittgenstein, *Philosophical Investigations*, sect. 116.

3. Jürgen Moltmann, *God in Creation: An Ecological Doctrine of Creation*, trans. Margaret Kohl (London: S.C.M., 1985), 35; cf. 13-40, 57-60, 215-75.

expression of the love of God. . . . The very existence of the world is an expression of the goodness of God."[4]

Other exponents of Christian theology may express this relationality in different ways. Some, for example, stress the role of being created in the image of God (Gen. 1:26-27). Several of the earlier Church Fathers stand within these horizons, including Irenaeus, Tertullian, Origen, and Lactantius. Some make much of the distinction between the image and likeness of God. Irenaeus, Tertullian, and Origen ascribe *image* (Hebrew צלם, *tselem*) to divine creation of humankind, but *likeness* (Hebrew דמות, *d^emuth*) to human potentiality or destiny, namely to what human beings may *become*.[5] On the other hand, most modern exegetes understand these verses as an example of Hebrew parallelism, namely as virtually synonymous terms.[6] Origen writes that "in their first creation humankind received the dignity of the *image* of God, but the fulfilment of the *likeness* is reserved for the final consummation . . . through the imitation of God."[7] Lactantius appears to be the first to argue that we owe "what is due" (in modern parlance, a sense of due respect for the human) "because humankind is the image of God."[8]

The axiom that to understand *being human* depends on understanding the human *in relation to God* finds expression in Calvin, Schleiermacher, Barth, Pannenberg, Moltmann, Balthasar, Rahner, and many others.[9] Recently F. LeRon Shults has placed new emphasis upon this in his *Reforming Theological Anthropology*.[10] He traces the effects of the philosophical tradition of "substance" from

4. Pannenberg, *Systematic Theology*, vol. 2, 19 and 21.

5. Irenaeus, *Against Heresies* III:23:2 and V:38:1-2; Tertullian, *Against Marcion* II:4, and *On Baptism* 5; Origen, *On First Principles* III:4:1.

6. Cf. Bruce Vawter, *On Genesis: A New Reading* (New York: Doubleday, 1977), 54-57; and Claus Westermann, *Genesis 1–11: A Commentary*, trans. J. J. Scullion (London: SPCK, 1984), 154-55.

7. Origen, *On First Principles* II:4:1, trans. from *Sources Chrétiennes*, vol. 268, ed. H. Crouzel and M. Simonetti (Paris: Cerf, 1980).

8. Lactantius, *The Divine Institutes*, VI:10:1.

9. J. Calvin, *Institutes*, I:1:1-3; Friedrich Schleiermacher, *The Christian Faith*, trans. H. R. Mackintosh and J. S. Stewart (Edinburgh: T&T Clark, rpt. 1989), 238-354; Barth, *Church Dogmatics*, III:2, sects. 43, 19-54; 44, 55-202; and 45, 303-24; Pannenberg, *Systematic Theology*, vol. 2, 9-21 and elsewhere; Moltmann, *God in Creation*, 13-40, 57-60, and 215-79; and Jürgen Moltmann, *Man: Christian Anthropology in the Conflicts of the Present*, trans. John Sturdy (London: SPCK, 1974), 1-21 and 105-17; Hans Urs von Balthasar, *Theo-Drama*, vol. 2, 175-334 and esp. 335-430, and vol. 3, 283-92 and 447-61; and Karl Rahner, *Foundations of Christian Faith: An Introduction to the Idea of Christianity*, trans. W. V. Dych (New York: Crossroad, 1978 and 2004), 24-106. See further G. C. Berkouwer, *Man: The Image of God*, trans. D. W. Jellema, Studies in Dogmatics (Grand Rapids: Eerdmans, 1962), throughout; Otto Weber, *Foundations of Dogmatics*, trans. D. R. Guder, 2 vols. (Grand Rapids: Eerdmans, 1983), vol. 1, 529-80; and in stark terms Helmut Thielicke, *The Evangelical Faith*, trans. G. W. Bromiley, 3 vols. (Grand Rapids: Eerdmans, 1974), vol. 1, 312-404.

10. F. LeRon Shults, *Reforming Theological Anthropology: After the Philosophical Turn to Relationality* (Grand Rapids and Cambridge, U.K.: Eerdmans, 2003), throughout.

Aristotle, through its revival in the medieval period, to the thinking of Descartes, Locke, and others virtually up to Hegel. Kant, however, offers the beginnings of a new perspective by adding a subcategory of "relation" to his main table of categories, and Shults regards this as "a major adjustment."[11] But Hegel went decisively further, and undertook "rigorous reflection on the ultimate relationality, the relation between the infinite and the finite."[12] In spite of his well-known differences from Hegel, Kierkegaard, Shults argues, also saw relationality as a key concept.

Shults traces the theme of relationality more positively through C. S. Peirce, Martin Heidegger, Jean-Paul Sartre, A. N. Whitehead, and rightly through the Jewish philosophers Martin Buber and Emmanuel Levinas. This was never alien to Christian doctrine. Quite the reverse: it stems from the very heart of biblical traditions. Shults writes, "Relationality has long been a staple of Christian theology."[13] He sees his present task as "to retrieve and refigure the relational thought-forms of the biblical tradition that can help us respond to late modern anthropological self-understanding."[14]

Shults is less alone in this task than he appears to imply or to imagine. Stanley Grenz, to name only one example, adopts "relationality" as a key theme of a whole book on this subject, primarily on the basis of an explicitly Trinitarian theology.[15] Moreover, neither Barth (as Shults notes) nor Moltmann nor Pannenberg can be accused of making it other than central in their discussions of the human. Writing from the standpoint of Reformed theology, Shults demonstrates the centrality of this category for Calvin. Calvin, he suggests, said considerably more than the widely known sentence, "Without knowledge of God there is no knowledge of self." Calvin insists that this knowledge is reciprocal: "Without knowledge of the self there is no knowledge of God"; and adds that by knowing God and knowing ourselves humankind faces "God's majesty."[16] Shults also includes among his dialogue partners especially Schleiermacher, Barth, and Pannenberg. The emphasis upon "reciprocity" in Schleiermacher, he argues, is valid, but has received undue neglect or misunderstanding, not least in non-specialist treatments.[17]

I am inclined to agree with Shults' verdict on Schleiermacher, and in my lecture handouts in the University of Nottingham I headed Schleiermacher's

11. Shults, *Reforming*, 21; cf. 11-34.

12. Shults, *Reforming*, 24.

13. Shults, *Reforming*, 33.

14. Shults, *Reforming*, 33.

15. Stanley J. Grenz, *The Social God and the Relational Self: A Trinitarian Theology of the Imago Dei* (Louisville and London: Westminster John Knox, 2001)

16. Calvin, *Institutes of the Christian Religion*, I:1:1-3 (Shults uses the translation by F. L. Battles); and Shults, *Reforming*, 1.

17. Shults, *Reforming*, 97-116.

sections in *The Christian Faith* that Shults discusses (namely 6-11), "Understanding in Relation to the Other."[18] I also noted this theme of reciprocity in his *Speeches*, his *Hermeneutics*, and his *Celebration of Christmas*. In the *Speeches* Schleiermacher rejects "miserable love of system" because it "rejects what is strange" and leaves "the other" out of account.[19] A key point in *The Christian Faith*, as Shults observes, is that in Part II the "explication" of human consciousness depends on a relationship to "God-consciousness." Schleiermacher writes, "We have the consciousness of sin whenever God-consciousness . . . determines our self-consciousness as pain."[20] On the other hand, in Chapter 13.3 (below) I express reserve over Schleiermacher's account of a "fall" and of the nature of human sin.

Shults concludes that theological anthropology articulates the gospel of grace, through which, by the Holy Spirit, humankind can rest in the presence of divine majesty disclosed as divine love. *This approach, in effect, seeks to establish a hermeneutical horizon of understanding for a doctrine of the human.* For understanding *the human* cannot be adequate unless it arises *in relation to the "Other."* This "Other," Shults concludes, "cannot be divorced from a trembling fascination with the human 'other' . . . through interaction with other persons . . . in which the boundaries of self and other are explored, negotiated, transgressed, or reified."[21]

This hermeneutical horizon, however, is different from those of most non-theistic inquiries into the human condition. More familiar starting points at the "foreign" end of the spectrum might include, for example, questions concerning what constitutes *being human* within the horizons of medical technology. Advances in research in embryology force upon us questions about the status of the embryo, and such questions often (although not always) remain restricted within bio-physical horizons of understanding. Bio-physical questions *also* remain of critical importance within Christian or theistic horizons, as in the case, for example, of questions about the emergence of the "primitive streak" as a *possible* threshold of being human. At a bio-physical level the primitive streak may seem to provide a necessary condition for the most rudimentary stage in the formation of a human nervous system, but its significance for wider questions about the beginnings of life still requires careful evaluation at all levels.

Parallel questions in the context of aging and the ending of life also often receive answers in strictly bio-physical terms. This applies not least in situations in which a human person has lost many of their normal faculties for living life with dignity. If a human person appears to be unable to respond to any external stim-

---

18. Schleiermacher, *Christian Faith* (2d edn.), 26-60.

19. Friedrich Schleiermacher, *On Religion: Speeches to Its Cultured Despisers,* trans. John Oman (London: Kegan Paul, Trench, and Trübner, 1893), 55.

20. Schleiermacher, *Christian Faith,* sect. 66, 27; cf. Part II, sects. 62-105, 259-475.

21. Shults, *Reforming,* 2.

ulus, and is claimed to have sunk to a virtually vegetative state, what determines whether or when a life-support machine may be turned off? When might a cessation of life-extending drugs constitute pre-emptive euthanasia? Does the existence of signed consent forms or "a living will" influence debates about what it is to be "a human person" in such a condition? On what basis would such debates include notions of "human dignity" in a theistic or nontheistic context?

Christian and theological horizons of understanding are always broader, never narrower, than naturalistic or merely bio-physical ways of understanding. Bio-physical questions are clearly to be included, but they do *not exhaustively* define Christian horizons of understanding. Any ethic that is almost exclusively consequential also needs to be placed within the *broader* horizons of deontological questions.

Some scholars seem to suggest that Christian horizons of understanding the human might be *incommensurable* with those from within naturalistic or exclusively bio-physical horizons. But this term is too lightly and too readily used, especially by those with overly strong sympathies with postmodern thought. For several years I was privileged to serve as a member of the Human Fertilization and Embryology Authority, appointed by the British Secretary of State for Health. In addition to inspecting clinics, evaluating requests for treatment licenses and research licenses, proactively exploring ethical issues, and overseeing the daily working of the Parliamentary Human Fertilization and Embryology Act (1990), we also had a duty to listen to, and to enter into dialogue with, a wide range and variety of groups and interests in public life. These ranged from "pro-life" groups who regarded every embryo from its earliest moment, whether damaged or whole, as fully human with an absolute right to life, through to research scientists desperate for "spare" embryos in the hope of thereby curing horrendous genetic diseases; patients desperate for fertility treatment; and clinicians with a variety of proactive agenda. In no case did I find biblical and Christian horizons of understanding so *radically* different from any of these as to render *any* kind of progressive, negotiating dialogue impossible. In the event the twenty-one members of the Government-appointed Authority provided (at least during my term of membership) a superb model of responsible hermeneutical listening, sensitivity, and dialogue in the interests of stable and informed public life. This was not always the case when we sometimes met with external pressure groups.

Some questions required members of the Authority to seek to stand within the horizons of "the other." Unless one seeks, for example, to enter into the horizons of disabled persons discussing the possible "screening out" of imperfect embryos, or agonized parents longing for the privilege and gift of parenthood, *hermeneutics* comes to be replaced by brittle, abstract, *a priori* systems. We have already discussed the varied shape and role of systems in relation to doctrine in Part II, 8.3, above. These horizons, however, are not definitive or absolute. To yield to the pleas of personal grief at the impossibility of treatment where informed consent has not been given, for example, would be to step outside the horizons of future scenarios concerning the well-being of future cases or even generations, and perhaps make one hard case in the present the arbiter for setting in motion unthinkable consequences for others in the future. But this brings us to the very heart of hermeneutics. For it is precisely the point of Schleiermacher's neglected maxim: "In interpretation it is essential that one be able *to step out of one's own frame of mind* into that of the author," or, here, of the *"other."*[22]

This relates to what Dilthey had in mind when he formulated his unfairly criticized notion that "re-experiencing" or "re-living" *(nacherleben)* the experiences of "the other" involves cultivating our powers of *imagination, feeling, empathy, aspiration, and flexibility* in such a way that we *can enter* "the mental life of another person." "Empathy" *(Hineinversetzen)* and "transposition" *(Transposition)* help us to share the horizons of understanding that shape the perceptions and judgments of another.[23]

All the same, to reject the view that some of these horizons of understanding are *incommensurable* is not to deny that blockages in understanding arise from time to time when "home" horizons of understanding meet with foreign horizons. Blockages may be perceived on both sides. Yet often there may appear to be an *overlapping* of horizons, and such overlap does not mean an *assimilation* of horizons, as I have repeatedly urged in Parts I and II. We find utterly unconvincing the defeatist and radically sceptical claims of Jean-François Lyotard with respect to the "differend" that in such dialogue the "idioms" of one will inevitably be assimilated and suppressed by the other in what he calls covert violence.[24] This is no more than a radically postmodern *assertion* that hermeneutics, in the sense of the term shared by Betti, Gadamer, and Ricoeur, is simply a sham. It would exclude many major thinkers discussed in this book as working under sheer illusion.

A *spectrum* of hermeneutical understanding and mutual engagement emerges. At the positive end of the spectrum, in response to those who suspect Schleiermacher and Dilthey of undue "psychologizing," Paul Ricoeur reminds us that with imagination we can project "possible worlds" that open up extensions of understanding: "Wherever there is a situation, there is an horizon which can be *contracted or enlarged*" (my italics).[25] Donald Capps constructively appropriates Ricoeur's model of hermeneutics in the service of pastoral care and counsel.[26] At the end of the spectrum where "distance" predominates (also in the context of pastoral counseling) Deborah van Deusen Hunsinger underlines Barth's

---

22. Schleiermacher, *Hermeneutics*, 42.

23. Dilthey, *Gesammelte Schriften*, Bd. 7, 213-14.

24. Jean-François Lyotard, *The Differend,* trans. G. van den Abbeele (Manchester: Manchester University Press, 1990).

25. Ricoeur, "The Task of Hermeneutics," in *Hermeneutics and the Human Sciences*, 62.

26. Donald Capps, *Pastoral Care and Hermeneutics* (Philadelphia: Fortress, 1984), 18-25 (on Ricoeur), 37-60, and throughout on pastoral care.

refusal to transpose the analogy of faith into an analogy of being in order to stress the distinctive role of divine *grace* as the point of entry into self-knowledge.[27] She quotes Hans Frei's doctrine that theology and culture remain "logically diverse, even when they reside in the same breast."[28]

Where horizons of understanding begin far apart (but not irretrievably so), a hermeneutic of Christian doctrine will seek to identify both points at which horizons substantially overlap (even if they never wholly converge) and also distinctive understandings that arise from within the broader and more comprehensive horizons of understanding in Christian doctrine.

This is *not*, however, to appeal to a "principle of correlation," especially as found in Paul Tillich. The principle of correlation faces at least five difficulties.[29] First, it tends to be static rather than working with moving, expanding horizons. Second, it works with generalizing typologies concerning which Tillich's critics quickly point out that the "questions" are artificially distorted or "loaded" by anticipating theological "answers." Third, it reduces everything to the "nearer" or overlapping end of the spectrum, and gives little weight to "distance" or to where "home" horizons differ most radically from "foreign" ones. Fourth, should more theological and less theological horizons of understanding condition each other in *total mutuality?* This impinges on the second criticism. Tillich writes, "The method of correlation explains the contents of the Christian faith through existential questions and theological answers in *mutual interdependence.*"[30] Fifth, whereas hermeneutical horizons often shape conceptual grammar, Tillich works almost entirely at the level of pre-conceptual symbols, based on a Jungian and quasi-naturalistic philosophy of language.[31]

Tillich seeks to do justice to divine transcendence and otherness in his own distinctive way. Indeed, it is precisely because he believes that conceptual language about God as "the most perfect" Being is inadequate that he bases everything on symbols. He writes, "When applied to God superlatives become diminutives. They place him on the level of other beings while elevating him

---

27. Deborah van Deusen Hunsinger, *Theology and Pastoral Counseling: A New Interdisciplinary Approach* (Grand Rapids: Eerdmans, 1995), 113-21; cf. 122-50.

28. Cited from "An Afterword to Eberhard Busch's Biography of Barth," in Hunsinger, *Theology*, 6.

29. "Five" is not exhaustive: I have not mentioned Tillich's devaluing of history.

30. Tillich, *Systematic Theology*, vol. 1, 68 (my italics).

31. Paul Tillich, "The Religious Symbol," in S. Hook (ed.), *Religious Experience and Truth* (Edinburgh: Oliver & Boyd, 1962), 301-22. Among well-known critics, Kenneth Hamilton argues that Tillich dissipates away what is distinctively "Christian" and kerygmatic in the Christian gospel: Kenneth Hamilton, *The System and the Gospel* (London: S.C.M., 1963). Hamilton writes, "To see Tillich's system as a whole is to see that it is incompatible with the Christian gospel" (227). This may be an overstatement, but it indicates justified disquiet about his method of correlation. Cf. also T. A. O'Meara and C. D. Weisser (eds.), *Paul Tillich in Catholic Thought* (London: Darton, Longman & Todd, 1965).

above all of them."[32] Traditional language, by contrast, "transforms the infinity of God into a finiteness which is merely an extension of the categories of finitude."[33] All the same, Tillich's method of correlation places him at some considerable distance from Christian thinkers in relation to horizons of understanding brought to bear upon a Christian doctrine of the human. Bernard Martin is a sympathetic expositor of Tillich, but his specialist study *Paul Tillich's Doctrine of Man* reveals how far Tillich stands here from Calvin, Barth, Moltmann, Pannenberg, and arguably even from Schleiermacher. Human finitude is defined *not primarily in relation to God* but in "the fact that his being is limited by nonbeing."[34] The "basic structure of man's being" is found in "the self-world correlation," not in terms of relationality to God.[35] By contrast Daniel Migliore writes, "Knowledge of God and knowledge of ourselves are intertwined. We cannot know God without being shocked into a new self-recognition, and we cannot know our true humanity without a new awareness of who God is."[36]

9.2. Horizons of Understanding:
Second Example, a Hermeneutic of Communal Framework

As Heyduck reminded us (above), the high-water mark of individualism occurs in the West from the period of the seventeenth century to late modernity in the later twentieth century, still with a strong legacy even today. In the late nineteenth century it dominated Liberal Protestantism, not least with Harnack's notion of "the infinite value of the human soul." From within the social sciences an instructive historical, philosophical, and sociological study of individualism has been provided by Steven Lukes.[37]

By contrast, in biblical studies in the early part of the twentieth century a number of biblical scholars were urging the importance of "corporate solidarity," especially in the earlier books of the Old Testament. Some cited passages, notably in Joshua, Judges and 1 and 2 Samuel, to urge this case. In 1926 Johannes Pedersen expressed this in unguarded, even extravagant terms. He argued that the individual was regarded as a center of power that extends far beyond the contours of the body, to mingle with that of the family and family property; the tribe and tribal provisions; to form "a psychic whole."[38]

---

32. Tillich, *Systematic Theology,* vol. 1, 261.

33. Tillich, *Systematic Theology,* vol. 2, 6.

34. Bernard Martin, *Paul Tillich's Doctrine of Man* (London: Nisbet, 1966), 92; cf. 92-111.

35. Martin, *Man,* 83; cf. 83-92. He cites Tillich, *Systematic Theology,* vol. 1, 182-89.

36. Migliore, *Faith Seeking,* 120.

37. Steven Lukes, *Individualism* (Oxford: Blackwell, 1973), throughout.

38. Johannes Pedersen, *Israel: Its Life and Culture,* 2 vols. (London and Copenhagen: Oxford University Press, 1926).

Such extravagant and questionable language would provoke a critical reaction some fifty years later.[39] Meanwhile, however, it reflected an early twentieth-century view of Israelite life. Writing in 1911, H. Wheeler Robinson appealed to the four phenomena of blood revenge, Levirate marriage, paternal absolution, and corporate responsibility to substantiate such an emphasis.[40] The practices of blood revenge (2 Sam. 14:7; 15:3; 21:1-14), and especially Levirate marriage (Deut. 25:5), led Wheeler Robinson to assume that (in the latter case) "a man is regarded as identical with his dead brother."[41] The absolute right of a father to dispose the life a son or daughter (Gen. 22, Abraham; Jacob, Gen. 42:37; Jephthah, Judg. 11:29-30) was thought to question the individual status of the latter. More to the point for modern ears, the story of the accountability of Israel as a whole for the sin of Achan, and his subsequent exposure by tribe, clan, and family (Josh. 7:24-26), seems to confirm Robinson's picture of corporate *responsibility*.

Rogerson points out that Wheeler Robinson oscillates between a notion of corporate representation and corporate responsibility. The former finds expression in the alternating uses of "I" and "we" in the Psalms and in the Servant Songs (Isa. 42–63).[42] But Robinson and Pedersen unnecessarily ascribe the influence of a "primitive" mentality in ancient Israel, in accordance with the anthropologies of such writers as Lévy-Bruhl. Aubrey Johnson even ascribes a corporately "extended" personality in terms of time as well as space.[43] This theme persisted in Old Testament scholarship until the third quarter of the twentieth century.

In more moderate forms, however, the appeal to a new, discredited anthropology does not invalidate the role of a *communal and corporate conception of humankind or of Israel alongside that of an emphasis upon the individual*.[44] What is a *foreign horizon* to all biblical traditions is the *individualism* of Western modernity. Wolff calls attention to the alternating "I" and "we" in narrative recitals of faith: "A wandering Aramaean was my ancestor, and *he* went down into Egypt. . . . The Egyptians treated *us* harshly and afflicted *us*. . . . Thus *we* cried to Yahweh, the God of *our* fathers. . . . He brought *us* out. . . . And now *I* bring the first of the ground, which thou, O Yahweh, hast given *me*" (Deut. 26:5-10).[45]

39. John W. Rogerson, "The Hebrew Conception of Corporate Personality," *JTS* 21 (1980) 1-16; repr. in B. Lang (ed.), *Anthropological Approaches in the Old Testament* (Philadelphia: Fortress, 1985), 43-59. Rogerson's own target is primarily Wheeler Robinson. See further J. R. Porter, "The Legal Aspects of Corporate Personality in the Old Testament," *Vetus Testamentum* 15 (1965) 361-68.

40. H. Wheeler Robinson, *The Christian Doctrine of Man* (Edinburgh: T&T Clark, 1911), 27-30.

41. Robinson, *Man*, 29.

42. Otto Eissfeldt, "The Ebed-Jahweh in Isaiah xl–lv," *Expository Times* 44 (1933) 261-68.

43. A. R. Johnson, *The One and the Many in the Israelite Conception of God* (Cardiff: Cardiff University Press, 1961).

44. See Hans Walter Wolff, *Anthropology of the Old Testament*, trans. Margaret Kohl (London: S.C.M., 1974), 214-22.

45. Wolff, *Anthropology*, 216 (his italics)

In different epochs of Israel's history, Wolff continues, the fate of the individual was largely the fate of his people. *Individuals* as such first emerge as those expelled from society (like Achan, Josh. 7:24-26 or like someone who does something "not done in Israel," Deut. 17:12). On Ps. 25:1-21, he comments, "The word 'lonely' *(yāchidh)* means here the misery of segregation and isolation, which implies wretchedness and affliction."[46] In 1 Sam. 21:1 "Why are you alone, and no one with you," he adds, "'Alone' *(lᵉbad)* here means much the same as separated, cut off, for *bad* is the part which has been split off from the whole."[47]

Nevertheless the individual may also stand out as one called and chosen. The call of Abraham separates him from the crowd: "Go from your country and from your kindred, and from your father's house . . ." (Gen. 12:1). The story of Jacob also "Tells of a great loneliness . . . (Gen. 32:24, 25, 29). . . . Every story of election is first the story of a sitting apart."[48] Jeremiah bears alone the burden of a call to prophetic ministry in which he, too, is excluded as a laughingstock (Jer. 20:7-8), just as Ezekiel also stands alone (Ezek. 2:3-5).

Eichrodt comments on Ezekiel's call, "The choice of this particular man as a prophet in itself runs counter to practically every human presupposition. . . . The messenger of God must be prepared to encounter hostility, contempt, and actual bodily injury."[49] In these examples God deals with persons *as individuals;* but this is a far cry from modern Western *individualism.*

The New Testament writings largely share this emphasis upon "a people." A major thesis in Tom Holland's recent work on Paul is that Paul's "letters are not about what God has done or is doing for a Christian. They are about what God has done or is doing for his covenant people, the church."[50] More than fifty years ago John A. T. Robinson derived a "corporate" understanding and exposition of Paul and his epistles largely from Paul's use of the term *body* (σῶμα, *sōma*), tracing the probable origins of the theme to Paul's encounter with Christ on the road to Damascus in which "Why are you persecuting *me?*" (Acts 9:4-5 and 22:7-8) revealed Christ and Christians *"not as an individual but as the Christian community"* (Robinson's italics).[51] Robinson makes the point that the very phrase *"members* of the body" (Greek μέλη, *melē*) is largely misunderstood within the

---

46. Wolff, *Anthropology,* 217. A. Weiser, *The Psalms: A Commentary,* trans. H. Hartwell (London: S.C.M., 1962), calls Ps. 25 "The lamentation of a passive soul earnest in its piety . . . composed in the quiet of a lonely life" (23).

47. Wolff, *Anthropology,* 217.

48. Wolff, *Anthropology,* 219.

49. Walther Eichrodt, *Ezekiel: A Commentary,* trans. C. Quinn (London: S.C.M., 1970), 61-62.

50. Tom Holland, *Contours of Pauline Theology: A Radical New Survey of the Influences on Paul's Biblical Writings* (Fearn, Scotland: Mentor/Focus, 2004), 40.

51. John A. T. Robinson, *The Body: A Study in Pauline Theology* (London: S.C.M, 1952), 58; see also 78-79.

context of Western individualism. "Members" of a club are individuals who subscribe to it and take part in its functions. "Members" of Christ are, for Paul, constituent elements of the "in-Christ" corporeity. Hence in my commentary I have usually translated μέλη *(mele)* as *limbs* of Christ.[52]

It would distract us from our main argument to trace the detailed research of New Testament specialists on this aspect. Margaret Mitchell and Dale Martin underline the importance of Pauline language about *the body* as a socio-political and corporate term, while Lionel Thornton underlines *fellowship* or *communal participation* (κοινωνία, *koinōnia*) as a fundamental trans-individual dimension, and from Albert Schweitzer to the present many emphasize the corporate dimension of *"in Adam"* and *"in Christ"* (Rom. 5:12-20; 1 Cor. 15:22, 23 and 49-52; cf. Rom. 8:1-2, and elsewhere).[53] Weiss distinguishes between different senses of "in Christ," but among these he identifies "belonging to Christ, being *bound together with* him and *the brethren*" (my italics).[54] After discussing the force of "in Christ" in Paul, James Dunn concludes, "We can hardly avoid speaking of the community which understood itself not only from the gospel . . . but also from the shared experience of Christ, which bonded them as one."[55]

This belongs to a different "world" from the individualism of Western modernity and post-Enlightenment language about the *rights* of the individual and individual autonomy. This is not to deny that a segment of overlap exists with the horizons of John Locke on "rights," and of Liberal Protestant writers in the mold of Harnack on the value of the individual soul. But the horizons of understanding within which questions are asked about the nature of *being human* are hugely divergent and *largely foreign to biblical and Christian roots*. Although notions of reciprocal *duties* between the state and its citizens arguably originate in the ancient world, the concept of either natural rights or rights presupposed by a social contract emerges seriously only in the seventeenth and eighteenth centuries. It is not, therefore, part of a historic Christian doctrine of being human.

Thomas Hobbes (1588-1679) understood "rights" to be based upon a voluntary transference of power to a king or government for the sake of personal and general

52. Anthony C. Thiselton, *The First Epistle to the Corinthians: A Commentary on the Greek Text,* NIGTC (Grand Rapids: Eerdmans and Carlisle: Paternoster, 2000), 989-1013.

53. M. M. Mitchell, *Paul and the Rhetoric of Reconciliation* (Tübingen: Mohr, 1991); Dale B. Martin, *The Corinthian Body* (New Haven, CT and London: Yale University Press, 1995), 3-61 and 94-105; L. S. Thornton, *The Common Life in the Body of Christ* (London: Dacre, 3d edn. 1950), 1-187 and 253-355; Albert Schweitzer, *The Mysticism of Paul the Apostle* (London: Black, 1931).

54. Johannes Weiss, *Earlier Christianity,* trans. F. C. Grant, 2 vols. (New York: Harper, 1959), vol. 2, 469.

55. James D. G. Dunn, *The Theology of Paul the Apostle* (Edinburgh: T&T Clark and Grand Rapids: Eerdmans, 1998), 401.

advantage. Since humankind is profoundly egoistic, Hobbes believed, human persons need to enable the state to intervene "for peace and defence of [the] self."[56] "Rights" are based not on human dignity, but because without the restraints of civilized government and society (to quote Hobbes's famous phrase) life for humankind was "solitary, poor, nasty, brutish, and short."[57]

A step nearer to the horizons of Christian doctrine occurs with John Locke (1632-1704). He appeals to "a law of nature" to restrain persons from "invading others' rights."[58] Locke, however, wrote not only as a philosopher but also as a Christian theist. His writings include a careful, commonsense exposition of the epistles of Paul, and in his second *Treatise of Government* he appealed not only to a law of nature but also to humankind's "being the workmanship of one omnipotent and infinitely wise Maker"; this offers a different basis for an individual's "right" to "life, liberty, and possessions."[59]

Yet Locke is ambiguous. On one side his arguments are firmly embedded in Christian traditions and language about God, and he draws concerns about a balance between "order" and tolerance from "the judicious" Anglican divine, Richard Hooker (the well-used adjective is Locke's). Yet on the other side natural law seems at times to feature as a free-standing innate idea. Wolterstorff rightly speaks here of "a deep fissure in Locke's theory."[60]

Many see the inspiration of Locke behind Thomas Jefferson's formulation of the Declaration of Independence, although the free-standing "moral sense" theories of Shaftesbury and Hutcheson were probably also contributory factors. Initially notions of "rights" stood precariously on the border between Christian theism and the egalitarian, pragmatic politics of the secular Enlightenment. With the passing of years, the latter gained steady ascendancy over the former. As Helmut Thielicke observes, "rights" based on justice indeed reflects a legacy of Greco-Christian tradition, but in political contexts it becomes "filled with anthropocentric content" and pressed into the service of pragmatic self-interest and ideology, "for everything depends on the *way* in which we desire them."[61]

Sacvan Bercovitch and Robert Bellah, cited with approval by Roger Lundin, trace the steady descent from the Pietism of the late eighteenth century to the secular progressivism of the mid-twentieth century to settle into a pragmatic, semi-secularized individualism in America. Bercovitch writes, "They conse-

---

56. Thomas Hobbes, *Leviathan*, ed. M. Oakshott (Oxford: Blackwell, 1960), I:14; also II:17.

57. Hobbes, *Leviathan*, I:13.

58. John Locke, *Two Treatises of Government* (1790) ed. P. Laslett (Cambridge: Cambridge University Press, 1988), II:2, sects. 6-8.

59. Locke, *Two Treatises*, II:2, sect. 6.

60. Nicholas Wolterstorff, *John Locke and the Ethics of Belief* (Cambridge: Cambridge University Press, 1996), 138; see Locke, *Two Treatises*, II:5-6.

61. Helmut Thielicke, *Theological Ethics,* ed. W. H. Lazareth, 3 vols. (Grand Rapids: Eerdmans, 1979), vol. 2: *Politics,* 67-68.

crated the American present . . . and translated . . . sacred history into a metaphor for limitless secular improvement."[62] I have called attention to these sources in *Thiselton on Hermeneutics.*[63]

The emergence of a freestanding or pragmatic concern for the rights of individuals in abstraction from any theistic ground characterizes no less the effects of the Enlightenment in Europe. Francis Hutcheson (1694-1946) in Scotland and especially Jeremy Bentham (1748-1832) in England based concerns for individual rights on "the principle of utility." Bentham defined this in wholly consequentialist terms whereby "to augment or diminish the happiness of those whose interest is in question" formed the fundamental criticism of ethics. This applied to "every action of a private individual" as well as to governments. Bentham saw the community as "composed of individuals."[64] J. S. Mill observed that for Bentham "the world is a collection of persons, ever pursuing his separate interest or pleasure."[65] In this respect Bentham reflects a decisive stage in the emergence of modern individualism.

Nevertheless Immanuel Kant (1726-1804) places individual autonomy at the deepest moral level by making moral motivation and volition dependent wholly upon the absolute autonomy of the individual will.[66] Nothing is good except the good will. Although on one side he formulated the maxim that human persons must be treated as ends, not as means to some other end, Kant left no room for interpersonal considerations of affection, love, or relationality in the sense of the term used here. Only the categorical imperative of duty addressed to the individual has absolute moral status. The romantic poet Friedrich Schiller coined an ironic verse in criticism of this:

"Willingly serve I my friends, but I do it, alas, with affection.
Hence I am cursed with the doubt, virtue I have not attained."
"This is your only resource, you must stubbornly seek to abhor them
Then you can do with disgust that which the law may enjoin."[67]

62. Sacvan Bercovitch, *The Rites of Assent: Transformation in the Symbolic Construction of America* (New York: Routledge, 1993), 147; cf. Robert Bellah, *Habits of the Heart: Individualism and Commitment in American Life* (Berkeley, CA: University of California Press, 1985 and 1996), esp. 56-62; and Roger Lundin, *The Culture of Interpretation: Christian Faith and the Postmodern World* (Grand Rapids: Eerdmans, 1993), esp. 140-41.

63. Thiselton, *Thiselton on Hermeneutics*, 589-92.

64. Jeremy Bentham, *An Introduction to the Principles of Morals and Legislation* (1789), ed. J. H. Burns and H. L. A. Hart (London: Methuen, 1982), 2, sect. 7.

65. John Stuart Mill, "Essay on Bentham," in Mill, *Dissertations and Discussions* (London: Routledge, n.d.), vol. 1, 362.

66. Immanuel Kant, *Groundwork of the Metaphysics of Morals*, trans. Mary Gregor (Cambridge: Cambridge University Press, 1998).

67. This English rhythmic approximation to the German is cited in J. S. MacKenzie, *A Manual of Ethics* (London: University Tutorial Press, 1929), 159.

Wolfhart Pannenberg shows how far away notions of "autonomy" (in this individualistic sense) are situated from Christian horizons of understandings concerning being human. He observes, "In the nonobservance of the order of nature Augustine found an autonomy of the will that puts the self in the center and uses everything else as a means to the self as an end. This is pride, which makes the self the principle of all things and thus sets itself in the place of God."[68] This kind of "autonomy" is different from that of human maturity in relation to God. We need to become "what we ought to be," but in this process, "we can all too easily give our independence the form of an autonomy in which we put ourselves in the place of God."[69] Fundamentally, Pannenberg writes, "It is of the nature of our human form of life *to be 'eccentric' relative to other things and beings* in awareness of *a horizon that transcends our finitude. . . .* An expression for this is 'openness to the world.'"[70] In his *Anthropology in Theological Perspective* Pannenberg places in contrast "an opposition of the ego to itself" in the context of brokenness and distortion of the self, and the human destiny in God's purpose of "exocentricity . . . a being present *to the other*" (my italics).[71]

Jane Lockwood O'Donovan carries the story of human rights further with reference to the U.N. *Universal Declaration of Human Rights* (1948).[72] This includes the phrase: "Everyone, as a member of society, has the right to social security" (Art. 22) and "to a standard of living adequate for the health and well-being of himself and his family, including food, clothing, housing" (Art. 25). Human rights here have become statements of needs and *interests,* abstracted from any broader horizon of understanding concerning obligations or grounds. The language arguably generates a politics of *claim.* In Thielicke's words, this has become "cut off from the soil of faith" in which notions of rights based on justice "had their origin."[73]

Thielicke expresses concern that "the *way* in which men desire them [rights]" drifts into anthropocentric and pragmatic criteria of self-interest.[74] O'Donovan traces the actual effects of attempts by governments to implement this kind of Declaration, and laments their "debilitating effects on social moral

---

68. Pannenberg, *Systematic Theology,* vol. 2, 243.

69. Pannenberg, *Systematic Theology,* vol. 2, 265.

70. Pannenberg, *Systematic Theology,* vol. 2, 229 (my italics)

71. Wolfhart Pannenberg, *Anthropology in Theological Perspective,* trans. M. J. O'Connell (London and New York: T&T Clark/Continuum, 1985 and 2004), 85.

72. Joan Lockwood O'Donovan, "A Timely Conversation with *The Desire of Nations* in Civil Society, Nation and State," in Craig Bartholomew, J. Chaplin, Robert Song, and Al Wolters (eds.), *A Royal Priesthood: A Dialogue with Oliver O'Donovan, Scripture and Hermeneutic Series,* vol. 3 (Grand Rapids: Zondervan and Carlisle: Paternoster, 2002), 377-94, esp. 379-84. Cf. also Oliver O'Donovan, *The Desire of Nations: Rediscovering the Roots of Political Theology* (Cambridge: Cambridge University Press, 1996), esp. 276-84.

73. Thielicke, *Ethics,* vol. 2, 67.

74. Thielicke, *Ethics,* vol. 2, 68 (his italics).

agency," which undermine "legitimate . . . moral and spiritual understandings within society."[75] What *originated* largely within a *Christian horizon* of understanding has become abstracted into a *differently grounded individualism* and philosophy of claims and interests. At best, she concludes, these reflect the "penumbra" of the Christian gospel.[76] Oliver O'Donovan similarly speaks of the "reorientation of society to individual wants," with a consequent transposition of a number of moral problems, including that of individual suffering.[77] "Natural right" soon became transposed into a matter of autonomous self-interest for an individual's "own self-preservation."[78] The ethics of "rights," however, open up a complex domain into which we cannot enter further here.[79]

9.3. Horizons of Understanding:
Third Example, a Hermeneutic of the Human Condition

It is understandable that in the middle and late twentieth century a counter-reaction to the Victorian moralism of the late nineteenth century should have placed discussions of human sin in the most serious sense virtually off the agenda. Ill-informed assumptions about the meaning of such terms as "total depravity" in Augustinian or Reformed theology may have further encouraged this neglect in some circles. In the subheading above, I use "human condition" in a serious theological sense in contrast to more superficial or moralistic concerns only with human actions.

Sermons or talks in many churches, if they mention human sin at all, have too often tended to speak of human "failures" and to focus upon *individual actions* or sins of omission. Even some liturgical confessions sometimes focus on individual acts of commission or omission, rather than upon the human condition. Some still perceive the language of the "General Confession" in the Book of Common Prayer Order for Morning and Evening Prayer as an embarrassment: "There is no health in us: But Thou, O Lord, have mercy upon us miserable sinners." Some deem the "Prayer Book Confession" in the Communion Service even worse: "We bewail our manifold sins and wickedness. . . . The burden of them is intolerable."

---

75. Joan Lockwood O'Donovan, "Conversation," in *Royal Priesthood,* 392. O'Donovan's argument is complex and relates in part to anomalies and contradictions inherent in notions of "the civic nation." Our concern is simply the more specific one of noting an abstraction from horizons of understanding central to Christian traditions.

76. Joan Lockwood O'Donovan, "Conversation," 391.

77. Oliver O'Donovan, *The Desire of Nations,* 276-77.

78. Oliver O'Donovan, *The Desire of Nations,* 278.

79. Cf., e.g., H. L. A. Hart, "Are There Any Natural Rights?" *Philosophical Review* 64 (1995) 175-91.

On the other hand, trite anecdotes about "committing sins," often in the context of all-age worship, may have caused embarrassment in the opposite direction. They reduced human self-contradiction, alienation, and bondage to moralistic shortcomings of underperformance.

Against all this background Wolfhart Pannenberg judiciously writes, "The decay of the doctrine of the original sin led to the anchoring of the concept of sin in *acts* of sin, and finally the concept was reduced to the *individual* act" (my italics).[80] He asserts, "Misery is the lot of those who are deprived of the fellowship with God that is the destiny of human life. . . . To speak of human misery is better than using . . . 'lostness' when we are far from God. The term 'misery' sums up our detachment from God."[81]

If this is a valid horizon of understanding concerning the human condition, some might argue that it is so radically different from the horizons of understanding nurtured and shaped by individualism and pragmatic progressivism in the late modern West that no hermeneutical bridge can be constructed between the two. Certainly, however, these horizons are not to be regarded as incommensurable or nonnegotiable in relation to each other. I have already expressed scepticism about overly ready applications of incommensurability, whether between Wittgenstein's language games or in relation to the respective horizons of Pannenberg and Hume. A wide spectrum of theologies of sin has lived with the possibility of conversation from the era of Irenaeus and Tertullian to the present.[82] Differing concepts of sin, moreover, are bound up with different conceptions of divine grace.

In actuality *outside* Christian traditions the emergence of *postmodern* perspectives has paved the way for a very different account of being human; different both from the easy optimism of the 1960s and 1970s, and also from the neopragmatism and progressivism of the 1970s and 1980s. Even outside the churches a renewed interest has emerged in the incisive analysis of the corporate or structural human condition in the theological and socio-ethical writings of Reinhold Niebuhr and others in a similar vein. Niebuhr showed how readily self-deception and disguise could play an active role in promoting destructive attitudes and practices within corporate institutions and society.[83]

In society and in everyday life many at the end of the twentieth century and in the first decade of the twenty-first have felt *vulnerable and disempowered any*

---

80. Pannenberg, *Systematic Theology,* vol. 2, 234.

81. Pannenberg, *Systematic Theology,* vol. 2, 178-79.

82. See, e.g., the historical surveys in N. P. Williams, *The Ideas of the Fall and Original Sin: A Historical and Critical Study* (London and New York: Longmans, Green, 1929), and Reginald S. Moxon, *The Doctrine of Sin: A Critical and Historical Investigation into the Views of the Concept of Sin Held in Early Christian, Mediaeval and Modern Times* (London: Allen & Unwin, 1922).

83. Reinhold Niebuhr, *Moral Man and Immoral Society* (London: S.C.M., 1963 [also New York: Scribner, 1932]), esp. 1-230.

longer to control forces that minister to their welfare or to bring about their down-fall. People experience frustration and resentment at their own inability to pit their strength against forces beyond their control. Anger then leads to a *culture of blame,* which in turn generates a proliferation of *litigation.* Yet the constant cry for "compensation" in the face of what thirty years ago we should have called "just life" presupposes a cultural perception (real or imagined) of wrongdoing or wrongbeing on the part of other persons or of corporate institutions. Doctors, teachers, and local authorities are more at risk of being accused at law than ever before. More often, however, people rage against an anonymous "them"; "they" have set up a state of affairs in which the vulnerable perceive themselves as disadvantaged victims. "Discrimination" has largely lost its primary meaning of wise discernment or judicious evaluation; it has come to denote the victimizing of the marginalized and vulnerable.

The most incisive and prodigious writer on a hermeneutic of anonymous, disguised, and diffused power has been Michel Foucault (1926-84). Foucault approaches the problem of oppressive power in society initially through what I should call a hermeneutic of the social sciences, although Joseph Rouse calls it "the epistemic context" within which we come to understand the true imprint of the knowledge claimed, and power exercised, by social science and the institutions associated with it.[84]

In earlier historical eras, Foucault argues, power was transparent and centralized in the figure of a king or tribal chief. But power in the second half of the twentieth century operates through hidden "micro-practices," not least through the "humane" endeavors of social workers, psychiatrists, teachers, doctors, and "facilitating" bureaucrats and social scientists. In a memorable and widely quoted sentence Foucault writes, "Power is everywhere . . . because it comes from everywhere."[85] The "social-service" professions, perhaps innocent at first, become power-seeking, and they exercise formative power. Foucault speaks of "the smiling face in the white coat" as such an agent of power.

At the everyday pragmatic level, especially with the unprecedented rise of information technology, teachers, doctors, social scientists, and bureaucrats have information or "knowledge" on file and at their fingertips. In such institutions as prisons, hospitals, and the armed services such knowledge transparently serves as power. This has been mitigated to some degree in very recent years by "Freedom of Information" Acts of Parliament or government with reference to data in electronic format. But Foucault has in mind a deeper *hermeneutical* level of power-effects. The very *ways in which* social scientists *shape* jargon and *conceptual*

---

84. Joseph Rouse, "Power/Knowledge," in Gary Gutting (ed.), *The Cambridge Companion to Foucault* (Cambridge: Cambridge University Press, 1994), 93-94; cf. 92-114.

85. Michel Foucault, *History of Sexuality,* vol. 1: *An Introduction,* trans. R. Hurley (New York: Pantheon, 1978 [French, 1976]), 93.

grammar, organize classifications and typologies, and determine *what counts as* "knowledge" in the information flow becomes formative for the *identities* and forms of life of persons in society. "Epistemic fields," or recognized areas of what *counts as* knowledge, provide what Foucault calls "strategic alignments" of power, whereby individuals fall victim to the prior categorizations and value systems of a bureaucratic "regime."

No one can evade such control, for there is little or no room for rational dialogue and argument within such regimes. Effectively argument and reason collapse into a rhetoric of force through persuasion, pressure, and the "ordering" of society. Foucault distinguishes between the overt use of force in terms of public executions or in military occupation, and "subtle coercion" through "movements, gestures, attitudes."[86] Appropriate "surveillance" can convey "where and how to locate individuals . . . to supervise the conduct of such individuals, to assess it, to judge it. . . . It was a procedure aimed at knowing, mastering, and using." But this process has become increasingly disguised, and "organized as a multiple, automatic, and anonymous power."[87]

In his earlier work Foucault exposed the hermeneutical dimension of linguistic grammar or "classification" with particular reference to the notion of "normality" and madness. We tend to assume that it is "natural" to perceive madness as mental illness, to be cured or controlled by psychiatrists. But in his early works Foucault traces the historical evolution of very different *conceptions* or logical grammars of madness. In the ancient world societies viewed it as on a par with "animal," nonhuman intelligence, or in other contexts as a sign of inspiration by the gods. In the high "classical," rationalist age of the seventeenth and eighteenth centuries, madness was viewed as a moral fault that reduced humans to animal status, to be isolated and contained rather than cured. In terms of a typically postmodern epistemology (or, more strictly, anti-epistemology) Foucault regarded all these typifications as wholly *social constructions.* "Mental illness" was "invented" by nineteenth-century reformers.[88]

Once the door has been opened to radical social constructionism, however, clearly what human life *is* seems to be determined today by sociologists, social scientists, politicians, medical research scientists, and bureaucrats. Foucault sees every notion of normalcy or "the normal" as defined by such influences. He includes sexual "norms" and sexual deviancy emphatically within this horizon of understanding. In the "classical" era, he argues, sexual offenders were categorized and excluded to protect the bourgeois family. Shifting social constructions of ho-

---

86. Michel Foucault, *Discipline and Punish,* trans. A. Sheridan (New York: Pantheon, 1977 [French, 1975]), 137.

87. Foucault, *Discipline,* 143 and 177.

88. Michel Foucault, *Madness and Civilization,* trans. R. Howard (New York: Pantheon, 1965 [1st French edn. 1961]); cf. Gary Gutting, "Foucault and the History of Madness," in Gutting, *Foucault,* 47-70.

mosexuality, Foucault argues, made it *possible* only in the late twentieth century to understand gay relationships less in terms of "psychological traits" than as *"a way of life"* distinctive to the "gay."[89]

We cannot deny that concepts and the grammar of concepts are socially *conditioned*. Foucault demonstrates this from his surveys of the histories of concepts in *The Order of Things* as well as in his *History of Sexuality*.[90] But this is different from radical versions of social *construction*. These invite critical comments not only from a number of philosophers of language, but also from scientists and engineers in those traditions of research that presuppose the objective givenness of certain properties in the world, or even stable regularities among persons. Such a "totalizing" view of social construction as Foucault's seems to hold is itself capable of being seen as an anti-postmodern "grand narrative" of the most generalizing kind, as others have pointed out.

On the other hand, Foucault's diagnosis of a "turn" from time to time in the direction of society carries weight. History yields discontinuities as well as continuities. Social institutions such as prisons, schools, and hospitals, and scientific norms such as those relating to health and sanity, are themselves historically conditioned, and yet hugely control the lives of individuals. Individual vulnerability makes people "docile bodies," to use Foucault's term, in the face of social forces beyond their control.[91] "We are judged, condemned, classified . . . destined to a certain mode of living and desiring."[92]

Where does this lead for a hermeneutic of the human? This historical and social tour of the nature of power in the late twentieth century may cause us to revise our initial reactions concerning a supposed contrast between notions of sin as an individual act of underperformance or failure outside church traditions and the biblical traditions of *sin as a human condition* that has corporate, structural, and communal dimensions. Many postmodern understandings of the human as corporately under bondage to forces of power beyond the control of the individual have more in common with biblical perspectives than the shallow liberal theological optimism that speaks only of the infinite value of an individual "soul." Indeed, the overly hasty revisions of liturgies between 1960 and the early 1980s may seem to reflect a very fleeting and transient phase of such optimism about the capacity of the individual to view everything in terms of a controlled and private world. The biblical traditions and Augustine's em-

89. Foucault, "Friendship as a Way of Life," in S. Lotinger (ed.), *Foucault Live: Interviews 1966-84* (New York: Semiotext(e), 1989), cited by Arnold J. Davidson, "Ethics as Ascetics," in Gutting (ed.), *Foucault*, 125.

90. Michel Foucault, *The Order of Things*, trans. A. Sheridan (New York: Random House, 1970 [French *Les mots et les choses*, 1966]).

91. Foucault, *Discipline*, 138.

92. Michel Foucault, *Power/Knowledge: Selected Interviews and Other Writings, 1972-77*, ed. Colin Gordon (New York: Random House, 1981), 93.

phasis upon misdirected will may perhaps turn out to be less "foreign" in their realistic understanding of the human condition than many might at first sight have imagined before the end of the twentieth century and first decade of the twenty-first.

It is time, then, to look more closely at the horizons of understanding that emerge in relation to *being human* in biblical traditions, in the doctrines of the early church, and in the history of doctrine up to the present. The theme of *the human condition* requires two further chapters (10 and 11), or four more (10–13) if we include under this heading humankind under the spell of misdirected desire. For the hermeneutical implications are manifold. We shall begin in the next chapter by exploring more closely *creation* as a horizon of understanding for interpreting the human condition.

CHAPTER 10

Creation as a Horizon of Understanding
for Interpreting the Human Condition

10.1. Creation as a Horizon of Understanding in the Biblical Traditions

At the beginning of the previous chapter we noted the importance of the mutual relations between God and humankind for shaping Christian horizons of understanding concerning the human. We noted this emphasis in a number of writings from the earlier Church Fathers to Calvin, Barth, Pannenberg, and the recent study by Shults. We recalled Migliore's comment: "We cannot know our true humanity without new awareness of who God is."[1]

This issue becomes defined with greater precision in the context of three areas: the notion of human beings as the *creation of God;* the doctrine that human persons were or are *created in God's image;* and biblical and doctrinal language about *Christ* as bearing the undistorted *image of God as "true man."*

Hermeneutical starting points for language about creation often place the main emphasis less on a past act than with reference to the *present.* In a number of the Psalms the divine act of creation is applied not only to the creation of the world but to the creation of the present speaker. "It was you who formed my inward parts. . . . I praise you, for I am fearfully and wonderfully made" (Ps. 139:13-14). Weiser writes that the poet applies the idea of creation "to his own person . . . and the hymn takes the form of 'testimony' expressing both awe and trust. . . . He does not possess an independent being. . . . He can do nothing else but testify to God, praising him for his wondrous works."[2] Commenting on the typical hermeneutical settings for speaking of creation in Israel and the church,

---

1. Migliore, *Faith Seeking,* 120.
2. Weiser, *Psalms,* 804-5.

González writes, "Creation was important to them because in worship they praised God the Creator."[3]

Psalm 8 arguably outstrips even Ps. 139 not only in its widespread fame and use, but in the power and poetry with which it ascribes praise and glory to God as Creator, expressing breathless wonder at the stars of the night sky and at the glorious splendor of the sun-drenched day, and stopping in hushed awe to ask: "What are human beings that you are mindful of them, mortals that you care for them?" (Ps. 8:4). The psalmist declares, "How majestic is your name in all the earth! You have set your glory above the heavens . . . the work of your fingers, the moon and stars that you have established" (Ps. 8:1, 3). Yet amid all this breathtaking splendor, God has crowned humankind "with glory and honour; you have given them dominion over the works of your hands" (Ps. 8:5-6). The psalm ends with a repetition of exclamatory praise: "O Lord our Sovereign, how majestic is your name in all the earth!" (Ps. 8:9).

The hermeneutical horizons within which creation and humankind are evaluated are formed first and foremost as *praise and address to God.* When theologians use the fashionable but abstract term *relationality,* the hermeneutical dynamic begins with the "I-Thou" relationship of *address to* God. Nothing goes to the heart of "relationality" more directly than this. Paul Ricoeur reminds us that too readily and too easily we elevate declarative prophetic discourse or didactic propositional discourse over and above "the movement toward the second person. . . . In the psalms of thanksgiving where the uplifted soul thanks someone . . . human speech becomes invocation. It is addressed to God in the second person."[4]

Ricoeur is aware that the concerns of Martin Buber and Gabriel Marcel have found a place in Christian theology, although he does not wish to make everything hinge on "encounter." Nevertheless alongside the indirect communication of wisdom discourse and the role of declaration and narrative, "hymnic" discourse has its place. Here language about creation and created personhood assumes a primary horizon in the discourse of I-Thou address rather than in questions asked to satisfy historical curiosity about origins alone.

All the same, the two parallel creation accounts of Gen. 1:1–2:4 and 2:5-25 include not only a self-involving present aspect but also a backward look to divine action at the beginning of "human" time, when space-time, the universe, and human persons came into being through the free decision of God. As Moltmann and Pannenberg, among others, remind us, God's sovereign, unconstrained choice to create the world and humankind expressed *God's love:* "When we say that God created the world 'out of freedom', we must immediately add 'out of

---

3. Justo L. González, *A Concise History of Christian Doctrine* (Nashville: Abingdon, 2005), 38.

4. Ricoeur, "Toward a Hermeneutic of the Idea of Revelation," in Ricoeur, *Essays in Biblical Interpretation,* 89.

love."[5] This is a further expression of the need to place any understanding of what it is to be human within the horizons of how God chose to relate himself to humankind. Hans Wolff argues that relationality or *relationship* emerges especially from the traditions of Gen. 2:4-25, conventionally ascribed to the "Yahwist" (whether this term identifies a tradition or also a specific view about dating and origin).[6]

This tradition speaks of humankind's relationship *to God, to animals, and to "other" human persons* (man and woman; woman and man), as well as *to the earth.* Human beings are close to God, for God "breathed into [his] nostrils the breath of life" (Gen. 2:7b). Yet human beings are also "utterly earthly," for they are formed "from the dust of the ground" (Gen. 2:7a).[7] When other biblical writers take this up, however, horizons shift from sheer creatureliness to those of divine *love* and compassion. For God knows how fragile and vulnerable human beings are. Humans are in danger of slipping "back to dust" (Ps. 90:3), but God "knows how we were made; he remembers that we are dust" (Ps. 103:14). This entire psalm is one of praise: "Bless the LORD, O my soul, and all that is in me, bless his holy name . . . who forgives all your iniquity, who heals all your diseases, who redeems your life from the Pit, who crowns you with steadfast love and mercy" (Ps. 103:1, 3, 4). The Lord "has compassion. . . . For he knows how we were made; he remembers that we are dust" (Ps. 103:13-14).

The two Genesis traditions reflect a different but not contradictory hermeneutic. The *"Yahwist"* tradition may present a narrative of the past, but it is also pregnant with meaning for the present, and this the psalmists take up. Other passages also take up the relationship to the *"other,"* namely to humans as *social* beings. God did not create human beings to be lonely and solitary. This theme emerged in 9.2 above. The premise "It is not good that the man should be alone; I will make him a helper as his partner" (Gen. 2:18) leads on not immediately to the creation of Eve, but initially to the formation of "every animal of the field and bird of the air" (Gen. 2:19). Writers differ over whether placing the animals next implies that this represented a "false start," or whether their creation from the same substance as the man ("the ground," 2:19) suggests "how near the beasts stand to man."[8] Whichever view we take, the main point is that (in Vawter's words) "man's social nature is in view"; he is not to be a solitary individual but to enjoy *relationships* with God, with a fellow human, and with the animal world.

The climactic exclamation of Gen. 2:23, "Bone of my bone and flesh of my flesh," indicates the affinity and intimacy that man and woman can enjoy together. The "linguistic" commentary on 2:19 and 2:24 respectively indicates how

---

5. Moltmann, *God in Creation,* 35; cf. Pannenberg, *Systematic Theology,* vol. 2, 19 and 21.

6. Wolff, *Anthropology of the Old Testament,* 93-95.

7. Wolff, *Anthropology,* 93.

8. Vawter, *On Genesis,* 74, holds the former view; Wolff, *Anthropology,* 94, holds the latter view. The quotations are from each respectively.

much closer the interpersonal relationship of fellow humans is than their relation to the animal world. *Man* (Hebrew אָדָם, *'ādām*) is formed from the *ground*
(Hebrew אֲדָמָה, *'ᵃdāmâ*) as the animals and birds were (v. 19). *Man* (Hebrew אִישׁ,
'îsh) is related to *woman* (Hebrew אִשָּׁה, *'ishâ*) in both affinity and complementarity, or in kinship and difference.

We must be cautious in extrapolating more than is due from exegesis alone.
Yet this Yahwist tradition implies a man-woman relationality that most notably
Karl Barth, Dietrich Bonhoeffer, and others develop in ways that accord with
other biblical passages (e.g., 1 Cor. 11:3-16), and with Christian doctrine.[9] Barth
writes, "Man is to woman and woman to man supremely the other, the fellow-
man. . . . The encounter between them carries with it . . . in all their antithesis,
their relatedness, their power of mutual attraction and their reciprocal reference
the one to the other. . . . Here humanity has its proper focus . . . the freedom of
heart for the other. . . . To know nothing of this sphere is to know nothing of the I
and Thou and their encounter, and therefore of the human. . . . There is no being
of man above the being of male and female."[10] Wolff insists that such a portrait
emerges directly from the Old Testament. He writes, "It is only man and woman
together who make up a whole and useful person."[11]

The *"Priestly"* document of Gen. 1:1–2:4, on the other hand, reflects a different but not contradictory perspective. God's creative power brings order in
place of chaos, although the phrase "the earth was a 'formless void'" (Hebrew
תֹהוּ וָבֹהוּ, *tōhû wābōhû*) should not be taken to denote an "entity" or substance.
Gen. 1:1–2:4 does not imply a dualistic conflict along the lines of the Babylonian
creation myth *Enuma elish* in which Marduk utilizes the body of the goddess
Tiamat and battles with primeval chaos.[12] The contexts of allusions, for example, to "Leviathan" (Hebrew לִוְיָתָן, *liwyāthān*, Job 41:1; Pss. 74:24; 104:26; Isa.
27:1), or to the "sea serpent" or "dragon" (Hebrew תַּנִּין, *tannîn*, Ps. 74:13; Isa.
51:9; cf. Greek δράκων, *drakōn*, in Rev. 12:3-17; 20:2), underline not divine struggle but absolute divine sovereignty.[13] Pannenberg even expresses reservation
about Barth's use of "nothingness" rather than "nothing" for divine creation *ex*

9. Barth, *Church Dogmatics*, III:1, sect. 41, 2, 183-206; sect. 41, 3, 288-329; and Dietrich
Bonhoeffer, *Creation and Fall, Temptation: Two Biblical Studies* (London: SCM, 1959), 40-43 and
63-69.

10. Barth, *Church Dogmatics*, III:2, sect. 45, 288 and 289.

11. Wolff, *Anthropology of the Old Testament*, 95.

12. For ancient Near Eastern creation myths, see James B. Pritchard, *Ancient New Eastern
Texts Relating to the Old Testament* (Princeton, NJ: Princeton University Press, 2d edn. 1955), 3-155,
esp. 60-72 and 104-6.

13. Brevard Childs helpfully explains the category of "broken" myth in B. S. Childs, *Myth and
Reality in the Old Testament* (London: S.C.M., 1960, 2d edn. 1962), 31-43. For a critique of sup-
posed dependence on Babylonian sources, see W. G. Lambert, "A New Look at the Babylonian
Background of Genesis," *JTS* 16 (1965) 287-300, and Alan R. Millard, "A New Babylonian 'Genesis'
Story," *Tyndale Bulletin* 18 (1967) 3-18.

nihilo lest this should let in by the back door any part of an eternal antithesis or dualism.[14]

Two alleged hermeneutical barriers to "hearing" the horizons of understanding have sometimes been raised. First, some make certain suppositions about the status of Gen. 1:1–2:25 as "myth," sometimes also ascribed to Babylonian sources. Second, some urge that "contradictions" make any reconciliation between the "Yahwist" and "Priestly" traditions of Gen. 2:5-25 and Gen. 1:1–2:4 impossible.

Neither assumption is securely based. First, we have alluded to Brevard Childs's concept of "broken" myth (n. 12) in which he distinguishes between the *sources* and *forms* of imagery and the *function* of such imagery within the biblical texts. Second, George B. Caird has provided a careful discussion of myth in *semantic* terms, which builds upon Childs's view. Caird distinguishes between at least seven distinct senses in which writers use the term *myth* in interpreting the biblical writings. He argues, in effect, that the question "Is it myth?" is banal and pointless, unless this is based upon careful semantic explorations of the term "myth." He writes, "The thesis which I shall propose . . . is that myth and eschatology are used in the Old and New Testaments as metaphor systems for theological interpretations of historical events."[15]

In theory, some might define myth so broadly (for example, as self-involving language embedded in community traditions) that it would hardly matter for hermeneutical currency whether or not these passages were "myth." However, even with reference to the more specific sense of the term, Gerhard von Rad writes, "Israel was actually able to make a connection between Creation and saving history — not with a present conceived in terms of myth"; while Otto Eissfeldt insists, "A real myth presupposes at least two gods."[16] These concepts of myth do not apply to the Genesis material. The issue of myth turns out to be a pseudo-problem, then, for alleging some hermeneutical barrier to their speaking today, or their relevance to doctrine. There are no grounds for exaggerating the supposed foreign origins of this material for questioning the capacity of these biblical horizons of understanding to address today's world.

The second alleged hermeneutical obstacle relates to allegations of "contradictions" between the two Genesis traditions, often coupled with charges of "contradictions" between Genesis and modern science. As we have noted, allegations of "contradictions" often arise through distractions about ancient "sources" in contrast to a more nuanced appreciation of the literary art frequently involved in drawing upon *complementary* traditions to present a stereo-

---

14. Pannenberg, *Systematic Theology,* vol. 2, 14.

15. George B. Caird, *The Language and Imagery of the Bible* (London: Duckworth, 1980), 219.

16. Gerhard von Rad, *Old Testament Theology,* trans. D. M. G. Stalker, 2 vols. (Edinburgh: Oliver & Boyd, 1962), vol. 1, 136; and Otto Eissfeldt, *The Old Testament: An Introduction,* trans. P. R. Ackroyd (Oxford: Blackwell, 1966), 35.

scopic or polyphonic narrative. Robert Alter makes precisely this point with reference to the literary traditions behind 1 Sam. 16:1-14 and 1 Sam. 17. The former depicts the anointing and kingship of David from the perspective of *divine decree* and divine sovereignty. The latter, 1 Sam. 17 onward, describes the "brawling chaos" of the micro-narratives that implement the divine purpose, and places an emphasis upon the series of human events that eventually implement the divine decree.[17]

The "Priestly" traditions of Gen. 1:1–2:4 keep in view the *cosmic perspective* of the universe and the world, within which humankind has a privileged place. The Yahwist perspective explores *human relationality* with God and with fellow humans. Nevertheless, Wolff observes, the two traditions are at one on "three essential points. . . . Man belongs in immediate proximity to the animals; . . . man is differentiated from the animals; [and] it is only man and woman together who make up a whole and useful person."[18]

On supposed contradictions we refer back further to our discussion of Mikhail Bakhtin and our brief reference to symphonic truth in Balthasar. Some issues are simply too large and complex to be captured by a single shot of the camera. Indeed, the polyphonic or pluralist voices that proclaim divine creation are not confined to Gen. 1:1–2:25. Karl Barth observes that to try to understand the doctrine of creation only as it is presented "at the beginning of the Bible," and to tie up at this "hitching post," is to remain blind to what is attested "in the centre of the Bible."[19] By "the centre" Barth means not only the substantial passages in Job, Psalms, and Isaiah, but also the witness of the New Testament to the creation of all things through Jesus Christ. The Old Testament "heaven and earth" become "all things" through the creative agency of Christ (Greek τὰ πάντα, *ta panta,* John 1:3; πάντα δι' αὐτοῦ ἐγένετο, *panta di' autou egeneto,* Eph. 3:9; Col. 1:16; Heb. 1:3; Rev. 4:11; at least three or more distinct traditions).

Balthasar also distinguishes between the reductive monotone of a single voice and the harmonious polyphony of "symphony." Räisänen's rather sad argument that biblical "contradictions" prevent theological construction is exposed for what it is both by literary and doctrinal reflections that do better justice to multiple horizons of understanding.[20]

The Priestly tradition elucidates the orderedness and variety of divine creative acts, and also places an emphasis upon "the new" that other passages in the

17. Robert Alter, *The Art of Biblical Narrative* (New York: Basic Books, 1981), 154; cf. 147-53.

18. Wolff, *Anthropology,* 95.

19. Barth, *Church Dogmatics,* III:1, sect. 40, 23 and 24.

20. Hans Urs von Balthasar, *Truth Is Symphonic: Aspects of a Christian Pluralism,* trans. G. Harrison (San Francisco: Ignatius, 1987), 13, 37-73, 85-87, and throughout. In a very different vein, on the plurality and coherence of biblical texts, cf. Gabriel Josipovici, *The Book of God: A Response to the Bible* (New Haven, CT and London: Yale University Press, 1988), esp. 53-74, on Gen. 1:1–2:25.

Old and New Testaments take up. It is so widely known that the verb *to create* (Hebrew ברא, *bārā'*, Gen. 1:1; 1:21; 1:27; 2:3) is used exclusively with God as the subject (some 46 times) that Raymond Van Leeuwen expresses concern that the term has become theologically "overloaded."[21] Nevertheless characteristically it carries the nuance of creating new things, and this aspect finds expression in Isa. 42:5-7; 43:2; and especially 65:17.

The Priestly tradition also lays the foundation for the Christian doctrine of creation through the Spirit of God (NRSV, "wind of God," Gen. 1:2, but Hebrew רוח אלהים *rûach ᵉlōhim*, wind or spirit) and also creation through the Word of God (1:3, "God said . . . "; also 1:6; 1:9; 1:11; 1:14; 1:20; 1:24; 1:26).

Although Foerster argues that the Hebrew verb conveys a doctrine of *creatio ex nihilo*, Van Leeuwen rejects this view. However, he concedes that the word denotes "an absolute beginning of the universe as well as the absolute sovereignty of God in bringing reality into being."[22] The Priestly tradition underlines the transcendence of God, who creates by his free, sovereign will, dividing and "separating" reality into entities and forces as he chooses. The "Yahwist" tradition complements this transcendent vision with a more immanentist view of God, who shapes materials as the potter shapes clay. But this is no diminution of divine sovereignty (Jer. 18:1-11); quite the reverse.

In the light of all these factors about the two traditions and their relation to creation in the rest of the Bible, questions about differences from modern geological or biological sciences may indeed appear banal. Even in Genesis the dual traditions do not address the scientific question "How?" but focus upon divine purpose, divine order, divine love, and human creatureliness and relationality. John Polkinghorne writes, "Science is essentially asking, and answering, the question 'How?' By what manner of means do things come about? Religion, essentially, is asking, and answering, the question 'Why?' Is there a meaning and purpose behind what is happening?"[23]

Polkinghorne also goes further in asserting a different mode of language in speaking of divine action from speaking of empirical objects or events. God, he writes, "transcends us and our power to grasp him. . . . The language of theology is the language of symbol."[24] While this may not apply to all theological statements, it remains true of such areas as primal creation.[25] In spite of all this, the

---

21. Raymond C. Van Leeuwen, "ברא," in *New International Dictionary of Old Testament Theology and Exegesis*, ed. William A. VanGemeren, 5 vols. (Carlisle U.K.: Paternoster, 1997), vol. 1, 728-35, esp. 731: "*B-r-'* as a root is not a uniquely theological term" (732).

22. Van Leeuwen, "ברא," *Dictionary*, 732.

23. John Polkinghorne, *Quarks, Chaos, and Christianity: Questions to Science and Religion* (London: Triangle, 1994), 5-7; also in Ian G. Barbour, *Issues in Science and Religion* (London: S.C.M., 1966), 23-26.

24. John Polkinghorne, *Science and Creation* (Boston, MA: Shambhala, 1988), 94.

25. See further Robert J. Russell, Nancey Murphy, and C. J. Isham (eds.), *Quantum Cosmol-*

Priestly tradition does depict the creation of the world as a sequence of forms; light and darkness, water and earth, vegetation and stars, fish and birds, land animals and humans. Wolfhart Pannenberg aptly observes, "Modern science might change the order to some extent. It is astonishing, however, how much agreement there is to the fact of a sequence."[26] The placing of the stars later in the sequence than we should expect may well have the purpose of clarifying their lack of divine status in relation to polytheistic religions among Israel's neighbors. They are no more than lamps or signs for the seasons.[27]

It turns out, then, that *neither the two traditions of Gen. 1:1–2:25 nor the form of Gen. 1:1–2:4 in relation to modern science constitutes barriers to hermeneutical communicative understanding or alien horizons of understanding.* Indeed, the emphasis on the *"newness"* of divine *creativity* speaks relevantly to human experience in situations where individual persons or even humankind as such has lost control of human well-being and destiny. Arguably such phenomena as global warming and other massive economic, social, or ideological forces invite *creative change of a kind greater than mere correction or self-regulation. At the heart of the Christian doctrine of the human person stands the belief that God can impart new life, grant new birth, and bring about a new beginning through new creation.* Hence *it is "God . . . who created the heavens . . . who gives breath to the people . . ."* who can cause Israel (or the Servant) to be "a light to the nations, to open the eyes that are blind" (Isa. 42:5-7). It is the *God who has proven his creative power* who can "create new heavens and a new earth" (Isa. 65:17).

Paul the apostle takes up and applies this logic in 1 Cor. 15. The resurrection of the dead is comparable to an act of new creation. Paul expresses this view in Rom. 4:17: "the God in whom he [Abraham] believed gives life to the dead and calls into existence the things that do not exist" (Greek τὰ μὴ ὄντα, *ta mē onta*). The question "How are the dead raised? With what kind of body do they come?" (1 Cor. 15:35) is answered initially from an analogy with creation and the divine power to create multiform modes of existence: "Not all flesh is alike, but there is one flesh for human beings, another for animals, another for birds, another for fish. . . . the glory of the sun . . . the glory of the moon . . . star differs from star in glory. So it is with the resurrection of the dead" (1 Cor. 15:39-42a).

In my larger commentary on 1 Corinthians I repeated Barth's view that "the linchpin of Paul's whole argument" comes in 1 Cor. 15:34: "Some people have no knowledge of *God.*" The ground for belief in the possibility and conceivability of a resurrection mode of existence is "*the infinite resourcefulness of God* as already

---

ogy and the Laws of Nature: Scientific Perspectives on Divine Action, (Berkeley, CA: Center for Theology and the Natural Sciences, 2d edn. 1996), esp. 93-138; John Polkinghorne, *Science and Theology: An Introduction* (London: S.C.M. and Minneapolis: Fortress, 1998), esp. 25-48; I. G. Barbour, *Religion in the Age of Science* (London: S.C.M., 1990).

26. Pannenberg, *Systematic Theology*, vol. 2, 116; cf. 117-22.

27. Pannenberg, *Systematic Theology*, vol. 2, 117.

demonstrated in his sovereign power and wisdom as Creator. . . . A dead person cannot contribute to his or her *'being brought to life.'*"[28] The free, sovereign decision of God to assign to each his/her or its own body (Greek ἴδιον σῶμα) is expressed by "as he has chosen" (NRSV; Greek καθὼς ἠθέλησεν, *kathōs ēthelēsen,* 15:38).[29]

Numerous other passages in the New Testament bear directly on the doctrine of creation. In 1 Cor. 11:2-16, for example, Paul elaborates a complex dialectic of gender-distinctiveness and gender-complementarity on one side, and gender-reciprocity and gender-mutuality on the other. He derives this dialectic from the interaction between three horizons of understandings: that of the "order" of creation; that of eschatological promise; and that of the situation on the church in Corinth and of witness to the world.[30]

The "Trinitarian" agency of creation, and an emphasis upon Jesus Christ as "mediate" Creator, finds a clear and undisputable place in the New Testament writings among a plurality of theological voices. In the theology of the Fourth Gospel Jesus Christ the Logos is the Creator of all things: πάντα δι' αὐτοῦ ἐγένετο (*panta di' autou egeneto,* John 1:3). In Pauline theology it is Christ δι' οὗ τὰ πάντα (*di' hou ta panta,* 1 Cor. 8:6b; cf. Col. 1:15b-17). In the theology of the Epistle to the Hebrews it is through Christ that God made the worlds: δι' οὗ καὶ ἐποίησεν τοὺς αἰῶνας (*di' hou kai epoiēsen tous aiōnas,* Heb. 1:2b; cf. Heb. 2:10). The preposition *dia* occurs with the genitive in all these references, except for the accusative (δι' ὅν), also used in Heb. 2:10.

Barth, Moltmann, and Pannenberg among many others underline the importance and centrality of this Christological and elsewhere Trinitarian agency of creation, and their point is fundamental.[31] However, in the Church Fathers this emphasis arises especially in the context of establishing the deity of the Holy Spirit and of explicating Trinitarian doctrine. Hence we postpone a more detailed discussion of this aspect until 18.2 and 19. We may note, however, in a preliminary way Barth's particular concern on this issue. On the one hand, he writes, "The aim of creation is history. . . . God wills and creates the creature for the sake of His Son or Word."[32] On the other hand, creation is not only the ex-

28. Thiselton, *First Epistle,* 1256 (my italics in the *Commentary*). Cf. also Karl Barth, *The Resurrection of the Dead,* trans. H. J. Stenning (London: Hodder & Stoughton, 1933), 18.

29. Thiselton, *First Epistle,* 1264-65 includes a discussion of the use of the aorist. T. C. Edwards rightly argues that it denotes a purposive and sovereign act: not "as he wills," but "as he purposed."

30. Thiselton, *First Epistle,* 811-48; also Judith Gundry-Volf, "Gender and Creation in 1 Cor. 11:2-16: A Study of Paul's Theological Method," in J. Adna, S. J. Hafemann, and O. Hofius (eds.), *Evangelium, Schriftsauslegung, Kirche: Festschrift für Peter Stuhlmacher* (Göttingen: Vandenhoeck & Ruprecht, 1997), 151-71.

31. Barth, *Church Dogmatics,* III:1, sects. 40-41, 3-329; Moltmann, *God in Creation,* esp. 8-10 and 94-103, but throughout; and Pannenberg, *Systematic Theology,* vol. 2, 20-59.

32. Barth, *Church Dogmatics,* III:1, sect. 41, 59.

pression of divine love and grace, but the precondition of the outworking of God's purposes of grace through Christ in history.[33]

This does not remove us from the realm of biblical testimony. In broader terms Gerhard von Rad writes, "Creation is connected theologically with the saving history. . . . It was a great achievement that Israel was actually able to make a connexion between Creation and the saving history — and not . . . in terms of myth."[34] This emerges especially in Isa. 40–65. The God who created the heavens is "he who created you, who formed you"; hence, "Fear not, for I redeem you" (cf. Isa. 42:5; 43:1; 44:24b-28). Gerhard von Rad traces this theme beyond Isaiah to Pss. 74, 89, and elsewhere.[35] All of this simply underlines the major *hermeneutical* point in the last third of this section: the God of Jesus Christ and of Christian doctrine is the God who does *new things,* and who through Christ and by the Holy Spirit does new things on the basis of divine grace and *love.*

10.2. Creation as a Horizon for Understanding the Human Condition from Irenaeus to Barth

Prior to Irenaeus the subapostolic writings and early apologists include confessions of faith concerning creation, but they are not yet the beginnings of doctrine. The *Didache* (probably late first century) speaks of creation in the context of praise: "To you be glory for ever. You, Lord Almighty, did create all things (τὰ πάντα, *ta panta*) for your Name's sake, and gave food and drink to humankind for their enjoyment that they might give thanks to you."[36] Justin (c. 100–c. 165) reflects the Old and New Testament traditions when he calls God "Father, Creator, and Lord" and declares that all things were created through Christ.[37]

However, in accordance with our discussions of "dispositional" accounts of belief, doctrinal formulation received an impetus when Marcion and early gnostic sects began to propagate claims contrary to the biblical traditions. Marcion argued that the world was created by a Demiurge, and separated the identity of God the Father of Jesus Christ from that of the God of the Old Testament and Judaism. Gnostic writers expounded a radical dualism in which creation arose out of a struggle between rival forces. Within a horizon of understanding that postulates a radical dualism between good and evil, mind and matter, spirit and physical embodiment, they ascribe evil not to the human will, but to matter, or to

---

33. Barth, *Church Dogmatics,* III:1, sect. 40, 26-27.
34. Gerhard von Rad, *Old Testament Theology,* vol. 1, 136.
35. Gerhard von Rad, *Old Testament Theology,* vol. 1, 137-39.
36. *Didache* 10:2-3 (Greek, Loeb Classical Library, Apostolic Fathers 1, ed. K. Lake [London: Heinemann, 1965], 324).
37. Justin, *Second Apology* 6:1; Greek, Migne, *Patrologia Graeca,* vol. 6, 453A.

mere ignorance of the spirit realm.[38] Contrary to a notion of creation carrying with it the assurance of *being loved* by an *Almighty* God, the gnostic believed that humankind was imprisoned in an embodied state, and that "salvation" was a matter of flight and escape from this.

Here indeed are "foreign" horizons of understanding against which Irenaeus, Tertullian, and Hippolytus formulated Christian doctrinal beliefs. Christian doctrine affirmed God as sole Creator, and the body and "human" time as good gifts of God. By contrast, many gnostic systems of "spirituality" urged indifference to bodily life and bodily relationships. Worse, salvation became privatized, made inner and individual. *The Gospel of Thomas* includes the *logion:* "Jesus said, 'Blessed are the solitary and elect; for you shall find the kingdom.'"[39] Gärtner calls this "almost a gnostic creed."[40] *Pneuma* (spirit) and *hulē* (matter) are opposed as ontological principles.[41] We might have expected that Jewish traditions would have finally maintained the traditions of the Old Testament against gnosticism. But, as Roy Wilson reminds us, Judaism in Egypt and in Syria had come into contact with the cults of Isis and Astarte, and this paved the way for Jewish-gnostic syncretism. Wilson sets out the sources.[42]

From the very beginning Christian exponents of apostolic doctrine held a view of creation and of being human that was opposed to gnostic dualism.[43] Irenaeus and Tertullian explicitly declare their belief in the one God as Creator in opposition to gnostic ideas.

Irenaeus (c. 130–c. 200) attacks the gnostic notion of a preexistent "Aeon" who is supposedly "eternal and unbegotten" as a dualist principle alongside "God."[44] He writes, "God is Creator of the world, and Christians (and others) celebrate the praise of one God, the Maker of heaven and earth."[45] With Tertullian, Irenaeus is the first to formulate an explicit doctrine of creation *ex nihilo,* arguing that to postulate preexistent matter or the agency of "another god" depends on grossly distorting and mishandling Scripture.[46] He rejects the gnostic "heresy" that "creation was formed through the mother by the Demi-

---

38. A standard account of gnostic systems can be found in Hans Jonas, *The Gnostic Religion* (cited above), 42-99, 130-46, and 206-37.

39. *Gospel of Thomas, Logion* 49.

40. Bertil Gärtner, *The Theology of the Gospel of Thomas,* trans. E. J. Sharpe (London: Collins, 1961), 198.

41. *Gospel of Truth,* 31:1; *Exc. ex Theodosius* 51:1.

42. Roy McL. Wilson, *The Gnostic Problem: A Study of the Relations between Hellenistic Judaism and the Gnostic Heresy* (London: Mowbray, 1958), 37-49 and throughout.

43. For an account of the Patristic evidence of gnostic belief, see Werner Foerster, *Gnosis: A Selection of Gnostic Texts,* vol. 1: *Patristic Evidence,* trans. R. McL. Wilson (Oxford: Clarendon, 1972).

44. Irenaeus, *Against Heresies* I:1:1.

45. Irenaeus, *Against Heresies* II:9:1.

46. Irenaeus, *Against Heresies* II:10:1-4.

urge."[47] In accord with biblical traditions he asserts that God called creation into being, exhibiting his "goodness."[48]

Tertullian (c. 160–c. 225) provides an even more explicit example of a disposition to respond by asserting a belief when the belief is denied or attacked. Predictably he attacks Marcion for denying that "Almighty God" is "the Lord and Maker of the universe."[49] In his confrontation with Hermogenes, however, he formulates (with Irenaeus) a doctrine of creation *ex nihilo*. Matter does not exert co-eternally with God; nor does God create the universe as an emanation of himself. God is "sole God, having nothing else co-existent with him."[50] God created the universe "neither out of matter . . . nor out of God."[51] Tertullian draws not only on Gen. 1:1-27 but also on John 1:3 and other New Testament passages to conclude: "All things were made out of nothing."[52] Hermogenes, he dryly adds, alludes to matter as having "a condition like his own," namely "confused, formless, and void."

It would not be entirely correct to imply that the development of a Christian doctrine of creation proceeded without any deviation, Origen, for example, returns to the notion of preexistent matter.[53] On the other hand, the earlier Church Fathers remain adamantly opposed to a view of creation other than that expounded in these pages. Hippolytus, for example, distances himself radically from gnostic views of creation.[54] By the time that we reach Athanasius (c. 296-373) and Basil the Great (c. 330-79) we are on firm and established ground, on which these thinkers underline a clear-cut contrast between Creator and creatures, not least to emphasize that neither Jesus Christ nor the Holy Spirit is a "created" being, but in fact divine co-creators of the universe.[55] We shall return to these "Trinitarian" passages in our exploration of the doctrine of the Holy Spirit.

There is a broad parallel between the earlier Fathers' defense of the goodness of God and the goodness of the world in opposition to the gnostics, and the defense put forward by Augustine of Hippo (354-430) of the goodness of God of the world in opposition to the Manicheans. The Manicheans ascribed the source of sin to human embodiment. Augustine insists that the source of sin resides in

47. Irenaeus, *Against Heresies* I:17:1; Greek, Migne, *Patrologia Graeca*, vol. 7, 637A.

48. Irenaeus, *Against Heresies* IV:38:3; Greek, Migne, *Patrologia Graeca*, vol. 7, 1107B.

49. Tertullian, *Against Marcion* II:2.

50. Tertullian, *Against Hermogenes* 17:1.

51. Tertullian, *Against Hermogenes* 15:1.

52. Tertullian, *Against Hermogenes* 45.

53. Origen, *De Principiis* II:4.

54. Hippolytus, *Refutation of All Heresies* VIII:2-3.

55. Athanasius, *Epistles to Serapion* 1:21-27 (Greek, Migne, *Patrologia Graeca*, vol. 26, 581A-93C; Athanasius, *Against the Arians* 1:18 (Migne, *Patrologia Graeca*, vol. 26, 49A) and 2:27 (*Patrologia Graeca*, vol. 26, 204A); Basil, *On the Holy Spirit* 10:24 (Migne, *Patrologia Graeca*, 32, 109D-12B); 16:38-40 (Migne, *Patrologia Graeca*, vol. 32, 136A-44A); and 24:55 (Migne, *Patrologia Graeca*, vol. 32, 169B-72C).

the human will.[56] Against the Manicheans he roundly asserts, "*Omnis natura bonum est.*" [57] "Evil is not out of God *(ex Deo)*, nor co-eternal with God, but comes out of the free will of our nature, which was created good by him who is good."[58] God created the universe *ex nihilo.* God did not create an undifferentiated continuum.

In terms of what is sometimes called "the principle of plenitude" Augustine argues that God out of his love and goodness created a universe of infinite complexity and variety. Necessarily this may suggest inequality or unevenness to some, but differentiations and "order" or ranking *(ordinatio)* are part of the aesthetic creation of the world.[59] We cannot have sunshine without shadows. We cannot have fire that warms without fire that burns.[60] The world may offer a *potential* for the *possibility* of evil or blame, but it is good, and is a cause for blessing God in praise: "O all you creatures of the Lord, bless the Lord."

Thomas Aquinas writes of creation and creatureliness in broadly the same vein.[61] Thomas adds that the Creator, who is both the God of Abraham and the Father manifested in Christ, is "First Cause" *(prima causa)* of all things, and also "Final Cause" *(finalis causa).*[62] He writes, "God is the efficient, exemplary, and final cause of everything" *(omnium rerum).*[63] The creation of the world is an act of God as Trinity. Thomas writes, "In the Nicene Creed we profess that the Father is *the Creator of all things visible and invisible,* of the Son that *through him all things were made,* of the Holy Ghost that he is *the Lord and life-giver.*"[64] All of this "springs from each and all of his [God's] attributes . . . wisdom . . . mercy . . . extravagantly generous goodness" *(ad misericordiam et bonitatem se superabunditer diffundentem).*[65] Genesis tells us that God "separated" light from darkness, and so on: "Therefore the separation and multitude of things come from him," and all "were very good."[66] Thomas adds, "Consequently divine wisdom causes the distinctions and inequality of things for the perfection of the universe *(distinctionis rerum propter perfectionem universi, ita et inaequalitatis).*"[67] Finally, Aquinas follows Augustine in defining evil as "a certain absence of good" *(quaedam absentia boni),* or "as privation" *(sicut privatio)* of some positive attribute, related to the

---

56. Augustine, *City of God,* XII:6.
57. Augustine, *Enchiridion,* IV:13.
58. Augustine, *Confessions,* VII:3, 4, 5.
59. Augustine, *City of God,* XI:23.
60. Augustine, *City of God,* XII:4.
61. Thomas Aquinas, *Summa Theologiae,* Ia, Q. 44-47 and indirectly Qq. 48-49 (Latin and English: Blackfriars edn., vol. 8, ed. Thomas Gilby.
62. Aquinas, *Summa,* Ia, Q. 44, arts. 1-3 and 4 (Blackfriars edn., vol. 8, 5-23).
63. Aquinas, *Summa,* Ia, Q. 4, art. 4 (Blackfriars edn., vol. 8, 23).
64. Aquinas, *Summa,* Ia, Q. 45, art. 6:1 (Blackfriars edn., vol. 8, 51).
65. Aquinas, *Summa,* Ia, Q. 45, art. 6:3 (Blackfriars edn., vol. 8, 55).
66. Aquinas, *Summa,* Ia, Q. 47, arts. 1 and 2 (Blackfriars edn., vol. 8, 93 and 95).
67. Aquinas, *Summa,* Ia, Q. 47, art. 2 (Blackfriars edn., vol. 8, 99).

human will but given potential origination in the diversity and "inequality" of the world.[68] He explicitly appeals to Augustine for the origins of evil in the human will, and to Aristotle for the inevitability of the effects of diversity in the world.[69]

Different nuances occur in Duns Scotus and William of Ockham, but we need to keep our main focus in view. The Reformers endorsed all the features that emerged in mainline Christian doctrine from the biblical writings through to the Fathers, although, as Shults and others write, they place an enhanced emphasis on the hermeneutical horizon of the understanding of humanness in the light of divine relationality.

Calvin endorses the concept of divine creation "out of nothing."[70] Divine creation reflects "the paternal goodness of God towards the human race."[71] God created angels, but the wickedness of the devil was not by creation but by corruption.[72] Calvin places a strong emphasis on humankind as created in the image of God (to which we turn shortly).[73] He is also emphatic in insisting that God created the world "for the happiness of man."[74] "He created all things for the sake of man."[75] God has created a wonderful universe, full of evident tokens of his love, and this encourages or provokes humankind "to invocation, praise, and love."[76]

Humankind as created persons are called upon to respect their own personhood as beings endorsed with reason, intelligence, and will. Humankind is destined to reflect the glory of God, and to reflect the divine image. Torrance writes, "In Calvin's view the key to the whole doctrine of man in creation and destiny is the idea of thankful response to the unbounded grace of God. Nor can we understand the doctrine of creation unless we too are evoked to a grateful adoration of the perfections of God."[77] Humankind is endowed with dignity, but was created *"ex nihilo."*[78] Finally, Calvin anticipates a major theme in modern theology with his emphasis upon humankind's distinctive capacity to be *addressed* by the word of God in communicative and revelatory action. Humankind as created persons are to approach God not "with presumptuous curiosity," but to "contemplate him" when he draws near and communicates himself to us.[79]

68. Aquinas, *Summa,* Ia, Q. 48, arts. 1 and 3 (Blackfriars edn., vol. 8, 109 and 117).

69. Aquinas, *Summa,* Ia, Q. 49, art. 1:1 and Q. 48, art. 2 (Blackfriars edn., vol. 8, 117 and 113).

70. Calvin, *Institutes,* I:15:5.

71. Calvin, *Institutes,* I:14:2 (Beveridge edn., vol. 1, 142).

72. Calvin, *Institutes,* I:14:4-6 and 16 (Beveridge edn., vol. 1, 144-46 and 152-53).

73. Calvin, *Institutes,* I:14:3-4 (Beveridge edn., vol. 1, 162-65). See further Thomas F. Torrance, *Calvin's Doctrine of Man,* 35-82.

74. John Calvin, *Commentary on the Psalms,* trans. A. Golding et al., 3 vols. (London: Tegg, 1840), vol. 1, 72, on Ps. 8:6.

75. Calvin, *Institutes,* I:14:22 (Beveridge edn., vol. 1, 157).

76. Calvin, *Institutes,* I:14:22 (Beveridge edn., vol. 1, 157).

77. Torrance, *Calvin's Doctrine,* 25; Calvin, *Institutes,* I:2:1-3; I:14:20-22.

78. Calvin, *Institutes,* I:15:5 (Beveridge edn., vol. 1, 166).

79. Calvin, *Institutes,* I:5:9 (Beveridge edn., vol. 1, 57).

This emphasis became prominent in twentieth-century theology. In the nineteenth century Friedrich Schleiermacher stressed the central theme "that the world exists only in absolute dependence upon God."[80] However, unlike Augustine, Aquinas, Calvin, and Barth, he argued that the doctrine of the Trinity is not presupposed by this experience of utter dependence upon God.[81] Creation rests solely upon divine activity, and is "out of nothing": matter did not exist independently of God.[82] God's decision to create the world was entirely free, and was enacted "through a *free* decree."[83] Even so, "absolute dependence upon God coincides entirely with the view that all such things are conditioned and determined by the interdependence of Nature."[84] Schleiermacher is concerned to reconcile Christian doctrine with natural science and urges that in the interest of achieving this "we should abandon the idea of the absolutely supernatural."[85]

If we were to restrict our attention to Part I of *The Christian Faith* it might surprise us that Schleiermacher, with his acute hermeneutical awareness, would seem to offer only a self-evident, almost tautologous, account of creation, which even he acknowledges is "vague." Nevertheless he moves to elucidate a human religious consciousness of sin and grace in Part II of his works, and Shults, we noted, ranks this as a major contribution in terms of "relationality" to God. On the other hand, whether this directly emerges from his doctrine of *creation* is at best ambiguous, and at worst doubtful. Perhaps we need to recall that his hermeneutical awareness was focused on the "cultured despisers" of his day, who were still influenced by deism, and on others who were captivated by Hegel's speculative themes.

Several contemporary British writers have restored the more classical perspectives. George Pattison understands creation as "an act of self-expression or self-communication" on the part of God, which provides conditions for *communion* and *relationship* with God, although, he rightly adds, we must maintain "the distinction between Creator and creature that . . . came to be a hallmark of Christian thinking."[86] Alistair McFadyen argues that "in Christian doctrine creation begins with a primal letting-be . . . [which] has to be understood within the context of . . . the divinely chosen dialogue-partnership. God's choice is *for* humanity; that is, for humanity to be what it truly is, God's dialogue-partner."[87] He

80. Schleiermacher, *The Christian Faith,* Part I, sect. 36, 142.

81. Schleiermacher, *The Christian Faith,* Part I, sect. 37, 144.

82. Schleiermacher, *The Christian Faith,* sect. 41, 152 and 153.

83. Schleiermacher, *The Christian Faith,* sect. 41, 156.

84. Schleiermacher, *The Christian Faith,* sect. 46, 170; and sect. 47, 178-84.

85. Schleiermacher, *The Christian Faith,* sect. 47, 183.

86. George Pattison, *A Short Course in Christian Doctrine* (London: SCM, 2005), 50-51 (my italics); cf. also 52-73.

87. Alistair I. McFadyen, *The Call to Personhood: A Christian Theory of the Individual in Social Relationships* (Cambridge: Cambridge University Press, 1990), 20.

adds, "When grace . . . is met with thanksgiving . . . then human life has an undistorted structure."[88]

Colin Gunton offers a more detailed analysis. He urges that the Christian doctrine of creation includes all of the following six components: (i) the agency of the whole Trinity; (ii) creation *ex nihilo;* (iii) creation as an expression of God's love; (iv) God's interactive relation with the world and with humankind; (v) a concept of divine preservation; and (vi) continuity with history and the work of redemption.[89]

Karl Barth includes all of these in his account of creation in *Church Dogmatics.* In particular his strong emphasis upon divine address through the Word of God in Christ, Scripture, and preaching leads to an account of a covenantal relation between God and human persons as the goal of creation. Barth called covenant in this sense the "internal" basis of creation.[90] However, God's covenantal purposes of grace also constituted a prior condition for the free decision of God to create the world. Hence in this complementary sense covenant also constitutes the "external" basis of creation.[91] Barth writes, "The creature is no more its own goal and purpose than it is its own ground and beginning. . . . Its destiny lies entirely in the purpose of its Creator as the One who speaks and cares for it. . . . He wills and posits the creature . . . because He has loved it from eternity."[92]

Although creation is associated with covenant in many accounts of Barth's *Dogmatics,* and although in III:1 Barth makes this both a major heading and a major theme of section 41, we should be cautious about letting this theme so dominate that it obscures other aspects of his doctrine of creation. Both Moltmann and Pannenberg make incisive critiques of this covenantal aspect. Moltmann warmly supports and endorses the *Christological and Trinitarian horizon of understanding* that Barth brings, but regrets that Barth "did not take over the Reformed *ordo decretorum,* but made 'the covenant', not 'glory', the inner ground of creation."[93]

Pannenberg expresses reserve about too strong an emphasis upon seeing God's relation to the world "from the standpoint of the beginning, or rather of the divine foreknowledge that lies behind the beginning."[94] This, he argues, over-literalizes the notion of divine foreknowledge in "an unfittingly anthropomorphic" and temporally conditioned way. Why, he asks, cannot the very act of cre-

88. McFadyen, *Personhood,* 21.

89. Colin Gunton, "The Doctrine of Creation," in Colin Gunton (ed.), *The Cambridge Companion to Christian Doctrine* (Cambridge: Cambridge University Press, 1997), 141-44; cf. also 145-57.

90. Barth, *Church Dogmatics,* III:1, sect. 41:3, 228-329.

91. Barth, *Church Dogmatics,* III:1, sect. 41:2, 94-328.

92. Barth, *Church Dogmatics,* III:1, sect. 41:2, 94 and 95.

93. Moltmann, *God in Creation,* 81.

94. Pannenberg, *Systematic Theology,* vol. 2, 143.

ation, rather than an intermediate concept of covenant, serve "directly as an expression of the love of God?"[95] God's love in sending his Son (John 3:16) is surely not different in kind from his love in creating the world.

Barth's most distinctive horizon of understanding for interpreting creation includes his Trinitarian frame, relationality, and Christ as the true man, the instantiation of true humanness. This belongs to his treatment of humankind as created in the image of God, to which we turn in Chapter 11. Creation is not divorced from the realm and action of God's grace. Because God is Creator and the one who sustains life, Barth cites the Heidelberg Catechism: "I therefore trust, not doubting but He will care for my every need of body and soul, and turn to good all the evil that he sends me in the vale of woe . . . as an Almighty God . . . and faithful Father."[96]

10.3. Creation in Recent "Hermeneutical" Theologies: Moltmann and Pannenberg

The first section of this chapter considered the role of creation for understanding the human condition especially in the biblical traditions. The second section traced the development of historical doctrine from Irenaeus to Barth. In both sections "hermeneutical" horizons were implicit and internal, in the sense of shaping Christian understanding in accordance with appropriate horizons of understanding. However, a distinctive step forward occurs with Moltmann and Pannenberg because their hermeneutical concerns are more explicit and more consciously formulated. Further, they engage *communicatively* with the impact and currency of a doctrine of creation for *Christian traditions and other traditions alike.* They facilitate the communication of a doctrine of creation in *intelligible contexts* for those who may as yet fail to understand their meaning for Christian doctrine.

Moltmann and Pannenberg are probably the most explicit among theologians of today to formulate such a hermeneutic, although some others engage with this task. We shall mention much more briefly toward the end of this section the approaches of John Macquarrie, Alister McGrath, Hans Küng, and John Polkinghorne.

Jürgen Moltmann (b. 1926) and Wolfhart Pannenberg (b. 1928) approach creation and the human condition with hermeneutical resources. Moltmann has from the beginning sought to address changing horizons of understanding in relation to changing patterns of human life. His autobiographical reflections trace such hermeneutical concerns in earlier years.[97] Nothing in his doctrine of cre-

---

95. Pannenberg, *Systematic Theology*, vol. 2, 144.
96. Barth, *Church Dogmatics*, III:1, sect. 40, 39, citing *Heidelberg Catechism*, Q. 26.
97. Jürgen Moltmann, "My Theological Career," in Jürgen Moltmann, *History and the Triune*

ation reduces the testimony of the sweep of the biblical traditions, but he also extrapolates from these traditions themes that clearly address issues of our times. Examples include the ecological crisis and the need for an organic rather than mechanistic approach to the world, as well as other features that resonate with "questions that arise" within and outside Christian traditions today.[98]

Moltmann traces a purposive continuity through creation, new creation, and eschatological consummation, through the dynamic agency of the Holy Spirit, "in a forward perspective."[99] But this is also a horizon of understanding for interpreting the human condition. Moltmann writes, "What we call the environmental crisis is not merely a crisis in the natural environment of human beings. It is nothing less than a crisis in human beings themselves."[100] His emphasis upon the creative agency of the Holy Spirit relates intimately to renewal in human life, and he expresses this with reference to the work of the Trinity. He writes, "Creation is a Trinitarian process: the Father creates through the Son in the Holy Spirit."[101] He cites the groundwork of Basil the Great in this context. He continues, "This Spirit is poured out on everything that exists. . . . The Spirit preserves it, makes it live, and renews it."[102] The Spirit is a fountain of life: a divine wellspring.[103]

Moltmann affirms without compromise the orthodox, widely supported Christian doctrine concerning *"the difference between God and the world"* (his italics).[104] God is not to be identified simply with the immanent forces of fertility. Nevertheless mechanistic, causal models of God's relation with the world are "one-sided": God not only preserves, makes, and perfects, but also indwells, sympathizes, participates in, and delights in, things of creation in a relationship that allows room for "mutuality."[105] The term *perichorēsis,* more characteristic of the Eastern or Greek Fathers than of the Westerns or Latin Fathers, becomes a significant term in Moltmann's work on the Spirit and the Trinity.

This does not become reduced to an organic immanentalism. The Priestly writings, Moltmann recalls, use the Hebrew word בָּרָא *(bārā')* with the suggestion that "God's creative activity has no analogy."[106] God's free, sovereign choice led to the

---

God: Contributions to Trinitarian Theology, trans. John Bowden (London: S.C.M., 1991), 165-82; cf. Jürgen Moltmann, *Experiences of God* (London: S.C.M., 1980), esp. 1-18; and Moltmann, *The Crucified God,* 1-6. See further Jürgen Moltmann, *God for a Secular Society: The Public Relevance of Theology,* trans. Margaret Kohl (London: S.C.M., 1999).

98. Moltmann, *God in Creation: An Ecological Doctrine of Creation,* cited above.

99. Moltmann, *Creation,* 8; cf. 7-13, 60-65, 94-103, and 276-96.

100. Moltmann, *Creation,* xi.

101. Moltmann, *Creation,* 9.

102. Moltmann, *Creation,* 10.

103. See also Moltmann, *The Spirit of Life: A Universal Affirmation,* trans. Margaret Kohl (London: S.C.M., 1992), 8-14, 39-47, 114-19, and 269-89.

104. Moltmann, *Creation,* 13.

105. Moltmann, *Creation,* 14.

106. Moltmann, *Creation,* 73.

creation of the world: "Creation cannot be conceived of as an emanation from the supreme Being. . . . God created the world . . . out of love."[107] Humankind shares a destiny to bear God's image on earth, and "as *image* men and women correspond to the Creator. . . . It is an *analogia relationis.*"[108] We develop these themes in Chapter 11.

Moltmann expounds in distinctive and moving ways the "self-limitation" or "withdrawal" that is involved in God's act of creation *ex nihilo*. These themes find a place in Barth and Brunner, but they express the point differently. Moltmann writes, "Nicholas of Cusa, J. G. Hamann, Friedrich Oetinger . . . Emil Brunner and others all saw that when God permitted creation, this was the first act in the divine self-humiliation which reached its profoundest point in the cross of Christ."[109] The only way of conceiving an *"extra Deum"* is "the assumption of a self-limitation by God himself."[110] Moltmann explains: "God does not create merely by calling something into existence. . . . *He 'creates' by letting-be, by making room, and by withdrawing himself.*"[111] This "self-restricting" love finds expression in the "self-emptying" of God in Christ in Phil. 2:5-11. This theme can be found also among a number of British writers, including Alistair McFadyen, John Polkinghorne, and William Vanstone.[112]

Initial creation, Moltmann writes, has no prior conditions: it is *creatio ex nihilo*. *Creation in history* is a "laborious" creation of salvation out of the overcoming of disaster. The *eschatological creation* of the kingdom of glory, finally, "proceeds from the vanquishing of sin and death, that is to say, the annihilating Nothingness. . . . God's adherence to his resolve to create also means a resolve to save . . . the promise of the redeeming *annihilatio nihili*.[113] Augustine and Aquinas were well aware that to speak of God's creating the world is to raise issues about evil. Moltmann relates this "nothingness" to Auschwitz and to Hiroshima as part of an ongoing hermeneutical problem. We cannot separate all that is involved in the process of creation from the exposure of God's own self in his Son "to annihilating Nothingness on the cross, in order to gather that Nothingness into his eternal being."[114]

Creation, then, as Barth rightly asserted, is part of the theology of "God who gives life to the dead." This leads on to a renewed emphasis upon the Trinitarian doctrine of creation. The power of the Spirit is at work; yet, Moltmann rightly observes, "the Spirit always points away from himself towards the Son and the Fa-

---

107. Moltmann, *Creation*, 75.

108. Moltmann, *God in Creation*, 77.

109. Moltmann, *God in Creation*, 87.

110. Moltmann, *God in Creation*, 86.

111. Moltmann, *God in Creation*, 88 (my italics).

112. John Polkinghorne (ed.), *The Work of Love: Creation as Kenosis* (London: SPCK and Grand Rapids: Eerdmans, 2001), esp. 43-65 and 90-106. This volume was dedicated to the memory of William Vanstone. Cf. also McFadyen, *Personhood*, 17-44.

113. Moltmann, *God in Creation*, 90.

114. Moltmann, *God in Creation*, 93.

ther."[115] Moltmann also explores Trinitarian creation and God's self-limitation in *The Trinity and the Kingdom of God.*[116]

Wolfhart Pannenberg formulates no fewer than four horizons of understanding within which creation becomes a lens through which to perceive the human condition. All provide hermeneutical bridges that supply pathways between modern thought and the heart of biblical and doctrinal traditions.

A first pathway traces continuities between the creative power of God and God's saving work of *new creation in human history* and in the history of the world. A second pathway or bridge takes up the theme of *preservation,* which engages with questions and anxieties about decay, finitude, and the ravages of time. Karl Barth had spoken of God's holding us from "the abyss of non-being," but Pannenberg expresses reservations about whether this resists endowing "non-being" with the status of a dualistic entity apart from God.

A third horizon of understanding takes up the notion of "order" or "orderedness." This, we noted, plays a part in Augustine and in Aquinas. When new attention is given currently to chaos, randomness, and chance in the sciences, and to anarchy and radical pluralism in socio-political contexts, the hunger for order makes itself known with fresh urgency. Only those who live in protected security can afford to glamorize disorder and chaos.

Fourth, Pannenberg traces the links between created personhood and human subjectivity, not least in exposing the shallowness of behaviorist account of the human. We may briefly expand each of these four horizons of understanding or frames of reference.

(1) Creation is a sovereign, free, divine act, in no way comparable to the inner necessity of an immanental divine emanation. Pannenberg writes, "There is to be no violation of the distinction between God and creature."[117] The Scriptures, Pannenberg writes, "speak quite freely . . . of a variety of divine acts, e.g., the many acts (Ps. 78:11, *'ᵃlîlôth'*) that God causes his people to see (cf. Ps. 77:12), the great acts of God (Ps. 106:2, *gᵉbûrôth*)."[118] The "new things" that God's creative power brings about stand in continuity with the promise of new creation and the resurrection (Isa. 43:19; 45:7; 1 Cor. 15:35-44).[119] Since God chooses to exercise his sovereign power freely in creation and in new creation, "the creation of the world is an expression of the love of God"; but this is no less so in the promise of new creation, salvation in Christ, and resurrection.[120] Pannenberg insists that creation and new creation are effects not only of the same creative,

---

115. Moltmann, *God in Creation,* 97; cf. 94-103.

116. Jürgen Moltmann, *The Trinity and the Kingdom of God: The Doctrine of God,* trans. Margaret Kohl (London: S.C.M., 1981), 105-14.

117. Pannenberg, *Systematic Theology,* vol. 2, 33.

118. Pannenberg, *Systematic Theology,* vol. 2, 8.

119. Pannenberg, *Systematic Theology,* vol. 2, 12-19.

120. Pannenberg, *Systematic Theology,* vol. 2, 20-21.

formative, power, but also of the *same divine love,* manifested in and through God the Son.

(2) Pannenberg also attributes *preservation* to the reality of divine creation, although not merely in the sense of "unchanging conservation." It is "a living occurrence, continual creation, a constantly new creative fashioning that goes beyond what was given existence originally.... Creation, preservation, and overruling thus form a unity."[121] *Preservation is a further horizon of understanding for interpreting and understanding the human.* Within biblical traditions the themes of God's covenant of promise with Noah (Gen. 9:8-17) and of God's maintaining "the circle of the earth" (Ps. 96:10) explicate this theme. The Book of Common Prayer includes the collect "O God, the Creator and Preserver of all humankind...." In Pannenberg's theology true humanness is seen especially in relationship to the constancy and promise of divine faithfulness.[122] This tradition can also be traced from Augustine through Gregory to Thomas Aquinas.

This aspect of preservation provides a horizon within which to interpret the human condition that reaches beyond Christian traditions alone. The phenomenon of change and decay remains also a *philosophical* theme. We may trace it from Plato's reflection upon contingency, through existentialist notions of dread, anxiety, and *Angst* in Kierkegaard, Heidegger, and other existentialist writers, to cosmological speculation in physics concerning the Second Law of Thermodynamics and the principle of entropy.[123]

Today it also forms a *socio-political* theme. The capacity not only of nations but also of less stable terrorist groups to blow the world apart by nuclear devices or to destroy human health by biochemical means, gives poignancy and relevance to the theme of preservation. On top of all this, in ecological terms the looming crisis of global warming places "preservation" firmly on the agenda of every thinking human person. Pannenberg paints this on the broadest canvas. He writes, "Preservation is a presupposition of [human and creaturely] activity. Creatures also need God's cooperation in order to act."[124]

Many now perceive the humanistic secular progressivism that followed nineteenth-century evolutionary theories and the optimistic American pragmatism of much of the twentieth century as both shallow and hollow. The mindsets of both pragmatism and progressivism appear to be suffering decline, in spite of misguided rearguard actions disguised as radical postmodern decon-

---

121. Pannenberg, *Systematic Theology,* vol. 2, 34; cf. 35-46.

122. Pannenberg, *Systematic Theology,* vol. 2, 40.

123. Søren Kierkegaard, *The Concept of Dread,* trans. M. Lowrie (Princeton: Princeton University Press, 1944), and *The Sickness unto Death,* trans. W. Lowrie (Princeton: Princeton University Press, 1941); Martin Heidegger, *Being and Time,* trans. J. Macquarrie and E. Robinson (Oxford: Blackwell, 1973), esp. sect. 40, 225-28. On the future of the galaxy, see A. R. Peacocke, *Creation and the World of Science* (Oxford: Clarendon, 1979), 326-32.

124. Pannenberg, *Systematic Theology,* vol. 2, 37.

structionist "advances."[125] Again, to quote Pannenberg: "In the historical think-ing of our day providence has disappeared, but there is also doubt about prog-ress."[126] What he calls "the dulling effect of what is routine" raises critical questions about both preservation and new creation.[127] A horizon of under-standing that embraces them construes "the human" in different ways from hori-zons that exclude them.

(3) Following Augustine and Thomas Aquinas, Pannenberg relates a doc-trine of creation to *order* and *orderedness*. Like Aquinas, he relates this to the vari-ety, differences, and distinctiveness of objects and events within the created or-der. "Creaturely reality . . . is a plurality of creatures."[128] Patterns of events reflect unity and coherence as well as difference and distinctiveness. Time contributes a fundamental dimension to this interplay. "The irreversibility of time" makes possible "the unique nature of objects and events, which also exhibit patterns and potential unity."[129]

Pannenberg devotes considerable discussion to creation and time. Space and time, he argues, are gifts through which the Spirit of God exhibits his creative, formative agency and power.[130] We have already noted Pannenberg's comments on the sequential ordering of the creation account in the "Priestly" document of Gen. 1:1–2:3.[131]

Some may too readily take "orderedness" for granted to perceive it as a gift from God. However, this is not the case among peoples who are faced with anar-chy, instability, the breakdown of order, or even in the natural sciences the inter-play of order and randomness or uncertainty. As horizons of understanding, the "ordered" time and place may be perceived more readily as a manifestation of the faithfulness of the Creator. Only those so dulled by formal routine that they long for nothing but the "excitement" of disruptions of order could fail to see its ne-cessity for the flourishing, even continuance, of the human condition.

The Hebrew sense of wonder at God's keeping at bay the appointed bound-aries of the sea may be about to be rediscovered in the long-term effects of global warming. In the twenty-first century our civilization can no longer take for granted the boundaries of the oceans and the ordered climate needed for human flourishing. "Order" is shown, however, not only in the appointed boundaries of the oceans (Job 38:4-17), but also in the eschatological ordering of the new cre-ation (1 Cor. 15:23; cf. 1 Cor. 15:20-28; 38-45). "Order" remains a gift from God.

---

125. Cf. Richard Rorty, *Truth and Progress: Philosophical Papers*, vol. 3 (Cambridge: Cam-bridge University Press, 1998), esp. 1-42.

126. Pannenberg, *Anthropology*, 503.

127. Pannenberg, *Systematic Theology*, vol. 2, 46.

128. Pannenberg, *Systematic Theology*, vol. 2, 61; cf. 61-76.

129. Pannenberg, *Systematic Theology*, vol. 2, 65.

130. Pannenberg, *Systematic Theology*, vol. 2, 76-84 and 84-115.

131. Pannenberg, *Systematic Theology*, vol. 2, 115-36.

Pannenberg places creation in the context of eschatology as the widest possible horizon of understanding meaning.[132]

(4) Created personhood also entails a rejection of *behaviorist* theories that human persons are no more than stimulus-response mechanisms devoid of transcendental rationality. Especially in his *Anthropology in Theological Perspective*, Pannenberg exposes the reductionist character of the behaviorism of J. B. Watson and B. F. Skinner. Today the debate may assume a more sophisticated level in terms of competing claims about the respective roles of instrumental and transcendental reason. In crude terms, if the earlier behaviorists saw humankind as akin to animals, more recent versions of behaviorism see humankind as akin to computers or to robots. Pannenberg elaborates on the sociological or social versions of recent theories, ranging from G. H. Mead to J. Habermas, Helmuth Plessner, and Arnold Gehlen.[133]

This discussion leads Pannenberg to issues concerning the image of God. Similarly I have postponed any brief consideration of reductionist views of selfhood to Chapter 11 (11.3), which concerns the image of God.

Relatively most space has been given to Moltmann and Pannenberg as exemplifying suggestive and constructive hermeneutical approaches to the present subject. But they are not alone in this endeavor. John Macquarrie, for example, also explores models of creation with an eye to their hermeneutical significance for the meaning of the human condition.[134] One of my former Ph.D. candidates, Georgina Morley, has traced this aspect of Macquarrie's theology in a constructive and critical treatment.[135] The theme of divine self-giving is prominent in this work. Alister E. McGrath expounds a hermeneutically relevant doctrine of creation in his work *A Scientific Theology*, vol. 1: *Nature*.[136]

Especially in his more general writings, Hans Küng not only expounds a succinct Christian doctrine of creation, but also asks questions that concern many ordinary people as well as nontheists about creation and humanness.[137] Küng places biblical and doctrinal themes about creation in relation to questions about cosmology. These include the "Big Bang" hypothesis, and explore Edwin P. Hubble's conclusions from the red shifts of the spectrum lines of galaxies that our universe is still expanding. Küng observes, "There must have been a begin-

132. Pannenberg, *Systematic Theology*, vol. 2, 136-74; cf. Pannenberg, "Eschatology and the Experience of Meaning," in *Basic Questions*, vol. 3, 192-210.

133. Pannenberg, *Anthropology*, 28-42, and more broadly, 43-79.

134. John Macquarrie, *Principles of Christian Theology* (London: S.C.M., 1966), 200-218.

135. Georgina Morley, *The Grace of Being: John Macquarrie's Natural Theology* (Bristol, IN: Wyndham Hall, 2001); U.K. edition, *John Macquarrie's Natural Theology: The Grace of Being* (Aldershot: Ashgate, 2003).

136. Alister E. McGrath, *A Scientific Theology*, vol. 1: *Nature* (Edinburgh and New York: T&T Clark, 2001), esp. 135-240, but also throughout.

137. For example, in Hans Küng, *Does God Exist? An Answer for Today*, trans. E. Quinn (London: Collins/Fount, 1979), esp. 627-54, and Hans Küng, *Credo: The Apostles' Creed Explained for Today*, trans. John Bowden (London: S.C.M., 1993), 15-29.

ning in which all radiation and all matter were compressed into an almost indescribable primal fireball of infinitesimal size and the utmost density and heat."[138] He expounds in further detail the emergence of protons, neutrons, electrons, and positrons, the construction of atoms of hydrogen and helium, and refinements of the theory by A. A. Penrose and R. W. Wilson in 1964, and then after the discoveries of the U.S. research satellite COBE in 1992.

Yet Küng does not depend upon such theories for the meaning or truth of biblical and Christian accounts of creation. He is emphatically *not* trying to find "a home for God" among scientific theories. He is exploring scenarios: *possible* horizons of understanding within which a Christian doctrine of creation may be intelligible as thought-experiments. He retains the Christian doctrine that "the good God is the origin of each and every one. . . . The world as a whole and in detail, including night, matter, even lowly creatures, the human body and sexuality, is fundamentally good. . . . Human beings are the goal of the process of creation. . . . They are responsible for the care of their environment."[139]

Among British thinkers, John Polkinghorne, Thomas F. Torrance, and A. R. Peacocke explore scenarios that perform parallel hermeneutical functions. Peacocke traces the transformation of the scientific worldview (discussed in Part II, above), issues concerning chance reductionism, theories of evolution, and divine and human agency.[140] John Polkinghorne differentiates between "levels of explanation," in ways not irrelevant to the major contrast in hermeneutics between *Verstehen* and *Erklärung*.[141] As we noted above, Polkinghorne distinguishes between different kinds of questions, but also, like Küng, considers scenarios that relate to the *plausibility, not demonstration,* of theistic accounts of creation within a scientific horizon of understanding. We discussed the distinction between rationalistic "certainty" and fallibilist "reasonableness" in our discussion of Imre Lakatos and Nancey Murphy above in Chapter 8 (8.4).

Polkinghorne argues, for example, that a "very special universe" is needed to meet the conditions required for our carbon-based life. Its margin of "brute possibility" is around "one in a trillion": if the universe expands too quickly, . . . it will rapidly become too dilute for anything interesting to happen in it. . . . If it expands too slowly, it will re-collapse before anything interesting happens. . . . To make carbon in a star, three helium nuclei have to be made to stick together. . . . This is tricky. . . . Also, carbon is not enough, for life one needs a lot more ele-

---

138. Küng, *Credo*, 15; cf. *Does God Exist?* 635-42.

139. Küng, *Credo*, 20; cf. *Does God Exist?* 630-31, 639-40, and 650-59.

140. Peacocke, *Creation and the World of Science*, 52-85, 86-111, 131-86, and throughout. On "man's role in creation" cf. 294-316.

141. John Polkinghorne, *The Way the World Is* (London: Triangle, 1983), 16-19; cf. also *Quarks, Chaos, and Christianity: Questions to Science and Religion* (London: Triangle, 1994); and esp. *Science and Creation: The Search for Understanding* (London: S.P.C.K., 1988), and *Belief in God in the Age of Science* (New Haven, CT: Yale University Press, 1998).

ments."[142] What nontheists may ascribe to "lucky accidents" mount up to an implausible degree on the basis of sheer chance. Polkinghorne writes, "Lucky accidents mount up. If the force of gravity were slightly stronger, all stars would be blue giants; if a little weaker, red dwarfs. There is an infinitesimal, small balance between the competing effects of explosive expansion and gravitational contraction, . . . at the very earliest epoch . . . a deviation of one part in 10 to the sixtieth."[143] Richard Swinburne mounts similar arguments to good effect.[144]

Polkinghorne, we have said, carefully distinguishes between "how" questions characteristically asked in the natural sciences and "why" questions characteristic of theology. Even so, further levels of explanation and understanding may be distinguished.[145] For example, the impact of a symphony may be presented in acoustic terms through an oscilloscope. Frequencies of the waves may measure pitch; structure and shapes of waves may appear to quantify timber or tone. However, the questions posed by an artist or professional musician about a Beethoven symphony will operate at a different level from those of an acoustic technician. Gadamer amplifies this point in his hermeneutics: art and technology operate at different levels of explanation and understanding. Even so, this does not imply total "incommensurability"; a musician may find an oscilloscope useful within firm limits, even if music cannot be "reduced" to visual patterns of waveforms on a computer monitor.

In *The Work of Love: Creation as Kenosis,* to which we have already referred, several writers trace the theme of divine *kenosis* or self-giving as a quality that runs through the very grain of creation. Thus Holmes Rolston qualifies talk about "selfish genes" in terms of his preferred description, "cruciform nature."[146] Biological processes "give birth" through "labor," "regenerating always in travail. Something is always dying, and something is always living on. 'The whole creation has been groaning in travail together until now' (Rom. 8:22). . . . There is a kind of death that bears much fruit, like a seed fallen into the earth . . ." (John 12:26).[147] Arthur Peacocke writes that in the created order of bodily life "the stakes for joy and pain are, as it were, continually being raised," and this can become "a transformative principle."[148]

A number of key issues have yet to be addressed, but we have postponed them because we have not yet considered the questions raised by biblical and doctrinal language about humankind as created in the image of God. To this we now turn in a new chapter.

142. Polkinghorne, *Quarks,* 27 and 29.
143. Polkinghorne, *Science and Creation,* 22.
144. Richard Swinburne, *The Existence of God* (Oxford: Oxford University Press, 1979), 36.
145. Polkinghorne offers a simple example in *The Way the World Is,* 16-19.
146. Holmes Rolston, "Kenosis and Nature," in Polkinghorne (ed.), *The Work of Love,* 43-65.
147. Rolston, "Kenosis and Nature," in *The Work of Love,* 58.
148. Arthur Peacocke, "The Cost of New Life," in *The Work of Love,* 31; cf. 21-42.

CHAPTER 11

Being Human: Image of God, Relationality with Others, and Bodily and Temporal Life

11.1. Image of God as a Horizon of Understanding for Interpreting the Human Condition: Wisdom and Responsibility for the World

Just as a doctrine of creation derives from more than Gen. 1:1–2:35, an understanding of the image of God derives from more than Gen. 1:26-27 alone. On the other hand the Genesis account deserves to be given its appropriate weight: "God said, 'Let us make humankind in our image, according to our likeness (Hebrew בצלמנו כדמותנו, *b^{e}tsalmēnû kidmûtēnû*); and let them have dominion over the fish of the sea, and over the birds of the air, and over the cattle, and over all the wild animals of the earth, and over every creeping thing that creeps upon the earth! So God created humankind in his image; in the image of God (בצלם אלהים, *b^{e}tselem ^{e}lōhîm*) he created them; male and female he created them" (Gen. 1:26-27, NRSV). Gen. 5:1 and Gen. 9:6 repeat the application of "the likeness of God" to the descendants of Adam.

Clearly Ps. 8:4-6 reflects a similar tradition: "You have made them a little lower than God, and crowned them with glory and honor. You have given them dominion over the works of your hands, you have put all things under their feet: all sheep and oxen . . . the beasts of the field, the birds of the air, and the fish of the sea." Psalm 8 confirms the different status, or at least role, of humankind and the animal kingdom, but does not explicitly use the terms *tselem*, or *dĕmûth*. On the other hand, Raymond Van Leeuwen, among others, argues that it presupposes this.[1]

The New Testament writings speak of humankind as being God's image

---

1. Raymond C. Van Leeuwen, "Form, Image," *Dictionary of Old Testament Theology and Exegesis*, vol. 4, 645.

(εἰκών, *eikōn,* 1 Cor. 11:7, although here of ἀνήρ, *anēr, man*) and God's likeness (ὁμοίωσις, *homoiōsis,* Jas. 3:9). More characteristically Paul and the Epistle to the Hebrews speak of Christ as the image of God (εἰκὼν τοῦ θεοῦ, *eikōn tou Theou,* 2 Cor. 4:4; Col. 1:15; cf. Heb. 1:3). Heb. 2:6-9 takes up the theology of Ps. 8:4-6, but argues that whereas humankind fell short of its destiny to rule over the earth ("we do not yet see everything in subjection to them"), nevertheless "we do see Jesus . . . now crowned with glory and honor," that is, fulfilling in his person the destiny of the truly human. Other New Testament passages confirm this theme by suggesting that only derivatively through Christ can humankind rediscover a temporarily lost destiny by becoming "conformed to the image of [God's] Son" (συμμόρφους τῆς εἰκόνος τοῦ υἱοῦ αὐτοῦ, *summorphous tēs eikonos tou huiou autou,* Rom. 8:29; similarly 1 Cor. 15:49, "we shall carry the image of the man from heaven"; cf. 2 Cor. 3:10; Eph. 4:22-24; Phil. 3:21; Col. 3:10).

H. Gunkel has complained that the *imago Dei* plays a far greater part in Christian doctrine and systematic theology than the passages of the Old Testament warrant.[2] Gerhard von Rad, however, offers a convincing *reason* why allusions in the Old Testament remain infrequent. He writes, "The central point in OT anthropology is that man is dust and ashes before God, and that he cannot stand before His Holiness."[3] Hence "man's divine likeness" stands on the margins, but remains nevertheless "highly significant": humankind "is brought into a direct relationship with God."[4] The difficulty is a different one: because of the paucity of references "there is no other evidence in the OT as to the proper interpretation of the divine likeness."[5]

It is also the case that Irenaeus, Tertullian, and Origen, among others, nurture a tradition that draws a distinction between "image" and "likeness," whereas modern exegetes generally agree, largely on the basis of Hebrew parallelism, that the two terms in these contexts are virtually synonymous.[6] Bruce Vawter points out that the semantic range of דמות (*dᵉmûth, likeness*) is very wide, varying from "nothing more significant than a vague similitude" to "a model, a blueprint, an exact copy, as in 2 Kings 16:10." צלם (*tselem* or *ṣelem, image*) often refers to a forbidden image, or an idol, and frequently denotes a scriptural statue designed to represent that which it depicts.[7]

Tselem (or *ṣelem*) *image,* then, has close connections with the *prohibition*

---

2. Hermann Gunkel, *Genesis* (Göttingen: Vandenhoeck & Ruprecht, 1910), 99-101.

3. Gerhard von Rad, "Divine Likeness in the OT," in Gerhard Kittel (ed.), *Theological Dictionary of the New Testament (TDNT),* trans. G. W. Bromiley, 10 vols. (Grand Rapids: Eerdmans, 1964-76), vol. 2, 390.

4. Gerhard von Rad, *TDNT,* vol. 2, 390.

5. Gerhard von Rad, *TDNT,* vol. 2, 390.

6. Irenaeus, *Against Heresies* V:6:1 and V:16:2-3; cf. IV:Preface, 4 and IV:64:1; Tertullian, *On Baptism* 5; Origen, *De Principiis* III:4:1.

7. Bruce Vawter, *On Genesis: A New Reading* (Garden City, NY: Doubleday, 1977), 55.

against idols (in Num. 33:52; 2 Kings 11:18; 2 Chron. 23:17; Ezek. 7:20; Dan. 3:1-15 often also carved or hewn image, פֶּסֶל, or *pesel*, Exod. 20:4; Lev. 26:1; Deut. 4:16; 5:8). But *d^emûth, likeness,* is also used in a parallel way: "To whom, then, will you liken God? With what equal (*d^emûth*) can you confront him?" (Isa. 40:18). David Clines suggests partly on this basis that humankind was not created *"in"* God's image, but *as* God's image. Humankind is to be God's representation on earth, to show in an embodied mode "God's lordship over the lower orders of creation."[8]

In recent systematic theology Moltmann offers a parallel understanding. He writes, "Belief in the destiny of man to be made in the image of God is protected by the Old Testament's prohibition of images. Man is to make himself no image or likeness of God . . . (Exod. 20:4) because he himself and only he is intended to represent the image and likeness of God upon the earth."[9]

Two other preliminary points arise from Old Testament exegesis. First, *man and woman together* bear the image and likeness of God. Barth writes, "In the duality of man and woman . . . [humankind] is a copy and imitation of God . . . to reflect God's image . . . in this particular duality . . . as man and woman."[10] Barth acknowledges that Dietrich Bonhoeffer's *Creation and Fall* (German, 1933) provided an impetus to explore this further.[11] Phyllis Trible has also placed it on a firmer exegetical basis, acknowledging Barth in a brief footnote.[12] It is arguable, however, that this insight goes back at least to Gregory of Nazianzus. He applies the argument that man and woman together reflect God as his image in order to draw the inference that God is beyond sexual categorization as male or female.[13]

The second preliminary observation is that "images," for example of a king or a god, often served in the ancient Near East to denote the sovereignty of a king or god over a particular area.[14] In these terms notably Augustine, and especially Aquinas, speak of the image of God as denoting humankind's "superiority to other animals. . . . This superiority humankind owes to reason and intellect (*ad rationem et intellectum*)," although Aquinas also concedes that "there are as many sorts of resemblance or ways of sharing a form."[15]

8. David J. A. Clines, "The Image of God in Man," *Tyndale Bulletin* 19 (1968) 101, from 53-103.

9. Jürgen Moltmann, *Man: Christian Anthropology in the Conflicts of the Present,* trans. John Sturdy (London: S.P.C.K., 1974), 109. Karl Barth implies this idea, but it is overshadowed by his emphasis on humankind as "partners," *Church Dogmatics,* III:1, sect. 41:2, 183-91.

10. Barth, *Church Dogmatics,* III:1, sect. 41:2, 186.

11. Bonhoeffer, *Creation and Fall/Temptation* (cited above), 40-44 and 63-69.

12. Phyllis Trible, *God and the Rhetoric of Sexuality* (Philadelphia: Fortress, 1978), 12-30. Barth is acknowledged briefly in n. 74. Cf. Barth, *Church Dogmatics,* III:1, sect. 41, 2, 194 on Bonhoeffer.

13. Gregory of Nazianzus, *On the Making of Man,* 16:7-9: the bodily, but not the Divine, is "divided into male and female" (16:9). The "image" is seen also "in Christ Jesus," where "there is neither male nor female" (16:2). On Bonhoeffer's view see also Ann L. Nickson, *Bonhoeffer on Freedom* (Aldershot: Ashgate, 2002), 48-84.

14. Wolff, *Anthropology of the Old Testament,* 160-61.

15. Thomas Aquinas, *Summa Theologiae,* Ia, Q. 3, art. 1 and Q. 4, art. 3 (Blackfriars edn., vol.

Within the history of Christian doctrine three major emphases retain some kind of exegetical warrant, each of which carries with it intelligible horizons of understanding in relation to questions of today.

First, many have perceived *human reason or the capacity for cognitive judgment* as a characteristic that differentiates human persons from the animal kingdom, and a feature of being created in God's image. But this can hardly be identified with what Heidegger terms "calculative" reason, and Habermas "instrumental" reason. Humankind in social and interpersonal terms operates with a gift of *phronēsis* rather than *technē,* which includes the life-related *wisdom* of the Old Testament wisdom literature rather than simply the capacity to gather information, which may be shared in common perhaps with some animals and some forms of electronic devices. In terms of hermeneutical horizons of understanding, this raises questions about whether human selfhood involves more than Hume's notion of "reason as the slave of the passions," and includes cognition, interpersonal understanding, and continuities of judgment and understanding.

Older nineteenth-century biblical scholarship tended to interpret the role of νοῦς (Greek *nous, mind)* in Paul and in other writers in quasi-Platonic idealist terms that were foreign to Paul. H. J. Holtzmann and Otto Pfleiderer interpreted νοῦς *(nous)* as a point-of-contact *(Anknüpfungspunkt)* with the Spirit of God.[16] R. Reitzenstein overpainted the notion of spirit-mind in the idealist sense to such a degree as to invite legitimate criticism that he reads pantheism into Paul. Not surprisingly this provoked a overreaction to the effect that Paul placed little value on human reason.

The balance has been largely restored by G. Bornkamm, Robert Jewett, Stanley Stowers, and James Dunn. Bornkamm points out that reason does not always denote "the wisdom of the world." Paul's preaching called for conversion away from idols "to the true, reasoned knowledge of God."[17] He continues, "Paul speaks of reason . . . in order to convict the hearer of his guilt before God."[18] "Paul allots to reason and to the rationality of man an exceedingly important role for the self-understanding of the Christian and for all areas of life."[19] The style of the Pauline sermon is not simply that of a "revelation-speech," as if to declare an oracle without argument or appeal to rational judgment.[20] Pannenberg

---

2, 23 and 57). Cf. Augustine, *On the Trinity,* 14:6; and Aquinas, *Summa,* Ia, Q. 13, art. 5 and Q. 45, arts. 6-7 (Blackfriars edn., vol. 3, 57-59 and vol. 8, 51-59).

16. Otto Pfleiderer, *Paulinism: A Contribution to the History of Primitive Christian Theology,* trans. E. Peters, 2 vols. (London: Williams & Norgate, 1877), vol. 1, 47-67.

17. Günther Bornkamm, "Faith and Reason in Paul," in G. Bornkamm, *Early Christian Experience,* trans. Paul Hammer (London: S.C.M., 1969), 31; cf. 29-46.

18. Bornkamm, *Early Christian Experience,* 35.

19. Bornkamm, *Early Christian Experience,* 35.

20. Bornkamm, *Early Christian Experience,* 36.

makes a similar point: "In trusting in the Spirit, Paul in no way spared himself thinking and arguing."[21]

Robert Jewett provides a detailed account of the history of research into Paul's anthropological terms, and offers exegetical conclusions in the light of their conflict settings within Paul's letter. He offers a hermeneutically sensitive survey from F. C. Baur through to J. A. T. Robinson and David Stacey.[22] He concludes that Paul frequently advocates the use of the mind (νοῦς, *nous*) and cognitive judgment over against the claims of hyper-"spiritual" enthusiasts in Galatians and 1 and 2 Thessalonians. In Gal. 3:1 Paul addresses his readers as "foolish" (ἀνόητοι, *anoētoi*, not using one's mind) and "bewitched" (ἐβάσκανεν, *ebaskanen*, to exert an evil influence through the [evil] eye, bewitch).[23] To begin with the principle of grace and then to revert to the law is irrational. In 2 Thess. 2:2 the enthusiasts' claim that the Parousia has already occurred is equally irrational: they have been shaken "out of their right mind" (ἀπὸ τοῦ νοός, *apo tou nöos*). In 1 Thess. 5:12, 14 and 2 Thess. 3:15 Paul seeks to put them in the right mind (νουθετεῖν, *nouthetein*).[24] In 1 Cor. 14:5, 13, 15, 19, and 24, Paul places a very high value on *the use of the mind* in praising God in contrast to preconscious glossolalia.[25]

Stanley Stowers argues convincingly that Paul attacks not the use of reason or wisdom, but "worldly" reason and "worldly" wisdom.[26] Thus, for example, "Far from opposing faith . . . to reason, 1 Cor. 1:18–4:21 criticizes a lack of openness to that which is new and different, as well as epistemic vices such as conceit."[27] James Dunn rightly distances Paul from Greek notions of reason as "of a piece with the divine," but nevertheless urges, "The importance of 'mind' for Paul is easily documented" (Rom. 7:23, 25; 12:2; 14:5; 1 Cor. 14:14-15; Gal. 3:1-3).[28]

This is not the place to undertake a full-scale examination of reason in biblical traditions and in the history of Christian doctrine. We may note in passing, however, Pannenberg's convincing observations concerning Luther's critique of human reason. He writes, "The reason *(ratio)* of which Luther spoke was the

---

21. Pannenberg, *Basic Questions*, vol. 2, 35.

22. Robert Jewett, *Paul's Anthropological Terms: A Study of Their Use in Conflict Settings*, Arbeiten zur Geschichte des antiken Judentums und des Urchristentums 10 (Leiden: Brill, 1971), 358-90.

23. Jewett, *Anthropological Terms*, 373-74; cf. *BDAG* (3d edn.), 171.

24. Jewett, *Anthropological Terms*, 367-73.

25. See Thiselton, *First Epistle*, 1081-1130; and Gerd Theissen, *Psychological Aspects of Pauline Theology*, trans. J. P. Galvin (Edinburgh: T&T Clark, 1987), esp. 267-342.

26. Stanley K. Stowers, "Paul on the Use and Abuse of Reason," in D. L. Balch, E. Ferguson, and Wayne Meeks (eds.), *Greeks, Romans, and Christians: Essays in Honor of J. Malherbe* (Minneapolis: Augsburg, 1990), 253-86.

27. Stowers, "Reason," 261.

28. James D. G. Dunn, *The Theology of Paul the Apostle* (Edinburgh: T&T Clark, 1998), 74; cf. 73-75.

Aristotelian-Thomistic understanding of reason" according to which "reason and intellect are related to each other as movement and rest." Luther's sharp judgments upon reason are to be understood in the light of the technical status of reason found in Aristotle and Aquinas: "The contents of the Christian faith could not be derived from these *a priori* principles."[29]

If the capacity to deploy reason in the sense of cognitive judgment and wisdom is one implicate (among others) of bearing the image of God as creaturely human beings, a hermeneutical horizon of understanding for interpreting humanness comes into focus. Human rationality does not relate to "cleverness" in deploying information, but to a responsible reasonableness that transcends the merely instrumental reason postulated by David Hume *and today by a radically postmodern contextual relativism*. Theories that make "rationality" depend wholly on gender, class, education, and social situation devalue the reasonableness that belongs to the very givenness of *being human*. Even Wittgenstein, for all his valid recognition of plurality in life, believed that *being human* provided certain shared foundations for judgment that transcend a radical contextual relativism.[30] We shall explore below further "reductionist" views of human selfhood.

A second theme also emerges. Even on the basis of exegesis and context in Gen. 1:26-27 and Ps. 8:4-6 alone, language about the image of God clearly carries with it notions of *dominion over, or stewardship of, the animal kingdom and the resources of the earth,* although Westermann and others insist that this aspect is a *consequence* of the image of God.[31] The double-edged impact of the exponential progress of technology in our times has rendered this an immediate and highly sensitive hermeneutical issue. On one side, technology appears to many to promise a mastery of nature that will provide infinite resources of energy, massive prolongation of human life, and protection against destructive forces in the face of which humankind was powerless in bygone eras. On the other side, technology appears to be on the verge of overreaching its earlier promise, despoiling the resources of earth in ruthless sacrifices of the future in the name of demands for the present. It has, as it were, placed weapons of potential self-destruction in the hands of irresponsible agents.

Reinhold Niebuhr perceived this latter aspect as long ago as in 1941, four

---

29. Pannenberg, "Faith and Reason," in *Basic Questions,* vol. 2, 55-56; cf. 46-64.

30. For example, "Why can a dog feel fear but not remorse? . . . Only someone who can reflect on the past can repent" (Wittgenstein, *Zettel,* sects. 518-19). Wittgenstein writes, "The common behaviour of mankind is the system of reference by which we interpret an unknown language" (Wittgenstein, *Philosophical Investigations,* sect. 206). "What determines our judgements . . . is the whole hurly-burly of human actions" (*Zettel,* sect. 567). Only someone from another planet could fail to understand a person's shaking up and down and making "bleating noises" as *human* laughter.

31. Claus Westermann, *Genesis 1–11: A Commentary,* trans. J. C. Scullion (London: S.P.C.K., 1984), 154-55.

years before the release of atomic power for human destruction. He writes, "Sometimes this lust for power expresses itself in terms of man's conquest of nature, in which the legitimate freedom and mastery of man in the world of nature are corrupted into a mere exploitation of nature. Man's sense of dependence upon nature and his reverent gratitude toward the miracle of nature's perennial abundance are destroyed by his arrogant sense of independence and his greedy effort to overcome the insecurity of nature's rhythms and claims by garnering her stores with excessive zeal and beyond natural requirements. . . . Greed as a form of the will-to-power has been a particularly flagrant sin in the modern era. . . . This culture is constantly tempted to regard physical comfort and security as life's final good."[32] One of my jointly supervised Nottingham Ph.D. graduates, Mark Lovatt, has produced a sympathetic but critical study of this subject.[33]

Clearly this aspect begins to touch on the question of the sense in which "the fall" of humankind has distorted or damaged the original or purposed creation of human beings in the image of God. We consider this aspect in Chapters 12 and especially 13. In the history of Christian doctrine the gift of "dominion" is both celebrated with gratitude and regarded as a heavy responsibility that humankind has too readily often abused. The affirmation of humankind's responsibility for the earth and the animal kingdom occurs not only in Gen. 1:26-27 and Ps. 8:4-6, but also in Gen. 9:1-3, where after the flood a new beginning is made in which "the fear and dread of you shall rest on every animal of the earth . . . on every bird . . . on all the fish of the sea" (9.2).

Among the Church Fathers Lactantius stands out as associating the image of God (in his terminology *Dei simulacrum*) as implying respect for life, including that of fellow human beings, "united by the bond of being human." On the basis of bearing the divine image humankind "should protect, love and cherish" fellow humans.[34] Augustine is more typical of the Patristic era in reflecting that to be created in the image of God is to be "endowed with reason and intelligence, so that [humankind] might excel all the creatures of the earth, air, and sea, which were not so gifted."[35] The image of God is "the mind and reason."[36]

The exercise of responsibility for the world prior to the rise of industrialization, technology, and the electronic era seemed in past times to be synonymous with its rational ordering and derivative from divine power. Aquinas's specific consideration of "dominion over the fish of the sea" concludes with an allusion to "God's image because of [humankind's] intellect and reason (*intellectum et*

---

32. Reinhold Niebuhr, *The Nature and Destiny of Man: A Christian Interpretation*, 2 vols. (London: Nisbet, 1941), vol. 1, 203.

33. Mark F. Lovatt, *Confronting the Will-to-Power: A Reconsideration of the Theology of Reinhold Niebuhr* (Carlisle, U.K.: Paternoster, 2001), esp. 89-112 and 151-200.

34. Lactantius, *The Divine Institutes*, VI:1:1; cf. chs. 10–11.

35. Augustine, *The City of God*, XII:23:1.

36. Augustine, *Exposition of the Psalms*, Ps. 43:6.

rationem)."[37] In the second century B.C. creation in the image of God is associated with being "endowed with strength like [God's] own" to exercise "dominion over beasts and birds" (Sir. [Ecclus.] 17:3; cf. 17:1-13). Jerome Murphy-O'Connor comments, "The parallelism of v. 3 shows that here image is conceived in terms of power . . . a capacity for action. . . . This power is the basis of humanity's authority over the rest of creation (v. 2)."[38]

In terms of *a horizon of understanding for today,* then, on one side stands *God's commission to exercise power* for the orderly flourishing of the world; on the other side stands the seduction of transposing *power for* the world's good into raw *power over* the world for self-aggrandizement and the deification of the present over the future. Eberhard Jüngel expresses this issue incisively. He writes, "Human beings must continue to rule if the world is not to be destroyed. . . . It will be destroyed just as quickly if we cease to rule as if we rule violently in reckless self-centredness. What we need is a form of control which is capable of controlling itself."[39] To express the same point in different terms, humankind cannot responsibly opt out of its commission to be faithful stewards of the earth and of its animate and inanimate resources, but *stewardship* must not degenerate into *exploitation.*

Pannenberg presses these issues even further by exploring the nature and limits of human "sharing in the creative force that comes from God."[40] He concedes that this gift can be used badly and irresponsibly, and even that "creative participation in God's creative working does not of itself mean fellowship with God and his will."[41] Gen. 1:26-28, he urges, suggests taking responsibility for such creative participation, with a degree of independence or independent judgment. It "does not have in view a dominion of force but . . . includes caring for the continued existence (e.g.) of animals . . . (Gen. 6:19-20)."[42] To be "God's stewards" does not give *carte blanche* for "unrestricted exploitation of nature."

Medical technology, however, has pressed to the limit the issue of "creative participation in God's creative working." One urgent example arises in the field of human fertilization and embryology. In what circumstances, if any, can humankind share in co-creating life through *in vitro* fertilization, the use of stem cells, and the application of a daily-growing technological advance in embryology? Some Christian writers appeal to the legitimacy of "co-creation," while others perceive such as notion as human *hubris* in trespassing on ground reserved

---

37. Aquinas, *Summa Theologiae,* Ia, Q. 3, art. 1 (Blackfriars edn., vol. 2, 23).

38. Jerome Murphy-O'Connor, *Becoming Human Together: The Pastoral Anthropology of St. Paul* (Wilmington, DE: Glazier, 1982), 50.

39. Eberhard Jüngel, "Jüngel," in Jürgen Moltmann (ed.), *How I Have Changed My Mind: Reflections on Thirty Years of Theology,* trans. John Bowden (London: S.C.M., 1997), 11.

40. Pannenberg, *Systematic Theology,* vol. 2, 131.

41. Pannenberg, *Systematic Theology,* vol. 2, 131.

42. Pannenberg, *Systematic Theology,* vol. 2, 132.

for God alone. What are the boundaries and responsibilities of a commission to rule on behalf of God?

Even the socio-political sphere raises questions akin to this. After centuries of traditions in which kings and other leaders were perceived to exercise power by divine commission, some writers even reject the very notion of "hierarchy" in church and state. Which is the more faithful interpretation of the principle of "ordering" the world? Do Augustine, Aquinas, and Luther represent an ongoing core of Christian traditions, or did the "radical" left-wing Reformers anticipate egalitarian insights of the twenty-first century that call for a reinterpretation of this tradition?[43] Whether the area is that of political ethics or of medical ethics, the *hermeneutical horizons of "image of God" engage critically with horizons of today.*

11.2. Image of God: The Capacity for Relationship with God and with Fellow Humans as "Other"

We reach a third theme under "image of God." Most writers on *imago Dei* today tend to emphasize *relationality* or *the capacity to relate to others* as an even more fundamental feature of this theme than *reasonableness or rationality* and *dominion or responsible stewardship.* There remain, of course, other candidates. The role of *freedom,* for example, finds a place in the history of Christian doctrines of "image of God." However, this is presupposed, in effect, among the three major features that we have identified for discussion, and the complexities of discussions about freedom would unnecessarily detain and distract us from our main point.

Karl Barth characteristically expounds this theme of relationality in a manner that has shaped and influenced other theologies in the late twentieth century. We noted this when we discussed "relationality" as a horizon of understanding for interpreting the human in Chapter 10. But it is worth exploring the point further. Barth writes, "[God] willed the existence of a being which in all its non-deity and therefore its differentiation can be a real partner . . . capable of action and responsibility in relation to Him."[44] A fundamental "God-likeness" emerges "in the true confrontation and reciprocity which are actualized in the reality of an 'I' and a 'Thou.'"[45] In God's own being, Barth writes, there is a counterpart: "a

43. What are we to make, for example, of Otto Weber's comment, citing W. Zimmerli, "[Humankind's] being in the image of God issues in the 'call to feudal lordship'" (Otto Weber, *Foundations of Dogmatics,* vol. 1, 560)? A radically egalitarian approach might be found in Itumeleng J. Mosala, *Biblical Hermeneutics and Black Theology in South Africa* (Grand Rapids: Eerdmans, 1989).

44. Barth, *Church Dogmatics,* III:1, sect. 41:2, 184-85.

45. Barth, *Church Dogmatics,* III:1, sect. 41:2, 184.

genuine but harmonious self-encounter and self-discovery; a free co-existence and co-operation; an open confrontation and reciprocity."[46] The analogy between God and humankind, he continues, is simply the existence of the I and the Thou in confrontation. "In this way he [God] wills and creates man as a partner who is capable of entering into a covenant-relationship with himself."[47]

Against this background Barth expounds his suggestive accounts of the relation between male and female. Relationality finds special expression "in the differentiation and relationship of man and woman, the relation of sex . . . free to reflect God's image. . . . This is the particular dignity ascribed to the sex relationship . . . the great paradigm of everything that is to take place between him [humankind] and God, and also . . . between him and his fellows."[48]

Further, in place of the *analogia entis* of Thomas Aquinas (and of Emil Brunner), Barth poses a more dynamic *analogia relationis*. This issue plays a part in Barth's approach, but George Hunsinger warns us not to pin too much upon a single specific doctrine of analogy as characterizing Barth throughout.[49] In Barth's view divine creation and creation in the image of God provide *conditions for the possibility* of intercourse between God and humankind.[50] *But divine grace* and human response operate to *actualize* this in dynamic, eventful communication.[51]

On the other hand, Emil Brunner writes, "It is most ill advised, and inevitably leads to serious inconsistencies, to take the view that the idea of the *analogia entis* — common to the whole Christian tradition — must be rejected as specifically Catholic, Neo-Platonist, and therefore a 'foreign body' in Christian theology. Whatever the Creator makes bears the imprint of His Creator-Spirit in itself."[52] Brunner also stresses the importance of relationality as central to the meaning of the image of God: "As Holy Love . . . He shows me my relation to Himself. . . . Love can only impart itself where it is received in love. . . . Only an 'I' can answer a 'Thou' . . . can freely answer God."[53]

46. Barth, *Church Dogmatics*, III:1, sect. 41:2, 185.

47. Barth, *Church Dogmatics*, III:1, sect. 41:2, 185.

48. Barth, *Church Dogmatics*, III:1, sect. 41:2, 186.

49. George Hunsinger, *How to Read Karl Barth: The Shape of His Theology* (New York and Oxford: Oxford University Press, 1991) 6 and 7-20. See further Otto Weber, *Karl Barth's Church Dogmatics: An Introductory Report on Volumes I:1 to III:4*, trans. A. C. Cochrane (London: Lutterworth, 1953), 124-27; and Barth's further discussion in *Church Dogmatics* III:3, sect. 48, 49-57, and in Emil Brunner and Karl Barth, *Natural Theology*, trans. P. Fraenkel (London: Centenary, 1946); cf. Clifford Green, *Karl Barth* (Minneapolis: Fortress, 1991), 26-33.

50. Cf. W. A. Whitehouse, "Karl Barth on 'The Work of Creation,'" in Nigel Biggar (ed.), *Reckoning with Barth* (London and Oxford: Mowbray, 1988), 49; cf. 43-57.

51. See also Karl Barth, *Anselm: Fides Quaerens Intellectum*, trans. I. W. Robertson (London: SCM, 1960), 26-72.

52. Emil Brunner, *The Christian Doctrine of Creation and Redemption: Dogmatics II*, trans. Olive Wyon (London: Lutterworth, 1952), 22.

53. Brunner, *Doctrine of Creation*, 55-56; cf. 55-61 on the image of God.

An important point of substance lies behind each side in this debate, and this specific debate should not distract from the issues. Barth has laid the foundations in *Dogmatics* III:1, sect. 41, for his well-known exposition of human relationality in III:4, in which he addresses relations between man and woman, parents and children, and near and distant neighbors, as well as the need for a wider respect for life. Humankind, Barth argues, cannot "be man without woman or woman apart from man. . . . No other distinction between man and man goes so deep as that in which the human male and the human female are so utterly different from each other."[54] It does not distract from the principle of mutuality and reciprocity in difference *as a principle* simply because Barth expresses this as an abstract generalization or as if he were unaware that "masculinity" and "femininity" vary on a spectrum of difference in which each gender may exhibit qualities and dispositions characteristic in general terms of the other. He is addressing the structure of relations, not pronouncing about individual persons. Indeed, he gives attention to traditions on this subject deriving from Schleiermacher and from Roman Catholic doctrine.[55] In male-female relationship each gender discovers limitation, constraint, and their own creatureliness as well as freedom, glory, and mystery. The relation "sanctifies man by including his sexuality within his humanity, and challenging him even in his bodily nature . . . to be true man: to be a body, but not only a body."[56]

Accepting constraints relates closely to Barth's insistence that only Jesus Christ is "true man," to which we turn in 11.3. On the other hand, some of Barth's claims may remain controversial today, in the context of same-sex relations and gender-change. Barth writes, "God requires that [humankind] should be genuinely and fully, male or female, that he should acknowledge his sex instead of trying in some ways to deny it."[57] Once again, however, we should be cautious in both directions about applying this to specific instances. In the area of transgender surgery, for example, some claim that surgery restores a true sexuality that has been misidentified; but again this probably applies only to some, not to all, transgender instances. We shall return to issues of sexuality in 11.4.

Does Barth go further than this? Is he too specific? On one side he argues that man has no privilege or advantage over woman, and that woman "does not come short of man in any way."[58] He also makes a key concession to the effect that different ages and cultures have held different notions of what characterizes the qualities of *man* and *woman* respectively.[59] On the other hand, he emphatically asserts that this does not mean that the distinction between masculine be-

54. Barth, *Church Dogmatics*, III:4, sect. 54, 118.
55. Barth, *Church Dogmatics*, III:4, sect. 54, 121-29.
56. Barth, *Church Dogmatics*, III:4, sect. 54, 132.
57. Barth, *Church Dogmatics*, III:4, sect. 54, 149.
58. Barth, *Church Dogmatics*, III:4, sect. 54, 170-71.
59. Barth, *Church Dogmatics*, III:4, sect. 54, 154.

ing and feminine being must not be blurred on either side."[60] Indeed, he writes, "The dispensation and the conjunction of man and woman, of their sexual independence and sexual interrelationship is controlled by a definite order [and] must not be confused and interchanged."[61] Woman, in Barth's view, "has thus to follow the initiative which he [man] must take."[62] I have tried to steer a careful line on these sensitive issues in my larger commentary on 1 Cor. 11:2-16.[63]

We shall return to a more critical discussion in 11.4 when we consider human sexuality under "embodiment" and bodily life. The point here is to explore "relationality," or the capacity for relationship as part of the image of God in terms of encounter with "otherness," acceptance of constraint, and a reciprocal and mutual engagement of adjustment and learning. This is very different from a bland experience of a "relation" with a replicated or projected self. "Sameness" would not be an experience of *relationship*, but a narcistic preoccupation with the self.

Martin Buber's *I and Thou* provides a classic understanding of relationality. He coins "I-Thou" and "I-it" not only as relations but as selves or entities. The human "I," he writes, "is different" in the immediate context of an "I-Thou" relation from what the self would remain or become as a less personal "I" in the context of "the basic word *I-It*." . . . "There is no 'I' as such, but only the I of the basic word *I-You* and the I of the basic word I-It. When a man says 'I', he means one or the other."[64] Buber continues further, "Relation is reciprocity. My 'You' acts on me as I act on it."[65] "The language of objects captures only one corner of actual life. . . . In the beginning is the relation."[66] The human self, in other words, is transformed into *a different kind of self* when it engages with "the other" as "You," from the self who merely reflects on others at a distance as "objects" in the world.

Subject-to-subject relations nurture reciprocity, dialogue, mutuality, and respect for the "other." A nonrelational "I," Buber suggests, is not fully "human." Most of all, God is "the eternal Thou": he is always Subject who addresses us, never a mere object of human reflection.[67] There are resonances here with other Jewish philosophical thinkers, including Franz Rosenzweig and Emmanuel Levinas.

60. Barth, *Church Dogmatics*, III:4, sect. 54, 154.

61. Barth, *Church Dogmatics*, III:4, sect. 54, 168.

62. Barth, *Church Dogmatics*, III:4, sect. 54, 171.

63. Thiselton, *First Epistle*, 800-848.

64. Martin Buber, *I and Thou*, new trans. by Walter Kaufman (New York: Scribner, 1970), 53 and 54.

65. Buber, *I and Thou*, 67.

66. Buber, *I and Thou*, 69.

67. See further Martin Buber, *Between Man and Man*, trans. R. Gregor Smith (London: Collins, 1961); and Steven Kepnes, *The Text as Thou: Martin Buber's Dialogical Hermeneutics and Narrative Theology* (Bloomington, IN: Indiana University Press, 1993).

By the late twentieth century almost every major writer on "image of God" had come to address the issue of "relationality" as a key feature under this heading. Migliore writes, "*Being created in the image of God means that humans find their true identity in coexistence with each other and with all other creatures*" (his italics).[68] Human existence is "not individualistic but communal." Citing Buber, Migliore adds, "We live in dialogue."[69] He approves of Barth's emphasis on relationality, but expresses reservations about Barth's comments on male initiative and leadership, citing the contrary views of Paul Jewett and of the feminist writers Rosemary Radford Ruether and Letty Russell.[70]

Stanley Grenz has written recently also to extend "Trinitarian theology to anthropology," and to apply a doctrine of the "social" Trinity to human relationality.[71] The concept of human selfhood as subject-in-relation-to-subject emerged, he argues, in such writers as Martin Buber, Michael Polanyi, and John Macmurray, and deserves further exploration. God the Trinity as "Social" Trinity provides the horizon of understanding for interpreting the human self.[72] Grenz begins with an assessment of Hegel's influence upon Trinitarian theology, but insists that an emphasis upon "God as three subjectivities" goes back behind Hegel to Richard of St. Victor and to the Cappadocian Fathers.[73]

Grenz regrets Barth's hesitation about referring to God as "three persons." Barth is correct to suggest that if Christ were "another personality," Christ the Son of God would not and could not be the Father's self-revelation, and monotheism would have become tritheism. Grenz acknowledges that Karl Rahner also has reservations about the notion of a "social" Trinity, although Rahner expounds his argument mainly on the basis of divine immutability.[74] Nevertheless Grenz appeals to Pannenberg and Moltmann for their major critiques of Barth and Rahner in this area.[75]

Moltmann had related a theology of the human self to theologies of the Trinity more than twenty years before the appearance of Grenz's book. In his magisterial work *The Trinity and the Kingdom of God* Moltmann writes, "The modern culture of subjectivity has long since been in danger of turning into a '*culture of narcissism*' which makes the self its own prisoner and supplies it

---

68. Migliore, *Faith Seeking Understanding*, 125.

69. Migliore, *Faith Seeking Understanding*, 126.

70. Paul Jewett, *Man as Male and Female* (Grand Rapids: Eerdmans, 1975); Rosemary Radford Ruether, *Sexism and God Talk: Towards a Feminist Theology* (Boston: Beacon, 1983); and Letty Russell, *The Future of Partnership* (Philadelphia: Westminster, 1979).

71. Stanley J. Grenz, *The Social God and the Relational Self: A Trinitarian Theology of the Imago Dei* (Louisville and London: Westminster John Knox, 2001), 10.

72. This is the broad theme of Grenz's part I, 23-137.

73. Grenz, *Social God*, 29-36.

74. Karl Rahner, *The Trinity*, trans. Joseph Donceel (London: Burns & Oates, 1970). On Rahner, see Karen Kilby, *Rahner: Theology and Philosophy* (London: Routledge, 2004).

75. Grenz, *Social God*, 41-51.

merely *with self-repetitions and self-confirmations*."[76] He believes that accounts of God simply as "Absolute Subject," especially in Hegel and Fichte, have not entirely escaped this problem. "Trinity of substance" allows only for "three modes of being" rather than the development of "a social doctrine of the Trinity."[77] Understanding "relationships" and "communities" grows out of a fuller understanding of God as Trinity. Moltmann explicitly attacks a "metaphysical" notion of divine immutability and impassibility. He writes: "A God who cannot suffer cannot love either."[78]

Moltmann expands and defends this starting point. The heart of his relational approach is summed up in his appeal to the New Testament: "The New Testament talks about God by *proclaiming in narrative the relationships of the Father, the Son, and the Spirit, which are relationships of fellowship and are open to the world.*"[79] The "sending" of the Son appears in Rom. 8:3-4, Gal. 4:4, and elsewhere. Moltmann declares that in the cross, "'God' is forsaken by 'God.' . . . If the Father forsakes the Son, the Son does not merely lose his sonship. The Father loses his fatherhood as well." On the cross "the love that binds the one to the other is transformed into a dividing curse. It is only as the One who is forsaken and cursed that the Son is still the Son. It is only as the One who forsakes, who surrenders the other, that the Father is still present. Communicating love and responding love are alike transformed . . . into the suffering and endurance of death."[80]

In relation to Barth, Moltmann observes, "The God who reveals himself in three modes of being can no longer deploy subjectivity in his state-of-revelation, the Holy Spirit. The Spirit is merely a common bond of love linking the Father with the Son."[81] Barth presents "the doctrine of the Trinity" as monotheism within a horizon of understanding focused on divine sovereignty: Rahner also "conjures up the danger of a 'vulgar tritheism'" as a greater danger than Sabellianism, although, Moltmann believes, that Rahner is in danger of affirming it.[82]

We discuss Trinitarian doctrine in Chapter 19. We may note here, however, that Pannenberg is equally insistent that God embraces a self-differentiation of persons within the unity of the Godhead. He rejects a route to "the plurality" of the Trinitarian persons from the essence of one God on the ground that this leads inevitably to modalism or to subordinationism.[83] The starting point is the

76. Moltmann, *The Trinity*, 5 (my italics).
77. Moltmann, *The Trinity*, 13-19.
78. Moltmann, *The Trinity*, 38; cf. 39-60.
79. Moltmann, *The Trinity*, 64 (my italics); cf. 65-90.
80. Moltmann, *The Trinity*, 80.
81. Moltmann, *The Trinity*, 142.
82. Moltmann, *The Trinity*, 144.
83. Pannenberg, *Systematic Theology*, vol. 1, 298; cf. 259-336.

revelation of God in Jesus Christ. This involves "*the reciprocal self-distinction of the Father, Son and Spirit as the concrete form of Trinitarian relations*" (his italics).[84] Pannenberg declares, "Precisely by distinguishing himself from the Father ... he [Jesus Christ] showed himself to be the Son of God and one with the Father who sent him (John 10:30)."[85] The Father is Father only as he is so in relation to the Son."[86] In the history of the economy of salvation biblical and Christian traditions affirm "the dependence of the Trinitarian persons upon one another. ... In their intratrinitarian relations the persons depend on one another in respect of their deity as well as their personal being."[87]

Clearly, Pannenberg and Moltmann are driving influences behind Grenz's *Social God* (2001). The application of their approach to the "image of God," their critique of Barth and Rahner, and their recovery of *perichoresis* in the Cappadocian Fathers and the Eastern Church reflect this influence.[88] With Moltmann, Grenz seeks to provide a safeguard against narcissism through "relationality," and with Pannenberg and Pannenberg's focus on public history he seeks a safeguard against undue preoccupation with "inwardness." Grenz identifies a problematic dimension in Augustine in this respect, in contrast to the more outward-looking focus on "communion" in John Zizioulas and other Eastern Orthodox writers.[89] He quotes Catherine Mowry LaCugna's comment: "Personhood in the Augustinian tradition has mainly to do with individual consciousness. ... The journey of the soul toward God is a journey inward. ... This makes the social, communal, toward-another character of personhood rather difficult to see."[90]

Like many other writers Grenz traces the origins of this trend in Descartes, Locke, and other rationalists and empiricists. It is worth our recalling that Archbishop William Temple, with his well-known social awareness, could describe Descartes's solitary starting point "shut up alone in a stove" as perhaps "the most disastrous moment in the history of Europe"; and a "*faux pas*" of monumental proportions.[91]

Grenz writes, "The elevation of the autonomous self to the center of the philosophical agenda gave birth to ... 'the transcendental pretense' of moder-

84. Pannenberg, *Systematic Theology*, vol. 1, 308.

85. Pannenberg, *Systematic Theology*, vol. 1, 310.

86. Pannenberg, *Systematic Theology*, vol. 1, 310.

87. Pannenberg, *Systematic Theology*, vol. 1, 329.

88. Cf. Grenz, *Social God*, 10-11, 33-37, 43-55, and 162-240.

89. Grenz, *Social God*, 63-64; cf. 51-57. see also John D. Zizioulas, *Being as Communion: Studies in Personhood and the Church*, Contemporary Greek Theologians 4 (Crestwood, NY: St. Vladimir's Seminary Press, 1984), and John D. Zizioulas, "Human Capacity and Human Incapacity: A Theological Exploration of Personhood," *Scottish Journal of Theology* 28 (1975) 401-48.

90. Catherine Mowry LaCugna, *God for Us: The Trinity and Christian Life* (San Francisco: Harper, 1992), 247.

91. William Temple, *Nature, Man, and God* (London: Macmillan, 1940), 57.

nity."[92] We have already traced the debilitating effects of such individualism for doctrine in our discussion of Heyduck's *The Recovery of Doctrine*. We also noted that Paul the apostle thought largely in corporate and communal terms. Krister Stendahl's celebrated essay "The Apostle Paul and the Introspective Conscience of the West" underlines the huge difference in this particular matter between Paul and Augustine.[93] In the religious sphere Grenz notes the effects of this inwardness and individualism in terms of the widespread resort to therapeutic and psychological models of "spiritual" journeying.[94]

The struggle between theological or hermeneutical models of spiritual growth on one side and pastoral counseling and more individualistic and "inner" therapeutic ones on the other does indeed form part of a horizon of understanding through which many questions engage us today. Charles Gerkin attacks "therapeutic" models of pastoral counseling as militating against "hermeneutical" models of interpersonal theological action.[95] In spite of a valid emphasis in recent biblical hermeneutics on communities of interpretation, some have even returned to a so-called "new" hermeneutical paradigm of "autobiographical" biblical reading.[96] By contrast Grenz undertakes a critique of the "autobiographical" self, the self-reliant self, the willful self, and the individualist subjectivity that lends to the dissolution of the relational, responsible self, which reflects the image of God in a Trinitarian perspective.[97]

Grenz acknowledges that Augustine's complex writings yield, ambivalently, both an individualist "inner" self and traces of a relational self. But the "birth" of the relational *imago Dei*, he argues, emerges with the Reformers. Fundamentally this is because Luther (with other Reformers) "locates all soteriological resonances outside the human person."[98] Their emphasis lies on a restored, re-created image of God in the belief that the original image and likeness was "lost" through human sin.[99]

92. Grenz, *Social God*, 72.

93. Krister Stendahl, "The Apostle Paul and the Introspective Conscience of the West" (1961 and 1963), repr. in K. Stendahl, *Paul among Jews and Gentiles* (London: S.C.M., 1977 and Philadelphia: Fortress, 1976), 78-96.

94. Grenz, *Social God*, 82-97.

95. Charles V. Gerkin, *The Living Human Document: Re-Visioning Pastoral Counseling in a Hermeneutical Mode* (Nashville: Abingdon, 1983); cf. also David Capps, *Pastoral Care and Hermeneutics* (Philadelphia: Fortress, 1984).

96. Ingrid Rosa Kitzberger (ed.), *Autobiographical Biblical Criticism: Between Text and Self* (Leiden: Deo, 2002).

97. Grenz, *Social God*, 98-137.

98. Grenz, *Social God*, 163.

99. Luther's view is complex. Fallen humanity stands under "the dominion of sin" (Martin Luther, *The Bondage of the Will*, 278-84). But in Martin Luther, *The Disputation concerning Man* (to which Grenz alludes), Luther also insists that human reason is rather "confirmed" than lost after the Fall, albeit for *a posteriori*, not *a priori* knowledge (Theses 9 and 10). Yet humankind is deceived and under the power of the devil (Theses 18-25).

We shall return to issues about whether or how the image of God is "lost" through human sin in Chapters 12 and 13. This was a complex issue for Luther and Calvin, but Grenz rightly concludes that their main emphasis comes not "from the fallen state of humankind but from the restoration given in Christ who is the second Adam."[100] This led them to a fresh appraisal of "image of God" not as "a static structure of human nature" but in terms of "the human person standing in right relationship with God and thereby mirroring the divine."[101]

David Cairns identifies Brunner's work as having a huge impact on mid-twentieth-century thought in this area.[102] Like Kierkegaard, Brunner sees the heart of language about the image of God in terms of the aphorism, "Love can only impart itself where it is received in love."[103] God wills human freedom to make this possible, which places a responsibility upon humankind. Hence Brunner writes, "Responsibility is part of the unchangeable structure of man's being."[104] But since humankind does not give glory to God, but seeks self-glory, the image of God becomes "lost."[105] Only Jesus Christ is the "true" human person, the true *imago Dei*, through whom "man once more receives God's Primal Word of Love; once more the divine image *(Urbild)* is reflected in him; the lost image is restored."[106]

Brunner insists, "Image of God is conceived *not as self-existing substance but as a relation*."[107] It is not something that "man possesses . . . *in himself*," like "a 'spark' from the Divine Spirit."[108] As an explanatory model Brunner distinguishes between the *"formal"* image of God according to which *humankind always stands before God as responsible and accountable to God*, and the *"material"* image according to which the *human relationship will be fully actualized*. The formal responsibility "cannot be lost"; but the material destiny can become "a lost destiny."[109]

Grenz expounds image of God in Christological and eschatological terms also, and applies "difference" and "bonding" in relationship to gender. To be "male and female" is to be "sexually differentiated and hence relational creatures."[110] He concludes, "Sexuality lies at the heart of human identity."[111] "Dif-

---

100. Grenz, *Social God*, 169. (Paul prefers the "last" Adam, 1 Cor. 15:45.)

101. Grenz, *Social God*, 170.

102. David Cairns, *The Image of God in Man* (London: S.C.M., 1953), 146; Grenz, *Social God*, 175-77; cf. Brunner, *Doctrine of Creation*, "The Image of God and Creation," 55-61.

103. Brunner, *Doctrine of Creation*, 56.

104. Brunner, *Doctrine of Creation*, 57.

105. Brunner, *Doctrine of Creation*, 58.

106. Brunner, *Doctrine of Creation*, 59.

107. Brunner, *Doctrine of Creation*, 59 (my italics).

108. Brunner, *Doctrine of Creation*, 60 (his italics).

109. Brunner, *Doctrine of Creation*, 61.

110. Grenz, *Social God*, 269.

111. Grenz, *Social God*, 301.

ference" and "bonding" together reflect the nature of God as Trinity, and of true humanness as imaging or reflecting that relationality. We return to gender issues in 11.3 and 11.4.

Alistair McFadyen's *The Call to Personhood* runs broadly parallel with Grenz's concerns, but with surprisingly little dialogue with Brunner, Pannenberg, or Moltmann. The image of God, McFadyen repeats, is "paradigmatically male and female," and human life is "dialogical" in both its "vertical" and "horizontal" dimensions, namely with God and with fellow human beings.[112] This is "a permanent and indestructible structure" at the level of ontology.[113] Christian understandings of the Fall recognize that at a practical level "the concrete conditions of human communication have become overbearingly distorted."[114] The restoration of the image of God reflects the inter-personal Trinitarian frame of divine grace.

Call and *communication* constitute the horizon of understanding within which McFadyen interprets image of God and human personhood. More specifically his "chief concern is to describe individual identity in terms of response."[115] This response is *to the call of discipleship, to the acceptance of responsibility, and to engagement in social formation.* Echoing a theme that we discussed above in Chapter 3, and to which we return in 11.4, McFadyen writes, "Social life and communication are founded on *bodiliness,* and interpersonal communication is both a social and a bodily activity . . . anchored firmly in a *social* world."[116]

These themes of bodiliness and relationality are integrally related to Christ, who serves as a paradigm of the truly human. Pannenberg identifies this issue in the following terms: "*Only in the light of the incarnation of the eternal Son . . .* can we say that the relation of the creature to the Creator finds *its supreme and final realization in humanity.*"[117] David Ford expounds this theme in the context of interpersonal relations.[118]

11.3. Christ as the Image of God and the Gift of Embodied Human Life

If God purposed humanity to reflect his deity and selfhood within the space-time conditions of the world as God's image, then Karl Barth's formulation is valid: "Jesus is man as God willed and created him. What constitutes true human nature in us depends upon what it is in him. We derive wholly from Jesus not

112. Alistair I. McFadyen, *The Call to Personhood: A Christian Theory of the Individual in Social Relationships* (Cambridge: Cambridge University Press, 1990), 39.

113. McFadyen, *Personhood,* 41.

114. McFadyen, *Personhood,* 43.

115. McFadyen, *Personhood,* 47.

116. McFadyen, *Personhood,* 77 (first italics mine; second and third, his).

117. Pannenberg, *Systematic Theology,* vol. 2, 175 (my italics).

118. David F. Ford, *Self and Salvation: Being Transformed* (Cambridge: Cambridge University Press, 1999).

merely our potential and actual relation to God, but even our human nature as such."[119] Jesus Christ is the paradigm case of the truly human. Humankind, apart from Christ, Barth believes, "in supreme unfaithfulness takes sides against God his Creator in contradiction against himself."[120] So how can humanity as such fully reflect God as God's image? By contrast, Jesus is the "Man for God."[121] Jesus is "real" man because he is called and chosen to bear God's image, and perfectly reflects God's being.[122] It may be tempting to set in contrast Barth's Jesus the "Man for God" with Dietrich Bonhoeffer's Jesus the "Man for Others." But Barth also describes Jesus as "Man for other men."[123] He writes, "The solidarity with which Jesus binds Himself to His fellows is wholly real."[124]

This view is not confined to Barth or to Barthian traditions. Jerome Murphy-O'Connor writes, "In order to find the true and essential nature of humanity he [Paul] did not look to his contemporaries but to *Christ, for he alone embodied the authenticity of humanity*" (my italics).[125] Murphy-O'Connor appeals to several New Testament passages for the notion that Christ is the image of God: Christ is "the image of the invisible God" (Col. 1:15); "Christ, who is the image of God . . . the light of the knowledge of the glory of God in the face of Jesus Christ" (2 Cor. 4:4-6); "being in the image of God, Christ did not use it to his own advantage . . ." (Phil. 2:6-7).

In a semipopular commentary on Philippians one writer sets out the respective narratives of Adam and Christ in parallel columns to exhibit Christ as what Alan Richardson termed "Adam in reverse," and the restorer of the image of God. Some are matching parallels: "made in the image of God . . . to be as God . . . found in fashion as a man . . ."; others are contrastive: "strove to be of reputation" is "made himself of no reputation"; "exalted himself" over against "humbled himself"; "disobedient to death" versus "obedient to death . . . God exalted him."[126]

A part-parallel can be found in the "recapitulation" themes (ἀνακεφα-λαίωσις, *anakephalaiōsis*), most notably of Irenaeus and Athanasius. The logic of Irenaeus is not quite the same as Paul's, but he writes that "What we had lost in Adam, namely being in the image and likeness of God, we might recover in

---

119. Barth, *Church Dogmatics*, III:2, sect. 43, 50.

120. Barth, *Church Dogmatics*, III:2, sect. 43, 26.

121. Barth, *Church Dogmatics*, III:1, sect. 44:1, 55 (title of this subsection).

122. Barth, *Church Dogmatics*, III:1, sect. 44:3, 132-202, esp. 160-70.

123. Barth, *Church Dogmatics*, III:1, sect. 45:1, 203-22.

124. Barth, *Church Dogmatics*, III:1, sect. 45:1, 211.

125. Murphy-O'Connor, *Becoming Human Together*, 45.

126. F. C. Synge, *Philippians and Colossians: Introduction and Commentary*, Torch (London: S.C.M., 1951), 29; cf. also Alan Richardson, *Introduction to the Theology of the New Testament* (London: S.C.M., 1958), 245. Richardson writes, "Christ repairs the damage wrought by Adam" (245).

Christ Jesus," and he states even more explicitly, "the Lord . . . who is his Word recapitulated Adam in himself."[127] "Recapitulation" is less explicit in Athanasius, but many Patristic specialists say that it lies in the background. Athanasius refers explicitly to Col. 1:15 where Christ is the image of God, and implies that this offers a further gift to humankind in the disintegration of humanity's bearing the image of God.[128]

The most explicit evidence for the theme of Christ as bearer of the image of God and "Adam in reverse" comes in Heb. 2:5-13, which expounds the victory of Christ within the horizon of understanding reflected in Ps. 8:4-6. "Adam" failed to fulfill the human vocation of subduing the earth, or of taking responsibility for it, but *Jesus Christ fulfilled every aspect of the vocation of being truly human.* True humanness involved not simply active stewardship, but also first the acceptance of *the constraints of time and place.* Thus Jesus "learned" human *maturity through suffering* (cf. Greek παθημάτων τελειῶσαι, *pathēmatōn teleiōsai,* 2:10; cf. the aphorism πάθειν . . . μάθειν). Second, humanness requires, even on the part of Jesus, the need to *look to God in trust* (v. 13) Third, Jesus is the *pioneer or prototype* (ἀρχηγός, *archēgos,* v. 10) of the new humanity. Fourth, by fulfilling true destiny as exemplified in Ps. 8:4-6, Jesus is *crowned with glory* because of the suffering of death, and is willing to name others his brothers and sisters (vv. 9 and 11).[129] Attridge includes an excursus in his commentary on "The Christological Pattern," and calls Heb. 2:10-18 "the 'classic' Christian model of conceiving of the Incarnation and its effects."[130]

Jesus as "true" man is not only "the Man for God" and "the Man for Others" (as Barth and Bonhoeffer term it), but as the incarnate Word he is also the paradigm of *bodiliness, embodiment and temporality both as gift and as constraint.* The Epistle to the Hebrews speaks of his "perfection" in terms of *temporal growth and experience* (Heb. 2:10; 5:8); of his being subject to *conditions of place and time* that require the exercise of *"trust"* in God (2:13); of his sharing in the fragility of *"flesh and blood"* (2:14); and indeed of his becoming "like his brothers and sisters *in every respect."* This included testing and temptation, "yet without sin" (2:17, 18; 4:15). "He offered up prayers and supplications with loud cries and tears. . . . He learned obedience through what he suffered" (5:7-8).

---

127. Irenaeus, *Against Heresies* V:19:1 and V:21:10; cf. V:16:2; and V:34:2. Cf. also N. P. Williams, *The Ideas of the Fall and of Original Sin* (London and New York: Longmans, Green, 1929), 196-98, who calls these two passages a classical statement of the idea of 'Recapitulation'" (197, n. 3). See also Tertullian, *Against Marcion* V:17:1.

128. Athanasius, *On the Incarnation* 3, 4, and 12.

129. Expounded further in Anthony C. Thiselton, "Hebrews," in *Eerdmans Commentary on the Bible,* ed. J. D. G. Dunn and J. W. Rogerson (Grand Rapids: Eerdmans, 2003), 1457; cf. 1451-82. See further William L. Lane, *Hebrews,* 2 vols. (Dallas: Word Books, 1991) 42:67.

130. Harold W. Attridge, *The Epistle to the Hebrews,* Hermeneia (Philadelphia: Fortress, 1989), 79.

In Chapter 3 we discussed "embodiment" in the biblical writings in the context of *self-involvement, contingency,* and *public* criteria of meaning in hermeneutics. More is "at stake" in "taking a stand," in expressing belief in bodily life, than mere "inwardness." Christian apostolic traditions, unlike secret gnostic traditions, were open to the public world, and not merely private and inner, with disdain for the social and physical. At the cost of repeating an earlier quotation, we recall Käsemann's definition: "'Body' for Paul mean[s] . . . *that piece of the world which we ourselves are* and for which we bear responsibility because it was the earliest gift of our Creator to us."[131] Being part of the *world* in this way, Käsemann rightly adds, embraces our "ability to communicate," and (he might have added) to be recognized and identified as *us.* As such, *"bodily obedience . . . in the world of every day"* gives to the lordship of Christ *intelligible and credible "visible expression."* It makes the gospel "credible."[132]

In the present chapter I use the terms *"high stakes"* to denote *the enhanced opportunities, responsibilities, and capacity for intelligibility, credibility, and vulnerability that a bodily and temporal mode of life brings.* People may behave differently when they are "seen" from when they are in private: *visibility makes the daily transactions of relationality more concrete, and transparent,* and more real and more lasting in their impact.

God's gift of "human" time heightens the stakes further by imposing choices to act at the right or wrong moment, giving growing vitality and the experience of growth, but at the same time the increasing vulnerabilities of aging. Pietist religion speaks of "living out" a personal faith and creed, and the Epistle of James asks what other kind of faith than this would or could be authentic (Jas. 1:12, 19-27; 2:14-26; 3:9-18; 4:4-10; 5:8-11).

This is so central to biblical and Christian traditions that it may appear banal to labor the point. However, some traditions of philosophical thought elevate reason and the "inner" human spirit above the bodily, temporal, physical, and contingent. Paul values reason and its role in the context of Christian discipleship; but he also insists on the importance of what is done *"in the body"* (1 Cor. 6:12-20). Dale Martin expounds the differing worlds of discourse about the body that belong respectively to Platonists and Stoics, to the apostle Paul, and to the later era when "the boundaries between mind and body were redrawn by Descartes."[133] The Christian revaluation of the body begins with the revaluation imposed by the cross: "Making a crucified criminal the honored figure of devotion ran completely counter to common assumptions."[134]

All the same, even some of the earlier Fathers reverted to a different view.

---

131. Käsemann, *New Testament Questions of Today,* 135.

132. Käsemann, *New Testament Questions of Today,* 135; cf. 136-37.

133. Dale B. Martin, *The Corinthian Body* (New Haven, CT and London: Yale University Press, 1995), 4.

134. Martin, *Corinthian Body,* 59.

Tertullian insists, "We are the soul" (Latin *anima*); "without the soul *(anima)* we are only a carcass."[135] In spite of Paul's strong contrast between body (σῶμα, *sōma*) and flesh (σάρξ, *sarx*), Tertullian sees only spirit and soul on one side, and "flesh" on the other. He writes, "I see no other substances in man."[136] For some, Plato's legacy that the soul is divine still lurked in the background.[137] Origen explicitly identifies "the groaning of the whole creation in labor pains" and "bondage to decay" (Rom. 8:21-22) as "nothing else than the body."[138] Origen acknowledges that Christ "possessed flesh" as well as soul, but his discussion quickly moves into praise of the soul or spirit.[139] The capacity to suffer bodily illness or disease is associated with acts of sin.[140] When at last the psychical or "ordinary" body is raised as a "spiritual" body (1 Cor. 15:44), it is for Origen "the soul" that will be united with God.[141]

The biblical writers in general do not think in these dualist terms. The psychosomatic is so blurred that the Hebrew word regularly translated *soul*, נפש (*nephesh*), actually denotes *dead body* in Num. 9:6, 7, and 10. Pannenberg comments, "We know conscious and self-conscious life only as bodily life. . . . Soul and body [are] constitutive elements of the unity of human life that belong to one another and cannot be reduced to one another."[142] Tertullian and Origen are not typical of the Patristic writings. The second-century Christian writer Athenagoras declares that resurrection cannot be only of "the soul," because the soul is not the whole person.[143] The biblical writers anticipate some aspects of our modern medical and psychiatric emphasis upon the psychosomatic unity of human persons. *Embodiment* is one of the Creator's gifts to his creatures that God deemed "very good" (Gen. 1:31).

Hermeneutical horizons of understanding emerge at two different levels here. One concerns a shift away from the rationalist dualism of Descartes on one side and from the reductionist empiricism of Hume on the other. The second concerns the "high stakes" bound up with bodily and temporal human life in such contexts as those of love and sexuality, power and control, the use of money, and human attitudes to time.

We have space to glance at the influence of dualist and naturalistic or positivist traditions only briefly. In his *Anthropology in Theological Perspective* Pannenberg explores the problems of behaviorism and other reductionist ac-

---

135. Tertullian, *Against Praxeas* 5.
136. Tertullian, *Against Marcion* V:16.
137. Plato, *Republic* 611E.
138. Origen, *De Principiis* I:7:5.
139. Origen, *De Principiis* II:8:2.
140. Origen, *De Principiis* II:10:6.
141. Origen, *De Principiis* III:6 6.
142. Pannenberg, *Systematic Theology*, vol. 2, 181-82.
143. Athenagoras, *The Resurrection of the Dead* 15.

counts of the human condition.[144] Eric Mascall also considers naturalistic explanations of the human self, arguing that naturalistic theories of evolution and other reductionist approaches cannot fully account for the uniqueness of human beings.[145] Among conservative writers of the early twentieth century, James Orr includes some incisive arguments against materialist and nontheist accounts of human personhood that (if accepted) would "deface" the divine image.[146]

In contemporary thought Jürgen Moltmann combines a strongly biblical and theological account of the human, but relates this to questions that arise within nontheistic thought.[147] John Macquarrie reminds us that to take human "embodiedness" seriously does not leave us with the two unacceptable alternatives of Descartes or Gilbert Ryle.[148] Karl Rahner expounds the dignity and freedom of human beings as those who are community builders, able to respond to moral law and having the capacity for Christ-centered living.[149] Helmut Thielicke attacks an exclusively biological view of humankind on one side, and the elevation of the creaturely to the status of the divine on the other.[150]

The era of stimulus-response behaviorism foundered on the self-contradictory character of the very argument that supposedly supports it. This applies both to J. B. Watson's version and to that of B. F. Skinner. If "rationality" is to be reduced to bioneurological processes, on what basis can the advocate of such a view claim to offer a "rational" rather than a rhetorical argument? Such an argument is reminiscent of Ayer's Logical Positivism (even with later modification), where his principle of verification or "verifiability" failed its own criteria. It failed either to be empirically verifiable or to constitute a merely formal, logically "internal" proposition or tautology.[151]

All the same, David Hume still has his followers in spite of carefully formulated critiques by C. A. Campbell, H. D. Lewis, and others. Hume argues on the basis of his own empiricist premises that the self merely denotes a succession of

---

144. Pannenberg, *Anthropology*, 27-79.

145. Eric L. Mascall, *The Importance of Being Human: Some Aspects of the Christian Doctrine of Man* (London: Oxford University Press, 1959), 1-36 and throughout.

146. James Orr, *God: Image in Man and Its Defacement in the Light of Modern Denials*, (London: Hodder & Stoughton, 2d ed. 1905), throughout.

147. Moltmann, *Man*, esp. 1-45.

148. John Macquarrie, *In Search of Humanity: A Theological and Philosophical Approach* (London: S.C.M., 1982), 47-58 and throughout.

149. Rahner, "The Dignity and Freedom of Man," in *Theological Investigations*, vol. 2, 235-63.

150. Helmut Thielicke, *Man in God's World*, trans. J. W. Doberstein (London: Clarke, 1967), 37-57.

151. A. J. Ayer, *Language, Truth and Logic* (London: Gollancz, 2d edn. 1946). Among numerous critiques, too many to list, see, e.g., H. J. Paton, *The Modern Predicament* (London: Allan & Unwin, 1955), 32-46; William P. Alston, *Divine Nature and Human Language* (Ithaca and London: Cornell University Press, 1989); and Richard Swinburne, *The Coherence of Theism* (Oxford: Oxford University Press, rev. ed. 1997).

perceptions of experiences or objects. We perceive impressions, ideas, or emotions, but there is no underlying structure that ties these together as a stable, continuing self. Hume writes, "For my part, when I enter most intimately into what I call *myself*, I always stumble on some particular perception or other. . . . I never catch myself without a perception, and never can observe anything but the perception."[152] If someone else, he adds, claims to perceive a continued entity that he calls *himself*, "there is no such principle in me" (loc. cit.).

C. A. Campbell stands initially within Hume's horizons in order to demonstrate their inadequacy. He explores how we might perceive (for example) of the striking of Big Ben at nine o'clock. We hear it striking. "A moment later I (the same subject) hear it striking again." If there is no continuous, stable self, how does the self distinguish between hearing Big Ben strike *nine* o'clock, and having nine perceptions of the clock's appearing to strike *one* o'clock? Only a stable self that embodies continuity can hold together the clock's striking *as striking nine o'clock*.[153] Campbell expands his argument about the continuity of the self over some two hundred pages in his Part I before turning to the nature of God in Part II. Like Bernard Lonergan, whose work we have discussed, Campbell explores the necessary condition for *cognitive judgments*. H. D. Lewis similarly demonstrates the stability and depth of human selfhood in a way that resists reductionist explanations.[154]

It might be argued that Campbell and Lewis respond to Hume on the basis of an unnecessarily idealist "metaphysical" view of the self. However, P. F. Strawson's influential work *Individuals* argues that the ability to identify persons or "particulars" *over a period of time* presupposes that the perception and judgments of the human self are more than subjective constructs of the mind. The concept of *person* is logically "primitive": it *irreducibly* combines the logic of *spatially locatable, embodied* beings with a logic of *personal agency and action*.[155] *Bodily* or *material* predicates (M-predicates) are predicated *simultaneously and interactively* with *personal*, consciousness-related predicates (P-predicates). Strawson attacks both behaviorism and Cartesian dualism, through explicating an irreducible conceptual logic of *persons*.[156] This provides a constructive hermeneutical horizon of understanding for our exposition of the *bodily and temporal* nature of human persons, who nevertheless are called to *responsibility and personal agency* in relation to others.

152. David Hume, *A Treatise of Human Nature*, ed. L. A. Selby-Bigge (Oxford: Clarendon, 1951), I:4:6, 252.

153. C. A. Campbell, *On Selfhood and Godhood* (London: Allan & Unwin and New York: Macmillan, 1957), 76.

154. H. D. Lewis, *The Elusive Mind* (London: Allan & Unwin and New York: Macmillan, 1969), 15-44 and 237-74.

155. Peter F. Strawson, *Individuals: An Essay in Descriptive Metaphysics* (London: Methuen, 1959), 15-116.

156. Strawson, *Individuals*, esp. 98-116.

Our second formulation of a hermeneutical horizon of understanding emerges through the notion that *bodily* and *temporal* human life constitutes a precondition for living in community with "high stakes." In some respects this is a questionable notion, for we do not experience consciousness other than in "bodily" settings. But in many biblical passages *bodily* life assumes a higher profile than in other contexts.

Käsemann, we have recalled twice already, sees bodiliness as the precondition for a credible and intelligible Christian discipleship that may be communicated to others. In this context Paul enjoins Christians in Rome, "Present your *bodies* (Greek τὰ σώματα ὑμῶν, *ta sōmata humōn*, i.e., your *whole selves, as visible beings in the public domain*) as a living sacrifice, holy and acceptable to God" (Rom. 12:1).[157] Their Christian living is to be distinctive, visible, and communicable, "not conformed to this world . . . but transformed by the renewing of your minds" (Rom. 12:2).

1 Cor. 6:12-20 provides an even more illuminating example. "The section demonstrates, once again, the inseparability of Christian identity and Christian lifestyle [and] the importance of the body and bodily actions."[158] The link with ch. 5 and 6:1-11 is clear: issues of "boundaries" in greed, grasping, and power, and in sexual self-gratification that is "off limits" exhibit an undeniable, concrete expression of Christian or un-Christian lifestyle *within the public domain*. The body is "for the Lord" (1 Cor. 6:14a), and the Lord "for the body" (6:14b). "Your members" (limbs and organs) are limbs and organs (μέλη, *melē*) of Christ (6:15). "Your body is a temple of the Holy Spirit" (6:19). "Glorify God *in your body*" (6:20). The fact that some later Uncial MSS add "and in your spirit" (C[3], D[2], Ψ, 1739mg, Syriac versions, the Vulgate, and AV/KJV) reveals how easily the importance of the bodily could be missed or even suppressed in the history of traditions.

11.4. Emotion, Sexuality, and Other Gifts
That Raise the Stakes for Living

We have already spoken of *embodiedness and time* as *"raising the stakes"* for what it is to be a human being. The phrase "high stakes" comes from the Church of England Doctrine Commission Report *Being Human*, to which I contributed together with the other dozen-or-so members of the Commission who wrote it.[159]

---

157. Cf. Charles E. B. Cranfield, *The Epistle to the Romans: A Critical and Exegetical Commentary*, 2 vols., ICC (Edinburgh: T&T Clark, 1975 and 1979), vol. 2, 595-601; and James D. G. Dunn, *Romans*, 2 vols., WBC (Dallas: Word, 1988), vol. 2, 708-10.

158. Thiselton, *First Epistle*, 459.

159. Church of England Doctrine Commission, *Being Human: A Christian Understanding of Personhood Illustrated with Reference to Power, Money, Sin, and Time* (London: Church Publishing, 2003), 7-11.

John Macquarrie has formulated another way of expressing these "high stakes" in his book *In Search of Humanity.* He points out that *"embodiedness"* provides "possibility for transcendence," although these are also "inseparable from possibilities of regression. . . . Human beings are . . . embodied in a material substrate which can be both supportive and threatening."[160]

On one side bodily life makes possible the experience of sensations: sight, sound, touch, taste, smell, warmth, cool breezes, or whatever. On the other side embodiment exposes us to disease, injury, death, and subjection to subpersonal forces.[161] Nevertheless in Hebrew thought within the Old Testament, life *without the body,* especially in the context of descent of a soul or a spirit to Sheol, was thought of as life under radically *reduced* conditions: here a person "could hardly be said to 'live,'" but simply "existed" in a "bloodless, juiceless way, the 'shade' or shadow of his former self."[162] Those in Sheol or Hades greet a newly arrived dead person or "shade" with the word, "You too become as weak as we; you have become like us! Your pomp is brought down to Sheol" (Isa. 14:10-11). In this context "a living dog is better than a dead lion" (Eccles. 9:4). This is a far cry from Plato's notion that the self regains its free dignity and freedom when it is "released" from the body.

Biblical traditions amplify and explicate the dimensions of "bodily" life with a wide and varied vocabulary that is used to denote emotions and the complexity of what today we call psychosomatic life. In his *Anthropology of the Old Testament* Hans Walter Wolff still maintains the catalogue of psycho-physiological terms that fascinated such earlier writers as Wheeler Robinson and Pedersen, albeit with more care and critical caution. Aspects of the self that denote sensations of need or desire come under such terms as throat, neck, and so forth.[163] The Hebrew בשׂר *(bāśār),* flesh, denotes humankind in community; "man in his bodily aspect"; humans in relationship; humans as weak and vulnerable (Job 10:4; 2 Chron. 32:8; Ps. 78:38-39; and Isa. 40:6); but it may also denote the capacity for extreme sensitivity and sympathy: "I will take away their heart of stone and give them a heart of flesh" (בשׂר, *bāśār,* Ezek. 11:19 and 36:26).[164] Inner organs of the body, especially לב *(lēbh) heart,* כליות *(kᵉlāyôth)* kidneys, *and* מעים *(mēˁîm) bowels,* may denote either physiological functions or depths of emotion. "My *liver* is poured out in the ground" is parallel with "my *eyes* are spent weeping, and my *bowels* are in turmoil" (Lam. 2:11). The verse conveys "measureless grief."[165] "My *heart* was embittered, and I was sharply pricked in the *kidneys*" (Ps. 73:21)

160. John Macquarrie, *In Search of Humanity: A Theological and Philosophical Approach* (London: S.C.M., 1982), 47; cf. 47-58 and 83-95.

161. Cf. Macquarrie, *Humanity,* 55.

162. C. Ryder Smith, *The Bible Doctrine of Salvation* (London: Epworth, 2d edn. 1946), 92.

163. Wolff, *Anthropology,* 10-25.

164. Wolff, *Anthropology,* 28; cf. 26-31.

165. Wolff, *Anthropology,* 63-66.

conveys "the most violent spiritual emotions . . . agonizing hours of doubt and mental distress."[166] *Bowels* may denote deep anguish and distress, or compassion and love (Song 5:4; Jer. 4:19).

In the New Testament *love* is not used primarily to convey an emotional state. In 1 Cor. 13:4-7 it is a manifestation of a *desire and will to seek the best for the other.* Hence Paul defines its dynamic in terms of showing *patience* and *kindness* (13:4a); refraining from envy, from bragging, and from promoting one's own supposed importance (13:4b). It is a matter of not behaving with discourtesy or with bad manners (13:5a); and not being preoccupied with self-interest (13:5b). It avoids being exasperated and pique; does not reckon up people's faults; rightly acclaims truth: and never tires of giving support to others (13:6-7).[167] In *this* passage love has more to do with generous judgments, will, and habits of action than with emotion.

Nevertheless in many other passages *heart* denotes strong emotion and yearning or longing. Paul speaks of his "heart's desire and prayer" (Rom. 10:1), and of writing "in anguish of heart" (2 Cor. 2:4). The heart is also capable of self-deception and comes very close to anticipating modern notions of the unconscious and subconscious (Rom. 2:16; 1 Cor. 4:5; 14:25).[168] When God's love is shed abroad "in our hearts" by the Holy Spirit (Rom. 5:5), this engages with the depths of our being.

Once again, John Macquarrie provides a magisterial exposition of the "high stakes" for better or worse of embodiedness in relation to human emotions. We need to allow emotions to be active because thereby "we can learn to be more sensitive to certain kinds of situation, and we can learn to control emotions like anger."[169] Moreover, he argues, emotions are more than inner moods. They point beyond themselves, and, as he argues elsewhere with reference to Schleiermacher and to Heidegger, they have ontological and referential significance as well as psychological content. Some are affirmative: "trust, contentment, joy, affection. Others are negative and opposite to these — suspicion, dissatisfaction, sorrow, resentment."[170] Hence: "The deliverances of the emotions need to be subjected to the critical scrutiny of reason. But our understanding of the human salvation will be vastly impoverished if the testimony of the emotions is neglected."[171] Even some of the "negative" emotions can stir us to healthy and beneficial action. These principles become extended in Moltmann's moving and penetrating material on "the Sorrow of God."[172]

---

166. Weiser, *The Psalms,* 512-13.

167. These phrases reflect my translation and exegesis of this passage, Thiselton, *First Epistle,* 1046-60.

168. Thiselton, *Psychological Aspects,* 59-117 and 292-342.

169. Macquarrie, *Humanity,* 56.

170. Macquarrie, *Humanity,* 57.

171. Macquarrie, *Humanity,* 57.

172. Moltmann, *The Trinity and the Kingdom of God,* 36-60 and elsewhere.

I turn now to some specific issues of these "high stakes" that result from placing together "relationality" and "bodiliness." Clearly *human sexuality* represents such an issue, and a hermeneutical horizon of understanding for interpreting the nature of the human. We recall Barth's emphasis upon relationality and "otherness" in the male-female relationship, and Grenz's conclusions about "bonding" and "difference." Grenz elaborates this theme in the final quarter of his book, stressing sexual differentiation and mutuality.[173] The key, he argues, is not subordination or hierarchy but mutual support. He cites Claus Westermann's comment on Gen. 2:18, "The man is created by God in such a way that he needs the help of a partner; hence mutual help is an essential part of human existence."[174]

This finds a parallel in Eccles. 4:9-10, "Two are better than one. . . . For if they fall, one will lift up the other." Grenz relates this to bodily life: "Being a human means being an embodied creature, and *embodiment entails being male or female*. Sexuality, therefore, includes the various dimensions of being in the world and relating to it as persons embodied as male or female."[175] "Sexuality is the dynamic that forms the basis of the uniquely human drive toward bonding."[176]

Grenz urges that as sexual beings "humans are fundamentally incomplete in themselves," although he extends this to include the notion that all persons find completion in community.[177] God as Trinity, he suggests, reflects this dialectic of incompleteness, bonding, and communal completion, although the church rightly, he notes, rejects any notion that God is sexual in any literal sense: "God is neither male nor female . . . the God of the Bible is beyond sexual distinctions."[178] Grenz alludes to Dietrich Bonhoeffer's observation that "belonging to one another" finds its deepest expression in terms of human sexuality.[179] All of this finds its expression through participation in the divine dynamic of love.[180]

The Church of England Doctrine Commission Report takes this further in practical terms for everyday life. The model for understanding sexuality is "God's own engagement with the world. . . . God desires and accepts love as well as giving it. God chooses not to be self-contained but deeply involved with the others God has made to be his partners in the world."[181] But the possibility of sexual intimacy brings "high stakes" because on one side "it is used to express the passion-

---

173. Grenz, *Social God*, 267-336.
174. Westermann, *Genesis 1–11*, 227; Grenz, *Social God*, 275.
175. Grenz, *Social God*, 272.
176. Grenz, *Social God*, 273.
177. Grenz, *Social God*, 280.
178. Grenz, *Social God*, 293.
179. Dietrich Bonhoeffer, *Creation and Fall/Temptation*, 62; cf. also 35-38.
180. Grenz, *Social God*, 332.
181. Church of England Doctrine Commission, *Being Human*, 85.

ate delight in each other and the passionate commitment to each other that God and God's people can experience."[182] On the other side, however, sexual intimacy can bring "disappointment and pain, even [the] jealousy and anger of God's wounded love for his unfaithful bride."[183] "Sexual engagement is mutually involving. It entails give-and-take, desire and delight, loss of control and self-surrender, the assumption of responsibility for each other."[184] Thus "the self-revelation and self-surrender of sexual engagement is particularly risky," for there are possibilities of joy, delight, and fulfillment, but also of pain, cruelty, perversion, and exploitation.[185] There is the glimpse of paradise, but also the risk of the wilderness.

Marriage brings the risk and the high stakes into sharpest focus. Paul is astonishingly ahead of his time in recognizing that sexual intimacy can give pleasure not only to man but also to woman (in contrast to the prevailing view of the times that the function of woman was to give one-sided pleasure to man). He stresses the *mutuality and reciprocity of the sexual relationship within marriage* (1 Cor. 7:3-6).[186] The initial comment of ch. 7, "It is good for a man not to have physical intimacy with a woman," is without doubt (to my mind) a quotation from a maxim circulated by some in Corinth.[187] Paul responds to the quotation with the words "Stop depriving each other (μὴ ἀποστερεῖτε, *mē apostereite*, present imperative) of what is due in marriage except perhaps by mutual agreement for a specific span of time" (1 Cor. 7:5). The married relationship takes precedence even over the parent-child relationship of each partner to their parents (Gen. 2:24). The symbolism of woman's creation from the man's rib (Gen. 2:21-22) reflects the character of sameness and difference that we have discussed with reference to Barth, Bonhoeffer, Brunner, and Grenz.

Nevertheless once again the contrast between the delight brought by many marriages and the darkness and suffering brought by others within a broken world points yet again to the high stakes involved in *bodily* life with its sexual dimensions. The report *Being Human* speaks of the consumer approach to sexuality in our day: "Sex has become one of the main idols of our time," and this commerce-laden approach explores sexual attractiveness "out of the context of relationships," often implying "such an inflated notion of sexual pleasure that the reality of sexual union can seem disappointing in relation to the fantasy."[188]

Sexual relations make it possible for some to exercise manipulative power over others. If a marriage ends in separation, painful and destructive conse-

182. *Being Human*, 85.
183. *Being Human*, 85.
184. *Being Human*, 86.
185. *Being Human*, 86.
186. See Thiselton, *First Epistle*, 503-10.
187. For evidence, see Thiselton, *First Epistle*, 493-502.
188. *Being Human*, 92.

quences arise not only for the couple, but for children, grandparents, and society. The relative security of marriage can make it easier for one partner to take the other for granted, or to resent change or development in the other.

Sexuality is a gift from the Creator designed not only to give happiness and delight, but also to allow the self to discover and to develop its own identity in relation to *"the other."* All the same, *"the other"* must presuppose a genuine mutuality and reciprocity. Simone de Beauvoir wrote in 1949, "Humanity is male, and man defines woman not in herself but as relative to him. . . . He is the subject. . . . She is the other."[189] But this is not what Christian theologians intend by "the other." Karl Barth writes, "Each sex has to realise that it is questioned by the other. . . . Neither the one nor the other can be content with his own sexuality or heedlessly work out his sexually conditioned capacities, needs, interests, tendencies, joys and sorrows. Man is unsettled by woman, and woman by man."[190] In Barth's view marriage "fixes and makes concrete" this experience for a particular man and a particular woman in a life-partnership that is the focus of "what is sought and striven for in genuine love."[191]

Sexuality, then, is a gift of God, and a paradigm case of relationality. Thereby it magnifies and raises the profile and the stakes of how we treat others and how others treat us in their mutuality with us and in their differences from us. But human sexuality in the setting of embodiment and bodiliness is not the only dimension of life that operates with this kind of effect. *The capacity of humankind to take responsibility for the world* (or to have "dominion" over it) *brings with it the gift of power, and the use of power constitutes a second axis of enhanced profile and higher stakes in our relations with fellow humans.*

If humankind is destined to reflect what *God* is like, human persons need *not only show love* and (as we have said) "to choose" *not to be self-contained* but deeply involved with . . . others; humankind is called to *exercise power and wisdom for the flourishing of all creation,* just as God exercises his rule. "If Christians are 'participants in the divine nature' (2 Pet. 1:4) and if power belongs to the divine nature, then Christians, and potentially all humanity, may share that power."[192] Nevertheless within a broken and fallen world "domination, the imposition of the will of one agent," also finds expression as an abuse, or distorted form, of power. In a careful conceptual study Gijsbert Van den Brink distinguishes between *power over* and *power to* or *power for,* which we often call *empowerment.* He writes, "Power is generally conceived here [i.e., in political theory] as power over persons rather than as power to do (or bring about)

189. Simone de Beauvoir, *The Second Sex,* "Introduction," repr. in E. Marks and Isabelle de Courtivron (eds.), *New French Feminism: An Anthology* (New York: Schocken and Hemel Hempstead: Harvester, 1981), 44; cf. 41-56.

190. Barth, *Church Dogmatics* III:4, sect. 54:1, 167.

191. Barth, *Church Dogmatics* III:4, sect. 54:1, 182 and 187.

192. Report, *Being Human,* 33.

things."[193] One major problem, he explains, is that we often disguise the desire for *power over people* as power *to* accomplish things. On the other hand, "All forms of power which we usually exercise in order to obtain some *specified outcome* . . . are more adequately formulated in terms of 'power *to*.'"[194] Conceptual clarification is therefore required.

Power, Van den Brink argues, is a dispositional concept, that is, instances of power are usually perceived in terms of their effects. But power is different from cause and from influence, even if it overlaps. It also differs from authority, which is a relational social phenomenon.[195] In its application to the nature of God, Van den Brink enumerates various problems in the use of the term *omnipotence*. In particular the logical paradoxes generated by *omnipotence* are well known. Rather than drawing upon Latin, more metaphysical tradition of *omnipotens*, he finds the Greek and biblical term παντοκράτωρ (*pantokratōr*), Almighty (2 Cor. 6:18; Rev. 1:8; 4:8; 11:17; 15:3; 16:7, 14; 19:25; 21:22), altogether more constructive and less potentially liable to mislead us.[196]

I do not have space to trace the differing concepts and uses of power revealed in the history of social relations and political action. One example discussed in the Report is that of Niccolò Machiavelli's *The Prince* (1513, published in 1532).[197] Luther's firm action in the face of the Peasants' Revolt (1524-26) is another example. Reinhold Niebuhr incisively demonstrates the ambiguity of human power. He writes, "Each principle of communal organization — the organisation of power and the balance of power — contains possibilities of contradicting the law of brotherhood. [It] may easily degenerate into tyranny. . . . Again, the principle of the balance of power is always pregnant with the possibility of anarchy."[198] Mark Lovatt (to whose work on Niebuhr we have already referred) assesses Niebuhr's theology of power against the background of human evil, in the face of which Niebuhr urges realism about the balances of the problem.[199] In some situations, especially with corporate bodies, "selflessness is self-defeating."[200]

In the report *Being Human* we accept that God commissions some, perhaps all, to exercise whatever power we or they may have for the flourishing of good. Some Christian officeholders may seek to opt out on the basis of a false humility, claiming that they merely share everyone else's questions. Yet God commissioned kings, judges, and prophets to act with courage and for good.

---

193. Gijsbert Van den Brink, *Almighty God: A Study of the Doctrine of Divine Omnipotence* (Kampen: Kok Pharos, 1993), 120.

194. Van den Brink, *Almighty God*, 121.

195. Van den Brink, *Almighty God*, 125-34.

196. Van den Brink, *Almighty God*, 134-84; cf. 204-75.

197. Report, *Being Human*, 42-44.

198. Niebuhr, *The Nature and Destiny of Man*, vol. 2, 267-68.

199. Lovatt, *Confronting the Will-to-Power*, 170-85.

200. Lovatt, *Confronting the Will-to-Power*, 171.

Nevertheless, on the other side, the power of the cross is far from a worldly power. Paul redefines it in Christ-like terms. At one level "power is made perfect in weakness" (2 Cor. 12:9), namely when a Christian has reached the end of his or her resources and trusts wholly in God (2 Cor. 1:9). *Power*, like *sexuality* and *bodiliness, raises the stakes for what kinds of human beings we are.* As Van den Brink reminds us, like belief the use of power is dispositional, that is, seen and experienced tangibly and visibly by its effects in the public domain. It may be accepted as a trust, or abused for self-aggrandizement and the oppression of the weak and unprotected.

The development of civilizations had led to the use of *money as our instrument of power* and of the quest for the *security of the self.* The biblical writings abound in warnings against the misuse of wealth. Like power itself, money may be used positively for human flourishing as a unit of exchange in place of goods, land, and property. The Report states, "Money is not the problem; we are the problem. It is not money that defines us theologically or spiritually, but our personal attitudes."[201] One problem, especially in our times, is the risk of equating a person's value or worth with the extent of their financial gain in the system of money. Profiles from business transactions are not always of the same order as the demonstrable contributions of craftsmen or farmers in earlier generations.

The most dramatic phenomenon of today is the explosion of credit. In moderation, drawing on credit permits the purchase of houses and the expansion of businesses. But today exponential advances of credit promote the use of wealth *in the present* drawn against *future* projections that may or may not materialize.[202] The present is becoming increasingly mortgaged to the future, which demonstrates the link between relationality, power, *and time.* The use of huge sums for a variety of insurance premiums and medical procedures makes possible what the Report calls "the fantasy of a risk-free life," as if humankind could hold old age, finitude, and mortality at bay.[203]

Yet there is a core of continuity in the biblical traditions and Christian doctrine. Concern for the poor, the destitute, the fatherless, and the widow is overwhelming in biblical traditions and Christian doctrine. The poor are a special concern of God's, for they live on the edge of destitution, with no economic security. "You shall not worry or oppress a resident alien, for you were aliens in the land of Egypt" (Exod. 22:21). "Because the poor are deported, because the needy groan, I will now rise up, says the LORD" (Ps. 12:5). James writes, "Religion that is pure . . . is this: to care for orphans and widows in their distress, and to keep oneself unstained by the world" (Jas. 1:27). Here, once again, we see the importance

---

201. Report, *Being Human,* 57.

202. See Peter Selby, *Grace and Mortgage: The Language of Faith and the Debt of the World* (London: Darton, Longman & Todd, 1997).

203. Report, *Being Human,* 74.

of the dispositional character of belief (introduced in 2.2). What people do with their pocketbook or purse *exhibits in the bodily world of action* what his or her faith *amounts to; how it is lived out.*

Just as sexuality, power, and money raise the profile and the stakes of "bodily" relationality, so *the gift of time* does the same. The most obvious example is that without the gift of time we could not practice and exhibit what we might call "the temporal virtues." *Faithfulness,* for example, presupposes the passing of a solid period of time for this virtue to be exercised and to become apparent. As Moltmann, Pannenberg, and Ricoeur all urge, the experience of time is a precondition for *memory, hope, recollection, faithfulness, and promise.*[204]

With the rise of rapid-return consumerism and the influence of postmodern perspectives, the nontheistic world threatens to diminish God's gift of time and even to turn it into a curse. Deadlines exert pressure on many victims today, whether in industry, commerce, or research programs. Relentless pressure makes an enemy of time. For the unemployed, the sick, or the destitute, time hangs heavily. The report *Being Human* acknowledges that Christians fall prey to these trends: to "a frantic busyness, a fear of novelty, a chronic impatience, a denial of death."[205]

By contrast, God's gift of time grants human persons the preconditions for the cultivation of the temporal virtues: patience and ability to wait; faithfulness to love and support through good and ill; resolve to trust when the future remains hidden. "'Taking time' is part of the nature of things. Trees take years to grow into their full stature. . . . Children take time to develop and grow," but too often we "allow ourselves to be dominated by clocks."[206] The liturgical year, with its observance of Sunday and its seasons of Advent, Christmas, Lent, Easter, Ascension Day, Whitsun, Trinity, and other Festivals offers a stable yearly and weekly rhythm that nurtures the passing of time within an overall linear, purposive, onward pattern.

We are left with a residual question on which Barth, Pannenberg, and others spend considerable attention. If *time* belongs as distinctively to the created order as *space and bodiliness,* does this imply that the world is temporal and that God is "timeless"? We address this question in 22.5. Here we make only a brief anticipatory comment.

If God were "timeless" in any absolute sense, it would be difficult to see where divine purpose would operate, without God's being dependent on the existence of the world. The biblical traditions ascribe successions of actions of God. However, God is not *conditioned* by time; rather, God is the *ground of the possibil-*

---

204. Cf. Jürgen Moltmann, *Experiences in Theology: Ways and Forms of Christian Theology,* trans. Margaret Kohl (London: S.C.M., 2000), 28-42; Pannenberg, *Systematic Theology,* vol. 2, 84-102; cf. vol. 1, 436-39; Ricoeur, *Time and Narrative,* vol. 1, 52-90 and vol. 3, 99-240.

205. Report, *Being Human,* 108.

206. Report, *Being Human,* 112 and 113.

ity of time. It may be constructive, therefore, to borrow Heidegger's term *temporality (Zeitlichkeit)* to denote the *transcendental* conditions for the *possibility* of time in speaking of God's relation to sequence, purpose, and change.

Physics and sociology contribute two further dimensions to this debate. Physics after Einstein suggests the indissoluble connection between the gift of *place, space, or embodiment* and the gift of *time.* It is difficult to imagine these as qualitatively different orders of gifts. Sociological research further suggests that human beings in practice distinguish regularly between chronological or astronomical time, measured by the clock, and "human" time, which is time as it is subject to social and human shaping and conditioning. It is not only the case that the same period of clock time passes rapidly in some situations and slowly in others. "Human time" becomes a social instrument of power and control. The employee waits for the employer to see him or her; the employer does not wait for the employee. Some impose deadlines; others have to meet deadlines. The structure of human time is as much a structure of power as money is. Even churches may find themselves managing or even manipulating time scales imposed upon others.

Nevertheless time is no less a gift from God through which to exhibit discipleship, growth, and honest virtue than bodiliness is. These two dimensions within which bodily and temporal life is lived are ways in which God enhances opportunity for relationships and the delight of being human, albeit within the constraints of limitations and divine "orderedness."

It now becomes apparent why the theme of Christ as the Image of God remains fundamental to any horizons of understanding for interpreting the human. Jesus Christ submitted himself fully to the *constraints* of time and place. The messianic temptations (Matt. 4:1-11; Luke 4:1-13) constitute a paradigmatic example of the temptation to take a shortcut that would violate the constraints of place, time, and suffering, to bring the timing of things to a head without the slow march to the cross. This would not have served the messianic calling in God's way or in God's time. Yet God's timing is not burdensome. Christians are called to place themselves within the grand temporal narrative of God's purposes enacted in history and in the world, from which they derive their identity and role. Within this grand narrative belong the "little narratives" of daily life. Here bodiliness or embodiment and time provide the preconditions not only to enjoy the fullness of life, but also, as Käsemann urges, to make Christian discipleship meaningful, credible, and communicable.

CHAPTER 12

The Hermeneutics of Misdirected Desire: The Nature of Human Sin

12.1. Horizons That Generate a Preunderstanding of the Multiform Nature of Sin

A massive gulf seems to be set between widespread notions of sin characteristic of more liberal Christian churches and those of traditions reflected by Paul, Augustine, Calvin, and more conservative or traditional churches. In the late nineteenth and early twentieth centuries, as we noted in 9.3, liberal theology reached its peak partly in reaction to a Victorian moralism and perhaps an excessive preoccupation with future judgment. Even up to the late 1960s churches and liturgies were producing forms of confessions of sin that in effect redefined sin as mistaken acts, failures, or falling short. The Church of England Alternative Service Book of 1980 did not wholly escape this fashion. However, this reintroduced unwittingly a *moralistic* understanding of sin by the back door. In biblical traditions the whole human condition is involved, including misdirected desire and the disruption of a relationship with God.

Pannenberg rightly speaks of "the dissolution of the traditional doctrine of sin, especially the idea of original sin," and plausibly suggests that "the decay of the doctrine" led to anchoring the concept of sin in "*acts* of sin," finally "reduced to the *individual* act."[1] However, even if part of the biblical vocabulary for sin called attention to this aspect, especially Hebrew חטא (*chāṭā'*), sometimes *to fall short* or *to miss the mark*, other vocabulary, for example, פשע (*pāsha'*), *to rebel*, opened up deeper aspects of human sin.

New levels of human thought and experience both inside and outside the

---

1. Pannenberg, *Systematic Theology*, vol. 2, 232 and 234 (my italics).

church have now overtaken the older liberal sensitivities. These derive not simply from Karl Barth's theology of crisis in the wake of World War I, but also initially Bultmann's use of existentialist analyses of the human condition in the mid-twentieth century; the insights of nontheist existentialist writers; Paul Ricoeur on human deception and fallibility; and then as we noted in 9.3, the rise of *postmodern* views of *the self as victim of forces beyond its control.* Bultmann draws on an existentialist hermeneutic to fill out a preunderstanding that the self-reliant, self-trusting human condition of "inauthentic" existence becomes trapped within inexorable processes generated by cause-effect, law-governed bondage to a past. When he combines this with a version of nineteenth-century Lutheranism, a very bleak picture of "man under sin" emerges.[2] It is not entirely surprising that one well-known exponent of mid-century English Liberalism, Denis Nineham, finds Bultmann so out of step with his [Nineham's] view of supposed "modern thought" that he declares, "In the last resort Bultmann too is a Biblicist."[3]

Toward the end of his career Bultmann acknowledged the validity of Macquarrie's criticism that his use of existentialism and of Heidegger had been "one-sided." Nevertheless, he replies, "Heidegger's analysis of existence has become for me fruitful for hermeneutics, that is, for the interpretation of the New Testament and of the Christian faith."[4] The hermeneutical horizon in question is not simply a matter of drawing upon some resonating or common vocabulary. Hermeneutics goes deeper than this. Following the earlier philosophies of Hegel and Dilthey, Bultmann finds in Heidegger the dual resources of an exposition of two phenomena. First he draws from him a notion of *historicity (Geschichtlichkeit), historicality,* or *radical historical finitude conditioned by one's pregiven place within the historical process.* Second, he derives from him the goal of *de-objectifying* a tradition formulated in spatio-temporal terms inherited from Aristotle, as if everything concerned "objective" states of affairs.

Historicity for Bultmann, as for Heidegger, implies the "being-there" *(Dasein)* of humankind within a *pregiven temporal horizon* of understanding.[5] *Deobjectification* implies the recognition that humankind is characterized by *Existenz* in which the person who is uniquely "me" *(Jemeinigkeit)* is constituted by the *effects of my prior understandings, stances, and decisions.* A human being does not survey the world in detached, abstract terms, but as one who already

---

2. Bultmann, *Theology of the New Testament,* vol. 1, 227-69. On the influence of *nineteenth-century* Lutheranism see Thiselton, *The Two Horizons,* 212-18 and more broadly 205-51.

3. Denis E. Nineham, *The Use and Abuse of the Bible: A Study of the Bible in an Age of Rapid Cultural Change* (London: Macmillan, 1976), 221.

4. Rudolf Bultmann, "Reply," in Charles W. Kegley, *The Theology of Rudolf Bultmann* (London: S.C.M., 1966), 275.

5. Heidegger, *Being and Time* Part I, sects. 9-13, 67-90. For a fuller exposition see Thiselton, *The Two Horizons,* 143-87, esp. 143-54.

"resides" within his or her nearest world *(Umwelt),* constituted by his or her "thrownness" *(Geworfenheit)* into it, and by its preshaped possibilities and constraints.[6] Heidegger writes, "The person is not a Thing, not a substance, not an object. . . . Man's being is not something we can simply compute by adding together . . . body, soul, and spirit."[7] He comments further, "Thus hermeneutic also becomes a 'hermeneutic' in the sense of working out the conditions on which the possibility of any ontological investigation depends."[8] It is thus a *transcendental* hermeneutic.

Heidegger's world is not the dualistic and substantival world of Descartes or of the British empiricists. *Dasein* (in other words, human being within pregiven horizons and a pregiven "world") is, in Heidegger's technical terms, "*thrown possibility* through and through" (his italics).[9] The existential structure of humankind is "projection" *(Entwurf),* in which the temporal dimensions and horizons of the past and future are fundamental. Heidegger comes near to the edge of Christian theology here, at least in his language: "Only because it *is* what it becomes (or alternatively does not become) can it say to itself, 'Become what you are,' and say it with understanding."[10]

This leads not only to an affirmation of the human condition amid the horizons of *time,* but also to an affirmation of the hermeneutical circle as a vehicle of understanding and interpretation.[11] Bare assertion, or bare description, abstracted from its hermeneutical frame, is a "derivative mode of interpretation."[12]

Further major themes of *Being and Time* include the "falling" *(Verfallen)* of *Dasein,* care *(Sorge),* and dread or anxiety *(Angst)* that generates fear *(Furcht). Dasein* faces death; or *"Being toward death as a possibility"* (Heidegger's italics).[13] This leads on to reflection upon "authentic *existentiell* possibility" and "authentic potentiality-for-being" within the conditions, constraints, and possibilities of temporality *(Zeitlichkeit),* and reflections concerning "the inauthentic future."[14]

Bultmann finds in all this a hermeneutical horizon or conceptual frame within which to understand Paul's contrast between humankind under the power of sin and humankind under divine grace. *The power of sin closes in human possibilities,* and renders humankind a prisoner of past decisions and past

6. Heidegger, *Being and Time,* Part I, sects. 14-24, 91-148; cf. Thiselton, *The Two Horizons,* 154-61.

7. Heidegger, *Being and Time,* sect. 10, 74.

8. Heidegger, *Being and Time,* Introduction, Part II, 62.

9. Heidegger, *Being and Time,* sect. 31, 183. Cf. Thiselton, *The Two Horizons,* 163-66.

10. Heidegger, *Being and Time,* sect. 31, 186; cf. 185.

11. Heidegger, *Being and Time,* sect. 32, 188-95. Cf. Thiselton, *The Two Horizons,* 166-68.

12. Heidegger, *Being and Time,* sect. 33, 195-203.

13. Heidegger, *Being and Time,* Part II, sect. 53, 306.

14. Heidegger, *Being and Time,* Part II, sects. 54-71, 312-423; cf. Thiselton, *The Two Horizons,* 169-87.

attitudes. It is existence under the law. By contrast, Bultmann writes, "Freedom is nothing else than being open for the genuine [authentic] future, *letting oneself be determined by the future.* So Spirit may be called the power of futurity."[15] In Rom. 5–7 Paul expounds the themes of human bondage to divine wrath, to death, and to the law, which Bultmann perceives as more intelligible and weighty in the light of existential hermeneutics.

To live "in the flesh," or to set one's mind on the things of the flesh (Rom. 8:7), is "to trust in one's self as being able to procure life by the use of the earthly and through one's own strength and accomplishments."[16] It denotes "the self-reliant attitude of the man who puts his trust in his own strength."[17] But thereby a human being is thrown under "the power of sin," which "forces all men without exception into slavery" (Rom. 3:23; cf. 3:9, 19; Gal. 3:22)."[18] Humankind is now caught up in *a vicious circle of bondage.* The law operates on the basis of what a person has become or has done *in the past up to the present.* The Spirit offers the possibility of being determined by the *future,* and lifted out of the cause-effect nexus that ties human persons to an imprisoning past.

As a hermeneutical *model* (and a model of *one aspect* only) Bultmann engages creatively with humanity's awareness *that past attitudes and decisions have blocked off paths to the future that would otherwise still lie open before them.* This is the tragic aspect of life, and it has been brilliantly exposed as such not only by Heidegger but also by a multitude of philosophers, artists, and novelists in the existentialist tradition from Kierkegaard and Dostoyevsky to Franz Kafka, Karl Jaspers, Jean-Paul Sartre, and Albert Camus. It is a feature of tragedy in literature that a key character draws onward toward an *unavoidable doom,* but often *under the illusion that he or she can control their destiny.* Bultmann transposes what might have been perceived as a narrow preoccupation with sin and the Jewish law into a wider model of doomed human existence, struggling to battle with superior forces "in one's own strength," but to no avail. By drawing upon temporal horizons of understanding, and upon Heidegger's notions of possibility, anxiety, historicity, and modes of being, Bultmann has added force, meaning, and credibility to Paul's portrait of humankind "under sin."

Nevertheless, because his approach is "one-sided," Bultmann's obsession with *deobjectification* has also eroded away the *grounds* of the possibility of new life. Even the Holy Spirit becomes less an active agent than a mode of human existence, namely "the power of futurity." In other words, the price for this deobjectification is that of transposing description, states of affairs, and public history into address, call, symbol, and myth. It would be tedious to repeat the

---

15. Rudolf Bultmann, *Theology of the New Testament,* vol. 1, 335.
16. Bultmann, *Theology,* vol. 1, 239.
17. Bultmann, *Theology,* vol. 1, 240.
18. Bultmann, *Theology,* vol. 1, 249.

detailed critique of Bultmann on myth that I (and others) have presented elsewhere.[19]

All the same, in spite of these very serious criticisms, Bultmann leaves a suggestive hermeneutics for our understanding of the vocabulary by means of which Paul denotes the human condition. Thus Bultmann writes, "'Body' and 'soul' do not refer to *parts* of man . . . but rather always mean man as a whole, with respect to some specific possibility of his being."[20]

Bultmann is not alone in exploring an existentialist hermeneutic. John Macquarrie endorses the view that humankind is not to be thought of in terms of "properties," but in terms of modes of existence oriented toward the past or the future.[21] Further, he draws on Heidegger's view of being-toward-death to explicate fallen human existence. He writes, "It is for fallen existence that death appears as the great evil that must be covered up. But if the transition is made from an inauthentic to an authentic existence, death is not changed; what is changed is the attitude towards death."[22] This is no longer the attitude of trying to flee from death or to cover it up, but an acceptance of death. Thereby a hitherto "senseless succession" of present moments attains a unity and potential meaning.

Paul Tillich also argues that theology has received "tremendous gifts from existentialism."[23] For him its analysis of finitude and human anxiety provides one of several hermeneutical bridges for theology. On the other hand, it is arguable that Tillich allows this existential analysis to become too dominant, so that a process of assimilation rather than of hermeneutics takes place under the methodological constraints of his principle of correlation. As Gadamer warns us, the two horizons that mark different understandings can never reach a total correspondence or one-to-one match. He writes, "The hermeneutic task consists in not covering up this tension by attempting a naïve assimilation of the two but in consciously bringing it out."[24] We do not suggest that Tillich's principle of correlation is "naïve"; but it is too generalizing and overly ready to lose the irreducible distinctiveness of Christian theology. Hans Frei goes further, and acutely observes, "The issue is one of compatibility . . . a compatibility that is, at the outset at least, in question."[25] For Tillich, even more than Bultmann, *dehistoricizes* the narrative of the human condition. He sees the biblical narratives of the Fall in Gen. 3 as "the profoundest and richest expression of man's awareness of his exis-

19. Thiselton, *The Two Horizons*, 252-92.

20. Rudolf Bultmann, *Existence and Faith: Shorter Writings of Rudolf Bultmann,* ed. Schubert Ogden (London: Collins/Fontana, 1964), 153.

21. Macquarrie, *An Existentialist Theology: A Comparison of Heidegger and Bultmann* (London: S.C.M., 1955, rpt. 1973), 32 and elsewhere.

22. John Macquarrie, *Studies in Christian Existentialism* (London: S.C.M., 1966), 236.

23. Paul Tillich, *Theology of Culture* (New York: Galaxy, 1964), 126.

24. Gadamer, *Truth and Method*, 306.

25. Hans W. Frei, *Types of Christian Theology* (New Haven, CT: Yale, 1992), 31.

tential estrangement and . . . transition from essence to existence"; but he does not even concede "a loose fit" with any event that may or may not have transpired.[26] The level of discourse is that of timeless symbolism. At the same time Tillich sees the symbol of the "fall" as resulting for humankind in "the power of separating himself from God."[27] It is the end of "dreaming innocence."[28]

This resonates, to be sure, with very many thinking people today because "destiny and freedom, tragedy and responsibility, are interwoven in every human being from early childhood on and in all social and political groups in the history of mankind."[29] Tillich perceives the tensions entailed in trying to do justice to each aspect. He argues that these tensions can readily be seen in Augustine's attempts to steer between Manichaeism and Pelagianism; in Luther's rejection of Erasmus; in the struggle between the Jansenists and the Jesuits; and in the conflict between liberal theology and neoorthodox theology. Christianity "cannot escape these tensions," Tillich concludes, but must also "acknowledge the tragic universality of estrangement and man's personal responsibility for it."[30]

In 9.3 we considered how the notion of "situatedness" within a pregiven socio-economic world offered a *postmodern* account of the vulnerability of human persons to social forces and structures beyond their control. We traced Michel Foucault's account of oppressive bureaucratic forces and officialdom, including "the smiling face in the white coat" of psychiatric and medical control of "norms" of conduct. J.-F. Lyotard goes even further. The "consensus" of a liberal democracy, he maintains, is a sham, for in conflicts between opposed views, the *"differend,"* as he calls it, always results in the assimilation of the language, agenda, and idioms of the weaker party into that of the stronger party. The party, group, or persons who "control" the discourse will not accommodate the weaker party, who perceive themselves victims of injustice or vested interests.[31] Even the "little narratives" of "local" concerns work themselves out as ruses of deceptive disguise. Human persons are vulnerable to irrationality, to randomness, and to the interests of the strong, and this finds expression in Lyotard's defense of the "the pagan ideal" and "terror." "Pagan" denotes here "a mode of action characterized by the impiety of proceeding without criteria."[32]

26. Tillich, *Systematic Theology,* vol. 2, 35.

27. Tillich, *Systematic Theology,* vol. 2, 37.

28. Tillich, *Systematic Theology,* vol. 2, 38-41.

29. Tillich, *Systematic Theology,* vol. 2, 44.

30. Tillich, *Systematic Theology,* vol. 2, 45.

31. Jean-François Lyotard, *The Differend: Phrases in Dispute,* trans. Georges Van Den Abbeele (Manchester: Manchester University Press, 1988), throughout. Cf. Jean-François Lyotard, *The Postmodern Condition: A Report on Knowledge,* trans. G. Bennington and B. Massumi (Manchester: Manchester University Press, 1984).

32. Bill Readings, *Introducing Lyotard: Art and Politics* (London: Routledge, 1991), xxxiii; and Honi Huber Haber, *Beyond Postmodern Politics: Lyotard, Rorty, Foucault* (New York and London: Routledge, 1994), 15-26.

Paul Ricoeur contributes substantially to these hermeneutical resources. He is not only the most significant exponent of hermeneutics alongside Gadamer; he also provides a bridge between phenomenology or existentialism and certain specific aspects of poststructuralist postmodernism, even though he is not strictly a postmodern thinker. The clearest account of how he stands as a historical bridge between these movements occurs in his "Intellectual Autobiography."[33] Between 1934 and 1939 he was heavily influenced by the existentialism of Karl Jaspers and the phenomenological existentialism of Gabriel Marcel, Maurice Merleau-Ponty, and Edmund Husserl. During the war years as a prisoner in Germany, he engaged more deeply with the philosophy of Husserl, Jaspers, and Heidegger, and began to prepare the ground for his *Voluntary and Involuntary*. In 1948 he published material on Marcel and on Jaspers, and in 1950 his *Philosophy of the Will*, volume I, *Voluntary and Involuntary*. Then in 1960 there followed the two-part continuation of *Philosophy of the Will: Finitude and Guilt:* Part I, *Fallible Man*; Part II, *The Symbolism of Evil*.[34] The theme of Part I was that *human frailty,* not necessarily evil, was the necessary effect of a finite will, but evil lies at hand because the human will is characterized by *fallibility,* with a strong capacity to do wrong.

Humankind is vulnerable to moral evil, and imagination, perception, and intention can readily be misdirected or deceived into situations of evil. Against Descartes and anticipating postmodern perspectives Ricoeur insists that the self is not transparent to itself or to others. There is an "otherness" *(alterité)* about one's body, other people, conscience, and (in his later *Oneself as Another*) even the self. In Part II, *The Symbolism of Evil*, Ricoeur explores the symbols of stain, of sin, and of *guilt,* including symbols of the Fall in tragic and Adamic myths. The symbols "gives rise to thought," or "set us thinking."[35] By 1965 Ricoeur had published his work on Freud, and this offered a model for certain aspects of hermeneutical awareness and hermeneutical interpretation, while at the same time underlining the obscurity of the self and its capacity for self-deception. Reflection and action are no longer the simple, transparent phenomena postulated in earlier, older, liberal theologies or liberal politics. Recognition of the opaqueness of the human self is one of the more positive insights of postmodern thought, although it is far from being an exclusively postmodern insight (Jer. 17:9; 1 Cor. 3:18). Ricoeur also shares the postmodern distrust of "totality" or rejection of plurality, recognizing "conflicts" of interpretations.

33. Paul Ricoeur, "Intellectual Autobiography," in Lewis E. Hahn (ed.), *The Philosophy of Paul Ricoeur* (Chicago and La Salle, IL: Open Court, 1995), 3-53.

34. Paul Ricoeur, *Philosophie de la Volonté: Finitude et Culpabilité:* I, *L'homme Fallible* (Paris: Aubier, 1960), trans. by C. A. Kebley as *Fallible Man* (Chicago: Regency, 1965); and II, *La symbolique du mal* (Paris: Aubier, 1960), trans. by E. Buchanan as *The Symbolism of Evil* (New York: Harper & Row, 1967; and Boston: Beacon Press, 1969).

35. Ricoeur, *Freud and Philosophy,* 543; and "Intellectual Autobiography," 17.

At the same time Ricoeur never surrendered a fundamental respect for the role of the human subject and the agency of the human self. More extreme versions of postmodernism, by contrast, sometimes bypass the role of the "speaking subject."[36] During the turbulent years of the late 1960s and 1970s in Paris he engaged with structuralism and poststructuralism, and shared seminars with Lacan and Derrida.[37] But the importance of the human subject, albeit in nothing like its Cartesian or empirical form, reappeared in his *Time and Narrative* (3 vols., French, 1983-85) and especially in *Oneself as Another* (French, 1990).[38] In this last work he revealed the complexity of the human self; its identity is not only one of "sameness" (Latin *idem*) that relates to "objectified" features of the self as a subject who speaks and acts, but also something more than self-identity (Latin *ipse;* French *ipséité*), namely a self-designation as speaker or agent. The French *même* permits an ambiguity that hovers between *same* and *self.* There is almost a "third" self or "another" in such experiences as the call of conscience.

Such a view of the complexity of the human selfhood, combined with deeply symbolic understandings of fallibility, self-deception, guilt, finitude, and evil, set the stage for a horizon of understanding that can encompass the multiformity of biblical traditions and vocabularies of sin and human alienation and brokenness. Sin is more than a matter of isolated acts of failure or error. What is at issue is the nature of the human self. Existentialism, postmodernity, and Ricoeur help us to adjust initial horizons of understanding that seek to interpret the human condition and the nature of human sin.

It is not the case that every aspect of postmodern thought is convincing. But it embodies certain insights that deserve attention and prove to be constructive for hermeneutics. Social, political, and natural disasters of the late twentieth and early twenty-first centuries provide fertile soil for a culture that is not only well aware of the vulnerability of humankind, but also recognizes the overwhelming force of structural and political systems beyond the control of the individual. The phenomena of escalating evil that brings oppression, hunger, poverty, unemployment, suffering, and violence to millions among the marginalized is more apparent today than perhaps in the mid-twentieth century. Such phenomena as global warming, terrorism, and in some cases the breakdown of civil and military order associated with former nation-states or empires nurtures a cast of mind different from that of the mid-century.

With the unmasking especially in secular postmodernity of various systems of truth or ethics as structures of *disguised power,* the concepts of human sin

36. Cf. Julia Kristeva's critique of Jacques Derrida in Julia Kristeva, "The System and the Speaking Subject," *Times Literary Supplement,* 12 October, 1973, 1249-52; repr. in Toril Moi (ed.), *The Kristeva Reader* (New York: Columbia University Press, 1986), 25-32.

37. Ricoeur, "Intellectual Autobiography," 17-35.

38. Paul Ricoeur, *Soi-même comme un autre* (Paris: Seuil, 1990), trans. by K. Blamey as *Oneself as Another* (Chicago: University of Chicago, 1992).

from the eighteenth century to the mid-twentieth century in terms of moralistic criteria no longer resonate with thinking persons as readily as they once did. In the present climate questions about alienation, broken relationships, self-damage, structural evil, deception, victimization, bondage, and wretchedness or "misery" carry more hermeneutical potential for understanding than older liberal notions of sin as mistakes and failures. In the next section we shall see that in this respect the biblical writings speak more readily to our day than to the moralism of earlier modernity. In particular we should be cautious not to sweep aside the Pauline and Augustinian emphases on sin as *misdirected desire*, and as a source of certain *irresistible effects*, not least the effects of *broken relationships*, broken hearts, and alienation.

12.2. Multiform Understandings of Sin in the Old and New Testaments

Within these horizons of understanding, simple accounts of human sin in terms of missing the mark may seem not only unduly legalistic but also to reflect a hermeneutics of pretended innocence. Older liberal theologies have often tried to seek support on the basis of the supposedly "milder" teaching of Jesus, in contrast to that of the Old Testament and Paul. But such a view is untenable.

Udo Schnelle writes of the beginnings of the gospels, "Jesus begins with the message of John the Baptist. John's proclamation is a preaching of judgment and repentance (cf. Matt. 3:2). For him it is not merely a question of moral improvement; the expressive βάπτισμα μετανοίας εἰς ἄφεσιν ἁμαρτιῶν ('baptism of repentance for the forgiveness of sins,' Mark 1:4) involves an anthropological presupposition: all of Israel, in its present state, is a 'collective disaster' and liable to judgement."[39] "All are sinners" (Luke 13:3).[40] Confession of personal and communal guilt is presupposed in the Lord's Prayer (Matt. 6:12; Luke 11:4). The parables of the unforgiving servant (Matt. 18:23-30) and of the Pharisee and the tax collector (Luke 18:10-14) underline the same point.

Jesus stands fully in continuity with the Old Testament traditions concerning human sin, and Paul, John, and Epistle to the Hebrews expound the same multidimensional vocabulary. John the Baptist's call for repentance, repeated by Jesus, is not fully reflected by a bare etymology of the Greek term μετανοέω, which some render as *having regret* or *"an after-mind"* (μετά, *after*, with νοῦς, *mind*). On the contrary, it represents the usual LXX translation of the Hebrew שׁוּב (shûbh), *to turn away from, to turn back*, although it also overlaps with נחם (nācham), *to be penitent, to regret*. J. Behm insists that in many contexts the

---

39. Udo Schnelle, *The Human Condition: Anthropology in the Teachings of Jesus, Paul, and John*, trans. O. C. Dean (Edinburgh: T&T Clark, 1996), 23.
40. Schnelle, *Human Condition*, 24.

Greek term denotes *conversion*. John the Baptist preaches both the need for conversion and a baptism of conversion; a continuous repetition of "manifold exertions to throw off sin. . . . It is demanded of all, not just of notorious sinners (Luke 3:12-13) or Gentiles (Matt. 3:7ff.). It implies a change from within."[41] Jesus makes conversion "a fundamental requirement."[42]

This accords entirely with Würthwein's understanding of repentance and conversion in the Old Testament and in rabbinic Judaism. It is clearly expressed, for example, in Joel 2:12: "*Turn* to me with all your heart, and with fasting, with weeping, and mourning"; cf. Isa. 22:12-13.[43] "What counts is turning from the sinful nature as such. . . . Conversion to Yahweh must be oriented to Yahweh . . . as a turning of the whole existence to Yahweh"[44] (cf. Hos. 6:1-6; Isa. 30:15; Jer. 34:15). As the Old Testament reaches the brink of the exile and postexilic period, the word שׁוּב (*shûbh*) combines with מִן (*min*) to mean *to turn from*.[45] Clearly the presupposition of all this in the Old Testament, John the Baptist, and *Jesus* is that sin denotes more than an *act*; it reflects a *stance, attitude, mind-set, or state,* as well as *misdirected desire, will, habit, or interest*. This understanding is confirmed in recent studies. For example, H. Merklein writes that in the Synoptic gospels "*repentance* is first of all a turning away from sin (Mark 1:4-5). . . . It is both a turning away from former things . . . and an acknowledgement of the message and mission of Jesus."[46]

The biblical writings regularly use three groups of words to denote different aspects of human sin, both in Hebrew and in Greek, to call attention respectively to (i) the aspect of action or failure; (ii) a more deliberate action with more serious effects often entailing an attitude or desire; and (iii) a resultant state of sinfulness. The differences are pronounced but not clear-cut, depending on context.

(i) In Hebrew the verb חָטָא (*chāta'*) usually denotes "*to do wrong, to commit a mistake . . . error, to miss the mark, to miss the way,*" while its cognate noun חַטָא (*chattā'th*) more generally denotes *sin* or *error* (or, in some contexts, also sin offering).[47] Thus, Proverbs warns its readers, "One who moves too hurriedly *misses the way* (חוֹטֵא, *chōtē'*)." In 1 Sam. 26:21, Saul says to David, "I *have done wrong*

---

41. J. Behm, "μετανοέω and μετάνοια *(metanoia)* in the New Testament," in Gerhard Kittel (ed.), *TDNT*, vol. 4, 1001; cf. 999-1006.

42. Behm, "μετανοέω," *TDNT*, vol. 4, 1091.

43. E. Würthwein, "Repentance and Conversion in the Old Testament," in Kittel, *TDNT*, 4, 983; cf. 980-89.

44. Würthwein, "Repentance," *TDNT*, vol. 4, 983 and 985.

45. Würthwein, "Repentance," *TDNT*, vol. 4, 986.

46. H. Merklein, "μετανοέω" *(metanoeō)*, in Horst Balz and Gerhard Schneider (eds.), *Exegetical Dictionary of the New Testament*, 3 vols. (Grand Rapids: Eerdmans, 1981), vol. 2, 417; cf. 415-19.

47. F. Brown, S. R. Driver, and C. A. Briggs (eds.), *The New Hebrew and English Lexicon* (Lafayette, IN: Associated, 1980), 306; cf. 306-8. Cf. further Richard E. Averbeck, "חטא," in W. A. VanGemeren, *New International Dictionary of Old Testament Theology and Exegesis*, vol. 2, 93-103.

(חטאתי, *chāṭā'tî*), come back. . . . I have been a fool and a made a great mistake." Significantly Lev. 4:2ff. speaks of "unintentional" sin or sins of omission (תחטא, *techᵉṭā'*, Lev. 4:2; cf. Lev. 4:22, 27; 5:16; Num. 15:27, 28). In the Piel form of the verb the meaning can be that of *bearing a loss:* "*I bore the loss* myself" (Gen. 31:39). In the Hiphal form it often denotes simply *missing the mark.* "Every one could sling a stone at a hair and not *miss*" (יחטא, *yachᵉṭî'*, Judg. 20:16). This places the emphasis upon sin as (sometimes unintentional) acts or shortcomings, and tends to resonate with notions in some writers that sin can be corrected by knowledge and teaching alone.

(ii) The Hebrew verb פשע (*pāsha'*) denotes considerably more than this. The Hebrew lexicon Brown-Driver-Briggs, *The New Hebrew-English Lexicon* (1980 edition), translates it *to rebel, to trespass,* in its verbal form (usually the Qal in Hebrew), and translates the substantival form פשע (*pesha'*), as *transgression* or *rebellion.*[48] Typically Isaiah begins the Lord's lawsuit against Israel with the words: "I reared children and brought them up, but they have rebelled against me" (Hebrew פשעו, *pāsh'û*). Children who rebel against their parents undertake a willful act that *results in a broken relationship. Pesha'* is applied to the rebellion of groups or nations in warfare (1 Kings 12:19; 2 Kings 3:5, 7; 2 Chron. 10:19), but especially to transgressing against God. In Isa. 59:13 the prophet accuses Israel of "*transgressing* (פשע, *pāshōa'*) and denying the Lord, turning away from following our God." Watts comments, "*Rebelling* (פשע) is naturally a political word implying refusal to fulfill a vassal's obligations. That would be a crime against Persia. But the words that follow, *denying* (כחש) and *turning away* (נסוג) are directed against *Yahweh, their God.*"[49] This use of the word is typical of the prophets (cf. Isa. 43:27; Hos. 14:10; Amos 4:4;). In the prophetic literature it often denotes a *wilful or deliberate breach of relationship with God and act of self-assertion,* often stemming from *misdirected desire* for other supposed goals apart from God.

(iii) A third Hebrew term takes us even further into the heart of the matter concerning the human condition. The Hebrew noun עון (*'āwōn*) is translated *iniquity, guilt, punishment for iniquity,* or *consequences of iniquity,* usually in the sense of denoting a state or status.[50] The cognate verb עוה (*'āwâ*) means *to do wrong* in the Qal form, but in the Niphal it means *to be disturbed, to be distressed,* and in the Hiphal *to pervert.* The Qal occurs in 2 Sam. 7:14, "When he commits iniquity, I will punish him" (cf. 2 Sam. 19:19; 24:17; 2 Kings 8:47; Ps. 106:6). In Job 33:37, however, it more explicitly denotes *perverting:* "I sinned, and perverted what was right." This nuance also occurs in Jeremiah: "the plaintive weeping of Israel's children [is heard] because they have perverted their way" (Jer. 3:21, העוו, *heᵉwû*). Here the sorrow, brokenness, or "misery" of the human condition is directly perceived as a

---

48. Brown-Driver-Briggs, *The New Hebrew-English Lexicon,* 833, cols. i and ii.

49. John D. W. Watts, *Isaiah 34–66* (Waco, TX: Word, 1987), 283.

50. Brown-Driver-Briggs, *The New Hebrew-English Lexicon,* 833, col. ii and 731, cols. i and ii.

damaged condition, resulting from wrongdoing. In Prov. 12:8 the Hebrew verb, this time in the Niphal, denotes a state of mind: "a perverse mind is despised" (NRSV). In Lam. 3:9 the Piel of the verb is used adjectivally to denote *crooked* paths.

This does not exhaust the Hebrew vocabulary for sin and evil, but provides the contours of its main dimensions. Further surveys that discuss general terms for sin or evil and specific metaphors for "willful error," "rebellion and treachery," and "opposites" can readily be found elsewhere.[51] The vocabulary for human sin in the New Testament is both more wide-ranging and more fluid. In very broad terms πλάνη *(plane),* "wandering from the path of truth, error," and ἁμαρτία *(hamartia),* "a departure from either human or divine standards of uprightness," appear at first sight to reflect the notion of human as a mistaken action, error, or failure that misses the mark, like *chattā'th.*[52] However, even this assumption would be too hasty.

The third (2000) edition of BDAG does not leave the matter there. ἁμαρτία *(hamartia)* is not simply a departure from divine or human standing (meaning 1); it also denotes "a *state* of being sinful, sinfulness."[53] Further, this "state of being sinful" acts as "a destructive evil power" as in Sir. 27:10; Rom. 5:12; 6:6; 6:14; Gal. 3:22, and elsewhere in Paul. Human persons can become "enslaved to sin" (Rom. 6:6); indeed, "sold into slavery under sin" (Rom. 7:14). There is an inner principle, internal process, or "law" of sin that brings serious consequences and entraps the sinner as its "captive" (Rom. 7:23). Not only Paul, but also other New Testament writers speak of sin (ἁμαρτία, *hamartia*) as a force that deceives humankind and thereby "hardens" them (Heb. 3:13). Even the more innocent-looking, πλᾶνη *(plane), error,* also denotes "delusion, deceit, deception to which one is subject."[54] The Jewish leaders want to guard against any "deception" (NRSV) about Jesus' being raised from the dead (Matt. 27:64). Paul assures the church in Thessalonica that his preaching does not spring from self-deception, self-interest, or "deceit" (1 Thess. 2:3).

It might be tempting to imagine that ἀνομία *(anomia)* denotes simply *lawlessness* in the sense of committing acts that fall short of the standards of the law. However, BDAG defines the meaning in terms of a *human state* or the *human condition:* "state or condition of being disposed to what is lawless . . . the product of a lawless disposition."[55] Paul speaks of human limbs and organs serving ἀνομία *(anomia)* as its slaves (Rom. 6:19). John states that everyone who commits sin is guilty of *anomia* (1 John 3:4). The *"lawless one"* in 2 Thess. 2:3 "exalts himself above every so-called God and takes his seat in the temple of God, declaring himself to be God."

51. Cf., e.g., C. Ryder Smith, *The Bible Doctrine of Sin and the Ways of God with Sinners* (London: Epworth, 1953), 15-36.

52. The quotations are from Danker-Bauer's 3d (2000) edn., BDAG, 50-51 and 822.

53. BDAG, 51, col. i.

54. BDAG, 822, cols. i and ii.

55. BDAG, 85, cols. i and ii.

Other Greek terms used in the New Testament correspond more clearly to the Hebrew words פֶּשַׁע (*pasha'*) and עָוֹן (*'āwōn*) or עָוָה (*'āwâ*). παράβασις (*parabasis*) may denote derivations from a norm, but it also denotes "*transgression.*"[56] In Rom. 2:23 it denotes a way of dishonoring God; in Rom. 5:14 it refers to the transgression of Adam. Yet it is an arguably "weaker" term in many contexts than παράπτωμα (*paraptōma*), which denotes an offense or a habit of wrongdoing. It denotes an offense against God in Wis. 10:1 and Rom. 5:15, 17-18; cf. Gal. 6:1. ἀδικία (*adikia*) is broader than *injustice*. In common with פֶּשַׁע (*p-sh-'*) it may denote an act, but in common with עָוָה (*'āwâ* or *āwōn*) it brings about harm or injury, especially in the form ἀδίκημα (*adikēma*).[57]

It is of course hazardous to undertake studies of vocabulary without noting how synonymy or difference is governed by context, which is why we have instantiated these provisional generalizations with reference to specific passages. What emerges from such studies is a fluidity in the use of the terms, but that between them they emphasize the respective dimensions of human sin as *manifold or multiform, including* an understanding of sin as actions that entail consequences. These are in the first place a breach of fellowship with God, emphasized in particular by the notion of "rebellion," and in the second place an aspect of self-destruction or distortion of the self, found especially in the Niphal form of עָוָה (*'āwâ*). Bonsirven rightly observes that in using such a wide-ranging vocabulary for human sin, Paul the apostle speaks of *sin* (singular) or sinfulness rather than a list of "*sins.*"[58]

The New Testament writers frequently speak of *desire* or *desires* (ἐπιθυμία, *epithumia*, 37 times) and its verbal form (ἐπιθυμεῖν, *epithumein*, 16 times), whether of good desires (Luke 22:15; Phil. 1:23; Heb. 6:11) or bad desires (Mark 4:19; John 8:44; Rom. 1:24; 1 Cor. 10:6). *Epithumia* is used in a bad sense thirty-one times, typically in Paul as desires of the flesh (σάρξ, *sarx*, Rom. 13:14; Gal. 5:16; 1 John 2:16). But, as Ryder Smith observes, in such contexts neither *desire* nor *flesh* in ordinary English usage conveys what is at issue. Smith proposes to translate the Greek in these contexts as *to set one's heart upon,* to denote the deliberate *choice* of such desire.[59] A substantial amount of research literature underlines Paul's emphasis upon *craving* in 1 Cor. 10:6. Collier in particular argues that "craving for evil things" (ἐπιθυμητὰς κακῶν, *epithumētas kakōn*, v. 6) has controlling significance and the utmost force for the whole of 1 Cor. 10:1-13.[60] This coheres with Pannenberg's important comment that whatever supposed shortcomings might be attributed to Augustine, "the classical significance of Au-

---

56. BDAG, 758-59.

57. BDAG, 20-21.

58. Joseph Bonsirven, *Theology of the New Testament,* trans. J. F. Tye (London: Burns & Oates, 1963), 254-62 and 275-78; cf. 52-59.

59. Smith, *Doctrine of Sin,* 162.

60. G. D. Collier, "That We Might Not Crave Evil: The Structure and Argument of 1 Cor. 10:1-13," *JSNT* 55 (1994) 55-75.

gustine for the Christian doctrine of sin consists in the fact that *he viewed and analyzed the Pauline link between sin and desire more deeply than Christian theology had hitherto managed to do*" (my italics).[61]

The remaining term that requires careful understanding and interpretation in the New Testament is a particular use of the word *flesh* (σάρξ, *sarx*). Sometimes the word denotes no more than physical flesh in the physiological sense (1 Cor. 15:39, of a substance: "not all flesh is the same flesh"). It also denotes human weakness, like the Hebrew בשׂר (*bāsār;* see, e.g., 1QS 9:4; Gal. 4:13). In some passages it refers to what is *external* (Gal. 6:12-13; Phil. 3:3-4). These uses are widely endorsed in Pauline scholarship.[62] However, Paul in particular employs the term also in a more theological way. In its most explicitly theological meaning and context it denotes (in Bultmann's words) "a turning away from the Creator . . . and a turning towards the creation — and to do that is to trust in one's self as being able to procure life by the use of the earthly and through one's own strength and accomplishments. It is in this sense, then, that 'fixing the mind on the things of the flesh' is to be at war against God (Rom. 8:7)."[63] In Phil. 3:3-7 and elsewhere, he adds, to live *according to the flesh* "is the self-reliant attitude of the man who puts his trust in his own strength."[64]

Sceptics may suggest that Bultmann is simply imposing a "Lutheran" interpretation onto Paul, and shortly we shall consider the claims of Stendahl and Sanders that interpreters too often do this. However, the contextual and exegetical evidence supports Bultmann's view on this specific matter, and several scholars who are not distinctively "Lutheran" reach similar conclusions on exegetical grounds. J. A. T. Robinson, an Anglican bishop and Cambridge academic who is not "Lutheran," comments, "The flesh . . . represents human self-sufficiency" (1 Cor. 3:21, "Glorying in human persons"; 2 Cor. 1:9, "trusting in ourselves"; or elsewhere "boasting," καυχᾶσθαι, *kaukāsthai*).[65]

Similarly, writing from within a Methodist tradition Robert Jewett points out that life "according to the flesh" in such conflict settings as that of Galatians denotes self-reliance either in relation to obedience to law, or, in the opposite direction, in antinomian self-indulgence.[66] The key, he writes, is the contrast "between boasting in the cross and boasting in the circumcised flesh."[67] This is evi-

---

61. Pannenberg, *Systematic Theology*, vol. 2, 241 and 242. On 1 Cor. 10:1-3 cf. also Thiselton, *First Epistle*, 717-49.

62. Alexander Sand, *Der Begriff "Fleische" in den paulinischen Hauptbriefen*, Biblische Untersuchungen h. Otto Kurr, Bd. 2 (Regensburg: F. Pustet, 1967), 125-217; Robert Jewett, *Paul's Anthropological Terms*, 49-166; and Dunn, *Paul*, 62-70.

63. Bultmann, *Theology of the New Testament*, vol. 1, 239.

64. Bultmann, *Theology of the New Testament*, vol. 1, 240.

65. J. A. T. Robinson, *The Body: A Study in Pauline Theology* (London: S.C.M., 1952), 25-26.

66. Jewett, *Paul's Anthropological Terms*, 95-116.

67. Jewett, *Anthropological Terms*, 99.

denced especially in Gal. 6:13-14, "shifting one's boast from the cross of Christ (Gal. 6:14) to the circumcised flesh (6:13)." The flesh, then, Jewett writes, signifies more than "weakness"; "it lures [humankind] to substitute his own good for God's. . . . The flesh presents to the libertinist objects of desire which man is to satisfy (5:16). . . . These objects lure man on. . . . They seem to offer man exactly what the law and circumcision offered — life."[68]

This approach presupposes a more serious but also more resonant hermeneutical horizon of understanding in relation to today's world. *Desire* in a market culture of consumerism stands nearer to the center of most people's agenda in the modern or postmodern West than talk about "missing the mark," when many are quite indifferent to aiming at some supposed standard or norm of acceptability. Moreover, *disappointed desire* is a widespread experience, not because what was desired was beyond reach, but because what has been desired and obtained fails to bring what it seemed to promise. In many cases, for example, credit or power to borrow may be almost without limit, but often the purchase of some coveted product merely generates a desire for more of the same, or for something different. Paul's language about sin's offering "wages" that turn out to be disastrous resonates with widespread experiences today of disenchantment and disillusion (Rom. 6:23, "the 'wages' of sin is death"). "Sin deceived me" (Rom. 7:11).

Krister Stendahl seeks to disengage Paul from interpretations that ascribe to him the outworking of a troubled conscience. Such a view is often based on an autobiographical understanding of Rom. 7:19, "I do not the good that I want to do." Stendahl argues that in Luther's struggle with his conscience "it is exactly at this point that we can discern the most drastic difference between Luther and Paul, between the sixteenth century and the first century."[69] Where he does speak of his own consciousness, Paul writes: "I am not aware of anything against myself" (1 Cor. 4:4) or of being "blameless as touching righteousness of the law" (Phil. 3:6). Stendahl does not imply that Paul fails to take sin seriously. It is, rather, that human sin is an objective matter of a wrong condition and wrong relationship with God, rather than that which depends on the findings of inner consciousness or conscience. Only God can pronounce a definitive verdict; self-assessment is a fallible and unreliable guide, and Paul is not at all obsessed with guilt in the sense of introspective anxiety. Further, the "I" of Rom. 7:14 alludes to corporate Israel, or to corporate humankind, whether with reference to corporate Christian experience or otherwise. Stendahl writes, "No one could ever deny that ἁμαρτία, *sin,* is a crucial word in Paul's terminology. . . . It is much harder to gauge how Paul subjectively experienced the power of sin in his life."[70]

---

68. Jewett, *Anthropological Terms,* 103-4.

69. Krister Stendahl, "The Apostle Paul and the Introspective Conscience of the West," originally in *Harvard Theological Review* 56 (1963) 199-215; conveniently repr. in Stendahl, *Paul among Jews and Gentiles* (London: SCM, 1977), 78-96.

70. Stendahl, "Introspective Conscience," *HTR* 56 (1963), 208.

This suggests that an appeal to a tortured conscience is not always, if at all, the best hermeneutical horizon of understanding with which to approach the subject, at least in Paul. Indeed, where Paul uses the Greek word most often translated *conscience* (συνείδησις, *suneidēsis*), many Pauline specialists argue that the Greek term denotes not conscience but self-awareness.[71] Even if the word were to denote *conscience,* Paul's use does not correspond with the usual use of the term either in Stoicism or in the modern West. Paul is much more concerned with *misdirected desire,* a *broken relationship with God,* and the effects of *self-damage.* His concern is with what Pannenberg calls human *"misery."* Pannenberg observes, "The term 'misery' sums up our detachment from God."[72]

This does not emerge exclusively from Paul. We have already noted the role of *turning from,* and *turning to,* in the message of Jesus. The Johannine writings reflect sharper dualisms than the Synoptics: light and darkness, vision and blindness, life and death, spirit and flesh, truth and falsehood. "Human persons loved *darkness* (σκότος, *skotos*) rather than light" (John 3:19; cf. 1 John 1:6); "He [Satan] has *blinded their eyes*" (τυφλόω, *tuphloō,* John 12:40; cf. 1 John 2:11); "If he [someone] keeps my sayings, he shall *never see death*" (θάνατος, *thanatos,* John 8:51-52; cf. John 5:24; 1 John 3:14; 5:16-17). "That which is born of the flesh is *flesh . . .*" (σάρξ, *sarx,* John 3:6; cf. 1 John 2:16); the Spirit of truth (John 15:26; 16:7-9; cf. John 1:14, 17; 3:21; 8:32; 14:6) (ἀλήθεια, *alētheia*) and its rejection.

In the first half of the twentieth century rash and unguarded assertions were made about the origins of such dualisms in "Hellenistic" and even gnostic sources, rather than in the words of Jesus. But with the parallel examples of such dualisms in the Qumran writings in discoveries dating from 1948, such speculations were exposed as unduly premature and mistaken.[73] More recently this has been further confirmed by the work of Martin Hengel and others in demonstrat-

---

71. R. A. Horsley, "Consciousness and Freedom among the Corinthians: 1 Corinthians 8–9," *Catholic Biblical Quarterly* 40 (1978) 574-89; Peter D. Gooch, "'Conscience' in 1 Corinthians 8 and 10," *New Testament Studies* 33 (1987) 244-54; P. D. Gardner, *The Gifts of God and the Authentication of a Christian: An Exegetical Study of 1 Corinthians 8–11* (Lanham, MD: University Press of America, 1994), 42-54; Thiselton, *First Epistle,* 640-45; cf. H.-J. Eckstein, *Der Begriff Syneidesis bei Paulus* (Tübingen: Mohr, 1983), 35-135.

72. Pannenberg, *Systematic Theology,* vol. 2, 179.

73. See James H. Charlesworth (ed.), *John and Qumran* (London: Geoffrey Chapman, 1972), esp. "Johannine Dualism," 18-35. On *truth,* see 1QH 4:14; 6:7-9; 7:14; 11:9-11; 1QS 1:11-13; 5:10; CD 13:10; John 8:31-32; 14:6; 16:13-15; 17:16-18. A clear example of dualism in the Dead Sea Scrolls comes in 1QS 3:13–4:26: "a Spirit of *truth*" and "a spirit of *perversity*"; a spring of *darkness* and a Presence of *Light;* and a destiny of *reward* or *punishment.* See Charlesworth, *John and Qumran,* 76-106; and for another view in 1QS 3:13–4:26, A. R. C. Leaney, *The Rule of Qumran and Its Meaning* (London: S.C.M., 1966), 53-56. Leaney cites 1QS 3:18 (two spirits); 3:20 (light and darkness); 3:21 (angel of darkness deceives), and 4:4 (spirit of wisdom), all with Old Testament roots.

ing that no such sharp boundary between Hellenism and Judaism existed as had been formerly presupposed.[74]

In the Fourth Gospel sin is also frequently placed in a Christological context. If Jesus Christ is *light, life,* and *truth* (John 1:3-5; 14:6), the very coming of Christ *sheds light upon* (the more characteristic meaning of φωτιζω, *phōtizō,* than "en-lightens," NRSV) a world that stands under the darkness of human sin (John 1:9). The metaphor of *hunger* and *thirst* (John 6:35; cf. John 4:10-14) underlines the il-lusion brought about by *misdirected desire.* The Paraclete will continue the min-istry of Jesus in exposing (ἐλέγχειν, *elenchein*) the sin of the world (John 16:8). John places human sin in a cosmic, objective, structural, and Christological con-text, which again provides a horizon of understanding that does not depend upon falling short of ethical norms or on a tortured conscience, both of which have tended to slip from public awareness in the twenty-first century.

The Epistle to the Hebrews may appear at first sight to present a narrow fo-cus on cultic, priestly, and sacrificial affairs. Nevertheless the fundamental ques-tion and theme of the epistle is one that lies deep within the heart of humankind: what conditions must a human being fulfill to *approach* or *draw near* (προσέπχομαι, *proserchomai*) to God (Heb. 10:22)? Sacrifice belongs to the framework of divine grace whereby human beings may *draw near* (ἐγγίζω, *engizō*) to God (Heb. 7:19). Where Paul speaks of *interpersonal relationships of alienation and reconciliation,* Hebrews speaks of *ability to enter into the divine presence,* to experience *access* to God. It presupposes that human sin has other-wise closed off this access. In hermeneutical terms, older liberal attempts to ex-press human sin in terms of ignorance, failure, or falling short are not only un-faithful to the multiform traditions of the biblical writings, but also less relevant to the concerns of a twenty-first century for whom moralist and legalistic con-cepts have less resonance than those of alienation, relationship, deception, vic-timization, bondage, and "misery."

12.3. Varying Horizons for Understandings of Human Sin from Irenaeus to Calvin

(1) *Irenaeus* (c. 130–c. 202), with roots in Asia Minor and subsequently Bishop of Lyons, holds together Eastern and Western traditions. In contrast to gnostic speculations that related human sin and evil to cosmological systems or to embodiedness, Irenaeus approached the issue existentially as a matter of chal-lenge to human growth. Like Clement of Alexandria he tended to associate sin with human weakness and lack of understanding. As we shall note more fully in

---

74. Martin Hengel, *Judaism and Hellenism: Studies in Their Encounter in Palestine during the Early Hellenistic Period,* trans. John Bowden (London: S.C.M., 1974).

12.4, he perceived Adam before the Fall as "a child, not yet . . . fully mature."[75] The struggle with sin provides an opportunity for moral discipline and growth in maturity. Nevertheless it would not be accurate to stop at this point with this widespread picture of Irenaeus. In the first Adam, Irenaeus writes, "we *offended against* [God]" (Greek προσεκόψαμεν, *prosekopsamen*).[76] In the second Adam, he continues, "we have been reconciled to him (ἀποκατηλλάγημεν, *apokatēllagēmen*)." Hence sin in Irenaeus *implies a broken relationship with God* that stands in need of reconciliation through the work of Christ. Moreover, the sin of Adam is depicted as "the grief of their wound" (Latin *dolor autem plagae est*) which brings death *(mors)*.[77] Popular notions, then, that Irenaeus teaches "a Fall upwards" are true only in part; in another respect they are misleading.[78]

(2) *Tertullian* (c. 160–c. 220/240) opposed not only gnostic cosmological and mythological dualist speculations, but also more specifically the teaching of Marcion. Marcion radicalized Paul's gospel of liberation from the demands of the law, and portrayed God the Father of Jesus Christ as a figure opposed to the God of the Old Testament and the law. Tertullian attacked Marcion's view, but in so doing *tended toward implying a legalistic concept of human sin.*

The notions of sin as *falling short* and *disobedience* come to the fore, perhaps recalling Tertullian's former career as a lawyer. Yet this is only one part of the picture. As we shall note in 12.4, Tertullian introduced an explicitly "traducian" doctrine of the Fall, namely that "the soul" (Latin *anima*) is shaped by a fragment from the soul of the father, thereby transmitting "fallenness" from parent to child. The whole traducian chain ran from Adam to the present. Against the tradition of Plato Tertullian insists that "the soul" is corporeal.[79] He writes, "The soul was in the beginning associated with Adam's body, which grew . . . and so . . . became the germ of the whole of substance (i.e., of the soul) *(totius substantiae, ita et condicionis istius semen effecit)*.[80] Hence, although he gave prominence to the legalistic or moralistic aspect of sin as disobedience and falling short, Tertullian also speaks of the transmission of a *state* or *condition* of fallenness in the context of the Fall.

(3) *Clement of Alexandria* (c. 150-215) sees human sin as the result of three factors: ignorance, weakness, and free choice. Humankind is misled by the sup-

---

75. Irenaeus, *Demonstration of the Apostolic Preaching* 12–14.

76. Irenaeus, *Against Heresies* V:16:3 (Greek, Migne, *Patrologia Graeca*, vol. 7, 1168B); the translation comes from G. W. H. Lampe, *A Patristic Greek Lexicon* (Oxford: Clarendon, 1961), 1174, col. i.

77. Irenaeus, *Against Heresies* V:34:2.

78. Cf. N. P. Williams, *The Ideas of the Fall and of Original Sin*, 195. The most influential account of Irenaeus's view at "textbook" level is John Hick, *Evil and the God of Love* (London: Macmillan, 1966), 217-78.

79. Tertullian, *De Anima* 5–6.

80. Tertullian, *De Anima* 9; cf. also 36.

posed attraction of sin, but it is contrary to right reason. Sin is not the result of an Adamic "fall." Although he is understood to hold a "weak" view of sin as ignorance, Clement implies that it is *misdirected desire* for what masquerades as something desirable and attractive.

(4) *Origen* (185-254) does not offer a wholly systematic view of the nature of human sin. In his discourse on resurrection and judgement, however, he reaches the incisive insight that (in the language of modern logical grammar) punishment for human sin may be "internal" rather than external. In other words, just as the "reward" of repeated music practice is simply the capacity to play well, so when Paul speaks of human thoughts "accusing them when God will judge the secrets of humankind" (Rom. 2:15-16), Origen observes that "certain tortures are produced" not by divine intervention but "by the hurtful affection of sins themselves."[81]

Origen's more widely known comments come in the context of newborn babies. Even they need a sacrifice for sin, for "I was shapen in iniquity, and in sin did my mother conceive me" (Ps. 51:5). "They go astray as soon as they are born."[82]

On the other hand, in spite of Origen's standing as a creative theologian, it is precarious to view him as standing at the center of the development of Christian doctrine. On the basis of his belief in the justice of God in the face of differing situations in life and the being of good and evil angels, Origen postulated a *prenatal* "fall" to account for such differences, appealing to Plato's philosophy of the soul.[83] The relation of infant baptism to infant sin also attracted his innovative attention, but his views changed in different periods, and his theology was finally condemned by the Fifth Ecumenical Council in Constantinople in 553. In 12.4 we shall note Origen's theory of a "seminal presence" in Adam on the part of later generations.[84]

(5) *Athanasius* (296-373) brings us onto firm ground. He offers no systematic treatment of sin, but considers everything within the context of Christ and redemption.[85] In general he sees human sin as the *rejection of contemplation of God*. This removes it from a moralistic and linguistic framework, and reflects the biblical traditions that sin causes alienation or a breach of relationship with God that requires reconciliation. The narrative of Adam provides a model for the nature of human sin: it is "departing from the consideration of the one true God and from desire for him."[86] The misdirected desire for other things in place of God "began to be habituated in these desires, so that [sinners] were afraid to

---

81. Origen, *De Principiis* II:10:4.

82. Origen, *Against Celsus* 50.

83. Origen, *De Principiis* IV:1:16 and 23 and *Against Celsus* 7:50. Cf. Joseph W. Trigg, *Origen: The Bible and Philosophy in the Third Century* (London: S.C.M., 1983), 103-15.

84. Origen, *Commentary on Romans* 5; cf. *Commentary on John*, 20:21.

85. Athanasius, *Against the Asians* II:65-66; I:9:60; *On the Incarnation*, sects. 4-7, 10-11, and 20-21.

86. Athanasius, *Against the Heathen* 3:3.

leave them."[87] "Contemplation" of God gives way to "contemplation of the body" and taking pleasure in such contemplation; indeed, it becomes "falling in love with pleasures."[88]

Sin is also a matter of "turning back" and "becoming evil," and this incurs corruption or "decay" (φθόρα, *phthora*), which leads to death, and, in the instance of Adam, also to "loss of paradise."[89] Following the sin of Adam, sin escalates and "passes beyond all measure."[90] "No heed was paid to law," and violence, conflict, and war now follow.[91] Athanasius cites Paul's classic passage on the consequences of humanity's turning away from God and falling into bondage to self-destructive practices and habits ("the Pauline fall") in Rom. 1:26-32 (cf. 1:18-32).[92]

(6) *Gregory of Nyssa* (c. 330–c. 395) offers the fullest treatment of the Fall, at least among the Cappadocian Fathers (discussed further in 12.4). But his consideration of "Adam's sin" is not speculative; it is existential. For it is "our sin." Gregory argues that the image of God borne by the first humans included the capacity for free choice, but humankind now no longer possesses the gift of self-determination. Evil does not originate in God, but "arises in the [human] will. . . . Darkness supervenes on the removal of light; . . . the perverse will . . . has chosen the worse rather than the better."[93] Gregory adds that "the will chooses . . . the thing that pleases it."[94] The "bias towards evil conduct" is generated primarily by envy.[95] Humanity is "in its present evil condition," but the forces that inhibit choice of virtue can be overcome by the power not of humankind but of God.[96] This provides a bridge from the earlier Fathers to Augustine's emphasis upon sin as misdirected desire, which in turn brings dire consequences.

(7) *Augustine of Hippo* (354-430) held a complex theology that cannot readily be summarized, not least because, in accordance with a dispositional understanding of belief, he faces a variety of opponents at different stages of his career, and he emphasizes most the themes and beliefs that stand in contrast to those that he most opposes. Yet two key themes persist: *the primacy of God's grace,* and *an understanding of sin as misdirected desire that brings bondage and self-destructive consequences.*

In theory Augustine requires an entire chapter if we are to do justice to his

---

87. Athanasius, *Against the Heathen* 3:4.
88. Athanasius, *Against the Heathen* 4:1.
89. Athanasius, *On the Incarnation* 3:4; cf. 6:1.
90. Athanasius, *On the Incarnation* 5:3.
91. Athanasius, *On the Incarnation* 5:4.
92. Athanasius, *On the Incarnation* 5:8; cf. 6:1-10.
93. Gregory of Nyssa, *The Great Catechism* (otherwise, *Oratio Catechetica Magna*) 5.
94. Gregory, *Catechism* 5.
95. Gregory, *Catechism* 6.
96. Gregory, *Catechism* 6.

thought. But this would distract us from the main purpose of this study. All the same we may note differences of genre that affect accurate interpretation. The *Confessions* reflect a hermeneutical starting point grounded in personal experience as well as Scripture. *The City of God* presents a more "public" narrative of God's historical relations with the world. His treatise *On Free Will* attacked the Manichaeans, in part drawing on Platonist resources. *The Enchiridion* comes nearest to nonpolemical instruction. However, the anti-Pelagian writings, for example, *On Nature and Grace,* paint the plight and bondage of human sinners in strong, dark colors as a backcloth to the immeasurable all-sufficiency of God's grace, in contrast to the compromised doctrine of grace in Pelagius.

Sin, for Augustine, derives from the human *will.* In the *Confessions* he recalls his early childish indignation with adults for their "disobedience" in not being "slaves to my interests. . . . I would revenge myself upon them by weeping."[97] In adolescence the "single desire that dominated my search for delight was simply to love and be loved. . . . My misery seethed and followed the driving force of my impulses, abandoning you [God]."[98] Augustine recalls the perversity of misdirected desire in a well-known passage: "I stole something which I had in plenty. . . . My desire was to enjoy . . . merely the excitement of thieving and doing what was wrong. . . . Such was my heart."[99] Sin is a matter of *misdirected desire.*

This also leads to *bondage.* Augustine carefully examines the teaching of Paul on the incapacity of the law to deliver from sin (Rom. 7:5-24). In particular he offers an exegesis of Rom. 7:15-17, "What I hate I do."[100] He concludes with Paul, "In my flesh dwells no good thing" (Rom. 7:18).[101] In the background also lies a different concept of freedom of the will from that held by many of the Eastern Fathers. While they tended to define freedom as an ability to choose between two or more actions, Augustine defined freedom as the liberty of the will to implement its desires in action.

R. S. Moxon comments, "The only self-motion of the apostate will is in the direction of sin. . . . Without external help [grace] . . . there was no escape from the necessity of sin" even if "some degree of freedom of will exists in every man."[102] In his *Confessions,* Augustine writes, "I sighed for such freedom, but was bound . . . by the iron of my own choice. The enemy had a grip on my will and so made a chain for me."[103] The world "laid me down with a sweet drowsiness" so that when God through the Scriptures called him, "Arise, you who are asleep, rise

---

97. Augustine, *Confessions,* I:6:8 (Henry Chadwick's translation).

98. Augustine, *Confessions,* II:2:3-4.

99. Augustine, *Confessions,* II:4:9.

100. Augustine, *Against Two Letters of the Pelagians,* I:10.18.

101. Augustine, *Against Two Letters of the Pelagians,* I:10.19.

102. Reginald S. Moxon, *The Doctrine of Sin: A Critical and Historical Investigation* (London: Allen & Unwin, 1922), 82-83.

103. Augustine, *Confessions,* VIII:5:10.

from the dead" (Eph. 5:14), Augustine replied "Just a little longer, please"; for he was "captive to the law of sin" (Rom. 7:22).[104]

(8) In *the Latin West through the medieval period and up to and including the Reformation* Augustine's doctrine of sin dominated, or at least strongly influenced, most of the Western traditions. *Gregory the Great* (c. 540-604) largely followed Augustine, although he rejected his notion of "irresistible" grace. *Anselm* (1033-1109) expounded in particular the notion of sin as "*not rendering to God what is his due* (Latin *debitum*).[105] In stressing this Godward dimension he emphasized personhood and relationality, but the concept of owing what is due introduced a legalistic understanding at the same time. A person who does not render compensation for what he or she has "stolen" remains guilty *(in culpa)*. Honor taken away must be repaid.[106]

One apparent detail brought unhelpful consequences. Anselm and many in the Latin tradition mistranslated or misunderstood the Greek and Hebrew for *repentance*. In the biblical texts the term denotes "turning" (Hebrew שׁוּב, *shûbh*), but this was rendered into Latin as *poenitentia*, which too readily came to be understood as "penance" or even "penitential works." To be sure, Anselm believed that only the work of Christ, not penitential works, could satisfy the debt incurred to God's honor, but a misunderstanding prevailed until Martin Luther clarified and corrected the heart of this linguistic issue.

(9) *Thomas Aquinas* (1225-74) provides abundant material on the nature of sin. In the *Prima Secundae* of the *Summa Theologiae* he discusses "good habits" or "virtues" (Ia2ae, Qq. 55-70) and "evils habits" or "vices" (Ia2ae, Qq. 71-89). The latter is divided into "Sin" (Qq. 71-80); "Original Sin" (Qq. 81-85); and "Effects of Sin" (Qq. 86-89).[107]

Sin originates from *self-love*, and includes sin *against God*, sin *against oneself*, and sin *against one's neighbor*.[108] By grace, "God makes us virtuous, and directs us to himself."[109] Sin is rejection and violation of this purpose for which human beings were created. It proceeds from misdirected desire in which "the greater the desire, there is a greater sin."[110] It is also a "turning aside from the rule of reason."[111] It inflicts "injury" on both others and self, but to injure others is more sinful than self-harm.[112] Sin is an act, but this proceeds from human *desire and will*.[113]

104. Augustine, *Confessions*, VIII:5:12.
105. Anselm, *Cur Deus Homo*, I:11.
106. Anselm, *Cur Deus Homo*, I:13.
107. Blackfriars edition, vols. 25–27.
108. Aquinas, *Summa Theologiae*, Ia2ae, Q. 72, art. 4.
109. Aquinas, *Summa Theologiae*, Ia2ae, Q. 62, art. 1.
110. Aquinas, *Summa Theologiae*, Ia2ae, Q. 72, art. 6.
111. Aquinas, *Summa Theologiae*, Ia2ae, Q. 73, art. 7.
112. Aquinas, *Summa Theologiae*, Ia2ae, Q. 73, art. 9.
113. Aquinas, *Summa Theologiae*, Ia2ae, Q. 74. arts. 1 and 2.

Aquinas ranks various sins in seriousness, and goes beyond the biblical traditions in distinguishing between "venial" and "mortal" sins.[114] He follows Augustine in seeing sin and evil as "a privation of the good," mainly to avoid the notion that God created a "thing" called sin or evil; even if as *privatio* (privation, absence) it springs from the misdirected desire of the human will.[115] Sin may grow "through habit."[116] Pride and self-love are "the beginning of every evil."[117] Finally, the *effects* of sin include "corruption" in the order of the world. "The stain of sin . . . parts man from God," and "the debt of punishment" may include "falling from sin to sin."[118]

In hermeneutical terms Aquinas embodies many of the phrases and distinctions that resonate with liturgical language and practices in the Western church: sinning against *God, others, and the self;* sinning in thought, word, and deed; not loving God as we ought; seeking our own way rather than God's. Such a hermeneutical starting point resonates with those who understand and appropriate such categories. Yet more deeply Aquinas appropriates Augustine's insight (and that of others before him) that *misdirected desire,* especially in the illusory interests of self-love or self-gratification, sets in motion a chain of effects that mire the self more deeply in disillusion, disappointment, and self-harm.

As we noted above, desire, the incitement of desire, and the gratification of desire are all marks of consumerist, market-oriented societies. Augustine and Aquinas provide a diagnosis of a widespread malaise that offers a rational explanation for the sense of disillusion, disappointment, and frustration that marks much in early twenty-first-century society in the West and perhaps elsewhere.

(10) *Martin Luther* (1483-1546). It is difficult fully to appreciate Luther's concerns about the nature of human sin outside a hermeneutical horizon that juxtaposes law and grace. This springs not from introspective self-examination, but from Luther's fresh understanding of Romans and of Pauline and Johannine theology. Among his earliest works after his rediscovery of Romans the *Heidelberg Disputation* (1518) provides a constructive starting point. He writes, "The law says: 'Do this', but it is never done. Grace says, 'Believe in him', and everything is done."[119] Luther explicates this principle in the twenty-eight "Conclusions" of the *Heidelberg Disputation.* He begins with a series of quotations from Paul: the

---

114. Aquinas, *Summa Theologiae,* Ia2ae, Q. 74, arts. 8-10 and Q. 88.

115. Aquinas, *Summa Theologiae,* Ia2ae, Q. 75, arts. 1-4.

116. Aquinas, *Summa Theologiae,* Ia2ae, Q. 78, art. 2.

117. Aquinas, *Summa Theologiae,* Ia2ae, Q. 84, art. 2.

118. Aquinas, *Summa Theologiae,* Ia2ae, Qq. 85-87 respectively, esp. Q. 85, art. 3; Q. 86, art. 2; and Q. 87, arts. 2-3.

119. Martin Luther, *The Heidelberg Disputation,* trans. and ed. James Atkinson, in *Luther: Early Theological Works,* Library of Christian Classics 16 (London: S.C.M., 1962), Thesis 26, 278 (German WA, I, 351).

law "amplifies sins" (Rom. 5:20); when the commandment came, "sin revived" (Rom. 7:9), it is "the law of sin and death" (Rom. 8:2).[120]

How, Luther asks, can a person do good "in his own strength"? "There is none who does good" (Rom. 3:10).[121] He believed that Scripture clearly witnessed to human incapacity to do good without the motivation or act being touched by self-interest or sin: "There is not a righteous man who does good, and yet sinneth not (Eccl. 7:20)."[122] *Any taking away of glory from God* is *"wrongdoing."*[123]

Humankind presumes to glory in its selfhood, Luther insists, citing Paul: "professing themselves to be wise, they were made fools" (Rom. 1:22).[124] Human self-sufficiency makes people "hate the cross and sufferings . . . and the glory that goes with them"; there is a *theologia gloriae* and a *theologia crucis,* and sinful humanity without true knowledge of God "prefers works to sufferings, and glory to a cross."[125] "The theologian of glory says bad is good and good is bad; the theologian of the cross calls them by their proper name."[126]

In Luther's view a broken relationship with God was not simply an effect of 'sins' as such; a living relationship with God depends upon a personal appropriation of the truth of justification by grace alone. To be sure, conflict and temptation *(Anfechtung)* still mark the life of the Christian. Yet the Christian's dual status as *simul iustus et peccator* does not detract from "confidence in God's grace, so secure and certain that a man would stake his life on it a thousand times. . . . It makes a man glad and bold and happy in dealing with God and with all his creatures."[127] Such faith springs from grace and the Holy Spirit; humankind, unaided, cannot experience it.

In 1525 Luther produced *The Bondage of the Will (De servo arbitrio)* in opposition to Erasmus. He begins by asserting that Scripture is not so obscure as to prevent the formulation of basic doctrine or right action.[128] He reviews Erasmus's handling of biblical texts, and then expounds his own understanding of biblical traditions. He addresses the issue of free will. Rom. 1:18-32, Luther argues, reveals that "the more it [free will] endeavors the worse it grows."[129] Rom. 3:9ff. and 3:19ff., he continues, reveal "the universal dominion of sin," both in acts and in its power.[130] All humankind as sinners are "devoid of the glory of God" (Rom.

---

120. Luther, *Heidelberg Disputation,* Conclusion I, 281.
121. Luther, *Heidelberg Disputation,* Conclusion II, 282.
122. Luther, *Heidelberg Disputation,* Conclusion VI, 284.
123. Luther, *Heidelberg Disputation,* Conclusion IX, 288.
124. Luther, *Heidelberg Disputation,* Conclusion XIX, 290.
125. Luther, *Heidelberg Disputation,* Conclusion XXI, 291.
126. Luther, *Heidelberg Disputation,* Conclusion XXI, 291 (the heading).
127. Luther, *Preface to the Epistle to the Romans* (1522).
128. Luther, *On the Bondage of the Will,* 66-74 (WA, vol. 18, 606-9).
129. Luther, *Bondage,* 278 (W.A., 18, 760).
130. Luther, *Bondage,* 278-86 (W.A., 18, 760-64).

3:21-26), but the Christian through Christ may "glory in God."[131] Luther also cites the Johannine emphasis on the need for new birth.[132] Bondage to sin is compounded by humankind's lack of awareness of its true condition.

Critics of Luther often argue that he extended Augustinianism into "a relentless and iron determinism." N. P. Williams, for one, writes with barely restrained polemic: "The Lutherans are more emphatic and more violent even than Calvin and his followers. The title of Luther's treatise against Erasmus, *De servo arbitrio,* leaves room for no mistake."[133] Nevertheless in hermeneutical terms Luther follows Paul and John in formulating a conception of the human condition that serves as a corollary to the sovereign grace of God and the all-sufficiency of Christ. Varied understandings of human sin maintain a sensitive hermeneutical relationship to theologies of the cross. Other expositions of Luther may be equally passionate in the opposite direction.[134] Recently more positive assessments of Luther among several major Roman Catholic theologians bear witness to a wider appreciation of this theology.[135]

(11) *John Calvin* (1509-64). In his *Institutes of the Christian Religion* Calvin follows the order of the ecumenical creeds in expounding a doctrine of God in Book I and Christ in Book II, before considering other articles in Books III and IV. His section on the Fall, human sin, and free will comes in the first six chapters of Book II. Hence *the hermeneutical context* is that of expounding the person and work of Christ. This faithfully reflects the hermeneutical framework of Paul and John as well as many thinkers on the history of the doctrine. In the very first chapter of Book II Calvin reaffirms the need for "knowledge of ourselves." But he qualifies this by distinguishing between the mistake of measuring ourselves by ourselves and the wisdom of measuring ourselves in the light of *God's purpose* for us as human beings. Calvin writes, "It seems proper first to consider the end for which he [humankind] was created . . . and secondly to consider his faculties, or rather want of faculties — a want which, perceived, will annihilate all his confidence and cover him with confusion."[136]

Like Augustine and Luther, Calvin aims to show the initiative and all-sufficiency of the grace of God to humankind. Critics view this as the application

---

131. Luther, *Bondage,* 290-91 (W.A., 18, 768).

132. Luther, *Bondage,* 305-7 (W.A., 18, 778-79).

133. Williams, *The Ideas of the Fall and of Original Sin,* 433.

134. Cf. Gordon E. Rupp and Philip S. Watson (eds.), *Luther and Erasmus: Free Will and Salvation,* Library of Christian Classics (Philadelphia: Westminster, 1969), 1-32; James Atkinson, *The Great Light: Luther and the Reformation* (Grand Rapids: Eerdmans and Exeter, U.K.: Paternoster, 1968), 11-109; Heinrich Bornkamm, *Luther in Mid-Career,* trans. E. T. Bachmann (London: Darton, Longman, & Todd, 1983), esp. 417-58; Philip S. Watson, *Let God Be God: An Interpretation of the Theology of Martin Luther* (London: Epworth, 1947).

135. James Atkinson, *Martin Luther: Prophet to the Church Catholic* (Grand Rapids: Eerdmans and Exeter: Paternoster, 1983), esp. 21-39.

136. Calvin, *Institutes,* I:1:3, vol. 1, 212.

of a brittle logic, but it may equally be ascribed to the notion of doctrine as worship and celebration. In language shared by Calvin and pietism, it may be seen as a matter of "giving God the glory." God's grace provides everything needed, because, Calvin writes, citing Paul, "all have sinned . . . so grace might reign . . ." (Rom. 5:19-21).[137] Calvin speaks of human loss at the Fall of Adam, but not for the speculative purpose of exploring different definitions that various writers have adopted. His purpose is to underline that "the works of the flesh" are sin (Gal. 5:19; Rom. 5:12). "Their whole nature is, as it were, a seed-bed of sin and therefore cannot but be odious and abominable to God [Calvin later cites Eph. 2:3 alongside Rom. 1:18-32]. . . . There could be no condemnation without guilt."[138] He implies "total depravity" in the fullest sense of the term. He writes, "Everything which is in man from the intellect to the will . . . is defiled and pervaded with this concupiscence."[139]

We shall consider Calvin's comments about Adam, the Fall, and "original sin" in 13.2.[140] He considers the effects of sin along lines that are similar to those identified by Augustine and Luther. The "dominion" of sin, Calvin writes, "extends to the whole race."[141] Approvingly he comments, "Augustine hesitates not to call the will *a slave*."[142] It is perhaps II:3 that many find most difficult. Calvin states, "When the will is enchained as the slave of sin, it cannot make a movement towards goodness, far less steadily pursue it."[143] The will "fastens on with the strongest affection towards sin" (loc. cit.). However, he also writes, "Dragged by necessity to evil," the will "nevertheless sins voluntarily."[144] The logic may seem contradictory until we recall that, like Augustine, Calvin understands freedom not as the capacity to choose various options, but as the capacity to implement desire through will and action.

The hermeneutical context softens what may seem very harsh if it is viewed as a dogmatic abstraction, namely as a "problem" rather than as a "question that arises." This view of human bondage does *arise* in the context of the theology of redemption that Calvin expounds in Book II. As he expresses the matter in his commentary on Isaiah, "Unless we realize our hopeless misery, we shall never know how much we need the remedy which Christ brings, nor come to him with the fervent love we owe him. . . . Each must know himself condemned until he is vindicated by Christ."[145] Redemption remains the fundamental hermeneutical horizon of meaning for interpreting material about human sin.

---

137. Calvin, *Institutes*, I:1:6, vol. 1, 215.

138. Calvin, *Institutes*, I:1:8, vol. 1, 217-18.

139. Calvin, *Institutes*, I:1:8, vol. 1, 218.

140. Calvin, *Institutes*, I:1:5, vol. 1, 214, uses the term explicitly.

141. Calvin, *Institutes*, I:2:1, vol. 1, 222-23.

142. Calvin, *Institutes*, I:2:7, vol. 1, 229.

143. Calvin, *Institutes*, I:3:5, vol. 1, 253.

144. Calvin, *Institutes*, I:3:5, vol. 1, 253-54.

145. Calvin, *Commentary on Isaiah*, on 33:6. Cf. also Timothy George, *Theology of the Reformers* (Nashville: Broadman, and Leicester: Apollo, 1988), 213-23.

CHAPTER 13

Toward a Hermeneutic of the Fall and Collective Sin

13.1. A Hermeneutic of Biblical Texts Traditionally Interpreted as Theologies of the Fall

In the context of hermeneutics the main importance of a traditional doctrine of the Fall is to underline that human sin denotes not only actions but also *a human condition and state,* and that sin carries with it serious *effects,* often of a structural and corporate nature. Even a Christian doctrine of sin as misdirected desire remains incomplete if the effects of misdirected desire are not traced through to a *state* of consequent alienation and self-contradiction, and to what Pannenberg rightly calls the "misery" of humankind when the human relation with God, who is the source of all well-being, has become damaged or disrupted. Pannenberg writes, "Misery, then, is the lot of those who are deprived of the fellowship with God that is the destiny of human life."[1]

Exegetical scholarship also tends to evaluate differently those passages of the New Testament that have traditionally been used as supporting texts for the "Fall" in the full doctrinal sense of the term. The Johannine emphasis on blindness, self-deceit, and willful preference for the way of the self, and no less Paul's emphasis on the corporate solidarity of humankind "under sin," paint a serious picture of the plight and bondage of humankind that runs parallel with much in Christian doctrine. Nevertheless, an account of the fall *of Adam* does not appear in John or in the Synoptic gospels, and Paul mentions the word *Adam* (Greek Ἀδάμ) only in the well-known passages Rom. 5:14 and 1 Cor. 15:22, 45. Here the main point is the contrast between corporate solidarity "in Adam" and "being-in-Christ." Allusions to Adam in the New Testament occur otherwise only in 1 Tim. 2:13, Luke 3:58, and Jude 14, and these are hardly serious expositions of the

---

1. Pannenberg, *Systematic Theology,* vol. 2, 178.

Fall. Even in the Old Testament, apart from the Adam narratives themselves, *Adam* seems to occur only in Deut. 32:8, 1 Chron. 1:1, and Job 31:33; and none of these relates to the "Fall" of Adam.

This is not to minimize the seriousness of Rom. 5:12-21, Rom. 1:18-32, and other passages in Paul as a wholesale exposition of the universality of sin. It is to ask: what, for hermeneutics, is the function and scope of the Fall narratives in the New Testament, and do the articulations of doctrine from Irenaeus to Calvin and in modern theology reflect this biblical perspective?[2]

The major source of material about Adam before and after the entry of sin into the world, before the era of Irenaeus and Tertullian, is that of inter-testamental Jewish literature, especially Jewish apocalyptic. It also finds expression in rabbinic tradition and literature from the first century onward. One major hermeneutical context concerns the origin of, and responsibility for, evil, to which (for example) 2 Esdras and the *Syriac Apocalypse of Baruch* give very different answers. A second stream of thought is more speculative. In the next section (13:2) we consider traditions about Adam's original state (childlike innocence or godlike powers?), which receive considerable attention in apocalyptic and in rabbinic sources.

2 Esdras ascribes the responsibility for the sin that ravages humankind to Adam: "O Adam, what have you done? Although it was you who sinned, the fall was not yours alone but ours also who are your descendants" (2 Esdr. 7:118-19; cf. 2 Esdr 3:4-5). Baruch offers a different view: "Adam is therefore not the cause, save only of his own soul. But each of us has been the Adam of his own soul" (*2 Baruch* 54:19). Baruch recognizes that Adam brought sin into the world, and that the physiological consequences involved death (*2 Baruch* 54:15). However, there is no notion of transmitted sin or transmitted guilt. *The Apocalypse of Moses* ascribes the disobedience of animals to humankind to the fall of Adam (*Apocalypse of Moses* 10–11). The notion of the "fall" of creation at the entry of human sin has parallels in Rom. 8:19-23; "Creation (κτίσις, *ktisis*) was subjected to futility. . . ."

N. P. Williams argues that traces of the "fall" in Gen. 6:1-4 occur not only in *1 Enoch* 19:1 and *2 Baruch* 4:7, but in Jude 6, 7 and 2 Pet. 1:4, on the "corruption of the world through lust." However, he recognizes that the only "fall" narrative known to Paul is that of Gen. 3. In rabbinic literature, as W. D. Davies demonstrates, the conception of the יצר הרע (*yētser hā-rā'*) becomes a dominant description of sin as "the inclination to [do] evil," or "evil impulse." Paul would be familiar with this, but it does not constitute a doctrine of the Fall. There is also

---

2. Emil Brunner tends to overstate the case when he observes, "The whole historic picture of 'the first man' has been finally and absolutely destroyed for us today," since the status and definition of "historic picture" has been more carefully narrowed since the work of Hans Frei and others on "history-like" narrative (Brunner, *Man in Revolt*, 85).

an impulse to good *(yētser hā-tôbh),* and the "impulse" is broadly equivalent to the modern notion of "drives": without the יצר־הרע "no man would build a house, nor marry a wife, not beget children, nor engage in trade." Divine law can tame and guide the evil impulse, and it is not cited to account for the origin of sin.[3]

Several Pauline specialists see in Paul three "Pauline versions" of the Fall: Rom. 1:18-32, Rom. 5:12-21, and Rom. 7:7-13. To be sure, in each passage Paul affirms the universality of human sin. But equally, in each passage, he places the emphasis upon the *present* plight of humankind rather than offering an explanatory theory of how human sin arose. *The hermeneutical function of each of the three passages is to demonstrate the superabundance of divine grace and the cosmic significance of salvation in and through Christ.* This remains incontrovertible whether we adopt a so-called Lutheran approach of first establishing human need and then expounding divine grace, or whether we follow the "New Perspective on Paul" with E. P. Sanders, in which the coming of Christ takes the initial place and this then relates to the respective positions of Jews and Gentiles. If we interpret Romans and Paul along the lines of the "third wave" of N. T. Wright and Richard Hays, perceiving Paul's theology as a narrative of dealings with the world, the result in this respect remains the same.[4] The emphasis in each case is on *corporate solidarity,* for which Adam and Christ stand as paradigms or models for the old and new humanity respectively.

(1) Within this hermeneutical horizon Rom. 1:18-32 lays out the groundwork for including Gentiles and Jews alike as standing under sin and divine wrath, apart from their inclusion "in Christ." The law is perceived as incapable of addressing the plight of humankind, whether of Jews or Gentiles (Rom. 7:7-24). Within these horizons, to be "in Adam" is to be bound together in a doomed solidarity; to be "in Christ" is to share in the new, redeemed, humanity: "As all die in Adam, so all will be made alive in Christ" (1 Cor. 15:22). "The free gift is not like the effect of the one man's sin. . . . Death exercised dominion through that one: much more surely will those who receive abundance of grace and the free gift of righteousness exercise dominion in life through the one man, Jesus Christ" (Rom. 5:16-17).

James Dunn provides a judicious discussion of the role of Adam in Paul, and a careful discussion of the so-called "fall" passages: Rom. 1:18-32 (cf. Rom. 3:23); Rom 5:12-20; and Rom. 7:7-13 (cf. Rom. 8:19-22).[5] Dunn concludes, "Humankind has fallen when it thought to rise, has become foolish not wise, baser not superior. It has denied its likeness to God . . . and now falls short of what it might have

---

3. See W. D. Davies, *Paul and Rabbinic Judaism* (London: S.P.C.K., 2d edn. 1955), 20-26, for further documented references.

4. For an excellent short summary, see N. T. Wright, *Paul: Fresh Perspectives,* esp. "Fighting over Paul's Legacy: Perspectives Old, New and Different," 13-20.

5. James D. G. Dunn, *The Theology of Paul,* 79-101.

become. . . . It shares in a pervasive out-of-joint-ness, frustration, and futility with the rest of creation."[6] Although Gen. 2–3 finds its place among the sources that suggest and inspire these conclusions, the narrative of Adam does not stand alone, and the overall purpose in Paul's "fall" passages is to communicate the immeasurable generosity of grace by contrast.[7]

It is hardly disputed among New Testament scholars that Rom. 1:18-32 reflects parallels with such Hellenistic Jewish material as Wis. Sol. 7:1 and 9:2-3 and especially Wis. Sol. 14:8-31 and 15:8-13. Paul, in effect, recites material commonly found in Jewish synagogue homilies in the Diaspora, much of which attacks idolatry and ethical antinomianism among the Gentiles. But Paul appears to stand alongside the Jewish material, only to give it a decisive twist at the end: he asks, "Are Jews any better than Gentiles?" He declares, "You have no excuse, whoever you are, when you judge others, for in passing judgment you condemn yourself. . . . All who have sinned apart from the law will also perish apart from the law: and all who have sinned under the law will be judged by the law. . . . You that boast in the law, do you dishonor God by breaking the law? . . . For there is no distinction, since all have sinned and fall short of the glory of God" (Rom. 2:1, 12, 23; 3:22-23).

Paul does not invoke the "fall" as an explanation for the origin of evil in the past, but as an assertion of *the present, inclusive, cosmic, universal scope of the sinfulness of humankind as a single solidarity in the present,* to which no exception can be found. Jews and Gentiles stand *equally* doomed without *the free grace of God* through Christ. This leads on to 4:4-5: either the principle of *grace* rules all; or the principle of *works* rules all. God alone can "give life to the dead" (4:17), as the Abraham narrative demonstrates at every level. If anyone seeks a "Jewish" model, let that person note that Abraham relied not upon himself, but solely on *divine promise* (4:20).

(2) This brings us to the second so-called "version of the fall" in Paul, namely to Rom. 5:12-21.[8] Rom. 4:1–5:11 expound the sovereign, free, life-giving grace of God that alone brings life. For Christians this is "the grace in which we stand," that is, the determining of horizons of understanding and formation that shape us. Rom. 5:6-11 paves the way for the argument that grace is immeasurably

---

6. Dunn, *Paul,* 101.

7. Cf. also C. K. Barrett, *From First Adam to Last: A Study in Pauline Theology* (London: Black and New York: Scribner, 1962); Robin Scroggs, *The Last Adam: A Study in Pauline Anthropology* (Philadelphia: Fortress, 1966); and E. Brandenburger, *Adam und Christus: Exegetisch-religionsgeschichtliche Untersuchungen zu Röm. 5:12-21 (1 Kor. 15)* (Neukirchen: Neukirchener, 1962).

8. On Rom. 5:12-21 see esp. C. E. B. Cranfield, *The Epistle to the Romans,* ICC, 2 vols. (Edinburgh: T&T Clark, 1975), vol. 1, 269-95. Cf. also James D. G. Dunn, *Romans 1–8* (Dallas: Word, 1988), 269-303; and Joseph A. Fitzmyer, *Romans,* Anchor Bible (New York and London: Doubleday, 1992), 405-28.

more decisive than sin. Explicitly in Rom. 5:15, "the free gift is *not like* the trespass." In what respect is this true? Paul replies as follows: (1) death entered the world through sin, "and death spread to all because all sinned" (Rom. 5:12). (2) Death characterized the human order of existence whether before or after the coming of the law: "death exercised dominion from Adam to Moses," and then even under the law (5:14). (3) But the gift of grace is not simply like the rule of sin and death, for although death entered the world "through one man's trespass" (Rom. 5:15), "*much more* have the grace of God and the free gift in the grace of the one man . . . *abounded for the many*" (5: 15b). Its effects are "much more," and become manifest in "abundance" (5:16-17).

All of this provides the horizon of understanding for what might otherwise appear as if it were an abstract principle about the Fall: "Just as one man's trespass led to condemnation for all, so one man's act of righteousness leads to justification and life for all. Just as by one man's disobedience the many were made sinners, so by the one man's obedience the many will be made righteous" (Rom. 5:18-19). Law may provoke an increase in sin, but the effects of grace "abounded all the more" (Rom. 5:20), and in place of the dominion of death *grace* establishes a new "dominion" (5:21). In other words, *corporate solidarity cuts both ways:* if we complain about sharing the common liabilities of being "in Adam," how can we expect to share the common benefits of being "in Christ," which are *much more?*

In all of this argument the "fall" material constitutes a derivative analogy to explicate what it means to be "in Christ," although with the further corollary of what *not* to be "in Christ" amounts to. This would be to return to the Adam-character of humanity as it is and has been apart from Christ. The common assumption often made outside the Christian tradition that Paul and Christians teach that "Adam sinned, and we pay for it" is at odds with Paul's logic. Paul states, "Death spread to all *because all* have sinned" (Rom. 5:12).

C. E. B. Cranfield expresses the point with his customary judiciousness. He writes that as an objection it might be argued that "Adam must alone be responsible for our ruin." He continues, "But in answer to this it may be pointed out that Paul in this passage insists on the dissimilarity as well as on the similarity between Christ and Adam. . . . We have no right to insist that . . . Paul must necessarily have held that the guilt which is ours through Adam must also be quite independent of our sinning. . . . It is not necessary that the ways in which the consequences follow from the acts should also be exactly parallel."[9] The main emphasis is in "the effectiveness and unspeakable generosity of the divine grace. . . . The triumph of grace described in v. 20b was not itself the end of the matter. Its goal was the dispossession of the usurper sin and the replacement of its reign by the reign of grace."[10] This shapes the hermeneutics of the whole argu-

---

9. Cranfield, *Romans*, 278; cf. Dunn, *Romans 1–8*, 294-98.
10. Cranfield, *Romans*, 288 and 294.

ment in 5:12-21. Käsemann observes, "Paul is not speaking primarily of act and punishment, but of ruling powers . . . a sphere of lordship."[11]

(3) Rom. 7:7-13 (and 7:14-25) do not explicitly mention Adam and a "fall." However, most Pauline scholars reject the notion that "I" in these verses is primarily autobiographical, and some ascribe the identity of "I" to Adam by implication. Probably, as Cranfield suggests, "Paul is using the first person singular in a generalizing kind of way," but the narrative of Gen. 3 "was present to his mind."[12] Methodius, Theodore of Mopsuestia, and Theodoret believed that Paul was speaking in the name of Adam.[13] But even if this were so, the hermeneutical horizon concerns the role of the law in the history of salvation. The law is holy and given by God, but it cannot reverse the effects of sin or bring about a new order. As Dunn observes, Paul addresses the eschatological tension in which the process of salvation has still to reach its completion.[14]

13.2. The Fall and an Original State?
Patristic Thought and Reformation Theology

Many Patristic writers share Paul's hermeneutic, inasmuch as notions of "fall" perform a role within a larger exposition of divine grace and Christology. Yet some, in addition to this, explore what they regard as logical inferences from the Adam narratives that arguably find little or no support from Paul or from other biblical traditions. Equally a very small number offer virtually no doctrine of a fall at all. Clement of Alexandria, for example, appears to see no connection between sin and death, or between sin and its impact on freedom of choice, or the role of corporate solidarity in relation to this context of thought. Several controversial themes emerge, as follows.

(1) *Image and likeness.* In brief, it is well known that Irenaeus drew a distinction between *image* (Hebrew צלם, *tselem*; Greek εἰκών, *eikōn*) and *likeness* (Hebrew דמות, *dᵉmûth*; Greek ὁμοίωσις, *homoiōsis*) in Gen. 1:26-27.[15] Most exegetes today regard the two terms as virtually synonymous in this context, not least within the framework of Hebrew parallelism. Luther was aware of this exegetical issue, and from Luther onward any attempt to base a doctrine of sin or the Fall partly on this supposed distinction has been rightly regarded as lacking any firm exegetical basis.

(2) *Was the condition of humankind before the "fall" one of immature inno-*

---

11. Ernst Käsemann, *Commentary on Romans,* trans. G. W. Bromiley (Grand Rapids: Eerdmans, 1980), 150; cf. 139-58.

12. Cranfield, *Romans,* vol. 1, 342 and 343; cf. 340-70.

13. Methodius, *Discourse on the Resurrection,* II:1 (Migne, *Patrologia Graeca,* vol. 18, 296-98).

14. Dunn, *Romans 1–8,* 377; cf. 375-412.

15. Irenaeus, *Against Heresies,* V:6:1.

cence, or one of *"original righteousness,"* or simply *unspecified?* Once again, Irenaeus is a key thinker on this issue. He followed Tatian in suggesting that prior to any "fall" Adam was created as a child, imperfect and undeveloped. He writes, "Humankind was little, being but a child. It had to grow and reach full maturity. . . . Its mind was not yet fully mature, and thus humanity was easily led astray by the deceiver."[16] Even allowing for the emphasis that Christ "learned obedience through what he suffered" (Heb. 5:8), the notion that "Christ showed forth the image truly" (which Irenaeus affirms) seems to present a problem if for Christ to bear this image entails immaturity or naivety.[17] How in this case could such an "image and likeness" show the world what *God* is like, let alone exercise dominion over the earth? Some reply that "image of God" need not specify the "fullest degree" of representation of God's being, but in the case of Christ this seems strained.

Schleiermacher occupies an ambiguous position on this question. He declares, "Adam must have been sundered from God *before* his first sin, because otherwise how could he "have indulged his appetite in express disobedience to a divine command?"[18] Schleiermacher insists that to hold this view does not rest upon a "liberal" interpretation of the Genesis narrative, and it is embedded in his theory of the movement of humankind to a higher religious consciousness.[19] Predictably Schleiermacher's approach to the "fall" has its critics. Emil Brunner roundly asserts, even if a little harshly, "Schleiermacher is not dealing with sin at all, but with stages of development."[20]

On the other hand, the concept of *"original righteousness"* is also not without its critics. Pannenberg writes, "Little is left of the traditional dogma of a perfect first estate when we submit it to the test of biblical theology."[21] The notion of an originally "perfect" image found expression in Jewish apocalyptic and in rabbinic literature. Adam was said to have been created as "a second angel" (2 *Enoch* 30:11); his body filled the whole world (*Leviticus Rabbah* 18); when he sinned he lost "the lightness of the sun" (*Genesis Rabbah* 11; *Baba Batra* 58a; *Jerusalem Targum* to Gen. 2:7).[22] Ambrose, among the Church Fathers, is widely thought to

---

16. Irenaeus, *Demonstration of the Apostolic Teaching* 12, in L. M. Froidevaux (ed.), *Sources Chrétiennes* (Paris: Cerf, 1965), vol. 62, 52; older sources do not include the *Demonstration* since it was discovered only in the early twentieth century. See also *Demonstration* 13-14, and *Against Heresies* IV:64:1.

17. Irenaeus, *Against Heresies*, V:16:2; cf. III:32:1.

18. Schleiermacher, *The Christian Faith*, 295; cf. 292-304.

19. Schleiermacher, *The Christian Faith*, 296.

20. Emil Brunner, *Man in Revolt: A Christian Anthropology*, trans. Olive Wyon (London: Lutterworth, 1939), 124.

21. Pannenberg, *Systematic Theology*, vol. 2, 214.

22. Sources are cited by J. Jeremias in "Ἀδάμ," *TDNT*, vol. 1, 141; and by H. L. Strack and P. Billerbeck (eds.), *Kommentar zum Neuen Testament aus Talmud und Midrasch*, 6 vols. (Munich: Beck, from 1922), vol. 3, 254 and vol. 4, 892 and 964-65.

be the first Christian writer to explicate a full formulation of "original righteousness." He writes, "Adam was a heavenly being in paradise" (Latin *Adam cum in paradiso esset coelestis erat*).[23] He was "like an angel" resplendent with heavenly grace, and "would speak with God" *(loquebatur cum Deo)*.[24]

Ambrose was a powerful influence upon Augustine, and it is in Augustine that a concept of "original righteousness" becomes most developed, perhaps with a further reference to rabbinic traditions. Among the Greek Fathers, Chrysostom expounds Adam's paradisal state as an existence without pain.[25] Augustine speculates that prelapsarian Adam possessed outstanding intellectual gifts, by means of which he named the animals (Gen. 2:20).[26] This extended to the spiritual and moral realm: "Man's nature was created at first fruitless and without any sin."[27] But a flaw enters in, which "comes not from the blameless Creator but from that form of original sin *(ex originali peccato)* which was committed by free will *(liberum arbitrium)*. For this reason our guilty nature is liable to pay a just penalty."[28]

Athanasius came close to this idea, but showed a judicious caution about how much we can duly infer from the biblical texts. He explicitly rejects the view of Irenaeus that Adam before the Fall was like a child; he credits him with high intellectual and moral powers. How could he enjoy intercourse with God if he were not pure in heart and capable of such contemplation? This is almost a doctrine of original righteousness, but Athanasius is reluctant to formulate it as an explicit doctrine. Sin brings φθορά *(phthora)*, which Williams interprets as denoting "disintegration" in this context.[29] Athanasius sees the Fall as a relapse from a status of privilege into the state of nature, when processes of decay or corruption began.[30]

In the pre-Reformation and Reformation periods, Dominican writers affirmed an Augustinian doctrine of original righteousness, although Franciscans were more hesitant. Luther and Calvin underlined Augustine's doctrine. Calvin is clear about the consequences of the Fall. He writes, "This is the hereditary corruption to which early Christian writers gave the name of Original sin, meaning by the term the depravation of a nature formerly good and pure."[31] He concedes that there has been "much discussion" and controversy about this, including the claim

---

23. Ambrose, *Exposition: Sermons* 15:36, on Ps. 118.

24. References cited by N. P. Williams, *Ideas of the Fall*, 301.

25. Chysostom, *Homily on Genesis*, 16 (Migne, *Patrologia Graeca*, vol. 53, 126-27).

26. Cf. Augustine, *On the Trinity*, 13:7; and *On the Literal Meaning of Genesis*, 9:12:20.

27. Augustine, *On Nature and Grace*, 3 (3).

28. Augustine, *On Nature and Grace*, 3 (3), Latin *Corpus Scriptorum Ecclesiasticorum Latinorum*, vol. 60, ed. C. F. Urba and J. Zycha (Vienna: Tempsky, 1913), 235.

29. Williams, *Ideas of the Fall*, 260-61.

30. Athanasius, *On the Incarnation*, 6:1; cf. 3:4, 14 and 22:1-2.

31. Calvin, *Institutes*, II:1:5 (Beveridge edition, vol. 1, 214). Cf. II:1:5-11.

of "Pelagius with his profane fiction — that Adam sinned only to his own hurt, but did no hurt to his posterity"; but he continues: "The orthodox therefore, and more especially Augustine, laboured to show that we . . . bring an innate corruption from the very womb. . . . 'I was shapen in iniquity, and in sin did my mother conceive me' (Ps. 51:5). . . . All of us, therefore, descending from an impure seed, came into the world tainted with the contagion of sin . . . in God's sight defiled and polluted."[32]

Calvin expounds this further. He recognizes the hermeneutical context that provides the frame of reference in Paul: "all have sinned; even so might grace reign . . ." (Rom. 5:12, 21).[33] The whole of human nature, however, he continues, is "as it were a seed-bed of sin . . . abominable to God. . . . [It] constantly produces new fruits."[34] It is not enough even to say that original sin is "want of the original righteousness," for things have become out of hand. "All the parts of the soul were possessed by sin, ever since Adam revolted from the fountain of righteousness."[35] This corruption redefines what we can call "natural." This now includes "depraved habit," for human persons are "by nature the children of wrath (Eph. 2:3)."[36]

Otto Weber writes that in contrast to Semi-Pelagianism "the Reformers basically resumed the doctrine of Augustine."[37] However, in spite of his advocacy of "Reformed Theology," Weber concedes, "The concept of 'inherited sin' is a theological interpretation. The question is whether it is an adequate interpretation of the scriptural witness."[38] The biblical witness, he adds, does explicitly affirm the universality of sin, and in a few passages, especially in Rom. 5:12-21, "original sinfulness" as well as the universality of grace.[39] G. C. Berkouwer provides a more detailed exposition not only of Luther and Calvin on sin, but also of various Reformation confessions on this subject, in his *Dogmatics*. Berkouwer emphasizes the reality and universality of human *guilt*, but has reservations about such categories as "realism" and "federalism" within the complexities of Reformed theology.[40] Pannenberg rightly expresses reservations about speculations concerning the state of Adam before the Fall. Too much speculation, he writes, about "Adam's former state is simply assuming without prior proof that we may see the New Testament sayings about the image of God as on the same plane as those in the original story."[41]

---

32. Calvin, *Institutes*, II:1:5.

33. Calvin, *Institutes*, II:1:6.

34. Calvin, *Institutes*, II:1:8 (Beveridge edition, 218).

35. Calvin, *Institutes*, II:1:9.

36. Calvin, *Institutes*, II:1:11. Cf. further III:3:13; and IV:15:10.

37. Otto Weber, *Foundations of Dogmatics*, trans. D. L. Guder, 2 vols. (Grand Rapids: Eerdmans, 1981), vol. 1, 602.

38. Weber, *Dogmatics*, vol. 1, 596.

39. Weber, *Dogmatics*, vol. 1, 596-99.

40. G. C. Berkouwer, *Sin*, trans. Philip Holtrop, Studies in Dogmatics (Grand Rapids: Eerdmans, 1971), esp. 424-30, 441-84, and 536-39.

41. Pannenberg, *Systematic Theology*, vol. 2, 214.

(3) *The Controversy about Traducianism.* In the light of hermeneutics, the older controversy about the respective claims of traducianism and creationism may be said to take place outside the appropriate horizons of understanding within which biblical traditions affirm the universality, condition, and corporate solidarity of humankind under sin. At best it might be thought of as a speculative attempt at "explanation" rather than understanding. Its significance for hermeneutics is questionable when issues of genetic heredity and social environment no longer depend on speculative theories about "the soul." Speculations about a material "soul" are in any case foreign to the biblical writings.

Tertullian, the classic advocate of traducianism, is in a curious position. On one side he insists on a use of Scripture and apostolic tradition that is uncontaminated by philosophy; on the other side he depends heavily on Stoic philosophy for his materialistic view of the soul on which he depends for traducianism.

Tertullian appropriates the Stoic view that the "soul" (Latin *anima*) is a "corporeal" or quasi-material substance, for example, like "fiery breath" (Greek πνεῦμα πυροειδές, *pneuma puroeides*). It may appear that he takes up the biblical term "breath of life" (Latin *flatus vitae*), but he interprets this in a way that diverges from that of the biblical writers, in effect to denote an ethereal substance. Tertullian also bases his view on empirical evidence for what today we should call the psychosomatic unity of the self, but again, he conceived of distinct "parts" of the self rather than a biblical, unified self. He writes, "I call on the Stoics to help me. . . . The soul *(anima)* is a corporeal substance. . . . [It] shares the pain of the body . . . by wounds and sores, [but] the body too suffers with the soul . . . with anxiety, distress, or love."[42]

On this basis Tertullian argues for the transmission of original sin, stating that each generation is an offshoot or derivative *(tradux)* of the previous one. He alludes to the narrative of Eve and Adam's rib (Gen. 2:21-23) to argue that Eve also is "a *tradux* of Adam."[43]

Today many would argue that to locate the transmission of a sinful disposition in a quasi-physical "soul" is either a conceptual category mistake, or, worse, a concession to a behaviorist account of hereditary character traits solely in terms of genetic transmission. To account for sin in bio-genetic terms would not reflect biblical and Christian doctrine. Gregory of Nyssa alone among the Greek Fathers veers in the direction of traducian language.[44]

Subsequently it became an unfortunate distraction in some late nineteenth-century systematic theologies. On one side Charles Hodge addresses traducianism and concludes that it lacks scriptural warrant; but Augustus Hopkins

---

42. Tertullian, *Treatise on the Soul* (or *De anima*) 5.

43. Tertullian, *Treatise on the Soul* 36; cf. 6; and further N. P. Williams, *Ideas of the Fall*, 233-45.

44. Gregory of Nyssa, *De Hominis Opificio* 29 (Migne, *Patrologia Graeca*, vol. 44, 233-34).

Strong defends traducianism in a lengthy debate.[45] Hodge's concern was to protest on behalf of the creative role of the agency of God in each generation, while Strong is concerned to include hereditary factors among those that led to the universality of sin. The question for hermeneutics, however, is whether this is the most appropriate horizon of understanding within which to raise such questions given that it presupposes notions of the "soul" that biblical writers do not share. It offers an example of systematic theologians formulating free-floating "problems" in place of genuine "questions that arise" in a hermeneutical context. By contrast, Torrance reminds us that Calvin addresses questions that arise within biblical horizons. He notes, "Calvin refuses to enunciate a doctrine of sin . . . except in the context of grace."[46] This is true to the hermeneutics of the New Testament.

13.3. The Hermeneutics of Sin in Modern Thought from Schleiermacher to Niebuhr

In the early nineteenth century some sought to formulate a doctrine of human sin and the Fall that began from a different starting point from that of more traditional theologies.

(1) *Friedrich Schleiermacher* (1768-1834) has been interpreted in radically different ways. Moxon interprets Schleiermacher as formulating "a new method of approaching the subject of sin . . . namely that before we can investigate sin we must investigate the faculty that reveals it . . . God-consciousness."[47] He continues, "The sense of sin is the internal strife which arises in us owing to the inadequacy of our God-consciousness."[48]

This is so, but it can be perceived in two different ways. In the earlier years of the twentieth century many regarded Schleiermacher's emphasis on "consciousness" as a "psychological" or introspective approach. From the 1960s onward, however, there has been a growing appreciation that, in Macquarrie's words, "Otto's 'creaturely feeling', Schleiermacher's 'feeling of absolute dependence', and Tillich's 'ultimate concern' denote a dimension of ontological immediacy."[49] Macquarrie speaks of "the disclosive character of affective states."[50] He comments, "We misinterpret Schleiermacher unless we see that for him feeling refers

---

45. Charles Hodge, *Systematic Theology*, 3 vols. (New York: Scribner, 1871; rpt. Grand Rapids: Eerdmans, 1946), vol. 2, 68-76; cf. Augustus Hopkins Strong, *Systematic Theology* (London: Pickering & Inglis, 1907), 493-97.

46. Torrance, *Calvin's Doctrine of Man*, 83 (his italics).

47. Moxon, *The Doctrine of Sin*, 198.

48. Moxon, *The Doctrine of Sin*, 199.

49. John Macquarrie, *Studies in Christian Existentialism* (London: S.C.M., 1966), 37.

50. Macquarrie, *Christian Existentialism*, 41.

... 'to that which transcends intellect and will.' . . . It is an error . . . to accept the presupposition . . . that feeling is 'mere feeling', a subjective emotion."[51]

We noted above that at least one writer in the Reformed tradition defends Schleiermacher's emphasis upon consciousness on the ground that this is human consciousness *in the light of God's presence or action,* or, as Schleiermacher terms it, "God-consciousness." F. LeRon Shults argues that "reciprocal relationality" between God and human selfhood provides the "hermeneutical horizon" for Schleiermacher just as it does for Calvin.[52] Schleiermacher carefully examines to what it is that "a consciousness of absolute dependence" or "a feeling of absolute dependence" relates.[53] The better translation is used in the heading to sect. 4 of *The Christian Faith,* namely "the consciousness of being absolutely dependent" *(schlechthinig abhängig).*[54] The three key terms are *Gefühl, schlechthinig,* and *Abhängigkeit.* I anticipated LeRon Shults's interpretation in *New Horizons in Hermeneutics* in 1992, some ten years before his book, setting in parallel "consciousness of being absolutely dependent" and "being in a relationship with God." I stated, "Schleiermacher would have endorsed Calvin's dictum that knowledge of God and knowledge of ourselves are bound together by a mutual tie."[55]

A sense of sin, Schleiermacher writes, arises from a sense of the inadequacy of our God-consciousness. It can be evoked by experiences of either enhancement or distress: God can speak to us through our shortcomings, sufferings, or pain. In Part II he almost reaches a Pauline horizon of meaning by placing awareness of sin in relation to divine grace.

Yet a deep ambiguity also characterizes Schleiermacher's work. As Pannenberg observes, he "greatly oversimplified" the relation between immediacy in human consciousness and what is "beyond" in relationality with "feeling" as a general state.[56] Still more problematic is Schleiermacher's almost obsessional concern with development, even before the impact of the evolutionary theories proposed by Charles Darwin and Herbert Spencer. Could Paul or John have countenanced the notion that sin is a matter of "arrested development"? Emil Brunner offers a critical assessment that we noted earlier only in part. He writes, "His [Schleiermacher's] doctrine of 'Original Sin' comes to this, that at every new stage in his development man is hindered by previous stages. . . . Thus the problem of Original Sin *(Erbsünde)* is . . . turned in a completely new direction by means of an idealistic evolutionism with a strong naturalistic tinge. . . . Schleiermacher is not dealing with sin at all, but with stages of devel-

51. Macquarrie, *Christian Existentialism,* 32-33.
52. Shults, *Reforming Theological Anthropology,* 97; see 97-116.
53. Schleiermacher, *The Christian Faith,* Part I, sects. 3-5, esp. 12-13, 17, and 20-24.
54. Schleiermacher, *The Christian Faith,* Part I, sect. 4, 12.
55. Thiselton, *New Horizons in Hermeneutics,* 207; cf. 204-16 and, more broadly, 216-36.
56. Pannenberg, *Anthropology in Theological Perspective,* 252-53.

opment."[57] Brunner's statement may seem a little brutal, but it contains genuine force.

(2) *Albrecht Ritschl* (1822-89) is widely perceived as reacting against the traditional Augustinian approach to sin and the Fall. However, in a careful study of Ritschl, James Richmond attacks "the stereotype" whereby Ritschl is portrayed as essentially Pelagian. Richmond doubts whether Ritschl rejected any doctrine of original sin; whether he came close to rejecting human guilt other than as "guilty feelings"; and whether he understood sin primarily as ignorance, or as *sins* rather than *sin*.[58] Richmond regards the conventional picture as a caricature of Ritschl, even if it is still widespread.

In one respect Richmond's corrective is helpful. Ritschl's most important and constructive contribution to modern theologies of sin was to reinstate the biblical emphasis on the *corporate, structural, and communal* nature of sin. His two central concerns were justification by grace through faith, especially in Paul, and the kingdom of God, especially in the teaching of Jesus.[59] Sin is defined as whatever is contrary to the kingdom of God, and this "cannot be completely represented . . . within the framework of individual life. . . . The subject of sin is humanity as the sum of all individuals in so far as the selfish action of each individual person, involving . . . interaction with all others . . . leads to the association of individuals in common evil."[60] On the other hand, Ritschl's preoccupation with some of the themes of classical liberalism led to an inadequate eschatology and the absence of any "objective" notion of final judgment, as we contend in 22.4, although he does hold a notion of "internal" punishment, as we note below.

Perhaps surprisingly in view of his emphasis on justification by faith, the hermeneutical horizon of understanding within which Ritschl reached this conclusion has certain affinities, even in 1874, with what has come to be called the New Perspective on Paul, associated initially with E. P. Sanders a century later in 1977. Ritschl argued that to understand the nature of sin our starting point must be *not* the plight of humankind, but the kingdom of God and justification by grace. Sanders rejects the "Lutheran" or Bultmannian method of beginning with human sin. He writes, "Paul's thought did not run from plight to solution, but rather from solution to plight."[61] Sanders adds: "The contrast is not between self-reliance and reliance upon God . . . but between belonging to Christ and not

---

57. Brunner, *Man in Revolt*, 123-24.

58. James Richmond, *Ritschl: A Reappraisal: A Study in Systematic Theology* (London and New York, 1978), 124.

59. Albrecht Ritschl, *The Christian Doctrine of Justification and Reconciliation: The Positive Development of the Doctrine*, trans. H. R. Mackintosh and A. B. Macaulay (repr. Clifton, N.J: Reference Book Publishers, 1966), 10-11.

60. Ritschl, *Justification*, 335.

61. E. P. Sanders, *Paul and Palestinian Judaism: A Comparison of Patterns of Religion* (London: S.C.M., 1977), 443.

belonging to Christ. . . . Effort is not the sin; the sin is aiming towards *any* goal but being found 'in Christ' (Phil. 3:9)."[62] Ritschl, in part-parallel, suggests that it is not true that humankind has first to understand its sin, and then to seek forgiveness. He writes, "The only way in which the idea of sin can be formed at all is by comparison with the idea of the good."[63]

This may begin to point to weaknesses in Ritschl's theology. In spite of his strong emphasis upon justification and faith, he is also influenced by Kant's notions of the good, responsibility, duty, and moral struggle. Sin in the New Testament, Ritschl argues, is either a matter of ignorance or failure to resist "the kingdom of evil." Does sin become more a concept of ethical philosophy than of misdirected desire and a breach of fellowship with God? Moxon might arguably be said to retain the "stereotyping" that Richmond regards as a caricature. Moxon writes, "Ritschl boldly repudiates the old doctrine of Original Sin, and seeks to explain sinfulness by a development of the Pelagian idea of the 'influence of example', and finds sin entirely in man's environment. . . . Sin consists in the general lowering of moral judgement owing to . . . evil example and to the vast complexity of sinful action in the world."[64]

Yet there is some truth in both verdicts, and each qualifies the other. Richmond does succeed in showing that Ritschl is concerned that the traditional doctrine sometimes seems to go beyond strict exegesis. For example, does "I was brought forth in iniquity, and in sin did my mother conceive me" (Ps. 51:5), which is a confession, not a formulation of doctrine, genuinely bear the weight that Augustine and others place upon it?[65] Does Rom. 5:12-21 bear such a weight, especially when Augustine uses a Latin version that translates the Greek ἐφ' ᾧ πάντες *(eph' hō pantes)* by the Latin *in quo omnes,* thereby implying a notion of "seminal headship" (all have sinned *in the person of* Adam; Rom. 5:12; cf. 5:19). Dogmas or doctrine, Ritschl insisted, must be based only on clear statements of Scripture. This provides a constructive discipline for his hermeneutical horizons. Nevertheless, as Moxon is well aware, he brings empirical observations and the psychological and sociological theories of the mid-to-late nineteenth century as sources that also shape his own doctrine.

Ritschl also expounds a notion of the connection between sin and punishment as an existential or conceptually "internal" one. We noted that Origen, in effect, was the first to consider such a concept explicitly. "Punishment" comes not from external divine intervention, but is inherent in the very processes of sin as self-destructive action. It is a negative version of "virtue is its own reward," and perhaps again the figure of Kant stands in the background. In this respect

---

62. Sanders, *Paul,* 482.
63. Ritschl, *Justification,* 327.
64. Moxon, *Doctrine of Sin,* 200.
65. Richmond, *Ritschl,* 130.

Richmond considers the verdicts of a long list of conservative critics of Ritschl at best one-sided, at worst unfair. He cites James Orr, J. K. Mozley, and H. R. Mackintosh to the effect that "there is no idea of divine punishment" in Ritschl.[66]

The figure of Adam in Ritschl's thought is entirely mythical or representative of human collectivity. His hermeneutic of "Adam" in part anticipates the de-objectifying and existential interpretation of Bultmann's demythologizing, and he alludes to the work of J. G. Eichhorn, a predecessor at Göttingen, on myth. Whether in the end he reduces *guilt* as *an objective* situation to *consciousness* of guilt as a subjective experience remains an issue of contention and debate, although most writers probably regard the conclusion as affirmation.

The most constructive step, and valid hermeneutical horizon, urged by Ritschl was that of the *corporate and communal* dimension of sin, which is faithful to Paul, John, and the Old Testament.

(3) *Frederick R. Tennant* (1866-1957) promoted, by contrast, a *philosophical, empirical, and individualist* account of evil and sin. In this respect his work threatened to turn back the clock to the early nineteenth century. Like many other late nineteenth-century and early twentieth-century thinkers, he was unduly influenced by naturalistic evolutionary theories, and tempted to see everything in developmental terms. Tennant believed that anthropology had demonstrated that in its early evolution humankind was a creature of natural processes, and that a moral consciousness of sin, or of right or wrong, emerged only gradually. "Adam," once again, is a myth or symbol for humankind in its amoral infancy.

Tennant produced two books on sin in the early years of the twentieth century. *The Origin and Propagation of Sin* was his Cambridge University Hulsean lectures for 1901-2, and here he viewed sin in the light of evolutionary theory. His second book, *The Concept of Sin*, appeared in 1912.[67] Here he views sin as "moral imperfection," for which a human being is accountable to God.[68] But this excludes anything having to do with *the state* of humankind, and leaves aside theories about a figure of Adam. He writes, "Volition, and volition alone," is sinful; not what can be attributed to conditions of life or a person's environment.[69] The term *sin* applies only to "the fact of deliberate choosing the worse when a better course is both known and possible."[70]

Three standard criticisms have been brought against this approach. First, Tennant confuses sin with moralism and moral culpability. Where is the maxim

---

66. Richmond, *Ritschl,* 133.

67. Frederick R. Tennant, *The Concept of Sin* (Cambridge: Cambridge University Press, 1912); and Frederick R. Tennant, *The Origin and Propagation of Sin* (Cambridge: Cambridge University Press, 2d edn. 1908).

68. Tennant, *The Concept of Sin,* 245.

69. Tennant, *The Concept of Sin,* 246.

70. Tennant, *The Concept of Sin,* 247.

of Athanasius that sin is rejection of *contemplation of God,* or the emphasis on sin as a breach of *fellowship with God?* As E. J. Bicknell observes, he writes not as a theologian but as a moral philosopher.[71] Second, "his view of sin is purely individualistic."[72] Bicknell points out that both in the light of biblical scholarship and of political events, especially the First World War of 1914-18, "we have become familiar with the idea of corporate responsibility and corporate guilt," and Tennant's approach is "curiously out of date."[73] A third criticism arises more specifically in relation to Tennant's book *The Origin and Propagation of Sin.* Here Tennant attempted to formulate a doctrine of sin in the light of evolutionary theory. Again, in the light of the World War I and writing in 1923, Bicknell questions the empirical warrant for the notion that "man has not fallen; he is rising." The concept of sin that arises in the light of evolutionary theories ignores the place of misdirected desire, and human relationship with God.

It might seem surprising that in the process of "demythologizing" the figure of Adam, philosophers might not have entertained the hypothesis of whether humankind in direct encounter with the Creator might be different in kind from the emergence of the human within a context that lacks such engagement. In much philosophical discourse to trace the different inferences that may be drawn from theistic and nontheistic premises is part of the exercise. This would not demand a historical reconstruction of an Adam narrative, as Bicknell observes.[74] But to assume that naturalism and anthropology can provide a comprehensive evaluation of the Genesis narrative is to import *a priori* positivism into the equation.

(4) *Karl Barth* (1886-1968) does not formally discuss "the Pride and Fall of Man" until *Church Dogmatics,* IV:1, sect. 60. For only in the context of grace and judgment in the light of Christ is Barth ready to address the problem of sin.[75] *Only within the hermeneutical horizons of Jesus Christ as "true man" who is the image of God can the full dimensions of human sin be seen.* Sin emerges within these horizons of understanding as that which only God through Christ can remove. Only in the light of Jesus Christ who is both Lord and Servant in the humiliation of self-giving in the incarnation and in the cross can the nature of human sin in terms of self-sufficiency, unbelief, and pride, be exposed and understood for what it is.

Human sin is in the first place understood as *pride* not on the basis of empir-

---

71. E. J. Bicknell, *The Christian Idea of Sin and Original Sin in the Light of Modern Knowledge* (London and New York: Longmans, Green, 1923), 32-34.

72. Bicknell, *Christian Idea of Sin,* 32; cf. 34-37.

73. Bicknell, *Christian Idea of Sin,* 34; cf. 35.

74. Bicknell, *Christian Idea of Sin,* 98.

75. Barth, *Church Dogmatics,* IV:1, sect. 60, "The Pride and Fall of Man," 358-513; sect. 60:1 "The Man of Sin in the Light of the Obedience of the Son of God," 358-413; sect. 60:2, "The Pride of Man," 413-78; and sect. 60:3, "The Fall of Man," 478-513.

ical observation, but in the light of the trust of Jesus Christ, who placed himself in the hands of God for judgment, vindication, and grace, in relation to which humankind insists on making its own judgments. Humankind prefers not to be judged, but in the light of Christ human alienation and bondage appears as the consequence that indeed it is. Barth writes, "Who and what the man is who commits sin — man in his properties as a sinner . . . must derive from the Christological insight which is normative for the whole context."[76] "The fall of man . . . corresponds exactly to what we have learned to know as the essence of sin — the pride of man. 'Pride goes before a fall' — The proverb is true."[77]

We might wonder whether such a *general* category as *pride* does full justice to varied models of sin in the biblical writings as well as to the contingent and particularist nature of hermeneutics. Barth concedes, "The definition is not exhaustive," and he subsequently equates pride with "the breaking of the divine command," "entry into a state of lawlessness," and "self-alienation from . . . the majesty of God."[78] "Man sins in that he ignores and despises the redemptive significance of the divine command . . . and rejects the confidence that God is the source of all goodness and good in man. . . . What God wills is revealed in what He has done in Jesus Christ."[79] More specifically humankind was created to be in covenant partnership with God, and to be "open to God."[80] Specifically in and through Christ the work of "God the Reconciler" brings about "God with us."[81]

Clearly the term *pride* carries with it a breach of fellowship with God, distrust of God, and much else that emerges as readers work their way through *Dogmatics* IV:1. The most hermeneutically illuminating feature of Barth's work is his horizon of understanding in terms of God the Reconciler and the "real man" Jesus Christ. It is in relation to Jesus Christ that a variety of distinctive acts, desires, habits, and states of pride, distrust, unbelief, self-gratification, and breach of fellowship with God can be seen for what they really are. In linguistic terms *pride* as a catchword seems both too broad and too narrow. In theological terms, however, Barth shows in a masterly way that this term provides a key for unlocking the multiform dimensions of human sin especially in relation to the grace of God.

(5) *Emil Brunner* (1889-1966) shares two fundamental points of approach with Barth. First, he defines sin in relation to the purpose for which God created humankind, and this is seen most clearly in Jesus Christ. The well-known English title *Man in Revolt* is the equivalent in the English editions of *Der Mensch im Widerspruch,* or *Humankind in Contradiction,* that is, contradiction of the

76. Barth, *Church Dogmatics,* IV:1, sect. 60:3, 478.
77. Barth, *Church Dogmatics,* IV:1, sect. 60:3, 478.
78. Barth, *Church Dogmatics,* IV:1, sect. 60:2, 413 and 414.
79. Barth, *Church Dogmatics,* IV:1, sect. 60:2, 414-15.
80. Barth, *Church Dogmatics,* IV:1, sect. 60:2, 421; cf. IV:1, sect. 57:2, 22-66.
81. Barth, *Church Dogmatics,* IV:1, sect. 57:1, "God with us," 3-21.

"true and the actual man" of God's purposes. Brunner writes, "Through sin man has lost . . . his God-given nature."[82] Second, the very origin of sin, Brunner continues, is "the assertion of human independence over against God, the declaration of the rights of man's freedom as independent of God's will, the constitution of the autonomous reason, morality, and culture. . . ."[83] He adds, "This is presumption, arrogance . . . the actual, primal, sin."[84]

We noted above a contrast between Ritschl's emphasis upon the collective or communal nature of sin or evil and Tennant's shallow individualism. Brunner addresses with eloquence and judicious balance the individual and corporate dimensions of human sin. On one side, "I can only speak of myself," and Brunner appreciates Kierkegaard's reflections on the individual. On the other hand, "we are a unity bound together in a solidarity."[85] He continues: "The sin of Adam is the destruction of communion with God, which is at the same time the severance of this bond."[86] "Being against God" brings about "being against one another."

(6) *Reinhold Niebuhr* (1892-1971) brilliantly captures this corporate dimension of structural sin, preparing the way for issues of justice and sin in liberation theologies. Following his earlier interest in the social ideas of liberal Protestant theology, he abandoned liberal optimism and progressivism in the face of the harsh realities of corporate power in industry and politics.[87] In theological terms he reflects affinities with Calvin, Barth, Brunner and Bonhoeffer, but his penetrating analysis of the self-deception of structural sin constitutes a distinctive contribution to the subject.

"In every human group," Niebuhr writes, "there is . . . more unrestrained egoism than the individuals who compose the group reveal in their personal relationships."[88] Sin and evil are due not simply to inadequacies or mistakes in the social sciences. In the end, he asserts, "Conflict is inevitable, and in this conflict power must be challenged by power."[89] All social cooperation requires a measure of coercion. Democratic power is actually more coercive than most people realize.[90] It is sheer romanticism to assume that otherwise a national or large social group could achieve "a common mind." As economies change, disproportions in the possession of power emerge. Social philosophers, such as John Dewey, do not do justice to the complexities of societies or human selfhood.

---

82. Brunner, *Man in Revolt*, 94.
83. Brunner, *Man in Revolt*, 129.
84. Brunner, *Man in Revolt*, 130.
85. Brunner, *Man in Revolt*, 139-40.
86. Brunner, *Man in Revolt*, 141.
87. Reinhold Niebuhr, *Moral Man and Immoral Society: A Study in Ethics and Politics* (London: S.C.M., 1963 and New York: Scribner, 1932).
88. Niebuhr, *Moral Man*, xi-xii.
89. Niebuhr, *Moral Man*, xv.
90. Niebuhr, *Moral Man*, 4.

The key theme in Niebuhr's analysis in this book is the role of "self-deception and hypocrisy . . . an unvarying element in the moral life of all human beings."[91] One prime example is "the dishonesty of nations," who will perform acts of corporate self-interest to the disadvantage of others "for the sake of our nation." What is in reality selfish wears the disguise of altruism, "for the benefit of our people."[92] "The selfishness of nations is proverbial."[93] "Altruistic passion is sluiced into the reservoirs of nationalism with great ease."[94] But this same principle operates on behalf of social classes. It protects the interests and positions of privileged classes especially when "power . . . inheres in the ownership of the means of production."[95] However, there is no less "moral cynicism" at work in the seizing of power of the "proletarian class." Niebuhr suggests, "The exaltation of class loyalty as the highest form of altruism is a natural concomitant of the destruction of national loyalty."[96]

Niebuhr does not exempt religious groups or family connections from this attack. Indeed, what is most insidious is that groupings in religion do not merely strive for self-affirmation and power; they may even lead their followers into "preoccupation with the self." Religious leaders sometimes capitalize on "ego-centricity in man."[97] A person may undertake questionable conduct in business or at work "for the sake of the family." All this is a study in disguised self-interest at a corporate or structural level. Dietrich Bonhoeffer speaks of a kind of preaching that is designed to capitalize on a personal sense of guilt; and Moltmann expounds the structural injustices that lead to the oppression of the vulnerable.[98]

Niebuhr develops the theme of "man as a sinner" at a more strictly theological level in his two-volume *The Nature and Destiny of Man* (1941). He expounds "the egotism of individuals" and the "group pride" of communities.[99] The root of sin is "man's pride and will-to-power." The religious dimension is humankind's rebellion against God; their "effort to usurp the place of God. The moral and social dimension of sin is injustice. The ego which falsely makes itself the centre of existence in its pride and will-to-power inevitably subordinates other life to its will and thus does injustice to other life."[100]

Niebuhr sees this as what lies behind Paul's description of the abandoned

91. Niebuhr, *Moral Man*, 95.

92. Niebuhr, *Moral Man*, 83-112.

93. Niebuhr, *Moral Man*, 84.

94. Niebuhr, *Moral Man*, 91.

95. Niebuhr, *Moral Man*, 114; cf. 113-41.

96. Niebuhr, *Moral Man*, 152; cf. 142-68.

97. Niebuhr, *Moral Man*, 54.

98. Dietrich Bonhoeffer, *Letters and Papers from Prison: The Enlarged Edition*, ed. E. Bethge (London: SCM, 1971), 324-29 and 339-42; cf. Moltmann, *The Crucified God*, 291-338.

99. Niebuhr, *The Nature and Destiny of Man*, vol. 1, 190-255.

100. Niebuhr, *Nature*, 191.

world in Rom. 1:18-32: "their foolish heart was darkened." Humankind seeks freedom from anxiety, but looks to find it in self-assertion and control rather than in trust in the security of God.[101] "Man falls into pride when he seeks to raise his contingent existence to unconditioned significance."[102] This coheres with Paul's exposition of human self-glorification, and finds endorsement in Augustine, Luther, Aquinas, and Calvin.[103] Human complacency finds expression in the parable of the rich fool (Luke 12:19-20). Greed is a form of power in that modern technology seduces humankind into thinking that mastery of technological resources can eliminate insecurity. We have noted above that this reflects Paul's notion of living "according to the flesh."

Niebuhr contends that "the group is more arrogant, hypocritical, self-centred and more ruthless in the pursuit of its ends than the individual."[104] He alludes to the "egotism" of racial, natural, and socio-economic groups.[105] The state may readily assume the status of an idol, and elevate its authority and its demands into a kind of idolatry. It may breed "sinful pride and idolatrous pretensions."[106] The prophets attacked such self-exaltation in the place of God (Isa. 2:12, 17; 26:3). The Magnificat exults in the putting down of the mighty and the lifting up the humble (Luke 1:52-53).

If pride is the attempt to center life on the self, Niebuhr argues, preoccupation with desires on the part of the self may derive from sensuality.[107] He identifies sexual license, gluttony, extravagance, drunkenness, and abandonment to forms of physical desire under this heading. Yet self-love may take more disguised and subtle forms, and thereby avoid social disapproval. "Sensuality [is] a secondary consequence of man's rebellion against God."[108] It finds exposition in Paul, Augustine, Aquinas, and Luther. Sensuality is "the inordinate love for all creaturely and mutable values which results from the primal love of self, rather than love of God."[109]

Niebuhr has brilliantly expounded the destructive effects of structural sin, its origins in misdirected desire, and its status as a turning away from God. These are valid horizons of understanding, and they do justice to the biblical understanding of corporate solidarity, which Paul expounds under the rubric "in Adam" in Rom. 5:12-21, in going one's own way in Rom. 1:18-32, and in the inade-

---

101. Niebuhr, *Nature*, 195.

102. Niebuhr, *Nature*, 198.

103. Niebuhr, *Nature*, 199, where some documentation is included, e.g., Augustine, *City of God*, XII:13; XIV:13; Aquinas, *Summa Theologiae*, Ia, Q. 77, art. 4; Calvin, *Institutes*, II:4.

104. Niebuhr, *Nature*, 221-22.

105. Niebuhr, *Nature*, 222.

106. Niebuhr, *Nature*, 223.

107. Niebuhr, *Nature*, 242-55.

108. Niebuhr, *Nature*, 245.

109. Niebuhr, *Nature*, 247.

quacy of law and teaching in Rom. 7:7-13 and beyond. Johannine "blindness" underlines Niebuhr's diagnosis of the role of self-deception, especially in terms of corporate sin. Yet some dimensions of the subject require further explanation or supplementation, and these have invited certain criticisms especially from some feminist writers.

13.4. The Hermeneutics of Sin in Modern Thought from Feminist Writers to Pannenberg

(7) *Some Feminist Responses to Niebuhr.* Feminist writers have expressed appreciation of much of Niebuhr's work. As early as in 1960, however, Valerie Saiving argued that the temptations of woman *as woman* were not the same as those of man *as man,* and that Niebuhr's diagnosis and exposition of sin as pride, will-to-power, and self-assertiveness was generally applicable to men rather than to women. If we need a complementary account for women, she argued, this may be better expressed by such terms as "triviality, distractibility, and diffuseness, lack of an organizing center or focus, dependence on others for one's own self-definition," or negation of the self.[110]

In 1980 Judith Plaskow published a Yale doctoral dissertation that developed this critique in greater detail, this time in relation to Paul Tillich as well as to Niebuhr.[111] In the early era of feminist theology feminist writers came mainly from the United States, and Niebuhr and Tillich held special influence in American theology. Her general argument is that both thinkers have been unduly selective in what they have highlighted and in what they have omitted in their account of human sin, and that this selective process more readily addresses a male-orientated agenda of discourse than a universal one. Supposedly inclusive experience is really male experience. In particular calls to self-sacrifice merely make the imbalance worse, when women have little "self" left to sacrifice.

Daphne Hampson adds further material to this critique. She expresses appreciation of Niebuhr's contribution, not least in the context of National Socialism in Germany and capitalist industrialism in America. But the emphasis on sin as pride and sensuality belongs primarily to a male world. Man is more competitive than woman. The sin of woman is more readily that of "wanting to be rid of herself," as Kierkegaard understood better than Niebuhr.[112] Most of all, in spite of his concerns about social power and social justice, Niebuhr's main understanding of the human self remains one of individualization. He lacks a full social or rela-

---

110. Valerie Saiving, "The Human Situation: a Feminine View," *Journal of Religion* 40 (1960) 100-112.

111. Judith Plaskow, *Sex, Sin and Grace: Women's Experience and the Theologies of Reinhold Niebuhr and Paul Tillich* (Lanham, MD: University Press of America, 1980).

112. Daphne Hampson, *Theology and Feminism* (Oxford: Blackwell, 1990), 123.

tional sense of the human, in which relation to the other is part of what it is to be oneself. It is "monadic" rather then reflecting "an essential relationality."[113]

We have noted in the studies explored above that in addition to work by Karl Barth and Dietrich Bonhoeffer, more recent emphases in Germany by Jürgen Moltmann and Wolfhart Pannenberg, in America by Stanley Grenz, in France by Paul Ricoeur, and in Britain by John Macquarrie and Alistair McFadyen have served to correct this imbalance. However, this does not close the discussion. It has taken new forms, for example, in the work of Angela West, Mary Elise Lowe, and others.[114]

(8) *Paul Tillich* (1896-1965). It is understandable that some feminist writers should include Tillich alongside their critique of Niebuhr, since Tillich identifies sin, if not with pride, then with *"hubris."*[115] He writes, "Hubris is the self-elevation of man into the sphere of the divine."[116] It is not something "small . . . and average," but what tempts kings, priests, the wealthy, and the great. It leads, however, to tragic self-destruction, and attributes the divine to finite human culture and creativity.

The larger context of this is Tillich's reflections on "the fall" of Adam and humankind as "a symbol for the human situation universally, not as the story of an event that happened 'once upon a time'."[117] The heart of this human situation is "existential estrangement" and "the transition from essence to existence."[118] Some of his critics have argued that this is an abstract notion, without specific content.[119] But Tillich expounds the theme in terms of the existential experience of *Angst,* as part of "finite freedom." It reflects the tragic in human life, as Kierkegaard and others have perceived this. It entails "unbelief," in that humankind "turns away from God" and "turns toward himself . . . the separation of man's will from the will of God."[120]

The turn from the infinite to the finite may appear to be abstract in conception, but Tillich seeks to provide existential symbols of its significance. One major point throughout his writings is that to confuse the finite or penultimate with the ultimate is thereby to *fragment* reality; to treat parts as if they were the whole. This is Tillich's understanding of "the demonic": it splits the wholeness of reality,

113. Hampson, *Feminism,* 124.

114. Angela West, *Deadly Innocence: Feminism and the Mythology of Sin* (New York and London: Continuum, 1996); and Paul Sponheim, Mary M. Fulkerson, and Rosemary Radford Ruether, "Women and Sin: Responses to Mary Elise Lowe," *Dialog* 39 (2000) 229-36.

115. Tillich, *Systematic Theology,* vol. 2, 56-59.

116. Tillich, *Systematic Theology,* vol. 2, 57.

117. Tillich, *Systematic Theology,* vol. 2, 33.

118. Tillich, *Systematic Theology,* vol. 2, 35.

119. For example, David E. Roberts, "Tillich's Doctrine of Man," in Charles W. Kegley and Robert W. Bretall (eds.), *The Theology of Paul Tillich* (New York: Macmillan, 1964), 108-30, esp. 125-26 and 129-30; and Bernard Martin, *Paul Tillich's Doctrine of Man* (London: Nisbet, 1966), 112-40, esp. 134-40.

120. Tillich, *Systematic Theology,* vol. 2, 54.

and seduces us toward "parts" in place of the whole. Here we see the influence of Jung. However, in his effort to disengage sin and "the fall" from the moral realm, Tillich comes very close to making "sin" an inevitable entailment of human finitude. He lacks the concern evident, for example, in Paul Ricoeur to make a very clear distinction between finitude and human sin or evil.

(9) *G. C. Berkouwer* (1903-96). Berkouwer stands in the tradition of Reformed Theology and produced eighteen volumes of Studies in Dogmatics of which a number have been translated into English, including *Man and the Image of God,* and *Sin,* of which the latter represents two volumes in Dutch. His theology of sin and the Fall broadly reflects Calvin's, and in the modern era the work of H. Bavinck. In his section on the origin of sin he rejects dualist theories, and follows Augustine and Calvin in stressing the role of human will, especially as this proceeds from a mind-set rendered "foolish" and "senseless" through separation from God.[121] Berkouwer includes material on "the gravity of sin" with particular reference to Rom. 1:18-32 and 6:23, and, in addition to painting the backcloth of divine grace, expounds the presupposition of divine holiness.[122] He notes the multiplicity of biblical terms that denote sin in its various modes.

(10) *Karl Rahner* (1904-84). Rahner perceives the essence of sin in "an actualisation of transcendental freedom in rejection of God."[123] However, humankind does not reject God solely in an individual context. Although a human being is "a free subject," such freedom is clearly conditioned by "the free history of all the others who constitute his unique world of persons." Such a "world" also "inevitably bears the stamp of the history of the freedom of all other men."[124] "Original" sin does not denote a bio-physical transmission of sin or guilt. In Catholic doctrine, he adds, neither judicial imputation nor biological heredity is involved for such transmission to occur. The key point is that *if "I" am free, so are other human persons,* with the result that all human persons live within a corporeity or collectivity in which each is conditioned by others for his or her starting point in the world. Rahner adds a *hermeneutical* observation. Although Catholic doctrine retains the reality that the *term* "original sin" represents, we can, and should, talk about the matter itself without using this word. It carries too much misleading baggage.

(11) *Hans Küng* (b. 1928). Küng's discussion of "sin and death," "the wretchedness of sin," and "the ruin of man" occurs in the context of offering a Catholic response to Karl Barth's theology of justification by grace.[125] Without question Küng, with Paul and with Barth, places *grace* at the heart of his horizons of un-

---

121. Berkouwer, *Sin,* 140; cf. 130-48.

122. Berkouwer, *Sin,* 235-322.

123. Karl Rahner, *Foundations of Christian Faith,* trans. W. V. Dych (New York: Crossroad, 1978), 115.

124. Rahner, *Foundations,* 107.

125. Hans Küng, *Justification: The Doctrine of Karl Barth and a Catholic Reflection,* trans. Thomas Collins (London: Burns & Oates and Nelson, 1964), 141-80.

derstanding: "The more man stands under grace, the freer he becomes."[126] The servitude of the sinner, he insists, is not to be made light of or blurred; indeed, it is solidly grounded in the Catholic tradition, including Trent. The biblical writings also witness to a theological and sometimes even empirical link between sin and death. "Sin is a fall from the covenant, a fall from God. Man, whose whole existence depends on God's love, turns away in sin from the foundation of his existence, and thus this foundation is for him — lost."[127]

(12) *John D. Zizioulas* (b. 1931). As we might expect, we find echoes of the Greek Fathers and especially of Athanasius in the Orthodox theologian John Zizioulas. He writes, "From the point of view of ontology the fall consists in *the refusal to make being dependent on communion,* in a rupture between truth and communion" (his italics).[128] Like Athanasius he alludes to communion with God, but also to communion with fellow human beings.

Zizioulas argues that for the Greek Fathers the fall did not bring about a new situation, but revealed and actualized the potential dangers inherent in creatureliness. In particular humankind no longer gave priority to communion with one another and with God. This leads to an undue focus upon "*individuality* in ontology" (his italics).[129] In turn, this fragments human existence. Furthermore, it disrupts the connection between truth and action, and between truth and love. It loses the Johannine and biblical emphasis upon "doing the truth." This dual combination of individuality and theoretical truth leads to our making the individual self "the ultimate reference-point of existence," and this accords with the biblical condemnation of elevating the self into the place of God.[130]

(13) *Wolfhart Pannenberg* (b. 1928). Like Barth, Pannenberg establishes a hermeneutical horizon of understanding within which questions about "the dignity and misery of humanity" legitimately arise and are capable of receiving intelligible answers.[131] Fellowship with God is the destiny of humankind, and this finds definitive realization in the incarnation of the Son."[132] This provides a starting point for understanding both the dignity and misery of humanity. Pannenberg's choice of vocabulary bears out the fundamental importance of this appropriate hermeneutical frame. For the term *misery* might at first sight appear overdrawn until we read: "Misery, then, is the lot of those who are deprived of the fellowship with God that is the destiny of human life."[133] The contrast between being in com-

126. Küng, *Justification,* 176.
127. Küng, *Justification,* 146.
128. John D. Zizioulas, *Being as Communion: Studies in Personhood and the Church* (Crestwood, NY: St. Vladimir's Seminary Press, 1985), 102.
129. Zizioulas, *Communion,* 103.
130. Zizioulas, *Communion,* 105.
131. Pannenberg, *Systematic Theology,* vol. 2, 175-275.
132. Pannenberg, *Systematic Theology,* vol. 2, 176.
133. Pannenberg, *Systematic Theology,* vol. 2, 178.

munion, communication, and engagement with the source of life, grace, and all that is good, and being "deprived" of all that comes with God's grace suggests that misery is an appropriate term for what Paul describes as being "under wrath."

Yet there are other profound reasons why *misery* tells us more than most other terms about human sinfulness. Not only is it the case that "the term 'misery' sums up our detachment from God" more powerfully even than "lost."[134] The term underlines the nature of sin as involving *a state* as well as an action, especially the condition or state of *alienation.* "We can alienate ourselves from someone [through an act], and we can also be in *a state of alienation.*"[135] Pannenberg traces a line of continuity from alienation in the New Testament (Eph. 4:18; Col. 1:21) to the reinterpretation of Paul Tillich and of self-alienation in Hegel and Marx.

Pannenberg expressly recognizes that "the decay of the doctrine of original sin led to the anchoring of the concept of sin in *acts* of sin, and finally the concept was reduced to the *individual* act" (my italics).[136] As we have noted above, this leads to a shallow moralism and to a serious neglect of the structural and corporate dimensions of sin prominent in Paul and John, and among modern thinkers in Niebuhr. Pannenberg explicates the shallow individualism and moralism that opens up the possibility of giving hostages to those who view "sin" only as the discarding of conventions and to the critiques offered by Nietzsche and Freud. Against those who attack Christianity for its opposed obsession with an introspective dwelling on self-guilt, he declares, "Christian faith does not create the fact of sin but presupposes it."[137]

This leads to a consideration of responsibility for sin and its destructive effects. In our culture today we typically place the blame for all evils on others, sometimes on specific people, but also "preferably on anonymous structures and pressures in the social system"; yet "we alone . . . are now responsible."[138] Biblical traditions underline these destructive effects, and this is all the more important since all the destructive forces of sin and evil are not always apparent to everyone. The classical prophets of Israel took up these consequences, sometimes in expounding tragedies of self-destruction, sometimes in exposing the results of oppression and injustice. They also proclaimed the reason for God's limiting such consequences, namely the grace and protection of God, who restrains these effects.

Pannenberg is one of the few contemporary theologians who give adequate weight to the force of the varied Hebrew and Greek vocabularies for sin in the biblical writings. Sin is not merely failure, or missing the mark, but also *apostasy*

---

134. Pannenberg, *Systematic Theology,* vol. 2, 179.

135. Pannenberg, *Anthropology in Theological Perspective,* 267-93. Here Pannenberg traces the horizons of alienation in Marx, Freud, Peter and Brigitte Berger, Paul Tillich, and others, including the biblical writings.

136. Pannenberg, *Systematic Theology,* vol. 2, 234.

137. Pannenberg, *Systematic Theology,* vol. 2, 236.

138. Pannenberg, *Systematic Theology,* vol. 2, 237.

(Hebrew *pesha'*) and *transgression*. The biblical writers speak of "the wickedness of the heart" and pray for a clean heart (Ps. 51:10; Jer. 32:39; Ezek. 11:19; 36:26). This leads to the fundamental concept of sin as *misdirected desire*. Pannenberg recognizes that many direct serious criticisms against Augustine, but such criticism, he observes, "should not blind us to [his] extraordinary achievement" of developing Paul's diagnosis of sin in terms of misplaced *desire*.[139] Many modern writers dismiss Augustine with undue haste.

Moreover, Augustine rightly identifies human sin in terms of "autonomy of the will that puts the self in the centre and uses everything else as a means to the self as an end."[140] Pride, in this context, generates perverted desire: it seeks all that it desires on behalf of the self. In this respect it becomes an act, attitude, and habit of "excessive self-affirmation."[141] Perverted desire becomes a structural principle. It may become "fixation on the self."[142] Certain social contexts can escalate the destructive consequences of this, but sin is "the power that dwells within us" (Rom. 7:17). Sin has its origin in the individual "heart."[143] Sin is universal, but to ascribe this universality to "social context" is not enough. The problem of human persons is that "their primary concern is with themselves. . . . They lack their authentic identity. . . . They show that they are alienated from themselves."[144]

Pannenberg demonstrates that we cannot avoid the theme of human bondage: "All that we can choose is the way in which we will be ourselves, at least within limits."[145] But even this brings negative effects. He writes, "At work here is the implicit form of the absolute self-willing that alienates us from God, by putting the self in the place that is God's alone, even though the relation to God is not an object of decision."[146] Sin has "power" over us because it promises life. We seize it in the hope of a fuller life; but in the end it brings nothing but death (Rom. 7:11; cf. Rom. 3:23). Pannenberg observes, "The inner logic of the link between sin and death as Paul stated it arises on the presupposition that all life comes from God."[147]

Pannenberg has provided an incisive, coherent, and judicious account of this area of doctrine that draws on the biblical traditions and the history of theology and other thought. His exposition retains hermeneutical relevance and sensitivity to varied horizons of understanding. It provides a fitting climax to our historical survey.

---

139. Pannenberg, *Systematic Theology*, vol. 2, 241.
140. Pannenberg, *Systematic Theology*, vol. 2, 243.
141. Pannenberg, *Systematic Theology*, vol. 2, 243.
142. Pannenberg, *Systematic Theology*, vol. 2, 250 and 251.
143. Pannenberg, *Systematic Theology*, vol. 2, 256.
144. Pannenberg, *Anthropology in Theological Perspective*, 266.
145. Pannenberg, *Systematic Theology*, vol. 2, 260.
146. Pannenberg, *Systematic Theology*, vol. 2, 261.
147. Pannenberg, *Systematic Theology*, vol. 2, 266; cf. 265-75.

CHAPTER 14

Hermeneutics and Linguistic Currencies
of Theologies of the Cross

14.1. Starting Points for Hermeneutics:
Two Kinds of Horizons of Understanding

The search for hermeneutical starting points for the Christian proclamation of the cross has never been easy. On one side, in terms of doctrinal *content,* Paul defines the very nature of the gospel and the gospel message in terms of the cross. The gospel message *is* "the proclamation of the cross" (ὁ λόγος ὁ τοῦ σταυροῦ, *ho logos ho tou staurou,* 1 Cor. 1:18). He interrupts his greeting to the church in Galatia with the words "Christ — who gave himself for our sins to set us free . . . ," and comments a few verses later, "If anyone proclaims to you a contrary gospel, let that person be *anathema*" (Gal. 1:4, 8). All the same, Paul knows that "the message of the cross is folly (μωρία, *mōria*) to those who are on their way to ruin" (Gal. 1:18). To proclaim "a crucified Christ (an-arthrous form in the Greek, χριστὸν ἐσταυρωμένον, *Christon estaurōmenon*), is to the Jews an *affront* (σκάνδαλον, *skandalon*) and to the Gentiles *folly* (1 Cor. 1:23).

What causes difficulties for those outside the Christian church has not necessarily remained the same over the centuries. Martin Hengel's classic study of the crucifixion has brilliantly exposed the repulsive character not only of crucifixion itself, but also even of talking about crucifixion in the first century.[1] Justin, Hengel reminds us, describes the affront of such a message as madness (μανία, *mania*).[2] The cross was a sign of shame (αἰσχύνη, *aischunē*, Heb. 12:2), or, in the

---

1. Martin Hengel, *The Cross of the Son of God,* trans. John Bowden (London: S.C.M., 1986), which contains his separately published *Crucifixion* (London: S.C.M., 1976); now 93-188.

2. Justin, *Apology,* I:13:4.

language of Celsus, an "ignominious" death.[3] Greek and Roman historians perceived crucifixion not only as a "barbaric" form of death with its concomitant cruelties reflecting outright sadism, but as something inappropriate as an object of thought.[4] Hengel notes, "By the public display of a naked victim in a prominent place — at a crossroads, in the theatre, on high ground . . . — crucifixion also represented his uttermost humiliation. With Deut. 21:23 in the background, the Jew in particular was very aware of this."[5]

More recently Welborn has underlined the social stigma attached even to conversation that mentioned crucifixion or a cross. When he calls the cross "foolishness" Welborn writes, "Paul means to say that the message about the crucified Christ was regarded by the elite of his day as a coarse and vulgar joke."[6] Yet this does not even begin to come to terms with the standard second-century response: how can a *"god" die?*

In our day, as Jürgen Moltmann incisively observes, the problem is almost the reverse. The cross has been so overlaid with two thousand years of veneration that he writes (quoting H. J. Iwand), "We have surrounded the cross with roses. We have made a theory of salvation out of it. But that is not . . . the bleakness inherent in it. . . ."[7] Today the problem is not quite that of the first century. In one direction it is what Alan Richardson called the stumbling block of particularity, namely: why should the fate or salvation *of the world* hang on the words and deeds of *Jesus of Nazareth?* In another direction it is the language and logic associated with *sacrifice, judgment, expiation, and redemption.*

Hermeneutical reflection on the proclamation and theology of the cross of Christ brings to light that we are seeking to engage with *two different kinds of horizons of understanding.* In our chapter on being human and on the spell of misdirected desire these kinds of horizons were not so radically different as to call for special comment, but they invite it here. (i) A *first* horizon of understanding concerns *the initial preunderstanding or readiness to understand on the part of those who seek to understand.* (ii) A *second* horizon of understanding concerns *what the otherness of the subject matter demands,* if distortion is not to be introduced in processes of understanding, and violence is not to be done to it.

(i) The first kind of horizon of understanding relates first and foremost to exploring the possibility of discovering *preunderstandings (Vorverständnis)* that will allow the *prior or existing horizons* of people to find *a point of overlap or en-*

---

3. Origen, *Contra Celsum* 6:10.

4. Dio Cassius 7:2; 11:4; 63:13:2; Tacitus, *Annals* 14:33:2; cf. Hengel, *Cross,* 114-55.

5. Hengel, *Cross,* 179.

6. L. L. Welborn, *Paul, the Fool of Christ: A Study of 1 Corinthians 1–4 in the Comic-Philosophic Tradition,* JSNTSS 293 (London and New York: Continuum and T&T Clark, 2005), 2; and throughout.

7. Jürgen Moltmann, *The Crucified God: The Cross of Christ as the Foundation and Criticism of Christian Theology,* trans. R. A. Wilson and John Bowden (London: S.C.M., 1974), 36.

gagement with *that which has yet to be understood.* How can we identify horizons of understanding among those who need to understand which furnish points of anchorage or resonate with what is hitherto uncharted territory for them concerning the theology of the cross?

An older generation of New Testament scholars from the early to the mid-twentieth century used to suggest that Paul and the "Hellenistic" church discarded language about the kingdom of God and the dawn of the "last days" that had made perfect sense in a Jewish-Palestinian milieu in favor of a "Hellenistic" vocabulary of salvation, eternal life, lordship, and dying-and-rising with a god. Wilhelm Bousset's *Kyrios Christos,* first published in 1913 and translated into English only in 1970, provides a well-known example.[8] The earliest Christians, Bousset argued, used "Son of man" as a major title for Jesus, but since neither "Christ" nor "Son of man" retained self-evident currency on Hellenistic soil, the Pauline churches replaced these terms in effect, with that of "Lord" *(Kyrios).* Many of Bousset's assumptions have been undermined in more recent scholarship, especially his assumption of a sharp contrast between Jewish-Palestinian and Hellenistic-Gentile cultures and geographical boundaries. Hengel most notably has questioned this, as well as I. Howard Marshall.[9]

In exploring horizons of understanding for today *in this first sense* it may be relevant to review the debate about the so-called "New Perspective on Paul" concerning whether theologies of the cross are to be approached in the "Lutheran" tradition of beginning with *aspects of the human "plight"* of alienation and bondage and then working toward understanding the "solution" of the cross; or whether, according to E. P. Sanders, this hermeneutical process is untrue to Paul. Some hermeneutical strategies might avoid this polarity by approaching a theology of the cross through exploring a concept of *human solidarity,* which applies equally to being "in Adam" and "in Christ," irrespective of questions about sequence. More fundamental, however, as a hermeneutic is the notion that *someone else has done something for us that we are incapable of doing for ourselves.* This is not an uncommon experience in human life that is not specific to any single class, race, gender, or historical era, especially since everyone has been an infant. With the rise of liberation theologies and the exposure of an increasing multiplicity of oppressive regimes, *liberation from oppression* may also open doors of understanding that readily lead on to perceptions of the meaning of redemption and salvation.

These provide examples of *one kind* of horizon of understanding, namely one that might provide a *preunderstanding* for a fuller engagement with a theology of the cross.

---

8. Wilhelm Bousset, *Kyrios Christos: A History of the Belief in Christ from the Beginnings of Christianity to Irenaeus,* trans. John E. Steely (Nashville: Abingdon, 1970).

9. Martin Hengel, *Judaism and Hellenism,* trans. John Bowden, 2 vols. (Philadelphia: Fortress, 1974), and *Between Jesus and Paul* (Philadelphia: Fortress, 1983).

(ii) *In a second sense* an *appropriate horizon of understanding is also that within which subject matter assumes its proper context for a fruitful understanding that does not distort it or impose inappropriate questions upon it.* This is part of Gadamer's concern to "hear the other" on its own terms without imposing our own prior conceptual worlds upon it. To explore such a horizon is not the same enterprise as that which we have just outlined, although *both are legitimate hermeneutical tasks* for a hermeneutic of doctrine.

The New Testament writers firmly place an understanding of the work of Christ *within horizons of understanding drawn from the Old Testament.* It is useless to isolate questions about whether the death of Jesus Christ should be interpreted *as a sacrifice* without understanding how deeply it is embedded in Old Testament tradition concerning sacrifice, whether or not twenty-first-century readers of the New Testament dwell within such a horizon. More fundamentally than this, a theology of *divine grace* is absolutely paramount for reassessing the well-known arguments about expiation, propitiation, and related concepts. Wolfhart Pannenberg rightly and roundly asserts: "The fact that a later age may find it hard to understand traditional ideas *is not a sufficient reason for replacing them.* It simply shows how necessary it is to open up these ideas to later generations by interpretation, and thus keep their meaning alive. The problems that people have with ideas like expiation and representation (or substitution) in our secularized age rest less on any lack of forcefulness in the traditional terms than on the fact that *those who are competent to interpret them do not explain their context with sufficient forcefulness or clarity*" (my italics).[10]

It would be difficult to find two sentences that more powerfully urge the importance of doctrine and its communication in Christian teaching and preaching than these two of Pannenberg's. It underlines the need for us to explore horizons of understanding *in both senses of the term* in the following pages. In the second sense of *horizon* we need to retain a frame of reference that not only keeps in view the currency of such terms as representation, substitution, and participation *within their proper historical and logical-conceptual contexts* by respecting their logical or conceptual grammar within ongoing traditions. We also need to respect and to identify the decisive importance of their relation to a *doctrine of divine grace* and to the pattern of *narrative history, covenant, and eschatological promise* to which they also belong.

Perhaps most hermeneutically sensitive of all at present are three sets of interpretative issues that engage with *both* of the two kinds of horizons of understanding that are under discussion. One concerns the role of human experiences to which a theology of the cross has spoken, in the face of the New Perspective. What *hermeneutical* issues does this debate raise? The second concerns the hermeneutical necessity of approaching all questions of interpretation about the

10. Pannenberg, *Systematic Theology,* vol. 2, 422.

cross from the standpoint of divine grace, which is the frame of reference or the horizon brought to bear by the biblical writings throughout. The third arises from the variety of imagery used to interpret the work of Christ in the New Testament.

(a) *The "New Perspective" and the Debate about Plight and Solution.* The term "New Perspective" is of course now outdated, but it was widely used to identify the approach of E. P. Sanders to interpreting Paul in 1977. Some attribute the nomenclature to James Dunn.[11] The hermeneutical aspect of Sanders' perspective may be summed up in the following quotation from his *Paul and Palestinian Judaism,* to which we have briefly alluded already. Sanders writes, "It seems likely that Paul's thought did not run from [human] plight to solution, but rather from solution to plight. . . . Paul did not, while 'under the law', perceive himself to have a 'plight' from which he needed salvation."[12]

One reason for this is that Sanders argues that Judaism was itself a religion of grace for those who observed the Jewish law; sin arises not from obedience to the law as generating "Lutheran" pride or "works," but from those who outside the covenant failed to look to Christ as their means of grace and atonement. He explains Paul's view of Jewish "sin" in terms of misusing the law to exclude others. The starting point for a proclamation of the cross, Sanders insists, is Christ, not (in Bultmann's language) humankind "under sin." Paul's message is also one of *present* "participation" in Christ rather than of atonement for *past* sins. It is a "transference" theology: Christians are transferred from being "in Adam" to being "in Christ" (Rom. 5:12-21).[13] "Paul did not begin with sin . . . but with the opportunity for salvation. . . . Paul did not preach about man, but about God."[14]

This presents something of a dilemma for a hermeneutical approach to the work of Christ. Bonhoeffer long ago called into question approaches to "salvation" that identified and even exploited a sense of need or of sin. In *Letters and Papers from Prison* Bonhoeffer writes of this approach, "It looks to me like an attempt to put a grown-up man back into adolescence."[15] He writes of those who adopt it: "They set themselves to drive people to inward despair and then the game is in their hands. This is secularized Methodism. . . . The ordinary man . . . has neither the time nor the inclination to concern himself with existential despair. . . . The attack by Christian apologetic on the adulthood of the world is . . . ignoble, because it amounts to an attempt to exploit man's weakness for purposes that are alien to him and to which he has not fully assented."[16] Bonhoeffer's

---

11. James D. G. Dunn, "The New Perspective on Paul," *Bulletin of the John Rylands Library* 65 (1983) 95-122.

12. Sanders, *Paul and Palestinian Judaism,* 443; cf. 434-47.

13. Sanders, *Paul,* 455-515.

14. Sanders, *Paul,* 446.

15. Dietrich Bonhoeffer, *Letters and Papers from Prison,* ed. E. Bethge, trans. Reginald Fuller (London: S.C.M., 3d enl. edn. 1971), 327 (also 1953 smaller edn. 147).

16. Bonhoeffer, *Letters and Papers,* 326 and 327.

attack comes in the context of his exposition of his notion of "the world that has come of age."[17]

While his words about a certain manipulative style of evangelism deserve attention, some of Bonhoeffer's interpreters warn us not to press these comments too far. Gerhard Ebeling writes: "If I am not mistaken, Bonhoeffer's name is widely held today in such respect *in spite of* the strange things that are to be found in his last Tegel letters, and that they were not able to destroy the credit he had earlier acquired."[18] John Godsey describes Bonhoeffer's latest period as challenging, but also as one of "theological fragmentation" when he no longer thinks of the church and world as seeking God for "answers" or for self-protection, but as Lord of the world.[19] Anticipating Moltmann, Bonhoeffer insists that the church can be true to itself only "when it exists for others."[20] A culture of overdependency and satisfied needs leads to infantile regression. It also nurtures self-affirmation and thereby an identity that contradicts the cross itself, turning a *theologia crucis* into a *theologia gloriae*.

The New Perspective on Paul as initiated by Sanders is not without its critics. Martin Hengel, Roland Deines, and Francis Watson have provided strong, if not decisive, critiques of Sanders' portrayal of both Judaism and of Paul.[21] Sanders' work is also being overtaken or modified by a narrative approach associated especially with Richard Hays and N. T. Wright, who has coined the term "fresh perspectives" to denote a further stage of research and method.[22]

The horizon of understanding in the second sense, namely that which relates to what the subject matter demands, perhaps remains controversial. But this cannot be said of a horizon of understanding in the first sense, namely of that which

---

17. Bonhoeffer, *Letters and Papers,* 327; cf. 325-29.

18. Gerhard Ebeling, *Word and Faith,* trans. James W. Leitch (London: S.C.M., 1963), 101-2.

19. John D. Godsey, *The Theology of Dietrich Bonhoeffer* (London: S.C.M., 1960), 248-49 and 270-82.

20. Bonhoeffer, *Letters and Papers,* 300 and 381 (cf. shorter edn., 68 and 180). See also Moltmann, *The Crucified God,* 19-20, and Jürgen Moltmann, *The Church in the Power of the Spirit,* trans. Margaret Kohl (London: S.C.M., 1975), throughout.

21. Martin Hengel, with Roland Deines, *The Pre-Christian Paul,* trans. J. Bowden (London: S.C.M., 1991), emphasizes the centrality of grace, justification by grace, and the reversals of the cross in Paul, as well as defending the insights of Augustine and Luther as interpreters of Paul; Martin Hengel and Roland Deines, "E. P. Sanders, 'Common Judaism', Jesus and the Pharisees," *JTS* 46 (1995) 1-70, attacks Sanders' broad pattern of Judaism in terms of "lowest common denominator" and "status quo" religion. Francis Watson, *Paul and the Hermeneutics of Faith* (London and New York: T&T Clark and Continuum, 2004), develops his earlier paper "Not the New Perspective," delivered to the British New Testament Society at Manchester in September 2002, with further critical reflection and interpretations of Habakkuk (Hab. 1:3; 2:4; et al.), the Minor Prophets, and other Old Testament passages.

22. Cf. Richard B. Hays, *The Faith of Jesus Christ: The Narrative Substructure of Galatians 3:1–4:11* (Grand Rapids: Eerdmans, 2002), and N. T. Wright, *Paul: Fresh Perspectives* (London: S.P.C.K., 2005), and *Jesus and the Victory of God* (London: S.P.C.K., 1996).

relates to preunderstanding. A human experience of struggle, guilt, or alienation from God has been an ingredient in the revelation of the self in relation to God, as we argued in 9.1, 11.2, and 12.1. Divine grace through the work of Christ enhances and focuses this experience in such often-cited examples as those of Augustine, Luther, and John Wesley. It does not greatly matter that the popular stereotype of Luther's famous "Tower experience" tends to exaggerate or to caricature the role of "innerness" or introspection. Luther's engagement with preparation to give lectures on the Psalms (if we date the experience in 1513-15) and clearly his engagement with Rom. 1:16-17 (whether in 1513-15 or 1518-19) were potent factors in his transformation of understanding alongside his inner wrestling.[23] Luther acknowledges: "I felt that I was a sinner before God with an extremely distorted conscience. I could not believe that he was placated by my satisfaction. I did not love, yes, I hated the righteous God who punishes sinners, and secretly . . . I was angry with God. . . . I raged with a fierce and troubled conscience." At last, he continues, he came to engage with "He who through faith is righteous shall live." "Then I began to understand."[24]

John Wesley does not hesitate to speak of an experience that he dates on May 24, 1738, when he felt his heart "strangely warmed" as soul-searching and doubt gave way to the experience "I felt I did trust in Christ, Christ alone for salvation. . . . He had taken away my sins, even mine, and saved me from the law of sin and death."[25] This followed his reading of Luther's Preface to the Epistle to the Romans.

Vincent Taylor shows convincingly that especially in Paul there is a correlation between specific aspects of the human experience of sin, bondage, or alienation, and aspects of the saving work of Christ.[26] New Testament scholars agree that Paul and other New Testament writers use a variety of imagery to interpret a theology of the cross. But many passages appear to identify a core theme in speaking of the death of Jesus Christ as *"for us."* Joachim Jeremias comments: "By an increasing number of comparisons and images he [Paul] tries to make his hearers and readers understand the meaning of this "for us."[27]

This is helpful, but we may go further. If sin is seen in structural or corporate

23. Martin Luther, "Preface to the Complete Edition of Luther: Latin Writings," in *Luther's Works,* vol. 34, ed. and trans. L. W. Spitz (Philadelphia: Muhlenberg, 1960), 327-38; cf. John Dillenberger, *Martin Luther: Selection from His Writings, Edited with an Introduction* (New York: Doubleday, 1961), xvii-xviii.

24. Luther, *Luther's Works,* vol. 34, 337.

25. There are numerous editions of Wesley's writings. A respected edition is F. Baker et al. (eds.), *The Works of John Wesley,* 15 vols. (Oxford: Clarendon and Nashville: Abingdon, 1984 onward).

26. Vincent Taylor, *The Atonement in New Testament Teaching* (London: Epworth, 1940), 114-22.

27. Joachim Jeremias, *The Central Message of the New Testament* (London: S.C.M., 1965), 36.

terms as characterizing collective humanity fallen *"in Adam,"* then the work of Christ is perceived as that of the last or *eschatological Adam* who brings about being *"in Christ"* (Rom. 5:12-21; 1 Cor. 15:22, 23 and 45-49). Experiences of *bondage* or vulnerability to forces beyond human control find a correlation with *Christ as Victor* over such forces (Col. 2:15). Notions of facing *divine wrath or judgment* are matched by a theology of *reconciliation* through the work of Christ on the cross (Rom. 5:1-11).

We cannot exclude a horizon of understanding, then, that responds to questions about human plight in terms of the saving work of Christ. While Sanders' work invites respect in exploring a horizon of understanding in the *second* sense, its validity is by no means self-evident or beyond criticism, and Käsemann rightly warns us that if we press such approaches, we may end up replacing Paul's core concerns about justification by grace with issues of ecclesiology.

(b) *The Horizon of the Presupposition of Grace and the Nature of Divine Love.* Far more important than the above debate is the axiomatic starting point in all the writings of the New Testament on the grace of God. The work of Christ is first and foremost a sovereign initiative of God, which represents the action of God in Christ: *"God* was in Christ reconciling the world to himself, not counting their trespasses against them" (2 Cor. 5:19). Similarly, *"God* commends *his* love toward us in that while we were yet sinners Christ died for us" (Rom. 5:8). The Johannine witness to the words of Jesus communicates the same emphasis, *"God* so loved the world that he gave his only-begotten Son, so that whoever believes in him should not perish but may have eternal life" (John 3:16).

Donald M. Baillie strongly emphasized the themes of God and God's grace in and through Christ in his influential book published in the years after the Second World War, *God Was in Christ.*[28] The crucifixion of Jesus, he writes, "set man thinking . . . not simply about the love of Jesus, but of the love of God."[29] One might have expected that the death of Jesus would have taken away any confidence in the love of God, he continues. That this was not so was not simply due to the vindication of Jesus Christ in the resurrection, but largely to "the whole teaching of Jesus himself," and his application to himself of the prophecies of Isa. 40-55.[30] Paul reflects: "God did not spare his own Son, but gave him up for us all" (Rom. 8:32). He insists, "Throughout the whole of this New Testament material there is no trace of any contrast between the wrath of God and the love of Christ."[31]

Some from a conservative, reformed, or pietist background may suspect that radically conservative writers would not share this view. But Leon Morris, impeccably conservative in all respects, writes, "Sometimes in their anxiety to give

---

28. Donald M. Baillie, *God Was in Christ: An Essay on Incarnation and Atonement* (London: Faber & Faber, 1948).

29. Baillie, *God Was in Christ,* 184.

30. Baillie, *God Was in Christ,* 185-86.

31. Baillie, *God Was in Christ,* 186.

due emphasis to what Christ has done for us, evangelicals have unwittingly introduced a division into the Godhead. . . . Emphatically this is not the position taken up in the Bible."[32] Vincent Taylor underlines a similar point: "Any theory of the atonement which implies an opposition or enmity of the Father towards man which is overcome by the gracious work of Christ is, and must be, a perversion of Pauline teaching."[33] The New Testament passages just cited above speak for themselves. This is not a "liberal" gloss on these texts, but what the texts assert. Whether this suggests any conclusion to the debate about the use of the terms *expiation* and *propitiation* remains to be explored.

Baillie has touched on a sensitive nerve for a hermeneutic of preunderstanding. I recall in earlier years being approached by a sceptic who posed the question: would not any decent father do a horrible job himself rather than "sending his son" to do it on his behalf? I wish that Jürgen Moltmann's works had been available in those early days. Moltmann, more profoundly than Baillie, points the way forward to a response.

First, Moltmann rearticulates the question that entices and provokes a larger horizon of understanding. As he writes in *Experiences of God:* "What does Christ's cross really mean *for God himself?*"[34] He asks, "Was not God present in Jesus' sufferings 'seriously'?"[35] Moltmann distances himself from "a God who is eternally in love with himself, and there without any concern for others." Such a God would be an idol, but "from the cross I found access to the trinitarian life of God."[36] The problem of "Jesusology" of modern times is that it isolates Jesus of Nazareth from the Trinitarian reality of his identity, his awareness, his mission, and his life.[37] On the contrary, Moltmann writes, "If God has taken upon himself death on the cross, he has also taken upon himself all of life, and real life as it stands under death, law and guilt."[38]

This opens up a hermeneutic that resonates with those who are still to engage more fully with a theology of the cross. Today many ask, "Where was God at Auschwitz, at Hiroshima, in Vietnam, in ground-zero 9/11? Moltmann writes, "God himself hung on the gallows. . . . It must also be said that, like the cross of Christ, even Auschwitz . . . is taken up into the grief of the Father, the surrender of the Son, and the power of the Spirit."[39] "God allows himself to be forced out.

---

32. Leon Morris, *Glory in the Cross* (London: Hodder & Stoughton, 1966) 46-47; cf. Leon Morris, *The Cross in the New Testament* (Exeter, U.K.: Paternoster, and Grand Rapids: Eerdmans, 1965), 208-59.

33. Taylor, *Atonement,* 110.

34. Jürgen Moltmann, *Experiences of God* (London: S.C.M., 1980), 15 (my italics).

35. Moltmann, *Experiences of God,* 16.

36. Moltmann, *Experiences of God,* 16.

37. Moltmann, *The Crucified God,* 97-98.

38. Moltmann, *The Crucified God,* 272.

39. Moltmann, *The Crucified God,* 278.

God suffers, God allows himself to be crucified and is crucified, and in this consummates his unconditional love."[40] Elsewhere Moltmann explains that God allows himself to grieve and to suffer, for "a God who cannot suffer cannot love either."[41]

If God has *chosen* by free sovereign decree to bear sorrow and suffering, this is not strictly so-called "Patripassian heresy." It does not deny that God cannot be subjected to any *external* force that might *impose* suffering upon him against his will. Even within the rigorous logic with which Pannenberg writes, Pannenberg can speak of "a trinitarian description of the divine action in the event of reconciliation."[42] "We understand from both 2 Cor. 5:18-19 and the more passive formulation in Rom. 5:10 that in the death of Jesus, God the Father acted to reconcile the world."[43] The self-giving of the Son and the giving up of him by the Father "are saying the same thing in different ways."[44] The term "cooperation" or joint working describes the event. "The self-offering of the Son . . . and his being offered up by the Father are one and the same event and form a single process."[45]

(c) *The Variety of Metaphors and Images That Describe the Work of Christ.* We need not delay long on this undeniable point because we have discussed it above. Here we need comment only on the hermeneutical significance of this variety. Ian Ramsey among others has stressed the communicative effectiveness of a *variety* of images, symbols, metaphors, and other forms of language for setting up and initiating what he terms "disclosure situations." Language used in revelation and religion becomes "stretched" beyond its everyday uses when it conveys complex realities concerning God and God's dealing with the world. It retains everyday vocabulary (in this case, the language of reconciliation, liberation, victory, substitution), but *qualifies* such language, often by placing a term in conjunction with another that serves to cancel off a merely wooden or over-literalist meaning.[46]

This juxtaposition of a variety of mutually qualifying images, symbols, analogies, or even referential terms allows an understanding to "come alive," as when (in Ramsey's language) "the penny drops," or we say "Now I see!" or have what he calls an "Aha!" experience.[47] Sometimes we see a complex puzzle *as* a *Gestalt*, which offers a coherent picture in place of the atomistic pieces with which we began.[48] Fre-

---

40. Moltmann, *The Crucified God*, 248.

41. Moltmann, *The Trinity and the Kingdom of God*, 38.

42. Pannenberg, *Systematic Theology*, vol. 2, 437.

43. Pannenberg, *Systematic Theology*, vol. 2, 438.

44. Pannenberg, *Systematic Theology*, vol. 2, 439.

45. Pannenberg, *Systematic Theology*, vol. 2, 450.

46. Ian T. Ramsey, *Religious Language: An Empirical Placing of Theological Phrases* (London: S.C.M., 1957), esp. 19-48.

47. Ramsey, *Religious Language*, 23.

48. Ramsey, *Religious Language*, 24.

quently these "pieces" of the jigsaw serve as *models* of what lies on the edge of human language. We should not regard the use of models as second-best for conveying cognitive or ontological truth-claims. A large proportion of "break throughs" in the natural sciences have been achieved in recent years through the exploratory power of cognitive models.[49] Janet Martin Soskice argues convincingly that metaphors and models can put forward meaningful cognitive truth-claims.[50]

On the subject of the cross and the atonement Colin Gunton has contributed distinctive work in *The Actuality of Atonement*. He shows how the rationalism of the Enlightenment (especially Hegel) disparaged religious "representations" *(Vorstellungen)* as if only the concept *(Begriff)* were capable of conveying cognitive and critically rational communication.[51] However, in recent years the dynamics of metaphor have been rehabilitated, not least through such writings as those of Paul Ricoeur. In the sciences Ingolf Dalferth and Richard Boyd among others have shown how successive metaphors relating to understandings of the universe (for example, the overtaking of "machine" metaphors by "field" metaphors) undergird understanding and advance in physical and biological sciences.[52] Gunton concludes, "New language and discovery happen together."[53] Eberhard Jüngel advances this discussion further.[54]

It would anticipate later discussion to follow Gunton's arguments further at this point. He applies the theory of language already outlined to the variety of images and patterns of thinking about the atonement found in the biblical writings and in the respective expositions of them, including Aulén's exposition of divine "victory"; Anselm and the Latin Fathers on the justice of God and "satisfaction"; language of "sacrifice" in the Epistle to the Hebrews; and Athanasius and others on representation, substitution, and the work of the triune God.

All of these images, metaphors, or referential terms provide multiple horizons of meaning in both the first and the second senses of the two kinds of hermeneutical horizons described above. We shall now endeavor to explore further the theological and doctrinal content that these convey. Jüngel declares, "The cross of Jesus Christ is the ground and measure of the formation of metaphors which are

---

49. Ramsey, *Religious Language*, 49-71, and Ian T. Ramsey, *Models for Divine Activity* (London: S.C.M., 1973), throughout; also Ian T. Ramsey, *Words about God* (London: S.C.M., 1971).

50. Janet Martin Soskice, *Metaphor and Religious Language* (Oxford: Clarendon, 1985).

51. Colin E. Gunton, *The Actuality of Atonement: A Study of Metaphor, Rationality and the Christian Tradition* (Edinburgh: T&T Clark, 1988), 1-26.

52. Ingolf U. Dalferth, *Religiöse Rede von Gott* (Munich: Christian Kaiser, 1981); Richard Boyd, "Metaphor and Theory Change: What Is Metaphor For?" in A. Ortony (ed.), *Metaphor and Thought* (Cambridge: Cambridge University Press, 1979), 356-408.

53. Gunton, *Atonement*, 31.

54. Eberhard Jüngel, "Metaphorical Truth: Reflections on Theological Metaphor as a Contribution to a Hermeneutics of Narrative Theology," in E. Jüngel, *Theological Essays*, ed. John B. Webster, 2 vols. (Edinburgh: T&T Clark, 1989 and 1995), vol. 1, 16-71.

appropriate to God; . . . metaphorical language about God expands the horizons of the world in such a way that we may speak of the renewal of the world."[55]

14.2. Hard Currencies of Biblical Language: Redemption and Salvation

In financial currency-markets hard currencies are those that do not readily fluctuate with time or with changing conditions in other economies. Soft currencies may be so precarious in the eyes of investors or business concerns that their effective value may be restricted to operating within a given national economy but often not generally beyond it.

At first sight *grace, redemption,* and *salvation* appear to have a quasi-technical ring that restricts their communicative currencies to religion, or, worse, to religions in the ancient world. But this would amount to being distracted by *vocabulary* rather than by word *use*. Problems of unfamiliar vocabulary evaporate through ready explanation, provided that use and conceptual grammar are reasonably transparent. In *The Two Horizons* I took up Wittgenstein's observations about *public criteria of meaning* in the context of an ongoing Israelite tradition, to underline the hard currency of terms whose conceptual grammar had become a matter of cumulative public perception and understanding amid the regularities of the life and history of Israel. I wrote, "What redemption, for example, is, can best be seen not from 'my own experience' but from recurring salvation-patterns in the Exodus, the wilderness wanderings, the Judges, and so on. These model language-games are of course revised and corrected in the light of subsequent history, in accordance with the principle of the hermeneutical circle. . . . But Old Testament history provides a necessary starting-point for the elucidation of concepts."[56]

I illustrated the point from Wittgenstein's observations about public criteria of meaning and regularities within traditions. We shall refer to Wittgenstein again later in this section, but meanwhile we shall trace the currencies of meaning more concretely by considering specific examples.

(1) *Redemption, redeem,* and *redeemer* finds expression in the two Hebrew terms גאל *(gāʾal,* verb; *gōʾēl,* noun, *redeemer)* and פדה *(pādâ,* verb, *redeem, ransom; pᵉdûth I,* abstract noun, *ransom).*[57] The Exodus becomes a paradigmatic model of redemption, for it denotes an act of redemption *from* bondage and

---

55. Jüngel, "Metaphorical Truth," in *Essays,* vol. 1, 65 and 71.

56. Thiselton, *The Two Horizons,* 382.

57. Brown-Driver-Briggs, *The New Hebrew-English Lexicon* (Peabody, MA: Hendrickson, 1980), 145 and 804, cite many references. See also G. J. Botterweck, H. Ringgren, and H.-J. Fabry (eds.), *Theological Dictionary of the Old Testament,* vol. 2, trans. J. T. Willis (Grand Rapids: Eerdmans, 1974 onward), 350-55; Kittel, "λύω and Compounds," *TDNT,* vol. 4, 328-35; and *Dictionary of Old Testament Theology and Exegesis,* vol. 1, 789-94.

jeopardy in Egypt *to* a new life and new identity in the land of promise *by means of* a saving act by an agent who intervenes to bring about the new state of affairs. In Exod. 6:6 God promises, "I will redeem you (גאל, *gā'al*) with a stretched out arm" (cf. Exod. 15:13). This pattern of action is celebrated in worship and corporate recollection in the Psalms, for example, Pss. 77:15; 106:10.[58] Isaiah recalls God's redemptive act as a ground for the renewal of the divine promise (Isa. 43:1; 44:23; 48:20; 63:9).

In addition to this major theological salvific context the Hebrew words are also used to denote the redemption of family property (Lev. 25:25-28), houses (Lev. 25:29-34), and relatives in difficulty (Lev. 25:47-49). The noun גאל (*gō'ēl*) also has a special use, to denote a near kinsman or close relative who can redeem a near blood-relative from harm, penalty, or jeopardy. Israelites who sell themselves into slavery because of poverty still retain the right to redemption (*ge'ullâ*), if their brother, uncle, cousin, or another near blood-relative or redeemer (*gō'ēl*) buys the slave back out of slavery through the payment of a price.[59] Usually redemption denotes transference *from* a state of bondage or jeopardy *to* a state of well-being *by* a costly act.

The Hebrew word פדה (*pādhâ*), to ransom, to redeem, or to deliver, has a broader meaning than גאל (*gā'al*). It is used in Exod. 13:13 of redeeming the firstborn (cf. also Exod. 34:2). David speaks of God's redeeming Israel (2 Sam. 7:23) and his own life (2 Sam. 4:9). Deuteronomy maintains the tradition of God's redeeming Israel from slavery in Egypt (Deut. 7:8; 9:26; 13:5). The book of Psalms uses the Qal of the Hebrew verb fourteen times, especially in a personal plea, "Redeem me . . ." (Pss. 26:11; 69:18; 119:134). The prophets take up the traditions of Yahweh's act of redeeming Israel as his people (Isa. 31:11; Hos. 7:13; 13:14; Mic. 6:4).

The Septuagint renders פדה (*pādhâ*) by Greek forms of λυτρόω (*lutroō*) denoting especially the payment of a ransom price. But the New Testament uses the nouns λύτρον (*lutron*) in Mark 10:45 and Matt. 20:28 where Jesus explains his death as a "ransom for many," and ἀπολύτρωσις in Luke 21:28 to denote the redemption for which the disciples had eagerly waited, as well as in Rom. 3:24; 8:23; 1 Cor. 1:30; Eph. 1:7, 14; 4:30; Col. 1:14; and Heb. 9:15.[60] However, writers also use the verb ἐξαγοράζω (*exagorazō*) in Gal. 3:13; 4:5; Eph. 5:16; Col. 4:5 and ἀγοράζω (*agorazō*) in Rev. 5:9; 14:3, 4; and λυτρόω (*lutroō*) in Luke 4:21; Tit. 2:14; and 1 Pet. 1:18.[61]

Büchsel comments of ἐξαγοράζω (*exagorazō*), "In the NT the word is used of the redeeming and liberating act of Christ."[62] At first sight it looks as if the model of redemption in the Exodus is wholly maintained, and predictably many

---

58. Cf. Weiser, *The Psalms*, 532-33 and 681.

59. R. Hubbard, "The *gō'ēl* in Ancient Israel: The Theology of an Israelite Institution," *Bulletin for Biblical Research* 1 (1991) 3-19.

60. F. Büchsel, "λύω . . . ἀπολύτρωσις," in Kittel (ed.), *TDNT*, vol. 4, 335-56.

61. F. Büchsel, "ἀγοράζω, ἐξαγοράζω," in Kittel (ed.), *TDNT*, vol. 1, 124-28.

62. Büchsel, *TDNT*, vol. 1, 126.

writers in Liberation Theology seize upon this aspect. Thus J. Severino Croatto declares, "The Exodus has been characterized as an event of political, social liberation at the people level . . . and its deep meaning remained 'recollected' in the 'credos' . . . of faith."[63] In very broad terms the Exodus paradigm remains a founding model for a horizon of understanding within which to perceive the meaning of *redeem* and *redemption*. However, the New Testament writers *qualify* the salvific model with a sociological one. This is the model of release from slavery to an oppressive master to the lordship of a new master or *Kurios*.

This may appear to press the model "from bondage to freedom by purchase-price" more strongly. Adolf Deissmann drew on research on Hellenistic religions to urge an understanding of *freedom* based on this model, in order to rescue it from "the stupendous force of dogmatic traditions" about "redemption."[64] Deissmann cited parallels that depicted the manumissions of slaves through "purchase" by Hellenistic deities on inscriptions found mainly at Delphi but also elsewhere, including, for example, at Physcus ("sale to Athene"), at Amphesia ("sale to Asclepius"), and at Cos ("sale to Adrastia").[65] The usual form was to date the certification and inscribe: "N.M. sold to the Pythian Apollo a male slave named XY at a price of z minae, for freedom."[66] Deissmann sees precisely this pattern in 1 Cor. 6:20, "You were bought with a price" (cf. Rom. 7:20-21; 1 Cor. 7:23; Gal. 4:1-7; 5:1). Paul, Deissmann concludes, uses "the very formula of the records."[67]

More recent scholarship, however, has challenged Deissmann's arguments. The transaction in Paul's theology involved a price *not for freedom* but for *change of ownership*. Dale B. Martin convincingly writes, "Most scholars have agreed that Deissmann's explanation of *buy* (ἀγοράζειν, *agorazein*) to mean redemption *from* slavery by social manumission must be rejected. *Priasthai*, not *agorazein*, is the word most commonly used in these contracts. *Agorazein* refers . . . to the ordinary sale of a slave by one owner to another owner. When Christ buys a person, the salvific element of the metaphor is to a higher level of slavery (as the slave of Christ)."[68] The key point here is that in the mid-first century in the Roman world what slavery *amounted to* depended entirely on the nature and character of the

---

63. J. Severino Croatto, *Exodus: A Hermeneutics of Freedom*, trans. Salvator Attanasio (Maryknoll, NY: Orbis, 1981), 80.

64. Adolf Deissmann, *Light from the Ancient East: The New Testament Illustrated by Recently Discovered Texts of the Greco-Roman World*, trans. L. R. M. Strachan (London: Hodder & Stoughton, 1927), 319 and 319-31.

65. Examples are cited in Deissmann, *Light*, 319-23.

66. Deissmann, *Light*, 322.

67. Deissmann, *Light*, 324.

68. Dale B. Martin, *Slavery as Salvation* (New Haven, CT: Yale University Press, 1990), 63 and xvi-xvii. This is also argued convincingly by S. S. Bartschy, *Μᾶλλον Χρῆσαι: First-Century Slavery and the Interpretation of 1 Cor. 7:21* (Missoula: Scholars, 1973), 121-25; and C. Wolff, *Der erste Brief des Paulus an die Korinther* (Leipzig: Evangelische Verlagsanstalt, 1996), 131-32; and others.

slave's *Kyrios* or lord and the purpose for which the slave had been purchased. Many who were able-bodied, numerate, and literate perceived the option of voluntary selling of themselves into slavery *under the right master* as an opportunity for *advancement.* They lived under the protection of their lord, and might well be more secure and well-provided-for than they might have been as freelance individuals. We shall amplify these claims when we come to explore what it means to confess Christ as one's Lord *(Kyrios)* in 17.1.[69]

We need to add one caveat. In the Patristic era some fastened on the pseudo-question of *to whom* the price of redemption might be paid. But there is not a one-to-one correspondence between the metaphor and the use of the word in transactions relating to Roman slavery. The imagery is rooted in the Hebrew background of פדה and גאל as redemption *from* jeopardy *to* security *by* a costly act. The *costliness* of redemption in Christ denotes *cost,* but *not* always, and not here, cost paid *to* some third party. The Arians made the parallel mistake of assuming that *Son* as applied to Christ carried *exactly* the semantic content as it does in the case of *human* sons, drawing the mistaken inference that Christ was "born before" God his Father. But the term *Son* as applied to Christ *overlaps* with *son* in everyday language; it is not an exact match. Hence, we reach, again with Ian Ramsey, the conclusion that *redemption* through Christ is an adequate *model,* but with appropriate *qualification.* Origen and Gregory of Nyssa speak of a ransom paid to the devil.[70] But Gregory of Nazianzus firmly rejects this notion, and most of the Fathers do not consider it.[71]

In hermeneutical terms, the meaning of *redemption* and *redeem* has been built up through a history and tradition of uses in a public world (in the Exodus, the history of Israel, and the Greco-Roman world), and its meaning has become thoroughly transparent and intelligible within these horizons of understanding.

(2) *Savior, save, salvation:* again, the currency of uses of these words emerges first within the public world of the history of Israel, most notably in the early texts that recount the narratives of the Judges. Old Testament specialists generally agree that the book of Judges portrays certain repeated cycles of events. Hans Küng describes this as "a constant alternation of fall, punishment and forbearance," especially in Judg. 2:13-23.[72] The cycle operates as follows: (i) "The Israelites did what was evil in the sight of the LORD" (Judg. 2:11); (ii) "The anger of the LORD was kindled against Israel, and he gave them over to plunderers who plundered them" (2:14); (iii) "They were in great distress" (2:15); (iv) "Then the LORD raised up judges, who delivered them [NRSV: Hebrew ישׁ, *yāsha'*, *saved* them]

---

69. Meanwhile, cf. Thiselton, *First Epistle,* 474-79 and 544-65, and Thomas Wiedemann, *Slavery: Greece and Rome,* New Surveys 19 (Oxford: Oxford University Press, 1977), esp. 1-46.

70. Origen, *Commentary on Romans,* 2:13: *Commentary on Exodus,* 6:9; cf. *Commentary on Matthew,* 13:8 and 16:8. Gregory of Nyssa, *Great Catechism* 22-26.

71. Gregory of Nazianzus, *Orations* 45:22.

72. Küng, *Justification,* 148.

from the power of those who plundered them" (2:16); (v) "But whenever the judge died, they would relapse and behave worse than their ancestors" (2:19). The same or a similar cycle is repeated in Judg. 3:7-11: (i) Israel sins; (ii) God is provoked to anger; (iii) God sells them into the power of their enemy; (iv) Israel cries to the Lord; (v) *God raised up a deliverer or a savior* (מוֹשִׁיעַ, *môshîaʿ*, from *yāshaʿ*) who *saves* them (יָשַׁע, *yāshaʿ*, 3:9); (vi) "The land had rest for forty years, when Othniel the judge died."

The successive judges Othniel (Judg. 3:1-11), Ehud (3:15-30), Deborah (4:4–5:31), Gideon (6:1–8:25), Abimelech (9:1-59), Tola (10:1-2), Jair (10:3-5), Jephthah (11:1–12:7), and, after three more, Samson (13:1–16:31) serve as models or paradigms of *saviors* who *save* or deliver Israel from the consequences of their willful breaches of loyalty to God. The Hebrew verb יָשַׁע (*yāshaʿ*) means *to deliver* or *to save* in the Hiphal; in the intransitive or reflexive Niphal it may denote *to live in abundance, to make spacious, to make sufficient* (Deut. 33:29; Isa. 45:17; Jer. 30:7), or *to be liberated, to be saved* (Isa. 30:15; 45:22; 64:4; Jer. 4:14; 8:20; 17:14; Pss. 80:4, 8, 20; 119:117), including being saved *from* (מִן, *min*). Heroic leaders who save Israel are called *saviours* (מוֹשִׁיעַ, *môshîaʿ*). In Isa. 43:11 God himself is the *Savior* (cf. Isa. 45:15, 21; Hos. 13:4). In some contexts the verb may denote to give victory (1 Sam. 25:26, 33), or to gain victory (1 Sam. 14:6; 17:47). The cognate noun יֶשַׁע (*yēshaʿ*) denotes *deliverance, rescue, salvation, safety,* or *welfare*. In Ps. 27:1 the psalmist exclaims, "Yahweh is my light and my *salvation*."[73]

The traditions of Israel's life thus provide what Ludwig Wittgenstein would view as model language-games. Model "language-games" serve as "objects of comparison" that throw light on the facts of our language "by way not only of similarities, but also of dissimilarities."[74] "Salvation" is not an unduly technical or esoteric term. Wittgenstein observes, "One learns the games by watching others play."[75] Hermeneutical horizons and questions become "problems" when we transfer language "*outside* a particular language-game," or when "language *goes on holiday*"; a language game consists of "language and the actions into which it is woven," in contrast to linguistic abstractions, like "an engine idling."[76] The Old Testament texts and life of Israel provide the public horizons of understanding in terms of which the vocabulary and language uses of the New Testament that relate to the work of Christ can be understood.

In the New Testament *salvation* (σωτηρία, *sōtēria*) is used some forty-two

---

73. All of these terms and classifications are from Brown-Driver-Briggs, *Lexicon* (1980 edn.), 446-47; cf. also Botterweck and Ringgren, *Theological Dictionary of the Old Testament,* 6:441-63; John F. A. Sawyer, *Semantics in Biblical Research: New Methods of Defining Hebrew Words for Salvation* (London: S.C.M., 1972); and W. VanGemeren, *New International Dictionary of Old Testament Theology and Exegesis,* vol. 2, 556-62.

74. Wittgenstein, *Philosophical Investigations,* sect. 130.

75. Wittgenstein, *Investigations,* sect. 54.

76. Wittgenstein, *Investigations,* sect. 38 and 7 (his italics).

times, of which just under half occur in Paul, seven occur in Hebrews, and four in Luke. The noun σωτήρ *(sōtēr), savior,* occurs twenty-four times, sometimes of Jesus Christ, but usually of God as Savior. In Paul the verb *to save* functions in semantic opposition to ἀπόλλυμι *(apollumi), to destroy,* or ἀπολλυμαι *(apollumai), to be lost, to perish, to be in a state of ruin.*[77] In Paul the verb and its participial forms often occur in the present tense. Thus in 1 Cor. 1:18 he sets in contrast "those who are on their way to ruin" (present middle articular participle, τοῖς μὲν ἀπολλυμένοις, *tois men apollumenois)* with "us who are on our way to salvation" (τοῖς δὲ σῳζομένοις ἡμῖν, *tois de sōzomenois hēmin).*

Implicitly this points to the well-known "three tenses of salvation" in Paul and elsewhere in the New Testament. Anderson Scott structured his entire book on Paul's theology around these "three tenses" as a methodological principle, and more recently G. B. Caird's *New Testament Theology* structures a chapter in the same way.[78] Like people in a lifeboat rescued from a sinking ship, they were saved when they left the sinking ship; they are in the process of being saved as they are carried to the shore; they will be saved when they finally step onto *terra firma.* These temporal distinctions have practical significance for Christian lifestyle. Christians put their trust in promises and pledges of future salvation, and do not judge the glory of the future consummation by what they perceive in an imperfect church and fallen world in the present. They are warned against the presumption of behaving like those who think that they have already "arrived" (1 Cor. 4:8-13). Their present pilgrimage is sober, joyful, and confident, but they remain vulnerable to temptation and the need for self-discipline and the assistance of present constraints.

14.3. Other Effective Hard Currencies: Reconciliation, Mediation, and Approach

Where Paul speaks of *reconciliation* with God (Greek καταλλαγή, *katallagē)*, the Epistle to the Hebrews speaks of *drawing near* to the divine presence (Greek προσέρχομαι, *proserchomai)*. Both terms are relatively transparent in meaning, almost as much in the twenty-first century as in the first. Each term presupposes something that stands in the way unless or until an interpersonal relationship of reconciliation or invitation to approach has been established. The Greek term without the compound form involving the preposition as a prefix (ἀλλάσσω, *allassō,* rather than *katallassō)* derives from the notion of *making otherwise*

---

77. Cf. Foerster Werner, "σῴζω," in Kittel, *TDNT,* vol. 7, 992 and 980-1024.

78. C. Anderson Scott, *Christianity according to St. Paul* (Cambridge: Cambridge University Press, 1927, 2d edn. 1961); George B. Caird with L. D. Hurst, *New Testament Theology* (Oxford: Clarendon, 1995), ch. 4, "The Three Tenses of Salvation," 118-35.

(ἄλλος, *other*) a previous situation, *to alter, to give in exchange.*[79] *Reconciliation* presupposes a former situation of *alienation*, of *hostility;* the invitation to *draw near* presupposes a situation of *exclusion* or *distance.*

It is of no great moment that the term καταλλαγή (*katallagē*) has no precise linguistic ancestry in the Old Testament in explicit terminology, although the idea is sometimes conveyed by כפר (*kāphar*), *to cover, to make atonement.* Since sin in the Old Testament, and especially in the prophets, entails a rebellious breach of relationship, the multiplicity of terms that convey the idea of putting the situation right imply *reconciliation.* But Paul explicates the theological significance of reconciliation with God through the use of a term that in everyday life denotes the reconciliation of husband and wife where there has been ill will, of friends who have fallen out, of contending parties at law, and in other interpersonal or social contexts. It denotes fundamentally "re-establishment of an interrupted or broken relationship."[80]

Because he emphasizes the initiative and grace of God in making reconciliation with humankind, Paul describes the event of reconciliation as one that human beings receive (καταλλαγὴν λαμβάνειν, *katallagēn lambanein*, Rom. 5:11). The previous verse is striking: εἰ γὰρ ἐχθροὶ ὄντες κατηλλάγημεν τῷ θεῷ διὰ τοῦ θανάτου τοῦ υἱοῦ αὐτοῦ: "for if while we were enemies we were reconciled with God through the death of his Son, [much more surely having been reconciled will we be saved by his life]" (Rom. 5:10). Humankind are said to have been *enemies* of God.[81] God proved his love for us "while we were still sinners" (Rom. 5:8). Karl Barth explicates this reconciliation first of all as *God with us:* He writes, "'God with us' is the core of the Christian message."[82] Barth views the relationship with the Old Testament background primarily in terms of covenant: "Reconciliation is the fulfilment of the covenant between God and man. 'Reconciliation' is the restitution, the resumption, of a fellowship which once existed but was then threatened by dissolution."[83] "God with us" (Immanuel, Matt. 1:23) is "the fulfilment of the broken covenant."[84] Cranfield offers a helpful clarification of the logic of Rom. 5:10. He writes, "The point made is that since God has already done the really difficult thing, that is, justified impious sinners, we may be

79. Friedrich Büchsel, "ἀλλάσσω, καταλλάσσω," in Kittel, *TDNT,* vol. 1, 251; cf. 251-59; Danker and Bauer in BDAG (3d edn. 2000), 45-46 and 521; J. Dupont, *La réconciliation dans la théologie de saint Paul* (Paris and Bruges: Descleé de Brouwer, 1953); Ernst Käsemann, *Perspectives on Paul,* trans. Margaret Kohl (London: S.C.M., 1971), 32-59; and I. H. Marshall, "The Meaning of Reconciliation," in R. A. Guelich (ed.), *Unity and Diversity in New Testament Theology: Essays in Honour of G. E. Ladd* (Grand Rapids: Eerdmans, 1978), 117-32.

80. BDAG, 521.

81. See Dunn, *Romans 1–8,* 268-69.

82. Barth, *Church Dogmatics,* IV:1, ch. 13, sect. 57, 1, 4; cf. 3-21.

83. Barth, *Church Dogmatics,* IV:1, ch. 13, sect. 57, 2, 22; cf. 22-66.

84. Barth, *Church Dogmatics,* IV:1, ch. 13, sect. 57, 3, 67-78.

absolutely confident that he will do what is by comparison very easy, namely, save from his wrath at the last those who are already righteous in his sight."[85]

This is brought about, Barth continues, through "the humiliation of the Son of God" in which the incarnation as "the Word made flesh" takes Jesus on behalf of humankind "into a far country."[86] In accordance with the derivation of the Greek word, Barth understands reconciliation as involving "an exchange" in which God in Christ *becomes* alienated, so that humankind may *become* the righteousness of God. He comments, "The love of God in Jesus Christ is decisively, fundamentally, and comprehensively his coming together with all men and their coming together with him. . . . It has been accomplished by God in his free grace defying and overcoming the sin of man."[87]

A further classic passage occurs in 2 Cor. 5:18-20. Ralph Martin, who has both published *Reconciliation* and produced a commentary on 2 Corinthians, concludes that the background and setting of these verses is "traditional material already in existence," especially in the light of its kerygmatic idioms (for example, "act as ambassadors," "entreat," "beg"), which Paul adapts in the light of the pastoral situation in Corinth.[88] The literary structure, he comments, suggests that it is "a carefully prepared piece of soteriological credo," namely part of a confessional statement that Paul fully endorses, but which is also pre-Pauline. In his commentary on this passage Martin notes the parallel with Rom. 5:1-11, and calls these verses "the quintessence" of Paul's argument. A new order has come into being through the love of Christ, "the advent of the new creation" (cf. 2 Cor. 5:17).[89]

Victor Furnish points out that the material on which Paul draws expresses three key principles: (i) *God* was reconciling the world to himself; (ii) *Christ* is the agent of reconciliation; and (iii) reconciliation includes *not charging* sinners with their trespasses.[90] Paul, in adapting the material to his pastoral needs, stresses that this act and state of reconciliation characterizes the nature of the *new creation* (2 Cor. 5:17). Furnish concludes, "The radical theocentrism of Paul's thought is apparent here."[91]

C. K. Barrett treads a careful path through the classic theological controversy concerning whether this reconciliation is one-sided (humankind reconciled to God) or two-sided (each reconciled to the other). He writes, "To reconcile is to end a relation of enmity, and to substitute for it one of peace and goodwill. It is

85. Cranfield, *Romans,* vol. 1, 266.

86. Barth, *Church Dogmatics,* IV:1, ch. 13, sect. 59, 1, 173 and 157-210.

87. Barth, *Church Dogmatics,* IV:1, ch. 13, sect. 58, 2, 103.

88. Ralph P. Martin, *Reconciliation: A Study of Paul's Theology* (London: Marshall, Morgan, & Scott, 1981), 94.

89. Ralph P. Martin, *2 Corinthians* (Dallas: Word, 1986), 145-46.

90. Victor P. Furnish, *II Corinthians,* Anchor Bible (New York: Doubleday, 1984), 334.

91. Furnish, *II Corinthians,* 335.

not necessarily implied that the enmity existed on one side only, but it is plainly stated that in this case the initiative to reconciliation was God's."[92]

James Denney, who wrote nearly a century ago, is at pains to stress that reconciliation denotes much more than a psychological state of goodwill on the part of humankind. On the basis of Pauline exegesis he asserts: "The work of reconciliation, in the sense of the New Testament, is a work which is *finished . . .* before the gospel is preached. . . . It is a work . . . *outside of us,* in which God so deals in Christ with the sin of the world that it shall no longer be a barrier between Himself and man. . . . Reconciliation is not something which is doing; it is something which is done."[93] Pannenberg and many others express caution about such an unqualified "objective" interpretation, since it leaves room for the notion that God is reconciled to humankind rather than initiating an ongoing work in which humankind learns to live in reconciliation with God.[94] We shall postpone any firm conclusion about this question until we discuss expiation and propitiation in 15.2. Denney's concern, however, is to show that reconciliation deals with the problem of humanity *under God's wrath,* which has a firm place within the Old and New Testaments, as well as to emphasize the *all-sufficiency and once-for-all character* of the work of Christ. John R. Taylor well expounds Denney's theology as a theology centered in the cross, but equally a theology of the love of God.[95] Meanwhile Barrett's careful comments remain worthy of continued reflection.

The imagery and conceptual grammar of *mediation and approach or access* is characteristic of the Epistle to the Hebrews, although it is not restricted to this epistle. Like *redemption* and *salvation,* it has a publicly intelligible tradition and horizon of understanding in the Old Testament. Ryder Smith expounds clearly and movingly what it was for Moses to stand as the agent of mediation in the narrative of Exodus. Moses, he writes, "was a societary man or nothing"; his work was "vicarious," reflecting both long agony over the people verging on despair, and his "unity with the people," no less.[96] Moses' corporate solidarity with the people of Israel was such that while he admitted before God that "this people have sinned a great sin," he asks on their behalf for divine forgiveness but astonishingly adds: "and if not, blot *me,* I pray thee, out of the book which thou hast written" (Exod. 32:31-32). Sometimes Moses stood as mediator facing and addressing Israel on behalf of God, and teaching them to obey God's commandments. At other times, when Israel sinned, Moses stood as mediator alongside Is-

92. C. K. Barrett, *The Second Epistle to the Corinthians* (London: Black, 1973), 175.

93. James Denney, *The Death of Christ: Its Place and Interpretation in the New Testament* (London: Hodder & Stoughton, 1912), 145-46.

94. Pannenberg, *Systematic Theology,* vol. 2, 403-16.

95. John Randolph Taylor, *God Loves Like That: The Theology of James Denney* (London: S.C.M., 1962), esp. 46-62.

96. C. Ryder Smith, *The Bible Doctrine of Salvation: A Study of the Atonement* (London: Epworth, 2d edn. 1946), 27.

rael facing and addressing God, pleading Israel's cause before God. When Moses sought to mediate, Smith comments, *"he was as a man who is torn in two. His unity with the people was so vital that he was ready to die for them; yet he could not forsake Jehovah with them. It is the tension between these two passions that is the hallmark of saviors"* (my italics).[97]

Moses constitutes a paradigm case for *mediation* for the currency of language, just as the judges were paradigms of what it means to be *saviors*. But the judges also acted as mediating agents between God and Israel, and Elijah also provides a paradigmatic model of the mediation. As a *prophet,* Elijah exercises "descending" mediation, "standing between" God and the people, to bring the word of God from God to the people. He also stands alongside the people, to serve as "ascending" mediator like a *priest,* to intercede on behalf of the people, to bring the people's word to God. Elijah, Ryder Smith concludes, was also "two men in one, and the two struggled with each other."[98]

It appears that God "spoke to no one face to face" except to Moses (Deut. 34:10). Yet prophets and the high priest continue the work of mediation. As concepts of mediation and divine transcendence developed over the centuries, by the time of the Targums the divine *shekinah (dwelling place),* divine *yekara (glory),* divine *memra* or *logos (word or utterance),* and divine *chokmah (wisdom),* together the Spirit of God and the angel(s) of God, came to be thought of as mediating figures through whom humankind might encounter the holy God. Such mediating agencies, however, appear already in the Old Testament. We need mention only the tent and the cloud (Exod. 33:7-11); the angel of the Lord (Exod. 14:19; Isa. 63:9); "the appearance of the likeness of the glory of the LORD" (Ezek. 1:28); the Spirit (Isa. 63:10-11); God's word (Ps. 107:20; Isa. 55:10-11); and God's wisdom (Prov. 8:5-11, 22-30). All these act as agencies or agents of divine action, and yet they are inseparable from God's presence. It is no accident that in the prologue to the Fourth Gospel we read, "The *word* (ὁ λόγος, *logos) dwelt* (ἐσκήνωσεν, *eskēnōsen*) among us, and we beheld his *glory* (τὴν δόξαν αὐτοῦ, *tēn doxan autou)*" (John 1:14). The light of God's *glory* is revealed in the *face* of Jesus Christ (2 Cor. 4:6). Paul proclaims "a crucified Christ" who is God's *wisdom* (1 Cor. 1:26).

All this entails an axiom: humankind possesses no "natural" or *a priori* right to enter and approach the immediate presence of God. *Approach to God cannot be taken for granted* unless a *mediator* opens the way and "stands between." On the Mount of Transfiguration God's *glory* appears and surrounds the three chosen figures, *Jesus, Moses,* and *Elijah.* Commentators generally agree that the cloud, the divine voice, the shining face, and in Luke also the glory, reflect the *Shekinah* of God (Matt. 17:2-6; Mark 9:43-48; Luke 9:28-36).[99] Although many

---

97. Smith, *Salvation,* 32-33.
98. Smith, *Salvation,* 33.

believe that Moses and Elijah represent respectively the law and the prophets, this does not exclude an implicit notion of mediation as embodying glory and suffering. A fulfillment of the role of the Suffering Servant in Isa. 42:1-4, 49:1-6, 50:6-11, and ch. 53 also indicates mediating agency on the part of Christ.

Paul provides a second example of the costly willingness of Moses to give up his life if this enables his mediation to be effective. In the very costly exclamation of Rom. 9:2-3, so great is Paul's identification with Israel, and so grieved is he by their unbelief, that he exclaims, "I could wish that I myself were accursed and cut off from Christ, for the sake of my people, my kindred according to the flesh." He pleads on Israel's behalf as "ascending" mediator; but he also declares God's judgment and grace as "descending" prophetic mediator on behalf of God.

Nevertheless it is in the Epistle to the Hebrews that a full theology of mediation comes to most distinctive expression. Admittedly the specific term μεσίτης (mesitēs) occurs only three times in Hebrews (Heb. 8:6; 9:15; 12:24) of the five times total in the New Testament (Gal. 3:19, 20; 1 Tim. 2:5). But the term as such is also lacking from the Old Testament, although rabbinic literature uses the term. Yet mediation is presupposed in Moses, Elijah, Paul, and other persons, and in the word of God, the wisdom of God, the angel of God, and the Spirit of God. Where μεσίτης does occur, it denotes "one who mediates between two parties to remove a disagreement or reach a common goal."[100] The three passages in Hebrews all explicitly call Jesus "the mediator of a better (or new) covenant."

Jesus as Mediator makes it possible for humankind to "draw near" to God: προσερχώμεθα οὖν μετὰ παρρησίας τῷ θρόνῳ τῆς χάριτος (proserchōmetha oun meta parrēsias tō thronō tēs charitos), "let us approach [or draw near to] the throne of grace with boldness" (Heb. 4:16). Heb. 1:1-13 has established beyond question that Jesus, the Son of God, can represent God to humankind. He fulfills the qualifications of both prophet and priest. God has spoken decisively through his Son (1:2). His Son, moreover, is co-creator of the universe, the radiance or shining forth of God's glory, and the exact imprint of God's essence (ἀπαύγασμα τῆς δόξης καὶ χαρακτὴρ τῆς ὑποστάσεως αὐτοῦ, apaugasma tēs doxēs kai charaktēr tēs hypostaseōs autou, Heb. 1:3). No reader can doubt that Jesus Christ "more than" represents God. Indeed, as the Son of God he eclipses even Moses, who was merely the servant of God (Heb. 3:1-6)

Yet Jesus stands equally in solidarity with humankind. He is the last Adam (Heb. 2:5-9); he calls humankind his brothers and sisters (2:11); and in his earthly

---

99. Donald A. Hagner, *Matthew 14–28* (Dallas: Word, 1995), 490-91; C. E. B. Cranfield, *The Gospel according to St. Mark,* Cambridge Greek Testament (Cambridge: Cambridge University Press, 1963), 294-96; Luke T. Johnson, *The Gospel of Luke,* Sacra Pagina (Collegeville, MN: Liturgical Press/Glazier, 1991), 152-56; Joel B. Green, *The Gospel of Luke,* NICNT (Grand Rapids: Eerdmans, 1997), 376-85; Joseph A. Fitzmyer, *The Gospel according to Luke, I–IX,* Anchor Bible (New York: Doubleday, 1981), 791-804.

100. BDAG, 634; cf. A. Oepke, "μεσίτης," in Kittel, *TDNT,* vol. 4, 598-624.

life he needed to place his *trust* in God as much as did any other human being (2:13). Jesus became "like his brothers and sisters in every respect . . . yet without sin" (2:17; 4:15). He cried to God with "supplications, loud cries and tears" (5:7). All this lays the foundation for the saving work of Christ as the great High Priest of the new covenant, one with God and one with humankind, and we return to these themes in 17.3, where we consider the Christology of Hebrews.

14.4. Multiple Concepts and Images in the New Testament as Models and Qualifiers

The comment of Jeremias (noted above) that the New Testament uses a variety of images to interpret the work of Christ should not surprise us, since it surpasses the power of any *single* model to convey its complexity.[101] On this basis there is truth in the maxim: "Theories of the atonement are right in what they affirm and wrong in what they deny." Gunton and Pannenberg similarly stress the significance of this pluriformity of models. They point out that each gives rise to a different history of interpretation.[102] Yet they function conjointly to qualify single models, or to cancel off certain unwanted overtones in other models. Isolated models that appear to claim comprehensiveness risk pressing one aspect of interpretation at the cost of underplaying others. This accords with Ramsey's formulation of his approach in terms of models and qualifiers.

Colin Gunton rightly criticizes the narrow reductionism of Enlightenment rationalism that, under the spell of an older view of the natural sciences, dismissed the capacity of metaphors and models to convey cognitive truth-claims and ontological states of affairs. Such a view of natural science is now outdated. Eberhard Jüngel's work on metaphor in this context substantiates the claims of Ricoeur, Gunton, Janet Martin Soskice, and others about the validity of metaphor to convey such cognitive truth. Furthermore, *"indirect" communication may stimulate imagination and participatory involvement,* which is relevant to language about the cross of Christ and Christ's atoning work. Garrett Green has fruitfully explored the role of metaphor and imagination in communicating truth that is also participatory and self-involving.[103]

Jeremias selects four models or "themes" that interpret the work of Christ, each of which communicates truth, but each of which also qualifies other models. He distinguishes between the following: (1) the cultic theme of *sacrifice;* (2) the socio-economic theme of *purchase and redemption;* (3) the legal theme of

---

101. Jeremias, *Central Message*, 31-50.

102. Pannenberg, *Systematic Theology,* vol. 2, 423, and Gunton, *Actuality of the Atonement*, 36-43.

103. Garrett Green, *Imagining God: Theology and the Religious Imagination* (Grand Rapids: Eerdmans, 1989), throughout.

forensic categories; and (4) what he calls "ethical substitution." We shall outline these now, but then in Chapter 15 explore how they function *together* in theological interpretation.

(1) *The cultic theme of sacrifice.* In the more specific sense of the term, *sacrifice* has its roots especially in the Levitical system of the Old Testament.[104] But it is also used in a broader context of giving the self for the benefit of others. In 1 Cor. 5:7 Paul speaks of Christ's death as that of the Passover lamb "sacrificed for us" (τὸ πάσχα ἡμῶν ἐτύθη Χριστός, *to pascha hēmōn etuthē Christos*). The verb ἐτύθη makes the translation "paschal lamb" (NRSV, REB, NIV) decisive as against "our Passover" (AV/KJV, NJB).[105] In this context Paul reminds his readers in Corinth that the sacrifice of Christ has released them from bondage to the past to a new order of existence characterized by purity of lifestyle. Christ, like the Passover sacrifice, has delivered them from "their Egypt."[106]

A more specific nuance of meaning occurs in Rom. 3:24-25. Here Paul declares that his Christian readers are "now *justified* by his *grace* as a gift, through the *redemption* that is in Christ Jesus, whom God has put forward as *a sacrifice of atonement*" (NRSV; Greek ὃν προέθετο ὁ θεὸς ἱλαστήριον διὰ [τῆς] πίστεως ἐν τῷ αὐτοῦ αἵματι, *hon proetheto ho theos hilastērion dia* [*tēs*] *pistěōs en tō autou haimati*).

We are not yet ready to debate the contested meaning of ἱλαστήριον (*hilastērion*), since this can be done only within appropriate horizons of understanding, not by lexicography and semantics alone.[107] The point here is that *sacrifice* provides *one* way among others of communicating how the work of Christ was *"for us."* Moreover, this is only one of several references to "expiatory" or "propitiatory" sacrifice (depending on our interpretation of ἱλαστήριον). In 2 Cor. 5:21 Paul states that "For our sake [again, the *'for us'* theme] God *made Christ to be sin*" (NRSV; Greek ὑπὲρ ἡμῶν ἁμαρτίαν ἐποίησεν, *huper hēmōn hamartian epoiēsen*). Again the meaning is controversial, and Whiteley urges that it is too easy to read this verse in the light of some prior theory of the atonement.[108] Whiteley hesitates to translate ἁμαρτίαν as *sin offering*. On the other hand, Leon Morris approaches the verse from a different angle and explicitly attacks Whiteley's view. He writes, "All the verbal juggling in the world cannot make 'made sin' mean "took upon himself human nature," which is Whiteley's

104. Jeremias, *Central Message*, 32-36.

105. D. O. Wenthe, "An Exegetical Study of 1 Cor. 5:7b," *The Spring Fielder* 38 (1974) 134-60.

106. Cf. Thiselton, *First Epistle to the Corinthians*, 403-8.

107. See Cranfield, *Romans*, vol. 1, 203-18; Dunn, *Romans 1–8*, 167-83; Käsemann, *Romans*, 91-101; and Anders Nygren, *Commentary on Romans*, trans. C. C. Rasmussen (London: S.C.M., 1952), 154-62. See also esp. M. Barth, *Was Christ's Death a Sacrifice?* SJT Occasional Papers 9 (Edinburgh: Oliver & Boyd, 1961), and Leon L. Morris, "The Meaning of ἱλαστήριον in Romans 3:25," *New Testament Studies* 2 (1955-56) 33-43.

108. D. E. H. Whiteley, *The Theology of St. Paul* (Oxford: Blackwell, 2d edn. 1974), 136.

interpretation.[109] On the other hand, Furnish rejects the translation *"sin offering"* (as in Lev. 4:25, 29) on the ground that it does not fit the context, although he recognizes that it may reflect the background of Isa. 53:6, 9: "The LORD has laid on him the iniquity of us all" (cf. 1 Pet. 2:22).[110]

The Synoptic gospels speak of Christ's "pouring out his blood for many": τὸ αἷμά μου . . . τὸ περὶ πολλῶν ἐκχυννόμενον (*to haima mou . . . to peri pollōn ekchunnomenon*, Matt. 26:28; parallel Mark 14:24; Luke 22:20). But while this is "sacrificial" in the broader sense of the term, an allusion to a Levitical sacrifice is not explicit. Similarly, the Johannine reference to "the lamb of God who takes away the sin of the world" (ὁ ἀμνὸς τοῦ θεοῦ, *ho amnos tou theou*, John 1:29) could just possibly imply a sacrificial lamb, but admits of other interpretations depending partly on whether the context is that of Johannine thought or the narrative situation portrayed.

The matter is different again in the Epistle to the Hebrews, where the argument is dominated by the concept of Jesus as High Priest who sacrifices himself as a perfect offering to open the way of approach to God in a decisive and unrepeatable way: διὰ δὲ τοῦ ἰδίου αἵματος εἰσῆλθεν ἐφάπαξ *(dia de tou idiou haimatos eisēlthen ephapax),* "through his own blood he entered once and for all into the Holy Place" (Heb. 9:12). Here and throughout Heb. 9:1–10:18 the emphasis on sacrifice is explicit and unmistakable.[111]

(2) *Language relating to purchase and redemption.* We have already discussed the place of this kind of language in 14.2. The verb ἀγοράζω *(agorazō),* to purchase, is used in 1 Cor. 6:20: ἠγοράσθητε γὰρ τιμῆς *(ēgorasthēte gar timēs),* "for you were bought with a price." We noted that this term underlines the *costliness* of redemption rather than implying any notion that would permit the question, "To whom is the price paid?" We also noted that this word group implied redemption or purchase *from* a condition of jeopardy or of oppressive servitude, *to* ownership and protection by a new Lord, who here is Jesus Christ. We explore this *Kyrios* concept further in 17.1.

(3) The *forensic* theme is drawn from criminal law. Jeremias comments: "All those passages referring to Isa. 53, the chapter about the Suffering Servant who carried the punishment inflicted because of our transgressions, belong here, as for instance Rom. 4:25 ('He was delivered for our offences'). A particularly impressive image . . . is used in Col. 2:14, 'God has cancelled the writ issued against us which enumerated the statutes we had violated, and destroyed it by nailing it

109. Morris, *The Cross in the New Testament,* 221.

110. Furnish, *II Corinthians,* 341 and 351.

111. M. E. Isaacs, "Priesthood and the Epistle to the Hebrews," *Heythrop Journal* 38 (1997) 51-62; G. Stählin, "ἅπαξ" *(hapax, ephapax), TDNT,* vol. 1, 381-84; Anthony C. Thiselton, "Hebrews," in J. W. Rogerson and J. D. G. Dunn (eds.), *Eerdmans Commentary on the Bible* (Grand Rapids: Eerdmans, 2003), 1467-69.

to the cross."[112] This states, Jeremias concludes, that Christ *suffered the death penalty that we deserved. Our human* sins are inscribed on the *titulus* of the cross.

Some writers concede that it is legitimate to speak of *substitution* in these two passages, but reject the traditional Reformation term *penal* substitution. Yet we saw in 14.1 that *the cross* and *crucifixion* belong to the conceptual domain of punishment for crimes. The antipathy toward using *penal* is understandable if or when this one aspect is overpressed, as if no other concept qualified it. Equally the term *penal substitution* becomes misleading if it is abstracted from its proper hermeneutical horizon of divine *grace* as an overarching understanding. Vincent Taylor judiciously observes, "Everyone desires a better word than *penal*, but until we find it we ought not to abandon it [simply] because it has been used in ways that revolt the conscience, or under the delusion that we can accept better for the consequences of sin by invoking the operation of an inevitable law of cause and effect in the moral universe rather than the activity of God."[113] Taylor rejects, therefore, Albrecht Ritschl's insistent argument that Christ suffered affliction, but not penalty.[114] However, he also makes a further subtle distinction between *becoming involved in the punishment of others* and *being punished*.[115]

Gal. 3:13 arguably comes within this forensic category, along with Rom. 4:25 and Col. 4:14. It is generally agreed that the immediate frame of references for interpreting this verse derives from the allusion to Deut. 21:23: "Cursed is everyone who hangs on a tree."[116] Whiteley, once again, sees this passage as a matter of Christ's self-identification with sinners, but misses the conceptual nuance discussed by Taylor.[117] F. F. Bruce, however, offers a more thorough exegesis of the Greek text and Deuteronomic background, exploring Deut. 27:26 in conjunction with Deut. 21:23. The "curse" of Deut. 27:26 was pronounced at the end of a covenant renewal ceremony upon one who had broken the covenant. Bruce writes, "Paul probably uses ἐπικατάρατος (in preference to the LXX κεκατηραμένος) when quoting Deut. 21:23 here by way of assimilation to his quotation of Deut. 27:26 in Gal. 3:10. . . . The curse which Christ 'became' was his people's curse. . . . The death which he died *was their death*." Citing C. K. Barrett on 2 Cor. 5:21, Bruce concludes, "He [Christ] came to stand in that relation with God which is normally the result of sin, estranged from God, and the object of his wrath."[118]

---

112. Jeremias, *Central Message*, 36-37.

113. Taylor, *Atonement*, 130.

114. Ritschl, *Justification and Reconciliation*, 311-12.

115. Taylor, *Atonement*, 129.

116. Christopher D. Stanley, *Paul and the Language of Scripture: Citation Technique in the Pauline Epistles and Contemporary Literature*, SNTSMS 69 (Cambridge: Cambridge University Press, 1992), 245-48.

117. Whiteley, *Theology of St. Paul*, 137-38; cf. also 83-85.

118. F. F. Bruce, *The Epistle to the Galatians*, NIGTC (Grand Rapids: Eerdmans and Carlisle,

(4) Finally, Jeremias identifies and expounds a fourth theme of *"ethical substitution,* consisting in Christ's vicarious obedience." However, he concedes that there may be only two examples of this in Paul: Rom. 5:18-19 and Gal. 4:4-5. In Rom. 5:18-19 Paul declares, "Through the obedience of this one man . . . many will become righteous." In Gal. 4:4-5 he writes, "Christ became a slave of the law in order to redeem those who were slaves of the law." Jeremias observes that while these four images and themes are all different, "the same intention" underlines them, namely to illustrate the *"for us"* effect of Christ's work.[119]

(5) Other themes occur in the New Testament, and these clearly extend this selective list. As is well known, Gustaf Aulén draws attention to the *victory* theme, with the "warrior" background in the Old Testament and allusions to victory and conquest in the New Testament.[120] This model clearly features in the Synoptic gospels. In Mark 3:27 Jesus tells his audience, "No one can enter a strong man's house and plunder his property without first tying up the strong man; then the house can be plundered." The context reveals that this alludes to the conquest by Jesus over the power of evil. Indeed, the very heart of the message of proclaiming and bringing near *the reign of God* is itself a victory motif. Jesus brings victory over bondage and death. Here is an important fifth model alongside the four that Jeremias discusses especially in Paul.

The importance of a multiple-model approach has been noted in the context of Ian Ramsey's philosophy of models and qualifiers, but this is further reinforced in more recent theological interpretation by Joel Green and Mark Baker.[121] They write, "Atonement theology is capable of being represented in a variety of ways. In fact, a plurality of metaphors has been used in Christian communities since the beginning of the Christian movement."[122] They rightly make the point that has become a major theme in hermeneutics of "interest" that it is essential "that we decenter our own self-interests so as to be addressed by the text as 'other.'"[123] Sometimes a desire to legitimate and to defend one's own ecclesial tradition can influence what weight we give as interpreters to each respective model.

One of several merits of the work by Green and Baker is that they do *not exclude* the role of any biblical model, but rather the reverse: it is by employing the full repertoire of biblical models that the truth of the work of Christ can best be

---

U.K.: Paternoster, 1982), 165 and 166; cf. C. K. Barrett, *A Commentary on the Second Epistle to the Corinthians* (London: Black, 1973), 180.

119. Jeremias, *Central Message,* 38.

120. Cf. Gustaf Aulén, *Christus Victor: An Historical Study of the Three Main Types of the Idea of the Atonement,* trans. A. G. Hebert (London: S.P.C.K., 1931, rpt. 1970).

121. Joel B. Green and Mark D. Baker, *Recovering the Scandal of the Cross: Atonement in New Testament and Contemporary Contexts* (Downers Grove, IL: InterVarsity Press, 200).

122. Green and Baker, *Scandal of the Cross,* 109.

123. Green and Baker, *Scandal of the Cross,* 110.

communicated to the church and to the world. Thus "sacrifice" could not be excluded without excluding the Epistle to the Hebrews and much else besides. Nevertheless they remain sensitive to the concerns of feminist writers about the difficulty of the overtones of "penal substitution." They cite the feminist writer Rita Nakashima Brock, who expresses concern about nuances of "child abuse" and "the shadow of the punitive father."[124]

This is precisely why we have emphasized not only a multi-model approach, but also the horizon of understanding opened up by Jürgen Moltmann in *The Crucified God* and other works. Within the horizon of Moltmann's work, the problem of "child abuse" can hardly arise. However, this begins to embark upon issues of interpretation, which is the subject matter of our next chapter.

---

124. Green and Baker, *Scandal of the Cross*, 91, from Rita Nakashima Brock, "And a Little Child Will Lead Us: Christology and Child Abuse," in Joanne Carlson Brown and Carole R. Bohn, *Christianity's Patriarchy and Abuse: A Feminist Critique* (New York: Pilgrim, 1989), 53.

CHAPTER 15

The Hermeneutics of the Work of Christ: Interpreting Biblical Material

15.1. Horizons of Understanding and Logical Grammar: Representation, Participation, Identification, and Substitution

A considerable degree of conceptual confusion vitiates many of the older modern debates concerning the use and validity of the terms *representation, participation, identification, and substitution* as ways of understanding the work of Christ. Much controversy surrounds especially the term *substitution,* which we now consider.

Since he defends the use of the term "penal," it may seem surprising that Vincent Taylor expresses strong reservations about *substitution.* He writes, "It is best to avoid the word *substitution* and to describe the work of Christ as *representative* in character."[1] Whiteley has similar reservations about *substitution,* for which he prefers the term *participation.*[2] Other writers, however, rightly insist that in its appropriate place *substitution* remains an indispensable term. One such writer is Eberhard Jüngel. In his essay "The Mystery of Substitution" he enters into conversation with Heinrich Vogel.[3] The "mystery" of the substitutionary work of Jesus Christ, Jüngel observes approvingly, has a key position in the very theological life of Vogel.[4] Jüngel places particular emphasis upon Mark 10:45: "The Son of Man came into the world to give his life as a ransom for [Greek λύτρον ἀντί, *lutron anti*] many." In Matt. 26:28 and in Gal. 3:13 the Greek prepositions are περί *(peri)* and ὑπέρ *(huper)* respectively.

The three prepositional phrases, Jüngel writes, "express the fact that one per-

---

1. Taylor, *Atonement,* 126 (my italics).

2. Whiteley, *Theology of St. Paul,* 130-37.

3. Eberhard Jüngel, *Ideological Essays II,* ed. J. B. Webster and trans. A. Neufeldt-Fest and J. B. Webster (Edinburgh: T&T Clark, 1995), 145-62.

4. Jüngel, *Essays II,* 147.

son has done or suffered something on behalf of, that is, in place of, other persons."[5] What was done or suffered in *place* of others is a negative event from which the other is *spared*" (his italics).[6] At the same time the phrase carries a positive meaning of *favor to the benefit of* those concerned. This is further bound up with the central theological motif of "Christ alone," *solus Christus*. This aspect, Jüngel concludes, provides a more faithful understanding than Bonhoeffer's reservations about substitution. The key theological axiom, Jüngel asserts, is: *"In the person of Jesus Christ God took our human place"* (his italics).[7] *This does not extend only to the death of Christ:* "Jesus Christ's whole being [is] a substitutionary existence."[8] Neither Schleiermacher nor Bultmann, Jüngel argues, can fully endorse Vogel's succinct "*He came in our place — that* is the mystery of the incarnation of the Son" (his italics).[9] Not only the New Testament but also the Nicene Creed should be interpreted in this way. Vogel sees himself as standing in the tradition of Gregory of Nazianzus's dictum "What is not taken on, is not also saved. But what is united with God will also be saved."[10]

In *exegetical* and *theological* terms this seems conclusive. However, there is more to be said from the standpoint of both *hermeneutics* and *logical implication*. We recall our discussions of Lakatos and Nancey Murphy in 8.4 to the effect that polemical "positions" sometimes achieve less than an ongoing "research program" in which adjustments and refinements may serve to move us beyond polemical "positions."

I suggest that much of this controversy lies under the spell of a logical confusion that fails to distinguish between two orders of effects in relation to the work of Christ. We suggested in 14.1 that an initial hermeneutic must include the notion that *divine grace* "achieves for a person *what that person cannot do for themselves*." This is a foundational principle of the meaning of the cross. Those who are "dead" cannot contribute to their life or salvation (see the discussion of resurrection in 22.3). However, the question of how grace is *received and appropriated* carries us to a different level of discussion. The keenest diagnosis of a widespread conceptual confusion comes from J. K. S. Reid, in his work *Our Life in Christ*. Reid formulates the principle that we need "to do justice to that certain difference which distinguishes Christ from those who benefit from what he does."[11] For example, he cites James Denney's observation: "Christ died for our sins. *That death* we do not die" (his italics).[12] P. T.

5. Jüngel, *Essays II*, 152.
6. Jüngel, *Essays II*, 152.
7. Jüngel, *Essays II*, 155.
8. Jüngel, *Essays II*, 156.
9. Jüngel, *Essays II*, 157.
10. Jüngel, *Essays II*, 161.
11. J. K. S. Reid, *Our Life in Christ* (London: S.C.M., 1963), 89.
12. James Denney, *Studies in Theology* (London: Hodder & Stoughton, 1894), 126; cf. Denney, *Death of Christ*, 237.

Forsyth, Reid continues, expressed the point even more succinctly: "He [Christ] saved us by his difference from us."[13]

Even so, Forsyth and Denney take different views about the application of the terms *representation* and *substitution* as well as *participation,* and this prompts Reid to adopt their common point of departure to make a constructive hermeneutical and logical distinction. Reid writes, "On the one hand . . . men participate in benefits acquired for them by Jesus Christ, and by his work and grace they are admitted to possession of what otherwise could never be theirs . . . forgiveness, or reconciliation, or simply salvation. *Here is where a rule of contrariety operates: Christ wins those benefits for us who had himself no need of them and has himself no part in them.* The New Testament is full of references to such benefits" (my italics).[14] Reid offers more examples: "because he [Christ] died, we live; because he suffered, we rejoice; because he was reckoned guilty, we are reckoned innocent; because he was condemned, we are acquitted."[15]

However, Reid also elucidates what is "on the other hand." There are *other* benefits, he writes, "in which *our participation is subject to a quite different rule of correspondence:* he confers some things upon us which he himself may be said to enjoy. Thus because he lives, we shall live also; because he conquers, we too are in all things conquerors; because he reigns, we shall reign with him; and so on."[16] Some benefits are *pro nobis;* others are *in nobis.* Reid might have said considerably more in this context about dying and being raised with Christ. He might also have added a further dimension by exploring *identification with Christ,* which is the key to Paul's theology of baptism as well as to resurrection and salvation. Yet Reid, like Jüngel, shows conclusively that *we cannot abandon the term substitution,* even if it is to be *complemented* by working out in what contexts *representation, participation, and identification also serve as further necessary explanatory terms.*

It would be simplistic to assign all *in nobis* benefits as due to the agency of the Holy Spirit, and all *pro nobis* benefits as due to the work of Christ alone. Once again, Moltmann and Pannenberg demonstrate in what specific ways the cross is both distinctively the work of *Christ* and at the same time a work of *God as Trinity.*[17] Within this framework or horizon of understanding *participation in the life of the triune God* becomes central to salvation, albeit distinctively through *the work of Christ as the ground of its possibility,* and through *the agency of the Holy Spirit as its actualization.* Lionel Thornton writes of participation in Christ in terms of identification with Christ, participation in the *koinōnia* of the Spirit,

---

13. P. T. Forsyth, *The Cruciality of the Cross* (London: Independent, 1909), 85.

14. Reid, *Our Life in Christ,* 90-91.

15. Reid, *Our Life in Christ,* 91.

16. Reid, *Our Life in Christ,* 91.

17. Pannenberg, *Systematic Theology,* vol. 2, 405-6 and 437-54; Moltmann, *The Crucified God,* 200-290; Moltmann, *The Trinity and the Kingdom of God,* 1-28, 151-77; among other writings.

partakers of the love of God the Father, sharers in Christ's victory, partakers derivatively in Christ's sonship, and participants in new birth and resurrection.[18]

In Part I above, we argued that a hermeneutic of doctrine should take full account of the concrete, contingent, bodily, and temporal dimensions in drama and narrative. The danger of attending too exclusively to such terms as "identification" as abstract theological formulae is that their role within the living, dynamic, dramatic narrative of the New Testament becomes lost from view. Thereby their hermeneutical currency becomes debased and reduced.

Clearly such passages as Mark 2:15, "Many tax collectors and sinners sat down at table with Jesus and his disciples," together with the question of the Pharisees, "Why does he eat with tax collectors and sinners?" speak eloquently of the *identification* of Jesus with the needy and sinful. "Those who are well have no need of a physician, but those who are sick; I came not to call the righteous, but sinners to repentance" (Mark 2:16-17). "The man receives sinners and eats with them" (Luke 15:2). The hermeneutical currency of *identification* comes to light in such living, dramatic contexts.

It might be thought that such passages refer only to the ministry of Jesus as a whole, rather than specifically to his work on the cross, even if both together constitute "the saving work of Christ." A hermeneutics of narrative time may suggest otherwise. In his *Narrative Discourse* Gérard Gennette discusses strategies of narrative time in terms of the deployment of variation in sequence, speed, frequency of retellings, and duration.[19] Many classic novels and popular detective stories have made these devices familiar. How could the narrative of Charles Dickens' *Great Expectations* or of Agatha Christie's detective mysteries operate without flashbacks (analepses) or prospective flashforwards (prolepses) in place of a wooden chronological portrayal of every event as it occurs in the strict sequence of "clock time"? *Narrative* time does not always follow the sequence or precise speed of *natural* time.

The Gospel of Mark employs such devices as changes of tempo to convey a specific point about the purpose of the ministry and death of Jesus. The early chapters begin at a very rapid, almost frantic pace. The Greek word *immediately* or *next* (*euthus*) characterizes the fast pace as one event follows rapidly upon another. However, the pace slows when Jesus comes to Jerusalem. Wesley Kort writes, "The pace of this (first) section is very quick. . . . The pace slows remarkably as Jesus moves toward Jerusalem. . . . The day of the crucifixion is carefully measured . . . detailed by the hour."[20] *The events of the passion are portrayed, in effect, in slow motion.*

18. Lionel Thornton, *The Common Life in the Body of Christ* (London: Dacre, 3d edn. 1950), Part I, 5-220.

19. Gérard Genette, *Narrative Discourse: An Essay in Method,* trans. J. E. Lewin (Ithaca, NY: Cornell University Press, 1980), chs. 4–6, and Gérard Genette, *Narrative Discourse Re-Visited,* trans. J. E. Lewin (Ithaca, NY: Cornell University Press, 1988), 33-37.

20. Wesley A. Kort, *Story, Text and Scripture: Literary Interests in Biblical Narrative* (University Park, PA: Pennsylvania University Press, 1988), 44.

The deliberate effect is to show that the *entire life and ministry of Jesus is oriented toward the cross and passion as its culmination and ultimate focus.*

Thus the whole ministry of Jesus through his words and deeds *witnesses to his identification with sinners.* As Son of Man Jesus represents humankind as a corporate figure also. The horizon of meaning that makes it possible to understand this life process is the cross and the resurrection. Within this horizon the terms *substitution, identification, representation,* and *participation* are no mere abstractions reflecting "problems" drawn from the epistles, but draw living currency from the whole of the New Testament.

15.2. Horizons of Understanding and Logical Grammar: Expiation and Propitiation

If an elucidation of conceptual grammar can help us to clarify the respective meanings and practical force of representation, participation, identification, and substitution, this applies all the more to attempts to bring order out of the classic controversies concerning the translation of ἱλαστήριον *(hilastērion),* variously rendered as *expiation, propitiation, means of dealing with sin,* or *mercy seat* in Rom. 3:25. The term occurs only here and in Heb. 9:25 in the New Testament, although the cognate form ἱλασμός *(hilasmos)* occurs in 1 John 2:2; 4:10; and the verb ἱλάσκομαι *(hilaskomai)* in Luke 18:13 and Heb. 2:17. The English versions and commentators translate the Greek variously (in Rom. 3:25) as *sacrifice of atonement* (NRSV, NIV); *a sacrifice for reconciliation* (NJB); *a means of expiating sin* (REB); *expiation* (RSV); *propitiation* (AV/KJV); *means of propitiation* (Moffatt); *means of dealing with sin* (Barrett); and *mercy seat* (Nygren).[21]

The LXX reflects the Hebrew כפרת *(kappōreth),* which is a cognate form of כפר, *to cover over sin.* The more usual Piel form כפר *(kipper)* denotes "cover over, pacify, make propitiation, propitiate" in certain contexts, and the noun כפרת *(kappōreth)* relates to *expiation* in such contexts as Exod. 25:16; 31:7; Lev. 16:2, 13; or alternatively to the slab of gold placed on top of the ark of testimony, which became the *place of meeting* or *mercy seat* in the Holy of Holies (Num. 7:89; 1 Chron. 28:11).[22] This last is the meaning of ἱλαστήριον *(hilastērion)* in Heb. 9:5. In nonbiblical Greek the verb denotes both *to propitiate* or *to placate,* and *to expiate* or *to cover sin,* for example, through some compensation or gift. The meaning in the LXX is debated, but many follow Dodd's maxim that the meaning *to propitiate* "is practically unknown where God is the object."[23]

21. C. K. Barrett, *The Epistle to the Romans* (London: Black, 1957, 2d edn. 1962), 72; Nygren, *Romans,* 156-58, where he alludes to Exod. 25:22, which portrays the *mercy seat* as the "place of meeting" between God and Israel.

22. Brown, Driver, and Briggs, *The New Hebrew-English Lexicon* (new edn. 1980), 497-98.

23. C. H. Dodd, *The Epistle of Paul to the Romans* (London: Hodder & Stoughton, 1932), 54-56.

The linguistic and lexicographical discussion is complex, even at times tortuous, and appears (to this writer) indecisive. C. H. Dodd set a trend by insisting that any notion of *propitiating* God undermined a Christian doctrine of grace. He wrote, "In accordance with biblical usage, therefore, the substantive (*hilastērion*) would mean not *propitiation,* but 'a means by which guilt is annulled.' . . . *Propitiation* is misleading."[24] The logical model is that of "removing defilement . . . [having] the value, so to speak, of a disinfectant."[25] C. K. Barrett endorses this: "The common Greek meaning 'to propitiate' becomes practically impossible when, as sometimes happens, God is the subject of the verb. God cannot be said to propitiate man: he cleanses, forgives man, and expiates (wipes out) his sin. Derivatives of the form before us here (in τήριος) generally refer to the means by which, or place where, an action is carried out. . . . Christ crucified was set forth as an 'expiatory person' or as an 'expiatory agency.'"[26]

Leon Morris, H. Ridderbos, and David Hill argue against Dodd for the meaning *propitiation* in this verse.[27] Morris scrutinizes every stage of Dodd's arguments, including the relation between the Hebrew and LXX, with close exegetical attention to Old Testament passages. He urges that *propitiation* does form part of the LXX meaning, although he also firmly agrees with Dodd "that propitiation in the crude sense is not possible with the God of Israel."[28] Morris includes at least one theological issue to which Dodd gives inadequate attention. He writes, "Wrath may be thought of especially as wrath against the loved ones. . . . It is against such a background that the Old Testament idea of propitiation is to be studied. . . . That wrath is the wrath of a loving father who yearns for his children. . . ."[29] Dodd, as is widely known, perceives divine wrath in "internal" terms as a process of cause and effect in a moral universe. This is a useful insight, but not a comprehensive one.

A careful and balanced linguistic and theological study comes from my former Sheffield colleague, David Hill. He examines each of the Hebrew and Greek uses of the terms in their proper contexts, underlining the point that "if . . . the meaning 'propitiation' is accepted, we rightly emphasize the *personal* nature of the breach with God caused by sin. . . . From God's love comes the means of averting the consequences of sin."[30] Moreover, the horizon of understanding (my term) for interpreting Rom. 3:25 is the opening chapters of the epistle with their single, dominating purpose of showing that all lie under the condemnation and

---

24. Dodd, *Romans,* 55.

25. Dodd, *Romans,* 54.

26. Barrett, *Romans,* 77.

27. H. Ridderbos, *Paul: An Outline of His Theology* (Grand Rapids: Eerdmans, 1975), 189-90; Leon Morris, *Apostolic Preaching of the Cross* (London: Tyndale, 1955), 136-60 and 161-85.

28. Morris, *Apostolic Preaching,* 153.

29. Morris, *Apostolic Preaching,* 159; cf. 161-85.

30. David Hill, *Greek Words and Hebrew Meanings: Studies in the Semantics of Soteriological Terms,* SNTSMS 5 (Cambridge: Cambridge University Press, 1967), 37-38 (my italics); 23-48.

wrath of God. The specific alternative of *mercy seat* in the context of the Day of Atonement faces the difficulty that, unlike Heb. 9:5, "the epistle to the Romans does not move in the sphere of Levitical symbolism."[31] The occurrence of the term in 4 Maccabees may also support the interpretation *"propitiation."* This may provide a more relevant background than the Day of Atonement.[32]

Cranfield and Dunn judiciously argue that neither expiation nor propitiation should be excluded. Cranfield exposes certain gaps in Dodd's arguments, and concludes: "What Paul's statement that God purposed Christ as a propitiatory victim means is that God, because in His mercy He willed to forgive sinful man, and being truly merciful, *willed to forgive them righteously*, that is, without in any way condoning their sin, *purposed to direct against His own very self* in the person of His Son the full weight of that righteous wrath which they deserved."[33] Cranfield's discussion of the issues is extensive.[34]

Is Dunn, then, correct when he laments, "an unnecessary polarizing of alternatives"?[35] This is precisely the issue that a hermeneutical elucidation of the logical and conceptual grammar of the terms addresses. Dodd bases his interpretation largely on the need to avoid any notion of "appeasing God" that would in his view undercut the initiative of divine grace. But this is a straw man that no one disputes *provided that we emphasize that the entire process springs from grace.* On the other hand, Cranfield's view concerning God's *"directing against His own very self"* wrath or what would be involved in self-chosen propitiation can become intelligible only within the kind of horizon of understanding that Moltmann has set forth in *The Crucified God* and *The Trinity and the Kingdom of God*, as well as Pannenberg's insistence on grace through the work of Christ as *Trinitarian* action. Both of these are masterly contributions to the hermeneutics of the subject, and promise to move the debate out from its well-worn grooves of either/or.

There is some justification for Dunn's describing the debate as an "older dispute."[36] But it may be "older" because in older debates the term "righteousness" has become too readily confused with a debate about "retributory justice," which does not accord very well even with Luther's understanding of "righteousness" in Romans. On Rom. 3:26 εἰς, τὸ εἶναι αὐτὸν δίκαιον καὶ δικαιοῦντα τὸν ἐκ πίστεως Ἰησοῦ, "that he himself is righteous and that he justifies the one who has faith in Jesus" (NRSV), many conservative writers repeat Denney's comment: "Something is done which enables God to justify the ungodly who believe in Jesus, and at the same time to appear signally and conspicuously a righteous God."[37]

---

31. Hill, *Greek Words*, 40.
32. Hill, *Greek Words*, 45-48.
33. Cranfield, *Romans*, vol. 1, 217 (my italics).
34. Cranfield, *Romans*, vol. 1, 205-18.
35. Dunn, *Romans 1–8*, 171.
36. Dunn, *Romans 1–8*, 171.
37. Denney, *The Death of Christ*, 167.

Denney was writing in 1912, when before the First World War the notion of the upright headmaster administering moral discipline still found favor with many. Today we might speak more meaningfully of *divine integrity*. Joel Green and Mark Baker, whose work we noted in the last chapter on the use of multiple models, offer suggestive comments about the interpretation put forward by Charles Hodge. Hodge, they point out, "read the Bible through the lens of the criminal justice system of his era," and pinned everything on a model that today raises sensitivities especially among feminist writers about "child abuse" and "patriarchy."[38]

Yet the nineteenth-century concern to place a heavy emphasis upon jurisprudence and theories of punishment should not lead us to *exclude* every issue about *divine self-consistency and integrity,* to which the model of propitiation may point, however relative it may be to other models that *qualify* it. The deeds of God are bound up with the character and reputation of God's *"name."* In Deuteronomy God chooses a place to cause his name to dwell (Hebrew שֵׁם, *shēm*) (Deut. 12:11; 14:23; 16:11). This name publicly proclaims his *glory* and *righteousness* (Pss. 102:15, 21; 103:1; 106:3, 8; 115:1; Isa. 12:4; 57:15; 63:16).[39] God's name is to be hallowed (Matt. 6:9; par. Luke 11:2) and glorified (John 12:28). The *righteousness* of God (Hebrew צֶדֶק, *tsedeq;* Greek δικαιοσύνη, *dikaiosunē*) can sometimes denote justice, but NJB often translates this term as *integrity:* "Let him weigh me on accurate scales, then he, God, will recognize my *integrity*" (Job 31:6); "Judge me, Yahweh, as my uprightness and my *integrity* deserve" (Ps. 7:8, NJB). David Reimer observes, "Righteousness . . . becomes a sort of verbal shorthand for *something true about God, . . .* behaviour that accord(s) with some standard."[40] Here perhaps it conveys the notion of *"being true to oneself."*

This also provides an appropriate horizon of understanding for the logical and conceptual currency of the *wrath* of God. It is often forgotten that the semantic opposite of love is not indifference to wrath. It is well established that many children will attempt to provoke parental wrath as a sign that the parent *cares* about them and what they do. C. H. Dodd combines a brilliant insight and a mistakenly reductionist depersonalization of the concept of the wrath of God in Rom. 1:18-32 when he claims that it is used not to describe the attitude of God to man, but to describe an inevitable process of "cause and effect in a moral universe."[41] The positive insight is the perception that *sometimes* the conceptual grammar of *wrath* is "internal": sin brings *its own* consequences, and God some-

---

38. Green and Baker, *Scandal of the Cross,* 146; cf. 91-97 and 147-52.

39. In the Targums *Shekinah* (or, more strictly in Aramaic, *Shekinta*), alongside *memra',* "word," and *y^eqārâ,* "glory," serve as public manifestation of the transcendent God, whose name also reflects his character; see also Hans Bietenhard, "ὄνομα," in Kittel, *TDNT,* vol. 5, 253-83.

40. David J. Reimer, "צֶדֶק," in William VanGemeren (ed.), *New International Dictionary of Old Testament Theology and Exegesis,* vol. 3, 746; cf. 744-69.

41. Dodd, *Romans,* 23.

times permits these to work out their own processes without the need for intervention. However, this may not *exhaustively* describe the conceptual grammar of divine wrath. Would a parent who *never* showed anger at the self-destructive actions of a child genuinely be *not only loving* but *also showing love in integrity*?

Does the "jealousy" of God (Exod. 20:5; 34:14; Deut. 4:24) underline his absolute love for his people? It is not "possessiveness" in the negative sense, for in Ezek. 16:42 the ultimate punishment is for God "to turn away my jealousy from you and be calm." Eichrodt comments, "Israel is brought face to face with his God and his wonderful will to love. . . . Ezekiel is, of course, standing on the shoulders of Hosea and Jeremiah. . . . He is unable to resist employing so bold an image. [They were] led . . . to immerse themselves in the same God's wonderful assurance of his love. . . . He [Ezekiel] tries to make us realize what depths of alienation from God, defying all human efforts at improvements, are laid open by the breaking of a relationship of love and trust."[42] It is nothing like the "optimism" of the Deuteronomist. Ezekiel presents "an explosion of a set of tensions which now exert unbearable pressure. . . . all hitherto hopes . . . are broken in pieces."[43]

The horizons of understanding projected by Jürgen Moltmann are closer to those of Ezekiel than are Dodd's. Moltmann writes of "the experience of the nearness of God in the god-forsaken one, of the divineness of God in the crucified and dead Christ . . . a new totality which annihilates the total *nihil*."[44] Only from within the "vacuum" of the "undisguised harshness of the deadliness of death as compared with the promise of life" does the "victory of praise" emerge.[45] Again, the key to a productive horizon of understanding is "the reverse question" to the usual one: "What does Christ's cross really mean for God himself?"[46] For Moltmann, as for Luther, the "visible being of God is the passion and cross of Christ."[47] God is to be experienced through a *theologia crucis,* not a *theologia gloriae.* Moltmann writes, "God suffers, God allows himself to be crucified and is crucified, and in this consummates his unconditional love. . . . The crucifixion [takes place] as an event of love for the Son and the grief of the Father . . . an event within the Trinity."[48] Moltmann writes, "Even Auschwitz is taken up into the grief of the Father, the surrender of the Son, and the power of the Spirit."[49] In a later work Moltmann writes that a God without sorrow is an "inhuman God," and declares, "A God who cannot suffer cannot love either."[50]

---

42. Walther Eichrodt, *Ezekiel: A Commentary,* trans. C. Quin (London: S.C.M., 1970), 210-13.
43. Eichrodt, *Ezekiel,* 212.
44. Moltmann, *Theology of Hope,* 198.
45. Moltmann, *Theology of Hope,* 210.
46. Moltmann, *Experience of God,* 15.
47. Moltmann, *The Crucified God,* 214.
48. Moltmann, *The Crucified God,* 248-49.
49. Moltmann, *The Crucified God,* 278.
50. Moltmann, *The Trinity and the Kingdom of God,* 38.

The logic of these statements relates broadly but certainly not precisely to the logic of Cranfield's comments on Rom. 3:25 noted above. Without condoning their sin, Cranfield writes, God "purposed to direct against His own very Self in the person of His Son the full weight of that righteous wrath which they deserved."[51] The logic is not the same, for Moltmann speaks of divine anguish, grief, and affliction where Cranfield more readily speaks of "wrath." All the same anguish at the self-destructive will of a loved one may suggest the very tension and self-contradiction that Eichrodt describes in Ezek. 16, and to which Paul seems to allude in Rom. 1:18-32.

It would be unwise to pursue this argument too far, and it requires careful qualification. Pannenberg asserts, "The world must be reconciled to God, not God to the world."[52] Yet within a Trinitarian framework, and within the horizon of "God was in Christ" (2 Cor. 5:19), granted that *everything* about the cross is an *act of God,* the phenomenon of *God's self-involvement* and participation in the self-contradiction of the cross hardly *excludes* a "Godward" dimension that has been initiated by the grace of God himself. To love humankind and to cover sin with "righteousness" might be Paul's equivalent to "acting with integrity," namely to act without retracting the promises and warnings that run through all covenantal traditions from Deuteronomy to the New Testament.

Rom 3:26 implies not that a God of grace is compromised by acting as a vengeful headmaster seeking a scapegoat, but that a God of grace *takes upon himself what it costs to stand by his promises and warnings,* while reconciling the world to himself. Dunn is right, however: expiation and propitiation do not offer an either-or. If we do not totally *exclude* what propitiation (qualified by other models) points to, this *also presupposes* the reality of *expiation.* Nevertheless, on its own *expiation* risks losing something, not least the *personal* dimension of the action. Finally, the adequacy, legitimacy, validity, and force of each term *depend on the horizons of understanding* within which each is used, and their conceptual grammar.

One further factor suggests that *integrity* should have a place in this atonement vocabulary. The centrality of God's own action of grace in and through Christ has often been linked with a use of the verb *must* (Greek δεῖ, *dei, it is necessary that*). This use needs careful logical clarification. In the Synoptic gospels Jesus declares, "The Son of Man *must* (δεῖ, *dei*) suffer much" (Mark 8:31; par. Luke 9:22); "It was necessary (δεῖ, *dei*) for Christ to suffer" (Acts 17:3). The term is used in popular debate more often than in the biblical writings, as in the conservative riposte: "God *must* punish sin." A simple conceptual clarification is required if this is not to mislead us. No external compulsion can be laid upon God. Hence many reject "God must . . ." sentences out of hand. However, this is a classic instance of

---

51. Cranfield, *Romans,* vol. 1, 217.
52. Pannenberg, *Systematic Theology,* vol. 1, 437.

the kind of logical confusion discussed and clarified by Gilbert Ryle.[53] When we say "Justice compels me to . . . ," we are making a hypostasis out of an abstraction. It is simply clumsy shorthand for "if I wish to behave justly, I have no option but to. . . ." Similarly, "God must . . ." or "Jesus must . . ." is always to be explicated in terms of a conditional clause: "If God wills to be true to his promise, he has committed himself already to follow this course of action." If Jesus wills to live out the role assigned to him by his Father and to embody the suffering-vindication pattern of the Scriptures, his only course is to go all the way to the cross. As we shall see in 16.2, Anselm was ahead of the game. He saw that "must" expressed "internal" fittingness and what was entailed in divine consistency.

15.3. Being "in Christ":
The Hermeneutics of Justification by Grace through Faith

Several hermeneutical and conceptual issues arise from attempts to understand the meaning of justification by grace in Paul, and its relation to the same theme in James and Jesus. (1) How is a person righteous and "counted" righteous by God, and simultaneously a sinner? The Reformation aphorism *simul iustus et peccator,* or *semper peccator, semper penitens, semper iustus,* looks *prima facie* like a self-contradictory proposition.[54] (2) What is the role of *faith* if everything comes from sheer *grace* that is given "without strings"? (3) How does Paul's theology of justification by grace relate to the outright condemnation of "faith without works" in James? "Faith apart from works is barren (ἀργή, *argē,* idle, Jas. 2:14, 17, 18). Is this a "contradiction"? (4) Is justification by grace a distinctively "Pauline" doctrine, supposedly absent from the teaching of Jesus and the gospels? I broadly addressed the first three of these questions in *The Two Horizons,* but here I approach them within the horizon of understanding of "being-in-Christ," which did not feature adequately in my earlier discussion.[55]

We begin, therefore, with a preliminary consideration of the Pauline language concerning "being *in Christ,*" which is itself a central description of the Christian condition of salvation as the effect of the work of Christ. In purely linguistic terms the Greek ἐν Χριστῷ ('Ιησοῦ), *en Christō (Iēsou),* denotes one of several things, depending on its context. Johannes Weiss distinguished five: (i) as a shorthand term for "because Christ has come" (Rom. 3:24); (ii) a representative

---

53. Gilbert Ryle, "Systematically Misleading Expressions," *Proceedings of the Aristotelian Society* 32 (1931-32) 139-70, also repr. in Antony Flew (ed.), *Logic and Language,* first series (Oxford: Blackwell, 1951).

54. On Luther's wording see P. Stuhlmacher, *Gerechtigkeit Gottes bei Paulus* (Göttingen: Vandenhoeck & Ruprecht, 1965), 19-23, and Gordon Rupp, *The Righteousness of God: Luther Studies* (London: Hodder & Stoughton, 1953), 225 and 255.

55. Thiselton, *Two Horizons,* 415-27.

use parallel with "in Adam" (1 Cor. 15:22); (iii) as a simple preposition, for example, "glory in Christ" (1 Cor. 1:31); (iv) as an instrumental use (1 Thess. 4:1); and (v) in a "mystical" sense, as in "I can do all things in Christ, who strengthens me" (Phil. 4:13).[56] Adolf Deissmann attempted to make an experiential-mystical understanding of the term the controlling one, but this does not bear scrutiny, not least because Paul's most characteristic uses of the phrases are applied to *all* believers. Wikenhauser observes, "This union [union with Christ] is not something which only Paul has attained. It is true of all Christians without exception."[57] In any case, Paul is normally reticent about "mystical" experiences (2 Cor. 12:1-7).

Albert Schweitzer paved the way for understanding Paul's most explicitly theological use of the phrase by expounding it in terms of *sharing the eschatological status* of Christ through *participation in Christ's death and resurrection.* It denotes "assuming the resurrection mode of existence before the general resurrection of the dead takes place."[58] Thus typically in this sense Paul writes, "If anyone is *in Christ* (ἐν Χριστῷ, *en Christō*) there is [or he or she is] a new creation" (2 Cor. 5:17). "There is therefore now no condemnation for those are in Christ Jesus" (Rom. 8:1).

This clearly overlaps with what Weiss calls the representative use: "As in Adam all die, so will all be made alive in Christ" (1 Cor. 15:22). This representative use presupposes a notion of corporate solidarity, namely sharing the privileges (on the positive side) and the liabilities (on the negative side) of the "in Adam" or "in Christ" solidarity. Russell Shedd expounds this theme in Paul with considerable exegetical detail.[59] It is not altogether fair when critics attack the Reformers for using language of legal imputation or fiction when they speak of being "clothed" in the righteousness of Christ, for what else does Paul mean when he says: "Put on (ἐνδύω, *enduō, be clothed with*) the Lord Jesus Christ" (Rom. 13:14), or "For as many of you have put on (ἐνδύω, *enduō*) Christ" (Gal. 3:27)? The point of this language is to denote *a condition or status which is derived from that of Christ.* James Dunn considers the varied uses and contexts of the eighty-three occurrences of "in Christ" in Paul, rightly stressing the importance of each context. In general, he concludes, it denotes the way in which the community derives what it is "from the shared experience of Christ, which bonded them as one."[60]

The concept of having-died-with Christ and sharing with Christ the resurrection mode of existence prior to the general resurrection is not, as Schweitzer attempted to argue, an entirely different conceptual grammar from that of justi-

56. Weiss, *Earliest Christianity,* vol. 2, 468-69, including note.

57. A. Wikenhauser, *Pauline Mysticism: Christ in the Mystical Teaching of St. Paul,* trans. J. Cunningham (Freiberg: Herder, 1960), 93.

58. Albert Schweitzer, *The Mysticism of Paul the Apostle,* trans. W. Montgomery (London: Black, 1931), 101; cf. 101-76.

59. Russell P. Shedd, *Man in Community: A Study of St. Paul's Application of Old Testament and Early Jewish Conceptions of Human Solidarity* (London: Epworth, 1958), 126-205.

60. Dunn, *Paul,* 401; cf. 396-401.

fication by grace, but precisely what *follows from* "being in Christ." Being in Christ is the horizon of understanding within which the various "problems" associated with justification by grace through faith alone becomes simply questions that receive intelligible answers.

One more comment arises from viewing justification by grace within the context of union with Christ. Paul's contrast between being "in Adam" and being "in Christ" is fundamentally a *structural or corporate* one between two solidarities or orders of existence. But traditionally interpretations of justification by grace through faith have tended to be overly individualistic. A new, corporate, communal, and more "situational" approach has emerged in Liberation Theology especially from José P. Miranda. He argues that Paul's view of the human condition in Rom. 1:18-32 is one of *adikia*, unrighteousness or communal injustice, which includes oppression and exploitation.[61] The law cannot put this right. But the gospel of Christ and kingdom of God bring about a change of situation, which carries with it "putting things right," including restoring social justice.[62] Aspects of Miranda's exegesis may perhaps be questioned, for example, whether his concept of faith is Paul's. Nevertheless he has broadened the horizons of understanding with which to approach the subject, and has shown close relation between Paul and the Old Testament prophets and the teaching of Jesus. We now return to our four questions.

(1) First, the main verb associated with justification, namely Greek δικαιόω *(dikaioō)*, means *"to render a favorable verdict, to vindicate,"* or in some contexts *"to put things right,"* or *"to put in a right relationship with. . . ."*[63] The Hebrew of the Old Testament to which the Greek largely corresponds also denotes the action of a judge pronouncing a verdict. In the Hiph'il of צדק *(ts-d-q)* the verb may mean broadly *to do justice, to declare righteous, to justify, to vindicate.*[64] *To do justice,* in practical terms, is often to *put things right.* The noun form δικαιοσύνη *(dikaiosunē)* may denote justice or righteousness. Ziesler argues that the noun denotes "real righteousness, with no 'as if' about it," but also concedes that it is "the language of relationships and denotes a right relation to God."[65] How then do we judge between "really" righteous and "counted as righteous"? Ziesler observes, "If God looks on believers only as they are found in Christ, he may properly declare them righteous — for in him — and only in him — they are righteous and therefore ought to be acquitted, there is nothing fictional here."[66]

61. José P. Miranda, *Marx and the Bible: A Critique of the Philosophy of Oppression,* trans. J. Eagleson (Maryknoll, NY: Orbis, 1974 and London: S.C.M., 1977), 160-72.

62. Miranda, *Marx,* 201-29.

63. *BDAG,* 3d edn. 2000, 249.

64. *BDB* (new edn. 1980), 842-43.

65. John A. Ziesler, *The Meaning of Righteousness in Paul: A Linguistic and Theological Enquiry,* SNTSMS 20 (Cambridge: Cambridge University Press, 1972), 8.

66. Ziesler, *Righteousness,* 169.

In *The Two Horizons* I drew a distinction between the believer's status or condition within an *eschatological* framework, and the status of believers within the framework of *law and historical processes*. I have only recently come to realize that in broad terms I was following my distinguished predecessor in my Nottingham Chair, Alan Richardson. Richardson also argues that while the Christian's righteousness is real, and not fiction, this righteousness is primarily that of an *eschatological status*.[67] Against F. Prat's contention that Protestant interpretations constitute a *contradiction* ("How can the false be true, or how can God declare true what he knows to be false?"), I argued that while *propositions* can be detached from a context and generate "contradictions," this cannot be said of *verdictive* speech-acts, or of "onlooks" of "*seeing . . . as . . .*" within a specific frame, context, or horizon.[68] Wittgenstein observed that "seeing . . . as . . ." all depends "on the *system* to which the sign [or picture, or utterance] belongs."[69] It is not a "contradiction" to see a drawing *as* a jumble of lines, and then (when told that it relates to a radio) to perceive it *as* a circuit diagram.[70] I explored Wittgenstein's conceptual grammar of "seeing . . . as . . . " and Donald Evans' logical grammar of "onlooks." Evans writes, "'Looking on *x* as *y*' involves placing it within a structure, organisation, or scheme. This often involves the *ascription of a status . . . to x*" (my italics).[71]

Neither Wittgenstein nor Evans has in mind our present subject. But Wittgenstein includes a variety of supporting observations that bear on it, and Evans even adds that sometimes different "onlooks" (or looking on *x* as *y*) may derive from the difference between a present and "futural" structural context. If "being in Christ" means to share Christ's resurrection status in advance of the general resurrection, and if, as Weiss declares, the divine verdict "put right" or "declared righteous" is strictly "a pre-dating of what is really an *eschatological* act," *the logic of the juxtaposition* simul iustus et peccator *becomes transparent:* the believer *remains a sinner strictly within the context or framework of the ongoing course of everyday historical processes,* and insofar as any notion of still being "under the law" is concerned. Nevertheless, "in Christ," who has been raised from the dead as the "last" or "eschatological" Adam, *within the framework and horizon of eschatological existence Christians share the status of Christ as those declared righteous, put right with God,* and "blameless (*unimpeachable;* Greek ἀνεγκλήτους, *anenklētous*) on the day of our Lord Jesus Christ" (1 Cor. 1:8).

67. Alan Richardson, *Introduction to the Theology of the New Testament* (London: S.C.M., 1958), 236-40.

68. Thiselton, *Two Horizons,* 417; cf. F. Prat, *The Theology of St. Paul,* 2 vols. (London: Burns, Oates, & Washbourne, 1945), vol. 2, 247.

69. Wittgenstein, *Zettel,* sect. 228 (his italics).

70. Wittgenstein, *Zettel,* sect. 201.

71. Donald D. Evans, *The Logic of Self-Involvement: A Philosophical Study of Everyday Language with Special Reference to the Christian Use of Language about God as Creator* (London: S.C.M., 1963), 127; cf. 124-41.

The eschatological reality is "brought forward" to characterize the present status of believers. However, they remain, in empirical or historical terms, still "on the way to the salvation" (present participle σῳζομένοις, *sōzomenois*, 1 Cor. 1:18), and the everyday conduct described in 1 Cor. 3:1 through to 1 Cor. 14:40 includes jealousy, strife, envy, inappropriate relationships, misdirected desire, and self-gratification. Yet these sinners are "holy." The Christian is indeed *simul iustus et peccator.*

(2) Yet if all this comes as sheer gift ("What do you have that you did not receive?" 1 Cor. 4:7; "The free gift is not like the trespass," Rom. 5:15), why is a special role also assigned to *faith?* Whiteley is correct to observe that at a popular level there is sometimes a tendency to regard faith as "another kind of work"; as if to imply that normal cards of moral achievement are no value, but faith is like a "trump card" that provides a "work" of a "spiritual" kind, of a higher order than "moral" works. He is also right to insist that for Paul faith was "in no sense a work."[72] Faith *in this context* is the believer's *appropriation of the gift of righteousness,* and this has the effect of *bringing forward the eschatological verdict* *"rightwised" or "not guilty" into the present.* Paul Tillich formulated the point very well in his formula: it is *accepting* that *we are accepted.*[73]

Schweitzer and Weiss pave the way for other interpreters when they observe that this righteousness "belongs strictly speaking" to the future, but also becomes effective in the present. Weiss calls it a "pre-dating" of an eschatological act.[74] Bultmann and Barrett both speak of the "paradoxical" nature of an eschatological verdict that is pronounced in the present.[75] Stuhlmacher, Kertelge, and C. Müller also call attention to the apocalyptic context of this judicial verdict.[76] Tillich's formulation in terms of "acceptance" coheres well with our earlier discussion of dispositional accounts of belief. Faith is not an "intellectual" work, as Bultmann, too, rightly insists. But it includes the *disposition to respond* to accusations (by the self, by others, or by agencies of any kind) of guilt and divine condemnation with an *active response of confidence and trust.* Being in Christ is its ontological *ground;* dispositional response is part of its *appropriation in daily life.* We need to recall, however, that the New Testament and Paul use the word "faith" (πίστις, *pistis*) in a variety of ways, and that the concept expounded in these paragraphs applies only to its use in the context of being-in-Christ and to the appropriation of justification by grace.

72. Whiteley, *Theology of St. Paul,* 162 and 164.

73. Tillich, *Systematic Theology,* vol. 3, 238-42.

74. Schweitzer, *Mysticism,* 203; and Weiss, *Earliest Christianity,* vol. 2, 502.

75. Bultmann, *Theology of the New Testament,* vol. 1, 276; Barrett, *Romans,* 75.

76. Stuhlmacher, *Gerechtigkeit;* Karl Kertelge, *Rechtfertigung bei Paulus: Studien zur Struktur und zum Bedeutungsgehalt des Paulinischen Rechtfertigungs Begriffs* (Münster: Aschendorff, 2d edn. 1967), 112-60; C. Müller, *Gottes Gerechtigkeit und Gottes Volk,* FRLANT 86 (Göttingen: Vandenhoeck & Ruprecht, 1964).

(3) How does Paul's doctrine relate to apparently contradictory statements in the Epistle of James? James writes, "What good is it, my brothers and sisters, if you say you have faith but do not have works? Can faith save you?" (Jas. 2:14). The very contrast of a different universe of discourse underlines the crucial importance of *horizons of understanding* in doctrine. The conceptual grammar of both *faith* and *works* in James is rendered very different from their conceptual grammar in Paul by virtue of a different hermeneutical agenda, different questions, and different horizons. The differences are so great that the term *contradiction* (which would presuppose that terms are used with the same meaning) cannot apply. Jeremias is on the way to making this point when he speaks of their difference of concerns.[77]

James attacks "faith alone" when *faith* denotes an intellectual assent to the truth-claims of monotheism. Hence "even the demons believe — and shudder" (Jas. 2:19). Dibelius writes, "James . . . cannot possibly be concerned about a theologically refined concept of faith."[78] But there is more to this than a different "definition." Peter Davids comments that what James condemns is "claiming to have faith" when this makes no difference *to life and action,* as James's two "parables" or instantiations reveal (attitudes to the poor, Jas. 2:14-17; and the argument from Abraham, 2:21-26).[79] Once again, this is precisely what *dispositional* accounts of belief expose. If there are no practical circumstances in which faith or belief *"make a difference"* that is observable in practical conduct, *in what* does the faith or belief *consist?* James's appeal to "works" amounts to an exposition of a dispositional view of faith within the constraints of first-century conceptual grammar. Paul's language about the active *appropriation* of an eschatological verdict does not come within the terms in which James sets out the debate.

Paul's concept of faith is also self-involving and expressed in the public domain in terms of how a "rightwised" Christian will seek to live. Huge stretches of his epistles address how this faith that has appropriated Christ and the gospel in and through union with Christ is to be "lived out" in everyday "bodily" discipleship.

(4) Any claim that the doctrine of justification by grace is peculiar to Paul and absent from Jesus is breathtaking in its simplistic misreading of Jesus. We have only to consider "the parables of reversal" to see the degree of misperception that is involved in such a verdict. Part of the reason for such a mistake is the overlay of two thousand years of traditions that tend to have the effect of removing the original shock of such parables of sheer grace and reversal of human expectations of supposed "justice."

---

77. J. Jeremias, "Paul and James," *Expository Times* 65 (1955) 368-71.

78. M. Dibelius and H. Greeven, *James: A Commentary on the Epistle of James,* trans. M. Williams, Hermeneia (Philadelphia: Fortress, 1975), 151.

79. Peter H. Davids, *The Epistle of James: A Commentary on the Greek Text,* NIGTC (Grand Rapids: Eerdmans and Carlisle, U.K.: Paternoster, 1982), 119-34.

In Luke 18:9-14 Jesus tells of a Pharisee who went to the temple to pray, and gave thanks to God that his profession, lifestyle, or "reserved occupation" enabled him to study the law, to avoid ceremonial defilement, to elude the company of thieves and rogues, to practice fasting, and to tithe his income to the most minute detail. The thanksgiving is understandable and genuine. Only after centuries of Western Christian traditions could a reader suggest that it is duplicitous or hypocritical. A tax collector now appears "standing far off" with downcast eyes, beating his breast, and saying only a very short, little prayer: "God, be merciful to me, a sinner!" Now comes the shock: "*This man* went down to his home justified (Greek, δεδικαιωμένος, *dedikaiōmenos*) *rather than the other*" (18:14). In the vocabulary of literary theory this exhibits "defamiliarization" and a dramatic reversal of audience expectations.

Grace is as shocking to *Jesus'* audience as it is to Paul's audience in Corinth.[80] It does violence to the parable to see "justification" as a reward for a penitential humility. The "sinner" simply casts himself upon God's mercy, and makes no other claim. He does not say, "See how sorry I am!"

Similar hermeneutical dynamics characterize the parable of the laborers in the vineyard (Matt. 20:1-16).[81] The parable is told in such a way that the audience *expects* that those who have worked for a full day and have borne the heat of the sun will receive more than those who were employed only for the last, cool, evening hour. It is a simple matter of *justice*. Consternation erupts among the audience when it transpires that *all* are given a full day's wage. The employer in the parable explains that the "pay" does not reflect their "works" or what they are thought *to deserve*. The punch line of the parable is: "Do you begrudge *my generosity?*" — or "Are you envious because I am generous?" (NRSV, Matt. 20:15). *Grace* has eclipsed justice, and this is as offensive as the "affront" of the cross proclaimed by Paul in 1 Cor. 1:18-25. Eta Linnemann writes, "What appeared as a breach in the ordered system of justice, was in truth the appearance of *goodness*."[82]

Since the parables are widely regarded as the bedrock of authentic sayings of Jesus, we may cite one more example from this genre, namely the twin parable of the prodigal son and the resentful brother (Luke 15:11-32). J. D. Crossan notes that in Luke the setting of the lost son is shared with that of the parable of the lost coin and the lost sheep (Luke 15:1-32), namely the indignant "murmuring" of the Pharisees and the scribes: "This man receives *sinners* and eats with them."

80. John Dominic Crossan, *The Dark Interval: Towards a Theology of Story* (Niles, IL: Argus, 1975), 101-2, and John Dominic Crossan, *In Parables: The Challenge of the Historical Jesus* (New York: Harper & Row, 1973), 68-69; Walter Wink, *The Bible in Human Transformation: Toward a New Paradigm for Biblical Study* (Philadelphia: Fortress, 1973), 42-43.

81. Cf. Ernest Fuchs, *Studies of the Historical Jesus,* trans. A. Scobre (London: S.C.M., 1864), 32-38 and 154-56.

82. Eta Linnemann, *Parables of Jesus: Introduction and Exposition* (London: S.P.C.K., 1965), 86.

Crossan captures the heart of the response made by Jesus: "Can you imagine, asks Jesus, a vagabond and wastrel son being feted by his father, and a dutiful and obedient son left out in the cold?"[83] Robert Funk comments on the hermeneutical function of this parable: "The word of grace and the deed of grace divide the audience into younger and elder sons — into sinners and Pharisees. . . . They either rejoice because they are glad to be dependent on grace, or they are offended because they want justice on top of grace. . . . They are horrified."[84]

These examples should be enough to discredit attempts to drive a wedge between Jesus and Paul on this subject and on the priority of grace. Parables such as that of the new wine and old wineskins, and the new patch on old clothing, show that Jesus, no less than Paul, proclaims new creation, not simply reformation (Mark 2:21-22). However, the *deeds* of Jesus are decisive here: Jesus has table fellowship with tax collectors and "sinners." His actions corroborate his words of grace, and it is the Pharisees and scribes who are most often the critics of his actions. Paul faithfully reflects the words and deeds of Jesus.

The broader theme of "being-in-Christ" also has parallels (even if not the same idiom) with the Fourth Gospel and Johannine theology. Believers derive their identity from the Vine of which they are branches, and the Vine as a whole *is* Jesus Christ. The branches are "in me" (John 15:2) and "abide in" Jesus (15:4, 5, 7-16). Jesus is the "bread of Life" (John 6:35), whose "flesh and blood" believers "eat and drink" (6:53). From him believers derive resurrection (6:54), and "live forever" (15:58). In the High Priestly Prayer, believers are "in" Christ, and Christ "in" them (John 17:10-24).

In spite of differences of logic and conceptual imagery the dimensions of participation, corporate solidarity, identification, and even substitution appear in John. Certainly the theme of new creation, rather than reformation, is prominent, even if new birth takes the place of death and resurrection (John 3:3-21). The Jesus of the Fourth Gospel declares, "The hour has come for the Son of Man to be glorified. Very truly I tell you, unless a grain of wheat falls into the earth and dies, it remains just a single grain; but if it dies, it bears much fruit" (John 12:23-24). It is hardly reading too much from the simile and symbol of "fruit," whether in these verses or in the Vine discourse, to see close resonances with "being-in-Christ" in Paul. In both cases believers share the very identity, destiny, life, and status of Christ.

It would be appropriate here to consider the complementary writing of the Epistle to the Hebrews. However, Hebrews presents a model in which reflection on the person and work of Christ is inseparable. We shall therefore return to this epistle in our next chapter on Christology.

---

83. Crossan, *In Parables*, 74.

84. Robert W. Funk, *Language, Hermeneutic and Word of God* (New York: Harper & Row, 1966), 16 and 17.

CHAPTER 16

Hermeneutical Factors in the History
of the Doctrine of the Atonement

16.1. The Special Significance of the Apostolic Fathers
and Early Christian Apologists

Ian Henderson distinguishes between two kinds of interpretation in hermeneutics.[1] There is the kind of interpretation that characterizes the reading of a text that is written in code. Once we have decoded the message, we can throw away the original. The other model is more akin to interpreting a work of art or a masterpiece. The hermeneutical process assists the understanding of the original, but the original remains the key to which we constantly return.

We have argued that all the conceptual, metaphorical, and analogical forms of communication that occur in the New Testament to convey understandings of the work of Jesus Christ qualify one another as a whole and as a plurality. Yet this does not suggest any reducibility of the "core" of the apostolic traditions that interpret and transmit a doctrine of the work of Jesus Christ. Over against any tendency to play down the substitutionary nature of the death of Christ as a sacrifice "for our sins" (albeit alongside the themes of representation, identification, and participation), the subapostolic and early Patristic writings are striking in their repetition of this core understanding, even when the gospel has moved (with some exceptions) from Jewish to Greco-Roman soil.

(1) Admittedly *the Epistle of Barnabas,* for example, the dating of which is uncertain but probably between 70 and 150, speaks out of a context that might lead us to expect some account of sacrificial imagery. It attacks Judaism and animal sacrifice, seeing its fulfillment in the sacrifice of Christ. Nevertheless it not

---

1. Ian Henderson, *Myth in the New Testament* (London: S.C.M., 1952), 31.

355

only places a direct quotation of Isa. 53:5-7 in the context of the substitutionary death of Christ, but also goes further than this. We read: "The Lord endured to give his flesh to utter destruction in order that we should be made holy through the forgiveness of sins, which is by the sprinkling of his blood" (παραδοῦναι τὴν σάρκα εἰς καταφθοράν, ἵνα τῇ ἀφέσει τῶν ἁμαρτιῶν ἁγνισθῶμεν, ὅ ἔστιν ἐν τῷ αἵματι τοῦ ῥαντίσματος αὐτοῦ).² Then Barnabas continues, "For the scripture concerning him relates partly to Israel, partly to us, and it speaks thus: 'He was wounded for our transgressions and bruised for our iniquities, by his stripes we are healed" (τῷ μώλωπι αὐτοῦ ἡμεῖς ἰάθημεν, Barnabas 5:2). This theme does not disappear: "the Lord endured to suffer for our life" (περὶ τῆς ψυχῆς, 5:5). Another passage portrays Christ "as a sacrifice for our sins" (ὑπὲρ τῶν ἡμετέρων ἁμαρτιῶν . . . προσφέρειν θυσίαν, huper tou hēmeterōn hamartiōn . . . prospherein thusian) and thereby as a "type" (ὁ τύπος, tupos) of the Isaac event in Gen. 22:1-14 (Barnabas 7:3).

(2) 1 Clement can be more accurately dated at c. 96. Clement of Rome is concerned about church order and unity. But he alludes to the work of Christ explicitly in 1 Clement 49:6. After expounding the gift of the love of God and love in action (1 Cor. 13:6-7), he concludes, "For the sake of the love that He had toward us, Jesus Christ our Lord gave his blood by the will of God for us, his flesh for our flesh (τὴν σάρκα ὑπὲρ τῆς σαρκὸς ἡμῶν, tēn sarka huper tēs sarkos hēmōn), and his life for our lives (καὶ τὴν ψυχὴν ὑπὲρ τῶν ψυχῶν ἡμῶν, kai tēn psychēn huper tōn psychōn hēmōn)" (1 Clement 49:6). Clement also writes, "Let us gaze steadfastly upon the blood of Christ, and know that it is precious to his Father, since it was shed for our salvation."³

(3) Polycarp, Bishop of Smyrna (c. 69–c. 155), frequently quotes passages from the New Testament, and, if Irenaeus is right, provides a direct link between John, Irenaeus, and other leaders in Asia and probably Rome. In his Epistle to the Philippians he quotes 1 Pet. 2:22 and 24. He writes, "In the pledge (ἀρραβών, arrabōn) of our righteousness. . . . Christ Jesus, 'who bore our sins in his own body on the tree (ἀνήνεγκεν ἡμῶν τὰς ἁμαρτίας τῷ ἰδίῳ σώματι ἐπὶ τὸ ξύλον), who did no sin, neither was guile found in his mouth,' endured all things for our sake, that we might live in him" (Polycarp, To the Philippians 8:1). This, again, is not an isolated reference. In his opening paragraphs he writes of "Christ, who endured" for our sins, even to the suffering of death, and whom God raised up (ὑπὲρ τῶν ἁμαρτιῶν, hyper tōn hamartiōn, Polycarp, To the Philippians 1:20).

(4) Ignatius, Bishop of Antioch (c. 35-107) on his way to martyrdom in Rome, exhibited a passion for martyrdom that reflected a theology of identification with Christ in his death and resurrection. Ignatius repeats Paul's declaration

2. Barnabas 5:1.

3. 1 Clement 7:4; cf. also "redemption (λύτρωσις, lutrōsis) through the blood of the Lord" (1 Clement 12:7).

(1 Cor. 1:18-25), "The cross is an affront (σκάνδαλον, *skandalon*) to unbelievers, but to us salvation and eternal life" (*To the Ephesians* 18:1). Through "our God, Jesus the Christ, . . . conceived by Mary by the dispensation of God, as well as by the seed of David, and of the Holy Spirit, the old kingdom was destroyed . . ." (Ignatius, *To the Ephesians* 18:2 and 19:3). The sign of an immovable faith, he concludes, is to be "nailed to the cross of Christ" (Ignatius, *To the Smyrnaeans* 1:1).

Ignatius coins other similes and novel metaphors: "There is one Physician . . . who is God and man" (*To the Ephesians* 7:2). Christians may be "carried up to the heights by the engine of Jesus Christ, that is, the cross, using the Holy Spirit as a rope" (*To the Ephesians* 9:1). In his most widely celebrated saying he implores the church of Rome not to intervene in his martyrdom: "I am God's wheat, and I am ground by the teeth of the wild beasts that I may be found pure bread of Christ. . . . Then I shall be truly a disciple of Christ" (*To the Romans* 4:1-2). But he retains more traditional language: Christ died "for our sake, so that, believing in his death, you may escape death" (Ignatius, *To the Trallians* 2:2; cf. *To the Smyrnaeans* 6:1).

(5) *Justin Martyr* (c. 100–c. 165), among the early Apologists, aims to write as a Christian philosopher to defend the faith with proof of its reasonableness. Hence his language about the cross is all the more striking. He states a substitutionary doctrine of the atonement explicitly. Alluding to Gal. 3:13, he writes: "Although a curse lies in the law against persons who are crucified ('Εν τῷ νόμῳ κατάρα κεῖται κατὰ τῶν σταυρωμένων ἀνθρώπων), yet no curse lies on the Christ of God by whom all that have committed things worthy of a curse are saved."[4] Justin continues, "For the whole human race will be found to be under a curse" (ὑπὸ κατάραν, *hupo kataran*).[5] Justin first cites Deut. 27:26, and then also Deut. 21:23. Our hope, he concludes, rests upon Christ, because God foresaw, and made provision for, what would come to pass, although in this context Justin also perceives it as a prediction of Jewish "curses" against Jesus. Hence he shows how God *removes* the curse.[6]

Justin also formulates symbolic and metaphorical language that has featured in popular Christian devotion over the centuries. Moses cast a *"tree"* into the bitter waters of Marah, with the result that the waters became sweet (Exod. 15:23). A righteous man is like a *"tree"* planted by the waters that causes everything to flourish (Ps. 1:3).[7] Elisha, by casting a *wooden* stick into the Jordan, recovered the blade of an axe, "just as Christ, by being crucified on a *tree* . . . has redeemed us" (*Dialogue with Trypho* 86). However, elsewhere Justin returns to straightforward propositional statements: "By his blood Christ cleanses those who believe in

---

4. Justin, *Dialogue with Trypho* 94.
5. Justin, *Dialogue* 95.
6. Justin, *Dialogue* 96.
7. Justin, *Dialogue* 86.

him."[8] "The Passion of Christ is the mystery by means of which humankind is saved by God."[9]

(6) The anonymous second-century *Epistle to Diognetus* includes four chapters (7–10) on the revelation of the love of God in Christ. They include the confession, "He himself took on himself the burden of our sins. He himself delivered over his own Son as a ransom for us (λύτρον ὑπὲρ ἡμῶν, *lutron huper hēmōn*), the Holy One for the wicked, the innocent for the guilty, the just for the unjust, the incorruptible for the corruptible, the immortal for the mortal: for what else could cover our sins (τὰς ἁμαρτίας ἡμῶν ἠδυνήθη καλύψαι, *tas hamartias hēmōn ēdunēthē kalupsai*) than his righteousness? In whom could we lawless and impious people be justified (δικαιωθῆναι, *dikaiōthēnai*) but in the Son of God only? O sweet exchange! (ὦ τῆς γλυκείας ἀνταλλαγῆς, *ō tēs glukeias antallagēs*)! O unexpected blessing that the wickedness of many should be covered (κρυβῇ, *krubē*) by the righteous One."[10]

(7) *Melito of Sardis* (d. c. 190) writes of the person of Christ as "by nature God and man" (φύσει θεὸς ὢν καὶ ἄνθρωπος, *phusei theos ōn kai anthrōpos*); he then describes the work of Christ in terms of the substitutionary analogy or type of the ram who was substituted in Gen. 22:1-10 to allow "Isaac to be loosed from his bonds. This ram, being put to death, ransomed Isaac. In like manner the Lord, being slain, saved us; and being bound, set us free; being sacrificed, he became our ransom."[11]

The period of the subapostolic writings and the early Christian Apologists is utterly striking in dispelling the myth that the development of Christian doctrine almost disappeared from sight during the so-called "tunnel period," and re-emerged as something different from the New Testament and apostolic doctrine in the Patristic period from Irenaeus (c. 130-200), Clement of Alexandria (c. 150–c. 215) and Tertullian (c. 160–c. 225) onward into the third century with Hippolytus and Origen. The second-century *Epistle to Diognetus* paves the way for the emphasis in Donald Baillie and especially in Moltmann that *God as God* bears human sin in and through Jesus Christ. The second-century Apologists expound this in explicitly vicarious and substitutionary terms, as well as through the language of representation, participation, self-involvement, and identification. The well-known words that begin "O sweet exchange" point to Luther, Calvin, and the Reformers, with their emphasis upon the "covering" of sin and the *gift* of righteousness. The *Epistle of Barnabas* and the very early *1 Clement* convey both participatory and substitutionary understandings of the death of Christ. Theologies of sacrifice and atonement are not hurriedly left behind as embarrassments that belong only to the world of the Old Testament. They are carried

---

8. Justin, *Apology* I:32.
9. Justin, *Dialogue* 74.
10. *Epistle to Diognetus* 9.
11. Melito of Sardis, *Fragments* 1 and 2.

forward with fresh force. It is well to heed the themes of this period before quasi-sociological explanations about power play, politics, and Greco-Roman influences enter into the picture to claim reductive socio-political pressures for the shaping of this doctrine in the Patristic church.

All the same, the apostolic and subapostolic traditions find continued expression in Irenaeus, Clement of Alexandria, and Tertullian. Irenaeus, for example, speaks of the love and forgiveness of God through Christ, appropriating Paul's passage about "blotting out the handwriting of our debt by 'fastening it to the cross' (Col. 2:15) so that by means of a tree . . . we may obtain remission of our debt" (*per quam 'delevit chirographum' debito nostri, et 'affixit illud Cruci' . . . per lignum accipiamas nostri debiti remissionem*).[12]

What humankind "lost" through a *tree* (Gen. 3:1-7), Irenaeus writes, has been regained and made manifest through a *tree*.[13] "By his own blood . . . he [Christ] gave himself as a redemption for those who had been led into captivity. . . . The omnipotent God . . . did righteously redeem . . . his own property. . . . The Lord thus has redeemed us through his own blood, giving his life for our lives, and his flesh for our flesh *(sanguino suo . . . redimens nos redemptionem semetipsum dedit pro his qui in captivitatem ducti sunt)*."[14] Irenaeus continues, "He redeems us righteously from it [apostasy] by his own blood . . . graciously *(suo sanguine redimens nos ab ea . . . benigne)*."[15] We discussed Irenaeus's use of the term "recapitulation" (Greek ἀνακεφαλαίωσις; Latin *recapitulatio*) in an earlier chapter.[16]

Clement of Alexandria, with all his emphasis upon acceptable intellectual "gnosticism" and Christ as a teacher of wisdom, alludes to the sacrifice of Isaac (Gen. 22:1-10) to explain the work of Christ as a sacrificial offering that renders us "redeemed from destruction by the Lord's blood" (τοὺς αἵματι κυρίου ἐκ φθορᾶς λελυτρωμένους, *tous haimati Kuriou ek phthorās lelutrōmenous*).[17] Christ suffered "in order that by his Passion we might live."[18]

Tertullian quotes the work of the Suffering Servant in Isa. 53, reminding a Christian reader who is tempted to flee persecution that "God spared not his own Son for you, that he might be made a curse for us, because 'Cursed is he who hangs on a tree' (Gal. 3:13) — He who was led as a sacrifice, like a lamb before its shearer (Isa. 53:7), so opened he not his mouth, but gave his back to scourges . . . delivered up to the death of the cross . . . that he might redeem us from our sins. . . . It cost the Lord his own blood."[19] Against Marcion, Tertullian insists that

---

12. Irenaeus, *Against Heresies* V:17:2, 3 (Latin, Migne, *Patrologia Graeca*, vol. 7, col. 1170).
13. Irenaeus, *Against Heresies* V:17:3.
14. Irenaeus, *Against Heresies* V:1:1 (Latin, Migne, *Patrologia Graeca*, vol. 7, col. 1121).
15. Irenaeus, *Against Heresies* V:2:1 (Latin, Migne, *Patrologia Graeca*, vol. 7, col. 1124).
16. Irenaeus, *Against Heresies* IV:6:2.
17. Clement of Alexandria, *Paedagogus* I:5.
18. Clement, *Stromata* IV:7.
19. Tertullian, *On Flight in Persecution* 12.

Christ truly did suffer, and quotes the pre-Pauline paradosis from 1 Cor. 15:3-4: "how that Christ died for our sins. . . ."[20] "In Christ's death . . . lies the whole weight and fruit of the name Christian." If it is denied, "God's entire work is subverted" *(totum Christiani nominis et pondus et fructus mors Christi).*[21]

16.2. The Hermeneutical Issues Raised by Anselm's Approach

It has become almost a matter of convention, especially since the publication of Gustaf Aulén's *Christus Victor,* to trace three or sometimes four main "theories of the atonement" in the history of Christian thought. This ground has been traveled frequently, but in the case of Anselm and the Reformers (even if not to the same degree as in the case of Abelard and Schleiermacher) there is still scope for further evaluation, especially in the light of sympathetic clarifications of Anselm's concerns by Barth and by Balthasar.

Two creative contributions in recent years deserve particular note. One has been Jürgen Moltmann's underlining that the mission and even the suffering of Jesus Christ remain a saving work of *God.* Other writers, including Baillie, have explored this approach, but none has done so within such a deeply *participatory* and *Trinitarian* horizon of understanding as Moltmann. God as the Father of Jesus Christ and the co-working of the Holy Spirit are involved in each stage of the action. The notion of God's merely "sending" his Son as if then to stand aside observing the Son doing a work *in his place* is as misguided as Arian misunderstandings about the implications of the word "Son." Anselm's approach may perhaps be less distant from Moltmann's than many seem to imply, and we shall consider Anselm very shortly.

A second creative contribution has been that of Colin Gunton in showing that the multifaceted character of diverse biblical models, metaphors, and concepts *adds to,* rather than subtracts from, the function of the major models and metaphors. Again, Gunton is not the only writer to call attention to this. Ian Ramsey's seminal work on models and qualifiers, which we have discussed already, provides a fertile background to Gunton's approach.

Many writers begin by treating Anselm (1033-1109) as a source of "problems" rather than first *listening* to the questions that he is asking and addressing. Initially a *hermeneutics* of doctrine will first listen, then explore the hori-

---

20. Tertullian, *Against Marcion* III:8.

21. Tertullian, *Against Marcion,* III:8. Although such sources as R. S. Franks, *The Work of Christ: A Historical Study of Christian Doctrine* (London and Edinburgh: Nelson, 1962), survey a range of sources in the early period, a useful collection of "core" material can also be found in an older conservative writer. See Nathaniel Dimock with H. G. Grey, *The Doctrine of the Death of Christ: In Relation to the Sin of Man, the Condemnation of the Law, and the Dominion of Satan* (London: Stock, 1903), Appendix iii-xcii.

zons of understanding within which Anselm's questions make best sense, and then attempt to evaluate his approach in relation to the New Testament, to the history of Christian doctrine, and to the coherence of truth as it developed up to today.

In the first chapter of Book I of *Why God Became Man*, Boso entreats Anselm, "I beg you to show me . . . what necessity and reason led God, although he is almighty, to take upon him the loneliness and weakness of human nature in order to renew it."[22] Anselm is hesitant to offer an answer to so profound a question, but lays down certain axioms that lead *in the direction of* an answer. They may not seem conclusive to unbelievers, but *a doctrine of God demands them*. In chapter 5 Anselm writes: "The redemption of man could be accomplished by no one *except God*," for only *God* can put right the damage caused by human sin.[23] Humankind has sold itself into the bondage of sin, as Augustine has declared (Rom. 7:14-23).[24] However, this does not, as some have implied, give to the devil, rather than to God, any "rights" over humankind, and God alone has the right to redeem humankind. But for the passion of Christ, "the handwriting of the decree" (Col. 2:14) stands against us.[25]

In chapters 8–10 Anselm turns to the *grace* that prompts redemption. In keeping with the meaning of grace as undeserved love, God "stoops" and "humbles himself" as an act of pure divine will, which in itself provides adequate reason for any act of God. The Father "spared not his own Son, but delivered him up for us all" (Rom. 8:32), while the Son came "to do the will of him who sent him" (John 6:38).[26]

Boso inquires into Christ's volunteering "obedience": how is Christ free and yet also constrained to offer *obedience*? Anselm insists, "God did not compel Christ to die, when there was no sin in him, but Christ freely underwent death . . . on account of his obedience in maintaining justice."[27] "The Father wills his death, while he himself [Christ] prefers to suffer death rather than leave the human race unsaved."[28] In chapter 10 Anselm enters the universe of discourse in which we have already argued that language that uses "must" in relation to the death of Christ takes the form of a *logical* condition implying an *internal* "must": *it explicates conditions entailed in God's choosing to act consistently*. God "cannot" (for example) claim to be trustworthy and true, and also tell a lie. It is the "must" of *internal logic, not* of *external compulsion*. Hence, Anselm writes, "We shall at-

---

22. Anselm, *Cur Deus Homo*, trans. E. R. Fairweather and repr. as *Why God Became Man* in E. R. Fairweather (ed.), *A Scholastic Miscellany: Anselm to Ockham*, Library of Christian Classics 10 (London: S.C.M., and Philadelphia: Westminster, 1956), 102, from 100 to 193.

23. Anselm, *Why God Became Man*, Bk. I, ch. 5, 105-6.

24. Anselm, *Why God*, I, 7, 108.

25. Anselm, *Why God*, I, 7, 109.

26. Anselm, *Why God*, I, 8, 110-11; cf. Matt. 26:39; John 14:31; Phil. 2:8-9.

27. Anselm, *Why God*, I, 9, 113; cf. John 14:31; 18:11.

28. Anselm, *Why God*, I, 9, 115.

tribute to God nothing that is at all unfitting . . . nothing that is in the least degree unseemly can be acknowledged in God."[29]

Chapters 11–15 now expound a key issue. Anselm writes, "To sin is the same thing as *not to render his due to God*" (my italics).[30] The debt that we owe is not to be subject to the will of God, and therefore involves the violation of his honor. To restore the honor due requires "some kind of restitution that will please him who was dishonored. . . . Everyone who sins must repay to God the honour that he has taken away, and this is the satisfaction that every sinner ought to make to God."[31]

It is Anselm's "satisfaction" approach rather than Calvin's "penal substitution" approach that first explicates the role of "justice" and "punishment" in this context. Anselm writes, "It is not fitting for God to do anything unjustly. . . . It does not belong to his freedom or kindness or will to forgive unpunished the sinner who does not repay to God what he took away."[32] "God maintains nothing more justly than the honour of his dignity. . . . The honour that was taken away must be repaid, or punishment will follow."[33] Punishment of sinners, to pay what is "owed" to God, restores God's honor. If God did not maintain his honor, "God would seem to fail in his direction of the world."[34]

Chapters 16–18 consider the relation of this to the world of angels, while chapters 19–24 elaborate the seriousness and consequences of human sin. The final chapter of Book I and the whole of Book II consider why the "payment" and satisfaction of God's honor are undertaken and fully performed by Christ. The argument reaches a major turning point in the key axiom in Book II, chapter 6: "*Only a God-Man can make the satisfaction by which man is saved*" (my italics).[35] Anselm fully integrates the person and work of Christ: "*No one but God can make this satisfaction. . . . But no one ought to make it, except him;* otherwise man does not make satisfaction."[36] Boso is said to express satisfaction that he has understood a great truth in response to his inquiry.

Chapters 7–12 now expound the theme of Christ's representation of humankind as true man. Christ is one with sinners yet without sin. He wills to lay down his life as true man. Finally, in chapters 13 through to 22 Anselm shows that Christ's death "outweighs all sins," however great and numerous, even as one and the same death.[37] The effects of the work of Christ are universal, applying to all

29. Anselm, *Why God*, I, 10, 118; cf. Gilbert Ryle's "Systematically Misleading Expressions," in his *Dilemmas*, which we cited above to explicate this issue.

30. Anselm, *Why God*, I, 11, 119 (my italics).

31. Anselm, *Why God*, I, 11, 119.

32. Anselm, *Why God*, I, 12, 121.

33. Anselm, *Why God*, I, 13, 122.

34. Anselm, *Why God*, I, 15, 124; cf. ch. 14, 123.

35. Anselm, *Why God*, II, 6, 150.

36. Anselm, *Why God*, II, 6, 151.

37. Anselm, *Why God*, II, esp. 14-15, 163-65.

generations. Last of all, Anselm returns to the logic of necessity or "must," distinguishing between "external" necessity and that which flows from the divine character as God.[38] In this context we may recall that Anselm formulated the ontological argument for the existence of God.[39] Whether or not it constitutes a strictly philosophical argument or whether, as Barth insists, it represents a Christian confession of faith, Anselm's dialogue raised issues about the status of logical and contingent necessity that arguably escaped some of the logical difficulties about existence as a predicate later unwittingly imported by Descartes, and attacked by Kant and Bertrand Russell.[40]

Anselm concludes *Why God Became Man* with an argument often overlooked by those who sharply dismiss concepts of "imputed" righteousness today. He writes, "If the Son willed to give to another what is owing to himself, could the Father rightly fail him, or deny it to the other?"[41] "How great and how just God's mercy is."[42]

One major issue of interpretation and understanding is the extent to which the "Godward" aspect of expiation, propitiation, or sacrifice should receive the strong emphasis that Anselm places upon it. We discussed this issue in detail with reference to expiation and propitiation in Paul, especially in Rom. 3:25-26. The question is frequently formulated as one of appeasing God's wrath, but we have argued that what Paul terms "God's righteousness" (in Anselm, very broadly "God's honor") might more readily be understood within the horizons of today's world in terms of divine *integrity*. This would cohere very well with Anselm's notion of what is "fitting" in terms not of external compulsion, but of the internal coherence and consistency of the divine nature.

Anselm also boldly raises the question of whether God in Christ has freedom to "give" what Christ's vicarious suffering has won to whomever God in Christ chooses to make a recipient of this purchased gift, irrespective of any logic of "imputation. To some degree Anselm anticipates the fundamental, ultimate question raised by Moltmann: is the arbiter of truth and meaning what the work of Christ means *to humankind,* or what it means *to God?* Moltmann asks: "What does Christ's cross mean to God himself?"[43]

Yet critics of Anselm regularly regard his interpretation as a context-relative

38. Anselm, *Why God,* II, 17, 172-76 and ch. 18, 176-79.

39. Anselm, *Proslogion: With a Reply on Behalf of the Fool by Gaunilo,* trans. M. J. Charlesworth (Oxford: Clarendon, 1965); also in E. R. Fairweather, *A Scholastic Miscellany,* 69-93.

40. Karl Barth, *Fides Quaerens Intellectum: Anselm's Proof of the Existence of God in the Context of His Theological Scheme,* trans. I. W. Robertson (London: S.C.M., 1960).

41. Anselm, *Why God,* II, 19, 180.

42. Anselm, *Why God,* II, 20, 181.

43. Jürgen Moltmann, *Experiences of God,* trans. Margaret Kohl (London: S.C.M., 1980), 15; and Moltmann, *History and the Triune God,* 122.

understanding, limited, first, by its "Latin" legacy from Tertullian and Cyprian and through to Augustine, and most especially limited, second, by notions of "degrees of honour" paid to dignitaries in the eleventh- and twelfth-century feudal system of paying honor to those "higher" within a socio-political hierarchy. The "Latin" tinge is also perceived as reaching back to the quasi-legalistic view of Tertullian of sin as a "debt." But frequently such critiques fail to take full account of the logical integration of Anselm's view of the person and work of Christ.

R. S. Franks, for example, offers three classic criticisms. (1) He sees a logical confusion between satisfaction to an injured party in private law, which depends on the pleasure of the injured party, and the standpoint of public law. (2) Anselm, Franks claims, is supposedly inconsistent in appealing to the categories of merit and satisfaction. (3) An appeal to the role of the person of Christ operates, Franks argues, "in a way fundamentally different from its principal use in antiquity."[44] Are these, however, the genuinely fundamental issues that Anselm's reinterpretation raises?

Even a writer as sophisticated as Daniel Migliore repeats the oversimplified caricature: "Grace is made conditional on satisfaction."[45] But as we observed earlier in our discussion of expiation, grace is the originating motive-force that initially sets the act of "satisfaction" in motion. It is unfair to ask of Anselm, "Is conditional grace still grace?" It is never conditional for humankind; and we should hesitate to describe the intra-Trinitarian purposes of how God chooses to sustain and to maintain his own integrity as "conditional." Anselm is fully aware of the fine nuances of logical, contingent, internal, and external "necessity."

What seems to have troubled many writers in recent years is the affront to egalitarian socio-political attitudes suggested by "degrees" of debt in relation to grades of honor. But the uniqueness of God's dignity, majesty, glory, and honor does not stand or fall with Anselm's feudal analogies. Moreover, the notion of "debt" does not necessarily entail "legalism." The Lord's Prayer includes the petition ἄφες ἡμῖν τὰ ὀφειλήματα ἡμῶν (aphes hēmin ta opheilēmata hēmōn, Matt. 6:12), forgive us our debts; even if Luke 11:4 has τὰς ἁμαρτίας ἡμῶν, our sins, in parallel. Karl Barth comments, "Man is God's debtor. He is a debtor who cannot pay. God has to excuse him. . . . The way in which it is put by Anselm of Canterbury (Cur Deus homo, I, 11, 13, 14) is very accurate and complete. . . . Man as man is bound Deo reddere quod debet . . . the one great honour which he can render to God. . . . He has dishonoured God. . . . God forgives us our sins, giving up his Son in our place."[46]

Hans Urs von Balthasar provides one of the most profound understandings of the hermeneutics of Anselm's approach to the work of Christ. Balthasar re-

---

44. R. S. Franks, The Work of Christ, 140-42.
45. Migliore, Faith Seeking Understanding, 153.
46. Barth, Church Dogmatics, IV:1, sect. 60:3, 485-86.

assesses "the central concept of *debere.*" He writes, "God is simply free. . . . Not the least necessity saddles God's freedom if he decides freely *(sponte)* to save lost mankind."[47] However, "Man has violated God's glory in that 'he has taken away from God whatever he has planned to make out of human nature.'"[48] When humankind wills what it ought, it honors God. But this universe of discourse about debt and honor, Balthasar argues, this "so-called doctrine of satisfaction will have about it nothing of the 'juristic.'" On the contrary, he is at pains to defend himself against any idea of a God of justice, "who would so delight in or stand in need of the blood of the innocent that apart from his death he would not pardon the guilty. . . . It is not a matter of reckoning, but of inner, *ontological* union. . . . The accent is placed on the covenant . . . and on *the obligation God has placed on himself by his decision* that man should remain an authentic partner. That is the understanding of grace."[49] God, Balthasar declares, has "freely bound himself. . . . Anselm's theory cannot be understood juristically."[50]

Colin Gunton suggests that Balthasar has overstated his point. He insists, "There is something of the 'juristic' in so far as Anselm is drawing upon a legal metaphor. . . ."[51] Nevertheless Gunton concedes that Balthasar correctly understands Anselm's "real concern" as with "the relation between creator and creature, not . . . abstract justice."[52] It is a matter of divine governance of the world *as God.* What is at stake is *the "order" of the universe. This is part of the horizon of understanding for a hermeneutic of the doctrine of the work of Christ alongside the priority, sovereignty, and initiative of divine grace.*[53] Emil Brunner offers Anselm rather faint praise, but his assertion that Anselm does not offer a *comprehensive* theological interpretation of the cross of Christ cannot be denied. The issue is rather the other way around. Does not Anselm explicate insights that must be retained as part of a fuller understanding of the atonement? Many critics too readily fasten upon a medieval context as unduly context-relative, and miss the heart of Anselm's larger concerns. These concerns are indispensable for a hermeneutics of the work of Christ.

47. Hans Urs von Balthasar, *The Glory of the Lord: A Theological Aesthetics,* trans. A. Louth et al. and ed. Joseph Fessio and John Riches, 6 vols. (Edinburgh: T&T Clark, 1984-91), vol. 2, *Studies in Theological Style: Clerical Styles,* 245-46.

48. Balthasar, *Glory,* vol. 2, 246-47.

49. Balthasar, *Glory,* vol. 2, 249-50.

50. Balthasar, *Glory,* vol. 2, 250.

51. Gunton, *The Actuality of Atonement,* 91.

52. Gunton, *Actuality,* 91; cf. further 87-96.

53. See further E. R. Fairweather, "Incarnation and Atonement: An Anselmian Response to Aulén's *Christus Victor,*" *Canadian Journal of Theology* 7 (1861) 167-75; and John McIntyre, *St. Anselm and His Critics: A Re-interpretation of the Cur Deus Homo* (Edinburgh: Oliver & Boyd, 1964).

16.3. From Abelard to the Reformers and Aulén:
Further Issues and Horizons

Peter Abelard (alternatively Abailard, 1079-1142) is frequently viewed as the paradigmatic expositor of a "moral influence" theory or interpretation of the atonement. Especially in his *Exposition of Romans* he does not interpret the death of Christ as expiation nor as a ransom. It is not understood as a sacrifice or propitiation or satisfaction, but simply as a supreme exhibition and demonstration of the love of God. The effects of the death are *entirely directed toward humankind*. The purpose of the cross was to melt the human heart. The love of God remains the central theme, although there are also echoes of Clement of Alexandria's emphasis upon the incarnation as a proclamation of divine wisdom to humankind. The work of Christ imparts wisdom and understanding. For didactic purposes (for the word generally is unacceptably ambiguous), it has often been described as a *"subjective"* theological interpretation of the cross.

An excerpt from the operative part of Abelard's *Exposition of Romans* can also be conveniently found in translation in *A Scholastic Miscellany*.[54] Abelard follows Paul in understanding grace as "a free and spiritual gift of God."[55] However, he immediately provides a gloss on the justice or righteousness of God that is open to question. On Rom. 3:19-26 he comments, "'The showing of his justice' — *that is, his love. . . .*"[56] Abelard seeks to defend this synonymous understanding on the basis of a temporal context. He comments, "In this time of grace — that is, of love *(amor)*. . . . So when he speaks of . . . God's righteousness in this time of grace . . . he clearly intimates how he first understood this righteousness to be a love *(caritas)* which perfectly meets the needs of man of our time, which is the time of grace."[57] The first stage of the argument is to treat *righteousness* or *justice* as a *synonym for love (amor* or *caritas)*.

The second stage is to carry the attack to those who argue that the death of Christ is redemption from the dominion of Satan. On the contrary, Abelard argues correctly, the devil has no "rights" over humankind. Further, however, the death of Christ does not signify deliverance from punishment. Abelard writes, "How cruel and wicked it seems that anyone should demand the blood of an innocent person as the price for anything . . . still less that God should consider the death of his Son so agreeable that by it he should be reconciled to the whole world."[58]

The third and concluding stage follows. Abelard writes: "By word and exam-

---

54. Peter Abailard, *Exposition of the Epistle to the Romans (An Excerpt from the Second Book)*, in E. R. Fairweather (ed.), *A Scholastic Miscellany*, 276-87.

55. Abailard, *Exposition*, in *Miscellany*, 279.

56. Abailard, *Exposition*, 279.

57. Abailard, *Exposition*, 279.

58. Abailard, *Exposition*, 283; cf. 280-83.

ple even unto death, he [Christ] has more fully bound us to himself by love, with the result that our hearts should be enkindled by such a gift of divine grace . . . [that we] should not shrink from enduring anything for him."[59] This "redemption" takes the form of "that deeper affection *(dilectio)* in us which . . . frees us from slavery to sin . . . so that we do all things out of love."[60] In this sense, "the love of God is poured into our hearts by the Holy Spirit" (Rom. 5:5).

Many interpreters will endorse the classic summary of Abelard offered by Franks: "He has reduced the whole process of redemption to one single clear principle, viz. the manifestation of God's love to us in Christ, which awakens an answering love in us. Out of this principle Abelard endeavours to explain all other points of view."[61] Franks adds that there are also isolated references in Abelard to Christ's death as a sacrifice, but this need not imply an expiatory sacrifice rather than simply the voluntary laying down of a life. Gustaf Aulén asserts that Abelard sought "to blaze a trail" in a quite different direction from that of Anselm and of Anselm's "Latin" predecessors from Tertullian to Augustine, to emphasize "that Christ is the great Teacher and Example, who arouses responsive love in man."[62]

The impact of the love of God in Christ upon the human heart finds a significant place in the meaning of the cross. But Emil Brunner, among others, is scathing, in effect, in his attack on the exclusion in Abelard's interpretation of *how the death of Christ is in any sense an act of God.* Brunner insists, "Between this death and that of Socrates, the only difference is one of degree, not of principle. The death of Jesus is a sublime and noble martyrdom . . . human love at its highest point. . . . The divine love is manifested. . . . But thinkers of this type have no idea that this . . . represents an actual objective transaction, in which God actually *does* something . . . which is absolutely necessary."[63] When he refers to "thinkers of this type" Brunner is tracing back a line from the late nineteenth century, namely from Ritschl and Schleiermacher, and back through the Socinians to Abelard. Brunner raises a hermeneutical question. He claims that they are "anxious to understand the meaning of the Cross of Christ. But . . . they have completely *failed* to understand the Cross."[64]

A few lines from Brunner cannot be enough to dismiss this tradition, but the issue of hermeneutics does raise a serious problem. Initially it might appear that a "liberal" approach more readily wins a sympathetic hearing on the part of what Brunner calls "rationalistic idealistic" conceptions of religion, and what Schleiermacher calls the "cultured despisers" of religion. But at a deeper and more reflec-

59. Abailard, *Exposition*, 283.
60. Abailard, *Exposition*, 284.
61. Franks, *The Work of Christ*, 146.
62. Aulén, *Christus Victor*, 112.
63. Brunner, *The Mediator*, 439.
64. Brunner, *The Mediator*, 438 (my italics).

tive stage, can this approach genuinely address the *purpose* of such a costly death, and explain how it relates to *God?* Most undergraduates in theology have heard the critical parable: if a stranger jumps off a pier with the words "this is to show you how much I love you," the sheer pointlessness, lack of *logic,* and *irrationality* of such a costly action stares us in the face. At best, as Brunner suggests, we may perhaps see it alongside, for example, the death of Socrates as a tragic but heroic death. The difficulty is that this leaves *so much* that is embedded in the biblical writings and in the history of Christian thought unexplained. *Too much* is turned into a needless blind alley or cul-de-sac that credibility loses more than it gains.

Further, this approach overlooks hermeneutical concerns in a more primary sense. Appropriate horizons of understanding for interpreting the work of Christ cannot exclude its status *as an act of God in Christ.* Moreover, it takes place, as Anselm and Calvin insist, in the context in *God's governance of the world order.* Hence the very aim of this approach, namely to let *human moral conscience* become the arbiter of the freedom of God to choose how to act, lets in by the back door a much more serious problem for moral conscience than that alleged to emerge at the hands of Anselm or the Reformers. The agony of Jesus Christ has the status of a moral *gesture,* and the *Trinitarian* horizon of understanding of the cross, so convincingly and thoroughly understood by Barth, Balthasar, Pannenberg, and Moltmann, becomes lost from view. A hermeneutic of doctrine will leave room for the impact of divine love in Christ; but what the Abelard-Socinus-Ritschl tradition *excludes* cannot be omitted without knocking the heart out of the doctrine.

(3) *The Reformers.* Martin Luther (1483-1546) offers a classic exposition of a substitutionary theology of the atonement, especially in his *Commentary on Galatians.* However, care needs to be exercised about selecting any particular source as a guide to the whole of Luther's enormous range of writings. *The Formula of Concord* (1580) recognized Luther's two *Catechisms* (1529), the *Augsburg Confession* (1530), and Luther's *Schmalkald Articles* (1537). Part II of the *Schmalkald Articles* declares, "Here the first and principal article is: that Jesus Christ, our Lord and God, died for our sins and rose again for our righteousness (Rom. 4:24); and that he alone is the Lamb of God who takes away the sins of the world (John 1:30); and that God has laid upon him the iniquities of us all (Isa. 53:4). All have sinned (Rom. 3:23); and are justified freely without works or their own merits by his grace through the redemption which is in Christ Jesus, in his blood (Rom. 3:24). . . . We must be certain of this doctrine and have no doubt at all of it."[65]

Whether Luther fully subscribes to a "penal" theory and to notions of "satisfaction" has been disputed. R. S. Franks and Philip Watson argue that "satisfac-

---

65. Martin Luther, *The Schmalkald Articles,* trans. W. R. Russell (Minneapolis: Augsburg/ Fortress, 1995), II.

tion" plays little or no part in Luther's theology of the work of Christ. His use of the term, together with language about "merit," emerges, they argue, only in the context of polemic against the Catholicism of the time and theologies of legalism.[66] Luther also draws on the model of Christ's victory over "the powers," as Aulén is eager to point out.[67]

Nevertheless *the substitutionary motif* remains dominant. Luther writes, "Christ was not only crucified and died, but sin also (through the love of the Divine majesty) was laid upon him. . . . And this is a singular consolation for all the godly, so to clothe Christ with our sins, and to wrap him in my sins, and the sins of the whole world, and so to behold him bearing all our iniquities. . . . If he be the Lamb of God ordained from everlasting to take away the sins of the world, if he be so wrapped . . . in our sins that he became accursed for us. . . . God laid our sins not upon us but upon his Son, Christ, that he bearing the punishment thereof might be our peace, and that by his stripes we might be healed."[68]

On the other hand, Luther does not stress the role of substitution in such a way that it excludes the central role of *identification with Christ,* or the *participatory,* representative, and self-involving dimensions of Christ's work and its appropriation by faith. This emerges in the early *Heidelberg Disputation* of 1518: "In Christ crucified is the true theology and knowledge of God. . . . God is not to be found except in sufferings and in the cross."[69] The believer is identified with and involved in the way of the cross. The Christian shares in Christ's death and resurrection. All the same, since, as Luther expresses it, "we could never be delivered from it [the effects of sin and "curse" of the law] by our own power, [the Father] sent his only Son into the world and laid upon him the sins of all men. . . . By this means the whole world is purged and cleansed from all sins, and so delivered from death."[70]

John Calvin (1498-1552) formulates his approach to the work of Christ mainly in the *Institutes,* Book II, chapters 6–17, as well as in his commentaries. Calvin introduces a fundamental principle: "God never showed himself propitious to his ancient people, nor gave them any hope of grace, without a Mediator."[71] In Calvin's view the effective work of mediators, including Moses and David under the old covenant, was based upon an anticipation of the work of Christ as Mediator.

---

66. Philip S. Watson, *Let God Be God: An Interpretation of the Theology of Martin Luther* (London: Epworth, 1947), 188-22; and Franks, *Work of Christ*, 288-300.

67. Martin Luther, *Luthers Werke: Briefwechsel, Bd. XI, 1, Januar, 1545–März, 1546,* Kritische Gesamtausgabe (Weimar: H. Böhlaus Nachfolger, 1948), 432-33 (abbreviated as WA).

68. Martin Luther, *A Commentary on St. Paul's Epistle to the Galatians,* trans. Philip S. Watson (London: James Clarke, 1953), 271.

69. Luther, *The Heidelberg Disputation* 20 and 21, in *Luther: Early Theological Works,* Library of Christian Classics 16, ed. J. Atkinson (London: SCM, 1962), 291.

70. Luther, *Galatians,* 272 (also WA, vol. 40, 437-38).

71. Calvin, *Institutes,* II:6:2 (Beveridge edn., vol. 1, 294).

The sacrificial system of the Old Testament was similarly ordained and willed by God as that which led up to its fulfillment in the sacrifice of Christ. The *sacrificial* nature of Christ's death and Christ's role as *Mediator* are therefore more than merely two themes or images among others; they are *paradigmatic* for any "core" understanding of the work of Christ as the fulfillment of promise in the Old Testament and as the definitive ordinances of God, on which the efficacy of *grace* in the Old Testament depended.[72]

Calvin declares, "The only end [or reason] given in scripture for the Son of God voluntarily assuming our nature and receiving it as a command from the Father is that he might propitiate the Father to us by becoming a victim [or sacrifice]."[73] "To redeem us from this curse [of sin in relation to the law] Christ was made a curse for us (Deut. 21:23, compared with Gal. 3:13; 4:4)."[74] In language that hints at Reid's distinction (above) between correspondence and contrariety, Calvin points out that since humanity is "dead in your sins . . ." (Col. 2:13), *only Christ can do for humankind what humankind cannot do for itself.* Calvin writes, "His eternal sacrifice, once offered, had abolished those daily sacrifices."[75]

In the *Institutes,* Book II, chapter 12 Calvin relates together the person and work of Christ in ways not dissimilar to Anselm. Issues of "necessity" arise from *within* the will of God "by divine decree," not from any external compulsion.[76] However, the work of Jesus Christ as both true God and true man emerges more fundamentally within the horizon of mediation rather than satisfaction. Calvin does not shrink from emphasizing (against Osiander) the genuine humanness of Christ, citing Heb. 4:15, "He was in all points tempted like as we are, yet without sin."[77] Book II, chapters 13-14, continue to expound a "two natures" Christology, and chapter 15 then expounds the threefold work of Christ as prophet, priest, and king.

In chapter 16 of Book II Calvin returns to the theme of Christ as Redeemer. He begins with the all-sufficiency of the work of Christ. He writes, "Condemned, dead, and lost in ourselves, we must in him seek righteousness, deliverance, life and salvation."[78] Article 6 explicitly addresses "why Christ was crucified": it was in "bearing, by substitution, the curse due to sin. . . . He made his soul אשם (*'āshām*), i.e., a propitiatory victim for sin (as the prophet says, Isa. 53:5, 10) on which the guilt and penalty being in a manner laid, ceases to be imputed to us. . . . 'He made him to be sin for us' . . . (2 Cor. 5:21)."[79]

---

72. Calvin, *Institutes,* II:6:4; II:7:1-5, and II:9:1-3.
73. Calvin, *Institutes,* II:12:4 (Beveridge edn., vol. 1, 403).
74. Calvin, *Institutes,* II:7:15 (Beveridge edn., vol. 1, 311).
75. Calvin, *Institutes,* II:7:17 (Beveridge edn., vol. 1, 312-13).
76. Calvin, *Institutes,* II:12:1 (Beveridge edn., vol. 1, 400-401).
77. Calvin, *Institutes,* II:12:7 (Beveridge edn., vol. 1, 406); further II:13:1-3; 14:1-8.
78. Calvin, *Institutes,* II:16:1 (Beveridge edn., vol. 1, 434).
79. Calvin, *Institutes,* II:16:6 (Beveridge edn., vol. 1, 439).

This is probably the clearest commitment to a theology of penal substitution in the history of the doctrine of the work of Christ. However, even Calvin includes the phrase "in a manner," as if to imply that more might be said, and elsewhere in the *Institutes* and in his *Commentaries* he speaks of bearing the cross in identification with Christ. He writes, "Every one of them [Christian disciples] must 'take up his cross' (Matt. 16:24)."[80] Christians must share adversity, as Christ did.[81]

Calvin's horizon of understanding is the frame of reference brought to bear by the Old Testament themes of grace, law, mediation, and sacrifice. The issue identified by Anselm and today by Moltmann, "What did the cross of Christ mean to God?" is presupposed rather than explicitly stated. But contrary to his popular image, Calvin is more clearly an expositor of Scripture than a "hermeneutical" theologian. His comment that he wrote the *Institutes* all the better to keep "doctrine" from interfering with exegesis in his commentaries is vindicated by the *Institutes*.

A hermeneutic of a doctrine of the cross will need to ask: given the buildup of conceptual grammar arising from God's self-revelation and his dealings with Israel, are these ordinances to be viewed as irreducible paradigms or as dispensable concepts when we seek to formulate appropriate horizons of understanding for interpreting the work of Christ today? For Calvin, the Mosaic sacrifices are types that both interpret, and are interpreted by, the antitype and "archetype" of Christ.[82]

(4) *Gustaf Aulén.* Aulén begins his Uppsala Lectures of 1930, published as *Christus Victor,* by examining critically a widespread view that the Patristic church had no developed theology of the atonement, but that formulations of a doctrine began with Anselm, were drastically reformulated by Abelard, and then reformulated once again by the Reformers, notably by Calvin. Aulén rejects such a reconstruction. The early church, he argues, did formulate a doctrine of the atonement, and this was different in emphasis from that of Anselm, Abelard, or the Reformers. At its heart was "the old mythological account of Christ's work as a victory over the devil," which, he claims, Anselm repressed or squeezed out.[83]

Aulén classifies the approaches of Anselm and Abelard respectively as "objective" and "subjective" theories of the atonement. The former involve what Aulén calls "a changed attitude on the part of *God*"; the latter involve only a change of attitude on the part of *humankind*.[84] Aulén expresses this in the overgeneralized and unguarded way that many have used it, but it is not strictly accu-

---

80. Calvin, *Institutes,* II:8:1 (Beveridge edn., vol. 2, 16).

81. Calvin, *Institutes,* II:8:8-11 (Beveridge edn., vol. 2, 21-24).

82. Calvin, *Institutes,* II:16:6 (Beveridge edn., vol. 1, 439).

83. Gustaf Aulén, *Christus Victor: An Historical Study of the Three Main Types of the Idea of the Atonement,* trans. A. G. Hebert (London: SPCK and New York: Macmillan, 1931), 18.

84. Aulén, *Christus Victor,* 18.

rate, and tends to load the dice against Anselm and Calvin. Within a hermeneutical horizon of grace God's attitude does *not* "change"; *his purposes were and are always gracious;* but God *implements* this grace on the basis of the work of Christ with righteousness, consistency, and *integrity* in ways that define his dealings with the world.

The last two centuries, Aulén writes, reflect the coexistence of these two types, the objective and the subjective. Anselm and Calvin represent the former. The subjective is represented first by Socinianism, and then in the modern period by the Enlightenment, Schleiermacher, and Ritschl. But both, Aulén continues, ignore the "dramatic" theme of "the Atonement as a Divine conflict and victory; Christ — Christus Victor — fights against and triumphs over the evil powers of the world, the 'tyrants' under which mankind is in bondage and suffering, and in Him God reconciles the world to Himself."[85]

Aulén concedes that this theme is not the only way of understanding the atonement. However, this "dramatic" view is a special type, which portrays "a *continuous* Divine work" (his italics) in contrast to the "finished" work of Christ as an offering made to God by Christ as "a *discontinuous* Divine work."[86] He terms the first of these two views "the dualist-dramatic" or "classic" view; and the second, the "objective" or "Latin" type of approach. He attacks the tendency to confuse these two, especially in the nineteenth century.

Liberal theologians, Aulén argues, backed away from the "classic" view because it appeared too "mythological."[87] Dualism seemed to suggest a view of demonic forces unworthy of theism. Perhaps too optimistically from his point of view, he predicted a radical shift toward his "classic" view, first in the light of reassessments of the history of doctrine by Harnack and others, and second, in the light of reassessments of Luther, whom he attempts to place within the "classic" rather than "objective" model of thinking.

Predictably Aulén draws on the theology of Irenaeus, whose work we briefly reviewed in 16.1. He describes as "typical" such passages from Irenaeus as the following: "He who is the almighty Word and true man, in redeeming us reasonably *(rationabiliter)* by His blood, gave Himself as the ransom for those who had been carried into captivity. . . . He redeemed that which was His own, not by violence, but by persuasion."[88] Irenaeus clearly believes that the purpose of the work of Christ is "that he might destroy sin, overcome death, and give life to humankind *(ut occideret quidem peccatum, evacuaret autem mortem, et vivificaret hominem)*."[89] Adam became "the devil's possession, and the devil held him under his

---

85. Aulén, *Christus Victor,* 20.

86. Aulén, *Christus Victor,* 21-22.

87. Aulén, *Christus Victor,* 26.

88. Aulén, *Christus Victor,* 43; Irenaeus, *Against Heresies* V:1:1, cited in part in our discussion above.

89. Irenaeus, *Against Heresies,* III:18:7.

power. . . . [But] he who had taken man captive was himself taken captive by God, and man was set free from the bondage of condemnation."[90] Aulén claims that the victory motif "stands in the centre of Irenaeus' thought."[91]

Be that as it may, in our discussion of the Apostolic Fathers and early Christian Apologists, we noted that Irenaeus also uses other models of the atonement, and we may question whether the victory motif is the most prominent theme in other second-century writers. Colin Gunton, among others, questions the centrality of the role of this approach within the New Testament. Wesley Carr, Gunton notes, casts doubt on the use made of Col. 2:13, which is one of the key passages to which Aulén appeals.[92]

The case may well be stronger with reference to Origen, Gregory of Nyssa, and Gregory of Nazianzus. Origen portrays Christ as overcoming the power of demons both in his ministry and by his death, and sees the church as still at war with demonic forces.[93] But there is no "payment" to Satan.[94] Gregory of Nyssa propounded the infamous fishhook analogy, whereby Satan seized the bait of the humanity of the crucified Christ, thereby to experience defeat at the hands of his disguised divinity.[95]

Gregory of Nazianzus also understood the death of Christ as bringing about the defeat of evil powers. But he very firmly rejects Gregory of Nyssa's notion of payment *to* Satan. He writes, "To whom was that Blood offered that was shed for us, and why was it shed? . . . We were detained in bondage by the Evil One, sold under sin. . . . I ask, to whom was this offered? If to the evil one, away with such *hubris* (φεῦ τῆς ὕβρεως, *pheu tēs hubreōs*). . . . A ransom which consists of God himself . . . *if to the Father, how?* Humanity must be sanctified by the humanity of God, that he might deliver us himself, and overcome the tyrant and draw us to himself by the mediation of his Son."[96]

Aulén's claims that in spite of such criticisms, "the idea of a transaction with the devil . . . was firmly established in the early church." But this is a matter of dispute, and should be treated with caution. The theme of victory over the devil is indeed a "firmly established" theme at a certain level, but what kind of victory is in view? George Caird argues that the "victory" of the martyrs in the book of Revelation is achieved by renouncing property, status, security, or even life in loyalty to Christ. This is a different kind of victory. Caird writes more generally,

---

90. Irenaeus, *Against Heresies*, III:23:1.

91. Aulén, *Christus Victor*, 37.

92. Gunton, *Actuality of Atonement*, 55; cf. Wesley Carr, *Angels and Principalities: The Background, Meaning, and Development of the Pauline Phrase 'hai archai kai hai exousiai,'* NTSMS (Cambridge: Cambridge University Press, 1981), 168-76.

93. Origen, *Against Celsus* 1:31, 7:17, and 8:44.

94. Origen, *Commentary on Matthew*, 16:8.

95. Gregory of Nyssa, *Great Catechism* 22–27.

96. Gregory of Nazianzus, *Orations* 45:22; cf. 39:13.

"Satan's strongest hold over the human race is gained through moral lapse. He is 'the spirit that is now at work in the sins of disobedience' (Eph. 2:2)... . Satan operates through the corrupted institutions of Church and state."[97] "Victory" is the progressive drama of the transformation of the vicious circle of sin and structural evil into righteousness, integrity, and love, and this has as much to do with Abelard's vision as with Aulén's.

To be fair to his aims, however, Aulén perceives the victory motif as offering a middle way between the subjectivism and liberalism of the Abelard-Socinus-Schleiermacher-Ritschl approach and the "objective" approach of Anselm, at least in terms of "satisfaction." Aulén rightly criticizes the older liberal "Jesus *versus* Paul" argument as reflecting respectively the "subjective" and "objective" models.[98] Both Jesus and Paul saw the work of Jesus Christ as "a ransom for many" (Mark 10:45); as "redemption through his blood" (Eph. 1:7); as "a ransom for all" (1 Tim. 2:6); and as "eternal redemption" (Heb. 9:12).[99]

Yet Aulén, as we have noted, does not claim exclusiveness or universality for this way of approach. He allows, for example, that the Epistle to the Hebrews regards the sacrifice of Christ both as God's own act of sacrifice and as a sacrifice offered to God, although he insists (controversially) that this double emphasis is "always alien to the Latin type."[100] In the end he allows that the New Testament expresses its doctrine "with many variations of outward form." His aim here is to deny special privilege either to the "Latin" or to the "Liberal" form.[101] In particular he seeks to argue that we should view Luther as a strong advocate of the "classical" model.[102]

This last claim contains some truth, but seems also one-sidedly overstated. Aulén stands on firmer ground when he claims that the "classic" idea almost dropped out of sight, leaving an overly polarized debate between "objective" and "subjective" views. Each approach has significant hermeneutical impact, and each operates within distinctive horizons of understanding. *Conflict and victory* do indeed remain fundamental aspects of salvation and of the Christian life, and attempts to rob baptismal liturgy of the imagery of "fighting under Christ's banner as his soldiers" owes more to political correctness than to healthy doctrine. Yet the conflict motif can be romanticized in ways alien to the hermeneutical horizons of the New Testament, and the conflict theme does not seem as dominant as Aulén claims. Even more to the point, he does not do justice to Anselm or to Calvin in noting their emphasis upon the self-involvement of both God and humankind in the "transaction" of the atonement. It is false simply to describe their

---

97. George Caird with L. D. Hurst, *New Testament Theology* (Oxford: Clarendon, 1994), 110.

98. Aulén, *Christus Victor*, 77-89.

99. Aulén, *Christus Victor*, 89.

100. Aulén, *Christus Victor*, 93.

101. Aulén, *Christus Victor*, 94-96.

102. Aulén, *Christus Victor*, 119-38; cf. 139-49.

approach as "objective" without more ado. We may recall Wittgenstein's warning about the capacity of "a drop of grammar" to conceal a whole philosophy or doctrine. Aulén has to some extent been seduced (if not guilty of seducing others) by his overgeneralizing schematic terminology. In Part I we have regularly warned against this in the interests of hermeneutical particularity.

Our survey of the subapostolic writings and the early Christian Apologists suggested that the theme of *vicarious sacrifice* marked a core of continuity with the New Testament, even if this is by no means the only central core of continuity. We also noted that, in accordance with the logic explicated by J. K. S. Reid, *substitutionary* concepts in no way *exclude* the role of identification, participation, and representation. Rather, these understandings belong together. This is what Aulén's portrait of Calvin seems to miss, although he readily sees it in Luther.

Abelard's approach reminds us to keep the *love of God* in the center. More strictly, *love and grace* provide the overarching horizon of understanding for everything else about the work of Christ. But to stress this horizon is to take the first step without embarking further on the journey. Anselm and Calvin show that divine integrity and the divine governance of the world also form part of a necessary horizon of understanding. Today, in the early twenty-first century, Moltmann has enlarged that horizon in further needed directions. He writes, "I no longer asked what the cross of Christ means for human beings, but *also* asked what the cross of the Son of God means for God himself, whom he called 'my Father.' I found an answer to this question in the perception of the deep *suffering* of God, which is bound up with the death of the Son in Golgotha and becomes manifest in him. It is the suffering of a boundless love."[103]

Here is the most fundamental hermeneutical horizon in both senses of the word "horizon." It places the doctrine of the work of Christ fully within the doctrine of divine grace and within the doctrine of the Trinity, from which it derives its theological truth and intelligibility. It also provides a horizon of hermeneutical communication within which those who seek a fuller understanding may engage with "questions that arise" where they already stand.

---

103. Jürgen Moltmann, *History and the Triune God: Contributions to Trinitarian Theology,* trans. John Bowden (London: S.C.M., 1991), 122. See also Moltmann, *Experiences of God,* 15.

CHAPTER 17

Hermeneutical Approaches to Christology

17.1. "Jesus is Lord":
Existential Hermeneutic and/or Ontological Truth-Claims?

"Problems" in modern Christological debates sometimes seem to reveal a deep chasm between the universe of discourse in which some New Testament specialists operate and that of many systematic theologians. Part of the difference of approach may relate to the difference between "Christologies from below," in which many New Testament specialists look to historical reconstruction to trace the words and deeds of Jesus of Nazareth, and "Christologies from above," in which formulations of doctrine may begin with the mission and person of Christ in Trinitarian terms, in which the incarnation intervenes between a state of pre-existence and restored glory.

Thus Maurice Wiles speaks of the need to tell "two stories . . . a human story . . . and also a mythological story of God's total self-giving." He continues, "We may interweave these two stories. . . . But we do not need — indeed, in this analysis we would be wrong — to tie these two stories together."[1]

The difference between Christologies "from below" and "from above" contributes to the problem, but does not account for the whole problem. A number of distinguished systematic theologians in fact begin with a Christology "from below" and bring to bear a horizon of understanding that explicates this in terms of fuller Trinitarian Christology. The most outstanding example of this is Pannenberg's Christology. He writes, "The concept of the incarnation is a relevant expression of the implied significance of the *coming and history of Jesus.* . . .

---

1. Maurice F. Wiles, "Does Christology Rest on a Mistake?" *Religious Studies* 6 (1970) 69-76; repr. in S. W. Sykes and J. P. Clayton (eds.), *Christ, Faith and History: Cambridge Studies in Christology* (Cambridge: Cambridge University Press, 1972), 9; cf. 3-12.

This means that the human and historical reality of Jesus of Nazareth can be appropriately understood only in the light of his coming from God. . . . Hence we cannot regard a Christology from below as ruling out completely the classical Christology of the incarnation."[2] Moltmann, too, declares, "The New Testament talks about God by proclaiming *in narrative* the relationships of the Father, the Son, and the Spirit, which are relationships of fellowship and *open to the world*" (my italics).[3]

A more serious contributory factor is the relegation to the category of "myth" any attempt in the New Testament to portray *trans*empirical realities that take place *within* the world. Such language is self-contradictory only if we begin with a positivist or naturalistic *worldview.* This is not quite the same as holding a positivist *ontology,* for a writer such as Bultmann may speak of God as more than a merely human projection, but not of God's action *within a naturalistic world order.*

Historically this goes back in part to Kant's notion of God as a presupposition of the world rather than as an agent who acts in the world. In part, through David F. Strauss it can be traced back to Hegel's contrast between *Vorstellung, representation,* in religion, and *Begriff,* critical *concept,* in philosophy. Strauss perceived of *myth* as that which conveyed ideas represented in narrative form. Today, thanks largely to Paul Ricoeur, Hans Frei, and a number of literary theorists, a deeper appreciation of the complex modes of narrative forms has emerged. Meanwhile, however, some New Testament specialists appear still trapped in Bultmann's mid-twentieth-century past, maintaining in Bultmann's words that "the New Testament represents the Christ-occurrence as a mythological occurrence."[4] To the extent to which he is "the Son of God, a pre-existent, divine being," Christ is "to that extent a mythical figure." Since he is also portrayed as "a concrete figure of history," Bultmann concludes, "we have here a unique combination of history and myth."[5]

I have discussed Bultmann's different understandings of *myth* in considerable detail elsewhere.[6] However, to sharpen the present argument we may recall that Bultmann deploys three distinct understandings of myth, and that these are not necessarily compatible.

(i) The most significant, which Bultmann derived in part from Hans Jonas

2. Pannenberg, *Systematic Theology,* vol. 2, 288.

3. Moltmann, *The Trinity and the Kingdom of God,* 64.

4. Rudolf Bultmann, "New Testament and Mythology: The Problems of Demythologizing the New Testament Proclamation," in Rudolf Bultmann, *New Testament and Mythology and Other Basic Writings,* selected, ed. and trans. by Schubert M. Ogden (Philadelphia: Fortress, 1984) 32; also in Hans-Werner Bartsch (ed.), *Kerygma and Myth,* trans. R. H. Fuller, 2 vols. (London: S.P.C.K., 2d edn., vol. 1, 1964 and vol. 2, 1962), vol. 1, 34.

5. Bultmann, *New Testament and Mythology,* 32; also in *Kerygma and Myth,* vol. 1, 34.

6. Thiselton, *The Two Horizons,* 205-92.

and Martin Heidegger, arises from the attempt *to describe in objectifying language what can (or should) be expressed in nonobjectifying or deobjectifying terms.* It would have avoided endless confusion if Bultmann had renamed his program one of "deobjectification." He writes, "The real *purpose* of myth is not to present an objective picture of the world as it is. . . . Myth should be interpreted . . . existentially."[7]

(ii) A second understanding amounts to little more and little less than the use of *analogy,* or even *imagery.* Bultmann writes, "Mythology is the use of imagery to express the other-worldly in terms of this world, and the divine in terms of human life."[8]

(iii) The third understanding moves from issues of conceptual or linguistic *mode* to that of alleged *content.* Bultmann explains, "The world is a three-storey structure with earth in the middle, heaven above it, and hell below it. Heaven is the dwelling place of God and of heavenly figures."[9] University of Nottingham philosopher Ronald W. Hepburn demonstrated the confusing and logically self-defeating effect of mixing definitions of form with definitions of content in this way.[10]

The incisive criticisms that have been articulated over the years of Bultmann's uses of the term *myth* should have alerted Maurice Wiles and others to the overly loose and unhelpful currency of the term in the context of Christology. Nevertheless this approach does shed light on hermeneutical issues in the present discussion by pointing to the *role of the existential or self-involving understanding of language* about Christ. It is less helpful on language about Christ *that serves ontological truth-claims.* The first relates primarily to *hermeneutics;* the second relates also to *doctrinal statements.*

This brings us to the first of several concrete examples, and concerns first *confessions of Christ as Lord* (κύριος, *Kurios*). In Part I we saw that early Christian *confessions* played a major part in the expression of *beliefs* especially as early Christian creeds. Bultmann, following Johannes Weiss, is correct to observe that what the currency of language about the lordship of Christ *actually means* is best perceived, at least initially, in what it is for the Christian believer to be *the slave of Christ.* Weiss writes, "What it [the confession "Jesus is Lord"] means in a practical religious sense will best be made clear through the correlative concept of 'servant' or 'slave' of Christ."[11]

To call Jesus "Lord," another writer comments, involves for Paul "surrender,

7. Bultmann, in *Kerygma and Myth,* vol. 1, 10; also *New Testament and Mythology,* 9.

8. Bultmann, in *Kerygma and Myth,* vol. 1, 10, n. 2; also *New Testament and Mythology,* 42, n. 5.

9. Bultmann, *New Testament and Mythology,* 1; also in *Kerygma and Myth,* vol. 1, 1.

10. Ronald W. Hepburn, "Demythologizing and the Problem of Validity," in A. Flew and A. MacIntyre (eds.), *New Essays in Philosophical Theology* (London: S.C.M., 1955), 227-42.

11. Weiss, *Earliest Christianity,* vol. 2, 458.

obedience, reverence, trust, and grateful love."[12] As I have argued elsewhere, we should not be misled by understandably pejorative nuances of the term *slave* in the first century or today. In the first-century Roman world, the nature and conditions of slavery *depended hugely on the character of the slave owner, the purpose for which the slave was purchased or acquired, and the role assigned to the slave* within the household.[13]

Bultmann rightly affirms a *hermeneutical* horizon within which the lordship of Christ is seen in terms of the Christian experiences of trust, commitment, and freedom. He cites Rom. 14:7-9: "We do not live to ourselves, and we do not die to ourselves. If we live, we live to the Lord, and if we die, we die to the Lord; so, then, whether we live or whether we die, we are the Lord's. For to this end Christ died and lived again, so that he might be Lord of both the dead and the living." Bultmann writes that on this basis "the believer . . . no longer 'belongs to himself'. He no longer bears the care of himself, for his own life, but lets this care go, yielding himself entirely to the grace of God."[14] *This is the self-involving or existential hermeneutic of the term.*

Even part of the Old Testament background resonates with this aspect. As Weiss and Beardslee stress, to be compelled into the service of God was thought to be of greater honor and freedom than to be a mere "independent" individual, solely responsible for one's own care, security, and circumstances.[15] The slave of a person of note often enjoyed more security, honor, well-being, and safety than a "free" individual without a patron or protector, although clearly a menial slave was merely a "thing" (Latin *res*) at the disposal of a master.

All the same, does *Kurios* convey no cognitive content? Does it make no ontological truth-claim? Clearly, as Dunn observes, "Jesus' Lordship was central for Paul. . . . He summarizes his gospel as the preaching of Jesus Christ as Lord (2 Cor. 4:5). . . . In 1 Cor. 12:3 he uses the confession 'Jesus is Lord' as the decisive test of whether inspiration is from the Holy Spirit or not."[16] Since the confession "Jesus is Lord" serves in effect as a criterion of being a Christian, this must include more than assenting to an intellectual head-belief about the status of Jesus Christ. To this extent Bultmann's view that it is an existential confession receives corroboration. Nevertheless the meaning of the confession *cannot be cashed out exhaustively and without remainder in existential terms.* In the early apostolic

12. H. A. A. Kennedy, *The Theology of the Epistles* (London: Duckworth, 1919), 84.

13. Thiselton, *First Epistle to the Corinthians*, 475-79, 534-40, and esp. 562-65. Other writers to whom these pages refer include Dale Martin, *Slavery as Salvation* (New Haven and London: Yale University Press, 1990), esp. 63-68, and Thomas Wiedemann, *Greek and Roman Slavery* (London: Groom Helm, 1981) and *Slavery, Greece and Rome* (Oxford: Oxford University Press, 1997).

14. Bultmann, *Theology of the New Testament*, vol. 1, 331.

15. Weiss, *Earliest Christianity*, vol. 2, 459; William A. Beardslee, *Human Achievement and Divine Vocation in the Message of Paul* (Naperville, IL: Allenson and London: S.C.M., 1961), 98.

16. Dunn, *Paul the Apostle*, 245.

preaching of Acts 2:36 Peter concluded his sermon on the Day of Pentecost with the declaration, "*God has made him both Lord* and Messiah," in vindicating his death in the act of his resurrection.[17]

The tradition of Rom. 1:3-4, which is probably pre-Pauline, is parallel with Acts 2:36. Dunn writes, "Exaltation to Lordship, we might say, was the other side of the coin of the appointment to sonship 'in power' (Rom. 1:4). Thus Rom. 10:9: the confession that 'Jesus is Lord' was the public expression of belief that 'God raised him from the dead'. 'Jesus is Lord' by virtue of resurrection from the dead. Or again, Rom. 14:9 [states]: 'it was for this purpose that Christ died and lived again *(ezēsen)*, in order that he might be Lord over both the dead and living.'"[18] The conclusive parallel is Phil. 2:6-11, which declares, "Therefore *God* has exalted him to the heights and bestowed on him the name that is above every name" (v. 9).

It recalls Bultmann's roots in nineteenth-century Lutheran Pietism that what he articulates runs closely parallel to the words of a currently fashionable song or chorus of the charismatic renewal movement: "*We* build him a throne." This expresses very well the cash-currency of practical Christian discipleship, but it ignores the *ontological* truth-basis that *God* "builds him a throne," as if Christ's lordship were to depend upon the church. The former would be empty unless the latter were *also* true.

Further to this, the earliest Christian communities did not stop short at "confessing" Jesus as Lord without tracing *continuities and grounds* for such a confession in the history of God's saving acts in the Old Testament and the life of Israel. One example is the use of Ps. 110:1, not least in the Epistle to the Hebrews.[19] Christ sits at the "right hand" of God as one honored by God as executive agent and authority for the implementation of the divine will and purpose (Rom. 8:34; Eph. 1:20; Heb. 1:3, 13; cf. 1:5-13). The phrase "calling on the name of the Lord" in fulfillment of Joel 2:32 came to occupy a special place in the New Testament (Acts 2:21; Rom. 10:13; 1 Cor. 1:2). Dunn comments, "The Lord Jesus is now envisaged as fulfilling the role of the Lord. In short, Paul seems to have had no qualms about transferring God's role in eschatological salvation to the risen Jesus," although Dunn stops short of an "identification" of Jesus as Yahweh as implying an oversimplified hermeneutics.[20] The creedal form of 1 Cor. 8:5-6 pro-

---

17. Cf. Oscar Cullmann, *Christology of the New Testament,* trans. S. C. Guthrie and C. A. M. Hall (London: S.C.M., 1959, 2d edn. 1963), 203-4 on this passage.

18. Dunn, *Paul,* 245.

19. See D. M. Hay, *Glory at the Right Hand: Psalm 110 in Early Christianity,* SBLMS 18 (Nashville: Abingdon, 1973); and L. Cerfaux, *Christ in the Theology of St. Paul,* trans. G. Webb and A. Walker (Freiburg: Herder, 1959), throughout.

20. Dunn, *Paul,* 250 and 250, n. 82, on D. B. Capes, *Old Testament Yahweh Texts in Paul's Christology,* WUNT II, 47 (Tübingen: Mohr, 1992), 123. See further Fitzmyer, *Romans,* 593, on the title "Lord of all" in Rom. 10:12, and Dunn, *Paul,* 250-60.

vides evidence of how closely Paul construes "one God, the Father" with "one Lord Jesus Christ," especially against the background of the *Shema'* of Deut. 6:4 (discussed further in 19.1, on the Trinity).

Bultmann's existential approach, then, contains a half-truth. Hurtado comments, "The earliest and key innovation in Christianity was not the use of certain honorific titles or other Christological rhetoric. Rather, it was the nature of the religious *praxis* of early and influential groups."[21] Nevertheless Bultmann's statement "The pre-existence of Christ . . . is not only irrational but utterly meaningless" devalues such examples as Paul's deliberate inclusion of Phil. 2:8-11, whether or not it was pre-Pauline in origin.[22] To regard preexistence as a first-century code for divine foreordaining or divine initiative goes beyond the evidence.

The test case for addressing the ontological or existential status of Christological truth-claims emerged in response to the World Council of Churches' inquiry to Bultmann about the validity of their axiom or criterion of "churches which acknowledge Jesus Christ as God and Saviour." How does Bultmann regard this? Bultmann concedes that Jesus is explicitly acknowledged as "God" in the confession of Thomas in John 20:28; but, he adds, nowhere else. In a more specific response to their inquiry he declared, "The formula 'Christ is God' is false in every sense in which God is understood as an entity which can be objectivized whether it is understood in an Arian or Nicene . . . sense. It is correct if 'God' is understood as the event of God's acting."[23] The "decisive question" is whether the titles tell us about "the nature of Jesus [by] objectifying him in his being in himself or whether they speak of him in his significance for man for faith."[24] On the same page Bultmann asks, "Does he help me because he is God's Son, or is he Son of God because he helps me?" Bultmann is content with those confessions that are self-involving, but rejects those that are, in effect, metaphysical. Neither the humanity nor the deity of Jesus Christ, he insists, can be "interpreted as a φύσις" *(phusis, nature)* rather than *"Christus pro me."*[25] Very little of this is entirely distinctive to Bultmann's Christology. It is part of a wider, generalized, assumption about "objectification" held in various quarters. Hence Bultmann argues in the same vein that the resurrection of Jesus Christ has no reality at all "independently of faith." The Easter event is "*nothing other* than the rise of faith in the risen one . . . not an objective event" (my italics).[26]

---

21. Hurtado, *One God, One Lord,* 124.

22. Bultmann, in *Kerygma and Myth,* vol. 1, 34-35; also Rudolf Bultmann, *Jesus Christ and Mythology* (New York: Scribner, 1958 and London: S.C.M., 1960), 16-17.

23. Rudolf Bultmann, "The Christological Confession," in *Essays Philosophical and Theological,* trans. C. G. Greig (London: S.C.M., 1995), 287; cf. 273-91.

24. Bultmann, *Essays,* 280.

25. Bultmann, *Essays,* 287.

26. Bultmann, in *Kerygma and Myth,* vol. 1, 42.

Disastrous consequences derive from what amounts to a linguistic and logical confusion, which stems initially from Bultmann's misguided commitment to an overly narrow philosophy of language drawn largely from neo-Kantianism and Heidegger. It is true that language concerning God, or (better) *from* God, is self-involving. Bultmann is right to urge: "To speak of God's act means to speak at the same time of my own existence."[27] Much of the New Testament concerns, or even conveys, "our being addressed by God here and now."[28] We have argued for self-involving, formative, and transformative language throughout almost every chapter of this volume. But does it follow (except specifically in Kant's philosophy and in Neo-Kantian traditions) that "it is not permitted to understand God's act as a phenomenon in the world apart from an *existentiell* encounter with it?"[29]

As I have argued many times in many places, the authenticity of the call and address of God through Jesus of Nazareth depends not simply on a voluntarist account of language, but *on the promise that certain states of affairs are the case, or are true*.[30] Jesus has the authority to forgive sins because he derives this authority *from God*. Indeed, the misunderstanding is one of *hermeneutics*, which Bultmann transposes illegitimately into a question of *truth*. It is true that the *hermeneutical* currency of "Jesus is Lord" is best perceived in terms of how believers manifest trust and obedience to Jesus as Lord. But the *basis* for this hermeneutical resonance is not self-generated. That is why Bultmann's "left-wing" critics, Karl Jaspers, Fritz Buri, and Herbert Braun, ask why "God" should be, on Bultmann's showing, any more than a nonobjectifying human projection or cipher for human values.[31]

Jaspers argues that Bultmann has misunderstood the nature of myth, and insists on the arbitrarily retained doctrine of justification by faith. Why stop there?[32] Indeed, too many writers to count have urged (i) the implausibility of a form-critical approach that proposes every possible *Sitz im Leben* except a need for *description* or *information;* and (ii) the arbitrary stopping point of a program

27. Bultmann, in *Kerygma and Myth*, vol. 1, 196.

28. Bultmann, in *Kerygma and Myth*, vol. 1, 196-97.

29. Bultmann, in *Kerygma and Myth*, vol. 1, 196.

30. Thiselton, *New Horizons in Hermeneutics*, 283-303; Thiselton, *Thiselton on Hermeneutics*, 75-117 and 131-49; Thiselton, *The Promise of Hermeneutics*, 144-52 and 223-40; and elsewhere.

31. Cf. Fritz Buri, *How Can We Speak Responsibly of God?* trans. H. H. Oliver (Philadelphia: Fortress, 1968); Fritz Buri, *Thinking Faith: Steps on the Way to a Philosophical Theology*, trans. H. H. Oliver (Philadelphia: Fortress, 1968); Karl Jaspers and Rudolf Bultmann, *Myth and Christianity: An Inquiry into the Possibility of Religion without Myth*, trans. R. J. Hoffman (Amherst, NY: Prometheus, 2005).

32. See Jaspers and Bultmann, *Myth and Christianity*, Part I; and on the arbitrary "scope" of demythologizing, John Macquarrie, *The Scope of Demythologizing: Bultmann and His Critics* (London: S.C.M., 1960), 102-244; David Cairns, *A Gospel without Myth: Bultmann's Challenge to the Preacher* (London: S.C.M., 1960).

of demythologization that simply declares "Here I stand" when critics press Bultmann about public criteria of meaning, the relation between event and interpretation, and incompatible notions of myth.[33] On top of all this, Bultmann seems to be unable or unwilling to distinguish between the kind of de-objectifying promoted by Fritz Buri and Herbert Braun, and the very different critique of static objectification urged by Eberhard Jüngel in his dialogue with Helmut Gollwitzer and others in his exposition of an analogy of event or analogy of coming, which we discuss in 19.3 on the language of divine transcendence.

Yet, when all has been said, Bultmann rescues *a neglected part of the hermeneutical "point"* of much Christological language, even if we must look elsewhere for its grounding in more credible truth-claims.

Kathryn Tanner offers an incisive and constructive diagnosis of how and why many "modern" Christologies come to grief on the basis of misleading judgments concerning the nature and application of epistemology. She writes, "In contemporary theology, following Immanuel Kant, this affirmation of the *pro me* suffers, one might say, a subjectivist epistemological swerve, which moves away from its use in Luther. . . . The *pro me* for Luther concerned a dimension of the reality of Christ's working. . . . Now, however, the *pro me* falls simply on the side of human apprehension. . . . The non-objectifying language about God . . . is apparently a precondition for appropriate Christian attitudes towards God." But we lose thereby an "extrospective" emphasis.[34]

17.2. Jesus, God and Man: Modern Debates, and a Dual Background in the Old Testament and Judaism

In her astute essay on some of the problems of "modern" Christologies Kathryn Tanner identifies more than the damaging effects imposed by importing epistemologies based too heavily on subjective human consciousness. We have noted how this influences Bultmann; but as she points out, it also strongly influenced Schleiermacher and many other modern Christologies, each giving undue privilege to the self-consciousness of the "I." Tanner also traces a "humanistic and this-worldly outlook" that perceives the true humanity of Jesus as "purportedly endangered by the emphasis on Christ's divinity in the creeds and high Christologies of the early church."[35] This problem is compounded by overly restrictive criteria

33. On the role of "knowledge" of Jesus in the earliest church, see Graham N. Stanton, *Jesus of Nazareth in New Testament Preaching*, SNTSMS 27 (Cambridge: Cambridge University Press, 1974), throughout. On the relation to form criticism see further Giovanni Miegge, *Gospel and Myth in the Thought of Rudolf Bultmann*, trans. Stephen Neil (London: Lutterworth, 1960), 1-61.

34. Kathryn Tanner, "Jesus Christ," in Colin E. Gunton, *The Cambridge Companion to Christian Doctrine* (Cambridge: Cambridge University Press, 1997), 253 and 254; cf. 245-72.

35. Tanner, "Jesus Christ," 246.

concerning historical reconstructions of the life, teaching, and works of Jesus; and by insufficiently self-critical notions of historical conditionedness.[36]

The first of these points is the subject of this section; Tanner's remaining points emerge again in the next section of this chapter. First, without doubt some modern Christologies explicate the genuine humanity of Jesus Christ in ways that offer a necessary hermeneutical corrective to features of the person of Christ that are largely neglected in more popular presentations of Christ in churches and in lecture rooms. One such example is John A. T. Robinson's *The Human Face of God*.[37] This reflects his conviction, earlier expressed in *Christ, Faith and History*, that "Jesus was not a hybrid," a "God-man" in the sense of a "sort of bat-man, or centaur, an unnatural conjunction of two strange species."[38]

In this particular respect Robinson is true to the creeds. We do not declare: "half-man, half-God," but "true man, true God." Thus Robinson attacks two distorted pictures of Jesus of Nazareth, one, as it were, on each side. One is the picture of "God in disguise." This picture squeezes out the *humanity* of Jesus. The other is "Jesus the perfect man," since a "perfect" man hardly seems to be "the likes of us."[39] Like most writers on Christology in the second half of the twentieth century, he makes much of Schweitzer's dictum that "each generation simply sees its own Christ." Nevertheless he believes that "critically controlled," historical scholarship can provide needed safeguards against this.[40]

Robinson considers doctrinal developments over the first four or five centuries, and sees some merit in early adoptionist Christology, because at least this did not compromise the humanity of Jesus Christ. However, he argues, when "divine *foreordination*" becomes "translated as the *pre-existence* of Christ," pressure on Christ's genuine humanity begins to be exerted.[41] He laments the fact that while the church was always on the watch against overemphasizing the humanity, "an over-emphasis on the divinity . . . [was] comfortably accommodated within orthodoxy."[42] Hence, he argues, while Apollinarius and Eutyches were condemned, a "docetic streak" runs through almost the whole of Alexandrian Christology.

Robinson cites Clement of Alexandria: "It would be ridiculous to imagine that the body of the Redeemer . . . had the usual needs of man" (*Stromata* 6:9; cf. 3:7). He cites Athanasius: "The Word disguised himself by appearing in a body. . . . By the works he did in the body [he] showed himself to be not man, but

36. Tanner, "Jesus Christ," 246-51.

37. John A. T. Robinson, *The Human Face of God* (London: S.C.M., 1973).

38. John A. T. Robinson, "Need Jesus Have Been Perfect?" in Sykes and Clayton (eds.), *Christ, Faith and History*; cf. 39-52.

39. Robinson, *Human Face*, 3.

40. Robinson, *Human Face*, 15.

41. Robinson, *Human Face*, 37 (my italics).

42. Robinson, *Human Face*, 38.

God the Word" (*De Incarnatione* 16:18). Cyril of Alexandria claimed that Jesus permitted his flesh to weep a little, "although it was in its nature tearless and incapable of grief" (*Commentary on John, 7*).[43] Robinson concludes that in general the Church Fathers, and especially the Alexandrians, ignored "what for us is the *sine qua non* of personal existence, namely the nexus of biological, historical, and social relationships with our fellow-men and with the universe."[44] The upshot was also to view Jesus as having no sexuality. Robinson writes, "The church appeared to present him as sexless," which for most people today, he urges, is a way of saying that Jesus was not fully human.[45]

The attribute of "perfection" compounds the problem. When we speak of Jesus as "*the* man" (discussed in 11.3 with reference to Barth, Brunner, and Bonhoeffer) this "paradoxically undercuts his humanity . . . making him an unreal figure with the static perfection of flawless porcelain, rather than a man of flesh and blood."[46] Jesus Christ has become too readily "the complete man of renaissance humanism, the all-rounder of whom it could be said, 'You name it: he's got it.'"[47]

The Epistle to the Hebrews presents Jesus Christ as "growing" in his maturity or perfection: "he learned obedience in the school of suffering" (Heb. 2:10; 5:9; 7:28). But "both the static and the sexless Jesus are powerful versions today of the cardboard Christ."[48] Jesus, Robinson continues, shared the same unconscious drives and libido as ordinary men and women. He was genuinely tempted: "Really to feel the pull of evil, one must see it as more attractive than the good."[49] Perhaps too harshly he dismisses P. T. Forsyth's discussion of this as a mere quibble.[50] Jesus felt the loves and hates of social estrangements as "a Jew of his time."[51]

Robinson remains tireless in his critique of Patristic models and idioms. He rightly criticizes the notion that different "parts" or different "natures" of Christ operate in his ministry in different times and situations. Irenaeus seems to move beyond Scripture in suggesting that "When he was being tempted and crucified and dying, the Logos remained quiescent."[52] Robinson calls Cyril "a master of the double switch." To Cyril Jesus Christ "will belong both to know and to seem

---

43. Robinson further cites Cyril of Alexandria, *De Trinitate* 10:24, in which eating is "a concession," not a real need; and Aquinas, *Summa Theologiae*, III, 15:7, 2 (*Human Face*, 40, nn. 13 and 14).

44. Robinson, *Human Face*, 41.

45. Robinson, *Human Face*, 64.

46. Robinson, *Human Face*, 68.

47. Robinson, *Human Face*, 70.

48. Robinson, *Human Face*, 80.

49. Robinson, *Human Face*, 91.

50. See P. T. Forsyth, *The Reason and Place of Jesus Christ* (London: Independent, 1909), 303.

51. Robinson, *Human Face*, 93.

52. Irenaeus, *Against Heresies* III:19:3; Robinson, *Human Face*, 111.

53. Cyril, *Apologia against Theodoret*, anathema 4.

not to know."[53] Yet the Fathers rejected any "split personality" notion: "For the one and only Christ is not twofold" *(diplous)*. Athanasius promoted a "double agency" concept: "He [Jesus] spat in human fashion, yet his spittle was charged with deity, for therewith he caused the eyes of the man born blind to recover their sight."[54]

Although he expresses the point perhaps too sweepingly, Robinson is right to see Platonic and perhaps Aristotelian notions of causality behind this desire for exaggerated specificity. All the same, when he reverts to the model of "two stories" promoted in Cambridge Studies in Christology, Robinson does not solve all or even most of the difficulties. Rather than speak of "two natures," he declares, "we must use two languages, man-language and God-language."[55] Only thus can we avoid "making Jesus a sort of centaur or bat-man."[56] "What we are talking about," he writes, [expressed in English spelling rather than in American English spelling] "is not two storeys but two stories."[57] To mix the "God-story" (the metaphysical) with the "man-story" (the historical) is to commit "category confusion."[58]

This, however, lets the cat out of the bag; it betrays the adoption of another, unsubstantiated agenda. The "upper storey," or God-story, has become explicitly associated with the *"mythological"* in contrast to the *"historico-scientific."* Here is an Anglo-Saxon version of Bultmann's irreconcilable dualism between this world and beyond; between report and address; between God and history. Perhaps the early Church Fathers were less foolish than Robinson appears to suggest in their fears that if they isolated the "humanity" of Jesus *alone in the public realm of verifiable (or falsifiable) history,* an erosion of the so-called "mythological," or the transcendent, begins to take place. We may readily agree with Robinson that we need to restore the portrayal of Jesus of Nazareth as fully and truly human, not half-human. This merits urgent and rigorous attention. The quotations from Irenaeus, Clement, and Cyril that Robinson cites expose fundamental weaknesses that verge on "separating" the two natures. Nevertheless, another problem lurks in the background with Robinson: where is the anchorage of the *"God-*story," of God in Christ, *in the public realm of ontological truth-claims?*

Maurice Wiles is clearly aware of a weakness at the level of ontology in his "two stories" model. He expounds the two stories, in part as if one story can stand the test of "science," while the other is "a frankly mythological story," and he comments: "To ask for some further ontological justification . . . would be to succumb to the category mistake of confusing the human historical story with

54. Athanasius, *Epistle to Serapion* 4:14.
55. Robinson, *Human Face*, 113.
56. Robinson, *Human Face*, 115; repeated from *Christ, Faith and History,* 39.
57. Robinson, *Human Face*, 117.
58. Robinson, *Human Face*, 118.

the divine mythological story."[59] On the other hand, Peter Baelz seeks to modify Wiles' implicit dualism. He writes, "It is a mistake to believe that they [the two "stories"] are utterly divorced from each other, or that there are no relations of a logical kind between them."[60] He offers a more sophisticated account of the relation between "scientific" and "theological" truth-claims than appears in Wiles or Robinson. The two "stories" *overlap.*

The extraordinary "looseness" and flexibility of such a "historical fit" emerges in Don Cupitt's essay "One Jesus, Many Christs?"[61] It is of course par for the course to concede that "some writers, like Seeley and Rénan, assimilate Jesus to the spirit of their own time. . . . Other writers, of whom Kierkegaard and Schweitzer are examples, emphasize the strangeness of Jesus."[62] It plays exactly into the hands of the critique expressed by Kathryn Tanner (above) when Cupitt continues, "The way he [Jesus] is Christ for me may be very different from the way he is Christ for some other person. . . . He [Christ] himself is not troubled by being many Christs."[63] The example might have been prepared especially to make Tanner's point. It is left to Graham Stanton in this volume to provide a more careful account of criteria that relate to the reading of the narratives of the gospels, although to address the "two stories" model falls outside his immediate purpose.[64]

Are there ways of achieving Robinson's *aim* (which genuinely reflects the "very man" of the creeds) without subscribing to a method that seems in danger of reducing ontological truth-claims into a contrived dualism between empirical events in history and "myth" as a vague, ill-defined category for acts of God in Christ that cannot be reduced to empirical verification or falsification?

I suggest two provisional and tentative ways forward in this chapter. The first is to trace the hermeneutical horizons of understanding that led to perceptions of the person and work of Jesus Christ as *both God and man,* albeit initially as *distinct promissory narratives of expectation,* but with more probability of interweaving them than those of history and myth.

(i) *Prophetic expectation* looked forward to the coming of a *figure who would receive an unprecedented anointing by the Holy Spirit* (Hebrew מָשִׁיח, *māshîach;*

---

59. Maurice F. Wiles, "Does Christology Rest on a Mistake?" in Sykes and Clayton (eds.), *Christ, Faith and History,* 11; cf. 10 (and 3-12).

60. Peter Baelz, "A Deliberate Mistake?" in Sykes and Clayton (eds.), *Christ, Faith and History,* 23; cf. 13-34.

61. Don Cupitt, "One Jesus, Many Christs?" in Sykes and Clayton (eds.), *Christ, Faith and History,* 131-44.

62. Cupitt, "One Jesus," 133.

63. Cupitt, "One Jesus," 143.

64. Graham N. Stanton, "The Gospel Tradition and Early Christological Reflection," in Sykes and Clayton (eds.), *Christ, Faith and History,* 191-204. Cf. more fully Stanton, *Jesus of Nazareth in New Testament Preaching* (cited above).

Aramaic, מְשִׁיחָא, meshîaʾ; Greek ὁ Χριστός, ho Christos, the anointed one), at times identified with the eschatological prophet "like Moses."

(ii) *Apocalyptic expectation* had become so disenchanted with the capacity of any human being, even an anointed king, to bring in the eschatological reign of God that the apocalyptists came to believe that *only God himself* could intervene in history in such a way as to inaugurate the new age and the new creation.

A second way forward is to seek a model *within the New Testament* where the highest possible Christology, including an *explicit identification of Jesus Christ as God, coheres within the same writing* with the *fullest possible explication of the humanness of Jesus* as fulfilling in every respect the status of being truly human. The one writing that places these two together without an apparent "category mistake" or category confusion is *the Epistle to the Hebrews.* Each of these two approaches provides horizons of understanding and hermeneutical resonances.

(1) The first type of promissory expectation arises largely from the prophets. Moltmann writes, "Jesus' history as the Christ does not begin with Jesus himself. It begins with the *rûach*/the Holy Spirit. It is the coming of the Spirit, the creative breath of God: in this Jesus comes forward as 'the anointed one' *(māsiach, christos),* proclaims the gospel of the kingdom with power, and convinces many with the signs of the new creation."[65] It is the power of the creative Spirit of God who through Jesus brings liberty and salvation. The Spirit "descends upon" Jesus at his baptism (Mark 1:10; par. Matt. 3:16; Luke 3:22), and "drove him" (Mark 1:12) or "led him" (Matt. 4:1; Luke 4:1) into the wilderness to be "tempted" for the testing and equipping of his messianic vocation. "Israel's messianic history of promise" provides "the presupposition of every christology," and Christology develops "out of the Jewish contours of the messianic promise."[66]

Moltmann acknowledges freely that "this allows us to comprehend the messianic mission of the earthly Jesus, which was neglected in the christological dogma of Nicaea."[67] To this extent he echoes one of the main concerns of John Robinson. However, the activity of the Holy Spirit would be left out of account, except in purely phenomenological terms, under the critical straightjacket of the strictly empirical or "scientific" reconstruction of the history of Jesus. Moltmann observes, "It looks as if by doing this we were coming close to 'the Jesus of history'. But this impression is deceptive. The gospels . . . tell the story of his life in the light of his resurrection and his presence in the Spirit of God. This, I believe, may even be said of Q, which says nothing about Easter. . . ."[68] What emerges

---

65. Jürgen Moltmann, *The Way of Jesus Christ: Christology in Messianic Dimensions,* trans. Margaret Kohl (London: S.C.M., 1990), 73.

66. Moltmann, *The Way of Jesus Christ,* 73-74.

67. Moltmann, *The Way,* 74.

68. Moltmann, *The Way,* 75.

from the gospels is "the experience of the presence of *the whole Christ* in the Spirit . . . in all his words and acts."[69]

Pannenberg likewise asserts, "The apostolic proclamation of Jesus of Nazareth as the Son of God began with his earthly coming, his fate at the end of his earthly path, and the divine action in raising him from the dead."[70] The Messiahship of Jesus is "the core of the NT witness and the basis of dogmatic statements about his person."[71] But the notion of God's "sending" the Son implies his preexistence, and we cannot neglect "the total character of the coming of Jesus and his history in order to find a basis for confession of his deity."[72] Stephen Sykes criticizes this approach as offering a Christology "from below" on the grounds that to include futurity and resurrection transposes it into a Christology "from above."[73] But this is hardly a decisive or wholly convincing criticism (see 17.5), on the basis of Moltmann's narrative context.

(2) A clear distinction between the prophetic expectation of an anointed human agent and the apocalyptic hope of divine intervention is introduced succinctly by Albert Schweitzer in his work on Paul, and by D. S. Russell on apocalyptic.[74] The preexilic and exilic prophets, he writes, expect a Messiah of David's line to come as the God-anointed ruler, endowed with wisdom and power, to rule the great kingdom. Haggai and Zechariah (c. 550 B.C.) see such a leader in Zerubbabel.[75] But Danielic eschatology is different. God himself brings about cosmic catastrophe. The book of *Enoch* develops this further. At first the more apocalyptic strand seems to "thrust aside" the prophetic, but then the *Psalms of Solomon* (c. 63 B.C.) move back to the prophetic with full force.[76] An anointed human leader purges Jerusalem of all "Latin" peoples, "Blessed is he who shall live in that day" (*Psalms of Solomon* 17:44). Jesus heralds, and speaks of, the reign of *God* appropriately to this extent as the apocalyptic hope and expectation. Nevertheless, "The Messiah, all unsuspected by the Scribes, lives at first in the person of Jesus humbly among men. . . . Although David's son, He is David's Lord."[77]

H. H. Rowley comments, "The apocalyptists did not for a moment imagine

---

69. Moltmann, *The Way*, 76 (his italics).

70. Pannenberg, *Systematic Theology*, vol. 2, 278.

71. Pannenberg, *Systematic Theology*, vol. 2, 279.

72. Pannenberg, *Systematic Theology*, vol. 2, 280; cf. 277-97.

73. Stephen W. Sykes, "Appendix: On Pannenberg's Christology 'From below,'" in Sykes and Clayton (eds.), *Christ, Faith and History*, 72. There is remarkably little interaction with Continental European Christology in this volume.

74. Albert Schweitzer, *The Mysticism of Paul the Apostle*, trans. W. Montgomery (London: Black, 1931), 76-88; and D. S. Russell, *The Method and Message of Jewish Apocalyptic 200 BC–AD 100* (London: S.C.M., 1964), 304-32.

75. Schweitzer, *Mysticism*, 76; cf. Russell, *Apocalyptic*, 305-6.

76. Schweitzer, *Mysticism*, 78-79 and Russell, *Apocalyptic*, 317-19.

77. Schweitzer, *Mysticism*, 83.

that the kingdom of God would be established by human means. It could be established only by a divine act. It would be a stone cut without hands that would become the mountain, or one like a Son of Man coming on the clouds of heaven."[78] "They did not believe in the power of the evil present to generate the longed-for morrow. . . . Their spring of hope was in God alone."[79]

Yet there is room alongside this for a commissioned and anointed leader to prepare the way. In spite of many criticisms brought against John Calvin's exposition of the person and work of Christ as prophet, priest, and king performing the work of mediator, the *Zadokite Document* of Qumran looks forward to a Messiah who will be both priest and king, "the Messiah of Aaron and Israel" (*Zadokite* [or *Damascus*] *Document* [*CD*] 14:19; 19:10; cf. 12:23).[80] "Belief in a priestly leader and kingly leader would find precedent in the joint leadership of Joshua and Zerubbabel" (Zech. 3–4).[81] It would not be surprising for these two figures and offices to merge in their fulfillment in Jesus Christ. After all, the New Testament makes it clear that *both* the *prophetic* tradition of the *obedient* righteous Servant and the *priestly* tradition of the Servant who is led *as a sacrifice* to the slaughter (Isa. 53:2-12) were jointly and together fulfilled in the person and work of Jesus Christ.

What begins to emerge is that the "two stories" model comes to grief because it does not begin far enough back in *the continuous and providential ordering of the history of Israel,* the Old Testament, and prophetic, priestly, and apocalyptic expectation and promise. In some cases (for example, Cupitt's) it is reduced to *fragmentary narratives of individual consciousness and experiences,* which entirely loses the continuity and anchorage of biblical narrative as a story of divine "ordering" from creation and the Exodus through the words and deeds of Jesus to the resurrection and Pentecost, and beyond. It is precisely this larger narrative that provides the horizon of understanding for interpreting Christ in the Epistle to the Hebrews.[82] That is why there is no tension or "category mistake" when the Epistle to the Hebrews places side by side the highest Christology in the New Testament with the clearest emphasis in the New Testament on the humanness.

---

78. H. H. Rowley, *The Relevance of Apocalyptic: A Study of Jewish and Christian Apocalypses from Daniel to Revelation* (London: Lutterworth, 1944), 157.

79. Rowley, *Apocalyptic,* 153.

80. Cited in Russell, *Apocalyptic,* 320-21.

81. Russell, *Apocalyptic,* 321. For further examples and themes see Joseph Klausner, *The Messianic Idea in Israel: From Its Beginning to the Completion of the Mishnah,* translated from the third Hebrew edn. by W. F. Stinespring (London: Allen & Unwin, 1956), 2-245 (Old Testament); 246-387 (Apocrypha and Pseudepigrapha); and 388-518 (rabbinic Judaism).

82. See Anthony C. Thiselton, "Human Being, Relationality and Time in Hebrews, 1 Corinthians, and Western Thought," in *Ex Auditu* 13 (1997-98) 76-95; rpt. in *Thiselton on Hermeneutics,* 727-46.

17.3. Jesus, God and Man:
The Distinctive Contribution of the Epistle to the Hebrews

In his careful and illuminating study *Jesus, God and Man* Raymond E. Brown concludes that "there are a number of passages in the New Testament which *imply* that Jesus is divine," but only three that explicitly use *theos* (θεός, *God*) of Jesus."[83] The former include John 10:30, "I and the Father are one"; 14:9, "He who has seen me has seen the Father"; John 8:24, 28, 56 ("the absolute use of *egō eimi*, 'I am'"); Phil. 2:6-7, "in the form of God"; and Col. 1:15, "the image of the invisible God." The latter are Heb. 1:8-9, "Your throne, O God, is forever. . . . Therefore, God, your God, has anointed you . . ."; John 1:1, "and the Word was God"; and John 20:28, "Thomas said . . . 'My Lord and my God.'"

Clearly John and Hebrews are major sources of "high" Christologies. But what is remarkable about Hebrews is that in comparison with other New Testament writings it has *both* the highest and most explicit declarations of the deity of Jesus Christ *and* the clearest and most deliberate expressions of the humanness of Jesus Christ. The writer of the Epistle to the Hebrews is a master theologian, a sensitive pastor, and a fine expository preacher of texts and themes from the Old Testament. It is essential for the writer's theology of priesthood, representation, and mediation that Christ is portrayed as genuinely human, and thereby able to represent humankind in priestly mediation to God, and equally portrayed as sharing in deity to represent God to humankind in prophetic mediation and address. *Jesus Christ is both "ascending" Mediator on behalf of humankind and "descending" Mediator on behalf of God.*

Nevertheless, in effect anticipating the later creeds and Chalcedon, this writer nowhere suggests that Jesus Christ is half-man and/or half-God. On one side, Jesus, as truly human, is portrayed as suffering weakness, as learning maturity through suffering, as calling men and women his brothers and sisters, and as experiencing the need that humans experience to trust in God (Heb. 2:7-13). "He had to become like his brothers and sisters in every respect, so that he might be a merciful and faithful high priest . . ." (Heb. 2:17). "He himself was tested by what he suffered" (2:18). "For we do not have a high priest who is unable to sympathize with our weaknesses (ταῖς ἀσθενείαις ἡμῶν) but have one who in every respect has been tested as we are, yet without sin (πεπειρασμένον δὲ κατὰ πάντα καθ' ὁμοιότητα χωρὶς ἁμαρτίας, *pepeirasmenon de kata panta kath' homoiotēta chōris hamartias*)" (Heb. 4:15).

Still more acutely the writer to the Hebrews continues, "In the days of his flesh, Jesus offered up prayers and supplications, with loud cries and tears, to the one who was able to save him from death. . . . Although he was a Son, he learned

---

83. Raymond E. Brown, *Jesus, God and Man: Modern Biblical Reflections* (London and Dublin: Geoffrey Chapman, 1968) 23.

obedience through what he suffered" (Heb. 5:7-8). "Consider him who endured such hostility against himself from sinners" (Heb. 12:3). "Jesus suffered outside the city gate. . . . Let us go and bear the abuse he endured" (13:13). In his classic older study of Christology H. R. Mackintosh writes, "Nowhere in the New Testament is the humanity of Christ set forth so movingly."[84] Vincent Taylor observes, "Much more than St. Paul he [the writer] assigns the greatest importance to the Gospel story . . . because he believes that Christ's . . . perfect humanity [was] essential to his mission."[85]

"Loud cries and tears" is almost certainly an allusion to Gethsemane (Heb. 5:7; Mark 14:32-36; par. Matt. 26:36-38). The maxim about "learning through suffering" (Greek *pathein . . . mathein . . .*) underlines the point that Jesus' being the Son of God did not make things easier for him: "Jesus was not exempt from the common law that learning comes by suffering."[86] As in the messianic temptations in the Synoptic gospels (Matt. 4:1-11; par. Luke 4:1-13), Jesus in Hebrews accepts the *constraints* of everyday human life. This includes the experience of genuine temptation *(pepeirasmenon,* 4:15; NRSV, *tested,* with marginal note *tempted;* NJB, *put to the test;* NIV, AV/KJV, and Ellingworth, *tempted;* Attridge, *tried).*[87] *Tempted* coheres better with the writer's emphasis upon Jesus' wholly sharing what it is to be human, as Ellingworth observes. An older commentator, B. F. Westcott, addresses scepticism about the genuineness of such temptation for a "sinless" person: "Only one who has not yielded to sin can know the fullest degree of the strength of temptation — for he who sins yields to temptation before it has revealed the greatest possible force . . . he who falls yields before the last strain."[88]

The passage in Heb. 2:5-18 that takes up and applies Ps. 8:4-6 to Jesus portrays Jesus as both thoroughly human, but also, in the words of Karl Barth already cited in 11.3 above, "Jesus is man as God willed and created him. . . . The nature of the man Jesus is the key to the problem of the human. This man is *man.*"[89] Historical Christologies sometimes ask, "Was Jesus truly human?" Barth and Hebrews reverse the question: given that Jesus was the paradigm of true humanness, are we, the readers, truly human?

Nevertheless the astonishing contribution of this epistle is to place all this

84. H. R. Mackintosh, *The Doctrine of the Person of Jesus Christ* (Edinburgh: T&T Clark, 1913), 79.

85. Vincent Taylor, *The Person of Christ in New Testament Teaching* (New York and London: Macmillan, 1958), 91.

86. F. F. Bruce, *The Epistle to the Hebrews* (London: Marshall and Grand Rapids: Eerdmans, 1964), 103.

87. H. W. Attridge, *Commentary on the Epistle to the Hebrews,* Hermeneia (Philadelphia: Fortress, 1989), 140; Paul Ellingworth, *The Epistle to the Hebrews: A Commentary on the Greek Text,* NIGTC (Grand Rapids: Eerdmans and Carlisle: Paternoster, 1993), 268-69.

88. B. F. Westcott, *The Epistle to the Hebrews: The Greek Text* (New York and London: Macmillan, 3d edn. 1903) in 4:15.

89. Barth, *Church Dogmatics* III:2, sect. 43, 50.

alongside what is probably (with the Fourth Gospel) the "highest" Christology of the deity of Jesus Christ in the entire New Testament. If, for one moment, the claim that to emphasize the deity of Jesus Christ is to undermine his humanity, or that to emphasize his humanity would be to detract from deity, how does it come about that Hebrews gives both the highest possible profile, without apparent tension? Does the point made by John Robinson depend for its force upon abstracting the person of Jesus Christ from the hermeneutical horizons that constitute its "home" language-game or frame of reference?

As Raymond Brown declares, the ascription of deity to Jesus Christ in Heb. 1:8-9 is explicit: "Your throne, O God, is forever and ever. . . ."[90] Heb. 1:3 is astonishingly explicit: "He [Jesus Christ] is the reflection of God's glory and the exact imprint of God's very being (χαρακτὴρ τῆς ὑποστάσεως αὐτοῦ, *charaktēr tēs hupostaseōs autou*), and sustains all things by his powerful word." The Greek word χαρακτήρ *(charaktēr)* denotes a die-stamp or engraving, while ὑπόστασις *(hupostasis)* means "the essential or basic structure/nature of an entity, substantial nature, essence, actual being, reality."[91] Montefiore comments that this "outright assertion" of deity does not merely mean that Jesus "resembles certain aspects" of God, but that he expresses and reveals "what it is that makes God be God."[92] It is tempting to compare Rudolf Bultmann's rash assertion that it is "false" to call Jesus "God" as if to say what he is "in himself" (above, 17.1) with this biblical writer's use of *hupostasis, charaktēr,* and *apaugasma (being, die-stamp, reflection,* or *radiance,* v. 3).

The following verses (1:8-14), like the Prologue of John, explicate the axiom "*God* has spoken" (1:1) in terms of speech through the Son (1:2a) as Creator of the world (1:2b), worshiped by the angels (1:6), and established as King: "Your throne, O God, is for ever and ever; and the righteous scepter is the scepter of your kingdom" (1:8). "They will perish, but you remain" (1:11). Christ is portrayed here as "descending" Mediator, with striking resonances with Wisdom Christology, in which Jesus Christ is identified as the "hypostasis" of God in the form of Divine Wisdom and Divine Word.[93] In Prov. 8:30 Wisdom stands beside God in a preexistent role as master worker, through whom God created the worlds.

The parallels between Christ, Word, and Wisdom are "unmistakable."[94]

---

90. Brown, *Jesus, God and Man,* 23.

91. Bauer-Danker-Arndt-Gingrich, *Greek-English Lexicon,* 3d edn. (2000), 1040; BDAG include Heb. 1:3 under this classification.

92. Hugh W. Montefiore, *A Commentary on the Epistle to the Hebrews* (London: Black, 1964), 35.

93. James D. G. Dunn, *Christology in the Making* (London and Philadelphia: S.C.M., 1980), 206-7, "a striking expression of Wisdom Christology."

94. Barnabas Lindars, *The Theology of the Letter to the Hebrews* (Cambridge: Cambridge University Press, 1991) 31-35; cf. Anthony T. Hanson, *Jesus Christ in the Old Testament* (London: SPCK, 1965), 48-82.

These "hypostases" also include God's *glory* in the Old Testament and in Judaism, mirrored in Christ as *the radiance of God's glory* (Heb. 1:3a; Wis. 9:26; also Wis. 7:21-27; 9:2). If we place these classic texts beside Heb. 1:1-3; 1 Cor. 8:6; and Col. 1:16-17, we are not far from the world of the Nicene Creed: "God from God, light from light, God from true God . . . of one being with the Father; through him [Christ] all things were made." In Jüngel's evocative language, Christ is to be called "the Place of the Conceivability of God."[95]

In this context the phrase "at the right hand of God" comes into its own in Hebrews and in the ecumenical creeds. Ellingworth and Vanhoye see it as the centerpiece of a chiastic structure in Hebrews.[96] The writer clearly uses Ps. 110:4, which appears in Heb. 1:13 as the climax of the seven quotations from the Old Testament in 1:3-13. Related themes emerge from the citations of Ps. 2:7; and 110:1; and some regard Hebrews as a homiletical reflection or midrash on Ps. 110 in the light of Christology.[97] While some modern Christologies find it difficult to reconcile "true God" and "true man," as John Macquarrie observes, "the author of Hebrews seeks to reconcile the two codes . . . through the concept of priesthood."[98]

This brings us to a critical point in our argument. Jesus is never explicitly called "God" in the Synoptic gospels. I have argued elsewhere that the effectiveness of the speech-acts of Jesus to convey authentic literation, empowerment, forgiveness, new life, commissioning, and promise *presuppose what is not explicitly stated.*[99] Until *by lifestyle and deeds, and above all by the cross and resurrection,* Jesus has manifested in the public domain what words alone could never have conveyed without misunderstanding, Jesus shows reserve in making oral claims about himself, preferring to focus on the reign of *God.* The earlier epistles of Paul, however, begin to make explicit statements about Jesus Christ as mediate Creator and Lord (1 Cor. 8:6; Rom. 9:5), by the early and middle 50s. Even so, the fact that the most explicit or weighty expression about the deity of Jesus Christ comes broadly in the later writings of the New Testament (especially Hebrews, Titus, John, 1 John and 2 Peter) suggests a problem. Raymond Brown writes, "If we date New Testament times from 30 to 100, quite clearly the use of 'God' for Je-

---

95. E. Jüngel, *God and the Mystery of the World: On the Foundation of the Theology of the Crucified One,* trans. D. L. Guder (Edinburgh: T&T Clark, 1983), 152; cf. 152-69.

96. Ellingworth, *Hebrews,* 95-98; A. Vanhoye, *Structure and Message of the Epistle to the Hebrews* (Rome: Pontifical Biblical Institute, 1989), 25-76.

97. G. W. Buchanan, *To the Hebrews,* Anchor Bible 36 (Garden City, N.Y.: Doubleday, 1972).

98. John Macquarrie, *Jesus Christ in Modern Thought* (London: S.C.M. and Philadelphia: Trinity Press International, 1990), 125.

99. Thiselton, "Christology in Luke, Speech-Act Theory, and the Problem of Dualism in Christology," in Joel B. Green and Max Turner (eds.), *Jesus of Nazareth: Lord and Christ* (Grand Rapids: Eerdmans, 1994), 453-72; repr. in Thiselton, *Thiselton on Hermeneutics,* 99-166; and further in *Thiselton on Hermeneutics,* 117-29 and "A Retrospective Re-appraisal," 131-49.

sus belongs to the second half of the period, and becomes frequent only towards the end of the period."[100]

Why might this be the case? Brown offers a convincing *hermeneutical* explanation and understanding. He writes, "The most plausible explanation is that in the earliest stage of Christianity the *Old Testament heritage dominated* the use of the title 'God'; hence 'God' was a title *too narrow to be applied to Jesus. It referred strictly to the Father of Jesus,* to the God to whom he prayed. Gradually . . . 'God' was understood to be a broader term."[101] God had revealed so much of himself in Jesus that 'God' could (indeed had to) include both the Father and the Son. Liturgical and devotional practices hastened this broader understanding. Thus Rom. 9:5, Tit. 2:13, 2 Pet. 1:1, and 1 John 5:20 are doxologies. In 1.2 and 3.1 of this study we argued that worship and doxology constitute fundamental and primary expressions of Christian doctrine.

This *hermeneutical* understanding remains more credibly anchored in the "home" horizons of the New Testament itself than purely *historical* speculations about the development of a "two-stage" Christology into a "three-stage" Christology, or, still less convincing, of the effects of pressures from the Greek world to transpose narratives of the earthly Jesus into mythological or metaphysical terms. Indeed, it was precisely such speculation that initiated the disastrous debates of the late eighteenth century, the whole of the nineteenth century, and the first two-thirds of the twentieth century about "the Jesus of history and the Christ of faith." In his brilliant and incisive critique (endorsed by Hans Küng) Karl-Josef Kuschel calls these "Failed Conversations of Yesterday."[102] Yet any approach to the doctrine of the person of Christ is still, at least for the present, to some extent obligated to explore what lessons arise from this unhappy and largely unproductive cul-de-sac, if only to avoid repeating its mistakes and to note hermeneutical issues that arise. To diagnose sources of hermeneutical malaise belongs to a hermeneutics of doctrine only a little less than exploring positive hermeneutical resources and insights.

17.4. The Jesus of History and the Christ of Faith: A Failed Debate within Reductionist Horizons

This largely confused and destructive debate was sparked off by Hermann Samuel Reimarus (1694-1768) and Gotthold Ephraim Lessing (1729-1781). Reimarus expressed extreme scepticism about a Christian doctrine of Jesus Christ as true God and true man, and attacked reports of the miracles of Jesus as unreliable,

---

100. Brown, *Jesus, God and Man,* 31.

101. Brown, *Jesus, God and Man,* 33-34.

102. Kuschel, *Born before All Time? The Dispute over Christ's Origin,* trans. John Bowden (London: S.C.M., 1992), 35-175; cf. Küng's Foreword, xvii-ix.

not least because "Jesus himself could not perform miracles where people had not faith beforehand. . . . Nothing was easier than to invent as many miracles as they pleased. . . . It is always a sign that a doctrine or history possesses no depth of authenticity when one is obliged to resort to miracles in order to prove its truth."[103] The apostles were "chiefly men of lower class" and "induced by ambitious motives . . . to follow Jesus"; and "the new doctrine of the apostles was an undoubted fabrication."[104] Sections 54-60 of the *Fragments* trace the alleged "fabrication" of the resurrection and the allegedly manipulative power-play that marked the beginnings of the apostolic church.

Reimarus combined aspects of Hume's scepticism with Enlightenment rationalism and deism.[105] G. E. Lessing gained access to his unpublished manuscripts through the family of Reimarus, and from among a huge amount of unpublished material Lessing published sections of it anonymously over a period from 1774 to 1778. Lessing agreed with Reimarus that the human testimony to the events of the historical life of Jesus was inadequate and unreliable. In 1777 he published "On the Proof of Spirit and Power," the title of which derived from Origen. Origen had argued that the authenticity of the Spirit and power of Christian faith could be demonstrated. Lessing replied that he was "no longer in the same situation as Origen's," because he had access only to "human reports of Spirit and power."

This gave rise to Lessing's notorious axiom: "If no historical truth can be demonstrated, then, nothing can be demonstrated by means of historical truths. That is: *accidental truths of history can never become the proof of necessary truths of reason. . . . That, then, is the great ugly ditch* (der garstige breite Graben) *which I cannot cross.*"[106]

The terms *necessary* and *accidental* expose the nature of Lessing's problem and agenda. *Necessary* truths are those that are *logically certain* because they follow *deductively* from an axiomatic promise; they are *analytically or formally true.* Only the tradition of "high" rationalism from Descartes to deism, and the tradition promoted by Lessing, seriously expected and demanded that truths of religion should be of the same order as logically demonstrable truths.

Our discussion above of "foundationalism" brought into the open the distinction between the "strong" foundationalism of high rationalism and the

---

103. Hermann Samuel Reimarus, *Reimarus: Fragments,* ed. Charles H. Talbert and trans. R. S. Fraser (London: S.C.M., 1971 and Philadelphia: Fortress, 1970), sect. 48, 232-33, and sect. 49, 234.

104. Reimarus, *Fragments,* 13, 240-41, and 243.

105. On Reimarus see Charles H. Talbert, "Introduction" to the *Fragments,* 1-43; Colin Brown, *Jesus in European Protestant Thought, 1778-1860* (Grand Rapids: Baker, 1985), 1-56; Colin Brown, *Miracles and the Critical Mind* (Grand Rapids: Eerdmans and Carlisle: Paternoster, 1984), 170-90; and Alistair E. McGrath, *The Making of Modern German Christology: From the Enlightenment to Pannenberg* (Oxford: Blackwell, 1986), 14-19.

106. Gotthold Ephraim Lessing, *Lessing's Theological Writings,* ed. Henry Chadwick (London: Black, 1956), 52-53 (my italics).

"weak" or "soft" foundationalism of reasonableness and plausibility within a fallibilist framework. Lessing was in actuality formulating the obvious: historical reconstruction of the life of Jesus could never, in the nature of the case, match the criteria required for the *necessary* truths of *deductive* logic. History yields accidental or *contingent* truths. However, our discussions of Torrance in 8.1, of Lonergan and Pannenberg in 8.2 and 8.3, and of Lakatos and Murphy in 8.4 show how *un*reasonably overdrawn and "hyperrationalist" Lessing's demands were.

Colin Brown captures the mood of Lessing's concerns, but perhaps almost overgenerously understates it. He writes, "History is so full of uncertainties that it cannot match the self-evident compelling power of purely rational argument."[107] Whether or not history is "so full of uncertainties," historical reconstruction could never belong to the same order of truth or certainty as that of logical necessity. In his careful study *Lessing's "Ugly Ditch"* Gordon Michalson shows that for Lessing the "ditch" was broadened not only because of the *temporal* gap, which Lessing cites when he alludes to Origen; but also, second, because of a *metaphysical* gap, which is of a different order from the problem of temporal distance. This involves Leibniz's distinction between contingent and necessary truths. But there is also a third contributory factor to the ditch or gap. Lessing implies an *"existential gap"* concerning the difficulties of *religious appropriation*.[108]

Lessing viewed the teachings of Jesus as of a different order from the supposed history or life of Jesus, which embodied, for example, accounts of miracles. Of the latter Lessing writes, "I deny that they can and should bind me to the very least faith in the other teachings of Christ."[109] Michalson comments that here "theology gradually becomes *hermeneutical* virtually without remainder."[110] The upshot of Lessing's work, summed up in his famous dictum, was to shake the confidence of thinkers and writers in historical reconstructions of lives of Jesus, especially when coupled with quasi-positivist or naturalistic assumptions of Reimarus on one side, and later Albert Schweitzer's sceptical conclusions in *The Quest of the Historical Jesus*. As Macquarrie observes, historical truths "would not have the universality that the true rationalist seeks."[111]

Kuschel perceives that the "history and faith" gulf identified by Lessing gives rise to yet another "ugly ditch." He writes, "Lessing saw a gulf between the language of the New Testament and the language of dogmatics."[112] It provoked a gulf between the universe of discourse characteristic of biblical scholarship and

---

107. Brown, *Miracles and the Critical Mind*, 111; cf. 110-11.

108. Gordon E. Michalson, *Lessing's "Ugly Ditch": A Study of Theology and History* (University Park, PA and London: Pennsylvania State University Press, 1985), 8-20.

109. Lessing, *Lessing: Theological Writings*, 53.

110. Michalson, *Lessing's "Ugly Ditch,"* 18 (my italics). Cf. also Daniel Fuller, *Easter Faith and History* (London: Tyndale and Grand Rapids: Eerdmans, 1965), 27-49.

111. Macquarrie, *Jesus Christ in Modern Thought*, 178.

112. Kuschel, *Born before All Time?* 30.

the universe of discourse characteristic of doctrine or systematic theology. He declares, *"That is the problem of all modern theology"* (my italics).[113] Kuschel points out that although the break or gulf finds classic expression in Protestant theology (for example, between the dogmatics of Karl Barth and the exegesis of Rudolf Bultmann), this is "also of fundamental significance for Catholic theology."[114] A major issue is the perception of the "pre-existence of Christ as a 'problem'; Rahner, Küng, Kasper, Schillebeeckx and Sobrino all address the Chalcedonian two natures christology" as that which has been put in question.

In the chronological development of the "Jesus of history" and "Christ of faith" debate, Immanuel Kant (1724-1804) stood as an ambivalent figure. In light of his *Religion within the Limits of Reason* (1791), Macquarrie is right to describe his approach as "Rationalist Christology."[115] Nevertheless Kant also sought to define the *limits* of human reason and the absolute status of moral value. This included the moral value of the teaching of Jesus, which thus transcended the realm of reason. Indeed, "reasoning" involved a measure of human construction or shaping that reveals Lessing's concept of reason as simplistic.

By naming Jesus Christ as an "archetype" Kant placed the figure of Jesus beyond the strictly empirical realm. As Macquarrie argues, Kant held the notion of Christ as an archetype who "has *come down* to us from heaven and has assumed our humanity . . . an acknowledgement of 'revelation' and even something like 'incarnation', like the *descendit* of the Nicene Creed."[116] On the other hand, Kant's very convictions about the limits of thought and the disjunction between "God" and the empirical realm leave more than a hint of docetism at the same time.

The Christology of Friedrich Schleiermacher (1768-1834) also contains ambiguities, but in the midst of ambiguities his work embodies at least five constructive features.

(i) First, Schleiermacher *holds together* issues relating to *the person and work of Christ*. We have noted the importance of this in Anselm in 16.2.

(ii) Schleiermacher never abandoned his early pietist conviction that the center of Christian faith and divine grace lies in *the experience of a personal relationship with God*. Hence he writes in *The Christian Faith*: *"The Redeemer (Erlöser) is like all men in virtue of the identity of human nature, but distinguished from them all by the constant potency of His God-consciousness, which was a veritable existence of God in Him"* (his italics).[117]

(iii) The Redeemer also follows the biblical traditions in seeing Jesus as "free from all sinfulness." But contrary to some more recent writers, this in no way questions for Schleiermacher his being truly human.

---

113. Kuschel, *Born before All Time?* 30.
114. Kuschel, *Born before All Time?* 31.
115. Macquarrie, *Jesus Christ in Modern Thought*, 175-91.
116. Macquarrie, *Jesus Christ in Modern Thought*, 184.
117. Schleiermacher, *The Christian Faith*, Part II, sect. 94, 385.

(iv) Schleiermacher struggles to avoid the two "opposite" errors of docetism and Ebionitism. Against docetism, Jesus Christ lived "a true human life."[118] Against Ebionitism, the God-consciousness of Jesus did not simply "emerge," and it was "not imperfect."[119] Against docetism, Jesus "had to develop gradually in human fashion into a really manifest consciousness."[120]

(v) Schleiermacher explored in soteriological terms the identity and role of Jesus Christ as "the Second Adam." This brings and constitutes "a new spiritual life."[121] The coming of Christ is a new and creative event.

If there are also ambiguities in Schleiermacher's work, these arise in part from his intense desire to take with the fullest seriousness the Enlightenment critique of Christian dogmatics (in spite of Strauss's later jibe about "the last churchly Christology"). In relation to "lives of Jesus," he does not believe that the New Testament term "Son of God" implied divine nature. While not denying the possibility of "miracle," he also tends to diffuse the term, sometimes to denote *any* manifestation of divine presence, action, or initiative. The "entry" of Jesus Christ as Redeemer into "the corporate life of sinfulness" without originating *from* it constitutes a "miraculous fact" *(eine wunderbare Erscheinung)*, but only if and when "miracle" has been properly and broadly defined.[122] He rejects notions of a miraculous "virgin birth" if this is taken to exclude "male activity" as sharing in the conception of Jesus.[123]

The more serious problem, however, is that Schleiermacher in the end tends to define the God-consciousness of Jesus as different from that of other persons *only, or no more than, in degree.* He writes, "There must reside in human nature the possibility of taking up the divine into itself, just as did happen in Christ. The *possibility* of this resides in human nature, so that the actual implanting therein of the divine element must be a purely divine . . . act."[124] Macquarrie calls this Christology "humanistic," for Schleiermacher "has promised to expound the incarnation as a natural fact."[125] Schleiermacher, then, firmly rejects a "two natures" Christology. These, he argues, cannot coexist in a single person. Moreover, Christian orthodoxy makes this even more difficult by understanding Jesus Christ *both* as having two natures *and* as sharing a single essence with the Father and the Holy Spirit as Trinity.[126] In 19.1 we note that his Trinitarian doctrine, taking up a mere twenty pages at the end of his long work, is very disappointing.

---

118. Schleiermacher, *The Christian Faith*, Part II, sect. 93, 381; further, Part I, sect. 22, 99-101.

119. Schleiermacher, *The Christian Faith*, Part II, sect. 97, 398; cf. Part I, sect. 22.

120. Schleiermacher, *The Christian Faith*, Part II, sect. 93, 381.

121. Schleiermacher, *The Christian Faith*, Part II, sect. 94, 389.

122. Schleiermacher, *The Christian Faith*, Part II, sect. 93, 381.

123. Schleiermacher, *The Christian Faith*, Part II, sect. 97, 403.

124. Schleiermacher, *The Christian Faith*, Part I, sect. 13, 64.

125. Macquarrie, *Jesus Christ in Modern Thought*, 208.

126. Schleiermacher, *The Christian Faith*, Part II, sect. 96, 392-98; cf. sects. 170-172, 738-51.

If Lessing and Kant have veered away from the "history" side of the gulf, Schleiermacher has struggled to keep Christology anchored in history. Whereas Kant thinks primarily as a philosopher, Schleiermacher's mind-set is perhaps more closely that of a New Testament scholar even than that of a systematic theologian, in spite of his teaching almost every theological subdiscipline except the Old Testament.

G. W. F. Hegel (1770-1831) reverses the situation, once again. Hegel understands the incarnation of Jesus Christ "from above" as the climactic moment in the historical and dialectical process of the unfolding of Absolute Spirit *(Geist)*. In Christ the Absolute becomes "Other." *The eternal Idea* becomes concrete in the human figure of Jesus of Nazareth.

Hegel opposed Schleiermacher's Christology as both too "churchly" and too closely tied to the Romanticism of the time, which, in Hegel's view, placed too much emphasis on psychological and subjective processes. No mere "feeling," even if it was a feeling *of* what lay beyond, could be adequate for ontological truth-claims. Philosophical reflection demands a more critical and rigorous method than that which relied on "representations" *(Vorstellungen)* in religion; critical thought worked with the concept *(Begriff)*.

Hegel understood the incarnation in conceptual terms as part of the dialectic of the life of God as Absolute. His *hermeneutical horizon of understanding* appears in his section on "the necessity of the religious standpoint" in the first volume of *Lectures on the Philosophy of Religion*.[127] Hegel writes, "Religion is the consciousness of what is *in and for itself true*, in contrast to sensuous, finite truth, and to sense perceptions. Accordingly it is a rising above . . . what is immediate, sensuous, individual . . . a going out and on to the Other."[128]

Thus *truth* relates *not to contingent history,* but to *the dialectic of Spirit or Mind (Geist)*. "Spirit in its finiteness is consciousness. . . . Nature is only appearance."[129] But, Hegel continues, "the abrogation of this finiteness constitutes the religious standpoint, where God is Object of consciousness as absolute Power . . . as representing the unfolding of the natural and spiritual universe . . . in progressive movement."[130] "Religion is not a transaction of man . . . but the absolute Idea itself . . . in its consciousness of itself" in relation to "what is *other* than itself."[131]

Within this horizon of understanding, Hegel conceives of the incarnation of Jesus Christ as a phenomenon of *divine self-differentiation* within the ongoing dialectic of Absolute Spirit. Hegel writes, "Undoubtedly the infinite idea of the In-

127. Georg W. F. Hegel, *Lectures on the Philosophy of Religion,* trans. from the 2d German edn. by E. B. Spiers and J. B. Sanderson, 3 vols. (London: Kegan, Paul, Trench, Trübner, 1895), vol. 1, 105-15.

128. Hegel, *Philosophy of Religion,* vol. 1, 106.

129. Hegel, *Philosophy of Religion,* vol. 1, 111.

130. Hegel, *Philosophy of Religion,* vol. 1, 113.

131. Hegel, *Philosophy of Religion,* vol. 1, 206.

carnation" constitutes "that speculative central point" of this dialectical process.[132] Hegel observes in his *Phenomenology of Mind* that "The Good, the Righteous, the Holy . . . have their support in this central point, and only *are* when consciousness goes back into thought . . . revealed [when] the divine nature is the same as the human."[133] Peter Hodgson explains, "The *possibility* of such an incarnation is based on the general concept of 'incarnation' meaning . . . the ideal unity or implicit identity of divine and human spirit . . . 'the universal divine idea.'"[134]

This does not imply that the earthly story is of no relevance to Hegel. The concrete, contingent career of Jesus forms part of Hegel's Christology. But it is not the horizon of understanding within which it gains its currency. *God, as it were, becomes "other" in Jesus Christ.* The death of Jesus Christ is a shameful, tragic event. The history of Jesus Christ (contrary later to Strauss) "is not taken merely as a myth . . . but as something perfectly historical."[135] "When the fullness of time was come, God sent His Son, i.e., when Spirit had entered so deeply into itself as to lessen its infinitude."[136] "The death of Christ is the central point round which all else turns, . . . the death of Christ does away with the human side of Christ's nature, . . . the Other-Being or otherness is . . . transfigured. . . . *God has died, God is dead.*"[137] But "God maintains himself in the process . . . the death of death. . . . God comes to life again, and these things are reversed."[138] Death is finitude; resurrection *is "absorption of natural finitude"* and belongs to the realm of Spirit as Spirit.[139] The era of the Spirit is the reconciling synthesis that overcomes the antithesis or "otherness" of Christ's suffering and death. Hegel cannot refrain from making a polemical quip that in his view Catholic liturgy and doctrine remain trapped in the negative "antithesis" of the Mass, while Protestant theology moves on to the realm of the resurrection, the infinite, and the Spirit.

In terms of Lessing's "ugly ditch" Hegel sees Christology as an episode in a divine unfolding of divine life "from above." Kierkegaard's ironic critique concerning a "theocentric" viewpoint has some force here. Although the life and death of Jesus remains fundamental for Hegel, his horizon of understanding pri-

---

132. Hegel, *Philosophy of Religion*, vol. 1, 151.

133. Georg W. F. Hegel, *The Phenomenology of Mind*, trans. J. B. Baillie (New York: Harper, 1967), 759-60.

134. Peter C. Hodgson, "Georg Wilhelm Friedrich Hegel," in Ninian Smart et al. (eds.), *Nineteenth-Century Religious Thought in the West*, 3 vols. (Cambridge: Cambridge University Press, 1985), vol. 1, 103; cf. 81-121.

135. Hegel, *Philosophy of Religion*, vol. 1, 146.

136. Hegel, *Philosophy of Religion*, vol. 3, 112.

137. Hegel, *Philosophy of Religion*, vol. 3, 86, 87, 89, and 91.

138. Hegel, *Philosophy of Religion*, vol. 3, 91.

139. Hegel, *Philosophy of Religion*, vol. 3, 93.

marily concerns Spirit and Idea. Nevertheless Hegel's boldness of vision has bequeathed a legacy of hermeneutical resources for later formulations of Christology and of the Trinity. The self-differentiation between Christ, the Spirit, and God the Father plays a seminal role in later distinctive developments on the part especially of Moltmann and Pannenberg, and "the death of death" becomes a further resource for Moltmann's hermeneutic of hope and Christology. Hence Hegel merits our attention in a *hermeneutics* of doctrine as a pioneer of formulations that come into their own only in the late twentieth century.

It is otherwise, however, with David F. Strauss (1808-1874). In hermeneutical terms Strauss moves from confusion to sheer bankruptcy as his work develops. His legacy for hermeneutics is to leave a trail of well-marked pitfalls to avoid.

In common with other "left-wing" pupils and critics of Hegel, including Feuerbach, Strauss turns Hegel's approach upside down. Initially his protest is valid. How could Hegel claim that the universal Absolute Spirit reached a new stage of consciousness or thought specifically in the person of Jesus Christ unless he had undertaken a more rigorous critical historical inquiry into the identity, words, and deeds of Jesus of Nazareth? The pendulum would swing once again *to history.* Otherwise Strauss showed an initial sympathy with Hegel and even, temporarily, with Schleiermacher. However, he soon went his own way with the publication of a first edition of his notorious *The Life of Jesus* (1835-36), written at the early age of twenty-seven.

Strauss regarded the historically reconstructed life of Jesus as owing much to the category of *myth.* He understood *myth* to denote the communication of *ideas* cast into the form of *historical narrative.*[140] He began from the "history" side of Lessing's ugly ditch, but also drawing on Hegel's distinction between *Vorstellung* (representation) and *Begriff* (concept) regarded the history of the life of Jesus as determined more by loose "representations" of ideas than by genuinely rigorous or authentic historical reports. Myth, for Strauss was, in Macquarrie's words, "a production of spirit . . . on the level of picture thinking, what Hegel called *Vorstellung.*"[141] Strauss increasingly came to attack the authenticity of the "supernatural" events that supposedly surrounded the life of Jesus. These, he argued, were "read back" from the second century.

"Historical myths," in Strauss's view, are those in which historical events have become transposed into miraculous marvels, as, for example, in the event of the baptism of Jesus. They are not conscious inventions, but often portray Jesus through the lenses of miraculous events associated with figures, occurrences, and expectations found in the Old Testament, and current in Judaism during the

---

140. David F. Strauss, *The Life of Jesus Critically Examined,* ed. Peter C. Hodgson, Lives of Jesus Series (Philadelphia: Fortress, 1972), sects. 15-16.

141. Macquarrie, *Jesus Christ in Modern Thought,* 225; similarly Alistair McGrath, *The Making of Modern German Christology,* 34-38; and Claude Welch, *Protestant Thought in the Nineteenth Century,* 2 vols. (New Haven, CT: Yale University Press, 1972 and 1985), vol. 1, 148-49.

time of Jesus. There are certain historical facts "behind" much of this material, but to reconstruct these can seldom go beyond conjecture.

This has moved a long way from the Christology of church doctrine, and Strauss presses this point. He writes, "Conceived in respect of an individual, a God-man, the attributes and functions that the church's doctrine ascribes to Christ are contradictory."[142] Notions of the virgin birth and the miracle worker are irrelevant both to nonmythical historical reconstruction and to Christian faith. The notion of an individual, however, who in his death and resurrection (in a mythical sense) participates in the divine human life of the race by the negation of naturalness and sensuousness, the negation of negation, "offers a way to spiritual life."[143]

The earlier editions of Strauss's *Life of Jesus* made an enormous impact. Hans Frei makes a key point when he writes, "He shifted the terms in which it [Life-of-Jesus research and Christology] would be carried on thereafter: *he assured the priority of the historical over the conceptual argument in the attack on traditional Christology*" (my italics).[144]

Over his lifetime Strauss revised his *Life of Jesus* a number of times, both to accommodate criticism and to express his changing views. In the first edition he had discounted the Gospel of John as a reliable historical source. In the third edition (1838-39) he went part of the way to meet the intense criticism that his work provoked by conceding the *possibility* that the Fourth Gospel might contain some authentic historical material. Strauss became better known to English-speaking audiences when George Eliot (Mary Ann Evans) translated the fourth edition (1840) into English in 1846. There is an allusion to her awareness of wider Continental scholarship when her main character in *Middlemarch* (1871), Dorothea, warns Edward Casaubon not to exhaust his health on merely replicating work already done in Continental Europe.

By 1872 Strauss had effectively renounced Christianity, answering his question "Are we still Christian?" in the negative, in *The Old Faith and the New*. Jesus had become a remote figure who cannot be decisive for us. Strauss rejected as misplaced his earlier optimism that we can have Christian faith in Jesus whether or not the major historical foundations have been chipped away. Alistair McGrath sums up the dilemma that Strauss created and that finally defeated him: "Faith must either collapse or else must be reinterpreted by dissociating the dogmatic principle of incarnation from the claim that the idea had been fully embodied in a concrete historical individual, Jesus of Nazareth."[145] Strauss had dismissed Schleiermacher's Christology as a last attempt to make "the churchly

---

142. Strauss, *Life of Jesus*, sect. 149, 780.

143. Strauss, *Life of Jesus*, sect. 149, 780.

144. Hans Frei, "David Friedrich Strauss," in Ninian Smart et al. (eds.), *Nineteenth-Century Religious Thought*, vol. 1, 224; cf. 215-60.

145. McGrath, *The Making of Modern German Christology*, 38.

Christ" acceptable to the modern world. But whether he put anything in its place except "Failed Conversations of Yesterday" may be seriously doubted.

F. C. Baur (1792-1860) had been Strauss's mentor in spite of the fact that many of Baur's publications postdated those that Strauss published in very early years. Baur was disappointed in Strauss, especially in the lack of rigor in his historical method. Baur also approached Christology from the *historical* side of Lessing's "ugly ditch" (in spite of his late dating of some so-called "catholic" writings of the New Testament). W. G. Kümmel describes Baur's approach as "a total historical perspective," whether to Jesus, Paul, or the later "catholic" Acts and epistles.[146]

Yet sooner or later a reaction was bound to occur, and one of the most radical was that of Martin Kähler (1835-1912). Under the often-cited title, *Der sogenannte historische Jesus und der geschichtliche, biblische Christus, The So-Called Historical Jesus and the Historic, Biblical Christ,* Kähler argued that the "historical" Jesus of modern authors "conceals from us the living Christ."[147] "I regard the entire Life-of-Jesus movement as a blind alley."[148] The "real" Christ is not that of New Testament historical scholarship with all its mere probabilities and uncertainties. (We might sympathize with Kähler when, unlike most systematic theologians and philosophers, very few biblical specialists say, "This is true," but their highest accolade is "This is almost certain." I doubt whether I can plead entire innocence of using this convention on occasion.) In his memorable aphorism Kähler declared, *"This real Christ is the Christ who is preached"* (his italics).[149]

Kähler was strongly influenced by the theology of the Reformation. On one side he saw the guild of New Testament scholarship as a new "papacy"; they appeared to control what ordinary Christian people could believe with integrity. On the other he believed that the need to master or to subscribe to sophisticated techniques of historical reconstruction and hypotheses constituted a form of justification by intellectual "works." This latter view finds a prominent place in the thought of Rudolf Bultmann. Kähler further paves the way for Bultmann's contrast between *Historie* as *past* history, or *objectified* history, and *Geschichte* as that which carries present historical *significance* "for me."

This last distinction reveals that we cannot actually live in Kähler's dreamland. Christian doctrine rejects docetism, and hermeneutics entails contingency, temporality, embodiment, and above all linguistic currency and truth-claims in the public domain. We explored these points in Chapters 3 and 4 of Part I, as well

146. W. G. Kümmel, *The New Testament: The History of the Investigation of Its Problems,* trans. S. M. Gilmour and Howard C. Kee (London: S.C.M., 1973 and Nashville: Abingdon, 1972), 136; cf. 127-43.

147. Martin Kähler, *The So-Called Historical Jesus and the Historic, Biblical Christ,* ed. and trans. Carl E. Braaten (Philadelphia: Fortress, 1964), 16.

148. Kähler, *The So-Called Historical Jesus,* 16.

149. Kähler, *The So-Called Historical Jesus,* 66.

as in such sections as 2.1, 5.2, and 6.2. As John Macquarrie comments on Bultmann, how could we talk of dying and rising with Christ unless Christ actually died and was raised?[150]

Apart from Bultmann, perhaps the one remaining major figure among those who set the agenda that turned out to be the "blind alley" was Albert Schweitzer, and his *The Quest of the Historical Jesus* (German *Von Reimarus zu Wrede*, 1906). Like Strauss and Baur he approached the "historical" side of Lessing's gulf but simultaneously undermined confidence among ordinary Christian believers in what such an approach might achieve.[151] Schweitzer himself believed that the life-of-Jesus research in Germany was "the greatest achievement of German theology," but conceded its negative effect on doctrine. It "cleared the site for a new edifice."[152] Schweitzer argued that initially all the exponents of what we now call "the first quest," writers from Reimarus (c. 1774) to Wrede (1901), *had shaped the figure of the "historical" Jesus largely in accord with their prior methods, interests, and assumptions.* Schweitzer argued, "Before Reimarus no one had attempted to form a historical conception of the life of Jesus."[153] He expresses admiration for the power of Reimarus's writing and his perception of the importance of eschatology for Jesus, but Reimarus misunderstood eschatology as a proclamation of a "political" Messiah.[154] Schweitzer also expresses a degree of admiration for Strauss, but recalls that Strauss turned his back on any compromise with church doctrine, and reconciled himself to giving up both teaching and the Christian faith.[155] Bruno Bauer adopted a literary method, but saw the "history" of Jesus as caught amidst the "pitched battle" between John and the Synoptic gospels. His work of 1840 was a "sceptical" life of Jesus.[156] Ernest Rénan provided "the first life of Jesus for the Catholic world," but constructed it largely "with his artistic imagination."[157] He portrayed a living figure, but one that reflected the Romanticist imagination of the time: a simple Galilean rabbi, "a winsome teacher who offered forgiveness to all . . . a noble pioneer."[158] Rénan professes to write a "scientific" work, but replaces rigor with "the highly coloured phrases of the novelist."[159]

Wilhelm Bousset and Johannes Weiss, Schweitzer concedes, raise more serious issues to be reckoned with. These include especially Weiss's appreciation of

---

150. John Macquarrie, "Philosophy and Theology in Bultmann's Thought," in Charles W. Kegley (ed.), *The Theology of Rudolf Bultmann* (London: S.C.M., 1966), 141.

151. Albert Schweitzer, *The Quest of the Historical Jesus: A Critical Study of Its Progress from Reimarus to Wrede*, trans. W. Montgomery (London: Black, 3d edn. 1854 [1st Eng. edn. 1910]).

152. Schweitzer, *Quest*, 1.

153. Schweitzer, *Quest*, 13.

154. Schweitzer, *Quest*, 16 and 23.

155. Schweitzer, *Quest*, 68-96.

156. Schweitzer, *Quest*, 137-60.

157. Schweitzer, *Quest*, 181; cf. 180-92.

158. Schweitzer, *Quest*, 185 and 187.

159. Schweitzer, *Quest*, 191.

eschatology. Yet behind their mutual disagreements with each other the limits of historical method begin to appear.[160] The "historical" Jesus "will not be a Jesus Christ to whom the religion of the present can subscribe."[161] On his last page Schweitzer writes his well-known sentence: "He comes to us as One unknown, without a name, as of old, by the lake-side. . . . He speaks to us the same word, Follow thou me!"[162]

Schweitzer set the stage for Rudolf Bultmann. On one side Bultmann's *History of the Synoptic Tradition* appears to focus upon historical reconstruction. But it is not a reconstruction of the *life of Jesus*. In *Jesus and the Word* Bultmann writes, "We can now know almost nothing about the life and personality of Jesus, since the early Christian sources show no interest in either, are moreover fragmentary and often legendary, and other sources do not exist."[163] The Synoptic traditions embody not historical reports as such, but *testimony, kerygma, confession, and address.* It is a valid inference, Bultmann concedes, to believe *that* Jesus existed, *that* he called disciples to follow him, and *that* he was crucified. But the *"what"* of further narrative belongs to the realm of *kerygma* rather than objective history. He adds that whoever reads Schweitzer's brilliant *Quest* "must vividly realize this."[164]

Criticisms of Bultmann's approach are now too well known to bear further repetition. We have alluded already to Graham Stanton's work in which he asks whether Luke alone among early Christians wanted to provide or to possess "an orderly account of the events that have been fulfilled among us, just as they were handed on to us by those who from the beginning were eyewitnesses . . ." (Luke 1:1-2).[165] The literature is now too vast to cite without repetition. As is also well known, even Bultmann's former pupils, Ernst Käsemann, G. Bornkamm, and Ernst Fuchs, inaugurated a "new Quest" in which inferences about Jesus could be drawn from accounts of an interweaving of words and actions.[166] Käsemann's essay "The Problem of the Historical Jesus" (1953) urged in particular the need to avoid docetism.

The blind alley of "failed questions of yesterday" provides an example of various approaches from Lessing to Bultmann in which hermeneutical horizons

---

160. Schweitzer, *Quest,* 241-49; cf. 222-68.

161. Schweitzer, *Quest,* 396-97.

162. Schweitzer, *Quest,* 401.

163. Rudolf Bultmann, *Jesus and the Word,* trans. Louise F. Smith and E. Lantero (London: Collins/Fontana and New York: Scribner, 1958), 14.

164. Bultmann, *Jesus,* 14.

165. Stanton, *Jesus of Nazareth in New Testament Preaching;* cf. also Graham N. Stanton, *The Gospels and Jesus* (Oxford: Oxford University Press, 1989).

166. Ernst Käsemann, *Essays on New Testament Themes,* trans. A. R. Allenson (London: S.C.M., 1964), esp. 15-47; and Ernst Fuchs, *Studies of the Historical Jesus,* trans. A. Scobie (London: S.C.M., 1964).

were never adequately examined. If hermeneutics featured at all, interpretation was regarded as shaped by nineteenth-century assumptions about historical method, which were often positivist. Positivism was disguised as a "value-neutral" historical approach. The *twofold* historical conditioning of *both the text and the modern interpreter or reader* was ignored or suppressed, and played little or no part in inquiry. Like many blind alleys in the history of thought, they served to cry out for a radically new and different approach. This may be found partly in what has come to be known as "the third quest," but more especially in the approach of Wolfhart Pannenberg.

17.5. Broader Hermeneutical Horizons: The Third Quest and Wolfhart Pannenberg

The debate that began with Reimarus and Lessing and proceeded through Strauss and Schweitzer to Rudolf Bultmann is in general a history of "talking past" the real hermeneutical issues. Yet to trace this debate still remains *de rigueur* for New Testament Christology, since many of its inbuilt assumptions, first, about historical method, second, about myth, third, about a supposedly "malleable" historical Jesus, and fourth about what can be believed by "modern man," still shaped many discussions in the second half of the twentieth century. To cite two examples only, the book of essays *The Myth of God Incarnate* (1977) and some (although clearly not all) of the Cambridge essays *Christ, Faith and History* still seem to live in this Lessing-to-Bultmann world of concepts and criteria.[167] Many of the essays in *The Myth of God* tediously repeated them as axioms of "historical" scholarship.[168] Don Cupitt understated this when he wrote, "The themes of the present volume are not novel."[169]

Meanwhile, from the 1950s through to the 1970s the so-called New Quest appeared to bring history into the debate more fruitfully, with an emphasis upon the deeds of Jesus and an interweaving between word and event. Fuchs and Ebeling made progress in the area of hermeneutical theory by exploring Heidegger's notion of a projected "world" especially in the parables of Jesus. I have explored what came to be called the New Hermeneutic elsewhere, and do not need to comment further on this aspect.[170] In the end, however, Ernst Fuchs, at least, still viewed the

---

167. John Hick (ed.), *The Myth of God Incarnate* (London: S.C.M., 1977).

168. Hick (ed.), *Myth of God*, 8-9, 37 (Frances Young, once again, "the two stories" as an alternative dualism); 140-41 (Don Cupitt); 146-65 (Maurice Wiles); and 196-200 (Denis Nineham).

169. Don Cupitt, "The Christ of Christendom," in Hick, *Myth of God*, 137; cf. 133-47.

170. Thiselton, *Thiselton on Hermeneutics*, 417-40, 463-88, and 515-21; the first of these is reprinted from "The Parables as Language Event: Some Comments on Fuchs' Hermeneutics in the Light of Linguistic Philosophy," in *Scottish Journal of Theology* 23 (1970) 437-68; also Thiselton, *The Two Horizons*, 205-92 and 342-56.

resurrection as an intralinguistic event, and although he and Ebeling developed a broader hermeneutics, their contribution to Christology and to the faith and history debate never fulfilled its initial promise. N. T. Wright and James D. G. Dunn perceive the movement as having little lasting value, and are not alone in perceiving its value as transitory rather than permanent.[171]

Genuinely broader hermeneutical horizons have the effect of redirecting the debate on Christology into more permanently constructive directions through the emergence of two newer movements. The first has come, or is coming, to be known as the "third quest." N. T. Wright, who associates himself with this approach, offers a clear and helpful account of its origins and distinctive features.[172] He includes among earlier exponents of what developed into this newer approach George B. Caird, Martin Hengel, Ben Meyer, Otto Betz, and Bruce Chilton. He also cites more recent work from E. Sanders, Gerd Theissen, Anthony Harvey, Ben Witherington, and James Charlesworth, among others.[173] These writers seek historical truth about Jesus, but they are wiser than earlier modern writers in the critical tools and methods that they use. They rightly perceive that to call a text "literary" or "theological" does not thereby diminish its status as a historical source, and indeed that all three dimensions should be considered together.

Several new steps are significant. Whereas the "old" quest asked questions from within narrower horizons of meaning that excluded virtually *a priori* certain theological understandings of acts of God, this "third" quest works from within multiple horizons of understanding. Wright enumerates some of them. How does Jesus fit into Judaism? What were Jesus' aims? Why did Jesus die? How did the early church begin?[174] On top of all these, and in relation to all of these *together:* how does this genuinely historical research "relate to the contemporary church and world?"[175] There is an *openness* to these horizons of understandings that is *profoundly hermeneutical.* It coheres entirely with the pleas for openness from Gadamer, Betti, and Ricoeur, and in this it differs substantially from the *closed* assumptions of most of the agenda in the "old" quest. Wright observes, "If we play the game properly — if, that is, we leave the meanings of 'divine' and 'human' as unknowns until we have looked at the material — then there can be no advance prediction of what the result may look like."[176]

The words *"no advance prediction"* exactly and precisely sum up Gadamer's

---

171. N. T. Wright, *Jesus and the Victory of God: Christian Origins and the Question of God,* vol. 2 (London: SPCK, 1996), 23-25; Dunn, *Jesus Remembered: Christianity in the Making,* vol. 1 (Grand Rapids and Cambridge: Eerdmans, 2003), 78-85.

172. Wright, *Jesus and the Victory of God,* 83-124.

173. Wright, *Jesus,* 84, cites a longer list of names.

174. Wright, *Jesus,* 91-113.

175. Wright, *Jesus,* 117.

176. Wright, *Jesus,* 121.

central concern, which Ricoeur also endorses. Indeed, the phrase might almost have been borrowed from Gadamer. *Openness* to understand *on the terms of that which we seek to understand rather than imposing* a priori *a preconstructed conceptual grid of "closed" assumptions or conceptual grammar upon the terms of the inquiry* describes and fulfills the central aim of *Truth and Method*.

James Dunn's *Jesus Remembered* (2003) adds significantly to the development of the "third quest." Dunn traces the negative effects of the flight from dogma that characterized the Enlightenment and its consequent return to a "Neo-Liberal" Jesus. The exclusion of "miracle" as an *a priori* by the Deists, Reimarus, and Strauss has little to do with the search for a viable, open, and accurate historical method.[177] Dunn further surveys the Liberal "lives" of Rénan and Harnack, and the collapse of the "liberal" Jesus with Schweitzer. He concedes that the old Quest leaves "markers" for future reflection, but he turns to fresh resources. With Wright, Dunn recognizes *both* the "Jewishness" of Jesus *and* the need for *a more open hermeneutical horizon.* In a substantial chapter on hermeneutics he considers historical distance, the hermeneutical circle, the encounter with texts, and historically effective or "historically effected" consciousness in Gadamer.[178]

Nothing has been needlessly sacrificed to a supposed "ditch" between the Jesus of history and the Christ of faith. Dunn and Wright, among others, work within more appropriate, more comprehensive, hermeneutical horizons.

A closely related movement or subset within this newer approach among biblical specialists arises from a growing interest in the "theological" interpretation of the biblical writings. This consciously does not absorb biblical studies into dogmatics, but seeks to let the biblical text speak for itself. The journal *Ex Auditu* reflects these aims, and the series of eight volumes (to date) published in the international Scripture and Hermeneutics series similarly seeks to promote these concerns.[179] Rather than seeking to shape the biblical text into the image of the "modern" biblical interpreter, these two networks consciously desire the formative effects of texts to have a transformative impact *upon them.* But this is not undertaken uncritically. With Ricoeur, these two groups seek to employ a hermeneutic of suspicion and retrieval. At the time of writing I understand that the Society of Biblical Literature is in process of recognizing a group of this kind on the theological interpretation of Scripture.

We have placed all of this approach under the broad heading of the "third quest" in the specific context of Christology. However, another major and even

---

177. Dunn, *Jesus Remembered*, 25-29.

178. Dunn, *Jesus Remembered*, 99-136.

179. The two most recent volumes are Craig G. Bartholomew, Joel B. Green, and Anthony C. Thiselton (eds.), *Reading Luke: Interpretation, Reflection, and Formation*, Scripture and Hermeneutics 6 (Carlisle, U.K.: Paternoster and Grand Rapids: Zondervan, 2005) and Craig G. Bartholomew et al. (eds.), *Canon and Biblical Interpretation* (Grand Rapids: Zondervan, 2006 and Carlisle: Paternoster, 2007).

more decisive force in redirecting the course of the older debate is Wolfhart Pannenberg's approach to Christology. His *hermeneutical horizons are larger, wider, and more comprehensive* than the more restricted ones of those who begin by excluding *a priori* any approach to history except a positivist one. Pannenberg firmly rejects a scepticism derived from Hume or from deism about the supposedly coextensive boundaries of empirical inquiry, the created order, and divine action.

Pannenberg's starting point for Christology is typically open. Against Kähler he does not reduce the reality of Christ to the church's "proclamation" or its "faith" in contrast to history and to what transpires in the public domain. Against positivism he does not restrict the investigation of history only to what fits within a nontheistic or naturalistic frame, horizon of meaning, or truth-claim. He writes, "History is the most comprehensive horizon of Christian theology. All theological questions and answers are meaningful only within the framework of the history which God has with humanity and through humanity with his whole creation — the history moving toward a future still hidden from the world, but already revealed in Jesus Christ."[180] This presupposition, he writes, must be defended both against Bultmann's existentialism and "on the other side against the thesis developed by Martin Kähler . . . that the real context of faith is suprahistorical."[181]

Pannenberg *begins* with a Christology in the context of public history "from below." He writes, "The apostolic proclamation of Jesus of Nazareth as the Son of God began with his earthly coming, his fate at the end of his earthly path, and the divine action in raising him from the dead."[182] Some (cf. Sykes's comment in n. 73) have argued that the very allusion to the resurrection renders this not genuinely a Christology "from below." But against the reductive positivism of some biblical scholars Pannenberg insists that we engage with biblical texts concerning "the total character of the coming of Jesus and his history."[183] Indeed, if we consider the horizon of understanding that shaped the interpretation of Jesus in the earliest communities, the Old Testament and apocalyptic expectations (as we argued in 17.2) play their part in shaping an authentic understanding of Jesus, and the expectation of resurrection, or at least of divine vindication, is part and parcel of the latter. We cannot simply replace that horizon with an alien frame derived from positivism or from some other "modern" philosophy. As Pannenberg observes in an early essay, event and meaning are *intertwined* as a whole.[184]

180. Pannenberg, "Redemptive Event and History," in *Basic Questions in Theology*, vol. 1, 15.
181. Pannenberg, *Basic Questions*, vol. 1, 15.
182. Pannenberg, *Systematic Theology*, vol. 2, 278.
183. Pannenberg, *Systematic Theology*, vol. 1, 280.
184. Pannenberg, "The Revelation of God in Jesus of Nazareth," in James M. Robinson and John B. Cobb, *New Frontiers in Theology*: vol. 3, *Theology as History* (New York: Harper & Row, 1967), 120; cf. 101-33.

The early 1967 essay to which we have just alluded sets out the programmatic approach that Pannenberg develops more fully in his later writings. Jesus Christ, he writes, "stood in a tradition that expected the coming of . . . God."[185] He shared the Israelite tradition of his hearers. When he called his disciples, "Jesus did not demand trust in his person without giving reasons for it."[186] This understanding of Jesus arose from his place within a horizon of understanding already established by the Old Testament and Judaism. Anticipations of universality emerge because the God of Israel is also Creator of the World. Jesus transformed Jewish tradition "from within," even if a "non-Jewish conception of the one unknown God" was transformed "from without" by the biblical heritage as shaped by Jesus.[187]

The second stage of Pannenberg's argument derives from the expectation of God's reign as a future act of God. *The truth and meaning of events emerge "only in the light of the End"* (my italics).[188] In the resurrection of Jesus Christ a *cosmic* event of the last days occurred.[189] A preliminary understanding of Jesus and divine purpose becomes possible in the interrelation between prophetic words, events, and expectation and the coming of Jesus, whom God raises from the dead. "The eschatological event which binds history into a whole brings about final knowledge of God."[190] *There is no separation between history and faith:* "We must reinstate today the original unity of facts and their meaning."[191] Pannenberg writes further, "Knowledge is not a stage beyond faith, but leads into faith."[192] Faith as based upon the trustworthiness of that to which it is directed. Hence "Christian faith must not be equated with a merely subjective conviction that would allegedly compensate for the uncertainty of an historical knowledge about Jesus."[193] This is a devastating comment on the "Christ of faith" versus "Jesus of history" debate, and on those who think it enough to sustain faith by "two stories," the relationship between which remains far from clear.

Arguably it does not do full justice to Pannenberg's thought to trace through this early essay, since in his later work he adds qualifications and additions to this basic argument. In particular he recognizes that a "Christology from below" needs a stronger emphasis before we proceed stage by stage to a fuller understanding of the "whole" Christ as the revelation of God. He expresses this stron-

185. Pannenberg, "Revelation of God in Jesus," 102.
186. Pannenberg, "Revelation," 103.
187. Pannenberg, "Revelation," 108.
188. Pannenberg, "Revelation," 113.
189. Pannenberg, "Revelation," 114-17.
190. Pannenberg, "Revelation," 122.
191. Pannenberg, "Revelation," 127.
192. Pannenberg, "Revelation," 129.
193. Pannenberg, "Revelation," 131.

ger emphasis upon "Christology from below" both in *Jesus — God and Man* and in his *Systematic Theology*.[194]

In his *Systematic Theology* Pannenberg writes, "If *Christology from below* does not manage to develop material alternatives to confession of the deity of Christ but shows that this confession, and consequently the concept of the incarnation, is a relevant expression of the implied significance of the coming and history of Jesus, then this means that the human and historical reality of Jesus of Nazareth can appropriately be understood only in the light of *his coming from God*."[195] Elsewhere in the same volume he writes, "Christology must get behind the confessional statements and titles of the primitive Christian tradition, reaching for the foundation to which these point. . . . This foundation is the history of Jesus."[196] All the same, Pannenberg insists that the resurrection of Jesus Christ "cannot be excluded for a full understanding of Christology."[197] The link between the apostolic proclamation and the history of Jesus, Pannenberg continues, receives full meaning "only if we include the primitive Christian witness to the resurrection of Jesus as the raising of Jesus to a form of fellowship with God that legitimates his pre-Easter work."[198] Only the resurrection confers upon him the status of *Kurios*. It is in the light of the resurrection that the "sending" of the Son is seen *in terms of his preexistence and not merely that of divine initiation*. The necessary horizon of understanding includes also "his coming from God."[199] Mark L. Y. Chan, one of my Nottingham doctoral graduates, has provided an excellent discussion of these issues that brings together Christology, hermeneutics, and Pannenberg's constructive theology.[200]

Far from these being later retrospective readings back from the late first century or even from the second century, Pannenberg comments, "these elements are already in the *pre-Pauline traditions and Kerygma*." Further, he writes, "The first Christians could not have successfully preached the resurrection of Jesus if his body had been intact in the tomb."[201] The event of the resurrection "implies already a claim to historicity. . . . The event took place in this world, namely in the tomb of Jesus in Jerusalem before the visit of the women."[202] Within the setting of apocalyptic expectation this *also* has cosmic significance: "If Jesus had

---

194. Wolfhart Pannenberg, *Jesus — God and Man*, trans. L. L. Wilkins and D. A. Priebe (London: S.C.M., 1968) and *Systematic Theology*, vol. 2, 277-323.

195. Pannenberg, *Systematic Theology*, vol. 2, 288 (my italics).

196. Pannenberg, Systematic Theology, vol. 2, 281.

197. Pannenberg, *Jesus — God and Man*, 88-106; cf. *Systematic Theology*, vol. 2, 352-59.

198. Pannenberg, *Systematic Theology*, vol. 2, 283.

199. Pannenberg, *Systematic Theology*, vol. 2, 288.

200. Mark L. Y. Chan, *Christology from Within and Ahead: Hermeneutics, Contingency, and the Quest for Transcontextual Criteria in Christology* (London and Boston: Brill, 2001), 222-60; cf. also 209-22.

201. Pannenberg, *Systematic Theology*, vol. 2, 358; cf. 359.

202. Pannenberg, *Systematic Theology*, vol. 2, 359 and 360.

been raised, the end of the world had begun."[203] This approach, Pannenberg argues, reflects legitimate historical method more adequately than that of positivist historians who approach the text with the *a priori* preconceived assumption that "dead men do not rise."[204]

Many of these assertions reflect horizons of understanding that we noted as appropriate ones in the first half of this chapter. The role of hermeneutics for Christology remains decisive. A hermeneutical horizon cannot but *begin* with the earthly Jesus in the light of Old Testament promise and Jewish expectation. But we have argued especially in Part I that horizons of understanding are capable of movement and expansion. "Understanding" is a *process* in which initial assumptions become corrected and re-formed. Pannenberg's approach to Christology takes full account of the relations between history, theology, and hermeneutics. Within the expanding horizon of understanding that he establishes, the persistent problem of faith and history becomes dissipated and recast. His Christology forms part of a wider and more comprehensive Christian theology. Mark Chan speaks of its role within Pannenberg's "eschatological Trinitarian ontology."[205]

203. Pannenberg, *Jesus — God and Man*, 85.
204. Pannenberg, *Jesus — God and Man*, 109.
205. Chan, *Christology from Within and Ahead*, 260.

CHAPTER 18

The Holy Spirit:
Scripture, History, Experience, and Hermeneutics

18.1. Horizons Shaped by the Beyond Within,
Extended by Christology and Eschatology

A number of writers have referred to the "self-effacing" reticence of the Holy Spirit. J. E. Fison writes, "His [the Spirit's] work is not to advertise but to efface Himself in . . . the *kenosis* of the Spirit."[1] This is very different, he comments, "from what is quickly perverted into an un-Christian . . . cocksureness" on the part of some who speak very many words about the Spirit.[2] N. Q. Hamilton and G. S. Hendry make parallel observations: the Holy Spirit characteristically sheds light upon Christ, not upon himself.[3] In the Paraclete sayings of the Fourth Gospel, "The Spirit will not speak on his own initiative (ἀφ' ἑαυτοῦ, *aph' heautou*). . . . He will glorify me, because he will take what is mine (ἐκ τοῦ ἐμοῦ, *ek tou emou*, from me) and will declare [this] to you" (John 16:13-14).

Might this raise a particular difficulty for an attempt to provide a hermeneutic of the doctrine of the Holy Spirit? How do we distinguish between phenomena in the public world that some or many ascribe to the agency of the Holy Spirit and that which genuinely springs from the Holy Spirit? This raises both difficulties and a transparent need to try to address the questions of meaning and understanding that are involved.

1. J. E. Fison, *The Blessing of the Holy Spirit* (London and New York: Longmans, Green, 1950), 22-23; cf. 72 and 210. See also H. Wheeler Robinson, *The Christian Experience of the Holy Spirit* (London: Nisbet, 1928) 83-4.

2. Fison, *Holy Spirit*, 15.

3. N. Q. Hamilton, *The Holy Spirit and Eschatology in St. Paul*, Scottish Journal of Theology Occasional Papers (Edinburgh: Oliver & Boyd, 1957), 3-16; and G. S. Hendry, *The Holy Spirit in Christian Theology* (London: S.C.M., 1965), 14-24.

A second set of questions arises from the dual or even multiple meanings of the Hebrew term רוח *(rûach)* and Greek word πνεῦμα *(pneuma)*, which should often be translated as *Spirit* (of God) but sometimes also denotes *spirit* [of a human being], and/or *wind* or *breath*. In some passages the meaning is contested. Thus some translate τῷ πνεύματι ζέοντες *(tō pneumati zeontes)* in Rom. 12:11 as "in ardour of spirit" (NEB) or "fervent in spirit" [human spirit] (AV/KJV); others translate it: "aglow with the Spirit" [of God] (RSV). Sadly, the NRSV has returned to an earlier translation than the RSV to render it "be ardent in spirit," and similarly NJB renders the Greek "an eager spirit." However, the REB has advanced on the earlier NEB of which it is a revision to translate the clause "aglow with the Spirit." NRSV and REB have inverted the translations of their respective predecessors in opposite directions. To compound this further, R. B. Hoyle and BDAG demonstrate the very wide range of meanings that πνεῦμα *(pneuma)* could convey in the Hellenistic world of Paul's day.[4]

A third factor invites mention. Until the early 1970s, as Moltmann observes, it was customary to introduce discussions or books on the doctrine of the Holy Spirit with some complaint about the widespread "forgetfulness of the Spirit."[5] Yet from the 1970s to the present "forgetfulness of the Spirit" has given way in many circles "to a positive obsession with the Spirit," although among this talk and literature "a new paradigm in pneumatology has not yet emerged."[6] Astonishingly even in spite of a resurgence of concern about the person of the Holy Spirit, we still hear widespread use of the neuter pronoun "it" in English when people speak of the Spirit, and the relationship between language about Christ and language about the Holy Spirit seems far from clear. Some even understand "the Lord is the Spirit" (2 Cor. 3:17) to be an "is" of identity rather of exegetical denotation (cf. Exod. 34:34).[7]

Fourth, one further reason for a hermeneutical lack of clarity is that, alongside the theological "reticence" or "kenosis" of the Holy Spirit, it is in the nature of the contrast of conceptual grammar or logic between the unseen and empirical to exacerbate this first difficulty. Like the wind, the activity of the Holy Spirit is most clearly to be seen from the Spirit's effects. Just as the wind is invisible but powers the movement of sailing ships, sways the trees, or breaks down hedges, so the invisible agency of the Holy Spirit brings love, assurance of sonship, new birth, the capacity to confess Christ as Lord, self-control, and the unity of Christians (John 31:5-8; 1 Cor. 12:3; Gal. 5:25; Eph. 4:3) as visible effects. But if, like the

4. R. Birch Hoyle, *The Holy Spirit in St. Paul* (London: Hodder & Stoughton, 1927), 175-81, and BDAG, 832-37.

5. Moltmann, *The Spirit of Life,* 1.

6. Moltmann, *The Spirit,* 1.

7. Hendry, *Holy Spirit,* 14-17; Vincent Taylor, *The Person of Christ in New Testament Teaching* (London: Macmillan, 1958), 54.

wind, the Spirit, as it were, "blows" where he chooses (John 3:8), can we deductively or invariably move from effect to cause in every possible case?

Fifth, the adjectival form πνευματικός (pneumatikos, that which appertains to the Spirit, spiritual), and the adverbial form πνευματικῶς (pneumatikōs, in a manner prompted by the Spirit, spiritually) have suffered serious exegetical and hermeneutical abuse. To be sure, these are occurrences of the adjectival and adverbial forms in Greek literature in which spiritual refers to a property of the human spirit in contrast to bodily (Plutarch, Moralia 129C; Hierocles, 27, 483). But in the New Testament, as F. W. Danker (BDAG, 3d edn.) comments, the word occurs "in the great majority of cases in reference to the divine πνεῦμα" (pneuma).[8] Indeed, in 1 Corinthians the church in Corinth tended to use the adjective "spiritual" to denote a "high-status" human achievement deserving of admiration, while Paul is obliged to redefine the term as denoting the agency and formative influence of God the Holy Spirit.[9] "Spirituality," for Paul and for John, never denotes a self-induced feeling-state of exulted awareness, but rather the effect of a transforming agency from the Holy Spirit.

The appropriate hermeneutical horizon of understanding for the truth and the communication of the doctrine of the Holy Spirit derives primarily from Old Testament traditions. These, in turn, become modified in the light of the Christological, corporate, and eschatological horizons in the New Testament. In the Old Testament the Spirit of God is not an immanental force like the world soul of the Stoics, but a transcendent, life-giving power from beyond. The presence and power of the Holy Spirit have rightly been characterized as "the Beyond Who Is Within." Paul reminds the church in Corinth that the Spirit is not the animating world-soul or "spirit of the world," but the transcendent, holy τὸ πνεῦμα τὸ ἐκ τοῦ θεοῦ (to pneuma to ek tou theou), the Spirit who comes forth from (ἐκ, ek) God (1 Cor. 2:12).

Bultmann observes that in Paul pneuma is not equivalent to the German Geist (spirit or mind) or to the English spirit in the Greek Platonic, idealist sense, but "πνεῦμα is the miraculous divine power that stands in contrast to all that is human."[10] Similarly, E. Schweizer writes, "In 1 Cor. 2:13-15 the πνευματικός (pneumatikos) is the man who knows God's saving work by virtue of the Spirit of God, while the ψυχικός (psuchikos) is blind thereto."[11]

Paul can be fully understood only within the horizons of understanding and expectation generated by the Old Testament and Judaism. W. D. Davies writes, "The Pauline doctrine of the Holy Spirit is only fully comprehensible in the light

---

8. BDAG, 837, col. i.

9. I argue this at length in Thiselton, First Epistle, 224-95 (on 2:6–3:4); 900-989 (on 12:1-11); 1074-1130 (14:1-25); and 1257-80 (15:35-44).

10. Bultmann, Theology, vol. 1, 153.

11. Eduard Schweizer, "πνεῦμα," in G. Kittel (ed.), TDNT, vol. 6, trans. G. W. Bromiley (Grand Rapids: Eerdmans, 1968), 436; cf. 332-453.

of rabbinic expectations of the Age to Come as an Age of the Spirit and of the community of the Spirit."[12] The Old Testament sets the agency of the Spirit of God apart from the human in terms of the "otherness," transcendence, and power that characterizes such agency. Baumgärtel begins his section on "Spirit of God" in the Old Testament and Judaism by citing the force of Isa. 31:3: "The Egyptians are אָדָם (*'ādām, man*), and not אֵל (*'ēl, God*), and their horses are בָשָׂר (*bāśār, flesh*), and not רוּחַ (*rûach, spirit*)." He comments, "בָשָׂר [*bāśār, flesh*] is earthly frailty and impotence, and its bearer is אָתָם [*'ādām, man*], while רוּחַ [*rûach, spirit*] is absolute power and majesty, and its bearer is אֵל [*'ēl, God*]."[13] Lindsay Dewar makes a similar point about this passage.[14]

This sets the tone for acts of the Spirit in the Old Testament. The Spirit is transcendent power. The Spirit of God turns the desert into a paradise, and makes it a place of justice (Isa. 32:15-17). The Spirit guarded Israel's cattle from marauders and wild beasts in the wilderness and gave them rest (Isa. 63:14). "The Spirit of the LORD rushed upon Samson, and he tore the lion apart barehanded as one might tear apart a kid" (Judg. 14:6). Similarly, "The Spirit of the LORD rushed upon Samson, and the ropes that were on his arms became like flax that has caught fire, and his bonds melted off his hands. Then he found a fresh jawbone of a donkey . . . and with it he killed a thousand men" (Judg. 15:14-15). E. F. Scott comments, "The effects of the Spirit were inexplicable because they belonged to the heavenly order, over against the earthly and human."[15] C. H. Powell makes a parallel point: the Spirit "does not belong to him whose native sphere is that of *bāśār*."[16]

A pattern begins to emerge according to which the Spirit "falls upon," or is "given to," certain elected individuals to perform tasks that they could not have performed only in their own strength. Sometimes the Spirit makes possible the exercise of gifts of leadership or military prowess: "The Spirit of the LORD came upon Othniel . . . he went out to war . . . and his hand prevailed . . ." (Judg. 3:10). "The Spirit of the LORD took possession of Gideon, and he sounded the trumpet . . ." (Judg. 6:34). Sometimes the Spirit of God gave a special gift of craftsmanship (to Bezalel, Exod. 31:3). The Spirit gave to Balaam the gift of wisdom or second sight (Num. 24:2). The Spirit caused Saul to experience "a prophetic frenzy" (1 Sam. 19:23). The gift of the Spirit for Moses and the seventy elders was to equip them for administrative oversight, wisdom, and leadership (Num. 11:17). Through the Spirit Joseph received the ability to interpret dreams (Gen. 41:38).

The gift of life, to which Moltmann accords special attention, associates the

12. W. D. Davies, *Paul and Rabbinic Judaism* (London: S.P.C.K., 2d edn. 1955), 217.

13. Friedrich Baumgärtel, "πνεῦμα (Old Testament and Judaism)," in Kittel, *TDNT*, vol. 6, 365 (cf. 359-68).

14. Lindsay Dewar, *The Holy Spirit and Modern Thought* (London: Mowbray, 1959), 5.

15. Ernest F. Scott, *The Spirit in the New Testament* (London: Hodder & Stoughton, 1923), 18.

16. Cyril H. Powell, *The Biblical Concept of Power* (London: Epworth, 1963), 26.

Spirit of God closely with God the Creator. The psalmist writes, "When you send forth your Spirit, they are created; and you renew the face of the ground" (Ps. 104:30). The *rûach* of God who moved on the surface of the waters in Gen. 1:2 is more likely to denote *the Spirit* of God (with Barrett, Dewar, and Pannenberg) than simply *wind* (NRSV, NJB), although *wind* remains possible.[17] The verse may reflect a wordplay. Barrett perceives here the imagery of a brooding or hovering bird (cf. Deut. 32:11), in which the Spirit of God broods over sheer chaos to bring forth life and order.[18] Vawter comments, "The wind of divine proportions might also be 'the spirit [i.e., the life-giving breath] of God' moving on the waters."[19] Moltmann includes this verse under the heading "Spirit — the Divine Energy of Life."[20]

The transcendence of the Spirit of God receives further emphasis from the association between *rûach* and *holy* or *holiness* (קדש, q-d-sh) in several passages. "Take not your Holy Spirit from me" (Ps. 51:13) reflects the Hebrew "Spirit of [God's] holiness." In Isa. 63:10, 13, "They grieved his Holy Spirit. . . . He put his Holy Spirit among them entails קדש (*qōdesh*) in the sense of "apartness, sacredness." One example of this use is to denote "places set apart as sacred by God's presence."[21] The verb קדש (*qādash*) means "to set apart, consecrate . . . be hallowed."[22] Hence God's holiness, John Webster writes, is "God's sheer irreducible particularity as *this One* who is and acts *thus*. God's name is his incomparability, his uniqueness."[23]

God's anointing of kings, prophets, and in special cases the Servant of Isa. 42–53 and "messianic" figures qualifies them to perform holy tasks in the power of the Spirit. The Servant is one of whom God says, "I have put my Spirit upon him" (Isa. 42:1). Jesus applies Isa. 61:1-2 to himself in the synagogue sermon of Luke 4:18-19: "The Spirit of the Lord God is upon me, because the Lord has anointed me. He has sent me to bring good news to the oppressed; to bind up the brokenhearted; to proclaim liberty to the captives and release to the prisoners, to proclaim the year of the LORD's favor." Hosea the prophet is "a man of the Spirit" (Hos. 9:7). The Spirit given to Elijah "rests upon Elisha" (2 Kings 2:15). Micah is "full of God's Spirit" (Mic. 3:8). The classic prophecy concerning the dynasty of King David finds expression in Isa. 11:1-5: "The Spirit of the LORD shall rest on

17. Cf. C. K. Barrett, *The Holy Spirit and the Gospel Tradition* (London: S.P.C.K., 1958), 18; Pannenberg, *Systematic Theology*, vol. 2, 55; Dewar, *Holy Spirit*, 5; on the other interpretation, Vawter, *On Genesis*, 40-41; Moltmann, *Spirit of Life*, 40-42.

18. Barrett, *Holy Spirit*, 18.

19. Vawter, *On Genesis*, 41.

20. Moltmann, *Spirit of Life*, 40.

21. Quotations from Brown-Driver-Briggs, *The New Hebrew-English Lexicon* (1980 edn.), 871; cf. 871-73.

22. Brown-Driver-Briggs (1980), 872.

23. John Webster, *Holiness* (Grand Rapids: Eerdmans, 2003), 36; cf. 31-52.

him: the Spirit of wisdom and understanding, the Spirit of counsel and might . . ." (11:2).

Although the main emphasis in the Old Testament falls upon the gift of the Spirit as transcendent anointing or empowerment for specific individuals called to perform particular tasks, a communal emphasis also begins to emerge. Ezekiel prophesies that the "dry bones" of the exiled community of Israel shall come to life as a living body through the Spirit of God (Ezek. 37:9). God's Spirit will also bring transformation, renewal, and obedience as the Spirit from beyond is placed "within" (Ezek. 36:27). Other communal references include Isa. 44:3-5 and Joel 2:28, the prophecy to which Peter alludes as being fulfilled on the Day of Pentecost.

This is precisely the hermeneutical horizon within which the New Testament theologies of the Holy Spirit emerge. It also forms a communicative horizon for conveying the meaning of a Christian doctrine of the Holy Spirit. *Both* the *more individual* model of *the gift of the Spirit as empowerment for special tasks* and the *more communal* model of *the gift of the Spirit as empowerment for a transformed and renewed life and lifestyle continue into the New Testament, but with Christological and eschatological extensions and qualifications.* Floyd Filson writes concerning this continuity in the New Testament: "It is likewise true that chosen individuals are given the Spirit for specific tasks; but this does not mean that some are left without the Spirit. Each is given the Spirit. . . . This again reflects the eschatological mood of the New Testament. . . . This was expected in the last days."[24]

With reference to the New Testament, N. Q. Hamilton calls Christology "the key to pneumatology."[25] The anointing by the Holy Spirit that becomes the gift of all Christians corporately is derived from the Christological anointing of Christ by the Spirit to bring in the reign of God. We hardly need to recall that the Hebrew or Aramaic *Messiah* and the Greek *Christos* denote the *Anointed One.* Thus the gift of the Spirit to a chosen individual for a specified task remains the Christological foundation for every Christian communal and individual experience of the Holy Spirit. Hence in Paul's words, "Anyone who does *not have the Spirit of Christ* does *not belong to him. But If Christ is in you, . . .* the Spirit is life. . . . If the Spirit of him who raised Jesus from the dead dwells in you, he *who raised Christ from the dead will give life to your mortal bodies also through his Spirit that dwells in you"* (Rom. 8:9-11).

James Dunn comments, "Rom. 8:9 rules out the possibility *both* of a non-Christian possessing the Spirit and of a Christian *not* possessing the Spirit."[26]

---

24. Floyd V. Filson, *The New Testament against Its Environment* (London: S.C.M., 1950), 78.

25. Hamilton, *The Holy Spirit and Eschatology,* 3.

26. James D. G. Dunn, *Baptism in the Holy Spirit: A Re-examination of the New Testament Teaching on the Gift of the Spirit in Relation to Pentecostalism Today* (London: S.C.M., 1970), 95; cf. also James D. G. Dunn, *Jesus and the Spirit: A Study of the Religious and Charismatic Experience of Jesus and the First Christians as Reflected in the New Testament* (London: S.C.M., 1975), 310-16.

Elsewhere he writes, "That the Spirit is thus to be seen as the defining mark of the Christian is put in blunt terms in Rom. 8:9. . . . In this verse . . . Paul provides the nearest thing to a definition of a Christian (someone who is 'of Christ')."[27] Like sonship, "being-in-Christ" is the foundation for receiving the gift of the Spirit. Yet Paul also appears to assert a reverse causal relationship between being-in-Christ and receiving the Holy Spirit. No less an important "definition" of being a Christian occurs in 1 Cor. 12:3: "No one can say 'Jesus is Lord' except by the Holy Spirit." We suggest that *Rom. 8:9-10 expresses the causal relationship in logical or theological terms:* to be in Christ lays the theological foundation for receiving the Spirit. But *1 Cor. 12:3 expresses the causal relationship in contingent or experiential terms:* it is impossible to acknowledge the full lordship of Christ over one's life unless the Holy Spirit has moved and empowered the Christian to make and to live out this confession.

Other New Testament passages support both sides of this reciprocal relationship. Gal. 4:6 expresses logical or theological causality: "Because you are children [NRSV; Greek, sons] God has sent the Spirit of his Son into our hearts, crying, 'Abba! Father!'" Both Christian reception of the Spirit and Christian sonship (in a non-gender-exclusive sense) are derived logically and theologically from Christ the Anointed One and from Christ the Son. Even here, however, implicitly the Holy Spirit prompts and actualizes filial consciousness and intimacy, as Swete suggests.[28] Albert Schweitzer comments that the Spirit is the "life-principle of His [Christ's] personality."[29] Gal. 5:25 attributes not only the cause of Christian existence but its *actualization* to the agency of the Holy Spirit: "If we live by the Spirit, let us also be guided [or walk] by the Spirit" (NRSV). (NEB suggests "source of life" and "course of life.") N. Q. Hamilton writes, "The Spirit is not just the beginning but the ground of this whole existence in Christ."[30] Eduard Schweizer clarifies the issue further: "πνεῦμα (*pneuma*, the Spirit) establishes this existence of the believer and is no longer regarded as a purely supplementary miraculous power. . . . In this light it is easy to see why the extraordinary nature of the manifestations can no longer be a decisive criterion."[31]

The controversial allusion to "baptism in the Spirit" invites interpretation in this Christological context. Paul writes, "In the one Spirit we were all baptized into one body — Jews or Greeks, slaves or free — and we were all made to drink of one Spirit" (1 Cor. 12:13). James Dunn points out that this is the only passage in the New Testament that speaks explicitly of baptism in the Spirit. He comments

27. Dunn, *Paul the Apostle*, 423; cf. 413-41.
28. Cf. Henry B. Swete, *The Holy Spirit in the New Testament* (London: Macmillan, 1921), 204-6.
29. Schweitzer, *Mysticism*, 165.
30. Hamilton, *Holy Spirit and Eschatology*, 12-13.
31. Schweizer, "πνεῦμα," *TDNT*, vol. 6, 425.

that unless we use "semantic sleight-of-hand" . . . there is no alternative to the conclusion that the baptism of the Spirit is what made the Corinthians members of the Body of Christ, that is, Christian."[32]

Moreover, baptism need not *in itself* specify water baptism: Paul sometimes uses βαπτίζειν *(baptizein)* in a literal sense to denote water baptism, but sometimes also metaphorically to denote being-in-Christ.[33] Emphatically he concludes that there is "no thought of a second gift of the Spirit," either here or elsewhere in Paul.[34]

To the transcendent and Christological horizons we must add the horizon of eschatology. More than half a dozen writers insist, "The Holy Spirit is the key to the Christian doctrine of the End"; or alternatively, "All the tension of the intermediate situation in which the 'new man' finds himself receives precise expression in Paul's doctrine of the Spirit."[35] Hamilton observes, "The Holy Spirit enables the believers to wait in a way appropriate to the future righteousness."[36] Thus Paul writes, "Not only creation but we ourselves who have the firstfruits of the Spirit groan inwardly while we wait (ἀπεκδεχόμενοι, *apekdechomenoi*) for adoption, the redemption of our bodies" (Rom. 8:23). The use of ἀπαρχή *(aparchē, firstfruits)* in this verse expounds the gift of the Holy Spirit as "a sign of what is to come."[37] Paul uses ἀρραβών *(arrabon*, deposit or guarantee) in the same way that 2 Cor. 5:5 does; God "has given us the Spirit as a guarantee" (i.e., of more of the same, or better, to come). This Greek word is elsewhere translated as *"first installment"* (2 Cor. 1:22). Cullmann writes, "The Holy Spirit is nothing else than the anticipation of the end in the present."[38] Hamilton heads his chapter on this subject, "The Spirit and the Eschatological Tension."[39]

Commenting on these verses and on ἀρραβών *(arrabon, first installment)* and ἀπαρχή *(aparchē, firstfruits)*, Hamilton writes that the center of gravity in relation to the Holy Spirit "lies in the future."[40] This reaches its climax in the concept of a resurrection mode of existence animated and characterized by the agency of the Holy Spirit (σῶμα πνευματικόν, *sōma pneumatikon*, 1 Cor. 15:44). I have expounded this understanding of "spiritual body" in detail in my larger commentary on 1 Corinthians, and this approach finds convincing support in

---

32. Dunn, *Baptism in the Holy Spirit*, 129; cf. 127-30.

33. Dunn, *Baptism in the Holy Spirit*, 130.

34. Dunn, *Baptism in the Holy Spirit*, 136; cf. 137-38.

35. Fison, *Holy Spirit*, 4; and Ethelbert Stauffer, *New Testament Theology*, trans. John Marsh (London: S.C.M., 1955), 166. Cf. Barrett, *Holy Spirit*, 160-61; Weiss, *Earliest Christianity*, vol. 2, 445; Whiteley, *Theology of St. Paul*, 126-27; Hamilton, *Holy Spirit*, throughout.

36. Hamilton, *Holy Spirit*, 34.

37. Schweizer, "πνεῦμα," *TDNT*, vol. 6, 422.

38. Cullmann, *Christ and Time*, 72.

39. Hamilton, *Holy Spirit*, 26-40.

40. Hamilton, *Holy Spirit*, 17-40 and 79.

the researches of N. T. Wright.[41] Wright convincingly and rightly defines *sōma pneumatikon* as "a body animated by, enlivened by, the Spirit of the true God . . . the *result* of the Spirit's work."[42] Pannenberg also constructively places Rom. 8:11 alongside 1 Cor. 15:42-44, and describes the resurrection mode of existence as "a life wholly permeated by the divine Creator Spirit *(sōma pneumatikon)*."[43]

These three horizons of understanding, namely the transcendent, the Christological, and the eschatological, provide firmer markers for interpretation and communication than vague notions of "spirituality" in the sense of the term often used with little critical rigor today. The experience of the Holy Spirit is not to be identified simply with intermittent "invasions" of spectacular phenomena, but with an empowerment to live out "being-in-Christ" in Christlike attitudes and conduct, often with awareness that this empowerment is "given" rather than achieved.

As Fison observes, "Without a true doctrine of the Holy Spirit, Christianity always goes hard or soft."[44] He explains: reliance upon secondhand institutions, sometimes in the direction of legalism, overly high sacramentalism, or authoritarianism based upon church-constructed norms, can make the church become hard. Alternatively, an illusion of freedom without the moral transformation and sanctification of the Spirit can make the church go soft in self-indulgent self-affirmation.

Paul found both distortions, especially the second, in Corinth, where "spirituality" risked becoming a self-constructed illusory phenomenon (1 Cor. 3:1-4). We have yet to consider, however, a number of issues that relate more explicitly to Christian doctrine, including those of gifts of the Spirit, the personhood of the Spirit, and other issues in the rest of the New Testament and in the Church Fathers.

18.2. The Spirit's Formation of Christ:
Personhood, Community, Gifts, Holiness

The agency and actions of the Holy Spirit are creative, life giving, formative, and transformative. To speak of the Spirit's "formation of Christ" is to address two levels of the work of the Holy Spirit. In accordance with expectations in the Old Testament and in the four gospels, the Holy Spirit anoints Jesus Christ and gives to him empowerment and "formation" for his messianic task of bringing in the

---

41. Thiselton, *First Epistle*, 1257-1301, esp. 1267-81; and N. T. Wright, *The Resurrection of the Son of God: Christian Origins and the Question of God*, vol. 3 (London: S.P.C.K., 2003), 340-56; cf. 361-69.

42. Wright, *Resurrection*, 354.

43. Pannenberg, *Systematic Theology*, vol. 3, 622.

44. Fison, *Holy Spirit*, 31.

reign of God, and of dying and being raised for the redemption of his people. After the resurrection and Pentecost, the Spirit is "poured out" upon the people of God to form Christ in them as those who are "in Christ." The pattern of the Spirit's work is Christomorphic, as John and the Church Fathers emphasize. The latter move toward an increasingly Trinitarian horizon of understanding in interpreting the person and work of the Holy Spirit.

H. B. Swete begins his study of *The Holy Spirit in the New Testament* with a consideration of the conception and birth of Jesus. In the Third Gospel Mary's question to the angel invites the response, "The Holy Spirit will come upon you, and the power of the Most High will overshadow you; therefore the child to be born will be holy; he will be called the Son of God" (Luke 1:35).[45] Matthew's setting is different, but he nevertheless relates that Mary conceived the child "ἐκ πνεύματος ἁγίου, of, from, Holy Spirit" (Matt. 1:18-21). Swete insists, "The prepositional phrase represents, even more clearly than the words of St. Luke, that the Spirit was the source of the vitalizing energy which gave life to the embryo. . . . The Spirit is seen presiding over the beginnings of a new creation."[46]

No less decisive is the event of the baptism of Jesus. The baptism of Jesus and the descent of the Holy Spirit find a place in all four gospels (Matt. 3:16; Mark 1:10; Luke 3:21-22; John 1:32-33). This marked a new era in the life of Jesus, in effect signifying the beginning of his messianic ministry in the formative power of the Spirit. Swete does not exaggerate the matter when he writes, "The chrism of the Spirit was received by our Lord not only with reference to His own needs, but that he might bestow it on all believers. The whole fountain of the Spirit is henceforth His, to shower upon His future Church."[47] Moltmann writes, "Jn. 3:34 describes this unique endowment with the Spirit as 'without measure.' . . . The Spirit makes Jesus 'the Kingdom of God in person.' . . . The energizing power of God is given him not for himself but for others: for the sick, the poor, sinners, the dying."[48]

The Spirit "drives" (Mark 1:12) or "leads" (Luke 4:1) Jesus into the desert for a period of testing, communion with God, and the distinctively "messianic" temptations (Matt. 4:1-11; Mark 1:12-13; Luke 4:1-13). Far from leading Jesus to perform "supernatural" or spectacular actions that would provide shortcuts to public acceptance and "success," Jesus, led by the Spirit, *accepts the constraints of his messianic humanness*. He will not reenact a Mosaic miracle of providing bread. He will not cast himself down from the temple platform into the valley of Hinnom to force God's hand to provide some miraculous action. He will not use the devil's methods to achieve a way forward without pain. In the theology of the Fourth

45. Swete, *The Holy Spirit in the New Testament*, 24-37.
46. Swete, *The Holy Spirit in the New Testament*, 31-32.
47. Swete, *The Holy Spirit in the New Testament*, 48.
48. Moltmann, *The Spirit of Life*, 61.

Gospel, although the Spirit gives new life and new birth (John 3:1-11), Jesus responds in obedience to the will of the Father, leaving his "glory" in the hands of the Father and the Spirit (John 16:14).

A degree of tension, although not contradiction, emerges between two different ways of interpreting the Spirit's manifestation in the Jesus of the first three gospels. In his *Jesus and the Spirit* Dunn concedes that manifestations of the miraculous do not constitute a criterion of the possession or actuality of the Spirit, but nevertheless perceives the ministry of Jesus as characterized by a "consciousness of supernatural power."[49] Jesus is not a magician, but he is a "charismatic." By contrast, C. K. Barrett and J. Fison discuss what Fison calls "the silence of the Sypnotists" about Jesus' manifestation of the Holy Spirit. Barrett asks, "Why do the Gospels say so little about the Spirit?"[50]

Barrett and Fison compare the reticence of the canonical prophets of the eighth and seventh centuries and the Synoptic writers to compare their experience of the Spirit with that of earlier seers. Jeremiah, for example, "never attributes his prophetic inspiration to the Spirit."[51] The gospels, Barrett writes, exhibit a tension between signs of the kingdom of God and the belief that such signs should not be sought for or emphasized.[52] Jesus, moreover, distinguishes between the "now" of his ministry and the "then" of fulfillment in the resurrection and Pentecost. He concludes, "Lack of glory and a sign of suffering were his Messianic vocation, *and part of his poverty was the absence of all the signs of the Spirit of God.* They would have been inconsistent with the office of a humiliated Messiah."[53] The response of Jesus to his messianic temptations provides one indication of this.

Fison endorses Barrett's conclusion. Apart from the early narrative of the conception and baptism of Jesus, he writes, one of the few peaks emerges in Jesus' citation of Isa. 61:1-2, "The Spirit of the Lord is upon me. . . ." The Synoptists show "reticence" about the Spirit.[54] Reflecting the work of Newton Flew, Fison argues that appeals to the Spirit could be misunderstood until Jesus had *lived out* the Christomorphic messianic vocation "in word and deed, and in humility, suffering, and service."[55] Fison presses this point for a Christian doctrine of the Holy Spirit today. Pentecost occurs only in the yonder side of Calvary: "The Holy Spirit at Pentecost does not go beyond the pattern of our Lord's life. . . . [The Spirit works] in the closest possible relationship with Christ."[56]

---

49. Dunn, *Jesus and the Spirit*, 75; cf. 68-92.
50. Fison, *Holy Spirit*, 81-102; Barrett, *The Holy Spirit and the Gospel Tradition*, 140-62.
51. Barrett, *Holy Spirit*, 146.
52. Barrett, *Holy Spirit*, 157.
53. Barrett, *Holy Spirit*, 158.
54. Fison, *Holy Spirit*, 95.
55. Fison, *Holy Spirit*, 94.
56. Fison, *Holy Spirit*, 120 and 121.

The Fourth Gospel brings this out clearly. In the Paraclete sayings in the Farewell Discourses, Jesus tells his disciples: "The Spirit of truth who comes from the Father will testify on my behalf" (John 15:26). "The Father will send [him] in my name" (John 14:26). "He will glorify me, because he will take what is mine and declare it to you" (John 16:14). The Spirit will be "another Advocate" (ἄλλον παράκλητον, *allon paraklēton*, John 14:15). The Holy Spirit will continue the witness and teaching of Jesus (John 14:26). Swete comments, "The Spirit was sent to reveal the Son."[57] Thus the Spirit's ministry will promote Christlike holiness: "He (ἐκεῖνος, *ekeinos*) will convict (ἐλέγξει, *elenxei*) the world in respect of sin, and of righteousness, and of judgement" (John 16:8-9). In the Fourth Gospel this applies especially to the sin of unbelief in Jesus Christ and the vindication of the righteousness of Christ.[58]

Paul takes up this notion of "the Christlikeness" of the action and effects of the Spirit in his classic formulation about "the fruit of the Spirit" in Gal. 5:22-23. The ninefold "fruit," which begins with love and ends with self-control, should typify "those who belong to Christ" (Gal. 5:24). As we noted above in discussing Robert Jewett's analysis of "flesh" (σάρξ, *sarx*) in Galatians, the opposite principle is that of self-assertion, whether in the form of libertinism or of legalism. In this respect "the written code kills, but the Spirit gives life" (2 Cor. 3:6). Bultmann rightly sets in contrast bondage to the law as entailing bondage to the cause-effect processes of the past with the liberty of the Spirit: "Freedom is nothing else than being open for the genuine future, letting oneself be determined by the future. So Spirit may be called the power of futurity."[59] In view of our earlier discussions of Bultmann and myth, however, we should add that the Spirit is *also more than this,* but *not less* than this.

Paul's account of so-called gifts of the Spirit (especially in 1 Cor. 12:1-11, 27-31; 14:1-40) underlines the Christomorphic purpose of these gifts within the setting of the community. First, he redefines the Corinthians' questions περὶ τῶν πνευματικῶν (*peri tōn pneumatikōn, about "spiritual" things, people, or gifts: masculine or neuter*) in terms of a parallel question about χαρίσματα (*charismata, freely bestowed gifts, gifts without strings,* 1 Cor. 12:1-11). Second, he points out that the criterion of receiving the Spirit is the capacity to confess, and to live out in practice, *the lordship of Christ* (12:3b). Certainly any notion of jealous or competitive "cursing" of a rival in the name of Christ could never come from the Spirit (1 Cor. 12:3a). Bruce Winter has recently shown that the allusion is probably to an implied *active* verb: "May Jesus grant a curse."[60]

---

57. Swete, *The Holy Spirit in the New Testament,* 153.

58. Swete, *The Holy Spirit,* 157-60.

59. Bultmann, *Theology,* vol. 1, 335.

60. Bruce Winter, "Religious Curses and Christian Vindictiveness: 1 Cor. 12–14," in Bruce Winter, *After Paul Left Corinth* (Grand Rapids: Eerdmans, 2001) 164-83. The translation of 1 Cor. 12:3 would be, "No one speaking through the agency of the Spirit of God says, 'Jesus grant a

Paul's third move is to point out that all gifts (χαρίσματα, *charismata*) given to believers by the Holy Spirit are given not for self-affirmation or self-glory but "for common advantage" (πρὸς τὸ συμφέρον, *pros to sumpheron*, 12:7) and "the building up of the community" (14:26). This lack of competitiveness, or in positive terms the mutual advantage, finds expression in the source of the gifts: "the same Spirit . . . the same Lord . . . the same God" (12:4). This passage is without doubt *implicitly "Trinitarian."*[61] Paul concludes the list of gifts in 12:8-10 with the comment, "All these things one and the same Spirit activates, appointing as he wills to each person individually" (12:11, my translation).

It is no accident that Paul places his reflections on the nature of love (1 Cor. 13:1-13) between chapters 12 and 14. Every phrase in chapter 13 reflects the situation in Corinth and is therefore a Pauline composition, but no doubt had been pre-prepared over a long enough period to be expressed in rhythmic, hymnic form. I have argued this elsewhere with reference to the literature on the subject.[62] The "resonating jar" and "reverberating cymbal" (13:1) reflect the self-advertising "noise" characteristic of a Corinthian mind-set. The need to wait patiently (13:4; cf. 11:20-21) and to exercise courtesy by avoiding "ill-mannered impropriety" (13:5) reflect both discourtesy at the Lord's Supper and holding the floor or interrupting in the use of prophetic speech or tongues in public worship (14:27-33). The golden rule is love: *to seek the best for the other.* This applies especially to the use of gifts of the Spirit "for the building up of the community" (14:26).[63]

We shall return to the question of the nature of specific gifts of the Spirit in 18.4. Our purpose in this section is to underline the Christomorphic and communal nature of gifts of the Spirit. As in the Old Testament traditions, the Spirit may empower chosen individuals to perform special tasks, but these are always for the service of God and for the welfare of the community of the people of God.

Do the earliest traditions, including the biblical material, suggest any preliminary answers to questions about the *personhood* of the Holy Spirit? Bultmann rightly points out that language about the agency of the Holy Spirit in the New Testament takes a dual form. However, he draws questionable inferences from this. He writes, "In *animistic thinking, pneuma* is conceived of as an inde-

---

curse.'" The Greek contains no verb, usually translated "is cursed," but simply reads *Anathema Iēsous.* In recent years some twenty-seven ancient "curse tablets" were excavated from around Corinth, reflecting the practice of involving pagan deities to "curse rivals in love or in business or in litigation."

61. Thiselton, *First Epistle to the Corinthians,* 928-36; and esp. Thiselton, *Thiselton on Hermeneutics,* 287-304, from G. N. Stanton, B. Longenecker, and S. Barton (eds.), *The Holy Spirit and Christian Origins: Essays in Honour of James D. G. Dunn* (Grand Rapids: Eerdmans, 2004), 207-28.

62. Thiselton, *First Epistle,* 1026-39.

63. Cf. Thiselton, *First Epistle,* 1131-68.

pendent agent, a *personal* power. . . . In *dynamistic thinking*, on the contrary, *pneuma* appears as an *impersonal force* which fills a man like a fluid, so to say."[64]

Under the first category the Holy Spirit comes alongside *to help* (Greek συναντιλαμβάνεται, *sunantilambanetai*, Rom. 8:26). Similarly, the Spirit "*bears witness with* our Spirit" (τὸ πνεῦμα συμμαρτυρεῖ, *to pneuma summarturei*, Rom. 8:16). On the other hand, the Spirit "filled" the house at Pentecost (Acts 2:2) and can "fill" believers, like wine (Eph. 5:18). It is unfortunate that Bultmann interprets this as "differences in conception relating to the Spirit," which relate respectively to an Old Testament and Hellenistic background.[65] A different understanding emerges if we ask how these two forms of expression *function together*.

If we consider the so-called animistic or personal model and the dynamistic or substantival model *separately*, the result is to suggest a subpersonal view of the Spirit, or at least one that hovers ambivalently between viewing the Spirit as a person and as an impersonal power. If, however, we regard them as examples of Ian Ramsey's models and qualifiers (discussed in Part I), it emerges that *the model of personal agency is qualified by extrapersonal characteristics that suggest a suprapersonal agency*. The Holy Spirit is characterized by personhood, but this is a more-than-human personhood.

It is a piece of wooden literalism to suggest, with Paul Feine, that the ancient world did not know "our" strict concept of person. It is clear that the capacity to address, and to be addressed by, God, angels, or human beings *presupposes* what it means to conceive of such a conversation-partner as personal. The two-sided dialogue of address and response is more than the "personification" of natural phenomena in poetic contexts. Lindsay Dewar declares, "A careful examination of his [Paul's] epistles can leave us in no possible doubt that he thought of Him [the Holy Spirit] as fully personal — a 'he' and not an 'it'. It is unfortunate that in the Greek πνεῦμα *(spirit or Spirit)* is a neuter substantive, for this has led — or rather misled — the [KJV/]AV translation to render the expression τὸ πνεῦμα αὐτό as 'the Spirit itself' (Rom. 8:16) instead of 'the Spirit Himself' as it is correctly rendered in the RV."[66] (The NRSV avoids the issue by translating "that very Spirit.")

Barth, as is well known, dissents from the use of the word *person*, but this relates more closely to Trinitarian issues. Apart from the note below, we discuss this in the next chapter.[67] Some argue for a masculine pronoun on the basis of ἐκεῖνος in the Paraclete discourses as well as the masculine of παράκλητος

---

64. Bultmann, *Theology*, vol. 1, 155 (most italics Bultmann's, some mine).

65. Bultmann, *Theology*, vol. 1, 155 and 157.

66. Dewar, *Holy Spirit*, 71.

67. Barth, *Church Dogmatics*, I:1, sect. 12, 2, 469-73. Barth insists on the term "mode of being," on the ground that to speak of the Trinity as "three persons" risks tritheism. Moltmann offers a decisive critique of this in *The Trinity and the Kingdom of God*, 139-44, and in a different way Pannenberg offers a strong critique in *Systematic Theology*, vol. 1, 300-327.

(paraklētos). Some argue for a feminine pronoun on the basis of the grammatical feminine of the Hebrew רוח *(rûach)*. But James Barr has convincingly demonstrated the irrelevance of the false assumption "that the grammatical structure of a language reflects the thought structure of those speaking it. . . . The clearest example is grammatical gender. . . . No one would suppose that the Turks, because they nowhere distinguish gender in their language, not even in personal pronouns, . . . are deficient in their concept of sexual difference; nor would we seriously argue that the French have extended their legendary erotic interests into the linguistic realm by forcing every noun to be either masculine or feminine."[68] "Grammatical gender . . . cannot be taken to reflect a thought pattern."[69] A moment's reflection will remind us that in Greek τέκνον *(teknon,* child) is neuter; but this does not imply a subpersonal or impersonal view of children. Many inanimate objects are masculine or feminine in the arbitrary categorizations of grammar.

The ultimate reason for ascribing personhood to the Holy Spirit lies in the unique intimacy between the Holy Spirit as a personal Agent and Jesus Christ, and between the Holy Spirit and God the Father. Athanasius and Basil rightly extrapolate from the New Testament that these intersubjective, interpersonal, perichoretic relations are different in kind even from the relation between God and such divine hypostases as *personified* Wisdom, Word, or the Face of God. We discuss this in the next section (18.3).

The very term *Holy* Spirit not only calls attention to the work of the Holy Spirit in sanctification and formation of ethical character, but also underlines the co-working of Father, Son, and Spirit in such passages as 1 Cor. 12:4-6. The bestowal and apportionment of the *charismata* result from the joint decree and implementation of "the same Spirit . . . the same Lord . . . the same God, who activates them." Both Moltmann and Pannenberg rightly place the gift and experience of the Spirit within such a Trinitarian frame.[70]

Fison elaborates the practical consequences of depersonalizing the Holy Spirit in such a way that the Spirit ceases to be a formative agent in the growth of Christlike holiness. He writes, "There is an inevitable tendency to objectify God in the safe world of It, the world which man can handle and manipulate by *gnōsis*, magic, or rule of thumb."[71] In Ps. 51:11, he points out, "the Holy Spirit" is precisely parallel to "Thy presence."[72] We noted Webster's comment that *holiness* (Hebrew קדש, *q-d-sh*) characterizes God *as God,* and as *this* God. Basil of Caesarea refers to the Holy Spirit as "having his subsistence of God . . . the fount

68. James Barr, *The Semantics of Biblical Language* (Oxford: Oxford University Press, 1961), 39.

69. Barr, *Semantics,* 40; cf. 41-45.

70. Moltmann, *The Spirit of Life,* 39-77; and Pannenberg, *Systematic Theology,* vol. 3, 1-21.

71. Fison, *Holy Spirit,* 38.

72. Fison, *Holy Spirit,* 42.

of holiness; . . . he is holy by nature (φύσει ἅγιον, *phusei hagion*) even as the Father is holy by nature, and as the Son is holy by nature."[73]

Karl Barth holds together the work of the Holy Spirit and the efficacy and appropriation of the divine Word: "The Holy Spirit . . . cannot be separated from the Word."[74] He writes, "The Holy Spirit is very generally God himself. . . . [Yet] the Holy Spirit is not identical with Jesus Christ, with the Son or Word of God."[75] Even 2 Cor. 3:17, "The Lord is the Spirit," is not an "identification." As other writers, including G. S. Hendry and Taylor, state, it means that in the Old Testament to which Paul refers (Exod. 34:34), "the Lord" denotes the Spirit.[76] The Spirit enables believers to witness to God's revelation in Christ.[77] No less characteristically, Barth writes, the Holy Spirit is known to the churches of the New Testament "directly in his holiness. They are continually questioned as to their own sanctification by Him . . . because He is no other than the presence and action of Jesus Christ Himself."[78] Moltmann broadens this process of "sanctification" to include "rediscovering the sanctity of life and the divine mystery of creation, and defending them from life's manipulation, the secularization of nature, and the destruction of the world through human violence."[79] Holiness is not a merely "privatized" style of life. "If whatever God has made and loves is holy, then life is holy in itself, and to live life with love and joy means sanctifying it."[80]

18.3. The Deity of the Holy Spirit: The Church Fathers and a Trinitarian Horizon

Initially in the period after the New Testament the subapostolic writings presuppose, rather than expound, many of the traditional biblical themes relating to the work of the Holy Spirit. Clement of Rome understands the work of the Spirit to include the inspiration of Scripture, in particular inspiring the words of Isa. 53 to refer to Christ. He cites Isa. 53:1-12, including "it is he who bears our sins," and declares, "The Holy Spirit spoke concerning him [Christ]" (*1 Clement* 16:2-4). The Holy Spirit speaks through Ps. 34:11-17 (*1 Clement* 22:1). Clement speaks of the Spirit's being "poured out" (ἔκχυσις, *ekchusis, 1 Clement* 2:2) upon Christians in fullness.

---

73. Basil, *Letters* 125:3; Greek from *St. Basil: The Letters*, ed. R. Deferrari, Heb. Classical Library, 4 vols. (London: Heinemann, 1938) vol. 2, 266.

74. Barth, *Church Dogmatics*, I:1, sect. 5, 150.

75. Barth, *Church Dogmatics*, I:1, sect. 12, 1, 450 and 451.

76. Hendry, *The Holy Spirit*, 24; and Taylor, *The Person of Christ*, 54.

77. Barth, *Church Dogmatics*, I:1, sect. 12, 1, 454.

78. Barth, *Church Dogmatics*, IV:2, sect. 64, 4, 322-23.

79. Moltmann, *The Spirit of Life*, 171; cf. 171-79.

80. Moltmann, *The Spirit of Life*, 176.

Ignatius also includes an allusion to the agency of the Holy Spirit in the miraculous conception of Jesus Christ: "Our God, Jesus the Christ, was conceived by Mary (ἐκυοφορήθη ὑπὸ Μαρίας, *ekuophorēthē hupo Marias*) by the dispensation of God and, on the one hand, from the seed of David, on the other hand, of the Holy Spirit (ἐκ σπέρματος μὲν Δαυείδ, πνεύματος δὲ ἁγίου, *ek spermatos men Daueid, pneumatos de hagiou*) (Ignatius, *To the Ephesians* 18:2).[81] The church, as God's building, is carried up to God "by the engine of Jesus Christ, the cross, using as a rope the Holy Spirit" (Ignatius, *To the Ephesians* 9:1). Among the sub-apostolic writings, the *Didache* is the first, apart from Matt. 28:19, to use the threefold Trinitarian name in baptism. H. B. Swete suggests that this reflects liturgical use by the first half of the second century, rather than simply a replication of Matt. 28.[82]

The agency and initiative of the Holy Spirit in the incarnation of Jesus Christ remain present as a theme from Matthew and Luke through Ignatius of Antioch into the early Christian Apologists and Irenaeus. Aristides speaks of Jesus Christ, the Son of God, "having come down from heaven in the Holy Spirit for the salvation of humankind" (Aristides, *Apology*, 15, ἐν πνεύματι ἁγίῳ, *en pneumati hagiō*). Justin continues the tradition of the Spirit's inspiring the prophetic Scriptures (*Dialogue with Trypho* 7). The Spirit is the Spirit who gives understanding (*Dialogue with Trypho* 39).

Irenaeus anticipates the phrase of the later ecumenical creeds, "the Holy Spirit, who spoke through the prophets," in his exposition of the apostolic "rule of faith" in the form of a creed.[83] In Book V of *Against Heresies* he repeats the tradition of Matthew, Luke, Ignatius, and Aristides that "the Holy Spirit came upon Mary. . . . Therefore, what she gave birth to was holy and the Son of the Most High."[84] God the Father, the Son, and the Holy Spirit were co-workers in the creation of the universe. Against the Valentinian gnostics Irenaeus affirms that God created humankind in his own image, "moulded by his hands, that is, by the Son and the [Holy] Spirit" (*per manus eius plasmatus est, i.e., per Filium et Spiritum, quibus et dixit, Faciemus hominem*).[85] Swete infers that "as the Hands of God, they [the Son and the Spirit] are Divine and co-equal."[86] This is not explicitly stated, but it is arguably *presupposed*, or alternatively may be *inferred* from Irenaeus. The preexistence of the Holy Spirit is also an implicit presupposition.

The apostolic tradition preserved by Irenaeus continues in Novatian, Hippolytus, and Cyprian, but the gnostics, Tertullian, and Origen raise wider is-

81. The Greek text is that of *Apostolic Fathers* (2 vols.), Loeb Classical library, ed. K. Lake (London: Heinemann, 1915).

82. Henry B. Swete, *The Holy Spirit in the Ancient Church* (London: Macmillan, 1912), 17-18.

83. Irenaeus, *Against Heresies* I:10:1.

84. Irenaeus, *Against Heresies* V:1:3.

85. Irenaeus, *Against Heresies* IV:Preface, 4.

86. Swete, *The Holy Spirit in the Ancient Church*, 88.

sues. Gnostic writings speak of the Spirit in ways more akin to the misunderstandings in Corinth that Paul rejects than to apostolic traditions. To be *pneumatikos* is to achieve a higher status than that of "ordinary" *(psychical)* believers. Moreover, some gnostic writings digress into ascribing a gender, usually female, to the Spirit. *The Gospel of Philip* rejects the tradition of Matthew, Luke, Ignatius, and others about the Holy Spirit's role in the conception of Jesus on the ground that "a woman" could not conceive a child in a woman.[87] *The Gospel of Thomas* implies at one point that the Spirit is the mother of Jesus.[88] However, elsewhere it portrays Jesus as "making Mary male" on the ground that she may then become "living spirit like you males."[89] Clearly this departs from the mainline tradition of a Christian doctrine of the Holy Spirit, even if the gnostic gospels also preserve versions of some more traditional material.

Tertullian during his Montanist stage, together with Montanists, raises issues about *Spirit and order.* For Paul the apostle the work of the Holy Spirit *brings about* order (1 Cor. 14:6-12, 20-23, 27-33a, 40), and this accords with the Spirit's bringing order out of chaos at creation (Gen. 1:2; see above). Tertullian, on the other hand, contrasts "the Church of the Spirit" with "the Church which consists of a number of bishops." The former, but not the latter, can "forgive sins . . . by means of a spiritual person."[90] Those who upset "new prophecies" from Montanus and Priscilla and Maximilian (in the interests of tradition and order) are merely unspiritual or "psychical."[91] The Holy Spirit "advances" believers toward "better things."[92] The Spirit inspires "ecstasy . . . rapture . . . whenever an interpretation of tongues has occurred."[93] In the face of the Bishop of Rome's withdrawal of recognition of Montanism, Praxeas helped "the devil in Rome, drove away prophecy . . . and put to flight the Paraclete."[94]

In more traditional terms, Novatian continues the teaching that the Holy Spirit was active both in the prophets of the Old Testament on specific occasions and in the apostles of the New Testament "always." The apostles received gifts that "this same Spirit distributes . . . to the Church."[95] The Holy Spirit brings new birth.[96] The Spirit sanctifies the people of God and maintains church order. He "restrains insatiable desires . . . reckless impulses . . . links love, binds together affections, keeps down sects, orders the rule of truth, overcomes heretics . . . guards

---

87. *The Gospel of Philip,* logion 18.
88. *The Gospel of Thomas,* logion 101.
89. *The Gospel of Thomas,* logion 114.
90. Tertullian, *On Modesty* 21.
91. Tertullian, *On Fasting* 1.
92. Tertullian, *On the Veiling of Virgins* 1.
93. Tertullian, *Against Marcion* V:8.
94. Tertullian, *Against Praxeas* 1.
95. Novatian, *Treatise concerning the Trinity* 29.
96. Novatian, *Treatise concerning the Trinity* 29.

the Gospel."[97] His indwelling brings holiness. Hippolytus diverges from Tertullian and the Montanists even more radically. The Holy Spirit works especially through the *offices* of the church, and through all "who believe aright."[98] The Spirit authenticates and empowers the ordination of bishops, presbyters, and deacons, as well as the appointment of lay confessors. The invocation of the Holy Spirit in and for ordination, in the form of prayer for the Spirit, features in Hippolytus.[99]

More about the relation between the Spirit and church order in Hippolytus and the wider setting of the debate about Monarchian views of the Trinity can be found with reference to the views of Praxeas, Noetus, and Sabellius, most conveniently in the work of H. B. Swete and Stanley Burgess.[100] Significant advances in explicating an understanding of the deity of the Holy Spirit within a Trinitarian framework came initially, although only in part, with Origen, and then more fully with Athanasius and with Basil.

This most creative phase was precipitated by the so-called Pneumatomachian controversy, which concluded with responses from Gregory of Nazianzus, as well as Basil, and in less detail from Gregory of Nyssa. Our arguments in 2.2 about "dispositional" accounts of belief once again reveal their relevance. These controversies were not merely matters of power play to be explained solely in socio-political terms, but expressions of orthodox belief brought into play publicly in response to their denials. This situation accords with the very nature of what it is *to believe,* especially as understood in dispositional terms.

Origen reflects on the person and work of the Holy Spirit especially in *De Principiis* I:3 and II:7 (c. 230) and in parts of his *Commentary on John* (c. 231). He begins his major theological treatise with the assertion that the apostles "handed down that the Holy Spirit is associated with the Father and the Son in honour and dignity."[101] On the other hand, Origen concedes that it is not yet clearly known "whether he is begotten *(natus)* or unbegotten *(innatus),* or whether he is to be understood as Son of God or not."[102] But he places an emphasis upon the threefold co-naming together of the Spirit with the Father and the Son in liturgical settings of worship, and this becomes significant for the subsequent direction of doctrinal development up to Basil and beyond. All knowledge of God the Father, whom the Son reveals, "is made known to us in the Holy Spirit." Origen alludes in this context to 1 Cor. 2:10.

Yet Origen cannot or does not advance to the point at which Athanasius and Basil affirm the co-equal status of God as Father, Son, and Holy Spirit. As Mi-

---

97. Novatian, *Treatise concerning the Trinity* 29.

98. Hippolytus, *The Apostolic Tradition* 1:3-4.

99. Hippolytus, *The Apostolic Tradition* 7:2-5; cf. also 3:1-7.

100. Swete, *The Holy Spirit in the Ancient Church,* 101-2; and Stanley M. Burgess, *The Holy Spirit: Ancient Christian Traditions* (Peabody, MA: Hendrickson, 1984), 78-84; cf. 62-70.

101. Origen, *De Principiis* I:Preface, 4 (Greek in Migne, *Patrologia Graeca,* vol. 11, 117 C).

102. Origen, *De Principiis* I:3:4 (in Migne, *Patrologia Graeca,* vol. 11, 149A).

chael Haykin argues in his careful and constructive study of the Holy Spirit in Origen, Athanasius, and the Cappadocian Fathers, Origen's main concern, especially in his *Commentary on John*, is "not the affirmation of the Spirit's divinity, but the demonstration of the reality of the Spirit's *distinct existence.*"[103] Thus, Haykin writes, "while the Son and the Spirit belong within the divine sphere, they are definitely inferior to the Father," although this "inferiority" may be "only economic and not ontological."[104] There are indeed three distinct persons within the Godhead, but Origen wishes to take with full seriousness the Johannine language, "The Father who sent me is greater than I" (John 14:28).[105] Reflecting on the Johannine Prologue (John 1:1-14), Origen writes, "The Holy Spirit is . . . first in rank of all the things brought into being by the Father through Christ."[106] In his system of philosophical metaphysics, it is arguable that the Son and the Spirit are "middle beings."[107]

A hundred years later, in the era of Athanasius and Basil, it became necessary to refine this very broad understanding of the Holy Spirit, when Serapion, Bishop of Thmuis, wrote to Athanasius to inform him of a group of Christians who held inadequate or derogatory views of the Spirit. Athanasius replied in his *Letters to Serapion* (A.D. 358-59), which became a landmark for the Christian doctrine of the Holy Spirit. The names "Tropici" and "Pneumatomachi" were given to the group in question. The heart of the issue at stake was that the Tropici insisted on regarding the Holy Spirit as a "creature" (κτίσμα, *ktisma, a created being*).

In his *First Letter* Athanasius insists that the Holy Spirit is no more a creature than Christ is. How could the Trinity consist of Creator and creature? This is a blasphemy against the Son of God.[108] It is "to speak evil of the Holy Spirit."[109] Athanasius cites biblical support with *responsible exegesis*. If the Holy Spirit were only a creature, Paul would not have named him alongside the Father and the Son in such a passage as 1 Cor. 12:4-7. Athanasius also pays particular attention to 1 Cor. 12:13, as well as to 1 Cor. 2:11-12; 3:16-17; and 10:4; and to 2 Cor. 13:13. He consciously addresses the issues as a faithful interpreter of the New Testament and as a faithful guardian of apostolic tradition.[110] The Holy Spirit is depicted in Scrip-

---

103. Michael A. G. Haykin, *The Spirit of God: The Exegesis of 1 and 2 Corinthians in the Pneumatomachian Controversy of the Fourth Century, Vigiliae Christianae,* Supplement XXVII (Leiden and New York: Brill, 1994) 15.

104. Haykin, *Spirit,* 16.

105. Origen, *Commentary on John,* 13:25 (Migne, *Patrologia Graeca,* vol. 14, 441B).

106. Origen, *Commentary on John,* 2:10 (Migne, *Patrologia Graeca,* vol. 14, 128B).

107. Cf. Joseph Wilson Trigg, *Origen: The Bible and Philosophy in the Third-Century Church* (London: S.C.M., 1985 and Louisville: John Knox, 1983), 95-103 and throughout.

108. Athanasius, *Letters to Serapion,* 1:10 (Migne, *Patrologia Graeca,* vol. 26, 556C). The most convenient English edition is C. R. B. Shapland (ed.), *The Letters of Saint Athanasius concerning the Holy Spirit* (London: Epworth, 1951).

109. Athanasius, *Letters to Serapion* 3:7 (Migne, *Patrologia Graeca,* vol. 26, 636D).

110. Athanasius, *Letters to Serapion* 1:33 (Migne, *Patrologia Graeca,* vol. 26, 605C-D).

ture as a fountain (πηγή, *pēgē*) and river (ποταμός, *potamos*) of life, and as the light (φῶς, *phōs*) and radiance (ἀπαύγασμα, *apaugasma*) of God. These images also feature in Christian tradition, for example, in Hippolytus. The "fountain-river" suggests an unbroken continuity of being from the Father in the Son, and in 1 Cor. 12:13 Paul speaks of believers as being "made to drink" of the Spirit, and of the spiritual rock that was Christ.

On the basis of 1 Cor. 2:12 (τὸ πνεῦμα τὸ ἐκ τοῦ θεοῦ, *to pneuma to ek tou theou*) and other passages the Holy Spirit, far from being a created being, proceeds *from* God. Creatures were created "from nothing" (ἐξ οὐκ ὄντων, *ex ouk ontōn;* the Holy Spirit derives from "the being" of God (ἀλλ᾽ ἐκ τοῦ θεοῦ, *all᾽ ek tou theou*).[111] The stage is set for the respective descriptions of *Jesus Christ* the Son as uniquely *"begotten, not made,"* and of the *Holy Spirit* as *"proceeding"* from God. Athanasius draws upon the image of a flowing fountain or river that simply "comes" from its source. The holiness of the Holy Spirit (1 Cor. 3:16-17 and 6:11) also underlines the Spirit's unique derivation from God, who alone is holy.[112] Finally, Athanasius explicates the Trinitarian implications of 1 Cor. 12:4-6 and 2 Cor. 13:13, "What is true of the unified activity of the Spirit and the Son is also true of the activity of the whole Trinity."[113]

Basil succeeded Eusebius as Bishop of Caesarea in 370. The *pneumatomachi* had already been active in Asia Minor, and initially Basil was eager to avoid a schism. This concern aroused some suspicion of Basil himself, and he became caught between polemics from both sides. Whereas Athanasius had stressed the unity of the triune God, Basil expounded above all the divine holiness of the Holy Spirit. The "Holy" Spirit is one with the "holy" God. His treatise *On the Spirit* appeared in about 373 as a result of long reflection on the subject and the need to clarify his position.[114] It contributed decisively to the expansion of the Third Article of the Nicene Creed at the Council of Constantinople in 381.

The end of the first chapter of *On the Spirit* will resonate immediately today with all who use the liturgical threefold doxology or *Gloria* of the mainline Christian churches: "Glory be to the Father, and to the Son, and to the Holy Spirit. . . ." Basil writes, "when praying with the people and using the full doxology . . . 'with (συν, *sun*) the Son together with the Holy Spirit,' . . . I was attacked by some present on the ground that I was introducing novel and . . . mutually contradictory terms."[115] Basil replies first by tracing the mistaken origins of his opponents' views, and then by turning to exegesis of biblical passages. Further-

---

111. Athanasius, *Letters to Serapion* 3:2 (Migne, *Patrologia Graeca*, vol. 26, 628B).

112. Athanasius, *Letters to Serapion* 1:31 (Migne, *Patrologia Graeca*, vol. 26, 601B).

113. Haykin, *The Spirit*, 94; cf. Athanasius, *Letters to Serapion* 1:30 (Migne, *Patrologia Graeca*, vol. 26, 600A-C).

114. A convenient English edition is David Anderson (ed. and trans.), *St. Basil the Great: On the Holy Spirit* (Crestwood, NY: St. Vladimir's Seminary Press, 1980).

115. Basil, *On the Spirit* 1:3.

more, the practice of the threefold invocation of God as Father, Son, and Holy Spirit in the act of baptism confirms that this direction of thought is valid.[116]

In an important part of a sustained argument Basil points out that to speak of the Holy Spirit as "proceeding from" God finds support both in the Fourth Gospel (John 15:26, which uses ἐκ, *ek*) and in Paul (1 Cor. 2:10-12, which also uses ἐκ τοῦ θεοῦ, *ek tou theou*).[117] Christians also invoke the Spirit as *"Lord and life,"* and *"Giver of life."*[118] Basil also calls the Spirit *"the Giver of life"* in *Against Eunomius*.[119] He argues that the Holy Spirit is divine because he *shares in all the action properly ascribable only to God:* "The Spirit knows 'the deep things of God' [1 Cor. 2:10-11]. . . . The Spirit gives life . . . raised Christ from the dead . . . comes 'that we might know the things freely given by God' [1 Cor. 2:12]."[120] The Spirit is inseparable from the actions of the Father and the Son (1 Cor. 12:4-6).[121] Basil pays special attention to 1 Cor. 12:13: ἐν ἑνὶ πνεύματι ἡμεῖς πάντες εἰς ἓν σῶμα ἐβαπτίσθημεν, "by [or in] one Spirit we were all baptized into one body." He regards this as conclusively demonstrating the inseparable co-working of the Father, the Son, and the Holy Spirit.[122] I have discussed these and other passages on Basil and Athanasius in *Thiselton on Hermeneutics*.[123]

Gregory of Nazianzus, Ambrose, and Augustine continue and develop these themes. They also insist, following Athanasius and Basil, that they are *genuine exegetical implicates* of the Paraclete passages in John and of passages about the Spirit especially in 1 Cor. 2:10-15 and other parts of the Pauline writings. Gregory argues that a "swarm" of biblical passages point to the deity of the Holy Spirit.[124] The Spirit is not a created being but "proceeds" (Greek πορεύω, *poreuō, proceed, come forth;* noun, ἐκπόρευσις, *ekporeusis, procession*) from the Father.[125] Again, both John 15:26 and 1 Cor. 2:12 may *together* influence this formulation, for Haykin observes, "The use of the preposition 'from within' (ἐκ, *ek*) instead of the Johannine 'from' (παρά, *para*) probably reflects the influence of 1 Cor. 2:12."[126] The "procession" of the Holy Spirit from the Father is parallel with, but not exchangeable with, the "generation" (γέννησις, *gennēsis*) of the Son. Gregory's use of the term (c. 380) enters the Niceno-Constantinopolitan Creed of 381.[127]

In the West Ambrose and Augustine share many of the themes and argu-

---

116. Basil, *On the Spirit* 15:35.
117. Basil, *On the Spirit* 9:22 (John 15:26); 24:56 (1 Cor. 2:10-12).
118. Basil, *On the Spirit* 13:29 and 24:56.
119. Basil, *Against Eunomius* 3:4 (Migne, *Patrologia Graeca*, vol. 29, 665A).
120. Basil, *On the Spirit* 24:56 (Migne, *Patrologia Graeca*, vol. 32, 172C).
121. Basil, *On the Spirit* 16:37.
122. Basil, *On the Spirit* 12:28 (Migne, *Patrologia Graeca*, vol. 32, 117A).
123. Thiselton, *Thiselton on Hermeneutics*, 287-304, esp. 299-304.
124. Gregory of Nazianzus, *Orations* 31:29.
125. Gregory, *Orations* 31:8.
126. Haykin, *The Spirit*, 217.
127. Cf. *Thiselton on Hermeneutics*, 301-2.

ments of the Cappadocian Fathers, Basil, and Gregory of Nazianzus (Gregory of Nyssa writes less explicitly on this subject). Writing on 1 Cor. 12:4-6 and 12:8-10, Ambrose declares, "If the Holy Spirit is of one will and operation with God the Father, he is also of one substance, since the Creator is known by his works. So, then, it is 'the same Spirit,' [Paul] says, 'the same Lord, the same God.'"[128] Language concerning "substance" may go beyond Paul, but Ambrose believes that he is extrapolating what Paul genuinely implies.

Augustine draws on a wider range of passages than Ambrose and the Cappadocian Fathers, and his thought is too complex to invite serious exploration within the scope and purpose of the present work. However, he repeats the core of the established doctrinal tradition. The Spirit is not a creature *(non creatura, sed creator)*; He is "the Creator Spirit who in the Trinity is distinctively called 'the Holy Spirit' . . . with whom is the Trinity, the Father, the Son, and the Holy Spirit . . . Creator *(cum quo est trinitas, pater et filius et spiritus sanctus . . . creator)*."[129] Augustine reflects that it may appear at times as if the Holy Spirit "alone were entirely sufficient" apart from the Son; but there can be no "separation" here, for God and the Spirit of God are one: Father, Son, and Holy Spirit work as one (1 Cor. 12:6).[130]

The Patristic era has established a firm and stable continuity between a responsible exegesis of the biblical material on the Holy Spirit and the developing Christian doctrine of the Spirit. Since the end of the nineteenth century, however, the early questions about "church order" and "gifts of the Spirit" raised by Tertullian have resurfaced again with new vigor and urgency. A wider context emerged of a century of concern for spiritual renewal. To this context we now turn.

18.4. Pentecostal Gifts Then and Now: Issues of History and Hermeneutics

It might have appeared that section 18.3 was simply a history of the Patristic doctrine of the Holy Spirit, rather than a hermeneutic of the doctrine of the Holy Spirit. However, we have needed to establish the main horizons of understanding within the church from the New Testament era to Augustine and the Cappadocian Fathers as a developing and stable doctrinal tradition for understanding the person and work of the Holy Spirit, based primarily on the New Testament. "Developments" that carried this tradition further emerged in accordance with a dispositional account of belief when situations arose in which others denied or distorted the doctrines that were genuinely implicit in the New Testament.

We need this firm marker to inquire now whether the new awakening of con-

---

128. Ambrose, *On the Holy Spirit* II:12:138-40.
129. Augustine, *The City of God*, 13:24; cf. also 14:4.
130. Augustine, *On the Holy Trinity*, I:8:18 and IV:20:29.

cerns for renewal by the Holy Spirit, which emerged largely (but not exclusively) from roots in the American revivals in the last two decades of the nineteenth century and first decade of the twentieth, brings *new* horizons of understanding and interpretation, or whether it *recovers "lost"* horizons from the New Testament and the earlier Church Fathers.

Further hermeneutical questions arise. The movement that began as "Pentecostalism," associated initially with Charles F. Parham (1873-1929) and with Joseph William Seymour (1870-1922), stresses the need for a fresh spiritual dynamism and holiness, but also the need to recover the "spiritual gifts" specified in Acts and in 1 Cor. 12–14. Most notably for Parham, these included "baptism in the Spirit" and healing. As this tradition moved into the major Christian traditions of Roman Catholic, Anglican, Lutheran, Presbyterian, Methodist, Baptist, and the like in the form of "the charismatic renewal" movement, baptism in the Holy Spirit and healing came to be emphasized in conjunction with other such gifts, including *glossolalia*, or speaking in tongues, and "interpreting" tongues, and in a so-called "third wave," a phenomenon of "power" evangelism.

These twentieth-century movements raise the question: is the new emphasis derived from a particular *exegesis* of New Testament passages, or does it relate to a shift of *doctrinal* emphasis? Does it honor the role and place of the Holy Spirit within the holy Trinity, or does it, even if unwittingly, abstract the work of the Holy Spirit from the Trinitarian and Christological framework that was so fundamental for the Church Fathers? On the other hand, does it reflect, rather than a distinctive exegesis or doctrine, a concern to cultivate certain *less formal styles of worship and phenomena* associated with the Spirit? An additional *cultural* question arises: does the appeal of the movement lie in a stronger and more serious spiritual commitment and dynamic? Or does it lie no less in impatience with tradition, "establishment," and "order" and a yearning for change, novelty, and instantaneousness, which in the late twentieth century resonates with a postmodern mind-set, even within the churches?

All of these questions must begin as open ones, capable of answers in any direction. Much will depend on hermeneutical issues, including that of the relation between "then" and "now." The first fundamental point that simply "arises" (in Gadamer's sense of the term) is the success of these movements in calling attention to the person and work of the Holy Spirit. We alluded to laments in earlier modern expositions of the doctrine of the Holy Spirit concerning the neglect of the doctrine. In both Catholic and Protestant circles many have called for the reversal of such neglect, since before the early years of the twentieth century. Pope Leo XIII demanded that pastors and preachers should "instruct their people more diligently and more fully about the Holy Spirit" in 1897.[131] Many trace the

---

131. In J. J. Wayne (ed.), *The Great Encyclical Letters of Pope Leo XIII* (New York: Benziger, 1903), 436.

new concerns about the work and gifts of the Spirit in newborn Pentecostalism indirectly from John and Charles Wesley and the Holiness movement, but most directly from the American revolutionist movement of such leaders as Dwight L. Moody and Charles Finney.[132]

Charles Parham is widely regarded as the founder of classical Pentecostalism. In 1901 he participated in revival meetings in Topeka, Kansas, at which speaking in tongues and an "outpouring" of the Spirit were experienced as a "Baptism of the Holy Spirit" and "second" blessing subsequent to coming to Christian faith. Parham formulated the classic four marks of Pentecostal theology and experience: salvation, baptism in the Holy Spirit, healing, and expectancy of the "second coming" of Christ. He declared, "We are . . . seeking to displace dead forms and creeds . . . with living, practical Christianity."[133] The experience of speaking in tongues was perceived as a direct fulfillment and replication of the apostolic experience narrated in Acts 2:1-12.

Another Pentecostalist leader, T. B. Barrett, insisted, "The Pentecostal revival seeks to return as much as possible to the doctrine, faith, and practice of original Christianity in all manners. . . . What really distinguishes us . . . is our definite claim to be baptized in the Holy Ghost in the same way as the 120 on the day of Pentecost, a Spirit baptism accompanied by the speaking in tongues, as was also the case on the other four occasions in the Acts" (Acts 2:1-12; 10:44-48; 11:15-18; 19:1-7).[134]

The concern to "restore" primitive apostolic faith and practice led to the use of the term "Restorationist." Parham believed that the tongues of Acts 2:1-12 were specifically *xenolalia, foreign* languages, rather than *glossolalia,* or *unintelligible* languages, perhaps in 1 Cor. 12:8-10 and 14:1-40. The former were especially significant for evangelism. The early Pentecostals also identified a theme that came to be elaborated in New Testament scholarship in the second half of the twentieth century, namely that in Acts Pentecost was presented or perceived as the reversal of the confusion of Babel.[135]

Joseph William Seymour represented a second initiating source in early Pentecostalism. The son of Afro-American slaves, he was pastor of the Azusa Street Mission in Los Angeles, and led there the Azusa Street Revival of 1906-8. The revival was marked by speaking in tongues, advent expectation, expectations

---

132. Donald Dayton, *The Theological Roots of Pentecostalism* (Lanham, MD: Scarecrow and Grand Rapids: Zondervan/Asbury, 1987), 28-60; and Walter J. Hollenweger, *The Pentecostals* (Peabody, MA: Hendrickson and London: S.C.M., 1972), 4-46.

133. Sarah Parham, *The Life of Charles Fox Parham: Founder of the Apostolic Faith Movement* (Joplin, MO: Hunter, 1930), 158. I am indebted to Sarah Ahn, one of my Nottingham Ph.D. graduates, for access to a number of sources for the development and theology of the Pentecostal tradition.

134. Cited in Nils Bloch-Hoell, *The Pentecostal Movement: Its Origins, Development, and Distinctive Character* (Oslo: Universitetsforlaget and London: Allen & Unwin, 1964), 1-2.

135. John C. O'Neil, *The Theology of Acts in Its Historical Setting* (London: SPCK, 1961).

of miracles, baptism in the Spirit, and vibrant singing. This "Black" Pentecostalism also carried with it a social concern for racial integration, in the tradition of the "Great Awakening" of the eighteenth century.[136]

Pentecostal traditions continue with vitality up to the present but have also fragmented into various groupings. The Assemblies of God, who trace their roots in part to Azusa Street and to Congregationalism, have become the largest Pentecostal tradition in America. The Elim Foursquare Gospel Church has Presbyterian roots. By the 1960s many of the characteristics of Pentecostal theologies of the Spirit had become absorbed *within,* rather than outside, the major churches, but often under the label of "the charismatic renewal movement." Some referred to this as "the second wave" of charismatic-Pentecostal theology and experience, or as neo-Pentecostalism. Initially during the 1960s, as Andrew Walker observes, there was often an anarchic or even maverick aspect among some of its leaders.[137]

By the 1970s, however, a more measured reflection had set in, many Roman Catholic churches also embraced the movement, and Cardinal Suenens lent support to it. Walker calls the decade from 1970 to 1980 "the golden era (to date) of the Renewal Movement."[138] In 1980 Kilian P. McDonnell had published a three-volume collection of doctrinal expositions and assessments from many of the more established churches, including Roman Catholic, Anglican, Lutheran, Presbyterian, and Methodist traditions.[139] During this decade a huge, exponential growth of neo-Pentecostalism churches took place especially in the two-thirds world.

In the earlier 1980s conflicting currents emerged. Many within the Renewal Movement itself expressed disquiet about personality-central "televangelists" who adopted a chat-show style in American television, and raised questions about pastoral oversight in "megachurches."[140] John Wimber placed a new emphasis upon "power evangelism," and in some countries "Restorationist" churches formed defensive doctrinal "networks."[141] At the same time other currents within the Renewal Movement were undertaking serious theological and exegetical reflection, and engaging in ecumenical dialogue. Peter Wagner used the term "third wave" to denote a more moderate, reflective, ecumenical stream within the Renewal Movement.

136. Walter J. Hollenweger, "The Black Roots of Pentecostalism," in A. H. Anderson and Walter J. Hollenweger (eds.), *Pentecostals after a Century: Global Perspectives on a Movement in Transition* (Sheffield: Sheffield Academic Press, 1999), 33-64.

137. Andrew Walker, "Pentecostalism and Charismatic Christianity," in Alistair McGrath (ed.), *Modern Christian Thought* (Oxford: Blackwell, 1993), 428-34.

138. Walker, "Pentecostalism," in *Modern Christian Thought,* 431.

139. Kilian P. McDonnell (ed.), *Presence, Power, and Praise: Documents on the Charismatic Renewal* 3 vols. (Collegeville, MN: Liturgical Press, 1980).

140. The television evangelists include such names as Jimmy Swaggert, Oral Roberts, Jim and Tammy Bakker, and Pat Robertson.

141. John Wimber, *Power Evangelism* (London: Hodder & Stoughton, 1985).

In the 1990s and the early years of the twenty-first century these cross-currents began to come together again. A vast literature emerged. Watson E. Mills produced a research bibliography on charismatic religion that included over two thousand research articles (1985).[142] Esther D. Schandorff compiled a two-volume bibliography of works on the Holy Spirit (1995), which lists some seven thousand books and articles, mainly on Pentecostal theology.[143] The *Journal of Pentecostal Theology,* published currently by Sage, was founded in 1993. In the issue current at the time of writing Christopher Stephenson discusses theological method and the relation between Pentecostal *spirituality, doctrine, and a rule of faith.*[144] In this same volume John Poirier and Scott Lewis discuss the inapplicability of postmodernist hermeneutics to Pentecostalist *hermeneutics.*[145]

Within the longer established denominations, many charismatic or "third-wave" exponents are nowadays less inclined to call for "baptism in the Spirit" as a "second stage" or "second blessing" after coming to faith. As we have noted, James Dunn's book *Baptism in the Spirit* has decisively demonstrated on exegetical grounds that the use of the phrase in Paul does not allude to a subsequent experience after initiation-conversion. On the other hand, an openness to receive and appropriate the gifts of the Holy Spirit in ways that bring "the charismatic vitality of the new life" has found a prominent place with front-line scholars of all Christian traditions. Jürgen Moltmann is one of the most respected and distinguished advocates of such openness, especially in his *The Spirit of Life* but also in other writings.[146]

Moltmann writes, "Call and endowment, *klēsis* and *charisma* belong together. . . . This means that every Christian is a charismatic, even if many people never live out their gifts."[147] Romans 12 contains gifts and tasks that we may call *"the everyday charismata of the lived life."*[148] These are shared among the congregation, but Moltmann hesitates to call them "supernatural." What is clear is that both the unity and the variety of the charismata are in view (1 Cor. 12–14). He writes, "There is no doubt at all that today the Pentecostal and charismatic congregations are growing everywhere," and these gifts may express themselves in *glossolalia* "just as intense pain is expressed by unrestrained weeping, or extreme

---

142. Watson E. Mills, *Charismatic Religion in Modern Research: A Bibliography* (Macon, GA: Mercer University Press, 1985).

143. Esther Dech Schandorff, *The Doctrine of the Holy Spirit: A Bibliography Showing Its Chronological Development,* American Theological Library Association Bibliography 28, 2 vols. (Lanham, MD: Scarecrow, 1995).

144. Christopher A. Stephenson, "The Rule of Spirituality and the Rule of Doctrine: A Necessary Relationship in Theological Method," *Journal of Pentecostal Theology* 15 (2006) 83-105.

145. *Journal of Pentecostal Theology,* vol. 15 (2006) 3-21.

146. Moltmann, *The Spirit of Life,* esp. 180-97.

147. Moltmann, *Spirit,* 180.

148. Moltmann, *Spirit,* 183 (his italics).

joy by jumping and dancing."[149] Sometimes, he suggests, more formal church services are impoverished by a lack of spontaneity and liberty, with restricted body language.

Prophetic speech, Moltmann continues, is "a special *charisma*" that may offer a liberating word "at the right time."[150] It may include personal testimony. Charismatic gifts also derive from believing "in the possible. . . .' All things are possible with God.'"[151] The *charismata* of the Spirit occur where faith replaces fear.[152] Moreover, just as Jesus healed many who were sick (Mark 1:32-35), miraculous healings were not only common in the ancient world; "we find them today too."[153] Moreover, Jesus did not heal all the sick (Mark 6:5). Healings cannot be "contrived"; "they happen when and where God wills it. There is no method for healings of this kind."[154] Sicknesses can sometimes relate to disrupted relationships and psychosomatic conditions, but those in need of healing may also call upon modern medicine. Jesus heals "by 'carrying' our sicknesses" (Matt. 8:17).[155]

Among his most memorable and formative comments, Moltmann observes that "the *charismata* of the handicapped life" are part of human *embodiment.*[156] While God can heal when he wills, it is also essential that the community of the church understands its identity to include *both the weak and the strong.* The disabled can bring and can be a *charisma* to the church: *"congregations without any disabled members are disabled and disabling congregations"* (my italics).[157] As the early Pentecostals claimed, the "pouring out" of the Spirit brings "energy" and "vibrancy," indeed "vitalizing energies."[158]

Without doubt Moltmann has expressed the heart of Pentecostal or "Charismatic Revival" theologies of the Holy Spirit in forms that find an acceptable and honored place in the more established Christian traditions. However, some concerns of an exegetical, doctrinal, and hermeneutical nature also remain. These arise when certain assumptions receive insufficiently critical assessment, and when some assumptions are not demanded by renewal or Pentecostal theologies as such, but have become added as cultural baggage.

Points of possible concern may perhaps relate to how understandings of speaking in tongues today relate to "kinds of tongues" in the New Testament; to the so-called "interpretation" of tongues; and to assumptions about the nature of

149. Moltmann, *Spirit,* 185.
150. Moltmann, *Spirit,* 186.
151. Moltmann, *Spirit,* 187.
152. Moltmann, *Spirit,* 188.
153. Moltmann, *Spirit,* 189.
154. Moltmann, *Spirit,* 190.
155. Moltmann, *Spirit,* 191.
156. Moltmann, *Spirit,* 192-93.
157. Moltmann, *Spirit,* 193.
158. Moltmann, *Spirit,* 195 and 196.

prophecy that go further than exegetical and historical evidence. Often such questions concern mainly the nature and degree of emphasis placed upon given interpretations. We may first consider these issues of emphasis, and then conclude this chapter by reconsidering hermeneutical questions about *glossolalia* and prophetic speech in a final section.

(1) An emphasis upon the ministry of the Holy Spirit reflects New Testament and Christian doctrine, provided that this is not abstracted and isolated from its Trinitarian frame. In such passages as 1 Cor. 12:4-7 and the Paraclete sayings of the Fourth Gospel (John 15:26; 16:12-14) the New Testament writers describe the work of the Holy Spirit as "co-working" with the Father and the Son. The Church Fathers likewise do not isolate the Spirit from a necessary Christological and Trinitarian context and horizon. It might be more constructive and less open to misunderstanding to speak of *Trinitarian* renewal rather than *Spirit* renewal. Otherwise a desire to honor the Spirit falls into a mirror image of "Jesusology" among those who seek to honor Jesus Christ.

(2) As Moltmann urges, an experience of *vitality, dynamism, power, and energy* faithfully reflects biblical and patristic interpretation. However, this can lead to *triumphalism,* and to the loss of a dimension of *pilgrimage, waiting, and self-discipline,* as Käsemann warns us. The glory of power and vitality invites a caveat about notions of premature "arrival" that may hint at an overrealized eschatology (1 Cor. 4:8-13; Heb. 4:1-16; 11:13, 39; 12:1-17).

(3) The delight that arises from an *intimate and personal relationship with God* through Jesus Christ in the Holy Spirit reflects the authentic witness of the Holy Spirit to sonship in Rom. 8:14 and Gal. 5:22. Yet, as most Pentecostal and charismatic writers recognize, this should not lead to an inward-looking *pietist individualism* but to a shared concern for the church and for the well-being of society and the world. Further, it does not imply the antiintellectualism or precritical approach often associated with personal pietism.

(4) *Newness of life* and orientation toward a moment-by-moment "walking in (or by) the Holy Spirit" reflects the New Testament and Patristic emphasis upon transformation and holiness. However, an awareness of the present and future, of *surprise and creative novelty,* invites a warning about the possible disregard of *tradition and history.* The Holy Spirit acts *in continuity with his own past work in earlier centuries.* Moreover, in the creation narratives (Gen. 1:1–2:25) and in 1 Cor. 14:40 the Holy Spirit brings *"order"* rather than chaos.

(5) While the Holy Spirit brings renewal of the heart, freedom, and spontaneity, he renews the *whole person.* The *mind* is no less part of human personhood, as are emotions and bodily action. Antiintellectualism has no *necessary* connection with renewal.

(6) The expectation of *healing,* as Moltmann empresses it, happens "when and where God wills it." It remains open to question whether terminology about the *"miraculous"* is the most accurate way of conveying God's almighty sover-

eignty to act in or through causal processes or otherwise, as God chooses. Too strong an emphasis on the *"supernatural"* gives hostages to the notions of a closed universe at the "lower" or "natural" level, as if to imply that God acts in two self-contained modes of sovereign action. In my commentary I have questioned whether ἐνεργήματα δυνάμεων (*energēmata dunameōn*, 1 Cor. 12:10) should be translated *the working of miracles* (NRSV, AV/KJV, and NJB) or *miraculous powers* (REB, NIV). I translate it *actively effective deeds of power* to avoid imposing a narrower and more specific category onto Paul than he explicitly uses.[159] *"Deeds of power"* does not *exclude* miracles, but neither does it *specify* them.

The Greek *energēmata* reflects 1 Cor. 12:6, and Calvin, among others, doubts whether it denotes *miracles* rather than *effective power*.[160] *Too weak an emphasis upon healing diminishes trust in the sovereignty of God; too strong an emphasis upon healing increases the anguish of the problem of evil and suffering for those* (and their loved ones) *who do not receive healing* by other than medical means.

Paul uses the plural form twice: *gifts* (plural) *of healings* (plural): Greek, χαρίσματα ἰαμάτων (*charismata iamatōn*, 12:9). Within the Pentecostal tradition Donald Gee declares that this should "not preclude" what he called "the merciful and manifold work of medical healing."[161] Similarly, Bengel insists that while they may include the miraculous, these gifts do not thereby exclude "natural remedies" *(per naturalia remedia)*.[162] Also from within Pentecostal traditions (like Gee) David Petts has argued that although "healing" is a mark of classical Pentecostalism, it may not always be granted in God's will, and that such passages as those that link healing with the saving work of Christ (Isa. 53:4) do not establish a universal "claim" to be healed.[163] McDonnell also documents several joint statements with Pentecostal or ecumenical churches that include the sentence, "We do not therefore regard 'divine healing' as being always miraculous . . . but also wish to express caution against giving wrong impressions and unnecessary distress through . . . laying too great a stress upon the faith of the individual who is seeking healing."[164] Two factors are those of eschatological timing and the

---

159. Thiselton, *First Epistle*, 939 and 952-56.

160. John Calvin, *The First Epistle of Paul to the Corinthians*, trans. D. W. Torrance (Edinburgh: Oliver & Boyd and St. Andrews, 1960), 262; also Helmut Thielicke, *The Evangelical Faith*, trans. G. Bromiley, 3 vols. (Grand Rapids: Eerdmans, 1974-82), vol. 3, 79.

161. Donald Gee, *Spiritual Gifts in the Work of Ministry Today* (Springfield, MO: Gospel, 1963).

162. J. A. Bengel, *Gnomon Novi Testamenti* (Stuttgart: Steinkopf, 1866 [1773]), 652.

163. David Petts, *Healing and Atonement* (Ph.D. diss., University of Nottingham, 1993).

164. McDonnell (ed.), *Presence, Power, Praise*, 305; cf. vol. 2, 22-36 and 182-220 for Methodist statements; vol. 3, 11-13 and 70-76, for Pope Paul VI; vol. 2, 379-80, for the Baptist Union of Great Britain and Ireland; vol. 2, 114-15 for the Southern Baptists of the USA; and vol. 2, 15-21 and 307-24 for Lutheran traditions.

communal exercise of faith. I have discussed these issues in my commentary on the Greek text, together with translating the term as a *generic* plural: *gifts of various kinds of healing*.[165]

(7) As we have noted (twice now), Dunn and others have questioned decisively the exegetical foundation for claims that *baptism in the Spirit* in 1 Cor. 12:13 denotes a "second stage" of personal Pentecost beyond the experience of identification in baptism in his death and resurrection (Rom. 6:7-11).[166] But does this imply that the claims of Parham, Seymour, and Barrett are wrong? We need to distinguish claims about the *exegetical basis* of using the *term* as they did from other claims about *the authenticity of the experience* denoted by the term. It would be presumptuous to deny that sometimes Christian believers "catch up" on an experience of Pentecostal power and holiness at a stage subsequent to their initial coming to faith. But if the term "baptism of the Spirit" is used to describe this, this is not Paul's use of the *term*. Such a claim would entail a misleading hermeneutic, based on a mistaken exegesis.

18.5. The Exegesis and Hermeneutics of Speaking in Tongues and Prophetic Speech

We turn finally to the gift of speaking in tongues, the so-called interpretation of tongues, and the gift of prophetic speech. We must first note that in 1 Cor. 12:10 Paul speaks of *species* of tongues or *kinds* of tongues (Greek γένη γλωσσῶν, *genē glōssōn*). Paul believes that there is more than one kind of gift of tongues. The gift in Acts 2:1-13 was probably of a different kind from that to which Paul refers in Corinth. Some argue that in Acts 2 the gift was for those who heard rather than for those who spoke (Acts 2:8).

Scholarly literature on the Pauline epistles proposes a wide range of possible understandings of speaking in tongues, of which we select the five most carefully argued as examples. These five suggest that the gift of tongues in 1 Corinthians denotes: (i) tongues as angelic speech (E. Earle Ellis and G. Dautzenberg);[167] (ii) tongues as the miraculous power to speak other languages (Chrysostom, Thomas Aquinas, Robert Gundry, and Christopher Forbes);[168]

---

165. Thiselton, *First Epistle*, 946-51.

166. Dunn, *Baptism in the Holy Spirit*, 109-13, 117-20, and 127-31; cf. Thiselton, *First Epistle*, 997-1001.

167. E. E. Ellis, *Prophecy and Hermeneutic in Early Christianity* (Grand Rapids: Eerdmans, 1978), 6-71; G. Dautzenberg, "Zum religionsgeschichtlichen Hintergrund der διακρίσεις πνευμάτων (1 Kor. 12:10)," *Biblische Zeitschrift* 15 (1971) 93-104.

168. Chrysostom, *Homilies on 1 Corinthians*, Hom. 29:5; R. H. Gundry, "'Ecstatic Utterance' (NEB)?" *JTS* 17 (1966) 299-307; C. Forbes, *Prophecy and Inspired Speech in Early Christianity and Its Hellenistic Environment*, WUNT II, 75 (Tübingen: Mohr, 1995), 57-65.

(iii) tongues as liturgical, archaic, or rhythmic formulations of speech (F. Bleek, C. F. G. Heinrici);[169] (iv) tongues as ecstatic speech (Tertullian; S. D. Currie; L. T. Johnson; H. Kleinknecht);[170] and (v) the release of preconscious or unconscious "welling up" of precognitive perceptions or experiences from an overcontrolled psyche (K. Stendahl; G. Theissen; F. D. Macchia, and broadly Max Turner and J. Moltmann).[171]

I have documented these arguments in my commentary on the Greek text of 1 Corinthians, including counterarguments put forward against the first four of these five understandings of speaking in tongues.[172] The view that I have long advocated since before 1979 is the fifth, which first occurred to me in the course of research on the words ἑρμηνεύω and διερμηνεύω in Philo and Josephus, from which it appeared that *to articulate* or *to put into words* was more frequent a meaning than *to interpret* in given contexts.[173] In the light of similar arguments from Stendahl, Theissen, and Macchia, I tried to refine and to modify my view especially in the light of the parallel with the "sighs too deep for words" in Rom. 8:26. This also comes close to Moltmann's view, cited above, concerning the release of almost inexpressible pain or joy, weeping or laughter. Weeping and laughter well up from the preconscious, preconceptual, precognitive mind, and spill out in sounds or in body language too deep for expression in neat propositional statements. Rather than repressing such deep expressions, Paul perceives it as a *liberating gift* of the Holy Spirit to "let it all out." This, as Theissen rightly argues, is healthier than bottling it up, or nailing it down.

Nevertheless Paul sees this phenomenon as more central to private praise in communion with God than to public worship (1 Cor. 14:2-12). The tongues of which *Paul* speaks are not communications to fellow believers, but are specifically addressed "to God" (14:2). This is where tongues *differ* from *prophetic*

169. C. F. G. Heinrici, *Der erste Sendschreiben des Apostel Paulus an die Korinther* (Göttingen: Vandenhoeck & Ruprecht, 1896), 376-94.

170. Tertullian, *Against Marcion* 5:8; S. D. Currie, "Speaking in Tongues," *Interpretation* 19 (1965) 274-94; H. Kleinknecht, *"pneuma"* (part), in G. Kittel (ed.), *TDNT*, vol. 6, 345-48.

171. Krister Stendahl, "Glossolalia — The NT Evidence," in K. Stendahl, *Paul among Jews and Gentiles* (London: S.C.M., 1977), 109-24; Gerd Theissen, *Psychological Aspects of Pauline Theology*, trans. J. P. Galvin (Edinburgh: T&T Clark, 1987), 74-114 and 292-341; A. C. Thiselton, *First Epistle*, 970-88, 1062-64, and 1094-1130, esp. 984-89; F. D. Macchia, "Groans Too Deep for Words: Toward a Theology of Tongues as Initial Evidence," *Asian Journal of Pentecostal Studies* 1 (1998) 149-73; and "Tongues and Prophecy: A Pentecostal Perspective," *Concilium* 3 (1996) 63-60; Max Turner, *The Holy Spirit and Spiritual Gifts: Then and Now* (Carlisle, U.K.: Paternoster, 1996), 227-39 and 303-14; cf. Moltmann, *Spirit of Life*, 185.

172. Thiselton, *First Epistle to the Corinthians*, 970-89 and 1096-1113.

173. Anthony C. Thiselton, "The 'Interpretation' of Tongues? A New Suggestion in the Light of Greek Usage in Philo and Josephus," *JTS* 30 (1979) 15-36; repr. in *Thiselton on Hermeneutics*, 247-85. Cf., e.g., Philo, *On the Migration of Abraham* 12:73, and 81; and Josephus, *Jewish War* 5:176 and 5:182.

speech, which is indeed intended to build up others (14:3-4). The "interpretation" of tongues becomes the subject of a prolonged reflection in 14:6-19. The key verse is 14:13: "One who speaks in a tongue should pray for the power [REB, ability] to interpret." Almost all the major versions (NRSV, REB, NIV, NASB, AV/KJV, NKJV) rightly understand Paul to be asking *the one who speaks in tongues* to make the utterance intelligible. The Greek does *not* include τις *(tis), someone:* no second person called an "interpreter" is involved. Only NJB hedges its bets by asking the person concerned to pray "that he may be given the interpretation," which might or might not be through a second person.

How then does the phrase traditionally rendered *"the interpretation of tongues"* (1 Cor. 12:10, NRSV) fit among the *charismata* of the Holy Spirit? Clearly if the gift of tongues provides release from repressed experiences of praise, joy, longing, or yearning for God, it also constitutes a genuine gift of the Spirit when such expressions can not only be released (through speaking in tongues) but also *put into words* for the *building up* of the church. These two gifts are almost complementary, and they become virtually sequential if both are given. An individual may still let the preconscious longings and yearnings spring up in glossolaliac praise in *individual communion* with God. In a *congregational* setting, however, it is an added gift if, as the believer begins to feel overwhelmed by a sense of divine awe and wonder, part or all of this comes into his or her conscious mind as capable of intelligible sharing with other Christians at worship. Then *both* the gift to "let it out" *and* the gift of putting it into intelligible speech become "gifts" of the Spirit respectively for private and public use.

The gift of *prophetic speech* also gives rise to a diversity of interpretations. C. K. Barrett, who offers less critical argument and evidence for his view than he otherwise normally offers, writes that it "was uttered in ordinary, though probably excited, perhaps ecstatic speech."[174] But this seems to go beyond the explicit evidence as at best an inference from a wider context. Some writers insist that prophetic speech came in short staccato outbursts. But John the Divine uses the term *"prophet"* or *prophetic speech* seven times to characterize his discourse in the book of Revelation (Rev. 1:3; 11:6; 19:10; 22:7, 10, 18, 19). Still more to the point Sandnes convincingly shows that Paul views his personal, apostolic ministry as prophetic, and he neither resorts to "thus says the Lord," nor restricts himself to short, staccato utterances, nor abandons rational discourse for which he has prepared in rigorous reflection.[175] There is no conclusive evidence that a prophecy must be any particular length, nor whether it is always expected to be ecstatic, nor that it need be unprepared and "spontaneous." The one universal criterion is

---

174. C. K. Barrett, *A Commentary on the First Epistle to the Corinthians* (London: Black, 2d edn. 1971), 286.

175. K. O. Sandnes, *Paul — One of the Prophets? A Contribution to the Apostle's Self-Understanding,* WUNT II, 43 (Tübingen: Mohr, 1991).

that it constitutes a message or address from God, not simply constructed by the speaker. But God may work through processes of preparatory reflection, just as God may work through unexpected, instant revelation. The former is perhaps more likely to be the "normal" mode of prophetic inspiration, especially since 1 Cor. 14:19, 23 associate prophetic speech with the conscious use of the mind (νοῦς, *nous*).

In my commentary on these verses I have included two extended additional Notes on prophetic speech.[176] The two Notes demonstrate how widely any horizon of understanding must be for a responsible hermeneutic of prophetic speech in the New Testament and today. The first Note considers detailed sources and documentation about possible Hellenistic or apocalyptic backgrounds; the Old Testament background; prophetic speech as pastoral preaching; prophets as leaders, and women prophets; and prophetic consciousness, prophetic fallibility, and prophetic testing. The second Note considers issues of a hermeneutical frame of reference; the goal of prophetic speech as building up, encouraging, and bringing comfort; the theory that prophecy denotes a creative or charismatic interpretation of Scripture; the respective arguments for "spontaneous" utterance or prepared preaching; and whether prophecy is addressed only to fellow believers or also to the wider world. 1 Cor. 14:23-25 envisages that prophetic speech brings *an unbeliever or inquirer to faith.* The passage about "strange tongues" (1 Cor. 14:21-22) serves to convey the point that nothing in worship should be so esoteric or unintelligible as to make Christians feel like "strangers" or like outsiders, as if they did not "belong" comfortably in their own "home," namely their church.

We cannot rehearse the arguments of some twenty pages again here. The upshot is to conclude with David Hill, Ulrich Müller, and Thomas Gillespie that in this context *prophetic speech denotes primarily applied pastoral preaching of the gospel,* whether long or short, whether prepared or spontaneous, and whether delivered in measured speech or with urgent passion.[177] The only two criteria are (i) that it should come from God as *address from God;* and (ii) that it should be an *intelligible, public, communicative act.*

Max Turner has also provided a careful study of prophecy among the gifts of the Holy Spirit in the New Testament, and compared it both sympathetically and critically with the phenomenon of prophecy today.[178] He recognizes the force of Sandnes's argument that since Paul includes prophetic discourse as part of his

---

176. Thiselton, *First Epistle,* 956-65 and 1087-94.

177. David Hill, *New Testament Prophecy* (London: Marshall, 1979), 110-40 and 193-213; Ulrich B. Müller, *Prophetie und Predigt im Neuen Testament Formgeschichtliche Untersuchungen zur urchristlichen Prophetie* (Gütersloh: Mohn, 1975); and Thomas W. Gillespie, *The First Theologians: A Study in Early Christian Prophecy* (Grand Rapids: Eerdmans, 1994).

178. Max Turner, *The Holy Spirit and Spiritual Gifts: Then and Now* (Carlisle, U.K.: Paternoster, 1996), 185-220 (New Testament) and 315-28 (now).

ministry, this reinforces the *gospel*-related aspect of prophetic speech, although Paul, he argues, "relativizes" prophetic authority in relation to apostolic authority.[179] Turner states, "With the exception of the eschatological prophecies, the rest are pastoral 'words' which articulate already known theology to specific circumstances, rather than offering new theological revelation."[180] Paul does not acquiesce to demands from the Corinthian prophets to decide the agenda for worship.[181]

I am less convinced than Turner in seeing both the New Testament and Pentecostalist-charismatic prophecy today as "oracular," although for both it is certainly perceived as revealed by God.[182] Both also grant a "mixed" authority to prophecy, since prophetic speech can be fallible and must therefore be tested.[183] Yet if prophecy in the New Testament is to a large degree pastoral preaching, it seems surprising to read that differences between prophecy in the New Testament today "do not appear to be material."[184] It is easier to accept that within the Renewal Movement a *range* of phenomena count as "prophetic," and that this includes within it a desire to hear and to convey the living voice of God, provided that its continuity with apostolic doctrine is tested. Our views are close, but perhaps not identical in emphasis.

We do not have space within the confines of this already lengthy chapter to examine passages in the Acts of the Apostles in the same detail. Nevertheless we offer a few observations. First, we have noted that the event relating to speaking in tongues on the Day of Pentecost may have had less to do with a mode of *speaking* than with a mode of *hearing* (Acts 2:6), and that this operated within the framework of bringing the whole people of God into a unity of co-sharing the Spirit (Acts 2:17-21; cf. Joel 2:28-29). Many exegetes and charismatic writers agree that not only is the gift of the Spirit *communal and eschatological;* it may also be perceived as a reversal of Babel (Gen. 11:1-9).

Second, a number of difficulties stand in the way of constructing a clear and precise picture. If the language was primarily communicative, why would Jews from the regions described in Acts 2:9-11 need any other language than Koine Greek, which was also spoken in "Galilee of the Gentiles" as the language of commerce?[185] The accusation of drunkenness might perhaps suggest a kind of *glosso-*

---

179. Turner, *Holy Spirit*, 215.
180. Turner, *Holy Spirit*, 219.
181. Turner, *Holy Spirit*, 220.
182. Turner, *Holy Spirit*, 316.
183. Turner, *Holy Spirit*, 321.
184. Turner, *Holy Spirit*, 327.
185. On the other hand, F. F. Bruce argues that "they recognized the indigenous languages and dialects of their own lands. The visitors from lands East . . . knew Aramaic, and those from lands West . . . knew Greek"; F. F. Bruce, *The Book of Acts* (London: Marshall, Morgan, & Scott and Grand Rapids: Eerdmans, 1965), 59.

lalia more akin to that of 1 Cor. 12:10 and 14:1-40 than to "foreign speech." On the other hand, Haenchen is not alone in interpreting Acts 2:4 to denote "to speak in a solemn or inspired way, but not ecstatic speech."[186]

The *source and effect* of these phenomena are clear. The coming of the Holy Spirit in power upon the apostolic circle and others is well summed up in its effect by Kilian McDonnell's title *Presence, Power, Praise*. As Turner notes, far from utilizing any Hellenistic concept of the Spirit, "the Spirit is the uniting motif and the driving force within the Lucan salvation history and provides the legitimation for the mission."[187] The deepest hermeneutical problem, which relatively few commentators touch with real care and depth, is whether this unique progress from Jerusalem to Rome recounts a nonrepeatable "founding" narrative, which is not intended to be a paradigm for subsequent generations. Such a genre would differ from the hortatory sections of Romans, 1 Corinthians, or the Epistle to the Hebrews, which clearly offer paradigms, models, and patterns for wider communities of the church.

Yet it would be rash to assume that the writings of Luke-Acts were other than *formative* for the wider church. Luke declares as a principle of continuity that the church continued to devote themselves "to the apostles' teaching and fellowship, to the breaking of bread and the prayers" (Acts 2:42). Where the patterns of the narrative reflect regularities in Acts, Luke appears to speak beyond a single nonrepeatable situation. In a recent volume under the title *Reading Luke*, a number of us sought to demonstrate that the Lucan writings are not merely informative but also *formative and transformative*.[188] In this volume Turner includes an essay on "Luke and the Spirit." The Gospel of Luke underlines the relation between Jesus Christ and the Spirit. The Acts of the Apostles links the exaltation of Jesus with "the intensification of God's reign and salvation, which transforms the community in ways hoped for in Luke 1-2."[189] This includes "empowering for mission *and* the renewal and transforming immanent Lordship of Jesus in and to the community."[190]

In response to much of the *phenomena* associated with the Holy Spirit both in the New Testament and in the church today we could do worse than repeat Karl Barth's key focus, which should guide our hermeneutics and never be lost. On 1 Cor. 12–14 he speaks of chapter 13 on love as indicating "a great passing away of all those things that are not love." He then declares: "What we are really con-

---

186. Ernst Haenchen, *The Acts of the Apostles: A Commentary*, trans. B. Noble and G. Shinn (Oxford: Blackwell, 1971), 168, n. 3.

187. Turner, *Holy Spirit*, 37.

188. Craig G. Bartholomew, Joel B. Green, and Anthony C. Thiselton (eds.), *Reading Luke: Interpretation, Reflection, Formation* (Carlisle, U.K.: Paternoster and Grand Rapids: Zondervan, 2005), 3-54 (Thiselton) and throughout.

189. Max Turner, "Luke and the Spirit," in *Reading Luke*, 280; cf. 267-93.

190. Max Turner, "Luke and the Spirit," in *Reading Luke*, 281.

cerned with is not *phenomena* in themselves, but with their *whence?* and *whither? to what do they point? to what do they testify?*"[191]

In *hermeneutical* terms clearly the horizons of understanding that shaped the discussion in 18.1 through to 18.3 are not the same as those that emerge in 18.4 and 18.5, although they overlap and complement each other. Where in 18.4–18.5 is the Holy Spirit whose "work is not to advertise but to efface Himself in . . . the *kenosis* of the Spirit," to glorify *Christ* as Lord of the Church?[192] *The hermeneutical paradox* here is that the more we engage with *signs* of the Holy Spirit, the more *we risk losing the very goal of the Holy Spirit's work,* namely to illuminate Christ, the cross, and the future resurrection as the heart of the gospel. It is time to respond to this in healthier theological terms by moving without more ado to a hermeneutic of *the Trinitarian God.*

---

191. Karl Barth, *The Resurrection of the Dead,* trans. H. J. Stenning (London: Hodder & Stoughton, 1933).

192. Cited in the first paragraph of this chapter from Fison, *The Blessing of the Holy Spirit,* 22-23

CHAPTER 19

The Hermeneutics of the Doctrine of God as Trinity

19.1. Hermeneutical Starting Points: The Relevance and Ambiguity of Experience

Chapters 17 on Christology and 18 on the Holy Spirit have already addressed questions about the deity of Christ and the deity of the Holy Spirit. Hence much of the groundwork for a Trinitarian theology has been covered not only by hermeneutical reflections on such passages as the Paraclete sayings in John 14–16 and such Pauline material as 1 Cor. 2:10-16 and 1 Cor. 12:4-7, but also in the exegesis and interpretation of those biblical passages on the part of Athanasius, Basil, and the other two Cappadocian Fathers. We also drew on Michael Haykin's excellent study of their exegesis of 1 and 2 Corinthians for their arguments about the deity of the Holy Spirit.[1]

Nevertheless, none of this addresses discussions of appropriate hermeneutical starting points for a doctrine of the Trinity. It has so far left aside issues about the unity of God as "one" amidst language about the deity and co-working of Christ and the Spirit.

Paul Fiddes rightly rejects a starting point that seems to afflict many, perhaps even the majority, of ordinary church people. He writes, "The doctrine [of the Trinity] is not stating the paradox that God is one being and three beings at the same time, or even that God is both 'one person' and 'three persons.'"[2] Even if we were to begin with an emphasis upon "one God," which we do not propose to do, Basil of Caesarea writes, "We confess one God not in number but in nature. . . . *God is not one in number.* . . . Number relates to quantity and . . . is of bodily nature."[3]

---

1. Haykin, *The Spirit of God,* esp. 59-201.

2. Paul Fiddes, *Participating in God: A Pastoral Doctrine of the Trinity* (Louisville: Westminster John Knox, 2000), 4.

3. Basil, *Letters* 8:2.

We propose two more fruitful hermeneutical starting points, followed by further hermeneutical supplements. We also argue that some traditional language about *being* and *substance* may well constitute a distraction or blind alley from a *hermeneutical* viewpoint, unless it can be very firmly placed within a horizon of understanding in which it is inseparable from *action, process, and revelation*, as Barth, Jüngel, and some others rightly insist.[4] There is a clear difference of judgment among theological thinkers about whether the increasing concern in the third, fourth, and fifth centuries for sharper terminological distinctions (often based upon philosophical categories) constitutes, as R. S. Franks suggests, "a technical advance," or whether, with Brunner, we perceive these as useful for their own times but as a hermeneutical distraction for today.[5]

The two *initial* hermeneutical horizons of understanding that are most appropriate as starting points are (i) that of *Christian experience* especially in prayer and worship, but suitably *interpreted, qualified, and constrained* in the light of biblical revelation; and (ii) *the narrative of the New Testament* as that of Jesus Christ in co-agency with God as the Father of Jesus and with the Holy Spirit as the anointing power of his ministry, self-surrender, and resurrection.

Moltmann and Pannenberg affirm the second of these starting points as the way into the subject, in contrast to the more static and often complex formulations of the Patristic church. Moltmann clarifies this distinction succinctly. He writes that whereas we may begin (with the New Testament) with the "history of Jesus the Son . . . as part of the history of the Father, the Son, and the Spirit," it is the case that "ever since Tertullian the Christian Trinity has always been depicted as belonging within the general concept of divine substance: *una substantia — tres personae*."[6] Worse, the early church "clung to the apathy axiom" associating suffering with transience and death. The latter has been tragic, because "A God who cannot suffer cannot love either."[7]

Pannenberg and Moltmann find the roots of the doctrine of the Trinity in

---

4. Barth, *Church Dogmatics*, I:2, ch. ii, Part 1, "The Triune God," sects. 8-12; and Eberhard Jüngel, *God's Being Is in Becoming: The Trinitarian Being of God in the Theology of Karl Barth. A Paraphrase*, trans. John Webster (Edinburgh: T&T Clark, 2001), esp. 13-53 and 75-139 (this is a revised translation of Eberhard Jüngel, *The Doctrine of the Trinity: God's Being Is in Becoming*, trans. Horton Harris [Edinburgh: Scottish Academic Press, 1976]).

5. Robert S. Franks, *The Doctrine of the Trinity* (London: Duckworth, 1953), 114; and Emil Brunner, *The Christian Doctrine of God: Dogmatics* vol. 1, trans. Olive Wyon (London: Lutterworth, 1949), 239. See further Vincent Brummer, *Atonement, Christology, and the Trinity: Making Sense of Christian Doctrine* (Aldershot, UK: Ashgate, 2005); John J. O'Donnell, *Trinity and Temporality: The Christian Doctrine of God in the Light of Process Theology and the Theology of Hope* (Oxford: Oxford University Press, 1983); Leonard Hodgson, *The Doctrine of the Trinity* (London: Nisbet, 1943); and David Brown, *The Divine Trinity* (London: Duckworth, 1985) esp. 219-44 and 272-309.

6. Moltmann, *The Trinity and the Kingdom of God*, 16.

7. Moltmann, *Trinity*, 23 and 38.

the narrative of Jesus of Nazareth, which cannot be understood other than in relation to God as the Father of Jesus and to the anointing and empowering of the Holy Spirit for his ministry.[8] As we have seen (p. 377), Moltmann writes (his italics): *"The New Testament talks about God by proclaiming in narrative the relationships of the Father, the Son, and the Spirit, which are relationships of fellowship and are open to the world."*[9] *Narrative,* as I have argued repeatedly elsewhere, provides an admirably fertile hermeneutic because it encourages self-involvement and entry into a projected "narrative world," and brings together word and deed in life-related ways.[10] However, we consider briefly, first, approaches to a doctrine of the Trinity within the horizon of experience.

Is "Christian experience" a reliable or appropriate hermeneutical horizon within which to begin? "Experience" offers a hermeneutical bridge, but if it is abstracted from Scripture, tradition, and reason, it is notoriously capable of unstable or diverse interpretation. Schleiermacher's principle of deriving doctrine from experience runs into severe problems in many areas. But he himself recognizes its especially problematic role in relation to the doctrines of the Trinity. He is sufficiently intimate with Kant's transcendental philosophy to recognize that the human mind categorizes, selects, and shapes what it *counts as* experience, while experience at a precognitive, intuitive, level has minimal resources to lead to critical judgments of such shaping.

Schleiermacher declares, "The Trinity . . . is not an immediate utterance concerning the Christian self-consciousness. . . . The encounter of an eternal distinction in the supreme Being is not an utterance concerning the religious consciousness, for from there it never could emerge."[11] In spite of his comments about the importance of a doctrine of the Trinity, Schleiermacher leaves this to some dozen or so pages at the end of his 750-page treatise, to which it forms hardly more than a postscript or tailpiece.[12]

"Experience," then, offers a reliable hermeneutical starting point only if it is regarded as a *provisional* way into the subject, in effect more strictly to yield *pre-understanding* or *preliminary* understanding rather than understanding itself (*Vorverständnis* rather than *Verstehen*). It remains subject to the "control" of engagement with the biblical narrative. As Moltmann writes, Trinitarian theology arises as an *"interpretative"* explication of the New Testament.[13]

This point of entry also relates to two further issues that we shall discuss in

---

8. Pannenberg, *Systematic Theology,* vol. 1, 259-77.

9. Moltmann, *Trinity,* 64.

10. Thiselton, *New Horizons in Hermeneutics,* 351-68 (on Ricoeur); 471-508 (on narrative); and 272-79 (on self-involvement); cf. Moltmann, *Trinity,* 61-96; and Pannenberg, *Systematic Theology,* vol. 1, 259-336.

11. Schleiermacher, *The Christian Faith,* Part II, sects. 170, 738, and 739.

12. Schleiermacher, *The Christian Faith,* Part II, "Conclusion," sects. 170-72, 738-51.

13. Moltmann, *Trinity,* 62-63.

19.2. First, certain "markers" or "signposts" are derived from the *response* to distortions or denials of beliefs, which emerge from the *dispositional character of belief* discussed in 2.1–2.3. Thus, while we shall try to avoid the later complexities of such terminological controversies as relate to οὐσία *(ousia)* and ὑπόστασις *(hupostasis)* in Greek and their relation to *substantia* and *persona* in Latin, it remains relevant to a hermeneutics of today to understand why Tertullian responded negatively to the "modalism" of Praxeas, and to the "dynamistic monarchianism" or subordinationism of Theodotus. Schleiermacher's language about whether human consciousness can or cannot experience divine centers of "consciousness" also invokes Karl Barth's sensitive concern about how far, if at all, such language can be even at best "analogical" if it is applied to God as Trinity. These issues are postponed until 19.2.

A constructive appeal to a hermeneutic of experience can be found in the Church of England Doctrine Commission Report of 1987, *We Believe in God*, of which I was a member and to which I was a contributor.[14] In particular we explored an approach to Trinitarian doctrine through the Christian experience of prayer. We might have said more, in retrospect, about the broader liturgical experience of worship. We did not explicitly mention George Lindbeck, but we began by arguing that to know certain linguistic "rules" about Trinitarian doctrine (for example, that we do not say, "God the Father died on the cross") is a far cry from *acknowledging* God as Trinity in life. At an uncritical, popular level, Karl Rahner's verdict is largely true, that many Christians are initially just "monotheist" in spite of their formal allegiance to creeds that state a Trinitarian doctrine of God.[15]

It is tempting, we conceded, to assume that prayer is a wholly *human* activity: or "all one's own doing." Nevertheless many Christians also witness to the experience of being *"prayed in"* or *prayed through,* especially when "we do not know how to pray as we ought" (Rom. 8:26a). Urges, promptings, and desires well up *as if from the Spirit who is "the Beyond Who Is Within,"* "the Spirit [who] bears witness with our spirit" (Rom. 8:16), prays through the believing Christian, and "intercedes with sighs too deep for words" (Rom. 8:26b).[16] Christians are, as it were, "caught up in divine conversation passing back and forth in and through the one who prays."[17] Christians come with confused or inarticulate longings, but find that the Holy Spirit bears witness in co-praying with the Christian to God as the Father who hears the cries of his children.

The Holy Spirit and God as our Father whom the Christian addresses are not perceived or understood as two distinct "centers of consciousness." Never-

---

14. Doctrine Commission of the Church of England, "God as Trinity: An Approach through Prayer," in *We Believe in God* (London: Church House Publishing, 1987), 104-21. We all endorsed this chapter, but Sarah Coakley did much of the groundwork.

15. Rahner, *Theological Investigations,* vol. 4, 79.

16. Doctrine Commission, "God as Trinity," in *We Believe in God,* 108.

17. Doctrine Commission, "God as Trinity," in *We Believe in God,* 108.

theless, in accordance with the teaching of Jesus Christ, we pray to *"Our Father"* (Matt. 6:9) or to *"Father"* (Luke 11:2). Christians know at the same time that to approach God is necessarily to approach God *"through Jesus Christ, our Lord"* (Heb. 4:14-16). If the *Holy Spirit* is at work in the heart of the Christian at prayer, this work has as its goal to glorify Christ (John 16:14), to reveal Christ (John 16:13-15), and to acknowledge Jesus as Lord (1 Cor. 12:3). All of this process amounts to "a participation in a divine dialogue" in which prayer is "incarnational." It involves *the agency of the Holy Spirit,* address *to God the Father,* and the glory and *mediation of God the Son.*[18] It is through the Holy Spirit that Christian believers share the distinctive prayer-cry of Jesus of Nazareth, *"Abba,* Father" (Mark 14:36; Rom. 8:15; Gal. 4:6; cf. Matt. 26:39; Luke 22:42).

In the language of the apostle Paul, the Holy Spirit actualizes what it is to be "in Christ," or "to have the mind of Christ" (1 Cor. 2:16). Paul writes, "It is no longer I who live, but Christ who lives in me" (Gal. 2:20). His pastoral goal is for the church "to be conformed to the image of God's Son" (Rom. 8:29). The longing for this experience and goal is not simply individualistic. Co-praying and co-longing characterize the Spirit's enlivening of the whole church, and this in turn spreads to the cosmic yearning of the whole created order to be freed from its bondage at the fulfillment of future hope and glory (Rom. 8:18-25).[19] We concluded, "The whole creation, inanimate as well as animate, is taken up in this trinitarian flow."[20]

The purpose of exploring this hermeneutical model is to try to show that a doctrine of the Trinity has *life-currency* for everyday Christian living, without having to appeal to hypothetical "problems" about the numerals "three" and "one," or to the polemical controversies and formulations of the third and fourth centuries. The doctrine is not an abstraction; nor is it primarily a matter of learning how to use "linguistic rules" (*pace* Lindbeck). This may be a derivative exercise for theologians, but does not reach the heart of the matter. Moreover, "experience-oriented" models do not operate in abstraction from biblical roots. As in the case of Christology in Luke 24:25-27 and 44-48, Scripture interprets Christian experience, and present experience, in turn, explicates what is implicit in Scripture.

---

18. Doctrine Commission, "God as Trinity," in *We Believe in God,* 109.

19. Rom. 8:19-22 combines apocalyptic imagery with poetic creativity; see Cranfield, *Epistle to the Romans,* vol. 1, 404-20; Ernst Käsemann, *Commentary on Romans,* trans. Geoffrey Bromiley (London: S.C.M., 1980), 230-39; and Ernst Käsemann, "The Cry for Liberty in the Worship of the Church," in Ernst Käsemann, *Perspectives on Paul,* trans. Margaret Kohl (London: S.C.M., 1971), 122-37.

20. Doctrine Commission, "God as Trinity," in *We Believe in God,* 111.

19.2. Hermeneutical Starting Points:
The New Testament Narrative of Trinitarian Co-Agency

As we noted above, Moltmann and Pannenberg adopt this approach.[21] It is un-deniable, even by the most rigorous critical criteria, that *Jesus* proclaimed the reign of *God*. J. Jeremias writes, "The central theme of the public proclamation of Jesus was the kingly reign of God."[22] Even in terms of the now infamous and largely discredited criterion of dissimilarity, this stands as bedrock of the Jesus tradition.[23] I. Howard Marshall also traces the centrality and significance of this theme.[24] However, most, if not all, of the language of Jesus about God in more personal contexts alludes to God as *Father*. Pannenberg sums up this point: "Je-sus called this God whose reign was near . . . the (heavenly) Father."[25]

H. F. D. Sparks submitted the sayings of Jesus about God as Father in the Synoptic gospels to careful critical examination.[26] Sparks rejects Harnack's inter-pretation of the universal Fatherhood of God and brotherhood of humankind, insisting, with T. W. Manson, that "Father" was used by Jesus primarily as an inti-mate, personal, often distinctively messianic relationship.[27] This "messianic" and personal use of the word occurs especially in Mark (Mark 8:38; 13:32; 14:36).[28] However, there are at very least five sayings common to Matthew and Luke that are widely agreed to be authentic, and these, too, witness to a relationship of inti-macy between Jesus and God as Father. Jesus "draws attention to the intimate and unique relationship which exists between the Father and himself."[29] Luke takes up the primary address of Jesus to "*Abba,* Father" (Mark 14:36) in Luke 22:42. In material peculiar to Luke we find the early question of the boy Jesus, "Did you not know that I must be in my Father's house?" (Luke 2:49). Jesus ad-dresses God twice in prayer from the cross as "Father" (Luke 23:24, 46). Matthew reproduces the three Markan texts intact, and in Matt. 12:50 changes Mark's "God" to "Father." The phrase "*my* Father" typically occurs in Matt. 20:23 and 26:29. Ten allusions to God as Father occur in the Sermon on the Mount.[30]

21. Moltmann, *Trinity,* 61-96; Pannenberg, *Systematic Theology,* vol. 1, 259-327.

22. Jeremias, Joachim, *New Testament Theology: Part I, The Proclamation of Jesus,* trans. John Bowden (London: S.C.M., 1971), 96.

23. Jeremias, *Proclamation,* 96-108.

24. I. Howard Marshall, *New Testament Theology: Many Witnesses, One Gospel* (Downers Grove, IL: InterVarsity Press, 2004), 59-67, 70-73, 77-82, and 133-39.

25. Pannenberg, *Systematic Theology,* vol. 1, 259.

26. H. F. D. Sparks, "The Doctrine of the Divine Fatherhood in the Gospels," in D. E. Nineham (ed.), *Studies in the Gospels: Essays in Memory of R. H. Lightfoot* (Oxford: Blackwell, 1967 [1955]), 241-62.

27. Sparks, "Fatherhood," 258-62.

28. Sparks, "Fatherhood," 243-46.

29. Sparks, "Fatherhood," 246.

30. Sparks, "Fatherhood," 251-55.

Jeremias expands this "intimate and unique" aspect identified by Sparks. He writes concerning Matt. 11:27 and parallel, "What Jesus wants to convey . . . is this: Just as a father talks to his son, just as he teaches him the letters of the Torah, just as he initiates him into the well-prepared secrets of his craft, just as he hides nothing from him and opens his heart to him as to no one else, so God has granted me knowledge of himself."[31] Jeremias continues, "All five strata of tradition in our gospels are unanimous in affirming that Jesus addressed God as 'my Father.'"[32] (The five are Mark, Q, M, L, and John.) It is the unanimous testimony of all five traditions that Jesus *always* used the words "Father," or "my Father," or *Abba*, except on the occasion when he was quoting Scripture as the words of his prayer (in Mark 15:34). At times Jesus extends the word to include God's fatherly care, but in such cases an index of a different use, such as "*your* Father," is found: "Do not be anxious what to say, for it is not you who speak but τὸ πνεῦμα τοῦ πατρὸς ὑμῶν (*to pneuma tou patros humōn*, the Spirit of your Father) in you who speaks" (Matt. 10:20, par. Luke 12:12). "Your Father" is several times used in addresses specifically to disciples (Matt. 6:26; par. Luke 12:24). Arthur Wainwright expounds this Father-Son relationship in the gospels and epistles as part of the groundwork for elucidating a doctrine of the Trinity within the New Testament.[33]

Pannenberg sums up the theological conclusion of this part of the narrative of the gospels. He writes, "The intimacy implied by invoking God as *Abba* typifies the relation of Jesus to God. . . . The idea of God as Father is by no means an arbitrary one, for which others might be substituted. . . . The fatherly relation of God to the king by an act of adoption gave the idea of God as Father a consistency which made it much more than a metaphor, but which also separated it from the mere idea of a family head."[34] Further, "the God of Jesus is none other than the God of Jewish faith according to the witness of the OT. He is the God of Abraham, Isaac, and Jacob (Matt. 12:26-27)."[35] Finally, "On the lips of Jesus 'Father' becomes a proper name for God."[36]

The narrative does not end there. By his resurrection from the dead, God declared Jesus to be the Son of God (Rom. 1:3-4). These verses doubtless belong to pre-Pauline tradition.[37]

No less striking is the repeated pattern of the narrative in the gospels that at every decisive point in the ministry of Jesus, God is at work not only as Father but in the person of the Holy Spirit. The Holy Spirit acts as initiating agent in the

31. Jeremias, *Proclamation*, 60.

32. Jeremias, *Proclamation*, 62.

33. Arthur W. Wainwright, *The Trinity in the New Testament* (London: SPCK, 1962), 41-50 and 171-95.

34. Pannenberg, *Systematic Theology*, vol. 1, 260 and 261.

35. Pannenberg, *Systematic Theology*, vol. 1, 260.

36. Pannenberg, *Systematic Theology*, vol. 1, 262.

37. A. M. Hunter, *Paul and His Predecessors* (London: S.C.M., 2d edn. 1961), 24-28.

conception of Jesus (Matt. 1:20; Luke 1:35); crucially the Holy Spirit descends upon Jesus at his baptism to anoint him for his messianic task, commencing with the trial of his messianic temptation. All four gospel traditions attest this (Matt. 3:16–4:1; Mark 1:10-12; Luke 3:21-22 and 4:1-2; John 1:32-34). The descent of the Spirit is intimately connected with the declaration "You are my beloved Son," as Moltmann and Pannenberg emphasize.[38] The "sending" formula brings together the Father's "sending" of the Son with the Son's anointing for his task by the Holy Spirit (John 2:16, 17; 6:29; 7:29, 8:42; 11:42; 17:3, 8, 18, 21, 23, 25; Acts 3:26; Rom. 8:3-4; Gal. 4:4; 2 John 4:9-10). Moltmann argues that the "sending formulas" are highly significant for preparing the way for a full doctrine of the Trinity. He expresses this in a schematic form. He writes, "In the history of the Son the Trinity means:

- The Father sends the Son through the Spirit.
- The Son comes from the Father in the power of the Spirit.
- The Spirit brings people into the fellowship of the Son with the Father."[39]

The biblical narrative does not reach completion until it reaches the critical moment of the crucifixion and exaltation in the resurrection. The agony in the Garden of Gethsemane is the prelude to the cross, in which Jesus is distressed and troubled, but pleads with his Father as *Abba* (Mk. 14:32-36). This agony, Moltmann comments, derives from "fear of separation from the Father, horror in the face of 'the death of God.'"[40] The "cup," he suggests, is abandonment by God: "The Father withdrawn, God is silent."[41] This may reflect the Hebrew idiom of Ps. 22:1, in accordance with which "Why have you forsaken me?" (למה עזבתני, *lāmâ ʿazabttāni*).[42] Moltmann refuses to disengage the work of God the Son from that of God the Father, even in such abandonment and separation. For he writes, "The Father suffers the death of the Son. So the pain of the Father corresponds to the death of the Son. And when in this descent into hell the Son loses the Father, then in this judgment the Father loses the Son. Here the innermost life of the Trinity is at stake."[43]

In the exaltation of Jesus Christ through the resurrection, however, the Easter witnesses saw "the glory of God in the face of Jesus Christ" (2 Cor. 4:6), as Jesus appeared in the likeness of God (2 Cor. 4:4), and as "the reflection of God's

38. Moltmann, *Trinity*, 65-71; Pannenberg, *Systematic Theology*, vol. 1, 266-68.

39. Moltmann, *Trinity*, 75.

40. Moltmann, *Trinity*, 76.

41. Moltmann, *Trinity*, 77.

42. Weiser, *Psalms*, 220-21, comments, "He sees only the abyss which separates him from God, and interprets the question as expressing *lament*. Sometimes, however, questions in Hebrew that ask "Why?" also express accusation.

43. Moltmann, *Trinity*, 81.

glory and the exact imprint of God's very being" (χαρακτὴρ τῆς ὑποστάσεως *charaktēr tēs hupostaseōs,* Heb. 1:3).[44] This raising takes place through the agency and activity of the Holy Spirit (Rom. 1:4; 8:11; 1 Pet. 3:18; cf. 1 Cor. 6:14). Moltmann writes: "The Father raises the Son through the Spirit; the Father reveals the Son through the Spirit; the Son is enthroned as Lord . . . through the Spirit."[45] In the lordship of the Son, he continues, the Father and the Spirit are co-agents; in the sending, surrender, and exaltation of the Son, the Father acts, the Son receives, and the Spirit is the means for actualizing the process. He sums up the point: "We find a Trinitarian co-working of Father, Son, and Spirit, but with changing patterns."[46]

Hans Urs von Balthasar makes a distinctive contribution to the reading of the biblical narratives of the gospel as a foundation for Trinitarian doctrine. He sets the passion of Christ within the broadest possible horizon of understanding. God the Father, he writes, "*is always* himself by giving himself. The Son, too, is always himself by allowing himself to be generated and by allowing the Father to do with him as he pleases. The Spirit is always himself by understanding his 'I' as the 'We' of Father and Son, by being 'expropriated' for the sake of what is most proper to them."[47] Rowan Williams alludes to the influence of "the great Russian thinker Sergius Bulgakov for this language of an eternal *kenosis* in the life of God which itself then makes possible the *kenosis* involved in creation. . . . God the Father pours out his divine life without remainders unto the Son; his identity is constituted in this act of giving away."[48]

In the narrative of the gospels this leads to a climactic *kenosis* not only in the agony of Good Friday, but also in the effects of the cry of dereliction from the cross through the reality of Holy Saturday. The self-giving and self-emptying of the Son reproduces the self-giving and *kenosis* of the Father. Holy Saturday finds Jesus, Son of God, with "the enemy," standing in the place of the lost, in both infinite difference from the Father and infinite obedience to the Father.[49] The "nothingness" and difference or distance of Holy Saturday prepares a space of creation and new creation enacted on Easter Day. Thus the dramatic narrative that we explored in Balthasar in 4.2 comes into its own as a hermeneutic in relation to an understanding of Trinitarian theology.

Pannenberg discusses precisely those biblical passages that feature in the

44. Cf. Moltmann, *Trinity,* 83-88.

45. Moltmann, *Trinity,* 88; cf. 89-96.

46. Moltmann, *Trinity,* 95.

47. Balthasar, *Theo-drama,* vol. 2, 256.

48. Rowan Williams, "Balthasar and the Trinity," in Edward T. Oakes and David Moss (eds.), *The Cambridge Companion to Hans Urs von Balthasar* (Cambridge: Cambridge University Press, 2004), 38; cf. 37-50.

49. Balthasar, *Theo-drama,* vol. 4, 319-32; and Hans Urs von Balthasar, *Heart of the World,* trans. Erasmo S. Leivà (San Francisco: Ignatius, 1979), 109-10.

gospels and epistles as foundation texts for interpretation in Athanasius and the Cappadocian Fathers, identified already in 18.3 above. These include especially Matt. 28:19, the baptismal formula, and those that witness to the cooperative work of the Trinity (1 Cor. 2:10-16; 12:4-7; 2 Cor. 13:13; and less directly Rom. 8:9-16; 1 Cor. 8:6; 15:45).[50] In explicating these passages in the context of Patristic theology Pannenberg takes up what he calls "Athanasius's most important argument — that the Father would not be the Father without the Son, and therefore that he was never without the Son."[51] The very term *Father* presupposes a relationship to an "other" as Son. Origen partially anticipates a glimpse of this when, as Haykin observes, he opposes strongly the notion that Father, Son, and Spirit are simply adjectival descriptions of temporary modes of being that the one God adopts for the implementations of the various stages of divine activity: creation, salvation, and sanctification.[52] All persons of the Trinity are involved in distinctive ways in each of their processes. Wainwright observes, "One thing is certain. The problem of the Trinity was being raised and answered in the New Testament."[53] It is a pity that he uses *problem* rather than *question.* Arguably it was a later perception of the Trinity as a "problem" that led to what Wainwright acknowledges as the impact of "Greek metaphysics" in a later era.[54]

19.3. Hermeneutical Supplements and Byways: God Who Is One Revealed in Action

Our two hermeneutical starting points, derived from Christian experience and the narrative of the New Testament, are only starting points. Our argument is that as a communicative hermeneutic of understanding, these set us on the right track in contrast to hypotheses about numerical puzzles or to such pedagogical images as shamrock. On the other hand, the New Testament narrative carries with it presuppositions derived from the Old Testament and shared initially by "Jewish" Christianity. The narrative of the New Testament extends backward with roots in the narrative experience of Israel. The two starting points considered so far might *risk verging on tritheism without this presupposed narrative.* For Israel the nature and identity of God is expressed in the *Shema'.* The confession "Yahweh is our God, YHWH is one" (Deut. 6:4) remains paramount. However, the Hebrew text יהוה אלהינו יהוה אחד (*Y-h-w-h*

---

50. Pannenberg, *Systematic Theology,* vol. 1, 267-74.

51. Athanasius, *Against the Asians* 1:29; cf. 14:34; Pannenberg, *Systematic Theology,* vol. 1, 273.

52. Haykin, *The Spirit of God,* 14. He cites Origen, *Commentary on Romans* 8:5 (Migne, *Patrologia Graeca,* vol. 14, 1169C); *Commentary on Titus* (Migne, *Patrologia Graeca,* 1304D-5A); and *Against Celsus* 8:12 (Migne, *Patrologia Graeca,* vol. 11, 1533A-C).

53. Wainwright, *Trinity,* 266.

54. Wainwright, *Trinity,* 267.

ᵉlōhēynu Y-h-w-h ʼechād) can be variously translated.[55] C. H. Gordon proposes, "Yahweh is our God, Yahweh is 'One.'"[56] M. Dahood suggests, "Yahweh our God is unique."[57] The translation "The LORD [YHWH] our God, the LORD [YHWH] is one" exactly corresponds with Jesus' declaration of the first commandment in Mark 12:29 (cf. the near parallels on love to God without distraction or divided interest in Matt. 22:37 and Luke 10:27). This assumes a probably pre-Pauline creedal form, 1 Cor. 8:6a: ἀλλὰ ἡμῖν εἷς θεὸς ὁ πατήρ, "but for us there is [only] one God, the Father."

Hermeneutics now begins to combine *a second cumulative narrative building up of an understanding of God as One* with formulations of belief that *draw also upon dispositional responses.* Any understanding of our first two starting points that might undermine the creed "God is one" would provoke a counterresponse that this would subvert the Old Testament roots of faith in the God of Abraham, Isaac, and Jacob; a faith that Jesus endorsed and confirmed (Mark 12:29) and Paul and pre-Pauline tradition corroborated (1 Cor. 8:1).

However, *one, same,* and *unique* have complex logical and conceptual grammar, as Wittgenstein observed. "One," he suggests, may have different meanings when it denotes a number on a numerical scale than in other contexts.[58] *Same* is more clearly fraught with problems: Wittgenstein observes, "'A thing is identical with itself' — There is no finer example of a useless proposition."[59] Basil of Caesarea, we noted, insists that neither "one" nor "three" has a numerical denotation when applied to God, since strictly we number only *objects* or "bodies."[60] What does "one God" denote in the *Shema*? We have noted that the Hebrew can be variously translated. Vriezen points out that the same grammatical construction is used in Exod. 36:13: "so that the tabernacle became . . . a *unity.*"[61] In the same way, Deut. 6:4-6 has an existential impact: "Because Yahweh is *one* (we might also say 'single'), the demand follows that Yahweh must be loved with *all one's heart,* with all one's soul, and with all one's might (literally 'multiplicity')." The oneness of God's being demands the heart."[62] The emphasis falls, as in Deut. 6:14, on "the unity and uniqueness" of God: "The unity of God is rooted on the

55. The Hebrew אחד *(ʼechād)* means *one* (Gen. 1:9; Exod. 12:49; Josh. 23:10); but also *one and the same* (Gen. 40:5; Job 31:15); or *only* or *alone* (1 Kings 4:19; Josh. 6:11); or *first* (Gen. 1:5; Exod. 39:10). See Brown-Driver-Briggs, *The New Hebrew-English Lexicon* (new 1980 edn., 25, col. ii–26 col. i).

56. C. H. Gordon, "His Name Is 'One,'" *Journal of Near Eastern Studies* 29 (1970) 198-99.

57. M. Dahood, in L. R. Fisher (ed.), *Ras Shamra Parallels* 1 (1972) 361. See further Peter C. Craigie, *The Book of Deuteronomy* (Grand Rapids: Eerdmans, 1976), 168-69.

58. Wittgenstein, *Philosophical Investigations,* sects. 552-53.

59. Wittgenstein, *Philosophical Investigations,* sect. 216; cf. sects. 226 ("the same"), 253-54, 556.

60. Basil, *Letters* 8:2.

61. T. C. Vriezen, *An Outline of Old Testament Theology* (Oxford: Blackwell, 1962), 175, n. 2.

62. Vriezen, *Old Testament Theology,* 175 (my italics); see further Gerhard von Rad, *Old Testament Theology,* vol. 1, 203-212, and vol. 2, 247-50.

uniqueness of the Being of God" (Vriezen's italics).[63] Indeed, Vriezen doubts whether at the stage of the Hebrew prophets "monotheism" is an appropriate term for this celebration of God's sole sovereignty.

This confession of faith has ontological or metaphysical implications. These occur in Deuteronomy: "Take to heart that the LORD is God in heaven above and on earth below; there is no other" (Deut. 4:39-40). In Isa. 40–55 this theme comes fully into its own: "God is with you only; there is no other" (Isa. 45:14; cf. 45:14-25). "There is no God besides me" (Isa. 45:21); "I am God, and there is no other" (45:22). There are nine such assertions in this single chapter. Nevertheless, as in Deuteronomy, the emphasis falls upon *God's saving work and action:* "YHWH is a God who delivers and rescues" (Isa. 45:21b). God is *incomparable* (Isa. 40:12-17).

If "one," however, carries with it an application in terms of the *one living God in action,* this is no different from the *unity of focus* in which God as Father, Son, and Holy Spirit are *one in action and self-giving* in 1 Cor. 12:4-7, where distinctive actions of Father, Son, and Spirit are also identified. The notion that *one is numerical* in Deut. 4:6 or Isa. 45:14-25 sets us off track into irrelevant speculative byways. Gerhard von Rad writes that when Israel confesses faith in the one God, "there is no question of its being due to a *philosophical* reduction of the multiplicity of numerous phenomena to the [world-]view of them as one."[64]

Trinitarian theology, then, cannot deny the roots shared by Jesus and the Old Testament. It is not a version of tritheism. However, God is one in *gracious action;* the hermeneutics of the *Shema* do not venture onto the ground of abstract or numerical speculation. Hence, whatever the requirements of *doctrine* at a more derivative or higher level of abstraction, at the level of *hermeneutics* two particular conclusions asserted by Pannenberg are of the utmost significance. He writes, "Any derivation of the plurality of trinitarian persons from the essence of the one God, whether it be viewed as spirit or love, leads into problems of either modalism on the one hand or subordinationism on the other. Neither, then, can be true to the intention of trinitarian dogma."[65]

A second comment provides a warning about the complexities of over-scholastic formulation of Trinitarian doctrine. Pannenberg points out, "Reformation theology lost the tighter systematic structuring that the doctrine of God has achieved in High Scholasticism because it took seriously its declaration that the Trinity is known only by revelation. This meant that it had to base what is said about the Trinity on Holy Scripture."[66] However, my Nottingham colleague

---

63. Vriezen, *Old Testament Theology,* 177; cf. 175-80.

64. Gerhard von Rad, *Old Testament Theology,* vol. 1, 211 (my italics to try to clarify his point).

65. Pannenberg, *Systematic Theology,* vol. 1, 298; this is not a merely hypothetical statement. Some studies do begin with the "essence" or "unity" of God. One well-known example is G. L. Prestige, *God in Patristic Thought* (London: Heinemann, 1936).

66. Pannenberg, *Systematic Theology,* vol. 1, 289.

Karen Kilby also argues that Thomas Aquinas regarded attempts to formulate too precise a doctrine of the Trinity as "theology reaching its limits."[67] Thomas, she argues, is content to consider proposals that neither he nor we can grasp.

This, then, raises a new question for a hermeneutic of a doctrine of the Trinity. Do the complex formulations of the third and fourth centuries constitute a hermeneutical resource or a hermeneutical byway or even distraction for an understanding of God as Trinity today, based primarily on the explication of Scripture? I argue that up to a certain point these may offer a derivative, supplemental, hermeneutical resource; beyond that point they may become a distraction. The potential of later formulations to become a resource derives from (i) their role as *expressions of belief generated by dispositional responses to denials or distortions* of beliefs maintained in apostolic traditions; and (ii) their safeguarding of the ontological status of Trinitarian truth-claims in a postmodern era when many make everything hinge upon confession claims on the part of the church.

In the second century these ontological formulations are fairly basic. Tertullian responded on one side to dynamistic Monarchianism or subordinationism, which is often ascribed to Theodotus, and on the other side to modalism, which Tertullian ascribed to Praxeas. As the years passed, modalism became known as Sabellianism. Whether Sabellius genuinely held a modalist belief, or whether he veered in this direction in an attempt to draw a line against it, is not our present concern. It remains a point of controversy among Patristic specialists.

Some historians of doctrine interpret these responses on the part of dispositional beliefs as polemics in the interest of power. But although many protagonists in the Patristic era were indisputably power seekers, sometimes even ruthlessly, and although manipulation occurred on both sides, to allow this to overshadow the theological issues of substance is to miss the theological and hermeneutical point. The record of responses that declare what is unacceptable serve not primarily to identify repressive or oppressive acts, but to identify "markers and signposts" in processes of doctrinal development. In the first of five successive Church of England Doctrine Commissions of which I have been a member and contributor, Anthony Harvey devoted an essay on theological method (which we all endorsed) under the very title "Markers and Signposts."[68] The church, Harvey (and the Commission) argued, "permits a substantial variety of emphasis and understanding among its members. . . . But this is *not* to say that there are *no limits to permissible formulations,* no frontiers beyond which the explorer cannot be authorized to go."[69] There are "the inevi-

---

67. Karen Kilby, "Aquinas, the Trinity, and the Limits of Understanding," *International Journal of Systematic Theology* 7 (2005) 414-27.

68. Anthony C. Harvey, "Markers and Signposts," in The Doctrine Commission of the Church of England, *Believing in the Church* (cited above, 1981), 286-302.

69. Harvey, "Markers," in *Believing,* 290 (my italics).

table boundary markers, provisional but definite . . . constraints which make creative action possible."[70]

Yet there are problems about such "markers" for hermeneutics. Far too readily they appear to exist as abstractions that identify "problems" disengaged from time. They can be misleading if they are abstracted from the chain of question-and-answer that first gave rise to them. Hence it is widely supposed that "tritheism" is off-limits because it does not do justice to a philosophically grounded monotheism. But Emil Brunner sums up the reason in the context of biblical tradition and Christian reflection: "If God himself did not become man in Jesus Christ, then His Revelation is not revelation."[71] The formula *una substantia* has no less to do with revelation and the unity of divine purpose and action than with any speculation about "Being." However, Brunner adds that in addition to "genuine Biblical thought" the orthodox doctrine of the Trinity as represented in the Athanasian Creed also drew upon "philosophical speculation which is remote from the Bible." He concludes, "The idea of '*una substantia*' has had a particularly disastrous influence."[72] To conceive of God as "Substance" undermines "the Biblical idea of the Absolute Subject. . . . This fatal idea . . . was a real disaster."[73]

Karl Barth asserts the dynamic, active horizon of understanding for any notion of what he calls the "unimpaired unity" of God no less clearly, for what is at stake in God's unity is not "substance" but "revelation." Divine revelation signifies "unimpaired unity, yet also in unimpaired distinction [as] Revealer, Revelation, and Revealedness."[74] It is in the context of active revelation that "we come up against the doctrine of the Trinity."[75] God, who can be known "only through God," makes himself known through Jesus Christ, who is the Word of God. This constitutes "The Root of the Doctrine of the Trinity."[76] God who reveals himself in this way, Barth continues in the next section, is "One in three distinctive modes of being subsisting in their mutual revelations: Father, Son, and Holy Spirit. It is thus that He is the Lord, i.e., the Thou who meets man's I . . . and therein reveals Himself to him as his God."[77]

Eberhard Jüngel points out how profoundly *hermeneutical*, in effect, Barth's modification of an approach through "substance" turns out to be. He writes, "If

70. Harvey, "Markers," in *Believing*, 291.

71. Emil Brunner, *The Christian Doctrine of God: Dogmatics*, vol. 1, trans. Olive Wyon (London: Lutterworth, 1949), 222; cf. 205-40.

72. Brunner, *Doctrine of God*, 239.

73. Brunner, *Doctrine of God*, 239.

74. Barth, *Church Dogmatics*, I:1, ch. 2, Part 1, "The Triune God," sect. 8, "God in his Revelation," 295; cf. 295-304.

75. Barth, *Church Dogmatics*, I:1, sect. 8, 2, 304.

76. Barth, *Church Dogmatics*, I:1, sect. 8, 2, 304-33.

77. Barth, *Church Dogmatics*, I:1, sect. 9, 348.

we take seriously the claim that, in Barth's sense, 'God's being *proceeds*,' then we shall have to begin our question concerning God's being not with the doctrine of God . . . but with the place where the particular path of the being of God as revelation is conceived. . . . This happens in the Christology of the *Church Dogmatics.* . . . Since it is God who reveals himself there, the doctrine of the Trinity is . . . 'the decisive part of the doctrine of God.'"[78] Jüngel explicitly states that Barth is here consciously making in his sequence of formulation "a *hermeneutical* decision of the greatest relevance"; it concerns "the treatment of hermeneutical problems."[79]

Part of the hermeneutical status of more complex models and metaphors that are used to explicate Trinitarian doctrine raises, as Barth and Jüngel emphasize, questions about the *status of analogical language.* How many of the technical terms used in the third, fourth, and fifth centuries are *closely* parallel with their linguistic currency when applied to human persons? Barth is troubled by Augustine's suggestion that there are "vestiges" of the Trinity everywhere, especially the idea that a human being has "some trace, however slight, of the Trinity . . . some image of the Trinity *(quandam trinitatis effigiem)*."[80] The process of perception, Augustine argues, yields three distinct elements: the eyes see an object; an object is presented to the senses; the mind attends to and evaluates what it sees. It is a single vision, but with "evident distinctions."[81] Barth asks whether this is not an application of *analogia entis* rather than of "the analogy of faith" because rather than deriving the doctrine of Trinity wholly from Christ and Christology it presupposes or suggests "a similarity between structures of created reality and the structure of the being of God, conceived as Trinity."[82] Jüngel rightly calls this "a *hermeneutical* problem" (his italics). Augustine, too, offers such analogies not as a way of *demonstrating* Trinitarian theology, but as a way of *understanding* it.[83]

Kelly discusses Augustine's principal Trinitarian analogy of love: in terms of lover *(amans)*, the object loved *(quod amatur)* and the love *(amor)* that unites the persons of the Trinity.[84] Augustine bases his approach on the Johannine axiom that "God is love" (1 John 4:8), and "love is from God" (1 John 4:9). The whole human person involves mind, memory, self-knowledge or understanding,

---

78. Eberhard Jüngel, *God's Being Is in Becoming: The Trinitarian Being of God in the Theology of Karl Barth, A Paraphrase*, trans. John Webster (Edinburgh: T&T Clark, 2001), 13 and 16 (his italics).

79. Jüngel, *God's Being Is in Becoming*, 16 (his italics).

80. Augustine, *On the Trinity*, XI:1; Barth, *Church Dogmatics*, I:1, sect. 8, 3, 334-35; cf. 336-47.

81. Augustine, *On the Trinity*, XI:2.

82. Jüngel, *God's Being Is in Becoming*, 17; cf. 17-27; and Barth, *Church Dogmatics*, I:1, sect. 8, 3, "Vestigium Trinitatis," 333-47.

83. Jüngel, *God's Being*, 17; cf. also Kelly, *Early Christian Doctrines*, 276-79 on Augustine's motivations and concerns in this context.

84. Augustine, *On the Trinity*, VIII:12, through to IX:2; cf. Kelly, *Doctrines*, 277.

and mind as knowing and loving. There are "not three lives but one life; not three minds, but one mind."[85] Nevertheless Augustine is aware that these analogies are no more than heuristic explorations. Hence, *on this basis*, as Jüngel also reminds us, Barth concedes that there is "something in" Augustine's approach, provided we stress that it is in no way "a matter of apologetics . . . not . . . human reason," but exploring on the basis of *revelation*.[86] In our own terminology, clearly for Jüngel and probably for Barth, such an approach is a "hermeneutical supplement," but if it is loosened from its anchorage in the self-revealing *action* of God and reified into a static ontology, it becomes a hermeneutical distraction.

Jüngel's exposition of Barth, as well as Barth's *Dogmatics* in its own right, helps us to address the question of what doctrinal developments after the close of the New Testament era provide additional hermeneutical resources, and what may be left more readily to historians of doctrine to chronicle as theological by-ways. Barth, Brunner, Jüngel, Pannenberg, and Moltmann are at one in understanding the biblical narrative of Christ in relation to the Father and to the Holy Spirit as the primary hermeneutical resource. Where corporate Christian experience accurately reflects the indicators of the biblical witness, this too may constitute a hermeneutical bridge, subject to the priority of the biblical narrative as defining the fundamental horizon of understanding.

Complexities arise when we examine the development of doctrine in the first five centuries of the church. Many of these terminological developments and refinements were needed *in their time*. Moreover, the *presupposition* of the biblical narrative, expressed in the *Shema'* and such early New Testament creeds as 1 Cor. 8:6, must be explicated to show *in what sense* the New Testament narratives imply Trinitarian rather than tritheistic faith.

It is here that, as Jüngel's translator, John Webster, points out, Jüngel comes into his own. This is because Jüngel has a triple interest in hermeneutics, in the status of metaphor and language, and in the significance of *presuppositions* that are often ontological and metaphysical, but not necessarily reified nor explicitly noticed. These operate beneath the surface of narratives or confessions of faith.[87] It would constitute a hermeneutical digression to explore every formulation of "God is one," or of *una substantia, unless this unity of divine Being is understood as part of the active process of divine Self-Revealing*. Hence for Jüngel "God's determination to be God in the movement of Jesus' historical existence entails God's passion. . . . The term 'becoming' is to provide a theological account of the being of God in which the trinitarian account of the being of God can *be* in self-surrender."[88] Jüngel's lan-

---

85. Augustine, *On the Trinity,* X; XVIII.

86. Barth, *Church Dogmatics,* I:1, sect. 8, 3, 341; and Jüngel, *God's Being,* 18-22.

87. John Webster, "Translator's Introduction," in Jüngel, *God's Being Is in Becoming,* ix-xxvi.

88. Webster, "Translator's Introduction," in *God's Being Is in Becoming,* xvii. Pannenberg's discussion of Moltmann may perhaps offer a part parallel: Pannenberg, *Systematic Theology,* vol. 1, 329.

guage is complex, but the sense in which we understand "process" and "event" requires special care and precision in this context. The terms have nothing to do with process thought in this context.

The formulations of the early church between the second and fifth centuries thus offer an uneven picture of hermeneutical resources that may supplement the two primary starting points. Some developments may lead us into byways that even set us on the wrong track.

The earliest responses to subordinationism and to modalism are sufficiently basic to serve as signposts along the way. Viewed through the lenses of a dispositional account of belief, the responses of the second-century church to the adoptionist dynamistic monarchianism of Thedotus, or on the opposite side to Praxeas, may serve as clarifications. Tertullian declares against Praxeas, "He says that the Father himself came down into the Virgin, was himself born of her, himself suffered, indeed was himself Jesus Christ."[89] Hence, Tertullian adds, we must now explore questions about Christ more carefully. Hippolytus similarly rejected belief-claims put forward by Noetus.[90] Whether or not he taught "modalism" in its unacceptable form, Sabellius found himself under attack from Callistus.[91] Athanasius, as Pannenberg points out, clearly develops proactive insights in the course of refuting opponents. For example, he argues that the Father cannot be thought of as "Father" without the Son, nor the Son as "Son" without the Father, and both in relation to the Holy Spirit.[92]

Some developments lead in unhelpful directions. We noted Barth's ambivalent verdict of part-approval and part-suspicion upon Augustine's notion of *vestigium trinitatis*. Many on one side perceive Augustine's "psychological" interpretation of the Trinity, including his analogy with being, knowledge, and love in human persons, as a high point of Patristic development. On the other side, Colin Gunton traces its negative effects not only upon understandings of the Trinity, but on theism and epistemology also. Gunton writes, "Augustine's legacy to his descendants was to locate the unknowability of God in the wrong place: not in the otherness of the personal, but in the Platonically conceived otherness — 'transcendence' — of the material or sensible and 'spiritual' or intelligible worlds. Whether that be the reason, the fact is that trinitarian theology has come into disrepute as being concerned chiefly with the defence and articulation of given and apparently paradoxical statements of dogma."[93]

All the same Gunton argues that *properly understood*, Trinitarian doctrine

---

89. Tertullian, *Against Praxeas* I:1; cf. V and VII.

90. Hippolytus, *Against the Heresy of Noetus*, XIV.

91. Cf. the interpretations of Kelly, *Early Christian Doctrines*, 121-23; and Franks, *Trinity*, 78-85.

92. Pannenberg, *Systematic Theology*, vol. 1, 279.

93. Colin Gunton, *The Promise of Trinitarian Theology* (Edinburgh: T&T Clark, 1991), 163; cf. 1-2.

can constitute a lynchpin in promoting the coherence and credibility of Christian theism. The Eastern Church, Gunton believes, held out the possibility of this, but Augustine and his Western successors "allowed the insidious return of a Hellenism in which being is not communion, but something underlying it. That is the matrix out of which the objectionable features of Western 'theism' have arisen."[94] Barth and Rahner have made us aware of this dualism between God's "being" and God's "becoming." A constructive theology of the Trinity, Gunton concludes, "will stress the *relations* with all dimensions of our reality" (my italics).[95] Only thus can we reconceive divine sovereignty and divine freedom.

Karl Rahner makes a related point when he laments the "isolation" of the doctrine of the Trinity. It has become almost a piece of self-contained technical doctrine, revolving around abstract problems concerning a "hypostatic axiom."[96] Rahner's widely known "axiom" is expressed differently: "The Trinity is a mystery of *salvation. . . . The 'economic' Trinity is the 'immanent' Trinity and the 'immanent' Trinity is the 'economic' Trinity*" (his italics).[97] The 'economic' Trinity is a formulation of the doctrine in which God as the Father, as the Son, and as the Holy Spirit takes responsibility for different aspects, or stages, of the process of creation and salvation. The 1662 Book of Common Prayer of the Church of England expresses this approach in its *Catechism* in the words: "First I learn to believe in God the Father who makes me and all the world. Second, in God the Son, who hath redeemed me and all mankind. Thirdly in God the Holy Spirit, who sanctified me and all the elect people of God." The "economic Trinity" whatever its adequacies or inadequacies, remains *relational:* God to God, and God to the world.

Yet a doctrine of the Trinity does *not depend* on creation or salvation. Hence, "*immanent* Trinity" calls attention to the persons of the Holy Trinity as *intrinsically* distinct, not simply extrinsically so in relation to the work of creation and redemption. Hence Rahner's correlation of the two implies an attempt to retain a genuinely theocentric ontology, but without collapsing the Trinitarian God's *relationality* to human experience into a merely "isolated" doctrine that remains remote from life. Rahner propounds *transcendental* questions about possibility, but he does not allow these to become abstractions.[98] He writes, "Jesus is not simply God in general, but the Son. . . . Hence there is at least *one* 'mission', *one* presence in the world, *one* reality of salvation history" (his italics).[99]

94. Gunton, *Trinitarian Theology*, 10.

95. Gunton, *Trinitarian Theology*, 119.

96. Karl Rahner, *The Trinity*, trans. Joseph Donceel (Tunbridge Wells, Kent: Burns & Oates, 1970), 10-15 and 24-30.

97. Rahner, *Trinity*, 21 and 22.

98. On Rahner's transcendental concerns, see Karen Kilby, *Karl Rahner: Theology and Philosophy* (London and New York: Routledge, 2004).

99. Rahner, *Trinity*, 23.

This provokes further questions about how we are to characterize the God whose *Being* is *also becoming*. Jüngel and Barth have raised questions about the limits of language. These are pressing in relation to God as Trinity. In a different context Wittgenstein warned us that "pictures" can be variously interpreted and can seduce us.[100] Whether images of shamrock and similar illustrative models encourage a "substance" conceptuality may be left aside, although the question is legitimate. They are symptomatic of more serious questions about the limits of language to describe the God who is "Beyond" as well as within.

19.4. The Hermeneutics of Divine Transcendence: Grace and Holy Love

The theology of Isa. 40–55 sums up the hermeneutical question: "'To whom will you compare me, or who is my equal?' says the Holy One" (Isa. 40:25). "'For my thoughts are not your thoughts, nor are your ways my ways,' says the LORD. 'For as the heavens are higher than the earth, so are my ways higher than your ways, and my thoughts than your thoughts'" (Isa. 55:8-9). The book of Job shares this emphasis upon divine transcendence and otherness: "Can you find out the deep things of God? Can you find out the limit of the Almighty? It is higher than heaven — what can you do? Deeper than Sheol — what can you know?" (Job 11:8). Such a view is not restricted to the Old Testament. Paul declares, "O the depth of the riches and wisdom and knowledge of God! How unsearchable are his judgments and how inscrutable his ways! For who has known the mind of the Lord? Or who has been his counselor?" (Rom. 11:33-34). *"Unsearchable"* (NRSV), Greek ἀνεξεραύνητος *(anexeraunētos)*, denotes what cannot be fathomed; *"inscrutable"* (NRSV), ἀνεξιχνίαστος *(anexichniastos)*, denotes what cannot be tracked, incomprehensible, *beyond anyone's grasp.*

Nevertheless in Isa. 55:8-9 the point of the emphasis upon God's otherness, difference, or utter *transcendence* is to show that whereas any normal human person would have given up on "the wicked," such is God's incomparable *free, sovereign grace* to the undeserving that in his *holy love* he will not give them up. Whybray comments that with respect to "the awesome approach of the holy God" human imaginings about what may happen remain "entirely irrelevant to the truth of the divine message."[101]

"To whom will you compare me?" poses the hermeneutical question concerning the limits of language. This is sometimes posed as if language encountered more constraints than thought. This preconception will not stand up in the

---

100. Wittgenstein, *Philosophical Investigations*, e.g., sects. 115-16, 139-40, and 291.

101. R. N. Whybray, *Isaiah 40–66*, New Century Bible Commentary (London: Oliphants, 1975), 193-94. Cf. H. Maldwyn Hughes, *The Christian Idea of God* (London: Duckworth, 1936), 58-79.

light of a rigorous philosophy of language. Amidst a longer set of observations about the question Wittgenstein asks, "What did the thought consist in, as it existed before expression?"[102] The limits of *thought* about God are broadly the same as those concerning *language* about God.

From the era of the Church Fathers onward the *via negativa* was regarded as a strategy that merited consideration. Clement of Alexandria coins a memorable hermeneutical model of communicative action: the speaker may throw a ball, he suggests, but if the hearer does not or cannot catch it dexterously, communication is void.[103] However, in the case of apprehending language concerning God, "We may reach somehow to a conception of the Almighty, becoming not what he *is* but what he *is not*."[104] "The Ruler of all [is] a being difficult to grasp and apprehend, even receding and withdrawing from him who pursues."[105] God cannot be embraced or declared in words.[106] Such devices as parables provide only "helps." Yet Clement then reaches the heart of the matter: "As the apostle John says, 'No one has seen God at any time, but the only-begotten God who is in the bosom of the Father — he has declared him'" (John 1:18).[107]

The possibility of respecting the transcendence of God by using the language of negation retained a place in Christian traditions. Origen declares that knowledge of God is "beyond the reach of human nature" except by divine grace, or more specifically through God the Son: "No one knows the Father except the Son" (Matt. 11:27; cf. John 14:9).[108] "God is beyond human comprehension and incapable of being measured."[109] Augustine declares that the being of God transcends language, but his theory of language leads (or misleads) him into saying, "God is more truly thought than he is uttered," although he partly redeems this by adding: "and God exists more truly than he is thought."[110]

In the first half of the sixth century Dionysius the Areopagite (Pseudo-Dionysius) allowed that positive language can be used of God (cataphatic language) provided that it was derived from revelation; otherwise the way of negation (apophatic language) has to be used to safeguard holiness, transcendence, and otherness.[111] He speaks of God as "superessential," or suprapersonal. The ninth-century translator of Dionysius (or Denys), John Scotus Erigena (c. 810-

---

102. Wittgenstein, *Philosophical Investigation*, sect. 335; cf. sects. 327-49.

103. Clement, *Stromata* II:6:2.

104. Clement, *Stromata* V:11:72.

105. Clement, *Stromata* II:2:6.

106. Clement, *Stromata* V:12, throughout.

107. Clement, *Stromata* V:12.

108. Origen, *Against Celsus* VII:44:1 and 43.

109. Origen, *De Principiis* I:1:5.

110. Augustine, *On the Trinity*, VII:4:7.

111. Dionysius, *Of the Divine Name* 1:1. See P. Rorem, *Pseudo-Dionysius: A Commentary on the Texts and an Introduction to Their Influence* (New York: Oxford University Press, 1993).

77) expanded this approach, urging that cataphatic affirmations concerning God were metaphorical, but apophatic negations were literal. Similar themes reappeared in Eckhart (Meister Eckhart) in the thirteenth century (c. 1260–c. 1327). The most "modern" aspect of Eckhart's work was his belief that since God transcended speech and thought, multiple linguistic strategies had to be employed, all of which were fallible and provisional, to point to God who is beyond the "God" of ordinary human discourse. Paradox and dialectic must be called into play.

Martin Luther propounds an especially illuminating way into the theme of divine transcendence, including thoughts in *The Bondage of the Will*. Where God is "Preached, revealed and offered to us," he writes, we cannot but "discuss God"; but in another way "Wherever God hides himself, and wills to be unknown to us, there we have no concern. . . . 'What is above us does not concern us' really holds good"; there is that in God which is "not preached, nor revealed, nor offered to us."[112] In the nineteenth century Kierkegaard (1813-55) emphasized the infinite qualitative difference between God and humankind. This was of such a radical nature that Jesus Christ, as the "God-man," constituted "an absolute paradox."[113] Against Hegel he insisted that no mere "spectator" viewpoint could gain a supposedly "theocentric" viewpoint. Only "indirect communication," paradox, and dialectic can be appropriate for Christian communication, for God is "other," and humankind is finite, contingent, and too readily self-deceived.[114]

In the early twentieth century Rudolf Otto (1869-1937) approached the subject of divine transcendence from a different angle, namely with an exploration of the numinous as "wholly other" in his book *The Idea of the Holy* (German, 1917).[115] Otto approached divine transcendence not, with Luther, Kierkegaard, and Barth, from the side of a theology of God, but from that of human experience, awe, wonder, the fear of God, and the sense of the holy. This coheres with aspects of biblical revelation, notably Isa. 6:1-5, "I saw the Lord . . . high and lofty. . . . Seraphs were in attendance and said, 'Holy, holy, holy, is the Lord of hosts.' . . . I said, 'Woe is me! I am lost. . . . My eyes have seen . . . the Lord of hosts.'" The first part of Otto's work expounds the theme of fearsome awe at the presence of "the Other"; the second part moves in to fascination and attraction

---

112. Luther, *On the Bondage of the Will* (edition cited above), 170 (Weimar edn., vol. 18, 685).

113. Søren Kierkegaard, *Philosophical Fragments*, ed. and trans. H. V. Hong and E. H. Hong (Princeton, NJ: Princeton University Press, 1985), 37-54, 65-66, and 95-105.

114. Søren Kierkegaard, *The Point of View for My Work as an Author*, ed. and trans. H. V. Hong and E. H. Hong (Princeton, NJ: Princeton University Press, 1998); *Training in Christianity and the Edifying Discourse*, trans. Walter Lowrie (Oxford: Oxford University Press, 1941); cf. also *Concluding Unscientific Postscript*, 97-99; and *Attack on "Christendom,"* 127.

115. Rudolf Otto, *The Idea of the Holy: An Inquiry into the Nonrational Factor in the Idea of the Divine and Its Relation to the Rational*, trans. J. W. Harvey (Oxford: Oxford University Press, 2d edn. 1950).

of the holy drawn by *holy love*.[116] The mystery of the humanness embraces both *mysterium tremendum* and *mysterium fascinosum* in a harmony of contrasts.

Almost in the same year (1916), in his early works prior to the first volume of *Church Dogmatics*, Karl Barth also speaks of God as "Wholly Other." Indeed, in his 1916 essay "The Strange New World within the Bible" Barth virtually rejects any notion of a hermeneutical bridge. You cannot come to the Bible, he declares, with *"your"* questions, since "it is not right human thoughts about God which form the content of the Bible, but the right divine thoughts about man."[117] God is not "religion," the church, or ethics, but "the mysterious 'other.'"[118] In the first essay, "The Righteousness of God" (also 1916), Barth declares, "[God's] will is not a corrected continuation of our own. It approaches us as a Wholly Other."[119] This theme is worked out in Barth's celebrated commentary on the Epistle to the Romans. Here he writes, "God . . . is distinguished qualitatively from man and from everything human, and must never be identified with anything we name or experience . . . as God."[120]

It would be a mistake to conclude that to emphasize that holy otherness of God springs exclusively from a tradition peculiar to Isaiah, Jeremiah, Paul, Augustine, Luther, Kierkegaard, and Barth. Paul Tillich is no less emphatic on this subject. He writes that if we apply to God such terms as "highest being" or even "most perfect" and "most powerful" being, "when applied to God superlatives become diminutives. They place him on a level with other beings while elevating him above all of them."[121] Hence Tillich insists that only symbols, not even analogies, can be used to speak of God. The only nonsymbolic statement about God that does not violate divine transcendence is to assert that God is "Being-itself."[122] Other thinkers engage with transcendence in other ways.[123]

Yet we argued that to speak of the Trinitarian God as *"Being"* rather than as *"Being-as-Becoming"* (with Jüngel) or as *Being-in-relation* (with Zizioulas) was a mistake. How, then, can we seek to arrive at a hermeneutic of divine transcendence that we may understand and communicate?

Jüngel and Zizioulas do in fact bring us nearer to the language of the biblical traditions. In the New Testament transcendence first of all finds expression in the

116. Otto, *Idea of the Holy*, chs. 1–5 and ch. 6 respectively.

117. Karl Barth, "The Strange New World within the Bible" in Barth, Karl, *The Word of God and the Word of Man*, translated by Douglas Horton (London: Hodder & Stoughton, n.d.) 43; cf. 29-50.

118. Barth, "Strange New World," in *Word of God*, 45; cf. 42.

119. Barth, "The Righteousness of God," in *Word of God*, 24; cf. 9-27.

120. Karl Barth, *The Epistle to the Roman*, trans. from the 6th edn. by E. C. Hoskyns (Oxford: Oxford University Press, 1933, rpt. 1968), 330-31 (on Rom. 9:1).

121. Tillich, *Systematic Theology*, vol. 1, 261.

122. Tillich, *Systematic Theology*, vol. 1, 262-71.

123. See Edward Farley, *The Transcendence of God: A Study in Contemporary Philosophical Theology* (London: Epworth, 1962). He includes Niebuhr, Tillich, Heim, and Hartshorne.

bodily enfleshment of Jesus Christ as the Word of God Incarnate, who is the *exact imprint and image of God* (Heb. 1:3; cf. John 1:14). Second, as Oscar Cullmann pointed out some fifty years ago, the imagery of the New Testament is not simply, if at all, spatial (relying on "above" to express divine transcendence), but even more primarily *temporal and eschatological.* Third, the living God of the Old Testament revealed himself in gracious actions that are presented in the mode of *temporal narrative,* not of abstract "attributes."

Jüngel includes an incisive chapter, "On the *Speakability* of God," in his *God as the Mystery of the World.*[124] He considers divine transcendence, mystery, and the problems of analogical language, and rejects any merely abstract or static vehicle of expression for this. Following Paul, he sees the center of Christian language in "the word of the cross" (1 Cor. 1:18-25). He writes, "The word of the cross is a proclamation which allows God to speak definitively. . . . *The word of the cross is the self-definition of God in human language*" (my italics).[125] On *this* basis (not on others) Jüngel *rejects* the notion that "God is incapable of definition."[126] Indeed, he traces the origins of this tradition not to Christian doctrine, but to pre-Socratic philosophical thought, to Plato, and to neo-Platonism. Through this route it enters the thought of Dionysius the Areopagite and a medieval way of negation.[127]

Jüngel allows that God is mystery, but disengages the New Testament understanding of mystery, which is positive but has been suppressed, from a "negative" understanding of mystery. Mystery as silence has more to do with Buddhist piety, and also devalues speech, failing to understand thought as "principle of order" and as "the principle which constitutes speech."[128] On the other hand, to resort to the use of analogy brings its own distinctive difficulties. Jüngel cites Barth's notorious remark (following the wording of the English translation of the "Preface" of *Church Dogmatics*): "I regard the *analogia entis* as the invention of the Antichrist, and I believe that because of it, it is impossible ever to become a Roman Catholic, all other reasons for not doing so being to my mind short-sighted and trivial."[129]

On the other hand, if analogy is used in a more "Protestant" way, disengaged from a philosophy of being, Jüngel allows that analogy as such is "indispensable."[130] Even in Aristotle, one use of analogy (the *analogia nominum*) may de-

---

124. Eberhard Jüngel, *God as the Mystery of the World: On the Foundation of the Theology of the Crucified One in the Dispute between Theism and Atheism,* trans. D. L. Guder (Edinburgh: T&T Clark, 1983), 226-98.

125. Jüngel, *God as the Mystery,* 229.

126. Jüngel, *God as the Mystery,* 231.

127. Jüngel, *God as the Mystery,* 231-45.

128. Jüngel, *God as the Mystery,* 253; cf. 250-55.

129. Jüngel, *God as the Mystery,* 262, n. 1; Barth, *Church Dogmatics,* I:1, "Preface," xiii.

130. Jüngel, *God as the Mystery,* 262, n. 1.

note simply a *metaphorical* transference in language *(epiphora)*. It rests on parity of *relations* between "two completely dissimilar entities."[131] A second use is that which has become familiar through Thomas Aquinas, namely that in which an *analogical* predication lies between *univocal* and *equivocal* predications.[132]

Jüngel distinguishes carefully between the analogy of *attribution* and both an analogy of *proportionality* and an analogy of *relation*.[133] In the end he concludes that it is possible to avoid "humanizing" God only "by using the pure analogy of relation . . . which preserves the absolute differentness of the things being related to each other."[134] "There can be no responsible talk about God without analogy."[135] Nevertheless the power of the word of the cross lies in "the event character of this event" of proclaiming the cross.[136] Hence what is "hermeneutically enabling" and grants "ontological release" is *"an analogy of advent"* (Jüngel's italics), which is central to the word of the cross and the "christological event."[137] Here metaphor and parable may take the form of *address,* and this witnesses to the personhood and relationality of the I-Thou relation between God and the world.[138]

The heart of the matter is that in and through the event of the cross of Christ "God's being is *thinkable again.*"[139] "God defined himself as love on the cross of Jesus. God is love (1 John 4:8). . . . His 'inner being' is itself a turning toward what is 'outside'.[140] The victory of the cross is "the creative 'standing into nothingness.' . . . God is eternally creative being, in that he *goes out of himself.*"[141] To speak of God as being *in this sense* is to declare and to *understand* that *God is love.* On this basis, "God is thinkable as one who speaks."[142] Jüngel gives further consideration to these issues elsewhere. He considers this whole discussion to be one of *hermeneutics;* for he concludes that the "conceivability" of God derives from the person and work of Jesus Christ, as focused in the cross and resurrection.[143]

The "backing" of the eventful character and narrative character of the *interweaving of the words and deeds* of Jesus coheres precisely with Wittgenstein's criteria concerning both stability and creativity and meaning and interpreta-

131. Jüngel, *God as the Mystery,* 267.
132. Cf. Aquinas, *Summa Theologiae,* Ia, Q. 13, arts. 3-6 (Blackfriars edn., vol. 3, 11-23).
133. Jüngel, *God as the Mystery,* 270-72.
134. Jüngel, *God as the Mystery,* 277.
135. Jüngel, *God as the Mystery,* 281.
136. Jüngel, *God as the Mystery,* 287.
137. Jüngel, *God as the Mystery,* 285, 286, and 288.
138. Jüngel, *God as the Mystery,* 287-89; cf. 11, 170-74, 203-4, 290, and 253-54.
139. Jüngel, *God as the Mystery,* 111 (his italics).
140. Jüngel, *God as the Mystery,* 220.
141. Jüngel, *God as the Mystery,* 224.
142. Jüngel, *God as the Mystery,* 289.
143. See also Jüngel, "Metaphysical Truth," in *Theological Essays,* vol. 1, 16-72, and "The World as Possibility and Actuality," loc. cit., 95-123, esp. 112.

tion.[144] The problem with Tillich's exclusive reliance upon symbols is that symbols and pictures can be "variously interpreted." In Wittgenstein's simile, actions in human life are like the gold that "backs" the paper currency of words and language.[145] Jesus *speaks* of the love of God, but also takes a towel and washes his disciples' feet; *speaks* of ransoming many, and *goes to the cross*. The language of "event" is not merely a Heideggerian escape from "propositions" into what threatens to become (in effect) human subjectivity; it is what provides propositions with the *truth-currency* of history and states of affairs in the inter-subjective public world. As Jüngel shows, we can in *this* way accord working currency to *"God is love,"* and to the *grace* of God.

Paul's testimony to the origins of "his" gospel focuses upon an understanding of God that has at its center the *grace* of God and "Christlikeness" of God. J. Jeremias and Seyoon Kim, among others, conclude that he "received it when on the road to Damascus God 'was pleased to reveal his Son to me, in order that I might preach him as the content of the gospel among the Gentiles'" (Gal. 1:16-17).[146] Jeremias calls Paul's experience on the road to Damascus "the key to Pauline theology," in which he reformulated a doctrine of the *grace* of God.[147]

Contrary to many widespread but ill-founded theories about a "psychological" preparation for Paul's call and conversion, Munck argued convincingly that "The Damascus experience comes without any preparation."[148] It comes out of the blue to "one who was to quite a special degree proof against the Gospel."[149] Placing the three Acts passages (Acts 9:3-9; 22:6-11; and 26:12-18) alongside Gal. 1:11-24, Munck concludes that "There is in the Damascus experience an element of compulsion that can be understood only in the assumption that Paul was not prepared for it."[150] He interprets Acts 26:14 to mean, "From now on you will have no discharge from the service that I, Christ, have now laid on you."[151] Paul was also utterly overwhelmed that God should choose him, "the least of all the apostles, unfit to be called an apostle, because I persecuted the church of God; but by the *grace* of God I am what I am" (1 Cor. 15:9-10).

In Galatians the *grace* of God (χάρις, *charis*) is expressed largely in personal terms (Gal. 1:15; 2:9), but not entirely so (Gal. 1:6; 5:4). 1 and 2 Corinthians in-

144. Wittgenstein, *Philosophical Investigations*, sects. 7-37; and 96-133; cf. *The Blue and Brown Books*, 20-49.

145. Wittgenstein, *Blue and Brown Books*, 49.

146. Seyoon Kim, *The Origin of Paul's Gospel* (Grand Rapids: Eerdmans and Tübingen: Mohr, 1981), 2; cf. 3-31, 51-66, and throughout.

147. Joachim Jeremias, *Der Schlüssel zur Theologie des Apostels Paulus* (Stuttgart: Calwer, 1971).

148. Johannes Munck, *Paul and the Salvation of Mankind*, trans. Frank Clarke (London: S.C.M., 1959), 13.

149. Munck, *Paul*, 15.

150. Munck, *Paul*, 20.

151. Munck, *Paul*, 21.

clude the personal dimension (1 Cor. 3:10; 15:10), but also as a broader gift of God (1 Cor 4:7; 12:4-11; 2 Cor. 1:12, 4:15; 6:1; 8:1, 6-9; 9:8, 14; 12:9). In Romans the grace of God is even more prominent: (Rom. 1:5; 3:24; 4:4, 16; 5:2, 15-21; 6:1, 14-15; 11:5-6; 12:3-6; 15:15). The later epistles take up the theme, and if Ephesians is perceived as a summary or focus of Paul's concerns, the epistle is full of allusions to grace (Eph. 1:6-7; 2:5-8; 3:2, 7-8; 4:7, 29).

The Fourth Gospel distinctively locates the grace of God in the person of Christ. The Logos is embodied in Jesus Christ, "full of grace and truth" (John 1:14). Grace mediated from God through Christ becomes *"grace"* piled upon *"grace"* (χάριν ἀντὶ χάριτος, *charin anti charitos,* John 1:16). "Grace and truth came through Jesus Christ" (John 1:17). In the body of the Fourth Gospel *love* becomes a dominant theme. God *loves* the world (John 3:16); God *loves* the Son (John 3:35; cf. 15:9); Jesus *loves* his own (John 13:1; 13:34; 14:21)

The Pauline and Johannine characterization of God as *grace* and *love* in eventful *action* stands in continuity with God's self-revelation to Israel. The Hebrew noun חֵן (*chēn*) and verb חָנַן (*chānan*), as in Exod. 33:19, "I will be *gracious* to whom I will be *gracious,* and will show mercy on whom I will show mercy," denotes *grace that is free and sovereign,* as this verse suggests. Brown-Driver-Briggs, *The New Hebrew-English Lexicon,* notes the typical context of showing *undeserved favor* by a superior to an inferior, alongside *grace.*[152] In a more extended lexicographical discussion H.-J. Fabry argues that over the sixty-seven uses of חֵן (*chēn*) in the Old Testament the two "basic meanings [are] 'grace' and 'favor' . . . a favorite expression of the Yahwist."[153] The grace of God, Fabry comments, may be conveyed as a *gift.* Above all "graciousness is a divine attribute. The adjective *channûn* is used almost exclusively of Yahweh in the Old Testament."[154] Yahweh is gracious and merciful, slow to anger, and abounding in steadfast love and faithfulness (Exod. 34:6; 2 Chron. 30:9; Neh. 9:17, 31; Pss. 86:15; 103:8; 111:4; 116:5; 145:8; Joel 2:13; Jonah 4:2).

The allusion to *steadfast love* calls to mind the Hebrew term for *covenant love* or *covenant grace,* namely חֶסֶד (*chesed*), often translated as *kindness,* or *loving-kindness* by KJV/AV. חֶסֶד occurs 245 times on the Old Testament, and is fundamentally a relational, interpersonal word.[155] The word "emphasizes the actional nature of *chesed.* . . . Yahweh 'sends' it . . . 'makes it great' . . . 'commands' it" (Pss. 89:8; 42:9; Jer. 31:33).[156] It denotes God's readiness to act on behalf of those whom he loves. It is also linked to the *covenant* notion of God's faithfulness in showing

---

152. Brown-Driver-Briggs, *The New Hebrew-English Lexicon* (new edn., 2000), 335-36.

153. H.-J. Fabry, חָנַן (*chānan*), חֵן (*chēn*), in Botterweck and Ringgren (eds.), *TDOT,* vol. 5, 22-36.

154. Fabry, חֵן, 30.

155. H.-J. Zobel, "חֶסֶד" (*chesed*), in Botterweck and Ringgren (eds.), *TDOT,* vol. 5, 36-64, esp. 46-7.

156. Zobel, "חֶסֶד," *TDOT,* 54.

lovingkindness. In a classic verse the biblical writer exclaims, "It is of the LORD's *chesed* that we are not consumed, because his compassions *(rach^amîm)* do not fail. They are new every morning. Great is thy faithfulness" (Lam. 3:22).

In addition to these two Hebrew terms the word for *love* (אהבה, *'ah^abâ*, noun, and אהב, *'āhab*, verb) occurs with very great frequency. Often the word denotes human love, either to God or to fellow human beings, but it also denotes divine love. Typically it denotes God's love to Israel (Deut. 7:8, 13; 23:6; 1 Kings 10:9; 2 Chron. 2:10; 9:8; Isa. 43:4; 48:14; Jer. 31:3; Hos. 3:1; 9:15; 11:1; 14:5; Mal. 1:2). The occurrences of these three major terms form part of the narrative of word and deed that builds the language functions (or language games) from which Paul, John, and other New Testament writers depict the sovereign grace and love of God in action, especially as it is focused and becomes "thinkable" in the person and actions of Jesus Christ.

Finally, one other contributory factor to the hermeneutics of divine *transcendence* has yet to be considered. Cullmann declares in *Christ and Time*, "Primitive Christian faith and thinking do not start from the spatial contrast between the Here and the Beyond, but from the time distinction between Formerly and Now and Then."[157] He concedes that the "spatial" imagery or metaphor plays a role, but the *temporal* contrast is "the essential thing." This emerges strikingly in Heb. 11:1, where "things not seen" include what is "unseen" because it has *not yet taken place*. The future is part of what is "other," and a holy source of transformative *promise*. This must be set alongside the hermeneutic of Jüngel and others as a contributory hermeneutical resource for speaking of the transcendence and holiness of God.

Hermeneutical models for the expression of *divine immanence* have recently become less problematic, provided that they are never reduced in such a way as to diminish divine transcendence. Moltmann's work on divine *perichoresis* must rank as one of the most creative hermeneutical advances in this area, together with the insights of Balthasar and others on the subject of divine *kenosis*.[158] In the context of feminist theology Sallie McFague has also explored a hermeneutic of divine immanence, calling attention to the role of organic rather than mechanistic models of divine action.[159] In a sequel to her earlier book she aims to hold together Christology and "embodiment" with issues of divine transcendence.[160]

In view of Moltmann's extensive work on *perichoresis* especially in *God in*

157. Oscar Cullmann, *Christ and Time: The Primitive Christian Conception of Time and History*, trans. Floyd V. Filson (London: S.C.M., 1951), 37.

158. Jürgen Moltmann, esp. *God in Creation: An Ecological Doctrine of Creation*, trans. Margaret Kohl (London: S.C.M., 1985); see also Balthasar, *Theo-drama*, vol. 4, 319-32.

159. Sallie McFague, *Models of God: Theology for an Ecological, Nuclear Age* (Philadelphia: Fortress, 1987).

160. Sallie McFague, *The Body of God: An Ecological Theology* (London: SCM, 1993), 27-64 and 159-96.

Creation, The Spirit of Life, and *The Trinity and Kingdom of God,* we need not delay further to explore a hermeneutic of divine immanence. Moltmann rightly returns to the theme that "creation is a trinitarian process: the Father creates through the Son in the Holy Spirit."[161] This opens the way for an understanding of God in the person of the Holy Spirit as "'poured out' on the whole creation," as "the fountain of life," albeit sustaining "*the difference* between God and the World" (Moltmann's italics).[162] Moltmann rightly moves from more mechanistic models of "maintaining" and "preserving" the world to more organic, interpersonal, and relational models such as "indwelling, sympathizing, participating . . . delighting in."[163]

Images of the latter kind more readily underline God's own often very costly *self-involvement* with the world and humankind. This, in turn, reopens the whole question of the "passion" of God. The classic Patristic doctrines of "impassibility, indivisibility . . . *ousia* . . . immutability" reflect the influence of Platonism more clearly than that of the Bible.[164] It is surprising that today, when so much has been written in criticism of the classical view, so-called "open theism" appears as an almost daring innovation, when its arguments usually follow not only the biblical narratives but the pioneering insights of Moltmann. The key to its validity rests not only on Moltmann's irrefutable dictum, "A God who cannot suffer cannot love either," but also upon the *covenantal* background and *theology of promise,* which stood at the heart of the theology of Luther and Calvin.[165] If the sovereign, transcendent God *freely chooses* or decrees to allow himself to suffer, this is an enhancement, not a diminution, of his sovereign freedom to choose how he will act.

It is necessary to try to formulate a hermeneutic of divine transcendence that coheres with, and supports, an understanding of God as holy and Other, while also revealing himself as the God who freely and sovereignly chooses to love in grace. Within this horizon of understanding, an understanding of divine immanence in terms of *perichoresis* and *kenosis* can only enhance the sovereign freedom of God as Other. This accords with Isa. 55:7-9: it is precisely *because* "'My thoughts are not your thoughts, nor are your ways my ways', says the LORD" that God "will abundantly pardon."

---

161. Moltmann, *God in Creation,* 9.

162. Moltmann, *God in Creation,* 11 and 13.

163. Moltmann, *God in Creation,* 14.

164. See the classic exposition in G. L. Prestige, *God in Patristic Thought* (London: S.P.C.K., 1952 [Heinemann, 1936]), 6-13, 25-27, 157-96.

165. Moltmann, *Trinity,* 38.

CHAPTER 20

The Church and Ministry in Hermeneutical Perspective

20.1. Hermeneutical Horizons:
Corporate, Communal, Theological-and-Institutional, Doxological

It is worth beginning with a retrospective glance back to Part I, and also to an earlier chapter in Part III. In 3.1, 4.2-3, and 9.2, we noted the communal framework of narrative confessions of faith and of other expressions of doctrine in the life of Israel and of the church. We noted in 3.1 that the confession of faith in Deut. 26:5-9, which begins in the first-person singular, "An Aramean ready to perish was my father," continues in the first-person *plural:* "The LORD brought *us* forth out of Egypt with a mighty hand. . . . He brought *us* into this place and gave *us* the land."

The logic of the plural is the same as that recited in the Passover: "When your son asks you, 'What do these testimonies mean?' you shall say, '*We* were Pharaoh's slaves in Egypt, and the LORD brought *us* out of Egypt with a mighty hand'" (Deut. 6:20-24). We also noted in 3.1 that Gerhard von Rad and G. E. Wright understand these as self-involving or participatory narrative recitals. Here the *identity* of the speakers becomes one with the *corporate* identity of historic Israel. These recitals constitute communal celebrations and communal acts of worship, and presuppose communal solidarity with the people of God in earlier centuries.

In the early twenty-first century such a horizon of understanding for exploring the nature of the church is often lost in narrower preoccupations with contemporary issues of ecclesiology, ecumenical statements, and local concerns. In the view of many ordinary churchpeople "the church" is the local congregation among whom they worship. Yet further from biblical horizons, in cultures where "nominal" Christianity is prevalent, "church" becomes a synonym for the building in which the local church meets. These considerations suggest that we need to reflect upon what questions need to be raised or at least reshaped as hermeneutical starting points. We suggest that four questions need to be explored, beginning with one that arises from the points just made.

(1) *Do we need to establish or to regain a horizon of understanding for approaching the nature of the church that is closer to the corporate and communal mind-set of the biblical writers and the early church than to the individualism that has characterized the West from the Enlightenment almost to the present?*

In 9.2 we explored the role of corporate solidarity in Israel. Although Johannes Pedersen and Wheeler Robinson overstated this, the balancing comments of J. W. Rogerson and H. W. Wolff still underline the corporate nature of much biblical thought about God's dealings with the world.[1] God called and elected *a people,* and the New Testament traditions unanimously regard the apostolic church as continuing this vocation to *corporate possession* and belonging, to *corporate identity* as God's people, to *corporate worship* as one people, and to *corporate responsibility* for witness and mission to the world. Geoffrey Wainwright rightly grounds this corporate dimension in *God's* own mission to the world through his people.[2]

In New Testament scholarship Tom Holland has recently placed new emphasis upon God's dealings with Christian believers as "a people" in Pauline thought. In 9.2 we cited Holland's comment that Paul's "letters are not about what God has done or is doing for a Christian. They are about what God has done or is doing for his covenant people, the church."[3] In his conclusion he writes, "We have also seen that Paul had a much more corporate view of man than is generally appreciated. This is in keeping with his Old Testament roots. . . . Focussing on this corporate framework of thought allows us to recognize the corporate dimensions of the argument in 1 Cor. 6:12-20. . . . Western expositions focus on the experience of individual believers whereas basic common sense ought to tell us that they were written to churches. . . . Their theology addresses the church's corporate experience of his God. . . . This corporate reading was to be a factor in the attempt to understand Paul's doctrine of justification . . . in the context of the Abrahamic covenant. . . . Its immediate focus is not on individual justification but the way Yahweh has delivered his people. . . ."[4]

Since ecclesiology raises sensitivities about vested interests of "churchmanship," the approach of Holland as a conservative evangelical writer may be compared with that of John A. T. Robinson as a more "catholic" Anglican, on some

---

1. John W. Rogerson, "The Hebrew Conception of Corporate Personality," *JTS* 21 (1980) 1-16, repr. in Lang (ed.), *Anthropological Approaches to the Old Testament* (Philadelphia: Fortress and London: SPCK, 1985), 43-59; and Wolff, *Anthropology of the Old Testament,* 214-22.

2. Geoffrey Wainwright, *Doxology: A Systematic Theology — The Praise of God in Worship, Doctrine, and Life* (London: Epworth, 1980), 122-46.

3. Tom Holland, *Contours of Pauline Theology,* 40 (cited above in 9.2).

4. Holland, *Contours,* 288-89.

matters liberal, on others conservative, and with Lionel Thornton who writes as a traditional "high" Anglo-Catholic. All three make the same point in different ways.

Robinson attacks the individualism that interprets what it is to be "members" (Greek μέλη, *melē*) of Christ's body, the church, on the analogy of being "members" who subscribe to a club.[5] "Members" of Christ are *constituent elements of the corporeity* of the body of Christ, better understood as "limbs of Christ" to reinvigorate the metaphor with its Pauline meaning.[6] Robinson presses the significance of Paul's experience of call, commission, and conversion as one in which Christ appeared to him with the words, "Why are you persecuting *me?*" (Acts 9:4-5; 22:7-8; 26:14-15) when he was in the process of persecuting *the church*. The church is the corporeity defined as being-in-Christ as one. It is not simply a group of fellow travelers going to the same destination, who enjoy one another's company, companionship, and support. John Bunyan's magnificent allegorical narrative *Pilgrim's Progress* offers a marvelous repertoire of imagery for the struggles, temptations, and victories of the individual Christian, but for all that it lacks any serious, biblical doctrine of the church as a corporate reality. Christian's "companions" in the allegory come and go as Christian battles on with variable support from fellow travelers.

Lionel Thornton has no lower doctrine of the church than Robinson, as the corporeity of all Christian believers who are "in Christ."[7] *Koinōnia* (κοινωνία, Acts 2:42; 1 Cor. 1:9; 10:16; 2 Cor. 6:14; 8:4; 9:13; 13:13; Phil. 1:5, 2:1; 3:10) denotes not simply "companionship," but "common and material interest and participation in a common object."[8] The cognate form *koinōnos* (κοινωνός, Matt. 23:30; par. Luke 5:10; 1 Cor. 10:18, 20; 2 Cor. 1:7; 8:23; Phlm. 17; Heb. 10:33; 1 Pet. 5:1) denotes *a joint shareholder or stockholder* who bears the common liabilities and advantages of participating in what is shared.[9] "Participation in" conveys κοινωνία *(koinōnia)* more adequately than "fellowship with" in most New Testament contexts.[10] In the portrayal offered by Luke-Acts of the earliest era of the church, believers were joint participants in "the apostles' teaching, κοινωνία, . . . the breaking of bread, and prayer" (Acts 2:42). Thornton structures this around the themes: Partakers of Christ; Partakers of the Spirit; Partakers of God's Love; Partakers of Christ's Victory; Partakers of Christ's Sonship. These lead on to the Consecration of the Church, the Resurrection of the Church, and other corporate themes. The profoundly *theological* understanding of the church that Thornton conveys is well summed up in the following sentences: "The hope of Israel went down into the

---

5. J. A. T. Robinson, *The Body: A Study in Pauline Theology,* esp. 58 and 78-79.

6. This is the translation in Thiselton, *First Epistle,* 989-1013.

7. Lionel S. Thornton, *The Common Life in the Body of Christ* (London: Dacre, 3d edn. 1950).

8. Thornton, *Common Life,* 31.

9. Thornton, *Common Life,* 71-77.

10. Thornton, *Common Life,* 71.

grave.... When the Messiah was in the tomb, Israel was in the tomb.... So, finally, ... *when Christ rose, the Church rose* from the dead" (my italics).[11]

Thornton's claims about κοινωνία *(koinōnia)* are lexicographically and exegetically sound. I have translated this term as "communal participation" in 1 Cor. 1:9 and elsewhere, and the research of J. Hainz, G. Panikulam, and others supports this.[12] At the same time Moltmann stresses both its *theological* dimension, because it denotes "the messianic way of life" lived "in the power of the Spirit," and the *practical* aspect of "fellowship among the congregation's rank and file" and "friendship ... from the 'grass-roots.'"[13] Moltmann describes the fellowship of the church as in principle "a fellowship of friends," in aim and task. He writes, "The church will not overcome its present crisis through reform of the administration of the sacraments, or from reform of its ministries. It will overcome the crisis through the rebirth of practical fellowship ... and friendship."[14]

(2) *Do biblical terms and phrases that draw attention to the communal and corporate nature of the church apply only to the church in the very widest "catholic" sense, or do they also apply to "local" churches? Is one of these a more "primary" unit than the other?*

In the Johannine writings and in the epistles as a whole we encounter such terms or phrases as *the vine and the branches* (John 15:1-11); *the sheep* and *the flock* (John 10:1-18); *the remnant* (Rom. 9:27; 11:5); *wild olive* (Rom. 11:17-24); *God's field, God's building,* and *God's temple* (1 Cor. 3:9-17); *the church of God* (1 Cor. 11:22); *the body of Christ* (1 Cor. 12:12-26; Eph. 1:23; 2:16; 4:4, 12; Col. 1:18); *the bride of Christ* (Eph. 5:25-26, 32; Rev. 21:2); or simply *the church* as such *(ekklēsia,* Matt. 16:18; Acts 8:1, 3; Gal. 1:13; Eph. 1:22; 3:10; 5:23-32; Col. 1:18).

To be sure, often *church (ekklēsia)* is used to denote a local congregation (Matt 18:17; Acts 13:1; Rom. 16:1; 1 Cor. 1:2; 16:19; Gal. 1:2; Phil. 4:15; 1 Thess. 1:1; Rev. 1:4). Sometimes the plural term *"churches"* underlines the local congregational meaning. But in 1 Cor. 1:2 the phrase τῇ ἐκκλησίᾳ τοῦ θεοῦ τῇ οὔσῃ ἐν Κορίνθῳ *(tē ekklēsia tou theou tē ousē en Korinthō,* to the church of God that is in Corinth, NRSV), as well as several near parallels *(the church at Cenchreae,* Rom. 16:1; *to the church of the Thessalonians,* 1 Thess. 1:1), is arguably ambiguous. Do these examples imply that a complete "church" exists at Corinth, Cenchreae, and Thessalonica?

K. L. Schmidt adopts a negative view, although his view remains open to

11. Thornton, *Common Life,* 282.

12. Thiselton, *First Epistle,* 103-5; J. Hainz, *Koinonia: "Kirche" als Gemeinschaft bei Paulus,* Biblische Untersuchungen (Regensburg: Pustet, 1982); and G. Panikulam, *Koinonia in the New Testament: A Dynamic Expression of Christian Life,* Analecta Biblica 85 (Rome: Pontifical Biblical Institute, 1979).

13. Jürgen Moltmann, *The Church in the Power of the Spirit: A Contribution to Messianic Ecclesiology,* trans. Margaret Kohl (London: S.C.M., 1977), 317; cf. 114-32, 272-75, and 314-17.

14. Moltmann, *Church,* 317.

question and debate. He insists that 1 Cor. 1:2 and 2 Cor. 1:1 do not denote "to the Corinthian congregation," but "the congregation, church, assembly, *as it is in Corinth*" (my italics).[15] Many of the themes of the epistle, he argues, "apply to the Church as a whole and not merely to the local congregation."[16] He declares, "The sum of the individual congregations does not produce the total community or the church."[17]

We cite Schmidt's view only to formulate the question, without yet implying an answer. Pannenberg points out that the question is more complex than we realize when we ask: "What is precisely the meaning of the term 'local church' for the primary units of the church's life? Are we speaking of the congregation assembled locally for the preaching of the Word and the Eucharist, or is 'local church' a term for the diocese subject to a bishop?"[18] The expansion of the size of dioceses over the years makes this a sharper question. We may extend it: is *a bishop a genuine mark of unity or identity independently of a wider college of bishops?* Is even a province genuinely translocal?

(3) *How does theological language about the church as the people of God in salvation-history or as the body and bride of Christ relate to sociological, empirical, and pragmatic language about the church as an institution, with its infrastructure for worship, service, and mission?*

The New Testament writers seem to hold these two dimensions together more clearly than often appears to be the case among some modern writers on the church, although there are important exceptions.

Karl Rahner, Wolfhart Pannenberg, and Robert Jenson all allude to the constructive concept of the church in Vatican II as *"uti sacramentum,"* "a sacrament as it were," and then more explicitly to "the church as the universal sacrament of salvation."[19] The church is a *visible sign* that "carries the mark of this world which will pass," and thereby is characterized in empirical terms by societal structures but also in theological terms as the pilgrim church en route to the final consummation. But the church must be distinguished from the kingdom or reign of God.[20] Rahner writes that the church is "the community of pilgrims," *not* "merely a static, unchanging instrument of salvation," as if it were without a history.[21] He

---

15. Karl L. Schmidt, "καλέω, κλῆσις, κλητός, ἐκκλησία," in *TDNT*, vol. 3, 506; cf. 469-536.

16. Schmidt, *TDNT*, vol. 3, 506.

17. Schmidt, *TDNT*, vol. 3, 506.

18. Pannenberg, *Systematic Theology*, vol. 3, 109.

19. Vatican II, *Lumen Gentium* (21 November 1964) 1:1, "The Mystery of the Church," in Austin P. Flannery (ed.), *Documents of Vatican II* (Grand Rapids: Eerdmans, 1975), 350; and *Lumen Gentium* 7:48, "The Pilgrim Church," 407. Cf. Robert Jenson, "The Church and the Sacraments," in Colin Gunton (ed.), *Cambridge Companion to Christian Doctrine*, 202; cf. 207-25.

20. Vatican II, *Lumen Gentium* 7:48, 408.

21. Karl Rahner, *Theological Investigations*, vol. 6: *Concerning Vatican Council II*, trans. Karl H. and Boniface Kruger (London: DLT, 1969), 298; cf. 295-312.

continues: "The Church . . . is living always on the proclamation of her own provisional status and of her historically advancing elimination in the coming kingdom of God towards which she is expectantly travelling as a pilgrim."[22]

Pannenberg also distinguishes clearly between the church and the kingdom of God in the context of future eschatology and present provisionality. The church was founded by the outpouring of the Holy Spirit on the Day of Pentecost (Acts 2:1-47). This founding event, Pannenberg writes, was not merely "an act of collective enthusiasm" but "the starting point of proclamation of the resurrection of the Crucified, and of his installation to a position of eschatological power as Son of God and *Kyrios*."[23] He continues: "The kingdom and the church are not herewith simply identical."[24] Further, "The church . . . is nothing apart from its function as an eschatological community and therefore as *an anticipatory sign of God's coming rule*."[25] As a *sign* or *sacrament* of final salvation, the church continues in pilgrimage *within the conditions of this world order*. The community of the people of God has its theological roots in the calling and history of Israel and in the Day of Pentecost, but it also has an "institutional" form, even though this institutional form certainly "does not control the presence of God's saving future."[26] Pannenberg endorses the formula of Vatican II: the church is "the mystery or sacrament of salvation."[27]

A common source for many writers (including Vatican II and Pannenberg) is Rudolf Schnackenburg's *God's Rule and Kingdom*, although the concept of the church as a sacrament goes back to Cyprian.[28] The church, Schnackenburg argues, is unlike the reign of God, in that the kingdom is not "built up" by human persons or believers. He cites the *Didache* prayer: "Rescue your Church from all evil . . . and bring her together from the four winds . . . into Thy Kingdom which Thou hast prepared for her."[29] John A. T. Robinson also argues for the importance of this point, urging that until we have more adequately clarified the relation between the church and the kingdom of God in the light of eschatology, we shall never arrive at a proper theology of the ministry.[30] Robinson argues that whereas the church should be subordinate to the kingdom and a function of it, and whereas the ministry should be a function of the church, the church has re-

22. Rahner, *Theological Investigations*, vol. 6, 298.

23. Pannenberg, *Systematic Theology*, vol. 3, 27.

24. Pannenberg, *Systematic Theology*, vol. 3, 30.

25. Pannenberg, *Systematic Theology*, vol. 3, 32.

26. Pannenberg, *Systematic Theology*, vol. 3, 37.

27. Pannenberg, *Systematic Theology*, vol. 3, 38.

28. Rudolf Schnackenburg, *God's Rule and Kingdom*, trans. J. Murray (London: Nelson, 1963), esp. 23-34; Cyprian, *Epistle* 69:6; and *On the Unity of the Church* 4.

29. *Didache* 1:5; Schnackenburg, *God's Rule*, 234.

30. John A. T. Robinson, "Kingdom, Church, and Ministry," in K. M. Carey (ed.), *The Historic Episcopate in the Fulness of the Church* (London: Dacre, 1954, 2d edn. 1960), 11-22.

versed the hierarchy and become subordinate to the ministry. He attacks the slogan *ubi episcopus, ibi ecclesia.*[31]

If, then, the church, in contrast to the kingdom, has needs, blemishes, fallibility, and existence as an "institution" in the world, we cannot ignore the social, ethical, political, and sociological aspects of the church as a structural organism. It is axiomatic among sociologists that any vision, however otherworldly, needs some kind of *infrastructure* to sustain its practical needs and fitness for its role within the world.

One compelling social analysis proposes a five-stage development of infrastructure as a *possibility* that may befall all visionary goals. In an initial stage a minimal infrastructure exists to insure such basic essentials as that of identifying and commissioning those who carry the vision and insuring adequate openings and communication for its implementation. As the vision embraces more people within it, a second stage of more complex organization emerges. Typically a third stage reflects an exact balance between the vision and resources for implementing it, including management of personnel and finance. In many cases a fourth stage develops in which the infrastructure begins to become top-heavy, which may even impede the vision. Finally, it is possible for a fifth stage to emerge in which *the infrastructure becomes an end in itself,* and the original vision is lost and forgotten. What began as a modest necessity turns into an end in itself that betrays the very purpose for which it was brought into being.

Dietrich Bonhoeffer and Jürgen Moltmann attack any concept or expression of the church in which the church becomes an end in itself. Bonhoeffer derives his eschatology from Christology. Since Jesus of Nazareth lived as "the Man for others," the church of Jesus Christ must be the servant church. Bonhoeffer writes, "The Church is her true self only when she exists for humanity. . . . She must take her part in the social life of the world, not lording it over men, but helping and serving them. She must tell men . . . what it means to live in Christ, to exist for others."[32] This is what lay behind Bonhoeffer's concern, often misunderstood, to avoid "the religious." The church must, with Jesus, "go to him *outside* the camp and bear the abuse he endured" (Heb. 13:13).

Pannenberg and Moltmann both understand the church as founded to serve the lordship of Christ, and inspired by the Holy Spirit for that end. Moltmann writes, "Ecclesiology can only be developed from Christology."[33] Because it participates in Christ's own mission, the church also shares this mission toward the coming of the kingdom.[34] Moltmann relates the being and empowerment of the

31. Robinson, "Kingdom," in *Historic Episcopate,* 18-19. See the fuller discussion in Richard P. McBrien, *The Church in the Thought of Bishop John Robinson* (London: S.C.M., 1966), 44-94.

32. Bonhoeffer, *Letters and Papers from Prison,* 166.

33. Moltmann, *Church,* 66.

34. Moltmann, *Church,* 75.

church *equally* to the agency of the Holy Spirit, as the title of his book implies. In fact, the basis is "the trinitarian theology of the cross." In this respect, Moltmann adds, both the emphasis on the cross of Christ in Reformed theology and upon the abundance of the Holy Spirit in Orthodox theology stand in need of complementation in the light of the other.[35] Moltmann devotes a section of his book to "The Church in the Trinitarian History of God."[36] In a profoundly theological statement of great *hermeneutical* significance he writes, "*It is not the church that has a mission of salvation to fulfil to the world; it is the mission of the Son and the Spirit through the Father that includes the church, creating a church as it goes on its way*" (my italics).[37]

Moltmann relates this theological truth to the "institutional" or sociological dimension of the church in a way that is entirely faithful to the witness of the New Testament. He continues, "It is not the church that administers the Spirit. . . . The Spirit 'administers' the church with the events of word and faith, sacrament and grace, offices and traditions."[38] The "practical" work of the church always proceeds on this ground: "Love participates in the history of God's suffering. . . . The true church is 'the church under the cross.' But . . . the church also participates in the history of the divine joy, . . . joy in the Spirit. . . . No ecclesiology should sink below this level."[39]

Moltmann adds two important justifications of these statements. First, in common with Schnackenburg, Pannenberg, and Robinson, he stresses that the church is moving toward the eschaton, and has not yet already arrived. It has yet to fulfill God's reign in the coming kingdom. Second, the church does not exist for itself and its own sake, any more than Christ came to serve himself. It exists to participate in God's mission to the world. This theme had already emerged in *Theology of Hope* and *The Crucified God*: "Whoever seeks to gain his life will lose it, but whoever loses his life will preserve it" (Mark 8:35).[40]

This theological evaluation of the church as an "institution" characterizes one of the many developments in Roman Catholic traditions that distinguish Vatican II from the earlier era of Vatican I and its ecclesiological peak in the late nineteenth century. Avery Dulles traces this shift of perspective clearly. *Lumen Gentium,* he points out, speaks of the church as "mystery, sacrament, Body of Christ, and People of God," and only toward the end addresses "the formal structures of ecclesiastical government."[41] By contrast, Dulles comments, "The bene-

---

35. Moltmann, *Church,* 37.

36. Moltmann, *Church,* 50-65.

37. Moltmann, *Church,* 64.

38. Moltmann, *Church,* 64.

39. Moltmann, *Church,* 65.

40. Cited in Moltmann, *The Crucified God,* 15.

41. Avery Dulles, *Models of the Church: A Critical Assessment of the Church in All Its Aspects* (Dublin: Gill & Macmillan, 2d edn. 1988), 35.

ficiaries of the Church, in the institutional model, are its own members. The Church . . . instructs them . . . for the sake of their eternal salvation."[42]

Dulles offers a succinct evaluation of the constructive and potentially destructive features of an "institutional" approach. The positive features include an emphasis upon the church's traditions, continuity with Christian origins, and corporate identity. On the other side, these can lead to clericalism, to an overconcern with judicial aspects of law, to overconcern about authority and jurisdiction, and to triumphalism.[43] Rahner questions the clericalism of the church. He writes, "The lifestyle especially of the higher clergy even today sometimes conforms too much to that of the 'managers' in secular society."[44]

(4) *What does the regular activity of the church in liturgy, prayer, worship, sacraments, and proclamation suggest about the nature of the church?*

If hermeneutics characteristically explores preunderstandings that reflect where people already are, for many Christians the experience of Sunday worship is the nearest to hand. The reading of Scripture, the recital of psalms, and the corporate repetition of such regular acts as the recital of the *Venite* (Ps. 95), the *Te Deum,* the *Magnificat* (Luke 1:46-55), the *Nunc Dimittis* (Luke 2:29-32), the *Gloria,* and the canon of the Eucharist or Communion (cf. 1 Cor. 11:23b-26) identify those who speak or sing as part of a community rooted in the history of divine saving acts in the history of Israel and the church from the exodus onward. The performative speech-act of ascribing glory to the Father, to the Son, and the Holy Spirit "as it was in the beginning, is now, and shall be forever" lifts those who offer praise from the transitoriness of the present moment to share in the eternal ascription of glory on the part of the whole communion of saints to the eternal God.

It becomes perhaps less of a danger for who those seriously participate in the liturgy of the church day by day or week by week to conceive of the church primarily as a sociological, local institution, imprisoned only in the contingent here and now of finance, appointments, management, and possible power play. Yet a yawning hermeneutical gap, at least in Western Protestantism, appears still to stand in need of being bridged. Many appear to perceive even the empowering work of the Holy Spirit as focused only on the present moments and the local concerns of "my community." Yet the Spirit's work proceeds both "vertically" through the centuries and "horizontally" across the worldwide church. This, however, leads us beyond hermeneutical starting points to themes that require further elucidation or evaluation.

---

42. Dulles, *Models,* 41.

43. Dulles, *Models,* 39-46.

44. Karl Rahner, *The Shape of the Church to Come,* trans. Edward Quinn (London: SPCK, 1974) 58.

20.2. Contributions of "Models" of the Church:
More on the Theological and Institutional

C. K. Barrett begins his Didsbury Lectures on the church and sacraments by formulating a "paradox." He declares, "In the New Testament the church is at the same time central and peripheral." Neither limb of the paradox can be neglected, he adds, without our falling into error.[45] Barrett continues, "There is no part of the New Testament that does not attach some kind of significance to the fellowship of the followers of Jesus, — but there is at the same time something provisional, temporary, penultimate, about who they are and what they do. . . . The fact is that the church is an eschatological monster, or prodigy, baffling description and definition."[46]

In a special "excursus" Pannenberg points out that the place of a doctrine of the church in systematic theology is ambiguous. He writes, "It is not self-evident that the concept of the church should be a separate dogmatic theme."[47] While "the marks of the church" (the church as *one, holy, catholic,* and *apostolic*) find their way into the catechetical lectures of Cyril of Jerusalem (c. 348-50), the doctrine of the church did not regularly become a separate area of doctrine prior to the Reformers. The Patristic and medieval church usually moved directly from Christology to the sacraments. Even the first edition of Calvin's *Institutes* (1536), Pannenberg reminds us, had no separate chapter on the church.[48] Whereas the kingdom of God is determinative, the church is characterized by provisionality.[49]

We have already argued that when it becomes difficult to use language with precision and transparency, Ian Ramsey's concept of models and qualifiers contributes a constructive resource. Avery Dulles recognizes the value of using "models" when we seek to understand the nature of the church. Just as difficulties arise when we seek to understand the atoning work of Christ under any exclusively *single* theme or category, so also in the case of ecclesiology almost any *single* explanatory model will predispose the user of the model to develop a theology of the church in a particular direction. In the mid-twentieth century, for example, many Anglo-Catholics within the Church of England regularly pressed the legitimate Pauline model of the church as the body of Christ to infer that as "an extension of the incarnation" the church possessed a status or absence of provisionality that many of their more Protestant counterparts in the Church of England would not be content to hold.

In accordance with his approach broadly within the horizons of Vatican II,

---

45. C. K. Barrett, *Church, Ministry and Sacraments in the New Testament* (Exeter, U.K.: Paternoster, 1985), 9.

46. Barrett, *Church,* 13.

47. Pannenberg, *Systematic Theology,* vol. 3, 21; cf. 21-27.

48. Pannenberg, *Systematic Theology,* vol. 3, 22.

49. Pannenberg, *Systematic Theology,* vol. 3, 25.

Dulles explores primarily the models set forth in *Lumen Gentium,* namely the church as *mystery, sacrament, body of Christ,* and *people of God.* He also expounds other models, including those of herald, servant, institution, and eschatological community. Dulles rightly comments, "The basic models of the Church have arisen in history as a result of the differing points of view, or horizons of believers and theologians of different ages and cultures. . . . Each of the models, self-evidently, has its own uses and limitations."[50] More problematic, he adds, is whether any of them turns out to be incompatible with another.

Dulles also makes a constructive comment that there is need for what we may call (in the terminology of this volume) a *hermeneutic of suspicion* (with Ricoeur) or a *hermeneutic of interest* (with Habermas). Some, he observes, "will be spontaneously drawn to certain models: Church officials have a tendency to prefer the institutional model; ecumenists, the community model; speculative theologians, the sacramental model; preachers and biblical scholars, the kerygmatic model; and secular activists, the servant model."[51] Repeating the maxim to which I have sometimes appealed in relation to theologies of atonement, Dulles declares that models are more likely to be valid in what they affirm than in what they might be taken to deny.

(i) Dulles regards *the institutional model* as facilitating a due recognition that the church needs to be *a structured community.* Such a community, he continues, would have to include a pastoral office equipped with authority to preside over the worship of the community as such, to prescribe the limits of tolerable dissent, and to represent the community in an official way.[52]

(ii) *The community model* emphasizes the need for both unity and loving relationships. We have noted Moltmann's strong emphasis upon this aspect.

(iii) *The sacramental model* calls attention to the church's function to be a *visible sign* and witness that points beyond itself to the reality of Christ and salvation.

(iv) *The kerygmatic model* of the church as herald of the gospel underlines its responsibility for gospel proclamation and communication of the faith in truth.

(v) *The servant model,* which Dulles still calls the "diaconal" model, points to the church's responsibly to exist not for itself but *for others* (as Bonhoeffer and Moltmann forcefully express it), and to serve the world.

Dulles does not simply enumerate these models, but also recognizes, in accordance with the principle expounded by Ian Ramsey, that these models require "qualification" and interaction, and cannot stand in isolation. He insists that the institutional model, while valid, must be subordinated to the communal life and mission of the church. Conversely, a communal emphasis alone might lead to an unchecked or "unhealthy spirit of enthusiasm in its search for religious experi-

---

50. Dulles, *Models,* 190.
51. Dulles, *Models,* 193.
52. Dulles, *Models,* 194.

ences or warm . . . relationships, [and] could lead to false expectations and impossible demands."[53] Each is incomplete in itself.

We earlier suggested that among the New Testament writings the theological nature of the church relates without undue tension to the empirical, structural, or sociological expressions of the church in the public domain. This is clearly the case in 1 Corinthians, where Paul, as we shall argue, sets forth what has come to be called "the marks of the church" in theological terms, while at the same time recognizing the importance of administrative and disciplinary oversight. We shall return to 1 Corinthians and to Paul.[54]

The Acts of the Apostles, once described by W. C. van Unnik in 1968 as a "storm center" of interpretation, continues to present substantial complexities for interpretation.[55] François Bovon has provided the most recent definitive and near-exhaustive critical discussion of scholarship on Luke-Acts from 1950 to the present, and covers some seven hundred pages of summaries and assessments.[56] At the beginning of this period Conzelmann argued that the chapters of Acts portrayed not the birth of the church as it actually happened, but an idealized picture of an unrepeatable era in the church's past, projected back from the author's time with a conscious sense of historical distance. Like F. C. Baur many years earlier, he drives a wedge between Acts and Paul.[57] In a further study, subsequent to *The Theology of St. Luke* (German *Die Mitte der Zeit*, 1954), Conzelmann linked Luke-Acts closely with the "Deutero-Pauline" Pastoral Epistles, observing: "The world becomes a place where the church is at home, a notion which Paul sharply rejected."[58] Ernst Käsemann also drew a contrast between the more eschatological emphasis of Paul and the church as a pilgrim people in Hebrews with Luke-Acts, commenting: "One does not write a history of the church if one daily expects the end of the world."[59]

It would be tedious and unnecessary to rehearse the numerous criticisms that have been brought against Conzelmann's conclusions over the last fifty years. I have mentioned his work simply to illustrate the complexity of the problem that faces interpreters of Luke-Acts. After Conzelmann, a whole series of

53. Dulles, *Models*, 195.

54. I have developed this point in Anthony C. Thiselton, "The Significance of Recent Research on 1 Corinthians for Hermeneutical Appropriation of This Epistle Today," *Neot.* 40 (2006) 91-123.

55. W. C. van Unnik, in L. E. Keck and J. L. Martyn (eds.), *Studies in Luke-Acts* (London: S.P.C.K., 1968), 18.

56. François Bovon, *Luke the Theologian: Fifty-five Years of Research (1950-2005)*, trans. largely by K. McKinney (Waco, TX: Baylor University Press, 2d rev. edn. 2006).

57. Hans Conzelmann, *The Theology of St. Luke*, trans. G. Buswell (London: Faber & Faber, 1960).

58. Hans Conzelmann, "Luke's Place in the Development of Early Christianity," in Keck and Martyn (eds.), *Studies*, 302-3; cf. 298-309.

59. Ernst Käsemann, *Essays on New Testament Themes* (London: S.C.M., 1964), 28.

writers have reshaped our understandings of the church in Luke-Acts. The most influential include Schweizer, Schnackenburg, Haenchen, Jervell, Roloff, Marshall, Reinhardt, and Barrett, as documented below.[60] Bovon offers admirable assessments of these writers. When all the trends, advances, reverses, and distractions have been taken into account, the Acts of the Apostles reflects all of the main models and themes discussed by Moltmann and by Dulles, with varying degrees of emphasis and contextual concern.

(1) The structure of Acts reflects the apostolic church as participant in *the mission* of Christ and the Holy Spirit. Whether, with Pannenberg, we view the foundation of the church on the Day of Pentecost as the proclamation of Christ as Lord (Acts 2:22-28) or, with Moltmann, as the pouring out of the Spirit (Acts 2:1-13), or, with both, the continuation of the mission of Jesus as the raised Christ, the movement from Jerusalem to Rome narrates the steady outreach and mission of the gospel. Setbacks and persecutions simply add impetus and power to the mission. R. R. Williams gave to his small popular commentary on Acts the subtitle: *Nothing Can Stop the Gospel.*[61]

The movement from Jerusalem to Rome does not represent, as J. Dupont claims, a movement from Jews to Gentiles. As Jervell argues, Luke retains the Jewish character of the church. W. G. Kümmel rightly suggests that Acts is structured "into five geographically determined sections in accordance with the missionary commission (Acts 1:8)."[62] The five stages of expansion and mission related respectively to Jerusalem (Acts 1:13–8:3); Samaria and the coast (8:4–11:18); Antioch and its mission (11:19–15:35); lands around the Aegean Sea (15:36-19:20); and from Jerusalem to Rome (19:21–28:31). In spite of persecution and trials, Luke ends his account of the church's mission under the Holy Spirit with the comment that the church proclaimed the reign of God and Jesus Christ "with all boldness and without hindrance" (Greek μετὰ παρρησίας ἀκωλύτως, *meta parrēsias akōlutōs*, Acts 28:31). P. Zingg emphasizes the use of the Greek imperfect to denote a steady, continuous *process of growth* (Acts 2:47; 5:14; 6:7; 9:31; 11:21; 12:24; 13:49; 16:5; 19:20) in contrast to the aorist for inciden-

---

60. Sources of particular relevance to the present chapter include Eduard Schweizer, *Church Order in the New Testament*, trans. F. Clarke (London: S.C.M., 1961), 34-51, 63-76, and 163-230; R. Schnackenburg, *The Church in the New Testament*, trans. W. J. O'Hara (London: Burns & Oates and Freiburg: Herder, 1965), 11-69 and 118-96; J. Jervell, *St. Luke and the People of God: A New Look at Luke-Acts* (Minneapolis: Augsburg, 1972); I. H. Marshall, *Luke: Historian and Theologian* (Exeter, U.K.: Paternoster, 1970) and *New Testament Theology* (Downers Grove, IL: InterVarsity Press, 2004), 155-208; Wolfgang Reinhardt, *Das Wachstum des Gottesvolkes* (Unpubl. diss. of 1995, summarized by Bovon, *Luke*, 553-54); and C. K. Barrett, *A Critical and Exegetical Commentary on the Acts of the Apostles*, 2 vols. (Edinburgh: T&T Clark, 1994 and 1998).

61. Ronald R. Williams, *Acts of the Apostles: "Nothing Can Stop the Gospel"* (London: S.C.M., 1953).

62. W. G. Kümmel, *Introduction to the New Testament* (London: S.C.M. and Nashville: Abingdon, 1966), 108.

tal events.[63] He also sees the process of this mission as originating in God's promise to Abraham concerning the blessing of all the earth through him (Gen. 12:3; 17:4-8; and especially 22:17-18). The church's mission carries forward that of Israel and of Christ to the world. François Bovon comments, "Luke's ecclesiology . . . is dynamic, doubly dynamic. First *in space* . . . it breaks through barriers, and then *in time* . . . growth takes place" (my italics).[64]

In 3.2 we drew attention to the importance for hermeneutics of embodiment and *place* with particular reference to the work of David Brown and John Inge. Francis Pereira's research, published as *Ephesus: Climax of Universalism in Luke-Acts,* carries this further within a perspective of mission in Acts.[65] In Ephesus Jews and Gentiles hear the word of God together for the first time (Acts 19:9-10; cf. 19:12-21). Harold Dollar develops a "multi-ethnic" notion of mission further in what he calls a "missiological hermeneutics."[66] Michael Goheen also formulates what he calls "a missional hermeneutic" of Luke-Acts in dialogue with David Bosch.[67] The very way in which Luke organizes the narrative structure, he concludes, is to underline the role of mission in the fulfillment of divine purposes for the world. This entails, for Bosch, "incarnating the Gospel in time" as part of the *missio Dei.*[68]

(2) Acts clearly reveals Luke's attention to *institutional* or *empirical* structures of the early church. Again, this meets with serious hermeneutical complexities. Those who, like Haenchen and Käsemann, date Acts late, and perceive it as reflecting the institutional interests of a church (in Conzelmann's phrase) "at home in the world," categorize Luke-Acts alongside the Pastoral Epistles as predictably concerned with *structures.* Those who see the earlier chapters of Acts as a historical account of its early years are inclined to pass over the institutional aspects too quickly. Through sustained engagement with Luke-Acts, I have long understood its main focus to be *the public domain.*

Luke's concern for the *public, visible, embodied domain of life* shows itself in many ways. Loveday Alexander's reassessment of the prologue to Luke-Acts (Luke 1:1-4; cf. Acts 1:1-3) points in this direction: Luke writes an ordered, reli-

---

63. P. Zingg, *Das Wachsen der Kirche: Beiträge zur Frage der lukanischen Redaktion und Theologie* (Göttingen: Vandenhoeck & Ruprecht, 1974), 3-74.

64. Bovon, *Luke the Theologian,* 460.

65. Francis Pereira, *Ephesus: Climax of Universalism in Luke-Acts: A Redactional Critical Study of Paul's Ministry in Ephesus* (Acts 18:23–20:1) (Anand, India: Gujarat Sahitya Prakash, 1983).

66. H. E. Dollar, *A Biblical-Missiological Exploration of the Cross-Cultural Dimensions in Luke-Acts* (San Francisco: Mellen Research University Press, 1993).

67. Michael Goheen, "A Critical Examination of David Bosch's Missional Reading of Luke," in C. G. Bartholomew, Joel B. Green, and Anthony C. Thiselton (eds.), *Reading Luke: Interpretation, Reflection, Formation* (Grand Rapids: Zondervan and Carlisle, U.K.: Paternoster, 2005), 229-66.

68. Goheen, in *Reading Luke,* 251-54.

able, publicly witnessed account in which eyewitnesses pass on a *publicly agreed* or "verified" tradition.[69] Discipleship becomes *public and visible* in such actions as the use of *money and possessions* and the importance of *place* (not merely symbolic place, as Conzelmann claims). The *dating* of events is expressed in terms of a triple system of temporal location in relation to the empire, local government, and religious leaders (Luke 3:1-2). Attitudes to the vulnerable and marginalized also reveal the *public* face of Christian discipleship. Luke is not, as Stephen Wilson shows, reacting against eschatology (as Käsemann and Conzelmann suggest), but against *inwardness*.[70] His concern about *the church as a visible, public, human structure,* alongside its status as *God's vehicle of mission,* is part and parcel of this.

The earliest era of the church focuses upon its geographical center in Jerusalem. From the very first, entry into the fellowship of believers requires not only inner repentance but the visible act of baptism (Acts 2:18). This has nothing to do with triumphalism. Schweizer writes, "Baptism is [in Acts 2:18] the profession of belonging to a despised band . . . not to a successful Church."[71] A decisive stage in the emergence of the church as separate from Judaism takes place with the speech of Stephen and the group of Hellenist leaders (Acts 6:3-6; 7:2-60; 8:15). Stephen's speech is a turning point in pressing the church's need to define itself consciously as different from an appendix to the synagogues, although James Burtchaell argues that the church initially reflected the institutional structures of the synagogue in its own way.[72]

No less significant, however, is the commission of the Seven διακονεῖν τραπέζαις, *diakonein trapezais* (NRSV *to wait on tables,* Acts 6:2). They are appointed (καταστήσομεν, *katastēsomen*) to do this task by and on behalf of the apostles (6:3). John Collins has strongly disputed the traditional English translation *to serve at tables,* with the further support of F. W. Danker in the third edition of *BDAG.*[73] Collins argues on the basis of both lexicographical evidence and exegesis that the verb διακονεῖν *(diakonein)* and the noun διακονία *(diakonia)* primarily denote the notion of a *go-between* rather than that of a *menial servant.* In 2 Cor. 3:7-9, *diakonia* seems to have more to do with *mediation* than with me-

---

69. Loveday Alexander, *The Preface to Luke's Gospel* (Cambridge: Cambridge University Press, 1993).

70. Wilson shows that Luke rejects *both* a wholly futurist *and* a wholly realized eschatology while retaining eschatological awareness for good pastoral reasons. Stephen G. Wilson, *The Gentiles and the Gentile Mission in Luke-Acts,* SNTSMS 23 (Cambridge: Cambridge University Press, 1973), 59-87.

71. Schweizer, *Church Order,* 41.

72. J. T. Burtchaell, *From Synagogue to Church: Public Services and Offices in the Earliest Christian Communities* (Cambridge: Cambridge University Press, 1992).

73. John N. Collins, *Diakonia: Reinterpreting the Ancient Sources* (New York and Oxford: Oxford University Press, 1990); John N. Collins, *Are All Christians Ministers?* (Collegeville, MN: Liturgical, 1992); and BDAG, 3d edn. (2000) 230-31.

nial or humble service.[74] Collins interprets Acts 6:1-6 to means that the Greek-speaking widows were neglected in the *ministry of the word* (not in the serving of meals or financial support), to which the apostles responded by appointing those who could *minister on their behalf* at a more local level (at tables) to release the apostles for wider public proclamation of the word.[75] If Collins is correct, *diakonein* denotes a *commissioned, authorized ministry on behalf of another,* as a *go-between,* with no *necessary* link with administering food or funds rather than the word of God.

We do not have space to examine Collins's arguments in detail, but there is a clear parallel between the respective status variations of slaves and that of the *diakonos.* In 17.1 we alluded to the status of slaves as ranging from one of a high dignity and honor to the menial status of a mere "thing" (Latin *res*), depending on the purpose for which they were purchased and the attitude and integrity of their master *(Kurios).* Similarly, the *diakonos* may participate in the dignity of the one whom he represents as deputy or go-between, and in the context of Acts 6:1-6 serve not as a social administrator but as a proclaimer of the word of God in a specific context or setting. The third edition (2000) of BDAG favors the meaning *one who functions as an intermediary* as its first category for the noun *diakonos* (Rom. 13:4; 1 Cor. 3:5; 2 Cor. 3:6; 6:4; 1 Thess. 3:2; 1 Tim. 1:12; Tit. 1:9), and *to function as an intermediary* or *to act as a go-between* for the verb *diakonein* (Matt. 20:28; Mark 10:45; 2 Cor. 8:19; 1 Pet. 1:12); and *service rendered in an intermediary capacity* for *diakonia* (Rom. 15:31; 2 Cor. 9:12). It describes Acts 6:2 as posing "a special problem" and opts for the meaning *care for, take care of.*[76] The lexicon adds: "*look after tables* can be understood as serving food at tables . . . but [it] more probably refers to *administrative responsibility.* . . . It may denote accounts."[77] BDAG also includes in other categorizations *one who gets something done at the behest of a superior,* or, in the case of *diakonia, performance of a service.*

The upshot of this complex discussion and research is to suggest that Acts 6:1-6 recounts an apostolic decision *to delegate* certain responsibilities to relieve ministerial, pastoral, or administrative loads. It is clearly *a decision of good management.* It marks the beginning of a necessary infrastructure, at the same time insuring lines of accountability to the apostles. The wider church was consulted about possible candidates ("select from among yourselves," Acts 6:3a), but the apostles retained the right of appointment and power of commission ("whom we may appoint to the task," 6:3b). The appointment was *collaborative* and collegial, and brought together the agency of the Holy Spirit and institutional needs. Schweizer underlines the gift of missionary preaching that marked out the Seven,

---

74. Collins, *Diakonia,* 204.

75. Collins, *Diakonia,* 230-31.

76. BDAG, 229-31: this is clearly a shift from the 2d edn. of 1979 (BAGD).

77. BDAG, 230, col. i.

but his assertion that they were not subordinate to the Twelve predates the lexicographical research on *go-between* and *intermediary*.[78]

The sending of Peter and John to "regularize" the mission to Samaria (Acts 8:14-17) through prayer, the laying on of hands, and the gift of the Holy Spirit combines a *theological* concern for the gospel with an *institutional* concern for structural continuity between the apostles and mother church of Jerusalem and the new Samaritan response to the work of God. This passage has given rise to multiple interpretations, often reflecting the prior denominational commitments of interpreters. N. Adler stresses the link between the mother church in Jerusalem, the apostolic laying on of hands, and the Samaritans.[79] Käsemann emphasizes apostolic authority, but only as the late redactional activity of Luke. Lampe stresses the link between baptism and the gift of the Holy Spirit; while Schweizer strongly resists the notion that the laying on of hands "transmits" the Holy Spirit, who comes as sheer gift, not *ex opere operato*.[80]

François Bovon points out that a certain continuity exists in the relation between the Holy Spirit and the laying on of hands in Acts 8:14-17, Acts 8:18-20 (Simon Magus), Acts 10:44-47 (Cornelius), Acts 11:16 and 13:3, and Acts 18:24-28 and 19:2-6 (the disciples of John the Baptist at Ephesus). Each involves "certain human rites" in the context of prayer for, or the gift of, the Holy Spirit, and Luke sees the Holy Spirit "at work in the transmission [of the Christian heritage] itself (Acts 1:2)."[81] In other words, Luke holds together the theological character of the church as participant in the mission of the Holy Spirit under the lordship of Christ and "institutional," visible, or empirical phenomena that constitute the "public" face of the church in the world.

Paul holds these two aspects together with special clarity in 1 Corinthians. The church is a translocal reality ("called to be saints together with all those who in every place call on the name of our Lord Jesus Christ," 1 Cor. 1:2). The church belongs to God (possessive genitive, 1 Cor. 1:2a), and is en route to future salvation (1:7; and present participles in 1:18-25). It is God's building and God's field (1 Cor. 3:9), and the shrine of the Holy Spirit (3:16, where *temple* is corporate, in contrast to 6:19 where it is both corporate and individual).[82] The church entails communal participation in the blood of Christ (1 Cor. 10:16), and continues the mission of Israel ("*our* ancestors . . . ," 10:1-13). It is founded upon common, pre-Pauline apostolic traditions, as Anders Eriksson well argues (1 Cor. 11:2; 11:23;

---

78. Schweizer, *Church Order*, 49.

79. N. Adler, *Taufe und Handauflegung: Eine exegetisch theologische Untersuchung von Apg. 8:14-17* (Münster: Aschendorf, 1951).

80. G. W. H. Lampe, "The Holy Spirit in the Writings of St. Luke," in D. E. Nineham (ed.), *Studies in the Gospels: Essays in Memory of R. H. Lightfoot* (Oxford: Blackwell, 1955), 159-200; and Schweizer, "πνεῦμα," in *TDNT*, vol. 6, 413-15.

81. Bovon, *Luke the Theologian*, 261-62 and 270-71.

82. Thiselton, *First Epistle*, 301-18; cf. 474-75.

15:3).[83] A dialectic of unity and diversity springs from the unmerited gifts (Greek χαρίσματα, *charismata*) of the Holy Spirit (1 Cor. 12:4-11, 27-31; 14:1-40). The church is the body of Christ (12:12-26). As a corporate entity it cannot dispense with, or make to feel unwanted, supposedly "weaker" limbs or members (1 Cor. 12:21-26). No genuine Christian, on the other hand, is to feel inferior or not needed (12:14-20). A monochrome, utterly uniform organism would not *be* a "body" (1 Cor. 12:19). On the other hand, an organism in conflict with itself would not survive as a body: all "were made to drink of one Spirit" (12:13).[84]

Nevertheless Paul recognizes the need for modest "management." As an ἀρχιτέκτων (*architektōn*, 1 Cor. 3:10), Paul assumes the role of one who in first-century Greco-Roman business would establish and implement building contracts, coordinate the workforce, and maintain an overview and oversight of the building work. The *architektōn* would often have a small team of "co-workers," which was precisely Paul's own policy of collaborative leadership. The so-called charismatic gifts described in 12:1–14:40 are "charismatic" only in the sense that they are not earned. Some gifts may have an aspect of "spontaneity," but ἀντιλήμψεις (*antilēmpseis*, 1 Cor. 12:28) almost certainly denotes what I have translated as *kinds of administrative support*.[85] This leads on precisely and coherently to κυβερνήσεις (*kubernēseis*) in 12:29, which I have translated as *the ability to formulate strategies* (for the church).[86] The noun from which this term derives denotes a *steersperson* or *pilot* (cf. Acts 27:11; Rev. 18:17). Margaret Mitchell confirms that it often denotes "rulership," and there are little grounds for accepting Gordon Fee's comments that it cannot allude to an administrative task.[87]

A less controversial "administrative" term comes in Paul's use of ὑπηρέτης (*hupēretēs*) and especially οἰκονόμος (*oikonomos*) in 1 Cor. 4:1-2. The former term covers a variety of ways of serving, ranging in the first century from *household servant* to *junior officer* or *subordinate* (REB). The latter term *oikonomos* is frequently translated *steward*, but today this meaning has shifted from Paul's main point. In contemporary papyri the Greek word often denotes *estate manager, treasurer*, or one who has responsibility for *managing a household budget*.[88] BDAG (3d edn. 2000) places as its first category of meaning for οἰκονόμος

---

83. Anders Eriksson, *Traditions as Rhetorical Proof: Pauline Argumentation in 1 Corinthians* (Stockholm: Almqvist & Wiksell, 1998), throughout.

84. On the body in 1 Corinthians, see Thiselton, *First Epistle*, 989-1024; and Dale Martin, *The Corinthian Body* (New Haven, CT: Yale University Press, 1993), 3-61 and 94-103.

85. Thiselton, *First Epistle*, 1019-21.

86. Thiselton, *First Epistle*, 1021-22.

87. Margaret M. Mitchell, *Paul and the Rhetoric of Reconciliation* (Tübingen: Mohr and Louisville: Westminster/Knox, 1992), 163; cf. Gordon D. Fee, *First Epistle to the Corinthians* (Grand Rapids: Eerdmans, 1987), 622.

88. Moulton and Milligan, *Vocabulary of the Greek Testament*, 442-43; and Thiselton, *First Epistle*, 335-37.

(oikonomos) manager of a household or estate, steward, manager (Luke 12:42; 1 Cor. 4:2; Luke 16:1, 3, the dishonest manager). Even its second and third catego-ries are: *treasurer* and *one who is entrusted with management administration.*[89] Similarly, BDAG suggests for οἰκονομία *(oikonomia) responsibility of manage-ment, management of a household . . . the work of an estate manager.*[90]

We do not have space to explore the Pauline epistles further, although we shall consider the Pastoral Epistles in the next and final section of this chapter, on ministry. While we have considered the models of *mission* and *institution*, we have already overlapped with other models proposed by Avery Dulles, namely those of *community, sacrament* or *visible sign, kerygmatic herald,* and *servant* for the world.

Clearly the model of *community* plays a major role in both Acts and Paul. Acts 2:42: "They devoted themselves to the apostles' teaching and fellowship, to the breaking of bread and prayer," and Acts 2:44: "All who believed were together and had all things in common," were programmatic for the Jerusalem church of Acts 1:15–8:3. The Council of Jerusalem (Acts 15:6-31) served both to preserve communal bonds and to maintain structural or institutional unity. Paul likewise calls those who are the church "to love one another with mutual affection, out-doing one another in showing honor" (Rom. 12:10). He declares, "If one member [of the body] suffers, all suffer with it; if one member is honored, all rejoice to-gether with it" (1 Cor. 12:26). The famous hymn or meditation on love addresses precisely these issues in the church at Corinth (1 Cor. 13:1-13).[91]

The model of the church as a *mutually supportive community* runs through-out the New Testament. In the Johannine writings, as Raymond Brown points out, the prayer of Jesus "that they may be one" (John 17:22) points to the commu-nity of fellow believers, while love for one's fellow believers appears in 15:12 as well as in John 13:12-15; 17:11, and also in the image of the flock (John 10:16). In the epistles 1 John 2:19 describes anti-Christs as those who have cut themselves off from the Christian community.[92] Stephen Smalley perceives love among Chris-tians as the theme of 1 John 4:7–5:4.[93] The concept of the church as the *pilgrim people of God* drawing support from one another in a hostile world finds clear ex-pression in the Epistle to the Hebrews. In their different ways Ernst Käsemann and Robert Jewett explicate this.[94]

---

89. BDAG, 698.

90. BDAG, 697-98.

91. Thiselton, *First Epistle,* 1027-30 and 1046-60.

92. Raymond E. Brown, *The Gospel according to John,* Anchor Bible, 2 vols. (London: Chap-man, 1971 and New York: Doubleday, 1966), cviii-cix.

93. Stephen S. Smalley, *1, 2, and 3 John* (Waco, TX: Word, 1984), 232-72.

94. Ernst Käsemann, *The Wandering People of God: An Investigation of the Letter to the He-brews,* trans. R. A. Harrisville and I. L. Sandberg (Minneapolis: Augsburg, 1984), 17-24, 48-63, and 167-73; and Robert Jewett, *Letter to Pilgrims: A Commentary on the Epistle to the Hebrews* (New York: Pilgrim, 1981), esp. 1-17.

Yet in both Johannine theology and in Hebrews there is also a place for *church order*. As Raymond Brown reminds us, in John 21:15-17 Peter is entrusted with pastoral care over the flock; in John 4:35-38 and 12:20 the disciples have a role in mission; and in John 20:23 the church, represented through the apostles, has authority to retain or remit sins.[95] In Heb. 13, love within the community (Heb. 13:10) is complemented by the injunction to "remember your leaders. . . . Obey your leaders and submit to them, for they are keeping watch over your souls" (Heb. 13:7 and 17).

A comprehensive catalogue of "models" would extend far beyond the selection explored by Dulles. We have not yet tapped one of the most "ecclesial" writings of the canon, namely Ephesians, in which the church features as a central theme. The church is conceived in Eph. 1:23 as *the body of Christ* and "the fullness of him who fills all in all." In Eph. 2:12-16 the church is *one people*, in whom "the dividing wall, that is, hostility" (2:14) has been abolished, to become *one body* (2:16). The remainder of that chapter uses a diversity of further images or models: the church is *"home"* for Christians; they are *"citizens* with the saints, and members of *the household of God,* built on the foundation of the apostles and prophets. . . . In Christ the whole structure is joined together, and grows into a *holy temple* in the Lord . . . a *dwelling place for God"* (Eph. 2:19-22). To the church Christ distributes gifts that determine related ministries: "The gifts that he gave were that some would be apostles, some prophets, some evangelists, some pastors and teachers, to equip the saints for the work of ministry, for building up the body of Christ" (Eph. 4:11-12). In whichever way we construe the syntax of "for the work of ministry," as in 1 Cor. 12:12-26, to be the *church* requires that all these roles and ministries need to function as one, for the common goal of *building* what is still in progress until the definitive consummation of the kingdom of God.

A final comment needs to be made on the model of the church as *sacrament*.[96] We discuss the nature of sacraments in the next chapter, Chapter 21. Here, the church serves as a sacrament in the broadest sense of the term, to denote the empirical, visible, embodied, public reality that points to, and explicates, the inward, spiritual truth of the gospel. No Protestant can take exception to the notion that the function of the church is to embody the gospel as a witness to the truth of the gospel, precisely *by pointing beyond itself.* Indeed, this model is a highly "Protestant" reminder of what Tillich and others call the "penultimate" status of the church that points to the ultimacy of God.[97] If we need New Testament support for this, we need only recall that the church is witness to Christ and the cross (Luke 24:48; Acts 1:8; 5:32; Heb. 12:1); as ambassadors to represent

95. Brown, *Gospel*, vol. 1, cx.
96. As in *Lumen Gentium* 1:1 and 7:48.
97. On the provisionality of the church, cf. also Rahner, *Theological Investigations,* vol. 6, 298.

Christ to others (2 Cor. 5:20); and the body of Christ who, in Käsemann's words (discussed above), makes discipleship credible and communicable.

20.3. The "Marks" of the Church and the Ministry of the Church: Apostleship

It is impossible to approach questions about the marks of the church in isolation from questions about the ministry, and vice versa, even as an issue of hermeneutics. Rahner, Pannenberg, and Moltmann, among others, all rightly subordinate questions about the ministry to questions about the church. Moltmann and Pannenberg remind us that confession of faith in the four "marks" (Latin *notae*) of the church as "one, holy, catholic, and apostolic" belong to the "Nicene" Creed of the Council of Constantinople (381).[98] But there is no comparable confession of faith about the nature of the ministry in the ecumenical creeds of the early church.

From earliest times, however, the ministry of the apostles and elders served to maintain *the identity* of the church as one, in the case of the apostles to exercise a transcontextual, translocal oversight that witnessed to its catholicity or universality, and through preaching and teaching to nurture its holiness and faithfulness to apostolic doctrine and traditions.

The First Epistle to the Corinthians constitutes a paradigm case for apostolic and ministerial nurture of the four marks of the church. These "marks," Moltmann insists, are not "criteria" in the sense that an unholy church cannot be called a church, but characteristics that are stated to be essential for the church as *"statements of faith"* (his italics).[99] They are essential characteristics because they derive from Christ as Lord of the church, and acknowledge "the uniting, sanctifying, comprehensive, and commissioning lordship of Christ."[100]

This coheres precisely with recent New Testament research on the nature of *apostleship*. An apostle is one who has been commissioned by Christ. But this does not necessarily strike an authoritarian note. On 1 Cor. 1:1, I commented, "The term points away from [Paul's] own personal wishes or initiative. . . . The term *apostle* entails witness to Christ, not simply in terms of knowledge or doctrine, but also in living out Christ's death and resurrection in practice."[101] Research on apostleship includes the following stages of thought.

(i) In the history of modern New Testament research F. C. Baur (1792-1860) regarded the supposed struggle between an alleged "Petrine" party and a "Pau-

---

98. Moltmann, *The Church in the Power of the Spirit*, 337-38; Pannenberg, *Systematic Theology*, vol. 3, 405-6.

99. Moltmann, *Church*, 338.

100. Moltmann, *Church*, 338.

101. Thiselton, *First Epistle*, 55-56.

line" party as fundamentally one of power based on claims to apostleship.[102] This power-related approach has been slow to die.

(ii) In the 1930s K. L. Rengstorf interpreted apostleship on the analogy of the rabbinic background relating to an official representative or delegate, who was known as one who was sent on behalf of another (שָׁלִיחַ, shālîach).[103] Rengstorf acknowledged that the model of agent should be supplemented by a second analogy of that between apostolic and prophetic call. Yet the rabbinic saying "A man's shālîach is like himself" (Berakoth 3:5) was understood to give grounds for a notion of "apostolic succession," which was promoted in the 1940s by Gregory Dix and A. G. Hebert.[104]

(iii) Predictably a reaction against such an interpretation set in, with decisive critiques from Mosbeck, Rigaux, Hans von Campenhausen, and C. K. Barrett.[105] As early as 1942 E. Käsemann produced a long essay on the "legitimacy" of apostleship, arguing that Paul's "charismatic" opponents in 1 and 2 Corinthians accused Paul of lacking the "signs" of an apostle. In response Paul insists that the "signs" of apostleship are not ecclesiological or "miraculous," but *Christological*.[106] Apostleship is defined in terms of exhibiting the mind (mind-set or stance) of Christ (1 Cor. 2:16). He writes, "The true sign of apostleship is not mighty works, nor ecstatic experiences but . . . service which lives out the cross."[107]

(iv) Käsemann's former pupil John H. Schütz (1975) endeavors to take up Käsemann's approach, but also in the light of Max Weber's sociological distinction between charismatic and institutional authority. He retains Käsemann's positive thesis of the cruciform nature of Paul's apostleship, but concludes with a more questionable claim that Paul's appeal to the Holy Spirit argues on virtually the same ground as that of his opponents. Paul, therefore, offers what amounts to an inconclusive, circular argument.[108]

(v) Rudolf Schnackenburg (1970) argues that Paul knew of no uniform concept of apostleship that embodied clear-cut criteria. But he rejects any attempt to

102. F. C. Baur, "Die Christuspartei in der Korinthischen Gemeinde . . . ," in *Tübinger Zeitschrift für Theologie* 4 (1831) 61-206.

103. Karl L. Rengstorf, "ἀπόστολος (apostolos)," in *TDNT*, vol. 1, 398-447, esp. 407-47.

104. Dom Gregory Dix, "Ministry in the Early Church," in Kenneth Kirk (ed.), *The Apostolic Ministry: Essays on the History and Doctrine of Episcopacy* (London: Hodder & Stoughton, 1946), 183-303; A. G. Hebert, in Kirk, *Ministry,* 493-533.

105. Hans von Campenhausen, *Ecclesiastical Authority and Spiritual Power in the Church of the First Three Centuries,* trans. J. A. Baker (London: Black, 1969), 30-54; H. Mosbeck, "*Apostolos* in the New Testament," *Studia Theologica* 2 (1949-50) 166-200; C. K. Barrett, *Signs of an Apostle* (London: Epworth, 1970), 12-16.

106. Ernst Käsemann, "Die Legitimität des Apostels," *ZNW* 41 (1942) 33-71.

107. Käsemann, "Die Legitimität," 40 and 61.

108. John H. Schütz, *Paul and the Anatomy of Apostolic Authority,* SNTSMS 26 (Cambridge: Cambridge University Press, 1975), 249-86.

play off the "charismatic" and "institutional" against each other, since this imposes anachronistic concepts or categories onto the New Testament.[109] Yet he concedes some guidelines. The apostles were witnesses to the resurrection of Christ, and soon became "a cohesive group." The group expanded to include such figures as Andronicus and Junia (traditionally known as Junias, Rom. 16:7; but on Junia, see Eldon Epp's recent discussion).[110] Like Käsemann, Schnackenburg rightly believes that 2 Cor. 3:1-6 and 12:11 imply that to be an apostle entailed appropriate *behavior* as witness to Christ. "Credentials" include *lifestyle*.

(vi) Bengt Holmberg (1978) emphasizes the *collaborative* nature of the ministry of apostles. Authority among the apostles was diffused in apostolic networks of transcontextual oversight.[111] This coheres convincingly with Anders Eriksson's significant research (1998) on the role of *shared, common, apostolic traditions* as a basis for common doctrine and ethics in the period of Paul's earlier epistles.[112] "Shared leadership," however, is different from the socio-political concept of "democracy," which even P. T. Forsyth, perhaps as a Congregationalist, seeks to infer as part of an ecclesiology, although to be fair to him more typically Forsyth also speaks of the need to "control" democracy in the light of the cross.[113]

(vii) Ernest Best (1986) reflects perhaps the most recent stage of research to date, although also largely anticipated by C. K. Barrett in 1970, and then supported in effect by J. A. Crafton (1991) and others.[114] Apostleship, Best argues, is misunderstood if it is placed only within a hermeneutic of understanding that is focused on "authority." Nevertheless the grounding of apostolic ministry derives from a distinctive apostolic status *as "founders"* of the communities and *as translocal overseers*. In the end, we might say, "the 'grammar' of apostleship rests upon the effectiveness and *transparency of this [apostolic] witness to that for the sake of which apostles were commissioned*."[115] Crafton emphasizes the transparency of apostolic *agency* in contrast to the personalities of apostolic *agents*. Apostles are transparent "windows" through which to see Christ.

---

109. Rudolf Schnackenburg, "Apostles before and during Paul's Time," in Ward Gasque and R. P. Martin (eds.), *Apostolic History and the Gospel: Essays Presented to F. F. Bruce* (Exeter, U.K.: Paternoster, 1970), 287-303.

110. Eldon Jay Epp, *Junia: The First Woman Apostle* (Minneapolis: Fortress, 2005), who offers strong evidence for reading *Junia* in Rom. 16:7.

111. B. Holmberg, *Paul and Power: The Structure of Authority in the Primitive Church as Reflected in the Pauline Epistles* (Lund: Gleerup, 1978), esp. 204-7.

112. Eriksson, *Traditions as Rhetorical Proof*, cited above.

113. P. T. Forsyth, *Lectures on the Church and the Sacraments* (London: Longmans, Green, 1917), 9-25.

114. Ernest Best, "Paul's Apostolic Authority," *JSNT* 27 (1986) 3-25; Barrett, *The Signs of an Apostle*, 36-46; J. A. Crafton, *The Agency of the Apostle*, JSNTSS 51 (Sheffield: Sheffield Academic Press, 1991), 53-103.

115. Thiselton, *First Epistle*, 673; cf. 55-68 and 663-75.

Such apostolic ministry is vital to the preservation of the four "marks" of the church: a church that expresses a translocal unity; a community growing in holiness; a people sharing the same history, destiny, and loyalty; and a community grounded in shared apostolic traditions, doctrine, and lifestyle of Christological and cruciform character. Without the primary founding witnesses to the death and resurrection of Christ, *the identity and continuity* of the church would have been at risk. James Smart observes that without the witness of the apostolic circle transmitted through Scripture, "soon the remembered Christ becomes an imagined Christ."[116] In our discussion of Christology we observed in 17.2 and 17.4 that many in modern times have appeared relatively untroubled by, indeed even to encourage, the notion of "many Christs."

Traditionally it has been assumed that this ministry of foundation witnesses characterized the role of "the Twelve" in the Acts of the Apostles. Hans von Campenhausen distinguished Luke's emphasis upon "the Twelve" as witnesses to the life and teaching of Jesus from Paul's broader conception of the apostolate.[117] E. Lohse argued for a first stage of development similar to Rengstorf's notion of the synagogue official as *shālîach,* followed by a second stage in which the apostolate became a more institutional ministry.[118] Interpretations of the election of Matthias (Acts 1:15-26) remain controversial. Many argue that a twelfth apostle was elected to serve with the eleven as part of a "founding college" of the church. G. Klein argues for an "institutional" understanding of the Twelve, and sees the threefold account of Paul's call and conversion in Acts as Luke's attempt to undermine any notion that Paul is an independent, "freelance" agent of the gospel.[119]

To draw such a picture from Gal. 1:11-24 would be a serious mistake, since Paul regularly insists that he receives and passes on a shared, apostolic, pre-Pauline tradition (cf. Rom. 1:3-4; 4:24; 10:9; 1 Cor. 11:23-26; 15:3-5; Phil. 2:6-11; 1 Thess. 4:1).[120] There is no reason to set Paul's consciousness of a "direct" call from God (Gal. 1:12-17; reflecting Jer. 1:4-5) against the action of the church in Antioch in recognizing, validating, and commissioning Paul for wider mission (Acts 13:1-3). This dual source of call, in which a sense of direct divine commission has to be recognized and affirmed by the church, has characterized the experience of "call" on the part of many or most who become ordained as clergy or in

116. James D. Smart, *The Strange Silence of the Birth of the Church* (London: S.C.M., 1970), 25.

117. Hans von Campenhausen, "Der urchristliche Apostelbegriff," *Studia Theologica* 1 (1947) 96-130.

118. E. Lohse, "Ursprung und Prägung des christlichen Apostolates," *Theologische Zeitschrift* 9 (1953) 259-75.

119. G. Klein, *Die Zwölf Apostel: Ursprung und Gehalt einer Idee* (Göttingen: Vandenhoeck & Ruprecht, 1961).

120. See Eriksson, *Traditions as Rhetorical Proof;* also A. M. Hunter, *Paul and His Predecessors* (London: S.C.M., 2d edn. 1961).

some other vocation. Luke recounts *both* the call of Paul "out of the blue" in Acts 9:3-9, 22:6-11; 26:12-19, which accords with Galatians, *and* his being set apart by the church, which accords with his respect for shared, transmitted, apostolic traditions. Luke easily holds these two sides together.

The ambiguous word here is "foundation." Paul alludes to *Christ as the only foundation* (1 Cor. 3:11). Hence the apostolate serves as a "foundation" (Eph. 2:20; cf. 1 Cor. 12:28) *not* in the sense that *the being of the church depends on the prior existence of the apostles,* but in the sense that *the apostolate provides a visible and public basis for the preservation and transmission of the church's recognizable identity and continuity as "apostolic."*

J. Roloff's more recent study of apostleship in Acts suggests that the apostolate itself is first grounded in Christ's lordship and commission, and the nature of the gospel itself. Then through participation in the mission of Christ and in salvation history apostleship makes concrete a continuity that becomes visible in the institution of the Lord's Supper and in apostolic traditions.[121] Apostolic "succession" is a *theological and Christological continuity* rather than an institutional and structural one. The upshot is to close much of the gap that many scholars have overstated between *apostle* in Paul and *apostle* in Luke-Acts. Roloff also rightly stresses the *living out* of apostleship in Christ-oriented διακονία *(diakonia).* Luke's emphasis on "the Twelve," he adds, was due partly to incipient gnostic appeals to secret, esoteric tradition.

Paul expresses this complementary balance *between too high a view of the ministry* and *too low a view of the ministry* in 1 Cor. 3:5-23. His argument provides a fundamental horizon of understanding both for apostleship and for other wider ministries. He begins by alluding to the apostolic persons of Apollos and himself in terms of a *neuter* pronoun: "*What* [Greek neuter, τί, *ti*] then is Apollos? What is Paul? *Servants* (διάκονοι, *diakonoi*) through whom you came to believe, as *the Lord* assigned to each" (1 Cor. 3:5, NRSV). Paul then holds together the contingent, specific series of actions on the part of ministers (conveyed by Greek aorists) with the fundamental, continuous process of giving life to the church, which God alone can do (conveyed by the Greek imperfect): "I planted, Apollos watered, but *God went on giving the increase*" (1 Cor. 3:6). Paul explicates the point: "So then neither the one who plants nor the one who waters is anything, but God who went on giving the increase" (1 Cor. 3:7). The context finds expression in 3:4: "When someone declares, 'I, for one, am one of Paul's people,' and another asserts, 'I, for my part, am for Apollos', are you not all too human?"[122]

Paul is equally concerned that by self-selecting the ministers whom they

---

121. J. Roloff, *Apostolat, Verkündigung, Kirche: Ursprung, Inhalt und Funktion des Kirchlichen Apostelamtes nach Paulus, Lukas, und den Pastoralbriefen* (Gütersloh: Gütersloher Verlagshaus/Mohn, 1965).

122. Thiselton, *First Epistle,* 286-303.

wish to follow and to hear, Christians in Corinth are "cheating themselves" out of *essential ministerial resources.* These are necessary as instrumental conditions for growth: "Let no one be self-deceived. . . . For all things are yours, whether Paul or Apollos or Cephas or the world or life . . . all are yours, and you are Christ's, and Christ is God's" (1 Cor. 3:18 and 22-23). On one side, ministers are mere instruments, and God is all; on the other side, ministers provide practical conditions for growth and "building up" within the church (1 Cor. 3:9b-17). Christ alone is the foundation (3:11); but the process of building requires pastoral, theological, and strategic oversight (the ἀρχιτέκτων, *architektōn;* see above, 3:10), and diverse roles on the part of ministers to resource other needs for the task.

Within this hermeneutic of understanding, ministry on the part of those commissioned and recognized by appropriate authority remains essential if the church is to remain or to become *one, holy, catholic, and apostolic.* On this reading of 1 Corinthians, ministers are not chosen on a competitive market-consumer basis by persons within a local congregation. I have argued elsewhere that this is a major issue for a theology of ministry in Corinth.[123] Corinth was a highly competitive city, preoccupied with success, business, market consumerism, and competitive rhetoric. The church there was still largely saturated with values drawn from this culture. Many in the local church deified "autonomy," and wished to choose their own leaders, their own ethics, their own theology, their own triumphalist interpretation of the gospel, and their own criteria of "spirituality." Paul has to redefine a number of their theological terms, not least "free," "all things are lawful," "we reign as kings," and "spiritual." From among scores of examples of recent research cited in the article to which I have referred, Pogoloff (1992), Moores (1995), Brown (1995), Hall (2004), and Welborn (2005) show how Paul's reproclamation of the cross transformed the Corinthian "world" and set forth "an understanding of the Church as one, holy, catholic, and apostolic."[124] David Hall states: "In both 1 and 2 Corinthians a contrast is drawn between two gospels and two lifestyles," and an understanding of the Holy Spirit that amounted to "a different Spirit."[125]

In the history of Christian thought the four "marks" of the church have

---

123. Thiselton, "The Significance of Recent Research on 1 Corinthians," in *Neot.* 40, n. 2 (2006) 91-123.

124. Thiselton, *Neot.* 40 (2006) 91, citing Stephen Pogoloff, *Logos and Sophia: The Rhetorical Situation of 1 Corinthians* (Atlanta: Scholars Press, 1992); John Moores, *Wrestling with Rationality in Paul: Romans 1–8 in a New Perspective,* JSNTMS 82 (Cambridge: Cambridge University Press, 1995); Alexandra Brown, *The Cross and Human Transformation: Paul's Apocalyptic Word in 1 Corinthians* (Minneapolis: Fortress, 1995); David R. Hall, *The Unity of the Corinthian Correspondence,* JSNTSS 251 (London and New York: T&T Clark, 2005); and L. L. Welborn, *Paul, the Fool of Christ: A Study of 1 Corinthians 1–4 in the Light of Comic-Philosophical Traditions,* JSNTSS 293 (London and New York: T&T Clark, 2002).

125. Hall, *Unity,* 163 and 183.

sometimes, on one side, been overstated as hard-edged criteria, but sometimes treated with insufficient seriousness. This applies to each of the four expected features of the church.

In some circles the unity or oneness of the church has been regarded as a purely theological, invisible mark of all who are "in Christ," and this is part of the grammar of the concept: "There is one body and one Spirit . . . one hope . . . one Lord, one faith, one baptism, one God . . ." (Eph. 4:3-5). Yet this epistle exhorts its readers to show eager concern not to let this unity splinter apart: σπουδάζοντες τηρεῖν τὴν ἑνότητα τοῦ πνεύματος, *spoudazontes tērein tēn henotēta tou pneumatos* (4:3). Robert Nelson discusses this concept of unity.[126] The unity of the church, however, is both given and lived out. Thornton cites the analogy of grafting in horticulture as Paul's example of being "united by growth" (Rom. 11:17).[127] Some writers apply a questionable hermeneutic as if to infer that prior, given oneness in Christ exonerates Christians from all obligation to make it visible in everyday life. Others place ecumenism at the top of the agenda so obsessively as to push other priorities out of the way.

The holiness of the church has also suffered misinterpretation in two opposite directions. The Donatists, to whom some might perhaps wish to add some of the Puritans, turned the legitimate call for holiness into a power-bid for exclusivity and division. On the other side, some traditions appear to interpret the holy only in moralistic terms, and to seek to assimilate the church of God into a quasi-secular arm of the social services. If the former trend is pressed so hard that it "unchurches" those who fail, this undermines the truth of justification by grace through faith, which recognizes that those who are the church are *simul iustus et peccator*. If the latter is unchallenged, holiness ceases to be that quality which transparently mediates the presence and glory of God.

In *Believing in the Church* the Doctrine Commission of the Church of England sought a middle way, arguing that there must be boundaries and limits to the church if it is not to lose its identity as the church (cf. 1 Cor. 5:1-5; 1 Tim. 4:1-16; 1 John 4:1-21), but these are often blurred and permeable rather than sharp and overly rigid boundaries. They serve a positive purpose to maintain the recognizable identity and credibility of the church. They defeat their purpose if they simply exclude anyone who is not like-minded, leaving the church as a group that provides only self-affirmation without challenge for its members. John Macquarrie sets the work of the Commission in context in a chapter on "The Anglican Theological Tradition."[128]

We have already considered the nature of *apostolicity* with particular refer-

---

126. J. Robert Nelson, *The Realm of Redemption: Studies in the Doctrine of the Church in Contemporary Protestant Theology* (London: Epworth, 1951), 200-210.

127. Thornton, *Common Life*, 61-65.

128. John Macquarrie, *Theology, Church, and Ministry* (London: SCM, 1986), 91-104.

ence to *apostleship* in Luke-Acts and in the Pauline epistles. We have also noted the transcontextual and translocal significance of *catholicity* especially with reference to Paul's disquiet concerning notions of "local" autonomy in Corinth. Yet over the centuries the actual currency of these two terms for the church of the day has often been disputed.

Apostolicity has usually been interpreted in terms of faithfulness to apostolic doctrine as revealed in the Scriptures and interpreted in the light of shared ecclesial traditions and the responsible use of Spirit-led reason. One source of debate has been that of different responses to the questions (i) "Is the authority of the apostles transferable?" and (ii) "What happens to the authority of the apostles after their deaths?" The formulations here are Brunner's.[129] Brunner offers firmly Protestant answers, namely, "no," to the first question, and in response to the second, "The Apostolate has validity only in one form: as the norm of the original tradition fixed in writing, the norm of the original witness of the New Testament."[130] Although earlier Catholic traditions held more mechanistic theories of apostolic succession, Vatican II still calls attention to a continuing apostolic role on the part of successors. The documents assert, "The apostles were careful to appoint successors in this hierarchically constituted society. . . . They made the ruling that on their death other proven men should take over their ministry."[131] More explicitly, *The Decree on the Pastoral Office of Bishops in the Church* states, "The bishops also have been designated by the Holy Spirit to take the place of the apostles as pastors."[132]

Pannenberg believes that differences regarding the nature of ministry among different ecclesiological tradition "now seem not to be insuperable," although he concedes that the issue of "who is authorized to give a valid ordination" still raises considerable difficulties, including what is "conferred" or "imparted" at ordination.[133] In Pannenberg's view, because *apostolicity* involves participation in the mission of Christ, "the church's holiness comes close to its apostolicity . . . to bear witness to the universal and definitive truth of the revelation of God as Jesus Christ."[134] This surely involves its catholicity as well.

Lesslie Newbigin recognized that at the level of the heart rather than the head, the traditions of the church tended to define continuity of catholic and apostolic faith in one of three, in effect competing, ways: (i) in terms of "institu-

---

129. Emil Brunner, *The Christian Doctrine of the Church, Faith, and the Consummations: Dogmatics* vol. 3, trans. David Cairns (London: Lutterworth, 1962), 49.

130. Brunner, *Doctrine of the Church*, 50 and 51.

131. Vatican II, *Lumen Gentium* (21 November 1964) 29:20, in Flannery (ed.), *Documents of Vatican II*, 371.

132. Vatican II, *Decree of the Pastoral Office of Bishops in the Church, Christus Dominus*, 28 October 1965, 2, in Flannery (ed.), *Documents of Vatican II*, 564.

133. Pannenberg, *Systematic Theology*, vol. 3, 399; cf. 398 and 397-431.

134. Pannenberg, *Systematic Theology*, vol. 3, 406.

tional" or hierarchical continuity through episcopal succession; (ii) in terms of faithfulness to apostolic doctrine as revealed in Scripture and faithfully proclaimed afresh; and (iii) in terms of a living experience and manifestation of the signs of the work of the Holy Spirit.[135] He associated these respectively with Roman Catholic, Protestant-Reformation, and Pentecostal mind-sets. Fifty years later, however, each tradition has to some degree shifted to embrace aspects of others, and these are no longer to be understood as alternative rather than complementary ways of safeguarding and discerning the continuity of the church's apostolicity and catholicity.

If we seek a *hermeneutic* that may do better justice to the transition from the New Testament to historical traditions, it is worth heeding Anthony T. Hanson's counsel to look not at abstract "problems" about ministry, but to see how ministry was *actually carried out* in the New Testament.[136] For example, whatever theoretical impressions we may receive from Gal. 1:11-24, in the event Paul works collaboratively with a host of colleagues, including Barnabas, Silvanus, Apollos, Timothy, Titus, Epaphras, Mark, Luke, Priscilla, Aquila, and many others, nine of whom are named among a plurality of "apostles."[137]

Whatever view we may take of the precise relation between apostles and *episkopoi,* both appear to have ministered as overseers beyond the context of a single city, town, or region. Both defend and maintain a translocal "orderedness." The third edition of the Greek lexicon BDAG (2000) comments: "*Episkopos* was taken over in Christian communities in reference to one who served as *overseer* or *supervisor,* with a special interest in guarding the apostolic tradition (Irenaeus, Origen, Hippolytus . . . Acts 20:28; Phil 1:1; Tit 1:7)."[138] In view of the fact that Roman Catholics, Orthodox, Lutherans, Anglicans, Methodists, and others exercise *episkopē* in different institutional ways and terms BDAG (Danker) comments that *bishop* may have become too loaded a term today to function as an *exact* equivalent. Nevertheless the key function of the *episkopos* in the New Testament and early Patristic literature is *to guard the apostolic faith* (Tit. 1:7), especially as part of a "college of bishops" or "overseers."

Gerd Theissen has popularized a contrast that may well be open to question, namely between "community organizers" and "itinerant charismatics." This is drawn in part from Weber's contrast between *charisma,* office, and functionalist theory.[139] To my mind, "traveling" ministries did not stand in transparent con-

---

135. Lesslie Newbigin, *The Household of Faith: Lectures on the Nature of the Church* (London: S.C.M., 1953), throughout.

136. Anthony T. Hanson, *The Pioneer Ministry* (London: S.C.M., 1961), 46.

137. Rom. 16:3, 9, 21; 1 Cor. 3:9; 2 Cor. 8:23; Phil. 2:25; 4:3; Col. 4:11; 1 Thess. 3:2; Phlm. 24.

138. BDAG, 379.

139. Gerd Theissen, *The First Followers of Jesus: A Sociological Analysis of the Earliest Christianity* (London: S.C.M., 1978); American edition: *Sociology of Early Palestinian Christianity* (Philadelphia: Fortress, 1978).

trast with "institutional order," but rather the reverse. As pastors, they nurtured a translocal or "catholic" "order" of doctrine, liturgy, and lifestyle. It is possible that Theissen's theory applies to an earlier era than Paul's. But too many writers uncritically impose Theissen's categories upon the middle and later years of the first century.

At all events the Pastoral Epistles constitute no mere inferior "descent" from the earlier Pauline epistles. After the key issues of the nature of the gospel had received clarification in Romans, 1 and 2 Corinthians, Galatians, and other earlier literature, the next step was to insure the *maintenance* of these hard-won traditions. This stage is in no way an *alternative* to mission; it is part of the conditions for preserving the vision in order to continue mission. Hence in the Pastoral Epistles an ἐπίσκοπος *(episkopos)* must be skilled to teach (διδακτικός *didaktikos,* 1 Tim. 3:2. This is repeated in *2 Clement* 2:36; in Irenaeus, *Against Heresies* IV:26:2; and later in Chrysostom with reference to preaching, *De Sacerdotio* VII:4:5). An *episkopos* must be *level-headed* or *stable* (νηφάλιος, *nēphalios,* 1 Tim. 3:2); *gracious* or *courteous* (ἐπιεικής, *epieikēs,* 1 Tim. 3:3); and *one who dislikes conflict* (ἄμαχος, *amachos,* 1 Tim. 3:3). An *episkopos* must also be κοσμίος *(kosmios),* which may either denote *an adornment to the church* or mean a *person or ordered mind and habits* (both meanings are possible, 1 Tim. 3:2). All of these qualities are appropriate for a senior pastor or bishop who is more in the public eye than more local ministers, and who oversees other pastors within a translocal region rather than a smaller locality. The "bishop" must be able *to teach* the apostolic faith with skill, wisdom, and integrity. Such a person needs to be *stable* in the face of conflicting cross-currents and fashions, or "winds of doctrine." As one who dislikes conflict, the capacity for conflict resolution may be required, and the theological role of "bishops" has consistently been perceived, at least in principle if not always in practice, as a focus of unity over the centuries.[140]

We have attempted to offer a hermeneutic of the doctrine of the church that shows that within the New Testament and in early theological development no tension exists in principle between the theological and institutional aspects of the church. Some kind of infrastructure is needed to implement the call of God to share in the mission of God, and to promote the theological vision that institutional factors serve. The incisive, critical question concerns whether and when infrastructure becomes first top-heavy and then may become an end in itself, serving only itself.

---

140. For a schematic list of the qualities required for *episkopoi, presbuteroi,* and *diakonoi* in the Pastorals see esp. William D. Mounce, *Pastoral Epistles,* WBC 46 (Nashville: Nelson, 2000), 155-60, with a useful bibliography on 149-52.

CHAPTER 21

The Hermeneutics of Word and Sacraments:
Baptism and the Lord's Supper or the Eucharist

21.1. Five Questions for Hermeneutics about Understanding the Sacraments

(i) The Emergence of the Term "Sacrament"

The term *sacrament* does not occur in the New Testament. C. K. Barrett rightly insists that although this fact is uncontested and widely known, the significance of this fact is widely overlooked in discussions of the sacraments.[1]

The word first enters Christian currency in c. A.D. 200, which is the approximate date of Tertullian's treatise *On Baptism*. The traditional translation of *On Baptism* 1:1 begins, "Here is our sacrament of water, in that by washing away of sins, we are set free . . ." (Latin *De sacramento aquae nostrae qua ablutis pristinae caecitatis in vitam aeternam liberamur*). However, in his critical edition of 1964 Ernest Evans translates this sentence, "*The sacred significance* of that water of ours in which sins . . . are washed away and we are set at liberty unto life eternal. . . ."[2] Yet in spite of this, Evans maintains in his Introduction, "By *sacramentum aquae nostrae* Tertullian means the sacrament of baptism," and cites other sources in Tertullian for further support.[3] In *Against Marcion* Tertullian writes: *nec alibi coniunctos (married persons) ad sacramentum baptismatis et eucharistiae admittens nisi. . . .*[4] Elsewhere Tertullian says that God wills all who are presbyters to be ready to undertake the duties of the sacraments

1. Barrett, *Church, Ministry, and Sacraments*, 55-57.
2. Ernest Evans (ed.), *Tertullian's Homily on Baptism: Introduction, Translation, and Commentary* (London: S.P.C.K., 1964), 4.
3. Evans (ed.), *Homily on Baptism*, "Introduction," xxxviii.
4. Tertullian, *Against Marcion* IV:35.

at all times: *omnes nos deus ita vult dispositos esse ut ubique sacramentis obeundis apti simus.*[5]

Some appeal to the origins of the Greek counterpart or equivalent to this sense of *sacrament,* namely μυστήριον *(mustērion).* But as Lampe's *Patristic Greek Lexicon* confirms, the earliest use of the term in this sense appears in the fourth century with Eusebius.[6]

Such scattered Patristic references, however, even if they soon come to represent an established consensus, stem from biblical foundations only in the light of retrospective interpretation of biblical understandings of baptism and the Eucharist or the Lord's Supper. Such postapostolic traditions may well be valid, but clearly they cannot constitute a hermeneutical starting point. Any theology of the sacraments as "sacraments" will be contingent on prior conclusions about the nature of baptism and the Lord's Supper, and on possible inferences drawn from the New Testament about the use of "embodied" words, actions, or speech-acts that use the physical or empirical to point beyond themselves to spiritual realities, events, or truths.

The absence of the actual *term sacrament* from the biblical writings contributes to the hermeneutic with which we begin. On the other hand, more positively, broader questions in semiotics and in philosophy of language concerning the currency of speech-acts and the preconditions for their efficacious functioning *do* provide a starting point for a hermeneutic of the sacraments. Recently Marvin Duffy has provided a careful critical study of "how ritual and sacraments work" in the light of speech-act theory in J. L. Austin, J. Habermas, and Louis-Marie Chauvet.[7] Duffy draws on wider speech-act theory, including that of Donald Evans, Richard Briggs, and Jean Ladrière, whose work was the subject of another of my Nottingham Ph.D. candidates, David Hilborn.[8] Duffy rightly stresses "self-implication" in the sacraments (cf. Evans on "self-involvement"), especially in the context of "those celebrating in the present bond with the founding community and the generations between then and now."[9] This reinforces the catholicity of the church, as Chauvet observes. As with "politeness theory," to which we alluded in Part I, Duffy explores the social grounding and social effects of speech-acts.

---

5. Tertullian, *On Exhortation to Chastity* 7.

6. G. W. H. Lampe, *A Patristic Greek Lexicon* (Oxford: Clarendon, 1961), 891-93, esp. 892-93, section F: Eusebius, *Demonstratio Evangelica* 9:6 (of baptism); Cyril of Jerusalem, *Catecheses* 19:1; Basil, *On the Spirit*, 66.

7. Marvyn Duffy, *How Language, Ritual, and Sacraments Work according to John Austin, Jürgen Habermas, and Louis-Marie Chauvet,* Tesi Gregoriana Serie Teologia 123 (Rome: Pontifical Gregorian University, 2005).

8. David Hilborn, *The Pragmatics of Liturgical Discourse* (Carlisle, U.K.: Paternoster, in the press).

9. Duffy, *Language, Ritual, and Sacraments,* 178; cf. 175-80.

(ii) Avoiding Imposing Prior Categorizations and Concepts

Gadamer, we have seen, insists on *openness* and on the need to avoid imposing prior categorizations and concepts onto the questions and subject matter that we seek to understand. He urges that we let the subject matter speak *on its own terms.* Questions that take some such form as "How many sacraments are there?" *presuppose* a whole way of looking at the relation between baptism, the Eucharist, ordination, marriage, and the wider use of symbolic objects and observable events. The argument must move in the reverse direction: *from* the contingent and particular *to* conclusions about such issues as those of definition.

Wittgenstein makes parallel points about "the particular case" and about how "a drop of grammar" embedded in a generalization can generate an entire way of looking at things. He observes in parenthesis: "(A whole cloud of philosophy condensed into a drop of grammar)."[10] We argued in Chapter 3 through to 6 that "classifying" or "category-ascribing" approaches doctrine in a way that is seriously at odds with hermeneutics, even if such respected thinkers as Lindbeck come nearer than they need to adopting this method. If this shapes an introduction or starting point, the damage is done, and the drop of grammar becomes irrevocably embedded within a horizon of understanding as a forgotten presupposition. Wittgenstein speaks of such embedded material as "removed from traffic" but as nevertheless belonging "to the scaffolding of our thought."[11]

For this reason a valid hermeneutic of understanding would ask not in the abstract, "How many sacraments are there?" but "How does a sacrament function and what might be its nature or status *within the following contexts:* (a) within a seven-sacrament system; (b) within a two "dominical" sacraments system; (c) within an "incarnational" life-as-sacramental system; (d) in relation to theology of baptism; (e) in relation to theology of Holy Communion; (f) in relation to questions about ordination and marriage; *and so on.* To follow this method is to respect hermeneutical particularity and to respond to *questions that arise* in their own right rather than to inherited abstract *"problems."*

(iii) Initial Horizons of Understanding: Baptism

Some horizons of understanding are embedded in the popular mind that to some degree are alien to the theologies of the biblical writings. Rudolf Schnackenburg considers one such example in his classic, near-definitive study *Baptism in the Thought of Paul.* It is a tribute to the fair-mindedness of this work that it bears the Catholic *Nihil Obstat* and *Imprimatur,* and has also been translated by a

---

10. Wittgenstein, *Philosophical Investigations,* II:xi, 222.
11. Wittgenstein, *On Certainty,* sects. 210 and 211.

leading British Baptist.[12] Schnackenburg discusses the theological significance of baptism especially in Paul under three themes: baptism as cleansing and regeneration; baptism as incorporation in Christ; and baptism as a salvation event of dying and being raised with Christ. Several factors combine to suggest that *"washing"* or *"cleansing"* is relatively peripheral in relation to the other two major themes.

Schnackenburg writes, "The washing away of sins does not represent the whole significance of becoming a Christian."[13] Some early texts do speak of baptism "for the forgiveness of sins" (Acts 2:38), but the emphasis upon being baptized "in the name of Christ" is more distinctive and more central. Indeed, one problem with this theme is that "the idea of cleansing in baptism also forms a bridge to ancient and widespread views of baptism in heathenism."[14] Schnackenburg does not mince his words. The balance of emphasis, he argues cogently, is found elsewhere. This may suggest the need to revise what for many constitutes the primary preunderstanding for arriving at an interpretation of the meaning of baptism.

(iv) A Parallel Hermeneutical Question about Infant Baptism

Many have defended each point of view in debates about believers' baptism and infant baptism. A classic debate took place between two New Testament specialists, Joachim Jeremias and Kurt Aland, in 1960-62.[15] Jeremias produced a study in which he examined the background of proselyte baptism and the *"oikos"* formula of household baptisms, which included Lydia (Acts 16:15), the jailer of Philippi (Acts 16:31-33), and Stephanas (1 Cor. 1:16; cf. 1 Cor. 16:15). He also explored other New Testament passages, and examined the development of baptism and infant baptism up to the end of the third century.[16]

Aland responded by arguing that these "households" did not necessarily include children, but rather, in their context, slaves and other adults. He argued that over the first two centuries the church imposed an age-limit on baptism, and

---

12. Rudolf Schnackenburg, *Baptism in the Thought of Paul,* trans. G. R. Beasley-Murray (Oxford: Blackwell, 1964).

13. Schnackenburg, *Baptism,* 7.

14. Schnackenburg, *Baptism,* 8.

15. Joachim Jeremias, *Infant Baptism in the First Four Centuries,* trans. David Cairns (London: S.C.M., 1960), from the 1958 German edn. with new material; Kurt Aland, *Did the Early Church Baptize Infants?* trans. G. R. Beasley Murray (London: S.C.M., 1962); and Joachim Jeremias, *The Origins of Infant Baptism: A Further Study in Reply to Kurt Aland,* trans. D. M. Burton (London: S.C.M., 1963).

16. These correspond broadly with the three main chapters in Jeremias, *Infant Baptism,* 19-87.

that infant baptism became an innovation only around 200-203.[17] Jeremias replied to Aland in a second study, reviewing their common agenda, household baptisms, and Aland's claims about an age-limit during the first two centuries. He challenged the supposed reason cited by Aland for delaying the baptism of children, and Aland's contention that baptismal policy changed around A.D. 200. He reaffirmed the situational significance of Jewish proselyte baptism and issues about Hellenistic mystery rites.[18]

Appeals to historical sources and to exegesis might appear to be inconclusive, since both sides tend to use the same data to argue their case. The real issue is a deeper one. It is *hermeneutical,* for, as Jeremias declares, the debate ultimately turns on *two different understandings of baptism.* Yet again the primary attention accorded to baptism as *cleansing* confuses the issue. Aland arguably gives hostages to fortune by suggesting that since baptism denotes washing or cleansing, the earliest church believed that baptism was unnecessary for infants. He writes: "Because children are innocent, they do not need baptism; they need it only when sinfulness awakens."[19] Jeremias has no difficulty in arguing that "washing" is only an aspect, and probably not the central aspect, of baptism.

A parallel hermeneutical divide comes between two different models or understandings represented respectively by Wheeler Robinson and by Oscar Cullmann. Robinson insists that "believers' baptism" is "a simple return to primitive Christian custom." He reasons: "It implies a *cleansing from sin*" (his italics); "Believers' Baptism emphasizes . . . the necessity and the individuality of *conversion*" (his italics); it is a *conscious* acceptance of his authority" (his italics).[20]

Cullmann, by contrast, begins with the theology of baptism in Rom. 6:1-11 as dying with Christ in terms of *new creation.* Baptism is not just "individual," but relates to "the individual inside the community."[21] Against Robinson's (and Barth's) supposition that the New Testament requires "consciousness," Cullmann insists that the emphasis falls on the saving action of Christ whether or not *"cognitio"* is involved.[22] It is not an act of "informing." Above all, Cullmann argues, "It is of the essence [of divine grace] that faith must *follow* as answer to the divine act"; faith is not a "precondition" of reception into covenant of grace *or grace would not be grace,* to which baptism bears witness.[23] In a study that has been unduly neglected, Pierre Marcel also argues that the priority of grace, a the-

---

17. Aland, *Did the Early Church Baptize Infants?* 53-74, 87-94, 101-2.

18. On proselyte baptism cf. Jeremias, *Infant Baptism,* 37.

19. Aland, *Did the Early Church Baptize Infants?* 106.

20. H. Wheeler Robinson, *Baptist Principles* (London: Carey Kingsgate, 4th edn. 1960), 11, 13, 17, and 23.

21. Oscar Cullmann, *Baptism in the New Testament,* trans. J. K. S. Reid (London: S.C.M., 1950), 29.

22. Cullmann, *Baptism,* 31.

23. Cullmann, *Baptism,* 33.

ology of covenant and covenant signs, and the parallel effectiveness of word and sacrament reach the heart of the debate about infant baptism.[24]

On the issue of "interpretation" of evidence, Cullmann rejects the notion that arguments from silence point only in one direction. He writes, "Those who dispute the Biblical character of infant baptism have therefore to reckon with the fact that *adult baptism for sons and daughters born of Christian parents . . . is even worse attested by the New Testament than infant baptism*" (Cullmann's italics). Here judgments about how changes of historical situation reshape hermeneutical understanding become inescapable.

It has not been the explicit aim of these paragraphs to press one side of the debate over against the other, but to expose the underlying *hermeneutical* complexities that underlie divergent traditions of understanding. The reduction of the debate about infant baptism to questions of "evidence" disregards the point that the hermeneutics of *what baptism means* brings us far nearer to the heart of this issue.

(v) Understandings of the Eucharist or the Lord's Supper Presuppose a Complexity of Hermeneutical Issues

My own convictions and beliefs about the meaning of the Lord's Supper provide an example. With many other scholars I believe that *the narrative of the Passover constitutes the appropriate and indispensable horizon of understanding* for interpreting the Lord's Supper and its words of institution. The meaning of "This is my body. . . . This is my blood" (Matt. 26:26-28; Mark 14:22-24; Luke 22:19-20 (v. 20, variant: "the new covenant in my blood"); 1 Cor. 11:24-25 (similar to Luke) is to my mind determined by the parallel "This is the bread of affliction" in the Passover *Seder*.[25] Here the *exegesis* of τοῦτο μού ἐστιν τὸ σῶμα τὸ ὑπὲρ ὑμῶν (*touto mou estin to sōma to huper humōn*, 1 Cor. 11:24) is inseparable from the *hermeneutical* function that it is judged to carry in a specific context or horizon of meaning. We discuss this further in 21.3.

---

24. Pierre C. Marcel, *The Biblical Doctrine of Infant Baptism: Sacrament of the Covenant of Grace*, trans. Philip E. Hughes (London: Clarke, 1953), 34-98 and throughout.

25. I argue this in Thiselton, "Was the Last Supper a Passover Meal? Significance for Exegesis," in *First Epistle to the Corinthians*, 871-82; see also F. J. Leenhardt, "This Is My Body," in Oscar Cullmann and Leenhardt, *Essays on the Lord's Supper*, trans. J. G. Davies (London: Lutterworth, 1958), 39-40. More broadly Otfried Hofius, "The Lord's Supper and the Lord's Supper Tradition: Reflections on 1 Cor. 11:23b-25," in Ben F. Meyer (ed.), *One Loaf, One Cup: Ecumenical Studies of 1 Cor. 11 and Other Eucharistic Texts*, Cambridge Conference of August 1988 (Macon, GA: Mercer University Press, 1988), 75-115; and Joachim Jeremias, *The Eucharistic Words of Jesus*, trans. Norman Perrin (London: S.C.M., 1966), 41-105. See also Oscar Cullmann and F. J. Leenhardt, *Essays on the Lord's Supper* (London: Lutterworth, 1958), especially Leenhardt.

The same principle applies to several other closely related exegetical and doctrinal issues. Do the words "not discerning the body" (1 Cor. 11:29) refer to the body of Christ as the church in Corinth, or to the body of Christ as signified or represented by the sacred elements of bread, or to both, or to something other or more? Can we be certain whether Johannine notions of "feeding" on the bread of life (John 6:35-37, 48-51) are specifically "Eucharistic," or whether allusions to feeding on Christ as the bread of life are symbolic or "sacramental" in a broader sense? Again, we cannot separate exegesis from hermeneutics.

One of the few entirely uncontroversial themes of the Eucharist or Lord's Supper is that of *unity* or *oneness*. Eucharistic liturgy and practice in all churches in every century presuppose the doctrinal and liturgical importance of 1 Cor. 10:16-17: "The cup of blessing" is "a sharing in the blood of Christ. . . . The bread that we break, is it not a sharing of the body of Christ? *Because there is one bread, we who are many are one body, for we all partake of the one bread*" (NRSV). Many versions of the Eucharistic canon include extracts from this passage or from *Didache* 9:4: "As the broken bread was scattered upon the mountains but was brought together and became one, so let thy Church be gathered together as one."

Virtually all traditions agree about the exegesis and emphasis of this theme, but is there more to be said about the *hermeneutical application?* John Zizioulas makes an incisive comment. Being *one*, he argues, concerns not only *social* divisions, "but *also natural* divisions (such as age, race, etc.). . . . There never was [in the early church] a celebration of the Eucharist especially for children, or for students etc., nor a Eucharist that could take place privately and individually. Such a thing would destroy precisely the catholic character of the eucharist which was *leiturgia*, i.e., a 'public work' for *all* Christians of the same city."[26] This seems axiomatic, but this *hermeneutical application* seems widely to have collapsed. It is entirely inappropriate to be asked to preside at a Communion "for the youth fellowship," or "for the Mother's Union," or to hear a fellow priest talk about having "his own altar." Nevertheless it happens. Perhaps this adds further force to the need for a *hermeneutic of doctrine that shapes practice and life.*

21.2. Hermeneutics and the Word of God, and Issues about Word and Sacrament

In the normal course of events this subject would require one of the longest chapters in the present book, as a large and sensitive topic in its own right. Karl Barth devoted two of the fourteen large volumes of the English edition of his *Church Dogmatics* to the doctrine of the Word of God. This includes an exposi-

---

26. Zizioulas, *Being as Communion*, 151-52 (his italics).

tion of a very broad theological and hermeneutical horizon of understanding within which "Word of God" is to be interpreted, focusing especially upon God's initiative and grace in self-revelation. As he comments later in II:1, "God is known through God, and through God alone."[27] Barth expounds the Word of God as the criterion of doctrine or dogmatics, and distinguishes between the Word of God in its primary sense as *God incarnate in Jesus Christ,* its second sense of the *witness of Scripture* as God's word written, and its third sense of the church's witness to Christ in the *proclamation* of the gospel.[28]

In this present study, however, I confine myself to a few paragraphs on the hermeneutics of a doctrine of Scripture and of the biblical writings because it would hardly be appropriate to replicate material already published in the five hundred pages of *The Two Horizons,* the seven hundred pages of *New Horizons in Hermeneutics,* or the eight hundred pages of *Thiselton on Hermeneutics.* All the same, since something must be said under this heading, I shall first offer a very brief preliminary comment on Barth, about whose work I may not have said enough in the three volumes mentioned, and shall then select for comment some fundamental axioms of a hermeneutic of the Word of God and its relation to the sacraments.

In contrast to popular misunderstandings of Barth, Barth declares that God may *speak* to us in multiple modes, including, for example, speaking "through Russian communism, a flute concerto, a blossoming shrub, or a dead dog."[29] The word of God includes preaching, and (in Barth's words) takes the form of "sacrament, i.e., the symbolic act which is carried through in the Church as directed by the biblical witness of revelation in accompaniment and confirmation of preaching."[30] It is *not* "self-exposition," focused on the preacher, the theologian, or, we might add, autobiographical tales of life in Vicarage or Manse.[31] The Bible provides "recollection" of God's past revelation as well as "expectation of His future revelation."[32] The "speech" of God is not mere "talk": *"The Word of God is itself the act of God"* (my italics).[33] In *action* it takes the form of "contingent contemporaneity" in "election, revelation, calling, separation, new birth," and "God's ruling action."[34] It enacts "a promise, a judgement, a claim."[35] Further, it is inseparable from *God's presence.*[36] Barth, in common with Zizioulas and the Orthodox tradition, stresses that the Word of God brings and makes possible *communion*

27. Barth, *Church Dogmatics,* II:1, sect. 27, 1, p. 179.

28. Barth, *Church Dogmatics,* I:1, sects. 1-2: pp. 3-45; and more especially sects. 3-4, pp. 47-124.

29. Barth, *Church Dogmatics,* I:1, sect. 3, 1, p. 55.

30. Barth, *Church Dogmatics,* I:1, sect. 3, 1, p. 56.

31. Barth, *Church Dogmatics,* I:1, sect. 3, 1, p. 64.

32. Barth, *Church Dogmatics,* I:1, sect. 4, 3, p. 111.

33. Barth, *Church Dogmatics,* I:1, sect. 5, 3, p. 143.

34. Barth, *Church Dogmatics,* I:1, sect. 5, 3, pp. 145 and 148.

35. Barth, *Church Dogmatics,* I:1, sect. 5, 3, p. 150.

36. Barth, *Church Dogmatics,* I:1, sect. 8, 1, pp. 295-304.

with God in relationality or relationship.[37] Yet revelation through the word is indirect and dialectical, for God is hidden, even if through Christ God is "ready" to be known in his chosen way and at the time of his choosing.[38]

A further aspect of Barth's exposition of a doctrine of the Word of God is his necessary emphasis upon its Trinitarian frame. Among recent expositors of Barth, Telford Work draws upon this aspect in Barth's thought, as well as other resources from Balthasar, Athanasius, and Augustine, to revivify a doctrine of the Word of God that is hermeneutically sensitive, without merely following the well-worn grooves of earlier discussions.[39]

We may now consider more broadly those aspects of a hermeneutics of the doctrine of the word of God that relate more distinctively to the sacraments.

(a) Both word and sacrament witness to Christ and to the gospel as *eventful enactments or actions*. It is not the case that the word is merely cognitive reflection while the sacraments are action. No less a sense of *expectation of an eventful happening should belong to the liturgy of the word* than in the liturgy of the sacrament, whether it be Eucharistic or baptismal. Both word and sacrament are actions and *events* of judgment and grace. Barth, Bultmann, Fuchs, and Ebeling appeal to "event" or "language event," with relatively good reason. But I have consistently preferred to explore the principles and terminology of self-involving *speech-action,* since speech-acts still depend transparently for their effectiveness for certain states of extralinguistic affairs being *ontologically the case.*[40] Bultmann, Fuchs, and Ebeling are too heavily influenced by Heidegger's view of language to see that existential force alone (as in Bultmann), or intralinguistic worlds alone (as in Fuchs), are inadequate as models of the dynamics of the word of God. God's word is grounded in ontology, even if in "Being as Becoming."

It is therefore regrettable that in a laudable desire to dignify and magnify the due *gravitas* of the presence of Christ in the Lord's Supper or the Eucharist and baptism, many churches often unwittingly downgrade the liturgy of the word as if it were somehow inferior to that of the sacraments. Both are complementary and simply enacted in different modes. This is one reason why Protestant traditions of doctrine within the Church of England have always resisted the wearing of "Eucharistic" vestments, which usually project a greater sense of weight and splendor above and beyond the cassock and surplice of the daily offices. The custom in some Presbyterian churches in Scotland of ceremonially placing the Bible in the pulpit as a formal liturgical act is one that is to be respected and envied.

---

37. Barth, *Church Dogmatics,* I:1, ch. 2, sects. 9-12, pp. 348-489; cf. Zizioulas, *Being as Communion,* 101-22.

38. Barth, *Church Dogmatics,* I:2, sects. 13-14, 1-121, and sect. 19, 457-537.

39. Telford Work, *Living and Active: Scripture in the Economy of Salvation* (Grand Rapids: Eerdmans, 2002).

40. From among these studies, see Thiselton, "Hermeneutics and Speech-Act Theory," in *Thiselton on Hermeneutics,* 51-149.

Whatever their differences, both Barth and Schleiermacher sought to nurture a *sense of expectancy* of an *eventful, transformative encounter* with the word of God in preaching.

(b) Among specialists in hermeneutics Paul Ricoeur has reminded us of the *multiform modes* of biblical discourse.[41] He points out that all too often we tend to privilege *didactic* and *prophetic* modes over others. We expect to be "taught"; we expect to be encouraged, confronted, or sometimes corrected and rebuked. Nevertheless the *psalmic* and hymnic literature *addresses God,* and thereby initiates, or continues, *dialogue* and *communion* with God as "Thou." It is interpersonal and intersubjective. *Wisdom* literature invites readers to *explore,* and leaves *questions,* and sometimes "answers," open-ended. Questions may stimulate creative thought and deeper engagement. Waismann comments that the question "is the first groping step . . . towards new horizons. . . . Questions lead us on and over the barriers of traditional opinions."[42] *Narrative* in Scripture projects "worlds" that we may enter and inhabit, and allows us to find meanings for our own personal "little" narratives when we insert "our" narrative into the larger grand narrative of God's dealings with the world.

Two consequences follow. First, when we relate these multiform modes to speech-action, our expectations of the manifold transforming effects of the word of God increase. William Tyndale, even in the premodern era, identified some eighteen modes of speech-acts performed by the Bible, The Bible, he wrote, *promises, names, appoints, declares, gives, condemns, curses, binds, kills, drives to despair, delivers, forgives, ministers life, wounds, blesses, heals, cures,* and *awakens.*[43] Second, this address *to* God in psalmic literature (and other writings) nurtures divine-human conversation, which in turn fosters divine-human *communion.* This is precisely what Calvin, Barth, Zizioulas, and most recently Jens Zimmermann identify as the major goal in the reading of Scripture.[44] If Hebrews 1–12 represents a homily, as is likely, this epistle provides a marvelous model of the multidimensional nature of preaching. Heb. 1:1-13 contains *exposition* of Old Testament passages with *creed, confession, hymn, praise, acclamation, argument,* and *celebration.* It is certainly not all "exhortation" or "teaching." To use Schleiermacher's metaphor, it catches fire, and "it strikes up the music."[45]

41. Ricoeur, *Essays on Biblical Interpretation,* 73-95.

42. F. Waismann, *The Principles of Linguistic Philosophy* (London: Macmillan and New York: St. Martin's Press, 1965), 405.

43. William Tyndale, "A Pathway into the Holy Scripture," in his *Doctrinal Treatises and Introduction to Different Portions of the Holy Scripture,* Parker Society Edition (Cambridge: Cambridge University Press, 1948), 8-12, 15, 17-18, and 21-23; cf. 7-29.

44. See further Zimmermann, *Recovering Theological Hermeneutics,* 18-19, 23-25 (on Barth), 34 (on Calvin), 63 (on Luther), 87-89, and 99.

45. F. D. E. Schleiermacher, *On Religion: Speeches to Its Cultured Despisers,* trans. John Oman (New York: Harper & Row, 1958), 119-20.

(c) *Scripture should be read, and the word of God heeded, with a hermeneutic of suspicion on guard against possible self-interests, including narcissistic desires for self-affirmation and approval without change.* Among the major exponents of hermeneutics Gadamer, Ricoeur, and Habermas are the most creative thinkers who address this subject. If readers *impose* their prior expectations and prior horizons of understandings upon biblical texts, especially their desires for self-affirmation and divine approval, only illusion and distortion will result.

Ricoeur and Habermas have written extensively on the self-deception of human beings, the fallibility of the human will, and the part played by self-affirming human "interests." Ricoeur draws on Freud to illustrate the principle, although not without an incisive critique of Freud's mechanistic worldview from the standpoint of theism. Gadamer shows how readily we as readers of texts can re-shape them into our own image by "premature assimilation." Thereby we lose the transforming and formative effect of engagement with the "other." I have explored Gadamer's approach to "formation" and Ricoeur's prescription for avoiding "narcissism" in 5.1 above.

It remains, before we conclude the present section, to add a few general observations about *sacraments,* especially in the light of our initial and provisional comments about the number and scope of sacraments. We noted that the term *sacrament,* in the technical theological and liturgical sense, first featured in Tertullian around 200-203. Since the Latin *sacramentum* also regularly denotes a *pledge* or *oath,* Christian sacraments soon came to be associated with God's *pledges* to remain faithful to his covenant *promise,* and the pledge of loyalty from Christian believers especially in baptism and the Eucharist.

The Reformers placed particular emphasis upon the sacraments as visible pledges of covenant promise, in parallel or analogy with the Old Testament covenant signs of circumcision and the Passover. Augustine defined sacraments as visible forms or signs of an invisible grace.[46] The 1662 English Book of Common Prayer defines a sacrament in its *Catechism* as "an outward and visible sign of an inward and spiritual grace given unto us, ordained by Christ himself as a means whereby we received the same and a pledge to assure us thereof." To the next catechetical question, "How many parts are there in a sacrament?" The answer given is: "Two: the outward visible sign and the inward spiritual grace." As far as I am aware, the Church of England has not yet formally approved any of the "revised" catechisms as an official alternative to, let alone replacement of, that of 1662.

Augustine and Aquinas understood the nature and functions of sacraments in the contexts of their respective theories of signs. Augustine additionally defined a sacrament as follows: "Signs, when they refer to divine things, are called 'sacraments'" (*"Signa, cum ad res divinas pertinent, sacramenta apellantur"*).[47] Robert

---

46. A variant parallel is found in Augustine, *City of God,* X:6; and *On Christian Doctrine,* II:1.
47. Augustine, *Epistles,* 138.

Markus, a Nottingham colleague, has provided an incisive and judicious account of Augustine's theory of signs, and its relation to theories of meaning.[48] He argues convincingly that the theory of signs underwent substantial changes during the two hundred years between Augustine and Gregory the Great, which in turn reflected a change of worldview between c. 400 and c. 600. Augustine discusses the nature of signs in *On Christian Doctrine*, Book II, where he recognizes that often the ambiguity of conventional signs may give rise to misunderstanding. In the case of Scripture, the interpretation of verbal signs requires the study of biblical languages as well as Christian wisdom.[49] Sacraments are based on conventional rather than natural representation, and even these need interpretation.

In due course Calvin developed and extended this principle to insist that sacraments should not be administered without the simultaneous ministry of the word. In the biblical writings, Calvin insists "any sign . . . was inseparably attached to doctrine, without which our eyes would gaze bewildered upon an unmeaning object."[50]

Hugh of St. Victor produced a classic treatise on the theology of the sacraments in the twelfth century. Not every sign, he argued, can be called a sacrament, even sacred writings, statues, or pictures. He writes, "A sacrament is a physical or material element set before the external senses, representing by likeness, signifying by its institution, and containing by sanctification, some invisible and spiritual grace."[51] The visible represents or communicates the invisible by likeness or analogy: it has been ordained or "instituted" by an appropriate authority to signify this communicative act; and its use has been sanctified or set apart for this purpose. Hugh of St. Victor thereby "narrows" or makes more specific a broader view of sacramental signs than Augustine implies. The generality of Augustine's view finds expression in his saying: *"sacramenta Novi Testamenti dant salutem; sacramenta Veteris Testamenti promiserunt Saluatorem."*[52]

Peter Lombard, a near contemporary of Hugh, modified the latter's definition to arrive at the standard medieval definition of sacraments as numbering seven, each of which conferred grace: baptism, confirmation, the Eucharist, penance, extreme unction, ordination, and marriage.[53] He broadly takes up Augustine's theory of signs on the basis of "likeness" and purpose, but he does not make much of the physical or visible element. Thomas Aquinas endorses the

48. Robert A. Markus, *Signs and Meanings: World and Text in Ancient Christianity* (Liverpool: Liverpool University Press, 1996), esp. chs. 3–4.

49. Augustine, *On Christian Doctrine*, II:1-16.

50. Calvin, *Institutes*, IV:14:4. See further Ronald S. Wallace, *Calvin's Doctrine of the Word and Sacrament* (Edinburgh: Oliver & Boyd, 1953), 72-81.

51. Hugh of St. Victor, *On Sacraments*, IX:2.

52. Augustine, *Commentary on the Psalms*, 73 ("The sacraments of the New Testament give salvation; the sacraments of the Old Testament promise the Saviour").

53. Peter Lombard, *Libri Sententiarum*, IV:1:4, ii.

number "seven," and this became widely accepted in the church of the thirteenth century.[54] The Council of Trent condemned under *anathema* any who would hold any more or less: *"aut esse plura vel pauciora quam septem."*[55]

Such a dogmatic adherence to *"seven"* presupposes a particular understanding and definition of *sacrament,* as we have noted. At first sight the English Book of Common Prayer appears no less dogmatic by insisting upon *two.* Nevertheless the Book of Common Prayer carries with it a clarificatory explanation that leaves room for other uses of the term. It offers qualifying phrases. In answer to the question in the catechism "How many sacraments hath *Christ ordained in his church?"* the catechumen answers, "Two only, as *generally necessary to salvation; that is to say, baptism and the Supper of the Lord."* No one could suggest that marriage or ordination is necessary for salvation; hence an implicit distinction within the seven allows for two as "dominical" or "gospel" sacraments The candidate then further identifies the "outward and visible sign" respectively as "water" and as "bread and wine." In the documents of Vatican II allusion to "the sacraments of faith" is followed by the qualification: "especially, that is to say, by baptism [and] . . . by the sacred mystery of the Eucharist, the pivot of all the other sacraments."[56]

By now it has become increasingly clear that irrespective of particular doctrinal beliefs, *three different uses of the word "sacrament" must be distinguished.*

(i) Most (or at least many) Protestant Churches speak of *the two "dominical" sacraments* as those that are ordained and *instituted by Christ* in the historic context of Scripture.

(ii) At the other end of the spectrum many use the term *sacramental* to denote in the very widest sense *any empirical, physical, or material object or event* in and through which they believe that God speaks and confers the grace of revelation and understanding. Washing or bathing on waking can be "sacramental" in the broad but diffused sense of conveying a concrete sign of the cleansing grace of God through a tactile and visible experience. No one would claim that this is "sacramental" in the "stronger" sense. But this may still give rise to ambiguity. Is the Fourth Gospel "sacramental" in the sense of conveying Eucharistic and perhaps baptismal allusions, or in the broader sense in which the Book of Signs (John 2:1–12:50) uses the signs of the miraculous deeds of Jesus Christ to point beyond themselves to spiritual realities.

(iii) Catholic and Orthodox traditions use the term *sacrament* in accordance with the growth of sacramental theology in the medieval period. Any *abstract* debate about *whether* ordination and marriage are "sacramental" is better avoided

54. Aquinas, *Summa Theologiae,* Part 3a, Q. 60-65, esp. Q. 61:3 (Blackfriars edn., vol. 56); cf. 3a, Q. 66-83, which includes baptism and the Eucharist.

55. *Council of Trent,* session 7, sect. 1.

56. Vatican II, "Sacred Liturgy," *Inter Oecumeneci* (26 September 1964), "Principles," 6, in Flannery (ed.), *Documents,* 46.

until it can be grounded in a hermeneutic of what "grace" is said to be conveyed. Other questions will contribute to a horizon of understanding: does the sacramental object or the sacramental dramatic action convey grace? Or does prayer that accompanies the sacramental action convey grace? Do both conjointly convey grace, and what is the role of the self-involving, participatory dimension, or appropriation through faith?

There may arguably be one exception to the above comments. Luther resisted the notion that *penance* could be described as a sacrament on the basis of a necessary return to the biblical understanding of repentance as *turning to God* rather than performing a rite. He insisted that the Greek μετανοεῖν reflected the Hebrew שׁוּב, *shûbh, to turn.*

Luther, Melanchthon, Calvin, and other Reformers understood the sacraments as *pledges or effective signs of divine promise.* In this respect they operate as the Word of God, not as that which was different in kind from the Word of God. Philip Melanchthon wrote, "The gospel is the promise of grace. The *locus* of signs is very closely related to *promises* as *seals which remind us of the promise,* and are certain witnesses to the divine will toward us, testifying that we shall certainly receive what God has promised."[57] Calvin defines a sacrament as "an external sign by which the Lord *seals* in our consciences his *promises* of good will toward us, in order to sustain the weakness of our faith, and we in turn testify our piety toward him" (my italics).[58] Calvin emphasizes the role of promise and divine word. He writes, "There never is a sacrament without an antecedent promise."[59] The truth of God, he adds, is already certain and needs no supplementation, but because of the weakness of our faith the sacrament is added "as a kind of appendix."[60] A sacrament is "word and sign" together, not "by magical incantation," but by a declaration of the gospel that should accompany the sign.[61]

Several practical liturgical effects follow. The sacraments should not be administered by "muttering the formula of consecration"; by using Latin for a congregation that does not understand Latin; by performing it "in a low grumble"; or by isolating it from the proclamation of the word of God. The background to Augustine's understanding whereby the Latin *sacramentum* was perceived as the counterpart to the Greek μυστήριον *(mustērion)* encouraged distortions in contrast to the notion of "*the promise* sealed by the sacrament. . . . The sacraments bring with them the clearest promises."[62] The Christian sacraments are parallels

---

57. Philip Melanchthon, *Loci Communes Rerum Theologicarum,* trans. and ed. Wilhelm Pauck, in *Melanchthon and Bucer,* Library of Christian Classics 19 (London: S.C.M. and Philadelphia: Westminster, 1969).

58. Calvin, *Institutes,* IV:14:1 (Beveridge edn., vol. 2, 491-92).

59. Calvin, *Institutes,* IV:14:3 (Beveridge edn., 492).

60. Calvin, *Institutes,* IV:14:3 (Beveridge edn., 492).

61. Calvin, *Institutes,* IV:14:4 (Beveridge edn., 493).

62. Calvin, *Institutes,* IV:14:5; cf. 3-4 (Beveridge edn., 493-94).

with the Old Testament covenantal signs, in which circumcision is a "seal" (Rom. 4:11). Above all, they are "sacramental signs of the covenants . . . symbols of cove-nant . . . digested and enacted by words."[63] They are "a pledge of his grace."[64]

It is a short step from this to the concept that Martin Bucer and Peter Martyr underline, namely that of the sacraments as *"visible words."* In the face of intense disagreement between Luther and Zwingli on the nature of the Lord's Supper (see 21.3), Martin Bucer sought to hold Reformation doctrines together. Com-pelled to flee from the European Continent, Peter Martyr came to Oxford in 1547 and Martin Bucer to Cambridge in 1549, both at the invitation of Archbishop Thomas Cranmer. Cranmer collaborated with them in the preparation of the 1552 edition of the Book of Common Prayer under Edward VI, which marked a high point of "Protestant" doctrine in the Church of England. Both undertook a careful examination not simply of "signs" in the broader tradition of Plato, which had influenced Augustine, but also especially of Old Testament covenant signs, signs in the New Testament, and the sacraments of baptism and Holy Communion. The latter are "visible words of God." Joseph McLelland and Peter Stephens expound the theological significance of this aspect for Peter Martyr and for Bucer.[65] In Bucer's view "the inward word" depends on the action of the Holy Spirit; "the outward word" was "the spoken word" of preaching and "the visible word" of baptism and Holy Communion.[66] But they are not "bare signs," "they offer what they show."[67] Hence the Prayer Book speaks of "effective" signs.

Gerhard Ebeling and Wolfhart Pannenberg discuss two finer points of inter-pretation. First, does the Reformers' emphasis upon *promise* render ambiguous what the sacraments "offer" in the present? Pannenberg reflects Luther's concern faithfully when (citing Ebeling) he writes, "The signifying nature of the sacra-mental presence of Christ and God's kingdom in baptism and in the Supper is an expression of the 'not yet' of our Christian life."[68] As we shall argue in 21.3 and 21.4, the Lord's Supper has the *eschatological* dimension of "until he comes." Bap-tism may be seen as an anticipation of the last judgment. As in justification by grace, there is a dual element of "now" and "not yet," and the Reformers were

63. Calvin, *Institutes*, IV:14:6 (Beveridge edn., 494).

64. Calvin, *Institutes*, IV:14:7 (Beveridge edn., 495). On the relation between the sacraments and the clear proclamation of the Word, see further Ronald S. Wallace, *Calvin's Doctrine of the Word and Sacrament*, 133-42.

65. See esp. Joseph C. McLelland, *The Visible Words of God: A Study in the Theology of Peter Martyr 1500-1562* (Edinburgh: Oliver & Boyd, 1957), and W. P. Stephens, *The Holy Spirit in the Theology of Martin Bucer* (Cambridge: Cambridge University Press, 1970), esp. "The Sacraments — the Visible Words," "Baptism — the Visible Word (1)," and "Holy Communion — the Visible Word (2)," 213-59.

66. Stephens, *Martin Bucer*, 208-20.

67. Martin Bucer, *Ephesians*, 104 (cited by Stephens, *Martin Bucer*, 219).

68. Pannenberg, *Systematic Theology*, vol. 3, 353; and Gerhard Ebeling, *Word of God and Tra-dition*, trans. S. H. Hooke (London: Collins, 1968), 225-35.

concerned that the *promissory* nature of the sacraments might become neglected or lost if too much emphasis were laid upon a cultic "here and now."

Second, the Reformers saw the sacraments as above all *proclaiming Christ and the gospel.* Yet a *proliferation* of signs and sacraments, and an emphasis upon the solemnity and mystery of sacraments in their own right, could unwittingly obscure Christ by directing too much attention to the signs themselves. Melanchthon points out that Christ is *the* sacrament. Hence Pannenberg observes that such overemphasis "pushed into the background the thought of sacramentality of Jesus Christ himself and his passion."[69]

The Lutheran and Reformation emphasis upon the sacraments as both pledges of divine promise and as visible words underlines constructively the continuity between word and sacrament. In Lutheran and Reformed circles these aspects continue to be emphasized. Robert Jenson and Daniel Migliore, for example, expound this theme in our own day, although in a recent more ecumenical study Jensen approaches the subject more broadly.[70] On the other hand, we may note two qualifications. First, the communal and corporate nature of sacraments is maintained within this theme only if we recall that the *Word of God,* as Christ, as Scripture, and as proclamation, is *addressed equally to the community:* of the whole church and of the congregation. Second, each of the five senses, including sight, is involved in sacramental reception, and the power of this *wholeness* of communication embraces also the preconscious and the precognitive dimensions of apprehension, which Jung, Jaspers, Tillich, and Ricoeur understand as contributing to the power of *symbols.* The Anglican Reformers emphasized divine agency and promise and the impact of sacramental signs by speaking of *effective signs* of grace.

21.3. Hermeneutical Issues about the Lord's Supper or Eucharist: Biblical and Historical Traditions

We begin with a brief clarification of terminology. It is an unfortunate accident of developing traditions that the three biblically derived terms *Eucharist, Holy Communion,* and *the Lord's Supper,* have come to be associated with certain "positions" on a spectrum of ecclesiologies. Additionally, the term *Mass* derives from the ecclesiastical Latin equivalent to *missa,* the dismissal at the end of the Latin Eucharist. Hence it belongs too distinctively to Roman Catholic tradition to serve wider, ecumenical usage. The other three terms indicate in practice pre-

---

69. Pannenberg, *Systematic Theology,* vol. 3, 348.

70. Robert Jenson, *Visible Words: The Interpretation and Practice of Christian Sacraments* (Philadelphia: Fortress, 1978); Migliore, *Faith Seeking Understanding,* 211; cf. 211-30; more recently Robert Jenson, "The Church and the Sacraments," in C. Gunton (ed.), *Cambridge Companion to Christian Doctrine,* 215-25.

ferred terms within a wide spectrum or range of ecclesiologies from Anglo-Catholic or Liberal Catholic traditions, which tend to favour *Eucharist;* through "central" or broader ecumenical traditions that tend to favor *Holy Communion;* to more conservative, Evangelical, or independent traditions, which tend to prefer *Lord's Supper.* Yet each of these three main terms is legitimate and carries biblical precedent. The Greek εὐχαριστήσας *(eucharistēsas)* features in the words of institution in pre-Paul apostolic traditions (1 Cor. 11:24), in the Synoptic gospels, and in the canons of most Eucharistic liturgies. The term *Communion* derives from (κοινωνία, *koinōnia*), *"sharing in* the blood of Christ . . . in the body of Christ" (1 Cor. 10:16). *The Lord's Supper* is a description used by Paul and in the church of Corinth (κυρῑακὸν δεῖπνον, *kuriakon deipnon,* 1 Cor. 11:20), where *deipnon* carries no particular reference to timing, but denotes the main meal of the day, usually, in its Corinthian context, after work in the evening. The English word *dinner* offers a comparison in both respects.

In 21.1 we suggested that among a complexity of hermeneutical questions perhaps the most central concerned the context or horizon of understanding within which we interpret the meaning of "this is my body" and "this is my blood" (Matt. 26:26-28; Mark 16:22-24; Luke 22:19-20; and 1 Cor. 11:24-25), or the Lukan and Pauline variant "this cup is the new covenant in my blood" and its wider context of "remembrance." τοῦτό ἐστιν τὸ σῶμά μου *(touto estin to sōma mou)* is identical in the three Synoptic accounts, with τοῦτό μού ἐστιν τὸ σῶμα *(touto mou estin to sōma)* in Paul, and the addition of τὸ ὑπὲρ ὑμῶν *(to huper humōn)* in Paul and Luke. Recently Anders Eriksson, and prior to him Otfried Hofius, have shown that these words are embedded in pre-Pauline common apostolic tradition and very soon became part of a formulaic liturgical narrative.[71]

Before we expound the heart of the matter, we need to address one potential distraction. From the 1920s to the 1960s Hans Lietzmann's work *Mass and Lord's Supper* (first edition 1926, with successive editions and appendices up to 1979) exercised considerable influence in promoting the notion of two very different types of traditions about the Eucharist.[72] Lietzmann argued that there were originally two "primitive types." The Roman liturgy of Hippolytus derived from the "Pauline type," in which the emphasis fell upon "proclaiming the Lord's death" (1 Cor. 11:26). Lietzmann also postulated a "Jerusalem type," which reflected a more joyous mood of celebration in fellowship meals, in which the emphasis fell upon communion with the raised, living Christ. This is supposedly described in Acts 2:46, and found its way into early Egyptian liturgies and in Serapion.

71. Eriksson, *Traditions as Rhetorical Proof: Pauline Argumentation in 1 Corinthians* (cited above), 100-134; Hofius, "The Lord's Supper and the Lord's Supper Traditions," in Meyer (ed.), *One Loaf, One Cup,* 75-115. See also A. B. McGowan, "Is There a Liturgical Text in This Gospel? The Institution Narratives and Their Early Interpretative Communities," *JBL* 118 (1999) 73-87.

72. Hans Lietzmann, *Mass and Lord's Supper: A Study in the History of the Liturgy,* with Introductions and Further Inquiry by R. D. Richardson (Leiden: Brill, 1979), esp. 172-86.

Lietzmann saw the origins of this second form in the *Haburah* (or *Chaburah*) meal.[73]

A. J. B. Higgins argued in favor of a modified form of Lietzmann's thesis, although he believed that *both* "types" went back to the very earliest times.[74] In English-speaking Anglican circles Gregory Dix promoted this general approach with considerable effect at the time.[75] Higgins drew positive conclusions from this approach. He argued that Jesus "founded" *together* both the community of the church as the messianic community and a focus on the new Passover as both a remembrance of his death and a celebration of his risen presence. The "real presence" of Christ in the Eucharist derives not from the Eucharistic elements but from recalling the sacrificial death of Christ as an event. The Eucharist looks forward to the final coming of the kingdom of God.[76]

Lietzmann's hypothesis has been developed in two quite different ways. E. Lohmeyer argued for an original dualism between a "Galilean" type (which approximated Lietzmann's "Jerusalem" type), and "Jerusalem" type (which approximated Lietzmann's "Pauline" type).[77] This implies a split within a tradition that Eriksson, Hofius, and others, more accurately understand as a single common apostolic tradition. By contrast Higgins tries to draw two "types" together, although his starting point remains unproven.

All this is hypothetical at best. Jeremias stands among an impressive array of more recent scholars who rightly question the foundations on which Lietzmann tried to build his theory. In particular Jeremias questions what is claimed about the *Haburah* (or *Chaburah*) meal. Lietzmann spoke of the meal as having "religious solemnity"; but Jeremias comments: "Every meal had 'religious solemnity' because of the grace that was always said." He declares, "Unfortunately it must be said . . . there here again we have an *ad hoc* conjecture for which there is absolutely no evidence."[78] Subsequent to the researches of Jeremias, I. Howard Marshall, among many others, has endorsed this critique of Lietzmann.[79]

Jeremias turns to more fruitful starting points to demonstrate that *the most constructive horizon of understanding for interpreting the Lord's Supper is the setting of the Passover.*[80] As we have noted, F. J. Leenhardt (1958) and O. Hofius (1988) strongly support this approach, and I have argued for it in my larger com-

---

73. Lietzmann, *Mass and Lord's Supper,* 193-209.

74. A. J. B. Higgins, *The Lord's Supper in the New Testament* (London: S.C.M., 1952), esp. 13-63.

75. Gregor Dix, *The Shape of the Liturgy* (London: S.C.M., 1943, 2d ed. 1945), esp. 50-70.

76. Higgins, *Lord's Supper,* 89.

77. Ernst Lohmeyer, "Das Abendmahl in der Urgemeinde," *JBL* 56 (1937) 217-52.

78. Joachim Jeremias, *The Eucharistic Words of Jesus,* 30; cf. 16-36.

79. I. Howard Marshall, *Last Supper and Lord's Supper* (Grand Rapids: Eerdmans, 1980) 108-23.

80. Jeremias, *Eucharistic Words,* 41-105.

mentary on the Greek text of 1 Corinthians. The *Mishnah* sets out an "order" or liturgy for the observance of the Passover in Judaism, the Passover *Seder* (or *tsēder*). The narrative of the Passover (Exod. 12:1-51) takes the form of *dramatic action* in which those who take part become *participants in the narrative world of,* and in effect *"relive," the drama of divine deliverance* from bondage in Egypt to live a new life as the redeemed people of God. Israel is to *recite and to celebrate* this history of God's saving acts of deliverance (Deut. 26:5). Exod. 12:25-27 declares: "When you come to the land that the LORD will give you, as he has promised, you shall keep this observance. And when your children say, 'What do you mean by this observance?' you shall say, 'It is the Passover sacrifice to the LORD. . . .'" "In every generation," the *Mishnah* declares, *"a man must so regard himself as if he came forth himself out of Egypt"* (M. *Pesaḥim* 10:5).[81]

In the Synoptic tradition Jesus directs his disciples to make preparations for him to eat the Passover with them (Matt. 26:17-19; Mark 14:14; Luke 22:7-13; cf. Luke 22:15).[82] Leenhardt convincingly dovetails the *Seder* or *tsēder* of the Passover with the words of institution of the Eucharist. The Jewish *Haggadah* (I follow Roth's edition) begins the *Seder* with the doxology: "Blessed art Thou, O Lord, our God, King of the universe, Creator of the produce of the vine — Blessed art Thou. . . ."[83] The Jewish "grace" is the counterpart to the phrase "after blessing [it]" (Matt. 26:26, NRSV; Mark 14:22, NRSV); and "when he had given thanks" (Luke 22:19 and 1 Cor. 11:24). It is unfortunate, if not barely excusable, that the NRSV inserts *"it,"* which is not in the Greek, on its own authority. In accord with the parallels in Luke and in Paul, Jesus *blesses God* for the bread as a Jewish "grace" or prayer of thanksgiving. To read it as a "consecration" of the elements is anachronistic exegesis. The NIV translates *gave thanks* even in the Matthean and Markan versions, which gives a better sense. NJB prudently translates "said the blessing," which reflects the Greek.

After the grace or "benediction" the *karpas* (like an *hors d'oeuvre* in the Passover meal) is dipped in salt water or vinegar, and distributed as a way of "recalling" the hyssop dipped in the blood of the first Passover sacrifice, with a second, benediction, "Blessed art Thou, O Lord, our God. . . ." The *Haggadah* then reads, "This is the bread of affliction that our forefathers ate in the land of Egypt": הָא לַחְמָא עַנְיָא דִּי־אֲכָלוּ אֲבָהָתָנָא בְּאַרְעָא דְמִצְרָיִם (*hā' lachmā' 'anya' diy-'akālû 'abānta' b^e'ārāts' d^emitsrāyîm*). Leenhardt describes this sequence at the Last Supper. He then notes the sudden departure from how the disciples had expected Jesus to continue. *"This is my body"* comes as "a surprise": it replaces the words,

---

81. The text can be found conveniently in Herbert Danby (ed.), *The Mishnah: Translated from the Hebrew with Introductions and Notes* (Oxford: Oxford University Press, 1933). The Tract *Pesaḥim* is on pp. 136-51, and *Pesaḥim* 10:6 on 151.

82. Cf. Jeremias, *Eucharistic Words,* 41-49.

83. Cecil Roth, *The Haggadah: New Edition with Notes,* Hebrew and English (London: Soncino, 1934), 8; cf. Jeremias, *Eucharistic Words,* 49-54.

"This is the bread of affliction."[84] This is the context for understanding these words.

The Passover *Seder* enables Jewish households *to participate in* the deliverance of the Passover *as if they were "there."* The Eucharist enables Christians *to participate in* the deliverance of the cross *as if they were "there."* They are *contemporaneous sharers in the drama.* The Black spiritual "Were you there when they crucified my Lord?" captures the mood very well.

This now provides a further hermeneutical horizon of understandings for τοῦτο ποιεῖτε εἰς τὴν ἐμὴν ἀνάμνησιν (*touto poieite eis tēn emēn anamnēsin, do this in "remembrance" of me,* 1 Cor. 11:24; 11:25; Luke 22:19). The meaning of the Greek ἀνάμνησις and the Hebrew זכר (*zēker, remembrance,* or *zākar, to remember*) has long been a source of controversy. Although it may include *calling to mind,* the Hebrew verb זכר (*zākar*) frequently denotes a *more objective, quasi-public act of bringing something into the present in such a way as to change a situation.* When Israel asks God "to remember the distress of his servants" (Lam. 3:19; cf. Exod. 32:13; Deut. 9:27; Ps. 20:4), this prayer expresses the plea that God will *act.*[85]

This interpretation raises a problem only in relation to the dubious use that such scholars as A. Bentzen, S. H. Hooke, and S. Mowinckel with their outdated "Myth and Ritual" approach have made of this more "objective" aspect. Bentzen presents "remembrance" as in effect a cultic *reenactment.* Needless to say, this put the clock back on any constructive debate between traditional Catholic notions of the Mass and Protestant understandings of the *"once for all"* nature of the sacrifice of Christ as ἐφάπαξ (*ephapax,* Rom. 6:10; Heb. 7:27; 9:12; 10:10).[86] In recent times there has been a steady convergence, probably on both sides, to the effect that the actual sacrifice of Christ remains *once for all,* but that its appropriation in the Eucharist involves a "realistic contemporaneity" on the part of the church, which is more than mere mental recollection as if in a Zwinglian sense.[87]

Such convergence in some measure can be found in the Anglican/Roman Catholic International Commission's (ARCIC) *"Windsor" Statement* of 1971. This *"Agreed Statement"* by Anglican and Roman Catholic members of the Commission declares on the sacrifice of Christ: "Christ's redeeming death and resurrection took place once and for all in history, Christ's death on the cross . . . was the one, perfect, and sufficient sacrifice for the sins of the world."[88] This is almost a word-for-word paraphrase of the Book of Common Prayer. The Document continues, "There can be no repetition of, or addition to, what was thus accom-

---

84. Leenhardt, "This Is My Body," in Cullmann and Leenhardt, *Essays,* 39-40.

85. Brown, Driver, and Briggs, *Hebrew-English Lexicon* (new edn. 1980), זכר, 269-71.

86. A. Bentzen, *King and Messiah,* trans. and ed. G. W. Anderson (Oxford: Blackwell, 2d edn. 1970), 12 and 72-80; cf. Mowinckel, *Psalmstudien,* 6 vols. (Oslo: Kristiania, 1921-24).

87. H. R. McAdoo and Alan Clark (cochairmen), Anglican/Roman Catholic International Commission, *Agreed Statement in Eucharistic Doctrine* (Windsor, 1971), II, 5.

88. ARCIC, *Agreed Statement,* II, 5.

plished once for all by Christ. . . . The Eucharist must not obscure this fundamental fact.[89] All the same, in the Eucharist the atoning work of Christ "is
proclaimed and made effective in the life of the Church. The notion of *memorial*,
as understood in the Passover celebration at the time of Christ — i.e., the *making
effective in the present of an event in the past* — has opened the way to a clearer
understanding of the relationship between Christ's sacrifice and the Eucharist."[90]
The Eucharistic memorial is no mere calling to mind of a past event or of its significance, but the church's effective proclamation of God's mighty acts.[91]

The Commission's joint report continues to use language to which we alluded in 21.2 about *"effective signs"* in sacramental actions. It declares, "Christ is
present and active," Christ's presence is "effectively signified by the bread and
wine."[92] The statement carefully asserts, "The bread and wine become the body
and blood of Christ by the action of the Holy Spirit." The report does not commit itself to specifying the *mode* of the Spirit's action, although it gives due place
to appropriation by faith. On the other hand, Vatican II is less encouraging and
deeply disappointing for Protestants. It reaffirms transubstantiation and declares
that the faithful "offer the sacred victim."[93]

Since the Passover places the Lord's Supper in a *covenantal* context, the notion of *promising assurance* also assumes a prominent place. Each participant in
the covenant gives a *pledge* to limit choices of free action: God chooses to be
faithful to his covenant promise; believers pledge themselves to serious acknowledgment of Christ's lordship. Hence Paul includes an uncompromising warning
of the possibility of perjury if this is not the driving force in participating in the
Lord' Supper (1 Cor. 11:27-33). It is like false witness. Archaeological research in
first-century Corinth, especially on two Roman villas at Anaploga in the outer
suburbs of the city, have shed a flood of light on how, by arranging the Supper
along the lines of ordinary Roman dining customs, this rite of unity and union
actually gave rise to the very reverse, and undermined its intention. Some were
treated like hangers-on or second-class citizens and located in the atrium, and
were probably served a lower grade of food and wine.[94]

---

89. ARCIC, *Agreed Statement*, II, 5.

90. ARCIC, *Agreed Statement*, II, 5 (my italics).

91. ARCIC, *Agreed Statement*, III, 6.

92. ARCIC, *Agreed Statement*, III, 10.

93. Vatican II, *Instruction on the Worship of the Eucharistic Mystery, Eucharisticum Mysterium*
(25 May 1967), 3C; cf. 3F (Flannery, *Documents*, 104).

94. Thiselton, *First Epistle to the Corinthians*, 849-99, esp. 858-66; J. Murphy-O'Connor, *St.
Paul's Corinth: Texts and Archaeology* (Wilmington, DE: Glazier, 1983) with a plan of a villa on 154-
55; J. Wiseman, "Corinth and Rome, I," in *Aufstieg und Niedergang der römischen Welt* 2:7:1 (1979),
esp. 528, cf. 438-548; and Bruce W. Winter, "Secular and Christian Responses to Corinthian Fam-
ines," *Tyndale Bulletin* 40, no. 1 (May 1989): 86-106. Some writers reject this interpretation of the
situation in Corinth, but most defend it. Tacitus witnesses to such dining customs as that of different locations and grades of food and wine.

Paul warns the church that the centrality of Christ has been undermined. The aim is for the whole church as one to be able to "proclaim" Christ: (i) that Christ died (the bread is broken), and (ii) that he died "for me/for us" (the bread is taken and eaten).[95] The phrase "without discerning the body" (1 Cor. 11:29) should not be reduced to the sense of "not respecting the church as Christ's body," although the context suggests that this may be *part* of the meaning. It alludes to an absence of understanding of what the Lord's Supper *means* and is *about:* it is the *Lord's* Supper, not a social occasion (1 Cor. 11:17, 20, 26, 33-34a). For those who *participate* as genuine *"sharers"* in the death and atoning work of Christ it remains an *effective sign of grace,* a *covenant promise,* and a *bond of union* (cf. 1 Cor. 10:16-17). Since to share in Christ's death is thereby to share also in resurrection (Rom. 6:1-11), this is also a celebration of the presence of the raised Christ.

We cannot yet conclude this exploration of hermeneutical questions that relate to the Eucharist without considering, even if briefly, the historical traditions of interpretation that have divided the church, especially since the Reformation. It has become customary to distinguish between four or five "classic" positions, which were once frozen in tradition but are now in a number of cases once again on the move.

(i) Thomas Aquinas (1225-74) and the Council of Trent (1545-63)

Thomas Aquinas formulated a formal doctrine of *transubstantiation* largely by means of appropriating the philosophical categories of Aristotle. Aristotle distinguished between the *substance* and *accidents* of object. An object might be said to have a substance or essence in which visible, contingent qualities inhered. Aquinas acknowledges his utilization of Aristotle's categories and Aristotle's theory of causality to address the dilemma: "It does not seem possible for the bread to be turned into the body of Christ."[96] But for Aristotle *change* is the "actuation" of that which is still in potentiality. Hence, on the one hand, "The complete *substance* of the bread is converted into the complete *substance* of Christ's body *(tota substantia panis convertitur in totam substantiam corporis Christi),* and the complete *substance* of the wine into the complete *substance* of Christ's blood."[97] But the "change" is *not in form (formalis)* but in substance *(substantialis).* Thus the *visible accidents* remain bread and wine: "There is no deception. . . . The acci-

95. Thiselton, *First Epistle,* 886-88; also Anthony C. Thiselton, *1 Corinthians: A Shorter Exegetical and Pastoral Commentary* (Grand Rapids: Eerdmans, 2005), 179-91, on the whole passage and its pastoral implications.
96. Aquinas, *Summa Theologiae,* 3a, Q. 75, art. 4 (Blackfriars edn., vol. 58, 69).
97. Aquinas, *Summa Theologiae,* 3a, Q. 75, art. 4 (Blackfriars edn., vol. 58, 73).

dents *(accidentia)*, which are the proper object for our sense to deal with, are genuinely there."[98]

Aquinas ascribes the moment of change to the "consecration" of the elements on the Communion Table. After this "the substantial form of the bread no longer remains."[99] The Council of Trent endorsed this doctrine of transubstantiation (1551) using the Aristotelian and Thomist distinction between substance and accidents. Vatican II appears still to endorse this standpoint. It declares, "Even in the reserved sacrament he (Christ) is to be adored because he is *substantially* present there through the conversion of bread and wine which . . . is most aptly called transubstantiation."[100]

(ii) Martin Luther (1483-1546)

Luther's view of the Lord's Supper must be distinguished on one side from Aquinas and on the other from both Calvin and especially Zwingli. Luther initially opposed transubstantiation on the ground that the theory of substance and accidents drew on an unscriptural philosophy and remained speculative, hypothetical, and unnecessary. He opposed it in his early writings (1520). Other Reformers were more hostile to this doctrine than Luther, who rejected its status as a *necessary* doctrine.[101]

Luther, more than Calvin, Cranmer, or Zwingli, emphasized that in Holy Communion the bread and wine is "the real flesh and real blood of Christ"; but against Aquinas he maintained that it also remains "real bread and real wine."[102] In his critique of Zwingli, Luther maintains that "This is my body" is the "is" (or *est*) of synecdoche, namely that the reality of Christ is so nearly identical with the vehicles of bread and wine that these may be identified with the latter without misrepresentation.[103] Luther believed that he did not dissent from Rome about the real presence of Christ in the Eucharist; only on whether the mode of Christ's presence could be so specifically described as a required doctrine.

Luther's criticisms of Zwingli were sharper. He writes, "It is the same devil

---

98. Aquinas, *Summa Theologiae*, 3a, Q. 75, art. 5 (Blackfriars edn., vol. 58, 77).

99. Aquinas, *Summa Theologiae*, 3a, Q. 75, art. 6 (Blackfriars edn., vol. 58, 79).

100. Vatican II, *Instruction on the Worship of the Eucharistic Mystery, Eucharisticum Mysterium* (25 May 1967), 3G (Flannery, ed., *Documents*, 104). On the other hand, ecumenical discussions continue. Cf. Alan Clark and Colin Davey (eds.), *Anglican/Roman Catholic Dialogue: The Work of the Preparatory Commission* (London and New York: Oxford University Press, 1974) and subsequent documents. On the other hand, cf. John Lawrence et al., *A Critique of Eucharistic Agreement* (London: S.P.C.K., 1975).

101. The point is elaborated in Pannenberg, *Systematic Theology*, vol. 3, 296-98.

102. Martin Luther, *On the Babylonian Captivity of the Church* (1520), in Henry Wace and Carl Buchheim (eds.), *Luther's Primary Works* (London: Murray, 1883 and Hodder & Stoughton, 1896), 147-48.

who now assails us through the fanatics. . . . They would like to make mere bread and wine as a symbol and memorial signs. . . . They will not grant that the Lord's body and blood are present, even though the plain, clear words stand right there: 'eat, this is my body.' . . . They say "The word 'is' must mean the same as 'represents,' as Zwingli writes. . . . There is no proof of representation . . . in the passage that they quote."[104]

(iii) John Calvin (1509-1564)

Calvin insisted, as we have already noted in 21.2, on the parity of word and sacrament as means of grace. The word must accompany the sacrament for the latter to be effective. Nevertheless "in regard to our sacraments, they present Christ the more clearly to us . . . the Supper of the Eucharist testifies that we are redeemed."[105] But Christ does not "give himself" only in the Lord's Supper: "He gives himself daily, when in the word of the gospel he allows himself to be partaken by us, in as much as he was crucified, when he seals that offer by the sacred mystery of the Supper, and when he accomplishes inwardly what he externally designates."[106] Calvin is "not satisfied" when all appropriation of the gospel is ascribed only to the work of the Holy Spirit rather than to the action of the living Christ.[107]

Calvin avoids any crude, localized notion that the presence of Christ remains tied to a location or to the elements. No distance of place can impede the presence and action of Christ.[108] He spends considerable time in a polemical refutation of transubstantiation, where his difference from Luther becomes most marked. This view makes the bread "but a mask" on the basis of a "fictitious" change in the elements.[109] Those who promote this view are "shamefully deluded by the imposition of Satan." This portrays Christ himself as "transmitted by the bodily mouth into the belly. . . . The cause of this brutish imagination was that consecration had the same effect with them as magical incantation."[110] Whereas Luther perceives Catholic doctrine as merely overly specific, Calvin perceives it as false and offensive. It undermines the nature of the sacraments as a word of promise to be received in faith.

Even in the Genevan Confession (1536) Calvin expounds the Lord's Supper

---

103. Cf. Weber, Foundations of Dogmatics, vol. 2, 624-25.

104. Martin Luther, Luther's Works, ed. J. Pelikan and H. J. Lehman, 55 vols. (Philadelphia: Fortress, 1943-86 ["American Edition"]), vol. 37, 18-19.

105. Calvin, Institutes, IV:14:22 (Beveridge edn., 507).

106. Calvin, Institutes, IV:17:5 (Beveridge edn., 560).

107. Calvin, Institutes, IV:17:7 (Beveridge edn., 561).

108. Calvin, Institutes, IV:17:10 (Beveridge edn., 563-64).

109. Calvin, Institutes, IV:17:13-14 (Beveridge edn., 565-66).

110. Calvin, Institutes, IV:17:15 (Beveridge edn., 567).

not only in positive terms as "the true spiritual communion which we have in his body and blood," but also in polemical terms as different from "the mass of the Pope [which] was a reprobate and diabolical ordinance, subverting the mystery of the Holy Supper . . . an idolatry condemned by God."[111] *The Genevan Catechism* (1545) is altogether more positive. The Lord's Supper "is not only food for our souls," but also brings "*promises* which he there gives us, and at the same time implements."[112]

(iv) Huldrych (or Ulrich) Zwingli (1484-1531)

Zwingli's approach to the Lord's Supper developed in the context of his belief that all gifts of grace to Christian believers come through the agency of the Holy Spirit, as well as an ecclesiology based on the incarnation of Christ. In both cases he distinguished between an "inner" content and external form. He argued that the assertion of a *literal* presence of Christ in the Eucharistic elements has no scriptural support. In terms of his theology as whole, like Calvin he placed a very strong emphasis upon the sovereignty of God and the supremacy of Scripture.[113] In 1525 the Roman Mass was abolished in Zurich, and Zwingli wrote two treatises on the Lord's Supper in defense of this. His work encountered fierce hostility equally from the Catholic authorities and from Luther.

In his treatise *On the Lord's Supper* Zwingli distinguishes "three groups" who believe that "we partake of the literal body and blood of Christ."[114] The first group believes that the bread and wine are "transubstantiated into that of the corporal body and blood"; others concede that the bread remains bread but "say that we eat the body of Christ under the bread"; others say that "we eat the body of Christ as it was in the resurrection."[115] In effect these reflect respectively the Roman, Lutheran, and "Renaissance" views. Zwingli rejects all of these as "falsehoods" that go beyond Scripture. It is the charge of going "beyond Scripture" that provokes Luther so intensely, who insists that "this is my body" is plain enough to see. Zwingli, to be sure, compares this with "I am the vine" (John 15:1) and other figurative, metaphorical, or symbolical uses of the very *to be*.[116] He in-

111. John Calvin, *The Genevan Confession of Faith* (1536, in J. K. S. Reid (ed.), *Calvin: Theological Treatises*, Library of Christian Classics 22 (London: S.C.M., 1954), Art. 16, 30.

112. Calvin, *The Catechism of the Church of Geneva*, "Concerning the Sacraments" in Reid (ed.) *Calvin*, 137; cf. 88-139.

113. G. W. Bromiley, "Introduction," in *Zwingli and Bullinger*, Library of Christian Classics 24 (Philadelphia: Westminster and London: S.C.M., 1953), 31-40 and 176-84.

114. Huldrych Zwingli, *On the Lord's Supper*, in Bromiley (ed.), *Zwingli and Bullinger*, art. 1, 188; cf. 185-238.

115. Zwingli, *On the Lord's Supper*, loc. cit., art. 1, 188.

116. Zwingli, *On the Lord's Supper*, loc. cit., art. 1, 190.

sists that this responds both to the Catholic and to the Lutheran view.[117] A conclusive argument, he believes, turns on the difference between a sign and that which a sign signifies. If the sacrament is a *sign*, "it is not the very body and blood of our Lord Jesus Christ."[118]

In Art. 2 Zwingli examines other biblical texts. In John 6:52-59, he argues, it is clear that "to eat the flesh" of Christ means to believe in Christ.[119] Indeed, John shows that the outward form is irrelevant: "the flesh profits nothing" (John 6:63). Only the action of the Holy Spirit can transform the physical or material into a means of grace. Article 3 explores further the biblical use of symbol and image, for example, "Behold, the Lamb of God, who takes away the sin of the world" (John 1:29). The fourth article addresses possible counterarguments. He claims to stand in continuity with the Bible and the Creeds.[120]

(v) Anglican Doctrine

During the critical era under discussion the best indicators of movement in Anglican doctrine remain the two editions of the Book of Common Prayer: the first edition of 1549; and more "Protestant" revision of 1552, influenced by Peter Martyr and Bucer as well as Cranmer. These can readily be compared in the text *The First and Second Prayer Books of Edward VI*.[121] The revisions to the 1552 Prayer Book resisted the *epiklesis* or invocation of the Spirit that had been retained in the 1549 Prayer of Eucharistic Consecration. The second Prayer Book of 1552 also removed prayers for the dead and Mass vestments. The latter suggested an *offering* of Christ's once-for-all sacrifice, and a difference of kind between word and sacrament. On the other hand, the 1549 Prayer Book had already declared: "*Christ our Pascall lambe is offered up for us, once for al, when he bare our sinnes on hys body upon the crosse*."[122] The "sacrifice" was "a sacrifice of praise"; not of Christ, but "of ourselves." In the Holy Communion God has "*vouchsafed to Feede us . . . with the spirtuall foode of the moste precious body and bloud of they sonne. . . .*"[123]

The 1549 Prayer Book omitted many details from the earlier Sarum Rite. These included "Hail Mary!"; the ritual approach to the sanctuary; censing and washing the hands prior to consecrating the elements; kissing the gospels and

---

117. Zwingli, *On the Lord's Supper,* loc. cit., art. 1, 191-93.

118. Zwingli, *On the Lord's Supper,* loc. cit., art. 1, 193.

119. Zwingli, *On the Lord's Supper,* loc. cit., art. 2, 199.

120. Zwingli, *On the Lord's Supper,* loc. cit., art. 14, 235-38.

121. *The First and Second Prayer Books of Edward VI* (New York: Dutton and London: Dent, 1910).

122. *The First and Second Prayer Books,* 224.

123. *The First and Second Prayer Books,* 227.

Communion Table; reference to the merits of the saints; making a sign of the cross with the Host; and various similar changes. The 1552 Edition introduced the "Black Rubric" at the end of the Communion service, which stated that kneeling was permissible only as *"the humble and gratefull acknowledgying of the benefites of Chryst"*; but it does not mean *"that any adoracion is doone . . . unto the Sacramentall bread or wyne . . . or essencial presence there keeping of Christ's naturall fleshe and bloude."*[124]

Anglican theology was always *in process*. It was never tied to some specific theologian or elaborate confession, although the Thirty-Nine Articles define markers, and Scripture remains the authoritative guide. In 1553 Queen Mary abolished the 1552 Prayer Book, but Elizabeth I restored a softened version in 1559. In the Elizabethan period Richard Hooker expounded a doctrine of the Lord's Supper in which "real presence" derived not from the consecrated elements of bread and wine, but from the Christian believer's *understanding, reception, and appropriation* of the *promissory word* of God *through* the elements. Hooker writes, "The real presence of Christ's most blessed body and blood is not therefore to be sought for in the sacrament, but in the worthy receiving of the sacrament."[125] This accords with biblical witness, Hooker urged, for "the fruit of the Eucharist in the participation of the body and blood of Christ" (1 Cor. 10:16-17).[126] With Luther, Melanchthon, and Calvin, he also places emphasis on "how Christ performeth his promise."[127] Peter Brooks and William Crockett provide further helpful material on Cranmer and the Anglican tradition.[128]

After a brief detour into the *Alternative Service Book* of 1980, which many English Anglicans regarded as typically "trendy" 1960s "dumbing down" of the Book of Common Prayer, the currently authorized *Common Worship* (2000) for the Church of England still recognizes the authority and use of the 1662 Book of Common Prayer, but also provides for variants in the Eucharistic canon and other parts of the liturgy in modern English. The doctrinal content, however, still broadly mirrors the Book of Common Prayer.

124. *The First and Second Prayer Books*, 393.

125. Richard Hooker, *The Works of Mr. Richard Hooker*, ed. John Keble, 3 vols. (Oxford: Clarendon, 7th edn. 1888), vol. 2, Book V, ch. 67, sect. 5, 352.

126. Hooker, *Works*, Book V, 67, 6, 353.

127. Hooker, *Works*, Book V, 67, 12, 361.

128. Peter Brooks, *Thomas Cranmer's Doctrine of the Eucharist: An Essay in Historical Development* (New York: Seabury, 1965); and William R. Crockett, "Holy Communion," in Stephen W. Sykes and John Booty (eds.), *The Study of Anglicanism* (London: S.C.M. and Philadelphia: Fortress, 1988), 272-83.

21.4. Baptism: The Problem of Diverse
Preunderstandings and Interpretations

We noted in 21.1 that the respective arguments for infant baptism and believers' baptism depend in hermeneutical terms less on straightforward controversies about evidence of this or that practice in the New Testament or the early church than upon fundamental differences of understanding about the very nature of baptism. Is the rite to be understood primarily, for example, as a covenantal and promissory embodied word and effective sign of grace, or is it to be understood as testimony to Christian discipleship expressed through public witness? Does the main emphasis fall upon baptism as a sign of divine initiative and grace, or upon baptism as a sign of human response to that grace? Does it operate in parallel with a word from God, or as a confession of faith? No doubt many would wish to avoid such a stark either/or, but the alternatives mark a direction of emphasis.

We began with biblical material. Rudolf Schnackenburg has constructively distinguished between three different horizons of understanding or theological emphases especially in Paul.[129] One concerns the notion of baptism as *"cleansing"* (Greek ἀπολούεσθαι, *apolouesthai, to have oneself washed, to wash;* and λουτρόν, *loutron, washing* or *bath*). The second is *"assignment to Christ,"* or *"incorporation into the body of Christ"* (βαπτίζειν εἰς Χριστόν, *baptizein eis Christon;* the translation is open to debate). The third is that of *"baptism as salvation event"* (σὺν Χριστῷ, *sun Christō, with Christ,* as in "buried with [Christ] by baptism into death," Rom. 6:4).

Schnackenburg is right to make much of the second two themes, and less of the first. A number of Baptist writers stress "cleansing" when the issue is that of the recipients of baptism, and (rightly) burial with Christ when the issue is the mode of baptism. Nevertheless, how reliable are Schnackenburg's exegetical foundations for the first of the three themes?

On the face of it Schnackenburg readily appeals to three main passages: 1 Cor. 6:11; Eph. 5:26; and Tit. 3:5.[130] But none of these speaks plainly or explicitly of baptism, without the additional need to appeal to interpretative assumptions. 1 Cor. 6:11 uses ἀπολούεσθαι, which NJB rightly renders *"you were washed clean"* to bring out the force of the Greek compound verb. Many exegetes describe this as an example of a "baptismal" aorist and repeat the bold assumption found in H. L. Goudge: "You were washed, i.e., in baptism."[131] But the context surely alludes to the whole broader event and experience of coming to Christian faith, within which "cleansing" takes place on several levels: by the blood of Christ, by

---

129. Rudolf Schnackenburg, *Baptism in the Thought of Paul* (cited above), 3-82.

130. Schnackenburg, *Baptism,* 3-17.

131. H. L. Goudge, *The First Epistle to the Corinthians,* Westminster (London: Methuen, 1903, 4th edn. 1915), 45.

the word of God, by baptism, or most probably by all three. Hence in a timely study James Dunn insists that we should speak here of a "conversion-initiation" context rather than too narrowly of a "baptismal" context.[132] The passage tells us more about becoming a Christian than about the nature and theology of baptism. Yet generations of scholars up to 1970 simply repeated the usual assumption based on no more than a repeated exegetical convention.

Eph. 5:26 presents a parallel scenario. It speaks of water, but the agents of cleansing are conjointly both the water and the divine word. It is no more specific to baptism than 1 Cor. 6:11. The image is applied to the church as a whole, not to individual believers, and (to quote Mitton) "part of the bride's preparation for marriage was careful bathing . . . [and] the cleansing needs also *the word*."[133] Mitton is no doubt right to see an allusion to baptism in the imagery as a whole, but its theology is subsumed within the dynamics of the point made by the total impact of the imagery.

Tit. 3:5 fares no better. William Mounce in his very detailed commentary acknowledges that most see an allusion here to baptism, but against this he writes that he "does not hold that the creed is thinking of baptism. λουτρόν *(loutron)* 'cleansing' is used many times . . . with no thought of the baptismal ritual, παλιγγενεσία *(palingenesia)*, 'regeneration,' is not technically 'rebirth,' and the references to John 3 and 1 Peter are irrelevant. . . . Nowhere was it [i.e., baptism] the agent of regeneration."[134]

Schnackenburg mentions 1 Pet. 3:21 in this context. Naturally enough the verse brings together baptism and water, as we should expect. Arguably the epistle is addressed to recently baptized Christians. But is the function of the water here *to cleanse*? The context (1 Pet. 1:20) speaks of *Noah's being saved by going through water.* For Noah the flood marked a transition between an old, doomed existence that stood under judgment and a new life that followed a great act of divine deliverance. Noah's "redemption" was parallel with that expounded in 1 Pet. 1:18-21. For Christian believers the transition of being redeemed entails "purification" (1:22), obedience, new birth (1:23), and the active agency of the living word of God (1:23-25). The concluding emphasis lies here: "the Word of the Lord endures forever" (1:25). E. G. Selwyn observes in his commentary on the Greek text: "It is reasonable to see here a reference to Christian *baptism as a new Exodus,* all the more in view of the allusion to the lamb 'without blemish and without spot', which immediately follows."[135]

132. James D. G. Dunn, *Baptism in the Holy Spirit,* 104; cf. 120-23 and 116-31.

133. C. Leslie Mitton, *Ephesians,* New Century Bible (London: Oliphants, 1976).

134. William D. Mounce, *Pastoral Epistles,* WBC (Nashville: Nelson, 2000), 448. Barrett detects here not baptism as "cleansing," but as "death and resurrection," and "putting on Christ as a garment"; C. K. Barrett, *The Pastoral Epistles,* New Clarendon Series (Oxford: Clarendon, 1963), 142.

135. E. G. Selwyn, *The First Epistle of Peter: The Greek Text* (London: Macmillan, 1947), 144 (my italics).

We need not press these points further. Schnackenburg is right to explore this aspect, but a survey of exegesis reveals how a hermeneutic depends upon unexamined exegetical traditions in this area. He is on stronger ground in his exposition of the other two major themes, "Assignment to Christ" relates especially to the phrase βαπτίζειν εἰς Χριστόν *(baptizein eis Christon)* and baptism as "salvation event" to dying, being buried, and being raised with Christ (σὺν Χριστῷ, *sun Christō*), especially in Rom. 6:1-11.

Schnackenburg rightly argues that although the preposition εἰς *(eis)* generally denotes movement toward a goal, in this baptismal context this preposition is more closely parallel with πιστεύειν εἰς *(pisteuein eis), to believe in,* in the sense of *direction* without movement.[136] This explains how the phrase in Gal. 3:27 coheres with its use in Rom. 6:3. In Gal. 3:27 the baptismal candidate *"puts on"* Christ like a new garment. Paul uses this image of "putting on" Christ in Rom. 13:14; Eph. 4:22-24; Col. 3:9-10; and elsewhere. In baptism the candidate "strips off" the old and "puts on" the new. This perspective traditionally has been held to support believers' baptism. This case is weakened only by the response that in a first-generation church we should expect this to be the norm, whatever adjustments may be made when children are born to parents who are already believers. The ancient liturgical tradition of turning west to renounce the works of the devil, and east to put on Christ, survives in the widespread custom today of turning east to recite the baptismal Creed. "Put off" and "put on" expresses the heart of baptismal doctrine.

Many versions translate εἰς *(eis)* as "into" in such phrases as "baptized into Christ" (NRSV, NIV, and KJV/AV for εἰς Χριστὸν ἐβαπτίσθητε, Gal. 3:27, although REB, "baptized into union with him," and NJB skillfully reconstruct the syntax). However, Schnackenburg insists: "Christ is not a 'sphere' into which we are plunged, but the personal Christ, with all that happened to Him; our baptism 'to Christ' has the goal of uniting us with this Christ and with everything that happened to him."[137] Others, for example, Flemington, argue in favor of the meaning "into." But Schnackenburg insists that we view each reference to baptism in its context.[138]

We do not have space to trace all of Schnackenburg's exegetical conclusions. He considers 1 Cor. 12:13 as a special example of "incorporation into the body of Christ."[139] His exposition of sharing in baptism as dying, being buried, and being raised with Christ faithfully expounds the *locus classicus* of Rom. 6:1-11. In terms of hermeneutics, this chapter explains how baptism denotes the event of identification with Christ in his death and resurrection "for us"/"for me," and

---

136. Schnackenburg, *Baptism*, 22-23.

137. Schnackenburg, *Baptism*, 25.

138. W. F. Flemington, *The New Testament Doctrine of Baptism* (London: S.P.C.K., 1957), 59-61.

139. Schnackenburg, *Baptism*, 26.

also the process of living out the life that new identity *begins*. This is the heart of the matter.[140]

The notion of pledging *allegiance* to Christ arises readily in this context. Indeed, baptism "in the Name of Christ" (with its parallel about baptism in allegiance to Moses in 1 Cor. 10:2) may partly explain the use of the preposition εἰς *(eis)* for the phrase *eis to onoma, in the name of*. Baptism is both Christological and related to salvation. Schnackenburg rightly observes: "Dying to the ruin wrought by the power of sin, with the goal of walking in a new life for God, is something different from the 'new birth' of the mystery religions."[141]

Günter Wagner has provided a comprehensive critique of mistaken attempts to claim that baptism in the New Testament was either derived from, or shaped by, alleged parallels with Hellenistic or oriental mystery religions.[142] The older theories of R. Reitzenstein and H. Wendland that Paul "borrowed" notions of sharing the fate and destiny of a god collapse with respect to linguistic issues and questions of dating. In contrast to the mystery religions, Wagner writes, in Paul the believer "is involved in the 'history' begun with Christ. . . . To be determined by the Christ-event really means to be involved in the eschatological event of the cross and resurrection (2 Cor. 5:14; Col. 3:3-4). . . . Through the 'body of Christ' the [baptized] has died to the law (Rom. 7:4). . . . Paul 'dies every day' (1 Cor. 15:31; cf. 2 Cor. 4:11-12; 11:23 . . . life ἐν Χριστῷ is sharing in the life of Christ in all of its phases . . . a being crucified with him (Rom. 6:6; Gal. 2:19) [and] being raised with Him (Col. 2:12; 3:1; Eph. 2:6)."[143]

C. F. D. Moule expounds this theme in eschatological terms in his essay "The Judgement Theme in the Sacraments."[144] He writes, "If Baptism is voluntary death, it is also a pleading guilty, an acceptance of the sentence."[145] It is, however, accepting a sentence of judgment that Christ invalidates and nails to the cross (Col. 2:14). In the Synoptic gospels Christ describes his coming death as a baptism (Mark 10:38; Luke 12:50). Christ's own baptism was "a sacrament of obedience — an anticipated death: our baptism is likewise an obedient acceptance of the situation caused by our sin and of the triumph over it."[146] Moule shares Luther's view that it is an "interim" institution looking toward the future and embodying *assurance and promise*. Alan Richardson, my sometime predecessor in

140. Schnackenburg, *Baptism*, 26-29.

141. Schnackenburg, *Baptism*, 59.

142. Günter Wagner, *Pauline Baptism and the Pagan Mysteries*, trans. J. P. Smith (Edinburgh: Oliver & Boyd, 1967), throughout.

143. Wagner, *Pauline Baptism*, 291-92.

144. C. F. D. Moule, "The Judgement Theme in the Sacraments," in W. D. Davies and D. Daube (eds.), *The Background to the New Testament and Its Eschatology: In Honour of C. H. Dodd* (Cambridge: Cambridge University Press, 1936), 464-81.

145. Moule, "Judgement Theme," in *Background*, 465.

146. Moule, "Judgement Theme," in *Background*, 466-67.

the University of Nottingham, holds the same view. He writes, "God's judgement on sin was executed in the baptism of death which Christ underwent. To be baptized is to accept God's verdict of 'guilty,' and so to be brought past the great assize and the final 'judgement.'"[147]

All four gospels portray baptism with this eschatological flavor. John the Baptist baptizes those who belong to those prepared for the last judgment (Matt. 3:1-12; Mark 1:4-8; Luke 3:1-17; John 1:19-27). The baptism of Jesus takes place in this context (Matt. 3:13-17; Mark 1:8-11; Luke 3:18-22; John 1:29-36). Oscar Cullmann speaks rightly of "the anchorage of baptism in the work of Christ. . . . Jesus is baptized in view of his death, which effects forgiveness of sins. . . . Jesus must unite himself in solidarity with his whole people, and go down himself to Jordan. . . . The baptism of Jesus points forward to . . . the Cross."[148] Hence, "Can you be baptized with the baptism that I am baptized with?" (Mark 10:38) alludes to death.

Another issue of interpretation arises from the extent to which we consider that baptism belongs within a communal context, or perceive it as more individually oriented. We earlier drew attention to Tom Holland's "corporate" exposition of Paul, which he explicitly applies to baptism.[149] The former can more readily accommodate infant baptism. Yet the core point is the parallel between the two sacraments instituted by Jesus Christ. *Both sacraments proclaim the death of Christ* and *anchor the gospel in the proclamation of the cross* (Rom. 6:1-11; 1 Cor. 11:23-26, especially v. 26). Both sacraments look forward to the eschaton.

147. Alan Richardson, *Introduction to the Theology of the New Testament* (London: S.C.M., 1958), 341.

148. Cullmann, *Baptism in the New Testament*, 14, 18, and 19.

149. Holland, *Contours of Pauline Theology*, 141-56.

CHAPTER 22

Eschatology: The Ultimate and Definitive
Hermeneutical Horizon of Meaning

22.1. Four Hermeneutical Starting Points:
Promise, Community, New Creation, and Apocalyptic

Four massive differences between biblical horizons of understanding for eschatology and the starting points adopted by many in everyday life today invite the formulation of four distinctive hermeneutical starting points for a biblical and Christian doctrine of the last things. The biblical writers do not begin with the potential of human selfhood or human consciousness to move to an understanding of, or belief in, eschatology. Biblical expectation and hope begins first of all with a hermeneutic of *divine promise.*

(i) Biblical horizons of understanding differ from other broader "religious" standpoints by grounding expectation and hope of future acts of God and human destiny *in a perceived gap between what God has promised and what has so far come about.* If God has pledged himself to perform or to provide what has not yet occurred, the immediate inference to be drawn is not that fulfillment is void, but that it is *not yet.* This forms the basis of the fundamental of *"not yet"* of biblical and Christian eschatology. It projects *hope* toward the future.

Moltmann, as we have noted, offers a timely and constructive exposition of this theme. He writes, "Presumption is a premature, self-willed anticipation of the fulfilment of what we hope for from God. Despair is the premature, arbitrary, anticipation of the non-fulfilment of what we hope for from God. Both forms of hopelessness, by anticipating the fulfilment or by giving up hope, cancel the wayfaring character of hope. They rebel against the patience in which hope trusts in the God of the promise."[1] "Expectation-thinking," Moltmann

---

1. Moltmann, *Theology of Hope,* 23.

comments, is "a new kind of thinking about the world," which is directed toward the future and "new things," and is unlike philosophical thinking about things in the present.[2]

Karl Rahner makes a broadly parallel point although in a different way in his essay "The Hermeneutics of Eschatological Assertions."[3] He points out that a hermeneutic that portrays future eschatological events as if they were a preview of continuing chronology or history "de-eschatologizes man himself. . . . The eschatological message becomes a statement which does not touch us at all at the moment. . . . If we lack an *a priori* horizon of an explicit nature, we do not allow Scripture to say what it really wishes to say."[4] Rahner continues, "The future must be really there; that is, it must be looked forward to . . . [as] still to come."[5]

(ii) The second substantial difference of horizon of understanding arises from the difference between the *individual* focus of much Western thought since the seventeenth and eighteenth centuries and the focus on *the world, creation, and community* that characterizes biblical eschatology.

One of the earlier works in the mid-twentieth century that elaborated the contrast was J. A. T. Robinson's *In the End, God. . . .* In contrast to thought about future destiny in the Western world, Robinson writes, "In the New Testament, on the other hand, the point around which hope and interest revolve is not the moment of death, but the day of the Parousia, or appearance of Christ in the glory of His Kingdom."[6] Hellenist cultures as they encountered the message of the New Testament, he observes, imposed upon it "an uneschatological view of history and an individualistic doctrine of the soul . . . the shift of emphasis which has produced the modern outlook. Whereas in primitive Christian thinking the moment of the individual's decease was entirely subordinated to the great Day of the Lord and the final judgement, in later thought it is the hour of death which becomes decisive."[7] Even the four traditional "last things," namely death, judgment, heaven and hell, are focused on the individual in contrast to "the great Last Thing" of the New Testament, which turns on the *cosmic, world events* of the *Parousia, the last judgment,* and *the resurrection of the dead.*

William Manson made a similar point, also in the 1950s. The "essence" of New Testament eschatology, he comments, is not a chronological projection of a series of events that follow the decease of an individual, but the broader understanding in which we "are impelled to think of all history and all life by reference

---

2. Moltmann, *Hope,* 35.

3. Rahner, "The Hermeneutics of Eschatological Assertions," in *Theological Investigations,* vol. 4, 323-46.

4. Rahner, "Hermeneutics," *Investigations,* 4, 328-29.

5. Rahner, "Hermeneutics," *Investigations,* 4, 333.

6. John A. T. Robinson, *In the End, God . . . : A Study of the Christian Doctrine of the Last Things* (London: James Clarke, 1950), 10.

7. Robinson, *In the End, God,* 11.

to an ultimate transcendent Event, an End towards which, under the judgment and mercy of God, the world is hastening."[8]

Moltmann places this perspective in a deeper *theological* understanding. The contrast is more than that between individual and communal or cosmic. Moltmann defines the biblical perspective as "the eschatological coming to pass of the faithfulness of God. . . . It points beyond itself, and even beyond Jesus, to the coming revelation of the glory of God. . . . Jesus . . . the Lord who appears as risen . . . appears in the foreglow of the coming, promised glory of God."[9] The "hermeneutics" of the biblical witness, he adds, concerns "the universal future of God for the world and for all men."[10] At the same time Moltmann makes the broader point that Manson and Rahner identify. This illuminates the present interaction of humankind *"in their relationship to the future"* (his italics).[11] In 18.1 we considered the work of the Holy Spirit within a situation of "eschatological tension." The Holy Spirit constitutes the "firstfruits" of a promised future, which is similar in kind but greater in glory than the present experience of the Spirit.

(iii) The nature of the hope, expectation, and promise of *the resurrection of the dead* clarifies this hermeneutical contrast beyond all doubt. Plato argued for the immortality of the soul on the ground that the nature of the soul was nonearthly and noncontingent, and therefore belonged to the eternal realm of Forms and Ideas. Paul places grounds for belief in the resurrection on an entirely different basis. The reason for confusion about the resurrection in Corinth (1 Cor. 15:2, εἰκῇ, *eikē, without due consideration*) derived from whether those in the church "had knowledge of God" (1 Cor. 15:34). The ground for belief is the *infinite resourcefulness of God as Creator to create anew a mode of existence appropriate for resurrection life, and the act of God in raising Jesus Christ,* as evidenced by witnesses (1 Cor. 15:3-6, 35-44).[12]

(iv) These three hermeneutical horizons, namely that of *promise* (and its relation to fulfillment), that of *community and cosmos,* and that of the sovereign *creative power of God* and new creation, come together as major features of *apocalyptic* thought within eschatology. This pattern of thought has influenced the eschatology of Jesus and Paul, as well as other material in the New Testament.

Some have understandable suspicions of appeals to apocalyptic, partly perhaps because of the false dawn associated with claims made on its behalf by Johannes Weiss and Albert Schweitzer, and partly because of what Klaus Koch

8. William Manson, *Eschatology,* Scottish Journal of Theology Occasional Papers (Edinburgh: Oliver & Boyd, 1953), 1.

9. Moltmann, *Hope,* 201.

10. Moltmann, *Hope,* 283.

11. Moltmann, *Hope,* 283.

12. Thiselton, *First Epistle to the Corinthians,* 1169-1313, esp. 1183-1206 and 1253-81; cf. Barth, *The Resurrection of the Dead,* 18; and H. A. A. Kennedy, *St. Paul's Conception of the Last Things* (London: Hodder & Stoughton, 1904), 243; cf. 222-341.

calls the "disquieting" features of nontheological apocalyptic.[13] Yet even the sometimes maverick claims of Schweitzer at the very least served to question the liberal pictures of Jesus conveyed by Ritschl and Harnack, and to query the foundations in which Walter Rauschenbusch would later seek to build a "social Gospel" of Jesus.[14] Weiss brought to the interpretation of Paul a recovery of Paul's emphasis on new creation, on the two ages of apocalyptic expectation, and a forward-looking perspective of maturity and hope.[15] History moves forward in accordance with the divine will; the promised future has yet to come to pass (1 Cor. 13:12); and the glory of the Lord stands in readiness to break into the present from the future.

Moltmann concedes the "ineffectiveness" of Weiss and Schweitzer to bring about a new beginning, but this was largely because they failed adequately to explore "Christian eschatology in the language of promise."[16] Hence it is not surprising that many expressed reservations about the role of apocalyptic for Jesus and Paul. Nevertheless a recovery emerged, in which Ernst Käsemann, Ulrich Wilckens, J. L. Martyn, and J. Christiaan Beker identified apocalyptic features within the theology of the New Testament, and Jürgen Moltmann, Wolfhart Pannenberg, and Gerhard Sauter expounded these features in systematic theology.[17] Koch observes, "Moltmann displays an insight into apocalyptic which is all too often lacking among specialist scholars."[18]

Biblical specialists frequently complain about the ambiguity of the term *apocalyptic*.[19] But many points in the teaching of Jesus and of Paul resonate with key themes in Christian eschatology and derive at least initially from axioms familiar in the apocalyptic literature of the day. Schweitzer observes, for example, that for Paul "the resurrection is not an isolated event. . . . [It is] the initial event of the rising of the dead in general."[20] Further, Jesus and Paul speak of *new creation* rather than human reformation (Mark 2:21-22; par. Matt. 9:16-17; Luke 5:36-38; 2 Cor. 5:17); the "old garment" (Mark 2:21) is like the things of "*this age*

---

13. Klaus Koch, *The Rediscovery of Apocalyptic,* trans. Margaret Kohl (London: S.C.M., 1972), 112-22.

14. On the history of research, see Norman Perrin, *The Kingdom of God in the Teaching of Jesus* (London: S.C.M., 1963), 14-57.

15. Weiss, *Earliest Christianity,* vol. 2, 433-35 and 523-45.

16. Moltmann, *Hope,* 41; cf. 37-42.

17. Ernst Käsemann, "On the Subject of Primitive Christian Apocalyptic," in Ernst Käsemann, *New Testament Questions of Today,* trans. W. J. Montague (London: S.C.M., 1969), 108-39; Beker, *Paul the Apostle,* 11-19, 135-81, and 351-68; Pannenberg, "The Revelation of God in Jesus of Nazareth," in Robinson and Cobb (eds.), *New Frontiers in Theology,* III: *Theology as History,* 101-33, and other works cited above; cf. *Systematic Theology,* vol. 3, 531-45.

18. Koch, *Rediscovery,* 108.

19. Barry B. Matlock, *Unveiling the Apocalyptic: Paul's Interpreters and the Rhetoric of Criticism,* JSNTSS 127 (Sheffield: Sheffield Academic Press, 1996).

20. Schweitzer, *Mysticism of Paul,* 98.

that are doomed to pass away" (1 Cor. 2:6); where Jesus speaks of demonic forces and asserts that only "a strong man can enter and plunder their house" (Mark 3:22-27; par. Matt. 12:25-29; Luke 11:16-22). Paul declares that "the god of this world has blinded their minds" (2 Cor. 4:4); Christ comes as deliverer to shepherd the oppressed flock (Matt. 15:24; Luke 19:10), and as physician to heal the sick (Mark 2:17); Paul speaks of "the present evil age" (Gal. 1:4), and Christ as "rescuing us (ἐρρύσατο, *errusato*) from the power of darkness and transferring us (μετέστησεν, *metestēsen*) into the kingdom of his beloved Son" (Col. 1:13).

It is hardly necessary to show how closely all this coheres with the mood and stance of apocalyptic. As Rowley observes, the apocalyptists never looked to the present and to the human situation "to generate the longed for tomorrow. . . . Their spring of hope was in God alone. . . . They knew nothing of the idea that man would steadily work his way upward on the stepping stones of his sins to the goal of his being. . . . He could rise only by the power of God."[21]

The significance of this mind-set for Christian eschatology is to underline and corroborate the three horizons of understanding identified above, especially that of divine *promise,* which *God fulfills in terms of his own sovereign choosing.* Hence eschatology entails looking to God both in terms of the future and in terms of present patient waiting. Furthermore, the *newness* of the inbreaking of the future, signified especially by the Holy Spirit as (in Bultmann's phrase) "the power of futurity," leads to what Moltmann perceives as the difference between the merely relatively new and *"the category Novum."*[22] He writes, "Just as the raised Christ does not *develop* out of the crucified and dead Christ, the *novum ultimum* — the ultimate new thing — does not *issue* from the history of the old."[23] Yet even the *novum* is not without any analogy, or we could not conceive of *that for which* we hope to any relative degree. "What is eschatologically new, itself creates its own continuity, since it does not annihilate the old but gathers it up and creates it anew. . . . '*This* mortal nature must put on immortality' (1 Cor. 15:53). The raised Christ is the crucified Christ and no other, but he is the crucified Christ in transfigured form."[24] God remains faithful to his creation.

These comments not only illuminate the eschatological hope, but also place in perspective a comparison that is sometimes offered between Moltmann and Pannenberg in their respective utilizations of apocalyptic patterns of thought. Klaus Koch and Michael Gilbertson in a more recent study suggest that while

---

21. H. H. Rowley, *The Relevance of Apocalyptic: A Study of Jewish and Christian Apocalypses from Daniel to Revelation* (London: Lutterworth, 1944), 141 and 155-56; cf. D. S. Russell, *The Method and Message of Jewish Apocalyptic, 200 B.C.–A.D. 100* (London: S.C.M., 1964), 104-51 and 205-303; and Koch, *Rediscovery,* 73-111.

22. Jürgen Moltmann, *The Coming of God: Christian Eschatology,* trans. Margaret Kohl (London: S.C.M., 1996), 27-29.

23. Moltmann, *Coming,* 28.

24. Moltmann, *Coming,* 29 (his italics).

Moltmann places relatively more emphasis upon the contrast and discontinuity between the old creation and the new, Pannenberg stresses their continuity and coherence. Gilbertson writes, "Pannenberg is concerned to emphasize the overall unity and coherence of history as the self-revelation of God . . . [as] ultimate horizons within which all events should be seen. Moltmann, on the other hand, is concerned to stress the *contradiction* between the coming reality of God and present historical reality" (his italics).[25]

Pannenberg does indeed perceive the continuity of history in terms of God's sovereign purpose, in which only the End can reveal the true meaning of the present. *The provisionality of present meaning* ("judge nothing before the time," 1 Cor. 4:5) is a fundamental theme of apocalyptic, for some things remain hidden in the present, and the definitive verdict awaits the end time when alone the completed picture will emerge for public understanding. Pannenberg also draws from apocalyptic the *universal* dimension of history and hermeneutic, which transcends the history of Israel and the church alone. However, is "contradiction" entailed in Moltmann's carefully measured statements about the *novum*? Moltmann usually prefers to speak of *"transformation"* of the world, the old, or history. Koch and Gilbertson signal only a difference of degree. Pannenberg and Moltmann complement rather than contradict each other. Each stresses the possibility of *novelty and surprise* as God's promises come to be fulfilled in unexpected ways. But each also stresses divine *faithfulness,* as God remains true to his promise.

22.2. Three Further Hermeneutical Horizons: Hope, the Grammar of Expectation, and Time: The "Imminence" of the Parousia

(v) *The discipline of waiting coupled with eager expectancy for the future.* This hermeneutic of understanding is far removed from the drive for *immediacy, instantaneousness, and instant gratification of desire* generated by the combined effect of socio-economic consumerism, the availability of massive financial credit, and an increasingly "postmodern" turn of mind. Almost unlimited credit draws upon, and uses up, the uncertain future for the desires of the present moment. Not only in the wealthier West but in many rising cultures, this stands in radical contrast with the ethos of Victorian England or of earlier American, European, and Japanese industrial economies, where many aimed to build foundations to last for future generations. This more solid mind-set has given way at the turn of the twenty-first century to a short-term philosophy of "enjoy it now; pay for it later."

25. Michael Gilbertson, *God and History in the Book of Revelation: New Testament Studies in Dialogue with Pannenberg and Moltmann,* SNTSMS 124 (Cambridge: Cambridge University Press, 2003), 143-44; cf. Koch, *Rediscovery,* 101-11.

Such horizons do not relate readily to an eschatology of "not yet" in which waiting is characterized not by resentment but by eager expectancy concerning what lies ahead. Postmodern consumerist cultures regard "waiting" as intolerable, and as a source of resentment or at best disappointed resignation.

The New Testament writers often "glory" in what is yet to come, but are more hesitant to express any hint of undue triumphalism about the present. Paul exclaims, "I consider that the sufferings of the present time are not worth comparing with the glory about to be revealed in us. For the creation waits with eager longing (Greek ἡ γὰρ ἀποκαραδοκία τῆς κτίσεως, *hē gar apokaradokia tēs ktiseōs*) for the revealing of the children of the God . . . in hope that creation itself will be set free from its bondage to decay, and will obtain the freedom of the glory of the children of God. We know that creation has been groaning in labor pains until now, and not only creation, but we ourselves who have the firstfruits (τὴν ἀπαρχήν, *tēn aparchēn*) of the Spirit, groan inwardly *while we wait . . . in hope. . . .* For who *hopes* for what is seen?" (Rom. 8:18-25).

Reference to Greek lexicons confirms that ἀποκαραδοκία *(apokaradokia)* denotes eager expectation in Rom. 8:19, as it does in Phil. 1:20, with the added nuance of painting an imaginative (δοκέω) scenario.[26] Grimm-Thayer takes up the component metaphors embedded in the rare word ἀποκαραδοκία, noting the meanings of κάρα *(kara)*, "head"; δοκέω *(dokeō)*, "to imagine or to watch"; with ἀπό *(apo)* as a directional or intensive compound. Taken as a whole, the verb embodies the compound metaphor *"to watch with head . . . outstretched."*[27] This does not constitute merely the kind of "etymologizing" that Barr reminds us says more about word history than word meaning, for contemporary readers would no doubt pick up the metaphorical force. Creation, we might say, *cranes its neck* to see what glory *will* be revealed *in* believers.

Paul sets this attitude of eager anticipation of the *future* in contrast to the "presumption" (as Moltmann calls it) of *premature* anticipation in Corinth: "Already you have become glutted! Already you have been 'made rich'! Without us you came to 'reign as kings'! — If only you did 'reign as kings', so that we, too, could reign as kings with you! For it seems to me that God has put us apostles on display as a grand finale, as those doomed to die" (1 Cor. 4:8-9). "Up to this very moment we have become, as it were, the world's scum, the scrapings from everyone's shoes" (4:13; my translation).[28] Barrett comments, "The Corinthians are behaving as if the age to come were already consummated, as if the saints had al-

---

26. BDAG, 112; J. H. Moulton and G. Milligan, *Vocabulary of the Greek Testament* (London: Hodder & Stoughton, [1930] 1952), 63: "those in Hades watch eagerly for the parousia of Christ."

27. J. H. Thayer, *Greek-English Lexicon of the New Testament* (Edinburgh: T&T Clark, 4th edn. 1901), 62-63.

28. Thiselton, *First Epistle to the Corinthians*, 344; the translation is defended and explained on 345-68.

ready taken over the kingdom (Dan. 7:18); for them there is no 'not yet' to qualify the 'already' of realised eschatology."[29]

What accounts for this dual attitude of joyous expectancy and disciplined patience? Pannenberg makes the fundamental point that hope, like faith, rests on *trust in the promises of God,* together with "a sense of the *incompleteness of life as it now is . . .* related to the confidence that it is oriented to its possible fulfilment."[30] Faith as trust "in God and in his promise is never apart from hope."[31] The interrelation between trustful faith and forward-looking hope finds a paradigm case in the faith of Abraham (Gen. 15:6 and Rom. 4:3). Typically, many of the Psalms express trustful hope (Pss. 43:5; 71:5, 14; 119:114). Believers "rejoice in the hope of the glory of God" (Rom. 5:2), and "wait for the hope of righteousness" (Gal. 5:5). In an objective sense that for which Christians hope is "laid up for [them] in heaven" (Col. 1:5; cf. Heb. 6:11, 18; 1 Pet. 1:3, 21; 3:15; 1 John 3:3). "Faith is the assurance of things hoped for" (Heb. 11:1).

This "not yet" also provides an ethical and practical dynamic for appropriating what lies ahead as the reign of God advances. This principle emerges in the very earliest writings of the Old Testament: "Be strong and courageous. . . . Go in to take possession of the land, . . . for I have given [it] to you, as I promised . . ." (Josh. 1:3, 9, 11).

Pannenberg explicates the distinctively Christian horizon of understanding this principle. Ernst Bloch comments that "the pressuring 'not yet' in the tendencies and latencies of material processes forms the ontological basis of the impulsive nature of life, of hunger, of dreams. Yet in these tendencies . . . perishing has its basis as well as becoming."[32] In other words, even within the flow of everyday life in general, the need to move on in the face of the "not yet" provides motivation and dynamic. There may be some parallel with the "drives" of the *yetser hā'-rā'* and *yetser hā'-tôbh* in rabbinic thought. But outside the promise of God that for which humankind strives and longs and yearns can prove to be disenchanting, disappointing, and illusory, and can turn to dust. For Christians, Paul declares, "Hope does not disappoint us, because God's love has been poured into our hearts through the Holy Spirit" (Rom. 5:5).

In this context it makes good sense for Neil Hamilton to speak of the Holy Spirit as bringing and being "the break-in of the future into the present."[33] The Holy Spirit is the firstfruits (ἀπαρχή, *aparchē*) or partial foretaste in the present of what lies in greater abundance in the future (Rom. 8:23). The Spirit is the "pledge," "down payment," or "earnest" (ἀρραβών, *arrabōn*) of that of which more will come in the future (2 Cor. 1:22; 5:5; cf. Eph. 1:14). Hence, in the present

29. C. K. Barrett, *First Epistle to the Corinthians* (London: Black, 2d edn. 1971), 109.
30. Pannenberg, *Systematic Theology,* vol. 3, 173.
31. Pannenberg, *Systematic Theology,* vol. 3, 173.
32. Pannenberg, *Systematic Theology,* vol. 3, 175.
33. Hamilton, *The Holy Spirit and Eschatology,* 24.

"the Spirit helps us in our weakness . . . intercedes with sighs too deep for words" (Rom. 8:26). To receive the Spirit is to receive the guarantee of future resurrection with Christ (Rom. 8:11).

Even in the Synoptic gospels a survey of what Jeremias calls "the reversals" of which Jesus speaks suggests that each of these can be understood in one or more of three distinct ways. Some *find fulfillment* from the ministry, death, and resurrection of Jesus Christ onward. Others begin *a process of initial fulfillment*, but do not fully reach fulfilment until the *Parousia* and resurrection of the dead. A third group remain "not yet" until the last day. All derive from *divine promise*, but all also depend on *divine timing*. Of these "reversals" Jeremias writes: "Conditions are reversed: what is hidden becomes manifest (Matt. 10:26); the poor become rich (Luke 6:20); the last are first (Mark 10:31); the small become great (Matt. 18:4); the hungry are filled (Luke 6:21); the weary find rest (Matt. 11:28); those who weep laugh (Luke 6:21); the mourners are comforted (Matt. 5:4); the sick are healed, blind receive their sight, lepers are cleansed, deaf hear (Matt. 11:5); prisoners are freed, the oppressed relieved (Luke 4:18); the lowly are exalted (Matt. 23:12; Luke 14:11; 18:14); the humble bear rule (Matt. 5:5); the members of the little flock become kings (Luke 12:32); and the dead live (Matt. 11:5)."[34]

(vi) An appropriate horizon of understanding for all of this depends also on an appreciation of *the conceptual grammar of expectation*. History witnesses to the disenchanted hopes of "millennial-minded" groups that predicted the Day of the Lord on a specific calendar date, and found themselves exposed as self-deceived. Yet can a hope or expectation that is *forever indefinite* genuinely inspire the joy, eagerness, and urgency of the kind that finds a place in the New Testament?

Many New Testament specialists still rehearse the threadbare theme that Jesus and Paul "expected" the Parousia during the lifetime of the first generation of Christians, but were proved to be wrong. The evidence for this is precarious. George B. Caird never accepted this piece of "critical doctrine," as he called it, and his impatience with it led him to an incisive exploration of what he termed "end-of-the-world metaphor." During the 1960s Caird collaborated on this subject with his fellow Oxford professor Stephen Ullmann, then Professor of Semantics. He concluded that while the New Testament often used metaphor in these contexts, the conclusions of many New Testament specialists betrayed little understanding or sensitivity concerning the use of metaphor in eschatology. Jesus expected the end of *the preresurrection* "world," or the end of the "world" *of Israel* as a nation. Sadly, much of Caird's work was not published until 1980, only four years before his untimely death, in *The Language and Imagery of the Bible*, but

---

34. Joachim Jeremias, *The Parables of Jesus*, trans. S. H. Hooke (London: S.C.M., rev. edn. 1963), 221-22.

had long since been formulated in oral lectures at Oxford.[35] Caird writes, "The biblical writers . . . regularly used end-of-the-world language metaphorically to refer to that which they knew was not the end of the world."[36]

Caird exposes the questionable nature of Bultmann's claims about Jesus' "mistake" without difficulty. On the one hand, Bultmann suggests that Jesus expected an imminent *Parousia* but was proved to have been mistaken since "history continued." On the other hand, Bultmann claims, "a belief in the temporal imminence of the end has no other function than to express the ultimate and transcendent function of a present decision."[37] But does Bultmann use "imminent" in a temporal or nontemporal sense? How can he have the argument both ways without changing the meaning of his terms?

We might argue a parallel point with reference to Paul's words: "*We* who are alive and who are left until the coming of the Lord will by no means precede those who have died" (1 Thess. 4:15). How could Paul be seen to take "expectation" seriously if he had said "*you* who are alive and remain," or even "*those* who are alive"? Ernest Best firmly dismisses such an argument.[38] But given that grammar and syntax *must imply* one of *two possible working assumptions,* and could not otherwise be expressed, *a hypothetical working presupposition should not be accorded the status of a proposition or assertion.* In a different context P. F. Strawson has argued this point rigorously. A. L. Moore is so firmly convinced of this that he attributes the belief that Paul expected the Parousia during his own lifetime to a mistaken acceptance "more through its frequent assertion than its sound evidence."[39] Paul knew that he frequently faced *violent death* (2 Cor. 11:23-27). He voiced equally the open assumption "*whether we live or die,* we are the Lord's" (Rom. 14:8; cf. 2 Cor. 5:9; Phil. 1:20-21).

These responses are valid, but do not quite reach the heart of this pseudo-controversy. Is "*expecting*" a "*mental state*" at all? More accurately, is it *primarily* a psychological process that goes on in the mind and *necessarily* entails *chronological* calculation or prediction? Wittgenstein's observations on the conceptual grammar of *to expect* suggest otherwise.

Just as what it is *to believe* is bound up with *attitudes, behavior, and disposition,* so also *to expect* "is embedded in a situation from which it takes its rise."[40]

---

35. George B. Caird, *The Language and Imagery of the Bible* (London: Duckworth, 1980), 131-200 and 243-71.

36. Caird, *Language and Imagery,* 256.

37. Caird, *Language and Imagery,* 254.

38. Ernest Best, *The First and Second Epistles to the Thessalonians* (London: Black, 1972), 194-96.

39. A. L. Moore, *1 and 2 Thessalonians* (London and Camden, NJ: Nelson, 1969), 70; see also A. L. Moore, *The Parousia in the New Testament,* Supplements to Novum Testamentum 13 (Leiden: Brill, 1966), 108-10.

40. Wittgenstein, *Zettel,* sect. 67.

Wittgenstein continues: "In order to understand the grammar of these states it is necessary to ask: 'What counts as a criterion for anyone's being in such a state?'"[41] No single thought, attitude, or action tells the whole story. However, Wittgenstein imagines what it would be like to expect a friend for tea at 4 o'clock. This may include: (i) seeing the friend's name in one's diary; (ii) preparing tea for two; (iii) wondering whether he will wish to smoke and finding an ashtray; (iv) putting out cigarettes; (v) beginning to feel impatient towards 4:30 if he has not arrived: "All this is called 'expecting.' . . . And there are endless variations to this process. . . . There is one single feature in common to all of them."[42] "Psychological" understandings of expectation as mental processes are not false, but they are "trivial" and miss "the *punctum saliens.*"[43]

If the expected person is a good friend who is more than welcome, expectation will manifest itself as *cheerfulness,* perhaps several days ahead of performing the actions described above. Sometimes *to expect* is not to hold any explicit propositional belief, but almost simply to feel "surprised if he did not come."[44] Fundamentally what it is *to expect* depends upon its *"surroundings"* and upon *behavior.*[45]

This describes how the New Testament writers seem to "expect" the fulfillment of divine promises, the Parousia of Jesus Christ, and the revelation of God's glory at the last day. They explicitly reject the notion that "expecting" has anything to do with chronological calculation (Mark 13:32; 1 Thess. 5:2; 2 Pet. 3:8-10). The logical currency of *expecting* the *eschaton* is shown by how Christians *live.* They live their lives as those accountable and responsible to God. They *live* as those whose vindication and final assurance of justification lies in a promised future. They *live* as those who look forward to the revelation of the crucified Christ in glory. But if this is the case, how does it make sense to apply the term "mistake" *to practical action* if this does not entail believing propositions about chronological duration?

Jesus states not only: "About that day and hour no one knows," but adds, "neither the angels of heaven nor the Son, but only the Father" (Mark 13:32; par. Matt. 24:36). Jesus speaks of expectation in terms of *attitude and action:* "Keep awake, for you do not know on what day your Lord is coming" (Matt. 24:42; cf. Luke 12:46). Paul tells the Christians in Thessalonica not to become preoccupied with speculations about the *Parousia* (2 Thess. 2:2-3). As in the case of a preg-

---

41. Wittgenstein, *Philosophical Investigations,* sect. 572.

42. Wittgenstein, *The Blue and Brown Books: Preliminary Studies for the "Philosophical Investigations"* (Oxford: Blackwell, 2d edn. 1969), 20.

43. Wittgenstein, *Zettel,* sect. 66.

44. Wittgenstein, *Philosophical Investigations,* sect. 582.

45. Wittgenstein, *Philosophical Investigations,* II:x, 191-92. See sects. 572-86; *Zettel,* sects. 58-68 and 71-77; and Ludwig Wittgenstein, *Philosophische Bemerkungen* (Oxford: Blackwell, 1964), sects. 21-31.

nancy, there may be signs of an imminent event, but this is not incompatible with being caught by surprise (1 Thess. 5:1-4). Christians are fundamentally in a state of readiness to meet Christ, whatever speculations may or may not be in the air (1 Thess. 5:5-11).

(vii) Finally, *the horizon of time* is of greater significance than *spatial* metaphors for offering a hermeneutical horizon for understanding faith and hope. Oscar Cullmann provides an illuminating comment on the definition of faith in Heb. 11:1. He writes, "Primitive Christian faith and thinking do not start from the spatial contrast between the Here and the Beyond, but from the time distinction between Formerly and Now and Then."[46] Cullmann recognizes that the spatial contrast between visible and invisible has a place, but "the essential thing" is the temporal dimension. Thus in Heb. 11:1 faith is "the assurance of things *hoped for*" and "the conviction of things not seen." Here that which is "not seen" refers to faith's apprehension of what is not "seen" *because it has not yet taken place*.

Whatever the different perspectives on time brought by John Marsh, James Barr, and others (which we consider in 22.5), this starting point accords with the eschatology of the Epistle to the Hebrews, and with much in the Synoptic gospels and in Paul.[47] It relates directly to the points made in 19.2 and 19.3 about *the event-character* of divine transcendence with reference to Jüngel's comments, in contrast to static categories exclusively of *being*.[48] The Epistle to the Hebrews, as I have argued elsewhere, is part of an ongoing *narrative* formulated in temporal terms, even if the author complements this with the spatial imagery of mediation and "access."[49] Since *covenant* constitutes one of the central themes of this epistle, the correlative concept of *promise* also becomes prominent, as we should expect. But, as Pannenberg points out, *faithfulness to promise* manifests itself only over a period of time. Neither God's proven faithfulness nor the readers' tested faithfulness can acquire working currency other than *through time*. Pannenberg writes, "Those who make a promise that they can keep only many years later . . . have to retain their identity if they are to meet the promise. Actions owe their unity to the *time-bridging* identity of their subject."[50]

The Epistle to the Hebrews holds together the vulnerability and constraints of the "not yet" of a pilgrim people in process of travel with "the steadfast an-

46. Oscar Cullmann, *Christ and Time: the Primitive Christian Conception of Time and History,* trans. F. V. Filson (London: S.C.M., 1951), 37.

47. Cf. John Marsh, *The Fulness of Time* (London: Nisbet, 1952); and James Barr, *Biblical Words for Time* (London: S.C.M., 1962).

48. Eberhard Jüngel, *The Doctrine of the Trinity: God's Being Is in Becoming,* trans. Horton Harris (Edinburgh: Scottish Academic Press, 1976), 5-41, and *God as the Mystery of the World,* esp. 152-298 (in contrast to 105-152).

49. Anthony C. Thiselton, "Human Being, Relationality and Time in Hebrews, 1 Corinthians, and Western Tradition," *Ex Auditu* 13 (1997) 76-95.

50. Pannenberg, *Systematic Theology,* vol. 2, 202 (my italics).

chor" (Heb. 6:19), the future hope (6:19), and the double guarantee of an oath (6:17). Heb. 11:1-39 movingly portrays the temporal succession of witnesses who "did not receive what was promised" (11:39) because the right time had not yet arrived. Jesus remains their model of faith in this respect, for he prayed in Gethsemane "with loud cries and tears" (Heb. 5:7) and was not exempt from the need to trust God (Heb. 2:13). As the mediating representative of humankind to God, he was a pioneer or trailblazer *(archēgos)* of humankind. E. Käsemann and Robert Jewett underline the temporal dimension of pilgrimage and journey, in contrast to the spatial dimensions of above and below in gnostic cosmologies.[51] To prepare for *heaven* is to travel toward the *homeland*.

C. K. Barrett expounds this theme in his essay, "The Eschatology of the Epistle to the Hebrews."[52] He notes that "entering into the [sabbath] rest" (Heb. 4:3) is in the present tense but that it also has future force: "The 'rest', precisely because it is God's, is both present and future: men enter it and must strive to enter it . . . a paradox which Hebrews shares with all primitive Christian eschatology."[53] Such is the motif of journey that Barrett entitles part of his essay: "The Pilgrim's Progress from the City of Destruction to the Celestial City."[54] In this present life Christians "have no abiding city; they seek one to come" (Heb. 13:14). God has "prepared" a city for them (11:16). They need patient endurance for the journey that lies ahead (Heb. 12:1). Yet the future "city that has foundations" lies ahead by virtue of *divine promise. Covenant promise* to Abraham in Hebrews (e.g., Heb. 11:13, 17, 33, 39) is no less a paradigm of faith and hope than it is for Paul in Rom. 4:13-25. Barrett comments, *"Promise* finds its correlative in *faith,* just as *city* finds its correlative in *pilgrimage"* (his italics).[55] He concludes, "The dawn of the new age has broken, though the full day has not yet come."[56]

Cullmann expresses a parallel point with reference to the New Testament as a whole. He writes, "The time tension is manifested in the Church through the continuance of sin, which nevertheless has already been defeated by the Spirit."[57] "Thus the Holy Spirit is nothing else than the anticipation of the end in the present."[58] This is expressed in such terms as the "firstfruits" of the Spirit (Rom. 8:23; cf. 2 Cor. 1:22; 5:5), as we have observed. It is unfortunate that so many writers

---

51. Robert Jewett, *Letter to Pilgrims: A Commentary on the Epistle to the Hebrews* (New York: Pilgrim, 1981); Ernst Käsemann, *The Wandering People of God* (Minneapolis: Augsburg, 1984).

52. C. K. Barrett, "The Eschatology of the Epistle to the Hebrews," in W. D. Davies and D. Daube (eds.), *The Background of the New Testament and Its Eschatology: Studies in Honour of Charles Harold Dodd* (Cambridge: Cambridge University Press, 1956), 363-93.

53. Barrett, "Eschatology," in *Background*, 372.

54. Barrett, "Eschatology," in *Background*, 373-83.

55. Barrett, "Eschatology," in *Background*, 380.

56. Barrett, "Eschatology," in *Background*, 391.

57. Cullmann, *Christ and Time*, 155.

58. Cullmann, *Christ and Time*, 72.

seem to speak almost glibly of "now" and "not yet" as if to rehearse a piece of technical critical dogma, rolled off the tongue and rehearsed in New Testament classes. For the earliest Christians it suggested a powerful dynamic of assured hope and action alongside a yearning for "completeness" and for that fuller experience of the Holy Spirit that is reserved for the end time and the resurrection. This can be recovered today.

22.3. The Hermeneutics of Language about the Resurrection: The Resurrection Mode of Existence

All of the horizons of understanding outlined above apply to interpreting the hope, future reality, and meaning of the resurrection of the dead. Above all, resurrection depends not upon some innate capacity of the human self, but upon *a promised, sovereign, gracious, and creative act of God*. It is an act of sheer grace, because like justification by grace resurrection is pure *gift*. Those who have died and are dead can make no contribution to their resurrection. "God *gives* (δίδωσιν, *didōsin*) it a body as he wills" (1 Cor. 15:38; cf. Rom. 4:16-25). "The promise rests on grace" (Rom. 4:16). It is a *sovereign* act because God accords a resurrection mode of existence καθὼς ἠθέλησεν (*kathōs ēthelēsen*, as he has willed, called by one writer "an aorist of sovereignty," 1 Cor. 15:38). It is *certain* because the ultimate ground of hope lies in the inexhaustible resources of divine wisdom and power to create a mode of being appropriate to the new resurrection environment in accordance with the versatility that God has already demonstrated. He demonstrated it when he brought into existence such a manifold and multiform creation (1 Cor. 15:34-44).

The more immediate ground of hope is also God's proven power shown in raising Jesus Christ from the dead by the agency of the Holy Spirit. This constitutes a pledge or promise of what is yet to come in the final resurrection of the dead: "If the Spirit of him who raised Jesus from the dead dwells in you, he who raised Christ from the dead will give life to your mortal bodies also through his Sprit that dwells in you" (Rom. 8:11). The reality of the resurrection of Jesus Christ is attested by pre-Pauline apostolic tradition and by many witnesses (1 Cor. 15:3-8).

Within the New Testament the *locus classicus* on the resurrection is 1 Corinthians 15. Hence the usual hermeneutical procedure suggests that we should first attempt to clarify *what questions* raised by some in Corinth Paul is first and foremost addressing. However, even if Paul is addressing questions or doubts raised in Corinth, this does not imply that this chapter is merely contingent upon such questions being asked. A hundred years of research on this epistle has not displaced the convictions of Luther, Calvin, and Barth that this chapter "forms not only the close and crown of the whole epistle, but also provides the key to its meaning from which light is shed onto the whole."[59] Luther declares, "Whoever denies this article must simultaneously deny far more . . . in brief, that God is God."[60] A person must either accept the resurrection of the dead, Luther comments, "or he must deny in a lump the Gospel and everything that is proclaimed of Christ and of God."[61]

(i) Some argue that a group in Corinth could not believe in any kind of postmortal existence. This view has been advocated by H. Grotius (1645), M. L. de Wette (1845), and more recently by W. Schmithals (1965).[62] One main argument is Paul's criticism of the Epicurean maxim "let us eat and drink, for tomorrow we die" (1 Cor. 15:32), and his statement, "if in this life only we have hope, we deserve pity" (15:17, 19). Disbelief in postmortal existence in the Greco-Roman world of the first century was probably more widespread than some assume.

(ii) From Chrysostom onward, with some support from Luther, many have argued that a number in Corinth believed that the resurrection had already occurred, even if as an "inner" experience (2 Tim. 2:18). Too many hold this view to name, but they include Munck, Wilckens, Käsemann, Barrett, and Becker.[63] Some perceive a proto-gnostic influence that implied a "spiritualized" resurrection. Others appeal to an overrealized eschatology (1 Cor. 4:8-13). But it is doubtful if this offers an *exhaustive* account of the problem, since the allusion in 15:12 to the maxim "there is *no* resurrection" seems unduly inappropriate if this is precisely the issue.[64]

(iii) Many argue that Hellenistic quasi-philosophical assumptions in Corinth made it difficult to accept any notion of *bodily* resurrection. Murphy-O'Connor, Strobel, Hoffmann, and Dale Martin are among many who see this as playing a major role in doubts in Corinth.[65] Pheme Perkins expounds the problem in relation to philosophical beliefs.[66] Within this view, some plausibly iden-

---

59. Barth, *The Resurrection of the Dead*, 11.

60. Martin Luther, *Luther's Works*, vol. 28: *Commentaries on 1 Corinthians 7 and 15 and Lectures on 1 Timothy*, ed. H. C. Oswald (St. Louis: Concordia, 1973), 95.

61. Luther, *Works*, vol. 28, 94. Cf. also John Calvin, *First Epistle to the Corinthians*, 312.

62. W. M. L. De Wette, *Kurze Erklärung der Briefe an die Korinther* (Leipzig: Weidmannsche Buchhandlung, 2d edn. 1845), 7; W. Schmithals, *Gnosticism in Corinth*, trans. John Steely (Nashville: Abingdon, 1971), 156.

63. Munck, *Paul and the Salvation of Mankind*, 165; Wilckens, *Weisheit und Torheit*, 11; Käsemann, *New Testament Questions*, 125-26; Barrett, *First Epistle*, 109; J. Becker, *Auferstehung der Toten in Urchristentum* (Stuttgart: Katholisches Bibelwerk, 1976), 74-76.

64. See D. W. Kuck, *Judgement and Community Conflict: Paul's Use of Apocalyptic Judgement Language in 1 Cor. 3:5–4:5* (Leiden: Brill, 1992), 27.

65. For example, P. Hoffmann, *Die Toten in Christus* (Münster: Aschendorff, 1966), 241-43; A. Strobel, *Der erste Brief an die Korinther*, Zürcher Bibelkommentare (Zürich: Theologischer, 1989), 226-27; Martin, *The Corinthian Body*, 104-36.

66. Pheme Perkins, *Resurrection: New Testament Witnesses and Contemporary Reflections* (London: Chapman, 1984), 221-27 and 431-46.

tify the problem as that of beginning with an anthropocentric starting point, rather than beginning with divine sovereignty and promise. Others, probably less plausibly, stress the problem that they may have conceived of the "body" as a crudely physical interpretation of σῶμα *(sōma)*. This may represent a *contributory factor* to any confusion between Paul and some in Corinth. As Jeremias insists, the issue for Paul was not the transformation of a physical mode of being into a nonbodily mode, but the need for a transformation of the sinful into the holy.[67]

(iv) It is likely that different groups in the church in Corinth found different aspects problematic. Indeed, if their horizons of understanding were other than those considered above in 22.1 and 22.2, it would scarcely be surprising if the second and third explanations contributed to a general climate of difficulty in understanding and appropriating belief in the resurrection of the dead. This would apply to those who had become Christians after Paul's departure from Corinth. Although he favored the second approach, Luther anticipated modern scholarship in suggesting that different groups faced different problems, and recently Margaret Mitchell and Anders Eriksson have defended this view.[68] In terms of *hermeneutics*, Paul's response addresses more than one question, and in addition to responding to contingent questions, Paul expounds a core of shared apostolic tradition.

We turn to the theology of the resurrection as Paul expounds it in 1 Cor. 15, although also in dialogue with other biblical material and with historical and modern Christian thought.

(1) Paul anchors and grounds the promise of the resurrection of the dead *in the promise and sovereign power of God, but he first exemplifies this in God's raising of Jesus Christ.* This is the one case of a resurrection that has occurred in advance of the general resurrection of the dead, and has been the object of public witness in the public world.

We may seriously misunderstand Paul's logic if we do not note, with M. E. Dahl, that Paul consistently uses the *passive voice* where the resurrection of Christ is in view. Dahl writes, "*God* is practically always the subject of 'resurrection' verbs in the N.T. . . . The vast majority of texts concerning ἐγείρω *(egeirō)* and ἀνίστημι *(anistēmi)* . . . in a transitive, active sense have God as subject, and Christ or man as object (Acts 3:15; 4:10; 5:30; 10:40; 13:30, 37; Rom. 4:21; 8:11 *(bis)*; 10:9; 1 Cor. 6:14; 15:15 *(bis)*; 2 Cor. 4:14; Gal. 1:1; Col. 2:12; 1 Thess. 1:10). . . . In nearly all other cases the verb is the passive — or middle — voice."[69] C. K.

67. J. Jeremias, "'Flesh and Blood Cannot Inherit the Kingdom of God' (1 Cor. 15:50)," *New Testament Studies* 2 (1955) 151-59.

68. Luther, *Luther's Works*, vol. 18, 59 (German, Weimar edn., vol. 36, 482); and Margaret Mitchell, *Paul and the Rhetoric of Reconciliation*, 177 and 287; Eriksson, *Traditions as Rhetorical Proof*, 236-37.

69. M. E. Dahl, *The Resurrection of the Body* (London: S.C.M., 1962), 96-97.

Barrett, F. J. Ortkemper, and W. Künneth also defend and expound this fundamental point.[70] Only in the Fourth Gospel (John 6:39-40, 54) is there any hint that Jesus Christ will raise "those whom God has given him" ("I will raise them up"; v. 54). But even here he does not speak of raising *himself,* and the broader context joins the agency of Jesus with that of the Father. *That* context concerns *Christology* rather than resurrection as such, and alludes to the mediate cause or channel rather than to the efficient cause or source of the resurrection event.

On this basis there can be no thought that resurrection derives from an innate capacity of the human self. Even in the case of Christ, it is the power of God through the Spirit that raises Christ. In the case of Christian believers, who are "in Christ," "the Spirit of him who raised Jesus from the dead . . . will give life to your mortal bodies . . ." (Rom. 8:11).

In 1 Cor. 15:3-11, as Eriksson cogently argues, Paul appeals to the shared beliefs and assumptions of the common pre-Pauline apostolic *kerygma* and creed.[71] The series of verbs ἀπέθανεν . . . ἐτάφη . . . ἐγήγερται . . . ὤφθη . . . (died . . . was buried . . . was raised . . . was seen [or appeared], 1 Cor. 15:3-5) represent a transmission or *paradosis* reflected in Rom. 4:24-25; 8:34; 10:9; and 14:9. In hermeneutical terms *they simultaneously assert propositional truth-claims* about Christ or states of affairs in the public world, *and serve as self-involving, participatory* speech-acts on the part of the apostolic community and those who confess them.[72]

An allusion to "the public world" brings us into immediate confrontation with interpretations of the resurrection of Christ by Bultmann, Hans Conzelmann, and W. Marxsen. On the other hand, Künneth, Pannenberg, and N. Thomas Wright share the view that a "public" event has occurred. Marxsen does not deny the resurrection of Christ in the very broad sense that a perception of the living Christ has occurred, even if *the mode of its perception* is allegedly unspecified.[73] Even the allusion to witnesses, Marxsen claims, is vague and unspecific. "See" may denote perceptual sight, as in "Oh, I see!" In view of instances when the aorist passive ὤφθη (*ōphthē*) has denoted theophanies, Marxsen insists (with Conzelmann) that it may signify here no more than an existential percep-

---

70. Barrett, *First Epistle,* 341; F. J. Ortkemper, *1 Korintherbrief* (Stuttgart: Verlag Katholisches Bibelwerk, 1993), 145; Walter Künneth, *The Theology of the Resurrection,* trans. J. W. Leitch (London: S.C.M., 1965), 111-49.

71. See Eriksson, *Traditions as Rhetorical Proof,* 86-97 and 232-78, for an excellent exposition of the principle; also J. N. D. Kelly, *Early Christian Creeds,* 16-29; Neufeld, *The Earliest Christian Confessions,* 42-51; Oscar Cullmann, *The Earliest Christian Confessions,* trans. J. K. S. Reid (London: Lutterworth, 1949), 10-47; and R. P. C. Hanson, *Tradition in the Early Church* (London: S.C.M., 1962), 8-17.

72. See Thiselton, *First Epistle to the Corinthians,* 1187-90.

73. W. Marxsen, *The Resurrection of Jesus of Nazareth,* trans. Margaret Kohl (Philadelphia: Fortress, 1970), 72.

tion, without reference to the public world. It implies, he believes (with Bultmann), little more than the evoking of faith. He writes, "The precise nature of the experience" is unclear.[74] The emphasis, in Marxsen view, is on present belief, not on a past occurrence.[75]

Künneth, Pannenberg, and Wright present more rigorous accounts of the relation between history and faith in this context, as well as some incisive exegetical comments. Each of these writers holds the "appearances" tradition firmly together with the "empty tomb" tradition. Pannenberg writes: "The first Christian could not have successfully preached the resurrection of Jesus if his body had been intact in the tomb. . . . We must assume that the tomb was in fact empty."[76] He concedes that the empty tomb as such does not constitute a "proof" of the resurrection, since other causes could in theory have been involved. Nevertheless it presents difficulties to theories about "hallucinations" or other subjective interpretations.[77] The allusions to the burial of Jesus within the primary apostolic tradition is not only an antidocetic inclusion with reference to his life and genuine death, but also reinforces an "antidocetic" view of his resurrection. The resurrection is a transformative event; but it also "took place in this world, namely in the tomb of Jesus in Jerusalem before the visit of the women. . . . Any assertion that an event took place in the past implies an historical claim and exposes itself to testing."[78]

Künneth places God's raising of Christ in the context of the miracle of life on which all life depends. He writes, "It is a primal miracle, like the creation of the world."[79] This coheres precisely with Paul's exposition of its theological grounds in 1 Cor. 15:35-49. This is one reason why, for Künneth, it misses the point simply to speak of it as a subjective theophany to a series of individuals. Wright makes a series of similar points.[80] It is not of the same order as ecstatic rapture, phantasy, or theophany. The account of the empty tomb, he insists, was included in the earliest apostolic tradition as well as the gospels.[81] It expresses "concern with the concrete, bodily resurrection . . . the clear safeguard against every spiritualizing tendency to evaporate the central declarations of the resurrection."[82]

(2) *Paul expounds the resurrection of the dead as sheer gift and sheer grace,*

---

74. Marxsen, *Resurrection*, 77, 106, 116-17, 124-25.

75. I discuss Marxsen in greater detail in *First Epistle*, 1197-1203.

76. Pannenberg, *Systematic Theology*, vol. 2, 358-59; see also N. T. Wright, *The Resurrection of the Son of God: Christian Origins and the Question of God*, vol. 3 (London: S.P.C.K., 2003), 12-31, 312-29, and 685-719.

77. Pannenberg, *Systematic Theology*, vol. 2, 359.

78. Pannenberg, *Systematic Theology*, vol. 2, 360.

79. Künneth, *The Theology of the Resurrection*, 75.

80. N. T. Wright, *The Resurrection of the Son of God*, 20-31 and 312-29; cf. Künneth, *The Theology of the Resurrection*, 84-86.

81. Künneth, *The Theology of the Resurrection*, 93.

82. Künneth, *The Theology of the Resurrection*, 97.

consonant with the very nature of the gospel. I have expounded this aspect more fully in the particular context of Luther and Barth on the resurrection.[83] Barth grounds this gift of grace entirely in what he calls the *"of God"* (1 Cor. 4:5), which constitutes "clearly the secret nerve" of the whole epistle.[84] Grace as sheer gift is no less prominent in 1 Corinthians than in Romans. For example, "What do you have that you did not receive?" (1 Cor. 4:7). "Spirituality" is not a matter of achievement but of the *gift* of the Spirit bringing the Spirit's *gifts* (χαρίσματα, *charismata*), Paul's preferred word, rather than πνευματικά *(pneumatika)*, the preferred word in Corinth (12:1–14:40).

This is why, as Moltmann observes, resurrection is a matter of "calling into existence the things that do not exist" (Rom. 4:17).[85] *That which is dead cannot contribute to its own rising.* Once again, resurrection is not a matter of "rising" but of "being raised." Moltmann thus rightly speaks of "the deadliness of death . . . a conquest of god-forsakenness."[86] In death, especially the death of the cross, we experience the "not yet" of hope.[87] Moltmann writes elsewhere: "Unless it apprehends the pain of the negative, Christian hope cannot be realistic and liberating."[88] Cullmann writes, "Only he who apprehends with the first Christians the horror of death, who takes death seriously as death, can comprehend the Easter exultation of the primitive Christian community and understand that the whole thinking of the New Testament is governed by belief in the Resurrection."[89]

While resurrection focuses upon the sovereign grace of *God,* the appropriation of the gift of resurrection, like the gift of justification by grace through faith, becomes actualized as *promise,* through *union with Christ.* As Moltmann writes, "The experience of the cross of Jesus means . . . the experience of the god-forsakenness of . . . an absolute *nihil.* . . . The experience of the appearance of the crucified one as the living Lord means . . . the nearness of God in the god-forsaken one . . . a new totality which *annihilates* the total *nihil.*"[90]

This is the hermeneutical horizon of understanding that reveals the closest possible parallel between resurrection and justification. In each case it is a matter of "Nothing in my hand I bring; simply to Thy cross I cling." It is impossible to "supplement" the gift and grace of God in either case, but in both cases "the yon-

---

83. Anthony C. Thiselton, "Luther on Barth on 1 Corinthians 15: Six Theses for Theology," in W. D. Stephens (ed.), *The Bible, the Reformation, and the Church: Essays in Honour of James Atkinson,* JSNTSS 105 (Sheffield: Sheffield Academic Press, 1995), 258-89; repr. in *Thiselton on Hermeneutics,* 769-92.

84. Barth, *Resurrection,* 18.

85. Moltmann, *Theology of Hope,* 145.

86. Moltmann, *Theology of Hope,* 211.

87. Moltmann, *Theology of Hope,* 172.

88. Moltmann, *The Crucified God,* 5.

89. Oscar Cullmann, *Immortality of the Soul or Resurrection of the Dead? The Witness of the New Testament* (London: Epworth, 1958), 26-27.

90. Moltmann, *Theology of Hope,* 198.

der side of the cross" derives from participation in Christ's resurrection. Christ "was delivered to death for our trespasses and raised for our justification" (Rom. 4:25). Justification by grace is strictly an eschatological event, an anticipation of the last judgment. In this respect its fundamental meaning is not only that of putting the believer in a *right relationship* with God, but also of *"putting to rights."* "Righteousness" comes into its own. Whether or not his book *Marx and the Bible* raises other more questionable claims, José P. Miranda's exposition of the social, structural, and communal characters of "putting things to rights" in justification by grace is valid.[91]

Luther makes much of Paul's insistence that without the resurrection "you are still in your sins" (1 Cor. 15:17).[92] On the other hand, in the light of the promised gift of resurrection, Paul exclaims, "Death, where is your sting? The sting of death is sin, and the power of sin is the law. But thanks be to God, who gives us the victory through our Lord Jesus Christ" (1 Cor. 15:55-57).[93] Luther writes, "Our Lord Christ brought it about that the venom and bites of the devil were deadened and completely swallowed up by him . . . who stripped him of all his might and power."[94] Schweitzer has also demonstrated the incompatibility of law and eschatology in apocalyptic. To be raised with Christ is to be raised out of the causal nexus of sin, law, and death, including the oppressive effects of sin, into the new creation (cf. Rom. 6:6-11).

Karl Barth makes a similar point. He writes, "The event of resurrection is the revelation of the sentence of God which is executed in this judgement; of the free resolve of his love . . . and therefore the righteousness of his judgement . . . in the giving of the Son . . . the righteousness which has come to man too."[95] The event of the resurrection, like justification, is God's "pronouncement in man's favour. . . . His word of power: 'Rise up and walk.'"[96] Even early Bultmann fully accepts Barth's linking of these aspects in his *Resurrection of the Dead*. He writes, "Death is not overcome for us by means of a pious frame of mind"; faith is "a waiting for what is promised."[97]

Confirmation of our discussion so far appears in the rhetorical structure of 1 Cor. 15. Paul first establishes the reality of the resurrection as a sovereign act of God exemplified and witnessed in the resurrection of Christ (15:1-11). Then he moves to a first *Refutatio* (15:12-19) in tracing the disastrous and unacceptable

91. José P. Miranda, *Marx and the Bible: A Critique of the Philosophy of Oppression*, trans. John Eagleson (London: S.C.M., 1977 and New York: Orbis, 1974), 160-250.

92. Luther, *Luther's Works*, vol. 28, 102 (WA, 36, 536).

93. Luther, *Luther's Works*, vol. 28, 204 (WA, 36, 681).

94. Luther, *Luther's Works*, vol. 28, 204 (WA, 36, 681).

95. Barth, *Church Dogmatics*, IV:1, sect. 61, 1, 514.

96. Barth, *Church Dogmatics*, IV:1, sect. 61, 1, 514.

97. Rudolf Bultmann, "Karl Barth, The Resurrection of the Dead," in R. Bultmann, *Faith and Understanding* vol. 1, trans. L. P. Smith (London: S.C.M., 1969), 68; cf. 66-94.

consequences for the gospel of denying the resurrection, followed by a first *Confirmatio* (15:20-34) of the resurrection of Christ as the foundation of present faith and endeavor and of eschatological promise. These sections correspond with our points (1) and (2) so far. Finally, from 15:35-58 Paul addresses the question: "How can 'the resurrection of the body' be intelligible and *conceivable?*" This is structured around a second *Refutatio* and second *Confirmatio*.[98]

(3) *The resurrection mode of existence carries with it "somatic" identity and capacity for communication, characterized by the fullness of the agency of the Holy Spirit, who promotes Christ-likeness, holiness, and glory within the new raised humanity.*

In addition to the multiple hermeneutical horizons of understanding already identified in this chapter, further issues of hermeneutics arise. These include: (a) What is the role of Paul's appeal to *God as Creator of the natural, created order* (15:35-41), and how does this relate to the three principles of *contrast, continuity, and transformation* (15:50-57)? The second cluster of questions gathers around: (b) "What is the precise meaning of σῶμα πνευματικόν *(sōma pneumatikon)* in 15:44, and how does it relate to the agency of the Holy Spirit and to bearing the image of Christ as the last Adam (15:49)?

(a) *The appeal to God as Creator (1 Cor. 15:35-41).* Barth rightly perceives that this section of Paul's argument concerns the *conceivability* of resurrection, which depends not at all upon whether we can imagine a resurrection state, but on whether *God's* resourceful creative powers will match the task of bringing such a mode of existence into being.[99] Luther makes a broadly similar point.[100] He writes, "Since He [God] once before created us from nothing, He can also again give us life from the grave and give the body a new form."[101] When he declares, "Some have no knowledge of God" (15:34), Paul implies that belief or unbelief in the resurrection is symptomatic of belief or unbelief in the sovereign power of God.

The analogy of God's creative action and the nature of creation provide three applications. First, in 1 Cor. 15:23 the notion of the "orderedness" of God's decrees and creation suggests that to believe that Christ *has been* raised, and that believers *will be* raised, is in no way strange or anomalous, for God raises "each in his own order: Christ the firstfruits, then at his coming those who belong to Christ. *Then* comes the end. . . . The *last* enemy to be destroyed is death . . ."

---

98. On the rhetorical structure see Thiselton, *First Epistle,* 1176-78; Eriksson, *Traditions as Rhetorical Proof,* 89-97; Mitchell, *Rhetoric,* 283-88; and Insawn Saw, *Paul's Rhetoric in 1 Corinthians 15* (Lewiston, NY: Mellen, 1995), 183-201.

99. Barth, *Resurrection,* 194-95; cf. the similar approach in A. Robertson and A. Plummer, *A Critical and Exegetical Commentary on the First Epistle of St. Paul to the Corinthians* (Edinburgh: T&T Clark, 1914), 368.

100. Luther, *Luther's Works,* vol. 28, 99 (WA, 35, 530).

101. Luther, *Luther's Works,* vol. 28, 182 (WA, 36, 650).

(15:23-28). God's purposes, as in creation, are ordered, and are unfolded in an ordered sequence.

Second, the created order itself reveals a threefold process of *contrast, continuity of identity,* and *transformation:* "What you sow does not come to life unless it dies. And as for what you sow, *you do not sow the body that is to be*" (1 Cor. 15:36-37). This alone should cause us to hesitate before interpreting *"body"* (15:38-44) only as *physical* body. A clear difference and contrast exists between the earthly body and the raised "body" (σῶμα, *sōma*) of the resurrection. Nevertheless, observation of earthly creation reveals that *continuity of identity survives through change of form.* If a seed is changed into corn, or a caterpillar into a butterfly, or an acorn into an oak tree, it is *that entity* which undergoes change, and which *retains its identity.* Yet at the same time the dramatic nature of the *transformation* (for example, from a caterpillar to a butterfly, or from an acorn to an oak tree) should not be understated. Similarly, the human mode of existence is "sown in dishonor . . . raised in glory" (15:43). To compromise either continuity or radical transformation would be a mistake. Luther writes, "It is really the work of God"; He will present us "as glorious and resplendent as He Himself is."[102]

Third, 1 Cor. 15:38-42 emphasizes *the proven, inexhaustible resources of the Creator God.* God has demonstrated already his extreme versatility in creating suitable modes of being for any environment and any need: the formation of fish for the sea; birds, for the air; the sun to warm the earth; the moon for the night; planets to move in the sky, and flaming gases of different magnitudes and places on the color spectrum: "There is one glory of the sun, and another glory of the moon, and another glory of the stars; indeed, *star differs from star in glory*" (15:41). Will God be unable to insure adequate diversity? Will God be stumped over issues of identity when a human face or a human voice can already be picked out from thousands upon thousands? Even an individual star is not an exact replica of another.

In spite of Hans Conzelmann's claims that 1 Cor. 15 constitutes a separate treatise, all this is integral with the rest of 1 Corinthians.[103] Has not Paul said the same thing about the unity and diversity of gifts given by the Spirit? "Each has his own particular gift from God" (ἕκαστος ἴδιον ἔχει χάρισμα ἐκ θεοῦ, *hekastos idion echei charisma ek tou theou,* 1 Cor. 7:7). "The Spirit apportions to each person his own particular gift, as he [the Spirit] wills (διαιροῦν ἰδίᾳ ἑκάστῳ καθὼς βούλεται, *diaroun idiā hekastō kathōs bouletai,* 12:11). Hence in 15:38: "God gives it a body as he has chosen, and to *each* kind of seed *its own body* (ἴδιον σῶμα, *idion sōma*)."

Paul regards the refusal to apply these lessons that are before everyone's eyes

---

102. Luther, *Luther's Works,* vol. 28, 187 (WA, 36, 637) and *Works,* 28, 190-91 (WA, 36, 662).

103. H. Conzelmann, *1 Corinthians: A Commentary,* Hermeneia (Philadelphia: Fortress, 1975), 249.

as a symptom of willful foolishness. His phrase ἄφρων σύ (*aphrōn su*, 15:36) is a strong use of rhetorical *exclamatio*. Barrett and NRSV translate it "Fool!" REB's "What stupid questions!" and NJB's/NIV's "How foolish" reduce the force of σύ, *you*. Kennedy observes that if we ask on what basis there remains a link between the earthly human self and the raised self of the resurrection, Paul provides "the only one [answer] we can expect him to give: 'the sovereign power of God.'"[104] The distinctiveness of identities or species and the creation of diversity find expression in Gen. 1:11-12. Richard Hays comments that what Paul aims to set before his readers is the *conceivability* of *diverse orders of being* on the basis of God's power to create. Hence God can create a *"sort of body . . . entirely outside our present experience."*[105]

(b) We may now inquire more specifically about *the meaning of σῶμα πνευματικόν (sōma pneumatikon)* in 15:44. We discussed the range of meanings of σῶμα, *sōma, "body"* in 3.2 and especially in 11.3. There we expressed agreement with Käsemann that σῶμα *(sōma)* denoted primarily for Paul *existence within a public, intersubjective context,* and that this included the expression and recognition of personal identity and "ability to communicate."[106] To be granted "bodily" existence is to live a public mode of being that makes possible the credibility of Christian discipleship and obedience to Christ as Lord in *visible, communicable,* and *intelligible* terms. This could not be conveyed by "private," inner, solipsistic or narcissistic states of mind or "spirit."

We cannot imagine what a celestial counterpart to these features of relational, intersubjective life might be in concrete terms. But this is of no consequence since it is God, not humankind, who has the task of designing and creating these resurrection modes of existence. Luther declares judiciously: "Do not keep asking how God will do this, or what form the body will receive, but be content to hear what God will do. Then leave it to Him what will become of it."[107]

The more urgent problem for Paul was how a sinful humanity can be fit to enter the immediate presence of the holy God. To be sure, in union with Christ believers will be "unimpeachable" on the last day (1 Cor. 1:8). But Paul addresses the totality of the transformed human being. At the resurrection, he declares, "What is sown in decay is raised in decay's reversal. It is sown in humiliation; it is raised in splendor. It is sown in weakness; it is raised in power. It is sown an ordinary human body; it is raised a body constituted by the [Holy] Spirit. If there is a body for the human realm, there is also a body for the realm of the Spirit. . . . The last Adam became a life-giving Spirit" (1 Cor. 15:42-45, my translation).[108]

---

104. H. A. A. Kennedy, *St. Paul's Conceptions of the Last Things* (London: Hodder & Stoughton, 1904), 243; cf. 222-341.

105. Richard B. Hays, *First Corinthians* (Louisville: Knox, 1997), 271.

106. Käsemann, *New Testament Questions of Today,* 135.

107. Luther, *Luther's Works,* vol. 28, 180 (WA, 36, 647).

108. I defend this translation in Thiselton, *First Epistle to the Corinthians,* 1270-84.

We reserve for the last section of this chapter a consideration of the dynamic, ongoing character of the resurrection life. We may note here, however, that the usual translations "perishable" and "imperishable" (NRSV, NJB, REB, NIV), ἐν φθορᾷ *(en phthorā)* and ἐν ἀφθαρσίᾳ *(en aphtharsia,* 15:42), are too static. The Greek term *phthora* denotes increasing weakness and decreasing strength, issuing in exhaustion and stagnation. It corresponds to the Hebrew שׁחת *(shāchat)* and חבל *(chēbel).* If this is correct, its semantic opposite would not be static "imperishability," but the glory of increasing capacities issuing in growing vitality.[109] The third edition of BDAG (2000) vividly and helpfully suggests *"breakdown of organic matter, dissolution, deterioration"* as its first meaning of φθορά, which precisely captures the essence of "ordinary human body," perhaps in the light of the principle of entropy.[110] BDAG rightly characterizes ἀφθαρσία as *"not being subject to decay,"* but adds the qualifying term "the state of not being subject to decay."[111] Having recognized the semantic opposition, it spoils the symmetry to denote the former as a *process* and the latter as a *state.* However, the entry under φθορά does go further than the second edition (BAGD, 1958).[112]

The second antithesis, ἐν ἀτιμίᾳ *(en atimiā), in humiliation,* and ἐν δόξῃ *(en doxē), in glory* (15:43), does not imply dishonor of the physical as such. Paul could not have endorsed such a notion. However, it *may* recall the associations of the earthly body with its past use as a tool for misdirected desire, or it *may* simply denote the lowly position or the *troublesomeness* of the earthly body (cf. the lowly state, in Phil. 3:21). The important term is its semantic opposite, *glory.* The biblical use of the term *glory* reflects the Hebrew כבות *(kābhôdh),* which suggests *weightiness* or *impressiveness.* But it is a polymorphic term, depending on *what it is that makes it impressive.* The Greek may also denote the *radiance* of a joyful face, as in the face of a bride in a "happy" wedding, or the face of a lover that *shines* radiantly.[113] Paul has just a moment ago used the term to denote the radiance of a star, but most characteristically it denotes the glory that suffuses the face in *face-to-face encounter with God* (2 Cor. 3:7-11; 3:18; cf. Phil. 3:21).

This provides corroborating evidence for interpreting the two sets of contrasts that follow as *weakness . . . power,* and *ordinary body . . . Spiritual body* (1 Cor. 15:44). This last term denotes *a mode of intersubjective existence animated and characterized by the agency and sanctifying action of the Holy Spirit.* The NRSV wrecks the contrast inexcusably by translating its semantic opposite σῶμα ψυχικόν *(sōma psuchikon)* as *physical body,* which is precisely *not* Paul's point, and introduces a new meaning at odds with 1 Cor. 2:6-16 and 3:1-4. In 1 Cor. 2:14

109. I argued this in an unpublished M.Th. thesis for the University of London in 1964.
110. BDAG, 1054-55.
111. BDAG, 135.
112. BGAD, 2d edn. 1958, 856. The second edition interprets *aphtharsia* as denoting primarily "incorruptibility, immortality," 125.
113. *BDAG,* 3d edn., 256-58.

the NRSV correctly renders ψυχικός as *unspiritual*, although I have rendered it *a person who lives on an entirely human level*. The contrast in both passages hinges on *openness to the power and action of the Holy Spirit*. Since the work of the Holy Spirit is to glorify Christ as Lord (cf. 1 Cor. 12:3), this also explains the Christological turn of the argument in chapters 2 and 16 and in 15:45-49.

To see the resurrection mode of existence as sustained and animated by the Holy Spirit entirely accords with the view that the Holy Spirit is the agent of the resurrection of Christ (Rom. 8:11). It also both underlines the transformative effect of the event of the resurrection of the dead, and responds to the interpretation of 15:50 by Jeremias in terms of sin and holiness. Moreover, it captures and explains the *dynamic* nature of the resurrection mode of existence as a movement *from glory to glory*. It is a source of surprise that relatively few, until recently, have expounded these verses in this way. It is probably due to blind-alley discussions on the part of older scholars such as Otto Pfleiderer about "pneuma-substance" and light-fabric, caused by reading through the spectacles of Hellenism rather than of the Old Testament.

Several of the Church Fathers observed what many modern commentators have missed. Irenaeus says that to be "spiritual" is to be "the handiwork of God," and Athanasius and Gregory of Nazianzus make parallel points.[114] Among recent writers, C. K. Barrett and N. T. Wright are among the minority who provide this valid interpretation. In 1 Cor. 15:44, Wright declares, Paul refers to "a body animated by, enlivened by, the Spirit of the true God."[115] Barrett describes the *sōma* as "the new body animated by the Spirit of God."[116]

22.4. Controversial Interpretations of the Parousia and of the Last Judgment

In contrast to the fallibility, ambiguities, and corrigible provisionality of judgments offered by humankind during the course of history, the final verdict of God expressed in the last judgment stands as a definitive evaluation of all life that cannot be revised. The very notion of "finality," even apart from the status of the verdict as God's, suggests, in Pannenberg's words, "the final horizon of the definitive meaning and therefore of the nature of all things and all events."[117]

The Old and New Testaments jointly witness to expectations of a final act of vindication and fulfillment of what has been incomplete. We have already discussed the logic of "expectation" and confusions about "the imminence of the

---

114. Irenaeus, *Against Heresies* V:6:1; cf. Athanasius, *Letters to Serapion* 1:22.

115. N. T. Wright, *The Resurrection of the Son of God*, 354; see 347-56 for an excellent discussion.

116. Barrett, *First Epistle to the Corinthians*, 372.

117. Pannenberg, *Systematic Theology*, vol. 3, 531.

Parousia" in 22.2. Further controversy arises over the precise form in which vindication and fulfillment or "closure" is expected to occur, and some writers doubt whether it is even an "occurrence" rather than a symbolic notion to denote completion. If, as we have argued, hope springs from a perceived gap between what God has promised and what God has so far brought about, this carries with it the expectation of an end time when such promises will finally have been fulfilled, and when the kingship of God becomes *unambiguously visible.*

In Old Testament expectation "the Day of the Lord" was perceived as a public event when God's kingship would become visible most conspicuously in the righting of wrongs. Since self-deception often heightens illusory perceptions of being sinned against rather than sinning, Amos exposes such illusions in Israel's longing for the Day of the Lord: "Alas, for you who desire the Day of the Lord. . . . It is darkness, not light" (Amos 5:18; cf. 5:20). Joel likewise depicts the Day of the Lord as "a day of darkness and gloom . . . [when] a great army comes . . . a flame of fire devouring the stubble. . . . The earth quakes, the heavens tremble. The sun and the moon are darkened. . . . The Day of the LORD is great, terrible indeed" (Joel 2:2-5, 19). Yet it is also at the Day of the Lord when, in Joel's words: "I will pour out my Spirit on all flesh; your sons and daughters shall prophesy . . ." (Joel 2:28).

It is here that a major cause of exegetical and interpretative controversy arises. In his sermon on the Day of Pentecost Peter declares that these "last days" prophesied by Joel are now fulfilled in the pouring out of the Holy Spirit "on all flesh" (Acts 2:17-21, citing Joel 2:10 and 28). How many of the expectations and promises that have been awaited are now fulfilled in the ministry, death, and resurrection of Jesus Christ and on the Day of Pentecost? How many remain outstanding until a final, public *Parousia?*

We have already considered the assumptions of Johannes Weiss and Albert Schweitzer about eschatology and the *Parousia,* together with Moltmann's critique of them. We also noted Jeremias's use of the category of "eschatology in *process of realization."* We enumerated a series of "reversals" identified by Jeremias, some of which were fulfilled in the ministry of Jesus, others of which were in process of fulfillment, while still others yet awaited fulfillment at the end time. Arthur Moore speaks of "the tension arising from the contrast between hidden and revealed lordship" as the tension "between 'now' and 'then.'"[118]

It is well known that in his emphasis upon "realized eschatology" C. H. Dodd propounded the hypothesis that Jesus applied to the "crisis" of his own preaching many of the "parables of crisis" that the evangelists and the church applied to the crisis of the *Parousia.* Dodd interpreted Mark 1:15, ἤγγικεν ἡ βασιλεία τοῦ θεοῦ (*ēngiken hē basileia tou theou*), to mean, "The kingdom of God *has come,*" rather than "is near."[119] Even the difficult declaration of Mark 9:1 ("There

118. Moore, *The Parousia in the New Testament,* 16-17.
119. C. H. Dodd, *The Parables of the Kingdom* (London: Nisbet, 1936), 44.

are some standing here . . .") is ascribed to a kingdom that has *already* come.[120] Those parables classified as parables of crisis include those of the faithful and unfaithful servants (Matt. 25:14-30; Luke 19:12-27), the wise and foolish virgins (Matt. 25:1-13), the thief at night (Matt. 24:43-44; Luke 12:39-40), and the waiting servants (Matt. 24:45-51). It is the early church, not Jesus, Dodd argues, who re-applied all of these to the need to be ready for the *Parousia*.[121] Jeremias followed Dodd with modifications.[122]

It is unnecessary to repeat the criticisms and counterarguments put forward by a generation of scholars. Norman Perrin, among others, has offered a convincing, if guarded, critique.[123] It is not the case, for example, that all the "reversals" entailed in the coming of the kingdom of God have taken place. The need for watchfulness remains. An eschatology of "now" and "not yet" not only permits but also *demands* the dual application of the parables in question both to the present and to the future. The early church and the canonical evangelists did not entirely misunderstand the intentions of Jesus. Further, in the parables of growth (the leaven, Matt. 13:13; Luke 13:20-21) and of the mustard seed (Mark 4:30-32; Matt. 13:31; Luke 13:18-19) the spread of the kingdom could not be said to have occurred exhaustively in the ministry of Jesus. In H. A. Guy's words, their "climax" remains in the future.[124]

J. A. T. Robinson's *Jesus and His Coming* achieved the status of a classic in its time.[125] He drew on the tradition of C. H. Dodd and T. F. Glasson to conclude: "No evidence is to be found that the *Parousia* expectation formed part of the earliest strata of Apostolic Christianity."[126] Jesus, he argues, did not expect a "second" coming. As a variant on "eschatology in process of realization," Robinson spoke of "a fully *inaugurated* eschatology: all is not yet summed up; yet all that is to be has now been set in motion."[127] Christ's finished work has yet to run its course.

Robinson subdivides eschatological expectations into three components. Jesus, he claims, understood "the *Parousia*" as both an act of *vindication* and an event of *visitation*. He writes, "Jesus is clearly claiming that God is going to vindicate him by [an] act of crowning deliverance."[128] With Dodd he interprets some of the passages often taken to imply this to mean something else. But he concedes

---

120. Dodd, *Parables*, 54.

121. Dodd, *Parables*, 54 and 174.

122. Jeremias, *Parables*, 48-63 and 169-80.

123. Perrin, *The Kingdom of God*, 64-78 and 81-86.

124. H. A. Guy, *The New Testament Doctrine of Last Things* (London: Oxford University Press, 1948), 49.

125. Robinson, *Jesus and His Coming: The Emergence of a Doctrine* (London: S.C.M., 1957).

126. Robinson, *Jesus*, 29.

127. Robinson, *Jesus*, 29-30.

128. Robinson, *Jesus*, 44.

that Mark 14:62 (par. Matt. 26:64; Luke 22:69), "You will see the Son of Man sitting at the right hand of power, and coming with the clouds of heaven," irreducibly requires this meaning.[129] Nevertheless Robinson also insists that "Jesus is not at this point speaking of a *coming from* God: . . . he is affirming his *vindication.*"[130] This is an "imminent" vindication: "the Sanhedrin is about to witness a dramatic reversal of judgement."[131] "Coming on the clouds" is not a *descent,* but an *ascent,* and it is about to occur. Hence, Robinson concludes, this act of divine vindication is an *enthronement.* It applies not to a "second" coming, but "to the moment of the *Resurrection* onwards; for there is never a suggestion that Jesus enters upon his triumph only at some *second* coming."[132]

Does this apply throughout the whole of the New Testament? Robinson agrees that "the early Church *did* expect a descent of Jesus on clouds from heaven, and that the Synoptic Evangelists shared that belief" (my italics).[133] But he questions whether this was what Jesus expected. Jesus, Robinson argues, understood that the *resurrection* constituted his *vindication,* and his own *earthly ministry,* as "God with us," constituted the divine *visitation.* Robinson also argues that the very earliest *kerygma* of the church, prior to the Synoptic evangelists and Paul (as in Acts 3:19-21), reflects the intention of Jesus. This cannot refer to a "second" coming, Robinson claims, because in this passage "Jesus is here still only the Christ-elect; the messianic age has yet to be inaugurated."[134]

One other component in Robinson's arguments has remained influential, even if, in my view, also precarious. This is his contention that the "coming" of Jesus Christ in *Maranatha, Our Lord, come* (1 Cor. 16:22), and possibly in "Come, Lord Jesus" (Rev. 22:20), "almost certainly has its context in the primitive Eucharist." He cites, "Behold, I stand at the door and knock. . . . I will come in to him and eat with him" (Rev. 3:20), as also "Eucharistic."[135] This deeschatologizes "coming," and renders more problematic than necessary the Eucharistic acclamation, "Christ will come again!"

Robinson's arguments are vulnerable to several criticisms, of which I formulated four in an early article published in 1976.[136] First, we do not question that *some* of the eschatological sayings of Jesus about the vindication of the Son of Man (e.g., Mark 9:1) allude to the resurrection and/or Pentecost. Some may al-

---

129. Robinson, *Jesus,* 43.

130. Robinson, *Jesus,* 45.

131. Robinson, *Jesus,* 46.

132. Robinson, *Jesus,* 51.

133. Robinson, *Jesus,* 52.

134. J. A. T. Robinson, "The Most Primitive Christology of All," in J. A. T. Robinson, *Twelve New Testament Studies* (London: S.C.M., 1962), 144; cf. *Jesus,* 28-29.

135. Robinson, *Jesus,* 27.

136. Anthony C. Thiselton, "The Parousia in Modern Theology: Some Questions and Comments," *Tyndale Bulletin* 27 (1976) 27-54, esp. 41-44.

lude to the prophecy of the fall of Jerusalem (probably Mark 13:1-23, but perhaps not Mark 13:23-32). Nevertheless there is no evidence, on the other side, that excludes the possibility of Jesus' understanding his dual or multiple applications of parabolic warnings to a series of "crises" that culminate in the "coming" of Christ in public vindication and in glory. George Caird spent more than twenty years in intensive exploration of the semantics of eschatological language (1962-84) and traces the problematic implications of the claims made by Schweitzer, Dodd, Jeremias, Bultmann, and others.[137] As we have noted in 22.2, Caird argues that the biblical writers could use and did use "end of the world" language in multiple applications.[138] The apocalyptic language of Mark 13:1-37 and Matt. 24:1-44 could well apply both to the fall of Jerusalem and to the end of the world, which would include the *public* coming of the Son of Man.[139]

Second, Robinson's exegesis of Acts 3:19-21 remains worse than precarious. C. F. D. Moule concludes, "It is simpler, surely, to interpret the crucial words to mean that Jesus is *already* recognized as the *previously* predestined Christ . . . who at the end is to be sent *back again* into the world" (his italics).[140] G. R. Beasley-Murray has questioned Robinson's exegesis of Mark 14:62 and other crucial passages.[141] A major theme of G. E. Ladd is that the "now" and "not yet" of eschatology is a unifying theme throughout the New Testament.[142]

Third, the contrast between "hidden" and "revealed" is best understood as a contrast between inner and private on the one hand, and the *public and universal* on the other. Several horizons of understanding explicated in 22.1 and 22.2, especially the context of apocalyptic, witness to an expectation that could not be described as exhaustively fulfilled in the resurrection of Christ and Pentecost without remainder. These are indeed cosmic turning points, but not public turning points that are universally visible to all peoples. In what Robinson acknowledges as the earliest of the epistles (A.D. 50), the symbolism of "a cry of command" and "the sound of God's trumpet" includes such a public dimension (1 Thess. 4:16-17). Robinson fully concedes the presence of the Advent hope in all of the epistles with the exception only of Galatians, Ephesians, Philemon, and 2 and 3 John.[143] He is content to use such New Testament language as "the *revealing* of our Lord Jesus Christ" and "the *day* of our Lord Jesus Christ" (1 Cor. 1:7-8). *"Revealing"*

---

137. Caird, *The Language and Imagery of the Bible,* 243-56.

138. Caird, *Language,* 256-57.

139. Caird, *Language,* 263-66.

140. C. F. D. Moule, "The Christology of Acts," in L. E. Keck and J. L. Martyn (eds.), *Studies in Luke-Acts* (London: S.P.C.K., 1968), 168.

141. G. R. Beasley-Murray, "Critical Review," in *JTS* 10 (1959) 134-40.

142. G. E. Ladd, *A Theology of the New Testament* (London: Lutterworth, 1974), 193-212, 298-310, 550-70, 619-32; and Ladd, "Eschatology and the Unity of New Testament Theology," *Expository Times* 82 (1971) 307-9.

143. Robinson, *Jesus,* 16-17.

(ἀποκάλυψις, *apokalupsis*) occurs in 2 Thess. 1:7; 1 Pet. 1:7, 13; 4:13; ἐπιφάνεια (*epiphaneia*), in 2 Thess. 2:8; 1 Tim. 6:14; 2 Tim. 4:1, 8; Tit. 2:13. *"The day of Christ"* (ἡμέρα, *hēmera*) occurs in Matt. 24:50; Mark 13:32; Luke 17:22-31; 1 Cor. 1:8; 5:5; 2 Cor. 1:14; Phil. 1:6, 10; 2:16; 1 Thess. 5:2-4; 2 Thess. 2:2. Robinson still retains reservations about using the word *coming* to denote the *Parousia*, although he has to recognize that in Paul and 2 Peter "the coming of the Lord" and "the day of the Lord" are equated (1 Thess. 4:15–5:11; 2 Pet. 3:1-10), and Hebrews speaks of Christ's "appearing a second time . . . to save those who are eagerly waiting for him" (Heb. 9:28).[144]

Fourth, to specify *coming* in such passages as 1 Cor. 16:20 as "Eucharistic" coming and presence is to go beyond the evidence. Although Lietzmann, Bornkamm, and Käsemann share this view, C. F. D. Moule and Anders Eriksson firmly reject it.[145] The only hint of "evidence" arises from a supposed parallel in *Didache* 10:6-7 and perhaps *Didache* 9:1. But to "read back" a Eucharistic context is no better than the older dubious practice of reading "baptismal aorists" into virtually every reference to the event of coming to faith. Sacramental theology does not need these questionable arguments; it can stand on its own feet. Moule applies his critique also to Rev. 22:20, which he applies to the future *Parousia* of Jesus Christ.

Arthur Moore provides a constructive contextual exegesis of those New Testament passages that allude to the *Parousia* in his book on this subject.[146] He rightly concludes, "Paul can encourage watchfulness, believing that the *Parousia* is near without necessarily believing that it would certainly come within a definite period of time."[147] This applies equally in Rom. 13:11-17; 15:19, 23; 1 Cor. 7:26; 15:12-34; 2 Cor. 5:1-10; Phil. 3:20; 4:5; and 1 and 2 Thessalonians, as well as in Mark 9:1; 13:30; 14:15 and elsewhere.[148] This fits well with our discussion of the conceptual grammar of expectation in Wittgenstein in 22.2.

Moore sums up the key point judiciously as follows: "Jesus and the early church as a whole based their future expectation upon the conviction that the End was in Jesus Christ (though hidden), and that therefore *the End in its manifest, unambiguous, universal form could not be far off;* but they persistently refused to allow the sense of nearness to be turned into a belief that the End would come within a certain number of years. . . . *They reckoned with the grace motif,* and realized that the time for repentance and faith could not be limited by man, and that the provision of God's mercy could not be measured nor forecast."[149]

---

144. Robinson, *Jesus,* 19.

145. C. F. D. Moule, "A Reconsideration of the Context of *Maranatha,*" in *New Testament Studies* 6 (1959-60) 302-10; and Eriksson, *Traditions,* 279-98. For wider documentation see Thiselton, *First Epistle to the Corinthians,* 1334-35 and 1347-52.

146. Moore, *The Parousia in the New Testament,* esp. 108-218.

147. Moore, *Parousia,* 117.

148. Moore, *Parousia,* 108-59.

149. Moore, *Parousia,* 207-8 (my italics).

This sane and balanced approach, based on responsible exegesis, does not flatten the various traditions within the New Testament as if to reduce their distinctive eschatological emphases into a monochrome landscape. In an early article that attacked Dodd's theory of development toward "realized eschatology" in Paul, John Lowe shows that Paul's emphasis varies in accordance with the pastoral needs that he addresses.[150] Eschatological expectation does not vanish in the later Prison Epistles: Philippians is full of it (Phil. 1:6, 10; 2:16; 4:5), while the early Epistle to the Galatians reflects little or none of this. There is no "steady evolution" here.[151] S. G. Wilson, as we noted, offers a similar comment about the eschatology of Luke-Acts. Luke calls attention to the "now" and to the "not yet" depending on the pastoral situation and respective understandings of his addressees.

When we move from exegetical questions and from the hermeneutics of the biblical writings to modern theology, we often find a more sweeping reinterpretation of the *Parousia* and last judgment, whether for good or for ill. Teilhard de Chardin emphasizes the unifying focus of what he terms the "Omega point" of the evolutionary process. On one side, this calls to mind the universality and wholeness in which God becomes "all in all" (1 Cor. 15:28). It provides a focus upon convergence and unification.[152] But on the other side, Teilhard seems to say little about the *Parousia* or the last judgment as such, even if he might suggest that these are implicit in the axiom "In Christ all things hold together" (Col. 1:17; cf. Eph. 1:10).

As we should expect, Paul Tillich understands this eschatological language as symbol. On one side, it is "the symbolic expression of the relation of the temporal to the eternal"; the symbol points to the fulfillment of humankind's creaturely yearnings, and to the end of provisionality and ambiguity.[153] On the other side, this language has nothing to do with "a catastrophe in time and space"; it is "an expression of our standing in every moment in face of the eternal."[154] Yet again: "we must look ahead to the end of history."[155] As Brian Hebblethwaite observes, for Tillich the *Parousia* is a symbol of "the sufficiency of God's sovereignty over the world and history and in the final supremacy of love over all the forces of self-love."[156]

---

150. John Lowe, "An Examination of Attempts to Detect Developments in St. Paul's Theology," *JTS* 42 (1941) 129-41.

151. Lowe, "Developments," *JTS* 42 (1941) 141.

152. Pierre Teilhard de Chardin, *The Phenomenon of Man* (New York: Harper & Row 1965) and *The Future of Man* (New York: Harper & Row, 1964).

153. Tillich, *Systematic Theology,* vol. 3, 421.

154. Tillich, *Systematic Theology,* vol. 3, 421.

155. Tillich, *Systematic Theology,* vol. 3, 422.

156. Brian Hebblethwaite, *The Christian Hope* (London: Marshall, Morgan & Scott, 1984), 150.

James P. Martin devotes a full-length study to examining the reasons for a steady dissolution of eschatology and a theology of the last judgment, from Kant, Hegel, and the Enlightenment onward. This reaches a climax, he argues, in the middle and later nineteenth century with Ritschl. As a backcloth, and by way of contrast, Martin first outlines the traditional orthodoxy of the Reformation and post-Reformation Confessionalism. He writes, "the *Parousia* and the Last Judgement were viewed as one event. . . . This followed the pattern of the Creeds."[157] Nevertheless, he argues, the Reformers tended to neglect the genre of *apocalyptic,* and attention to this might have sustained orthodox eschatology more readily when it later came under question and suffered erosion. The most positive feature of Reformation eschatology, Martin suggests, was to underline the close relation of eschatology to Christ as Judge and Savior. Calvin tended to use the term *"glorification"* for the consummation of all things.[158] Another closely related theme was the *manifestation of what had been hidden.*

This dialectic of the hidden and the manifest, we suggest, leads to a valid *conceptual grammar of the last judgment.* The judgment is not primarily a matter of awarding prizes or penalties as such, but a public manifestation of the truth, in which self-deception and fallible judgment have been stripped away, because they are no longer possible to hide by pretense or behind private individualism. In the words of Hans Küng, "All that exists . . . has a provisional character. . . . My nontransparent ambivalent existence and the deeply discordant history of humanity demand a final transparency, a revelation of a definitive meaning."[159]

This stands in continuity with the beginning of a process undertaken by the Holy Spirit in "convicting" the believers and the world of sin (John 16:7-11), and the public declaration of the "putting right" or "justification" that hitherto had to be appropriated in advance only *by faith.* At the same time, the orthodoxy of the Reformation did not evaporate the last judgment in terms of its anticipation wholly in history or in the present but appealed to the clearly future references of such passages as 1 Cor. 3:13 and 2 Cor. 5:10.

Calvin perceived the contemplation of the last judgment not primarily as a resource for intimidation and fear, but as a means of *grace* that would lead believers and others to understand the worthlessness of their "works," and thereby to flee to Christ to seek the justification of sheer grace through faith. Calvin writes, "Our conscience must be called to the judgement-seat of God. . . . Then only shall we clearly perceive what the value of our works is."[160] Christ assumes the role of Judge not only because he is King but also because he acquits believers who are in Christ of their sins. Calvin comes close to anticipating the theme ex-

157. James P. Martin, *The Last Judgement in Protestant Theology from Orthodoxy to Ritschl* (Edinburgh: Oliver & Boyd, 1963), 4.

158. Martin, *Last Judgement,* 6; Calvin, *Institutes,* III:9:5; also III:25, 1-12.

159. Hans Küng, *Eternal Life?* trans. Edward Quinn (London: Collins, 1984), 261; cf. 259-64.

160. Calvin, *Institutes,* III:12:5 (Beveridge edn., vol. 2, 64).

pounded by C. F. D. Moule and Alan Richardson that justification by grace and baptism are anticipations of the last judgment. Moule writes, "Baptism is a pleading guilty . . . [to be] brought past the great assize, past the final judgement of the last day."[161]

In 15.2 we considered whether "wrath" could ever be a sign of love. It is widely assumed that the opposite of love is wrath. But the opposite of love, we argued there, is *not wrath but indifference.* Loving parents who express disapproval when a beloved child insists on some self-damaging course of action would be showing more, rather than less, loving concern than parents who simply shrugged their shoulders. Sometimes parents may hide their concern if the child needs to learn from mistakes. But *the grace* of wrath guards against the notion that God is indifferent to self-destructive acts, even if such a concept has all but dissipated away today.

Martin traces how, from the era of deism and the Enlightenment onward, the realities of eschatology and judgment evaporated not only for philosophical reasons but also because this was felt to be incompatible with love. Martin sees this trend as reaching a peak in Albrecht Ritschl. Pannenberg also traces the decline of eschatology from the Enlightenment to Hegel and Schleiermacher, although Martin insists that the climax comes with Ritschl.[162] Martin writes, "The methodological reduction of eschatology in the nineteenth century reached its climax in the theology of Albrecht Ritschl, where there is no Last Judgement and indeed no idea of judgement at all. . . . The Kingdom of God for Ritschl is an immanent reality within this world. . . . Ritschl rejects wrath in the New Testament by rejecting the idea of holiness in the New Testament."[163]

The history of "the last things" from the Enlightenment through Hegel and Schleiermacher to Ritschl demonstrates the difficulty of reaching an understanding of eschatology without appropriate hermeneutical horizons of understanding. The genuine recovery of the horizons of apocalyptic in Pannenberg and Moltmann has been a decisive turning point, along the multiple horizons that we identified in 22.1 and 22.2.

Although the term is used specifically in its biblical sense, Moltmann shows decisively the fundamental importance of recovering the understanding of *Judge* that pervades the Old Testament as well as apocalyptic. The judge is one who *"puts things to rights,"* which is especially urgent for the weak, for the oppressed, for widows and orphans, and for all who possess neither the strength nor institutional resources to put matters right for themselves.[164] In 14.1 and 14.2, we traced the steady historical buildup of the conceptual currency of what it is *"to save"*

---

161. C. F. D. Moule, "The Judgement Theme in the Sacraments," in Davies and Daube (eds.), *Background to the New Testament,* 465 and 467.

162. Pannenberg, *Systematic Theology,* vol. 3, 532-36; Martin, *Last Judgement,* 129-208.

163. Martin, *Last Judgement,* 196, 199, and 203.

164. Moltmann, *The Coming of God,* 235-56.

and *"to be a savior"* through the linguistic transparency of what it was *to be a judge* who rescued Israel in the days of *the Judges.*

Moltmann writes, "Originally hope for the Last Judgement was a hope cherished by the victims of world history, a hope that the divine justice would triumph over their oppressors and murderers."[165] So often, he observes, is the idea of God poisoned that "it is high time to discover *the gospel of God's judgement* and to awaken *joy in God's coming righteousness and justice*" (his italics).[166] God deeply *involves himself* in the last judgment, which is "the *apokatastasis pantōn,* the restoration of all things, when God is 'all in all'. Here 'At the name of Jesus every knee shall bow, and every tongue confess him Lord, to the glory of God the Father' (Phil. 2:10-11)."[167] This is the culmination of *the trust that has placed everything in God's hands.*

22.5. The Transformation of Time, and Symbols of Sharing in Promised Glory

Among the hermeneutical conditions for even contemplating releasing the imagination to catch a glimpse of the promised destiny of the resurrection mode of existence as sharing in the divine glory of "heaven," the nature of symbol and a reappraisal of notions of time take their place alongside other horizons of understanding.

Robert Gundry writes, "Symbolic language fills the book of Revelation as it fills other apocalyptic literature. We may therefore presume that the description of the New Jerusalem in Rev. 21:1–22:5 deals in symbolism. Our presumption is rewarded when we read of the city's coming down out of heaven, stretching out and up to unheard-of dimensions, having gates that each consist of a single pearl, being paved with gold that can be seen through, and so on. Such language invites symbolic interpretation."[168] Symbols both resonate with the depths of the self at a precognitive level, and point beyond themselves to what may transcend conceptual formulation.

Yet two perils beset the use of symbol. One is the need for an explanatory or suspicious hermeneutical axis that offers relative "control" against flights of unwarranted fancy, including flight from biblical tradition. The other derives from the "timeless" nature of symbol, in contrast to typology or narrative. We need to ask about the relation between promised glory and time.

165. Moltmann, *Coming,* 235.
166. Moltmann, *Coming,* 235.
167. Moltmann, *Coming,* 236-38.
168. Robert H. Gundry, "The New Jerusalem: People as Place, Not Place as People," in Robert H. Gundry, *The Old Is Better: New Testament Essays in Support of Traditional Interpretations* (Tübingen: Mohr Siebeck, 2005), 399; cf. 399-411.

Celestial glory is symbolically presented under the image of city life. This suggests not static rest, but dynamic, ongoing movement. Certainly the Epistle to the Hebrews offers a dialectical qualifier to limit this model: "A sabbath rest still remains for the people of God" (Heb. 4:9; cf. 4:4; 4:8; 4:10). For weary pilgrims the thought of traveling forever and ever would seem more like a betrayal of promised glory if there were no promise of rest.[169] How can future glory be both action and rest?

Eternal rest within the static realm of Plato's timeless Forms or Ideas would not cohere with the self-revealed nature of *the living God* who does "new things." This does not present a biblical vision. At the risk of overpressing an anthropomorphic analogy, we suggest that it also raises the existential specter of the intolerable and inglorious unadulterated boredom of being forever and forever frozen in the final frame of a film, video, or drama.

Moltmann reminds us that the resurrection mode of existence and "the new heavens and the new earth" are characterized by the newness of a *novum* that does not merely "grow out of" the old. It is a new creation. Nevertheless, it *"takes up" and transforms, rather than discards, the old.* Gilbertson comments similarly on the eschatology of the book of Revelation: "Although there is discontinuity with the old earth, there is clearly also continuity."[170] This might be taken to suggest *neither a continuation of human time or space-time as we know it, nor a complete cessation or destruction of human time or space-time as we know it.*

This suggests a possible way forward in the face of controversial debates about the nature of the *eternal,* both in relation to the eternity of *God* and in relation to the eternity of *eternal life.* Traditionally three philosophical views have been put forward.[171] In the light of Augustine's valid dictum, "God created the world not in time *(in tempore)* but with time *(cum tempore),*" many infer that eternity denotes *timelessness.* Time and space-time belong to the realm of the created order, which in philosophical terms implies the contingent and empirical. But this raises questions about whether or not the being of God can be *conceptually* located within this realm.

Some believe that the "timeless" view receives confirmation from the fact that time and space are two dimensions of the same reality in the theory of relativity. According to this theory, *time* accelerates or decelerates depending on the direction and degree of *spatial* motion in the case of an object at extreme velocity. If it is inconceivable that space was "there" before any act of divine creation, how would it be possible to claim something different about time?

The Greco-Roman milieu of the Patristic era encouraged thought in which

---

169. Cf. H. W. Attridge, "Let Us Strive to Enter That Rest," *HTR* 73 (1980) 279-88.

170. Gilbertson, *God and History in the Book of Revelation,* 107.

171. Two brief but helpful philosophical discussions can be found in William L. Craig, "God, Time, and Eternity," *Religious Studies* 14 (1979) 497-503; and E. Stump and N. Kretzmann, "Eternity," *Journal of Philosophy* 78 (1981) 429-58.

time and change were ascribed to realm of "mere appearance," and this was coupled with the theological doctrine that God was "immutable." Supposedly any change in God could be taken to imply that either a previous state or a subsequent state was less than "perfect." For Plato reality was "Being," not "becoming." But this sits uncomfortably and uneasily with the Hebrew-Christian view of the God who makes promises (Exod. 12:25; Deut. 1:11), who devises purposes, and who reconsiders and revises plans of action (Judg. 2:18; Jer. 15:6). Hence Jüngel (rightly in my view) expounds the theme that for God "Being is in Becoming."

If we move from philosophical discussion to the arguments of biblical specialists, we discover as much disagreement among them as among philosophers. We may note as sample views those of Cullmann, Marsh, and Barr. Oscar Cullmann rejects the "timeless" interpretation of eternal reality in favor of what amounts to *temporal everlastingness*. For Plato, he comments, time is merely "the *copy* of eternity. . . . Primitive Christianity knows nothing of timelessness. . . . Eternity, which is possible only as an attribute of God, is time — Or to put it better, what we call 'time' is nothing but a part . . . of this same unending duration of God's time."[172] This αἰών *(aiōn), age,* denotes a limited division of time. Eternity is "everlastingly continuing time"; time is "limited time."[173] "Time and eternity share this time quality. . . . The 'eternal' God is . . . 'he who is, who was, and who will be' (Rev. 1:4)."[174]

Other biblical specialists, however, dissent from Cullmann. John Marsh argues that we should not be misled by the fact that Hebrew poets used a temporal term עלם, *'ôlām* (equivalent to the Greek αἰών, *aiōn*), to denote *eternity*.[175] The plural idiom "into the ages of the ages" is an attempt to use inadequate symbols to denote something which is not-time. Marsh declares, "Eternity . . . is qualitatively different from time."[176] The Gospel of John depicts "the intrusion of eternity into time," and the eternal is related to the temporal in other than temporal ways.[177] The vision of the book of Revelation is of "the Lamb . . . slain from the foundation of the world" (Rev. 13:8).[178]

James Barr attacks both Cullmann and Marsh for basing their arguments upon *word* studies rather than upon biblical *statements*. Cullmann draws more than is legitimate, he argues, from studies of αἰών, καιρός, and χρόνος.[179] But

172. Cullmann, *Christ and Time,* 61 and 62.

173. Cullmann, *Christ and Time,* 62.

174. Cullmann, *Christ and Time,* 63; cf. 64-68.

175. John Marsh, *The Fulness of Time* (London: Nisbet, 1952), 29-32. But cf. Brown-Driver-Briggs, *Hebrew-English Lexicon* (new edn. 1980), 761-63 for a far wider list of meanings.

176. Marsh, *Fulness,* 139.

177. Marsh, *Fulness,* 143 and 144.

178. Marsh, *Fulness,* 147.

179. James Barr, *Biblical Words for Time* (London: S.C.M., 1962, 2d edn. 1969), 47-81 (1st edn.), 50-85 (2d edn.).

Marsh and John A. T. Robinson fall under the same methodological critique.[180] "The fault is one that Cullmann shares with his critic Marsh."[181] Barr plausibly argues that Genesis appears to imply that when God created the universe, God created time, and he considers that this undermines Cullmann's case.[182] All the same, it would do Barr an injustice to infer that his view of eternity is simply "timeless." He argues that "before" the creation of the world "there was not something other than time, but time of another kind," even if no biblical evidence for this could be produced.[183] There is at least "some case" for thinking of eternity "as a reality other than time."

Before we explore this further, we must consider a third major concept of eternity found in philosophical thought. Boethius suggests, in the words of Henry Chadwick, that "as time is to eternity, so the circle is to the centre. . . . For us, events fall into past, present, and future time. God is outside time. For him the knowledge of temporal events is an eternal knowledge in the sense that all is a simultaneous present."[184] Thomas Aquinas follows this path. He writes, "His [God's] eternity includes all times."[185] This is probably the majority view, since it accommodates the notion of divine immutability that Aquinas wishes to retain. Nevertheless, each of these views is vigorously defended.

Within the horizons of understanding set out for an interpretation of eschatology, however, the notion of continuity and contrast between the old and new creation suggests *neither timelessness nor everlastingness,* but *a transformation of human time as we know it into God's time.* Moltmann rightly speaks of "a change in the transcendental conditions of time."[186] All that we have said in previous chapters and in 22.3 about *somatic* existence, bodiliness, purpose, narrative, and temporality suggests that a "timeless" existence would be a *reduced* mode of existence, devoid of all adventure, of new purposes, of memory and hope, of anticipation, development, excitement, and surprises. Can this be what the *living* God has prepared for his people and for his creation, which is *"raised in power, raised in glory"* (1 Cor. 15:44)?

Everlastingness fares no better. This notion would fail to reassure those who fear that "promotion" to the glory of heaven would turn out to be the very reverse: an endless repetition of repeated hymns of praise, sung over and over again. Apart from the sense of existential disappointment generated by such a scenario, it is implausible to think that God created the universe "within" rather than "with" time and space-time. Can we even conceive of *measured* time before

---

180. Barr, *Words for Time*, 20-46 (1st edn.), 21-49 (2d edn.).
181. Barr, *Words for Time*, 80 (1st edn.), 85 (2d edn.).
182. Barr, *Words for Time*, 145 (1st edn.), 151 (2d edn.).
183. Barr, *Words for Time*, loc. cit.
184. Henry Chadwick, *Boethius* (Oxford: Clarendon, 1981), 242 and 246.
185. Aquinas, *Summa Theologiae*, Ia, Q. 10, art. 2.
186. Moltmann, *The Coming of God*, 26.

such objects as the astronomical bodies existed to make chronological or "natural" time possible?

"God's time" would constitute a precondition for narrative experience, succession, purpose, novelty, faithfulness, and the "temporal virtues" discussed above. Strictly it might be more accurate to speak of the transcendental conditions for time as *temporality (Zeitlichkeit* in contrast to *Zeit*).[187] Lest this should appear to be wholly theoretical or speculative, we should recall how many versions and conceptions of time additional to astronomically measured "clock time" we experience in everyday life. I have discussed this elsewhere; hence here I merely summarize.[188] Seymour Chatman and Gérard Genette have shown the critical importance of differences between "clock time" and *narrative time* in such devices as flashbacks, flash forwards, variations of pace, and so on in novels, plays, or what Ricoeur calls refigured narrative. The Gospel of Mark rushes ahead at high speed until it reaches a transition in Mark 8:27-38, where Peter confesses Jesus as the Christ. The next section proceeds at a steadier pace. The passion narrative tells the events of the cross in slow motion. Mark does not use "natural" or "chronological" time in strictly equal speed or pace because he wants to show that the passion dominates the purpose of the ministry of Jesus and Mark's narrative point of view. In sociological and socio-economic terms, the manner in which we divide the day, how we perceive time, and who has to wait for whom in an employment hierarchy speak volumes about social or economic status.[189]

Time and space as we know them are unlikely to feature as a dimension of celestial glory, because the new creation is a transformed mode of existence. *Transformed time as God's time*, together with life in a *somatic mode of existence*, will permit the possibilities of "bodiliness" without its present constraints. This may provide a focus of *hope* because it would *enhance* but *not reduce* a mode of glory. To pass *from glory to glory* would not be an eternal *fortissimo*, but a crescendo of wonder and praise. What is fundamental about "body," we have seen in earlier chapters, is the capacity for *intersubjective relationality*, entailing intersubjective recognition, intersubjective identity, and intersubjective communication. We have seen from our exploration of 1 Cor. 15:38-49 that the transformed self will have been delivered from sin and shame, and therefore have nothing to fear from recognition; and that it will be a *transformed* self as capable of retaining a continuity of identity as, in the light of Paul's analogies from creation, an oak tree would from an acorn.

187. Heidegger, *Being and Time*, 351-52 (German, 304-5).

188. Anthony C. Thiselton, with Roger Lundin and Clarence Walhout, *The Promise of Hermeneutics* (Grand Rapids: Eerdmans and Carlisle, U.K.: Paternoster, 1999), 183-208.

189. See esp. Robert H. Lauer, *Temporal Man: The Meaning and Uses of Social Time* (New York: Praeger, 1981), 1-51 and throughout. Cf. further W. E. Moore, *Scarce Resource: Man, Time and Society* (New York: Wiley, 1963); and Alvin Toffler, *Future Shock* (New York: Random, 1970).

Gundry expounds the *communal* nature of the *"New Jerusalem"* as the people of God rather than a dwelling place. The New Jerusalem, he argues, denotes the redeemed saints themselves. The New Jerusalem is the Bride of the Lamb (Rev. 19:7-8). The Bride of Christ (Rev. 18:23; 21:2, 9; 22:17; cf. Eph. 5:25-28) is identified as the saints who have suffered and who cry, "Amen. Come, Lord Jesus!" (Rev. 22:21).[190] The New Jerusalem is *holy* because it denotes the perfected people of God (Rev. 21:2, 8; 22:11-15), who have become transformed through the formative agency of the Holy Spirit (1 Cor. 15:44). The qualities expressed in symbol apply to the saints as *persons.* Gundry comments, "Sheer happiness characterizes the city, a happiness unadulterated by tears, pain, or death — elements in the old creation that have peculiar poignancy for those facing persecution to the death by the beast (Rev. 21:4; cf. 7:12-17)."[191]

Language about the New Jerusalem draws on a repertoire of symbols that reach through to the depths of the human psyche in ways that surpass conceptual analogy or simile. Jung, Tillich, and Ricoeur have expounded this capacity of symbol to reach through to preconscious, preconceptual levels of the human mind.[192] Northrop Frye writes, "City, mountain, river, garden, tree, oil, fountain, bread, wine, bride, sheep . . . recur so often that they clearly indicate some kind of unifying principle."[193]

Mathias Rissi traces the Old Testament and apocalyptic background to the use of these symbols especially in Rev. 21:1-27 and 22:1-5.[194] The *mountain* looks back to Isa. 2:1-4 and its expansion in Isa. 60:11-14, as well as to other passages. The mountain, like the New Jerusalem, will "become the place of continual encounter with God: 'The sun shall be no more your light by day, nor for brightness shall the moon give you light by night; but *the* LORD *shall be your everlasting light,* and *your God will be your glory'* (Isa. 60:19)."[195] In accordance with our hermeneutic in 22.1 Rissi writes, "The heart and centre of this hope is the covenant promise of the presence of God in the midst of his people."[196] In much apocalyptic and in other intertestamental writings the *symbols* of glory point to the reality that is *God himself,* who radiates glory as if from multiform jewels: sapphires, emeralds, gold, beryls, and rubies. The "streets" of the city cry, "Hallelujah!" (Tob. 13:16-18). The

190. Gundry, "The New Jerusalem," in *The Old Is Better,* 401-2.

191. Gundry, "The New Jerusalem," 404.

192. See, e.g., Wayne Rollins, *Jung and the Bible* (Atlanta: John Knox, 1983), 18-20; Paul Tillich, *Dynamics of Faith* (London: Allen & Unwin, 1957), 42-47; and Ricoeur, *Freud and Philosophy,* 93-94, 420, and throughout; *Interpretation Theory,* 55-57; and *The Conflict of Interpretations,* 287-334.

193. Northrop Frye, *The Great Code: The Bible and Literature* (New York and London: Harcourt Brace Jovanovich, 1982), xiii.

194. Mathias Rissi, *The Future of the World: An Exegetical Study of Revelation 19:11–22:15* (London: S.C.M., 1972), esp. 41-83.

195. Rissi, *Future of the World,* 43.

196. Rissi, *Future of the World,* 46.

basis for praise is the fulfillment of covenant promise (2 *Baruch* 4:3-6), which is the dwelling of God himself with and among humankind.

Rev. 21:1-2 takes up Isa. 65:17. The abolition of the sea (21:1) symbolizes the abolition of confusion, of isolation, of the primeval sea monster Leviathan or Antichrist, and of death.[197] Isa. 65:16-17 declares: "the former troubles are forgotten." Thus the vision of Rev. 21:1-6 continues: "God will dwell with them . . . and he will wipe every tear from their eyes. Death will be no more; mourning and crying and pain will be no more, for the first things have passed away" (Rev. 21:3-4). Rissi writes: "The church's assurance is grounded in God's own promise. God explicitly orders the seer to confirm that these words are trustworthy. . . . These same statements also characterize the words of Jesus, who is 'the word of God' in person (Rev. 1:5; 3:7, 14; 19:13)."[198] Since they radiate the glory *of God*, the jewels of the New Jerusalem shine with transparent light. This radiant glory is the medium in which the raised and perfected saints live. In fulfillment of Ezek. 43:1-17, the glory of God shines forth and fills the temple, and makes the mountain holy.

The gift of water speaks powerfully of the very deepest longings finding satisfaction: "To the thirsty I will give water as a gift from the spring of the water of life" (Rev. 21:6). "Living" water, or inexhaustibly running water, was more precious in an oriental desert culture than containers of water that could run dry. The high mountain, a symbol of transcendent divine presence, manifests "the glory of God and radiance like a precious rare jewel, like jasper, clear as crystal" (Rev. 21:11).

Like the promises of God, none of this can be shaken, for solid walls surround and protect it (21:14). The "restoration of all things" brings access at the end time to the tree of life: "The leaves of the tree are for the healing of the nations" (22:2). The symbol of the New Jerusalem (21:1-27) leads on to the archetypal symbol of paradise (22:1-5), the garden of delight and happiness into which nothing harmful can enter (22:3). There is no death, no mourning, no pain, no isolation from God or from others in the deluded subjectivity of narcissistic loneliness and self-absorption.

Rissi writes, "If death is not the end, then the grief and the mourning does not have to be endless either. . . . If we believe that the dead experience resurrection, then hope leads us out of the abyss of fear, and makes us free. We look beyond the graves and the partings in our life to that future of God's in which 'every tear shall be wiped away' and 'death shall be on more.'"[199] But what sustains the glory of it all is the glory of the living, ongoing, sovereign, gracious God. The saints and angels will praise and worship God not only for what he has already

---

197. George B. Caird, *The Revelation of St. John the Divine* (London: Black, 1966), 262; David E. Aune, *Revelation 17–22* (Nashville: Nelson, 1998); Rissi, *Future of the World*, 457.

198. Rissi, *Future of the World*, 58.

199. Rissi, *Future of the World*, 125.

done through Christ and through the Holy Spirit, but also for what God is yet to do, which exceeds all imagining.

The wonderful priestly or Aaronic blessing of Lev. 6:24-26 begins: "The LORD bless you and keep you; the LORD *make his face to shine upon you* and be gracious to you." David Ford comments on "face." He writes, "We are given our faces. We have no choice about them, and inheritance together with social formation determines much about them. Yet we seem to have some freedom with them and perhaps in the long run significantly form them through our habits of living. . . . Each face is individual yet it is also a primary locus for relating to others and the world. The face as relating, welcoming, incorporating others is fundamental to social life. . . . Faces can interanimate each other and at the same time seem to become more fully and distinctively themselves."[200]

To see God "face to face" amid the interanimating faces of all the saints is to share in the divine glory. In Ford's language, God's salvation of "abundance" is enacted in the "the loving face" and "the singing self."[201] "Then we will see face to face" (1 Cor. 13:12), "with unveiled faces seeing the glory of the Lord . . . , transformed from one degree of glory to another" (2 Cor. 3:18). "When he is revealed, we will be like him, for we will see him as he is" (1 John 3:2).

200. David F. Ford, *Self and Salvation: Being Transformed* (Cambridge: Cambridge University Press, 1999), 19.

201. Ford, *Salvation,* 119 and 120.

Bibliography

Abraham, William J., *Waking from Doctrinal Amnesia* (Nashville: Abingdon, 1986).

Aland, Kurt, *Did the Early Church Baptize Infants?* translated by G. R. Beasley-Murray (London: S.C.M., 1962).

Alexander, Loveday, *The Preface to Luke's Gospel* (Cambridge: Cambridge University Press, 1993).

Allenbach, J., Benoit, A., and Bertrand, D. A., et al. (eds.), *Biblia Patristica: Index des Citations et Allusions Bibliques dans la Littérature Patristique*, 7 vols. to date (Paris: Éditions du Centre National de la Recherche, 1975-2000).

Alston, William P., *Divine Nature and Human Language* (Ithaca and London: Cornell University Press, 1989).

Alter, Robert, *The Art of Biblical Narrative* (New York: Basic Books, 1981).

Anderson, A. H., and Hollenweger, Walter J. (eds.), *Pentecostals after a Century: Global Perspectives on a Movement in Transition* (Sheffield: Sheffield Academic Press, 1999).

Anderson, David (ed. and trans.), *St. Basil the Great: On the Holy Spirit* (Crestwood, NY: St. Vladimir's Press, 1980).

Anselm, *Why God Became Man,* in E. R. Fairweather (ed.), *A Scholastic Miscellany: Anselm to Ockham,* Library of Christian Classics 10 (London: S.C.M. and Philadelphia: Westminster, 1956).

Aparece, Pederito A., *Teaching, Learning, and Community: An Examination of Wittgensteinian Themes Applied to the Philosophy of Education,* Tesi Gregoriana 22 (Rome: Pontifical Gregorian University, 2005).

Apel, Karl-Otto, *Towards a Transformation of Philosophy,* translated by G. Adey and D. Frisby (London and Boston: Routledge & Kegan Paul, 1980).

_____, *Understanding and Explanation: A Transcendental-Pragmatic Perspective,* translated by Georgia Warnke (Cambridge, MA: MIT Press, 1984).

Apostolic Fathers, edited by K. Lake, Loeb Classical Library, 2 vols. (London: Heinemann, 1915).

Aquinas, Thomas, *Summa Theologiae,* Latin and English, Blackfriars edn., 60 vols. (London: Eyre & Spottiswood and New York: McGraw & Hill, 1963 onward).

Astley, Jeff, *The Philosophy of Christian Religious Education* (Birmingham, AL: Religious Education Press, 1994).

Atkinson, James, *Martin Luther: Prophet to the Church Catholic* (Grand Rapids: Eerdmans and Exeter, U.K.: Paternoster, 1983).

Attridge, H. W., "Let Us Strive to Enter That Rest," *HTR* 73 (1980) 279-88.

_____, *Commentary on the Epistle to the Hebrews*, Hermeneia (Philadelphia: Fortress, 1989).

Aulén, Gustaf, *The Faith of the Christian Church*, translated by E. H. Wahlstrom and G. E. Arden (London: S.C.M., 1954).

_____, *Christus Victor: An Historical Study of the Three Main Types of the Idea of the Atonement*, translated by A. G. Hebert (London: SPCK and New York: Macmillan, 1931, rpt. 1970).

Austin, John L., *How to Do Things with Words*, edited by J. O. Urmson (Oxford: Clarendon, 1962).

Avis, Paul D. L., *The Church in the Theology of the Reformers* (London: Marshall, Morgan & Scott, 1981).

Baillie, Donald M., *God Was in Christ: An Essay on Incarnation and Atonement* (London: Faber & Faber, 1948).

Bakhtin, Mikhail M., *The Dialogic Imagination: Four Essays*, edited by Michael Holquist and translated by Caryl Emerson and Michael Holquist (Austin: University of Texas Press, 1981).

_____, *Problems of Dostoevsky's Poetics*, edited and translated by Caryl Emerson (Minneapolis: University of Minnesota Press, 1984).

Balla, Peter, *Challenges to New Testament Theology: An Attempt to Justify the Enterprise* (Peabody, MA: Hendrickson, 1997).

Balthasar, Hans Urs von, *Heart of the World*, translated by Erasmo S. Leivà (San Francisco: Ignatius, 1979).

_____, *The Glory of the Lord: A Theological Aesthetics*, translated by A. Louth and others and edited by Joseph Fessio and John Riches, 6 vols. (Edinburgh: T&T Clark, 1984-91).

_____, *Truth Is Symphonic: Aspects of a Christian Pluralism*, translated by G. Harrison (San Francisco: Ignatius, 1987).

_____, *Theo-Drama: Theological Dramatic Theory*, translated by G. Harrison, 5 vols. (San Francisco: Ignatius, 1988-98).

Barbour, Ian G., *Religion in the Age of Science* (London: S.C.M., 1990).

_____, *Religion and Science: Historical and Contemporary Issues* (London: S.C.M., 1998).

Barfield, Owen, "Poetic Diction and Legal Fiction," in Max Black (ed.), *The Importance of Language* (Englewood Cliffs, NJ: Prentice-Hall, 1962).

Barr, James, *The Semantics of Biblical Language* (Oxford: Oxford University Press, 1961).

_____, *Biblical Words for Time* (London: S.C.M., 1962; 2d edn. 1969).

Barrett, C. K., "The Eschatology of the Epistles to the Hebrews," in W. D. Davies and D. Daube (eds.), *The Background of the New Testament and Its Eschatology: Studies in Honour of Charles Harold Dodd* (Cambridge: Cambridge University Press, 1956), 363-93.

_____, *The Holy Spirit and the Gospel Tradition* (London: SPCK, 1958).

_____, *The Signs of an Apostle* (London: Epworth, 1970).

_____, *A Commentary on the Second Epistle to the Corinthians* (London: Black, 1973).

_____, *Church, Ministry and Sacraments in the New Testament* (Exeter, U.K.: Paternoster, 1985).

_____, *A Critical and Exegetical Commentary on the Acts of the Apostles,* 2 vols. (Edinburgh: T&T Clark, 1994 and 1998).

Barth, Karl, *The Word of God and the Word of Man,* translated by Douglas Horton (London: Hodder & Stoughton, 1928).

_____, *The Resurrection of the Dead,* translated by H. J. Stenning (London: Hodder & Stoughton, 1933).

_____, *Church Dogmatics,* edited by G. W. Bromiley and T. F. Torrance, 14 vols. (Edinburgh: T&T Clark, 1957-75).

Barth, M., *Was Christ's Death a Sacrifice?* Scottish Journal of Theology Occasional Papers (Edinburgh: Oliver & Boyd, 1961).

Bartholomew, Craig G., Green, Joel B., and Thiselton, Anthony C. (eds.), *Reading Luke: Interpretation, Reflection, and Formation,* Scripture and Hermeneutics 6 (Carlisle, U.K.: Paternoster and Grand Rapids: Zondervan, 2005).

_____ et al. (eds.), *Canon and Biblical Interpretation,* Scripture and Hermeneutics 7 (Grand Rapids: Zondervan, 2006 and Carlisle, U.K.: Paternoster, 2007).

Bartsch, Hans-Werner (ed.), *Kerygma and Myth,* translated by R. H. Fuller, 2 vols. (London: SPCK, 2d edn., vol. 1, 1964 and vol. 2, 1962).

Bauckham, Richard J., *Bible and Mission: Christian Witness in a Postmodern World* (Carlisle, U.K.: Paternoster, 2003).

_____, and Drewery, Benjamin (eds.), *Scripture, Tradition and Reason: A Study in the Criteria of Doctrine, Essays in Honour of Richard P. C. Hanson* (London and New York: Continuum/T&T Clark, 2004).

Bauer, W., and Danker, F. W., *A Greek-English Lexicon of the New Testament and Other Early Christian Literature,* translated, edited, and revised by W. F. Arndt, F. W. Gingrich, and F. W. Danker [BDAG] (Chicago: University of Chicago Press, 3d edn. 2000).

Bauman, Zygmunt, *Hermeneutics and Social Science: Approaches to Understanding* (London: Hutchinson, 1978).

Beauvoir, Simone de, *The Second Sex,* "Introduction," reprinted in E. Marks and Isabelle de Courtivron (eds.), *New French Feminisms: An Anthology* (New York: Schocken, 1981), 41-56.

Becker, J., *Auferstehung der Toten in Urchristentum* (Stuttgart: Katholisches Bibelwerk, 1976).

Beilby, James, *Epistemology as Theology: An Evaluation of Plantinga's Religious Epistemology* (Aldershot, U.K. and Burlington, VT: Ashgate, 2005).

Beker, J. Christiaan, *Paul the Apostle: The Triumph of God in Life and Thought* (Edinburgh: T&T Clark, 1980).

Bellah, Robert N., *Habits of the Heart: Individualism and Commitment in American Life* (Berkeley, CA: University of California Press, 1996).

Benco, Stephen, *The Meaning of* Sanctorum Communio (Naperville, IL: Allenson and London: S.C.M., 1964).

Bercovitch, Sacvan, *The Rites of Assent: Transformation in the Symbolic Construction of America* (New York: Routledge, 1993).

Berkhof, Hendrikus, *Christian Faith: An Introduction to the Study of the Faith,* translated by S. Woudstra (Grand Rapids: Eerdmans, 1979).

Berkouwer, G. C., *Man: The Image of God,* translated by D. W. Jellema, Studies in Dogmatics (Grand Rapids: Eerdmans, 1962).

_____, *Sin,* translated by Philip Holtrop, Studies in Dogmatics (Grand Rapids: Eerdmans, 1971).

Best, Ernest, "Paul's Apostolic Authority," *Journal for the Study of the New Testament* 27 (1986) 3-25.

Betti, Emilio, *Die Hermeneutik als allgemeine Methodik der Geisteswissenschaften* (Tübingen: Mohr, 1962).

_____, *Auslegungslehre als Methodik der Geisteswissenschaften* (Tübingen: Mohr, 1967, abridged in one vol.).

Bicknell, E. J., *The Christian Idea of Sin and Original Sin in the Light of Modern Knowledge* (London and New York: Longmans, Green, 1923).

Bloch-Hoell, Nils, *The Pentecostal Movement: Its Origins, Development, and Distinctive Character* (Oslo: Universitetsforlaget and London: Allen & Unwin, 1964).

Bonhoeffer, Dietrich, *Creation and Fall/Temptation: Two Biblical Studies,* translated by J. C. Fletcher and E. Bethge (New York: Macmillan and London: S.C.M., 1959).

_____, *Letters and Papers from Prison,* edited by E. Bethge and translated by Reginald Fuller (London: S.C.M., 3d enl. edn. 1971).

_____, *Meditation on the Word,* translated by D. M. Gracie (Cambridge, MA: Cowley, 1986).

Bonsirven, Joseph, *Theology of the New Testament,* translated by J. F. Tye (London: Burns & Oates, 1963).

Botterweck, G. J., Ringgren, H., and Fabry, H.-J. (eds.), *Theological Dictionary of the Old Testament,* translated by J. T. Willis (Grand Rapids: Eerdmans, 1974 onward).

Bourdieu, Pierre, *Language and Symbolic Power,* edited by J. Thompson and translated by G. Raymond (Cambridge, MA: Harvard University Press, 1991).

Bovon, François, *Luke the Theologian: Fifty-five Years of Research (1950-2005),* translated largely by K. McKinney (Waco, TX: Baylor University Press, 2d rev. edn. 2006).

Bowker, John, "Religions as Systems," in Doctrine Commission of the Church of England, *Believing in the Church: The Corporate Nature of Faith* (Carlisle, U.K.: SPCK, 1981), 159-89.

Boyd, Richard, "Metaphor and Theory Change: What Is Metaphor For?" in A. Ortony (ed.), *Metaphor and Thought* (Cambridge: Cambridge University Press, 1979), 356-408.

Briggs, Richard S., *Words in Action: Speech Act Theory and Biblical Interpretation, Toward a Hermeneutic of Self-Involvement* (Edinburgh and New York: T&T Clark, 2001).

Brooks, Peter, *Thomas Cranmer's Doctrine of the Eucharist: An Essay in Historical Development* (New York: Seabury, 1965).

Brown, Alexandra, *The Cross and Human Transformation: Paul's Apocalyptic Word in 1 Corinthians* (Minneapolis: Fortress, 1995).

Brown, Clifford A., *Jung's Hermeneutic of Doctrine: Its Theological Significance,* American Academy of Religion Dissertation Series 22 (Chico, CA: Scholars Press, 1981).

Brown, Colin, *Miracles and the Critical Mind* (Grand Rapids: Eerdmans and Carlisle, U.K.: Paternoster, 1984).

_____, *Jesus in European Protestant Thought 1778-1860* (Grand Rapids: Baker, 1985).

Brown, David, *The Divine Trinity* (La Salle, IL: Open Court and London: Duckworth, 1985).

Brown, David, *God and the Enchantment of Place: Reclaiming Human Experience* (Oxford: Oxford University Press, 2004).

Brown, F., Driver, S. R., and Briggs, C. A. (eds.), *The New Hebrew and English Lexicon* (Lafayette, IN: Associated Publishers, 1980).

Brown, Penelope, and Levinson, Stephen C., *Politeness: Some Universals in Language Usage,* Studies in Interactional Sociolinguistics 4 (Cambridge: Cambridge University Press, 1987).

Brown, Raymond E., *Jesus, God and Man: Modern Biblical Reflections* (London and Dublin: Geoffrey Chapman, 1968).

_____, *The Gospel according to John,* Anchor Bible, 2 vols. (London: Chapman, 1971 and New York: Doubleday, 1966).

Bruce, F. F., *The Epistle to the Galatians,* NIGTC (Grand Rapids: Eerdmans and Carlisle, U.K.: Paternoster, 1982).

Brueggemann, Walter, *The Land: Place as Gift, Promise and Challenge in Biblical Faith* (London: SPCK, 1978).

Brummer, Vincent, *Atonement, Christology, and the Trinity: Making Sense of Christian Doctrine* (Aldershot, UK: Ashgate, 2005).

Brunner, Emil, *Man in Revolt: A Christian Anthropology,* translated by Olive Wyon (London: Lutterworth, 1939).

_____, and Barth, Karl, *Natural Theology,* translated by P. Fraenkel (London: Centenary, 1946).

_____, *The Christian Doctrine of God: Dogmatics I,* translated by Olive Wyon (London: Lutterworth, 1949).

_____, *The Christian Doctrine of Creation and Redemption: Dogmatics II,* translated by Olive Wyon (London: Lutterworth, 1952).

_____, *The Christian Doctrine of the Church, Faith, and the Consummation: Dogmatics III,* translated by David Cairns (London: Lutterworth, 1962).

Buber, Martin, *Between Man and Man,* translated by R. Gregor Smith (London: Collins, 1961).

_____, *I and Thou,* translated by Ronald Gregor Smith (Edinburgh: T&T Clark, 1984).

Bultmann, Rudolf, *Theology of the New Testament,* translated K. Grobel, 2 vols. (London: S.C.M., 1952 and 1955).

_____, "The Christological Confession," in *Essays Philosophical and Theological,* translated by C. G. Greig (London: S.C.M., 1955), 273-91.

_____, *Jesus and the Word,* translated by Louise F. Smith and E. Lantero (London: Collins/ Fontana and New York: Scribner, 1958).

_____, *Jesus Christ and Mythology* (New York: Scribner, 1958 and London: S.C.M., 1960).

_____, *Existence and Faith: Shorter Writings of Rudolf Bultmann,* edited by Schubert Ogden (London: Collins/Fontana, 1964).

_____, "Karl Barth, The Resurrection of the Dead," in R. Bultmann, *Faith and Understanding,* vol. 1, translated by L. P. Smith (London: S.C.M., 1969).

_____, "New Testament and Mythology: The Problems of Demythologizing the New Testament Proclamation," in Rudolf Bultmann, *New Testament and Mythology and Other Basic Writings,* selected, edited, and translated by Schubert M. Ogden (Philadelphia: Fortress, 1984).

Burgess, Stanley M., *The Holy Spirit: Ancient Christian Traditions* (Peabody, MA: Hendrickson, 1984).

Buri, Fritz, *How Can We Speak Responsibly of God?* translated by H. H. Oliver (Philadelphia: Fortress, 1968).

_____, *Thinking Faith: Steps on the Way to a Philosophical Theology,* translated by H. H. Oliver (Philadelphia: Fortress, 1968).

Burnaby, John, *The Belief of Christendom: A Commentary on the Nicene Creed* (London: SPCK, 1959).

Burtchaell, J. T., *From Synagogue to Church: Public Services and Offices in the Earliest Christian Communities* (Cambridge: Cambridge University Press, 1992).

Caird, George B., *The Language and Imagery of the Bible* (London: Duckworth, 1980).

_____, with Hurst, L. D., *New Testament Theology* (Oxford: Clarendon, 1994).

Cairns, David, *The Image of God in Man* (London: S.C.M., 1953).

Calvin, John, *The Genevan Confession of Faith* (1536), in J. K. S. Reid (ed.), *Calvin: Theological Treatises,* Library of Christian Classics 22 (London: S.C.M., 1954).

_____, *Institutes of the Christian Religion,* translated by H. Beveridge, 2 vols. (London: James Clarke, 1957).

Campbell, C. A., *On Selfhood and Godhood* (London: Allan & Unwin and New York: Macmillan, 1957).

Campenhausen, Hans von, "Der urchristliche Apostelbegriff," *Studia Theologica* 1 (1947) 96-130.

_____, *Ecclesiastical Authority and Spiritual Power in the Church of the First Three Centuries,* translated by J. A. Baker (London: Black, 1969).

_____, "Das Bekenntnis im Urchristentum," *ZNW* 63 (1972) 210-53.

Capes, D. B., *Old Testament Yahweh Texts in Paul's Christology,* WUNT II, 47 (Tübingen: Mohr, 1992).

Capps, Donald, *Pastoral Care and Hermeneutics* (Philadelphia: Fortress, 1984).

Carr, Wesley, *Angels and Principalities: The Background, Meaning, and Development of the Pauline Phrase* 'hai archai kai hai exousiai,' SNTSMS (Cambridge: Cambridge University Press, 1981).

Cerfaux, L., *Christ in the Theology of St. Paul,* translated by G. Webb and A. Walker (Freiburg: Herder, 1959).

Chadwick, Henry, *Boethius* (Oxford: Clarendon, 1981).

Chan, Mark L. Y., *Christology from Within and Ahead: Hermeneutics, Contingency, and the Quest for Transcontextual Criteria in Christology* (London and Boston: Brill, 2001).

Chardin, Pierre Teilhard de, *The Phenomenon of Man* (New York: Harper & Row, 1965).

Charles, R. H., *A Critical History of the Future Life in Israel, in Judaism, and in Christianity* (London: Black, 2d edn. 1913).

Childs, Brevard S., *Myth and Reality in the Old Testament* (London, S.C.M., 1960, 2d edn. 1962).

_____, *Exodus: A Commentary* (London: S.C.M., 1974).

_____, *Old Testament Theology in a Canonical Context* (Philadelphia: Fortress and London: S.C.M., 1985).

Clark, Alan, and Davey, Colin (eds.), *Anglican/Roman Catholic Dialogue: The Work of the Preparatory Commission* (London and New York: Oxford University Press, 1974).

Clark, Katrina, and Holmquist, Michael, *Mikhail Bakhtin* (Cambridge, MA: Harvard University Press, 1984).

Clayton, John P., *The Concept of Correlation: Paul Tillich and the Possibility of a Mediating Theology* (Berlin: Walter de Gruyter, 1980).

Clines, David, J. A., "The Image of God in Man," *Tyndale Bulletin* 19 (1968) 53-103.

Collins, John N., *Diakonia: Reinterpreting the Ancient Sources* (New York and Oxford: Oxford University Press, 1990).

_____, *Are All Christians Ministers?* (Collegeville, MN: Liturgical Press, 1992).

Corrington, Richard S., *The Community of Interpreters: On the Hermeneutics of Nature and the Bible in the American Philosophical Tradition,* Studies in American Biblical Hermeneutics 3 (Macon, GA: Mercer University Press, 1987).

Crafton, J. A., *The Agency of the Apostle,* JSNTSS 51 (Sheffield: Sheffield Academic Press, 1991).

Craig, William L., "God, Time, and Eternity," *Religious Studies* 14 (1979) 497-503.

Craigie, Peter C., *The Book of Deuteronomy* (Grand Rapids: Eerdmans, 1976).

Cranfield, Charles E. B., *The Epistle to the Romans: A Critical and Exegetical Commentary,* 2 vols., ICC (Edinburgh: T&T Clark, 1975 and 1979).

Croatto, J. Severino, *Exodus: A Hermeneutics of Freedom,* translated by Salvator Attanasio (Maryknoll, NY: Orbis, 1981).

Crockett, William R., "Holy Communion," in Stephen W. Sykes and John Booty (eds.), *The Study of Anglicanism* (London: S.C.M. and Philadelphia: Fortress, 1988), 272-83.

Crowe, Frederick E., *Lonergan* (London: Geoffrey Chapman, 1992).

Cullmann, Oscar, *The Earliest Christian Confessions,* translated by J. K. S. Reid (London: Lutterworth, 1949).

_____, *Baptism in the New Testament,* translated by J. K. S. Reid (London: S.C.M., 1950).

_____, *Christ and Time: The Primitive Christian Conception of Time and History,* translated by Floyd V. Filson (London: S.C.M., 1951).

_____, and Leenhardt, F. J., *Essays on the Lord's Supper* (London: Lutterworth, 1958).

_____, *Immortality of the Soul or Resurrection of the Dead? The New Testament Witness* (London: Epworth, 1958).

_____, *Christology of the New Testament,* translated by S. C. Guthrie and C. A. M. Hall (London: S.C.M., 1959, 2d edn. 1963).

Curtis, William A., *A History of Creeds and Confessions of Faith in Christendom and Beyond* (Edinburgh: T&T Clark, 1911).

Dahl, M. E., *The Resurrection of the Body* (London: S.C.M., 1962).

Dalferth, Ingolf U., *Religiöse Rede von Gott* (Munich: Christian Kaiser, 1981).

Danby, Herbert (ed.), *The Mishnah: Translated from the Hebrew with Notes* (Oxford: Clarendon, 1933).

Danker, Frederick W., *Creeds in the Bible* (St. Louis: Concordia, 1966).

Dautzenberg, G., "Zum religionsgeschichtlichen Hintergrund der διακρίσεις πνευμάτων (1 Kor. 12:10)," *Biblische Zeitschrift* 15 (1971) 93-104.

Davies, W. D., *Paul and Rabbinic Judaism* (London: SPCK, 2d edn. 1955).

Dayton, Donald, *The Theological Roots of Pentecostalism* (Lanham, MD: Scarecrow and Grand Rapids: Zondervan/Asbury, 1987).

Denney, James, *The Death of Christ: Its Place and Interpretation in the New Testament* (London: Hodder & Stoughton, 1912).

Descartes, René, *The Philosophical Writings of Descartes,* edited and translated by J. Cottingham and others, 3 vols. (Cambridge: Cambridge University Press, 1984-91).

Dewar, Lindsay, *The Holy Spirit and Modern Thought* (London: Mowbray, 1959).

Dibelius, M., and Greeven, H., *James: A Commentary on the Epistle of James,* translated by M. Williams, Hermeneia (Philadelphia: Fortress, 1975).

Dilthey, Wilhelm, *Gesammelte Schriften,* Bd. V: Die Geistige Welt: Einleitung in die Philosophie des Lebens (Leipzig and Berlin: Teubner, 1927).

_____, *Gesammelte Schriften,* Bd. VII: *Die Aufbau der Geschichtlichen Welt in den Geisteswissenschaften* (Leipzig and Berlin: Teubner, 1927).

_____, *Selected Writings*, edited and translated by H. P. Rickman (Cambridge: Cambridge University Press, 1976).

Dimock, Nathaniel, with Grey, H. G., *The Doctrine of the Death of Christ: In Relation to the Sin of Man, the Condemnation of the Law, and the Dominion of Satan* (London: Stock, 1903).

_____, *The Doctrine of the Sacraments in Relation to the Doctrines of Grace* (London and New York: Longmans, Green, 1908).

Dix, Gregory, *The Shape of the Liturgy* (London: S.C.M., 1943, 2d edn. 1945).

_____, "Ministry in the Early Church," in Kenneth Kirk (ed.), *The Apostolic Ministry: Essays on the History and Doctrine of Episcopacy* (London: Hodder & Stoughton, 1946).

Doctrine Commission of the Church of England, *Believing in the Church: The Corporate Nature of Faith* (London: SPCK, 1981).

_____, "God as Trinity: An Approach through Prayer," in *We Believe in God* (London: Church House Publishing, 1987).

_____, *Being Human: A Christian Understanding of Personhood with Reference to Power, Money, Sex, and Time* (London: Church House Publishing, 2003).

Dodd, Charles H., *The Apostolic Preaching and Its Developments* (London: Hodder & Stoughton, 2d edn. 1944).

Duffy, Marvyn, *How Language, Ritual, and Sacraments Work according to John Austin, Jürgen Habermas, and Louis-Marie Chauvet*, Tesi Gregoriana Serie Teologia 123 (Rome: Pontifical Gregorian University, 2005).

Dulles, Avery, *Models of the Church: A Critical Assessment of the Church in All Its Aspects* (Dublin: Gill & MacMillan, 2d edn. 1988).

Dunn, James D. G., *Baptism in the Holy Spirit: A Re-examination of the New Testament Teaching on the Gift of the Spirit in Relation to Pentecostalism Today* (London: S.C.M., 1970).

_____, *Jesus and the Spirit: A Study of the Religious and Charismatic Experience of Jesus and the First Christians as Reflected in the New Testament* (London: S.C.M., 1975).

_____, *Christology in the Making* (London and Philadelphia: S.C.M., 1980).

_____, "The New Perspective on Paul," *Bulletin of the John Rylands Library* 65 (1983) 95-122.

_____, *Romans*, 2 vols., Word Biblical Commentary (Dallas: Word Books, 1988).

_____, *The Theology of Paul the Apostle* (Edinburgh: T&T Clark and Grand Rapids: Eerdmans, 1998).

_____, *Jesus Remembered: Christianity in the Making*, vol. 1 (Grand Rapids and Cambridge: Eerdmans, 2003).

Dupont, J., *La réconciliation dans la théologie de Saint Paul* (Paris and Bruges: Desclée de Brouwer, 1953).

Eastwood, Cyril, *The Priesthood of All Believers: An Examination of the Doctrine from the Reformation to the Present Day* (London: Epworth, 1960).

Ebeling, Gerhard, *Word and Faith*, translated by James W. Leitch (London: S.C.M., 1963).

_____, *Word of God and Tradition*, translated by S. H. Hooke (London: Collins, 1968).

_____, *Introduction to a Theological Theory of Language*, translated by R. A. Wilson (London: Collins, 1973).

Eissfeldt, Otto, "The Ebed-Jahweh in Isaiah xl–lv," *Expository Times* 44 (1933) 261-68.

Ellis, E. E., *Prophecy and Hermeneutic in Early Christianity* (Grand Rapids: Eerdmans, 1978).

Epp, Eldon Jay, *Junia: The First Woman Apostle* (Minneapolis: Fortress, 2005).

Eriksson, Anders, *Traditions as Rhetorical Proof: Pauline Argumentation in 1 Corinthians,* Coniectanea Biblica, New Testament Series 29 (Stockholm: Almqvist & Wiksells, 1998).

Evans, Donald D., *The Logic of Self-Involvement: A Philosophical Study of Everyday Language with Special Reference to the Christian Use of Language about God as Creator* (London: S.C.M., 1963).

_____ (ed.), *Tertullian's Homily on Baptism: Introduction, Translation, and Commentary* (London: SPCK, 1964).

Fairweather, E. R., "Incarnation and Atonement: An Anselmian Response to Aulén's Christus Victor," *Canadian Journal of Theology* 7 (1861) 167-75.

Farley, Edward, *The Transcendence of God: A Study in Contemporary Philosophical Theology* (London: Epworth, 1962).

Feyerabend, Paul, *Against Method* (London: Verso, 3d edn. 1993).

Fiddes, Paul, *Participating in God: A Pastoral Doctrine of the Trinity* (Louisville: Westminster/John Knox, 2000).

Fison, J. E., *The Blessing of the Holy Spirit* (London and New York: Longmans, Green, 1950).

Fitzmyer, Joseph A. (ed.), *The Biblical Commission's Document "The Interpretation of the Bible in the Church": Text and Commentary* (Rome: Editrice Pontificio Instituto Biblico, 1995); also text only, Pontifical Biblical Commission *The Interpretation of the Bible in the Church* (Sherbrooke, QC: Éditions Paulines, 1994).

Flannery, Austin P. (ed.), *Documents of Vatican II* (Grand Rapids: Eerdmans, 1975).

Flemington, W. F., *The New Testament Doctrine of Baptism* (London: SPCK, 1957).

Flew, R. Newton, *Jesus and His Church: A Study of the Idea of the Ecclesia in the New Testament* (London: Epworth, 1938).

Forbes, C., *Prophecy and Inspired Speech in Early Christianity and Its Hellenistic Environment,* WUNT II, 75 (Tübingen: Mohr, 1995).

Ford, David F., *Self and Salvation: Being Transformed* (Cambridge: Cambridge University Press, 1999).

Forsyth, P. T., *The Cruciality of the Cross* (London: Independent Press, 1909).

_____, *The Person and Place of Jesus Christ* (London: Independent Press, 1909).

_____, *Lectures on the Church and the Sacraments* (London: Longmans, Green, 1917).

Foucault, Michel, *Madness and Civilization,* translated by R. Howard (New York: Pantheon, 1965).

_____, *The Order of Things,* translated by A. Sheridan (New York: Random, 1970).

_____, *History of Sexuality,* vol. 1: *An Introduction,* translated by R. Hurley (New York: Pantheon, 1978).

_____, *Discipline and Punish,* translated by A. Sheridan (New York: Pantheon, 1977).

_____, *Power/Knowledge: Selected Interviews and Other Writings 1972-77,* edited by Colin Gordon (New York: Random, 1981).

Fowl, Stephen E., *The Story of Christ in the Ethics of Paul: An Analysis of the Function of the Hymnic Material in the Pauline Corpus,* JSNTSS 36 (Sheffield: Sheffield Academic Press, 1990).

_____, *Engaging Scripture: A Model for Theological Interpretation* (Oxford: Blackwell, 1998).

Franks, Robert S., *The Doctrine of the Trinity* (London: Duckworth, 1953).

_____, *The Work of Christ: A Historical Study of Christian Doctrine* (London and Edinburgh: Nelson, 1962).

Frei, Hans, *The Eclipse of Biblical Narrative: A Study in Eighteenth and Nineteenth Century Hermeneutics* (New Haven, CT: Yale University Press, 1974).

Bibliography

Frei, Hans, *Types of Christian Theology* (New Haven, CT: Yale University Press, 1992).

Frye, Northrop, *The Great Code: The Bible and Literature* (New York and London: Harcourt Brace Jovanovich, 1982).

Fuchs, Ernst, *Studies of the Historical Jesus,* translated by A. Scobie (London: S.C.M., 1964).

Fuller, Daniel, *Easter Faith and History* (London: Tyndale and Grand Rapids: Eerdmans, 1965).

Funk, Robert W., *Language, Hermeneutic and Word of God* (New York: Harper & Row, 1966).

Gadamer, Hans-Georg, *Kleine Schriften,* 4 vols. (Tübingen: Mohr, 1967-77).

_____, *Philosophical Hermeneutics,* translated and edited by David E. Linge (Berkeley: University of California Press, 1976).

_____, *Dialogue and Dialectic: Eight Hermeneutical Studies on Plato* (New Haven, CT: Yale University Press, 1980).

_____, *Reason in the Age of Science,* translated by F. Lawrence (Cambridge, MA: MIT Press, 1981).

_____, *Truth and Method,* translated by J. Weinsheimer and D. G. Marshall (London: Sheed & Ward, 2d rev. Eng. edn. 1989).

_____, *Hans-Georg Gadamer on Education, Poetry, and History: Applied Hermeneutics* (Albany, NY: State University of New York Press, 1992).

_____, "Reflections on My Philosophical Journey," in Lewis E. Hahn (ed.), *The Philosophy of Hans-Georg Gadamer* (Chicago and La Salle: Open Court, 1997), 3-63.

_____, *Hermeneutics, Religion, and Ethics,* translated by J. Weinsheimer (New Haven, CT and London: Yale University Press, 1999).

Gee, Donald, *Spiritual Gifts in the Work of Ministry Today* (Springfield, MO: Gospel, 1963).

Geffré, Claude, *The Risk of Interpretation: On Being Faithful to Christian Tradition in a Non-Christian Age,* translated by David Smith (New York: Paulist, 1987).

Gehring, Hans-Ulrich, *Schriftprinzip und Rezeptionsästhetik: Rezeption in Martin Luther's Predigt und bei Hans Robert Jauss* (Neukirchen-Vluyn: Neukirchener, 1999).

Genette, Gérard, *Narrative Discourse: An Essay in Method,* translated by J. E. Lewin (Ithaca, NY: Cornell University Press 1980).

_____, *Narrative Discourse Re-Visited,* translated by J. E. Lewin (Ithaca, NY: Cornell University Press, 1988).

George, Timothy, *Theology of the Reformers* (Nashville: Broadman, and Leicester: Apollos, 1988).

Gerkin, Charles V., *The Living Human Document: Re-Visioning Pastoral Counselling in a Hermeneutical Mode* (Nashville: Abingdon, 1983).

Gilbertson, Michael, *God and History in the Book of Revelation: New Testament Studies in Dialogue with Pannenberg and Moltmann,* SNTSMS 124 (Cambridge: Cambridge University Press, 2003).

Gillespie, Thomas W., *The First Theologians: A Study in Early Christian Prophecy* (Grand Rapids: Eerdmans, 1994).

Godsey, John D., *The Theology of Dietrich Bonhoeffer* (London: S.C.M., 1960).

Goheen, Michael, "A Critical Examination of David Bosch's Missional Reading of Luke," in C. G. Bartholomew, Joel B. Green, and Anthony C. Thiselton (eds.), *Reading Luke: Interpretation, Reflection, Formation* (Grand Rapids: Zondervan and Carlisle, U.K.: Paternoster, 2005), 229-66.

González, Justo L., *A Concise History of Christian Doctrine* (Edinburgh: Alban Books, 2006 and Nashville: Abingdon, 2005).

Gordon C. H., "His Name Is 'One,'" *Journal of Near Eastern Studies* 29 (1970) 198-99.

Green, Garrett, *Imagining God: Theology and the Religious Imagination* (Grand Rapids: Eerdmans, 1989).

Green, Joel B., *The Theology of the Gospel of Luke* (Cambridge: Cambridge University Press, 1995).

_____, and Baker, Mark D., *Recovering the Scandal of the Cross: Atonement in New Testament and Contemporary Contexts* (Downers Grove, IL: InterVarsity, 2000).

Grenz, Stanley J., and Franke, John R., *Beyond Foundationalism: Shaping Theology in a Postmodern Context* (Louisville: Westminster/John Knox, 2001).

Grenz, Stanley J., *The Social God and the Relational Self: A Trinitarian Theology of the Imago Dei* (Louisville and London: Westminster John Knox, 2001).

Grillmeier, A., "The Reception of Chalcedon in the Roman Catholic Church," *Ecumenical Review* 22 (1970) 383-411.

Grobel, Kendrick, *The Gospel of Truth: A Valentinian Meditation on the Gospel, Translation from the Coptic and Commentary* (London: A. & C. Black and Abingdon, 1960).

Gundry, Robert H., *Sōma in Biblical Theology with Emphasis on Pauline Anthropology*, SNTSMS 29 (Cambridge: Cambridge University Press, 1976).

_____, "The New Jerusalem: People as Place, Not Place as People," in Robert H. Gundry, *The Old Is Better: New Testament Essays in Support of Traditional Interpretations* (Tübingen: Mohr Siebeck, 2005), 399-411.

Gundry-Volf, Judith, "Gender and Creation in 1 Cor. 11:2-16: A Study of Paul's Theological Method," in J. Adna, S. J. Hafemann, and O. Hofius (eds.), *Evangelium, Schriftsauslegung, Kirche: Festschrift für Peter Stuhlmacher* (Göttingen: Vandenhoeck & Ruprecht, 1997), 151-71.

Gunton, Colin E., *The Actuality of Atonement: A Study of Metaphor, Rationality and the Christian Tradition* (Edinburgh: T&T Clark, 1988), 1-26.

_____, *The Promise of Trinitarian Theology* (Edinburgh: T&T Clark, 1991).

_____, "The Doctrine of Creation," in Colin Gunton (ed.), *The Cambridge Companion to Christian Doctrine* (Cambridge: Cambridge University Press, 1997), 145-57.

Guy, H. A., *The New Testament Doctrine of Last Things* (London: Oxford University Press, 1948).

Haber, Honi Huber, *Beyond Postmodern Politics: Lyotard, Rorty, Foucault* (New York and London: Routledge, 1994).

Habermas, Jürgen, *The Theory of Communicative Action: The Critique of Functionalist Reason*, translated by T. McCarthy, 2 vols. (Cambridge: Polity, 1987).

Hainz, J., *Koinonia: "Kirche" als Gemeinschaft bei Paulus*, Biblische Untersuchungen (Regensburg: Pustet, 1982).

Hall, David R., *The Unity of the Corinthian Correspondence*, JSNTSS 251 (London and New York: T&T Clark, 2005).

Hamilton, N. Q., *The Holy Spirit and Eschatology in St. Paul*, Scottish Journal of Theology Occasional Papers (Edinburgh: Oliver & Boyd, 1957).

Hanfling, Oswald, *Wittgenstein's Later Philosophy* (London: Macmillan, 1989).

Hanson, Anthony T., *The Pioneer Ministry* (London: S.C.M., 1961).

_____, *Jesus Christ in the Old Testament* (London: SPCK, 1965).

_____, *Grace and Truth: A Study in the Doctrine of the Incarnation* (London: SPCK, 1975).

Hanson, R. P. C., *Tradition in the Early Church* (London: S.C.M., 1962).

Harnack, Adolf von, *What Is Christianity?* translated by T. B. Saunders (London: Ernest Benn, 5th edn. 1958).

Hart, H. L. A., "Are There Any Natural Rights?" *Philosophical Review* 64 (1995) 175-91.

Harvey, Anthony C., "Markers and Signposts," in The Doctrine Commission of the Church of England, *Believing in the Church* (cited above, 1981), 286-302.

Hauerwas, Stanley, *A Community of Character: Towards a Constructive Christian Ethic* (Notre Dame, IN: University of Notre Dame Press, 4th edn. 1986).

Hay, D. M., *Glory at the Right Hand: Psalm 110 in Early Christianity,* SBLMS 18 (Nashville: Abingdon, 1973).

Haykin, Michael A. G., *The Spirit of God: The Exegesis of 1 and 2 Corinthians in the Pneumatomachian Controversy of the Fourth Century,* Supplement to *Vigiliae Christianae* 27 (Leiden and New York: Brill, 1994).

Hays, Richard B., *The Faith of Jesus Christ: The Narrative Substructure of Galatians 3:1–4:11* (Grand Rapids: Eerdmans, 2002).

Hebblethwaite, Brian, *The Christian Hope* (London: Marshall, Morgan & Scott, 1984).

Hegel, Georg W. F., *Lectures on the Philosophy of Religion,* translated by E. B. Spiers and J. B. Sanderson, 3 vols. (London: Kegan Paul, Trench, Trübner, 1895).

———, *The Phenomenology of Mind,* translated with Notes by J. B. Baillie (New York: Harper & Row, 1967).

Heidegger, Martin, *An Introduction to Metaphysics,* translated by Ralph Manheim (New Haven, CT and London: Yale University Press, 1959).

———, *Being and Time,* translated by J. Macquarrie and E. Robinson (Oxford: Blackwell, 1962).

———, *On the Way to Language,* translated by P. Hertz (New York: Harper & Row, 1971).

———, "The Origin of the Work of Art," in *Heidegger, Poetry, Language, and Thought,* translated by A. Hofstadter (New York: Harper & Row, 1971), 15-87.

Heim, Karl, *The Transformation of the Scientific World View,* translated by N. H. Smith (London: S.C.M., 1953).

Heisenberg, Werner, *Physics and Philosophy: The Revolution in Modern Science* (London: Allen & Unwin, 1959).

Henderson, Ian, *Myth in the New Testament* (London: S.C.M., 1952).

Hendry, G. S., *The Holy Spirit in Christian Theology* (London: S.C.M., 1965).

Hengel, Martin, *Judaism and Hellenism: Studies in Their Encounter in Palestine during the Early Hellenistic Period,* translated by John Bowden (London: S.C.M. and Philadelphia: Fortress, 1974).

———, *The Cross of the Son of God,* translated by John Bowden (London: S.C.M., 1986).

———, with Deines, Roland, *The Pre-Christian Paul,* translated by J. Bowden (London: S.C.M., 1991).

———, and Deines, Roland, "E. P. Sanders, 'Common Judaism', Jesus and the Pharisees," *JTS* 46 (1995) 1-70.

Heyduck, Richard, *The Recovery of Doctrine in the Contemporary Church: An Essay in Philosophical Ecclesiology* (Waco, TX: Baylor University Press, 2002).

Hick, John (ed.), *The Myth of God Incarnate* (London: S.C.M., 1977).

Higgins, A. J. B., *The Lord's Supper in the New Testament* (London: S.C.M., 1952).

High, Dallas M., *Language, Persons and Beliefs: Studies in Wittgenstein's Philosophical Investigations and Religious Use of Language* (New York: Oxford University Press, 1967).

Hill, David, *Greek Words and Hebrew Meanings: Studies in the Semantics of Soteriological Terms,* SNTSMS 5 (Cambridge: Cambridge University Press, 1967).

_____, *New Testament Prophecy* (London: Marshall, 1979).

Hill, Edmund, *Being Human: A Biblical Perspective* (London: Chapman, 1984).

Hobbes, Thomas, *Leviathan,* edited by M. Oakshott (Oxford: Blackwell, 1960).

Hodge, Charles, *Systematic Theology,* 3 vols. (New York: Scribner, 1871).

Hodgson, Leonard, *The Doctrine of the Trinity* (London: Nisbet, 1943).

Hoffmann, P., *Die Toten in Christus* (Münster: Aschendorff, 1966).

Hofius, Otfried, "The Lord's Supper and the Lord's Supper Tradition: Reflections on 1 Cor. 11:23b-25," in Ben F. Meyer (ed.), *One Loaf, One Cup: Ecumenical Studies of 1 Cor. 11 and Other Eucharistic Texts,* Cambridge Conference of August 1988 (Macon, GA: Mercer University Press, 1988), 75-115.

Holland, Tom, *Contours of Pauline Theology: A Radical New Survey of the Influences on Paul's Biblical Writings* (Fearn, Scotland: Mentor/Focus, 2004).

Hollenweger, Walter J., *The Pentecostals* (Peabody, MA: Hendrickson and London: S.C.M., 1972).

Holmberg, B., *Paul and Power: The Structure of Authority in the Primitive Church as Reflected in the Pauline Epistles* (Lund: Gleerup, 1978).

Holmquist, Michael, *Dialogism: Bakhtin and His World* (London and New York: Routledge, 1990).

Hooker, Richard, *Of the Laws of Ecclesiastical Polity,* arranged by John Keble and revised by R. W. Church, 3 vols. (Oxford: Clarendon, 7th edn. 1888).

Hoyle, R. Birch, *The Holy Spirit in St. Paul* (London: Hodder & Stoughton, 1927).

Hughes, H. Maldwyn, *The Christian Idea of God* (London: Duckworth, 1936).

Hume, David, *A Treatise of Human Nature,* edited by L. A. Selby-Bigge (Oxford: Clarendon, 1951).

Hunsinger, Deborah van Deusen, *Theology and Pastoral Counselling: A New Interdisciplinary Approach* (Grand Rapids: Eerdmans, 1995).

Hunsinger, George, *How to Read Karl Barth: The Shape of His Theology* (New York and Oxford: Oxford University Press, 1991).

Hunter, A. M., *Paul and His Predecessors* (London: S.C.M., 2d edn. 1961).

Hurtado, Larry W., *One God, One Lord: Early Christian Devotion and Ancient Jewish Monotheism* (London and New York: T&T Clark, 2d edn. 1998).

_____, *Lord Jesus Christ: Devotion to Jesus in Earliest Christianity* (Grand Rapids: Eerdmans, 2005).

Inge, John, *A Christian Theology of Place* (Aldershot, UK: Ashgate, 2003).

Jaspers, Karl, and Bultmann, Rudolf, *Myth and Christianity: An Inquiry into the Possibility of Religion without Myth,* translated by R. J. Hoffman (Amherst, NY: Prometheus, 2005).

Jauss, Hans Robert, "The Alterity and Modernity of Mediaeval Literature," in *New Literary History* 10 (1978-79) 181-229.

_____, *Toward an Aesthetic of Reception,* translated by T. Bahti, Theory and History of Literature 2 (Minneapolis: University of Minnesota Press, 1982).

_____, *Question and Answer: Forms of Dialogic Understanding,* translated by M. Hays, Theological History of Literature 68 (Minneapolis: University of Minnesota Press, 1989).

_____, *Wege des Verstehens* (Munich: Fink, 1994).

Jenson, Robert, *Visible Words: The Interpretation and Practice of Christian Sacraments* (Philadelphia: Fortress, 1978).

_____, "The Church and the Sacraments," in Colin Gunton (ed.), *Cambridge Companion on Christian Doctrine* (Cambridge: Cambridge University Press, 1997), 207-25.

Jeremias, Joachim, *Infant Baptism in the First Four Centuries,* translated by David Cairns (London: S.C.M., 1960).

_____, *The Origins of Infant Baptism: A Further Study in Reply to Kurt Aland* translated by D. M. Burton (London: S.C.M., 1963).

_____, *The Parables of Jesus,* translated by S. H. Hooke (London: S.C.M., rev. edn. 1963).

_____, *The Central Message of the New Testament* (London: S.C.M., 1965).

_____, *The Eucharistic Words of Jesus,* translated by Norman Perrin (London: S.C.M., 1966).

_____, *New Testament Theology:* Part I, *The Proclamation of Jesus,* translated by John Bowden (London: S.C.M., 1971).

_____, *Der Schlüssel zur Theologie des Apostels Paulus* (Stuttgart: Calwer, 1971).

Jewett, Paul K., *Man as Male and Female* (Grand Rapids: Eerdmans, 1975).

_____, *Infant Baptism and the Covenant of Grace* (Grand Rapids: Eerdmans, 1978).

Jewett, Robert, *Paul's Anthropological Terms: A Study of their Use in Conflict Settings,* Arbeiten zur Geschichte des antiken Judentums und des Urchristentums 10 (Leiden: Brill, 1971).

_____, *Letter to Pilgrims: A Commentary on the Epistle to the Hebrews* (New York: Pilgrim, 1981).

Johnson, A. R., *The One and the Many in the Israelite Conception of God* (Cardiff, Wales: Cardiff University Press, 1961).

Johnston, Paul, *Wittgenstein: Rethinking the Inner* (London and New York: Routledge, 1993).

Jonas, Hans, *The Gnostic Religion* (Boston: Beacon, 2d rev. edn. 1963).

Jones, Malcolm, *Dostoevsky and the Dynamics of Religious Experience* (London: Anthem, 2005).

Jones, O. R. (ed.), *The Private Language Argument* (London: Macmillan, 1971).

Jüngel, Eberhard, *God as the Mystery of the World: On the Foundation of the Theology of the Crucified One in the Dispute between Theism and Atheism,* translated by D. L. Guder (Edinburgh: T&T Clark, 1983).

_____, "Jüngel," in Jürgen Moltmann (ed.), *How I Have Changed My Mind: Reflections on Thirty Years of Theology,* translated by John Bowden (London: S.C.M., 1997).

_____, *Theological Essays,* edited by John B. Webster, 2 vols. (Edinburgh: T&T Clark, 1989 and 1995).

_____, *God's Being Is in Becoming: The Trinitarian Being of God in the Theology of Karl Barth. A Paraphrase,* translated by John Webster (Edinburgh: T&T Clark, 2001).

Kähler, Martin, *The So-Called Historical Jesus and the Historic, Biblical Christ,* edited and translated by Carl E. Braaten (Philadelphia: Fortress, 1964).

Kant, Immanuel, *Groundwork of the Metaphysics of Morals,* translated by Mary Gregor (Cambridge: Cambridge University Press, 1998).

Käsemann, Ernst, "Die Legitimität das Apostels," *ZNW* 2 (1942) 33-71.

_____, *Essays on New Testament Themes,* translated by A. R. Allenson (London: S.C.M., 1964).

_____, "On the Subject of Primitive Christian Apocalyptic," in E. Käsemann, *New Testament Questions of Today,* translated by W. J. Montague (London: S.C.M., 1969), 108-37.

_____, *Perspectives on Paul,* translated by Margaret Kohl (London: S.C.M., 1971).

_____, *The Wandering People of God: An Investigation of the Letter to the Hebrews,* translated by R. A. Harrisville and I. L. Sandberg (Minneapolis: Augsburg, 1984).

_____, *Commentary on Romans,* translated by G. W. Bromiley (Grand Rapids: Eerdmans, 1980).

Kelly, J. N. D., *Early Christian Creeds* (London: Longman, 3d edn. 1972).

Kelsey, David, *The Uses of Scripture in Recent Theology* (London: S.C.M., 1975).

Kennedy, H. A. A., *St. Paul's Conceptions of the Last Things* (London: Hodder & Stoughton, 1904).

Kepnes, Steven, *The Text as Thou: Martin Buber's Dialogical Hermeneutics and Narrative Theology* (Bloomington, IN: Indiana University Press, 1993).

Kerr, Fergus, *Theology after Wittgenstein* (Oxford: Blackwell, 1986).

Kertelge, Karl, *Rechtfertigung bei Paulus: Studien zur Struktur und zum Bedeutungsgehalt des Paulinischen Rechtfertigungs Begriffs* (Münster: Aschendorff, 2d edn. 1967).

Kierkegaard, Søren, *Concluding Unscientific Postscript to the Philosophical Fragments,* English translation by D. Swenson and W. Lowrie (Princeton: Princeton University Press, 1941).

_____, *The Sickness unto Death,* translated by W. Lowrie (Princeton, NJ: Princeton University Press, 1941).

_____, *The Concept of Dread,* translated by M. Lowrie (Princeton, NJ: Princeton University Press, 1944).

_____, *Philosophical Fragments,* edited and translated by H. V. Hong and E. H. Hong (Princeton, NJ: Princeton University Press, 1985).

_____, *The Point of View for My Work as an Author,* edited and translated by H. V. Hong and E. H. Hong (Princeton, NJ: Princeton University Press, 1998).

Kilby, Karen, *Karl Rahner: Theology and Philosophy* (London and New York: Routledge, 2004).

_____, "Aquinas, the Trinity, and the Limits of Understanding," *International Journal of Systematic Theology* 7 (2005) 414-27.

Kim, Seyoon, *The Origin of Paul's Gospel* (Grand Rapids: Eerdmans and Tübingen: Mohr, 1981).

Kittel, Gerhard, and Friedrich, Gerhard, *Theological Dictionary to the New Testament,* translated by G. W. Bromiley, 10 vols. (Grand Rapids: Eerdmans, 1964-76).

Klausner, Joseph, *The Messianic Idea in Israel: from Its Beginning to the Completion of the Mishnah,* translated from the third Hebrew edition by W. F. Stinespring (London: Allen & Unwin, 1956).

Klein, G., *Die Zwölf Apostel: Urspung und Gehalt einer Idee* (Göttingen: Vandenhoeck & Ruprecht, 1961).

Knowles, Robert, *Anthony Thiselton and the Grammar of Hermeneutics: The Search for a Unified Theory* (University of Cardiff Ph.D. contracted with Ashgate for publication).

Koch, Klaus, *The Rediscovery of Apocalyptic,* translated by Margaret Kohl (London: S.C.M., 1972).

Kort, Wesley A., *Story, Text and Scripture: Literary Interests in Biblical Narrative* (University Park, PA and London: Pennsylvania State University Press, 1988).

Kramer, Werner, *Christ, Lord, Son of God* (London: S.C.M., 1966).

Kretzmann, N., "Eternity," *Journal of Philosophy* 78 (1981) 429-58.

Kripke, Saul A., *Wittgenstein on Rules and Private Language* (Oxford: Blackwell, 1982).

Krister Stendahl, "The Apostle Paul and the Introspective Conscience of the West," *HTR* 56 (1963) 199-215, reprinted in Krister Stendahl, *Paul among Jews and Gentiles* (London: S.C.M., 1977).

Kuhn, Thomas S., *The Structure of Scientific Revolutions* (Chicago: Chicago University Press, 2d rev. ed. 1970 [1st edn. 1962]).

———, *The Essential Tension: Selected Studies in a Scientific Tradition and Change* (Chicago: University of Chicago Press, 1977).

Kümmel, W. G., *The New Testament: The History of the Investigation of Its Problems,* translated by S. M. Gilmour and Howard C. Kee (London: S.C.M., 1973 and Nashville: Abingdon, 1972).

Küng, Hans, *Eternal Life?* translated by Edward Quinn (London: Collins, 1984).

———, and Tracy, David (eds.), *Paradigm Change in Theology: A Symposium for the Future,* translated by Margaret Köhl (Edinburgh: T&T Clark, 1989).

———, *Credo, the Apostles' Creed Explained for Today,* translated by John Bowden (London: S.C.M., 1993).

Künneth, Walter, *The Theology of the Resurrection,* translated by J. W. Leitch (London: S.C.M., 1965).

Kuschel, H.-J. *Born before All Time? The Dispute over Christ's Origin,* translated by John Bowden (London: S.C.M., 1992).

LaCugna, Catherine Mowry, *God for Us: The Trinity and Christian Life* (San Francisco: Harper, 1992).

Ladd, G. E., "Eschatology and the Unity of New Testament Theology," *Expository Times* 82 (1971) 307-9.

———, *A Theology of the New Testament* (London: Lutterworth, 1974).

Laeuchli, Samuel, *The Language of Faith: An Introduction to the Semantic Dilemma of the Early Church* (London: Epworth, 1962).

Laidlaw, John, *The Bible Doctrine of Man* (Edinburgh: T&T Clark, 1895).

Lakatos, Imre, and Musgrave, Alan (eds.), *Criticism and the Growth of Knowledge* (Cambridge: Cambridge University Press, 1970).

———, *Proofs and Refutations: The Logic of Mathematical Discovery,* edited by J. Worrall and E. Zahar (Cambridge: Cambridge University Press, 1976, with additional material from 1963-64).

———, *Mathematics, Science, and Epistemology: Philosophical Papers,* edited by J. Worrall and Gregory Currie, 2 vols. (Cambridge: Cambridge University Press, 1978), vol. 2.

———, and Feyerabend, Paul, *For and Against Method: Including Lakatos's Lectures on Scientific Method and the Lakatos-Feyerabend Correspondence,* edited by M. Motterlini (Chicago and London: University of Chicago Press, 1999).

Lampe, G. W. H., "The Holy Spirit in the Writings of St. Luke," in D. E. Nineham (ed.), *Studies in the Gospels: Essays in Memory of R. H. Lightfoot* (Oxford: Blackwell, 1955), 159-200.

———, *A Patristic Greek Lexicon* (Oxford: Clarendon, 1961).

Larvor, Brendan, *Lakatos: An Introduction* (London and New York: Routledge, 1998).

Lash, Nicholas, *Change in Focus: A Study of Doctrinal Change and Continuity* (London: Sheed & Ward, 1973).

———, "What Might Martyrdom Mean?" in Nicholas Lash, *Theology on the Way to Emmaus* (London: S.C.M., 1986), 75-92.

Laurer, Robert H., *Temporal Man: The Meaning and Uses of Social Time* (New York: Praeger, 1981).

Lawrence, John, et al., *A Critique of Eucharistic Agreement* (London: SPCK, 1975).

Leenhardt, F. J., "This Is My Body," in Oscar Cullmann and Leenhardt, *Essays on the Lord's Supper,* translated by J. G. Davies (London: Lutterworth, 1958), 39-40.

Lessing, Gotthold Ephraim, *Lessing's Theological Writings,* edited by Henry Chadwick (London: Black, 1956).

Lewis, H. D., *The Elusive Mind* (London: Allan & Unwin and New York: Macmillan, 1969).

Lietzmann, Hans, *Mass and Lord's Supper: A Study in the History of the Liturgy,* with Introductions and Further Inquiry by R. D. Richardson (Leiden: Brill, 1979).

Lin, Hong-Hsin, *The Relevance of Hermeneutical Theory in Heidegger, Gadamer, Wittgenstein, and Ricoeur for the Concept of Self in Adult Education* (Nottingham Ph.D. diss., August 1998).

Lindbeck, George A., *The Nature of Doctrine: Religion and Theology in a Postliberal Age* (Philadelphia: Westminster Press and London: SPCK, 1984).

Locke, John, *An Essay Concerning Human Understanding,* edited by Peter H. Nidditch (Oxford: Clarendon edn., Oxford University Press, 1975).

_____, *Two Treatises of Government,* edited by P. Laslett ([1790]; Cambridge: Cambridge University Press, 1988).

Lohse, E., "Ursprung und Prägung des christlichen Apostolates," *Theologische Zeitschrift* 9 (1953) 259-75.

Lonergan, Bernard, *Method in Theology* (London: Darton, Longman & Todd, 1972).

_____, *Insight: A Study of Human Understanding* (New York and London: Harper & Row, 1978.

Longenecker, Bruce W. (ed.), *Narrative Dynamics in Paul: A Critical Assessment* (Louisville and London: Westminster/John Knox Press, 2002).

Lovatt, Mark F. W., *Confronting the Will-To-Power: A Reconsideration of the Theology of Reinhold Niebuhr* (Carlisle, U.K.: Paternoster, 2001).

Lowe, John, "An Examination of Attempts to Detect Developments in St. Paul's Theology," *JTS* 42 (1941) 129-41.

Lundin, Roger, *The Culture of Interpretation: Christian Faith and the Postmodern World* (Grand Rapids: Eerdmans, 1993).

Luther, Martin, *Luther's Works,* edited by J. Pelikan and H. J. Lehman, 55 vols. (Philadelphia: Fortress, 1943-86).

_____, *A Commentary on St. Paul's Epistle to the Galatians,* translated by Philip S. Watson (London: James Clarke, 1953).

_____, *The Bondage of the Will,* translated by J. I. Packer and O. R. Johnston (London: Clark, 1957).

_____, "Preface to the Complete Edition of Luther: Latin Writings," in *Luther's Works,* vol. 34: *The Career of the Reformer,* edited and translated by Lewis W. Spitz (Philadelphia: Muhlenberg Press, 1960) 327-38.

_____, *Luther: Early Theological Works,* translated and edited by James Atkinson, Library of Christian Classics 16 (London: S.C.M. and Philadelphia: Westminster, 1962).

_____, *The Schmalkald Articles,* translated by W. R. Russell (Minneapolis: Augsburg/Fortress, 1995).

Lyotard, Jean-François, *The Postmodern Condition: A Report on Knowledge,* translated by G. Bennington and B. Massumi (Manchester: Manchester University Press, 1984).

_____, *The Differend: Phrases in Dispute,* translated by Georges Van Den Abbeele (Manchester: Manchester University Press, 1988).

Macchia, F. D., "Groans Too Deep for Words: Toward a Theology of Tongues as Initial Evidence," *Asian Journal of Pentecostal Studies* 1 (1998) 149-73.

_____, "Tongues and Prophecy: A Pentecostal Perspective," *Concilium* 3 (1996) 63-69.

Mackintosh, H. R., *The Doctrine of the Person of Jesus Christ* (Edinburgh: T&T Clark, 1913).

Macquarrie, John, *An Existentialist Theology: A Comparison of Heidegger and Bultmann*, London: S.C.M., 1955, rpt. 1973).

_____, *The Scope of Demythologizing: Bultmann and His Critics* (London: S.C.M., 1960).

_____, *Principles of Christian Theology* (London: S.C.M., 1966; 2d edn. 1977).

_____, *Studies in Christian Existentialism* (London: S.C.M., 1966).

_____, *In Search of Humanity: A Theological and Philosophical Approach* (London: S.C.M., 1982).

_____, *Theology, Church, and Ministry* (London: S.C.M., 1986).

_____, *Jesus Christ in Modern Thought* (London: S.C.M. and Philadelphia: Trinity Press International, 1990).

Manson, William, *Eschatology*, Scottish Journal of Theology Occasional Papers (Edinburgh: Oliver & Boyd, 1953).

Marcel, Pierre C., *The Biblical Doctrine of Infant Baptism: Sacrament of the Covenant of Grace*, translated by Philip E. Hughes (London: Clarke, 1953).

Mascall, Eric L., *The Importance of Being Human: Some Aspects of the Christian Doctrine of Man* (London: Oxford University Press, 1959).

Markus, Robert A., *Signs and Meanings: World and Text in Ancient Christianity* (Liverpool: Liverpool University Press, 1996).

Marsh, John, *The Fulness of Time* (London: Nisbet, 1952).

Marshall, Bruce D., *Trinity and Truth* (Cambridge: Cambridge University Press, 2000).

Marshall, I. Howard, *The Origins of New Testament Christology* (Leicester: Inter-Varsity Press, 1976).

_____, "The Meaning of Reconciliation," in R. A. Guelich (ed.), *Unity and Diversity in New Testament Theology: Essays in Honour of G. E. Ladd* (Grand Rapids: Eerdmans, 1978), 117-32.

_____, *Last Supper and Lord's Supper* (Grand Rapids: Eerdmans, 1980).

_____, *New Testament Theology: Many Witnesses, One Gospel* (Downers Grove, IL: InterVarsity Press, 2004).

Martin, Bernard, *Paul Tillich's Doctrine of Man* (London: Nisbet, 1966).

Martin, Dale B., *Slavery as Salvation* (New Haven, CT: Yale University Press, 1990).

_____, *The Corinthian Body* (New Haven, CT and London: Yale University Press, 1995).

Martin, James P., *The Last Judgement in Protestant Theology from Orthodoxy to Ritschl* (Edinburgh: Oliver & Boyd, 1963).

Martin, Ralph P., *Reconciliation: A Study of Paul's Theology* (London: Marshall, Morgan, & Scott, 1981).

Marxsen, W., *The Resurrection of Jesus of Nazareth*, translated by Margaret Kohl (Philadelphia: Fortress, 1970).

Matlock, Barry B., *Unveiling the Apocalyptic: Paul's Interpreters and the Rhetoric of Criticism*, JSNTSS 127 (Sheffield: Sheffield Academic Press, 1996).

McAdoo, H. R., and Clark, Alan (Co-Chairmen), Anglican/Roman Catholic International Commission, *Agreed Statement in Eucharistic Doctrine* (Windsor, 1971).

McBrien, Richard P., *The Church in the Thought of Bishop John Robinson* (London: S.C.M., 1966).

McDonnell, Kilian P. (ed.), *Presence, Power, and Praise: Documents on the Charismatic Renewal,* 3 vols. (Collegeville, MN: Liturgical Press, 1980).

McFadyen, Alistair I., *The Call to Personhood: A Christian Theory of the Individual in Social Relationships* (Cambridge: Cambridge University Press, 1990).

McFague, Sallie, *Models of God: Theology for an Ecological, Nuclear Age* (Philadelphia: Fortress, 1987).

_____, *The Body of God: An Ecological Theology* (London: S.C.M., 1993).

McGrath, Alister E., *The Making of Modern German Christology: From the Enlightenment to Pannenberg* (Oxford: Blackwell, 1986).

_____, *The Genesis of Doctrine: A Study in the Foundations of Doctrinal Criticism* (Oxford: Blackwell, 1990).

_____, *A Scientific Theology,* vol. 1: *Nature* (Edinburgh and New York: T&T Clark, 2001).

McIntyre, John, *St. Anselm and His Critics: A Re-interpretation of the* Cur Deus Homo (Edinburgh: Oliver & Boyd, 1964).

McLelland, Joseph C., *The Visible Words of God: A Study in the Theology of Peter Martyn 1500-1562* (Edinburgh: Oliver & Boyd, 1957).

Melanchthon, Philip, *Loci Communes Rerum Theologicarum,* translated and edited by Wilhelm Pauck, in *Melanchthon and Bucer,* Library of Christian Classics 19 (London: S.C.M. and Philadelphia: Westminster, 1969).

Michalson, Gordon E., *Lessing's "Ugly Ditch": A Study of Theology and History* (University Park, PA and London: Pennsylvania State University Press, 1985).

Miegge, Giovanni, *Gospel and Myth in the Thought of Rudolf Bultmann,* translated by Stephen Neill (London: Lutterworth, 1960).

Migliore, Daniel L., *Faith Seeking Understanding: An Introduction to Christian Theology* (Grand Rapids: Eerdmans, 1991).

Migne, J. P. (ed.), *Patrologiae Cursus Completus,* Patrologia Graeca (Paris: Garnier, 1857-66).

Miranda, José P., *Marx and the Bible: A Critique of the Philosophy of Oppression,* translated by John Eagleson (London: S.C.M., 1977 and New York: Orbis, 1974).

Moberly, R. W. L., "Yahweh Is One: The Translation of the *Shema*," Supplements to Vetus Testamentum 41 (1990) 209-15.

_____, *Prophecy and Discernment* (Cambridge: Cambridge University Press, 2006).

Moltmann, Jürgen, *Theology of Hope,* translated by J. Leitch (London: S.C.M., 1967).

_____, *The Crucified God: The Cross of Christ as the Foundation and Criticism of Christian Theology,* translated by R. A. Wilson and John Bowden (London: S.C.M., 1974).

_____, *Man: Christian Anthropology in the Conflicts of the Present,* translated by John Sturdy (London: SPCK, 1974).

_____, *The Church in the Power of the Spirit: A Contribution to Messianic Ecclesiology,* translated by Margaret Kohl (London: S.C.M., 1977).

_____, *The Open Church: Invitation to a Messianic Lifestyle,* translated by M. Douglas Meeks (London: S.C.M., 1978); also published as *The Passion for Life: A Messianic Lifestyle* (Philadelphia: Fortress, 1978).

_____, *The Trinity and the Kingdom of God: The Doctrine of God,* translated by Margaret Kohl (London: S.C.M., 1981).

_____, *God in Creation: An Ecological Doctrine of Creation,* translated by Margaret Kohl (London: S.C.M., 1985).

_____, *The Way of Jesus Christ: Christology in Messianic Dimensions,* translated by Margaret Kohl (London: S.C.M., 1990).

_____, *History and the Triune God: Contributions to Trinitarian Theology,* translated by John Bowden (London: S.C.M., 1991).

_____, *The Spirit of Life: A Universal Affirmation,* translated by Margaret Kohl (London: S.C.M., 1992).

_____, *The Coming of God: Christian Eschatology,* translated by Margaret Kohl London: S.C.M., 1996).

_____, *Experiences in Theology: Ways and Forms of Christian Theology,* translated by Margaret Kohl (London: S.C.M., 2000).

Moore, A. L., *The Parousia in the New Testament,* Supplements to Novum Testamentum 13 (Leiden: Brill, 1966).

Moore, W. E., *Scarce Resource: Man, Time and Society* (New York: Wiley, 1963).

Moores, John, *Wrestling with Rationality in Paul: Romans 1–8 in a New Perspective,* JSNTMS 82 (Cambridge: Cambridge University Press, 1995).

Morley, Georgina, *The Grace of Being: John Macquarrie's Natural Theology* (Bristol, IN: Wyndham Hall Press, 2001 and Aldershot: Ashgate, 2003).

Morris, Leon, *The Apostolic Preaching of the Cross* (London: Tyndale, 1955).

_____, "The Meaning of ἱλαστήριον in Romans 3:25," *New Testament Studies* 2 (1955-56) 33-43.

_____, *The Cross in the New Testament* (Exeter, U.K.: Paternoster and Grand Rapids: Eerdmans, 1965).

Morson, Gary Saul, and Emerson, Caryl, *Mikhail Bakhtin: Creation of a Prosaics* (Stanford, CA: Stanford University Press, 1990).

Mosala, Itumeleng J., *Biblical Hermeneutics and Black Theology in South Africa* (Grand Rapids: Eerdmans, 1989).

Mosbeck, H., "*Apostolos* in the New Testament," *Studia Theologica* 2 (1949-50) 166-200.

Moule, C. F. D., "The Judgement Theme in the Sacraments," in W. D. Davies and D. Daube (eds.), *The Background to the New Testament and its Eschatology: In Honour of C. H. Dodd* (Cambridge: Cambridge University Press, 1936), 464-81.

_____, "The Christology of Acts," in L. E. Keck and J. L. Martyn (eds.), *Studies in Luke-Acts* (London: SPCK, 1968).

Moulton, J. H., and Milligan, G., *Vocabulary of the Greek Testament* (London: Hodder & Stoughton, [1930] 1952).

Mounce, William D., *Pastoral Epistles,* WBC 46 (Nashville: Thomas Nelson, 2000).

Moxon, Reginald S., *The Doctrine of Sin: A Critical and Historical Investigation into the Views of the Concept of Sin Held in Early Christian, Mediaeval and Modern Times* (London: Allen & Unwin, 1922).

Müller, Ulrich B., *Prophetie und Predigt im Neuen Testament: Formgeschichtliche Untersuchungen zur urchristlichen Prophetie* (Gütersloh: Mohn, 1975).

Munck, Johannes, *Paul and the Salvation of Mankind,* translated by Frank Clarke (London: S.C.M., 1959).

Murphy, Nancey, *Theology in the Age of Scientific Reasoning,* Cornell Studies in the Philosophy of Religion (Ithaca and London: Cornell University Press, 1990).

_____, *Beyond Liberalism and Fundamentalism: How Modern and Post-Modern Philosophy Set the Theological Agenda,* Rockwell Lecture Series (London and New York: Continuum/Trinity International, 1996).

Murphy-O'Connor, Jerome, *Becoming Human Together: The Pastoral Anthropology of St. Paul* (Wilmington: Glazier, 1982).

Nelson, J. Robert, *The Realm of Redemption: Studies in the Doctrine of the Nature of the Church in Contemporary Theology* (London: Epworth, 1951; 6th edn. 1963).

Neufeld, Dietmar, *Reconceiving Texts as Speech Acts: An Analysis of 1 John,* Biblical Interpretation Monograph Series 7 (Leiden and New York: Brill, 1994).

Neufeld, Vernon H., *The Earliest Christian Confessions,* NTTS 5 (Leiden: Brill and Grand Rapids: Eerdmans, 1963).

Neunheuser, Burkhard, *Baptism and Confirmation,* translated by J. J. Hughes (London: Burns & Oates and Freiburg: Herder, 1964).

Newbigin, Leslie, *The Household of Faith: Lectures on the Nature of the Church* (London: S.C.M., 1953).

Newlands, George, *Theology of the Love of God* (London: Collins, 1980).

Niebuhr, Reinhold, *Moral Man and Immoral Society* (London: S.C.M., 1963 [also New York: Scribner, 1932]).

_____, *Moral Man and Immoral Society: A Study in Ethics and Politics* (London: S.C.M., 1963 and New York: Scribner, 1932).

_____, *The Nature and Destiny of Man: A Christian Interpretation,* 2 vols. (London: Nisbet, 1941).

Nineham, Denis, E., *The Use and Abuse of the Bible: A Study of the Bible in an Age of Rapid Cultural Change* (London: Macmillan, 1976).

Nürnberger, Klaus, *Theology of the Biblical Witness* (Münster and London: LIT, 2002).

Nygren, Anders, *Commentary on Romans,* translated by C. C. Rasmussen (London: S.C.M., 1952).

_____, *Meaning and Method: Prolegomena to a Scientific Philosophy of Religion and a Scientific Theology* (London: Epworth, 1972).

O'Donnell, John J., *Trinity and Temporality: The Christian Doctrine of God in the Light of Process Theology and the Theology of Hope* (Oxford: Oxford University Press, 1983).

O'Donovan, Joan Lockwood, "A Timely Conversation with *The Desire of Nations* in Civil Society, Nation and State," in Craig Bartholomew, J. Chaplin, Robert Song, and Al Wolters (eds.), *A Royal Priesthood, A Dialogue with Oliver O'Donovan,* Scripture and Hermeneutic Series 3 (Grand Rapids: Zondervan and Carlisle, U.K.: Paternoster, 2002).

O'Donovan, Oliver, *The Desire of Nations: Rediscovering the Roots of Political Theology* (Cambridge: Cambridge University Press, 1996).

O'Meara, T. A., and Weisser, C. D. (eds.), *Paul Tillich in Catholic Thought* (London: Darton, Longman & Todd, 1965).

Orr, James, *God's Image in Man and Its Defacement in the Light of Modern Denials* (London: Hodder & Stoughton, 2d edn. 1905).

Osborne, Grant R., *The Hermeneutical Spiral: A Comprehensive Introduction to Biblical Interpretation* (Downers Grove, IL: InterVarsity Press, 1991).

Otto, Rudolf, *The Idea of the Holy: An Inquiry into the Nonrational Factor in the Idea of the Divine and Its Relation to the Rational,* translated by J. W. Harvey (Oxford: Oxford University Press, 2d edn. 1950).

Pagels, Elaine, *The Johannine Gospel in Gnostic Exegesis: Heracleon's Commentary on John* (Nashville and New York: Abingdon, 1973).

Panikulam, G., *Koinonia in the New Testament: A Dynamic Expression of Christian Life,* Analecta Biblica 85 (Rome: Biblical Institute Press, 1979).

Pannenberg, Wolfhart, "The Revelation of God in Jesus of Nazareth," in James M. Robinson and John B. Cobb, *New Frontiers in Theology:* III, *Theology as History* (New York: Harper & Row, 1967), 101-33.

_____, *Jesus — God and Man,* translated by L. L. Wilkins and D. A. Priebe (London: S.C.M., 1968).

_____, *Basic Questions in Theology,* translated by G. H. Kehm and R. Wilson, 3 vols. (London: S.C.M., 1970-73).

_____, *Theology and the Philosophy of Science,* translated by F. McDonagh (Philadelphia: Westminster, 1976).

_____, *Anthropology in Theological Perspective,* translated by M. J. O'Connell (London and New York: T&T Clark/Continuum, 1985 and 2004).

_____, *Systematic Theology,* translated by G. W. Bromiley, 3 vols. (Grand Rapids: Eerdmans and Edinburgh: T&T Clark, 1991-98).

_____, "Theological Appropriation of Scientific Understandings," in C. R. Albright and J. Haugen (eds.), *Beginning with the End: God, Science, and Wolfhart Pannenberg* (Chicago: Open Court, 1997).

Pattison, George, *A Short Course in Christian Doctrine* (London: S.C.M., 2005).

Peacocke, A. R., *Creation and the World of Science* (Oxford: Clarendon, 1979).

_____, *Theology for a Scientific Age: Being and Becoming — Natural and Divine* (Oxford: Blackwell, 1990).

Perkins, Pheme, *Resurrection: New Testament Witnesses and Contemporary Reflections* (London: Chapman, 1984).

Perrin, Norman, *The Kingdom of God in the Teaching of Jesus* (London: S.C.M., 1963).

Peters, Ted, *God — the World's Future: Systematic Theology for a Postmodern Era* (Minneapolis: Fortress, 1992).

Petts, David, *Healing and Atonement,* University of Nottingham Ph.D. (Nottingham: University of Nottingham, 1993).

Plantinga, Alvin, and Wolterstorff, Nicholas, *Faith and Rationality* (Notre Dame, IN: University of Notre Dame Press, 1983).

Plaskow, Judith, *Sex, Sin and Grace: Women's Experience and the Theologies of Reinhold Niebuhr and Paul Tillich* (Lanham, MD: University Press of America, 1980).

Pogoloff, *Logos and Sophia: The Rhetorical Situation of 1 Corinthians* (Atlanta: Scholars, 1992).

Polkinghorne, John, *The Way the World Is* (London: Triangle, 1983).

_____, *Science and Creation: The Search for Understanding* (Boston, MA: Shambhala, 1988 and London: SPCK, 1988).

_____, *Quarks, Chaos, and Christianity: Questions to Science and Religion* (London: Triangle, 1994).

_____, *Science and Theology: An Introduction* (London: S.C.M. and Minneapolis: Fortress, 1998).

_____ (ed.), *The Work of Love: Creation as Kenosis* (London: SPCK and Grand Rapids: Eerdmans, 2001).

_____, *Belief in God in an Age of Science* (New Haven, CT: Yale University Press, 2003).

Porter, J. R., "The Legal Aspects of Corporate Personality in the Old Testament," *Vetus Testamentum* 15 (1965) 361-68.

Powell, Cyril H., *The Biblical Concept of Power* (London: Epworth, 1963).

Prestige G. L., *God in Patristic Thought* (London: SPCK, 1952).

Price, H. H., *Belief*, Muirhead Library of Philosophy (London: Allen & Unwin and New York: Humanities, 1969).

Quash, Ben, "Hans Urs von Balthasar," in David F. Ford (with Rachel Muirs), *The Modern Theologians* (Oxford: Blackwell, 3d edn. 2005), 106-23.

_____, *Theology and the Drama of History*, Cambridge Studies in Christian Doctrine (Cambridge: Cambridge University Press, 2005).

Rad, Gerhard von, *Old Testament Theology*, translated by D. M. G. Stalker, 2 vols. (Edinburgh and London: Oliver & Boyd, 1962), vol. 1.

Rahner, Karl, *Theological Investigations*, 22 vols. (English, London: Darton, Longman & Todd and New York: Seabury/Crossroad, 1961-91).

_____, *The Church and the Sacraments* (New York: Herder & Herder, 1963).

_____, *The Trinity*, translated by Joseph Donceel (Tunbridge Wells and London: Burns & Oates, 1970).

_____, *The Shape of the Church to Come*, translated by Edward Quinn (London: SPCK, 1974).

_____, *Foundations of Christian Faith: An Introduction to the Idea of Christianity*, translated by W. V. Dych (New York: Crossroad, 1978 and 2004).

_____, and Thüsing, Wilhelm, *A New Christology*, translated by David Smith and V. Green (London: Burns & Oates, 1980).

Räisänen, Heikki, *Challenges to Biblical Interpretation: Collected Essays 1991-2000*, Biblical Interpretation Series 59 (London and Boston: Brill, 2001).

Ramsey, Ian T., *Religious Language: An Empirical Placing of Theological Phrases* (London: S.C.M., 1957).

_____, *Models for Divine Activity* (London: S.C.M., 1973).

_____, *Words about God* (London: S.C.M., 1971).

Readings, Bill, *Introducing Lyotard: Art and Politics* (London: Routledge, 1991).

Reid, J. K. S., *Our Life in Christ* (London: S.C.M., 1963).

Reimarus, Hermann Samuel, *Reimarus: Fragments*, edited by Charles H. Talbert and translated by R. S. Fraser (London: S.C.M., 1971 and Philadelphia: Fortress, 1970).

Rengstorf, Karl L., "ἀπόστολος" *(apostolos)*, in G. Kittel (ed.), *TDNT*, vol. 1, 398-447.

Rhees, Rush, *Discussions of Wittgenstein* (London: Routledge and Kegan Paul, 1970).

Richardson, Alan, *Creeds in the Making: A Short Introduction to the History of Christian Doctrine* (London: S.C.M., 1935).

_____, *Introduction to the Theology of the New Testament* (London: S.C.M., 1958).

Richmond, James, *Ritschl: A Reappraisal*, A Study in Systematic Theology (London and New York: Collins, 1978).

Ricoeur, Paul, *The Symbolism of Evil* (New York: Harper & Row, 1967 and Boston: Beacon, 1969).

_____, *Freud and Philosophy: An Essay on Interpretation*, translated by D. Savage (New Haven, CT and London: Yale University Press, 1970).

_____, *The Conflict of Interpretations: Essays in Hermeneutics*, edited by Don Ihde (Evanston, IL: Northwestern University Press, 1974).

_____, *Interpretation Theory: Discourse and the Surplus of Meaning* (Fort Worth: Texas Christian University Press, 1976).

_____, *Essays on Biblical Interpretation*, edited by Lewis S. Mudge (London: SPCK, 1981 and Minneapolis: Fortress, 1980).

_____, *Hermeneutics and the Human Sciences,* edited and translated by John B. Thompson (Cambridge: Cambridge University Press, 1981).

_____, *Time and Narrative,* translated by K. McLaughlin and D. Peliauer, 3 vols. (Chicago and London: University of Chicago Press, 1984-88).

_____, *Oneself as Another,* translated by Kathleen Blamey (Chicago and London: University of Chicago Press, 1992).

_____, "Intellectual Autobiography," in Lewis E. Hahn (ed.), *The Philosophy of Paul Ricoeur* (Chicago and La Salle, IL: Open Court, 1995), 3-53.

Ridderbos, *Paul: An Outline of His Theology* (Grand Rapids: Eerdmans, 1975).

Rissi, Mathias, *The Future of the World: An Exegetical Study of Revelation 19:11–22:15* (London: S.C.M., 1972).

Ritschl, Albrecht, *The Christian Doctrine of Justification and Reconciliation: The Positive Development of the Doctrine,* translated by H. R. Mackintosh and A. B. Macaulay (reprint, Clifton, NJ: Reference Book Publishers, 1966).

Robinson, H. Wheeler, *The Christian Experience of the Holy Spirit* (London: Nisbet, 1928).

_____, *The Christian Doctrine of Man* (Edinburgh: T&T Clark, 1911).

_____, *Baptist Principles* (London: Carey Kingsgate, 4th edn. 1960).

Robinson, James M., "Hermeneutics Since Barth," in James M. Robinson and John B. Cobb Jr. (eds.), *New Frontiers in Theology: II, The New Hermeneutic* (New York and London: Harper & Row, 1964), 1-77.

Robinson, John A. T., *In the End, God . . . A Study of the Christian Doctrine of the Last Things* (London: James Clarke, 1950).

_____, *The Body: A Study in Pauline Theology* (London: S.C.M., 1952).

_____, "Kingdom, Church, and Ministry," in K. M. Carey (ed.), *The Historic Episcopate in the Fulness of the Church* (London: Dacre, 1954, 2d edn. 1960), 11-22.

_____, *Jesus and His Coming: The Emergence of a Doctrine* (London: S.C.M., 1957).

_____, "The Most Primitive Christology of All," in J. A. T. Robinson, *Twelve New Testament Studies* (London: S.C.M., 1962), 144.

_____, "Need Jesus Have Been Perfect?" in Stephen W. Sykes and J. P. Clayton (eds.), *Christ, Faith and History: Cambridge Studies in Christology* (Cambridge: Cambridge University Press, 1972), 39-52.

_____, *The Human Face of God* (London: S.C.M., 1973).

Rogerson, John W., "The Hebrew Conception of Corporate Personality," *JTS* 21 (1980) 1-16, reprinted in Lang (ed.), *Anthropological Approaches,* 43-59.

Rollins, Wayne, *Jung and the Bible* (Atlanta: John Knox, 1983).

Roloff, J., *Apostolat, Verkündigung, Kirche: Ursprung, Inhalt und Funktion des Kirchlichen Apostelamtes nach Paulus, Lukas, und den Pastoralbriefen* (Gütersloh: Gütersloher Verlagshaus/Mohn, 1965).

Rorem, P., *Pseudo-Dionysius: A Commentary on the Texts and an Introduction to Their Influence* (New York: Oxford University Press, 1993).

Rorty, Richard, *Philosophy and the Mirror of Nature* (Princeton, NJ: Princeton University Press, 1979).

_____, *Truth and Progress: Philosophical Papers,* vol. 3 (Cambridge: Cambridge University Press, 1998).

Roth, Cecil, *The Haggadah: New Edition with Notes,* Hebrew and English (London: Soncino, 1934).

Rowley, H. H., *The Relevance of Apocalyptic: A Study of Jewish and Christian Apocalypses from Daniel to Revelation* (London: Lutterworth, 1944).

Ruether, Rosemary Radford, *Sexism and God Talk: Toward a Feminist Theology* (Boston: Beacon, 1983).

Rupp, Gordon, *The Righteousness of God: Luther Studies* (London: Hodder & Stoughton, 1953).

_____, and Watson, Philip S. (eds.), *Luther and Erasmus: Free Will and Salvation*, Library of Christian Classics (Philadelphia: Westminster, 1969).

Rush, Ormond, *The Reception of Doctrine: An Appropriation of Hans Robert Jauss' Reception Aesthetics and Literary Hermeneutics*, Tesi Gregoriana, Serie Teologia 19 (Rome: Pontifical Gregorian University, 1997).

Russell, D. S., *The Method and Message of Jewish Apocalyptic 200 B.C.–A.D. 100* (London: S.C.M., 1964).

Russell, Letty, *The Future of Partnership* (Philadelphia: Westminster, 1979).

Russell, Robert J., Murphy, Nancey, and Isham, C. J. (eds.), *Quantum Cosmology and the Laws of Nature: Scientific Perspectives on Divine Action* (Berkeley, CA: Center for Theology and the Natural Sciences and Vatican City: Vatican Observatory Publications, 2d edn. 1996).

Ryle, Gilbert, "Systematically Misleading Expressions," *Proceedings of the Aristotelian Society* 32 (1931-32) 139-70.

_____, *The Concept of Mind* (London: Hutchinson, 1949 and Penguin Books, 1963).

Saiving, Valerie, "The Human Situation: A Feminine View," *Journal of Religion* 40 (1960) 100-112.

Salmon, George, *The Infallibility of the Church* (London: John Murray, 1888, 2d edn. 1890).

Sanders, E. P., *Paul and Palestinian Judaism: A Comparison of Patterns of Religion* (London: S.C.M., 1977).

Sandnes, K. O., *Paul — One of the Prophets? A Contribution to the Apostle's Self-Understanding*, WUNT II (Tübingen: Mohr, 1991).

Sarot, Marcel (ed.), *The Future as God's Gift: Explorations in Christian Eschatology* (Edinburgh: T&T Clark, 2000).

Saw, Insawn, *Paul's Rhetoric in 1 Corinthians 15* (Lewiston, NY: Mellen, 1995).

Sawyer, John F. A., *Semantics in Biblical Research: New Methods of Defining Hebrew Words for Salvation* (London: S.C.M., 1972).

Scalise, Charles J., *Hermeneutics as Theological Prolegomena: A Canonical Approach*, Studies in American Hermeneutics 8 (Macon, GA: Mercer University Press, 1994).

Schandorff, Esther Dech, *The Doctrine of the Holy Spirit: A Bibliography Showing Its Chronological Development*, ATLA Bibliography 28, 2 vols. (Lanham, MD: Scarecrow, 1995).

Schillebeeckx, E., *Christ, the Sacrament of Encounter with God* (London: Sheed & Ward, 1963).

Schilling, Harold K., *The New Consciousness in Science and Religion* (London: S.C.M., 1973).

Schleiermacher, F. D. E., *On Religion: Speeches to Its Cultured Despisers*, translated by John Oman (New York: Harper & Row, 1958).

_____, *Hermeneutics: The Handwritten Manuscripts*, edited by H. Kimmerle and translated by J. Duke and J. Forstman; AAR Text and Translation 1; (Missoula: Scholars. 1977).

_____, *The Christian Faith*, translated by H. R. Mackintosh and J. S. Stewart (Edinburgh: T&T Clark, rpt. 1989).

Schmidt, Karl L., "καλέω, κλῆσις, κλητός, ἐκκλησία," in G. Kittel (ed.), *TDNT*, vol. 3, 469-536.

Schmithals, W., *Gnosticism in Corinth*, translated by John Steely (Nashville: Abingdon, 1971).

Schnackenburg, Rudolf, *God's Rule and Kingdom*, translated by J. Murray (London: Nelson, 1963).

_____, *Baptism in the Thought of Paul*, translated by G. R. Beasley-Murray (Oxford: Blackwell, 1964).

_____, *The Church in the New Testament*, translated by W. J. O'Hara (London: Burns & Oates and Freiburg: Herder, 1965).

_____, "Apostles before and during Paul's Time," in Ward Gasque and R. P. Martin (eds.), *Apostolic History and the Gospel: Essays Presented to F. F. Bruce* (Exeter, U.K.: Paternoster, 1970).

Schnelle, Udo, *The Human Condition: Anthropology in the Teachings of Jesus, Paul, and John*, translated by O. C. Dean (Edinburgh: T&T Clark, 1996).

Schütz, John H., *Paul and the Anatomy of Apostolic Authority*, SNTSMS 26 (Cambridge: Cambridge University Press, 1975).

Schweitzer, Albert, *The Mysticism of Paul the Apostle*, translated by W. Montgomery (London: Black, 1931).

_____, *The Quest of the Historical Jesus: A Critical Study of Its Progress from Reimarus to Wrede*, translated by W. Montgomery (London: Black, 3d edn. 1954 [1st Eng. edn. 1910]).

Schweizer, Eduard, *Church Order in the New Testament*, translated by F. Clarke (London: S.C.M., 1961).

_____, "πνεῦμα," in G. Kittel (ed.), *TDNT*, vol. 6, translated by G. W. Bromiley (Grand Rapids: Eerdmans, 1968), 332-453.

Scott, C. Anderson, *Christianity according to St. Paul* (Cambridge: Cambridge University Press, 1927, 2d edn. 1961).

Scott, Ernest F., *The Spirit in the New Testament* (London: Hodder & Stoughton 1923).

Scroggs, Robin, *The Last Adam: A Study in Pauline Anthropology* (Philadelphia: Fortress, 1966).

Searle, John, *Intentionality: An Essay in the Philosophy of Mind* (Cambridge: Cambridge University Press, 1983).

Seeberg, A., *Der Katechismus der Urchristenheit* (1903; reprinted, Munich: Kaiser, 1966).

Selwyn, E. G., *The First Epistle of Peter: The Greek Text* (London: Macmillan, 1947).

Shapland, C. R. B. (ed.), *The Letters of Saint Athanasius concerning the Holy Spirit* (London: Epworth, 1951).

Shedd, Russell P., *Man in Community: A Study of St. Paul's Application of Old Testament and Early Jewish Conceptions of Human Solidarity* (London: Epworth, 1958).

Shults, F. LeRon, *Reforming Theological Anthropology: After the Philosophical Turn to Relationality* (Grand Rapids and Cambridge, U.K.: Eerdmans, 2003).

Simon, Ulrich, *Heaven in the Christian Tradition* (London: Rockliff, 1958).

_____, *The Ascent to Heaven* (London: Barrie & Rockliff, 1961).

_____, *The End Is Not Yet: A Study in Christian Eschatology* (London: Nisbet, 1964).

Skemp, J. B., *The Greeks and the Gospel* (London: Carey Kingsgate, 1964).

Smalley, Stephen S., *1, 2, 3 John*, WBC (Waco, TX: Word, 1984).

Smart, James D., *The Strange Silence of the Birth of the Church* (London: S.C.M., 1970).

Smith, C. Ryder, *The Bible Doctrine of Salvation: A Study of the Atonement* (London: Epworth Press, 2d edn. 1946).

_____, *The Bible Doctrine of Sin and the Ways of God with Sinners* (London: Epworth, 1953).

Sobrino, Jon, *Christology at the Crossroads: A Latin American Approach,* translated by John Drury (London: S.C.M., 1978).

Soskice, Janet Martin, *Metaphor and Religious Language* (Oxford: Clarendon, 1985).

Sowers, Stanley K., "Paul on the Use and Abuse of Reason," in D. L. Balch, E. Ferguson, and Wayne Meeks (eds.), *Greeks, Romans, and Christians: Essays in Honor of J. Malherbe* (Minneapolis: Augsburg, 1990) 253-86.

Sparks, H. F. D., "The Doctrine of the Divine Fatherhood in the Gospels," in D. E. Nineham (ed.), *Studies in the Gospels: Essays in Memory of R. H. Lightfoot* (Oxford: Blackwell, 1967 [1955]).

Sponheim, Paul, *God — The Question and the Quest* (Philadelphia: Fortress, 1985).

_____, Ruether, Rosemary Radford, and Fulkerson, Mary McClintoch, "Women and Sin: Responses to Mary Elise Lowe," *Dialog* 39 (2000) 229-36.

Stanley, Christopher D., *Paul and the Language of Scripture: Citation Technique in the Pauline Epistles and Contemporary Literature,* SNTSMS 69 (Cambridge: Cambridge University Press, 1992).

Stanton, Graham N., *Jesus of Nazareth in New Testament Preaching,* SNTSMS 27 (Cambridge: Cambridge University Press, 1974).

_____, *The Gospels and Jesus* (Oxford: Oxford University Press, 1989).

Stauffer, Ethelbert, *New Testament Theology,* translated by John Marsh (New York and London: Macmillan, 1955).

Stendahl, Krister, "The Apostle Paul and the Introspective Conscience of the West" (1961 and 1963), reprinted in K. Stendahl, *Paul among Jews and Gentiles* (London: S.C.M., 1977 and Philadelphia: Fortress, 1976).

_____, "Glossolalia — The NT Evidence," in K. Stendahl, *Paul among Jews and Gentiles* (London: S.C.M., 1977).

Stephens, W. P., *The Holy Spirit in the Theology of Martin Bucer* (Cambridge: Cambridge University Press, 1970).

Stephenson, Christopher A., "The Rule of Spirituality and the Rule of Doctrine: A Necessary Relationship in Theological Method," *Journal of Pentecostal Theology* 15 (October 2006) 83-105.

Sternberg, Meir, *The Poetics of Biblical Narrative: Ideological Literature and the Drama of Reading* (Bloomington: Indiana University Press, 1985).

Stewart, Jacqui A., *Reconstructing Science and Theology in Postmodernity: Pannenberg, Ethics, and the Human Sciences* (Aldershot, U.K. and Burlington, VT: Ashgate, 2000).

Strauss, David F., *The Life of Jesus Critically Examined,* edited by Peter C. Hodgson, Lives of Jesus (Philadelphia: Fortress, 1972).

Strobel, A., *Der erste Brief an die Korinther,* Zürcher Bibelkommentare (Zürich: Theologischer, 1989).

Strong, A. H., *Systematic Theology,* 3 vols. (1907; reprinted, London: Pickering & Inglis, 1965).

Stroup, George, *The Promise of Narrative Theology* (London: S.C.M., 1984 [John Knox, 1981]).

Stuhlmacher, P., *Gerechtigkeit Gottes bei Paulus* (Göttingen: Vandenhoeck & Ruprecht, 1965).

Stump, E., "Eternity," *Journal of Philosophy* 78 (1981) 429-58.

Swete, Henry B., *The Holy Spirit in the Ancient Church* (London: Macmillan, 1912).

_____, *The Holy Spirit in the New Testament* (London: Macmillan, 1921).

Swinburne, Richard, *The Existence of God* (Oxford: Oxford University Press, 1979).

_____, *The Coherence of Theism* (Oxford: Oxford University Press, rev. edn. 1997).

Sykes, S. W., and Clayton, J. P. (eds.), *Christ, Faith and History: Cambridge Studies in Christology* (Cambridge: Cambridge University Press, 1972).

Tanner, Kathryn, "Jesus Christ," in Colin E. Gunton, *The Cambridge Companion to Christian Doctrine* (Cambridge: Cambridge University Press, 1997), 245-72.

Taylor, John Randolph, *God Loves like That: The Theology of James Denney* (London: S.C.M., 1962).

Taylor, Vincent, *The Atonement in New Testament Teaching* (London: Epworth, 1940).

_____, *The Person of Christ in New Testament Teaching* (New York and London: Macmillan, 1958).

Temple, William, *Nature, Man, and God* (London: Macmillan, 1940).

Tennant, Frederick R., *The Origin and Propagation of Sin* (Cambridge: Cambridge University Press, 2d edn. 1908).

_____, *The Concept of Sin* (Cambridge: Cambridge University Press, 1912).

Thayer, J. H., *Greek-English Lexicon of the New Testament* (Edinburgh: T&T Clark, 4th edn. 1901).

Theissen, Gerd, *The First Followers of Jesus: A Sociological Analysis of the Earliest Christianity* (London: S.C.M., 1978); American edition: *Sociology of Early Palestinian Christianity* (Philadelphia: Fortress, 1978).

Thielicke, Helmut, *Man in God's World,* translated by J. W. Doberstein (London: Clarke, 1967).

_____, *The Evangelical Faith,* translated by G. Bromiley, 3 vols. (Grand Rapids: Eerdmans, 1974-82), vol. 3.

_____, *Theological Ethics,* edited by W. H. Lazareth, 3 vols. (Grand Rapids: Eerdmans, 1979).

Thiselton, Anthony C., "The Parousia in Modern Theology: Some Questions and Comments," *Tyndale Bulletin* 27 (1976) 27-54.

_____, *The Two Horizons: New Testament Hermeneutics and Philosophical Description* (Grand Rapids: Eerdmans and Exeter, U.K.: Paternoster, 1980).

_____, *New Horizons in Hermeneutics: The Theory and Practice of Transforming Biblical Reading* (Grand Rapids: Zondervan and Carlisle, U.K.: Paternoster, 1992).

_____, "Christology in Luke, Speech-Act Theory, and the Problem of Dualism in Christology," in Joel B. Green and Max Turner (eds.), *Jesus of Nazareth: Lord and Christ* (Grand Rapids: Eerdmans, 1994).

_____, *Interpreting God and the Postmodern Self: On Meaning, Manipulation, and Promise* (Edinburgh: T&T Clark and Grand Rapids: Eerdmans, 1995).

_____, "Luther on Barth on 1 Corinthians 15: Six Theses for Theology," in W. P. Stephens (ed.), *The Bible, the Reformation, and the Church: Essays in Honour of James Atkinson,* JSNTSS 105 (Sheffield: Sheffield Academic Press, 1995), 258-89; reprinted in *Thiselton on Hermeneutics,* 769-92.

_____, with Lundin, Roger, and Walhout, Clarence, *The Promise of Hermeneutics* (Grand Rapids: Eerdmans and Carlisle, U.K.: Paternoster, 1999).

_____, *The First Epistle to the Corinthians: A Commentary on the Greek Text,* NIGTC series (Grand Rapids: Eerdmans and Carlisle, U.K.: Paternoster, 2000).

_____, "'Reading Luke' as Interpretation, Reflection and Formation," in Craig Bartholomew, Joel B. Green, and Anthony C. Thiselton (eds.), *Reading Luke: Interpretation, Reflection, Formation,* Scripture and Hermeneutics Series 6 (Carlisle, U.K.: Paternoster and Grand Rapids: Zondervan, 2005), 3-52.

_____, _1 Corinthians: A Shorter Exegetical and Pastoral Commentary_ (Grand Rapids: Eerdmans, 2006).

_____, "The Significance of Recent Research on 1 Corinthians for Hermeneutical Appropriation of This Epistle Today," in _Neot._ 40 (2006) 91-123.

_____, _Thiselton on Hermeneutics: Collected Works and New Essays_, Contemporary Thinkers on Religion (Aldershot, U.K.: Ashgate and Grand Rapids: Eerdmans, 2006).

Thomson, John B., _The Ecclesiology of Stanley Hauerwas: A Christian Theology of Liberation_ (Aldershot and London, and Burlington, VT: Ashgate, 2003).

Thornton, L. S., _The Common Life in the Body of Christ_ (London: Dacre, 3d edn. 1950).

Tilley, Terrence W., _The Evils of Theodicy_ (Washington, DC: Georgetown University Press, 1991).

Tillich, Paul, _Systematic Theology_, 3 vols. (Chicago: University of Chicago Press, 1951-64 and London: Nisbet 1953-64).

_____, _Dynamics of Faith_ (London: Allen & Unwin, 1957).

_____, _Theology of Culture_ (New York: Galaxy, 1964).

_____, _Ultimate Concern: Dialogues with Students_, edited by D. Mackenzie Brown (London: S.C.M., 1965).

Todorov, Tzvetan, _Mikhail Bakhtin: The Dialogical Principle_, translated by W. Godzich, Theory and History of Literature 12 (Minneapolis: University of Minnesota Press, 1984).

Torrance, Alan J., _Persons in Communion: Trinitarian Description and Human Participation_ (Edinburgh: T&T Clark, 1996).

Torrance, Thomas F., _Theological Science_ (London and New York: Oxford University Press, 1969).

_____, _God and Rationality_ (London and New York: Oxford University Press, 1971).

_____, _The Trinitarian Faith: The Evangelical Theology of the Ancient Catholic Church_ (Edinburgh: T&T Clark, 1988).

_____, _Divine Meaning: Studies in Patristic Hermeneutics_ (Edinburgh: T&T Clark, 1995).

Tovey, Derek, _Narrative Art and Act in the Fourth Gospel_, JSNTSS 151 (Sheffield: Sheffield Academic Press, 1997).

Tracy, David, _The Analogical Imagination: Christian Theology and the Culture of Pluralism_ (London: S.C.M., 1981).

_____, _Plurality and Ambiguity: Hermeneutics, Religion, Hope_ (London: S.C.M., 1987).

_____, _Blessed Rage for Order: The New Pluralism in Theology_ (San Francisco: Harper & Row, 1988 and Chicago: University of Chicago Press, 1996).

_____, "Hermeneutical Reflections in the New Paradigm," in Hans Küng and David Tracy (eds.), _Paradigm Change in Theology_, cited above, 34-62.

Travis, Stephen H., _Christ and the Judgment of God: Divine Retribution in the New Testament_ (London: Marshall Pickering, 1986).

Trible, Phyllis, _God and the Rhetoric of Sexuality_ (Philadelphia: Fortress, 1978).

Trigg, Joseph Wilson, _Origen: The Bible and Philosophy in the Third-Century Church_ (London: S.C.M., 1985 and Louisville: John Knox, 1983).

Turner, Max, _The Holy Spirit and Spiritual Gifts: Then and Now_ (Carlisle, U.K.: Paternoster, 1996).

Turner, Philip, "Tolerable Diversity and Ecclesial Integrity: Communion or Federation?" in _The Journal of Anglican Studies_ 1:2 (2003) 24-46.

Tyndale, William, _Doctrinal Treatises and Introduction to Different Portions of the Holy Scripture_, Parker Society Edition (Cambridge: Cambridge University Press, 1948).

Van den Brink, Gijsbert, *Almighty God: A Study of the Doctrine of Divine Omnipotence* (Kampen: Kok Pharos, 1993).

VanGemeren, W. A. (ed.), *New International Dictionary of Old Testament Theology and Exegesis*, 5 vols. (Grand Rapids: Zondervan, 1997).

Vanhoozer, Kevin (ed.), *The Trinity in a Pluralistic Age: Theological Essays on Culture and Religion* (Grand Rapids: Eerdmans, 1997).

_____, *Is There a Meaning in This Text?* (Grand Rapids: Zondervan, 1998).

_____, *The Drama of Doctrine: A Canonical-Linguistic Approach to Christian Theology* (Louisville: Westminster/John Knox Press, 2005).

Van Huyssteen, J. Wentzel, *Essays in Postfoundationalist Theology* (Grand Rapids and Cambridge: Eerdmans, 1997).

Vatican II, *Lumen Gentium* (21 November 1964), in Austin P. Flannery (ed.), *Documents of Vatican II* (Grand Rapids: Eerdmans, 1975).

_____, *Decree of the Pastoral Office of Bishops in the Church, Christus Dominus* (28 October 1965), in Austin P. Flannery (ed.), *Documents of Vatican II* (Grand Rapids: Eerdmans, 1975).

_____, *Instruction on the Worship of the Eucharistic Mystery, Eucharisticum Mysterium* (25 May 1967), in Austin P. Flannery (ed.), *Documents of Vatican II* (Grand Rapids: Eerdmans, 1975).

Vawter, Bruce, *On Genesis: A New Reading* (New York: Doubleday, 1977).

Vriezen, T. C., *An Outline of Old Testament Theology*, translated by the author (Oxford: Blackwell, 1962).

Wagner, Günter, *Pauline Baptism and the Pagan Mysteries*, translated by J. P. Smith (Edinburgh: Oliver & Boyd, 1967).

Wainwright, Arthur W., *The Trinity in the New Testament* (London: SPCK, 1962).

Wainwright, Geoffrey, *Doxology: A Systematic Theology: The Praise of God in Worship, Doctrine, and Life* (London: Epworth, 1980).

Walker, Andrew, "Pentecostalism and Charismatic Christianity," in Alistair McGrath (ed.), *Modern Christian Thought* (Oxford: Blackwell, 1993) 428-34.

Wallace, Ronald S., *Calvin's Doctrine of the Word and Sacrament* (Edinburgh: Oliver & Boyd, 1953).

Warnke, Georgia, *Gadamer: Hermeneutics, Tradition and Reason* (Cambridge: Polity, 1987).

Watson, Francis, *Paul and the Hermeneutics of Faith* (London and New York: T&T Clark and Continuum, 2004).

Watson, Philip S., *Let God Be God: An Interpretation of the Theology of Martin Luther* (London: Epworth, 1947).

Wayne, J. J. (ed.), *The Great Encyclical Letters of Pope Leo XIII* (New York: Benziger, 1903).

Weber Otto, *Karl Barth's Church Dogmatics: An Introductory Report on Volumes I:1 to III:4*, translated by A. C. Cochrane (London: Lutterworth, 1953).

_____, *Foundations of Dogmatics*, translated by D. L. Guder, 2 vols. (Grand Rapids: Eerdmans, 1981 and 1983).

Webster, John B., *Eberhard Jüngel: An Introduction to his Theology* (Cambridge: Cambridge University Press, 1986).

_____, *Holiness* (Grand Rapids: Eerdmans, 2003).

Weinsheimer, Joel C., *Gadamer's Hermeneutics: A Reading of Truth and Method* (New Haven, CT and London: Yale University Press, 1985).

Weiser, A., *The Psalms: A Commentary*, translated by H. Hartwell (London: S.C.M., 1962).

Weiss, Johannes, *Earliest Christianity* (earlier English title, *History of Primitive Christianity*), English edited by F. C. Grant, 2 vols. (New York: Harper, 1959).

Welborn, L. L., *Paul, the Fool of Christ: A Study of 1 Corinthians 1–4 in the Comic-Philosophic Tradition*, JSNTSS 293 (London and New York: Continuum and T&T Clark, 2005).

Welch, Claude, *Protestant Thought in the Nineteenth Century*, 2 vols. (New Haven: Yale, 1972 and 1985).

Wells, Samuel, *Improvisation: The Drama of Christian Ethics* (London: SPCK, 2004).

Wengst, K., *Christologische Formeln und Lieder des Urchristentums* (Gütersloh: Gütersloher, 1972).

West, Angel, *Deadly Innocence: Feminism and the Mythology of Sin* (New York and London: Continuum, 1996).

Westermann, Claus, *Genesis 1–11: A Commentary*, translated by J. Scullion (London: SPCK, 1984).

Whitehouse, W. A., "Karl Barth on 'the Work of Creation,'" in Nigel Biggar (ed.), *Reckoning with Barth* (London and Oxford: Mowbray, 1988), 43-57.

Whiteley, D. E. H., *The Theology of St. Paul* (Oxford: Blackwell, 2d edn. 1974).

Whybray, R. N., *Isaiah 40–66*, New Century Bible (London: Oliphants, 1975).

Wiedemann, Thomas, *Greek and Roman Slavery* (London: Groom, Helm, 1981).

_____, *Slavery: Greece and Rome*, New Surveys 19 (Oxford: Oxford University Press, 1997).

Wikenhauser, A., *Pauline Mysticism: Christ in the Mystical Teaching of St. Paul*, translated by J. Cunningham (Freiberg: Herder, 1960).

Wiles, Maurice F., "Does Christology Rest on a Mistake?" *Religious Studies* 6 (1970) 69-76.

Williams D. J., *Paul's Metaphors — Their Context and Character* (Peabody, MA: Hendrickson, 1999).

Williams, N. P., *The Ideas of the Fall and Original Sin: A Historical and Critical Study* (London and New York: Longmans, Green, 1929).

Williams, Rowan, *On Christian Theology* (Oxford: Blackwell, 2000).

_____, "Balthasar and the Trinity," in Edward T. Oakes and David Moss (eds.), *The Cambridge Companion to Hans Urs von Balthasar* (Cambridge: Cambridge University Press, 2004), 37-50.

Williamson, Hugh, *The Lord Is King: A Personal Rediscovery* (Nottingham: Crossway, 1993).

Wilson, Roy McL., *The Gnostic Problem: A Study of the Relations between Hellenistic Judaism and the Gnostic Heresy* (London: Mowbray, 1958).

Wilson, Stephen G., *The Gentiles and the Gentile Mission in Luke-Acts*, SNTSMS 23 (Cambridge: Cambridge University Press, 1973).

Wimber, John, *Power Evangelism* (London: Hodder & Stoughton, 1985).

Wink, Walter, *The Bible in Human Transformation: Toward a New Paradigm for Biblical Study* (Philadelphia: Fortress, 1973).

Winter, Bruce, "Religious Curses and Christian Vindictiveness: 1 Cor. 12–14," in Bruce Winter, *After Paul Left Corinth* (Grand Rapids: Eerdmans, 2001), 164-83.

Wittgenstein, Ludwig, *Philosophische Bemerkungen* (Oxford: Blackwell, 1964).

_____, *Philosophical Investigations*, German and English (Oxford: Blackwell, 2d edn. 1967).

_____, *The Blue and Brown Books: Preliminary Studies for the "Philosophical Investigations"* (Oxford: Blackwell, 2d edn. 1969).

_____, *Zettel*, edited and translated by G. E. M. Anscombe and G. H. von Wright, German and English (Oxford: Blackwell, 1967).

_____, *On Certainty — Über Gewissheit,* edited by G. E. M. Anscombe and G. H. von Wright, German and English (Oxford: Blackwell, 1969).

_____, *Culture and Value,* German and English translated by Peter Winch, edited by G. H. von Wright (Oxford: Blackwell, 2d edn. 1978).

_____, *Remarks on the Philosophy of Psychology,* edited by G. E. M. Anscombe, G. H. von Wright, and H. Nyman, translated by A. E. M. Anscombe, C. G. Luckhardt, and M. A. E. Aue, 2 vols. (Oxford: Blackwell, 1980).

_____, *Wittgenstein's Lectures on Philosophical Psychology, 1946-47* (Hemel Hempstead, U.K.: Harvester Wheatsheaf, 1988).

_____, *Philosophical Occasions: 1912-1951,* edited by J. Klagge and A. Nordmann (Indianapolis and Cambridge: Hackett, 1993).

Wolff, Hans Walter, *Anthropology of the Old Testament,* translated by Margaret Kohl (London: S.C.M., 1974).

Wolterstorff, Nicholas, *Divine Discourse: Philosophical Reflections on the Claim that God Speaks* (Cambridge: Cambridge University Press, 1985).

_____, *John Locke and the Ethics of Belief* (Cambridge: Cambridge University Press, 1996).

Wood, W. Jay, *Epistemology: Becoming Intellectually Virtuous* (Downers Grove: InterVarsity Press and Leicester: Apollos, 1998).

Work, Telford, *Living and Active: Scripture in the Economy of Salvation* (Grand Rapids: Eerdmans, 2002).

Wright, G. Ernest, *God Who Acts: Biblical Theology as Recital* (London: S.C.M., 1952).

Wright, N. T., "How Can the Bible Be Authoritative?" *Vox Evangelica* 21 (1991) 1-20.

_____, *Jesus and the Victory of God: Christian Origins and the Question of God,* vol. 2 (London: SPCK, 1996).

_____, *The Resurrection of the Son of God: Christian Origins and the Question of God,* vol. 3 (London: SPCK, 2003).

_____, *Paul: Fresh Perspectives* (London: SPCK, 2005).

Young, Frances, *The Art of Performance: Towards a Theology of Holy Scripture* (London: Darton, Longman & Todd, 1990).

Ziesler, John A., *The Meaning of Righteousness in Paul: A Linguistic and Theological Enquiry,* SNTSMS 20 (Cambridge: Cambridge University Press, 1972).

Zimmermann, Jens, *Recovering Theological Hermeneutics: An Incarnational-Trinitarian Theory of Interpretation* (Grand Rapids: Baker Academic, 2004).

Zingg, P., *Das Wachsen der Kirche: Beiträge zur Frage der lukanischen Redaktion und Theologie* (Göttingen: Vandenhoeck & Ruprecht, 1974).

Zizioulas, John D., "Human Capacity and Human Incapacity: A Theological Exploration of Personhood," *Scottish Journal of Theology* 28 (1975) 401-48.

_____, *Being as Communion: Studies in Personhood and the Church,* Contemporary Greek Theologians 4 (Crestwood, NY: St. Vladimir's Seminary Press, 1985).

Zwingli, Huldrych, *On the Lord's Supper,* translated and edited by Geoffrey W. Bromiley, in *Zwingli and Bullinger,* Library of Christian Classics 24 (Philadelphia: Westminster and London: S.C.M., 1953), 185-238.

Index of Names

Funk, Robert W., 354
Furnish, Victor P., 327, 333

Gadamer, Hans-Georg, xvii, xix, xxi, 3-8, 57,
    59-60, 71-72, 81-87, 90-104, 106, 109-15, 121-
    23, 129, 131-32, 139-40, 145-48, 151-58, 161,
    168, 170, 178, 183, 222, 261, 263, 312, 408-9,
    511, 519
Gärtner, Bertil, 208
Gee, Donald, 443
Geffré, Claude, 110
Gehlen, Arnold, 220
Genette, Gérard, 67, 340, 578
Gerkin, Charles V., 238
Giddens, Anthony, 54
Gilbertson, Michael, 545-46, 575
Gilkey, Langdon, 105
Gillespie, Thomas W., 447
Glasson, T. F., 567
Godsey, John D., 314
Goheen, Michael, 492
Gollwitzer, Helmut, 383
González, Justo L., 5-8, 63, 199
Gordon, C. H., 44, 461
Goudge, H. L., 536
Green, Garrett, 331
Green, Joel B., 335, 344
Gregory of Nazianzus, 225, 235, 237, 276, 323,
    338, 373, 432-33, 435-36, 451, 460, 565
Gregory of Nyssa, 235, 237, 276, 292, 323, 373,
    432-33, 436, 451, 460
Gregory the Great, 218, 278, 520
Grenz, Stanley J., 131, 180, 235, 237-40, 250-51,
    304
Grillmeier, A., 102-3
Grondin, Jean, 122
Grotius, H., 555
Gundry, Robert H., 47, 444, 574, 579
Gunkel, Hermann, 224
Gunton, Colin E., 213, 319, 331, 360, 365, 373,
    467-68
Guy, H. A., 567

Habermas, Jürgen, 86, 104, 109, 114, 120, 139-
    40, 157-58, 161, 220, 226, 489, 510, 519
Haenchen, Ernst, 449, 491-92
Hahn, Ferdinand, 46
Hainz, J., 482
Hall, David R., 504
Hall, Thor, 107
Hamann, J. G., 216
Hamilton, N. Q., 414, 419-21, 548
Hampson, Daphne, 303-4

Hanson, Anthony T., 507
Harnack, Adolf, 13, 34-37, 50, 107, 185, 188,
    372, 409, 456, 544
Harvey, Anthony C., 408, 463-64
Harvey, David, 54
Hauerwas, Stanley, xviii-xix, 67
Haykin, Michael A. G., 433, 435, 451, 460
Hays, Richard B., 285, 314, 563
Heal, Jane, 170
Hebblethwaite, Brian, 571
Hebert, A. G., 500
Hegel, Georg W. F., 56-57, 72-73, 76, 112, 134-
    35, 138-39, 141, 153, 159, 180, 212, 235-36,
    258, 307, 319, 377, 400-402, 471, 572-73
Heidegger, Martin, 50, 52, 54, 66, 72, 106, 121-
    23, 140, 158, 161, 180, 218, 226, 249, 256,
    258-61, 263, 378, 382, 475, 517
Heinrici, C. F. G., 445
Heisenberg, Werner, 148
Henderson, Ian, 355
Hendry, G. S., 414-29
Hengel, Martin, 36, 272, 309-11, 314, 408
Hepburn, Ronald W., 378
Herder, J. G., 57
Hermogenes, 209
Heyduck, Richard, xviii-xix, 21, 73, 106, 126-
    29, 131, 133, 149, 185, 238
Hick, John, 157
Higgins, A. J. B., 526
High, Dallas M., 19, 32-33
Hilborn, David, 510
Hill, David, 342, 447
Hippolytus, 208-9, 358, 430, 432, 434, 467, 525
Hobbes, Thomas, 188-89
Hodge, Charles, 6, 66-67, 76, 79, 164, 292-93,
    344
Hodgson, Peter C., 401
Hoffmann, P., 555
Hofius, Otfried, 45, 525-26
Holland, Tom, 187, 480, 540
Holmberg, B., 501
Holmquist, Michael, 142
Holtzmann, H. J., 226
Hooke, S. H., 528
Hooker, Richard, 141, 189, 535
Hoyle, R. Birch, 415
Hubble, Edwin P., 220
Hugh of St. Victor, 520
Hume, David, 56, 132, 150, 161, 163, 171-72,
    193, 226, 228, 244-46, 396, 410
Hunsinger, Deborah van Deusen, 183-84
Hunsinger, George, 232
Hunter, A. M., 14

Index of Subjects

Index of Scripture and Other Ancient Sources